COMPILATION OF SELECTED
AEROSPACE LAWS
VOLUME 1: TITLE 49 UNITED STATES CODE

As amended through Public Law 118-158, Enacted December 21, 2024

Prepared By M. TWINCHEK

2025

Forward

This Compilation of Selected Aerospace Laws is a resource for those interested in U.S. laws governing civil aerospace. This compilation includes laws governing civil aviation, aviation safety, airport improvement, the Federal Aviation Administration(FAA), the National Transportation Safety Board, aviation security, essential air service, commercial airlines, general aviation, unmanned aircraft systems, aviation labor, international aviation, commercial space transportation, air traffic management, and general FAA operations.

The materials included comes from publicly available, open source information, prepared for the public by the Office of the Legislative Counsel of the U.S. House of Representatives and the Office of the Law Revision Counsel.

Items listed as a Statute Compilation do not appear in the U.S. Code or that have been classified to a title of the U.S. Code that has not been enacted into positive law. Each Statute Compilation incorporates the amendments made to the underlying statute since it was originally enacted and are current as of the date noted.

This compilation is not an official document and should not be cited as evidence of any law. The official version of Federal law is found in the United States Statutes at Large and in the U.S. Code, the legal effect of which is established in sections 112 and 204, respectively, of title 1, United States Code.

A special thanks is extended to the Office of Law Revision Counsel and the House Office of the Legislative Counsel for providing the U.S. Code and statute compilations; and to the Government Publications Office for hosting and making these available for use to the public. An additional thank you is offered to the staff of the House and Senate Committees who were gracious in responding to inquiries and providing background infor-

i

mation on the legislation included.

Questions and comments may be directed to:
M. Twinchek
Email: mtwinchek@outlook.com

Contents

SELECTED PROVISIONS OF

TITLE 49 U.S.C.
— TRANSPORTATION

CURRENT THROUGH PUBLIC LAW 118-158

SUBTITLE I
DEPARTMENT OF TRANSPORTATION

TITLE 49—TRANSPORTATION

This title was enacted by Pub. L. 95–473, §1, Oct. 17, 1978, 92 Stat. 1337; Pub. L. 97–449, §1, Jan. 12, 1983, 96 Stat. 2413; Pub. L. 103–272, July 5, 1994, 108 Stat. 745

* * * * * * *

5

SUBTITLE I—DEPARTMENT OF TRANSPORTATION

* * * * * * *

CHAPTER 1—ORGANIZATION

* * * * * * *

§101. PURPOSE

(a) The national objectives of general welfare, economic growth and stability, and security of the United States require the development of transportation policies and programs that contribute to providing fast, safe, efficient, and convenient transportation at the lowest cost consistent with those and other national objectives, including the efficient use and conservation of the resources of the United States.

(b) A Department of Transportation is necessary in the public interest and to—

(1) ensure the coordinated and effective administration of the transportation programs of the United States Government;

(2) make easier the development and improvement of coordinated transportation service to be provided by private enterprise to the greatest extent feasible;

(3) encourage cooperation of Federal, State, and local governments, carriers, labor, and other interested persons to achieve transportation objectives;

(4) stimulate technological advances in transportation, through research and development or otherwise;

(5) provide general leadership in identifying and solving transportation problems; and

(6) develop and recommend to the President and Congress transportation policies and programs to achieve transportation objectives considering the needs of the public, users, carriers, industry, labor, and national defense.

(Pub. L. 97–449, §1(b), Jan. 12, 1983, 96 Stat. 2414; Pub. L. 102–240, title VI, §6018, Dec. 18, 1991, 105 Stat. 2183.)

§102. DEPARTMENT OF TRANSPORTATION

(a) The Department of Transportation (referred to in this section as the "Department") is an executive department of the United States Government at the seat of Government.

(b) The head of the Department is the Secretary of Transportation (referred to in this section as the "Secretary"). The Secretary is appointed by the President, by and with the advice and consent of the Senate.

(c) The Department has a Deputy Secretary of Transportation appointed by the President, by and with the advice and consent of the Senate. The Deputy Secretary—

(1) shall carry out duties and powers prescribed by the Secretary; and

(2) acts for the Secretary when the Secretary is absent or unable to serve or when the office of Secretary is vacant.

(d) The Department has an Under Secretary of Transportation for Policy appointed by the President, by and with the advice and consent of the Senate. The Under Secretary shall provide leadership in the development of policy for the Department, supervise the policy activities of Assistant Secretaries with primary responsibility for aviation, international, and other transportation policy development and carry out other powers and duties prescribed by the Secretary. The Under Secretary acts for the Secretary when the Secretary and the Deputy Secretary are absent or unable to serve, or when the offices of Secretary and Deputy Secretary are vacant.

(e) ASSISTANT SECRETARIES; GENERAL COUNSEL.—

(1) APPOINTMENT.—The Department has 8 Assistant Secretaries and a General Counsel, including—

(A) an Assistant Secretary for Aviation and International Affairs, an Assistant Secretary for Governmental Affairs, an Assistant Secretary for Research and Technology, an Assistant Secretary for Transportation Policy, and an Assistant Secretary for Aviation Consumer Protection, who shall each be appointed by the President, with the advice and consent of the Senate;

(B) an Assistant Secretary for Budget and Programs who shall be appointed by the President;

(C) an Assistant Secretary for Administration, who shall be appointed by the Secretary, with the approval of the President;

(D) an Assistant Secretary for Tribal Government Affairs, who shall be appointed by the President; and

(E) a General Counsel, who shall be appointed by the President, with the advice and consent of the Senate.

(2) DUTIES AND POWERS.—The officers set forth in paragraph (1) shall carry out duties and powers prescribed by the Secretary. An Assistant Secretary or the General Counsel, in the order prescribed by the Secretary, acts for the Secretary when the Secretary, Deputy Secretary, and Under Secretary of Transportation for Policy are absent or unable to serve, or when the offices of the Secretary, Deputy Secretary, and Under Secretary of Transportation for Policy are vacant.

(f) OFFICE OF TRIBAL GOVERNMENT AFFAIRS.—

(1) ESTABLISHMENT.—There is established in the Department an Office of Tribal Government Affairs, under the Assistant Secretary for Tribal Government Affairs—

(A) to oversee the tribal self-governance program under section 207 of title 23;

(B) to plan, coordinate, and implement policies and programs serving Indian Tribes and Tribal organizations;

(C) to coordinate Tribal transportation programs and activities in all offices and administrations of the Department; and

(D) to be a participant in any negotiated rulemakings relating to, or having an impact on, projects, programs, or funding associated with the Tribal transportation program under section 202 of title 23.

(2) RESERVATION OF TRUST OBLIGATIONS.—

(A) RESPONSIBILITY OF SECRETARY.—In carrying out this title, the Secretary shall be responsible to exercise the trust obligations of the United States to Indians and Indian tribes to ensure that the rights of a tribe or individual Indian are protected.

(B) PRESERVATION OF UNITED STATES RESPONSIBILITY.—Nothing in this title shall absolve the United States from any responsibility to Indians and Indian tribes, including responsibilities derived from the trust relationship and any treaty, executive order, or agreement between the United States and an Indian tribe.

(g) OFFICE OF CLIMATE CHANGE AND ENVIRONMENT.—

(1) ESTABLISHMENT.—There is established in the Department an Office of Climate Change and Environment to plan, coordinate, and implement—

(A) department-wide research, strategies, and actions under the Department's statutory authority to reduce transportation-related energy use and mitigate the effects of climate change; and

(B) department-wide research strategies and actions to address the impacts of climate change on transportation systems and infrastructure.

(2) CLEARINGHOUSE.—The Office shall establish a clearinghouse of solutions, including cost-effective congestion reduction approaches, to reduce air pollution and transportation-related energy use and mitigate the effects of climate change.

(h) INTERAGENCY INFRASTRUCTURE PERMITTING IMPROVEMENT CENTER.—

(1) DEFINITIONS.—In this subsection:

(A) CENTER.—The term "Center" means the Interagency Infrastructure Permitting Improvement Center established by paragraph (2).

(B) PROJECT.—The term "project" means a project authorized or funded under—

(i) this title; or

(ii) title 14, 23, 46, or 51.

(2) ESTABLISHMENT.—There is established within the Office of the Secretary a center, to be known as the "Interagency Infrastructure Permitting Improvement Center".

(3) PURPOSES.—The purposes of the Center shall be—

(A) to implement reforms to improve interagency coordination and expedite projects relating to the permitting and environmental review of major transportation infrastructure projects, including—

(i) developing and deploying information technology tools to track project schedules and metrics; and

(ii) improving the transparency and accountability of the permitting process;

(B)(i) to identify appropriate methods to assess environmental impacts; and

(ii) to develop innovative methods for reasonable mitigation;

(C) to reduce uncertainty and delays with respect to environmental reviews and permitting; and

(D) to reduce costs and risks to taxpayers in project delivery.

(4) EXECUTIVE DIRECTOR.—The Center shall be headed by an Executive Director, who shall—

(A) report to the Under Secretary of Transportation for Policy;

(B) be responsible for the management and oversight of the daily activities, decisions, operations, and personnel of the Center; and

(C) carry out such additional duties as the Secretary may prescribe.

(5) DUTIES.—The Center shall carry out the following duties:

(A) Coordinate and support implementation of priority reform actions for Federal agency permitting and reviews.

(B) Support modernization efforts at the operating administrations within the Department and interagency pilot programs relating to innovative approaches to the permitting and review of transportation infrastructure projects.

(C) Provide technical assistance and training to Department staff on policy changes, innovative approaches to project delivery, and other topics, as appropriate.

(D) Identify, develop, and track metrics for timeliness of permit reviews, permit decisions, and project outcomes.

(E) Administer and expand the use of online transparency tools providing for—

(i) tracking and reporting of metrics;

(ii) development and posting of schedules for permit reviews and permit decisions;

(iii) the sharing of best practices relating to efficient project permitting and reviews; and

(iv) the visual display of relevant geospatial data to support the permitting process.

(F) Submit to the Secretary reports describing progress made toward achieving—

(i) greater efficiency in permitting decisions and review of infrastructure projects; and

(ii) better outcomes for communities and the environment.

(6) INNOVATIVE BEST PRACTICES.—

(A) IN GENERAL.—The Center shall work with the operating administrations within the Department, eligible entities, and other public and private interests to develop and promote best practices for innovative project delivery.

(B) ACTIVITIES.—The Center shall support the Department and operating administrations in conducting environmental reviews and permitting, together with project sponsor technical assistance activities, by—

(i) carrying out activities that are appropriate and consistent with the goals and policies of the Department to improve the delivery timelines for projects;

(ii) serving as the Department liaison to—

(I) the Council on Environmental Quality; and

(II) the Federal Permitting Improvement Steering Council established by section 41002(a) of the Fixing America's Surface Transportation Act (42 U.S.C. 4370m–1(a));

(iii) supporting the National Surface Transportation and Innovative Finance Bureau (referred to in this paragraph as the "Bureau") in implementing activities to improve delivery timelines, as described in section 116(f), for projects carried out under the programs described in section 116(d)(1) for which the Bureau administers the application process;

(iv) leading activities to improve delivery timelines for projects carried out under programs not administered by the Bureau by—

(I) coordinating efforts to improve the efficiency and effectiveness of the environmental review and permitting process;

(II) providing technical assistance and training to field and headquarters staff of Federal agencies with respect to policy changes and innovative approaches to the delivery of projects; and

(III) identifying, developing, and tracking metrics for permit reviews and decisions by Federal agencies for projects under the National Environmental Policy Act of 1969 (42 U.S.C. 4321 et seq.).

(C) NEPA COMPLIANCE ASSISTANCE.—

(i) IN GENERAL.—Subject to clause (ii), at the request of an entity that is carrying out a project, the Center, in coordination with the appropriate operating administrations within the Department, shall provide technical assistance relating to compliance with the applicable requirements of the National Environmental Policy Act of 1969 (42 U.S.C. 4321 et seq.) and applicable Federal authorizations.

(ii) ASSISTANCE FROM THE BUREAU.—For projects carried out under the programs described in section 116(d)(1) for which the Bureau administers the application process, the Bureau, on request of the entity carrying out the project, shall provide the technical assistance described in clause (i).

(i) CHIEF TRAVEL AND TOURISM OFFICER.—

(1) ESTABLISHMENT.—There is established in the Office of the Secretary of Transportation a position, to be known as the "Chief Travel and Tourism Officer".

(2) DUTIES.—The Chief Travel and Tourism Officer shall collaborate with the Assistant Secretary for Aviation and International Affairs to carry out—

(A) the National Travel and Tourism Infrastructure Strategic Plan under section 1431(e) of Public Law 114–94 (49 U.S.C. 301 note); and

(B) other travel- and tourism-related matters involving the Department of Transportation.

(j) OFFICE OF AVIATION CONSUMER PROTECTION.—

(1) ESTABLISHMENT.—There is established in the Department an Office of Aviation Consumer Protection (in this subsection referred to as the "Office") to administer and enforce the aviation consumer protection and civil rights authorities provided to the Department by statute, including the authorities under section 41712—

(A) to assist, educate, and protect passengers; and

(B) to monitor compliance with, conduct investigations relating to, and enforce, with support of attorneys in the Office of the General Counsel, including by taking appropriate action to address violations of aviation consumer protection and civil rights.

(2) LEADERSHIP.—The Office shall be headed by the Assistant Secretary for Aviation Consumer Protection (in this subsection referred to as the "Assistant Secretary").

(3) TRANSITION.—Not later than 180 days after funding is appropriated for an Office of Aviation Consumer Protection headed by an Assistant Secretary, the Office of Aviation Consumer Protection that is a unit within the Office of the General Counsel of the Department which is headed by the Assistant General Counsel for Aviation Consumer Protection shall cease to exist. The Secretary shall determine which employees are necessary to fulfill the responsibilities of the new Office of Aviation Consumer Protection and such employees shall be transferred from the Office of the

General Counsel, as appropriate, to the newly established Office of Aviation Consumer Protection.

(4) COORDINATION.—The Assistant Secretary shall coordinate with the General Counsel appointed under subsection (e)(1)(E), in accordance with section 1.26 of title 49, Code of Federal Regulations (or a successor regulation), on all legal matters relating to—

(A) aviation consumer protection; and

(B) the duties and activities of the Office described in subparagraphs (A) through (C) [1] of paragraph (1).

(5) ANNUAL REPORT.—The Assistant Secretary shall submit to the Secretary, who shall submit to Congress and make publicly available on the website of the Department, an annual report that, with respect to matters under the jurisdiction of the Department, or otherwise within the statutory authority of the Department—

(A) analyzes trends in aviation consumer protection, civil rights, and licensing;

(B) identifies major challenges facing passengers; and

(C) addresses any other relevant issues, as the Assistant Secretary determines to be appropriate.

(6) FUNDING.—There is authorized to be appropriated $12,000,000 for fiscal year 2024, $13,000,000 for fiscal year 2025, $14,000,000 for fiscal year 2026, $15,000,000 for fiscal year 2027, and $16,000,000 for fiscal year 2028 to carry out this subsection.

(Pub. L. 97–449, §1(b), Jan. 12, 1983, 96 Stat. 2414; Pub. L. 98–557, §26(a), Oct. 30, 1984, 98 Stat. 2873; Pub. L. 103–272, §4(j)(1), July 5, 1994, 108 Stat. 1365; Pub. L. 107–295, title II, §215(a), (c), Nov. 25, 2002, 116 Stat. 2101, 2102; Pub. L. 109–59, title I, §1119(l), Aug. 10, 2005, 119 Stat. 1189; Pub. L. 110–140, title XI, §1101(a), Dec. 19, 2007, 121 Stat. 1756; Pub. L. 112–166, §2(k)(1), Aug. 10, 2012, 126 Stat. 1286; Pub. L. 114–94, div. A, title VI, §6011(a), Dec. 4, 2015, 129 Stat. 1568; Pub. L. 117–58, div. A, title IV, §14009, div. B, title V, §§25009(a), 25018(b), Nov. 15, 2021, 135 Stat. 651, 852, 875; Pub. L. 118–63, title V, §501, May 16, 2024, 138 Stat. 1186.)

[1] So in original. Paragraph (1) does not contain a subparagraph (C).

* * * * * * *

§106. FEDERAL AVIATION ADMINISTRATION

(a) IN GENERAL.—The Federal Aviation Administration is an administration in the Department of Transportation.

(b) ADMINISTRATION LEADERSHIP.—

(1) ADMINISTRATOR.—

(A) IN GENERAL.—The head of the Administration is the Administrator, who shall be appointed by the President, by and with the advice and consent of the Senate.

(B) QUALIFICATIONS.—The Administrator shall—

(i) be a citizen of the United States;

(ii) not be an active duty member of the Armed Forces;

(iii) not have retired from the Armed Forces within the 7 years preceding nomination; and

(iv) have experience in organizational management and a field directly related to aviation.

(C) FITNESS.—In appointing an individual as Administrator, the President shall consider the fitness of such individual to carry out efficiently the duties and powers of the office.

(D) TERM OF OFFICE.—The term of office for any individual appointed as Administrator shall be 5 years.

(E) REPORTING CHAIN.—Except as provided in subsection (f) or in other provisions of law, the Administrator reports directly to the Secretary of Transportation.

(2) DEPUTY ADMINISTRATOR.—

(A) IN GENERAL.—The Administrator has a Deputy Administrator, who shall be appointed by the President.

(B) QUALIFICATIONS.—The Deputy Administrator shall—

(i) be a citizen of the United States; and

(ii) have experience in organizational management and a field directly related to aviation.

(C) FITNESS.—In appointing an individual as Deputy Administrator, the President shall consider the fitness of the individual to carry out efficiently the duties and powers of the office, including the duty to act for the Administrator when the Administrator is absent or unable to serve, or when the office of Administrator is vacant.

(D) REPORTING CHAIN.—The Deputy Administrator reports directly to the Administrator.

(E) DUTIES.—The Deputy Administrator shall carry out duties and powers prescribed by the Administrator.

(F) COMPENSATION.—

(i) ANNUAL RATE OF BASIC PAY.—The annual rate of basic pay of the Deputy Administrator shall be set by the Secretary but shall not exceed the annual rate of basic pay payable to the Administrator.

(ii) EXCEPTION.—A retired regular officer of the Armed Forces serving as the Deputy Administrator is entitled to hold a rank and grade not lower than that held when appointed as the Deputy Administrator and may elect to receive—

(I) the pay provided for the Deputy Administrator under clause (i); or

(II) the pay and allowances or the retired pay of the military grade held.

(iii) REIMBURSEMENT OF EXPENSES.—If the Deputy Administrator elects to receive compensation described in clause (ii)(II), the Administration shall reimburse the appropriate military department from funds available for the expenses of the Administration.

(3) LEADERSHIP OF THE ADMINISTRATION DEFINED.—In this section, the term "leadership of the Administration" means—

(A) the Administrator under paragraph (1); and

(B) the Deputy Administrator under paragraph (2).

(c) ASSISTANT ADMINISTRATOR FOR RULEMAKING AND REGULATORY IMPROVEMENT.—There is an Assistant Administrator for Rulemaking and Regulatory Improvement who shall be appointed by the Administrator and shall—

(1) be responsible for developing and managing the execution of a regulatory agenda for the Administration that meets statutory and Administration deadlines, including by—

(A) prioritizing rulemaking projects that are necessary to improve safety;

(B) establishing the regulatory agenda of the Administration; and

(C) coordinating with offices of the Administration, the Department, and other Federal entities as appropriate to improve timely feedback generation and approvals when required by law;

(2) not delegate overall responsibility for meeting internal timelines and final completion of the regulatory activities of the Administration outside the Office of the Assistant Administrator for Rulemaking and Regulatory Improvement;

(3) on an ongoing basis, review the regulations of the Administration in effect to—

(A) improve safety;

(B) reduce undue regulatory burden;

(C) replace prescriptive regulations with performance-based regulations, as appropriate;

(D) prevent duplicative regulations; and

(E) increase regulatory clarity and transparency whenever possible;

(4) make recommendations for the review of the Administrator under subsection (f)(3)(C)(ii);

(5) receive, coordinate, and respond to petitions for rulemaking and for exemption as provided for in subpart A of part 11 of title 14, Code of Federal Regulations, and provide an initial response to a petitioner not later than 30 days after the receipt of such a petition—

(A) acknowledging receipt of such petition;

(B) confirming completeness of such petition;

(C) providing an initial indication of the complexity of the request and how such complexity may impact the timeline for adjudication; and

(D) requesting any additional information, as appropriate, that would assist in the consideration of the petition;

(6) track the issuance of exemptions and waivers by the Administration to sections of title 14, Code of Federal Regulations, and establish a methodology by which to determine if it would be more efficient and in the interest of the public to amend a rule to reduce the future need of waivers and exemptions; and

(7) promulgate regulatory updates as determined more efficient or in the best interest of the public under paragraph (6).

(d) [Reserved].

(e) PROHIBITION ON CONFLICTING PECUNIARY INTERESTS.—

(1) IN GENERAL.—The leadership of the Administration may not have a pecuniary interest in, or hold a financial interest in, an aeronautical enterprise or engage in another business, vocation, or employment.

(2) TEACHING.—Notwithstanding paragraph (1), the Deputy Administrator may not receive compensation for teaching without prior approval of the Administrator.

(3) FINANCIAL INTEREST DEFINED.—In this subsection, the term "financial interest"—

(A) means—

(i) any current or contingent ownership, equity, or security interest;

(ii) any indebtedness or compensated employment relationship; or

(iii) any right to purchase or acquire any such ownership, equity, or security interest, including a stock option; and

(B) does not include securities held in an index fund.

(f) AUTHORITY OF THE SECRETARY AND THE ADMINISTRATOR.—

(1) AUTHORITY OF THE SECRETARY.—Except as provided in paragraphs (2) and (3), the Secretary of Transportation shall carry out the duties and powers, and controls the personnel and activities, of the Administration. In exercising duties, powers, and authorities that are assigned to the Secretary or the Administrator under this title, neither the Secretary nor the Administrator may submit decisions for the approval of, or be bound by the decisions or recommendations of, a committee, board, council, or organization that is—

(A) established by executive order; or

(B) not explicitly directed by legislation to review the exercise of such duties, powers, and authorities by the Secretary or the Administrator.

(2) AUTHORITY OF THE ADMINISTRATOR.—The Administrator—

(A) is the final authority for carrying out all functions, powers, and duties of the Administration relating to—

(i) the appointment and employment of all officers and employees of the Administration (other than Presidential and political appointees);

(ii) the acquisition, establishment, improvement, operation, maintenance, security (including cybersecurity), and disposal of property, facilities, services, and equipment of the Administration, including all elements of the air traffic control system owned by the Administration;

(iii) except as otherwise provided in paragraph (4), the promulgation of regulations, rules, orders, circulars, bulletins, and other official publications of the Administration; and

(iv) any obligation imposed on the Administrator, or power conferred on the Administrator, by the Air Traffic Management System Performance Improvement Act of 1996 (or any amendment made by that Act);

(B) shall offer advice and counsel to the President with respect to civil aviation, any matter for which the Administrator is the final authority under subparagraph (A), any duty carried out by the Administrator pursuant to paragraph (3), or the provisions of this title, or the appointment and qualifications of any officer or employee of the Administration to be appointed by the President or as a political appointee;

(C) may delegate, and authorize successive redelegations of, to an officer or employee of the Administration any function, power, or duty conferred upon the Administrator, unless such delegation is prohibited by law; and

(D) except as otherwise provided for in this title, and notwithstanding any other provision of law, shall not be required to coordinate, submit for approval or concurrence, or seek the advice or views of the Secretary or any other officer or employee of the Department of Transportation on any matter with respect to which the Administrator is the final authority.

(3) DUTIES AND POWERS OF THE ADMINISTRATOR.—

(A) IN GENERAL.—The Administrator shall carry out—

(i) the duties and powers of the Secretary under this subsection related to aviation safety (except duties and powers related to transportation, packaging, marking, or description of hazardous material) and stated in—

(I) subsections (c) and (d) of section 1132;

(II) sections 40101(c), 40103(b), 40106(a), 40108, 40109(b), 40113(a), 40113(c), 40113(d), 40113(e), 40114(a), and 40117;

(III) chapter 443;

(IV) chapter 445, except sections 44502(a)(3), 44503, and 44509;

(V) chapter 447, except sections 44721(b) and 44723;

(VI) chapter 448;

(VII) chapter 451;

(VIII) chapter 453;

(IX) section 46104;

(X) subsections (d) and (h)(2) of section 46301, section 46303(c), sections 46304 through 46308, section 46310, section 46311, and sections 46313 through 46320;

(XI) chapter 465;

(XII) chapter 471;

(XIII) chapter 475; and

(XIV) chapter 509 of title 51; and

(ii) such additional duties and powers as may be prescribed by the Secretary.

(B) APPLICABILITY.—Section 40101(d) applies to the duties and powers specified in subparagraph (A).

(C) TRANSFER.—Any of the duties and powers specified in subparagraph (A) may only be transferred to another part of the Department if specifically provided by law or in a reorganization plan submitted under chapter 9 of title 5.

(D) ADMINISTRATIVE FINALITY.—A decision of the Administrator in carrying out the duties or powers specified in subparagraph (A) is administratively final.

(4) REGULATIONS.—

(A) IN GENERAL.—

(i) ISSUANCE OF REGULATIONS.—In the performance of the functions of the Administrator and the Administration, the Administrator is authorized to issue, rescind, and revise such regulations as are necessary to carry out those functions. The issuance of such regulations shall be governed by the provisions of chapter 5 of title 5.

(ii) PETITIONS FOR RULEMAKING.—The Administrator shall act upon all petitions for rulemaking no later than 6 months after the date such petitions are filed by dismissing such petitions, by informing the petitioner of an intention to dismiss, or by issuing a notice of proposed rulemaking or advanced notice of proposed rulemaking.

(iii) RULEMAKING TIMELINE.—The Administrator shall issue a final regulation, or take other final action, not later than 16 months after the last day of the public comment period for the regulations or, in the case of an advanced notice of proposed rulemaking, if issued, not later than 24 months after the date of publication in the Federal Register of notice of the proposed rulemaking.

(iv) REPORTING REQUIREMENT.—On February 1 and August 1 of each year the Administrator shall submit to the Committee on Transportation and Infrastructure of the House of Representatives and the Committee on Commerce, Science, and

Transportation of the Senate a letter listing each deadline the Administrator missed under this subparagraph during the 6-month period ending on such date, including an explanation for missing the deadline and a projected date on which the action that was subject to the deadline will be taken.

(B) APPROVAL OF SECRETARY OF TRANSPORTATION.—

(i) IN GENERAL.—The Administrator may not issue, unless the Secretary of Transportation approves the issuance of the regulation in advance, a proposed regulation or final regulation that—

(I) is likely to result in the expenditure by State, local, and Tribal governments in the aggregate, or by the private sector, of $250,000,000 or more (adjusted annually for inflation beginning with the year following the date of enactment of the FAA Reauthorization Act of 2024) in any year; or

(II) is significant.

(ii) SIGNIFICANT REGULATIONS.—For purposes of this paragraph, a regulation is significant if the Administrator, in consultation with the Secretary (as appropriate), determines that the regulation—

(I) will have an annual effect on the economy of $250,000,000 or more (adjusted annually for inflation beginning with the year following the date of enactment of the FAA Reauthorization Act of 2024);

(II) raises novel or serious legal or policy issues that will substantially and materially affect other transportation modes; or

(III) adversely affects, in a substantial and material way, the economy, a sector of the economy, productivity, competition, jobs, the environment, public health or safety, or a State, local, or Tribal government or community.

(iii) EMERGENCY REGULATION.—

(I) IN GENERAL.—In an emergency as determined by the Administrator, the Administrator may issue a final regulation described in clause (i) without prior approval of the Secretary.

(II) OBJECTION.—If the Secretary objects to a regulation issued under subclause (II) [1] in writing not later than 5 days (excluding Saturday, Sundays, and legal public holidays) after the issuance, the Administrator shall immediately rescind such regulation.

(iv) OTHER REGULATIONS.—The Secretary may not require that the Administrator submit a proposed or final regulation to the Secretary for approval, nor may the Administrator submit a proposed or final regulation to the Secretary for approval, if the regulation—

(I) does not require the approval of the Secretary under clause (i) (excluding a regulation issued under clause (iii)); or

(II) is a routine or frequent action or a procedural action.

(v) TIMELINE.—The Administrator shall submit a copy of any proposed or final regulation requiring approval by the Secretary under clause (i) to the Secretary, who shall either approve the regulation or return the regulation to the Administrator with comments not later than 30 days after receiving the regulation. If the Secretary fails to approve or return the regulation with comments to the Administrator not later than 30 days after receiving such regulation, the regulation shall be deemed to have been approved by the Secretary.

(C) PERIODIC REVIEW.—

(i) IN GENERAL.—For any significant regulation issued after the date of enactment of the FAA Reauthorization Act of 2024, in addition to the review requirements established under section 5.13(d)of title 49, Code of Federal Regulations, the Administrator shall review any significant regulation 3 years after the effective date of such regulation.

(ii) DISCRETIONARY REVIEW.—The Administrator may review any regulation that has been in effect for more than 3 years.

(iii) SUBSTANCE OF REVIEW.—In performing a review under clause (i) or (ii), the Administrator shall determine if—

(I) the cost assumptions supporting the regulation were accurate;

(II) the intended benefit of the regulation is being realized;

(III) the need remains to continue such regulation as in effect; and

(IV) the Administrator recommends updates to such regulation based on the review criteria specified in section 5.13(d) of title 49, Code of Federal Regulations.

(iv) REVIEW MANAGEMENT.—Any periodic review of a regulation under this subparagraph shall be managed by the Assistant Administrator for Rulemaking and Regulatory Improvement, who may task an advisory committee or the Management Advisory Council established under subsection (p) to assist in performing the review.

(5) DEFINITION OF POLITICAL APPOINTEE.—For purposes of this subsection, the term "political appointee" means any individual who—

(A) is employed in a position listed in sections 5312 through 5316 of title 5 (relating to the Executive Schedule);

(B) is a limited term appointee, limited emergency appointee, or noncareer appointee in the Senior Executive Service, as defined under paragraphs (5), (6), and (7), respectively, of section 3132(a) of title 5; or

(C) is employed in a position in the executive branch of the Government of a confidential or policy-determining character under schedule C of subpart C of part 213 of title 5 of the Code of Federal Regulations.

(g) [reserved].

(h) TECHNICAL CENTER FOR ADVANCED AEROSPACE.—

(1) IN GENERAL.—There is established within the Administration a technology center to support the advancement of aerospace safety and innovation which shall be known as the "William J. Hughes Technical Center for Advanced Aerospace" (in this subsection referred to as the "Technical Center") that shall be used by the Administrator and, as permitted by the Administrator, other governmental entities, academia, and the aerospace industry.

(2) MANAGEMENT.—The activities of the Technical Center shall be managed by a Director.

(3) ACTIVITIES.—The activities of the Technical Center shall include—

(A) developing and stimulating technology partnerships with and between industry, academia, and other government agencies and supporting such partnerships by—

(i) liaising between external persons and offices of the Administration interested in such work;

(ii) providing technical expertise and input, as appropriate; and

(iii) providing access to the properties, facilities, and systems of the Technical Center through appropriate agreements;

(B) managing technology demonstration grants awarded by the Administrator;

(C) identifying software, systems, services, and technologies that could improve aviation safety and the operations and management of the air traffic control system and working with relevant offices of the Administration to consider the use and integration of such software, systems, services, and technologies, as appropriate;

(D) supporting the work of any collocated facilities and tenants of such facilities, and to the extent feasible, enter into agreements as necessary to utilize the facilities, systems, and technologies of such collocated facilities and tenants;

(E) managing the facilities of the Technical Center; and

(F) carrying out any other duties as determined appropriate by the Administrator.

(i) The Deputy Administrator shall carry out duties and powers prescribed by the Administrator. The Deputy Administrator acts for the Administrator when the Administrator is absent or unable to serve, or when the office of the Administrator is vacant.

(j) CIVIL AEROMEDICAL INSTITUTE.—There is established within the Federal Aviation Administration an institute to conduct civil aeromedical research under section 44507 of this title. Such institute shall be known as the "Civil Aeromedical Institute". Research conducted by the institute should take appropriate advantage of capabilities of other government agencies, universities, or the private sector.

(k) AUTHORIZATION OF APPROPRIATIONS FOR OPERATIONS.—

(1) SALARIES, OPERATIONS, AND MAINTENANCE.—There is authorized to be appropriated to the Secretary of Transportation for salaries, operations, and maintenance of the Administration—

(A) $12,729,627,000 for fiscal year 2024;

(B) $13,055,000,000 for fiscal year 2025;

(C) $13,354,000,000 for fiscal year 2026;

(D) $13,650,000,000 for fiscal year 2027; and

(E) $13,954,000,000 for fiscal year 2028.

Such sums shall remain available until expended.

(2) AUTHORIZED EXPENDITURES.—Out of amounts appropriated under paragraph (1), the following expenditures are authorized:

(A) Such sums as may be necessary for fiscal years 2012 through 2015 to carry out and expand the Air Traffic Control Collegiate Training Initiative.

(B) Such sums as may be necessary for fiscal years 2012 through 2015 for the completion of the Alaska aviation safety project with respect to the 3 dimensional mapping of Alaska's main aviation corridors.

(C) Such sums as may be necessary for fiscal years 2012 through 2015 to carry out the Aviation Safety Reporting System and the development and maintenance of helicopter approach procedures.

(D) Not more than the following amounts for commercial space transportation activities:

(i) $75,938,000 for fiscal year 2023.

(ii) $42,018,000 for fiscal year 2024.

(iii) $52,985,000 for fiscal year 2025.

(iv) $59,044,000 for fiscal year 2026.

(v) $65,225,000 for fiscal year 2027.

(vi) $71,529,000 for fiscal year 2028.

(3) ADMINISTERING PROGRAM WITHIN AVAILABLE FUNDING.—

(A) IN GENERAL.—Notwithstanding any other provision of law, in each of fiscal years 2024 through 2028, if the Secretary determines that the funds appropriated under paragraph (1) are insufficient to meet the salary, operations, and maintenance expenses of the Federal Aviation Administration, as authorized by this section, the Secretary shall reduce nonsafety-related activities of the Administration as necessary to reduce such expenses to a level that can be met by the funding available under paragraph (1).

(B) PRIORITIZATION.—In reducing non-safety-related activities of the Administration under subparagraph (A), the Secretary shall prioritize such reductions from amounts other than amounts authorized under this subsection, section 48101, or section 48103.

(C) SUNSET.—This paragraph shall cease to be effective on October 1, 2028.

(l) PERSONNEL AND SERVICES.—

(1) OFFICERS AND EMPLOYEES.—Except as provided in subsections (a) and (g) of section 40122, the Administrator is authorized, in the performance of the functions of the Administrator, to appoint, transfer, and fix the compensation of such officers and employees, including attorneys, as may be necessary to carry out the functions of the Administrator and the Administration. In fixing compensation and benefits of officers and employees, the Administrator shall not engage in any type of bargaining, except to the extent provided for in section 40122(a), nor shall the Administrator be bound by any requirement to establish such compensation or benefits at particular levels.

(2) EXPERTS AND CONSULTANTS.—The Administrator is authorized to obtain the services of experts and consultants in accordance with section 3109 of title 5.

(3) TRANSPORTATION AND PER DIEM EXPENSES.—The Administrator is authorized to pay transportation expenses, and per diem in lieu of subsistence expenses, in accordance with chapter 57 of title 5.

(4) USE OF PERSONNEL FROM OTHER AGENCIES.—The Administrator is authorized to utilize the services of personnel of any other Federal agency (as such term is defined under section 551(1) of title 5).

(5) VOLUNTARY SERVICES.—

(A) GENERAL RULE.—In exercising the authority to accept gifts and voluntary services under section 326 of this title, and without regard to section 1342 of title 31, the Administrator may not accept voluntary and uncompensated services if such services are used to displace Federal employees employed on a full-time, part-time, or seasonal basis.

(B) INCIDENTAL EXPENSES.—The Administrator is authorized to provide for incidental expenses, including transportation, lodging, and subsistence, for volunteers who provide voluntary services under this subsection.

(C) LIMITED TREATMENT AS FEDERAL EMPLOYEES.—An individual who provides voluntary services under this subsection shall not be considered a Federal employee for any purpose other than for purposes of chapter 81 of title 5, relating to compensation for work injuries, and chapter 171 of title 28, relating to tort claims.

(6) CONTRACTS.—The Administrator is authorized to enter into and perform such contracts, leases, cooperative agreements, or other transactions as may be necessary to carry out the functions of the Administrator and the Administration. The Administrator may enter into such contracts, leases, cooperative agreements, and other transactions with any Federal agency (as such term is defined in section 551(1) of title 5) or any instrumentality of the United States, any State, territory, or possession, or political subdivision thereof, any other governmental entity, or any person, firm, association, corporation, or educational institution, on such terms and conditions as the Administrator may consider appropriate.

(7) PROHIBITION ON CERTAIN PERFORMANCE-BASED INCENTIVES.—No employee of the Administration shall be given an award, financial incentive, or other compensation, as a result of actions to meet performance goals related to meeting or exceeding schedules, quotas, or deadlines for certificates issued under section 44704.

(m) COOPERATION BY ADMINISTRATOR.—With the consent of appropriate officials, the Administrator may, with or without reimbursement, use or accept the services, equipment, personnel, and facilities of any other Federal agency (as such term is defined in section 551(1) of title 5) and any other public or private entity. The Administrator may also cooperate with appropriate officials of other public and private agencies and instrumentalities concerning the use of services, equipment, personnel, and facilities. The head of each Federal agency shall cooperate with the Administrator in making the services, equipment, personnel, and facilities of the Federal agency available to the Administrator. The head of a Federal agency is authorized, notwithstanding any other provision of law, to transfer to or to receive from the Administration, with or without reimbursement, supplies, personnel, services, and equipment other than administrative supplies or equipment.

(n) ACQUISITION.—

(1) IN GENERAL.—The Administrator is authorized—

(A) to acquire (by purchase, lease, condemnation, or otherwise), construct, improve, repair, operate, and maintain—

(i) air traffic control facilities and equipment;

(ii) research and testing sites and facilities; and

(iii) such other real and personal property (including office space and patents), or any interest therein, within and outside the continental United States as the Administrator considers necessary;

(B) to lease to others such real and personal property; and

(C) to provide by contract or otherwise for eating facilities and other necessary facilities for the welfare of employees of the Administration at the installations of the Administration, and to acquire, operate, and maintain equipment for these facilities.

(2) TITLE.—Title to any property or interest therein acquired pursuant to this subsection shall be held by the Government of the United States.

(o) TRANSFERS OF FUNDS.—The Administrator is authorized to accept transfers of unobligated balances and unexpended balances of funds appropriated to other Federal agencies (as such term is defined in section 551(1) of title 5) to carry out functions transferred by law to the Administrator or functions transferred pursuant to law to the Administrator on or after the date of the enactment of the Air Traffic Management System Performance Improvement Act of 1996.

(p) MANAGEMENT ADVISORY COUNCIL.—

(1) ESTABLISHMENT.—The Administrator shall establish an advisory council which shall be known as the Federal Aerospace Management Advisory Council (in this subsection referred to as the "Council").

(2) MEMBERSHIP.—The Council shall consist of 13 members, who shall consist of—

(A) a designee of the Secretary of Transportation;

(B) a designee of the Secretary of Defense;

(C) 5 members representing aerospace and technology interests, appointed by the Administrator;

(D) 5 members representing aerospace and technology interests, appointed by the Secretary of Transportation; and

(E) 1 member, appointed by the Secretary of Transportation, who is the head of a union representing air traffic control system employees.

(3) QUALIFICATIONS.—No officer or employee of the Federal Government may be appointed to the Council under subparagraph (C) or (D) of paragraph (2).

(4) FUNCTIONS.—

(A) IN GENERAL.—

(i) ADVISE; COUNSEL.—The Council shall provide advice and counsel to the Administrator on issues which affect or are affected by the activities of the Administrator.

(ii) RESOURCE.—The Council shall function as an oversight resource for management, policy, spending, and regulatory matters under the jurisdiction of the Administrator.

(iii) SUBMISSIONS TO ADMINISTRATION.—With respect to Administration management, policy, spending, funding, data management and analysis, safety initiatives, international agreements, activities of the International Civil Aviation Organization, and regulatory matters affecting the aerospace industry and the national airspace system, the Council may—

(I) regardless of whether solicited by the Administrator, submit comments, recommended modifications, proposals, and supporting or dissenting views to the Administrator; and

(II) request the Administrator include in any submission to Congress, the Secretary, or the general public, and in any submission for publication in the Federal Register, a description of the comments, recommended modifications, and dissenting or supporting views received from the Council under subclause (I).

(iv) REASONING.—Together with a Council submission that is published or described under clause (iii)(II), the Administrator may provide the reasons for any differences between the views of the Council and the views or actions of the Administrator.

(v) COST-BENEFIT ANALYSIS.—The Council shall review the rulemaking cost-benefit analysis process and develop recommendations to improve the analysis and ensure that the public interest is fully protected.

(vi) PROCESS REVIEW.—The Council shall review the process through which the Administration determines to use advisory circulars, service bulletins, and other externally facing guidance and regulatory material.

(B) MEETINGS.—The Council shall meet not less than 3 times annually or at the call of the chair or the Administrator.

(C) ACCESS TO DOCUMENTS AND STAFF.—The Administrator may give the Council appropriate access to relevant documents and personnel of the Administration, and the Administrator shall make available, consistent with the authority to withhold commercial and other proprietary information under section 552 of title 5 (commonly known as the "Freedom of Information Act"), cost data associated with the acquisition and operation of air traffic service systems.

(D) DISCLOSURE OF COMMERCIAL OR PROPRIETARY DATA.—Any member of the Council who receives commercial or other proprietary data as provided for in this paragraph from the Administrator shall be subject to the provisions of section 1905 of title 18, pertaining to unauthorized disclosure of such information.

(5) APPLICATION OF CHAPTER 10 OF TITLE 5.—Chapter 10 of title 5 does not apply to—

(A) the Council;

(B) such aviation rulemaking committees as the Administrator shall designate; or

(C) such aerospace rulemaking committees as the Secretary shall designate.

(6) ADMINISTRATIVE MATTERS.—

(A) TERMS.—Members of the Council appointed under paragraph (2)(C) shall be appointed for a term of 3 years.

(B) TERM FOR AIR TRAFFIC CONTROL REPRESENTATIVE.—The member appointed under paragraph (2)(E) shall be appointed for a term of 3 years, except that the term of such individual shall end whenever the individual no longer meets the requirements of paragraph (2)(E).

(C) VACANCY.—Any vacancy on the Council shall be filled in the same manner as the original appointment, except that any member appointed to fill a vacancy occurring before the expiration of the term for which the predecessor of the member was appointed shall be appointed for the remainder of that term.

(D) CONTINUATION IN OFFICE.—A member of the Council whose term expires shall continue to serve until the date on which the successor of the member takes office.

(E) REMOVAL.—Any member of the Council appointed under paragraph (2) may be removed for cause by whomever makes the appointment.

(F) CHAIR; VICE CHAIR.—The Council shall elect a chair and a vice chair from among the members appointed under subparagraphs (C) and (D) of paragraph (2), each of whom shall serve for a term of 1 year. The vice chair shall perform the duties of the chair in the absence of the chair.

(G) TRAVEL AND PER DIEM.—Each member of the Council shall be paid actual travel expenses, and per diem in lieu of subsistence expenses when away from the usual place of residence of the member, in accordance with section 5703 of title 5.

(H) DETAIL OF PERSONNEL FROM THE ADMINISTRATION.—The Administrator shall make available to the Council such staff, information, and administrative services and assistance as may reasonably be required to enable the Council to carry out the responsibilities of the Council under this subsection.

(q) AIRCRAFT NOISE OMBUDSMAN.—

(1) ESTABLISHMENT.—There shall be in the Administration an Aircraft Noise Ombudsman.

(2) GENERAL DUTIES AND RESPONSIBILITIES.—The Ombudsman shall—

(A) be appointed by the Administrator;

(B) serve as a liaison with the public on issues regarding aircraft noise; and

(C) be consulted when the Administration proposes changes in aircraft routes so as to minimize any increases in aircraft noise over populated areas.

(3) NUMBER OF FULL-TIME EQUIVALENT EMPLOYEES.—The appointment of an Ombudsman under this subsection shall not result in an increase in the number of full-time equivalent employees in the Administration.

(r) CHIEF OPERATING OFFICER.—

(1) IN GENERAL.—

(A) APPOINTMENT.—There shall be a Chief Operating Officer for the air traffic control system who is appointed by the Administrator and subject to the authority of the Administrator.

(B) QUALIFICATIONS.—The Chief Operating Officer shall have a demonstrated ability in management and knowledge of or experience in aviation.

(C) TERM.—The Chief Operating Officer shall be appointed for a term of 5 years.

(D) REMOVAL.—The Chief Operating Officer shall serve at the pleasure of the Administrator, except that the Administrator shall make every effort to ensure stability and continuity in the leadership of the air traffic control system.

(E) VACANCY.—Any individual appointed to fill a vacancy in the position of Chief Operating Officer occurring before the expiration of the term for which the individual's predecessor was appointed may be appointed for either the remainder of the term or for a full term.

(2) COMPENSATION.—

(A) IN GENERAL.—The Chief Operating Officer shall be paid at an annual rate of basic pay to be determined by the Administrator. The annual rate may not exceed the annual compensation paid under section 102 of title 3. The Chief Operating Officer shall be subject to the post-employment provisions of section 207 of title 18 as if the position of Chief Operating Officer were described in section 207(c)(2)(A)(i) of that title.

(B) BONUS.—In addition to the annual rate of basic pay authorized by subparagraph (A), the Chief Operating Officer may receive a bonus for any calendar year not to exceed 30 percent of the annual rate of basic pay, based upon the Administrator's evaluation of the Chief Operating Officer's performance in relation to the performance goals set forth in the performance agreement described in paragraph (3).

(3) ANNUAL PERFORMANCE AGREEMENT.—The Administrator and the Chief Operating Officer shall enter into an annual performance agreement that sets forth measurable organization and individual goals for the Chief Operating Officer in key operational areas. The agreement shall be subject to review and renegotiation on an annual basis and shall include responsibility for—

(A) the state of good repair of the air traffic control system;

(B) the continuous improvement of the safety and efficiency of the air traffic control system; and

(C) identifying services and solutions to increase the safety and efficiency of airspace use and to support the safe integration of all airspace users.

(4) ANNUAL PERFORMANCE REPORT.—The Chief Operating Officer shall prepare and transmit to the Secretary of Transportation, the Committee on Transportation and Infrastructure of the House of Representatives, and the Committee on Commerce, Science, and Transportation of the Senate an annual management report containing the annual performance agreement required under paragraph (3), an assessment of the performance of the Chief Operating Officer in relation to the performance goals in the performance agreement for the previous year, and such other information as may be prescribed by the Administrator.

(5) RESPONSIBILITIES.—The Administrator may delegate to the Chief Operating Officer any authority of the Administrator and shall delegate, at a minimum the following:

(A) STRATEGIC PLANS.—To implement the strategic plan of the Administration for the air traffic control system in order to further—

(i) a mission and objectives;

(ii) standards of performance relative to such mission and objectives, including safety, efficiency, and productivity;

(iii) annual and long-range strategic plans;

(iv) methods of the Administration to accelerate air traffic control modernization and improvements in aviation safety related to air traffic control; and

(v) plans to integrate new entrant operations into the national airspace system and associated action items.

(B) OPERATIONS.—To oversee the day-to-day operational functions of the Administration for air traffic control, including—

(i) modernization of the air traffic control system;

(ii) increasing productivity or implementing cost-saving measures;

(iii) training and education; and

(iv) the management of cost-reimbursable contracts.

(C) BUDGET.—To—

(i) develop a budget request of the Administration related to the air traffic control system;

(ii) submit such budget request to the Administrator; and

(iii) ensure that the budget request supports the agency's annual and long-range strategic plans for air traffic control services.

(6) UNFUNDED CAPITAL INVESTMENT NEEDS REPORT.—

(A) IN GENERAL.—Not later than 10 days after the date on which the budget of the President for a fiscal year is submitted to Congress pursuant to section 1150 of title 31,[2] the Administrator shall submit to the Secretary, the Committee on Transportation and Infrastructure of the House of Representatives, and the Committee on Commerce, Science, and Transportation of the Senate a report on any unfunded capital investment needs of the air traffic control system.

(B) CONTENTS OF BRIEFING.—In providing the report under subparagraph (A), the

Administrator shall include, for each unfunded capital investment need, the following:

(i) A summary description of such unfunded capital investment need.

(ii) The objective to be achieved if such unfunded capital investment need is funded in whole or in part.

(iii) The additional amount of funds recommended in connection with such objective.

(iv) The Budget Line Item Program and Budget Line Item number associated with such unfunded capital investment need, as applicable.

(v) Any statutory requirement associated with such unfunded capital investment need, as applicable.

(C) PRIORITIZATION OF REQUIREMENTS.—The briefing required under subparagraph (A) shall present unfunded capital investment needs in overall urgency of priority.

(D) UNFUNDED CAPITAL INVESTMENT NEED DEFINED.—In this paragraph, the term "unfunded capital investment need" means a program that—

(i) is not funded in the budget of the President for the fiscal year as submitted to Congress pursuant to section 1105 of title 31;

(ii) is for infrastructure or a system related to necessary modernization or sustainment of the air traffic control system;

(iii) is listed for any year in the most recent National Airspace System Capital Investment Plan of the Administration; and

(iv) would have been recommended for funding through the budget referred to in subparagraph (A) by the Administrator if—

(I) additional resources had been available for the budget to fund the program, activity, or mission requirement; or

(II) the program, activity, or mission requirement has emerged since the budget was formulated.

(7) AIR TRAFFIC CONTROL SYSTEM DEFINED.—In this section, the term "air traffic control system" has the meaning such term has under section 40102(a).

(s) CHIEF TECHNOLOGY OFFICER.—

(1) IN GENERAL.—

(A) ESTABLISHMENT.—There shall be a Chief Technology Officer for the air traffic control system that shall report directly to the Chief Operating Officer of the air traffic control system.

(B) APPOINTMENT.—The Chief Technology Officer shall be appointed by the Administrator.

(C) MINIMUM QUALIFICATIONS.—The Chief Technology Officer shall have—

(i) at least 10 years experience in engineering management, systems management, or another relevant technical management field; and

(ii) knowledge of or experience in the aviation industry.

(2) RESPONSIBILITIES.—The responsibilities of the Chief Technology Officer shall include—

(A) ensuring the proper operation, maintenance, and cybersecurity of technology systems relating to the air traffic control system across all offices of the Administration;

(B) coordinating the implementation, operation, maintenance, and cybersecurity of technology programs relating to the air traffic control system with the aerospace industry and other Federal agencies;

(C) reviewing and providing advice to the Secretary, the Administrator, and the Chief Operating Officer on the Administration's budget, cost-accounting system, and benefit-cost analyses with respect to technology programs relating to the air traffic control system;

(D) consulting with the Administrator on the Capital Investment Plan of the Administration prior to its submission to Congress;

(E) developing an annual air traffic control system technology operation and maintenance plan that is consistent with the annual performance targets established under paragraph (4); and

(F) ensuring that the air traffic control system architecture remains, to the maximum extent practicable, flexible enough to incorporate future technological advances developed and directly procured by the Administration, aircraft operators, or other private providers of information and services related to air traffic management.

(3) COMPENSATION.—

(A) IN GENERAL.—The Chief Technology Officer shall be paid at an annual rate of basic pay to be determined by the Administrator, in consultation with the Chief Operating Officer. The annual rate may not exceed the annual compensation paid under section 102 of title 3.

(B) POST-EMPLOYMENT.—The Chief Technology Officer shall be subject to the postemployment provisions of section 207 of title 18 as if the position of Chief Technology Officer were described in section 207(c)(2)(A)(i) of such title.

(C) BONUS.—In addition to the annual rate of basic pay authorized by subparagraph (A), the Chief Technology Officer may receive a bonus for any calendar year not to exceed 30 percent of the annual rate of basic pay, based upon the Administrator's evaluation of the Chief Technology Officer's performance in relation to the performance targets established under paragraph (4).

(4) ANNUAL PERFORMANCE TARGETS.—

(A) IN GENERAL.—The Administrator and the Chief Operating Officer, in consultation with the Chief Technology Officer, shall establish measurable annual performance targets for the Chief Technology Officer in key operational areas.

(B) REPORT.—The Administrator shall transmit to the Committee on Transportation and Infrastructure of the House of Representatives and the Committee on Commerce, Science, and Transportation of the Senate a report describing the annual performance targets established under subparagraph (A).

(5) ANNUAL PERFORMANCE REPORT.—The Chief Technology Officer shall prepare and transmit to the Secretary of Transportation, the Committee on Transportation and Infrastructure of the House of Representatives, and the Committee on Commerce, Science, and Transportation of the Senate an annual report containing—

(A) detailed descriptions and metrics of how successful the Chief Technology Officer was in meeting the annual performance targets established under paragraph (4); and

(B) other information as may be requested by the Administrator and the Chief Operating Officer.

(t) OFFICE OF WHISTLEBLOWER PROTECTION AND AVIATION SAFETY INVESTIGATIONS.—

(1) ESTABLISHMENT.—There is established in the Federal Aviation Administration (in this subsection referred to as the "Agency") the Office of Whistleblower Protection and Aviation Safety Investigations (in this subsection referred to as the "Office").

(2) DIRECTOR.—

(A) APPOINTMENT.—The head of the Office shall be the Director, who shall be appointed by the Secretary of Transportation.

(B) QUALIFICATIONS.—The Director shall have a demonstrated ability in investigations and knowledge of or experience in aviation.

(C) TERM.—The Director shall be appointed for a term of 5 years.

(D) VACANCIES.—Any individual appointed to fill a vacancy in the position of the Director occurring before the expiration of the term for which the individual's predecessor was appointed shall be appointed for the remainder of that term.

(E) LIMITATION OF DUTIES.— The Director may only perform duties of the Director described in paragraph (3)(A).

(3) COMPLAINTS AND INVESTIGATIONS.—

(A) AUTHORITY OF DIRECTOR.—The Director shall—

(i) receive complaints and information submitted by employees of persons holding certificates issued under title 14, Code of Federal Regulations (if the certificate holder does not have a similar in-house whistleblower or safety and regulatory noncompliance reporting process established under or pursuant to a safety management system) and employees of the Agency concerning the possible existence of an activity relating to a violation of an order, a regulation, or any other provision of Federal law relating to aviation safety;

(ii) assess complaints and information submitted under clause (i) and determine whether a substantial likelihood exists that a violation of an order, a regulation, or any other provision of Federal law relating to aviation safety has occurred;

(iii) based on findings of the assessment conducted under clause (ii), make recommendations to the Administrator of the Agency, in writing, regarding further investigation or corrective actions;

(iv) receive allegations of whistleblower retaliation by employees of the Agency;

(v) coordinate with and provide all necessary assistance to the Office of Investigations and Professional Responsibility, the inspector general of the Department of Transportation, and the Office of Special Counsel on investigations relating to whistleblower retaliation by employees of the Agency; and

(vi) investigate allegations of whistleblower retaliation by employees of the Agency that have been delegated to the Office by the Office of Investigations and Professional Responsibility, the inspector general of the Department of Transportation, or the Office of Special Counsel.

(B) DISCLOSURE OF IDENTITIES.—The Director shall not disclose the identity of an individual who submits a complaint or information under subparagraph (A)(i) unless—

(i) the individual consents to the disclosure in writing; or

(ii) the Director determines, in the course of an investigation, that the disclosure is required by regulation, statute, or court order, or is otherwise unavoidable, in which case the Director shall provide the individual reasonable advanced notice of the disclosure.

(C) INDEPENDENCE OF DIRECTOR.—The Secretary, the Administrator, or any officer or employee of the Agency may not prevent or prohibit the Director from initiating, carrying out, or completing any assessment of a complaint or information submitted under subparagraph (A)(i) or from reporting to Congress on any such assessment.

(D) ACCESS TO INFORMATION.—In conducting an assessment of a complaint or information submitted under subparagraph (A)(i), the Director shall have access to all records, reports, audits, reviews, documents, papers, recommendations, and other material of the Agency necessary to determine whether a substantial likelihood exists that a violation of an order, a regulation, or any other provision of Federal law relating to aviation safety may have occurred.

(4) RESPONSES TO RECOMMENDATIONS.—Not later than 60 days after the date on which the Administrator receives a report with respect to an investigation, the Administrator shall respond to a recommendation made by the Director under paragraph (3)(A)(iii) in writing and retain records related to any further investigations or corrective actions taken in response to the recommendation.

(5) INCIDENT REPORTS.—If the Director determines there is a substantial likelihood that a violation of an order, a regulation, or any other provision of Federal law relating to aviation safety has occurred that requires immediate corrective action, the Director shall report the potential violation expeditiously to the Administrator and the Inspector General of the Department of Transportation.

(6) REPORTING OF CRIMINAL VIOLATIONS TO INSPECTOR GENERAL.—If the Director has reasonable grounds to believe that there has been a violation of Federal criminal law, the Director shall report the violation expeditiously to the Inspector General.

(7) DEPARTMENT OF TRANSPORTATION OFFICE OF THE INSPECTOR GENERAL PEER REVIEW.—

(A) IN GENERAL.—Not later than 2 years after the date of enactment of the FAA Reauthorization Act of 2024, and every 5 years thereafter, the inspector general of the Department of Transportation shall perform a peer review of the Office of Whistleblower Protection and Aviation Safety Investigations.

(B) PEER REVIEW SCOPE.—In completing the peer reviews required under this paragraph, the inspector general shall, to the extent appropriate, use the most recent peer review guides published by the Council of the Inspectors General on Integrity and Efficiency Audit Committee and Investigations Committee.

(C) REPORTS TO CONGRESS.—Not later than 90 days after the completion of a peer review required under this paragraph, the inspector general shall submit to the Committee on Transportation and Infrastructure of the House of Representatives and the Committee on Commerce, Science, and Transportation of the Senate a description of any actions taken or to be taken to address the results of the peer review.

(8) WHISTLEBLOWER OMBUDSMAN.—

(A) IN GENERAL.—Within the Office, there shall be established the position of Whistleblower Ombudsman.

(B) OMBUDSMAN QUALIFICATIONS.—The individual selected as Ombudsman shall have knowledge of Federal labor law and demonstrated government experience in human resource management and conflict resolution.

(C) DUTIES.—The Ombudsman shall carry out the following duties:

(i) Educate Administration employees about prohibitions against materially adverse acts of retaliation and any specific rights or remedies with respect to those retaliatory actions.

(ii) Serve as an independent confidential resource for Administration employees to discuss any specific retaliation allegation and available rights or remedies based on the circumstances, as appropriate.

(iii) Coordinate with Human Resource Management, the Office of Accountability and Whistleblower Protection, the Office of Professional Responsibility, and the Office of the Chief Counsel, as necessary.

(iv) Coordinate with the Office of the Inspector General of the Department of Transportation's Whistleblower Protection Coordinator and the Office of the Special Counsel, as necessary.

(v) Conduct outreach and assist in the development of training within the Agency to mitigate the potential for retaliation and promote timely and appropriate processing of any protected disclosure or allegation of materially adverse acts of retaliation.

(Pub. L. 97–449, §1(b), Jan. 12, 1983, 96 Stat. 2416; Pub. L. 98–216, §2(2), Feb. 14, 1984, 98 Stat. 5; Pub. L. 100–591, §5(a), Nov. 3, 1988, 102 Stat. 3013; Pub. L. 101–508, title IX, §9106, Nov. 5, 1990, 104 Stat. 1388–355; Pub. L. 101–604, title I, §101(c), Nov. 16, 1990, 104 Stat. 3068; Pub. L. 102–581, title I, §104, Oct. 31, 1992, 106 Stat. 4877; Pub. L. 103–272, §§4(j)(3), 5(m)(4), July 5, 1994, 108 Stat. 1365, 1375; Pub. L. 103–305, title I, §103, title II, §201, Aug. 23, 1994, 108 Stat. 1571, 1581; Pub. L. 104–264, title I, §103(a), title II, §§223(a), 224–230, 276(c), title XII, §1210, Oct. 9, 1996, 110 Stat. 3216, 3229–3234, 3282; Pub. L. 104–287, §5(1), Oct. 11, 1996, 110 Stat. 3388; Pub. L. 105–102, §3(c)(3), Nov. 20, 1997, 111 Stat. 2215; Pub. L. 106–6, §4, Mar. 31, 1999, 113 Stat. 10; Pub. L. 106–181, title I, §103(a), title III, §§302(a)–(c), 303, 305, 306, 307(c)(1), title VII, §701, Apr. 5, 2000, 114 Stat. 66, 115–118, 121, 123, 124, 126, 154; Pub. L. 106–528, §8(a), Nov. 22, 2000, 114 Stat. 2522; Pub. L. 107–71, title I, §101(c)(3), (d), Nov. 19, 2001, 115 Stat. 602, 603; Pub. L. 108–176, title I, §103(a),(b), title II, §§201–204, 224(c), Dec. 12, 2003, 117 Stat. 2495, 2496, 2522–2526, 2528; Pub. L. 110–330, §6, Sept. 30, 2008, 122 Stat. 3719; Pub. L. 111–12, §6, Mar. 30, 2009, 123 Stat. 1458; Pub. L. 111–69, §6, Oct. 1, 2009, 123 Stat. 2055; Pub. L. 111–116, §6, Dec. 16, 2009, 123 Stat. 3032; Pub. L. 111–153, §6, Mar. 31, 2010, 124 Stat. 1085; Pub. L. 111–161, §6, Apr. 30, 2010, 124 Stat. 1127; Pub. L. 111–197, §6, July 2, 2010, 124 Stat. 1354; Pub. L. 111–216, title I, §105, Aug. 1, 2010, 124 Stat. 2350; Pub. L. 112–30, title II, §206, Sept. 16, 2011, 125 Stat. 359; Pub. L. 112–91, §6, Jan. 31, 2012, 126 Stat. 4; Pub. L. 112–95, title I, §103, title II, §203, 204, title III, §§306(b), 341, Feb. 14, 2012, 126 Stat. 16, 37, 61, 78; Pub. L. 112–166, §2(k)(2), Aug. 10, 2012, 126 Stat. 1286; Pub. L. 113–188, title XV, §1501(a), Nov. 26, 2014, 128 Stat. 2023; Pub. L. 114–55, title I, §103, Sept. 30, 2015, 129 Stat. 523; Pub. L. 114–141, title I, §103, Mar. 30, 2016, 130 Stat. 323; Pub. L. 114–190, title I, §1103, July 15, 2016, 130 Stat. 618; Pub. L. 115–63, title I, §103, Sept. 29, 2017, 131 Stat. 1170; Pub. L. 115–141, div. M, title I, §103, Mar. 23, 2018, 132 Stat. 1047; Pub. L. 115–254, div. B, title I, §113, title V, §§545(a), 564, div. K, title I, §1991(a), Oct. 5, 2018, 132 Stat. 3200, 3374, 3385, 3626; Pub. L. 116–260, div. V, title I, §§114, 133(a), (b), Dec. 27, 2020, 134 Stat. 2333, 2353, 2355; Pub. L. 117–286, §4(a)(302), (c)(46), Dec. 27, 2022, 136 Stat. 4339, 4359; Pub. L. 117–328, div. Q, §104, Dec. 29, 2022, 136 Stat. 5253; Pub. L. 118–15, div. B, title II, §2203, Sept. 30, 2023, 137 Stat. 84; Pub. L. 118–34, title I, §103, Dec. 26, 2023, 137 Stat. 1114; Pub. L. 118–41, title I, §103, Mar. 8, 2024, 138 Stat. 22; Pub. L. 118–63, title I, §103, title II, §§201, 202(a), 203–204(b), 206(g), 210–214, 216, May 16, 2024, 138 Stat. 1034–1041, 1045, 1049–1054.)

---

[1] So in original. Probably should be "subclause (I)".

[2] So in original. Probably should be "section 1105 of title 31,".

* * * * * * *

§114. Transportation Security Administration

(a) In General.—The Transportation Security Administration shall be an administration of the Department of Homeland Security.

(b) Leadership.—

(1) Head of transportation security administration.—

(A) Appointment.—The head of the Administration shall be the Administrator of the Transportation Security Administration (referred to in this section as the "Administrator"). The Administrator shall be appointed by the President, by and with the advice and consent of the Senate.

(B) Qualifications.—The Administrator must—

(i) be a citizen of the United States; and

(ii) have experience in a field directly related to transportation or security.

(C) Term.—Effective with respect to any individual appointment by the President, by and with the advice and consent of the Senate, after the date of enactment of the TSA Modernization Act, the term of office of an individual appointed as the Administrator shall be 5 years. The term of office of an individual serving as the Administrator on the date of enactment of the TSA Modernization Act shall be 5 years beginning on the date that the Administrator began serving.

(2) Deputy administrator.—

(A) Appointment.—There is established in the Transportation Security Administration a Deputy Administrator, who shall assist the Administrator in the management of the Transportation Security Administration. The Deputy Administrator shall be appointed by the President.

(B) Vacancy.—The Deputy Administrator shall be Acting Administrator during the absence or incapacity of the Administrator or during a vacancy in the office of Administrator.

(C) Qualifications.—The Deputy Administrator must—

(i) be a citizen of the United States; and

(ii) have experience in a field directly related to transportation or security.

(3) Chief counsel.—

(A) Appointment.—There is established in the Transportation Security Administration a Chief Counsel, who shall advise the Administrator and other senior officials on all legal matters relating to the responsibilities, functions, and management of the Transportation Security Administration.

(B) Qualifications.—The Chief Counsel must be a citizen of the United States.

(c) Limitation on Ownership of Stocks and Bonds.—The Administrator may not own stock in or bonds of a transportation or security enterprise or an enterprise that makes equipment that could be used for security purposes.

(d) Functions.—The Administrator shall be responsible for security in all modes of transportation, including—

(1) carrying out chapter 449, relating to civil aviation security, and related research and development activities; and

(2) security responsibilities over other modes of transportation that are exercised by

the Department of Transportation.

(e) SCREENING OPERATIONS.—The Administrator shall—

(1) be responsible for day-to-day Federal security screening operations for passenger air transportation and intrastate air transportation under sections 44901 and 44935;

(2) develop standards for the hiring and retention of security screening personnel;

(3) train and test security screening personnel; and

(4) be responsible for hiring and training personnel to provide security screening at all airports in the United States where screening is required under section 44901, in consultation with the Secretary of Transportation and the heads of other appropriate Federal agencies and departments.

(f) ADDITIONAL DUTIES AND POWERS.—In addition to carrying out the functions specified in subsections (d) and (e), the Administrator shall—

(1) receive, assess, and distribute intelligence information related to transportation security;

(2) assess threats to transportation;

(3) develop policies, strategies, and plans for dealing with threats to transportation security;

(4) make other plans related to transportation security, including coordinating countermeasures with appropriate departments, agencies, and instrumentalities of the United States Government;

(5) serve as the primary liaison for transportation security to the intelligence and law enforcement communities;

(6) on a day-to-day basis, manage and provide operational guidance to the field security resources of the Administration, including Federal Security Managers as provided by section 44933;

(7) enforce security-related regulations and requirements;

(8) identify and undertake research and development activities necessary to enhance transportation security;

(9) inspect, maintain, and test security facilities, equipment, and systems;

(10) ensure the adequacy of security measures for the transportation of cargo;

(11) oversee the implementation, and ensure the adequacy, of security measures at airports and other transportation facilities;

(12) require background checks for airport security screening personnel, individuals with access to secure areas of airports, and other transportation security personnel;

(13) work in conjunction with the Administrator of the Federal Aviation Administration with respect to any actions or activities that may affect aviation safety or air carrier operations;

(14) work with the International Civil Aviation Organization and appropriate aeronautic authorities of foreign governments under section 44907 to address security concerns on passenger flights by foreign air carriers in foreign air transportation;

(15) establish and maintain a National Deployment Office as required under section 44948 of this title; and

(16) carry out such other duties, and exercise such other powers, relating to transportation security as the Administrator considers appropriate, to the extent authorized by law.

(g) NATIONAL EMERGENCY RESPONSIBILITIES.—

(1) IN GENERAL.—Subject to the direction and control of the Secretary of Homeland Security, the Administrator, during a national emergency, shall have the following responsibilities:

(A) To coordinate domestic transportation, including aviation, rail, and other surface transportation, and maritime transportation (including port security).

(B) To coordinate and oversee the transportation-related responsibilities of other departments and agencies of the Federal Government other than the Department of Defense and the military departments.

(C) To coordinate and provide notice to other departments and agencies of the Federal Government, and appropriate agencies of State and local governments, including departments and agencies for transportation, law enforcement, and border control, about threats to transportation.

(D) To carry out such other duties, and exercise such other powers, relating to transportation during a national emergency as the Secretary of Homeland Security shall prescribe.

(2) AUTHORITY OF OTHER DEPARTMENTS AND AGENCIES.—The authority of the Administrator under this subsection shall not supersede the authority of any other department or agency of the Federal Government under law with respect to transportation or transportation-related matters, whether or not during a national emergency.

(3) CIRCUMSTANCES.—The Secretary of Homeland Security shall prescribe the circumstances constituting a national emergency for purposes of this subsection.

(h) MANAGEMENT OF SECURITY INFORMATION.—In consultation with the Transportation Security Oversight Board, the Administrator shall—

(1) enter into memoranda of understanding with Federal agencies or other entities to share or otherwise cross-check as necessary data on individuals identified on Federal agency databases who may pose a risk to transportation or national security;

(2) establish procedures for notifying the Administrator of the Federal Aviation Administration, appropriate State and local law enforcement officials, and airport or airline security officers of the identity of individuals known to pose, or suspected of posing, a risk of air piracy or terrorism or a threat to airline or passenger safety;

(3) in consultation with other appropriate Federal agencies and air carriers, establish policies and procedures requiring air carriers—

(A) to use information from government agencies to identify individuals on passenger lists who may be a threat to civil aviation or national security; and

(B) if such an individual is identified, notify appropriate law enforcement agencies, prevent the individual from boarding an aircraft, or take other appropriate action with respect to that individual; and

(4) consider requiring passenger air carriers to share passenger lists with appropriate Federal agencies for the purpose of identifying individuals who may pose a threat to aviation safety or national security.

(i) VIEW OF NTSB.—In taking any action under this section that could affect safety, the Administrator shall give great weight to the timely views of the National Transportation Safety Board.

(j) ACQUISITIONS.—

(1) IN GENERAL.—The Administrator is authorized—

(A) to acquire (by purchase, lease, condemnation, or otherwise) such real property, or any interest therein, within and outside the continental United States, as the Administrator considers necessary;

(B) to acquire (by purchase, lease, condemnation, or otherwise) and to construct, repair, operate, and maintain such personal property (including office space and patents), or any interest therein, within and outside the continental United States, as the Administrator considers necessary;

(C) to lease to others such real and personal property and to provide by contract or otherwise for necessary facilities for the welfare of its employees and to acquire, maintain, and operate equipment for these facilities;

(D) to acquire services, including such personal services as the Secretary of Homeland Security determines necessary, and to acquire (by purchase, lease, condemnation, or otherwise) and to construct, repair, operate, and maintain research and testing sites and facilities; and

(E) in cooperation with the Administrator of the Federal Aviation Administration, to utilize the research and development facilities of the Federal Aviation Administration.

(2) TITLE.—Title to any property or interest therein acquired pursuant to this subsection shall be held by the Government of the United States.

(k) TRANSFERS OF FUNDS.—The Administrator is authorized to accept transfers of unobligated balances and unexpended balances of funds appropriated to other Federal agencies (as such term is defined in section 551(1) of title 5) to carry out functions assigned by law to the Administrator.

(l) REGULATIONS.—

(1) IN GENERAL.—The Administrator is authorized to issue, rescind, and revise such regulations as are necessary to carry out the functions of the Administration.

(2) EMERGENCY PROCEDURES.—

(A) IN GENERAL.—Notwithstanding any other provision of law or executive order (including an executive order requiring a cost-benefit analysis), if the Administrator determines that a regulation or security directive must be issued immediately in order to protect transportation security, the Administrator shall issue the regulation or security directive without providing notice or an opportunity for comment and without prior approval of the Secretary.

(B) REVIEW BY TRANSPORTATION SECURITY OVERSIGHT BOARD.—Any regulation or security directive issued under this paragraph shall be subject to review by the Transportation Security Oversight Board established under section 115. Any regulation or security directive issued under this paragraph shall remain effective for a period not to exceed 90 days unless ratified or disapproved by the Board or rescinded by the Administrator.

(3) FACTORS TO CONSIDER.—In determining whether to issue, rescind, or revise a regulation under this section, the Administrator shall consider, as a factor in the final determination, whether the costs of the regulation are excessive in relation to the enhancement of security the regulation will provide. The Administrator may waive requirements for an analysis that estimates the number of lives that will be saved by the

regulation and the monetary value of such lives if the Administrator determines that it is not feasible to make such an estimate.

(4) AIRWORTHINESS OBJECTIONS BY FAA.—

(A) IN GENERAL.—The Administrator shall not take an aviation security action under this title if the Administrator of the Federal Aviation Administration notifies the Administrator that the action could adversely affect the airworthiness of an aircraft.

(B) REVIEW BY SECRETARY.—Notwithstanding subparagraph (A), the Administrator may take such an action, after receiving a notification concerning the action from the Administrator of the Federal Aviation Administration under subparagraph (A), if the Secretary of Transportation subsequently approves the action.

(m) PERSONNEL AND SERVICES; COOPERATION BY ADMINISTRATOR.—

(1) AUTHORITY OF ADMINISTRATOR.—In carrying out the functions of the Administration, the Administrator shall have the same authority as is provided to the Administrator of the Federal Aviation Administration under subsections (l) and (m) of section 106.

(2) AUTHORITY OF AGENCY HEADS.—The head of a Federal agency shall have the same authority to provide services, supplies, equipment, personnel, and facilities to the Administrator as the head has to provide services, supplies, equipment, personnel, and facilities to the Administrator of the Federal Aviation Administration under section 106(m).

(n) PERSONNEL MANAGEMENT SYSTEM.—

(1) IN GENERAL.—The personnel management system established by the Administrator of the Federal Aviation Administration under section 40122 shall apply to employees of the Transportation Security Administration, or, subject to the requirements of such section, the Administrator may make such modifications to the personnel management system with respect to such employees as the Administrator considers appropriate, such as adopting aspects of other personnel systems of the Department of Homeland Security.

(2) MERITORIOUS EXECUTIVE OR DISTINGUISHED EXECUTIVE RANK AWARDS.—Notwithstanding section 40122(g)(2) of this title, the applicable sections of title 5 shall apply to the Transportation Security Administration personnel management system, except that—

(A) for purposes of applying such provisions to the personnel management system—

(i) the term "agency" means the Department of Homeland Security;

(ii) the term "senior executive" means a Transportation Security Administration executive serving on a Transportation Security Executive Service appointment;

(iii) the term "career appointee" means a Transportation Security Administration executive serving on a career Transportation Security Executive Service appointment; and

(iv) The [1] term "senior career employee" means a Transportation Security Administration employee covered by the Transportation Security Administration Core Compensation System at the L or M pay band;

(B) receipt by a career appointee or a senior career employee of the rank of Meritorious Executive or Meritorious Senior Professional entitles the individual to a lump-sum payment of an amount equal to 20 percent of annual basic pay, which shall be in addition to the basic pay paid under the applicable Transportation Security Administration pay system; and

(C) receipt by a career appointee or a senior career employee of the rank of Distinguished Executive or Distinguished Senior Professional entitles the individual to a lump-sum payment of an amount equal to 35 percent of annual basic pay, which shall be in addition to the basic pay paid under the applicable Transportation Security Administration pay system.

(3) DEFINITION OF APPLICABLE SECTIONS OF TITLE 5.—In this subsection, the term "applicable sections of title 5" means—

(A) subsections (b), (c) and (d) of section 4507 of title 5; and

(B) subsections (b) and (c) of section 4507a of title 5.

(o) AUTHORITY OF INSPECTOR GENERAL.—The Transportation Security Administration shall be subject to chapter 4 of title 5 and other laws relating to the authority of the Inspector General of the Department of Homeland Security.

(p) LAW ENFORCEMENT POWERS.—

(1) IN GENERAL.—The Administrator may designate an employee of the Transportation Security Administration or other Federal agency to serve as a law enforcement officer.

(2) POWERS.—While engaged in official duties of the Administration as required to fulfill the responsibilities under this section, a law enforcement officer designated under paragraph (1) may—

(A) carry a firearm;

(B) make an arrest without a warrant for any offense against the United States committed in the presence of the officer, or for any felony cognizable under the laws of the United States if the officer has probable cause to believe that the person to be arrested has committed or is committing the felony; and

(C) seek and execute warrants for arrest or seizure of evidence issued under the authority of the United States upon probable cause that a violation has been committed.

(3) GUIDELINES ON EXERCISE OF AUTHORITY.—The authority provided by this subsection shall be exercised in accordance with guidelines prescribed by the Administrator, in consultation with the Attorney General of the United States, and shall include adherence to the Attorney General's policy on use of deadly force.

(4) REVOCATION OR SUSPENSION OF AUTHORITY.—The powers authorized by this subsection may be rescinded or suspended should the Attorney General determine that the Administrator has not complied with the guidelines prescribed in paragraph (3) and conveys the determination in writing to the Secretary of Homeland Security and the Administrator.

(q) AUTHORITY TO EXEMPT.—The Administrator may grant an exemption from a regulation prescribed in carrying out this section if the Administrator determines that the exemption is in the public interest.

(r) NONDISCLOSURE OF SECURITY ACTIVITIES.—

(1) IN GENERAL.—Notwithstanding section 552 of title 5, the Administrator shall prescribe regulations prohibiting the disclosure of information obtained or developed in

carrying out security under authority of the Aviation and Transportation Security Act (Public Law 107–71) or under chapter 449 of this title if the Administrator decides that disclosing the information would—

(A) be an unwarranted invasion of personal privacy;

(B) reveal a trade secret or privileged or confidential commercial or financial information; or

(C) be detrimental to the security of transportation.

(2) AVAILABILITY OF INFORMATION TO CONGRESS.—Paragraph (1) does not authorize information to be withheld from a committee of Congress authorized to have the information.

(3) LIMITATION ON TRANSFERABILITY OF DUTIES.—Except as otherwise provided by law, the Administrator may not transfer a duty or power under this subsection to another department, agency, or instrumentality of the United States.

(4) LIMITATIONS.—Nothing in this subsection, or any other provision of law, shall be construed to authorize the designation of information as sensitive security information (as defined in section 1520.5 of title 49, Code of Federal Regulations)—

(A) to conceal a violation of law, inefficiency, or administrative error;

(B) to prevent embarrassment to a person, organization, or agency;

(C) to restrain competition; or

(D) to prevent or delay the release of information that does not require protection in the interest of transportation security, including basic scientific research information not clearly related to transportation security.

(S) TRANSPORTATION SECURITY STRATEGIC PLANNING.—

(1) IN GENERAL.—The Secretary of Homeland Security shall develop, prepare, implement, and update, as needed—

(A) a National Strategy for Transportation Security; and

(B) transportation modal security plans addressing security risks, including threats, vulnerabilities, and consequences, for aviation, railroad, ferry, highway, maritime, pipeline, public transportation, over-the-road bus, and other transportation infrastructure assets.

(2) ROLE OF SECRETARY OF TRANSPORTATION.—The Secretary of Homeland Security shall work jointly with the Secretary of Transportation in developing, revising, and updating the documents required by paragraph (1).

(3) CONTENTS OF NATIONAL STRATEGY FOR TRANSPORTATION SECURITY.—The National Strategy for Transportation Security shall include the following:

(A) An identification and evaluation of the transportation assets in the United States that, in the interests of national security and commerce, must be protected from attack or disruption by terrorist or other hostile forces, including modal security plans for aviation, bridge and tunnel, commuter rail and ferry, highway, maritime, pipeline, rail, mass transit, over-the-road bus, and other public transportation infrastructure assets that could be at risk of such an attack or disruption.

(B) The development of risk-based priorities, based on risk assessments conducted or received by the Secretary of Homeland Security (including assessments conducted under the Implementing Recommendations of the 9/11 Commission Act of 2007) across all transportation modes and realistic deadlines for addressing security needs associated with those assets referred to in subparagraph (A).

(C) The most appropriate, practical, and cost-effective means of defending those assets against threats to their security.

(D) A forward-looking strategic plan that sets forth the agreed upon roles and missions of Federal, State, regional, local, and tribal authorities and establishes mechanisms for encouraging cooperation and participation by private sector entities, including nonprofit employee labor organizations, in the implementation of such plan.

(E) A comprehensive delineation of prevention, response, and recovery responsibilities and issues regarding threatened and executed acts of terrorism within the United States and threatened and executed acts of terrorism outside the United States to the extent such acts affect United States transportation systems.

(F) A prioritization of research and development objectives that support transportation security needs, giving a higher priority to research and development directed toward protecting vital transportation assets. Transportation security research and development projects shall be based, to the extent practicable, on such prioritization. Nothing in the preceding sentence shall be construed to require the termination of any research or development project initiated by the Secretary of Homeland Security or the Secretary of Transportation before the date of enactment of the Implementing Recommendations of the 9/11 Commission Act of 2007.

(G) A 3- and 10-year budget for Federal transportation security programs that will achieve the priorities of the National Strategy for Transportation Security.

(H) Methods for linking the individual transportation modal security plans and the programs contained therein, and a plan for addressing the security needs of intermodal transportation.

(I) Transportation modal security plans described in paragraph (1)(B), including operational recovery plans to expedite, to the maximum extent practicable, the return to operation of an adversely affected transportation system following a major terrorist attack on that system or other incident. These plans shall be coordinated with the resumption of trade protocols required under section 202 of the SAFE Port Act (6 U.S.C. 942) and the National Maritime Transportation Security Plan required under section 70103(a) of title 46.

(4) SUBMISSION OF PLANS.—

(A) IN GENERAL.—The Secretary of Homeland Security shall submit the National Strategy for Transportation Security, including the transportation modal security plans and any revisions to the National Strategy for Transportation Security and the transportation modal security plans, to appropriate congressional committees not less frequently than April 1 of each even-numbered year.

(B) PERIODIC PROGRESS REPORT.—

(i) REQUIREMENT FOR REPORT.—Each year, in conjunction with the submission of the budget to Congress under section 1105(a) of title 31, United States Code, the Secretary of Homeland Security shall submit to the appropriate congressional committees an assessment of the progress made on implementing the National Strategy for Transportation Security, including the transportation modal security plans.

(ii) CONTENT.—Each progress report submitted under this subparagraph shall include, at a minimum, the following:

(I) Recommendations for improving and implementing the National Strategy for Transportation Security and the transportation modal and intermodal security plans that the Secretary of Homeland Security, in consultation with the Secretary of Transportation, considers appropriate.

(II) An accounting of all grants for transportation security, including grants and contracts for research and development, awarded by the Secretary of Homeland Security in the most recent fiscal year and a description of how such grants accomplished the goals of the National Strategy for Transportation Security.

(III) An accounting of all—

(aa) funds requested in the President's budget submitted pursuant to section 1105 of title 31 for the most recent fiscal year for transportation security, by mode;

(bb) personnel working on transportation security by mode, including the number of contractors; and

(cc) information on the turnover in the previous year among senior staff of the Department of Homeland Security, including component agencies, working on transportation security issues. Such information shall include the number of employees who have permanently left the office, agency, or area in which they worked, and the amount of time that they worked for the Department of Homeland Security.

(iii) Written explanation of transportation security activities not delineated in the national strategy for transportation security.—At the end of each fiscal year, the Secretary of Homeland Security shall submit to the appropriate congressional committees a written explanation of any Federal transportation security activity that is inconsistent with the National Strategy for Transportation Security, including the amount of funds to be expended for the activity and the number of personnel involved.

(C) Classified material.—Any part of the National Strategy for Transportation Security or the transportation modal security plans that involve information that is properly classified under criteria established by Executive order shall be submitted to the appropriate congressional committees separately in a classified format.

(D) Appropriate congressional committees defined.—In this subsection, the term "appropriate congressional committees" means the Committee on Transportation and Infrastructure and the Committee on Homeland Security of the House of Representatives and the Committee on Commerce, Science, and Transportation, the Committee on Homeland Security and Governmental Affairs, and the Committee on Banking, Housing, and Urban Affairs of the Senate.

(5) Priority Status.—

(A) In general.—The National Strategy for Transportation Security shall be the governing document for Federal transportation security efforts.

(B) Other plans and reports.—The National Strategy for Transportation Security shall include, as an integral part or as an appendix—

(i) the current National Maritime Transportation Security Plan under section 70103 of title 46;

(ii) the report required by section 44938 of this title;

(iii) transportation modal security plans required under this section;

(iv) the transportation sector specific plan required under Homeland Security Presidential Directive–7; and

(v) any other transportation security plan or report that the Secretary of Homeland Security determines appropriate for inclusion.

(6) COORDINATION.—In carrying out the responsibilities under this section, the Secretary of Homeland Security, in coordination with the Secretary of Transportation, shall consult, as appropriate, with Federal, State, and local agencies, tribal governments, private sector entities (including nonprofit employee labor organizations), institutions of higher learning, and other entities.

(7) PLAN DISTRIBUTION.—The Secretary of Homeland Security shall make available and appropriately publicize an unclassified version of the National Strategy for Transportation Security, including its component transportation modal security plans, to Federal, State, regional, local and tribal authorities, transportation system owners or operators, private sector stakeholders, including nonprofit employee labor organizations representing transportation employees, institutions of higher learning, and other appropriate entities.

(t) TRANSPORTATION SECURITY INFORMATION SHARING PLAN.—

(1) DEFINITIONS.—In this subsection:

(A) APPROPRIATE CONGRESSIONAL COMMITTEES.—The term "appropriate congressional committees" has the meaning given that term in subsection (s)(4)(E).

(B) PLAN.—The term "Plan" means the Transportation Security Information Sharing Plan established under paragraph (2).

(C) PUBLIC AND PRIVATE STAKEHOLDERS.—The term "public and private stakeholders" means Federal, State, and local agencies, tribal governments, and appropriate private entities, including nonprofit employee labor organizations representing transportation employees.

(D) TRANSPORTATION SECURITY INFORMATION.—The term "transportation security information" means information relating to the risks to transportation modes, including aviation, public transportation, railroad, ferry, highway, maritime, pipeline, and over-the-road bus transportation, and may include specific and general intelligence products, as appropriate.

(2) ESTABLISHMENT OF PLAN.—The Secretary of Homeland Security, in consultation with the program manager of the information sharing environment established under section 1016 of the Intelligence Reform and Terrorism Prevention Act of 2004 (6 U.S.C. 485), the Secretary of Transportation, and public and private stakeholders, shall establish a Transportation Security Information Sharing Plan. In establishing the Plan, the Secretary of Homeland Security shall gather input on the development of the Plan from private and public stakeholders and the program manager of the information sharing environment established under section 1016 of the Intelligence Reform and Terrorism Prevention Act of 2004 (6 U.S.C. 485).

(3) PURPOSE OF PLAN.—The Plan shall promote sharing of transportation security information between the Department of Homeland Security and public and private stakeholders.

(4) CONTENT OF PLAN.—The Plan shall include—

(A) a description of how intelligence analysts within the Department of Homeland Security will coordinate their activities within the Department and with other Federal, State, and local agencies, and tribal governments, including coordination with existing modal information sharing centers and the center described in section 1410 of the Implementing Recommendations of the 9/11 Commission Act of 2007;

(B) the establishment of a point of contact, which may be a single point of contact within the Department of Homeland Security, for each mode of transportation for the sharing of transportation security information with public and private stakeholders, including an explanation and justification to the appropriate congressional committees if the point of contact established pursuant to this subparagraph differs from the agency within the Department of Homeland Security that has the primary authority, or has been delegated such authority by the Secretary of Homeland Security, to regulate the security of that transportation mode;

(C) a reasonable deadline by which the Plan will be implemented; and

(D) a description of resource needs for fulfilling the Plan.

(5) COORDINATION WITH INFORMATION SHARING.—The Plan shall be—

(A) implemented in coordination, as appropriate, with the program manager for the information sharing environment established under section 1016 of the Intelligence Reform and Terrorism Prevention Act of 2004 (6 U.S.C. 485); and

(B) consistent with the establishment of the information sharing environment and any policies, guidelines, procedures, instructions, or standards established by the President or the program manager for the implementation and management of the information sharing environment.

(6) ANNUAL REPORT ON PLAN.—The Secretary of Homeland Security shall annually submit to the appropriate congressional committees a report containing the Plan.

(7) SECURITY CLEARANCES.—The Secretary of Homeland Security shall, to the greatest extent practicable, take steps to expedite the security clearances needed for designated public and private stakeholders to receive and obtain access to classified information distributed under this section, as appropriate.

(8) CLASSIFICATION OF MATERIAL.—The Secretary of Homeland Security, to the greatest extent practicable, shall provide designated public and private stakeholders with transportation security information in an unclassified format.

(u) ENFORCEMENT OF REGULATIONS AND ORDERS OF THE SECRETARY OF HOMELAND SECURITY.—

(1) APPLICATION OF SUBSECTION.—

(A) IN GENERAL.—This subsection applies to the enforcement of regulations prescribed, and orders issued, by the Secretary of Homeland Security under a provision of chapter 701 of title 46 and under a provision of this title other than a provision of chapter 449 (in this subsection referred to as an "applicable provision of this title").

(B) VIOLATIONS OF CHAPTER 449.—The penalties for violations of regulations prescribed and orders issued by the Secretary of Homeland Security or the Administrator under chapter 449 of this title are provided under chapter 463 of this title.

(C) Nonapplication to certain violations.—

(i) Paragraphs (2) through (5) do not apply to violations of regulations prescribed, and orders issued, by the Secretary of Homeland Security under a provision of this title—

(I) involving the transportation of personnel or shipments of materials by contractors where the Department of Defense has assumed control and responsibility;

(II) by a member of the armed forces of the United States when performing official duties; or

(III) by a civilian employee of the Department of Defense when performing official duties.

(ii) Violations described in subclause (I), (II), or (III) of clause (i) shall be subject to penalties as determined by the Secretary of Defense or the Secretary of Defense's designee.

(2) Civil penalty.—

(A) In general.—A person is liable to the United States Government for a civil penalty of not more than $10,000 for a violation of a regulation prescribed, or order issued, by the Secretary of Homeland Security under an applicable provision of this title.

(B) Repeat violations.—A separate violation occurs under this paragraph for each day the violation continues.

(3) Administrative imposition of civil penalties.—

(A) In general.—The Secretary of Homeland Security may impose a civil penalty for a violation of a regulation prescribed, or order issued, under an applicable provision of this title. The Secretary shall give written notice of the finding of a violation and the penalty.

(B) Scope of civil action.—In a civil action to collect a civil penalty imposed by the Secretary of Homeland Security under this subsection, a court may not re-examine issues of liability or the amount of the penalty.

(C) Jurisdiction.—The district courts of the United States shall have exclusive jurisdiction of civil actions to collect a civil penalty imposed by the Secretary of Homeland Security under this subsection if—

(i) the amount in controversy is more than—

(I) $400,000, if the violation was committed by a person other than an individual or small business concern; or

(II) $50,000 if the violation was committed by an individual or small business concern;

(ii) the action is in rem or another action in rem based on the same violation has been brought; or

(iii) another action has been brought for an injunction based on the same violation.

(D) Maximum penalty.—The maximum civil penalty the Secretary of Homeland Security administratively may impose under this paragraph is—

(i) $400,000, if the violation was committed by a person other than an individual or small business concern; or

(ii) $50,000, if the violation was committed by an individual or small business concern.

(E) NOTICE AND OPPORTUNITY TO REQUEST HEARING.—Before imposing a penalty under this section the Secretary of Homeland Security shall provide to the person against whom the penalty is to be imposed—

(i) written notice of the proposed penalty; and

(ii) the opportunity to request a hearing on the proposed penalty, if the Secretary of Homeland Security receives the request not later than 30 days after the date on which the person receives notice.

(4) COMPROMISE AND SETOFF.—

(A) The Secretary of Homeland Security may compromise the amount of a civil penalty imposed under this subsection.

(B) The Government may deduct the amount of a civil penalty imposed or compromised under this subsection from amounts it owes the person liable for the penalty.

(5) INVESTIGATIONS AND PROCEEDINGS.—Chapter 461 shall apply to investigations and proceedings brought under this subsection to the same extent that it applies to investigations and proceedings brought with respect to aviation security duties designated to be carried out by the Secretary of Homeland Security.

(6) DEFINITIONS.—In this subsection:

(A) PERSON.—The term "person" does not include—

(i) the United States Postal Service; or

(ii) the Department of Defense.

(B) SMALL BUSINESS CONCERN.—The term "small business concern" has the meaning given that term in section 3 of the Small Business Act (15 U.S.C. 632).

(7) ENFORCEMENT TRANSPARENCY.—

(A) IN GENERAL.—The Secretary of Homeland Security shall—

(i) provide an annual summary to the public of all enforcement actions taken by the Secretary under this subsection; and

(ii) include in each such summary the docket number of each enforcement action, the type of alleged violation, the penalty or penalties proposed, and the final assessment amount of each penalty.

(B) ELECTRONIC AVAILABILITY.—Each summary under this paragraph shall be made available to the public by electronic means.

(C) RELATIONSHIP TO THE FREEDOM OF INFORMATION ACT AND THE PRIVACY ACT.—Nothing in this subsection shall be construed to require disclosure of information or records that are exempt from disclosure under sections 552 or 552a of title 5.

(v) AUTHORIZATION OF APPROPRIATIONS.—There are authorized to be appropriated to the Transportation Security Administration for salaries, operations, and maintenance of the Administration—

(1) $7,849,247,000 for fiscal year 2019;

(2) $7,888,494,000 for fiscal year 2020; and

(3) $7,917,936,000 for fiscal year 2021.

(w) LEADERSHIP AND ORGANIZATION.—

(1) IN GENERAL.—For each of the areas described in paragraph (2), the Administrator of the Transportation Security Administration shall appoint at least 1 individual who shall—

(A) report directly to the Administrator or the Administrator's designated direct report; and

(B) be responsible and accountable for that area.

(2) AREAS DESCRIBED.—The areas described in this paragraph are as follows:

(A) Aviation security operations and training, including risk-based, adaptive security—

(i) focused on airport checkpoint and baggage screening operations;

(ii) workforce training and development programs; and

(iii) ensuring compliance with aviation security law, including regulations, and other specialized programs designed to secure air transportation.

(B) Surface transportation security operations and training, including risk-based, adaptive security—

(i) focused on accomplishing security systems assessments;

(ii) reviewing and prioritizing projects for appropriated surface transportation security grants;

(iii) operator compliance with surface transportation security law, including regulations, and voluntary industry standards; and

(iv) workforce training and development programs, and other specialized programs designed to secure surface transportation.

(C) Transportation industry engagement and planning, including the development, interpretation, promotion, and oversight of a unified effort regarding risk-based, risk-reducing security policies and plans (including strategic planning for future contingencies and security challenges) between government and transportation stakeholders, including airports, domestic and international airlines, general aviation, air cargo, mass transit and passenger rail, freight rail, pipeline, highway and motor carriers, and maritime.

(D) International strategy and operations, including agency efforts to work with international partners to secure the global transportation network.

(E) Trusted and registered traveler programs, including the management and marketing of the agency's trusted traveler initiatives, including the PreCheck Program, and coordination with trusted traveler programs of other Department of Homeland Security agencies and the private sector.

(F) Technology acquisition and deployment, including the oversight, development, testing, evaluation, acquisition, deployment, and maintenance of security technology and other acquisition programs.

(G) Inspection and compliance, including the integrity, efficiency and effectiveness of the agency's workforce, operations, and programs through objective audits, covert testing, inspections, criminal investigations, and regulatory compliance.

(H) Civil rights, liberties, and traveler engagement, including ensuring that agency employees and the traveling public are treated in a fair and lawful manner consistent with Federal laws and regulations protecting privacy and prohibiting discrimination and reprisal.

(I) Legislative and public affairs, including communication and engagement with internal and external audiences in a timely, accurate, and transparent manner, and development and implementation of strategies within the agency to achieve congressional approval or authorization of agency programs and policies.

(3) NOTIFICATION.—The Administrator shall submit to the appropriate committees of Congress—

(A) not later than 180 days after the date of enactment of the TSA Modernization Act, a list of the names of the individuals appointed under paragraph (1); and

(B) an update of the list not later than 5 days after any new individual is appointed under paragraph (1).

(x) TRANSPORTATION SECURITY PREPAREDNESS PLAN.—

(1) IN GENERAL.—Not later than two years after the date of the enactment of this subsection, the Secretary of Homeland Security, acting through the Administrator, in coordination with the Chief Medical Officer of the Department of Homeland Security, and in consultation with the partners identified under paragraphs (3)(A)(i) through (3)(A)(iv), shall develop a transportation security preparedness plan to address the event of a communicable disease outbreak. The Secretary, acting through the Administrator, shall ensure such plan aligns with relevant Federal plans and strategies for communicable disease outbreaks.

(2) CONSIDERATIONS.—In developing the plan required under paragraph (1), the Secretary, acting through the Administrator, shall consider each of the following:

(A) The findings of the survey required under section 6411 of the National Defense Authorization Act for Fiscal Year 2022.

(B) The findings of the analysis required under section 6414 of the National Defense Authorization Act for Fiscal Year 2022.

(C) The plan required under section 6415 of the National Defense Authorization Act for Fiscal Year 2022.

(D) All relevant reports and recommendations regarding the Administration's response to the COVID–19 pandemic, including any reports and recommendations issued by the Comptroller General and the Inspector General of the Department of Homeland Security.

(E) Lessons learned from Federal interagency efforts during the COVID–19 pandemic.

(3) CONTENTS OF PLAN.—The plan developed under paragraph (1) shall include each of the following:

(A) Plans for communicating and collaborating in the event of a communicable disease outbreak with the following partners:

(i) Appropriate Federal departments and agencies, including the Department of Health and Human Services, the Centers for Disease Control and Prevention, the Department of Transportation, the Department of Labor, and appropriate interagency task forces.

(ii) The workforce of the Administration, including through the labor organization certified as the exclusive representative of full- and part-time non-supervisory Administration personnel carrying out screening functions under section 44901 of this title.

(iii) International partners, including the International Civil Aviation Organization and foreign governments, airports, and air carriers.

(iv) Public and private stakeholders, as such term is defined under subsection (t)(1)(C).

(v) The traveling public.

(B) Plans for protecting the safety of the Transportation Security Administration workforce, including—

(i) reducing the risk of communicable disease transmission at screening checkpoints and within the Administration's workforce related to the Administration's transportation security operations and mission;

(ii) ensuring the safety and hygiene of screening checkpoints and other workstations;

(iii) supporting equitable and appropriate access to relevant vaccines, prescriptions, and other medical care; and

(iv) tracking rates of employee illness, recovery, and death.

(C) Criteria for determining the conditions that may warrant the integration of additional actions in the aviation screening system in response to the communicable disease outbreak and a range of potential roles and responsibilities that align with such conditions.

(D) Contingency plans for temporarily adjusting checkpoint operations to provide for passenger and employee safety while maintaining security during the communicable disease outbreak.

(E) Provisions setting forth criteria for establishing an interagency task force or other standing engagement platform with other appropriate Federal departments and agencies, including the Department of Health and Human Services and the Department of Transportation, to address such communicable disease outbreak.

(F) A description of scenarios in which the Administrator should consider exercising authorities provided under subsection (g) and for what purposes.

(G) Considerations for assessing the appropriateness of issuing security directives and emergency amendments to regulated parties in various modes of transportation, including surface transportation, and plans for ensuring compliance with such measures.

(H) A description of any potential obstacles, including funding constraints and limitations to authorities, that could restrict the ability of the Administration to respond appropriately to a communicable disease outbreak.

(4) DISSEMINATION.—Upon development of the plan required under paragraph (1), the Administrator shall disseminate the plan to the partners identified under paragraph (3)(A) and to the Committee on Homeland Security of the House of Representatives and the Committee on Homeland Security and Governmental Affairs and the Committee on Commerce, Science, and Transportation of the Senate.

(5) REVIEW OF PLAN.—Not later than two years after the date on which the plan is disseminated under paragraph (4), and biennially thereafter, the Secretary, acting through the Administrator and in coordination with the Chief Medical Officer of the Department of Homeland Security, shall review the plan and, after consultation with the partners identified under paragraphs (3)(A)(i) through (3)(A)(iv), update the plan as appropriate.

(Added Pub. L. 107–71, title I, §101(a), Nov. 19, 2001, 115 Stat. 597; amended Pub. L. 107–296, title XVI, §1601(b), title XVII, §1707, Nov. 25, 2002, 116 Stat. 2312, 2318; Pub. L. 108–7, div. I, title III, §351(d), Feb. 20, 2003, 117 Stat. 420; Pub. L. 108–458, title IV, §4001(a), Dec. 17, 2004, 118 Stat. 3710; Pub. L. 110–53, title XII, §§1202, 1203(a), title XIII, §1302(a), title XV, §1503(a), Aug. 3, 2007, 121 Stat. 381, 383, 390, 425; Pub. L. 110–161, div. E, title V, §568(a), Dec. 26, 2007, 121 Stat. 2092; Pub. L. 111–83, title V, §561(c)(1), Oct. 28, 2009, 123 Stat. 2182; Pub. L. 114–301, §2(d), Dec. 16, 2016, 130 Stat. 1514; Pub. L. 115–254, div. K, title I, §§1903, 1904(a), (b)(1), 1905, 1909, 1988(c), Oct. 5, 2018, 132 Stat. 3543, 3544, 3546, 3549, 3623; Pub. L. 117–81, div. F, title LXIV, §6412(a), Dec. 27, 2021, 135 Stat. 2409; Pub. L. 117–286, §4(b)(95), Dec. 27, 2022, 136 Stat. 4353.)

---

[1] *So in original. Probably should not be capitalized.*

§115. TRANSPORTATION SECURITY OVERSIGHT BOARD

(a) IN GENERAL.—There is established in the Department of Homeland Security a board to be known as the "Transportation Security Oversight Board".

(b) MEMBERSHIP.—

(1) NUMBER AND APPOINTMENT.—The Board shall be composed of 7 members as follows:

(A) The Secretary of Homeland Security, or the Secretary's designee.

(B) The Secretary of Transportation, or the Secretary's designee.

(C) The Attorney General, or the Attorney General's designee.

(D) The Secretary of Defense, or the Secretary's designee.

(E) The Secretary of the Treasury, or the Secretary's designee.

(F) The Director of National Intelligence, or the Director's designee.

(G) One member appointed by the President to represent the National Security Council.

(2) CHAIRPERSON.—The Chairperson of the Board shall be the Secretary of Homeland Security.

(c) DUTIES.—The Board shall—

(1) review and ratify or disapprove any regulation or security directive issued by the Administrator of the Transportation Security Administration under section 114(l)(2) within 30 days after the date of issuance of such regulation or directive;

(2) facilitate the coordination of intelligence, security, and law enforcement activities affecting transportation;

(3) facilitate the sharing of intelligence, security, and law enforcement information affecting transportation among Federal agencies and with carriers and other transportation providers as appropriate;

(4) explore the technical feasibility of developing a common database of individuals who may pose a threat to transportation or national security;

(5) review plans for transportation security;

(6) make recommendations to the Administrator regarding matters reviewed under paragraph (5).

(d) QUARTERLY MEETINGS.—The Board shall meet at least quarterly.

(e) CONSIDERATION OF SECURITY INFORMATION.—A majority of the Board may vote to close a meeting of the Board to the public, except that meetings shall be closed to the public whenever classified,[1] sensitive security information, or information protected in accordance with section 40119(b), will be discussed.

(Added Pub. L. 107–71, title I, §102(a), Nov. 19, 2001, 115 Stat. 604; amended Pub. L. 107–296, title IV, §426(a), Nov. 25, 2002, 116 Stat. 2186; Pub. L. 111–259, title IV, §411, Oct. 7, 2010, 124 Stat. 2725; Pub. L. 115–254, div. K, title I, §1991(b), Oct. 5, 2018, 132 Stat. 3626.)

[1] *So in original. The word "information" probably should be inserted.*

* * * * * * *

CHAPTER 3—GENERAL DUTIES AND POWERS

SUBCHAPTER I—DUTIES OF THE SECRETARY OF TRANSPORTATION

SUBCHAPTER II—ADMINISTRATIVE

SUBCHAPTER III—MISCELLANEOUS

SUBCHAPTER I—DUTIES OF THE SECRETARY OF TRANSPORTATION

§301. LEADERSHIP, CONSULTATION, AND COOPERATION

The Secretary of Transportation shall—

(1) under the direction of the President, exercise leadership in transportation matters, including those matters affecting national defense and those matters involving national or regional emergencies;

(2) provide leadership in the development of transportation policies and programs, and make recommendations to the President and Congress for their consideration and implementation;

(3) coordinate Federal policy on intermodal transportation and initiate policies to promote efficient intermodal transportation in the United States;

(4) promote and undertake the development, collection, and dissemination of technological, statistical, economic, and other information relevant to domestic and international transportation;

(5) consult and cooperate with the Secretary of Labor in compiling information regarding the status of labor-management contracts and other labor-management problems and in promoting industrial harmony and stable employment conditions in all modes of transportation;

(6) promote and undertake research and development related to transportation, including noise abatement, with particular attention to aircraft noise, and including basic highway vehicle science;

(7) consult with the heads of other departments, agencies, and instrumentalities of the United States Government on the transportation requirements of the Government, including encouraging them to establish and observe policies consistent with maintaining a coordinated transportation system in procuring transportation or in operating their own transport services;

(8) consult and cooperate with State and local governments, carriers, labor, and other interested persons, including, when appropriate, holding informal public hearings; and

(9) develop and coordinate Federal policy on financing transportation infrastructure, including the provision of direct Federal credit assistance and other techniques used to leverage Federal transportation funds.

(Pub. L. 97–449, §1(b), Jan. 12, 1983, 96 Stat. 2418; Pub. L. 102–240, title V, §5002(a), title VI, §6017, Dec. 18, 1991, 105 Stat. 2158, 2183; Pub. L. 105–178, title I, §1504, June 9, 1998, 112 Stat. 251.)

§302. POLICY STANDARDS FOR TRANSPORTATION

(a) The Secretary of Transportation is governed by the transportation policy of sections 10101 and 13101 of this title in addition to other laws.

(b) This subtitle and chapters 221 and 315 of this title do not authorize, without appropriate action by Congress, the adoption, revision, or implementation of a transportation policy or investment standards or criteria.

(c) The Secretary shall consider the needs—

(1) for effectiveness and safety in transportation systems; and

(2) of national defense.

(d)(1) It is the policy of the United States to promote the construction and commercialization of high-speed ground transportation systems by—

(A) conducting economic and technological research;

(B) demonstrating advancements in high-speed ground transportation technologies;

(C) establishing a comprehensive policy for the development of such systems and the effective integration of the various high-speed ground transportation technologies; and

(D) minimizing the long-term risks of investors.

(2) It is the policy of the United States to establish in the shortest time practicable a United States designed and constructed magnetic levitation transportation technology capable of operating along Federal-aid highway rights-of-way, as part of a national transportation system of the United States.

(e) INTERMODAL TRANSPORTATION.—It is the policy of the United States Government to encourage and promote development of a national intermodal transportation system in the United States to move people and goods in an energy-efficient manner, provide the foundation for improved productivity growth, strengthen the Nation's ability to compete in the global economy, and obtain the optimum yield from the Nation's transportation resources.

(Pub. L. 97–449, §1(b), Jan. 12, 1983, 96 Stat. 2419; Pub. L. 98–216, §2(2), Feb. 14, 1984, 98 Stat. 5; Pub. L. 102–240, title I, §1036(a), title V, §5001, Dec. 18, 1991, 105 Stat. 1978, 2158; Pub. L. 103–272, §5(m)(6), July 5, 1994, 108 Stat. 1375; Pub. L. 104–88, title III, §308(a), Dec. 29, 1995, 109 Stat. 946.)

§303. POLICY ON LANDS, WILDLIFE AND WATERFOWL REFUGES, AND HISTORIC SITES

(a) It is the policy of the United States Government that special effort should be made to preserve the natural beauty of the countryside and public park and recreation lands, wildlife and waterfowl refuges, and historic sites.

(b) The Secretary of Transportation shall cooperate and consult with the Secretaries of the Interior, Housing and Urban Development, and Agriculture, and with the States, in developing transportation plans and programs that include measures to maintain or enhance the natural beauty of lands crossed by transportation activities or facilities.

(c) APPROVAL OF PROGRAMS AND PROJECTS.—Subject to subsections (d) and (h), the Secretary may approve a transportation program or project (other than any project for a park road or parkway under section 204 of title 23) requiring the use of publicly owned land of a public park, recreation area, or wildlife and waterfowl refuge of national, State, or local significance, or land of an historic site of national, State, or local significance (as determined by the Federal, State, or local officials having jurisdiction over the park, area, refuge, or site) only if—

(1) there is no prudent and feasible alternative to using that land; and

(2) the program or project includes all possible planning to minimize harm to the park, recreation area, wildlife and waterfowl refuge, or historic site resulting from the use.

(d) DE MINIMIS IMPACTS.—

(1) REQUIREMENTS.—

(A) REQUIREMENTS FOR HISTORIC SITES.—The requirements of this section shall be considered to be satisfied with respect to an area described in paragraph (2) if the Secretary determines, in accordance with this subsection, that a transportation program or project will have a de minimis impact on the area.

(B) REQUIREMENTS FOR PARKS, RECREATION AREAS, AND WILDLIFE OR WATERFOWL REFUGES.—The requirements of subsection (c)(1) shall be considered to be satisfied with respect to an area described in paragraph (3) if the Secretary determines, in accordance with this subsection, that a transportation program or project will have a de minimis impact on the area. The requirements of subsection (c)(2) with respect to an area described in paragraph (3) shall not include an alternatives analysis.

(C) CRITERIA.—In making any determination under this subsection, the Secretary shall consider to be part of a transportation program or project any avoidance, minimization, mitigation, or enhancement measures that are required to be implemented as a condition of approval of the transportation program or project.

(2) HISTORIC SITES.—With respect to historic sites, the Secretary may make a finding of de minimis impact only if—

(A) the Secretary has determined, in accordance with the consultation process required under section 306108 of title 54, United States Code,[2] that—

(i) the transportation program or project will have no adverse effect on the historic site; or

(ii) there will be no historic properties affected by the transportation program or project;

(B) the finding of the Secretary has received written concurrence from the applicable State historic preservation officer or tribal historic preservation officer (and from the Advisory Council on Historic Preservation if the Council is participating in the consultation process); and

(C) the finding of the Secretary has been developed in consultation with parties consulting as part of the process referred to in subparagraph (A).

(3) PARKS, RECREATION AREAS, AND WILDLIFE OR WATERFOWL REFUGES.—With respect to parks, recreation areas, or wildlife or waterfowl refuges, the Secretary may make a finding of de minimis impact only if—

(A) the Secretary has determined, after public notice and opportunity for public review and comment, that the transportation program or project will not adversely affect the activities, features, and attributes of the park, recreation area, or wildlife or waterfowl refuge eligible for protection under this section; and

(B) the finding of the Secretary has received concurrence from the officials with jurisdiction over the park, recreation area, or wildlife or waterfowl refuge.

(e) SATISFACTION OF REQUIREMENTS FOR CERTAIN HISTORIC SITES.—

(1) IN GENERAL.—The Secretary shall—

(A) align, to the maximum extent practicable, the requirements of this section with the requirements of the National Environmental Policy Act of 1969 (42 U.S.C. 4321 et seq.) and section 306108 of title 54, including implementing regulations; and

(B) not later than 90 days after the date of enactment of this subsection, coordinate with the Secretary of the Interior and the Executive Director of the Advisory Council on Historic Preservation (referred to in this subsection as the "Council") to establish procedures to satisfy the requirements described in subparagraph (A) (including regulations).

(2) AVOIDANCE ALTERNATIVE ANALYSIS.—

(A) IN GENERAL.—If, in an analysis required under the National Environmental Policy Act of 1969 (42 U.S.C. 4321 et seq.), the Secretary determines that there is no feasible or prudent alternative to avoid use of a historic site, the Secretary may—

(i) include the determination of the Secretary in the analysis required under that Act;

(ii) provide a notice of the determination to—

(I) each applicable State historic preservation officer and tribal historic preservation officer;

(II) the Council, if the Council is participating in the consultation process under section 306108 of title 54; and

(III) the Secretary of the Interior; and

(iii) request from the applicable preservation officer, the Council, and the Secretary of the Interior a concurrence that the determination is sufficient to satisfy subsection (c)(1).

(B) CONCURRENCE.—If the applicable preservation officer, the Council, and the Secretary of the Interior each provide a concurrence requested under subparagraph (A)(iii), no further analysis under subsection (c)(1) shall be required.

(C) PUBLICATION.—A notice of a determination, together with each relevant concurrence to that determination, under subparagraph (A) shall—

(i) be included in the record of decision or finding of no significant impact of the Secretary; and

(ii) be posted on an appropriate Federal website by not later than 3 days after the date of receipt by the Secretary of all concurrences requested under subparagraph (A)(iii).

(3) ALIGNING HISTORICAL REVIEWS.—

(A) IN GENERAL.—If the Secretary, the applicable preservation officer, the Council, and the Secretary of the Interior concur that no feasible and prudent alternative exists as described in paragraph (2), the Secretary may provide to the applicable preservation officer, the Council, and the Secretary of the Interior notice of the intent of the Secretary to satisfy subsection (c)(2) through the consultation requirements of section 306108 of title 54.

(B) SATISFACTION OF CONDITIONS.—To satisfy subsection (c)(2), the applicable preservation officer, the Council, and the Secretary of the Interior shall concur in the treatment of the applicable historic site described in the memorandum of agreement or programmatic agreement developed under section 306108 of title 54.

(f) REFERENCES TO PAST TRANSPORTATION ENVIRONMENTAL AUTHORITIES.—

(1) SECTION 4(F) REQUIREMENTS.—The requirements of this section are commonly referred to as section 4(f) requirements (see section 4(f) of the Department of Transportation Act (Public Law 89–670; 80 Stat. 934) as in effect before the repeal of that section).

(2) SECTION 106 REQUIREMENTS.—The requirements of section 306108 of title 54 are commonly referred to as section 106 requirements (see section 106 of the National Historic Preservation Act of 1966 (Public Law 89–665; 80 Stat. 917) as in effect before the repeal of that section).

(g) BRIDGE EXEMPTION FROM CONSIDERATION.—A common post-1945 concrete or steel bridge or culvert (as described in 77 Fed. Reg. 68790) that is exempt from individual review under section 306108 of title 54 shall be exempt from consideration under this section.

(h) RAIL AND TRANSIT.—

(1) IN GENERAL.—Improvements to, or the maintenance, rehabilitation, or operation of, railroad or rail transit lines or elements thereof that are in use or were historically used for the transportation of goods or passengers shall not be considered a use of a historic site under subsection (c), regardless of whether the railroad or rail transit line or element thereof is listed on, or eligible for listing on, the National Register of Historic Places.

(2) EXCEPTIONS.—

(A) IN GENERAL.—Paragraph (1) shall not apply to—

(i) stations; or

(ii) bridges or tunnels located on—

(I) railroad lines that have been abandoned; or

(II) transit lines that are not in use.

(B) CLARIFICATION WITH RESPECT TO CERTAIN BRIDGES AND TUNNELS.—The bridges and tunnels referred to in subparagraph (A)(ii) do not include bridges or tunnels located on railroad or transit lines—

(i) over which service has been discontinued; or

(ii) that have been railbanked or otherwise reserved for the transportation of goods or passengers.

(Pub. L. 97–449, §1(b), Jan. 12, 1983, 96 Stat. 2419; Pub. L. 100–17, title I, §133(d), Apr. 2, 1987, 101 Stat. 173; Pub. L. 109–59, title VI, §6009(a)(2), Aug. 10, 2005, 119 Stat. 1875; Pub. L. 113–287, §5(p), Dec. 19, 2014, 128 Stat. 3272; Pub. L. 114–94, div. A, title I, §§1301(b), 1302(b), 1303(b), title XI, §11502(b), Dec. 4, 2015, 129 Stat. 1376, 1378, 1690.)

[1] *So in original. The words ", United States Code" probably should not appear.*

§303A. DEVELOPMENT OF WATER TRANSPORTATION

(a) POLICY.—It is the policy of Congress—

(1) to promote, encourage, and develop water transportation, service, and facilities for the commerce of the United States; and

(2) to foster and preserve rail and water transportation.

(b) DEFINITION.—In this section, "inland waterway" includes the Great Lakes.

(c) REQUIREMENTS.—The Secretary of Transportation shall—

(1) investigate the types of vessels suitable for different classes of inland waterways to promote, encourage, and develop inland waterway transportation facilities for the commerce of the United States;

(2) investigate water terminals, both for inland waterway traffic and for through traffic by water and rail, including the necessary docks, warehouses, and equipment, and investigate railroad spurs and switches connecting with those water terminals, to develop the types most appropriate for different locations and for transferring passengers or property between water carriers and rail carriers more expeditiously and economically;

(3) consult with communities, cities, and towns about the location of water terminals, and cooperate with them in preparing plans for terminal facilities;

(4) investigate the existing status of water transportation on the different inland waterways of the United States to learn the extent to which—

(A) the waterways are being used to their capacity and are meeting the demands of traffic; and

(B) water carriers using those waterways are interchanging traffic with rail carriers;

(5) investigate other matters that may promote and encourage inland water transportation; and

(6) compile, publish, and distribute information about transportation on inland waterways that the Secretary considers useful to the commercial interests of the United States.

(Pub. L. 103–272, §4(j)(6)(A), July 5, 1994, 108 Stat. 1366.)

§304. APPLICATION OF CATEGORICAL EXCLUSIONS FOR MULTIMODAL PROJECTS

(a) DEFINITIONS.—In this section, the following definitions apply:

(1) COOPERATING AUTHORITY.—The term "cooperating authority" means a Department of Transportation operating administration or secretarial office that has expertise but is not the lead authority with respect to a proposed multimodal project.

(2) LEAD AUTHORITY.—The term "lead authority" means a Department of Transportation operating administration or secretarial office that has the lead responsibility for compliance with the National Environmental Policy Act of 1969 (42 U.S.C. 4321 et seq.) with respect to a proposed multimodal project.

(3) MULTIMODAL PROJECT.—The term "multimodal project" has the meaning given the term in section 139(a) of title 23.

(b) EXERCISE OF AUTHORITIES.—The authorities granted in this section may be exercised for a multimodal project, class of projects, or program of projects that are carried out under this title or title 23.

(c) APPLICATION OF CATEGORICAL EXCLUSIONS FOR MULTIMODAL PROJECTS.—In considering the environmental impacts of a proposed multimodal project, a lead authority may apply categorical exclusions designated under the National Environmental Policy Act of 1969 (42 U.S.C. 4321 et seq.) in implementing regulations or procedures of a cooperating authority for a proposed multimodal project, subject to the conditions that—

(1) the lead authority makes a determination, with the concurrence of the cooperating authority—

(A) on the applicability of a categorical exclusion to a proposed multimodal project; and

(B) that the project satisfies the conditions for a categorical exclusion under the National Environmental Policy Act of 1969 (42 U.S.C. 4321 et seq.) and this section;

(2) the lead authority follows the implementing regulations of the cooperating authority or procedures under that Act; and

(3) the lead authority determines that—

(A) the proposed multimodal project does not individually or cumulatively have a significant impact on the environment; and

(B) extraordinary circumstances do not exist that merit additional analysis and documentation in an environmental impact statement or environmental assessment required under that Act.

(d) COOPERATING AUTHORITY EXPERTISE.—A cooperating authority shall provide expertise to the lead authority on aspects of the multimodal project in which the cooperating authority has expertise.

(Pub. L. 97–449, §1(b), Jan. 12, 1983, 96 Stat. 2419; Pub. L. 112–141, div. A, title I, §1314(a), July 6, 2012, 126 Stat. 547; Pub. L. 114–94, div. A, title I, §1310, Dec. 4, 2015, 129 Stat. 1397.)

§304A. ACCELERATED DECISIONMAKING IN ENVIRONMENTAL REVIEWS

(a) IN GENERAL.—In preparing a final environmental impact statement under the National Environmental Policy Act of 1969 (42 U.S.C. 4321 et seq.), if the lead agency modifies the statement in response to comments that are minor and are confined to factual corrections or explanations of why the comments do not warrant additional agency response, the lead agency may write on errata sheets attached to the statement, instead of rewriting the draft statement, subject to the condition that the errata sheets—

(1) cite the sources, authorities, and reasons that support the position of the agency; and

(2) if appropriate, indicate the circumstances that would trigger agency reappraisal or further response.

(b) SINGLE DOCUMENT.—To the maximum extent practicable, the lead agency shall expeditiously develop a single document that consists of a final environmental impact statement and a record of decision, unless—

(1) the final environmental impact statement makes substantial changes to the proposed action that are relevant to environmental or safety concerns; or

(2) there is a significant new circumstance or information relevant to environmental concerns that bears on the proposed action or the impacts of the proposed action.

(c) ADOPTION AND INCORPORATION BY REFERENCE OF DOCUMENTS.—

(1) AVOIDING DUPLICATION.—To prevent duplication of analyses and support expeditious and efficient decisions, the operating administrations of the Department of Transportation shall use adoption and incorporation by reference in accordance with this subsection.

(2) ADOPTION OF DOCUMENTS OF OTHER OPERATING ADMINISTRATIONS.—An operating administration or a secretarial office within the Department of Transportation may adopt a draft environmental impact statement, an environmental assessment, or a final environmental impact statement of another operating administration for the use of the adopting operating administration when preparing an environmental assessment or final environmental impact statement for a project without recirculating the document for public review, if—

(A) the adopting operating administration certifies that the proposed action is substantially the same as the project considered in the document to be adopted;

(B) the other operating administration concurs with such decision; and

(C) such actions are consistent with the requirements of the National Environmental Policy Act of 1969 (42 U.S.C. 4321 et seq.).

(3) INCORPORATION BY REFERENCE.—An operating administration or secretarial office within the Department of Transportation may incorporate by reference all or portions of a draft environmental impact statement, an environmental assessment, or a final

environmental impact statement for the use of the adopting operating administration when preparing an environmental assessment or final environmental impact statement for a project if—

(A) the incorporated material is cited in the environmental assessment or final environmental impact statement and the contents of the incorporated material are briefly described;

(B) the incorporated material is reasonably available for inspection by potentially interested persons within the time allowed for review and comment; and

(C) the incorporated material does not include proprietary data that is not available for review and comment.

(Added Pub. L. 114–94, div. A, title I, §1311(a), Dec. 4, 2015, 129 Stat. 1398.)

§305. Transportation investment standards and criteria

(a) Subject to sections 301–304 of this title, the Secretary of Transportation shall develop standards and criteria to formulate and economically evaluate all proposals for investing amounts of the United States Government in transportation facilities and equipment. Based on experience, the Secretary shall revise the standards and criteria. When approved by Congress, the Secretary shall prescribe standards and criteria developed or revised under this subsection. This subsection does not apply to—

(1) the acquisition of transportation facilities or equipment by a department, agency, or instrumentality of the Government to provide transportation for its use;

(2) an inter-oceanic canal located outside the 48 contiguous States;

(3) defense features included at the direction of the Department of Defense in designing and constructing civil air, sea, or land transportation;

(4) foreign assistance programs;

(5) water resources projects; or

(6) grant-in-aid programs authorized by law.

(b) A department, agency, or instrumentality of the Government preparing a survey, plan, or report that includes a proposal about which the Secretary has prescribed standards and criteria under subsection (a) of this section shall—

(1) prepare the survey, plan, or report under those standards and criteria and on the basis of information provided by the Secretary on the—

(A) projected growth of transportation needs and traffic in the affected area;

(B) the relative efficiency of various modes of transportation;

(C) the available transportation services in the area; and

(D) the general effect of the proposed investment on existing modes of transportation and on the regional and national economy;

(2) coordinate the survey, plan, or report—

(A) with the Secretary and include the views and comments of the Secretary; and

(B) as appropriate, with other departments, agencies, and instrumentalities of the Government, States, and local governments, and include their views and comments; and

(3) send the survey, plan, or report to the President for disposition under law and procedure established by the President.

(Pub. L. 97–449, §1(b), Jan. 12, 1983, 96 Stat. 2420.)

* * * * * * *

SUBTITLE II
OTHER GOVERNMENT AGENCIES

SUBTITLE II—OTHER GOVERNMENT AGENCIES

* * * * * * *

CHAPTER 11—NATIONAL TRANSPORTATION SAFETY BOARD

SUBCHAPTER I—GENERAL

SUBCHAPTER II—ORGANIZATION AND ADMINISTRATIVE

SUBCHAPTER III—AUTHORITY

SUBCHAPTER IV—ENFORCEMENT AND PENALTIES

---

[1] *Section catchline amended by Pub. L. 118–63 without corresponding amendment of chapter analysis.*

SUBCHAPTER I—GENERAL

§1101. DEFINITIONS

(a) IN GENERAL.—In this chapter:

(1) ACCIDENT.—The term "accident" includes damage to or destruction of vehicles in surface or air transportation or pipelines, regardless of whether the initiating event is accidental or otherwise.

(2) STATE.—The term "State" means a State of the United States, the District of Columbia, Puerto Rico, the Virgin Islands, American Samoa, the Northern Mariana Islands, and Guam.

(b) APPLICABILITY OF OTHER DEFINITIONS.—Section 2101(23) of title 46 and section 40102(a) of this title shall apply to this chapter.

(Pub. L. 103–272, §1(d), July 5, 1994, 108 Stat. 746; Pub. L. 106–424, §2, Nov. 1, 2000, 114 Stat. 1883; Pub. L. 115–232, div. C, title XXXV, §3541(b)(17), Aug. 13, 2018, 132 Stat. 2324; Pub. L. 118–63, title XII, §1203, May 16, 2024, 138 Stat. 1422.)

SUBCHAPTER II—ORGANIZATION AND ADMINISTRATIVE

§1111. GENERAL ORGANIZATION

(a) ORGANIZATION.—The National Transportation Safety Board is an independent establishment of the United States Government.

(b) APPOINTMENT OF MEMBERS.—The Board is composed of 5 members appointed by the President, by and with the advice and consent of the Senate. Not more than 3 members may be appointed from the same political party. At least 3 members shall be appointed on the basis of technical qualification, professional standing, and demonstrated knowledge in accident reconstruction, safety engineering, human factors, transportation safety, or transportation regulation.

(c) TERMS OF OFFICE AND REMOVAL.—The term of office of each member is 5 years. An individual appointed to fill a vacancy occurring before the expiration of the term for which the predecessor of that individual was appointed, is appointed for the remainder of that term. When the term of office of a member ends, the member may continue to serve until a successor is appointed and qualified. The President may remove a member for inefficiency, neglect of duty, or malfeasance in office.

(d) CHAIRMAN AND VICE CHAIRMAN.—The President shall designate, by and with the advice and consent of the Senate, a Chairman of the Board. The President also shall designate a Vice Chairman of the Board. The terms of office of both the Chairman and Vice Chairman are 3 years. When the Chairman is absent or unable to serve or when the position of Chairman is vacant, the Vice Chairman acts as Chairman.

(e) DUTIES AND POWERS OF CHAIRMAN.—The Chairman is the chief executive and administrative officer of the Board. Subject to the general policies and decisions of the Board, the Chairman shall—

(1) appoint and supervise officers and employees, other than regular and full-time employees in the immediate offices of another member, necessary to carry out this chapter;

(2) fix the pay of officers and employees necessary to carry out this chapter;

(3) distribute business among the officers, employees, and administrative units of the Board; and

(4) supervise the expenditures of the Board.

(f) QUORUM.—Three members of the Board are a quorum in carrying out duties and powers of the Board.

(g) OFFICES, BUREAUS, AND DIVISIONS.—The Board shall establish offices necessary to carry out this chapter, including an office to investigate and report on the safe transportation of hazardous material. The Board shall establish distinct and appropriately staffed bureaus, divisions, or offices to investigate and report on accidents involving each of the following modes of transportation:

(1) aviation.

(2) highway and motor vehicle.

(3) rail and tracked vehicle.

(4) pipeline.

(5) marine.

(h) CHIEF FINANCIAL OFFICER.—The Chairman shall designate an officer or employee of the Board as the Chief Financial Officer. The Chief Financial Officer shall—

(1) report directly to the Chairman on financial management and budget execution;

(2) direct, manage, and provide policy guidance and oversight on financial management and property and inventory control; and

(3) review the fees, rents, and other charges imposed by the Board for services and things of value it provides, and suggest appropriate revisions to those charges to reflect costs incurred by the Board in providing those services and things of value.

(i) BOARD MEMBER STAFF.—Each member of the Board shall select and supervise regular and full-time employees in his or her immediate office as long as any such employee has been approved for employment by the designated agency ethics official under the same guidelines that apply to all employees of the Board. Except for the Chairman, the appointment authority provided by this subsection is limited to the number of full-time equivalent positions, in addition to 1 senior professional staff at a level not to exceed the GS 15 level and 1 administrative staff, allocated to each member through the Board's annual budget and allocation process.

(j) SEAL.—The Board shall have a seal that shall be judicially recognized.

(k) OPEN MEETINGS.—

(1) IN GENERAL.—The Board shall be deemed to be an agency for purposes of section 552b of title 5.

(2) NONPUBLIC COLLABORATIVE DISCUSSIONS.—

(A) IN GENERAL.—Notwithstanding section 552b of title 5, a majority of the members may hold a meeting that is not open to public observation to discuss official agency business if—

(i) no formal or informal vote or other official agency action is taken at the meeting;

(ii) each individual present at the meeting is a member or an employee of the Board;

(iii) at least 1 member of the Board from each political party is present at the meeting, if applicable; and

(iv) the General Counsel of the Board is present at the meeting.

(B) DISCLOSURE OF NONPUBLIC COLLABORATIVE DISCUSSIONS.—Except as provided under subparagraphs (C) and (D), not later than 2 business days after the conclusion of a meeting under subparagraph (A), the Board shall make available to the public, in a place easily accessible to the public—

(i) a list of the individuals present at the meeting; and

(ii) a summary of the matters, including key issues, discussed at the meeting, except for any matter the Board properly determines may be withheld from the public under section 552b(c) of title 5.

(C) SUMMARY.—If the Board properly determines a matter may be withheld from the public under section 552b(c) of title 5, the Board shall provide a summary with as much general information as possible on each matter withheld from the public.

(D) ACTIVE INVESTIGATIONS.—If a discussion under subparagraph (A) directly relates to an active investigation, the Board shall make the disclosure under subparagraph (B) on the date the Board adopts the final report.

(E) PRESERVATION OF OPEN MEETINGS REQUIREMENTS FOR AGENCY ACTION.—Nothing in this paragraph may be construed to limit the applicability of section 552b of title 5 with respect to a meeting of the members other than that described in this paragraph.

(F) STATUTORY CONSTRUCTION.—Nothing in this paragraph may be construed—

(i) to limit the applicability of section 552b of title 5 with respect to any information which is proposed to be withheld from the public under subparagraph (B)(ii); or

(ii) to authorize the Board to withhold from any individual any record that is accessible to that individual under section 552a of title 5.

(Pub. L. 103–272, §1(d), July 5, 1994, 108 Stat. 746; Pub. L. 106–424, §10, Nov. 1, 2000, 114 Stat. 1886; Pub. L. 109–443, §9(a), (d), Dec. 21, 2006, 120 Stat. 3301; Pub. L. 115–254, div. C, §1112(a), (b), Oct. 5, 2018, 132 Stat. 3436.)

§1112. SPECIAL BOARDS OF INQUIRY ON AIR TRANSPORTATION SAFETY

(a) ESTABLISHMENT.—If an accident involves a substantial question about public safety in air transportation, the National Transportation Safety Board may establish a special board of inquiry composed of—

(1) one member of the Board acting as chairman; and

(2) 2 members representing the public, appointed by the President on notification of the establishment of the special board of inquiry.

(b) QUALIFICATIONS AND CONFLICTS OF INTEREST.—The public members of a special board of inquiry must be qualified by training and experience to participate in the inquiry and may not have a pecuniary interest in an aviation enterprise involved in the accident to be investigated.

(c) AUTHORITY.—A special board of inquiry has the same authority that the Board has under this chapter.

(Pub. L. 103–272, §1(d), July 5, 1994, 108 Stat. 747.)

§1113. ADMINISTRATIVE

(a) GENERAL AUTHORITY.—(1) The National Transportation Safety Board, and when authorized by it, a member of the Board, an administrative law judge employed by or assigned to the Board, or an officer or employee designated by the Chairman of the Board, may conduct hearings to carry out this chapter, administer oaths, and require, by subpoena or otherwise, necessary witnesses and evidence.

(2) A witness or evidence in a hearing under paragraph (1) of this subsection may be summoned or required to be produced from any place in the United States to the designated place of the hearing. A witness summoned under this subsection is entitled to the same fee and mileage the witness would have been paid in a court of the United States.

(3) A subpoena shall be issued under the signature of the Chairman or the Chairman's delegate but may be served by any person designated by the Chairman.

(4) If a person disobeys a subpoena, order, or inspection notice of the Board, the Board may bring a civil action in a district court of the United States to enforce the subpoena, order, or notice. An action under this paragraph may be brought in the judicial district in which the person against whom the action is brought resides, is found, or does business. The court may punish a failure to obey an order of the court to comply with the subpoena, order, or notice as a contempt of court.

(b) ADDITIONAL POWERS.—(1) The Board may—

(A) procure the temporary or intermittent services of experts or consultants under section 3109 of title 5;

(B) make agreements and other transactions necessary to carry out this chapter without regard to section 6101(b) to (d) of title 41;

(C) use, when appropriate, available services, equipment, personnel, and facilities of a department, agency, or instrumentality of the United States Government on a reimbursable or other basis;

(D) confer with employees and use services, records, and facilities of State and local governmental authorities;

(E) appoint advisory committees composed of qualified private citizens and officials of the Government and State and local governments as appropriate;

(F) accept voluntary and uncompensated services notwithstanding another law;

(G) accept gifts of money and other property;

(H) make contracts with nonprofit entities to carry out studies related to duties and powers of the Board;

(I) negotiate and enter into agreements with individuals and private entities and departments, agencies, and instrumentalities of the Government, State and local governments, and governments of foreign countries for the provision of facilities, accident-related and technical services or training in accident investigation theory and techniques, and require that such entities provide appropriate consideration for the reasonable costs of any facilities, goods, services, or training provided by the Board;

(J) notwithstanding section 1343 of title 31, acquire 1 or more small unmanned aircraft (as defined in section 44801) for use in investigations under this chapter; and

(K) notwithstanding section 3301 of title 41, acquire training on emerging transportation technologies if such training—

(i) is required for an ongoing investigation; and

(ii) meets the criteria under section 3304(a)(7)(A) of title 41.

(2) The Board shall deposit in the Treasury amounts received under paragraph (1)(I) of this subsection to be credited as offsetting collections to the appropriation of the Board. The Board shall maintain an annual record of collections received under paragraph (1)(I) of this subsection.

(c) SUBMISSION OF CERTAIN COPIES TO CONGRESS.—When the Board submits to the President or the Director of the Office of Management and Budget a budget estimate, budget request, supplemental budget estimate, other budget information, a legislative recommendation, prepared testimony for congressional hearings, or comments on legislation, the Board must submit a copy to Congress at the same time. An officer, department, agency, or instrumentality of the Government may not require the Board to submit the estimate, request, information, recommendation, testimony, or comments to another officer, department, agency, or instrumentality of the Government for approval, comment, or review before being submitted to Congress. The Board shall develop and approve a process for the Board's review and comment or approval of documents submitted to the President, Director of the Office of Management and Budget, or Congress under this subsection.

(d) LIAISON COMMITTEES.—The Chairman may determine the number of committees that are appropriate to maintain effective liaison with other departments, agencies, and instrumentalities of the Government, State and local governmental authorities, and independent standard-setting authorities that carry out programs and activities related to transportation safety. The Board may designate representatives to serve on or assist those committees.

(e) INQUIRIES.—The Board, or an officer or employee of the Board designated by the Chairman, may conduct an inquiry to obtain information related to transportation safety after publishing notice of the inquiry in the Federal Register. The Board or designated officer or employee may require by order a department, agency, or instrumentality of the Government, a State or local governmental authority, or a person transporting individuals or property in commerce to submit to the Board a written report and answers to requests and questions related to a duty or power of the Board. The Board may prescribe the time within which the report and answers must be given to the Board or to the designated officer or employee. Copies of the report and answers shall be made available for public inspection.

(f) REGULATIONS.—The Board may prescribe regulations to carry out this chapter.

(g) OVERTIME PAY.—

(1) IN GENERAL.—Subject to the requirements of this section and notwithstanding paragraphs (1) and (2) of section 5542(a) of title 5, for an employee of the Board whose basic pay is at a rate which equals or exceeds the minimum rate of basic pay for GS–10 of the General Schedule, the Board may establish an overtime hourly rate of pay for the employee with respect to work performed at the scene of an accident (including travel

to or from the scene) and other work that is critical to an accident investigation in an amount equal to one and one-half times the hourly rate of basic pay of the employee. All of such amount shall be considered to be premium pay.

(2) LIMITATION ON OVERTIME PAY TO AN EMPLOYEE.—An employee of the Board may not receive overtime pay under paragraph (1), for work performed in a calendar year, in an amount that exceeds 15 percent of the annual rate of basic pay of the employee for such calendar year.

(3) LIMITATION ON TOTAL AMOUNT OF OVERTIME PAY.—The Board may not make overtime payments under paragraph (1) for work performed in any fiscal year in a total amount that exceeds 1.5 percent of the amount appropriated to carry out this chapter for that fiscal year.

(4) BASIC PAY DEFINED.—In this subsection, the term "basic pay" includes any applicable locality-based comparability payment under section 5304 of title 5 (or similar provision of law) and any special rate of pay under section 5305 of title 5 (or similar provision of law).

(h) STRATEGIC WORKFORCE PLAN.—

(1) IN GENERAL.—The Board shall develop a strategic workforce plan that addresses the immediate and long-term workforce needs of the Board with respect to carrying out the authorities and duties of the Board under this chapter.

(2) ALIGNING THE WORKFORCE TO STRATEGIC GOALS.—In developing the strategic workforce plan under paragraph (1), the Board shall take into consideration—

(A) the current state and capabilities of the Board, including a high-level review of mission requirements, structure, workforce, and performance of the Board;

(B) the significant workforce trends, needs, issues, and challenges with respect to the Board and the transportation industry;

(C) with respect to employees involved in transportation safety work, the needs, issues, and challenges, including accident severity and risk, posed by each mode of transportation, and how the Board's staffing for each transportation mode reflects these aspects;

(D) the workforce policies, strategies, performance measures, and interventions to mitigate succession risks that guide the workforce investment decisions of the Board;

(E) a workforce planning strategy that identifies workforce needs, including the knowledge, skills, and abilities needed to recruit and retain skilled employees at the Board;

(F) a workforce management strategy that is aligned with the mission of the Board, including plans for continuity of leadership and knowledge sharing;

(G) an implementation system that addresses workforce competency gaps, particularly in mission-critical occupations; and

(H) a system for analyzing and evaluating the performance of the Board's workforce management policies, programs, and activities.

(3) PLANNING PERIOD.—The strategic workforce plan developed under paragraph (1) shall address a 5-year forecast period, but may include planning for longer periods based on information about emerging technologies or safety trends in transportation.

(4) PLAN UPDATES.—The Board shall update the strategic workforce plan developed under paragraph (1) not less than once every 5 years.

(5) Relationship to strategic plan.—The strategic workforce plan developed under paragraph (1) may be developed separately from, or incorporated into, the strategic plan required under section 306 of title 5.

(6) Availability.—The strategic workforce plan under paragraph (1) and the strategic plan required under section 306 of title 5 shall be—

(A) submitted to the Committee on Transportation and Infrastructure of the House of Representatives and the Committee on Commerce, Science, and Transportation of the Senate; and

(B) made available to the public on a website of the Board.

(i) Non-accident-related Travel Budget.—

(1) In general.—The Board shall establish annual fiscal year budgets for non-accident-related travel expenditures for each Board member.

(2) Notification.—The Board shall notify the Committee on Transportation and Infrastructure of the House of Representatives and the Committee on Commerce, Science, and Transportation of the Senate of any non-accident-related travel budget overrun for any Board member not later than 30 days of such overrun becoming known to the Board.

(Pub. L. 103–272, §1(d), July 5, 1994, 108 Stat. 747; Pub. L. 106–424, §§3(a), (b)(1), 4, Nov. 1, 2000, 114 Stat. 1883, 1884; Pub. L. 109–443, §9(e)–(g), Dec. 21, 2006, 120 Stat. 3301; Pub. L. 111–350, §5(o)(2), Jan. 4, 2011, 124 Stat. 3853; Pub. L. 115–254, div. C, §1112(c)–(e), Oct. 5, 2018, 132 Stat. 3437, 3438; Pub. L. 118–63, title XII, §§1204(a), 1205–1207(a), May 16, 2024, 138 Stat. 1422–1424.)

§1114. Disclosure, availability, and use of information

(a) General.—(1) Except as provided in subsections (b), (c), (d), and (f) of this section, a copy of a record, information, or investigation submitted or received by the National Transportation Safety Board, or a member or employee of the Board, shall be made available to the public on identifiable request and at reasonable cost. This subsection does not require the release of information described by section 552(b) of title 5 or protected from disclosure by another law of the United States.

(2) The Board shall deposit in the Treasury amounts received under paragraph (1) to be credited to the appropriation of the Board as offsetting collections.

(b) Certain Confidential Information.—(1) In general.—The Board may disclose confidential information described in section 1905 of title 18, including trade secrets, only—

(A) to another department, agency, or instrumentality of the United States Government when requested for official use;

(B) to a committee of Congress having jurisdiction over the subject matter to which the information is related, when requested by that committee;

(C) in a judicial proceeding under a court order that preserves the confidentiality of the information without impairing the proceeding; and

(D) to the public to protect health and safety after giving notice to any interested person to whom the information is related and an opportunity for that person to comment in writing, or orally in closed session, on the proposed disclosure, if the delay resulting from notice and opportunity for comment would not be detrimental to health and safety.

(2) Information disclosed under paragraph (1) of this subsection may be disclosed only

in a way designed to preserve its confidentiality.

(3) PROTECTION OF VOLUNTARY SUBMISSION OF INFORMATION.—Notwithstanding any other provision of law, neither the Board, nor any agency receiving information from the Board, shall disclose voluntarily provided safety-related information if that information is not related to the exercise of the Board's accident or incident investigation authority under this chapter and if the Board finds that the disclosure of the information would inhibit the voluntary provision of that type of information.

(c) COCKPIT RECORDINGS AND TRANSCRIPTS.—

(1) CONFIDENTIALITY OF RECORDINGS.—Except as provided in paragraph (2), the Board may not disclose publicly any part of a cockpit voice or video recorder recording or transcript of oral communications by and between flight crew members and ground stations related to an accident or incident investigated by the Board.

(2) EXCEPTION.—Subject to subsections (b) and (g), the Board shall make public any part of a transcript, any written depiction of visual information obtained from a video recorder, or any still image obtained from a video recorder the Board decides is relevant to the accident or incident—

(A) if the Board holds a public hearing on the accident or incident, at the time of the hearing; or

(B) if the Board does not hold a public hearing, at the time a majority of the other factual reports on the accident or incident are placed in the public docket.

(3) REFERENCES TO INFORMATION IN MAKING SAFETY RECOMMENDATIONS.—This subsection does not prevent the Board from referring at any time to cockpit voice or video recorder information in making safety recommendations.

(d) SURFACE VEHICLE RECORDINGS AND TRANSCRIPTS.—

(1) CONFIDENTIALITY OF RECORDINGS.—Except as provided in paragraph (2), the Board may not disclose publicly any part of a surface vehicle voice or video recorder recording or transcript of oral communications by or among drivers, train employees, or other operating employees responsible for the movement and direction of the vehicle or vessel, or between such operating employees and company communication centers, related to an accident investigated by the Board.

(2) EXCEPTION.—Subject to subsections (b) and (g), the Board shall make public any part of a transcript, any written depiction of visual information obtained from a video recorder, or any still image obtained from a video recorder the Board decides is relevant to the accident—

(A) if the Board holds a public hearing on the accident, at the time of the hearing; or

(B) if the Board does not hold a public hearing, at the time a majority of the other factual reports on the accident are placed in the public docket.

(3) REFERENCES TO INFORMATION IN MAKING SAFETY RECOMMENDATIONS.—This subsection does not prevent the Board from referring at any time to voice or video recorder information in making safety recommendations.

(e) DRUG TESTS.—(1) Notwithstanding section 503(e) of the Supplemental Appropriations Act, 1987 (Public Law 100–71, 101 Stat. 471), the Secretary of Transportation shall provide the following information to the Board when requested in writing by the Board:

(A) any report of a confirmed positive toxicological test, verified as positive by a medical review officer, conducted on an officer or employee of the Department of Transportation under post-accident, unsafe practice, or reasonable suspicion toxicological testing requirements of the Department, when the officer or employee is reasonably associated with the circumstances of an accident or incident under the investigative jurisdiction of the Board.

(B) any laboratory record documenting that the test is confirmed positive.

(2) Except as provided by paragraph (3) of this subsection, the Board shall maintain the confidentiality of, and exempt from disclosure under section 552(b)(3) of title 5—

(A) a laboratory record provided the Board under paragraph (1) of this subsection that reveals medical use of a drug allowed under applicable regulations; and

(B) medical information provided by the tested officer or employee related to the test or a review of the test.

(3) The Board may use a laboratory record made available under paragraph (1) of this subsection to develop an evidentiary record in an investigation of an accident or incident if—

(A) the fitness of the tested officer or employee is at issue in the investigation; and

(B) the use of that record is necessary to develop the evidentiary record.

(f) FOREIGN INVESTIGATIONS.—

(1) IN GENERAL.—Notwithstanding any other provision of law, neither the Board, nor any agency receiving information from the Board, shall disclose records or information relating to its participation in foreign aircraft accident investigations; except that—

(A) the Board shall release records pertaining to such an investigation when the country conducting the investigation issues its final report or 2 years following the date of the accident, whichever occurs first; and

(B) the Board may disclose records and information when authorized to do so by the country conducting the investigation.

(2) SAFETY RECOMMENDATIONS.—Nothing in this subsection shall restrict the Board at any time from referring to foreign accident investigation information in making safety recommendations.

(g) PRIVACY PROTECTIONS.—Before making public any still image obtained from a video recorder under subsection (c)(2) or subsection (d)(2), the Board shall take such action as appropriate to protect from public disclosure any information that readily identifies an individual, including a decedent.

(Pub. L. 103–272, §1(d), July 5, 1994, 108 Stat. 749; Pub. L. 104–291, title I, §§102, 103, Oct. 11, 1996, 110 Stat. 3452; Pub. L. 106–424, §§3(b)(2), 5(a), (b), Nov. 1, 2000, 114 Stat. 1884, 1885; Pub. L. 115–254, div. C, §1104(a), Oct. 5, 2018, 132 Stat. 3429; Pub. L. 118–63, title XII, §1208(a), May 16, 2024, 138 Stat. 1424.)

§1115. TRAINING

(a) DEFINITION.—In this section, "Institute" means the Transportation Safety Institute of the Department of Transportation and any successor organization of the Institute.

(b) USE OF INSTITUTE SERVICES.—The National Transportation Safety Board may use, on a reimbursable basis, the services of the Institute. The Secretary of Transportation shall make the Institute available to—

(1) the Board for safety training of employees of the Board in carrying out their duties and powers; and

(2) other safety personnel of the United States Government, State and local governments, governments of foreign countries, interstate authorities, and private organizations the Board designates in consultation with the Secretary.

(c) FEES.—(1) Training at the Institute for safety personnel (except employees of the Government) shall be provided at a reasonable fee established periodically by the Board in consultation with the Secretary. The fee shall be paid directly to the Secretary, and the Secretary shall deposit the fee in the Treasury. The amount of the fee—

(A) shall be credited to the appropriate appropriation (subject to the requirements of any annual appropriation); and

(B) is an offset against any annual reimbursement agreement between the Board and the Secretary to cover all reasonable costs of providing training under this subsection that the Secretary incurs in operating the Institute.

(2) The Board shall maintain an annual record of offsets under paragraph (1)(B) of this subsection.

(d) TRAINING OF BOARD EMPLOYEES AND OTHERS.—The Board may conduct training of its employees in those subjects necessary for the proper performance of accident investigation and in those subjects furthering the personnel and workforce development needs set forth in the strategic workforce plan of the Board as required under section 1113(h). The Board may also authorize attendance at courses given under this subsection by other government personnel, personnel of foreign governments, and personnel from industry or otherwise who have a requirement for accident investigation training. The Board may require non-Board personnel to reimburse some or all of the training costs, and amounts so reimbursed shall be credited to the appropriation of the Board as offsetting collections.

(Pub. L. 103–272, §1(d), July 5, 1994, 108 Stat. 750; Pub. L. 104–291, title I, §104, Oct. 11, 1996, 110 Stat. 3453; Pub. L. 106–424, §3(b)(3), Nov. 1, 2000, 114 Stat. 1884; Pub. L. 118–63, title XII, §1204(b), May 16, 2024, 138 Stat. 1423.)

§1116. REPORTS, STUDIES, AND RETROSPECTIVE REVIEWS

(a) PERIODIC REPORTS.—The National Transportation Safety Board shall report periodically to Congress, departments, agencies, and instrumentalities of the United States Government and State and local governmental authorities concerned with transportation safety, and other interested persons. The report shall—

(1) advocate meaningful responses to reduce the likelihood of transportation accidents similar to those investigated by the Board; and

(2) propose corrective action to make the transportation of individuals as safe and free from risk of injury as possible, including action to minimize personal injuries that occur in transportation accidents.

(b) STUDIES, INVESTIGATIONS, AND OTHER REPORTS.—The Board also shall—

(1) carry out special studies and investigations about transportation safety, including avoiding personal injury;

(2) examine techniques and methods of accident investigation and periodically publish recommended procedures for accident investigations;

(3) prescribe requirements for persons reporting accidents and aviation incidents

that—

    (A) may be investigated by the Board under this chapter; or

    (B) involve public aircraft (except aircraft of the armed forces and the intelligence agencies);

    (4) evaluate, examine the effectiveness of, and publish the findings of the Board about the transportation safety consciousness of other departments, agencies, and instrumentalities of the Government and their effectiveness in preventing accidents; and

    (5) evaluate the adequacy of safeguards and procedures for the transportation of hazardous material and the performance of other departments, agencies, and instrumentalities of the Government responsible for the safe transportation of that material.

(c) ANNUAL REPORT.—The National Transportation Safety Board shall submit a report to Congress on July 1 of each year. The report shall include—

    (1) a statistical and analytical summary of the transportation accident investigations conducted and reviewed by the Board during the prior calendar year;

    (2) a survey and summary of the recommendations made by the Board to reduce the likelihood of recurrence of those accidents together with the observed response to each recommendation;

    (3) a list of each recommendation made by the Board to the Secretary of Transportation or the Commandant of the Coast Guard that was closed in an unacceptable status in the preceding 12 months, including—

        (A) any explanation the Board received from the Secretary or Commandant; and

        (B) any explanation from the Board as to why the recommendation was closed in an unacceptable status, including a discussion of why alternate means, if any, taken by the Secretary or Commandant to address the Board's recommendation were inadequate;

    (4) a detailed appraisal of the accident investigation and accident prevention activities of other departments, agencies, and instrumentalities of the United States Government and State and local governmental authorities having responsibility for those activities under a law of the United States or a State;

    (5) a description of the activities and operations of the National Transportation Safety Board Training Center during the prior calendar year;

    (6) a list of accidents, during the prior calendar year, that the Board was required to investigate under section 1131 but did not investigate and an explanation of why they were not investigated; and

    (7) a list of ongoing investigations that have exceeded the expected time allotted for completion by Board order and an explanation for the additional time required to complete each such investigation.

(d) RETROSPECTIVE REVIEWS.—

    (1) IN GENERAL.—Subject to paragraph (2), not later than June 1, 2019, and at least every 5 years thereafter, the Chairman shall complete a retrospective review of recommendations issued by the Board that are classified as open by the Board.

    (2) CONTENTS.—A review under paragraph (1) shall include—

        (A) a determination of whether the recommendation should be updated, closed, or reissued in light of—

            (i) changed circumstances;

(ii) more recently issued recommendations;

(iii) the availability of new technologies; or

(iv) new information making the recommendation ineffective or insufficient for achieving its objective; and

(B) a justification for each determination under subparagraph (A).

(3) REPORT.—Not later than 180 days after the date a review under paragraph (1) is complete, the Chairman shall submit to the Committee on Commerce, Science, and Transportation of the Senate and the Committee on Transportation and Infrastructure of the House of Representatives a report that includes—

(A) the findings of the review under paragraph (1);

(B) each determination under paragraph (2)(A) and justification under paragraph (2)(B); and

(C) if applicable, a schedule for updating, closing, or reissuing a recommendation.

(Pub. L. 103–272, §1(d), July 5, 1994, 108 Stat. 751; Pub. L. 115–254, div. C, §§1107(a), 1111(a), Oct. 5, 2018, 132 Stat. 3432, 3436; Pub. L. 118–63, title XII, §1209, May 16, 2024, 138 Stat. 1425.)

§1117. METHODOLOGY

(a) IN GENERAL.—Not later than 2 years after the date of enactment of the National Transportation Safety Board Reauthorization Act, the Chairman shall include with each investigative report in which a recommendation is issued by the Board a methodology section detailing the process and information underlying the selection of each recommendation.

(b) ELEMENTS.—Except as provided in subsection (c), the methodology section under subsection (a) shall include, for each recommendation—

(1) a brief summary of the Board's collection and analysis of the specific accident investigation information most relevant to the recommendation;

(2) a description of the Board's use of external information, including studies, reports, and experts, other than the findings of a specific accident investigation, if any were used to inform or support the recommendation, including a brief summary of the specific safety benefits and other effects identified by each study, report, or expert; and

(3) a brief summary of any examples of actions taken by regulated entities before the publication of the safety recommendation, to the extent such actions are known to the Board, that were consistent with the recommendation.

(c) ACCEPTABLE LIMITATION.—If the Board knows of more than 3 examples taken by regulated entities before the publication of the safety recommendation that were consistent with the recommendation, the brief summary under subsection (b)(3) may be limited to only 3 of those examples.

(d) EXCEPTION.—Subsection (a) shall not apply if the recommendation is only for a person to disseminate information on—

(1) an existing agency best practices document; or

(2) an existing regulatory requirement.

(e) RULE OF CONSTRUCTION.—Nothing in this section may be construed to require any change to a recommendation made by the Board before the date of enactment of the National Transportation Safety Board Reauthorization Act, unless the recommendation is a repeat recommendation issued on or after the date of enactment of such Act.

(f) SAVINGS CLAUSE.—Nothing in this section may be construed—

(1) to delay publication of the findings, cause, or probable cause of a Board investigation;

(2) to delay the issuance of an urgent recommendation that the Board has determined must be issued to avoid immediate loss, death, or injury; or

(3) to limit the number of examples the Board may consider before issuing a recommendation.

(Pub. L. 103–272, §1(d), July 5, 1994, 108 Stat. 751; Pub. L. 104–66, title II, §2151, Dec. 21, 1995, 109 Stat. 731; Pub. L. 109–443, §2(a)(1), Dec. 21, 2006, 120 Stat. 3297; Pub. L. 115–254, div. C, §1107(b)(1), Oct. 5, 2018, 132 Stat. 3432.)

§1118. AUTHORIZATION OF APPROPRIATIONS

(a) IN GENERAL.—

(1) AUTHORIZATIONS.—There is authorized to be appropriated for purposes of this chapter—

(A) $140,000,000 for fiscal year 2024;

(B) $145,000,000 for fiscal year 2025;

(C) $148,000,000 for fiscal year 2026;

(D) $151,000,000 for fiscal year 2027; and

(E) $154,000,000 for fiscal year 2028.

(2) AVAILABILITY.—Amounts authorized under paragraph (1) shall remain available until expended.

(b) EMERGENCY FUND.—The Board has an emergency fund of $2,000,000 available for necessary expenses of the Board, not otherwise provided for, for accident investigations. In addition, there are authorized to be appropriated such sums as may be necessary to increase the fund to, and maintain the fund at, a level not to exceed $4,000,000.

(c) FEES, REFUNDS, AND REIMBURSEMENTS.—

(1) IN GENERAL.—The Board may impose and collect such fees, refunds, and reimbursements as it determines to be appropriate for services provided by or through the Board.

(2) RECEIPTS CREDITED AS OFFSETTING COLLECTIONS.—Notwithstanding section 3302 of title 31, any fee, refund, or reimbursement collected under this subsection—

(A) shall be credited as offsetting collections to the account that finances the activities and services for which the fee is imposed or with which the refund or reimbursement is associated;

(B) shall be available for expenditure only to pay the costs of activities and services for which the fee is imposed or with which the refund or reimbursement is associated; and

(C) shall remain available until expended.

(3) REFUNDS.—The Board may refund any fee paid by mistake or any amount paid in excess of that required.

(Pub. L. 103–272, §1(d), July 5, 1994, 108 Stat. 752; Pub. L. 103–411, §2, Oct. 25, 1994, 108 Stat. 4236; Pub. L. 104–291, title I, §105, Oct. 11, 1996, 110 Stat. 3453; Pub. L. 106–424, §13, Nov. 1, 2000, 114 Stat. 1888; Pub. L. 108–168, §2, Dec. 6, 2003, 117 Stat. 2032; Pub. L. 109–443, §§8(a), (b)(1), (c), Dec. 21, 2006, 120 Stat. 3300; Pub. L. 115–254, div. C, §1103, Oct. 5, 2018, 132 Stat. 3429; Pub. L. 118–63, title XII, §1202, May 16, 2024, 138 Stat. 1422.)

§1119. Accident and safety data classification and publication

(a) In General.—Not later than 90 days after the date of the enactment of this section, the National Transportation Safety Board shall, in consultation and coordination with the Administrator of the Federal Aviation Administration, develop a system for classifying air carrier accident data maintained by the Board.

(b) Requirements for Classification System.—

(1) In general.—The system developed under this section shall provide for the classification of accident and safety data in a manner that, in comparison to the system in effect on the date of the enactment of this section, provides for safety-related categories that provide clearer descriptions of accidents associated with air transportation, including a more refined classification of accidents which involve fatalities, injuries, or substantial damage and which are only related to the operation of an aircraft.

(2) Public comment.—In developing a system of classification under paragraph (1), the Board shall provide adequate opportunity for public review and comment.

(3) Final classification.—After providing for public review and comment, and after consulting with the Administrator, the Board shall issue final classifications. The Board shall ensure that air travel accident covered under this section is classified in accordance with the final classifications issued under this section for data for calendar year 1997, and for each subsequent calendar year.

(4) Publication.—The Board shall publish on a periodic basis accident and safety data in accordance with the final classifications issued under paragraph (3).

(5) Recommendations of the administrator.—The Administrator may, from time to time, request the Board to consider revisions (including additions to the classification system developed under this section). The Board shall respond to any request made by the Administrator under this section not later than 90 days after receiving that request.

(c) Appeals.—

(1) Notification of rights.—In any case in which an employee of the Board determines that an occurrence associated with the operation of an aircraft constitutes an accident, the employee shall notify the owner or operator of that aircraft of the right to appeal that determination to the Board.

(2) Procedure.—The Board shall establish and publish the procedures for appeals under this subsection.

(3) Limitation on applicability.—This subsection shall not apply in the case of an accident that results in a loss of life.

(Added Pub. L. 104–264, title IV, §407(a)(1), Oct. 9, 1996, 110 Stat. 3257; amended Pub. L. 108–168, §5, Dec. 6, 2003, 117 Stat. 2034.)

SUBCHAPTER III—AUTHORITY

§1131. General authority

(a) General.—(1) The National Transportation Safety Board shall investigate or have investigated (in detail the Board prescribes) and establish the facts, circumstances, and cause or probable cause of—

(A) an aircraft accident the Board has authority to investigate under section 1132 of this title or an aircraft accident involving a public aircraft as defined by section 40102(a) of this title other than an aircraft operated by the Armed Forces or by an intelligence agency of the United States;

(B) a highway accident, including a railroad grade crossing accident, the Board selects, concurrent with any State investigation, in which case the Board and the relevant State agencies shall coordinate to ensure both the Board and State agencies have timely access to the information needed to conduct each such investigation, including any criminal and enforcement activities conducted by the relevant State agency;

(C) a railroad—

(i) accident in which there is a fatality or substantial property damage, except—

(I) a grade crossing accident or incident, unless selected by the Board; or

(II) an accident or incident involving a trespasser, unless selected by the Board; or

(ii) accident or incident that involves a passenger train, except in any case in which such accident or incident resulted in no fatalities or serious injuries to the passengers or crewmembers of such train, and—

(I) was a grade crossing accident or incident, unless selected by the Board; or

(II) such accident or incident involved a trespasser, unless selected by the Board;

(D) a pipeline accident in which there is a fatality, substantial property damage, or significant injury to the environment;

(E) a major marine casualty (except a casualty involving only public vessels) occurring on or under the navigable waters, internal waters, or the territorial sea of the United States as described in Presidential Proclamation No. 5928 of December 27, 1988, or involving a vessel of the United States (as defined in section 116 of title 46), under regulations prescribed jointly by the Board and the head of the department in which the Coast Guard is operating; and

(F) any other accident related to the transportation of individuals or property when the Board decides—

(i) the accident is catastrophic;

(ii) the accident involves problems of a recurring character; or

(iii) the investigation of the accident would carry out this chapter.

(2)(A) Subject to the requirements of this paragraph, an investigation by the Board under paragraph (1)(A)–(D) or (F) of this subsection has priority over any investigation by another department, agency, or instrumentality of the United States Government. The Board shall provide for appropriate participation by other departments, agencies, or instrumentalities in the investigation. However, those departments, agencies, or instrumentalities may not participate in the decision of the Board about the probable cause of the accident.

(B) If the Attorney General, in consultation with the Chairman of the Board, determines and notifies the Board that circumstances reasonably indicate that the accident may have been caused by an intentional criminal act, the Board shall relinquish investigative priority to the Federal Bureau of Investigation. The relinquishment of investigative priority by the Board shall not otherwise affect the authority of the Board to continue its investigation under this section.

(C) If a Federal law enforcement agency suspects and notifies the Board that an accident being investigated by the Board under subparagraph (A), (B), (C), or (D) of paragraph (1) may have been caused by an intentional criminal act, the Board, in consultation with the law enforcement agency, shall take necessary actions to ensure that evidence of the criminal act is preserved.

(3) This section and sections 1113, 1116(b), 1133, and 1134(a) and (c)–(e) of this title do not affect the authority of another department, agency, or instrumentality of the Government to investigate an accident under applicable law or to obtain information directly from the parties involved in, and witnesses to, the accident. The Board and other departments, agencies, and instrumentalities shall ensure that appropriate information developed about the accident is exchanged in a timely manner.

(b) ACCIDENTS INVOLVING PUBLIC VESSELS.—(1) The Board or the head of the department in which the Coast Guard is operating shall investigate and establish the facts, circumstances, and cause or probable cause of a marine accident involving a public vessel and any other vessel. The results of the investigation shall be made available to the public.

(2) Paragraph (1) of this subsection and subsection (a)(1)(E) of this section do not affect the responsibility, under another law of the United States, of the head of the department in which the Coast Guard is operating.

(c) ACCIDENTS NOT INVOLVING GOVERNMENT MISFEASANCE OR NONFEASANCE.—(1) When asked by the Board, the Secretary of Transportation or the Secretary of the department in which the Coast Guard is operating may—

(A) investigate an accident described under subsection (a) or (b) of this section in which misfeasance or nonfeasance by the Government has not been alleged; and

(B) report the facts and circumstances of the accident to the Board.

(2) The Board shall use the report in establishing cause or probable cause of an accident described under subsection (a) or (b) of this section.

(d) ACCIDENTS INVOLVING PUBLIC AIRCRAFT.—The Board, in furtherance of its investigative duties with respect to public aircraft accidents under subsection (a)(1)(A) of this section, shall have the same duties and powers as are specified for civil aircraft accidents under sections 1132(a), 1132(b), and 1134(a), (b), (d), and (f) of this title.

(e) ACCIDENT REPORTS.—The Board shall report on the facts and circumstances of each accident investigated by it under subsection (a) or (b) of this section. The Board shall make each report available to the public—

(1) in electronic form at no cost in a publicly accessible database on a website of the Board; and

(2) if the electronic form required in paragraph (1) is not printable, in printed form upon a reasonable request at a reasonable cost.

(f) TIMELINESS OF REPORTS.—If any accident report under subsection (e) is not completed within 2 years from the date of the accident, the Board shall submit to the Committee on Transportation and Infrastructure of the House of Representatives and the Committee on Commerce, Science, and Transportation of the Senate a report identifying such accident report and the reasons for which such report has not been completed. The Board shall report progress toward completion of the accident report to each such Committees every 90 days thereafter, until such time as the accident report is completed.

(Pub. L. 103–272, §1(d), July 5, 1994, 108 Stat. 752; Pub. L. 103–411, §3(c), Oct. 25, 1994, 108 Stat. 4237; Pub. L. 106–424, §§6(a), 7, Nov. 1, 2000, 114 Stat. 1885, 1886; Pub. L. 108–168, §7, Dec. 6, 2003, 117 Stat. 2034; Pub. L. 109–443, §9(b), (c), Dec. 21, 2006, 120 Stat. 3301; Pub. L. 115–254, div. C, §1113(b), Oct.

5, 2018, 132 Stat. 3438; Pub. L. 117–263, div. K, title CXVI, §11601(c)(3), Dec. 23, 2022, 136 Stat. 4146; Pub. L. 118–63, title XII, §§1210–1212, May 16, 2024, 138 Stat. 1425, 1426.)

§1132. CIVIL AIRCRAFT ACCIDENT INVESTIGATIONS

(a) GENERAL AUTHORITY.—(1) The National Transportation Safety Board shall investigate—

(A) each accident involving civil aircraft; and

(B) with the participation of appropriate military authorities, each accident involving both military and civil aircraft.

(2) A person employed under section 1113(b)(1) of this title that is conducting an investigation or hearing about an aircraft accident has the same authority to conduct the investigation or hearing as the Board.

(b) NOTIFICATION AND REPORTING.—The Board shall prescribe regulations governing the notification and reporting of accidents involving civil aircraft.

(c) PARTICIPATION OF SECRETARY.—The Board shall provide for the participation of the Secretary of Transportation in the investigation of an aircraft accident under this chapter when participation is necessary to carry out the duties and powers of the Secretary. However, the Secretary may not participate in establishing probable cause.

(d) ACCIDENTS INVOLVING ONLY MILITARY AIRCRAFT.—If an accident involves only military aircraft and a duty of the Secretary is or may be involved, the military authorities shall provide for the participation of the Secretary. In any other accident involving only military aircraft, the military authorities shall give the Board or Secretary information the military authorities decide would contribute to the promotion of air safety.

(Pub. L. 103–272, §1(d), July 5, 1994, 108 Stat. 753.)

§1133. REVIEW OF OTHER AGENCY ACTION

The National Transportation Safety Board shall review on appeal—

(1) the denial, amendment, modification, suspension, or revocation of a certificate issued by the Secretary of Transportation under section 44703, 44709, or 44710 of this title;

(2) the revocation of a certificate of registration under section 44106 of this title;

(3) a decision of the head of the department in which the Coast Guard is operating on an appeal from the decision of an administrative law judge denying, revoking, or suspending a license, certificate, document, or register in a proceeding under section 6101, 6301, or 7503, chapter 77, or section 9303 of title 46; and

(4) under section 46301(d)(5) of this title, an order imposing a penalty under section 46301.

(Pub. L. 103–272, §1(d), July 5, 1994, 108 Stat. 754.)

§1134. INSPECTIONS AND AUTOPSIES

(a) ENTRY AND INSPECTION.—An officer or employee of the National Transportation Safety Board—

(1) on display of appropriate credentials and written notice of inspection authority, may enter property where a transportation accident has occurred or wreckage from the accident is located and do anything necessary to conduct an investigation; and

(2) during reasonable hours, may inspect any record, including an electronic record, process, control, or facility related to an accident investigation under this chapter.

(b) INSPECTION, TESTING, PRESERVATION, AND MOVING OF AIRCRAFT AND PARTS.—(1) In investigating an aircraft accident under this chapter, the Board may inspect and test, to the extent necessary, any civil aircraft, aircraft engine, propeller, appliance, or property on an aircraft involved in an accident in air commerce.

(2) Any civil aircraft, aircraft engine, propeller, appliance, or property on an aircraft involved in an accident in air commerce shall be preserved, and may be moved, only as provided by regulations of the Board.

(c) AVOIDING UNNECESSARY INTERFERENCE AND PRESERVING EVIDENCE.—In carrying out subsection (a)(1) of this section, an officer or employee may examine or test any vehicle, vessel, rolling stock, track, or pipeline component. The examination or test shall be conducted in a way that—

(1) does not interfere unnecessarily with transportation services provided by the owner or operator of the vehicle, vessel, rolling stock, track, or pipeline component; and

(2) to the maximum extent feasible, preserves evidence related to the accident, consistent with the needs of the investigation and with the cooperation of that owner or operator.

(d) EXCLUSIVE AUTHORITY OF BOARD.—Only the Board has the authority to decide on the way in which testing under this section will be conducted, including decisions on the person that will conduct the test, the type of test that will be conducted, and any individual who will witness the test. Those decisions are committed to the discretion of the Board. The Board shall make any of those decisions based on the needs of the investigation being conducted and, when applicable, subsections (a), (c), and (e) of this section.

(e) PROMPTNESS OF TESTS AND AVAILABILITY OF RESULTS.—An inspection, examination, or test under subsection (a) or (c) of this section shall be started and completed promptly, and the results shall be made available.

(f) AUTOPSIES.—(1) The Board may order an autopsy to be performed and have other tests made when necessary to investigate an accident under this chapter. However, local law protecting religious beliefs related to autopsies shall be observed to the extent consistent with the needs of the accident investigation.

(2) With or without reimbursement, the Board may obtain a copy of an autopsy report performed by a State or local official on an individual who died because of a transportation accident investigated by the Board under this chapter.

(g) RECORDERS AND DATA.—In investigating an accident under this chapter, the Board may require from a transportation operator or equipment manufacturer or the vendors, suppliers, subsidiaries, or parent companies of such manufacturer, or operator of a product or service which is subject to an investigation by the Board—

(1) any recorder or recorded information pertinent to the accident;

(2) without undue delay, information the Board determines necessary to enable the Board to read and interpret any recording device or recorded information pertinent to the accident; and

(3) design specifications or data related to the operation and performance of the equipment the Board determines necessary to enable the Board to perform independent physics-based simulations and analyses of the accident situation.

(Pub. L. 103–272, §1(d), July 5, 1994, 108 Stat. 754; Pub. L. 115–254, div. C, §1105, Oct. 5, 2018, 132 Stat. 3431; Pub. L. 118–63, title XII, §1213, May 16, 2024, 138 Stat. 1426.)

§1135. SECRETARY OF TRANSPORTATION'S RESPONSES TO SAFETY RECOMMENDATIONS

(a) GENERAL.—When the National Transportation Safety Board submits a recommendation about transportation safety to the Secretary of Transportation, the Secretary shall give to the Board a formal written response to each recommendation not later than 90 days after receiving the recommendation. The response shall indicate whether the Secretary intends—

(1) to carry out procedures to adopt the complete recommendation;

(2) to carry out procedures to adopt a part of the recommendation; or

(3) to refuse to carry out procedures to adopt the recommendation.

(b) TIMETABLE FOR COMPLETING PROCEDURES AND REASONS FOR REFUSALS.—A response under subsection (a)(1) or (2) of this section shall include a copy of a proposed timetable for completing the procedures. A response under subsection (a)(2) of this section shall detail the reasons for the refusal to carry out procedures on the remainder of the recommendation. A response under subsection (a)(3) of this section shall detail the reasons for the refusal to carry out procedures.

(c) PUBLIC AVAILABILITY.—The Board shall make a copy of each recommendation and response available to the public—

(1) in electronic form at no cost in a publicly accessible database on a website of the Board; and

(2) if the electronic form required in paragraph (1) is not printable, in printed form upon a reasonable request at a reasonable cost.

(d) ANNUAL REPORT ON AIR CARRIER SAFETY RECOMMENDATIONS.—

(1) IN GENERAL.—The Secretary shall submit to Congress and the Board, on an annual basis, a report on the recommendations made by the Board to the Secretary regarding air carrier operations conducted under part 121 of title 14, Code of Federal Regulations.

(2) RECOMMENDATIONS TO BE COVERED.—The report shall cover—

(A) any recommendation for which the Secretary has developed, or intends to develop, procedures to adopt the recommendation or part of the recommendation, but has yet to complete the procedures; and

(B) any recommendation for which the Secretary, in the preceding year, has issued a response under subsection (a)(2) or (a)(3) refusing to carry out all or part of the procedures to adopt the recommendation.

(3) CONTENTS.—

(A) PLANS TO ADOPT RECOMMENDATIONS.—For each recommendation of the Board described in paragraph (2)(A), the report shall contain—

(i) a description of the recommendation;

(ii) a description of the procedures planned for adopting the recommendation or part of the recommendation;

(iii) the proposed date for completing the procedures; and

(iv) if the Secretary has not met a deadline contained in a proposed timeline developed in connection with the recommendation under subsection (b), an explanation for not meeting the deadline.

(B) REFUSALS TO ADOPT RECOMMENDATIONS.—For each recommendation of the Board described in paragraph (2)(B), the report shall contain—

(i) a description of the recommendation; and

(ii) a description of the reasons for the refusal to carry out all or part of the procedures to adopt the recommendation.

(Pub. L. 103–272, §1(d), July 5, 1994, 108 Stat. 755; Pub. L. 108–168, §6, Dec. 6, 2003, 117 Stat. 2034; Pub. L. 109–443, §2(b), Dec. 21, 2006, 120 Stat. 3298; Pub. L. 111–216, title II, §202, Aug. 1, 2010, 124 Stat. 2351; Pub. L. 111–249, §6(1), (2), Sept. 30, 2010, 124 Stat. 2628; Pub. L. 118–63, title XII, §§1214, 1220(a), May 16, 2024, 138 Stat. 1426, 1432.)

§1136. ASSISTANCE TO PASSENGERS INVOLVED IN AIRCRAFT ACCIDENTS AND FAMILIES OF SUCH PASSENGERS

(a) IN GENERAL.—As soon as practicable after being notified of an aircraft accident within United States airspace or airspace delegated to the United States involving an air carrier or foreign air carrier, resulting in any loss of life, and for which the National Transportation Safety Board will serve as the lead investigative agency, the Chairman of the Board shall—

(1) designate and publicize the name and phone number of a director of family support services who shall be an employee of the Board and shall be responsible for acting as a point of contact within the Federal Government for the families of passengers involved in the accident and a liaison between the air carrier or foreign air carrier and the families; and

(2) designate an independent nonprofit organization, with experience in disasters and posttrauma communication with families, which shall have primary responsibility for coordinating the emotional care, psychological care, and family support services of passengers involved in the accident and the families of such passengers.

(b) RESPONSIBILITIES OF THE BOARD.—The Board shall have primary Federal responsibility for facilitating the recovery and identification of fatally-injured passengers involved in an accident described in subsection (a).

(c) RESPONSIBILITIES OF DESIGNATED ORGANIZATION.—The organization designated for an accident under subsection (a)(2) shall have the following responsibilities with respect to passengers involved in the accident and the families of such passengers:

(1) To provide emotional care, psychological care, and family support services, in coordination with the disaster response team of the air carrier or foreign air carrier involved.

(2) To take such actions as may be necessary to provide an environment in which the families may grieve in private.

(3) To meet with passengers involved in the accident and the families of such passengers who have traveled to the location of the accident, to contact the families unable to travel to such location, and to contact all passengers and affected families regularly thereafter until such time as the organization, in consultation with the director of family support services designated for the accident under subsection (a)(1), determines that further assistance is no longer needed.

(4) To communicate with the passengers and families as to the roles of the

organization, government agencies, and the air carrier or foreign air carrier involved with respect to the accident and the post-accident activities.

(5) To arrange a suitable memorial service, in consultation with the families.

(d) PASSENGER LISTS.—

(1) REQUESTS FOR PASSENGER LISTS BY THE DIRECTOR OF FAMILY SERVICES.—

(A) REQUESTS BY DIRECTOR OF FAMILY SUPPORT SERVICES.—It shall be the responsibility of the director of family support services designated for an accident under subsection (a)(1) to request, as soon as practicable, from the air carrier or foreign air carrier involved in the accident a passenger list, which is based on the best available information at the time of the request.

(B) USE OF INFORMATION.—The director of family support services may not release to any person information on a list obtained under subparagraph (A), except that the director may, to the extent the director considers appropriate, provide information on the list about a passenger to—

(i) the family of the passenger; or

(ii) a local, Tribal, State, or Federal agency responsible for determining the whereabouts or welfare of a passenger.

(C) LIMITATION.—A local, Tribal, State, or Federal agency may not release to any person any information obtained under subparagraph (B)(ii), except if given express authority from the director of family support services.

(D) RULE OF CONSTRUCTION.—Nothing in subparagraph (C) shall be construed to preclude a local, Tribal, State, or Federal agency from releasing information that is lawfully obtained through other means independent of releases made by the director of family support services under subparagraph (B).

(2) REQUESTS FOR PASSENGER LISTS BY DESIGNATED ORGANIZATION.—

(A) REQUESTS BY DESIGNATED ORGANIZATION.—The organization designated for an accident under subsection (a)(2) may request from the air carrier or foreign air carrier involved in the accident a passenger list.

(B) USE OF INFORMATION.—The designated organization may not release to any person information on a passenger list but may provide information on the list about a passenger to the family of the passenger to the extent the organization considers appropriate.

(e) CONTINUING RESPONSIBILITIES OF THE BOARD.—In the course of its investigation of an accident described in subsection (a), the Board shall, to the maximum extent practicable, ensure that the families of passengers involved in the accident—

(1) are briefed, prior to any public briefing, about the accident, its causes, and any other findings from the investigation; and

(2) are individually informed of and allowed to attend any public hearings and meetings of the Board about the accident.

(f) USE OF AIR CARRIER RESOURCES.—To the extent practicable, the organization designated for an accident under subsection (a)(2) shall coordinate its activities with the air carrier or foreign air carrier involved in the accident so that the resources of the carrier can be used to the greatest extent possible to carry out the organization's responsibilities under this section.

(g) PROHIBITED ACTIONS.—

(1) ACTIONS TO IMPEDE THE BOARD.—No person (including a State or political subdivision) may impede the ability of the Board (including the director of family support services designated for an accident under subsection (a)(1)), or an organization designated for an accident under subsection (a)(2), to carry out its responsibilities under this section or the ability of passengers involved in the accident and the families of such passengers to have contact with one another.

(2) UNSOLICITED COMMUNICATIONS.—In the event of an accident involving an air carrier providing interstate or foreign air transportation and in the event of an accident involving a foreign air carrier that occurs within the United States, no unsolicited communication concerning a potential action for personal injury or wrongful death may be made by an attorney (including any associate, agent, employee, or other representative of an attorney) or any potential party to the litigation to an individual injured in the accident, or to a relative of an individual involved in the accident, before the 45th day following the date of the accident.

(3) PROHIBITION ON ACTIONS TO PREVENT CERTAIN CARE AND SUPPORT SERVICES.—No State or political subdivision thereof may prevent the employees, agents, or volunteers of an organization designated for an accident under subsection (a)(2) from providing emotional care, psychological care, and family support services under subsection (c)(1) in the 30-day period beginning on the date of the accident. The director of family support services designated for the accident under subsection (a)(1) may extend such period for not to exceed an additional 30 days if the director determines that the extension is necessary to meet the needs of the passengers and families and if State and local authorities are notified of the determination.

(h) DEFINITIONS.—In this section, the following definitions apply:

(1) AIRCRAFT ACCIDENT.—The term "aircraft accident" means any aviation disaster, regardless of its cause or suspected cause, for which the Board is the lead investigative agency.

(2) PASSENGER.—The term "passenger" includes—

(A) an employee of an air carrier or foreign air carrier aboard an aircraft;

(B) any other person aboard the aircraft without regard to whether the person paid for the transportation, occupied a seat, or held a reservation for the flight; and

(C) any other person injured or killed in the aircraft accident, as determined appropriate by the Board.

(3) PASSENGER LIST.—The term "passenger list" means a list based on the best available information at the time of a request, of the name of each passenger aboard the aircraft involved in the accident.

(i) STATUTORY CONSTRUCTION.—Nothing in this section may be construed as limiting the actions that an air carrier may take, or the obligations that an air carrier may have, in providing assistance to passengers involved in the aircraft accident and the families of such passengers.

(j) RELINQUISHMENT OF INVESTIGATIVE PRIORITY.—

(1) GENERAL RULE.—This section (other than subsection (g)) shall not apply to an aircraft accident if the Board has relinquished investigative priority under section 1131(a)(2)(B) and the Federal agency to which the Board relinquished investigative priority is willing and able to provide assistance to the victims and families of the

passengers involved in the accident.

(2) BOARD ASSISTANCE.—If this section does not apply to an aircraft accident because the Board has relinquished investigative priority with respect to the accident, the Board shall assist, to the maximum extent possible, the agency to which the Board has relinquished investigative priority in assisting families with respect to the accident.

(Added Pub. L. 104–264, title VII, §702(a)(1), Oct. 9, 1996, 110 Stat. 3265; amended Pub. L. 106–181, title IV, §401(a)(1), (b)–(d), Apr. 5, 2000, 114 Stat. 129; Pub. L. 108–168, §3(a), Dec. 6, 2003, 117 Stat. 2033; Pub. L. 115–254, div. C, §1109(c), Oct. 5, 2018, 132 Stat. 3434; Pub. L. 118–63, title XII, §1215(a), May 16, 2024, 138 Stat. 1427.)

§1137. AUTHORITY OF THE INSPECTOR GENERAL

(a) IN GENERAL.—The Inspector General of the Department of Transportation, in accordance with the mission of the Inspector General to prevent and detect fraud and abuse, shall have authority to review only the financial management, property management, and business operations of the National Transportation Safety Board, including internal accounting and administrative control systems, to determine compliance with applicable Federal laws, rules, and regulations.

(b) DUTIES.—In carrying out this section, the Inspector General shall—

(1) keep the Chairman of the Board and Congress fully and currently informed about problems relating to administration of the internal accounting and administrative control systems of the Board;

(2) issue findings and recommendations for actions to address such problems; and

(3) report periodically to Congress on any progress made in implementing actions to address such problems.

(c) ACCESS TO INFORMATION.—In carrying out this section, the Inspector General may exercise authorities granted to the Inspector General under subsections (a) and (c) of section 406 of title 5.

(d) AUTHORIZATIONS OF APPROPRIATIONS.—

(1) FUNDING.—There are authorized to be appropriated to the Secretary of Transportation for use by the Inspector General of the Department of Transportation such sums as may be necessary to cover expenses associated with activities pursuant to the authority exercised under this section.

(2) REIMBURSABLE AGREEMENT.—In the absence of an appropriation under this subsection for an expense referred to in paragraph (1), the Inspector General and the Board shall have a reimbursable agreement to cover such expense.

(Added Pub. L. 106–424, §12(a), Nov. 1, 2000, 114 Stat. 1887; amended Pub. L. 109–443, §4, Dec. 21, 2006, 120 Stat. 3299; Pub. L. 117–286, §4(b)(96), Dec. 27, 2022, 136 Stat. 4353.)

§1138. EVALUATION AND AUDIT OF NATIONAL TRANSPORTATION SAFETY BOARD

(a) IN GENERAL.—To promote economy, efficiency, and effectiveness in the administration of the programs, operations, and activities of the National Transportation Safety Board, the Comptroller General of the United States shall evaluate and audit the programs and expenditures of the Board. Such evaluation and audit shall be conducted as determined necessary by the Comptroller General or the appropriate congressional committees.

(b) RESPONSIBILITY OF COMPTROLLER GENERAL.—The Comptroller General shall evaluate and audit Board programs, operations, and activities, including—

(1) information management and security, including privacy protection of personally identifiable information;

(2) resource management;

(3) workforce development;

(4) procurement and contracting planning, practices and policies;

(5) the process and procedures to select an accident to investigate;

(6) the extent to which the Board follows leading practices in selected management areas; and

(7) the extent to which the Board addresses management challenges in completing accident investigations.

(c) APPROPRIATE CONGRESSIONAL COMMITTEES.—For purposes of this section the term "appropriate congressional committees" means the Committee on Commerce, Science, and Transportation of the Senate and the Committee on Transportation and Infrastructure of the House of Representatives.

(Added Pub. L. 109–443, §5(a), Dec. 21, 2006, 120 Stat. 3299; amended Pub. L. 113–188, title XV, §1502, Nov. 26, 2014, 128 Stat. 2025; Pub. L. 115–254, div. C, §1110, Oct. 5, 2018, 132 Stat. 3435; Pub. L. 118–63, title XII, §1221(a), May 16, 2024, 138 Stat. 1432.)

§1139. ASSISTANCE TO PASSENGERS INVOLVED IN RAIL PASSENGER ACCIDENTS AND FAMILIES OF SUCH PASSENGERS

(a) IN GENERAL.—As soon as practicable after being notified of a rail passenger accident within the United States involving a rail passenger carrier and resulting in any loss of life, and for which the National Transportation Safety Board will serve as the lead investigative agency, the Chairman of the Board shall—

(1) designate and publicize the name and telephone number of a director of family support services who shall be an employee of the Board and shall be responsible for acting as a point of contact within the Federal Government for the families of passengers involved in the accident and a liaison between the rail passenger carrier and the families; and

(2) designate an independent nonprofit organization, with experience in disasters and post-trauma communication with families, which shall have primary responsibility for coordinating the emotional care, psychological care, and family support services of passengers involved in the accident and the families of such passengers.

(b) RESPONSIBILITIES OF THE BOARD.—The Board shall have primary Federal responsibility for—

(1) facilitating the recovery and identification of fatally injured passengers involved in an accident described in subsection (a); and

(2) communicating with the families of passengers involved in the accident as to the roles, with respect to the accident and the post-accident activities, of—

(A) the organization designated for an accident under subsection (a)(2);

(B) Government agencies; and

(C) the rail passenger carrier involved.

(c) RESPONSIBILITIES OF DESIGNATED ORGANIZATION.—The organization designated for an accident under subsection (a)(2) shall have the following responsibilities with respect to passengers involved in the accident and the families of such passengers:

(1) To provide emotional care, psychological care, and family support services, in coordination with the disaster response team of the rail passenger carrier involved.

(2) To take such actions as may be necessary to provide an environment in which the families may grieve in private.

(3) To meet with passengers involved in the accident and the families of such passengers who have traveled to the location of the accident, to contact the families unable to travel to such location, and to contact all passengers and affected families periodically thereafter until such time as the organization, in consultation with the director of family support services designated for the accident under subsection (a)(1), determines that further assistance is no longer needed.

(4) To arrange a suitable memorial service, in consultation with the passengers and families.

(d) PASSENGER LISTS.—

(1) REQUESTS FOR PASSENGER LISTS BY THE DIRECTOR OF FAMILY SERVICES.—

(A) REQUESTS BY DIRECTOR OF FAMILY SUPPORT SERVICES.—It shall be the responsibility of the director of family support services designated for an accident under subsection (a)(1) to request, as soon as practicable, from the rail passenger carrier involved in the accident a passenger list, which is based on the best available information at the time of the request.

(B) USE OF INFORMATION.—The director of family support services may not release to any person information on a list obtained under subparagraph (A), except that the director may, to the extent the director considers appropriate, provide information on the list about a passenger to—

(i) the family of the passenger; or

(ii) a local, Tribal, State, or Federal agency responsible for determining the whereabouts or welfare of a passenger.

(C) LIMITATION.—A local, Tribal, State, or Federal agency may not release to any person any information obtained under subparagraph (B)(ii), except if given express authority from the director of family support services.

(D) RULE OF CONSTRUCTION.—Nothing in subparagraph (C) shall be construed to preclude a local, Tribal, State, or Federal agency from releasing information that is lawfully obtained through other means independent of releases made by the director of family support services under subparagraph (B).

(2) REQUESTS FOR PASSENGER LISTS BY DESIGNATED ORGANIZATION.—

(A) REQUESTS BY DESIGNATED ORGANIZATION.—The organization designated for an accident under subsection (a)(2) may request from the rail passenger carrier involved in the accident a passenger list.

(B) USE OF INFORMATION.—The designated organization may not release to any person information on a passenger list but may provide information on the list about a passenger to the family of the passenger to the extent the organization considers appropriate.

(e) CONTINUING RESPONSIBILITIES OF THE BOARD.—In the course of its investigation of an accident described in subsection (a), the Board shall, to the maximum extent practicable, ensure that the families of passengers involved in the accident—

(1) are briefed, prior to any public briefing, about the accident and any other findings from the investigation; and

(2) are individually informed of and allowed to attend any public hearings and meetings of the Board about the accident.

(f) Use of Rail Passenger Carrier Resources.—To the extent practicable, the organization designated for an accident under subsection (a)(2) shall coordinate its activities with the rail passenger carrier involved in the accident to facilitate the reasonable use of the resources of the carrier.

(g) Prohibited Actions.—

(1) Actions to impede the board.—No person (including a State or political subdivision thereof) may impede the ability of the Board (including the director of family support services designated for an accident under subsection (a)(1)), or an organization designated for an accident under subsection (a)(2), to carry out its responsibilities under this section or the ability of passengers involved in the accident and the families of such passengers to have contact with one another.

(2) Unsolicited communications.—No unsolicited communication concerning a potential action or settlement offer for personal injury or wrongful death may be made by an attorney (including any associate, agent, employee, or other representative of an attorney) or any potential party to the litigation, including the railroad carrier or rail passenger carrier, to an individual (other than an employee of the rail passenger carrier) injured in the accident, or to a relative of an individual involved in the accident, before the 45th day following the date of the accident.

(3) Prohibition on actions to prevent certain care and support services.—No State or political subdivision thereof may prevent the employees, agents, or volunteers of an organization designated for an accident under subsection (a)(2) from providing emotional care, psychological care, and family support services under subsection (c)(1) in the 30-day period beginning on the date of the accident. The director of family services designated for the accident under subsection (a)(1) may extend such period for not to exceed an additional 30 days if the director determines that the extension is necessary to meet the needs of the passengers and families and if State and local authorities are notified of the determination.

(h) Definitions.—In this section:

(1) Rail passenger accident.—The term "rail passenger accident" means any rail passenger disaster that—

(A) results in any loss of life;

(B) the Board will serve as the lead investigative agency for; and

(C) occurs in the provision of—

(i) interstate intercity rail passenger transportation (as such term is defined in section 24102); or

(ii) high-speed rail (as such term is defined in section 26105) transportation, regardless of its cause or suspected cause.

(2) Rail passenger carrier.—The term "rail passenger carrier" means a rail carrier providing—

(A) interstate intercity rail passenger transportation (as such term is defined in section 24102); or

(B) interstate or intrastate high-speed rail (as such term is defined in section 26105) transportation,

except that such term does not include a tourist, historic, scenic, or excursion rail carrier.

(3) Passenger.—The term "passenger" includes—

(A) an employee of a rail passenger carrier aboard a train;

(B) any other person aboard the train without regard to whether the person paid for the transportation, occupied a seat, or held a reservation for the rail transportation; and

(C) any other person injured or killed in a rail passenger accident, as determined appropriate by the Board.

(4) Passenger list.—The term "passenger list" means a list based on the best available information at the time of the request, of the name of each passenger aboard the rail passenger carrier's train involved in the accident. A rail passenger carrier shall use reasonable efforts, with respect to its unreserved trains, and passengers not holding reservations on its other trains, to ascertain the names of passengers aboard a train involved in an accident.

(i) Limitation on Statutory Construction.—Nothing in this section may be construed as limiting the actions that a rail passenger carrier may take, or the obligations that a rail passenger carrier may have, in providing assistance to the families of passengers involved in a rail passenger accident.

(j) Relinquishment of Investigative Priority.—

(1) General rule.—This section (other than subsection (g)) shall not apply to a rail passenger accident if the Board has relinquished investigative priority under section 1131(a)(2)(B) and the Federal agency to which the Board relinquished investigative priority is willing and able to provide assistance to the victims and families of the passengers involved in the accident.

(2) Board assistance.—If this section does not apply to a rail passenger accident because the Board has relinquished investigative priority with respect to the accident, the Board shall assist, to the maximum extent possible, the agency to which the Board has relinquished investigative priority in assisting families with respect to the accident.

(k) Savings Clause.—Nothing in this section shall be construed to abridge the authority of the Board or the Secretary of Transportation to investigate the causes or circumstances of any rail accident, including development of information regarding the nature of injuries sustained and the manner in which they were sustained for the purposes of determining compliance with existing laws and regulations or for identifying means of preventing similar injuries in the future, or both.

(Added Pub. L. 110–432, div. A, title V, §501(a), Oct. 16, 2008, 122 Stat. 4894; amended Pub. L. 114–94, div. A, title XI, §11316(a), Dec. 4, 2015, 129 Stat. 1676; Pub. L. 115–254, div. C, §1109(d), Oct. 5, 2018, 132 Stat. 3435; Pub. L. 118–63, title XII, §1215(c), May 16, 2024, 138 Stat. 1428.)

§1140. Information [1] individuals involved in accidents and families of such individuals

In the course of an investigation of an accident described in section 1131(a)(1), except an aircraft accident described in section 1136 or a rail passenger accident described in section

1139, the Board may, to the maximum extent practicable, ensure that individuals involved in accidents and the families of such individuals, and other individuals the Board deems appropriate—

(1) are informed as to the roles, with respect to the accident and the post-accident activities, of the Board;

(2) are briefed, before any public briefing, about the accident, its causes, and any other findings from the investigation; and

(3) are individually informed of and allowed to attend any public hearings and meetings of the Board about the accident.

(Added Pub. L. 115–254, div. C, §1109(e)(1), Oct. 5, 2018, 132 Stat. 3435; amended Pub. L. 118–63, title XII, §1215(e), May 16, 2024, 138 Stat. 1430.)

¹ *So in original. Probably should be followed by "for".*

SUBCHAPTER IV—ENFORCEMENT AND PENALTIES

§1151. AVIATION ENFORCEMENT

(a) CIVIL ACTIONS BY BOARD.—The National Transportation Safety Board may bring a civil action in a district court of the United States against a person to enforce section 1132, 1134(b) or (f)(1) (related to an aircraft accident), 1136(g)(2), or 1155(a) of this title or a regulation prescribed or order issued under any of those sections. An action under this subsection may be brought in the judicial district in which the person does business or the violation occurred.

(b) CIVIL ACTIONS BY ATTORNEY GENERAL.—On request of the Board, the Attorney General may bring a civil action in an appropriate court—

(1) to enforce section 1132, 1134(b) or (f)(1) (related to an aircraft accident), 1136(g)(2), or 1155(a) of this title or a regulation prescribed or order issued under any of those sections; and

(2) to prosecute a person violating those sections or a regulation prescribed or order issued under any of those sections.

(c) PARTICIPATION OF BOARD.—On request of the Attorney General, the Board may participate in a civil action to enforce section 1132, 1134(b) or (f)(1) (related to an aircraft accident), 1136(g)(2), or 1155(a) of this title.

(d) NOTIFICATION TO CONGRESS.—If the Board or Attorney General carry out such civil actions described in subsection (a) or (b) of this section against an airman employed at the time of the accident or incident by an air carrier operating under part 121 of title 14, Code of Federal Regulations, the Board shall immediately notify the Committee on Transportation and Infrastructure of the House of Representatives and the Committee on Commerce, Science, and Transportation of the Senate of such civil actions, including—

(1) the labor union representing the airman involved, if applicable;

(2) the air carrier at which the airman is employed;

(3) the docket information of the incident or accident in which the airman was involved;

(4) the date of such civil actions taken by the Board or Attorney General; and

(5) a description of why such civil actions were taken by the Board or Attorney

General.

(e) SUBSEQUENT NOTIFICATION TO CONGRESS.—Not later than 15 days after the notification described in subsection (d), the Board shall submit a report to or brief the Committee on Transportation and Infrastructure of the House of Representatives and the Committee on Commerce, Science, and Transportation of the Senate describing the status of compliance with the civil actions taken.

(Pub. L. 103–272, §1(d), July 5, 1994, 108 Stat. 756; Pub. L. 106–181, title IV, §401(a)(2), Apr. 5, 2000, 114 Stat. 129; Pub. L. 118–63, title XII, §1208(b), May 16, 2024, 138 Stat. 1424.)

§1152. JOINDER AND INTERVENTION IN AVIATION PROCEEDINGS

A person interested in or affected by a matter under consideration in a proceeding or a civil action to enforce section 1132, 1134(b) or (f)(1) (related to an aircraft accident), or 1155(a) of this title, or a regulation prescribed or order issued under any of those sections, may be joined as a party or permitted to intervene in the proceeding or civil action.

(Pub. L. 103–272, §1(d), July 5, 1994, 108 Stat. 756.)

§1153. JUDICIAL REVIEW

(a) GENERAL.—The appropriate court of appeals of the United States or the United States Court of Appeals for the District of Columbia Circuit may review a final order of the National Transportation Safety Board under this chapter. A person disclosing a substantial interest in the order may apply for review by filing a petition not later than 60 days after the order of the Board is issued.

(b) PERSONS SEEKING JUDICIAL REVIEW OF AVIATION MATTERS.—(1) A person disclosing a substantial interest in an order related to an aviation matter issued by the Board under this chapter may apply for review of the order by filing a petition for review in the United States Court of Appeals for the District of Columbia Circuit or in the court of appeals of the United States for the circuit in which the person resides or has its principal place of business. The petition must be filed not later than 60 days after the order is issued. The court may allow the petition to be filed after the 60 days only if there was a reasonable ground for not filing within that 60-day period.

(2) When a petition is filed under paragraph (1) of this subsection, the clerk of the court immediately shall send a copy of the petition to the Board. The Board shall file with the court a record of the proceeding in which the order was issued.

(3) When the petition is sent to the Board, the court has exclusive jurisdiction to affirm, amend, modify, or set aside any part of the order and may order the Board to conduct further proceedings. After reasonable notice to the Board, the court may grant interim relief by staying the order or taking other appropriate action when cause for its action exists. Findings of fact by the Board, if supported by substantial evidence, are conclusive.

(4) In reviewing an order under this subsection, the court may consider an objection to an order of the Board only if the objection was made in the proceeding conducted by the Board or if there was a reasonable ground for not making the objection in the proceeding.

(5) A decision by a court under this subsection may be reviewed only by the Supreme Court under section 1254 of title 28.

(c) ADMINISTRATOR SEEKING JUDICIAL REVIEW OF AVIATION MATTERS.—When the Administrator of the Federal Aviation Administration decides that an order of the Board under section 44703(d), 44709, or 46301(d)(5) of this title will have a significant adverse impact on carrying out this chapter related to an aviation matter, the Administrator may obtain judicial review of the order under section 46110 of this title. The Administrator shall be made a party to the judicial review proceedings. Findings of fact of the Board are conclusive if supported by substantial evidence.

(d) COMMANDANT SEEKING JUDICIAL REVIEW OF MARITIME MATTERS.—If the Commandant of the Coast Guard decides that an order of the Board issued pursuant to a review of a Coast Guard action under section 1133 of this title will have an adverse impact on maritime safety or security, the Commandant may obtain judicial review of the order under subsection (a). The Commandant, in the official capacity of the Commandant, shall be a party to the judicial review proceedings.

(Pub. L. 103–272, §1(d), July 5, 1994, 108 Stat. 756; Pub. L. 108–293, title VI, §622, Aug. 9, 2004, 118 Stat. 1063; Pub. L. 112–95, title III, §301(b), Feb. 14, 2012, 126 Stat. 56.)

§1154. DISCOVERY AND USE OF COCKPIT AND SURFACE VEHICLE RECORDINGS AND TRANSCRIPTS

(a) IN GENERAL.—(1) Except as provided by this subsection, a party in a judicial proceeding may not use discovery to obtain—

(A) any still image that the National Transportation Safety Board has not made available to the public under section 1114(c) or 1114(d) of this title;

(B) any part of a cockpit or surface vehicle recorder transcript that the National Transportation Safety Board has not made available to the public under section 1114(c) or 1114(d) of this title; and

(C) a cockpit or surface vehicle recorder recording.

(2)(A) Except as provided in paragraph (4)(A) of this subsection, a court may allow discovery by a party of a cockpit or surface vehicle recorder transcript if, after an in camera review of the transcript, the court decides that—

(i) the part of the transcript made available to the public under section 1114(c) or 1114(d) of this title does not provide the party with sufficient information for the party to receive a fair trial; and

(ii) discovery of additional parts of the transcript is necessary to provide the party with sufficient information for the party to receive a fair trial.

(B) A court may allow discovery, or require production for an in camera review, of a cockpit or surface vehicle recorder transcript that the Board has not made available under section 1114(c) or 1114(d) of this title only if the cockpit or surface vehicle recorder recording is not available.

(3) Except as provided in paragraph (4)(A) of this subsection, a court may allow discovery by a party of a cockpit or surface vehicle recorder recording, including with regard to a video recording any still image that the National Transportation Safety Board has not made available to the public under section 1114(c) or 1114(d) of this title, if, after an in camera review of the recording, the court decides that—

(A) the parts of the transcript made available to the public under section 1114(c) or 1114(d) of this title and to the party through discovery under paragraph (2) of this subsection do not provide the party with sufficient information for the party to receive a fair trial; and

(B) discovery of the cockpit or surface vehicle recorder recording, including with regard to a video recording any still image that the National Transportation Safety Board has not made available to the public under section 1114(c) or 1114(d) of this title, is necessary to provide the party with sufficient information for the party to receive a fair trial.

(4)(A) When a court allows discovery in a judicial proceeding of a still image or a part of a cockpit or surface vehicle recorder transcript not made available to the public under section 1114(c) or 1114(d) of this title or a cockpit or surface vehicle recorder recording, the court shall issue a protective order—

(i) to limit the use of the still image, the part of the transcript, or the recording to the judicial proceeding; and

(ii) to prohibit dissemination of the still image, the part of the transcript, or the recording to any person that does not need access to the still image, the part of the transcript, or the recording for the proceeding.

(B) A court may allow a still image or a part of a cockpit or surface vehicle recorder transcript not made available to the public under section 1114(c) or 1114(d) of this title or a cockpit or surface vehicle recorder recording to be admitted into evidence in a judicial proceeding, only if the court places the still image, the part of the transcript, or the recording under seal to prevent the use of the still image, the part of the transcript, or the recording for purposes other than for the proceeding.

(5) This subsection does not prevent the Board from referring at any time to cockpit or surface vehicle recorder information in making safety recommendations.

(6) In this subsection:

(A) RECORDER.—The term "recorder" means a voice or video recorder.

(B) STILL IMAGE.—The term "still image" means any still image obtained from a video recorder.

(C) TRANSCRIPT.—The term "transcript" includes any written depiction of visual information obtained from a video recorder.

(b) REPORTS.—No part of a report of the Board, related to an accident or an investigation of an accident, may be admitted into evidence or used in a civil action for damages resulting from a matter mentioned in the report.

(Pub. L. 103–272, §1(d), July 5, 1994, 108 Stat. 757; Pub. L. 106–424, §5(c)(1), Nov. 1, 2000, 114 Stat. 1885; Pub. L. 115–254, div. C, §1104(b), Oct. 5, 2018, 132 Stat. 3430.)

§1155. PENALTIES

(a) CIVIL PENALTY.—(1) A person violating section 1132, section 1134(b), section 1134(f)(1), section 1136(g), or section 1139(g) of this title or a regulation prescribed or order issued under any of those sections is liable to the United States Government for a civil penalty of not more than $1,000. A separate violation occurs for each day a violation continues.

(2) This subsection does not apply to a member of the armed forces of the United States or an employee of the Department of Defense subject to the Uniform Code of Military Justice when the member or employee is performing official duties. The appropriate military authorities are responsible for taking necessary disciplinary action and submitting to the National Transportation Safety Board a timely report on action taken.

(3) The Board may compromise the amount of a civil penalty imposed under this subsection.

(4) The Government may deduct the amount of a civil penalty imposed or compromised under this subsection from amounts it owes the person liable for the penalty.

(5) A civil penalty under this subsection may be collected by bringing a civil action against the person liable for the penalty. The action shall conform as nearly as practicable to a civil action in admiralty.

(b) CRIMINAL PENALTY.—A person that knowingly and without authority removes, conceals, or withholds a part of a civil aircraft involved in an accident, or property on the aircraft at the time of the accident, shall be fined under title 18, imprisoned for not more than 10 years, or both.

(Pub. L. 103–272, §1(d), July 5, 1994, 108 Stat. 758; Pub. L. 104–264, title VII, §702(b), Oct. 9, 1996, 110 Stat. 3267; Pub. L. 118–63, title XII, §1216(a), May 16, 2024, 138 Stat. 1431.)

* * * * * * *

SUBTITLE III
GENERAL AND INTERMODAL PROGRAMS

SUBTITLE III—GENERAL AND INTERMODAL PROGRAMS

* * * * * * *

CHAPTER 51—TRANSPORTATION OF HAZARDOUS MATERIAL

§5101. PURPOSE

The purpose of this chapter is to protect against the risks to life, property, and the environment that are inherent in the transportation of hazardous material in intrastate, interstate, and foreign commerce.

(Pub. L. 103–272, §1(d), July 5, 1994, 108 Stat. 759; Pub. L. 109–59, title VII, §7101(b), Aug. 10, 2005, 119 Stat. 1891.)

§5102. DEFINITIONS

In this chapter—

 (1) "commerce" means trade or transportation in the jurisdiction of the United States—

(A) between a place in a State and a place outside of the State;

(B) that affects trade or transportation between a place in a State and a place outside of the State; or

(C) on a United States-registered aircraft.

(2) "hazardous material" means a substance or material the Secretary designates under section 5103(a) of this title.

(3) "hazmat employee"—

    (A) means an individual—

        (i) who—

            (I) is employed on a full time, part time, or temporary basis by a hazmat employer; or

            (II) is self-employed (including an owner-operator of a motor vehicle, vessel, or aircraft) transporting hazardous material in commerce; and

        (ii) who during the course of such full time, part time, or temporary employment, or such self employment, directly affects hazardous material transportation safety as the Secretary decides by regulation; and

    (B) includes an individual, employed on a full time, part time, or temporary basis by a hazmat employer, or self employed, who during the course of employment—

        (i) loads, unloads, or handles hazardous material;

        (ii) designs, manufactures, fabricates, inspects, marks, maintains, reconditions, repairs, or tests a package, container, or packaging component that is represented, marked, certified, or sold as qualified for use in transporting hazardous material in commerce;

        (iii) prepares hazardous material for transportation;

        (iv) is responsible for the safety of transporting hazardous material; or

        (v) operates a vehicle used to transport hazardous material.

(4) "hazmat employer"—

    (A) means a person—

        (i) who—

             (I) employs or uses at least 1 hazmat employee on a full time, part time, or temporary basis; or

            (II) is self-employed (including an owner-operator of a motor vehicle, vessel, or aircraft) transporting hazardous material in commerce; and

        (ii) who—

             (I) transports hazardous material in commerce;

            (II) causes hazardous material to be transported in commerce; or

            (III) designs, manufactures, fabricates, inspects, marks, maintains, reconditions, repairs, or tests a package, container, or packaging component that is represented, marked, certified, or sold as qualified for use in transporting hazardous material in commerce; and

    (B) includes a department, agency, or instrumentality of the United States Government, or an authority of a State, political subdivision of a State, or Indian tribe, carrying out an activity described in clause (ii).

(5) "imminent hazard" means the existence of a condition relating to hazardous material that presents a substantial likelihood that death, serious illness, severe personal

injury, or a substantial endangerment to health, property, or the environment may occur before the reasonably foreseeable completion date of a formal proceeding begun to lessen the risk of that death, illness, injury, or endangerment.

(6) "Indian tribe" has the same meaning given that term in section 4 of the Indian Self-Determination and Education Assistance Act (25 U.S.C. 450b).

(7) "motor carrier"—

(A) means a motor carrier, motor private carrier, and freight forwarder as those terms are defined in section 13102; but

(B) does not include a freight forwarder, as so defined, if the freight forwarder is not performing a function relating to highway transportation.

(8) "National Response Team" means the National Response Team established under the National Contingency Plan established under section 105 of the Comprehensive Environmental Response, Compensation, and Liability Act of 1980 (42 U.S.C. 9605).

(9) "person", in addition to its meaning under section 1 of title 1—

(A) includes a government, Indian tribe, or authority of a government or tribe that—

(i) offers hazardous material for transportation in commerce;

(ii) transports hazardous material to further a commercial enterprise; or

(iii) designs, manufactures, fabricates, inspects, marks, maintains, reconditions, repairs, or tests a package, container, or packaging component that is represented, marked, certified, or sold as qualified for use in transporting hazardous material in commerce; but

(B) does not include—

(i) the United States Postal Service; and

(ii) in sections 5123 and 5124 of this title, a department, agency, or instrumentality of the Government.

(10) "public sector employee"—

(A) means an individual employed by a State, political subdivision of a State, or Indian tribe and who during the course of employment has responsibilities related to responding to an accident or incident involving the transportation of hazardous material;

(B) includes an individual employed by a State, political subdivision of a State, or Indian tribe as a firefighter or law enforcement officer; and

(C) includes an individual who volunteers to serve as a firefighter for a State, political subdivision of a State, or Indian tribe.

(11) "Secretary" means the Secretary of Transportation except as otherwise provided.

(12) "State" means—

(A) except in section 5119 of this title, a State of the United States, the District of Columbia, Puerto Rico, the Northern Mariana Islands, the Virgin Islands, American Samoa, Guam, and any other territory or possession of the United States designated by the Secretary; and

(B) in section 5119 of this title, a State of the United States and the District of Columbia.

(13) "transports" or "transportation" means the movement of property and loading, unloading, or storage incidental to the movement.

(14) "United States" means all of the States.

(Pub. L. 103–272, §1(d), July 5, 1994, 108 Stat. 759; Pub. L. 103–311, title I, §117(a)(1), Aug. 26, 1994, 108 Stat. 1678; Pub. L. 104–88, title III, §308(d), Dec. 29, 1995, 109 Stat. 947; Pub. L. 109–59, title VII, §§7102, 7126, Aug. 10, 2005, 119 Stat. 1892, 1909; Pub. L. 110–244, title III, §302(a), June 6, 2008, 122 Stat. 1618.)

§5103. GENERAL REGULATORY AUTHORITY

(a) DESIGNATING MATERIAL AS HAZARDOUS.—The Secretary shall designate material (including an explosive, radioactive material, infectious substance, flammable or combustible liquid, solid, or gas, toxic, oxidizing, or corrosive material, and compressed gas) or a group or class of material as hazardous when the Secretary determines that transporting the material in commerce in a particular amount and form may pose an unreasonable risk to health and safety or property.

(b) REGULATIONS FOR SAFE TRANSPORTATION.—(1) The Secretary shall prescribe regulations for the safe transportation, including security, of hazardous material in intrastate, interstate, and foreign commerce. The regulations—

(A) apply to a person who—

(i) transports hazardous material in commerce;

(ii) causes hazardous material to be transported in commerce;

(iii) designs, manufactures, fabricates, inspects, marks, maintains, reconditions, repairs, or tests a package, container, or packaging component that is represented, marked, certified, or sold as qualified for use in transporting hazardous material in commerce;

(iv) prepares or accepts hazardous material for transportation in commerce;

(v) is responsible for the safety of transporting hazardous material in commerce;

(vi) certifies compliance with any requirement under this chapter; or

(vii) misrepresents whether such person is engaged in any activity under clause (i) through (vi); and

(B) shall govern safety aspects, including security, of the transportation of hazardous material the Secretary considers appropriate.

(2) A proceeding to prescribe the regulations must be conducted under section 553 of title 5, including an opportunity for informal oral presentation.

(c) FEDERALLY DECLARED DISASTERS AND EMERGENCIES.—

(1) IN GENERAL.—The Secretary may by order waive compliance with any part of an applicable standard prescribed under this chapter without prior notice and comment and on terms the Secretary considers appropriate if the Secretary determines that—

(A) it is in the public interest to grant the waiver;

(B) the waiver is not inconsistent with the safety of transporting hazardous materials; and

(C) the waiver is necessary to facilitate the safe movement of hazardous materials into, from, and within an area of a major disaster or emergency that has been declared under the Robert T. Stafford Disaster Relief and Emergency Assistance Act (42 U.S.C. 5121 et seq.).

(2) PERIOD OF WAIVER.—A waiver under this subsection may be issued for a period of not more than 60 days and may be renewed upon application to the Secretary only after notice and an opportunity for a hearing on the waiver. The Secretary shall immediately revoke the waiver if continuation of the waiver would not be consistent with the goals

and objectives of this chapter.

(3) STATEMENT OF REASONS.—The Secretary shall include in any order issued under this section the reasons for granting the waiver.

(d) CONSULTATION.—When prescribing a security regulation or issuing a security order that affects the safety of the transportation of hazardous material, the Secretary of Homeland Security shall consult with the Secretary of Transportation.

(e) BIENNIAL REPORT.—The Secretary of Transportation shall submit to the Committee on Transportation and Infrastructure of the House of Representatives and the Senate Committee on Commerce, Science, and Transportation a biennial report providing information on whether the Secretary has designated as hazardous materials for purposes of chapter 51 of such title all by-products of the methamphetamine-production process that are known by the Secretary to pose an unreasonable risk to health and safety or property when transported in commerce in a particular amount and form.

(Pub. L. 103–272, §1(d), July 5, 1994, 108 Stat. 761; Pub. L. 103–311, title I, §117(a)(2), Aug. 26, 1994, 108 Stat. 1678; Pub. L. 103–429, §6(3), Oct. 31, 1994, 108 Stat. 4378; Pub. L. 107–296, title XVII, §1711(a), Nov. 25, 2002, 116 Stat. 2319; Pub. L. 109–59, title VII, §§7103, 7126, Aug. 10, 2005, 119 Stat. 1893, 1909; Pub. L. 109–177, title VII, §741, Mar. 9, 2006, 120 Stat. 272; Pub. L. 114–94, div. A, title VII, §7201, Dec. 4, 2015, 129 Stat. 1589.)

§5103A. LIMITATION ON ISSUANCE OF HAZMAT LICENSES

(a) LIMITATION.—

(1) ISSUANCE OF LICENSES.—A State may not issue to any individual a license to operate a motor vehicle transporting in commerce a hazardous material unless—

(A) "the Secretary of Homeland Security"; [1] has first determined, upon receipt of a notification under subsection (d)(1)(B), that the individual does not pose a security risk warranting denial of the license; or

(B) the individual holds a valid transportation security card issued under section 70105 of title 46.

(2) RENEWALS INCLUDED.—For the purposes of this section, the term "issue", with respect to a license, includes renewal of the license.

(b) HAZARDOUS MATERIALS DESCRIBED.—The limitation in subsection (a) shall apply with respect to any material defined as hazardous material by the Secretary of Transportation for which the Secretary of Transportation requires placarding of a commercial motor vehicle transporting that material in commerce.

(c) RECOMMENDATIONS ON CHEMICAL AND BIOLOGICAL MATERIALS.—The Secretary of Health and Human Services shall recommend to the Secretary of Transportation any chemical or biological material or agent for regulation as a hazardous material under section 5103(a) if the Secretary of Health and Human Services determines that such material or agent poses a significant risk to the health of individuals.

(d) BACKGROUND RECORDS CHECK.—

(1) IN GENERAL.—Upon the request of a State regarding issuance of a license under subsection (a)(1)(A) to an individual, the Attorney General—

(A) shall carry out a background records check regarding the individual; and

(B) upon completing the background records check, shall notify the Secretary of Homeland Security of the completion and results of the background records check.

(2) SCOPE.—A background records check regarding an individual under this subsection shall consist of the following:

(A) A check of the relevant criminal history data bases.

(B) In the case of an alien, a check of the relevant data bases to determine the status of the alien under the immigration laws of the United States.

(C) As appropriate, a check of the relevant international data bases through Interpol–U.S. National Central Bureau or other appropriate means.

(e) REPORTING REQUIREMENT.—Each State shall submit to the Secretary of Homeland Security, at such time and in such manner as the Secretary of Homeland Security may prescribe, the name, address, and such other information as the Secretary of Homeland Security may require, concerning—

(1) each alien to whom the State issues a license described in subsection (a); and

(2) each other individual to whom such a license is issued, as the Secretary of Homeland Security may require.

(f) ALIEN DEFINED.—In this section, the term "alien" has the meaning given the term in section 101(a)(3) of the Immigration and Nationality Act.

(g) BACKGROUND CHECKS FOR DRIVERS HAULING HAZARDOUS MATERIALS.—

(1) IN GENERAL.—

(A) EMPLOYER NOTIFICATION.—Not later than 90 days after the date of enactment of this subsection, the Director of the Transportation Security Administration, after receiving comments from interested parties, shall develop and implement a process for notifying hazmat employers designated by an applicant of the results of the applicant's background record check, if—

(i) such notification is appropriate considering the potential security implications; and

(ii) the Director, in a final notification of threat assessment,[2] served on the applicant [2] determines that the applicant does not meet the standards set forth in regulations issued to carry out this section.

(B) RELATIONSHIP TO OTHER BACKGROUND RECORDS CHECKS.—

(i) ELIMINATION OF REDUNDANT CHECKS.—An individual with respect to whom the Transportation Security Administration—

(I) has performed a security threat assessment under this section; and

(II) has issued a final notification of no security threat,

is deemed to have met the requirements of any other background check that is required for purposes of any Federal law applicable to transportation workers if that background check is equivalent to, or less stringent than, the background check required under this section.

(ii) DETERMINATION BY DIRECTOR.—Not later than 60 days after the date of issuance of the report under paragraph (5), but no later than 120 days after the date of enactment of this subsection, the Director shall initiate a rulemaking proceeding, including notice and opportunity for comment, to determine which background checks required for purposes of Federal laws applicable to transportation workers are equivalent to, or less stringent than, those required under this section.

(iii) FUTURE RULEMAKINGS.—The Director shall make a determination under the criteria established under clause (ii) with respect to any rulemaking proceeding to establish or modify required background checks for transportation workers initiated after the date of enactment of this subsection.

(2) APPEALS PROCESS FOR MORE STRINGENT STATE PROCEDURES.—If a State establishes its own standards for applicants for a hazardous materials endorsement to a commercial driver's license, the State shall also provide—

(A) an appeals process similar to and to the same extent as the process provided under part 1572 of title 49, Code of Federal Regulations, by which an applicant denied a hazardous materials endorsement to a commercial driver's license by that State may appeal that denial; and

(B) a waiver process similar to and to the same extent as the process provided under part 1572 of title 49, Code of Federal Regulations, by which an applicant denied a hazardous materials endorsement to a commercial driver's license by that State may apply for a waiver.

(3) CLARIFICATION OF TERM DEFINED IN REGULATIONS.—The term "transportation security incident", as defined in part 1572 of title 49, Code of Federal Regulations, does not include a work stoppage or other nonviolent employee-related action resulting from an employer-employee dispute. Not later than 30 days after the date of enactment of this subsection, the Director shall modify the definition of that term to reflect the preceding sentence.

(4) BACKGROUND CHECK CAPACITY.—Not later than October 1, 2005, the Director shall transmit to the Committee on Commerce, Science, and Transportation of the Senate and the Committees on Transportation and Infrastructure and Homeland Security of the House of Representatives a report on the implementation of fingerprint-based security threat assessments and the adequacy of fingerprinting locations, personnel, and resources to accomplish the timely processing of fingerprint-based security threat assessments for individuals holding commercial driver's licenses who are applying to renew hazardous materials endorsements.

(5) REPORT.—

(A) IN GENERAL.—Not later than 60 days after the date of enactment of this subsection, the Director shall transmit to the committees referred to in paragraph (4) a report on the Director's plans to reduce or eliminate redundant background checks for holders of hazardous materials endorsements performed under this section.

(B) CONTENTS.—The report shall—

(i) include a list of background checks and other security or threat assessment requirements applicable to transportation workers under Federal laws for which the Department of Homeland Security is responsible and the process by which the Secretary of Homeland Security will determine whether such checks or assessments are equivalent to, or less stringent than, the background check performed under this section; and

(ii) provide an analysis of how the Director plans to reduce or eliminate redundant background checks in a manner that will continue to ensure the highest level of safety and security.

(h) COMMERCIAL MOTOR VEHICLE OPERATORS REGISTERED TO OPERATE IN MEXICO OR CANADA.—

(1) IN GENERAL.—Beginning on the date that is 6 months after the date of enactment of

this subsection, a commercial motor vehicle operator registered to operate in Mexico or Canada shall not operate a commercial motor vehicle transporting a hazardous material in commerce in the United States until the operator has undergone a background records check similar to the background records check required for commercial motor vehicle operators licensed in the United States to transport hazardous materials in commerce.

(2) EXTENSION.—The Director of the Transportation Security Administration may extend the deadline established by paragraph (1) for a period not to exceed 6 months if the Director determines that such an extension is necessary.

(3) COMMERCIAL MOTOR VEHICLE DEFINED.—In this subsection, the term "commercial motor vehicle" has the meaning given that term by section 31101.

(Added Pub. L. 107–56, title X, §1012(a)(1), Oct. 26, 2001, 115 Stat. 396; amended Pub. L. 109–59, title VII, §§7104, 7105, 7126, Aug. 10, 2005, 119 Stat. 1894, 1909; Pub. L. 110–53, title XV, §1556(a), Aug. 3, 2007, 121 Stat. 475; Pub. L. 110–244, title III, §302(b), June 6, 2008, 122 Stat. 1618; Pub. L. 115–254, div. K, title I, §1978, Oct. 5, 2018, 132 Stat. 3618.)

[1] So in original. The quotation marks and semicolon probably should not appear.

[2] So in original. Comma probably should appear after "applicant".

§5104. REPRESENTATION AND TAMPERING

(a) REPRESENTATION.—A person may represent, by marking or otherwise, that—

(1) a package, component of a package, or packaging for transporting hazardous material is safe, certified, or complies with this chapter only if the package, component of a package, or packaging meets the requirements of each applicable regulation prescribed under this chapter; or

(2) hazardous material is present in a package, container, motor vehicle, rail freight car, aircraft, or vessel only if the material is present.

(b) TAMPERING.—No person may alter, remove, destroy, or otherwise tamper unlawfully with—

(1) a marking, label, placard, or description on a document required under this chapter or a regulation prescribed under this chapter; or

(2) a package, component of a package, or packaging, container, motor vehicle, rail freight car, aircraft, or vessel used to transport hazardous material.

(Pub. L. 103–272, §1(d), July 5, 1994, 108 Stat. 761; Pub. L. 103–311, title I, §117(b), Aug. 26, 1994, 108 Stat. 1678; Pub. L. 103–429, §6(4), Oct. 31, 1994, 108 Stat. 4378; Pub. L. 109–59, title VII, §7106, Aug. 10, 2005, 119 Stat. 1897.)

§5105. TRANSPORTING CERTAIN HIGHLY RADIOACTIVE MATERIAL

(a) DEFINITIONS.—In this section, "high-level radioactive waste" and "spent nuclear fuel" have the same meanings given those terms in section 2 of the Nuclear Waste Policy Act of 1982 (42 U.S.C. 10101).

(b) TRANSPORTATION SAFETY STUDY.—In consultation with the Secretary of Energy, the Nuclear Regulatory Commission, potentially affected States and Indian tribes, representatives of the rail transportation industry, and shippers of high-level radioactive waste and spent nuclear fuel, the Secretary shall conduct a study comparing the safety of using trains operated only to transport high-level radioactive waste and spent nuclear fuel with the safety of using other methods of rail transportation for transporting that waste and fuel. The Secretary shall submit to Congress not later than November 16, 1991, a report on the results of the study.

(c) SAFE RAIL TRANSPORTATION REGULATIONS.—Not later than November 16, 1992, after considering the results of the study conducted under subsection (b) of this section, the Secretary shall prescribe amendments to existing regulations that the Secretary considers appropriate to provide for the safe rail transportation of high-level radioactive waste and spent nuclear fuel, including trains operated only for transporting high-level radioactive waste and spent nuclear fuel.

(d) INSPECTIONS OF MOTOR VEHICLES TRANSPORTING CERTAIN MATERIAL.—(1) Not later than November 16, 1991, the Secretary shall require by regulation that before each use of a motor vehicle to transport a highway-route-controlled quantity of radioactive material in commerce, the vehicle shall be inspected and certified as complying with this chapter and applicable United States motor carrier safety laws and regulations. The Secretary may require that the inspection be carried out by an authorized United States Government inspector or according to appropriate State procedures.

(2) The Secretary may allow a person, transporting or causing to be transported a highway-route-controlled quantity of radioactive material, to inspect the motor vehicle used to transport the material and to certify that the vehicle complies with this chapter. The inspector qualification requirements the Secretary prescribes for an individual inspecting a motor vehicle apply to an individual conducting an inspection under this paragraph.

(Pub. L. 103–272, §1(d), July 5, 1994, 108 Stat. 762; Pub. L. 109–59, title VII, §§7107, 7126, Aug. 10, 2005, 119 Stat. 1897, 1909.)

§5106. HANDLING CRITERIA

The Secretary may prescribe criteria for handling hazardous material, including—

(1) a minimum number of personnel;

(2) minimum levels of training and qualifications for personnel;

(3) the kind and frequency of inspections;

(4) equipment for detecting, warning of, and controlling risks posed by the hazardous material;

(5) specifications for the use of equipment and facilities used in handling and transporting the hazardous material; and

(6) a system of monitoring safety procedures for transporting the hazardous material.

(Pub. L. 103–272, §1(d), July 5, 1994, 108 Stat. 763; Pub. L. 109–59, title VII, §7126, Aug. 10, 2005, 119 Stat. 1909.)

§5107. HAZMAT EMPLOYEE TRAINING REQUIREMENTS AND GRANTS

(a) TRAINING REQUIREMENTS.—The Secretary shall prescribe by regulation requirements for training that a hazmat employer must give hazmat employees of the employer on the safe loading, unloading, handling, storing, and transporting of hazardous material and emergency preparedness for responding to an accident or incident involving the transportation of hazardous material. The regulations—

(1) shall establish the date, as provided by subsection (b) of this section, by which the training shall be completed; and

(2) may provide for different training for different classes or categories of hazardous material and hazmat employees.

(b) BEGINNING AND COMPLETING TRAINING.—A hazmat employer shall begin the training of hazmat employees of the employer not later than 6 months after the Secretary prescribes the regulations under subsection (a) of this section. The training shall be completed within a reasonable period of time after—

(1) 6 months after the regulations are prescribed; or

(2) the date on which an individual is to begin carrying out a duty or power of a hazmat employee if the individual is employed as a hazmat employee after the 6-month period.

(c) CERTIFICATION OF TRAINING.—After completing the training, each hazmat employer shall certify, with documentation the Secretary may require by regulation, that the hazmat employees of the employer have received training and have been tested on appropriate transportation areas of responsibility, including at least one of the following:

(1) recognizing and understanding the Department of Transportation hazardous material classification system.

(2) the use and limitations of the Department hazardous material placarding, labeling, and marking systems.

(3) general handling procedures, loading and unloading techniques, and strategies to reduce the probability of release or damage during or incidental to transporting hazardous material.

(4) health, safety, and risk factors associated with hazardous material and the transportation of hazardous material.

(5) appropriate emergency response and communication procedures for dealing with an accident or incident involving hazardous material transportation.

(6) the use of the Department Emergency Response Guidebook and recognition of its limitations or the use of equivalent documents and recognition of the limitations of those documents.

(7) applicable hazardous material transportation regulations.

(8) personal protection techniques.

(9) preparing a shipping document for transporting hazardous material.

(d) COORDINATION OF TRAINING REQUIREMENTS.—In consultation with the Administrator of the Environmental Protection Agency and the Secretary of Labor, the Secretary shall ensure that the training requirements prescribed under this section do not conflict with or duplicate—

(1) the requirements of regulations the Secretary of Labor prescribes related to hazard communication, and hazardous waste operations, and emergency response that are contained in part 1910 of title 29, Code of Federal Regulations; and

(2) the regulations the Agency prescribes related to worker protection standards for hazardous waste operations that are contained in part 311 of title 40, Code of Federal Regulations.

(e) TRAINING GRANTS.—

(1) IN GENERAL.—Subject to the availability of funds under section 5128(c), the Secretary shall make grants under this subsection—

(A) for training instructors to train hazmat employees; and

(B) to the extent determined appropriate by the Secretary, for such instructors to train hazmat employees.

(2) ELIGIBILITY.—A grant under this subsection shall be made through a competitive process to a nonprofit organization that demonstrates—

(A) expertise in conducting a training program for hazmat employees; and

(B) the ability to reach and involve in a training program a target population of hazmat employees.

(f) TRAINING OF CERTAIN EMPLOYEES.—The Secretary shall ensure that maintenance-of-way employees and railroad signalmen receive general awareness and familiarization training and safety training pursuant to section 172.704 of title 49, Code of Federal Regulations.

(g) RELATIONSHIP TO OTHER LAWS.—(1) Chapter 35 of title 44 does not apply to an activity of the Secretary under subsections (a)–(d) of this section.

(2) An action of the Secretary under subsections (a)–(d) of this section and section 5106 is not an exercise, under section 4(b)(1) of the Occupational Safety and Health Act of 1970 (29 U.S.C. 653(b)(1)), of statutory authority to prescribe or enforce standards or regulations affecting occupational safety or health.

(h) EXISTING EFFORT.—No grant under subsection (e) shall supplant or replace existing employer-provided hazardous materials training efforts or obligations.

(i) COMMUNITY SAFETY GRANTS.—The Secretary shall establish a competitive program for making grants to nonprofit organizations for—

(1) conducting national outreach and training programs to assist communities in preparing for and responding to accidents and incidents involving the transportation of hazardous materials, including Class 3 flammable liquids by rail; and

(2) training State and local personnel responsible for enforcing the safe transportation of hazardous materials, including Class 3 flammable liquids.

(Pub. L. 103–272, §1(d), July 5, 1994, 108 Stat. 763; Pub. L. 103–311, title I, §§106, 119(c)(1)–(3), Aug. 26, 1994, 108 Stat. 1674, 1680; Pub. L. 109–59, title VII, §§7108, 7126, Aug. 10, 2005, 119 Stat. 1897, 1909; Pub. L. 112–141, div. C, title III, §33016, July 6, 2012, 126 Stat. 841; Pub. L. 114–94, div. A, title VII, §7301, Dec. 4, 2015, 129 Stat. 1594.)

§5108. REGISTRATION

(a) PERSONS REQUIRED TO FILE.—(1) A person shall file a registration statement with the Secretary under this subsection if the person is transporting or causing to be transported in commerce any of the following:

(A) a highway-route-controlled quantity of radioactive material.

(B) more than 25 kilograms of a Division 1.1, 1.2, or 1.3 explosive material in a motor vehicle, rail car, or transport container.

(C) more than one liter in each package of a hazardous material the Secretary designates as extremely toxic by inhalation.

(D) hazardous material in a bulk packaging, container, or tank, as defined by the Secretary, if the bulk packaging, container, or tank has a capacity of at least 3,500 gallons or more than 468 cubic feet.

(E) a shipment of at least 5,000 pounds (except in a bulk packaging) of a class of hazardous material for which placarding of a vehicle, rail car, or freight container is required under regulations prescribed under this chapter.

(2) The Secretary may require any of the following persons to file a registration statement with the Secretary under this subsection:

(A) a person transporting or causing to be transported hazardous material in commerce and not required to file a registration statement under paragraph (1) of this subsection.

(B) a person designing, manufacturing, fabricating, inspecting, marking, maintaining, reconditioning, repairing, or testing a package, container, or packaging component that is represented, marked, certified, or sold as qualified for use in transporting hazardous material in commerce.

(3) A person required to file a registration statement under this subsection may transport or cause to be transported, or design, manufacture, fabricate, inspect, mark, maintain, recondition, repair, or test a package, container packaging component, or container for use in transporting, hazardous material, only if the person has a statement on file as required by this subsection.

(4) The Secretary may waive the filing of a registration statement, or the payment of a fee, required under this subsection, or both, for any person not domiciled in the United States who solely offers hazardous materials for transportation to the United States from a place outside the United States if the country of which such person is a domiciliary does not require persons domiciled in the United States who solely offer hazardous materials for transportation to the foreign country from places in the United States to file registration statements, or to pay fees, for making such an offer.

(b) FORM, CONTENTS, AND LIMITATION ON FILINGS.—(1) A registration statement under subsection (a) of this section shall be in the form and contain information the Secretary requires by regulation. The Secretary may use existing forms of the Department of Transportation and the Environmental Protection Agency to carry out this subsection. The statement shall include—

(A) the name and principal place of business of the registrant;

(B) a description of each activity the registrant carries out for which filing a statement under subsection (a) of this section is required; and

(C) each State in which the person carries out any of the activities.

(2) A person carrying out more than one activity, or an activity at more than one location, for which filing is required only has to file one registration statement to comply with subsection (a) of this section.

(c) FILING.—Each person required to file a registration statement under subsection (a) shall file the statement in accordance with regulations prescribed by the Secretary.

(d) SIMPLIFYING THE REGISTRATION PROCESS.—The Secretary may take necessary action to simplify the registration process under subsections (a)–(c) of this section and to minimize the number of applications, documents, and other information a person is required to file under this chapter and other laws of the United States.

(e) COOPERATION WITH ADMINISTRATOR.—The Administrator of the Environmental Protection Agency shall assist the Secretary in carrying out subsections (a)–(g)(1) and (h) of this section by providing the Secretary with information the Secretary requests to carry out the objectives of subsections (a)–(g)(1) and (h).

(f) AVAILABILITY OF STATEMENTS.—The Secretary shall make a registration statement filed under subsection (a) of this section available for inspection by any person for a fee the Secretary establishes. However, this subsection does not require the release of information described in section 552(b) of title 5 or otherwise protected by law from disclosure to the public.

(g) FEES.—(1) The Secretary shall establish, impose, and collect from a person required to file a registration statement under subsection (a) of this section a fee necessary to pay for the costs of the Secretary in processing the statement.

(2)(A) In addition to a fee established under paragraph (1) of this subsection, the Secretary shall establish and impose by regulation and collect an annual fee. Subject to subparagraph (B) of this paragraph, the fee shall be at least $250 but not more than $3,000 from each person required to file a registration statement under this section. The Secretary shall determine the amount of the fee under this paragraph on at least one of the following:

(i) gross revenue from transporting hazardous material.

(ii) the type of hazardous material transported or caused to be transported.

(iii) the amount of hazardous material transported or caused to be transported.

(iv) the number of shipments of hazardous material.

(v) the number of activities that the person carries out for which filing a registration statement is required under this section.

(vi) the threat to property, individuals, and the environment from an accident or incident involving the hazardous material transported or caused to be transported.

(vii) the percentage of gross revenue derived from transporting hazardous material.

(viii) the amount to be made available to carry out sections 5108(g)(2), 5115, and 5116 of this title.

(ix) other factors the Secretary considers appropriate.

(B) The Secretary shall adjust the amount being collected under this paragraph to reflect any unexpended balance in the account established under section 5116(h) of this title. However, the Secretary is not required to refund any fee collected under this paragraph.

(C) The Secretary shall transfer to the Secretary of the Treasury amounts the Secretary of Transportation collects under this paragraph for deposit in the Hazardous Materials Emergency Preparedness Fund established under section 5116(h) of this title.

(3) FEES ON EXEMPT PERSONS.—Notwithstanding subsection (a)(4), the Secretary shall impose and collect a fee of $25 from a person who is required to register under this section but who is otherwise exempted by the Secretary from paying any fee under this section. The fee shall be used to pay the costs incurred by the Secretary in processing registration statements filed by such persons.

(h) MAINTAINING PROOF OF FILING AND PAYMENT OF FEES.—The Secretary may prescribe regulations requiring a person required to file a registration statement under subsection (a) of this section to maintain proof of the filing and payment of fees imposed under subsection (g) of this section.

(i) RELATIONSHIP TO OTHER LAWS.—(1) Chapter 35 of title 44 does not apply to an activity of the Secretary under subsections (a)–(g)(1) and (h) of this section.

(2)(A) This section does not apply to an employee of a hazmat employer.

(B) Subsections (a)–(h) of this section do not apply to a department, agency, or instrumentality of the United States Government, an authority of a State or political subdivision of a State, an Indian tribe, or an employee of a department, agency, instrumentality, or authority carrying out official duties.

(Pub. L. 103–272, §1(d), July 5, 1994, 108 Stat. 765; Pub. L. 103–311, title I, §§104, 117(a)(3), 119(d)(1),

Aug. 26, 1994, 108 Stat. 1673, 1678, 1680; Pub. L. 105–102, §2(3), Nov. 20, 1997, 111 Stat. 2204; Pub. L. 105–225, §7(b)(1), Aug. 12, 1998, 112 Stat. 1511; Pub. L. 109–59, title VII, §§7109(a)–(c), (e), (f), 7114(d)(3), 7126, Aug. 10, 2005, 119 Stat. 1897, 1898, 1900, 1909; Pub. L. 114–94, div. A, title VII, §7203(b)(1), Dec. 4, 2015, 129 Stat. 1591.)

§5109. MOTOR CARRIER SAFETY PERMITS

(a) REQUIREMENT.—A motor carrier may transport or cause to be transported by motor vehicle in commerce hazardous material only if the carrier holds a safety permit the Secretary issues under this section authorizing the transportation and keeps a copy of the permit, or other proof of its existence, in the vehicle. The Secretary shall issue a permit if the Secretary finds the carrier is fit, willing, and able—

(1) to provide the transportation to be authorized by the permit;

(2) to comply with this chapter and regulations the Secretary prescribes to carry out this chapter; and

(3) to comply with applicable United States motor carrier safety laws and regulations and applicable minimum financial responsibility laws and regulations.

(b) APPLICABLE TRANSPORTATION.—The Secretary shall prescribe by regulation the hazardous material and amounts of hazardous material to which this section applies. However, this section shall apply at least to transportation by a motor carrier, in amounts the Secretary establishes, of—

(1) a class A or B explosive;

(2) liquefied natural gas;

(3) hazardous material the Secretary designates as extremely toxic by inhalation; and

(4) a highway-route-controlled quantity of radioactive material, as defined by the Secretary.

(c) APPLICATIONS.—A motor carrier shall file an application with the Secretary for a safety permit to provide transportation under this section. The Secretary may approve any part of the application or deny the application. The application shall be under oath and contain information the Secretary requires by regulation.

(d) AMENDMENTS, SUSPENSIONS, AND REVOCATIONS.—(1) After notice and an opportunity for a hearing, the Secretary may amend, suspend, or revoke a safety permit, as provided by procedures prescribed under subsection (e) of this section, when the Secretary decides the motor carrier is not complying with a requirement of this chapter, a regulation prescribed under this chapter, or an applicable United States motor carrier safety law or regulation or minimum financial responsibility law or regulation.

(2) If the Secretary decides an imminent hazard exists, the Secretary may amend, suspend, or revoke a permit before scheduling a hearing.

(e) PROCEDURES.—The Secretary shall prescribe by regulation—

(1) application procedures, including form, content, and fees necessary to recover the complete cost of carrying out this section;

(2) standards for deciding the duration, terms, and limitations of a safety permit;

(3) procedures to amend, suspend, or revoke a permit; and

(4) other procedures the Secretary considers appropriate to carry out this section.

(f) SHIPPER RESPONSIBILITY.—A person offering hazardous material for motor vehicle transportation in commerce may offer the material to a motor carrier only if the carrier has a safety permit issued under this section authorizing the transportation.

(g) CONDITIONS.—A motor carrier may provide transportation under a safety permit issued under this section only if the carrier complies with conditions the Secretary finds are required to protect public safety.

(h) LIMITATION ON DENIAL.—The Secretary may not deny a non-temporary permit held by a motor carrier pursuant to this section based on a comprehensive review of that carrier triggered by safety management system scores or out-of-service disqualification standards, unless—

(1) the carrier has the opportunity, prior to the denial of such permit, to submit a written description of corrective actions taken and other documentation the carrier wishes the Secretary to consider, including a corrective action plan; and

(2) the Secretary determines the actions or plan is insufficient to address the safety concerns identified during the course of the comprehensive review.

(Pub. L. 103–272, §1(d), July 5, 1994, 108 Stat. 767; Pub. L. 109–59, title VII, §7126, Aug. 10, 2005, 119 Stat. 1909; Pub. L. 114–94, div. A, title VII, §7202, Dec. 4, 2015, 129 Stat. 1589.)

§5110. SHIPPING PAPERS AND DISCLOSURE

(a) PROVIDING SHIPPING PAPERS.—Each person offering for transportation in commerce hazardous material to which the shipping paper requirements of the Secretary apply shall provide to the carrier providing the transportation a shipping paper that makes the disclosures the Secretary prescribes in regulations.

(b) KEEPING SHIPPING PAPERS ON THE VEHICLE.—(1) A motor carrier, and the person offering the hazardous material for transportation if a private motor carrier, shall keep the shipping paper on the vehicle transporting the material.

(2) Except as provided in paragraph (1) of this subsection, the shipping paper shall be kept in a location the Secretary specifies in a motor vehicle, train, vessel, aircraft, or facility until—

(A) the hazardous material no longer is in transportation; or

(B) the documents are made available to a representative of a department, agency, or instrumentality of the United States Government or a State or local authority responding to an accident or incident involving the motor vehicle, train, vessel, aircraft, or facility.

(c) DISCLOSURE TO EMERGENCY RESPONSE AUTHORITIES.—When an incident involving hazardous material being transported in commerce occurs, the person transporting the material, immediately on request of appropriate emergency response authorities, shall disclose to the authorities information about the material.

(d) RETENTION OF PAPERS.—

(1) OFFERORS.—The person who provides the shipping paper under this section shall retain the paper, or an electronic format of it, for a period of 2 years after the date that the shipping paper is provided to the carrier, with the paper or electronic format to be accessible through the offeror's principal place of business.

(2) CARRIERS.—The carrier required to keep the shipping paper under this section,[1] shall retain the paper, or an electronic format of it, for a period of 1 year after the date that the shipping paper is provided to the carrier, with the paper or electronic format to be accessible through the carrier's principal place of business.

(3) AVAILABILITY TO GOVERNMENT AGENCIES.—Any person required to keep a shipping paper under this subsection shall, upon request, make it available to a Federal, State, or

[§5111. Repealed. Pub. L. 109–59, title VII,
§7111, Aug. 10, 2005, 119 Stat. 1899]

CHAPTER 51—TRANSPORTATION O
HAZARDOUS MATERIA

local government agency at reasonable times and locations.

(Pub. L. 103–272, §1(d), July 5, 1994, 108 Stat. 768; Pub. L. 103–311, title I, §115, Aug. 26, 1994, 108 Stat. 1678; Pub. L. 109–59, title VII, §§7110, 7126, Aug. 10, 2005, 119 Stat. 1898, 1909; Pub. L. 110–244, title III, §302(i), June 6, 2008, 122 Stat. 1618.)

[1] *So in original. Comma probably should not appear.*

[§5111. Repealed. Pub. L. 109–59, title VII, §7111, Aug. 10, 2005, 119 Stat. 1899]

Section, Pub. L. 103–272, §1(d), July 5, 1994, 108 Stat. 769, related to use of rail tank cars built before Jan. 1, 1971, to transport hazardous material in commerce.

§5112. Highway routing of hazardous material

(a) APPLICATION.—(1) This section applies to a motor vehicle only if the vehicle is transporting hazardous material in commerce for which placarding of the vehicle is required under regulations prescribed under this chapter. However, the Secretary by regulation may extend application of this section or a standard prescribed under subsection (b) of this section to—

(A) any use of a vehicle under this paragraph to transport any hazardous material in commerce; and

(B) any motor vehicle used to transport hazardous material in commerce.

(2) Except as provided by subsection (d) of this section and section 5125(c) of this title, each State and Indian tribe may establish, maintain, and enforce—

(A) designations of specific highway routes over which hazardous material may and may not be transported by motor vehicle; and

(B) limitations and requirements related to highway routing.

(b) STANDARDS FOR STATES AND INDIAN TRIBES.—(1) The Secretary, in consultation with the States, shall prescribe by regulation standards for States and Indian tribes to use in carrying out subsection (a) of this section. The standards shall include—

(A) a requirement that a highway routing designation, limitation, or requirement of a State or Indian tribe shall enhance public safety in the area subject to the jurisdiction of the State or tribe and in areas of the United States not subject to the jurisdiction of the State or tribe and directly affected by the designation, limitation, or requirement;

(B) minimum procedural requirements to ensure public participation when the State or Indian tribe is establishing a highway routing designation, limitation, or requirement;

(C) a requirement that, in establishing a highway routing designation, limitation, or requirement, a State or Indian tribe consult with appropriate State, local, and tribal officials having jurisdiction over areas of the United States not subject to the jurisdiction of that State or tribe establishing the designation, limitation, or requirement and with affected industries;

(D) a requirement that a highway routing designation, limitation, or requirement of a State or Indian tribe shall ensure through highway routing for the transportation of hazardous material between adjacent areas;

(E) a requirement that a highway routing designation, limitation, or requirement of one State or Indian tribe affecting the transportation of hazardous material in another State or tribe may be established, maintained, and enforced by the State or tribe establishing the designation, limitation, or requirement only if—

(i) the designation, limitation, or requirement is agreed to by the other State or tribe within a reasonable period or is approved by the Secretary under subsection (d) of this section; and

(ii) the designation, limitation, or requirement is not an unreasonable burden on commerce;

(F) a requirement that establishing a highway routing designation, limitation, or requirement of a State or Indian tribe be completed in a timely way;

(G) a requirement that a highway routing designation, limitation, or requirement of a State or Indian tribe provide reasonable routes for motor vehicles transporting hazardous material to reach terminals, facilities for food, fuel, repairs, and rest, and places to load and unload hazardous material;

(H) a requirement that a State be responsible—

(i) for ensuring that political subdivisions of the State comply with standards prescribed under this subsection in establishing, maintaining, and enforcing a highway routing designation, limitation, or requirement; and

(ii) for resolving a dispute between political subdivisions; and

(I) a requirement that, in carrying out subsection (a) of this section, a State or Indian tribe shall consider—

(i) population densities;

(ii) the types of highways;

(iii) the types and amounts of hazardous material;

(iv) emergency response capabilities;

(v) the results of consulting with affected persons;

(vi) exposure and other risk factors;

(vii) terrain considerations;

(viii) the continuity of routes;

(ix) alternative routes;

(x) the effects on commerce;

(xi) delays in transportation; and

(xii) other factors the Secretary considers appropriate.

(2) The Secretary may not assign a specific weight that a State or Indian tribe shall use when considering the factors under paragraph (1)(I) of this subsection.

(c) LIST OF ROUTE DESIGNATIONS.—

(1) IN GENERAL.—In coordination with the States, the Secretary shall update and publish periodically a list of currently effective hazardous material highway route designations.

(2) STATE RESPONSIBILITIES.—

(A) IN GENERAL.—Each State shall submit to the Secretary, in a form and manner to be determined by the Secretary and in accordance with subparagraph (B)—

(i) the name of the State agency responsible for hazardous material highway route designations; and

(ii) a list of the State's currently effective hazardous material highway route designations.

(B) FREQUENCY.—Each State shall submit the information described in subparagraph (A)(ii)—

(i) at least once every 2 years; and

(ii) not later than 60 days after a hazardous material highway route designation is established, amended, or discontinued.

(d) DISPUTE RESOLUTION.—(1) The Secretary shall prescribe regulations for resolving a dispute related to through highway routing or to an agreement with a proposed highway route designation, limitation, or requirement between or among States, political subdivisions of different States, or Indian tribes.

(2) A State or Indian tribe involved in a dispute under this subsection may petition the Secretary to resolve the dispute. The Secretary shall resolve the dispute not later than one year after receiving the petition. The resolution shall provide the greatest level of highway safety without being an unreasonable burden on commerce and shall ensure compliance with standards prescribed under subsection (b) of this section.

(3)(A) After a petition is filed under this subsection, a civil action about the subject matter of the dispute may be brought in a court only after the earlier of—

(i) the day the Secretary issues a final decision; or

(ii) the last day of the one-year period beginning on the day the Secretary receives the petition.

(B) A State or Indian tribe adversely affected by a decision of the Secretary under this subsection may bring a civil action for judicial review of the decision in an appropriate district court of the United States not later than 89 days after the day the decision becomes final.

(e) RELATIONSHIP TO OTHER LAWS.—This section and regulations prescribed under this section do not affect sections 31111 and 31113 of this title or section 127 of title 23.

(f) EXISTING RADIOACTIVE MATERIAL ROUTING REGULATIONS.—The Secretary is not required to amend or again prescribe regulations related to highway routing designations over which radioactive material may and may not be transported by motor vehicles, and limitations and requirements related to the routing, that were in effect on November 16, 1990.

(Pub. L. 103–272, §1(d), July 5, 1994, 108 Stat. 769; Pub. L. 109–59, title VII, §7126, Aug. 10, 2005, 119 Stat. 1909; Pub. L. 112–141, div. C, title III, §33013(a), July 6, 2012, 126 Stat. 839.)

§5113. UNSATISFACTORY SAFETY RATING

A violation of section 31144(c)(3) shall be considered a violation of this chapter, and shall be subject to the penalties in sections 5123 and 5124.

(Pub. L. 103–272, §1(d), July 5, 1994, 108 Stat. 771; Pub. L. 105–178, title IV, §4009(b), June 9, 1998, 112 Stat. 407; Pub. L. 109–59, title VII, §7112(a), Aug. 10, 2005, 119 Stat. 1899.)

§5114. AIR TRANSPORTATION OF IONIZING RADIATION MATERIAL

(a) TRANSPORTING IN AIR COMMERCE.—Material that emits ionizing radiation spontaneously may be transported on a passenger-carrying aircraft in air commerce (as defined in section 40102(a) of this title) only if the material is intended for a use in, or incident to, research or medical diagnosis or treatment and does not present an unreasonable hazard to health and safety when being prepared for, and during, transportation.

(b) PROCEDURES.—The Secretary shall prescribe procedures for monitoring and enforcing regulations prescribed under this section.

(c) NONAPPLICATION.—This section does not apply to material the Secretary decides does not pose a significant hazard to health or safety when transported because of its low order of radioactivity.

(Pub. L. 103–272, §1(d), July 5, 1994, 108 Stat. 772; Pub. L. 109–59, title VII, §7126, Aug. 10, 2005, 119 Stat. 1909.)

§5115. TRAINING CURRICULUM FOR THE PUBLIC SECTOR

(a) IN GENERAL.—In coordination with the Administrator of the Federal Emergency Management Agency, the Chairman of the Nuclear Regulatory Commission, the Administrator of the Environmental Protection Agency, the Secretaries of Labor, Energy, and Health and Human Services, and the Director of the National Institute of Environmental Health Sciences, and using existing coordinating mechanisms of the National Response Team and, for radioactive material, the Federal Radiological Preparedness Coordinating Committee, the Secretary of Transportation shall maintain, and update periodically, a current curriculum of courses, including online curriculum as appropriate, necessary to train public sector emergency response and preparedness teams in matters relating to the transportation of hazardous material. Only in developing the curriculum, the Secretary of Transportation shall consult with regional response teams established under the national contingency plan established under section 105 of the Comprehensive Environmental Response, Compensation, and Liability Act of 1980 (42 U.S.C. 9605), representatives of commissions established under section 301 of the Emergency Planning and Community Right-To-Know Act of 1986 (42 U.S.C. 11001), persons (including governmental entities) that provide training for responding to accidents and incidents involving the transportation of hazardous material, and representatives of persons that respond to those accidents and incidents.

(b) REQUIREMENTS.—The curriculum maintained and updated under subsection (a) of this section—

(1) shall include—

(A) a recommended course of study to train public sector employees to respond to an accident or incident involving the transportation of hazardous material and to plan for those responses;

(B) recommended courses and minimum number of hours of instruction necessary for public sector employees to be able to respond safely and efficiently to an accident or incident involving the transportation of hazardous material and to plan those responses; and

(C) appropriate emergency response training and planning programs for public sector employees developed with Federal financial assistance, including programs developed with grants made under section 126(g) of the Superfund Amendments and Reauthorization Act of 1986 (42 U.S.C. 9660a); and

(2) may include recommendations on material appropriate for use in a recommended course described in clause (1)(B) of this subsection.

(c) TRAINING ON COMPLYING WITH LEGAL REQUIREMENTS.—A recommended course described in subsection (b)(1)(B) of this section shall provide the training necessary for public sector employees to comply with—

(1) regulations related to hazardous waste operations and emergency response contained in part 1910 of title 29, Code of Federal Regulations, prescribed by the Secretary of Labor;

(2) regulations related to worker protection standards for hazardous waste operations contained in part 311 of title 40, Code of Federal Regulations, prescribed by the Administrator; and

(3) standards related to emergency response training prescribed by the National Fire Protection Association and such other voluntary consensus standard-setting organizations as the Secretary of Transportation determines appropriate.

(d) DISTRIBUTION AND PUBLICATION.—With the National Response Team—

(1) the Secretary shall distribute the curriculum and any updates to the curriculum to the regional response teams and all committees and commissions established under section 301 of the Emergency Planning and Community Right-To-Know Act of 1986 (42 U.S.C. 11001); and

(2) the Secretary may publish and distribute a list of programs and courses maintained and updated under this section and of any programs utilizing such courses.

(Pub. L. 103–272, §1(d), July 5, 1994, 108 Stat. 772; Pub. L. 103–429, §6(5), Oct. 31, 1994, 108 Stat. 4378; Pub. L. 109–59, title VII, §§7113, 7126, Aug. 10, 2005, 119 Stat. 1899, 1909; Pub. L. 109–295, title VI, §612(c), Oct. 4, 2006, 120 Stat. 1410; Pub. L. 112–141, div. C, title III, §33004(a), July 6, 2012, 126 Stat. 832; Pub. L. 114–94, div. A, title VI, §6013, Dec. 4, 2015, 129 Stat. 1570.)

§5116. PLANNING AND TRAINING GRANTS, MONITORING, AND REVIEW

(a) PLANNING AND TRAINING GRANTS.—(1) The Secretary shall make grants to States and Indian tribes—

(A) to develop, improve, and carry out emergency plans under the Emergency Planning and Community Right-To-Know Act of 1986 (42 U.S.C. 11001 et seq.), including ascertaining flow patterns of hazardous material on lands under the jurisdiction of a State or Indian tribe, and between lands under the jurisdiction of a State or Indian tribe and lands of another State or Indian tribe;

(B) to decide on the need for regional hazardous material emergency response teams; and

(C) to train public sector employees to respond to accidents and incidents involving hazardous material.

(2) To the extent that a grant is used to train emergency responders under paragraph (1)(C), the State or Indian tribe shall provide written certification to the Secretary that the emergency responders who receive training under the grant will have the ability to protect nearby persons, property, and the environment from the effects of accidents or incidents involving the transportation of hazardous material in accordance with existing regulations or National Fire Protection Association standards for competence of responders to accidents and incidents involving hazardous materials.

(3) The Secretary may make a grant to a State or Indian tribe under paragraph (1) of this subsection only if—

(A) the State or Indian tribe certifies that the total amount the State or Indian tribe expends (except amounts of the Federal Government) for the purpose of the grant will at least equal the average level of expenditure for the last 5 years; and

(B) any emergency response training provided under the grant shall consist of—

(i) a course developed or identified under section 5115 of this title; or

(ii) any other course the Secretary determines is consistent with the objectives of this section.

(4) A State or Indian tribe receiving a grant under this subsection shall ensure that planning and emergency response training under the grant is coordinated with adjacent States and Indian tribes.

(5) A training grant under paragraph (1)(C) may be used—

(A) to pay—

(i) the tuition costs of public sector employees being trained;

(ii) travel expenses of those employees to and from the training facility;

(iii) room and board of those employees when at the training facility; and

(iv) travel expenses of individuals providing the training;

(B) by the State, political subdivision, or Indian tribe to provide the training; and

(C) to make an agreement with a person (including an authority of a State, a political subdivision of a State or Indian tribe, or a local jurisdiction), subject to approval by the Secretary, to provide the training if—

(i) the agreement allows the Secretary and the State or Indian tribe to conduct random examinations, inspections, and audits of the training without prior notice;

(ii) the person agrees to have an auditable accounting system; and

(iii) the State or Indian tribe conducts at least one on-site observation of the training each year.

(6) The Secretary shall allocate amounts made available for grants under this subsection among eligible States and Indian tribes based on the needs of the States and Indian tribes for emergency response planning and training. In making a decision about those needs, the Secretary shall consider—

(A) the number of hazardous material facilities in the State or on land under the jurisdiction of the Indian tribe;

(B) the types and amounts of hazardous material transported in the State or on such land;

(C) whether the State or Indian tribe imposes and collects a fee for transporting hazardous material;

(D) whether such fee is used only to carry out a purpose related to transporting hazardous material;

(E) the past record of the State or Indian tribe in effectively managing planning and training grants; and

(F) any other factors the Secretary determines are appropriate to carry out this subsection.

(b) COMPLIANCE WITH CERTAIN LAW.—The Secretary may make a grant to a State under this section in a fiscal year only if the State certifies that the State complies with sections 301 and 303 of the Emergency Planning and Community Right-To-Know Act of 1986 (42 U.S.C. 11001, 11003).

(c) APPLICATIONS.—A State or Indian tribe interested in receiving a grant under this section shall submit an application to the Secretary. The application must be submitted at the time, and contain information, the Secretary requires by regulation to carry out the objectives of this section.

(d) GOVERNMENT'S SHARE OF COSTS.—A grant under this section is for 80 percent of the cost the State or Indian tribe incurs in the fiscal year to carry out the activity for which the grant is made. Amounts of the State or tribe under subsection (a)(3)(A) of this section are not part of the non-Government share under this subsection.

(e) MONITORING AND TECHNICAL ASSISTANCE.—In coordination with the Secretaries of Transportation and Energy, Administrator of the Environmental Protection Agency, and Director of the National Institute of Environmental Health Sciences, the Administrator of the Federal Emergency Management Agency shall monitor public sector emergency response planning and training for an accident or incident involving hazardous material. Considering the results of the monitoring, the Secretaries, Administrators, and Director each shall provide technical assistance to a State, political subdivision of a State, or Indian tribe for carrying out emergency response training and planning for an accident or incident involving hazardous material and shall coordinate the assistance using the existing coordinating mechanisms of the National Response Team and, for radioactive material, the Federal Radiological Preparedness Coordinating Committee.

(f) DELEGATION OF AUTHORITY.—To minimize administrative costs and to coordinate Federal financial assistance for emergency response training and planning, the Secretary may delegate to the Administrator of the Federal Emergency Management Agency, Director of the National Institute of Environmental Health Sciences, Chairman of the Nuclear Regulatory Commission, Administrator of the Environmental Protection Agency, and Secretaries of Labor and Energy any of the following:

(1) authority to receive applications for grants under this section.

(2) authority to review applications for technical compliance with this section.

(3) authority to review applications to recommend approval or disapproval.

(4) any other ministerial duty associated with grants under this section.

(g) MINIMIZING DUPLICATION OF EFFORT AND EXPENSES.—The Secretaries of Transportation, Labor, and Energy, Administrator of the Federal Emergency Management Agency, Director of the National Institute of Environmental Health Sciences, Chairman of the Nuclear Regulatory Commission, and Administrator of the Environmental Protection Agency shall review periodically, with the head of each department, agency, or instrumentality of the Government, all emergency response and preparedness training programs of that department, agency, or instrumentality to minimize duplication of effort and expense of the department, agency, or instrumentality in carrying out the programs and shall take necessary action to minimize duplication.

(h) ANNUAL REGISTRATION FEE ACCOUNT AND ITS USES.—The Secretary of the Treasury shall establish an account in the Treasury (to be known as the "Hazardous Materials Emergency Preparedness Fund") into which the Secretary of the Treasury shall deposit amounts the Secretary of Transportation transfers to the Secretary of the Treasury under section 5108(g)(2)(C) of this title. Without further appropriation, amounts in the account are available—

(1) to make grants under this section and section 5107(e);

(2) to monitor and provide technical assistance under subsection (e) of this section;

(3) to publish and distribute an emergency response guide; and

(4) to pay administrative costs of carrying out this section and sections 5107(e) and 5108(g)(2) of this title, except that not more than 2 percent of the amounts made available from the account in a fiscal year may be used to pay those costs.

(i) SUPPLEMENTAL TRAINING GRANTS.—

(1) In order to further the purposes of subsection (a), the Secretary shall, subject to the availability of funds and through a competitive process, make a grant or make grants to national nonprofit fire service organizations for the purpose of training instructors to conduct hazardous materials response training programs for individuals with statutory responsibility to respond to hazardous materials accidents and incidents.

(2) For the purposes of this subsection the Secretary, after consultation with interested organizations, shall—

(A) identify regions or locations in which fire departments or other organizations which provide emergency response to hazardous materials transportation accidents and incidents are in need of hazardous materials training; and

(B) prioritize such needs and develop a means for identifying additional specific training needs.

(3) Funds granted to an organization under this subsection shall only be used—

(A) to provide training, including portable training, for instructors to conduct hazardous materials response training programs;

(B) to purchase training equipment used exclusively to train instructors to conduct such training programs; and

(C) to disseminate such information and materials as are necessary for the conduct of such training programs.

(4) The Secretary may only make a grant to an organization under this subsection in a fiscal year if the organization enters into an agreement with the Secretary to provide training, including portable training, for instructors to conduct hazardous materials response training programs in such fiscal year that will use—

(A) a course or courses developed or identified under section 5115 of this title; or

(B) other courses which the Secretary determines are consistent with the objectives of this subsection;

for training individuals with statutory responsibility to respond to accidents and incidents involving hazardous materials. Such agreement also shall provide that training courses shall comply with Federal regulations and national consensus standards for hazardous materials response and be open to all such individuals on a nondiscriminatory basis.

(5) The Secretary may not award a grant to an organization under this subsection unless the organization ensures that emergency responders who receive training under the grant will have the ability to protect nearby persons, property, and the environment from the effects of accidents or incidents involving the transportation of hazardous material in accordance with existing regulations or National Fire Protection Association standards for competence of responders to accidents and incidents involving hazardous materials.

(6) Notwithstanding paragraphs (1) and (3), to the extent determined appropriate by the Secretary, a grant awarded by the Secretary to an organization under this subsection to conduct hazardous material response training programs may be used to train

individuals with responsibility to respond to accidents and incidents involving hazardous material.

(7) For the purposes of this subsection, the term "portable training" means live, instructor-led training provided by certified fire service instructors that can be offered in any suitable setting, rather than specific designated facilities. Under this training delivery model, instructors travel to locations convenient to students and utilize local facilities and resources.

(8) The Secretary may impose such additional terms and conditions on grants to be made under this subsection as the Secretary determines are necessary to protect the interests of the United States and to carry out the objectives of this subsection.

(j) ALERT GRANT PROGRAM.—

(1) ASSISTANCE FOR LOCAL EMERGENCY RESPONSE TRAINING.—The Secretary shall establish a grant program to make grants to eligible entities described in paragraph (2)—

(A) to develop a hazardous materials response training curriculum for emergency responders, including response activities for the transportation of crude oil, ethanol, and other flammable liquids by rail, consistent with the standards of the National Fire Protection Association; and

(B) to make the training described in subparagraph (A) available in an electronic format.

(2) ELIGIBLE ENTITIES.—An eligible entity referred to in paragraph (1) is a nonprofit organization that—

(A) represents first responders or public officials responsible for coordinating disaster response; and

(B) is able to provide direct or web-based training to individuals responsible for responding to accidents and incidents involving hazardous materials.

(3) FUNDING.—

(A) IN GENERAL.—To carry out the grant program under paragraph (1), the Secretary may use, for each fiscal year, any amounts recovered during such fiscal year from grants awarded under this section during a prior fiscal year.

(B) OTHER HAZARDOUS MATERIAL TRAINING ACTIVITIES.—For each fiscal year, after providing grants under paragraph (1), if funds remain available, the Secretary may use the amounts described in subparagraph (A)—

(i) to make grants under—

(I) subsection (a)(1)(C);

(II) subsection (i); and

(III) section 5107(e);

(ii) to conduct monitoring and provide technical assistance under subsection (e);

(iii) to publish and distribute the emergency response guide referred to in subsection (h)(3); and

(iv) to pay administrative costs in accordance with subsection (h)(4).

(C) OBLIGATION LIMITATION.—Notwithstanding any other provision of law, for each fiscal year, amounts described in subparagraph (A) shall not be included in the obligation limitation for the Hazardous Materials Emergency Preparedness grant program for that fiscal year.

(k) REPORTS.—The Secretary shall submit an annual report to the Committee on

Transportation and Infrastructure of the House of Representatives and the Committee on Commerce, Science, and Transportation of the Senate and make available the report to the public. The report submitted under this subsection shall include information on the allocation and uses of the planning and training grants under subsection (a) and grants under subsections (i) and (j) of this section and under subsections (e) and (i) of section 5107. The report submitted under this subsection shall identify the ultimate recipients of such grants and include—

(1) a detailed accounting and description of each grant expenditure by each grant recipient, including the amount of, and purpose for, each expenditure;

(2) the number of persons trained under the grant program, by training level;

(3) an evaluation of the efficacy of such planning and training programs; and

(4) any recommendations the Secretary may have for improving such grant programs.

(Pub. L. 103–272, §1(d), July 5, 1994, 108 Stat. 773; Pub. L. 103–311, title I, §§105, 119(a), (d)(2), (3), Aug. 26, 1994, 108 Stat. 1673, 1679, 1680; Pub. L. 103–429, §7(c), Oct. 31, 1994, 108 Stat. 4389; Pub. L. 104–287, §§5(8), 6(b), Oct. 11, 1996, 110 Stat. 3389, 3398; Pub. L. 109–59, title VII, §§7114(a)–(d)(2), (e), 7126, Aug. 10, 2005, 119 Stat. 1900, 1909; Pub. L. 109–295, title VI, §612(c), Oct. 4, 2006, 120 Stat. 1410; Pub. L. 112–141, div. C, title III, §33004(b), July 6, 2012, 126 Stat. 832; Pub. L. 114–94, div. A, title VII, §7203(a), (b)(2), Dec. 4, 2015, 129 Stat. 1589, 1591; Pub. L. 117–58, div. B, title VI, §26002, Nov. 15, 2021, 135 Stat. 882.)

§5117. Special Permits and Exclusions

(a) Authority To Issue Special Permits.—(1) As provided under procedures prescribed by regulation, the Secretary may issue, modify, or terminate a special permit authorizing a variance from this chapter or a regulation prescribed under section 5103(b), 5104, 5110, or 5112 of this title to a person performing a function regulated by the Secretary under section 5103(b)(1) in a way that achieves a safety level—

(A) at least equal to the safety level required under this chapter; or

(B) consistent with the public interest and this chapter, if a required safety level does not exist.

(2) A special permit issued under this section shall be effective for an initial period of not more than 2 years and may be renewed by the Secretary upon application for successive periods of not more than 4 years each or, in the case of a special permit relating to section 5112, for an additional period of not more than 2 years.

(b) Applications.—When applying for a special permit or renewal of a special permit under this section, the person must provide a safety analysis prescribed by the Secretary that justifies the special permit. The Secretary shall publish in the Federal Register notice that an application for a new special permit or a modification to an existing special permit has been filed and shall give the public an opportunity to inspect the safety analysis and comment on the application. The Secretary shall make available to the public on the Department of Transportation's Internet Web site any special permit other than a new special permit or a modification to an existing special permit and shall give the public an opportunity to inspect the safety analysis and comment on the application for a period of not more than 15 days. This subsection does not require the release of information protected by law from public disclosure.

(c) Applications To Be Dealt With Promptly.—The Secretary shall issue or renew a special permit or approval for which an application was filed or deny such issuance or renewal within 120 days after the first day of the month following the date of the filing of such application, or the Secretary shall make available to the public a statement of the reason why the Secretary's decision on a special permit or approval is delayed, along with an estimate of the additional time necessary before the decision is made.

(d) EXCLUSIONS.—(1) The Secretary shall exclude, in any part, from this chapter and regulations prescribed under this chapter—

(A) a public vessel (as defined in section 2101 of title 46);

(B) a vessel exempted under section 3702 of title 46 from chapter 37 of title 46; and

(C) a vessel to the extent it is regulated under the Ports and Waterways Safety Act of 1972 (33 U.S.C. 1221 et seq.).

(2) This chapter and regulations prescribed under this chapter do not prohibit—

(A) or regulate transportation of a firearm (as defined in section 232 of title 18), or ammunition for a firearm, by an individual for personal use; or

(B) transportation of a firearm or ammunition in commerce.

(e) LIMITATION ON AUTHORITY.—Unless the Secretary decides that an emergency exists, a special permit or renewal granted under this section is the only way a person subject to this chapter may be granted a variance from this chapter.

(f) INCORPORATION INTO REGULATIONS.—

(1) IN GENERAL.—Not later than 1 year after the date on which a special permit has been in continuous effect for a 10-year period, the Secretary shall conduct a review and analysis of that special permit to determine whether it may be converted into the hazardous materials regulations.

(2) FACTORS.—In conducting the review and analysis under paragraph (1), the Secretary may consider—

(A) the safety record for hazardous materials transported under the special permit;

(B) the application of a special permit;

(C) the suitability of provisions in the special permit for incorporation into the hazardous materials regulations; and

(D) rulemaking activity in related areas.

(3) RULEMAKING.—After completing the review and analysis under paragraph (1) and after providing notice and opportunity for public comment, the Secretary shall either institute a rulemaking to incorporate the special permit into the hazardous materials regulations or publish in the Federal Register the Secretary's justification for why the special permit is not appropriate for incorporation into the regulations.

(g) DISCLOSURE OF FINAL ACTION.—The Secretary shall periodically, but at least every 120 days—

(1) publish in the Federal Register notice of the final disposition of each application for a new special permit, modification to an existing special permit, or approval during the preceding quarter; and

(2) make available to the public on the Department of Transportation's Internet Web site notice of the final disposition of any other special permit during the preceding quarter.

(Pub. L. 103–272, §1(d), July 5, 1994, 108 Stat. 776; Pub. L. 103–311, title I, §120(a), Aug. 26, 1994, 108 Stat. 1680; Pub. L. 109–59, title VII, §§7115(a)(1), (b)–(g), 7126, Aug. 10, 2005, 119 Stat. 1901, 1909; Pub. L. 112–141, div. C, title III, §33012(c), July 6, 2012, 126 Stat. 839; Pub. L. 114–94, div. A, title VII, §7204,

Dec. 4, 2015, 129 Stat. 1592.)

§5118. HAZARDOUS MATERIAL TECHNICAL ASSESSMENT, RESEARCH AND DEVELOPMENT, AND ANALYSIS PROGRAM

(a) RISK REDUCTION.—

(1) PROGRAM AUTHORIZED.—The Secretary of Transportation may develop and implement a hazardous material technical assessment, research and development, and analysis program for the purpose of—

(A) reducing the risks associated with the transportation of hazardous material; and

(B) identifying and evaluating new technologies to facilitate the safe, secure, and efficient transportation of hazardous material.

(2) COORDINATION.—In developing the program under paragraph (1), the Secretary shall—

(A) utilize information gathered from other modal administrations with similar programs;

(B) coordinate with other modal administrations, as appropriate; and

(C) coordinate, as appropriate, with other Federal agencies.

(b) COOPERATION.—In carrying out subsection (a), the Secretary shall work cooperatively with regulated and other entities, including shippers, carriers, emergency responders, State and local officials, and academic institutions.

(c) COOPERATIVE RESEARCH.—

(1) IN GENERAL.—As part of the program established under subsection (a), the Secretary may carry out cooperative research on hazardous materials transport.

(2) NATIONAL ACADEMIES.—The Secretary may enter into an agreement with the National Academies to support research described in paragraph (1).

(3) RESEARCH.—Research conducted under this subsection may include activities relating to—

(A) emergency planning and response, including information and programs that can be readily assessed and implemented in local jurisdictions;

(B) risk analysis and perception and data assessment;

(C) commodity flow data, including voluntary collaboration between shippers and first responders for secure data exchange of critical information;

(D) integration of safety and security;

(E) cargo packaging and handling;

(F) hazmat release consequences; and

(G) materials and equipment testing.

(Added Pub. L. 112–141, div. C, title III, §33007(a), July 6, 2012, 126 Stat. 835; amended Pub. L. 114–94, div. A, title VI, §6014, Dec. 4, 2015, 129 Stat. 1570.)

§5119. UNIFORM FORMS AND PROCEDURES

(a) ESTABLISHMENT OF WORKING GROUP.—The Secretary shall establish a working group of State and local government officials, including representatives of the National Governors' Association, the National Association of Counties, the National League of Cities, the United States Conference of Mayors, the National Conference of State Legislatures, and the Alliance for Uniform Hazmat Transportation Procedures.

(b) PURPOSE OF WORKING GROUP.—The purpose of the working group shall be to develop uniform forms and procedures for a State to register, and to issue permits to, persons that transport, or cause to be transported, hazardous material by motor vehicle in the State.

(c) LIMITATION ON WORKING GROUP.—The working group may not propose to define or limit the amount of a fee a State may impose or collect.

(d) PROCEDURE.—The Secretary shall develop a procedure for the working group to employ in developing recommendations for the Secretary to harmonize existing State registration and permit laws and regulations relating to the transportation of hazardous materials, with special attention paid to each State's unique safety concerns and interest in maintaining strong hazmat safety standards.

(e) REPORT OF WORKING GROUP.—Not later than 18 months after the date of enactment of this subsection, the working group shall transmit to the Secretary a report containing recommendations for establishing uniform forms and procedures described in subsection (b).

(f) REGULATIONS.—Not later than 18 months after the date the working group's report is delivered to the Secretary, the Secretary shall issue regulations to carry out such recommendations of the working group as the Secretary considers appropriate. In developing such regulations, the Secretary shall consider the State needs associated with the transition to and implementation of a uniform forms and procedures program.

(g) LIMITATION ON STATUTORY CONSTRUCTION.—Nothing in this section shall be construed as prohibiting a State from voluntarily participating in a program of uniform forms and procedures until such time as the Secretary issues regulations under subsection (f).

(Pub. L. 103–272, §1(d), July 5, 1994, 108 Stat. 777; Pub. L. 104–287, §5(9), Oct. 11, 1996, 110 Stat. 3389; Pub. L. 109–59, title VII, §7116, Aug. 10, 2005, 119 Stat. 1901.)

§5120. INTERNATIONAL UNIFORMITY OF STANDARDS AND REQUIREMENTS

(a) PARTICIPATION IN INTERNATIONAL FORUMS.—Subject to guidance and direction from the Secretary of State, the Secretary of Transportation shall participate in international forums that establish or recommend mandatory standards and requirements for transporting hazardous material in international commerce.

(b) CONSULTATION.—The Secretary may consult with interested authorities to ensure that, to the extent practicable, regulations the Secretary prescribes under sections 5103(b), 5104, 5110, and 5112 of this title are consistent with standards and requirements related to transporting hazardous material that international authorities adopt.

(c) DIFFERENCES WITH INTERNATIONAL STANDARDS AND REQUIREMENTS.—This section—

(1) does not require the Secretary to prescribe a standard or requirement identical to a standard or requirement adopted by an international authority if the Secretary decides the standard or requirement is unnecessary or unsafe; and

(2) does not prohibit the Secretary from prescribing a safety standard or requirement more stringent than a standard or requirement adopted by an international authority if the Secretary decides the standard or requirement is necessary in the public interest.

(Pub. L. 103–272, §1(d), July 5, 1994, 108 Stat. 778; Pub. L. 109–59, title VII, §§7117, 7126, Aug. 10, 2005, 119 Stat. 1902, 1909.)

§5121. ADMINISTRATIVE

(a) GENERAL AUTHORITY.—To carry out this chapter, the Secretary may investigate, conduct tests, make reports, issue subpenas, conduct hearings, require the production of records and property, take depositions, and conduct research, development, demonstration, and training activities. Except as provided in subsections (c) and (d), after notice and an opportunity for a hearing, the Secretary may issue an order requiring compliance with this chapter or a regulation prescribed, or an order, special permit, or approval issued, under this chapter.

(b) RECORDS, REPORTS, AND INFORMATION.—A person subject to this chapter shall—

(1) maintain records and property, make reports, and provide information the Secretary by regulation or order requires; and

(2) make the records, property, reports, and information available for inspection when the Secretary undertakes an investigation or makes a request.

(c) INSPECTIONS AND INVESTIGATIONS.—

(1) IN GENERAL.—A designated officer, employee, or agent of the Secretary—

(A) may inspect and investigate, at a reasonable time and in a reasonable manner, records and property relating to a function described in section 5103(b)(1);

(B) except in the case of packaging immediately adjacent to its hazardous material contents, may gain access to, open, and examine a package offered for, or in, transportation when the officer, employee, or agent has an objectively reasonable and articulable belief that the package may contain a hazardous material;

(C) may remove from transportation a package or related packages in a shipment offered for or in transportation for which—

(i) such officer, employee, or agent has an objectively reasonable and articulable belief that the package may pose an imminent hazard; and

(ii) such officer, employee, or agent contemporaneously documents such belief in accordance with procedures set forth in guidance or regulations prescribed under subsection (e);

(D) may gather information from the offeror, carrier, packaging manufacturer or tester, or other person responsible for the package, to ascertain the nature and hazards of the contents of the package;

(E) as necessary, under terms and conditions specified by the Secretary, may order the offeror, carrier, packaging manufacturer or tester, or other person responsible for the package to have the package transported to, opened, and the contents examined and analyzed, at a facility appropriate for the conduct of such examination and analysis;

(F) when safety might otherwise be compromised, may authorize properly qualified personnel to assist in the activities conducted under this subsection; and

(G) shall provide to the affected offeror, carrier, packaging manufacturer or tester, or other person responsible for the package reasonable notice of—

(i) his or her decision to exercise his or her authority under paragraph (1);

(ii) any findings made; and

(iii) any actions being taken as a result of a finding of noncompliance.

(2) DISPLAY OF CREDENTIALS.—An officer, employee, or agent acting under this subsection shall display proper credentials, in person or in writing, when requested.

(3) SAFE RESUMPTION OF TRANSPORTATION.—In instances when, as a result of an inspection or investigation under this subsection, an imminent hazard is not found to exist, the Secretary, in accordance with procedures set forth in regulations prescribed under subsection (e), shall assist—

(A) in the safe and prompt resumption of transportation of the package concerned; or

(B) in any case in which the hazardous material being transported is perishable, in the safe and expeditious resumption of transportation of the perishable hazardous material.

(d) EMERGENCY ORDERS.—

(1) IN GENERAL.—If, upon inspection, investigation, testing, or research, the Secretary determines that a violation of a provision of this chapter, or a regulation prescribed under this chapter, or an unsafe condition or practice, constitutes or is causing an imminent hazard, the Secretary may issue or impose emergency restrictions, prohibitions, recalls, or out-of-service orders, without notice or an opportunity for a hearing, but only to the extent necessary to abate the imminent hazard.

(2) WRITTEN ORDERS.—The action of the Secretary under paragraph (1) shall be in a written emergency order that—

(A) describes the violation, condition, or practice that constitutes or is causing the imminent hazard;

(B) states the restrictions, prohibitions, recalls, or out-of-service orders issued or imposed; and

(C) describes the standards and procedures for obtaining relief from the order.

(3) OPPORTUNITY FOR REVIEW.—After taking action under paragraph (1), the Secretary shall provide for review of the action under section 554 of title 5 if a petition for review is filed within 20 calendar days of the date of issuance of the order for the action.

(4) EXPIRATION OF EFFECTIVENESS OF ORDER.—If a petition for review of an action is filed under paragraph (3) and the review under that paragraph is not completed by the end of the 30-day period beginning on the date the petition is filed, the action shall cease to be effective at the end of such period unless the Secretary determines, in writing, that the imminent hazard providing a basis for the action continues to exist.

(5) OUT-OF-SERVICE ORDER DEFINED.—In this subsection, the term "out-of-service order" means a requirement that an aircraft, vessel, motor vehicle, train, railcar, locomotive, other vehicle, transport unit, transport vehicle, freight container, potable tank, or other package not be moved until specified conditions have been met.

(e) REGULATIONS.—

(1) TEMPORARY REGULATIONS.—Not later than 60 days after the date of enactment of the Hazardous Materials Transportation Safety and Security Reauthorization Act of 2005, the Secretary shall issue temporary regulations to carry out subsections (c) and (d). The temporary regulations shall expire on the date of issuance of the regulations under paragraph (2).

(2) FINAL REGULATIONS.—Not later than 1 year after such date of enactment, the Secretary shall issue regulations to carry out subsections (c) and (d) in accordance with subchapter II of chapter 5 of title 5.

(3) MATTERS TO BE ADDRESSED.—The regulations issued under this subsection shall

address—

(A) the safe and expeditious resumption of transportation of perishable hazardous material, including radiopharmaceuticals and other medical products, that may require timely delivery due to life-threatening situations;

(B) the means by which—

(i) noncompliant packages that present an imminent hazard are placed out-of-service until the condition is corrected; and

(ii) noncompliant packages that do not present a hazard are moved to their final destination;

(C) appropriate training and equipment for inspectors; and

(D) the proper closure of packaging in accordance with the hazardous material regulations.

(f) FACILITY, STAFF, AND REPORTING SYSTEM ON RISKS, EMERGENCIES, AND ACTIONS.—(1) The Secretary shall—

(A) maintain a facility and technical staff sufficient to provide, within the United States Government, the capability of evaluating a risk related to the transportation of hazardous material and material alleged to be hazardous;

(B) maintain a central reporting system and information center capable of providing information and advice to law enforcement and firefighting personnel, other interested individuals, and officers and employees of the Government and State and local governments on meeting an emergency related to the transportation of hazardous material; and

(C) conduct a continuous review on all aspects of transporting hazardous material to decide on and take appropriate actions to ensure safe transportation of hazardous material.

(2) Paragraph (1) of this subsection does not prevent the Secretary from making a contract with a private entity for use of a supplemental reporting system and information center operated and maintained by the contractor.

(g) GRANTS AND COOPERATIVE AGREEMENTS.—The Secretary may enter into grants and cooperative agreements with a person, agency, or instrumentality of the United States, a unit of State or local government, an Indian tribe, a foreign government (in coordination with the Department of State), an educational institution, or other appropriate entity—

(1) to expand risk assessment and emergency response capabilities with respect to the safety and security of transportation of hazardous material;

(2) to enhance emergency communications capacity as determined necessary by the Secretary, including the use of integrated, interoperable emergency communications technologies where appropriate;

(3) to conduct research, development, demonstration, risk assessment, and emergency response planning and training activities; or

(4) to otherwise carry out this chapter.

(h) REPORT.—The Secretary shall, once every 2 years, prepare and make available to the public on the Department of Transportation's Internet Web site a comprehensive report on the transportation of hazardous materials during the preceding 2 calendar years. The report shall include—

(1) a statistical compilation of accidents and casualties related to the transportation of

hazardous material;

(2) a list and summary of applicable Government regulations, criteria, orders, and special permits;

(3) a summary of the basis for each special permit;

(4) an evaluation of the effectiveness of enforcement activities relating to a function regulated by the Secretary under section 5103(b)(1) and the degree of voluntary compliance with regulations;

(5) a summary of outstanding problems in carrying out this chapter in order of priority; and

(6) recommendations for appropriate legislation.

(Pub. L. 103–272, §1(d), July 5, 1994, 108 Stat. 779; Pub. L. 103–311, title I, §§108, 117(a)(2), Aug. 26, 1994, 108 Stat. 1674, 1678; Pub. L. 109–59, title VII, §§7118, 7126, Aug. 10, 2005, 119 Stat. 1902, 1909; Pub. L. 110–244, title III, §302(e), June 6, 2008, 122 Stat. 1618; Pub. L. 112–141, div. C, title II, §32501(c), title III, §33009(a), (b)(1), (c), July 6, 2012, 126 Stat. 803, 836, 837; Pub. L. 114–94, div. A, title VII, §7205, Dec. 4, 2015, 129 Stat. 1592.)

§5122. ENFORCEMENT

(a) GENERAL.—At the request of the Secretary, the Attorney General may bring a civil action in an appropriate district court of the United States to enforce this chapter or a regulation prescribed or order, special permit, or approval issued under this chapter. The court may award appropriate relief, including a temporary or permanent injunction, punitive damages, and assessment of civil penalties considering the same penalty amounts and factors as prescribed for the Secretary in an administrative case under section 5123.

(b) IMMINENT HAZARDS.—(1) If the Secretary has reason to believe that an imminent hazard exists, the Secretary may bring a civil action in an appropriate district court of the United States—

(A) to suspend or restrict the transportation of the hazardous material responsible for the hazard; or

(B) to eliminate or mitigate the hazard.

(2) On request of the Secretary, the Attorney General shall bring an action under paragraph (1) of this subsection.

(c) WITHHOLDING OF CLEARANCE.—(1) If any owner, operator, or individual in charge of a vessel is liable for a civil penalty under section 5123 of this title or for a fine under section 5124 of this title, or if reasonable cause exists to believe that such owner, operator, or individual in charge may be subject to such a civil penalty or fine, the Secretary of Homeland Security, upon the request of the Secretary, shall with respect to such vessel refuse or revoke any clearance required by section 60105 of title 46.

(2) Clearance refused or revoked under this subsection may be granted upon the filing of a bond or other surety satisfactory to the Secretary.

(Pub. L. 103–272, §1(d), July 5, 1994, 108 Stat. 780; Pub. L. 104–324, title III, §312(a), Oct. 19, 1996, 110 Stat. 3920; Pub. L. 109–59, title VII, §§7119, 7126, Aug. 10, 2005, 119 Stat. 1905, 1909; Pub. L. 109–304, §17(h)(1), Oct. 6, 2006, 120 Stat. 1709.)

§5123. CIVIL PENALTY

(a) PENALTY.—(1) A person that knowingly violates this chapter or a regulation, order, special permit, or approval issued under this chapter is liable to the United States Government for a civil penalty of not more than $75,000 for each violation. A person acts knowingly when—

(A) the person has actual knowledge of the facts giving rise to the violation; or

(B) a reasonable person acting in the circumstances and exercising reasonable care would have that knowledge.

(2) If the Secretary finds that a violation under paragraph (1) results in death, serious illness, or severe injury to any person or substantial destruction of property, the Secretary may increase the amount of the civil penalty for such violation to not more than $175,000.

(3) If the violation is related to training, a person described in paragraph (1) shall be liable for a civil penalty of at least $450.

(4) A separate violation occurs for each day the violation, committed by a person that transports or causes to be transported hazardous material, continues.

(b) HEARING REQUIREMENT.—The Secretary may find that a person has violated this chapter or a regulation prescribed or order, special permit, or approval issued under this chapter only after notice and an opportunity for a hearing. The Secretary shall impose a penalty under this section by giving the person written notice of the amount of the penalty.

(c) PENALTY CONSIDERATIONS.—In determining the amount of a civil penalty under this section, the Secretary shall consider—

(1) the nature, circumstances, extent, and gravity of the violation;

(2) with respect to the violator, the degree of culpability, any history of prior violations, the ability to pay, and any effect on the ability to continue to do business; and

(3) other matters that justice requires.

(d) CIVIL ACTIONS TO COLLECT.—The Attorney General may bring a civil action in an appropriate district court of the United States to collect a civil penalty under this section and any accrued interest on the civil penalty as calculated in accordance with section 1005 of the Oil Pollution Act of 1990 (33 U.S.C. 2705). In the civil action, the amount and appropriateness of the civil penalty shall not be subject to review.

(e) COMPROMISE.—The Secretary may compromise the amount of a civil penalty imposed under this section before referral to the Attorney General.

(f) SETOFF.—The Government may deduct the amount of a civil penalty imposed or compromised under this section from amounts it owes the person liable for the penalty.

(g) DEPOSITING AMOUNTS COLLECTED.—Amounts collected under this section shall be deposited in the Treasury as miscellaneous receipts.

(h) PENALTY FOR OBSTRUCTION OF INSPECTIONS AND INVESTIGATIONS.—

(1) The Secretary may impose a penalty on a person who obstructs or prevents the Secretary from carrying out inspections or investigations under subsection (c) or (i) of section 5121.

(2) For the purposes of this subsection, the term "obstructs" means actions that were known, or reasonably should have been known, to prevent, hinder, or impede an investigation.

(i) PROHIBITION ON HAZARDOUS MATERIAL OPERATIONS AFTER NONPAYMENT OF PENALTIES.—

(1) IN GENERAL.—Except as provided under paragraph (2), a person subject to the jurisdiction of the Secretary under this chapter who fails to pay a civil penalty assessed

under this chapter, or fails to arrange and abide by an acceptable payment plan for such civil penalty, may not conduct any activity regulated under this chapter beginning on the 91st day after the date specified by order of the Secretary for payment of such penalty unless the person has filed a formal administrative or judicial appeal of the penalty.

(2) EXCEPTION.—Paragraph (1) shall not apply to any person who is unable to pay a civil penalty because such person is a debtor in a case under chapter 11 of title 11.

(3) RULEMAKING.—Not later than 2 years after the date of enactment of this subsection, the Secretary, after providing notice and an opportunity for public comment, shall issue regulations that—

(A) set forth procedures to require a person who is delinquent in paying civil penalties to cease any activity regulated under this chapter until payment has been made or an acceptable payment plan has been arranged; and

(B) ensures [1] that the person described in subparagraph (A)—

(i) is notified in writing; and

(ii) is given an opportunity to respond before the person is required to cease the activity.

(Pub. L. 103–272, §1(d), July 5, 1994, 108 Stat. 780; Pub. L. 109–59, title VII, §§7120(a)–(c), 7126, Aug. 10, 2005, 119 Stat. 1905, 1906, 1909; Pub. L. 112–141, div. C, title III, §33010, July 6, 2012, 126 Stat. 837.)

[1] *So in original. Probably should be "ensure".*

§5124. CRIMINAL PENALTY

(a) IN GENERAL.—A person knowingly violating section 5104(b) or willfully or recklessly violating this chapter or a regulation, order, special permit, or approval issued under this chapter shall be fined under title 18, imprisoned for not more than 5 years, or both; except that the maximum amount of imprisonment shall be 10 years in any case in which the violation involves the release of a hazardous material that results in death or bodily injury to any person.

(b) KNOWING VIOLATIONS.—For purposes of this section—

(1) a person acts knowingly when—

(A) the person has actual knowledge of the facts giving rise to the violation; or

(B) a reasonable person acting in the circumstances and exercising reasonable care would have that knowledge; and

(2) knowledge of the existence of a statutory provision, or a regulation or a requirement required by the Secretary, is not an element of an offense under this section.

(c) WILLFUL VIOLATIONS.—For purposes of this section, a person acts willfully when—

(1) the person has knowledge of the facts giving rise to the violation; and

(2) the person has knowledge that the conduct was unlawful.

(d) RECKLESS VIOLATIONS.—For purposes of this section, a person acts recklessly when the person displays a deliberate indifference or conscious disregard to the consequences of that person's conduct.

(Pub. L. 103–272, §1(d), July 5, 1994, 108 Stat. 781; Pub. L. 109–59, title VII, §7121, Aug. 10, 2005, 119 Stat. 1906.)

§5125. PREEMPTION

(a) GENERAL.—Except as provided in subsections (b), (c), and (e) of this section and unless authorized by another law of the United States, a requirement of a State, political subdivision of a State, or Indian tribe is preempted if—

(1) complying with a requirement of the State, political subdivision, or tribe and a requirement of this chapter, a regulation prescribed under this chapter, or a hazardous materials transportation security regulation or directive issued by the Secretary of Homeland Security is not possible; or

(2) the requirement of the State, political subdivision, or tribe, as applied or enforced, is an obstacle to accomplishing and carrying out this chapter, a regulation prescribed under this chapter, or a hazardous materials transportation security regulation or directive issued by the Secretary of Homeland Security.

(b) SUBSTANTIVE DIFFERENCES.—(1) Except as provided in subsection (c) of this section and unless authorized by another law of the United States, a law, regulation, order, or other requirement of a State, political subdivision of a State, or Indian tribe about any of the following subjects, that is not substantively the same as a provision of this chapter, a regulation prescribed under this chapter, or a hazardous materials transportation security regulation or directive issued by the Secretary of Homeland Security, is preempted:

(A) the designation, description, and classification of hazardous material.

(B) the packing, repacking, handling, labeling, marking, and placarding of hazardous material.

(C) the preparation, execution, and use of shipping documents related to hazardous material and requirements related to the number, contents, and placement of those documents.

(D) the written notification, recording, and reporting of the unintentional release in transportation of hazardous material and other written hazardous materials transportation incident reporting involving State or local emergency responders in the initial response to the incident.

(E) the designing, manufacturing, fabricating, inspecting, marking, maintaining, reconditioning, repairing, or testing a package, container, or packaging component that is represented, marked, certified, or sold as qualified for use in transporting hazardous material in commerce.

(2) If the Secretary prescribes or has prescribed under section 5103(b), 5104, 5110, or 5112 of this title or prior comparable provision of law a regulation or standard related to a subject referred to in paragraph (1) of this subsection, a State, political subdivision of a State, or Indian tribe may prescribe, issue, maintain, and enforce only a law, regulation, standard, or order about the subject that is substantively the same as a provision of this chapter or a regulation prescribed or order issued under this chapter. The Secretary shall decide on and publish in the Federal Register the effective date of section 5103(b) of this title for any regulation or standard about any of those subjects that the Secretary prescribes. The effective date may not be earlier than 90 days after the Secretary prescribes the regulation or standard nor later than the last day of the 2-year period beginning on the date the Secretary prescribes the regulation or standard.

(3) If a State, political subdivision of a State, or Indian tribe imposes a fine or penalty the Secretary decides is appropriate for a violation related to a subject referred to in paragraph

(1) of this subsection, an additional fine or penalty may not be imposed by any other authority.

(c) COMPLIANCE WITH SECTION 5112(b) REGULATIONS.—(1) Except as provided in paragraph (2) of this subsection, after the last day of the 2-year period beginning on the date a regulation is prescribed under section 5112(b) of this title, a State or Indian tribe may establish, maintain, or enforce a highway routing designation over which hazardous material may or may not be transported by motor vehicles, or a limitation or requirement related to highway routing, only if the designation, limitation, or requirement complies with section 5112(b), and is published in the Department's hazardous materials route registry under section 5112(c).

(2)(A) A highway routing designation, limitation, or requirement established before the date a regulation is prescribed under section 5112(b) of this title does not have to comply with section 5112(b)(1)(B), (C), and (F).

(B) This subsection and section 5112 of this title do not require a State or Indian tribe to comply with section 5112(b)(1)(I) if the highway routing designation, limitation, or requirement was established before November 16, 1990.

(C) The Secretary may allow a highway routing designation, limitation, or requirement to continue in effect until a dispute related to the designation, limitation, or requirement is resolved under section 5112(d) of this title.

(d) DECISIONS ON PREEMPTION.—(1) A person (including a State, political subdivision of a State, or Indian tribe) directly affected by a requirement of a State, political subdivision, or tribe may apply to the Secretary, as provided by regulations prescribed by the Secretary, for a decision on whether the requirement is preempted by subsection (a), (b)(1), or (c) of this section or section 5119(f). The Secretary shall publish notice of the application in the Federal Register. The Secretary shall issue a decision on an application for a determination within 180 days after the date of the publication of the notice of having received such application, or the Secretary shall publish a statement in the Federal Register of the reason why the Secretary's decision on the application is delayed, along with an estimate of the additional time necessary before the decision is made. After notice is published, an applicant may not seek judicial relief on the same or substantially the same issue until the Secretary takes final action on the application or until 180 days after the application is filed, whichever occurs first.

(2) After consulting with States, political subdivisions of States, and Indian tribes, the Secretary shall prescribe regulations for carrying out paragraph (1) of this subsection.

(3) Subsection (a) of this section does not prevent a State, political subdivision of a State, or Indian tribe, or another person directly affected by a requirement, from seeking a decision on preemption from a court of competent jurisdiction instead of applying to the Secretary under paragraph (1) of this subsection.

(e) WAIVER OF PREEMPTION.—A State, political subdivision of a State, or Indian tribe may apply to the Secretary for a waiver of preemption of a requirement the State, political subdivision, or tribe acknowledges is preempted by subsection (a), (b)(1), or (c) of this section or section 5119(f). Under a procedure the Secretary prescribes by regulation, the Secretary may waive preemption on deciding the requirement—

(1) provides the public at least as much protection as do requirements of this chapter and regulations prescribed under this chapter; and

(2) is not an unreasonable burden on commerce.

(f) FEES.—(1) A State, political subdivision of a State, or Indian tribe may impose a fee related to transporting hazardous material only if the fee is fair and used for a purpose related to transporting hazardous material, including enforcement and planning, developing, and maintaining a capability for emergency response.

(2) A State or political subdivision thereof or Indian tribe that levies a fee in connection with the transportation of hazardous materials shall biennially report to the Secretary on—

(A) the basis on which the fee is levied upon persons involved in such transportation;

(B) the purposes for which the revenues from the fee are used;

(C) the annual total amount of the revenues collected from the fee; and

(D) such other matters as the Secretary requests.

(g) APPLICATION OF EACH PREEMPTION STANDARD.—Each standard for preemption in subsection (a), (b)(1), or (c), and in section 5119(f), is independent in its application to a requirement of a State, political subdivision of a State, or Indian tribe.

(h) NON-FEDERAL ENFORCEMENT STANDARDS.—This section does not apply to any procedure, penalty, required mental state, or other standard utilized by a State, political subdivision of a State, or Indian tribe to enforce a requirement applicable to the transportation of hazardous material.

(Pub. L. 103–272, §1(d), July 5, 1994, 108 Stat. 781; Pub. L. 103–311, title I, §§107, 117(a)(2), 120(b), Aug. 26, 1994, 108 Stat. 1674, 1678, 1681; Pub. L. 103–429, §6(6), Oct. 31, 1994, 108 Stat. 4378; Pub. L. 107–296, title XVII, §1711(b), Nov. 25, 2002, 116 Stat. 2320; Pub. L. 109–59, title VII, §§7122, 7123(a), 7126, Aug. 10, 2005, 119 Stat. 1907, 1909; Pub. L. 110–244, title III, §302(c), June 6, 2008, 122 Stat. 1618; Pub. L. 112–141, div. C, title III, §§33006(d), 33011, 33013(b), July 6, 2012, 126 Stat. 835, 838, 839.)

§5126. RELATIONSHIP TO OTHER LAWS

(a) CONTRACTS.—A person under contract with a department, agency, or instrumentality of the United States Government that transports hazardous material, or causes hazardous material to be transported, or designs, manufactures, fabricates, inspects, marks, maintains, reconditions, repairs, or tests a package, container, or packaging component that is represented as qualified for use in transporting hazardous material shall comply with this chapter, regulations prescribed and orders issued under this chapter, and all other requirements of the Government, State and local governments, and Indian tribes (except a requirement preempted by a law of the United States) in the same way and to the same extent that any person engaging in that transportation, designing, manufacturing, fabricating, inspecting, marking, maintaining, reconditioning, repairing, or testing that is in or affects commerce must comply with the provision, regulation, order, or requirement.

(b) NONAPPLICATION.—This chapter does not apply to—

(1) a pipeline subject to regulation under chapter 601 of this title; or

(2) any matter that is subject to the postal laws and regulations of the United States under this chapter or title 18 or 39.

(Pub. L. 103–272, §1(d), July 5, 1994, 108 Stat. 783; Pub. L. 103–311, title I, §117(a)(2), Aug. 26, 1994, 108 Stat. 1678; Pub. L. 109–59, title VII, §7124, Aug. 10, 2005, 119 Stat. 1908; Pub. L. 110–244, title III, §302(d), June 6, 2008, 122 Stat. 1618.)

§5127. Judicial Review

(a) Filing and Venue.—Except as provided in section 20114(c), a person adversely affected or aggrieved by a final action of the Secretary under this chapter may petition for review of the final action in the United States Court of Appeals for the District of Columbia or in the court of appeals for the United States for the circuit in which the person resides or has its principal place of business. The petition must be filed not more than 60 days after the Secretary's action becomes final.

(b) Judicial Procedures.—When a petition is filed under subsection (a), the clerk of the court immediately shall send a copy of the petition to the Secretary. The Secretary shall file with the court a record of any proceeding in which the final action was issued, as provided in section 2112 of title 28.

(c) Authority of Court.—The court has exclusive jurisdiction, as provided in subchapter II of chapter 5 of title 5, to affirm or set aside any part of the Secretary's final action and may order the Secretary to conduct further proceedings.

(d) Requirement for Prior Objection.—In reviewing a final action under this section, the court may consider an objection to a final action of the Secretary only if the objection was made in the course of a proceeding or review conducted by the Secretary or if there was a reasonable ground for not making the objection in the proceeding.

(Added Pub. L. 109–59, title VII, §7123(b), Aug. 10, 2005, 119 Stat. 1907.)

§5128. Authorization of appropriations

(a) In General.—There are authorized to be appropriated to the Secretary to carry out this chapter (except sections 5107(e), 5108(g)(2), 5113, 5115, 5116, and 5119)—

(1) $67,000,000 for fiscal year 2022;
(2) $68,000,000 for fiscal year 2023;
(3) $69,000,000 for fiscal year 2024;
(4) $70,000,000 for fiscal year 2025; and
(5) $71,000,000 for fiscal year 2026.

(b) Hazardous Materials Emergency Preparedness Fund.—From the Hazardous Materials Preparedness Fund established under section 5116(h), the Secretary may expend, for each of fiscal years 2022 through 2026—

(1) $39,050,000 to carry out section 5116(a);
(2) $150,000 to carry out section 5116(e);
(3) $625,000 to publish and distribute the Emergency Response Guidebook under section 5116(h)(3); and
(4) $2,000,000 to carry out section 5116(i).

(c) Hazardous Materials Training Grants.—From the Hazardous Materials Emergency Preparedness Fund established pursuant to section 5116(h), the Secretary may expend $5,000,000 for each of fiscal years 2022 through 2026 to carry out section 5107(e).

(d) Community Safety Grants.—Of the amounts made available under subsection (a) to carry out this chapter, the Secretary shall withhold $4,000,000 for each of fiscal years 2022 through 2026 to carry out section 5107(i).

(e) Credits to Appropriations.—

(1) Expenses.—In addition to amounts otherwise made available to carry out this

chapter, the Secretary may credit amounts received from a State, Indian tribe, or other public authority or private entity for expenses the Secretary incurs in providing training to the State, Indian tribe, authority or entity.

(2) AVAILABILITY OF AMOUNTS.—Amounts made available under this section shall remain available until expended.

(Pub. L. 103–272, §1(d), July 5, 1994, 108 Stat. 783, §5127; Pub. L. 103–311, title I, §§103, 119(b), (c)(4), Aug. 26, 1994, 108 Stat. 1673, 1680; renumbered §5128 and amended Pub. L. 109–59, title VII, §§7123(b), 7125, Aug. 10, 2005, 119 Stat. 1907, 1908; Pub. L. 110–244, title III, §302(f), June 6, 2008, 122 Stat. 1618; Pub. L. 112–141, div. C, title III, §33017, July 6, 2012, 126 Stat. 841; Pub. L. 113–159, title I, §1301, Aug. 8, 2014, 128 Stat. 1847; Pub. L. 114–21, title I, §1301, May 29, 2015, 129 Stat. 225; Pub. L. 114–41, title I, §1301, July 31, 2015, 129 Stat. 453; Pub. L. 114–73, title I, §1301, Oct. 29, 2015, 129 Stat. 575; Pub. L. 114–87, title I, §1301, Nov. 20, 2015, 129 Stat. 684; Pub. L. 114–94, div. A, title VII, §7101, Dec. 4, 2015, 129 Stat. 1588; Pub. L. 117–58, div. B, title VI, §26001, Nov. 15, 2021, 135 Stat. 881.)

* * * * * * *

SUBTITLE VI
MOTOR VEHICLE AND DRIVER
PROGRAMS

SUBTITLE VI—MOTOR VEHICLE AND DRIVER PROGRAMS

PART A—GENERAL

---

[1] *So in original. Probably should be "31100".*

PART A—GENERAL

* * * * * * *

CHAPTER 303—NATIONAL DRIVER REGISTER

Sec.

* * * * * * *

30305. Access to Register information.

* * * * * * *

§30305. ACCESS TO REGISTER INFORMATION

* * * * * * *

(b) REQUESTS TO OBTAIN INFORMATION.—

* * * * * * *

* * * * * * *

(8)(A) An individual who is seeking employment by an air carrier as a pilot may request the chief driver licensing official of a State to provide information about the individual under subsection (a) of this section to the prospective employer of the individual, the authorized agent of the prospective employer, or the Secretary of Transportation.

(B) An air carrier that is the prospective employer of an individual described in subparagraph (A), or an authorized agent of such an air carrier, may request and receive information about that individual from the National Driver Register through an organization approved by the Secretary for purposes of requesting, receiving, and transmitting such information directly to the prospective employer of such an individual or the authorized agent of the prospective employer. This paragraph shall be carried out in accordance with paragraphs (2) and (11) of section 44703(h) and the Fair Credit Reporting Act (15 U.S.C. 1681 et seq.).

(C) Information may not be obtained from the National Driver Register under this paragraph if the information was entered in the Register more than 5 years before the request unless the information is about a revocation or suspension still in effect on the date of the request.

* * * * * * *

(Pub. L. 103–272, §1(e), July 5, 1994, 108 Stat. 976; Pub. L. 104–264, title V, §502(b), Oct. 9, 1996, 110 Stat. 3262; Pub. L. 104–324, title II, §207(b), Oct. 19, 1996, 110 Stat. 3908; Pub. L. 105–102, §2(18), Nov. 20, 1997, 111 Stat. 2205; Pub. L. 105–178, title II, §2006(b), June 9, 1998, 112 Stat. 335; Pub. L. 108–375, div. A, title X, §1061, Oct. 28, 2004, 118 Stat. 2056; Pub. L. 114–94, div. A, title V, §5512, Dec. 4, 2015, 129 Stat. 1556; Pub. L. 115–254, div. B, title V, §563, Oct. 5, 2018, 132 Stat. 3384.)

* * * * * * *

SUBTITLE VII
AVIATION PROGRAMS

PART A
AIR COMMERCE AND SAFETY AIR COMMERCE AND SAFETY

SUBTITLE VII—AVIATION PROGRAMS

PART A—AIR COMMERCE AND SAFETY

SUBPART I—GENERAL

SUBPART II—ECONOMIC REGULATION

SUBPART III—SAFETY

SUBPART IV—ENFOTCEMENT AND PENALTIES

PART B—AIRPORT DEVELOPMENT AND NOISE

PART C—FINANCING

PART D—PUBLIC AIRPORTS

PART E—MISCELLANEOUS

PART A—AIR COMMERCE AND SAFETY

SUBPART I—GENERAL

CHAPTER 401—GENERAL PROVISIONS

§40101. POLICY

(a) ECONOMIC REGULATION.—In carrying out subpart II of this part and those provisions of subpart IV applicable in carrying out subpart II, the Secretary of Transportation shall consider the following matters, among others, as being in the public interest and consistent with public convenience and necessity:

(1) assigning and maintaining safety as the highest priority in air commerce.

(2) before authorizing new air transportation services, evaluating the safety implications of those services.

(3) preventing deterioration in established safety procedures, recognizing the clear intent, encouragement, and dedication of Congress to further the highest degree of safety in air transportation and air commerce, and to maintain the safety vigilance that has evolved in air transportation and air commerce and has come to be expected by the traveling and shipping public.

(4) the availability of a variety of adequate, economic, efficient, and low-priced services without unreasonable discrimination or unfair or deceptive practices.

(5) coordinating transportation by, and improving relations among, air carriers, and encouraging fair wages and working conditions.

(6) placing maximum reliance on competitive market forces and on actual and potential competition—

(A) to provide the needed air transportation system; and

(B) to encourage efficient and well-managed air carriers to earn adequate profits and attract capital, considering any material differences between interstate air transportation and foreign air transportation.

(7) developing and maintaining a sound regulatory system that is responsive to the needs of the public and in which decisions are reached promptly to make it easier to adapt the air transportation system to the present and future needs of—

(A) the commerce of the United States;

(B) the United States Postal Service; and

(C) the national defense.

(8) encouraging air transportation at major urban areas through secondary or satellite airports if consistent with regional airport plans of regional and local authorities, and if endorsed by appropriate State authorities—

(A) encouraging the transportation by air carriers that provide, in a specific market, transportation exclusively at those airports; and

(B) fostering an environment that allows those carriers to establish themselves and develop secondary or satellite airport services.

(9) preventing unfair, deceptive, predatory, or anticompetitive practices in air transportation.

(10) avoiding unreasonable industry concentration, excessive market domination, monopoly powers, and other conditions that would tend to allow at least one air carrier or foreign air carrier unreasonably to increase prices, reduce services, or exclude competition in air transportation.

(11) maintaining a complete and convenient system of continuous scheduled interstate air transportation for small communities and isolated areas with direct financial assistance from the United States Government when appropriate.

(12) encouraging, developing, and maintaining an air transportation system relying on actual and potential competition—

(A) to provide efficiency, innovation, and low prices; and

(B) to decide on the variety and quality of, and determine prices for, air transportation services.

(13) encouraging entry into air transportation markets by new and existing air carriers and the continued strengthening of small air carriers to ensure a more effective and competitive airline industry.

(14) promoting, encouraging, and developing civil aeronautics and a viable, privately-owned United States air transport industry.

(15) strengthening the competitive position of air carriers to at least ensure equality with foreign air carriers, including the attainment of the opportunity for air carriers to maintain and increase their profitability in foreign air transportation.

(16) ensuring that consumers in all regions of the United States, including those in small communities and rural and remote areas, have access to affordable, regularly scheduled air service.

(b) ALL-CARGO AIR TRANSPORTATION CONSIDERATIONS.—In carrying out subpart II of this part and those provisions of subpart IV applicable in carrying out subpart II, the Secretary of Transportation shall consider the following matters, among others and in addition to the matters referred to in subsection (a) of this section, as being in the public interest for all-cargo air transportation:

(1) encouraging and developing an expedited all-cargo air transportation system provided by private enterprise and responsive to—

(A) the present and future needs of shippers;

(B) the commerce of the United States; and

(C) the national defense.

(2) encouraging and developing an integrated transportation system relying on competitive market forces to decide the extent, variety, quality, and price of services provided.

(3) providing services without unreasonable discrimination, unfair or deceptive practices, or predatory pricing.

(c) GENERAL SAFETY CONSIDERATIONS.—In carrying out subpart III of this part and those provisions of subpart IV applicable in carrying out subpart III, the Administrator of the Federal Aviation Administration shall consider the following matters:

(1) the requirements of national defense and commercial and general aviation.

(2) the public right of freedom of transit through the navigable airspace.

(d) SAFETY CONSIDERATIONS IN PUBLIC INTEREST.—In carrying out subpart III of this part and those provisions of subpart IV applicable in carrying out subpart III, the Administrator shall consider the following matters, among others, as being in the public interest:

(1) assigning, maintaining, and enhancing safety and security as the highest priorities in air commerce.

(2) regulating air commerce in a way that best promotes safety and fulfills national defense requirements.

(3) encouraging and developing civil aeronautics, including new aviation technology.

(4) controlling the use of the navigable airspace and regulating civil and military operations in that airspace in the interest of the safety and efficiency of both of those operations.

(5) consolidating research and development for air navigation facilities and the installation and operation of those facilities.

(6) developing and operating a common system of air traffic control and navigation for military and civil aircraft.

(7) providing assistance to law enforcement agencies in the enforcement of laws related to regulation of controlled substances, to the extent consistent with aviation safety.

(e) INTERNATIONAL AIR TRANSPORTATION.—In formulating United States international air transportation policy, the Secretaries of State and Transportation shall develop a negotiating policy emphasizing the greatest degree of competition compatible with a well-functioning international air transportation system, including the following:

(1) strengthening the competitive position of air carriers to ensure at least equality with foreign air carriers, including the attainment of the opportunity for air carriers to maintain and increase their profitability in foreign air transportation.

(2) freedom of air carriers and foreign air carriers to offer prices that correspond to consumer demand.

(3) the fewest possible restrictions on charter air transportation.

(4) the maximum degree of multiple and permissive international authority for air carriers so that they will be able to respond quickly to a shift in market demand.

(5) eliminating operational and marketing restrictions to the greatest extent possible.

(6) integrating domestic and international air transportation.

(7) increasing the number of nonstop United States gateway cities.

(8) opportunities for carriers of foreign countries to increase their access to places in the United States if exchanged for benefits of similar magnitude for air carriers or the traveling public with permanent linkage between rights granted and rights given away.

(9) eliminating discrimination and unfair competitive practices faced by United States airlines in foreign air transportation, including—

(A) excessive landing and user fees;

(B) unreasonable ground handling requirements;

(C) unreasonable restrictions on operations;

(D) prohibitions against change of gauge; and

(E) similar restrictive practices.

(10) promoting, encouraging, and developing civil aeronautics and a viable, privately-owned United States air transport industry.

(f) STRENGTHENING COMPETITION.—In selecting an air carrier to provide foreign air transportation from among competing applicants, the Secretary of Transportation shall consider, in addition to the matters specified in subsections (a) and (b) of this section, the strengthening of competition among air carriers operating in the United States to prevent unreasonable concentration in the air carrier industry.

(Pub. L. 103–272, §1(e), July 5, 1994, 108 Stat. 1094; Pub. L. 104–264, title IV, §401(a), Oct. 9, 1996, 110 Stat. 3255; Pub. L. 106–181, title II, §201, Apr. 5, 2000, 114 Stat. 91.)

§40102. DEFINITIONS

(a) GENERAL DEFINITIONS.—In this part—

(1) "aeronautics" means the science and art of flight.

(2) "air carrier" means a citizen of the United States undertaking by any means, directly or indirectly, to provide air transportation.

(3) "air commerce" means foreign air commerce, interstate air commerce, the transportation of mail by aircraft, the operation of aircraft within the limits of a Federal airway, or the operation of aircraft that directly affects, or may endanger safety in, foreign or interstate air commerce.

(4) "air navigation facility" means a facility used, available for use, or designed for use, in aid of air navigation, including—

(A) a landing area;

(B) runway lighting and airport surface visual and other navigation aids;

(C) apparatus, equipment, software, or service for distributing aeronautical and meteorological information to air traffic control facilities or aircraft;

(D) communication, navigation, or surveillance equipment for air-to-ground or air-to-air applications;

(E) any structure, equipment, or mechanism for guiding or controlling flight in the air or the landing and takeoff of aircraft; and

(F) buildings, equipment, and systems dedicated to the national airspace system.

(5) "air transportation" means foreign air transportation, interstate air transportation, or the transportation of mail by aircraft.

(6) "aircraft" means any contrivance invented, used, or designed to navigate, or fly in, the air.

(7) "aircraft engine" means an engine used, or intended to be used, to propel an aircraft, including a part, appurtenance, and accessory of the engine, except a propeller.

(8) "airman" means an individual—

(A) in command, or as pilot, mechanic, or member of the crew, who navigates aircraft when under way;

(B) except to the extent the Administrator of the Federal Aviation Administration may provide otherwise for individuals employed outside the United States, who is directly in charge of inspecting, maintaining, overhauling, or repairing aircraft, aircraft engines, propellers, or appliances; or

(C) who serves as an aircraft dispatcher or air traffic control-tower operator.

(9) "airport" means a landing area used regularly by aircraft for receiving or discharging passengers or cargo.

(10) "all-cargo air transportation" means the transportation by aircraft in interstate air transportation of only property or only mail, or both.

(11) "appliance" means an instrument, equipment, apparatus, a part, an appurtenance, or an accessory used, capable of being used, or intended to be used, in operating or controlling aircraft in flight, including a parachute, communication equipment, and another mechanism installed in or attached to aircraft during flight, and not a part of an aircraft, aircraft engine, or propeller.

(12) "cargo" means property, mail, or both.

(13) "charter air carrier" means an air carrier holding a certificate of public convenience and necessity that authorizes it to provide charter air transportation.

(14) "charter air transportation" means charter trips in air transportation authorized under this part.

(15) "citizen of the United States" means—

(A) an individual who is a citizen of the United States;

(B) a partnership each of whose partners is an individual who is a citizen of the United States; or

(C) a corporation or association organized under the laws of the United States or a State, the District of Columbia, or a territory or possession of the United States, of which the president and at least two-thirds of the board of directors and other managing officers are citizens of the United States, which is under the actual control of citizens of the United States, and in which at least 75 percent of the voting interest is owned or controlled by persons that are citizens of the United States.

(16) "civil aircraft" means an aircraft except a public aircraft.

(17) "civil aircraft of the United States" means an aircraft registered under chapter 441 of this title.

(18) "conditional sales contract" means a contract—

(A) for the sale of an aircraft, aircraft engine, propeller, appliance, or spare part, under which the buyer takes possession of the property but title to the property vests in the buyer at a later time on—

(i) paying any part of the purchase price;

(ii) performing another condition; or

(iii) the happening of a contingency; or

(B) to bail or lease an aircraft, aircraft engine, propeller, appliance, or spare part, under which the bailee or lessee—

(i) agrees to pay an amount substantially equal to the value of the property; and

(ii) is to become, or has the option of becoming, the owner of the property on complying with the contract.

(19) "conveyance" means an instrument, including a conditional sales contract, affecting title to, or an interest in, property.

(20) "Federal airway" means a part of the navigable airspace that the Administrator designates as a Federal airway.

(21) "foreign air carrier" means a person, not a citizen of the United States, undertaking by any means, directly or indirectly, to provide foreign air transportation.

(22) "foreign air commerce" means the transportation of passengers or property by aircraft for compensation, the transportation of mail by aircraft, or the operation of aircraft in furthering a business or vocation, between a place in the United States and a place outside the United States when any part of the transportation or operation is by aircraft.

(23) "foreign air transportation" means the transportation of passengers or property by aircraft as a common carrier for compensation, or the transportation of mail by aircraft, between a place in the United States and a place outside the United States when any part of the transportation is by aircraft.

(24) "interstate air commerce" means the transportation of passengers or property by aircraft for compensation, the transportation of mail by aircraft, or the operation of aircraft in furthering a business or vocation—

(A) between a place in—

(i) a State, territory, or possession of the United States and a place in the District of Columbia or another State, territory, or possession of the United States;

(ii) a State and another place in the same State through the airspace over a place outside the State;

(iii) the District of Columbia and another place in the District of Columbia; or

(iv) a territory or possession of the United States and another place in the same territory or possession; and

(B) when any part of the transportation or operation is by aircraft.

(25) "interstate air transportation" means the transportation of passengers or property by aircraft as a common carrier for compensation, or the transportation of mail by aircraft—

(A) between a place in—

(i) a State, territory, or possession of the United States and a place in the District of Columbia or another State, territory, or possession of the United States;

(ii) Hawaii and another place in Hawaii through the airspace over a place outside Hawaii;

(iii) the District of Columbia and another place in the District of Columbia; or

(iv) a territory or possession of the United States and another place in the same territory or possession; and

(B) when any part of the transportation is by aircraft.

(26) "intrastate air carrier" means a citizen of the United States undertaking by any means to provide only intrastate air transportation.

(27) "intrastate air transportation" means the transportation by a common carrier of passengers or property for compensation, entirely in the same State, by turbojet-powered aircraft capable of carrying at least 30 passengers.

(28) "landing area" means a place on land or water, including an airport or intermediate landing field, used, or intended to be used, for the takeoff and landing of aircraft, even when facilities are not provided for sheltering, servicing, or repairing aircraft, or for receiving or discharging passengers or cargo.

(29) "large hub airport" means a commercial service airport (as defined in section 47102) that has at least 1.0 percent of the passenger boardings.

(30) "mail" means United States mail and foreign transit mail.

(31) "medium hub airport" means a commercial service airport (as defined in section 47102) that has at least 0.25 percent but less than 1.0 percent of the passenger boardings.

(32) "navigable airspace" means airspace above the minimum altitudes of flight prescribed by regulations under this subpart and subpart III of this part, including airspace needed to ensure safety in the takeoff and landing of aircraft.

(33) "navigate aircraft" and "navigation of aircraft" include piloting aircraft.

(34) "nonhub airport" means a commercial service airport (as defined in section 47102) that has less than 0.05 percent of the passenger boardings.

(35) "operate aircraft" and "operation of aircraft" mean using aircraft for the purposes of air navigation, including—

(A) the navigation of aircraft; and

(B) causing or authorizing the operation of aircraft with or without the right of legal control of the aircraft.

(36) "passenger boardings"—

(A) means, unless the context indicates otherwise, revenue passenger boardings in the United States in the prior calendar year on an aircraft in service in air commerce, as the Secretary determines under regulations the Secretary prescribes; and

(B) includes passengers who continue on an aircraft in international flight that stops at an airport in the 48 contiguous States, Alaska, or Hawaii for a nontraffic purpose.

(37) "person", in addition to its meaning under section 1 of title 1, includes a governmental authority and a trustee, receiver, assignee, and other similar representative.

(38) "predatory" means a practice that violates the antitrust laws as defined in the first section of the Clayton Act (15 U.S.C. 12).

(39) "price" means a rate, fare, or charge.

(40) "propeller" includes a part, appurtenance, and accessory of a propeller.

(41) "public aircraft" means any of the following:

(A) Except with respect to an aircraft described in subparagraph (E), an aircraft used only for the United States Government, except as provided in section 40125(b).

(B) An aircraft owned by the Government and operated by any person for purposes related to crew training, equipment development, or demonstration, except as provided in section 40125(b).

(C) An aircraft owned and operated by the government of a State, the District of Columbia, or a territory or possession of the United States or a political subdivision of one of these governments, except as provided in section 40125(b).

(D) An aircraft exclusively leased for at least 90 continuous days by the government of a State, the District of Columbia, or a territory or possession of the United States or a political subdivision of one of these governments, except as provided in section 40125(b).

(E) An aircraft owned or operated by the armed forces or chartered to provide transportation or other commercial air service to the armed forces under the conditions specified by section 40125(c). In the preceding sentence, the term "other commercial air service" means an aircraft operation that (i) is within the United States territorial airspace; (ii) the Administrator of the Federal Aviation Administration determines is available for compensation or hire to the public, and (iii) must comply with all applicable civil aircraft rules under title 14, Code of Federal Regulations.

(F) An unmanned aircraft that is owned and operated by, or exclusively leased for at least 90 continuous days by, an Indian Tribal government, as defined in section 102 of the Robert T. Stafford Disaster Relief and Emergency Assistance Act (42 U.S.C. 5122), except as provided in section 40125(b).

(42) "small hub airport" means a commercial service airport (as defined in section 47102) that has at least 0.05 percent but less than 0.25 percent of the passenger boardings.

(43) "spare part" means an accessory, appurtenance, or part of an aircraft (except an aircraft engine or propeller), aircraft engine (except a propeller), propeller, or appliance, that is to be installed at a later time in an aircraft, aircraft engine, propeller, or appliance.

(44) "State authority" means an authority of a State designated under State law—

(A) to receive notice required to be given a State authority under subpart II of this part; or

(B) as the representative of the State before the Secretary of Transportation in any matter about which the Secretary is required to consult with or consider the views of a State authority under subpart II of this part.

(45) "ticket agent" means a person (except an air carrier, a foreign air carrier, or an employee of an air carrier or foreign air carrier) that as a principal or agent sells, offers for sale, negotiates for, or holds itself out as selling, providing, or arranging for, air transportation.

(46) "United States" means the States of the United States, the District of Columbia, and the territories and possessions of the United States, including the territorial sea and the overlying airspace.

(47) "air traffic control system" means the combination of elements used to safely and efficiently monitor, direct, control, and guide aircraft in the United States and United States-assigned airspace, including—

(A) allocated electromagnetic spectrum and physical, real, personal, and intellectual property assets making up facilities, equipment, and systems employed to detect, track, and guide aircraft movement;

(B) laws, regulations, orders, directives, agreements, and licenses;

(C) published procedures that explain required actions, activities, and techniques used to ensure adequate aircraft separation;

(D) trained personnel with specific technical capabilities to satisfy the operational, engineering, management, and planning requirements for air traffic control; and

(E) systems, software, and hardware operated, owned, and maintained by third parties that support or directly provide air navigation information and air traffic management services with Administration approval.

(b) LIMITED DEFINITION.—In subpart II of this part, "control" means control by any means.

(Pub. L. 103–272, §1(e), July 5, 1994, 108 Stat. 1097; Pub. L. 103–305, title VI, §601(b)(2)(B), Aug. 23, 1994, 108 Stat. 1606; Pub. L. 103–411, §3(a), Oct. 25, 1994, 108 Stat. 4236; Pub. L. 103–429, §6(46), Oct. 31, 1994, 108 Stat. 4384; Pub. L. 105–137, §6, Dec. 2, 1997, 111 Stat. 2641; Pub. L. 106–181, title III, §301, title VII, §702(a), Apr. 5, 2000, 114 Stat. 115, 155; Pub. L. 108–176, title II, §225(a), title VIII, §807, Dec. 12, 2003, 117 Stat. 2528, 2588; Pub. L. 110–181, div. A, title X, §1078(a), Jan. 28, 2008, 122 Stat. 334; Pub. L. 112–95, title II, §205, Feb. 14, 2012, 126 Stat. 39; Pub. L. 115–254, div. B, title III, §355(a), Oct. 5, 2018, 132 Stat. 3305; Pub. L. 118–63, title II, §215, May 16, 2024, 138 Stat. 1054.)

§40103. SOVEREIGNTY AND USE OF AIRSPACE

(a) SOVEREIGNTY AND PUBLIC RIGHT OF TRANSIT.—(1) The United States Government has exclusive sovereignty of airspace of the United States.

(2) A citizen of the United States has a public right of transit through the navigable airspace. To further that right, the Secretary of Transportation shall consult with the Architectural and Transportation Barriers Compliance Board established under section 502 of the Rehabilitation Act of 1973 (29 U.S.C. 792) before prescribing a regulation or issuing an order or procedure that will have a significant impact on the accessibility of commercial airports or commercial air transportation for individuals with disabilities.

(b) USE OF AIRSPACE.—(1) The Administrator of the Federal Aviation Administration shall develop plans and policy for the use of the navigable airspace and assign by regulation or order the use of the airspace necessary to ensure the safety of aircraft and the efficient use of airspace. The Administrator may modify or revoke an assignment when required in the public interest.

(2) The Administrator shall prescribe air traffic regulations on the flight of aircraft

(including regulations on safe altitudes) for—

(A) navigating, protecting, and identifying aircraft;

(B) protecting individuals and property on the ground;

(C) using the navigable airspace efficiently; and

(D) preventing collision between aircraft, between aircraft and land or water vehicles, and between aircraft and airborne objects.

(3) To establish security provisions that will encourage and allow maximum use of the navigable airspace by civil aircraft consistent with national security, the Administrator, in consultation with the Secretary of Defense, shall—

(A) establish areas in the airspace the Administrator decides are necessary in the interest of national defense; and

(B) by regulation or order, restrict or prohibit flight of civil aircraft that the Administrator cannot identify, locate, and control with available facilities in those areas.

(4) Notwithstanding the military exception in section 553(a)(1) of title 5, subchapter II of chapter 5 of title 5 applies to a regulation prescribed under this subsection.

(c) FOREIGN AIRCRAFT.—A foreign aircraft, not part of the armed forces of a foreign country, may be navigated in the United States as provided in section 41703 of this title.

(d) AIRCRAFT OF ARMED FORCES OF FOREIGN COUNTRIES.—Aircraft of the armed forces of a foreign country may be navigated in the United States only when authorized by the Secretary of State.

(e) NO EXCLUSIVE RIGHTS AT CERTAIN FACILITIES.—A person does not have an exclusive right to use an air navigation facility on which Government money has been expended. However, providing services at an airport by only one fixed-based operator is not an exclusive right if—

(1) it is unreasonably costly, burdensome, or impractical for more than one fixed-based operator to provide the services; and

(2) allowing more than one fixed-based operator to provide the services requires a reduction in space leased under an agreement existing on September 3, 1982, between the operator and the airport.

(Pub. L. 103–272, §1(e), July 5, 1994, 108 Stat. 1101; Pub. L. 118–63, title V, §550(a), May 16, 2024, 138 Stat. 1212.)

§40104. PROMOTION OF CIVIL AERONAUTICS AND SAFETY OF AIR COMMERCE

(a) DEVELOPING CIVIL AERONAUTICS AND SAFETY OF AIR COMMERCE.—The Administrator of the Federal Aviation Administration shall encourage the development of civil aeronautics and safety of air commerce in and outside the United States.

(b) AIRPORT CAPACITY ENHANCEMENT PROJECTS AT CONGESTED AIRPORTS.—In carrying out subsection (a), the Administrator shall take action to encourage the construction of airport capacity enhancement projects at congested airports as those terms are defined in section 47175.

(c) EDUCATIONAL AND PROFESSIONAL DEVELOPMENT.—

(1) IN GENERAL.—In carrying out subsection (a), the Administrator shall support and undertake efforts to promote and support the education and professional development of current and future aerospace professionals.

(2) EDUCATIONAL MATERIALS.—Based on the availability of resources, the

Administrator shall—

(A) develop and distribute civil aviation information and educational materials; and

(B) provide expertise to State and local school administrators, college and university officials, and officers of other interested organizations and entities.

(3) CONTENT.—In developing the educational materials under paragraph (2), the Administrator shall ensure such materials, including presentations, cover topics of broad relevance, including—

(A) ethical decision-making and the responsibilities of aerospace professionals;

(B) managing a workforce, encouraging proper reporting of prospective safety issues, and educating employees on safety management systems; and

(C) responsibilities as a designee or representative of the Administrator.

(d) INTERNATIONAL ROLE AND ASSISTANCE OF THE FAA.—

(1) IN GENERAL.—In carrying out subsection (a), the Administrator shall promote and achieve global improvements in the safety, efficiency, and environmental effect of air travel by exercising leadership with the Administrator's foreign counterparts, in the International Civil Aviation Organization and its subsidiary organizations, and other international organizations and fora, and with the private sector.

(2) INTERNATIONAL PRESENCE.—The Administrator shall maintain an international presence to—

(A) assist foreign civil aviation authorities in—

(i) establishing robust aviation oversight practices and policies;

(ii) harmonizing international aviation standards for air traffic management, operator certification, aircraft certification, airports, and certificated or credentialed individuals;

(iii) validating and accepting foreign aircraft design and production approvals;

(iv) preparing for new aviation technologies, including powered-lift aircraft, products, and articles; and

(v) appropriately adopting continuing airworthiness information, such as airworthiness directives;

(B) encourage the adoption of United States standards, regulations, and policies;

(C) establish, maintain, and update bilateral or multilateral aviation safety agreements and the aviation safety information contained within such agreements;

(D) engage in bilateral and multilateral discussions as required under paragraph (5) and provide technical assistance as described in paragraph (6);

(E) validate foreign aviation products and ensure reciprocal validation of products for which the United States is the state of design or production;

(F) support accident and incident investigations, particularly such investigations that involve United States persons and certified products and such investigations where the National Transportation Safety Board is supporting an investigation pursuant to annex 13 of the International Civil Aviation Organization;

(G) support the international safety activities of the United States aviation sector;

(H) maintain valuable relationships with entities with aviation equities, including civil aviation authorities, other governmental bodies, non-governmental organizations, and foreign manufacturers; and

(I) perform other activities as determined necessary by the Administrator.

(3) INTERNATIONAL OFFICES.—In carrying out the responsibilities described in subsection (a), the Administrator—

(A) shall maintain international offices of the Administration;

(B) every 5 years, may review existing international offices to determine—

(i) the effectiveness of such offices in fulfilling the mission described in paragraph (2); and

(ii) the adequacy of resources and staffing to achieve the mission described in paragraph (2); and

(C) shall establish offices to address gaps identified by the review under subparagraph (B) and in furtherance of the mission described in paragraph (2), putting an emphasis on establishing such offices—

(i) where international civil aviation authorities are located;

(ii) where regional intergovernmental organizations are located;

(iii) in countries that have difficulty maintaining a category 1 classification through the International Aviation Safety Assessment program; and

(iv) in regions that have experienced substantial growth in aviation operations or manufacturing.

(4) BILATERAL AND MULTILATERAL ENGAGEMENT; TECHNICAL ASSISTANCE.—The Administrator shall—

(A) in consultation with the Secretary of State, engage bilaterally and multilaterally, including with the International Civil Aviation Organization, on an ongoing basis to bolster international collaboration, data sharing, and harmonization of international aviation safety requirements including through—

(i) sharing of continued operational safety information;

(ii) prioritization of pilot training deficiencies, including manual flying skills and flight crew training, to discourage over reliance on automation, further bolstering the components of airmanship;

(iii) encouraging the consideration of the safety advantages of appropriate Federal regulations, which may include relevant Federal regulations pertaining to flight crew training requirements; and

(iv) prioritizing any other flight crew training areas that the Administrator believes will enhance all international aviation safety; and

(B) seek to expand technical assistance provided by the Federal Aviation Administration in support of enhancing international aviation safety, including by—

(i) promoting and enhancing effective oversight systems, including operational safety enhancements identified through data collection and analysis;

(ii) promoting and encouraging compliance with international safety standards by counterpart civil aviation authorities;

(iii) minimizing cybersecurity threats and vulnerabilities across the aviation ecosystem;

(iv) supporting the sharing of safety information, best practices, risk assessments, and mitigations through established international aviation safety groups; and

(v) providing technical assistance on any other aspect of aviation safety that the Administrator determines is likely to enhance international aviation safety.

(5) BILATERAL AVIATION SAFETY AGREEMENTS.—

(A) IN GENERAL.—The Administrator shall negotiate, enter into, promote, enforce, evaluate the effectiveness of, and seek to update bilateral or multilateral aviation safety agreements, and the parts of such agreements, with international aviation authorities.

(B) PURPOSE.—The Administrator shall seek to enter into bilateral aviation safety agreements under this section to, at a minimum—

(i) improve global aviation safety;

(ii) increase harmonization of, and reduce duplicative, requirements, processes, and approvals to advance the aviation interests of the United States;

(iii) ensure access to international markets for operators, service providers, and manufacturers from the United States; and

(iv) put in place procedures for recourse when a party to such agreements fails to meet the obligations of such party under such agreements.

(C) SCOPE.—The scope of a bilateral aviation safety agreement entered into under this section shall, as appropriate, cover existing aviation users and concepts and establish a process by which bilateral aviation safety agreements can be updated to include new and novel concepts on an ongoing basis.

(D) CONTENTS.—Bilateral aviation safety agreements entered into under this section shall, as appropriate and consistent with United States law and regulation, include topics such as—

(i) airworthiness, certification, and validation;

(ii) maintenance;

(iii) operations and pilot training;

(iv) airspace access, efficiencies, and navigation services;

(v) transport category aircraft;

(vi) fixed-wing aircraft, rotorcraft, powered-lift aircraft, products, and articles;

(vii) aerodrome certification;

(viii) unmanned aircraft and associated elements of such aircraft;

(ix) flight simulation training devices;

(x) new or emerging technologies and technology trends; and

(xi) other topics as determined appropriate by the Administrator.

(E) RULE OF CONSTRUCTION.—Bilateral or multilateral aviation safety agreements entered into under this subsection shall not be construed to diminish or alter any authority of the Administrator under any other provision of law.

(7) [1] STRATEGIC PLAN.—The Administrator shall maintain a strategic plan for the international engagement of the Administration that includes—

(A) all elements of the report required under section 243(b) of the FAA Reauthorization Act of 2018 (49 U.S.C. 44701 note);

(B) measures to fulfill the mission described in paragraph (2);

(C) initiatives to attain greater expertise among employees of the Federal Aviation Administration in issues related to dispute resolution, intellectual property, and export control laws;

(D) policy regarding the future direction and strategy of the United States engagement with the International Civil Aviation Organization;

(E) procedures for acceptance of mandatory airworthiness information, such as airworthiness directives, and other safety-related regulatory documents, including procedures to implement the requirements of section 44701(e)(5);

(F) all factors, including funding and resourcing, necessary for the Administration to maintain leadership in the global activities related to aviation safety and air transportation;

(G) establishment of, and a process to regularly track and update, metrics to measure the effectiveness of, and foreign civil aviation authority compliance with, bilateral aviation safety agreements; and

(H) a strategic methodology to facilitate the ability of the United States aerospace industry to efficiently operate and export new aerospace technologies, products, and articles in key markets globally.

(e) PROMOTION OF UNITED STATES AEROSPACE STANDARDS, PRODUCTS, AND SERVICES ABROAD.—The Secretary shall take appropriate actions to—

(1) promote United States aerospace-related safety standards abroad;

(2) facilitate and vigorously defend approvals of United States aerospace products and services abroad;

(3) with respect to bilateral partners, utilize bilateral safety agreements and other mechanisms to improve validation of United States certificated aeronautical products, services, and appliances and enhance mutual acceptance in order to eliminate redundancies and unnecessary costs; and

(4) with respect to the aeronautical safety authorities of a foreign country, streamline validation and coordination processes.

(f) TRAVEL.—The Administrator and the Secretary of Transportation shall, in carrying out the responsibilities described in subsection (a), delegate to the appropriate supervisors of offices of the Administration the ability to authorize the domestic and international travel of relevant personnel who are not in the Federal Aviation Administration Executive System, without any additional approvals required, for the purposes of—

(1) promoting aviation safety, aircraft operations, air traffic, airport, unmanned aircraft systems, aviation fuels, and other aviation standards, regulations, and initiatives adopted by the United States;

(2) facilitating the adoption of United States approaches on such aviation standards and recommended practices at the International Civil Aviation Organization;

(3) supporting the acceptance of Administration design and production approvals by other civil aviation authorities;

(4) training Administration personnel and training provided to other persons;

(5) engaging with regulated entities, including performing site visits;

(6) activities associated with subsections (c) through (e); and

(7) other activities as determined by the Administrator.

(Pub. L. 103–272, §1(e), July 5, 1994, 108 Stat. 1102; Pub. L. 103–429, §6(47), Oct. 31, 1994, 108 Stat. 4384; Pub. L. 104–264, title IV, §401(b)(1), Oct. 9, 1996, 110 Stat. 3255; Pub. L. 108–176, title III, §303, title VIII, §813, Dec. 12, 2003, 117 Stat. 2533, 2590; Pub. L. 115–254, div. B, title II, §241, title V, §539(a), Oct. 5, 2018, 132 Stat. 3257, 3370; Pub. L. 116–260, div. V, title I, §119(f)(1), (2), Dec. 27, 2020, 134 Stat. 2342; Pub. L. 118–63, title III, §§356, 357(a), 358(a)–(c)(1), (d), 359, May 16, 2024, 138 Stat. 1114–1116, 1119, 1120.)

[1] So in original. No par. (6) has been enacted.

§40105. International negotiations, agreements, and obligations

(a) Advice and Consultation.—The Secretary of State shall advise the Administrator of the Federal Aviation Administration and the Secretaries of Transportation and Commerce, and consult with them as appropriate, about negotiations for an agreement with a government of a foreign country to establish or develop air navigation, including air routes and services. The Secretary of Transportation shall consult with the Secretary of State in carrying out this part to the extent this part is related to foreign air transportation.

(b) Actions of Secretary and Administrator.—(1) In carrying out this part, the Secretary of Transportation and the Administrator—

(A) shall act consistently with obligations of the United States Government under an international agreement;

(B) shall consider applicable laws and requirements of a foreign country; and

(C) may not limit compliance by an air carrier with obligations or liabilities imposed by the government of a foreign country when the Secretary takes any action related to a certificate of public convenience and necessity issued under chapter 411 of this title.

(2) This subsection does not apply to an agreement between an air carrier or an officer or representative of an air carrier and the government of a foreign country, if the Secretary of Transportation disapproves the agreement because it is not in the public interest. Section 40106(b)(2) of this title applies to this subsection.

(c) Consultation on International Air Transportation Policy.—In carrying out section 40101(e) of this title, the Secretaries of State and Transportation, to the maximum extent practicable, shall consult on broad policy goals and individual negotiations with—

(1) the Secretaries of Commerce and Defense;

(2) airport operators;

(3) scheduled air carriers;

(4) charter air carriers;

(5) airline labor;

(6) consumer interest groups;

(7) travel agents and tour organizers; and

(8) other groups, institutions, and governmental authorities affected by international aviation policy.

(d) Congressional Observers at International Aviation Negotiations.—The President shall grant to at least one representative of each House of Congress the privilege of attending international aviation negotiations as an observer if the privilege is requested in advance in writing.

(Pub. L. 103–272, §1(e), July 5, 1994, 108 Stat. 1102.)

§40106. Emergency powers

(a) Deviations From Regulations.—Appropriate military authority may authorize aircraft of the armed forces of the United States to deviate from air traffic regulations prescribed under section 40103(b)(1) and (2) of this title when the authority decides the deviation is essential to the national defense because of a military emergency or urgent military necessity. The authority shall—

(1) give the Administrator of the Federal Aviation Administration prior notice of the

deviation at the earliest practicable time; and

(2) to the extent time and circumstances allow, make every reasonable effort to consult with the Administrator and arrange for the deviation in advance on a mutually agreeable basis.

(b) SUSPENSION OF AUTHORITY.—(1) When the President decides that the government of a foreign country is acting inconsistently with the Convention for the Suppression of Unlawful Seizure of Aircraft or that the government of a foreign country allows territory under its jurisdiction to be used as a base of operations or training of, or as a sanctuary for, or arms, aids, or abets, a terrorist organization that knowingly uses the unlawful seizure, or the threat of an unlawful seizure, of an aircraft as an instrument of policy, the President may suspend the authority of—

(A) an air carrier or foreign air carrier to provide foreign air transportation to and from that foreign country;

(B) a person to operate aircraft in foreign air commerce to and from that foreign country;

(C) a foreign air carrier to provide foreign air transportation between the United States and another country that maintains air service with the foreign country; and

(D) a foreign person to operate aircraft in foreign air commerce between the United States and another country that maintains air service with the foreign country.

(2) The President may act under this subsection without notice or a hearing. The suspension remains in effect for as long as the President decides is necessary to ensure the security of aircraft against unlawful seizure. Notwithstanding section 40105(b) of this title, the authority of the President to suspend rights under this subsection is a condition to a certificate of public convenience and necessity, air carrier operating certificate, foreign air carrier or foreign aircraft permit, or foreign air carrier operating specification issued by the Secretary of Transportation under this part.

(3) An air carrier or foreign air carrier may not provide foreign air transportation, and a person may not operate aircraft in foreign air commerce, in violation of a suspension of authority under this subsection.

(Pub. L. 103–272, §1(e), July 5, 1994, 108 Stat. 1103.)

§40107. PRESIDENTIAL TRANSFERS

(a) GENERAL AUTHORITY.—The President may transfer to the Administrator of the Federal Aviation Administration a duty, power, activity, or facility of a department, agency, or instrumentality of the executive branch of the United States Government, or an officer or unit of a department, agency, or instrumentality of the executive branch, related primarily to selecting, developing, testing, evaluating, establishing, operating, or maintaining a system, procedure, facility, or device for safe and efficient air navigation and air traffic control. In making a transfer, the President may transfer records and property and make officers and employees from the department, agency, instrumentality, or unit available to the Administrator.

(b) DURING WAR.—If war occurs, the President by executive order may transfer to the Secretary of Defense a duty, power, activity, or facility of the Administrator. In making the transfer, the President may transfer records, property, officers, and employees of the Administration to the Department of Defense.

(Pub. L. 103–272, §1(e), July 5, 1994, 108 Stat. 1104.)

§40108. TRAINING SCHOOLS

(a) AUTHORITY TO OPERATE.—The Administrator of the Federal Aviation Administration may operate schools to train officers and employees of the Administration to carry out duties, powers, and activities of the Administrator.

(b) ATTENDANCE.—The Administrator may authorize officers and employees of other departments, agencies, or instrumentalities of the United States Government, officers and employees of governments of foreign countries, and individuals from the aeronautics industry to attend those schools. However, if the attendance of any of those officers, employees, or individuals increases the cost of operating the schools, the Administrator may require the payment or transfer of amounts or other consideration to offset the additional cost. The amount received may be credited to the appropriation current when the expenditures are or were paid, the appropriation current when the amount is received, or both.

(Pub. L. 103–272, §1(e), July 5, 1994, 108 Stat. 1104.)

§40109. AUTHORITY TO EXEMPT

(a) AIR CARRIERS AND FOREIGN AIR CARRIERS NOT ENGAGED DIRECTLY IN OPERATING AIRCRAFT.—(1) The Secretary of Transportation may exempt from subpart II of this part—

(A) an air carrier not engaged directly in operating aircraft in air transportation; or

(B) a foreign air carrier not engaged directly in operating aircraft in foreign air transportation.

(2) The exemption is effective to the extent and for periods that the Secretary decides are in the public interest.

(b) SAFETY REGULATION.—The Administrator of the Federal Aviation Administration may grant an exemption from a regulation prescribed in carrying out paragraphs (1) and (2) of section 40103(b) when the Administrator decides the exemption is in the public interest.

(c) OTHER ECONOMIC REGULATION.—Except as provided in this section, the Secretary may exempt to the extent the Secretary considers necessary a person or class of persons from a provision of chapter 411, chapter 413 (except sections 41307 and 41310(b)–(f)), chapter 415 (except sections 41502, 41505, and 41507–41509), chapter 417 (except sections 41703, 41704, 41710, 41713, and 41714), chapter 419, subchapter II of chapter 421, and sections 44909(a), 44909(b), and 46301(b) of this title, or a regulation or term prescribed under any of those provisions, when the Secretary decides that the exemption is consistent with the public interest.

(d) LABOR REQUIREMENTS.—The Secretary may not exempt an air carrier from section 42112 of this title. However, the Secretary may exempt from section 42112(b)(1) and (2) an air carrier not providing scheduled air transportation, and the operations conducted during daylight hours by an air carrier providing scheduled air transportation, when the Secretary decides that—

(1) because of the limited extent of, or unusual circumstances affecting, the operation of the air carrier, the enforcement of section 42112(b)(1) and (2) of this title is or would be an unreasonable burden on the air carrier that would obstruct its development and prevent it from beginning or continuing operations; and

(2) the exemption would not affect adversely the public interest.

(e) MAXIMUM FLYING HOURS.—The Secretary may not exempt an air carrier under this section from a provision referred to in subsection (c) of this section, or a regulation or term prescribed under any of those provisions, that sets maximum flying hours for pilots or copilots.

(f) SMALLER AIRCRAFT.—(1) An air carrier is exempt from section 41101(a)(1) of this title, and the Secretary may exempt an air carrier from another provision of subpart II of this part, if the air carrier—

(A)(i) provides passenger transportation only with aircraft having a maximum capacity of 55 passengers; or

(ii) provides the transportation of cargo only with aircraft having a maximum payload of less than 18,000 pounds; and

(B) complies with liability insurance requirements and other regulations the Secretary prescribes.

(2) The Secretary may increase the passenger or payload capacities when the public interest requires.

(3)(A) An exemption under this subsection applies to an air carrier providing air transportation between 2 places in Alaska, or between Alaska and Canada, only if the carrier is authorized by Alaska to provide the transportation.

(B) The Secretary may limit the number or location of places that may be served by an air carrier providing transportation only in Alaska under an exemption from section 41101(a)(1) of this title, or the frequency with which the transportation may be provided, only when the Secretary decides that providing the transportation substantially impairs the ability of an air carrier holding a certificate issued by the Secretary to provide its authorized transportation, including the minimum transportation requirement for Alaska specified under section 41732(b)(1)(B) of this title.

(g) EMERGENCY AIR TRANSPORTATION BY FOREIGN AIR CARRIERS.—(1) To the extent that the Secretary decides an exemption is in the public interest, the Secretary may exempt by order a foreign air carrier from the requirements and limitations of this part for not more than 30 days to allow the foreign air carrier to carry passengers or cargo in interstate air transportation in certain markets if the Secretary finds that—

(A) because of an emergency created by unusual circumstances not arising in the normal course of business, air carriers holding certificates under section 41102 of this title cannot accommodate traffic in those markets;

(B) all possible efforts have been made to accommodate the traffic by using the resources of the air carriers, including the use of—

(i) foreign aircraft, or sections of foreign aircraft, under lease or charter to the air carriers; and

(ii) the air carriers' reservations systems to the extent practicable;

(C) the exemption is necessary to avoid unreasonable hardship for the traffic in the markets that cannot be accommodated by the air carriers; and

(D) granting the exemption will not result in an unreasonable advantage to any party in a labor dispute where the inability to accommodate traffic in a market is a result of the dispute.

(2) When the Secretary grants an exemption to a foreign air carrier under this subsection,

the Secretary shall—

(A) ensure that air transportation that the foreign air carrier provides under the exemption is made available on reasonable terms;

(B) monitor continuously the passenger load factor of air carriers in the market that hold certificates under section 41102 of this title; and

(C) review the exemption at least every 30 days (or, in the case of an exemption that is necessary to provide and sustain air transportation in American Samoa between the islands of Tutuila and Manu'a, at least every 180 days) to ensure that the unusual circumstances that established the need for the exemption still exist.

(3) RENEWAL OF EXEMPTIONS.—

(A) IN GENERAL.—Except as provided in subparagraph (B), the Secretary may renew an exemption (including renewals) under this subsection for not more than 30 days.

(B) EXCEPTION.—The Secretary may renew an exemption (including renewals) under this subsection that is necessary to provide and sustain air transportation in American Samoa between the islands of Tutuila and Manu'a for not more than 180 days.

(4) CONTINUATION OF EXEMPTIONS.—An exemption granted by the Secretary under this subsection may continue for not more than 5 days after the unusual circumstances that established the need for the exemption cease.

(h) NOTICE AND OPPORTUNITY FOR HEARING.—The Secretary may act under subsections (d) and (f)(3)(B) of this section only after giving the air carrier notice and an opportunity for a hearing.

(Pub. L. 103–272, §1(e), July 5, 1994, 108 Stat. 1104; Pub. L. 104–287, §5(65), Oct. 11, 1996, 110 Stat. 3395; Pub. L. 115–254, div. B, title IV, §402, div. K, title I, §1991(c)(1), Oct. 5, 2018, 132 Stat. 3328, 3627; Pub. L. 118–63, title XI, §1101(d), May 16, 2024, 138 Stat. 1413.)

§40110. GENERAL PROCUREMENT AUTHORITY

(a) GENERAL.—In carrying out this part, the Administrator of the Federal Aviation Administration—

(1) to the extent that amounts are available for obligation, may acquire services or, by condemnation or otherwise, an interest in property, including an interest in airspace immediately adjacent to and needed for airports and other air navigation facilities owned by the United States Government and operated by the Administrator;

(2) may construct and improve laboratories and other test facilities; and

(3) may dispose of any interest in property for adequate compensation, and the amount so received shall—

(A) be credited to the appropriation current when the amount is received;

(B) be merged with and available for the purposes of such appropriation; and

(C) remain available until expended.

(b) PURCHASE OF HOUSING UNITS.—

(1) AUTHORITY.—In carrying out this part, the Administrator may purchase a housing unit (including a condominium or a housing unit in a building owned by a cooperative) that is located outside the contiguous United States if the cost of the unit is $300,000 or less.

(2) ADJUSTMENTS FOR INFLATION.—For fiscal years beginning after September 30, 1997, the Administrator may adjust the dollar amount specified in paragraph (1) to take

into account increases in local housing costs.

(3) CONTINUING OBLIGATIONS.—Notwithstanding section 1341 of title 31, the Administrator may purchase a housing unit under paragraph (1) even if there is an obligation thereafter to pay necessary and reasonable fees duly assessed upon such unit, including fees related to operation, maintenance, taxes, and insurance.

(4) CERTIFICATION TO CONGRESS.—The Administrator may purchase a housing unit under paragraph (1) only if, at least 30 days before completing the purchase, the Administrator transmits to the Committee on Transportation and Infrastructure of the House of Representatives and the Committee on Commerce, Science, and Transportation of the Senate a report containing—

(A) a description of the housing unit and its price;

(B) a certification that the price does not exceed the median price of housing units in the area; and

(C) a certification that purchasing the housing unit is the most cost-beneficial means of providing necessary accommodations in carrying out this part.

(5) PAYMENT OF FEES.—The Administrator may pay, when due, fees resulting from the purchase of a housing unit under this subsection from any amounts made available to the Administrator.

(c) DUTIES AND POWERS.—When carrying out subsection (a) of this section, the Administrator of the Federal Aviation Administration may—

(1) notwithstanding section 1341(a)(1) of title 31, lease an interest in property for not more than 20 years;

(2) consider the reasonable probable future use of the underlying land in making an award for a condemnation of an interest in airspace;

(3) construct, or acquire an interest in, a public building (as defined in section 3301(a) of title 40) only under a delegation of authority from the Administrator of General Services; and

(4) dispose of property under subsection (a)(3) of this section, except for airport and airway property and technical equipment used for the special purposes of the Administration, only under sections 121, 123, and 126 and chapter 5 of title 40.

(d) ACQUISITION MANAGEMENT SYSTEM.—

(1) IN GENERAL.—In consultation with such non-governmental experts in acquisition management systems as the Administrator may employ, and notwithstanding provisions of Federal acquisition law, the Administrator shall develop, implement, and periodically update an acquisition management system for the Administration that addresses the unique needs of the agency and, at a minimum, provides for—

(A) more timely and cost-effective acquisitions of equipment, services, property, and materials; and

(B) the resolution of bid protests and contract disputes related thereto, using consensual alternative dispute resolution techniques to the maximum extent practicable.

(2) APPLICABILITY OF FEDERAL ACQUISITION LAW.—The following provisions of Federal acquisition law shall not apply to the acquisition management system developed, implemented, and periodically updated pursuant to paragraph (1):

(A) Division C (except sections 3302, 3501(b), 3509, 3906, 4710, and 4711) of subtitle I of title 41.

(B) Division B (except sections 1704 and 2303) of subtitle I of title 41.

(C) The Federal Acquisition Streamlining Act of 1994 (Public Law 103–355). However, section 4705 of title 41 shall apply to the acquisition management system developed, implemented, and periodically updated pursuant to paragraph (1). For the purpose of applying section 4705 of title 41 to the system, the term "executive agency" is deemed to refer to the Federal Aviation Administration.

(D) The Small Business Act (15 U.S.C. 631 et seq.), except that all reasonable opportunities to be awarded contracts shall be provided to small business concerns and small business concerns owned and controlled by socially and economically disadvantaged individuals.

(E) The Competition in Contracting Act.

(F) Subchapter V of chapter 35 of title 31, relating to the procurement protest system.

(G) The Federal Acquisition Regulation and any laws not listed in subparagraphs (A) through (F) providing authority to promulgate regulations in the Federal Acquisition Regulation.

(3) Certain provisions of division B (except sections 1704 and 2303) of subtitle I of title 41.—Notwithstanding paragraph (2)(B), chapter 21 of title 41 shall apply to the acquisition management system developed, implemented, and periodically updated under paragraph (1) with the following modifications:

(A) Sections 2101 and 2106 of title 41 shall not apply.

(B) The Administrator shall adopt definitions for the acquisition management system that are consistent with the purpose and intent of the Office of Federal Procurement Policy Act, as in effect on October 9, 1996.

(C) After the adoption of those definitions, the criminal, civil, and administrative remedies provided under division B of subtitle I of title 41 apply to the acquisition management system.

(D) In the administration of the acquisition management system, the Administrator may take adverse personnel action under section 2105(c)(1)(D) of title 41 in accordance with the procedures contained in the Administration's personnel management system.

(4) Commercial products and services.—In implementing and updating the acquisition management system pursuant to paragraph (1), the Administrator shall, whenever possible—

(A) describe the requirements with respect to a solicitation for the procurement of supplies or services in terms of—

(i) functions to be performed;

(ii) performance required; or

(iii) essential physical and system characteristics;

(B) ensure that commercial services or commercial products may be procured to fulfill such solicitation, or to the extent that commercial products suitable to meet the needs of the Administration are not available, ensure that nondevelopmental items other than commercial products may be procured to fulfill such solicitation;

(C) provide offerors of commercial services, commercial products, and nondevelopmental items other than commercial products an opportunity to compete in any solicitation for the procurement of supplies or services;

(D) revise the procurement policies, practices, and procedures of the Administration to reduce any impediments to the acquisition of commercial products and commercial services;

(E) ensure that any procurement of new equipment takes into account the life cycle, reliability, performance, service support, and costs to guarantee the acquisition of equipment that is of high quality and reliability resulting in greater performance and cost-related benefits; and

(F) ensure that procurement officials—

(i) acquire commercial services, commercial products, or nondevelopmental items other than commercial products to meet the needs of the Administration;

(ii) in a solicitation for the procurement of supplies or services, state the specifications for such supplies or services in terms that enable and encourage bidders and offerors to supply commercial services or commercial products, or to the extent that commercial products suitable to meet the needs of the Administration are not available, to supply nondevelopmental items other than commercial products;

(iii) require that prime contractors and subcontractors at all levels under contracts with the Administration incorporate commercial services, commercial products, or nondevelopmental items other than commercial products as components of items supplied to the Administration;

(iv) modify procurement requirements in appropriate circumstances to ensure that such requirements can be met by commercial services or commercial products, or to the extent that commercial products suitable to meet the needs of the Administration are not available, nondevelopmental items other than commercial products; and

(v) require training of appropriate personnel in the acquisition of commercial products and commercial services.

(5) ADJUDICATION OF CERTAIN BID PROTESTS AND CONTRACT DISPUTES.—A bid protest or contract dispute that is not addressed or resolved through alternative dispute resolution shall be adjudicated by the Administrator through Dispute Resolution Officers or Special Masters of the Federal Aviation Administration Office of Dispute Resolution for Acquisition, acting pursuant to sections 46102, 46104, 46105, 46106 and 46107 and shall be subject to judicial review under section 46110 and to section 504 of title 5.

(e) PROHIBITION ON RELEASE OF OFFEROR PROPOSALS.—

(1) GENERAL RULE.—Except as provided in paragraph (2), a proposal in the possession or control of the Administrator may not be made available to any person under section 552 of title 5.

(2) EXCEPTION.—Paragraph (1) shall not apply to any portion of a proposal of an offeror the disclosure of which is authorized by the Administrator pursuant to procedures published in the Federal Register. The Administrator shall provide an opportunity for public comment on the procedures for a period of not less than 30 days beginning on the date of such publication in order to receive and consider the views of all interested parties on the procedures. The procedures shall not take effect before the 60th day following the

date of such publication.

(3) PROPOSAL DEFINED.—In this subsection, the term "proposal" means information contained in or originating from any proposal, including a technical, management, or cost proposal, submitted by an offeror in response to the requirements of a solicitation for a competitive proposal.

(Pub. L. 103–272, §1(e), July 5, 1994, 108 Stat. 1106; Pub. L. 103–429, §6(48), (80), Oct. 31, 1994, 108 Stat. 4384, 4388; Pub. L. 104–264, title XII, §1201, Oct. 9, 1996, 110 Stat. 3279; Pub. L. 106–181, title III, §307(b), title VII, §703, Apr. 5, 2000, 114 Stat. 125, 156; Pub. L. 107–217, §3(n)(5), Aug. 21, 2002, 116 Stat. 1302; Pub. L. 108–176, title II, §§222, 224(a), (b), Dec. 12, 2003, 117 Stat. 2527; Pub. L. 108–178, §4(k), Dec. 15, 2003, 117 Stat. 2642; Pub. L. 111–350, §5(o)(7), Jan. 4, 2011, 124 Stat. 3853; Pub. L. 112–95, title II, §§206, 210, Feb. 14, 2012, 126 Stat. 39, 44; Pub. L. 115–254, div. B, title V, §544, Oct. 5, 2018, 132 Stat. 3374; Pub. L. 118–63, title II, §§218(b), 228, title XI, §1101(e), (f), May 16, 2024, 138 Stat. 1055, 1062, 1413.)

§40111. MULTIYEAR PROCUREMENT CONTRACTS FOR SERVICES AND RELATED ITEMS

(a) GENERAL AUTHORITY.—Notwithstanding section 1341(a)(1)(B) of title 31, the Administrator of the Federal Aviation Administration may make a contract of not more than 5 years for the following types of services and items of supply related to those services for which amounts otherwise would be available for obligation only in the fiscal year for which appropriated:

(1) operation, maintenance, and support of facilities and installations.

(2) operation, maintenance, and modification of aircraft, vehicles, and other highly complex equipment.

(3) specialized training requiring high quality instructor skills, including training of pilots and aircrew members and foreign language training.

(4) base services, including ground maintenance, aircraft refueling, bus transportation, and refuse collection and disposal.

(b) REQUIRED FINDINGS.—The Administrator may make a contract under this section only if the Administrator finds that—

(1) there will be a continuing requirement for the service consistent with current plans for the proposed contract period;

(2) providing the service will require a substantial initial investment in plant or equipment, or will incur a substantial contingent liability for assembling, training, or transporting a specialized workforce; and

(3) the contract will promote the best interests of the United States by encouraging effective competition and promoting economies in operation.

(c) CONSIDERATIONS.—When making a contract under this section, the Administrator shall be guided by the following:

(1) The part of the cost of a plant or equipment amortized as a cost of contract performance may not be more than the ratio between the period of contract performance and the anticipated useful commercial life (instead of physical life) of the plant or equipment, considering the location and specialized nature of the plant or equipment, obsolescence, and other similar factors.

(2) The Administrator shall consider the desirability of—

(A) obtaining an option to renew the contract for a reasonable period of not more

175

than 3 years, at a price that does not include charges for nonrecurring costs already amortized; and

(B) reserving in the Administrator the right, on payment of the unamortized part of the cost of the plant or equipment, to take title to the plant or equipment under appropriate circumstances.

(d) ENDING CONTRACTS.—A contract made under this section shall be ended if amounts are not made available to continue the contract into a subsequent fiscal year. The cost of ending the contract may be paid from—

(1) an appropriation originally available for carrying out the contract;

(2) an appropriation currently available for procuring the type of service concerned and not otherwise obligated; or

(3) amounts appropriated for payments to end the contract.

(Pub. L. 103–272, §1(e), July 5, 1994, 108 Stat. 1107.)

§40112. MULTIYEAR PROCUREMENT CONTRACTS FOR PROPERTY

(a) GENERAL AUTHORITY.—Notwithstanding section 1341(a)(1)(B) of title 31 and to the extent that amounts otherwise are available for obligation, the Administrator of the Federal Aviation Administration may make a contract of more than one but not more than 5 fiscal years to purchase property, except a contract to construct, alter, or make a major repair or improvement to real property.

(b) REQUIRED FINDINGS.—The Administrator may make a contract under this section if the Administrator finds that—

(1) the contract will promote the safety or efficiency of the national airspace system and will result in reduced total contract costs;

(2) the minimum need for the property to be purchased is expected to remain substantially unchanged during the proposed contract period in terms of production rate, procurement rate, and total quantities;

(3) there is a reasonable expectation that throughout the proposed contract period the Administrator will request appropriations for the contract at the level required to avoid cancellation;

(4) there is a stable design for the property to be acquired and the technical risks associated with the property are not excessive; and

(5) the estimates of the contract costs and the anticipated savings from the contract are realistic.

(c) REGULATIONS.—The Administrator shall prescribe regulations for acquiring property under this section to promote the use of contracts under this section in a way that will allow the most efficient use of those contracts. The regulations may provide for a cancellation provision in the contract to the extent the provision is necessary and in the best interest of the United States. The provision may include consideration of recurring and nonrecurring costs of the contractor associated with producing the item to be delivered under the contract. The regulations shall provide that, to the extent practicable—

(1) to broaden the aviation industrial base—

(A) a contract under this section shall be used to seek, retain, and promote the use under that contract of subcontractors, vendors, or suppliers; and

(B) on accrual of a payment or other benefit accruing on a contract under this section to a subcontractor, vendor, or supplier participating in the contract, the payment or benefit shall be delivered in the most expeditious way practicable; and

(2) this section and regulations prescribed under this section may not be carried out in a way that precludes or curtails the existing ability of the Administrator to provide for—

(A) competition in producing items to be delivered under a contract under this section; or

(B) ending a prime contract when performance is deficient with respect to cost, quality, or schedule.

(d) CONTRACT PROVISIONS.—(1) A contract under this section may—

(A) be used for the advance procurement of components, parts, and material necessary to manufacture equipment to be used in the national airspace system;

(B) provide that performance under the contract after the first year is subject to amounts being appropriated; and

(C) contain a negotiated priced option for varying the number of end items to be procured over the period of the contract.

(2) If feasible and practicable, an advance procurement contract may be made to achieve economic-lot purchases and more efficient production rates.

(e) CANCELLATION PAYMENT AND NOTICE OF CANCELLATION CEILING.—(1) If a contract under this section provides that performance is subject to an appropriation being made, it also may provide for a cancellation payment to be made to the contractor if the appropriation is not made.

(2) Before awarding a contract under this section containing a cancellation ceiling of more than $100,000,000, the Administrator shall give written notice of the proposed contract and cancellation ceiling to the Committee on Commerce, Science, and Transportation of the Senate and the Committee on Transportation and Infrastructure of the House of Representatives. The contract may not be awarded until the end of the 30-day period beginning on the date of the notice.

(f) ENDING CONTRACTS.—A contract made under this section shall be ended if amounts are not made available to continue the contract into a subsequent fiscal year. The cost of ending the contract may be paid from—

(1) an appropriation originally available for carrying out the contract;

(2) an appropriation currently available for procuring the type of property concerned and not otherwise obligated; or

(3) amounts appropriated for payments to end the contract.

(Pub. L. 103–272, §1(e), July 5, 1994, 108 Stat. 1108; Pub. L. 104–106, div. E, title LVI, §5606, Feb. 10, 1996, 110 Stat. 700; Pub. L. 104–287, §5(9), Oct. 11, 1996, 110 Stat. 3389.)

§40113. ADMINISTRATIVE

(a) GENERAL AUTHORITY.—The Secretary of Transportation (or the Administrator of the Transportation Security Administration with respect to security duties and powers designated to be carried out by that Administrator or the Administrator of the Federal Aviation Administration with respect to aviation safety duties and powers designated to be carried out by that Administrator) may take action the Secretary, Administrator of the Transportation Security Administration, or Administrator of the Federal Aviation Administration, as appropriate, considers necessary to carry out this part, including conducting investigations, prescribing regulations, standards, and procedures, and issuing orders.

(b) HAZARDOUS MATERIAL.—In carrying out this part, the Secretary has the same authority to regulate the transportation of hazardous material by air that the Secretary has under section 5103 of this title. However, this subsection does not prohibit or regulate the transportation of a firearm (as defined in section 232 of title 18) or ammunition for a firearm, when transported by an individual for personal use.

(c) GOVERNMENTAL ASSISTANCE.—The Secretary (or the Administrator of the Federal Aviation Administration with respect to aviation safety duties and powers designated to be carried out by the Administrator) may use the assistance of the Administrator of the National Aeronautics and Space Administration and any research or technical department, agency, or instrumentality of the United States Government on matters related to aircraft fuel and oil, and to the design, material, workmanship, construction, performance, maintenance, and operation of aircraft, aircraft engines, propellers, appliances, and air navigation facilities. Each department, agency, and instrumentality may conduct scientific and technical research, investigations, and tests necessary to assist the Secretary or Administrator of the Federal Aviation Administration in carrying out this part. This part does not authorize duplicating laboratory research activities of a department, agency, or instrumentality.

(d) INDEMNIFICATION.—The Administrator of the Federal Aviation Administration may indemnify an officer or employee of the Federal Aviation Administration against a claim or judgment arising out of an act that the Administrator decides was committed within the scope of the official duties of the officer or employee.

(e) ASSISTANCE TO FOREIGN AVIATION AUTHORITIES.—

(1) SAFETY-RELATED TRAINING AND OPERATIONAL SERVICES.—The Administrator may provide safety-related training and operational services to foreign aviation authorities (whether public or private) with or without reimbursement, if the Administrator determines that providing such services promotes aviation safety or efficiency. The Administrator may also provide technical assistance related to all aviation safety-related training and operational services in connection with bilateral and multilateral agreements, including further bolstering the components of airmanship. The Administrator is authorized to participate in, and submit offers in response to, competitions to provide these services, and to contract with foreign aviation authorities to provide these services consistent with section 106(l)(6). To the extent practicable, air travel reimbursed under this subsection shall be conducted on United States air carriers.

(2) REIMBURSEMENT SOUGHT.—The Administrator shall actively seek reimbursement for services provided under this subsection from foreign aviation authorities capable of providing such reimbursement. The Administrator is authorized, notwithstanding any other provision of law or policy, to accept payments for services provided under this subsection in arrears.

(3) CREDITING APPROPRIATIONS.—Funds received by the Administrator pursuant to this section shall—

(A) be credited to the appropriation current when the amount is received;

(B) be merged with and available for the purposes of such appropriation; and

(C) remain available until expended.

(4) AUTHORIZATION OF APPROPRIATIONS.—There is authorized to be appropriated to the Administrator, $5,000,000 for each of fiscal years 2021 through 2023, to carry out this subsection. Amounts appropriated under the preceding sentence for any fiscal year shall remain available until expended.

(6) [1] TECHNICAL ASSISTANCE OUTSIDE OF AGREEMENTS.—In the absence of a bilateral or multilateral agreement, the Administrator may provide technical assistance and training under this subsection if the Administrator determines that—

(A) a foreign government would benefit from technical assistance pursuant to this subsection to strengthen aviation safety, efficiency, and security; and

(B) the engagement is to provide inherently governmental technical assistance and training.

(7) INHERENTLY GOVERNMENTAL TECHNICAL ASSISTANCE AND TRAINING DEFINED.—In this subsection, the term "inherently governmental technical assistance and training" means technical assistance and training that—

(A) relies upon or incorporates Federal Aviation Administration-specific program, system, policy, or procedural matters;

(B) must be accomplished using agency expertise and authority; and

(C) relates to—

(i) international aviation safety assessment technical reviews and technical assistance;

(ii) aerodrome safety and certification;

(iii) aviation system certification activities based on Federal Aviation Administration regulations and requirements;

(iv) cybersecurity efforts to protect United States aviation ecosystem components and facilities;

(v) operation and maintenance of air navigation system equipment, procedures, and personnel; or

(vi) training and exercises in support of aviation safety, efficiency, and security.

(f) APPLICATION OF CERTAIN REGULATIONS TO ALASKA.—In amending title 14, Code of Federal Regulations, in a manner affecting intrastate aviation in Alaska, the Administrator of the Federal Aviation Administration shall consider the extent to which Alaska is not served by transportation modes other than aviation, and shall establish such regulatory distinctions as the Administrator considers appropriate.

(Pub. L. 103–272, §1(e), July 5, 1994, 108 Stat. 1110; Pub. L. 103–305, title II, §202, Aug. 23, 1994, 108 Stat. 1582; Pub. L. 106–181, title I, §156(a), Apr. 5, 2000, 114 Stat. 89; Pub. L. 107–71, title I, §140(c), Nov. 19, 2001, 115 Stat. 641; Pub. L. 112–95, title II, §207, Feb. 14, 2012, 126 Stat. 39; Pub. L. 115–254, div. K, title I, §1991(c)(2), Oct. 5, 2018, 132 Stat. 3627; Pub. L. 116–260, div. V, title I, §119(g), Dec. 27, 2020, 134 Stat. 2342; Pub. L. 118–63, title II, §218(c), title III, §358(c)(2), May 16, 2024, 138 Stat. 1055, 1117.)

[1] *So in original. There is no par. (5).*

§40114. REPORTS AND RECORDS

(a) WRITTEN REPORTS.—(1) Except as provided in this part, the Secretary of Transportation (or the Administrator of the Federal Aviation Administration with respect to aviation safety duties and powers designated to be carried out by the Administrator) shall make a written report of each proceeding and investigation under this part in which a formal hearing was held and shall provide a copy to each party to the proceeding or investigation. The report shall include the decision, conclusions, order, and requirements of the Secretary or Administrator as appropriate.

(2) The Secretary (or the Administrator with respect to aviation safety duties and powers designated to be carried out by the Administrator) shall have all reports, orders, decisions, and regulations the Secretary or Administrator, as appropriate, issues or prescribes published in the form and way best adapted for public use. A publication of the Secretary or Administrator is competent evidence of its contents.

(b) PUBLIC RECORDS.—Except as provided in subpart II of this part, copies of tariffs and arrangements filed with the Secretary under subpart II, and the statistics, tables, and figures contained in reports made to the Secretary under subpart II, are public records. The Secretary is the custodian of those records. A public record, or a copy or extract of it, certified by the Secretary under the seal of the Department of Transportation is competent evidence in an investigation by the Secretary and in a judicial proceeding.

(Pub. L. 103–272, §1(e), July 5, 1994, 108 Stat. 1110.)

§40115. WITHHOLDING INFORMATION

(a) OBJECTIONS TO DISCLOSURE.—(1) A person may object to the public disclosure of information—

(A) in a record filed under this part; or

(B) obtained under this part by the Secretary of Transportation or State or the United States Postal Service.

(2) An objection must be in writing and must state the reasons for the objection. The Secretary of Transportation or State or the Postal Service shall order the information withheld from public disclosure when the appropriate Secretary or the Postal Service decides that disclosure of the information would—

(A) prejudice the United States Government in preparing and presenting its position in international negotiations; or

(B) have an adverse effect on the competitive position of an air carrier in foreign air transportation.

(b) WITHHOLDING INFORMATION FROM CONGRESS.—This section does not authorize information to be withheld from a committee of Congress authorized to have the information.

(Pub. L. 103–272, §1(e), July 5, 1994, 108 Stat. 1111.)

§40116. STATE TAXATION

(a) DEFINITION.—In this section, "State" includes the District of Columbia, a territory or possession of the United States, and a political authority of at least 2 States.

(b) PROHIBITIONS.—Except as provided in subsection (c) of this section and section 40117 of this title, a State, a political subdivision of a State, and any person that has purchased or leased an airport under section 47134 of this title may not levy or collect a tax, fee, head charge, or other charge on—

(1) an individual traveling in air commerce;

(2) the transportation of an individual traveling in air commerce;

(3) the sale of air transportation; or

(4) the gross receipts from that air commerce or transportation.

(c) AIRCRAFT TAKING OFF OR LANDING IN STATE.—A State or political subdivision of a State may levy or collect a tax on or related to a flight of a commercial aircraft or an activity or service on the aircraft only if the aircraft takes off or lands in the State or political subdivision as part of the flight.

(d) UNREASONABLE BURDENS AND DISCRIMINATION AGAINST INTERSTATE COMMERCE.—(1) In this subsection—

(A) "air carrier transportation property" means property (as defined by the Secretary of Transportation) that an air carrier providing air transportation owns or uses.

(B) "assessment" means valuation for a property tax levied by a taxing district.

(C) "assessment jurisdiction" means a geographical area in a State used in determining the assessed value of property for ad valorem taxation.

(D) "commercial and industrial property" means property (except transportation property and land used primarily for agriculture or timber growing) devoted to a commercial or industrial use and subject to a property tax levy.

(2)(A) A State, political subdivision of a State, or authority acting for a State or political subdivision may not do any of the following acts because those acts unreasonably burden and discriminate against interstate commerce:

(i) assess air carrier transportation property at a value that has a higher ratio to the true market value of the property than the ratio that the assessed value of other commercial and industrial property of the same type in the same assessment jurisdiction has to the true market value of the other commercial and industrial property.

(ii) levy or collect a tax on an assessment that may not be made under clause (i) of this subparagraph.

(iii) levy or collect an ad valorem property tax on air carrier transportation property at a tax rate greater than the tax rate applicable to commercial and industrial property in the same assessment jurisdiction.

(iv) levy or collect a tax, fee, or charge, first taking effect after August 23, 1994, exclusively upon any business located at a commercial service airport or operating as a permittee of such an airport other than a tax, fee, or charge wholly utilized for airport or aeronautical purposes.

(v) except as otherwise provided under section 47133, levy or collect a tax, fee, or charge, first taking effect after the date of enactment of this clause, upon any business located at a commercial service airport or operating as a permittee of such an airport that is not generally imposed on sales or services by that State, political subdivision, or authority unless wholly utilized for airport or aeronautical purposes.

(B) Subparagraph (A) of this paragraph does not apply to an in lieu tax completely used for airport and aeronautical purposes.

(e) OTHER ALLOWABLE TAXES AND CHARGES.—Except as provided in subsection (d) of this section, a State or political subdivision of a State may levy or collect—

(1) taxes (except those taxes enumerated in subsection (b) of this section), including property taxes, net income taxes, franchise taxes, and sales or use taxes on the sale of goods or services; and

(2) reasonable rental charges, landing fees, and other service charges from aircraft

operators for using airport facilities of an airport owned or operated by that State or subdivision.

(f) PAY OF AIR CARRIER EMPLOYEES.—(1) In this subsection—

(A) "pay" means money received by an employee for services.

(B) "State" means a State of the United States, the District of Columbia, and a territory or possession of the United States.

(C) an employee is deemed to have earned 50 percent of the employee's pay in a State or political subdivision of a State in which the scheduled flight time of the employee in the State or subdivision is more than 50 percent of the total scheduled flight time of the employee when employed during the calendar year.

(2) The pay of an employee of an air carrier having regularly assigned duties on aircraft in at least 2 States is subject to the income tax laws of only the following:

(A) the State or political subdivision of the State that is the residence of the employee.

(B) the State or political subdivision of the State in which the employee earns more than 50 percent of the pay received by the employee from the carrier.

(3) Compensation paid by an air carrier to an employee described in subsection (a) in connection with such employee's authorized leave or other authorized absence from regular duties on the carrier's aircraft in order to perform services on behalf of the employee's airline union shall be subject to the income tax laws of only the following:

(A) The State or political subdivision of the State that is the residence of the employee.

(B) The State or political subdivision of the State in which the employee's scheduled flight time would have been more than 50 percent of the employee's total scheduled flight time for the calendar year had the employee been engaged full time in the performance of regularly assigned duties on the carrier's aircraft.

(Pub. L. 103–272, §1(e), July 5, 1994, 108 Stat. 1111; Pub. L. 103–305, title I, §112(e), title II, §208, Aug. 23, 1994, 108 Stat. 1576, 1588; Pub. L. 104–264, title I, §149(b), Oct. 9, 1996, 110 Stat. 3226; Pub. L. 104–287, §5(66), Oct. 11, 1996, 110 Stat. 3395; Pub. L. 115–254, div. B, title I, §159(a), Oct. 5, 2018, 132 Stat. 3220.)

§40117. PASSENGER FACILITY CHARGES

(a) DEFINITIONS.—In this section, the following definitions apply:

(1) AIRPORT, COMMERCIAL SERVICE AIRPORT, AND PUBLIC AGENCY.—The terms "airport", "commercial service airport", and "public agency" have the meaning those terms have under section 47102.

(2) ELIGIBLE AGENCY.—The term "eligible agency" means a public agency that controls a commercial service airport.

(3) ELIGIBLE AIRPORT-RELATED PROJECT.—The term "eligible airport-related project" means any of the following projects:

(A) A project for airport development or airport planning under subchapter I of chapter 471.

(B) A project for terminal development described in section 47119(a).

(C) A project for costs of terminal development referred to in subparagraph (B) incurred after August 1, 1986, at an airport that did not have more than .25 percent of the total annual passenger boardings in the United States in the most recent calendar year for which data is available and at which total passenger boardings declined by at least 16 percent between calendar year 1989 and calendar year 1997.

(D) A project for airport noise capability planning under section 47505.

(E) A project to carry out noise compatibility measures eligible for assistance under section 47504, whether or not a program for those measures has been approved under section 47504.

(F) A project for constructing gates and related areas at which passengers board or exit aircraft. In the case of a project required to enable additional air service by an air carrier with less than 50 percent of the annual passenger boardings at an airport, the project for constructing gates and related areas may include structural foundations and floor systems, exterior building walls and load-bearing interior columns or walls, windows, door and roof systems, building utilities (including heating, air conditioning, ventilation, plumbing, and electrical service), and aircraft fueling facilities adjacent to the gate.

(G) A project for converting vehicles and ground support equipment used at a commercial service airport to low-emission technology (as defined in section 47102) or to use cleaner burning conventional fuels, retrofitting of any such vehicles or equipment that are powered by a diesel or gasoline engine with emission control technologies certified or verified by the Environmental Protection Agency to reduce emissions, or acquiring for use at a commercial service airport vehicles and ground support equipment that include low-emission technology or use cleaner burning fuels if the airport is located in an air quality nonattainment area (as defined in section 171(2) of the Clean Air Act (42 U.S.C. 7501(2))) or a maintenance area referred to in section 175A of such Act (42 U.S.C. 7505a) and if such project will result in an airport receiving appropriate emission credits as described in section 47139.

(H) A project at a small hub airport for a noise barrier where the day–night average sound level from commercial, general aviation, or cargo operations is expected to exceed 55 decibels as a result of new airport development.

(I) A project for the replacement of existing workspace elements (including any associated in-kind facility or equipment within or immediately adjacent to a terminal development or renovation project at such airport) related to the relocation of a Federal agency on airport grounds due to such terminal development or renovation project for which development costs are eligible costs under this section.

(4) GROUND SUPPORT EQUIPMENT.—The term "ground support equipment" means service and maintenance equipment used at an airport to support aeronautical operations and related activities.

(5) PASSENGER FACILITY CHARGE.—The term "passenger facility charge" means a charge imposed under this section.

(6) PASSENGER FACILITY REVENUE.—The term "passenger facility revenue" means revenue derived from a passenger facility charge.

(b) GENERAL AUTHORITY.—(1) Except as provided under subsection (l), the Secretary of Transportation may authorize under this section an eligible agency to impose a passenger facility charge of $1, $2, $3, $4, or $4.50 on each paying passenger of an air carrier or foreign air carrier boarding an aircraft at an airport the agency controls to finance an eligible airport-related project, including making payments for debt service on indebtedness incurred to carry out the project, to be carried out in connection with the airport or any other airport the agency controls.

(2) A State, political subdivision of a State, or authority of a State or political subdivision that is not the eligible agency may not regulate or prohibit the imposition or collection of a passenger facility charge or the use of the passenger facility revenue.

(3) A passenger facility charge may be imposed on a passenger of an air carrier or foreign air carrier originating or connecting at the commercial service airport that the agency controls.

(4) MAXIMUM COST FOR CERTAIN LOW-EMISSION TECHNOLOGY PROJECTS.—The maximum cost that may be financed by imposition of a passenger facility charge under this section for a project described in subsection (a)(3)(G) with respect to a vehicle or ground support equipment may not exceed the incremental amount of the project cost that is greater than the cost of acquiring a vehicle or equipment that is not low-emission and would be used for the same purpose, or the cost of low-emission retrofitting, as determined by the Secretary.

(5) DEBT SERVICE FOR CERTAIN PROJECTS.—In addition to the uses specified in paragraph (1), the Secretary may authorize a passenger facility charge imposed under paragraph (1) to be used for making payments for debt service on indebtedness incurred to carry out at the airport a project that is not an eligible airport-related project if the Secretary determines that such use is necessary due to the financial need of the airport.

(6) NOISE MITIGATION FOR CERTAIN SCHOOLS.—

(A) IN GENERAL.—In addition to the uses specified in paragraphs (1) and (5), the Secretary may authorize a passenger facility charge imposed under paragraph (1) at a large hub airport that is the subject of an amended judgment and final order in condemnation filed on January 7, 1980, by the Superior Court of the State of California for the county of Los Angeles, to be used for a project to carry out noise mitigation for a building, or for the replacement of a relocatable building with a permanent building, in the noise impacted area surrounding the airport at which such building is used primarily for educational purposes, notwithstanding the air easement granted or any terms to the contrary in such judgment and final order, if—

(i) the Secretary determines that the building is adversely affected by airport noise;

(ii) the building is owned or chartered by the school district that was the plaintiff in case number 986,442 or 986,446, which was resolved by such judgment and final order;

(iii) the project is for a school identified in 1 of the settlement agreements effective February 16, 2005, between the airport and each of the school districts;

(iv) in the case of a project to replace a relocatable building with a permanent building, the eligible project costs are limited to the actual structural construction costs necessary to mitigate aircraft noise in instructional classrooms to an interior noise level meeting current standards of the Federal Aviation Administration; and

(v) the project otherwise meets the requirements of this section for authorization of a passenger facility charge.

(B) ELIGIBLE PROJECT COSTS.—In subparagraph (A)(iv), the term "eligible project costs" means the difference between the cost of standard school construction and the cost of construction necessary to mitigate classroom noise to the standards of the Federal Aviation Administration.

(c) APPLICATIONS.—(1) An eligible agency must submit to the Secretary an application for authority to impose a passenger facility charge. The application shall contain information and be in the form that the Secretary may require by regulation.

(2) Before submitting an application, the eligible agency must provide reasonable notice to, and an opportunity for consultation with, air carriers and foreign air carriers operating at the airport. The Secretary shall prescribe regulations that define reasonable notice and contain at least the following requirements:

(A) The agency must provide written notice of individual projects being considered for financing by a passenger facility charge and the date and location of a meeting to present the projects to air carriers and foreign air carriers operating at the airport.

(B) Not later than 30 days after written notice is provided under subparagraph (A) of this paragraph, each air carrier and foreign air carrier operating at the airport must provide to the agency written notice of receipt of the notice. Failure of a carrier to provide the notice may be deemed certification of agreement with the project by the carrier under subparagraph (D) of this paragraph.

(C) Not later than 45 days after written notice is provided under subparagraph (A) of this paragraph, the agency must conduct a meeting to provide air carriers and foreign air carriers with descriptions of projects and justifications and a detailed financial plan for projects.

(D) Not later than 30 days after the meeting, each air carrier and foreign air carrier must provide to the agency certification of agreement or disagreement with projects (or total plan for the projects). Failure to provide the certification is deemed certification of agreement with the project by the carrier. A certification of disagreement is void if it does not contain the reasons for the disagreement.

(E) The agency must include in its application or notice submitted under subparagraph (A) copies of all certifications of agreement or disagreement received under subparagraph (D).

(F) For the purpose of this section, an eligible agency providing notice and an opportunity for consultation to an air carrier or foreign air carrier is deemed to have satisfied the requirements of this paragraph if the eligible agency limits such notices and consultations to air carriers and foreign air carriers that have a significant business interest at the airport. In the subparagraph, the term "significant business interest" means an air carrier or foreign air carrier that had no less than 1.0 percent of passenger boardings at the airport in the prior calendar year, had at least 25,000 passenger boardings at the airport in the prior calendar year, or provides scheduled service at the airport.

(3) Before submitting an application, the eligible agency must provide reasonable notice and an opportunity for public comment. The Secretary shall prescribe regulations that define reasonable notice and provide for at least the following under this paragraph:

(A) A requirement that the eligible agency provide public notice of intent to collect a passenger facility charge so as to inform those interested persons and agencies that may be affected. The public notice may include—

(i) publication in local newspapers of general circulation;

(ii) publication in other local media; and

(iii) posting the notice on the agency's Internet website.

(B) A requirement for submission of public comments no sooner than 30 days, and no later than 45 days, after the date of the publication of the notice.

(C) A requirement that the agency include in its application or notice submitted under subparagraph (A) copies of all comments received under subparagraph (B).

(4) After receiving an application, the Secretary may provide notice and an opportunity to air carriers, foreign air carriers, and other interested persons to comment on the application. The Secretary shall make a final decision on the application not later than 120 days after receiving it.

(d) LIMITATIONS ON APPROVING APPLICATIONS.—The Secretary may approve an application that an eligible agency has submitted under subsection (c) of this section to finance a specific project only if the Secretary finds, based on the application, that—

(1) the amount and duration of the proposed passenger facility charge will result in revenue (including interest and other returns on the revenue) that is not more than the amount necessary to finance the specific project;

(2) each project is an eligible airport-related project that will—

(A) preserve or enhance capacity, safety, or security of the national air transportation system;

(B) reduce noise resulting from an airport that is part of the system; or

(C) provide an opportunity for enhanced competition between or among air carriers and foreign air carriers;

(3) the application includes adequate justification for each of the specific projects; and

(4) in the case of an application to impose a charge of more than $3.00 for an eligible surface transportation or terminal project, the agency has made adequate provision for financing the airside needs of the airport, including runways, taxiways, aprons, and aircraft gates.

(e) LIMITATIONS ON IMPOSING CHARGES.—(1) An eligible agency may impose a passenger facility charge only—

(A) if the Secretary approves an application that the agency has submitted under subsection (c) of this section or a passenger facility charge imposition is authorized under subsection (l); and

(B) subject to reasonable terms the Secretary may prescribe to carry out the objectives of this section.

(2) A passenger facility charge may not be collected from a passenger—

(A) for more than 2 boardings on a one-way trip or a trip in each direction of a round trip;

(B) for the boarding to an eligible place under subchapter II of chapter 417 of this title for which essential air service compensation is paid under subchapter II;

(C) enplaning at an airport if the passenger did not pay for the air transportation which resulted in such enplanement, including any case in which the passenger obtained the ticket for the air transportation with a frequent flier award coupon without monetary payment;

(D) on flights, including flight segments, between 2 or more points in Hawaii;

(E) in Alaska aboard an aircraft having a seating capacity of less than 60 passengers; and

(F) enplaning at an airport if the passenger did not pay for the air transportation which resulted in such enplanement due to charter arrangements and payment by the

Department of Defense.

(f) LIMITATIONS ON CONTRACTS, LEASES, AND USE AGREEMENTS.—(1) A contract between an air carrier or foreign air carrier and an eligible agency made at any time may not impair the authority of the agency to impose a passenger facility charge or to use the passenger facility revenue as provided in this section.

(2) A project financed with a passenger facility charge may not be subject to an exclusive long-term lease or use agreement of an air carrier or foreign air carrier, as defined by regulations of the Secretary.

(3) A lease or use agreement of an air carrier or foreign air carrier related to a project whose construction or expansion was financed with a passenger facility charge may not restrict the eligible agency from financing, developing, or assigning new capacity at the airport with passenger facility revenue.

(g) TREATMENT OF REVENUE.—(1) Passenger facility revenue is not airport revenue for purposes of establishing a price under a contract between an eligible agency and an air carrier or foreign air carrier.

(2) An eligible agency may not include in its price base the part of the capital costs of a project paid for by using passenger facility revenue to establish a price under a contract between the agency and an air carrier or foreign air carrier.

(3) For a project for terminal development, gates and related areas, or a facility occupied or used by at least one air carrier or foreign air carrier on an exclusive or preferential basis, a price payable by an air carrier or foreign air carrier using the facilities must at least equal the price paid by an air carrier or foreign air carrier using a similar facility at the airport that was not financed with passenger facility revenue.

(4) Passenger facility revenues that are held by an air carrier or an agent of the carrier after collection of a passenger facility charge constitute a trust fund that is held by the air carrier or agent for the beneficial interest of the eligible agency imposing the charge. Such carrier or agent holds neither legal nor equitable interest in the passenger facility revenues except for any handling fee or retention of interest collected on unremitted proceeds as may be allowed by the Secretary.

(h) COMPLIANCE.—(1) As necessary to ensure compliance with this section, the Secretary shall prescribe regulations requiring recordkeeping and auditing of accounts maintained by an air carrier or foreign air carrier and its agent collecting a passenger facility charge and by the eligible agency imposing the charge.

(2) The Secretary periodically shall audit and review the use by an eligible agency of passenger facility revenue. After review and a public hearing, the Secretary may end any part of the authority of the agency to impose a passenger facility charge to the extent the Secretary decides that the revenue is not being used as provided in this section.

(3) The Secretary may set off amounts necessary to ensure compliance with this section against amounts otherwise payable to an eligible agency under subchapter I of chapter 471 of this title if the Secretary decides a passenger facility charge is excessive or that passenger facility revenue is not being used as provided in this section.

(i) REGULATIONS.—The Secretary shall prescribe regulations necessary to carry out this section. The regulations—

 (1) may prescribe the time and form by which a passenger facility charge takes effect;

 (2) shall—

(A) require an air carrier or foreign air carrier and its agent to collect a passenger facility charge that an eligible agency imposes under this section;

(B) establish procedures for handling and remitting money collected;

(C) ensure that the money, less a uniform amount the Secretary determines reflects the average necessary and reasonable expenses (net of interest accruing to the carrier and agent after collection and before remittance) incurred in collecting and handling the charge, is paid promptly to the eligible agency for which they are collected; and

(D) require that the amount collected for any air transportation be noted on the ticket for that air transportation; and

(3) may permit an eligible agency to request that collection of a passenger facility charge be waived for—

(A) passengers enplaned by any class of air carrier or foreign air carrier if the number of passengers enplaned by the carriers in the class constitutes not more than one percent of the total number of passengers enplaned annually at the airport at which the charge is imposed; or

(B) passengers enplaned on a flight to an airport—

(i) that has fewer than 2,500 passenger boardings each year and receives scheduled passenger service; or

(ii) in a community which has a population of less than 10,000 and is not connected by a land highway or vehicular way to the land-connected National Highway System within a State.

(j) Limitation on Certain Actions.—A State, political subdivision of a State, or authority of a State or political subdivision that is not the eligible agency may not tax, regulate, or prohibit or otherwise attempt to control in any manner, the imposition or collection of a passenger facility charge or the use of the revenue from the passenger facility charge.

(k) Competition Plans.—

(1) In general.—Beginning in fiscal year 2001, no eligible agency may impose a passenger facility charge under this section with respect to a covered airport (as such term is defined in section 47106(f)) unless the agency has submitted to the Secretary a written competition plan in accordance with such section. This subsection does not apply to passenger facility charges in effect before the date of the enactment of this subsection.

(2) Secretary shall ensure implementation and compliance.—The Secretary shall review any plan submitted under paragraph (1) to ensure that it meets the requirements of this section, and shall review its implementation from time-to-time to ensure that each covered airport successfully implements its plan.

(l) Passenger Facility Charge Streamlining.—

(1) In general.—

(A) Regulations.—The Secretary shall prescribe regulations to streamline the process for authorizing eligible agencies for airports to impose passenger facility charges.

(B) Passenger facility charge.—An eligible agency may impose a passenger facility charge of $1, $2, $3, $4, or $4.50 in accordance with the provisions of this subsection instead of using the procedures otherwise provided in this section.

(2) Notice and opportunity for consultation.—The eligible agency must provide

reasonable notice and an opportunity for consultation to air carriers and foreign air carriers in accordance with subsection (c)(2) and must provide reasonable notice and opportunity for public comment in accordance with subsection (c)(3).

(3) NOTICE OF INTENTION.—The eligible agency must submit to the Secretary a notice of intention to impose a passenger facility charge under this subsection. The notice shall include—

(A) information that the Secretary may require by regulation on each project for which authority to impose a passenger facility charge is sought;

(B) the amount of revenue from passenger facility charges that is proposed to be collected for each project; and

(C) the level of the passenger facility charge that is proposed.

(4) ACKNOWLEDGMENT OF RECEIPT AND INDICATION OF OBJECTION.—

(A) IN GENERAL.—The Secretary shall acknowledge receipt of the notice and indicate any objection to the imposition of a passenger facility charge under this subsection for any project identified in the notice within 60 days after receipt of the eligible agency's notice.

(B) PROHIBITED OBJECTION.—The Secretary may not object to an eligible airport-related project that received Federal financial assistance for airport development, terminal development, airport planning, or for the purposes of noise compatibility, if the Federal financial assistance and passenger facility charge collection (including interest and other returns on the revenue) do not exceed the total cost of the project.

(C) ALLOWED OBJECTION.—The Secretary may only object to the imposition of a passenger facility charge under this subsection for a project that—

(i) establishes significant policy precedent;

(ii) raises significant legal issues;

(iii) garners significant controversy, as evidenced by significant opposition to the proposed action by the applicant or other airport authorities, airport users, governmental agencies, elected officials, or communities;

(iv) raises significant revenue diversion, airport noise, or access issues, including compliance with section 47111(e) or subchapter II of chapter 475;

(v) includes multimodal components; or

(vi) serves no aeronautical purpose.

(5) AUTHORITY TO IMPOSE CHARGE.—Unless the Secretary objects within 30 days after receipt of the eligible agency's notice, the eligible agency is authorized to impose a passenger facility charge in accordance with the terms of its notice under this subsection.

(6) ACKNOWLEDGEMENT NOT AN ORDER.—An acknowledgement issued under paragraph (4) shall not be considered an order issued by the Secretary for purposes of section 46110.

(m) FINANCIAL MANAGEMENT OF CHARGES.—

(1) HANDLING OF CHARGES.—A covered air carrier shall segregate in a separate account passenger facility revenue equal to the average monthly liability for charges collected under this section by such carrier or any of its agents for the benefit of the eligible agencies entitled to such revenue.

(2) TRUST FUND STATUS.—If a covered air carrier or its agent fails to segregate passenger facility revenue in violation of the subsection, the trust fund status of such

revenue shall not be defeated by an inability of any party to identify and trace the precise funds in the accounts of the air carrier.

(3) PROHIBITION.—A covered air carrier and its agents may not grant to any third party any security or other interest in passenger facility revenue.

(4) COMPENSATION TO ELIGIBLE ENTITIES.—A covered air carrier that fails to comply with any requirement of this subsection, or otherwise unnecessarily causes an eligible entity to expend funds, through litigation or otherwise, to recover or retain payment of passenger facility revenue to which the eligible entity is otherwise entitled shall be required to compensate the eligible agency for the costs so incurred.

(5) INTEREST ON AMOUNTS.—A covered air carrier that collects passenger facility charges is entitled to receive the interest on passenger facility charge accounts if the accounts are established and maintained in compliance with this subsection.

(6) EXISTING REGULATIONS.—The provisions of section 158.49 of title 14, Code of Federal Regulations, that permit the commingling of passenger facility charges with other air carrier revenue shall not apply to a covered air carrier.

(7) COVERED AIR CARRIER DEFINED.—In this section, the term "covered air carrier" means an air carrier that files for chapter 7 or chapter 11 of title 11 bankruptcy protection, or has an involuntary chapter 7 of title 11 bankruptcy proceeding commenced against it, after the date of enactment of this subsection.

(n) USE OF REVENUES AT PREVIOUSLY ASSOCIATED AIRPORT.—Notwithstanding the requirements relating to airport control under subsection (b)(1), the Secretary may authorize use of a passenger facility charge under subsection (b) to finance an eligible airport-related project if—

(1) the eligible agency seeking to impose the new charge controls an airport where a $2.00 passenger facility charge became effective on January 1, 2013; and

(2) the location of the project to be financed by the new charge is at an airport that was under the control of the same eligible agency that had controlled the airport described in paragraph (1).

(Pub. L. 103–272, §1(e), July 5, 1994, 108 Stat. 1113; Pub. L. 103–305, title II, §§203, 204(a)(1), (b), Aug. 23, 1994, 108 Stat. 1582, 1583; Pub. L. 104–264, title I, §142(b)(2), title XII, §1202, Oct. 9, 1996, 110 Stat. 3221, 3280; Pub. L. 104–287, §5(67), Oct. 11, 1996, 110 Stat. 3395; Pub. L. 106–181, title I, §§105(a), (b), 135(a), (b), 151, 152(a), 155(c), Apr. 5, 2000, 114 Stat. 71, 83, 86–88; Pub. L. 108–176, title I, §§121(a)–(c), 122–123(d), 124, Dec. 12, 2003, 117 Stat. 2499–2502; Pub. L. 110–253, §3(c)(1), June 30, 2008, 122 Stat. 2417; Pub. L. 110–330, §5(a), Sept. 30, 2008, 122 Stat. 3718; Pub. L. 110–337, §1, Oct. 2, 2008, 122 Stat. 3729; Pub. L. 111–12, §5(a), Mar. 30, 2009, 123 Stat. 1458; Pub. L. 111–69, §5(a), Oct. 1, 2009, 123 Stat. 2055; Pub. L. 111–116, §5(a), Dec. 16, 2009, 123 Stat. 3032; Pub. L. 111–153, §5(a), Mar. 31, 2010, 124 Stat. 1085; Pub. L. 111–161, §5(a), Apr. 30, 2010, 124 Stat. 1127; Pub. L. 111–197, §5(a), July 2, 2010, 124 Stat. 1354; Pub. L. 111–216, title I, §104(a), Aug. 1, 2010, 124 Stat. 2349; Pub. L. 111–249, §5(a), Sept. 30, 2010, 124 Stat. 2628; Pub. L. 111–329, §5(a), Dec. 22, 2010, 124 Stat. 3567; Pub. L. 112–7, §5(a), Mar. 31, 2011, 125 Stat. 32; Pub. L. 112–16, §5(a), May 31, 2011, 125 Stat. 219; Pub. L. 112–21, §5(a), June 29, 2011, 125 Stat. 234; Pub. L. 112–27, §5(a), Aug. 5, 2011, 125 Stat. 271; Pub. L. 112–30, title II, §205(a), Sept. 16, 2011, 125 Stat. 358; Pub. L. 112–91, §5(a), Jan. 31, 2012, 126 Stat. 4; Pub. L. 112–95, title I, §§111(a)–(c)(1), 152(e)(1), Feb. 14, 2012, 126 Stat. 17, 18, 34; Pub. L. 114–190, title II, §2302, July 15, 2016, 130 Stat. 638; Pub. L. 115–254, div. B, title I, §121, div. B, title V, §539(b), Oct. 5, 2018, 132 Stat. 3201, 3370; Pub. L. 118–63, title VII, §§775, 776(a), May 16, 2024, 138 Stat. 1300.)

§40118. GOVERNMENT-FINANCED AIR TRANSPORTATION

(a) TRANSPORTATION BY AIR CARRIERS HOLDING CERTIFICATES.—A department, agency, or instrumentality of the United States Government shall take necessary steps to ensure that the transportation of passengers and property by air is provided by an air carrier holding a certificate under section 41102 of this title if—

(1) the department, agency, or instrumentality—

(A) obtains the transportation for itself or in carrying out an arrangement under which payment is made by the Government or payment is made from amounts provided for the use of the Government; or

(B) provides the transportation to or for a foreign country or international or other organization without reimbursement;

(2) the transportation is authorized by the certificate or by regulation or exemption of the Secretary of Transportation; and

(3) the air carrier is—

(A) available, if the transportation is between a place in the United States and a place outside the United States; or

(B) reasonably available, if the transportation is between 2 places outside the United States.

(b) TRANSPORTATION BY FOREIGN AIR CARRIERS.—This section does not preclude the transportation of passengers and property by a foreign air carrier if the transportation is provided under a bilateral or multilateral air transportation agreement to which the Government and the government of a foreign country are parties if the agreement—

(1) is consistent with the goals for international aviation policy of section 40101(e) of this title; and

(2) provides for the exchange of rights or benefits of similar magnitude.

(c) PROOF.—The Administrator of General Services shall prescribe regulations under which agencies may allow the expenditure of an appropriation for transportation in violation of this section only when satisfactory proof is presented showing the necessity for the transportation.

(d) CERTAIN TRANSPORTATION BY AIR OUTSIDE THE UNITED STATES.—Notwithstanding subsections (a) and (c) of this section, any amount appropriated to the Secretary of State or the Administrator of the Agency for International Development may be used to pay for the transportation of an officer or employee of the Department of State or one of those agencies, a dependent of the officer or employee, and accompanying baggage, by a foreign air carrier when the transportation is between 2 places outside the United States.

(e) RELATIONSHIP TO OTHER LAWS.—This section does not affect the application of the antidiscrimination provisions of this part.

(f) PROHIBITION OF CERTIFICATION OR CONTRACT CLAUSE.—(1) No certification by a contractor, and no contract clause, may be required in the case of a contract for the transportation of commercial products in order to implement a requirement in this section.

(2) In paragraph (1), the term "commercial product" has the meaning given such term in section 103 of title 41, except that it shall not include a contract for the transportation by air of passengers.

(g) TRAINING REQUIREMENTS.—The Administrator of General Services shall ensure that any contract entered into for provision of air transportation with a domestic carrier under this section requires that the contracting air carrier submits to the Administrator of General Services, the Secretary of Transportation, the Administrator of the Transportation Security Administration, the Secretary of Labor and the Commissioner of U.S. Customs and Border Protection an annual report regarding—

    (1) the number of personnel trained in the detection and reporting of potential severe forms of trafficking in persons and sex trafficking (as such terms are defined in paragraphs (11) and (12) of section 103 of the Trafficking Victims Protection Act of 2000 (22 U.S.C. 7102)), including the training required under section 44734(a)(4);

    (2) the number of notifications of potential human trafficking victims received from staff or other passengers; and

    (3) whether the air carrier notified the National Human Trafficking Hotline or law enforcement at the relevant airport of the potential human trafficking victim for each such notification of potential human trafficking, and if so, when the notification was made.

(Pub. L. 103–272, §1(e), July 5, 1994, 108 Stat. 1116; Pub. L. 103–355, title VIII, §8301(h), Oct. 13, 1994, 108 Stat. 3398; Pub. L. 104–287, §5(68), Oct. 11, 1996, 110 Stat. 3395; Pub. L. 104–316, title I, §127(d), Oct. 19, 1996, 110 Stat. 3840; Pub. L. 105–277, div. G, subdiv. A, title XII, §1225(h), title XIII, §1335(p), title XIV, §1422(b)(6), Oct. 21, 1998, 112 Stat. 2681–775, 2681–789, 2681–793; Pub. L. 108–176, title VIII, §806, Dec. 12, 2003, 117 Stat. 2588; Pub. L. 111–350, §5(o)(8), Jan. 4, 2011, 124 Stat. 3854; Pub. L. 115–232, div. A, title VIII, §836(g)(9), Aug. 13, 2018, 132 Stat. 1874; Pub. L. 115–425, title I, §111(a), Jan. 8, 2019, 132 Stat. 5475; Pub. L. 118–63, title XI, §1101(g), May 16, 2024, 138 Stat. 1413.)

§40119. SENSITIVE SECURITY INFORMATION

(a) DISCLOSURE.—

    (1) REGULATIONS PROHIBITING DISCLOSURE.—Notwithstanding the establishment of a Department of Homeland Security, the Secretary of Transportation, in accordance with section 552(b)(3)(B) of title 5, shall prescribe regulations prohibiting disclosure of information obtained or developed in ensuring security under this title if the Secretary of Transportation decides disclosing the information would—

      (A) be an unwarranted invasion of personal privacy;

      (B) reveal a trade secret or privileged or confidential commercial or financial information; or

      (C) be detrimental to transportation safety.

    (2) DISCLOSURE TO CONGRESS.—Paragraph (1) shall not be construed to authorize information to be withheld from a committee of Congress authorized to have such information.

    (3) RULE OF CONSTRUCTION.—Nothing in paragraph (1) shall be construed to authorize the designation of information as sensitive security information (as such term is defined in section 15.5 of title 49, Code of Federal Regulations) to—

      (A) conceal a violation of law, inefficiency, or administrative error;

      (B) prevent embarrassment to a person, organization, or agency;

      (C) restrain competition; or

      (D) prevent or delay the release of information that does not require protection in the interest of transportation security, including basic scientific research information not clearly related to transportation security.

    (4) LAW ENFORCEMENT DISCLOSURE.—Section 552a of title 5 shall not apply to

disclosures that the Administrator may make from the systems of records of the Federal Aviation Administration to any Federal law enforcement, intelligence, protective service, immigration, or national security official in order to assist the official receiving the information in the performance of official duties.

(b) TRANSFERS OF DUTIES AND POWERS PROHIBITED.—Except as otherwise provided by law, a duty or power under this section may not be transferred to another department, agency, or instrumentality of the Federal Government.

(Added Pub. L. 118–63, title II, §223(a), May 16, 2024, 138 Stat. 1060.)

§40120. RELATIONSHIP TO OTHER LAWS

(a) NONAPPLICATION.—Except as provided in the International Navigational Rules Act of 1977 (33 U.S.C. 1601 et seq.), the navigation and shipping laws of the United States and the rules for the prevention of collisions do not apply to aircraft or to the navigation of vessels related to those aircraft.

(b) EXTENDING APPLICATION OUTSIDE UNITED STATES.—The President may extend (in the way and for periods the President considers necessary) the application of this part to outside the United States when—

(1) an international arrangement gives the United States Government authority to make the extension; and

(2) the President decides the extension is in the national interest.

(c) ADDITIONAL REMEDIES.—A remedy under this part is in addition to any other remedies provided by law.

(Pub. L. 103–272, §1(e), July 5, 1994, 108 Stat. 1117.)

§40121. AIR TRAFFIC CONTROL MODERNIZATION REVIEWS

(a) REQUIRED TERMINATIONS OF ACQUISITIONS.—The Administrator of the Federal Aviation Administration shall terminate any acquisition program initiated after the date of the enactment of the Air Traffic Management System Performance Improvement Act of 1996 and funded under the Facilities and Equipment account that—

(1) is more than 50 percent over the cost goal established for the program;

(2) fails to achieve at least 50 percent of the performance goals established for the program; or

(3) is more than 50 percent behind schedule as determined in accordance with the schedule goal established for the program.

(b) AUTHORIZED TERMINATION OF ACQUISITION PROGRAMS.—The Administrator shall consider terminating, under the authority of subsection (a), any substantial acquisition program that—

(1) is more than 10 percent over the cost goal established for the program;

(2) fails to achieve at least 90 percent of the performance goals established for the program; or

(3) is more than 10 percent behind schedule as determined in accordance with the schedule goal established for the program.

(c) EXCEPTIONS AND REPORT.—

(1) CONTINUANCE OF PROGRAM, ETC.—Notwithstanding subsection (a), the

Administrator may continue an acquisitions program required to be terminated under subsection (a) if the Administrator determines that termination would be inconsistent with the development or operation of the national air transportation system in a safe and efficient manner.

(2) DEPARTMENT OF DEFENSE.—The Department of Defense shall have the same exemptions from acquisition laws as are waived by the Administrator under section 40110(d)(2) of this title when engaged in joint actions to improve or replenish the national air traffic control system. The Administration may acquire real property, goods, and services through the Department of Defense, or other appropriate agencies, but is bound by the acquisition laws and regulations governing those cases.

(3) REPORT.—If the Administrator makes a determination under paragraph (1), the Administrator shall transmit a copy of the determination, together with a statement of the basis for the determination, to the Committees on Appropriations of the Senate and the House of Representatives, the Committee on Commerce, Science, and Transportation of the Senate, and the Committee on Transportation and Infrastructure of the House of Representatives.

(Added Pub. L. 104–264, title II, §252, Oct. 9, 1996, 110 Stat. 3236; amended Pub. L. 106–181, title III, §307(c)(2), Apr. 5, 2000, 114 Stat. 126.)

§40122. FEDERAL AVIATION ADMINISTRATION PERSONNEL MANAGEMENT SYSTEM

(a) IN GENERAL.—

(1) CONSULTATION AND NEGOTIATION.—In developing and making changes to the personnel management system initially implemented by the Administrator of the Federal Aviation Administration on April 1, 1996, the Administrator shall negotiate with the exclusive bargaining representatives of employees of the Administration certified under section 7111 of title 5 and consult with other employees of the Administration.

(2) DISPUTE RESOLUTION.—

(A) MEDIATION.—If the Administrator does not reach an agreement under paragraph (1) or the provisions referred to in subsection (g)(2)(C) with the exclusive bargaining representative of the employees, the Administrator and the bargaining representative—

(i) shall use the services of the Federal Mediation and Conciliation Service to attempt to reach such agreement in accordance with part 1425 of title 29, Code of Federal Regulations (as in effect on the date of enactment of the FAA Modernization and Reform Act of 2012); or

(ii) may by mutual agreement adopt alternative procedures for the resolution of disputes or impasses arising in the negotiation of the collective-bargaining agreement.

(B) MID-TERM BARGAINING.—If the services of the Federal Mediation and Conciliation Service under subparagraph (A)(i) do not lead to the resolution of issues in controversy arising from the negotiation of a mid-term collective-bargaining agreement, the Federal Service Impasses Panel shall assist the parties in resolving the impasse in accordance with section 7119 of title 5.

(C) BINDING ARBITRATION FOR TERM BARGAINING.—

(i) ASSISTANCE FROM FEDERAL SERVICE IMPASSES PANEL.—If the services of the Federal Mediation and Conciliation Service under subparagraph (A)(i) do not lead to the resolution of issues in controversy arising from the negotiation of a term collective-bargaining agreement, the Administrator and the exclusive bargaining representative of the employees (in this subparagraph referred to as the "parties") shall submit their issues in controversy to the Federal Service Impasses Panel. The Panel shall assist the parties in resolving the impasse by asserting jurisdiction and ordering binding arbitration by a private arbitration board consisting of 3 members.

(ii) APPOINTMENT OF ARBITRATION BOARD.—The Executive Director of the Panel shall provide for the appointment of the 3 members of a private arbitration board under clause (i) by requesting the Director of the Federal Mediation and Conciliation Service to prepare a list of not less than 15 names of arbitrators with Federal sector experience and by providing the list to the parties. Not later than 10 days after receiving the list, the parties shall each select one person from the list. The 2 arbitrators selected by the parties shall then select a third person from the list not later than 7 days after being selected. If either of the parties fails to select a person or if the 2 arbitrators are unable to agree on the third person in 7 days, the parties shall make the selection by alternately striking names on the list until one arbitrator remains.

(iii) FRAMING ISSUES IN CONTROVERSY.—If the parties do not agree on the framing of the issues to be submitted for arbitration, the arbitration board shall frame the issues.

(iv) HEARINGS.—The arbitration board shall give the parties a full and fair hearing, including an opportunity to present evidence in support of their claims and an opportunity to present their case in person, by counsel, or by other representative as they may elect.

(v) DECISIONS.—The arbitration board shall render its decision within 90 days after the date of its appointment. Decisions of the arbitration board shall be conclusive and binding upon the parties.

(vi) MATTERS FOR CONSIDERATION.—The arbitration board shall take into consideration such factors as—

(I) the effect of its arbitration decisions on the Federal Aviation Administration's ability to attract and retain a qualified workforce;

(II) the effect of its arbitration decisions on the Federal Aviation Administration's budget; and

(III) any other factors whose consideration would assist the board in fashioning a fair and equitable award.

(vii) COSTS.—The parties shall share costs of the arbitration equally.

(3) RATIFICATION OF AGREEMENTS.—Upon reaching a voluntary agreement or at the conclusion of the binding arbitration under paragraph (2)(C), the final agreement, except for those matters decided by an arbitration board, shall be subject to ratification by the exclusive bargaining representative of the employees, if so requested by the bargaining representative, and the final agreement shall be subject to approval by the head of the agency in accordance with the provisions referred to in subsection (g)(2)(C).

(4) COST SAVINGS AND PRODUCTIVITY GOALS.—The Administration and the exclusive

bargaining representatives of the employees shall use every reasonable effort to find cost savings and to increase productivity within each of the affected bargaining units.

(5) ANNUAL BUDGET DISCUSSIONS.—The Administration and the exclusive bargaining representatives of the employees shall meet annually for the purpose of finding additional cost savings within the Administration's annual budget as it applies to each of the affected bargaining units and throughout the agency.

(b) EXPERT EVALUATION.—On the date that is 3 years after the personnel management system is implemented, the Administration shall employ outside experts to provide an independent evaluation of the effectiveness of the system within 3 months after such date. For this purpose, the Administrator may utilize the services of experts and consultants under section 3109 of title 5 without regard to the limitation imposed by the last sentence of section 3109(b) of such title, and may contract on a sole source basis, notwithstanding any other provision of law to the contrary.

(c) PAY RESTRICTION.—No officer or employee of the Administration may receive an annual rate of basic pay in excess of the annual rate of basic pay payable to the Administrator.

(d) ETHICS.—The Administration shall be subject to Executive Order No. 12674 and regulations and opinions promulgated by the Office of Government Ethics, including those set forth in section 2635 of title 5 of the Code of Federal Regulations.

(e) EMPLOYEE PROTECTIONS.—Until July 1, 1999, basic wages (including locality pay) and operational differential pay provided employees of the Administration shall not be involuntarily adversely affected by reason of the enactment of this section, except for unacceptable performance or by reason of a reduction in force or reorganization or by agreement between the Administration and the affected employees' exclusive bargaining representative.

(f) LABOR-MANAGEMENT AGREEMENTS.—Except as otherwise provided by this title, all labor-management agreements covering employees of the Administration that are in effect on the effective date of the Air Traffic Management System Performance Improvement Act of 1996 shall remain in effect until their normal expiration date, unless the Administrator and the exclusive bargaining representative agree to the contrary.

(g) PERSONNEL MANAGEMENT SYSTEM.—

(1) IN GENERAL.—In consultation with the employees of the Administration and such non-governmental experts in personnel management systems as he may employ, and notwithstanding the provisions of title 5 and other Federal personnel laws, the Administrator shall develop and implement, not later than January 1, 1996, a personnel management system for the Administration that addresses the unique demands on the agency's workforce. Such a new system shall, at a minimum, provide for greater flexibility in the hiring, training, compensation, and location of personnel.

(2) APPLICABILITY OF TITLE 5.—The provisions of title 5 shall not apply to the new personnel management system developed and implemented pursuant to paragraph (1), with the exception of—

(A) section 2302(b), relating to whistleblower protection, including the provisions for investigation and enforcement as provided in chapter 12 of title 5;

(B) sections 3304(f), to the extent consistent with the Federal Aviation Administration's status as an excepted service agency, 3308–3320, 3330a, 3330b,

3330c, and 3330d, relating to veterans' preference;

(C) chapter 71, relating to labor-management relations;

(D) section 7204, relating to antidiscrimination;

(E) chapter 73, relating to suitability, security, and conduct;

(F) chapter 81, relating to compensation for work injury;

(G) chapters 83–85, 87, and 89, relating to retirement, unemployment compensation, and insurance coverage;

(H) sections 1204, 1211–1218, 1221, and 7701–7703, relating to the Merit Systems Protection Board;

(I) subsections (b), (c), and (d) of section 4507 (relating to Meritorious Executive or Distinguished Executive rank awards) and subsections (b) and (c) of section 4507a (relating to Meritorious Senior Professional or Distinguished Senior Professional rank awards), except that—

(i) for purposes of applying such provisions to the personnel management system—

(I) the term "agency" means the Department of Transportation;

(II) the term "senior executive" means a Federal Aviation Administration executive;

(III) the term "career appointee" means a Federal Aviation Administration career executive; and

(IV) the term "senior career employee" means a Federal Aviation Administration career senior professional;

(ii) receipt by a career appointee or a senior career employee of the rank of Meritorious Executive or Meritorious Senior Professional entitles the individual to a lump-sum payment of an amount equal to 20 percent of annual basic pay, which shall be in addition to the basic pay paid under the Federal Aviation Administration Executive Compensation Plan; and

(iii) receipt by a career appointee or a senior career employee of the rank of Distinguished Executive or Distinguished Senior Professional entitles the individual to a lump-sum payment of an amount equal to 35 percent of annual basic pay, which shall be in addition to the basic pay paid under the Federal Aviation Administration Executive Compensation Plan; and

(J) subject to paragraph (4) of this subsection, section 6329, relating to disabled veteran leave.

(3) APPEALS TO MERIT SYSTEMS PROTECTION BOARD.—Under the new personnel management system developed and implemented under paragraph (1), an employee of the Administration may submit an appeal to the Merit Systems Protection Board and may seek judicial review of any resulting final orders or decisions of the Board from any action that was appealable to the Board under any law, rule, or regulation as of March 31, 1996. Notwithstanding any other provision of law, retroactive to April 1, 1996, the Board shall have the same remedial authority over such employee appeals that it had as of March 31, 1996.

(4) CERTIFICATION OF DISABLED VETERAN LEAVE.—In order to verify that leave credited to an employee pursuant to paragraph (2)(J) is used for treating a service-connected disability, that employee shall, notwithstanding section 6329(c) of title 5, submit to

the Assistant Administrator for Human Resource Management of the Federal Aviation Administration certification, in such form and manner as the Administrator of the Federal Aviation Administration may prescribe, that the employee used that leave for purposes of being furnished treatment for that disability by a health care provider.

(5) PAID PARENTAL LEAVE.—The Administrator shall implement a paid parental leave benefit for employees of the Administration that is, at a minimum, consistent with the paid parental leave benefits provided under section 6382 of title 5.

(6) EFFECTIVE DATE.—This subsection shall take effect on April 1, 1996.

(7) REMOTE POSITIONS.—

(A) IN GENERAL.—If the Administrator determines that a covered position has not been filled after multiple vacancy announcements and that there are unique circumstances affecting the ability of the Administrator to fill such position, the Administrator may consider, in consultation with the appropriate labor union, applicants for the covered position who apply under a vacancy announcement recruiting from the State or territory in which the position is based.

(B) COVERED POSITION DEFINED.—In this paragraph, the term "covered position" means a safety-critical position, to include personnel located at contract towers, based in Alaska, Hawaii, Puerto Rico, American Samoa, Guam, the Northern Mariana Islands, and the Virgin Islands.

(h) RIGHT TO CONTEST ADVERSE PERSONNEL ACTIONS.—An employee of the Federal Aviation Administration who is the subject of a major adverse personnel action may contest the action either through any contractual grievance procedure that is applicable to the employee as a member of the collective bargaining unit or through the Administration's internal process relating to review of major adverse personnel actions of the Administration, known as Guaranteed Fair Treatment, or under section 40122(g)(3).

(i) ELECTION OF FORUM.—Where a major adverse personnel action may be contested through more than one of the indicated forums (such as the contractual grievance procedure, the Federal Aviation Administration's internal process, or that of the Merit Systems Protection Board), an employee must elect the forum through which the matter will be contested. Nothing in this section is intended to allow an employee to contest an action through more than one forum unless otherwise allowed by law.

(j) DEFINITION.—In this section, the term "major adverse personnel action" means a suspension of more than 14 days, a reduction in pay or grade, a removal for conduct or performance, a nondisciplinary removal, a furlough of 30 days or less (but not including placement in a nonpay status as the result of a lapse of appropriations or an enactment by Congress), or a reduction in force action.

(Added Pub. L. 104–264, title II, §253, Oct. 9, 1996, 110 Stat. 3237; amended Pub. L. 106–181, title III, §§307(a), 308, Apr. 5, 2000, 114 Stat. 124, 126; Pub. L. 112–95, title VI, §§601, 602, 611, Feb. 14, 2012, 126 Stat. 109, 111, 117; Pub. L. 114–242, §2(a), (b), Oct. 7, 2016, 130 Stat. 978; Pub. L. 115–254, div. B, title V, §531, Oct. 5, 2018, 132 Stat. 3366; Pub. L. 116–283, div. A, title XI, §1103(c)(1), Jan. 1, 2021, 134 Stat. 3887; Pub. L. 118–63, title III, §342(b), May 16, 2024, 138 Stat. 1099.)

§40123. PROTECTION OF VOLUNTARILY SUBMITTED INFORMATION

(a) IN GENERAL.—Notwithstanding any other provision of law, including section 552(b)(3)(B) of title 5, neither the Administrator of the Federal Aviation Administration, nor any agency or third party receiving information from the Administrator, shall disclose voluntarily-provided safety or security related information if the Administrator finds that—

(1) the disclosure of the information would inhibit the voluntary provision of that type of information and that the receipt of that type of information aids in fulfilling the Administrator's safety and security responsibilities; and

(2) withholding such information from disclosure would be consistent with the Administrator's safety and security responsibilities.

(b) REGULATIONS.—The Administrator shall issue regulations to carry out this section.

(Added Pub. L. 104–264, title IV, §402(a), Oct. 9, 1996, 110 Stat. 3255; amended Pub. L. 118–63, title III, §354(a), May 16, 2024, 138 Stat. 1113.)

§40124. INTERSTATE AGREEMENTS FOR AIRPORT FACILITIES

Congress consents to a State making an agreement, not in conflict with a law of the United States, with another State to develop or operate an airport facility.

(Added Pub. L. 104–287, §5(69)(A), Oct. 11, 1996, 110 Stat. 3395, §40121; renumbered §40124, Pub. L. 105–102, §3(d)(1)(B), Nov. 20, 1997, 111 Stat. 2215.)

§40125. QUALIFICATIONS FOR PUBLIC AIRCRAFT STATUS

(a) DEFINITIONS.—In this section, the following definitions apply:

(1) COMMERCIAL PURPOSES.—The term "commercial purposes" means the transportation of persons or property for compensation or hire, but does not include the operation of an aircraft by the armed forces for reimbursement when that reimbursement is required by any Federal statute, regulation, or directive, in effect on November 1, 1999, or by one government on behalf of another government under a cost reimbursement agreement if the government on whose behalf the operation is conducted certifies to the Administrator of the Federal Aviation Administration that the operation is necessary to respond to a significant and imminent threat to life or property (including natural resources) and that no service by a private operator is reasonably available to meet the threat.

(2) GOVERNMENTAL FUNCTION.—The term "governmental function" means an activity undertaken by a government, such as national defense, intelligence missions, firefighting, search and rescue, law enforcement (including transport of prisoners, detainees, and illegal aliens), aeronautical research, biological or geological resource management (including data collection on civil aviation systems undergoing research, development, test, or evaluation at a test range (as such term is defined in section 44801)), infrastructure inspections, or any other activity undertaken by a governmental entity that the Administrator determines is inherently governmental.

(3) QUALIFIED NON-CREWMEMBER.—The term "qualified non-crewmember" means an individual, other than a member of the crew, aboard an aircraft—

(A) operated by the armed forces or an intelligence agency of the United States Government; or

(B) whose presence is required to perform, or is associated with the performance of, a governmental function.

(4) ARMED FORCES.—The term "armed forces" has the meaning given such term by section 101 of title 10.

(b) AIRCRAFT OWNED BY GOVERNMENTS.—An aircraft described in subparagraph (A), (B), (C), (D), or (F) of section 40102(a)(41) does not qualify as a public aircraft under such section when the aircraft is used for commercial purposes or to carry an individual other than a crewmember or a qualified non-crewmember.

(c) AIRCRAFT OWNED OR OPERATED BY THE ARMED FORCES.—

(1) IN GENERAL.—Subject to paragraph (2), an aircraft described in section 40102(a)(41)(E) qualifies as a public aircraft if—

(A) the aircraft is operated in accordance with title 10;

(B) the aircraft is operated in the performance of a governmental function under title 14, 31, 32, or 50 and the aircraft is not used for commercial purposes; or

(C) the aircraft is chartered to provide transportation or other commercial air service to the armed forces and the Secretary of Defense (or the Secretary of the department in which the Coast Guard is operating) designates the operation of the aircraft as being required in the national interest.

(2) LIMITATION.—An aircraft that meets the criteria set forth in paragraph (1) and that is owned or operated by the National Guard of a State, the District of Columbia, or any territory or possession of the United States, qualifies as a public aircraft only to the extent that it is operated under the direct control of the Department of Defense.

(d) SEARCH AND RESCUE PURPOSES.—An aircraft described in section 40102(a)(41)(D) that is not exclusively leased for at least 90 continuous days by the government of a State, the District of Columbia, or a territory or possession of the United States or a political subdivision of 1 of those governments, qualifies as a public aircraft if the Administrator determines that—

(1) there are extraordinary circumstances;

(2) the aircraft will be used for the performance of search and rescue missions;

(3) a community would not otherwise have access to search and rescue services; and

(4) a government entity demonstrates that granting the waiver is necessary to prevent an undue economic burden on that government.

(Added Pub. L. 106–181, title VII, §702(b)(1), Apr. 5, 2000, 114 Stat. 155; amended Pub. L. 110–181, div. A, title X, §1078(b), (c), Jan. 28, 2008, 122 Stat. 334; Pub. L. 112–141, div. C, title V, §35003, July 6, 2012, 126 Stat. 843; Pub. L. 115–254, div. B, title III, §355(b), Oct. 5, 2018, 132 Stat. 3305; Pub. L. 118–63, title IX, §923, May 16, 2024, 138 Stat. 1355.)

§40126. SEVERABLE SERVICES CONTRACTS FOR PERIODS CROSSING FISCAL YEARS

(a) IN GENERAL.—The Administrator of the Federal Aviation Administration may enter into a contract for procurement of severable services for a period that begins in 1 fiscal year and ends in the next fiscal year if (without regard to any option to extend the period of the contract) the contract period does not exceed 1 year.

(b) OBLIGATION OF FUNDS.—Funds made available for a fiscal year may be obligated for the total amount of a contract entered into under the authority of subsection (a).

(Added Pub. L. 106–181, title VII, §705(a), Apr. 5, 2000, 114 Stat. 157.)

§40127. PROHIBITIONS ON DISCRIMINATION

(a) PERSONS IN AIR TRANSPORTATION.—An air carrier or foreign air carrier may not subject a person in air transportation to discrimination on the basis of race, color, national origin, religion, sex, or ancestry.

(b) USE OF PRIVATE AIRPORTS.—Notwithstanding any other provision of law, no State or local government may prohibit the use or full enjoyment of a private airport within its jurisdiction by any person on the basis of that person's race, color, national origin, religion, sex, or ancestry.

(Added Pub. L. 106–181, title VII, §706(a), Apr. 5, 2000, 114 Stat. 157.)

§40128. OVERFLIGHTS OF NATIONAL PARKS

(a) IN GENERAL.—

(1) GENERAL REQUIREMENTS.—A commercial air tour operator may not conduct commercial air tour operations over a national park or tribal lands, as defined by this section, except—

(A) in accordance with this section;

(B) in accordance with conditions and limitations prescribed for that operator by the Administrator; and

(C) in accordance with any applicable air tour management plan or voluntary agreement under subsection (b)(7) for the park or tribal lands.

(2) APPLICATION FOR OPERATING AUTHORITY.—

(A) APPLICATION REQUIRED.—Before commencing commercial air tour operations over a national park or tribal lands, a commercial air tour operator shall apply to the Administrator for authority to conduct the operations over the park or tribal lands.

(B) COMPETITIVE BIDDING FOR LIMITED CAPACITY PARKS.—Whenever an air tour management plan limits the number of commercial air tour operations over a national park during a specified time frame, the Administrator, in cooperation with the Director, shall issue operation specifications to commercial air tour operators that conduct such operations. The operation specifications shall include such terms and conditions as the Administrator and the Director find necessary for management of commercial air tour operations over the park. The Administrator, in cooperation with the Director, shall develop an open competitive process for evaluating proposals from persons interested in providing commercial air tour operations over the park. In making a selection from among various proposals submitted, the Administrator, in cooperation with the Director, shall consider relevant factors, including—

(i) the safety record of the person submitting the proposal or pilots employed by the person;

(ii) any quiet aircraft technology proposed to be used by the person submitting the proposal;

(iii) the experience of the person submitting the proposal with commercial air tour operations over other national parks or scenic areas;

(iv) the financial capability of the person submitting the proposal;

(v) any training programs for pilots provided by the person submitting the proposal; and

(vi) responsiveness of the person submitting the proposal to any relevant criteria developed by the National Park Service for the affected park.

(C) NUMBER OF OPERATIONS AUTHORIZED.—In determining the number of authorizations to issue to provide commercial air tour operations over a national park, the Administrator, in cooperation with the Director, shall take into consideration the provisions of the air tour management plan, the number of existing commercial air tour operators and current level of service and equipment provided by any such operators, and the financial viability of each commercial air tour operation.

(D) COOPERATION WITH NPS.—Before granting an application under this paragraph, the Administrator, in cooperation with the Director, shall develop an air tour management plan in accordance with subsection (b) and implement such plan.

(E) TIME LIMIT ON RESPONSE TO ATMP APPLICATIONS.—The Administrator shall make every effort to act on any application under this paragraph and issue a decision on the application not later than 24 months after it is received or amended.

(F) PRIORITY.—In acting on applications under this paragraph to provide commercial air tour operations over a national park, the Administrator shall give priority to an application under this paragraph in any case in which a new entrant commercial air tour operator is seeking operating authority with respect to that national park.

(3) EXCEPTION.—Notwithstanding paragraph (1), commercial air tour operators may conduct commercial air tour operations over a national park under part 91 of title 14, Code of Federal Regulations if—

(A) such activity is permitted under part 119 of such title;

(B) the operator secures a letter of agreement from the Administrator and the national park superintendent for that national park describing the conditions under which the operations will be conducted; and

(C) the total number of operations under this exception is limited to not more than five flights in any 30-day period over a particular park.

(4) SPECIAL RULE FOR SAFETY REQUIREMENTS.—Notwithstanding subsection (c), an existing commercial air tour operator shall apply, not later than 90 days after the date of the enactment of this section, for operating authority under part 119, 121, or 135 of title 14, Code of Federal Regulations. A new entrant commercial air tour operator shall apply for such authority before conducting commercial air tour operations over a national park or tribal lands. The Administrator shall make every effort to act on any such application for a new entrant and issue a decision on the application not later than 24 months after it is received or amended.

(5) EXEMPTION FOR NATIONAL PARKS WITH 50 OR FEWER FLIGHTS EACH YEAR.—

(A) IN GENERAL.—Notwithstanding paragraph (1), a national park that has 50 or fewer commercial air tour operations over the park each year shall be exempt from the requirements of this section, except as provided in subparagraph (B).

(B) WITHDRAWAL OF EXEMPTION.—If the Director determines that an air tour management plan or voluntary agreement is necessary to protect park resources and values or park visitor use and enjoyment, the Director shall withdraw the exemption of a park under subparagraph (A).

(C) LIST OF PARKS.—

(i) IN GENERAL.—The Director and Administrator shall jointly publish a list each year of national parks that are covered by the exemption provided under this paragraph.

(ii) NOTIFICATION OF WITHDRAWAL OF EXEMPTION.—The Director shall inform the Administrator, in writing, of each determination to withdraw an exemption under subparagraph (B).

(D) ANNUAL REPORT.—A commercial air tour operator conducting commercial air tour operations over a national park that is exempt from the requirements of this section shall submit to the Administrator and the Director a report each year that includes the number of commercial air tour operations the operator conducted during the preceding 1-year period over such park.

(b) AIR TOUR MANAGEMENT PLANS.—

(1) ESTABLISHMENT.—

(A) IN GENERAL.—The Administrator, in cooperation with the Director, shall establish an air tour management plan for any national park or tribal land for which such a plan is not in effect whenever a person applies for authority to conduct a commercial air tour operation over the park. The air tour management plan shall be developed by means of a public process in accordance with paragraph (4).

(B) OBJECTIVE.—The objective of any air tour management plan shall be to develop acceptable and effective measures to mitigate or prevent the significant adverse impacts, if any, of commercial air tour operations upon the natural and cultural resources, visitor experiences, and tribal lands.

(C) EXCEPTION.—An application to begin or expand commercial air tour operations at Crater Lake National Park or Great Smoky Mountains National Park may be denied without the establishment of an air tour management plan by the Director of the National Park Service if the Director determines that such operations would adversely affect park resources or visitor experiences.

(2) ENVIRONMENTAL DETERMINATION.—In establishing an air tour management plan under this subsection, the Administrator and the Director shall each sign the environmental decision document required by section 102 of the National Environmental Policy Act of 1969 (42 U.S.C. 4332) which may include a finding of no significant impact, an environmental assessment, or an environmental impact statement and the record of decision for the air tour management plan.

(3) CONTENTS.—An air tour management plan for a national park—

(A) may prohibit commercial air tour operations over a national park in whole or in part;

(B) may establish conditions for the conduct of commercial air tour operations over a national park, including commercial air tour routes, maximum or minimum altitudes, time-of-day restrictions, restrictions for particular events, maximum number of flights per unit of time, intrusions on privacy on tribal lands, and mitigation of noise, visual, or other impacts;

(C) shall apply to all commercial air tour operations over a national park that are also within ½ mile outside the boundary of a national park;

(D) shall include incentives (such as preferred commercial air tour routes and altitudes, relief from caps and curfews) for the adoption of quiet aircraft technology by commercial air tour operators conducting commercial air tour operations over a national park;

(E) shall provide for the initial allocation of opportunities to conduct commercial air tour operations over a national park if the plan includes a limitation on the number of commercial air tour operations for any time period; and

(F) shall justify and document the need for measures taken pursuant to subparagraphs (A) through (E) and include such justifications in the record of decision.

(4) PROCEDURE.—In establishing an air tour management plan for a national park or tribal lands, the Administrator and the Director shall—

(A) hold at least one public meeting with interested parties to develop the air tour management plan;

(B) publish the proposed plan in the Federal Register for notice and comment and make copies of the proposed plan available to the public;

(C) comply with the regulations set forth in sections 1501.3 and 1501.5 through 1501.8 of title 40, Code of Federal Regulations (for purposes of complying with the regulations, the Federal Aviation Administration shall be the lead agency and the National Park Service is a cooperating agency);

(D) solicit the participation of any Indian tribe whose tribal lands are, or may be, overflown by aircraft involved in a commercial air tour operation over the park or tribal lands to which the plan applies, as a cooperating agency under the regulations referred to in subparagraph (C); and

(E) consult with the advisory group established under section 805 of the National Parks Air Tour Management Act of 2000 (49 U.S.C. 40128 note) and consider all advice, information, and recommendations provided by the advisory group to the Administrator and the Director.

(5) JUDICIAL REVIEW.—An air tour management plan developed under this subsection shall be subject to judicial review.

(6) AMENDMENTS.—The Administrator, in cooperation with the Director, may make amendments to an air tour management plan. Any such amendments shall be published in the Federal Register for notice and comment. A request for amendment of an air tour management plan shall be made in such form and manner as the Administrator may prescribe.

(7) VOLUNTARY AGREEMENTS.—

(A) IN GENERAL.—As an alternative to an air tour management plan, the Director and the Administrator may enter into a voluntary agreement with a commercial air tour operator (including a new entrant commercial air tour operator and an operator that has interim operating authority) that has applied to conduct commercial air tour operations over a national park to manage commercial air tour operations over such national park.

(B) PARK PROTECTION.—A voluntary agreement under this paragraph with respect to commercial air tour operations over a national park shall address the management issues necessary to protect the resources of such park and visitor use of such park without compromising aviation safety or the air traffic control system and may—

(i) include provisions such as those described in subparagraphs (B) through (E) of paragraph (3);

(ii) include provisions to ensure the stability of, and compliance with, the voluntary agreement; and

(iii) provide for fees for such operations.

(C) PUBLIC REVIEW.—The Director and the Administrator shall provide an opportunity for public review of a proposed voluntary agreement under this paragraph and shall consult with any Indian tribe whose tribal lands are, or may be, flown over by a commercial air tour operator under a voluntary agreement under this paragraph. After such opportunity for public review and consultation, the voluntary agreement may be implemented without further administrative or environmental process beyond that described in this subsection.

(D) TERMINATION.—

(i) IN GENERAL.—A voluntary agreement under this paragraph may be terminated at any time at the discretion of—

(I) the Director, if the Director determines that the agreement is not adequately protecting park resources or visitor experiences; or

(II) the Administrator, if the Administrator determines that the agreement is adversely affecting aviation safety or the national aviation system.

(ii) EFFECT OF TERMINATION.—If a voluntary agreement with respect to a national park is terminated under this subparagraph, the operators shall conform to the requirements for interim operating authority under subsection (c) until an air tour management plan for the park is in effect.

(c) INTERIM OPERATING AUTHORITY.—

(1) IN GENERAL.—Upon application for operating authority, the Administrator shall grant interim operating authority under this subsection to a commercial air tour operator for commercial air tour operations over a national park or tribal lands for which the operator is an existing commercial air tour operator.

(2) REQUIREMENTS AND LIMITATIONS.—Interim operating authority granted under this subsection—

(A) shall provide annual authorization only for the greater of—

(i) the number of flights used by the operator to provide the commercial air tour operations over a national park within the 12-month period prior to the date of the enactment of this section; or

(ii) the average number of flights per 12-month period used by the operator to provide such operations within the 36-month period prior to such date of enactment, and, for seasonal operations, the number of flights so used during the season or seasons covered by that 12-month period;

(B) may not provide for an increase in the number of commercial air tour operations over a national park conducted during any time period by the commercial air tour operator above the number that the air tour operator was originally granted unless such an increase is agreed to by the Administrator and the Director;

(C) shall be published in the Federal Register to provide notice and opportunity for comment;

(D) may be revoked by the Administrator for cause;

(E) shall terminate 180 days after the date on which an air tour management plan is established for the park or tribal lands;

(F) shall promote protection of national park resources, visitor experiences, and tribal lands;

(G) shall promote safe commercial air tour operations;

(H) shall promote the adoption of quiet technology, as appropriate; and

(I) may allow for modifications of the interim operating authority without further environmental review beyond that described in this subsection, if—

(i) adequate information regarding the existing and proposed operations of the operator under the interim operating authority is provided to the Administrator and the Director;

(ii) the Administrator determines that there would be no adverse impact on aviation safety or the air traffic control system; and

(iii) the Director agrees with the modification, based on the professional expertise of the Director regarding the protection of the resources, values, and visitor use and enjoyment of the park.

(3) NEW ENTRANT AIR TOUR OPERATORS.—

(A) IN GENERAL.—The Administrator, in cooperation with the Director, may grant interim operating authority under this paragraph to an air tour operator for a national park or tribal lands for which that operator is a new entrant air tour operator without further environmental process beyond that described in this paragraph, if—

(i) adequate information on the proposed operations of the operator is provided to the Administrator and the Director by the operator making the request;

(ii) the Administrator agrees that there would be no adverse impact on aviation safety or the air traffic control system; and

(iii) the Director agrees, based on the Director's professional expertise regarding the protection of park resources and values and visitor use and enjoyment.

(B) SAFETY LIMITATION.—The Administrator may not grant interim operating authority under subparagraph (A) if the Administrator determines that it would create a safety problem at the park or on the tribal lands, or the Director determines that it would create a noise problem at the park or on the tribal lands.

(C) ATMP LIMITATION.—The Administrator may grant interim operating authority under subparagraph (A) of this paragraph only if the air tour management plan for the park or tribal lands to which the application relates has not been developed within 24 months after the date of the enactment of this section.

(d) COMMERCIAL AIR TOUR OPERATOR REPORTS.—

(1) REPORT.—Each commercial air tour operator conducting a commercial air tour operation over a national park under interim operating authority granted under subsection (c) or in accordance with an air tour management plan or voluntary agreement under subsection (b) shall submit to the Administrator and the Director a report regarding the number of commercial air tour operations over each national park that are conducted by the operator and such other information as the Administrator and Director may request in order to facilitate administering the provisions of this section.

(2) REPORT SUBMISSION.—Not later than 90 days after the date of enactment of the FAA Modernization and Reform Act of 2012, the Administrator and the Director shall jointly issue an initial request for reports under this subsection. The reports shall be submitted to the Administrator and the Director with a frequency and in a format prescribed by the Administrator and the Director.

(e) EXEMPTIONS.—This section shall not apply to—

(1) the Grand Canyon National Park; or

(2) tribal lands within or abutting the Grand Canyon National Park.

(f) LAKE MEAD.—This section shall not apply to any air tour operator while flying over or near the Lake Mead National Recreation Area, solely as a transportation route, to conduct an air tour over the Grand Canyon National Park. For purposes of this subsection, an air tour operator flying over the Hoover Dam in the Lake Mead National Recreation Area en route to the Grand Canyon National Park shall be deemed to be flying solely as a transportation route.

(g) DEFINITIONS.—In this section, the following definitions apply:

(1) COMMERCIAL AIR TOUR OPERATOR.—The term "commercial air tour operator" means any person who conducts a commercial air tour operation over a national park.

(2) EXISTING COMMERCIAL AIR TOUR OPERATOR.—The term "existing commercial air tour operator" means a commercial air tour operator that was actively engaged in the business of providing commercial air tour operations over a national park at any time during the 12-month period ending on the date of the enactment of this section.

(3) NEW ENTRANT COMMERCIAL AIR TOUR OPERATOR.—The term "new entrant commercial air tour operator" means a commercial air tour operator that—

(A) applies for operating authority as a commercial air tour operator for a national park or tribal lands; and

(B) has not engaged in the business of providing commercial air tour operations over the national park or tribal lands in the 12-month period preceding the application.

(4) COMMERCIAL AIR TOUR OPERATION OVER A NATIONAL PARK.—

(A) IN GENERAL.—The term "commercial air tour operation over a national park" means any flight, conducted for compensation or hire in a powered aircraft where a purpose of the flight is sightseeing over a national park, within ½ mile outside the boundary of any national park (except the Grand Canyon National Park), or over tribal lands (except those within or abutting the Grand Canyon National Park), during which the aircraft flies—

(i) below a minimum altitude, determined by the Administrator in cooperation with the Director, above ground level (except solely for purposes of takeoff or landing, or necessary for safe operation of an aircraft as determined under the rules and regulations of the Federal Aviation Administration requiring the pilot-in-command to take action to ensure the safe operation of the aircraft); or

(ii) less than 1 mile laterally from any geographic feature within the park (unless more than ½ mile outside the boundary).

(B) FACTORS TO CONSIDER.—In making a determination of whether a flight is a commercial air tour operation over a national park for purposes of this section, the Administrator may consider—

(i) whether there was a holding out to the public of willingness to conduct a sightseeing flight for compensation or hire;

(ii) whether a narrative that referred to areas or points of interest on the surface below the route of the flight was provided by the person offering the flight;

(iii) the area of operation;

(iv) the frequency of flights conducted by the person offering the flight;

(v) the route of flight;

(vi) the inclusion of sightseeing flights as part of any travel arrangement package offered by the person offering the flight;

(vii) whether the flight would have been canceled based on poor visibility of the surface below the route of the flight; and

(viii) any other factors that the Administrator and the Director consider appropriate.

(5) NATIONAL PARK.—The term "national park" means any unit of the National Park System.

(6) TRIBAL LANDS.—The term "tribal lands" means Indian country (as that term is defined in section 1151 of title 18) that is within or abutting a national park.

(7) ADMINISTRATOR.—The term "Administrator" means the Administrator of the Federal Aviation Administration.

(8) DIRECTOR.—The term "Director" means the Director of the National Park Service.

(Added Pub. L. 106–181, title VIII, §803(a), Apr. 5, 2000, 114 Stat. 186; amended Pub. L. 108–176, title III, §323(a), Dec. 12, 2003, 117 Stat. 2541; Pub. L. 109–115, div. A, title I, §177, Nov. 30, 2005, 119 Stat. 2427; Pub. L. 112–95, title V, §501, Feb. 14, 2012, 126 Stat. 100; Pub. L. 112–141, div. C, title V, §35002, July 6, 2012, 126 Stat. 843; Pub. L. 115–254, div. B, title V, §539(c), Oct. 5, 2018, 132 Stat. 3370; Pub. L. 118–63, title VI, §628, May 16, 2024, 138 Stat. 1243.)

§40129. COLLABORATIVE DECISIONMAKING PILOT PROGRAM

(a) ESTABLISHMENT.—Not later than 90 days after the date of enactment of this section, the Administrator of the Federal Aviation Administration shall establish a collaborative decisionmaking pilot program in accordance with this section.

(b) DURATION.—Except as provided in subsection (k), the pilot program shall be in effect for a period of 2 years.

(c) GUIDELINES.—

(1) ISSUANCE.—The Administrator, with the concurrence of the Attorney General, shall issue guidelines concerning the pilot program. Such guidelines, at a minimum, shall—

(A) define a capacity reduction event;

(B) establish the criteria and process for determining when a capacity reduction event exists that warrants the use of collaborative decisionmaking among carriers at airports participating in the pilot program; and

(C) prescribe the methods of communication to be implemented among carriers during such an event.

(2) VIEWS.—The Administrator may obtain the views of interested parties in issuing the guidelines.

(d) EFFECT OF DETERMINATION OF EXISTENCE OF CAPACITY REDUCTION EVENT.—Upon a determination by the Administrator that a capacity reduction event exists, the Administrator may authorize air carriers and foreign air carriers operating at an airport participating in the pilot program to communicate for a period of time not to exceed 24 hours with each other concerning changes in their respective flight schedules in order to use air traffic capacity most effectively. The Administration shall facilitate and monitor such communication. The Attorney General, or the Attorney General's designee, may monitor such communication.

(e) SELECTION OF PARTICIPATING AIRPORTS.—Not later than 30 days after the date on which the Administrator establishes the pilot program, the Administrator shall select 2 airports to participate in the pilot program from among the most capacity-constrained airports in the Nation based on the Administration's Airport Capacity Benchmark Report 2001 or more recent data on airport capacity that is available to the Administrator. The Administrator shall select an airport for participation in the pilot program if the Administrator determines that collaborative decisionmaking among air carriers and foreign air carriers would reduce delays at the airport and have beneficial effects on reducing delays in the national airspace system as a whole.

(f) ELIGIBILITY OF AIR CARRIERS.—An air carrier or foreign air carrier operating at an airport selected to participate in the pilot program is eligible to participate in the pilot program if the Administrator determines that the carrier has the operational and communications capability to participate in the pilot program.

(g) MODIFICATION OR TERMINATION OF PILOT PROGRAM AT AN AIRPORT.—The Administrator, with the concurrence of the Attorney General, may modify or end the pilot program at an airport before the term of the pilot program has expired, or may ban an air carrier or foreign air carrier from participating in the program, if the Administrator determines that the purpose of the pilot program is not being furthered by participation of the airport or air carrier or if the Secretary of Transportation, with the concurrence of the Attorney General, finds that the pilot program or the participation of an air carrier or foreign air carrier in the pilot program has had, or is having, an adverse effect on competition among carriers.

(h) ANTITRUST IMMUNITY.—

(1) IN GENERAL.—Unless, within 5 days after receiving notice from the Secretary of the Secretary's intention to exercise authority under this subsection, the Attorney General submits to the Secretary a written objection to such action, including reasons for such objection, the Secretary may exempt an air carrier's or foreign air carrier's activities that are necessary to participate in the pilot program under this section from the antitrust laws for the sole purpose of participating in the pilot program. Such exemption shall not extend to any discussions, agreements, or activities outside the scope of the pilot program.

(2) ANTITRUST LAWS DEFINED.—In this section, the term "antitrust laws" has the meaning given that term in the first section of the Clayton Act (15 U.S.C. 12).

(i) CONSULTATION WITH ATTORNEY GENERAL.—The Secretary shall consult with the Attorney General regarding the design and implementation of the pilot program, including determining whether a limit should be set on the number of occasions collaborative decisionmaking could be employed during the initial 2-year period of the pilot program.

(j) EVALUATION.—

(1) IN GENERAL.—Before the expiration of the 2-year period for which the pilot program is authorized under subsection (b), the Administrator shall determine whether the pilot program has facilitated more effective use of air traffic capacity and the Secretary, with the concurrence of the Attorney General, shall determine whether the pilot program has had an adverse effect on airline competition or the availability of air services to communities. The Administrator shall also examine whether capacity benefits resulting from the participation in the pilot program of an airport resulted in capacity benefits to other parts of the national airspace system.

(2) OBTAINING NECESSARY DATA.—The Administrator may require participating air carriers and airports to provide data necessary to evaluate the pilot program's impact.

(k) EXTENSION OF PILOT PROGRAM.—At the end of the 2-year period for which the pilot program is authorized, the Administrator, with the concurrence of the Attorney General, may continue the pilot program for an additional 2 years and expand participation in the program to up to 7 additional airports if the Administrator determines pursuant to subsection (j) that the pilot program has facilitated more effective use of air traffic capacity and if the Secretary, with the concurrence of the Attorney General, determines that the pilot program has had no adverse effect on airline competition or the availability of air services to communities. The Administrator shall select the additional airports to participate in the extended pilot program in the same manner in which airports were initially selected to participate.

(Added Pub. L. 108–176, title IV, §423(a), Dec. 12, 2003, 117 Stat. 2552.)

§40130. FAA AUTHORITY TO CONDUCT CRIMINAL HISTORY RECORD CHECKS

(a) CRIMINAL HISTORY BACKGROUND CHECKS.—

(1) ACCESS TO INFORMATION.—The Administrator of the Federal Aviation Administration, for certification purposes of the Administration only, is authorized—

(A) to conduct, in accordance with the established request process, a criminal history background check of an airman in the criminal repositories of the Federal Bureau of Investigation and States by submitting positive identification of the airman to a fingerprint-based repository in compliance with section 217 of the National Crime Prevention and Privacy Compact Act of 1998 (34 U.S.C. 40316); and

(B) to receive relevant criminal history record information regarding the airman checked.

(2) RELEASE OF INFORMATION.—In accessing a repository referred to in paragraph (1), the Administrator shall be subject to the conditions and procedures established by the Department of Justice or the State, as appropriate, for other governmental agencies conducting background checks for noncriminal justice purposes.

(3) LIMITATION.—The Administrator may not use the authority under paragraph (1) to conduct criminal investigations.

(4) REIMBURSEMENT.—The Administrator may collect reimbursement to process the fingerprint-based checks under this subsection, to be used for expenses incurred, including Federal Bureau of Investigation fees, in providing these services.

(b) DESIGNATED EMPLOYEES.—The Administrator shall designate, by order, employees of the Administration who may carry out the authority described in subsection (a).

(Added Pub. L. 112–95, title VIII, §802(a), Feb. 14, 2012, 126 Stat. 118; amended Pub. L. 118–63, title XI, §1101(h), May 16, 2024, 138 Stat. 1413.)

§40131. NATIONAL AIRSPACE SYSTEM CYBER THREAT MANAGEMENT PROCESS

(a) ESTABLISHMENT.—The Administrator of the Federal Aviation Administration, in consultation with the heads of other agencies as the Administrator determines necessary, shall establish a national airspace system cyber threat management process to protect the national airspace system cyber environment, including the safety, security, and efficiency of air navigation services provided by the Administration.

(b) ISSUES TO BE ADDRESSED.—In establishing the national airspace system cyber threat management process under subsection (a), the Administrator shall, at a minimum—

(1) monitor the national airspace system for significant cybersecurity incidents;

(2) in consultation with appropriate Federal agencies, evaluate the cyber threat landscape for the national airspace system, including updating such evaluation on both annual and threat-based timelines;

(3) conduct national airspace system cyber incident analyses;

(4) create a cyber common operating picture for the national airspace system cyber environment;

(5) coordinate national airspace system significant cyber incident responses with other appropriate Federal agencies;

(6) track significant cyber incident detection, response, mitigation implementation, recovery, and closure;

(7) establish a process, or utilize existing processes, to share relevant significant cyber incident data related to the national airspace system;

(8) facilitate significant cybersecurity reporting, including through the Cybersecurity and Infrastructure Agency; and

(9) consider any other matter the Administrator determines appropriate.

(c) DEFINITIONS.—In this section:

(1) CYBER COMMON OPERATING PICTURE.—The term "cyber common operating picture" means the correlation of a detected cyber incident or cyber threat in the national airspace system and other operational anomalies to provide a holistic view of potential cause and impact.

(2) CYBER ENVIRONMENT.—The term "cyber environment" means the information environment consisting of the interdependent networks of information technology infrastructures and resident data, including the internet, telecommunications networks, computer systems, and embedded processors and controllers.

(3) CYBER INCIDENT.—The term "cyber incident" means an action that creates noticeable degradation, disruption, or destruction to the cyber environment and causes a safety or other negative impact on operations of—

(A) the national airspace system;

(B) civil aircraft; or

(C) aeronautical products and articles.

(4) CYBER THREAT.—The term "cyber threat" means the threat of an action that, if carried out, would constitute a cyber incident or an electronic attack.

(5) ELECTRONIC ATTACK.—The term "electronic attack" means the use of electromagnetic spectrum energy to impede operations in the cyber environment, including through techniques such as jamming or spoofing.

(6) SIGNIFICANT CYBER INCIDENT.—The term "significant cyber incident" means a cyber incident, or a group of related cyber incidents, that the Administrator determines is likely to result in demonstrable harm to the national airspace system of the United States.

(Added Pub. L. 118–63, title III, §393(a), May 16, 2024, 138 Stat. 1144.)

§40132. NATIONAL STRATEGIC PLAN FOR AVIATION WORKFORCE DEVELOPMENT

(a) IN GENERAL.—Not later than September 30, 2025, the Secretary of Transportation shall, in consultation with other Federal agencies and the Cooperative Aviation Recruitment, Enrichment, and Employment Readiness Council (in this section referred to as the "CAREER Council") established in subsection (c), establish and maintain a national strategic plan to improve recruitment, hiring, and retention and address projected challenges in the civil aviation workforce, including—

(1) any short-term, medium-term, and long-term workforce challenges relevant to the economy, workforce readiness, and priorities of the United States aviation sector;

(2) any existing or projected workforce shortages; and

(3) any workforce situation or condition that warrants special attention by the Federal Government.

(b) REQUIREMENTS.—The national strategic plan described in subsection (a) shall—

(1) take into account the activities and accomplishments of all Federal agencies that are related to carrying out such plan;

(2) include recommendations for carrying out such plan; and

(3) project and identify, on an annual basis, aviation workforce challenges, including any applicable workforce shortages.

(c) CAREER COUNCIL.—

(1) ESTABLISHMENT.—Not later than September 30, 2025, the Secretary, in consultation with the Administrator, shall establish a council comprised of individuals with expertise in the civil aviation industry to—

(A) assist with developing and maintaining the national strategic plan described in subsection (a); and

(B) provide advice to the Secretary, as appropriate, relating to the CAREER Program established under section 625 of the FAA Reauthorization Act of 2018, including as such advice relates to program administration and grant application selection, and support the development of performance metrics regarding the quality and outcomes of the Program.

(2) APPOINTMENT.—The CAREER Council shall be appointed by the Secretary from candidates nominated by national associations representing various sectors of the aviation industry, including—

(A) commercial aviation;

(B) general aviation;

(C) aviation labor organizations, including collective bargaining representatives of Federal Aviation Administration aviation safety inspectors, aviation safety engineers, and air traffic controllers;

(D) aviation maintenance, repair, and overhaul;

(E) aviation manufacturers; and

(F) unmanned aviation.

(3) TERM.—Each council member appointed by the Secretary under paragraph (2) shall serve a term of 2 years.

(d) NONDELEGATION.—The Secretary may not delegate any of the authorities or responsibilities under this section to the Administrator of the Federal Aviation

Administration.

(Added Pub. L. 118–63, title IV, §441(a), May 16, 2024, 138 Stat. 1184.)

§41101. REQUIREMENT FOR A CERTIFICATE

(a) GENERAL.—Except as provided in this chapter or another law—

(1) an air carrier may provide air transportation only if the air carrier holds a certificate issued under this chapter authorizing the air transportation;

(2) a charter air carrier may provide charter air transportation only if the charter air carrier holds a certificate issued under this chapter authorizing the charter air transportation; and

(3) an air carrier may provide all-cargo air transportation only if the air carrier holds a certificate issued under this chapter authorizing the all-cargo air transportation.

(b) THROUGH SERVICE AND JOINT TRANSPORTATION.—A citizen of the United States providing transportation in a State of passengers or property as a common carrier for compensation with aircraft capable of carrying at least 30 passengers, under authority granted by the appropriate State authority—

(1) may provide transportation for passengers and property that includes through service by the citizen over its routes in the State and in air transportation by an air carrier or foreign air carrier; and

(2) subject to sections 41309 and 42111 of this title, may make an agreement with an air carrier or foreign air carrier to provide the joint transportation.

(c) PROPRIETARY OR EXCLUSIVE RIGHT NOT CONFERRED.—A certificate issued under this chapter does not confer a proprietary or exclusive right to use airspace, an airway of the United States, or an air navigation facility.

(Pub. L. 103–272, §1(e), July 5, 1994, 108 Stat. 1118.)

§41102. GENERAL, TEMPORARY, AND CHARTER AIR TRANSPORTATION CERTIFICATES OF AIR CARRIERS

(a) ISSUANCE.—The Secretary of Transportation may issue a certificate of public convenience and necessity to a citizen of the United States authorizing the citizen to provide any part of the following air transportation the citizen has applied for under section 41108 of this title:

(1) air transportation as an air carrier.

(2) temporary air transportation as an air carrier for a limited period.

(3) charter air transportation as a charter air carrier.

(b) FINDINGS REQUIRED FOR ISSUANCE.—(1) Before issuing a certificate under subsection (a) of this section, the Secretary must find that the citizen is fit, willing, and able to provide the transportation to be authorized by the certificate and to comply with this part and regulations of the Secretary.

(2) In addition to the findings under paragraph (1) of this subsection, the Secretary, before issuing a certificate under subsection (a) of this section for foreign air transportation, must find that the transportation is consistent with the public convenience and necessity.

(c) TEMPORARY CERTIFICATES.—The Secretary may issue a certificate under subsection (a) of this section for interstate air transportation (except the transportation of passengers) or foreign air transportation for a temporary period of time (whether the application is for permanent or temporary authority) when the Secretary decides that a test period is desirable—

(1) to decide if the projected services, efficiencies, methods, and prices and the projected results will materialize and remain for a sustained period of time; or

(2) to evaluate the new transportation.

(d) FOREIGN AIR TRANSPORTATION.—The Secretary shall submit each decision authorizing the provision of foreign air transportation to the President under section 41307 of this title.

(Pub. L. 103–272, §1(e), July 5, 1994, 108 Stat. 1119.)

§41103. ALL-CARGO AIR TRANSPORTATION CERTIFICATES OF AIR CARRIERS

(a) APPLICATIONS.—A citizen of the United States may apply to the Secretary of Transportation for a certificate authorizing the citizen to provide all-cargo air transportation. The application must contain information and be in the form the Secretary by regulation requires.

(b) ISSUANCE.—Not later than 180 days after an application for a certificate is filed under this section, the Secretary shall issue the certificate to a citizen of the United States authorizing the citizen, as an air carrier, to provide any part of the all-cargo air transportation applied for unless the Secretary finds that the citizen is not fit, willing, and able to provide the all-cargo air transportation to be authorized by the certificate and to comply with regulations of the Secretary.

(c) TERMS.—The Secretary may impose terms the Secretary considers necessary when issuing a certificate under this section. However, the Secretary may not impose terms that restrict the places served or prices charged by the holder of the certificate.

(d) EXEMPTIONS AND STATUS.—A citizen issued a certificate under this section—

(1) is exempt in providing the transportation under the certificate from the requirements of—

(A) section 41101(a)(1) of this title and regulations or procedures prescribed under section 41101(a)(1); and

(B) other provisions of this part and regulations or procedures prescribed under those provisions when the Secretary finds under regulations of the Secretary that the exemption is appropriate; and

(2) is an air carrier under this part except to the extent the carrier is exempt under this section from a requirement of this part.

(Pub. L. 103–272, §1(e), July 5, 1994, 108 Stat. 1119; Pub. L. 103–429, §6(49), Oct. 31, 1994, 108 Stat. 4384.)

§41104. ADDITIONAL LIMITATIONS AND REQUIREMENTS OF CHARTER AIR CARRIERS

(a) RESTRICTIONS.—The Secretary of Transportation may prescribe a regulation or issue an order restricting the marketability, flexibility, accessibility, or variety of charter air transportation provided under a certificate issued under section 41102 of this title only to the extent required by the public interest. A regulation prescribed or order issued under this subsection may not be more restrictive than a regulation related to charter air transportation that was in effect on October 1, 1978.

(b) SCHEDULED OPERATIONS.—

(1) IN GENERAL.—Except as provided in paragraphs (3) and (4), an air carrier, including an indirect air carrier, may not provide, in aircraft designed for more than 9 passenger seats, regularly scheduled charter air transportation, for which the public is provided in advance a schedule containing the departure location, departure time, and arrival location of the flight, to or from an airport that—

(A) does not have an airport operating certificate issued under part 139 of title 14, Code of Federal Regulations (or any subsequent similar regulation); or

(B) has an airport operating certificate issued under part 139 of title 14, Code of Federal Regulations (or any subsequent similar regulation) if the airport—

(i) is a reliever airport (as defined in section 47102) and is designated as such in the national plan of integrated airports maintained under section 47103; and

(ii) is located within 20 nautical miles (22 statute miles) of 3 or more airports that each annually account for at least 1 percent of the total United States passenger enplanements and at least 2 of which are operated by the sponsor of the reliever airport.

(2) DEFINITION.—In this paragraph, the term "regularly scheduled charter air transportation" does not include operations for which the departure time, departure location, and arrival location are specifically negotiated with the customer or the customer's representative.

(3) EXCEPTION.—This subsection does not apply to any airport in the State of Alaska or to any airport outside the United States.

(4) WAIVERS.—The Secretary may waive the application of paragraph (1)(B) in cases in which the Secretary determines that the public interest so requires.

(c) ALASKA.—An air carrier holding a certificate issued under section 41102 of this title may provide charter air transportation between places in Alaska only to the extent the Secretary decides the transportation is required by public convenience and necessity. The Secretary may make that decision when issuing, amending, or modifying the certificate. This subsection does not apply to a certificate issued under section 41102 to a citizen of the United States who, before July 1, 1977—

(1) maintained a principal place of business in Alaska; and

(2) conducted air transport operations between places in Alaska with aircraft with a certificate for gross takeoff weight of more than 40,000 pounds.

(d) SUSPENSIONS.—(1) The Secretary shall suspend for not more than 30 days any part of the certificate of a charter air carrier if the Secretary decides that the failure of the carrier to comply with the requirements described in sections 41110(e) and 41112 of this title, or a regulation or order of the Secretary under section 41110(e) or 41112, requires immediate suspension in the interest of the rights, welfare, or safety of the public. The Secretary may act under this paragraph without notice or a hearing.

(2) The Secretary shall begin immediately a hearing to decide if the certificate referred to in paragraph (1) of this subsection should be amended, modified, suspended, or revoked. Until the hearing is completed, the Secretary may suspend the certificate for additional periods totaling not more than 60 days. If the Secretary decides that the carrier is complying with the requirements described in sections 41110(e) and 41112 of this title and regulations and orders under sections 41110(e) and 41112, the Secretary immediately may end the suspension period and proceeding begun under this subsection. However, the Secretary is not prevented from imposing a civil penalty on the carrier for violating the requirements described in section 41110(e) or 41112 or a regulation or order under section 41110(e) or 41112.

(Pub. L. 103–272, §1(e), July 5, 1994, 108 Stat. 1120; Pub. L. 106–181, title VII, §723, Apr. 5, 2000, 114 Stat. 165; Pub. L. 106–528, §8(c), Nov. 22, 2000, 114 Stat. 2522; Pub. L. 108–176, title VIII, §822, Dec. 12, 2003, 117 Stat. 2594.)

§41105. TRANSFERS OF CERTIFICATES

(a) GENERAL.—A certificate issued under section 41102 of this title may be transferred only when the Secretary of Transportation approves the transfer as being consistent with the public interest.

(b) CERTIFICATION TO CONGRESS.—When a certificate is transferred, the Secretary shall certify to the Committee on Commerce, Science, and Transportation of the Senate and the Committee on Transportation and Infrastructure of the House of Representatives that the transfer is consistent with the public interest. The Secretary shall include with the certification a report analyzing the effects of the transfer on—

(1) the viability of each carrier involved in the transfer;

(2) competition in the domestic airline industry; and

(3) the trade position of the United States in the international air transportation market.

(Pub. L. 103–272, §1(e), July 5, 1994, 108 Stat. 1121; Pub. L. 104–287, §5(9), Oct. 11, 1996, 110 Stat. 3389.)

§41106. AIRLIFT SERVICE

(a) INTERSTATE TRANSPORTATION.—(1) Except as provided in subsection (d) of this section, the transportation of passengers or property by CRAF-eligible aircraft in interstate air transportation obtained by the Secretary of Defense or the Secretary of a military department through a contract for airlift service in the United States may be provided only by an air carrier that—

    (A) has aircraft in the civil reserve air fleet or offers to place the aircraft in that fleet; and

    (B) holds a certificate issued under section 41102 of this title.

(2) The Secretary of Transportation shall act as expeditiously as possible on an application for a certificate under section 41102 of this title to provide airlift service.

(b) TRANSPORTATION BETWEEN THE UNITED STATES AND FOREIGN LOCATIONS.—Except as provided in subsection (d), the transportation of passengers or property by CRAF-eligible aircraft between a place in the United States and a place outside the United States obtained by the Secretary of Defense or the Secretary of a military department through a contract for airlift service shall be provided by an air carrier referred to in subsection (a).

(c) TRANSPORTATION BETWEEN FOREIGN LOCATIONS.—The transportation of passengers or property by CRAF-eligible aircraft between two places outside the United States obtained by the Secretary of Defense or the Secretary of a military department through a contract for airlift service shall be provided by an air carrier referred to in subsection (a) whenever transportation by such an air carrier is reasonably available.

(d) EXCEPTION.—When the Secretary of Defense decides that no air carrier holding a certificate under section 41102 is capable of providing, and willing to provide, the airlift service, the Secretary of Defense may make a contract to provide the service with an air carrier not having a certificate.

(e) CRAF-ELIGIBLE AIRCRAFT DEFINED.—In this section, "CRAF-eligible aircraft" means aircraft of a type the Secretary of Defense has determined to be eligible to participate in the civil reserve air fleet.

(Pub. L. 103–272, §1(e), July 5, 1994, 108 Stat. 1121; Pub. L. 106–398, §1 [[div. A], title III, §385(a), (b)], Oct. 30, 2000, 114 Stat. 1654, 1654A–87; Pub. L. 112–81, div. A, title III, §365, Dec. 31, 2011, 125 Stat. 1380.)

§41107. TRANSPORTATION OF MAIL

When the United States Postal Service finds that the needs of the Postal Service require the transportation of mail by aircraft in foreign air transportation or between places in Alaska, in addition to the transportation of mail authorized under certificates in effect, the Postal Service shall certify that finding to the Secretary of Transportation with a statement about the additional transportation and facilities necessary to provide the additional transportation. A copy of each certification and statement shall be posted for at least 20 days in the office of the Secretary. After notice and an opportunity for a hearing, the Secretary shall issue a new certificate under section 41102 of this title, or amend or modify an existing certificate under section 41110(a)(2)(A) of this title, to provide the additional transportation and facilities if the Secretary finds the additional transportation is required by the public convenience and necessity.

(Pub. L. 103–272, §§1(e), 4(k)(1), July 5, 1994, 108 Stat. 1121, 1370; Pub. L. 106–31, title VI, §6003, May 21, 1999, 113 Stat. 113.)

§41108. APPLICATIONS FOR CERTIFICATES

(a) FORM, CONTENTS, AND PROOF OF SERVICE.—To be issued a certificate of public convenience and necessity under section 41102 of this title, a citizen of the United States must apply to the Secretary of Transportation. The application must—

(1) be in the form and contain information required by regulations of the Secretary; and

(2) be accompanied by proof of service on interested persons as required by regulations of the Secretary and on each community that may be affected by the issuance of the certificate.

(b) NOTICE, RESPONSE, AND ACTIONS ON APPLICATIONS.—(1) When an application is filed, the Secretary shall post a notice of the application in the office of the Secretary and give notice of the application to other persons as required by regulations of the Secretary. An interested person may file a response with the Secretary opposing or supporting the issuance of the certificate. Not later than 90 days after the application is filed, the Secretary shall—

(A) provide an opportunity for a public hearing on the application;

(B) begin the procedure under section 41111 of this title; or

(C) dismiss the application on its merits.

(2) An order of dismissal issued by the Secretary under paragraph (1)(C) of this subsection is a final order and may be reviewed judicially under section 46110 of this title.

(3) If the Secretary provides an opportunity for a hearing under paragraph (1)(A) of this subsection, an initial or recommended decision shall be issued not later than 150 days after the date the Secretary provides the opportunity. The Secretary shall issue a final order on the application not later than 90 days after the decision is issued. However, if the Secretary does not act within the 90-day period, the initial or recommended decision on an application to provide—

(A) interstate air transportation is a final order and may be reviewed judicially under section 46110 of this title; and

(B) foreign air transportation shall be submitted to the President under section 41307 of this title.

(4) If the Secretary acts under paragraph (1)(B) of this subsection, the Secretary shall issue a final order on the application not later than 180 days after beginning the procedure on the application.

(5) If a citizen applying for a certificate does not meet the procedural schedule adopted by the Secretary in a proceeding, the Secretary may extend the period for acting under paragraphs (3) and (4) of this subsection by a period equal to the period of delay caused by the citizen. In addition to an extension under this paragraph, an initial or recommended decision under paragraph (3) of this subsection may be delayed for not more than 30 days in extraordinary circumstances.

(c) PROOF REQUIREMENTS.—(1) A citizen applying for a certificate must prove that the citizen is fit, willing, and able to provide the transportation referred to in section 41102 of this title and to comply with this part.

(2) A person opposing a citizen applying for a certificate must prove that the transportation referred to in section 41102(b)(2) of this title is not consistent with the public convenience and necessity. The transportation is deemed to be consistent with the public

convenience and necessity unless the Secretary finds, by a preponderance of the evidence, that the transportation is not consistent with the public convenience and necessity.

(Pub. L. 103–272, §1(e), July 5, 1994, 108 Stat. 1121.)

§41109. Terms of certificates

(a) GENERAL.—(1) Each certificate issued under section 41102 of this title shall specify the type of transportation to be provided.

(2) The Secretary of Transportation—

(A) may prescribe terms for providing air transportation under the certificate that the Secretary finds may be required in the public interest; but

(B) may not prescribe a term preventing an air carrier from adding or changing schedules, equipment, accommodations, and facilities for providing the authorized transportation to satisfy business development and public demand.

(3) A certificate issued under section 41102 of this title to provide foreign air transportation shall specify the places between which the air carrier is authorized to provide the transportation only to the extent the Secretary considers practicable and otherwise only shall specify each general route to be followed. The Secretary shall authorize an air carrier holding a certificate to provide foreign air transportation to handle and transport mail of countries other than the United States.

(4) A certificate issued under section 41102 of this title to provide foreign charter air transportation shall specify the places between which the air carrier is authorized to provide the transportation only to the extent the Secretary considers practicable and otherwise only shall specify each geographical area in which, or between which, the transportation may be provided.

(5) As prescribed by regulation by the Secretary, an air carrier other than a charter air carrier may provide charter trips or other special services without regard to the places named or type of transportation specified in its certificate.

(b) MODIFYING TERMS.—(1) An air carrier may file with the Secretary an application to modify any term of its certificate issued under section 41102 of this title to provide interstate or foreign air transportation. Not later than 60 days after an application is filed, the Secretary shall—

(A) provide the carrier an opportunity for an oral evidentiary hearing on the record; or

(B) begin to consider the application under section 41111 of this title.

(2) The Secretary shall modify each term the Secretary finds to be inconsistent with the criteria under section 40101(a) and (b) of this title.

(3) An application under this subsection may not be dismissed under section 41108(b)(1)(C) of this title.

(Pub. L. 103–272, §1(e), July 5, 1994, 108 Stat. 1123; Pub. L. 104–287, §5(70), Oct. 11, 1996, 110 Stat. 3396.)

§41110. Effective periods and amendments, modifications, suspensions, and revocations of certificates

(a) GENERAL.—(1) Each certificate issued under section 41102 of this title is effective from the date specified in it and remains in effect until—

(A) the Secretary of Transportation suspends or revokes the certificate under this section;

(B) the end of the period the Secretary specifies for an air carrier having a certificate of temporary authority issued under section 41102(a)(2) of this title; or

(C) the Secretary certifies that transportation is no longer being provided under a certificate.

(2) On application or on the initiative of the Secretary and after notice and an opportunity for a hearing or, except as provided in paragraph (4) of this subsection, under section 41111 of this title, the Secretary may—

(A) amend, modify, or suspend any part of a certificate if the Secretary finds the public convenience and necessity require amendment, modification, or suspension; and

(B) revoke any part of a certificate if the Secretary finds that the holder of the certificate intentionally does not comply with this chapter, sections 41308–41310(a), 41501, 41503, 41504, 41506, 41510, 41511, 41701, 41702, 41705–41709, 41711, 41712, and 41731–41742, chapter 419, subchapter II of chapter 421, and section 46301(b) of this title, a regulation or order of the Secretary under any of those provisions, or a term of its certificate.

(3) The Secretary may revoke a certificate under paragraph (2)(B) of this subsection only if the holder of the certificate does not comply, within a reasonable time the Secretary specifies, with an order to the holder requiring compliance.

(4) A certificate to provide foreign air transportation may not be amended, modified, suspended, or revoked under section 41111 of this title if the holder of the certificate requests an oral evidentiary hearing or the Secretary finds, under all the facts and circumstances, that the hearing is required in the public interest.

(b) ALL-CARGO AIR TRANSPORTATION.—The Secretary may order that a certificate issued under section 41103 of this title authorizing all-cargo air transportation is ineffective if, after notice and an opportunity for a hearing, the Secretary finds that the transportation is not provided to the minimum extent specified by the Secretary.

(c) FOREIGN AIR TRANSPORTATION.—(1) Notwithstanding subsection (a)(2)–(4) of this section, after notice and a reasonable opportunity for the affected air carrier to present its views, but without a hearing, the Secretary may suspend or revoke the authority of an air carrier to provide foreign air transportation to a place under a certificate issued under section 41102 of this title if the carrier—

(A) notifies the Secretary, under section 41734(a) of this title or a regulation of the Secretary, that it intends to suspend all transportation to that place; or

(B) does not provide regularly scheduled transportation to the place for 90 days immediately before the date the Secretary notifies the carrier of the action the Secretary proposes.

(2) Paragraph (1)(B) of this subsection does not apply to a place provided seasonal transportation comparable to the transportation provided during the prior year.

(d) TEMPORARY CERTIFICATES.—On application or on the initiative of the Secretary, the Secretary may—

(1) review the performance of an air carrier issued a certificate under section 41102(c) of this title on the basis that the air carrier will provide innovative or low-priced air transportation under the certificate; and

(2) amend, modify, suspend, or revoke the certificate or authority under subsection (a)(2) or (c) of this section if the air carrier has not provided, or is not providing, the transportation.

(e) CONTINUING REQUIREMENTS.—(1) To hold a certificate issued under section 41102 of this title, an air carrier must continue to be fit, willing, and able to provide the transportation authorized by the certificate and to comply with this part and regulations of the Secretary.

(2) After notice and an opportunity for a hearing, the Secretary shall amend, modify, suspend, or revoke any part of a certificate issued under section 41102 of this title if the Secretary finds that the air carrier—

(A) is not fit, willing, and able to provide the transportation authorized by the certificate and to comply with this part and regulations of the Secretary; or

(B) does not file reports necessary for the Secretary to decide if the carrier is complying with the requirements of clause (A) of this paragraph.

(f) ILLEGAL IMPORTATION OF CONTROLLED SUBSTANCES.—The Secretary—

(1) in consultation with appropriate departments, agencies, and instrumentalities of the United States Government, shall reexamine immediately the fitness of an air carrier that—

(A) violates the laws and regulations of the United States related to the illegal importation of a controlled substance; or

(B) does not adopt available measures to prevent the illegal importation of a controlled substance into the United States on its aircraft; and

(2) when appropriate, shall amend, modify, suspend, or revoke the certificate of the carrier issued under this chapter.

(g) RESPONSES.—An interested person may file a response with the Secretary opposing or supporting the amendment, modification, suspension, or revocation of a certificate under subsection (a) of this section.

(Pub. L. 103–272, §1(e), July 5, 1994, 108 Stat. 1123; Pub. L. 103–429, §6(50), Oct. 31, 1994, 108 Stat. 4384.)

§41111. SIMPLIFIED PROCEDURE TO APPLY FOR, AMEND, MODIFY, SUSPEND, AND TRANSFER CERTIFICATES

(a) GENERAL REQUIREMENTS.—(1) The Secretary of Transportation shall prescribe regulations that simplify the procedure for—

(A) acting on an application for a certificate to provide air transportation under section 41102 of this title; and

(B) amending, modifying, suspending, or transferring any part of that certificate under section 41105 or 41110(a) or (c) of this title.

(2) Regulations under this section shall provide for notice and an opportunity for each interested person to file appropriate written evidence and argument. An oral evidentiary hearing is not required to be provided under this section.

(b) WHEN SIMPLIFIED PROCEDURE USED.—The Secretary may use the simplified procedure to act on an application for a certificate to provide air transportation under section 41102 of this title, or to amend, modify, suspend, or transfer any part of that certificate under section 41105 or 41110(a) or (c) of this title, when the Secretary decides the use of the procedure is in the public interest.

(c) CONTENTS.—(1) To the extent the Secretary finds practicable, regulations under this section shall include each standard the Secretary will apply when—

(A) deciding whether to use the simplified procedure; and

(B) making a decision on an action in which the procedure is used.

(2) The regulations may provide that written evidence and argument may be filed under section 41108(b) of this title as a part of a response opposing or supporting the issuance of a certificate.

(Pub. L. 103–272, §1(e), July 5, 1994, 108 Stat. 1125.)

§41112. LIABILITY INSURANCE AND FINANCIAL RESPONSIBILITY

(a) LIABILITY INSURANCE.—The Secretary of Transportation may issue a certificate to a citizen of the United States to provide air transportation as an air carrier under section 41102 of this title only if the citizen complies with regulations and orders of the Secretary governing the filing of an insurance policy or self-insurance plan approved by the Secretary. The policy or plan must be sufficient to pay, not more than the amount of the insurance, for bodily injury to, or death of, an individual or for loss of, or damage to, property of others, resulting from the operation or maintenance of the aircraft under the certificate. A certificate does not remain in effect unless the carrier complies with this subsection.

(b) FINANCIAL RESPONSIBILITY.—To protect passengers and shippers using an aircraft operated by an air carrier issued a certificate under section 41102 of this title, the Secretary may require the carrier to file a performance bond or equivalent security in the amount and on terms the Secretary prescribes. The bond or security must be sufficient to ensure the carrier adequately will pay the passengers and shippers when the transportation the carrier agrees to provide is not provided. The Secretary shall prescribe the amounts to be paid under this subsection.

(Pub. L. 103–272, §1(e), July 5, 1994, 108 Stat. 1126.)

§41113. PLANS TO ADDRESS NEEDS OF FAMILIES OF PASSENGERS INVOLVED IN AIRCRAFT ACCIDENTS

(a) SUBMISSION OF PLANS.—Each air carrier holding a certificate of public convenience and necessity under section 41102 of this title shall submit to the Secretary and the Chairman of the National Transportation Safety Board a plan for addressing the needs of the families of passengers involved in any aircraft accident involving an aircraft of the air carrier and resulting in any loss of life.

(b) CONTENTS OF PLANS.—A plan to be submitted by an air carrier under subsection (a) shall include, at a minimum, the following:

(1) A plan for publicizing a reliable, toll-free telephone number, and for providing staff, to handle calls from the families of the passengers.

(2) A process for notifying the families of the passengers, before providing any public notice of the names of the passengers, either by utilizing the services of the organization designated for the accident under section 1136(a)(2) of this title or the services of other suitably trained individuals.

(3) An assurance that the notice described in paragraph (2) will be provided to the family of a passenger as soon as the air carrier has verified that the passenger was aboard

the aircraft (whether or not the names of all of the passengers have been verified) and, to the extent practicable, in person.

(4) An assurance that the air carrier will provide to the director of family support services designated for the accident under section 1136(a)(1) of this title, and to the organization designated for the accident under section 1136(a)(2) of this title, immediately upon request, a list (which is based on the best available information at the time of the request) of the names of the passengers aboard the aircraft (whether or not such names have been verified), and will periodically update the list.

(5) An assurance that the family of each passenger will be consulted about the disposition of all remains and personal effects of the passenger within the control of the air carrier.

(6) An assurance that if requested by the family of a passenger, any possession of the passenger within the control of the air carrier (regardless of its condition) will be returned to the family unless the possession is needed for the accident investigation or any criminal investigation.

(7) An assurance that any unclaimed possession of a passenger within the control of the air carrier will be retained by the air carrier for at least 18 months.

(8) An assurance that the family of each passenger will be consulted about construction by the air carrier of any monument to the passengers, including any inscription on the monument.

(9) An assurance that the treatment of the families of nonrevenue passengers (and any other victim of the accident, including any victim on the ground) will be the same as the treatment of the families of revenue passengers.

(10) An assurance that the air carrier will work with any organization designated under section 1136(a)(2) of this title on an ongoing basis to ensure that families of passengers receive an appropriate level of services and assistance following each accident.

(11) An assurance that the air carrier will provide reasonable compensation to any organization designated under section 1136(a)(2) of this title for services provided by the organization.

(12) An assurance that the air carrier will assist the family of a passenger in traveling to the location of the accident and provide for the physical care of the family while the family is staying at such location.

(13) An assurance that the air carrier will commit sufficient resources to carry out the plan.

(14) An assurance that, upon request of the family of a passenger, the air carrier will inform the family of whether the passenger's name appeared on a preliminary passenger manifest for the flight involved in the accident.

(15) An assurance that the air carrier will provide adequate training to the employees and agents of the carrier to meet the needs of survivors and family members following an accident.

(16) An assurance that the air carrier, in the event that the air carrier volunteers assistance to United States citizens within the United States with respect to an aircraft accident outside the United States involving any loss of life, will consult with the Board and the Department of State on the provision of the assistance.

(17)(A) An assurance that, in the case of an accident that results in any damage to a manmade structure or other property on the ground that is not government-owned, the air carrier will promptly provide notice, in writing, to the extent practicable, directly to the owner of the structure or other property about liability for any property damage and means for obtaining compensation.

(B) At a minimum, the written notice shall advise an owner (i) to contact the insurer of the property as the authoritative source for information about coverage and compensation; (ii) to not rely on unofficial information offered by air carrier representatives about compensation by the air carrier for accident-site property damage; and (iii) to obtain photographic or other detailed evidence of property damage as soon as possible after the accident, consistent with restrictions on access to the accident site.

(18) An assurance that, in the case of an accident in which the National Transportation Safety Board conducts a public hearing or comparable proceeding at a location greater than 80 miles from the accident site, the air carrier will ensure that the proceeding is made available simultaneously by electronic means at a location open to the public at both the origin city and destination city of the air carrier's flight if that city is located in the United States.

(c) CERTIFICATE REQUIREMENT.—The Secretary may not approve an application for a certificate of public convenience and necessity under section 41102 of this title unless the applicant has included as part of such application a plan that meets the requirements of subsection (b).

(d) LIMITATION ON LIABILITY.—An air carrier shall not be liable for damages in any action brought in a Federal or State court arising out of the performance of the air carrier in preparing or providing a passenger list, or in providing information concerning a preliminary passenger manifest, pursuant to a plan submitted by the air carrier under subsection (b), unless such liability was caused by conduct of the air carrier which was grossly negligent or which constituted intentional misconduct.

(e) AIRCRAFT ACCIDENT AND PASSENGER DEFINED.—In this section, the terms "aircraft accident" and "passenger" have the meanings such terms have in section 1136 of this title.

(f) STATUTORY CONSTRUCTION.—Nothing in this section may be construed as limiting the actions that an air carrier may take, or the obligations that an air carrier may have, in providing assistance to the families of passengers involved in an aircraft accident.

(Added Pub. L. 104–264, title VII, §703(a), Oct. 9, 1996, 110 Stat. 3267; amended Pub. L. 106–181, title IV, §402(a)(1)–(3), (5)–(c), Apr. 5, 2000, 114 Stat. 129, 130; Pub. L. 108–176, title VIII, §809(a), Dec. 12, 2003, 117 Stat. 2588; Pub. L. 115–254, div. C, §1109(a), Oct. 5, 2018, 132 Stat. 3434.)

CHAPTER 413—FOREIGN AIR TRANSPORTATION

§41301. REQUIREMENT FOR A PERMIT

A foreign air carrier may provide foreign air transportation only if the foreign air carrier holds a permit issued under this chapter authorizing the foreign air transportation.

(Pub. L. 103–272, §1(e), July 5, 1994, 108 Stat. 1126.)

§41302. PERMITS OF FOREIGN AIR CARRIERS

The Secretary of Transportation may issue a permit to a person (except a citizen of the United States) authorizing the person to provide foreign air transportation as a foreign air carrier if the Secretary finds that—

(1) the person is fit, willing, and able to provide the foreign air transportation to be authorized by the permit and to comply with this part and regulations of the Secretary; and

(2)(A) the person is qualified, and has been designated by the government of its country, to provide the foreign air transportation under an agreement with the United States Government; or

(B) the foreign air transportation to be provided under the permit will be in the public interest.

(Pub. L. 103–272, §1(e), July 5, 1994, 108 Stat. 1126.)

§41303. TRANSFERS OF PERMITS

A permit issued under section 41302 of this title may be transferred only when the Secretary of Transportation approves the transfer because the transfer is in the public interest.

(Pub. L. 103–272, §1(e), July 5, 1994, 108 Stat. 1127.)

§41304. Effective periods and amendments, modifications, suspensions, and revocations of permits

(a) GENERAL.—The Secretary of Transportation may prescribe the period during which a permit issued under section 41302 of this title is in effect. After notice and an opportunity for a hearing, the Secretary may amend, modify, suspend, or revoke the permit if the Secretary finds that action to be in the public interest.

(b) SUSPENSIONS AND RESTRICTIONS.—Without a hearing, but subject to the approval of the President, the Secretary—

(1) may suspend summarily the permits of foreign air carriers of a foreign country, or amend, modify, or limit the operations of the foreign air carriers under the permits, when the Secretary finds—

(A) the action is in the public interest; and

(B) the government, an aeronautical authority, or a foreign air carrier of the foreign country, over the objection of the United States Government, has—

(i) limited or denied the operating rights of an air carrier; or

(ii) engaged in unfair, discriminatory, or restrictive practices that have a substantial adverse competitive impact on an air carrier related to air transportation to, from, through, or over the territory of the foreign country; and

(2) to make this subsection effective, may restrict operations between the United States and the foreign country by a foreign air carrier of a third country.

(c) ILLEGAL IMPORTATION OF CONTROLLED SUBSTANCES.—The Secretary—

(1) in consultation with appropriate departments, agencies, and instrumentalities of the Government, shall reexamine immediately the fitness of a foreign air carrier that—

(A) violates the laws and regulations of the United States related to the illegal importation of a controlled substance; or

(B) does not adopt available measures to prevent the illegal importation of a controlled substance into the United States on its aircraft; and

(2) when appropriate, shall amend, modify, suspend, or revoke the permit of the carrier issued under this chapter.

(d) RESPONSES.—An interested person may file a response with the Secretary opposing or supporting the amendment, modification, suspension, or revocation of a permit under subsection (a) of this section.

(Pub. L. 103–272, §1(e), July 5, 1994, 108 Stat. 1127.)

§41305. Applications for permits

(a) FORM, CONTENTS, NOTICE, RESPONSE, AND ACTIONS ON APPLICATIONS.—(1) A person must apply in writing to the Secretary of Transportation to be issued a permit under section 41302 of this title. The Secretary shall prescribe regulations to require that the application be—

(A) verified;

(B) in a certain form and contain certain information;

(C) served on interested persons; and

(D) accompanied by proof of service on those persons.

(2) When an application is filed, the Secretary shall post a notice of the application in

the office of the Secretary and give notice of the application to other persons as required by regulations of the Secretary. An interested person may file a response with the Secretary opposing or supporting the issuance of the permit. The Secretary shall act on an application as expeditiously as possible.

(b) TERMS.—The Secretary may impose terms for providing foreign air transportation under the permit that the Secretary finds may be required in the public interest.

(Pub. L. 103–272, §1(e), July 5, 1994, 108 Stat. 1127.)

§41306. SIMPLIFIED PROCEDURE TO APPLY FOR, AMEND, MODIFY, AND SUSPEND PERMITS

(a) REGULATIONS.—The Secretary of Transportation shall prescribe regulations that simplify the procedure for—

(1) acting on an application for a permit to provide foreign air transportation under section 41302 of this title; and

(2) amending, modifying, or suspending any part of that permit under section 41304(a) or (b) of this title.

(b) NOTICE AND OPPORTUNITY TO RESPOND.—Regulations under this section shall provide for notice and an opportunity for each interested person to file appropriate written evidence and argument. An oral evidentiary hearing is not required to be provided under this section.

(Pub. L. 103–272, §1(e), July 5, 1994, 108 Stat. 1128.)

§41307. PRESIDENTIAL REVIEW OF ACTIONS ABOUT FOREIGN AIR TRANSPORTATION

The Secretary of Transportation shall submit to the President for review each decision of the Secretary to issue, deny, amend, modify, suspend, revoke, or transfer a certificate issued under section 41102 of this title authorizing an air carrier, or a permit issued under section 41302 of this title authorizing a foreign air carrier, to provide foreign air transportation. The President may disapprove the decision of the Secretary only if the reason for disapproval is based on foreign relations or national defense considerations that are under the jurisdiction of the President. The President may not disapprove a decision of the Secretary if the reason is economic or related to carrier selection. A decision of the Secretary—

(1) is void if the President disapproves the decision and publishes the reasons (to the extent allowed by national security) for disapproval not later than 60 days after it is submitted to the President; or

(2)(A) takes effect as a decision of the Secretary if the President does not disapprove the decision not later than 60 days after the decision is submitted to the President; and

(B) when effective, may be reviewed judicially under section 46110 of this title.

(Pub. L. 103–272, §1(e), July 5, 1994, 108 Stat. 1128.)

§41308. EXEMPTION FROM THE ANTITRUST LAWS

(a) DEFINITION.—In this section, "antitrust laws" has the same meaning given that term in the first section of the Clayton Act (15 U.S.C. 12).

(b) EXEMPTION AUTHORIZED.—When the Secretary of Transportation decides it is required by the public interest, the Secretary, as part of an order under section 41309 or 42111 of this title, may exempt a person affected by the order from the antitrust laws to the extent necessary to allow the person to proceed with the transaction specifically approved by the order and with any transaction necessarily contemplated by the order.

(c) EXEMPTION REQUIRED.—In an order under section 41309 of this title approving an agreement, request, modification, or cancellation, the Secretary, on the basis of the findings required under section 41309(b)(1), shall exempt a person affected by the order from the antitrust laws to the extent necessary to allow the person to proceed with the transaction specifically approved by the order and with any transaction necessarily contemplated by the order.

(Pub. L. 103–272, §1(e), July 5, 1994, 108 Stat. 1128.)

§41309. COOPERATIVE AGREEMENTS AND REQUESTS

(a) FILING.—An air carrier or foreign air carrier may file with the Secretary of Transportation a true copy of or, if oral, a true and complete memorandum of, an agreement (except an agreement related to interstate air transportation), or a request for authority to discuss cooperative arrangements (except arrangements related to interstate air transportation), and any modification or cancellation of an agreement, between the air carrier or foreign air carrier and another air carrier, a foreign carrier, or another carrier.

(b) APPROVAL.—The Secretary of Transportation shall approve an agreement, request, modification, or cancellation referred to in subsection (a) of this section when the Secretary finds it is not adverse to the public interest and is not in violation of this part. However, the Secretary shall disapprove—

(1) or, after periodic review, end approval of, an agreement, request, modification, or cancellation, that substantially reduces or eliminates competition unless the Secretary finds that—

(A) the agreement, request, modification, or cancellation is necessary to meet a serious transportation need or to achieve important public benefits (including international comity and foreign policy considerations); and

(B) the transportation need cannot be met or those benefits cannot be achieved by reasonably available alternatives that are materially less anticompetitive; or

(2) an agreement that—

(A) is between an air carrier not directly operating aircraft in foreign air transportation and a carrier subject to subtitle IV of this title; and

(B) governs the compensation the carrier may receive for the transportation.

(c) NOTICE AND OPPORTUNITY TO RESPOND OR FOR HEARING.—(1) When an agreement, request, modification, or cancellation is filed, the Secretary of Transportation shall give the Attorney General and the Secretary of State written notice of, and an opportunity to submit written comments about, the filing. On the initiative of the Secretary of Transportation or on request of the Attorney General or Secretary of State, the Secretary of Transportation may conduct a hearing to decide whether an agreement, request, modification, or cancellation is consistent with this part whether or not it was approved previously.

(2) In a proceeding before the Secretary of Transportation applying standards under subsection (b)(1) of this section, a party opposing an agreement, request, modification, or cancellation has the burden of proving that it substantially reduces or eliminates

competition and that less anticompetitive alternatives are available. The party defending the agreement, request, modification, or cancellation has the burden of proving the transportation need or public benefits.

(3) The Secretary of Transportation shall include the findings required by subsection (b)(1) of this section in an order of the Secretary approving or disapproving an agreement, request, modification, or cancellation.

(Pub. L. 103–272, §1(e), July 5, 1994, 108 Stat. 1129; Pub. L. 104–88, title III, §308(l), Dec. 29, 1995, 109 Stat. 948; Pub. L. 104–287, §5(71), Oct. 11, 1996, 110 Stat. 3396.)

§41310. DISCRIMINATORY PRACTICES

(a) PROHIBITION.—An air carrier or foreign air carrier may not subject a person, place, port, or type of traffic in foreign air transportation to unreasonable discrimination.

(b) REVIEW AND NEGOTIATION OF DISCRIMINATORY FOREIGN CHARGES.—(1) The Secretary of Transportation shall survey charges imposed on an air carrier by the government of a foreign country or another foreign entity for the use of airport property or airway property in foreign air transportation. If the Secretary of Transportation decides that a charge is discriminatory, the Secretary promptly shall report the decision to the Secretary of State. The Secretaries of State and Transportation promptly shall begin negotiations with the appropriate government to end the discrimination. If the discrimination is not ended in a reasonable time through negotiation, the Secretary of Transportation shall establish a compensating charge equal to the discriminatory charge. With the approval of the Secretary of State, the Secretary of the Treasury shall impose the compensating charge on a foreign air carrier of that country as a condition to accepting the general declaration of the aircraft of the foreign air carrier when it lands or takes off.

(2) The Secretary of the Treasury shall maintain an account to credit money collected under paragraph (1) of this subsection. An air carrier shall be paid from the account an amount certified by the Secretary of Transportation to compensate the air carrier for the discriminatory charge paid to the government.

(c) ACTIONS AGAINST DISCRIMINATORY ACTIVITY.—(1) The Secretary of Transportation may take actions the Secretary considers are in the public interest to eliminate an activity of a government of a foreign country or another foreign entity, including a foreign air carrier, when the Secretary, on the initiative of the Secretary or on complaint, decides that the activity—

(A) is an unjustifiable or unreasonable discriminatory, predatory, or anticompetitive practice against an air carrier; or

(B) imposes an unjustifiable or unreasonable restriction on access of an air carrier to a foreign market.

(2) The Secretary of Transportation may deny, amend, modify, suspend, revoke, or transfer under paragraph (1) of this subsection a foreign air carrier permit or tariff under section 41302, 41303, 41304(a), 41504(c), 41507, or 41509 of this title.

(d) FILING OF, AND ACTING ON, COMPLAINTS.—(1) An air carrier, computer reservations system firm, or a department, agency, or instrumentality of the United States Government may file a complaint under subsection (c) or (g) of this section with the Secretary of Transportation. The Secretary shall approve, deny, or dismiss the complaint, set the complaint for a hearing or investigation, or begin another proceeding proposing remedial action not later than 60 days after receiving the complaint. The Secretary may extend the period for acting for additional periods totaling not more than 30 days if the Secretary decides that with additional time it is likely that a complaint can be resolved satisfactorily through negotiations with the government of the foreign country or foreign entity. The Secretary must act not later than 90 days after receiving the complaint. However, the Secretary may extend this 90-day period for not more than an additional 90 days if, on the last day of the initial 90-day period, the Secretary finds that—

(A) negotiations with the government have progressed to a point that a satisfactory resolution of the complaint appears imminent;

(B) an air carrier or computer reservations system firm has not been subjected to economic injury by the government or entity as a result of filing the complaint; and

(C) the public interest requires additional time before the Secretary acts on the complaint.

(2) In carrying out paragraph (1) of this subsection and subsection (c) of this section, the Secretary of Transportation shall—

(A) solicit the views of the Secretaries of Commerce and State and the United States Trade Representative;

(B) give an affected air carrier or foreign air carrier reasonable notice and an opportunity to submit written evidence and arguments within the time limits of this subsection; and

(C) submit to the President under section 41307 or 41509(f) of this title actions proposed by the Secretary of Transportation.

(e) REVIEW.—(1) The Secretaries of State, the Treasury, and Transportation and the heads of other departments, agencies, and instrumentalities of the Government shall keep under review, to the extent of each of their jurisdictions, each form of discrimination or unfair competitive practice to which an air carrier is subject when providing foreign air transportation or a computer reservations system firm is subject when providing services with respect to airline service. Each Secretary and head shall—

(A) take appropriate action to eliminate any discrimination or unfair competitive practice found to exist; and

(B) request Congress to enact legislation when the authority to eliminate the discrimination or unfair practice is inadequate.

(2) The Secretary of Transportation shall report to Congress annually on each action taken under paragraph (1) of this subsection and on the continuing program to eliminate discrimination and unfair competitive practices. The Secretaries of State and the Treasury each shall give the Secretary of Transportation information necessary to prepare the report.

(f) REPORTS.—Not later than 30 days after acting on a complaint under this section, the Secretary of Transportation shall report to the Committee on Transportation and Infrastructure of the House of Representatives and the Committee on Commerce, Science, and Transportation of the Senate on action taken under this section on the complaint.

(g) ACTIONS AGAINST DISCRIMINATORY ACTIVITY BY FOREIGN CRS SYSTEMS.—The Secretary of Transportation may take such actions as the Secretary considers are in the public interest to eliminate an activity of a foreign air carrier that owns or markets a computer reservations system, or of a computer reservations system firm whose principal offices are located outside the United States, when the Secretary, on the initiative of the

Secretary or on complaint, decides that the activity, with respect to airline service—

(1) is an unjustifiable or unreasonable discriminatory, predatory, or anticompetitive practice against a computer reservations system firm whose principal offices are located inside the United States; or

(2) imposes an unjustifiable or unreasonable restriction on access of such a computer reservations system to a foreign market.

(Pub. L. 103–272, §1(e), July 5, 1994, 108 Stat. 1130; Pub. L. 104–287, §5(9), Oct. 11, 1996, 110 Stat. 3389; Pub. L. 106–181, title VII, §741, Apr. 5, 2000, 114 Stat. 174.)

§41311. GAMBLING RESTRICTIONS

(a) IN GENERAL.—An air carrier or foreign air carrier may not install, transport, or operate, or permit the use of, any gambling device on board an aircraft in foreign air transportation.

(b) DEFINITION.—In this section, the term "gambling device" means any machine or mechanical device (including gambling applications on electronic interactive video systems installed on board aircraft for passenger use)—

(1) which when operated may deliver, as the result of the application of an element of chance, any money or property; or

(2) by the operation of which a person may become entitled to receive, as the result of the application of an element of chance, any money or property.

(Added Pub. L. 103–305, title II, §205(a)(1), Aug. 23, 1994, 108 Stat. 1583.)

§41312. ENDING OR SUSPENDING FOREIGN AIR TRANSPORTATION

(a) GENERAL.—An air carrier holding a certificate issued under section 41102 of this title to provide foreign air transportation—

(1) may end or suspend the transportation to a place under the certificate only when the carrier gives at least 90 days notice of its intention to end or suspend the transportation to the Secretary of Transportation, any community affected by that decision, and the State authority of the State in which a community is located; and

(2) if it is the only air carrier holding a certificate to provide non-stop or single-plane foreign air transportation between 2 places, may end or suspend the transportation between those places only when the carrier gives at least 60 days notice of its intention to end or suspend the transportation to the Secretary and each community directly affected by that decision.

(b) TEMPORARY SUSPENSION.—The Secretary may authorize the temporary suspension of foreign air transportation under subsection (a) of this section when the Secretary finds the suspension is in the public interest.

(Added Pub. L. 103–429, §6(51)(A), Oct. 31, 1994, 108 Stat. 4384; amended Pub. L. 104–287, §5(72), Oct. 11, 1996, 110 Stat. 3396.)

§41313. PLANS TO ADDRESS NEEDS OF FAMILIES OF PASSENGERS INVOLVED IN FOREIGN AIR CARRIER ACCIDENTS

(a) DEFINITIONS.—In this section, the following definitions apply:

(1) AIRCRAFT ACCIDENT.—The term "aircraft accident" means any aviation disaster,

regardless of its cause or suspected cause, that occurs within the United States; and

(2) PASSENGER.—The term "passenger" has the meaning given such term by section 1136.

(b) SUBMISSION OF PLANS.—A foreign air carrier providing foreign air transportation under this chapter shall transmit to the Secretary of Transportation and the Chairman of the National Transportation Safety Board a plan for addressing the needs of the families of passengers involved in an aircraft accident that involves an aircraft under the control of the foreign air carrier and results in any loss of life.

(c) CONTENTS OF PLANS.—To the extent permitted by foreign law which was in effect on the date of the enactment of this section, a plan submitted by a foreign air carrier under subsection (b) shall include the following:

(1) TELEPHONE NUMBER.—A plan for publicizing a reliable, toll-free telephone number and staff to take calls to such number from families of passengers involved in an aircraft accident that involves an aircraft under the control of the foreign air carrier and results in any loss of life.

(2) NOTIFICATION OF FAMILIES.—A process for notifying, in person to the extent practicable, the families of passengers involved in an aircraft accident that involves an aircraft under the control of the foreign air carrier and results in any loss of life before providing any public notice of the names of such passengers. Such notice shall be provided by using the services of—

(A) the organization designated for the accident under section 1136(a)(2); or

(B) other suitably trained individuals.

(3) NOTICE PROVIDED AS SOON AS POSSIBLE.—An assurance that the notice required by paragraph (2) shall be provided as soon as practicable after the foreign air carrier has verified the identity of a passenger on the foreign aircraft, whether or not the names of all of the passengers have been verified.

(4) LIST OF PASSENGERS.—An assurance that the foreign air carrier shall provide, immediately upon request, and update a list (based on the best available information at the time of the request) of the names of the passengers aboard the aircraft (whether or not such names have been verified), to—

(A) the director of family support services designated for the accident under section 1136(a)(1); and

(B) the organization designated for the accident under section 1136(a)(2).

(5) CONSULTATION REGARDING DISPOSITION OF REMAINS AND EFFECTS.—An assurance that the family of each passenger will be consulted about the disposition of any remains and personal effects of the passenger that are within the control of the foreign air carrier.

(6) RETURN OF POSSESSIONS.—An assurance that, if requested by the family of a passenger, any possession (regardless of its condition) of that passenger that is within the control of the foreign air carrier will be returned to the family unless the possession is needed for the accident investigation or a criminal investigation.

(7) UNCLAIMED POSSESSIONS RETAINED.—An assurance that any unclaimed possession of a passenger within the control of the foreign air carrier will be retained by the foreign air carrier for not less than 18 months after the date of the accident.

(8) MONUMENTS.—An assurance that the family of each passenger will be consulted about construction by the foreign air carrier of any monument to the passengers built in

the United States, including any inscription on the monument.

(9) EQUAL TREATMENT OF PASSENGERS.—An assurance that the treatment of the families of nonrevenue passengers (and any other victim of the accident, including any victim on the ground) will be the same as the treatment of the families of revenue passengers.

(10) SERVICE AND ASSISTANCE TO FAMILIES OF PASSENGERS.—An assurance that the foreign air carrier will work with any organization designated under section 1136(a)(2) on an ongoing basis to ensure that families of passengers receive an appropriate level of services and assistance following an accident.

(11) COMPENSATION TO SERVICE ORGANIZATIONS.—An assurance that the foreign air carrier will provide reasonable compensation to any organization designated under section 1136(a)(2) for services and assistance provided by the organization.

(12) TRAVEL AND CARE EXPENSES.—An assurance that the foreign air carrier will assist the family of any passenger in traveling to the location of the accident and provide for the physical care of the family while the family is staying at such location.

(13) RESOURCES FOR PLAN.—An assurance that the foreign air carrier will commit sufficient resources to carry out the plan.

(14) SUBSTITUTE MEASURES.—If a foreign air carrier does not wish to comply with paragraph (10), (11), or (12), a description of proposed adequate substitute measures for the requirements of each paragraph with which the foreign air carrier does not wish to comply.

(15) TRAINING OF EMPLOYEES AND AGENTS.—An assurance that the foreign air carrier will provide adequate training to the employees and agents of the carrier to meet the needs of survivors and family members following an accident.

(16) CONSULTATION ON CARRIER RESPONSE NOT COVERED BY PLAN.—An assurance that, in the event that the foreign air carrier volunteers assistance to United States citizens within the United States with respect to an aircraft accident outside the United States involving any loss of life, the foreign air carrier shall consult with the Board and the Department of State on the provision of the assistance.

(17) NOTICE CONCERNING LIABILITY FOR MANMADE STRUCTURES.—

(A) IN GENERAL.—An assurance that, in the case of an accident that results in any damage to a manmade structure or other property on the ground that is not government-owned, the foreign air carrier will promptly provide notice, in writing, to the extent practicable, directly to the owner of the structure or other property about liability for any property damage and means for obtaining compensation.

(B) MINIMUM CONTENTS.—At a minimum, the written notice shall advise an owner (i) to contact the insurer of the property as the authoritative source for information about coverage and compensation; (ii) to not rely on unofficial information offered by foreign air carrier representatives about compensation by the foreign air carrier for accident-site property damage; and (iii) to obtain photographic or other detailed evidence of property damage as soon as possible after the accident, consistent with restrictions on access to the accident site.

(18) SIMULTANEOUS ELECTRONIC TRANSMISSION OF NTSB HEARING.—An assurance that, in the case of an accident in which the National Transportation Safety Board conducts a public hearing or comparable proceeding at a location greater than 80 miles from the accident site, the foreign air carrier will ensure that the proceeding is made available

simultaneously by electronic means at a location open to the public at both the origin city and destination city of the foreign air carrier's flight if that city is located in the United States.

(d) PERMIT AND EXEMPTION REQUIREMENT.—The Secretary shall not approve an application for a permit under section 41302 unless the applicant has included as part of the application or request for exemption a plan that meets the requirements of subsection (c).

(e) LIMITATION ON LIABILITY.—A foreign air carrier shall not be liable for damages in any action brought in a Federal or State court arising out of the performance of the foreign air carrier in preparing or providing a passenger list pursuant to a plan submitted by the foreign air carrier under subsection (c), unless the liability was caused by conduct of the foreign air carrier which was grossly negligent or which constituted intentional misconduct.

(Added Pub. L. 105–148, §1(a), Dec. 16, 1997, 111 Stat. 2681; amended Pub. L. 106–181, title IV, §403(a)–(c)(1), Apr. 5, 2000, 114 Stat. 130; Pub. L. 108–176, title VIII, §809(b), Dec. 12, 2003, 117 Stat. 2589; Pub. L. 115–254, div. B, title V, §539(d), div. C, §1109(b), Oct. 5, 2018, 132 Stat. 3370, 3434; Pub. L. 118–63, title XI, §1101(i), May 16, 2024, 138 Stat. 1413.)

CHAPTER 415—PRICING

§41501. ESTABLISHING REASONABLE PRICES, CLASSIFICATIONS, RULES, PRACTICES, AND DIVISIONS OF JOINT PRICES FOR FOREIGN AIR TRANSPORTATION

Every air carrier and foreign air carrier shall establish, comply with, and enforce—

(1) reasonable prices, classifications, rules, and practices related to foreign air transportation; and

(2) for joint prices established for foreign air transportation, reasonable divisions of those prices among the participating air carriers or foreign air carriers without unreasonably discriminating against any of those carriers.

(Pub. L. 103–272, §1(e), July 5, 1994, 108 Stat. 1132.)

§41502. ESTABLISHING JOINT PRICES FOR THROUGH ROUTES WITH OTHER CARRIERS

(a) JOINT PRICES.—An air carrier may establish reasonable joint prices and through service with another carrier. However, an air carrier not directly operating aircraft in air transportation (except an air express company) may not establish under this section a joint price for the transportation of property with a carrier subject to subtitle IV of this title.

(b) PRICES, CLASSIFICATIONS, RULES, AND PRACTICES AND DIVISIONS OF JOINT PRICES.—For through service by an air carrier and a carrier subject to subtitle IV of this title, the participating carriers shall establish—

(1) reasonable prices and reasonable classifications, rules, and practices affecting those prices or the value of the transportation provided under those prices; and

237

(2) for joint prices established for the through service, reasonable divisions of those joint prices among the participating carriers.

(c) STATEMENTS INCLUDED IN TARIFFS.—An air carrier and a carrier subject to subtitle IV of this title that are participating in through service and joint prices shall include in their tariffs, filed with the Secretary of Transportation, a statement showing the through service and joint prices.

(Pub. L. 103–272, §1(e), July 5, 1994, 108 Stat. 1132; Pub. L. 104–88, title III, §308(l), Dec. 29, 1995, 109 Stat. 948; Pub. L. 105–102, §2(22), Nov. 20, 1997, 111 Stat. 2205.)

§41503. ESTABLISHING JOINT PRICES FOR THROUGH ROUTES PROVIDED BY STATE AUTHORIZED CARRIERS

Subject to sections 41309 and 42111 of this title, a citizen of the United States providing transportation under section 41101(b) of this title may make an agreement with an air carrier or foreign air carrier for joint prices for that transportation. The joint prices agreed to must be the lowest of—

(1) the sum of the applicable prices for—

(A) the part of the transportation provided in the State and approved by the appropriate State authority; and

(B) the part of the transportation provided by the air carrier or foreign air carrier;

(2) a joint price established and filed under section 41504 of this title; or

(3) a joint price prescribed by the Secretary of Transportation under section 41507 of this title.

(Pub. L. 103–272, §1(e), July 5, 1994, 108 Stat. 1132.)

§41504. TARIFFS FOR FOREIGN AIR TRANSPORTATION

(a) FILING AND CONTENTS.—In the way prescribed by regulation by the Secretary of Transportation, every air carrier and foreign air carrier shall file with the Secretary, publish, and keep open to public inspection, tariffs showing the prices for the foreign air transportation provided between places served by the carrier and provided between places served by the carrier and places served by another air carrier or foreign air carrier with which through service and joint prices have been established. A tariff—

(1) shall contain—

(A) to the extent the Secretary requires by regulation, a description of the classifications, rules, and practices related to the foreign air transportation;

(B) a statement of the prices in money of the United States; and

(C) other information the Secretary requires by regulation; and

(2) may contain—

(A) a statement of the prices in money that is not money of the United States; and

(B) information that is required under the laws of a foreign country in or to which the air carrier or foreign air carrier is authorized to operate.

(b) CHANGES.—(1) Except as provided in paragraph (2) of this subsection, an air carrier or foreign air carrier may change a price or a classification, rule, or practice affecting that price or the value of the transportation provided under that price, specified in a tariff of the carrier for foreign air transportation only after 30 days after the carrier has filed, published, and posted notice of the proposed change in the same way as required for a tariff under subsection (a) of this section. However, the Secretary may prescribe an alternative notice requirement, of at least 25 days, to allow an air carrier or foreign air carrier to match a proposed change in a passenger fare or a charge of another air carrier or foreign air carrier. A notice under this paragraph must state plainly the change proposed and when the change will take effect.

(2) If the effect of a proposed change would be to begin a passenger fare that is outside of, or not covered by, the range of passenger fares specified under section 41509(e)(2) and (3) of this title, the proposed change may be put into effect only on the expiration of 60 days after the notice is filed under regulations prescribed by the Secretary.

(c) REJECTION OF CHANGES.—The Secretary may reject a tariff or tariff change that is not consistent with this section and regulations prescribed by the Secretary. A tariff or change that is rejected is void.

(Pub. L. 103–272, §1(e), July 5, 1994, 108 Stat. 1133.)

§41505. UNIFORM METHODS FOR ESTABLISHING JOINT PRICES, AND DIVISIONS OF JOINT PRICES, APPLICABLE TO COMMUTER AIR CARRIERS

(a) DEFINITION.—In this section, "commuter air carrier" means an air carrier providing transportation under section 40109(f) of this title that provides at least 5 scheduled roundtrips a week between the same 2 places.

(b) GENERAL.—Except as provided in subsection (c) of this section, when the Secretary of Transportation prescribes under section 41508 or 41509 of this title a uniform method generally applicable to establishing joint prices and divisions of joint prices for and between air carriers holding certificates issued under section 41102 of this title, the Secretary shall make that uniform method apply to establishing joint prices and divisions of joint prices for and between air carriers and commuter air carriers.

(c) NOTICE REQUIRED BEFORE MODIFYING, SUSPENDING, OR ENDING TRANSPORTATION.—A commuter air carrier that has an agreement with an air carrier to provide transportation for passengers and property that includes through service by the commuter air carrier over the commuter air carrier's routes and air transportation provided by the air carrier shall give the air carrier and the Secretary at least 90 days' notice before modifying, suspending, or ending the transportation. If the commuter air carrier does not give that notice, the uniform method of establishing joint prices and divisions of joint prices referred to in subsection (b) of this section does not apply to the commuter air carrier.

(Pub. L. 103–272, §1(e), July 5, 1994, 108 Stat. 1134.)

§41506. PRICE DIVISION FILING REQUIREMENTS FOR FOREIGN AIR TRANSPORTATION

Every air carrier and foreign air carrier shall keep currently on file with the Secretary of Transportation, if the Secretary requires, the established divisions of all joint prices for foreign air transportation in which the carrier participates.

(Pub. L. 103–272, §1(e), July 5, 1994, 108 Stat. 1134.)

§41507. AUTHORITY OF THE SECRETARY OF TRANSPORTATION TO CHANGE

PRICES, CLASSIFICATIONS, RULES, AND PRACTICES FOR FOREIGN AIR TRANSPORTATION

(a) GENERAL.—When the Secretary of Transportation decides that a price charged or received by an air carrier or foreign air carrier for foreign air transportation, or a classification, rule, or practice affecting that price or the value of the transportation provided under that price, is or will be unreasonably discriminatory, the Secretary may—

(1) change the price, classification, rule, or practice as necessary to correct the discrimination; and

(2) order the air carrier or foreign air carrier to stop charging or collecting the discriminatory price or carrying out the discriminatory classification, rule, or practice.

(b) WHEN SECRETARY MAY ACT.—The Secretary may act under this section on the Secretary's own initiative or on a complaint filed with the Secretary and only after notice and an opportunity for a hearing.

(Pub. L. 103–272, §1(e), July 5, 1994, 108 Stat. 1134.)

§41508. AUTHORITY OF THE SECRETARY OF TRANSPORTATION TO ADJUST DIVISIONS OF JOINT PRICES FOR FOREIGN AIR TRANSPORTATION

(a) GENERAL.—When the Secretary of Transportation decides that a division between air carriers, foreign air carriers, or both, of a joint price for foreign air transportation is or will be unreasonable or unreasonably discriminatory against any of those carriers, the Secretary shall prescribe a reasonable division of the joint price among those carriers. The Secretary may order the adjustment in the division of the joint price to be made retroactively to the date the complaint was filed, the date the order for an investigation was made, or a later date the Secretary decides is reasonable.

(b) WHEN SECRETARY MAY ACT.—The Secretary may act under this section on the Secretary's own initiative or on a complaint filed with the Secretary and only after notice and an opportunity for a hearing.

(Pub. L. 103–272, §1(e), July 5, 1994, 108 Stat. 1135.)

§41509. AUTHORITY OF THE SECRETARY OF TRANSPORTATION TO SUSPEND, CANCEL, AND REJECT TARIFFS FOR FOREIGN AIR TRANSPORTATION

(a) CANCELLATION AND REJECTION.—(1) On the initiative of the Secretary of Transportation or on a complaint filed with the Secretary, the Secretary may conduct a hearing to decide whether a price for foreign air transportation contained in an existing or newly filed tariff of an air carrier or foreign air carrier, a classification, rule, or practice affecting that price, or the value of the transportation provided under that price, is lawful. The Secretary may begin the hearing at once and without an answer or another formal pleading by the air carrier or foreign air carrier, but only after reasonable notice. If, after the hearing, the Secretary decides that the price, classification, rule, or practice is or will be unreasonable or unreasonably discriminatory, the Secretary may cancel or reject the tariff and prevent the use of the price, classification, rule, or practice.

(2) With or without a hearing, the Secretary may cancel or reject an existing or newly filed tariff of a foreign air carrier and prevent the use of a price, classification, rule, or practice when the Secretary decides that the cancellation or rejection is in the public

interest.

(3) In deciding whether to cancel or reject a tariff of an air carrier or foreign air carrier under this subsection, the Secretary shall consider—

(A) the effect of the price on the movement of traffic;

(B) the need in the public interest of adequate and efficient transportation by air carriers and foreign air carriers at the lowest cost consistent with providing the transportation;

(C) the standards prescribed under law related to the character and quality of transportation to be provided by air carriers and foreign air carriers;

(D) the inherent advantages of transportation by aircraft;

(E) the need of the air carrier and foreign air carrier for revenue sufficient to enable the air carrier and foreign air carrier, under honest, economical, and efficient management, to provide adequate and efficient air carrier and foreign air carrier transportation;

(F) whether the price will be predatory or tend to monopolize competition among air carriers and foreign air carriers in foreign air transportation;

(G) reasonably estimated or foreseeable future costs and revenues for the air carrier or foreign air carrier for a reasonably limited future period during which the price would be in effect; and

(H) other factors.

(b) SUSPENSION.—(1)(A) Pending a decision under subsection (a)(1) of this section, the Secretary may suspend a tariff and the use of a price contained in the tariff or a classification, rule, or practice affecting that price.

(B) The Secretary may suspend a tariff of a foreign air carrier and the use of a price, classification, rule, or practice when the suspension is in the public interest.

(2) A suspension becomes effective when the Secretary files with the tariff and delivers to the air carrier or foreign air carrier affected by the suspension a written statement of the reasons for the suspension. To suspend a tariff, reasonable notice of the suspension must be given to the affected carrier.

(3) The suspension of a newly filed tariff may be for periods totaling not more than 365 days after the date the tariff otherwise would go into effect. The suspension of an existing tariff may be for periods totaling not more than 365 days after the effective date of the suspension. The Secretary may rescind at any time the suspension of a newly filed tariff and allow the price, classification, rule, or practice to go into effect.

(c) EFFECTIVE TARIFFS AND PRICES WHEN TARIFF IS SUSPENDED, CANCELED, OR REJECTED.—(1) If a tariff is suspended pending the outcome of a proceeding under subsection (a) of this section and the Secretary does not take final action in the proceeding during the suspension period, the tariff goes into effect at the end of that period subject to cancellation when the proceeding is concluded.

(2)(A) During the period of suspension, or after the cancellation or rejection, of a newly filed tariff (including a tariff that has gone into effect provisionally), the affected air carrier or foreign air carrier shall maintain in effect and use—

(i) the corresponding seasonal prices, or the classifications, rules, and practices affecting those prices or the value of transportation provided under those prices, that were in effect for the carrier immediately before the new tariff was filed; or

(ii) another price provided for under an applicable intergovernmental agreement or understanding.

(B) If the suspended, canceled, or rejected tariff is the first tariff of the carrier for the covered transportation, the carrier, for the purpose of operations during the period of suspension or pending effectiveness of a new tariff, may file another tariff containing a price or another classification, rule, or practice affecting the price, or the value of the transportation provided under the price, that is in effect (and not subject to a suspension order) for any air carrier providing the same transportation.

(3) If an existing tariff is suspended or canceled, the affected air carrier or foreign air carrier, for the purpose of operations during the period of suspension or pending effectiveness of a new tariff, may file another tariff containing a price or another classification, rule, or practice affecting the price, or the value of the transportation provided under the price, that is in effect (and not subject to a suspension order) for any air carrier providing the same transportation.

(d) RESPONSE TO REFUSAL OF FOREIGN COUNTRY TO ALLOW AIR CARRIER TO CHARGE A PRICE.—When the Secretary finds that the government or an aeronautical authority of a foreign country has refused to allow an air carrier to charge a price contained in a tariff filed and published under section 41504 of this title for foreign air transportation to the foreign country—

(1) the Secretary, without a hearing—

(A) may suspend any existing tariff of a foreign air carrier providing transportation between the United States and the foreign country for periods totaling not more than 365 days after the date of the suspension; and

(B) may order the foreign air carrier to charge, during the suspension periods, prices that are the same as those contained in a tariff (designated by the Secretary) of an air carrier filed and published under section 41504 of this title for foreign air transportation to the foreign country; and

(2) a foreign air carrier may continue to provide foreign air transportation to the foreign country only if the government or aeronautical authority of the foreign country allows an air carrier to start or continue foreign air transportation to the foreign country at the prices designated by the Secretary.

(e) STANDARD FOREIGN FARE LEVEL.—(1)(A) In this subsection, "standard foreign fare level" means—

(i) for a class of fares existing on October 1, 1979, the fare between 2 places (as adjusted under subparagraph (B) of this paragraph) filed for and allowed by the Civil Aeronautics Board to go into effect after September 30, 1979, and before August 13, 1980 (with seasonal fares adjusted by the percentage difference that prevailed between seasons in 1978), or the fare established under section 1002(j)(8) of the Federal Aviation Act of 1958 (Public Law 85–726, 72 Stat. 731), as added by section 24(a) of the International Air Transportation Competition Act of 1979 (Public Law 96–192, 94 Stat. 46); or

(ii) for a class of fares established after October 1, 1979, the fare between 2 places in effect on the effective date of the establishment of the new class.

(B) At least once every 60 days for fuel costs, and at least once every 180 days for other costs, the Secretary shall adjust the standard foreign fare level for the particular foreign air transportation to which the standard foreign fare level applies by increasing or decreasing that level by the percentage change from the last previous period in the actual operating cost for each available seat-mile. In adjusting a standard foreign fare level, the Secretary may not make an adjustment to costs actually incurred. In establishing a standard foreign fare level and making adjustments in the level under this paragraph, the Secretary may use all relevant or appropriate information reasonably available to the Secretary.

(2) The Secretary may not decide that a proposed fare for foreign air transportation is unreasonable on the basis that the fare is too low or too high if the proposed fare is neither more than 5 percent higher nor 50 percent lower than the standard foreign fare level for the same or essentially similar class of transportation. The Secretary by regulation may increase the 50 percent specified in this paragraph.

(3) Paragraph (2) of this subsection does not apply to a proposed fare that is not more than—

(A) 5 percent higher than the standard foreign fare level when the Secretary decides that the proposed fare may be unreasonably discriminatory or that suspension of the fare is in the public interest because of an unreasonable regulatory action by the government of a foreign country that is related to a fare proposal of an air carrier; or

(B) 50 percent lower than the standard foreign fare level when the Secretary decides that the proposed fare may be predatory or discriminatory or that suspension of the fare is required because of an unreasonable regulatory action by the government of a foreign country that is related to a fare proposal of an air carrier.

(f) SUBMISSION OF ORDERS TO PRESIDENT.—The Secretary shall submit to the President an order made under this section suspending, canceling, or rejecting a price for foreign air transportation, and an order rescinding the effectiveness of such an order, before publishing the order. Not later than 10 days after its submission, the President may disapprove the order on finding disapproval is necessary for United States foreign policy or national defense reasons.

(g) COMPLIANCE AS CONDITION OF CERTIFICATE OR PERMIT.—This section and compliance with an order of the Secretary under this section are conditions to any certificate or permit held by an air carrier or foreign air carrier. An air carrier or foreign air carrier may provide foreign air transportation only as long as the carrier maintains prices for that transportation that comply with this section and orders of the Secretary under this section.

(Pub. L. 103–272, §1(e), July 5, 1994, 108 Stat. 1135.)

§41510. REQUIRED ADHERENCE TO FOREIGN AIR TRANSPORTATION TARIFFS

(a) PROHIBITED ACTIONS BY AIR CARRIERS, FOREIGN AIR CARRIERS, AND TICKET AGENTS.—An air carrier, foreign air carrier, or ticket agent may not—

(1) charge or receive compensation for foreign air transportation that is different from the price specified in the tariff of the carrier that is in effect for that transportation;

(2) refund or remit any part of the price specified in the tariff; or

(3) extend to any person a privilege or facility, related to a matter required by the Secretary of Transportation to be specified in a tariff for foreign air transportation, except as specified in the tariff.

(b) PROHIBITED ACTIONS BY ANY PERSON.—A person may not knowingly—

(1) pay compensation for foreign air transportation of property that is different from

the price specified in the tariff in effect for that transportation; or

(2) solicit, accept, or receive—

(A) a refund or remittance of any part of the price specified in the tariff; or

(B) a privilege or facility, related to a matter required by the Secretary to be specified in a tariff for foreign air transportation of property, except as specified in the tariff.

(Pub. L. 103–272, §1(e), July 5, 1994, 108 Stat. 1138.)

§41511. SPECIAL PRICES FOR FOREIGN AIR TRANSPORTATION

(a) FREE AND REDUCED PRICING.—This chapter does not prohibit an air carrier or foreign air carrier, under terms the Secretary of Transportation prescribes, from issuing or interchanging tickets or passes for free or reduced-price foreign air transportation to or for the following:

(1) a director, officer, or employee of the carrier (including a retired director, officer, or employee who is receiving retirement benefits from an air carrier or foreign air carrier).

(2) a parent or the immediate family of such an officer or employee or the immediate family of such a director.

(3) a widow, widower, or minor child of an employee of the carrier who died as a direct result of a personal injury sustained when performing a duty in the service of the carrier.

(4) a witness or attorney attending a legal investigation in which the air carrier is interested.

(5) an individual injured in an aircraft accident and a physician or nurse attending the individual.

(6) a parent or the immediate family of an individual injured or killed in an aircraft accident when the transportation is related to the accident.

(7) an individual or property to provide relief in a general epidemic, pestilence, or other emergency.

(8) other individuals under other circumstances the Secretary prescribes by regulation.

(b) SPACE-AVAILABLE BASIS.—Under terms the Secretary prescribes, an air carrier or foreign air carrier may grant reduced-price foreign air transportation on a space-available basis to the following:

(1) a minister of religion.

(2) an individual who is at least 60 years of age and no longer gainfully employed.

(3) an individual who is at least 65 years of age.

(4) an individual who has severely impaired vision or hearing or another physical or mental disability and an accompanying attendant needed by that individual.

(Pub. L. 103–272, §1(e), July 5, 1994, 108 Stat. 1139; Pub. L. 118–63, title V, §550(b), May 16, 2024, 138 Stat. 1212.)

CHAPTER 417—OPERATIONS OF CARRIERS

SUBCHAPTER I—REQUIREMENTS

SUBCHAPTER II—SMALL COMMUNITY AIR SERVICE

SUBCHAPTER III—REGIONAL AIR SERVICE INCENTIVE PROGRAM

[1] So in original. Does not conform to section catchline.

SUBCHAPTER I—REQUIREMENTS

§41701. Classification of air carriers

The Secretary of Transportation may establish—

(1) reasonable classifications for air carriers when required because of the nature of the transportation provided by them; and

(2) reasonable requirements for each class when the Secretary decides those requirements are necessary in the public interest.

(Pub. L. 103–272, §1(e), July 5, 1994, 108 Stat. 1140.)

§41702. Interstate air transportation

An air carrier shall provide safe and adequate interstate air transportation.

(Pub. L. 103–272, §1(e), July 5, 1994, 108 Stat. 1140.)

§41703. Navigation of foreign civil aircraft

(a) Permitted Navigation.—A foreign aircraft, not part of the armed forces of a foreign country, may be navigated in the United States only—

(1) if the country of registry grants a similar privilege to aircraft of the United States;

(2) by an airman holding a certificate or license issued or made valid by the United

States Government or the country of registry;

(3) if the Secretary of Transportation authorizes the navigation; and

(4) if the navigation is consistent with terms the Secretary may prescribe.

(b) REQUIREMENTS FOR AUTHORIZING NAVIGATION.—The Secretary may authorize navigation under this section only if the Secretary decides the authorization is—

(1) in the public interest; and

(2) consistent with any agreement between the Government and the government of a foreign country.

(c) PROVIDING AIR COMMERCE.—The Secretary may authorize an aircraft permitted to navigate in the United States under this section to provide air commerce in the United States. However, the aircraft may take on for compensation, at a place in the United States, passengers or cargo destined for another place in the United States only if—

(1) specifically authorized under section 40109(g) of this title; or

(2) under regulations the Secretary prescribes authorizing air carriers to provide otherwise authorized air transportation with foreign registered aircraft under lease or charter to them without crew.

(d) PERMIT REQUIREMENTS NOT AFFECTED.—This section does not affect section 41301 or 41302 of this title. However, a foreign air carrier holding a permit under section 41302 does not need to obtain additional authorization under this section for an operation authorized by the permit.

(e) CARGO IN ALASKA.—

(1) IN GENERAL.—For the purposes of subsection (c), eligible cargo taken on or off any aircraft at a place in Alaska in the course of transportation of that cargo by any combination of 2 or more air carriers or foreign air carriers in either direction between a place in the United States and a place outside the United States shall not be deemed to have broken its international journey in, be taken on in, or be destined for Alaska.

(2) ELIGIBLE CARGO.—For purposes of paragraph (1), the term "eligible cargo" means cargo transported between Alaska and any other place in the United States on a foreign air carrier (having been transported from, or thereafter being transported to, a place outside the United States on a different air carrier or foreign air carrier) that is carried—

(A) under the code of a United States air carrier providing air transportation to Alaska;

(B) on an air carrier way bill of an air carrier providing air transportation to Alaska;

(C) under a term arrangement or block space agreement with an air carrier; or

(D) under the code of a United States air carrier for purposes of transportation within the United States.

(Pub. L. 103–272, §1(e), July 5, 1994, 108 Stat. 1140; Pub. L. 108–176, title VIII, §808, Dec. 12, 2003, 117 Stat. 2588.)

§41704. TRANSPORTING PROPERTY NOT TO BE TRANSPORTED IN AIRCRAFT CABINS

Under regulations or orders of the Secretary of Transportation, an air carrier shall transport as baggage the property of a passenger traveling in air transportation that may not be carried in an aircraft cabin because of a law or regulation of the United States. The carrier is liable to pay an amount not more than the amount declared to the carrier by that passenger for actual loss of, or damage to, the property caused by the carrier. The carrier may impose reasonable charges and conditions for its liability.

(Pub. L. 103–272, §1(e), July 5, 1994, 108 Stat. 1141.)

§41705. DISCRIMINATION AGAINST INDIVIDUALS WITH DISABILITIES

(a) IN GENERAL.—In providing air transportation, an air carrier, including (subject to section 40105(b)) any foreign air carrier, may not discriminate against an otherwise qualified individual on the following grounds:

(1) the individual has a physical or mental impairment that substantially limits one or more major life activities.

(2) the individual has a record of such an impairment.

(3) the individual is regarded as having such an impairment.

(b) EACH ACT CONSTITUTES SEPARATE OFFENSE.—For purposes of section 46301, a separate violation occurs under this section for each individual act of discrimination prohibited by subsection (a).

(c) INVESTIGATION OF COMPLAINTS.—

(1) IN GENERAL.—The Secretary shall—

(A) not later than 120 days after the receipt of any complaint of a violation of this section or a regulation prescribed under this section, investigate such complaint; and

(B) provide, in writing, to the individual that filed the complaint and the air carrier or foreign air carrier alleged to have violated this section or a regulation prescribed under this section, the determination of the Secretary with respect to—

(i) whether the air carrier or foreign air carrier violated this section or a regulation prescribed under this section;

(ii) the facts underlying the complaint; and

(iii) any action the Secretary is taking in response to the complaint.

(2) PUBLICATION OF DATA.—The Secretary shall publish disability-related complaint data in a manner comparable to other consumer complaint data.

(3) REVIEW AND REPORT.—The Secretary shall regularly review all complaints received by air carriers alleging discrimination on the basis of disability and shall report annually to Congress on the results of such review.

(4) TECHNICAL ASSISTANCE.—Not later than 180 days after the date of the enactment of this subsection, the Secretary shall—

(A) implement a plan, in consultation with the Department of Justice, the United States Architectural and Transportation Barriers Compliance Board, and the National Council on Disability, to provide technical assistance to air carriers and individuals with disabilities in understanding the rights and responsibilities set forth in this section; and

(B) ensure the availability and provision of appropriate technical assistance manuals to individuals and entities with rights or responsibilities under this section.

(Pub. L. 103–272, §1(e), July 5, 1994, 108 Stat. 1141; Pub. L. 106–181, title VII, §707(a), Apr. 5, 2000, 114 Stat. 158; Pub. L. 108–176, title V, §503(d)(1), Dec. 12, 2003, 117 Stat. 2559; Pub. L. 118–63, title V, §§549, 550(c), May 16, 2024, 138 Stat. 1212.)

§41706. PROHIBITIONS AGAINST SMOKING ON PASSENGER FLIGHTS

(a) SMOKING PROHIBITION IN INTERSTATE AND INTRASTATE AIR TRANSPORTATION.—An individual may not smoke—

(1) in an aircraft in scheduled passenger interstate or intrastate air transportation; or

(2) in an aircraft in nonscheduled passenger interstate or intrastate air transportation, if a flight attendant is a required crewmember on the aircraft (as determined by the Administrator of the Federal Aviation Administration).

(b) SMOKING PROHIBITION IN FOREIGN AIR TRANSPORTATION.—The Secretary of Transportation shall require all air carriers and foreign air carriers to prohibit smoking—

(1) in an aircraft in scheduled passenger foreign air transportation; and

(2) in an aircraft in nonscheduled passenger foreign air transportation, if a flight attendant is a required crewmember on the aircraft (as determined by the Administrator or a foreign government).

(c) LIMITATION ON APPLICABILITY.—

(1) IN GENERAL.—If a foreign government objects to the application of subsection (b) on the basis that subsection (b) provides for an extraterritorial application of the laws of the United States, the Secretary shall waive the application of subsection (b) to a foreign air carrier licensed by that foreign government at such time as an alternative prohibition negotiated under paragraph (2) becomes effective and is enforced by the Secretary.

(2) ALTERNATIVE PROHIBITION.—If, pursuant to paragraph (1), a foreign government objects to the prohibition under subsection (b), the Secretary shall enter into bilateral negotiations with the objecting foreign government to provide for an alternative smoking prohibition.

(d) ELECTRONIC CIGARETTES.—

(1) INCLUSION.—The use of an electronic cigarette shall be treated as smoking for purposes of this section.

(2) ELECTRONIC CIGARETTE DEFINED.—In this section, the term "electronic cigarette" means a device that delivers nicotine to a user of the device in the form of a vapor that is inhaled to simulate the experience of smoking.

(e) REGULATIONS.—The Secretary shall prescribe such regulations as are necessary to carry out this section.

(Pub. L. 103–272, §1(e), July 5, 1994, 108 Stat. 1141; Pub. L. 106–181, title VII, §708(a), Apr. 5, 2000, 114 Stat. 159; Pub. L. 112–95, title IV, §401(a), Feb. 14, 2012, 126 Stat. 83; Pub. L. 115–254, div. B, title IV, §409, Oct. 5, 2018, 132 Stat. 3331.)

§41707. INCORPORATING CONTRACT TERMS INTO WRITTEN INSTRUMENT

To the extent the Secretary of Transportation prescribes by regulation, an air carrier may incorporate by reference in a ticket or written instrument any term of the contract for providing interstate air transportation.

(Pub. L. 103–272, §1(e), July 5, 1994, 108 Stat. 1141.)

§41708. REPORTS

(a) APPLICATION.—To the extent the Secretary of Transportation finds necessary to carry out this subpart, this section and section 41709 of this title apply to a person controlling an air carrier or affiliated (within the meaning of section 11343(c) of this title) with a carrier.

(b) REQUIREMENTS.—The Secretary may require an air carrier or foreign air carrier—

(1)(A) to file annual, monthly, periodical, and special reports with the Secretary in the form and way prescribed by the Secretary; and

(B) to file the reports under oath;

(2) to provide specific answers to questions on which the Secretary considers information to be necessary; and

(3) to file with the Secretary a copy of each agreement, arrangement, contract, or understanding between the carrier and another carrier or person related to transportation affected by this subpart.

(c) DIVERTED AND CANCELLED FLIGHTS.—

(1) MONTHLY REPORTS.—The Secretary shall require an air carrier referred to in paragraph (2) to file with the Secretary a monthly report on each flight of the air carrier that is diverted from its scheduled destination to another airport and each flight of the air carrier that departs the gate at the airport at which the flight originates but is cancelled before wheels-off time.

(2) APPLICABILITY.—An air carrier that is required to file a monthly airline service quality performance report pursuant to part 234 of title 14, Code of Federal Regulations, shall be subject to the requirement of paragraph (1).

(3) CONTENTS.—A monthly report filed by an air carrier under paragraph (1) shall include, at a minimum, the following information:

(A) For a diverted flight—

(i) the flight number of the diverted flight;

(ii) the scheduled destination of the flight;

(iii) the date and time of the flight;

(iv) the airport to which the flight was diverted;

(v) wheels-on time at the diverted airport;

(vi) the time, if any, passengers deplaned the aircraft at the diverted airport; and

(vii) if the flight arrives at the scheduled destination airport—

(I) the gate-departure time at the diverted airport;

(II) the wheels-off time at the diverted airport;

(III) the wheels-on time at the scheduled arrival airport; and

(IV) the gate-arrival time at the scheduled arrival airport.

(B) For flights cancelled after gate departure—

(i) the flight number of the cancelled flight;

(ii) the scheduled origin and destination airports of the cancelled flight;

(iii) the date and time of the cancelled flight;

(iv) the gate-departure time of the cancelled flight; and

(v) the time the aircraft returned to the gate.

(4) PUBLICATION.—The Secretary shall compile the information provided in the monthly reports filed pursuant to paragraph (1) in a single monthly report and publish such report on the Internet Web site of the Department of Transportation.

(Pub. L. 103–272, §1(e), July 5, 1994, 108 Stat. 1141; Pub. L. 112–95, title IV, §402(a), Feb. 14, 2012, 126 Stat. 83.)

§41709. RECORDS OF AIR CARRIERS

(a) REQUIREMENTS.—The Secretary of Transportation shall prescribe the form of records to be kept by an air carrier, including records on the movement of traffic, receipts and expenditures of money, and the time period during which the records shall be kept. A carrier may keep only records prescribed or approved by the Secretary. However, a carrier may keep additional records if the additional records do not impair the integrity of the records prescribed or approved by the Secretary and are not an unreasonable financial burden on the carrier.

(b) INSPECTION.—(1) The Secretary at any time may—

(A) inspect the land, buildings, and equipment of an air carrier or foreign air carrier when necessary to decide under subchapter II of this chapter or section 41102, 41103, or 41302 of this title whether a carrier is fit, willing, and able; and

(B) inspect records kept or required to be kept by an air carrier, foreign air carrier, or ticket agent.

(2) The Secretary may employ special agents or auditors to carry out this subsection.

(Pub. L. 103–272, §1(e), July 5, 1994, 108 Stat. 1142.)

§41710. TIME REQUIREMENTS

When a matter requiring action of the Secretary of Transportation is submitted under section 40109(a) or (c)–(h), 41309, or 42111 of this title and an evidentiary hearing—

(1) is ordered, the Secretary shall make a final decision on the matter not later than the last day of the 12th month that begins after the date the matter is submitted; or

(2) is not ordered, the Secretary shall make a final decision on the matter not later than the last day of the 6th month that begins after the date the matter is submitted.

(Pub. L. 103–272, §1(e), July 5, 1994, 108 Stat. 1142.)

§41711. AIR CARRIER MANAGEMENT INQUIRY AND COOPERATION WITH OTHER AUTHORITIES

In carrying out this subpart, the Secretary of Transportation may—

(1) inquire into the management of the business of an air carrier and obtain from the air carrier, and a person controlling, controlled by, or under common control with the carrier, information the Secretary decides reasonably is necessary to carry out the inquiry;

(2) confer and hold a joint hearing with a State authority; and

(3) exchange information related to aeronautics with a government of a foreign country through appropriate departments, agencies, and instrumentalities of the United States Government.

(Pub. L. 103–272, §1(e), July 5, 1994, 108 Stat. 1142.)

§41712. UNFAIR AND DECEPTIVE PRACTICES AND UNFAIR METHODS OF COMPETITION

(a) IN GENERAL.—On the initiative of the Secretary of Transportation or the complaint of an air carrier, foreign air carrier, air ambulance consumer (as defined by the Secretary of Transportation), or ticket agent, and if the Secretary considers it is in the public interest, the Secretary may investigate and decide whether an air carrier, foreign air carrier, or ticket agent has been or is engaged in an unfair or deceptive practice or an unfair method of competition in air transportation or the sale of air transportation. If the Secretary, after notice and an opportunity for a hearing, finds that an air carrier, foreign air carrier, or ticket agent is engaged in an unfair or deceptive practice or unfair method of competition, the Secretary shall order the air carrier, foreign air carrier, or ticket agent to stop the practice or method.

(b) E-TICKET EXPIRATION NOTICE.—It shall be an unfair or deceptive practice under subsection (a) for any air carrier, foreign air carrier, or ticket agent utilizing electronically transmitted tickets for air transportation to fail to notify the purchaser of such a ticket of its expiration date, if any.

(c) DISCLOSURE REQUIREMENT FOR SELLERS OF TICKETS FOR FLIGHTS.—

(1) IN GENERAL.—It shall be an unfair or deceptive practice under subsection (a) for any ticket agent, air carrier, foreign air carrier, or other person offering to sell tickets for air transportation on a flight of an air carrier to fail to disclose, whether verbally in oral communication or in writing in written or electronic communication, prior to the purchase of a ticket—

(A) the name of the air carrier providing the air transportation; and

(B) if the flight has more than one flight segment, the name of each air carrier providing the air transportation for each such flight segment.

(2) INTERNET OFFERS.—In the case of an offer to sell tickets described in paragraph (1) on an Internet Web site, disclosure of the information required by paragraph (1) shall be provided on the first display of the Web site following a search of a requested itinerary in a format that is easily visible to a viewer.

(Pub. L. 103–272, §1(e), July 5, 1994, 108 Stat. 1143; Pub. L. 106–181, title II, §221, Apr. 5, 2000, 114 Stat. 102; Pub. L. 111–216, title II, §210, Aug. 1, 2010, 124 Stat. 2362; Pub. L. 115–254, div. B, title IV, §419(b), Oct. 5, 2018, 132 Stat. 3336.)

§41713. PREEMPTION OF AUTHORITY OVER PRICES, ROUTES, AND SERVICE

(a) DEFINITION.—In this section, "State" means a State, the District of Columbia, and a territory or possession of the United States.

(b) PREEMPTION.—(1) Except as provided in this subsection, a State, political subdivision of a State, or political authority of at least 2 States may not enact or enforce a law, regulation, or other provision having the force and effect of law related to a price, route, or service of an air carrier that may provide air transportation under this subpart.

(2) Paragraphs (1) and (4) of this subsection do not apply to air transportation provided entirely in Alaska unless the transportation is air transportation (except charter air transportation) provided under a certificate issued under section 41102 of this title.

(3) This subsection does not limit a State, political subdivision of a State, or political authority of at least 2 States that owns or operates an airport served by an air carrier holding a certificate issued by the Secretary of Transportation from carrying out its proprietary powers and rights.

(4) TRANSPORTATION BY AIR CARRIER OR CARRIER AFFILIATED WITH A DIRECT AIR CARRIER.—

(A) GENERAL RULE.—Except as provided in subparagraph (B), a State, political subdivision of a State, or political authority of 2 or more States may not enact or enforce a law, regulation, or other provision having the force and effect of law related to a price, route, or service of an air carrier or carrier affiliated with a direct air carrier through common controlling ownership when such carrier is transporting property by aircraft or by motor vehicle (whether or not such property has had or will have a prior or subsequent air movement).

(B) MATTERS NOT COVERED.—Subparagraph (A)—

(i) shall not restrict the safety regulatory authority of a State with respect to motor vehicles, the authority of a State to impose highway route controls or limitations based on the size or weight of the motor vehicle or the hazardous nature of the cargo, or the authority of a State to regulate motor carriers with regard to minimum amounts of financial responsibility relating to insurance requirements and self-insurance authorization; and

(ii) does not apply to the transportation of household goods, as defined in section 13102 of this title.

(C) APPLICABILITY OF PARAGRAPH (1).—This paragraph shall not limit the applicability of paragraph (1).

(Pub. L. 103–272, §1(e), July 5, 1994, 108 Stat. 1143; Pub. L. 103–305, title VI, §601(b)(1), (2)(A), Aug. 23, 1994, 108 Stat. 1605, 1606; Pub. L. 105–102, §2(23), Nov. 20, 1997, 111 Stat. 2205.)

§41714. AVAILABILITY OF SLOTS

(a) MAKING SLOTS AVAILABLE FOR ESSENTIAL AIR SERVICE.—

(1) OPERATIONAL AUTHORITY.—If basic essential air service under subchapter II of this chapter is to be provided from an eligible point to a high density airport (other than Ronald Reagan Washington National Airport), the Secretary of Transportation shall ensure that the air carrier providing or selected to provide such service has sufficient operational authority at the high density airport to provide such service. The operational authority shall allow flights at reasonable times taking into account the needs of passengers with connecting flights.

(2) EXEMPTIONS.—If necessary to carry out the objectives of paragraph (1), the Secretary shall by order grant exemptions from the requirements of subparts K and S of part 93 of title 14, Code of Federal Regulations (pertaining to slots at high density airports), to air carriers using Stage 3 aircraft or to commuter air carriers, unless such an exemption would significantly increase operational delays.

(3) ASSURANCE OF ACCESS.—If the Secretary finds that an exemption under paragraph (2) would significantly increase operational delays, the Secretary shall take such action as may be necessary to ensure that an air carrier providing or selected to provide basic essential air service is able to obtain access to a high density airport.

(4) ACTION BY THE SECRETARY.—The Secretary shall issue a final order under this subsection on or before the 60th day after receiving a request from an air carrier for operational authority under this subsection.

(b) SLOTS FOR FOREIGN AIR TRANSPORTATION.—

(1) EXEMPTIONS.—If the Secretary finds it to be in the public interest at a high density airport (other than Ronald Reagan Washington National Airport), the Secretary may grant by order exemptions from the requirements of subparts K and S of part 93 of title

14, Code of Federal Regulations (pertaining to slots at high density airports), to enable air carriers and foreign air carriers to provide foreign air transportation using Stage 3 aircraft.

(2) SLOT WITHDRAWALS.—The Secretary may not withdraw a slot at Chicago O'Hare International Airport from an air carrier in order to allocate that slot to a carrier to provide foreign air transportation.

(3) EQUIVALENT RIGHTS OF ACCESS.—The Secretary shall not take a slot at a high density airport from an air carrier and award such slot to a foreign air carrier if the Secretary determines that air carriers are not provided equivalent rights of access to airports in the country of which such foreign air carrier is a citizen.

(4) CONVERSIONS OF SLOTS.—Effective May 1, 2000, slots at Chicago O'Hare International Airport allocated to an air carrier as of November 1, 1999, to provide foreign air transportation shall be made available to such carrier to provide interstate or intrastate air transportation.

(c) SLOTS FOR NEW ENTRANTS.—If the Secretary finds it to be in the public interest, the Secretary may by order grant exemptions from the requirements under subparts K and S of part 93 of title 14, Code of Federal Regulations (pertaining to slots at high density airports), to enable new entrant air carriers to provide air transportation at high density airports (other than Ronald Reagan Washington National Airport).

(d) SPECIAL RULES FOR RONALD REAGAN WASHINGTON NATIONAL AIRPORT.—

(1) IN GENERAL.—Notwithstanding sections 49104(a)(5) and 49111(e) of this title, or any provision of this section, the Secretary may, only under circumstances determined by the Secretary to be exceptional, grant by order to an air carrier currently holding or operating a slot at Ronald Reagan Washington National Airport an exemption from requirements under subparts K and S of part 93 of title 14, Code of Federal Regulations (pertaining to slots at Ronald Reagan Washington National Airport), to enable that carrier to provide air transportation with Stage 3 aircraft at Ronald Reagan Washington National Airport; except that such exemption shall not—

(A) result in an increase in the total number of slots per day at Ronald Reagan Washington National Airport;

(B) result in an increase in the total number of slots at Ronald Reagan Washington National Airport from 7:00 ante meridiem to 9:59 post meridiem;

(C) increase the number of operations at Ronald Reagan Washington National Airport in any 1-hour period by more than 2 operations;

(D) result in the withdrawal or reduction of slots operated by an air carrier;

(E) result in a net increase in noise impact on surrounding communities resulting from changes in timing of operations permitted under this subsection; and

(F) continue in effect on or after the date on which the final rules issued under subsection (f) become effective.

(2) LIMITATION ON APPLICABILITY.—Nothing in this subsection shall adversely affect Exemption No. 5133, as from time-to-time amended and extended.

(e) STUDY.—

(1) MATTERS TO BE CONSIDERED.—The Secretary shall continue the Secretary's current examination of slot regulations and shall ensure that the examination includes consideration of—

(A) whether improvements in technology and procedures of the air traffic control system and the use of quieter aircraft make it possible to eliminate the limitations on hourly operations imposed by the high density rule contained in part 93 of title 14 of the Code of Federal Regulations or to increase the number of operations permitted under such rule;

(B) the effects of the elimination of limitations or an increase in the number of operations allowed on each of the following:

(i) congestion and delay in any part of the national aviation system;

(ii) the impact of noise on persons living near the airport;

(iii) competition in the air transportation system;

(iv) the profitability of operations of airlines serving the airport; and

(v) aviation safety;

(C) the impact of the current slot allocation process upon the ability of air carriers to provide essential air service under subchapter II of this chapter;

(D) the impact of such allocation process upon the ability of new entrant air carriers to obtain slots in time periods that enable them to provide service;

(E) the impact of such allocation process on the ability of foreign air carriers to obtain slots;

(F) the fairness of such process to air carriers and the extent to which air carriers are provided equivalent rights of access to the air transportation market in the countries of which foreign air carriers holding slots are citizens;

(G) the impact, on the ability of air carriers to provide domestic and international air service, of the withdrawal of slots from air carriers in order to provide slots for foreign air carriers; and

(H) the impact of the prohibition on slot withdrawals in subsections (b)(2) and (b)(3) of this section on the aviation relationship between the United States Government and foreign governments, including whether the prohibition in such subsections will require the withdrawal of slots from general and military aviation in order to meet the needs of air carriers and foreign air carriers providing foreign air transportation (and the impact of such withdrawal on general aviation and military aviation) and whether slots will become available to meet the needs of air carriers and foreign air carriers to provide foreign air transportation as a result of the planned relocation of Air Force Reserve units and the Air National Guard at O'Hare International Airport.

(2) REPORT.—Not later than January 31, 1995, the Secretary shall complete the current examination of slot regulations and shall transmit to the Committee on Commerce, Science, and Transportation of the Senate and the Committee on Transportation and Infrastructure of the House of Representatives a report containing the results of such examination.

(f) RULEMAKING.—The Secretary shall conduct a rulemaking proceeding based on the results of the study described in subsection (e). In the course of such proceeding, the Secretary shall issue a notice of proposed rulemaking not later than August 1, 1995, and shall issue a final rule not later than 90 days after public comments are due on the notice of proposed rulemaking.

(g) WEEKEND OPERATIONS.—The Secretary shall consider the advisability of revising section 93.227 of title 14, Code of Federal Regulations, so as to eliminate weekend schedules from the determination of whether the 80 percent standard of subsection (a)(1) of that section has been met.

(h) DEFINITIONS.—In this section and sections 41715–41718 and 41734(h), the following definitions apply:

(1) COMMUTER AIR CARRIER.—The term "commuter air carrier" means a commuter operator as defined or applied in subpart K or S of part 93 of title 14, Code of Federal Regulations.

(2) HIGH DENSITY AIRPORT.—The term "high density airport" means an airport at which the Administrator limits the number of instrument flight rule takeoffs and landings of aircraft.

(3) NEW ENTRANT AIR CARRIER.—The term "new entrant air carrier" means an air carrier that does not hold a slot at the airport concerned and has never sold or given up a slot at that airport after December 16, 1985, and a limited incumbent carrier.

(4) SLOT.—The term "slot" means a reservation for an instrument flight rule takeoff or landing by an air carrier of an aircraft in air transportation.

(5) LIMITED INCUMBENT AIR CARRIER.—The term "limited incumbent air carrier" has the meaning given that term in subpart S of part 93 of title 14, Code of Federal Regulations; except that—

(A) "40" shall be substituted for "12" in sections 93.213(a)(5), 93.223(c)(3), and 93.225(h);

(B) for purposes of such sections, the term "slot" shall not include—

(i) "slot exemptions";

(ii) slots operated by an air carrier under a fee-for-service arrangement for another air carrier, if the air carrier operating such slots does not sell flights in its own name, and is under common ownership with an air carrier that seeks to qualify as a limited incumbent and that sells flights in its own name; or

(iii) slots held under a sale and license-back financing arrangement with another air carrier, where the slots are under the marketing control of the other air carrier; and

(C) for Ronald Reagan Washington National Airport, the Administrator shall not count, for the purposes of section 93.213(a)(5), slots currently held by an air carrier but leased out on a long-term basis by that carrier for use in foreign air transportation and renounced by the carrier for return to the Department of Transportation or the Federal Aviation Administration.

(6) REGIONAL JET.—The term "regional jet" means a passenger, turbofan-powered aircraft with a certificated maximum passenger seating capacity of less than 71.

(7) NONHUB AIRPORT.—The term "nonhub airport" means an airport that had less than .05 percent of the total annual boardings in the United States as determined under the Federal Aviation Administration's Primary Airport Enplanement Activity Summary for Calendar Year 1997.

(8) SMALL HUB AIRPORT.—The term "small hub airport" means an airport that had at least .05 percent, but less than .25 percent, of the total annual boardings in the United States as determined under the summary referred to in paragraph (7).

(9) MEDIUM HUB AIRPORT.—The term "medium hub airport" means an airport that each

year has at least .25 percent, but less than 1.0 percent, of the total annual boardings in the United States as determined under the summary referred to in paragraph (7).

(i) 60-DAY APPLICATION PROCESS.—

(1) REQUEST FOR SLOT EXEMPTIONS.—Any slot exemption request filed with the Secretary under this section or section 41716 or 41717 (other than subsection (c)) shall include—

(A) the names of the airports to be served;

(B) the times requested; and

(C) such additional information as the Secretary may require.

(2) ACTION ON REQUEST; FAILURE TO ACT.—Within 60 days after a slot exemption request under this section or section 41716 or 41717 (other than subsection (c)) is received by the Secretary, the Secretary shall—

(A) approve the request if the Secretary determines that the requirements of the section under which the request is made are met;

(B) return the request to the applicant for additional information relating to the request to provide air transportation; or

(C) deny the request and state the reasons for its denial.

(3) 60-DAY PERIOD TOLLED FOR TIMELY REQUEST FOR MORE INFORMATION.—If the Secretary returns under paragraph (2)(B) the request for additional information during the first 20 days after the request is filed, then the 60-day period under paragraph (2) shall be tolled until the date on which the additional information is filed with the Secretary.

(4) FAILURE TO DETERMINE DEEMED APPROVAL.—If the Secretary neither approves the request under paragraph (2)(A) nor denies the request under paragraph (2)(C) within the 60-day period beginning on the date the request is received, excepting any days during which the 60-day period is tolled under paragraph (3), then the request is deemed to have been approved on the 61st day, after the request was filed with the Secretary.

(j) EXEMPTIONS MAY NOT BE TRANSFERRED.—No exemption from the requirements of subparts K and S of part 93 of title 14, Code of Federal Regulations, granted under this section or section 41716, 41717, or 41718 may be bought, sold, leased, or otherwise transferred by the carrier to which it is granted, except through an air carrier merger or acquisition.

(k) AFFILIATED CARRIERS.—For purposes of this section and sections 41716, 41717, and 41718, an air carrier that operates under the same designator code, or has or enters into a code-share agreement, with any other air carrier shall not qualify for a new slot or slot exemption as a new entrant or limited incumbent air carrier at an airport if the total number of slots and slot exemptions held by the two carriers at the airport exceed 20 slots and slot exemptions.

(Added Pub. L. 103–305, title II, §206(a)(1), Aug. 23, 1994, 108 Stat. 1584; amended Pub. L. 104–287, §5(9), Oct. 11, 1996, 110 Stat. 3389; Pub. L. 105–66, title III, §345, Oct. 27, 1997, 111 Stat. 1449; Pub. L. 105–102, §2(24), Nov. 20, 1997, 111 Stat. 2205; Pub. L. 105–154, §2(a)(1)(C), (2), Feb. 6, 1998, 112 Stat. 3; Pub. L. 106–181, title II, §231(a), (d)(2)–(4), Apr. 5, 2000, 114 Stat. 106, 112; Pub. L. 112–95, title IV, §414(c), (d), Feb. 14, 2012, 126 Stat. 92.)

§41715. PHASE-OUT OF SLOT RULES AT CERTAIN AIRPORTS

(a) TERMINATION.—The rules contained in subparts S and K of part 93, title 14, Code of

Federal Regulations, shall not apply—

(1) after July 1, 2002, at Chicago O'Hare International Airport; and

(2) after January 1, 2007, at LaGuardia Airport or John F. Kennedy International Airport.

(b) STATUTORY CONSTRUCTION.—Nothing in this section and sections 41714 and 41716–41718 shall be construed—

(1) as affecting the Federal Aviation Administration's authority for safety and the movement of air traffic; and

(2) as affecting any other authority of the Secretary to grant exemptions under section 41714.

(c) FACTORS TO CONSIDER.—

(1) IN GENERAL.—Before the award of slot exemptions under sections 41714 and 41716–41718, the Secretary of Transportation may consider, among other determining factors, whether the petitioning air carrier's proposal provides the maximum benefit to the United States economy, including the number of United States jobs created by the air carrier, its suppliers, and related activities. The Secretary should give equal consideration to the consumer benefits associated with the award of such exemptions.

(2) APPLICABILITY.—Paragraph (1) does not apply in any case in which the air carrier requesting the slot exemption is proposing to use under the exemption a type of aircraft for which there is not a competing United States manufacturer.

(Added Pub. L. 106–181, title II, §231(b)(2), Apr. 5, 2000, 114 Stat. 108.)

§41716. INTERIM SLOT RULES AT NEW YORK AIRPORTS

(a) EXEMPTIONS FOR AIR SERVICE TO SMALL AND NONHUB AIRPORTS.—Subject to section 41714(i), the Secretary of Transportation shall grant, by order, exemptions from the requirements under subparts K and S of part 93 of title 14, Code of Federal Regulations (pertaining to slots at high density airports) to any air carrier to provide nonstop air transportation, using an aircraft with a certificated maximum seating capacity of less than 71, between LaGuardia Airport or John F. Kennedy International Airport and a small hub airport or nonhub airport—

(1) if the air carrier was not providing such air transportation during the week of November 1, 1999;

(2) if the number of flights to be provided between such airports by the air carrier during any week will exceed the number of flights provided by the air carrier between such airports during the week of November 1, 1999; or

(3) if the air transportation to be provided under the exemption will be provided with a regional jet as replacement of turboprop air transportation that was being provided during the week of November 1, 1999.

(b) EXEMPTIONS FOR NEW ENTRANT AND LIMITED INCUMBENT AIR CARRIERS.—Subject to section 41714(i), the Secretary shall grant, by order, exemptions from the requirements under subparts K and S of part 93 of title 14, Code of Federal Regulations (pertaining to slots at high density airports), to any new entrant air carrier or limited incumbent air carrier to provide air transportation to or from LaGuardia Airport or John F. Kennedy International Airport if the number of slot exemptions granted under this subsection to such air carrier with respect to such airport when added to the slots and slot exemptions held by such air carrier with respect to such airport does not exceed 20; except that the Secretary may grant not to exceed 4 additional slot exemptions at LaGuardia Airport to an incumbent air carrier operating at least 20 but not more than 28 slots at such airport as of October 1, 2004, to provide air transportation between LaGuardia Airport and a small hub airport or nonhub airport.

(c) STAGE 3 AIRCRAFT REQUIRED.—An exemption may not be granted under this section with respect to any aircraft that is not a Stage 3 aircraft (as defined by the Secretary).

(d) PRESERVATION OF CERTAIN EXISTING SLOT-RELATED AIR SERVICE.—An air carrier that provides air transportation of passengers from LaGuardia Airport or John F. Kennedy International Airport to a small hub airport or nonhub airport, or to an airport that is smaller than a nonhub airport, on or before the date of the enactment of this subsection pursuant to an exemption from the requirements of subparts K and S of part 93 of title 14, Code of Federal Regulations (pertaining to slots at high density airports), or where slots were issued to an air carrier conditioned on a specific airport being served, may not terminate air transportation for that route before July 1, 2003, unless—

(1) before October 1, 1999, the Secretary received a written air service termination notice for that route; or

(2) after September 30, 1999, the air carrier submits an air service termination notice under section 41719 for that route and the Secretary determines that the carrier suffered excessive losses, including substantial losses on operations on that route during any three quarters of the year immediately preceding the date of submission of the notice.

(Added Pub. L. 106–181, title II, §231(c), Apr. 5, 2000, 114 Stat. 109; amended Pub. L. 108–447, div. H, title I, §199, Dec. 8, 2004, 118 Stat. 3235.)

§41717. INTERIM APPLICATION OF SLOT RULES AT CHICAGO O'HARE INTERNATIONAL AIRPORT

(a) SLOT OPERATING WINDOW NARROWED.—Effective July 1, 2001, the requirements of subparts K and S of part 93 of title 14, Code of Federal Regulations, do not apply with respect to aircraft operating before 2:45 post meridiem and after 8:14 post meridiem at Chicago O'Hare International Airport.

(b) EXEMPTIONS FOR AIR SERVICE TO SMALL AND NONHUB AIRPORTS.—Effective May 1, 2000, subject to section 41714(i), the Secretary of Transportation shall grant, by order, exemptions from the requirements of subparts K and S of part 93 of title 14, Code of Federal Regulations (pertaining to slots at high density airports), to any air carrier to provide nonstop air transportation, using an aircraft with a certificated maximum seating capacity of less than 71, between Chicago O'Hare International Airport and a small hub or nonhub airport—

(1) if the air carrier was not providing such air transportation during the week of November 1, 1999;

(2) if the number of flights to be provided between such airports by the air carrier during any week will exceed the number of flights provided by the air carrier between such airports during the week of November 1, 1999; or

(3) if the air transportation to be provided under the exemption will be provided with a regional jet as replacement of turboprop air transportation that was being provided during the week of November 1, 1999.

(c) EXEMPTIONS FOR NEW ENTRANT AND LIMITED INCUMBENT AIR CARRIERS.—

(1) IN GENERAL.—The Secretary shall grant, by order, 30 exemptions from the requirements under subparts K and S of part 93 of title 14, Code of Federal Regulations, to any new entrant air carrier or limited incumbent air carrier to provide air transportation to or from Chicago O'Hare International Airport.

(2) DEADLINE FOR GRANTING EXEMPTIONS.—The Secretary shall grant an exemption under paragraph (1) within 45 days of the date of the request for such exemption if the person making the request qualifies as a new entrant air carrier or limited incumbent air carrier.

(d) SLOTS USED TO PROVIDE TURBOPROP SERVICE.—

(1) IN GENERAL.—Except as provided in paragraph (2), a slot used to provide turboprop air transportation that is replaced with regional jet air transportation under subsection (b)(3) may not be used, sold, leased, or otherwise transferred after the date the slot exemption is granted to replace the turboprop air transportation.

(2) TWO-FOR-ONE EXCEPTION.—An air carrier that otherwise could not use 2 slots as a result of paragraph (1) may use 1 of such slots to provide air transportation.

(3) WITHDRAWAL OF SLOT.—If the Secretary determines that an air carrier that is using a slot under paragraph (2) is no longer providing the air transportation that replaced the turboprop air transportation, the Secretary shall withdraw the slot that is being used under paragraph (2).

(4) CONTINUATION.—If the Secretary determines that an air carrier that is using a slot under paragraph (2) is no longer providing the air transportation that replaced the turboprop air transportation with a regional jet, the Secretary shall withdraw the slot being used by the air carrier under paragraph (2) but shall allow the air carrier to continue to hold the exemption granted to the air carrier under subsection (b)(3).

(e) INTERNATIONAL SERVICE AT O'HARE AIRPORT.—

(1) TERMINATION OF REQUIREMENTS.—Subject to paragraph (2), the requirements of subparts K and S of part 93 of title 14, Code of Federal Regulations, shall be of no force and effect at Chicago O'Hare International Airport after May 1, 2000, with respect to any aircraft providing foreign air transportation.

(2) EXCEPTION RELATING TO RECIPROCITY.—The Secretary may limit access to Chicago O'Hare International Airport with respect to foreign air transportation being provided by a foreign air carrier domiciled in a country to which an air carrier provides nonstop air transportation from the United States if the country in which that carrier is domiciled does not provide reciprocal airport access for air carriers.

(f) STAGE 3 AIRCRAFT REQUIRED.—An exemption may not be granted under this section with respect to any aircraft that is not a Stage 3 aircraft (as defined by the Secretary).

(g) PRESERVATION OF CERTAIN EXISTING SLOT-RELATED AIR SERVICE.—An air carrier that provides air transportation of passengers from Chicago O'Hare International Airport to a small hub airport or nonhub airport, or to an airport that is smaller than a nonhub airport, on or before the date of the enactment of this subsection pursuant to an exemption from the requirements of subparts K and S of part 93 of title 14, Code of Federal Regulations (pertaining to slots at high density airports), or where slots were issued to an air carrier conditioned on a specific airport being served, may not terminate air transportation service for that route for a period of 1 year after the date on which those requirements cease to apply to such airport unless—

(1) before October 1, 1999, the Secretary received a written air service termination notice for that route; or

(2) after September 30, 1999, the air carrier submits an air service termination notice under section 41719 for that route and the Secretary determines that the carrier suffered excessive losses, including substantial losses on operations on that route during the calendar quarters immediately preceding submission of the notice.

(Added Pub. L. 106–181, title II, §231(d)(1), Apr. 5, 2000, 114 Stat. 110.)

§41718. SPECIAL RULES FOR RONALD REAGAN WASHINGTON NATIONAL AIRPORT

(a) BEYOND-PERIMETER EXEMPTIONS.—The Secretary shall grant, by order, 24 exemptions from the application of sections 49104(a)(5), 49109, 49111(e), and 41714 of this title to air carriers to operate limited frequencies and aircraft on select routes between Ronald Reagan Washington National Airport and domestic hub airports and exemptions from the requirements of subparts K and S of part 93, Code of Federal Regulations, if the Secretary finds that the exemptions will—

(1) provide air transportation with domestic network benefits in areas beyond the perimeter described in that section;

(2) increase competition by new entrant air carriers or in multiple markets;

(3) not reduce travel options for communities served by small hub airports and medium hub airports within the perimeter described in section 49109; and

(4) not result in meaningfully increased travel delays.

(b) WITHIN-PERIMETER EXEMPTIONS.—The Secretary shall grant, by order, 20 exemptions from the requirements of sections 49104(a)(5), 49111(e), and 41714 of this title and subparts K and S of part 93 of title 14, Code of Federal Regulations, to air carriers for providing air transportation to airports within the perimeter established for civil aircraft operations at Ronald Reagan Washington National Airport under section 49109. The Secretary shall develop criteria for distributing slot exemptions for flights within the perimeter to such airports under this paragraph in a manner that promotes air transportation—

(1) by new entrant air carriers and limited incumbent air carriers;

(2) to communities without existing nonstop air transportation to Ronald Reagan Washington National Airport;

(3) to small communities;

(4) that will provide competitive nonstop air transportation on a monopoly nonstop route to Ronald Reagan Washington National Airport; or

(5) that will produce the maximum competitive benefits, including low fares.

(c) LIMITATIONS.—

(1) STAGE 3 AIRCRAFT REQUIRED.—An exemption may not be granted under this section with respect to any aircraft that is not a Stage 3 aircraft (as defined by the Secretary).

(2) GENERAL EXEMPTIONS.—

(A) HOURLY LIMITATION.—The exemptions granted—

(i) under subsections (a), (b), and (i) and departures authorized under subsection (g)(2) may not be for operations between the hours of 10:00 p.m. and 7:00 a.m.; and

(ii) under subsections (a), (b), (g), and (i) may not increase the number of operations at Ronald Reagan Washington National Airport in any 1-hour period during the hours between 7:00 a.m. and 9:59 p.m. by more than 5 operations.

(B) USE OF EXISTING SLOTS.—A non-limited incumbent air carrier utilizing an exemption authorized under subsection (g)(3) for an arrival permitted between the hours of 10:01 p.m. and 11:00 p.m. under this section shall discontinue use of an existing slot during the same time period the arrival exemption is operated.

(3) ALLOCATION OF WITHIN-PERIMETER EXEMPTIONS.—Of the exemptions granted under subsection (b)—

(A) without regard to the criteria contained in subsection (b)(1), six shall be for air transportation to small hub airports and nonhub airports;

(B) ten shall be for air transportation to medium hub and smaller airports; and

(C) four shall be for air transportation to airports without regard to their size.

(4) APPLICABILITY TO EXEMPTION NO. 5133.—Nothing in this section affects Exemption No. 5133, as from time-to-time amended and extended.

(d) APPLICATION PROCEDURES.—The Secretary shall establish procedures to ensure that all requests for exemptions under this section are granted or denied within 90 days after the date on which the request is made.

(e) APPLICABILITY OF CERTAIN LAWS.—Neither the request for, nor the granting of an exemption, under this section shall be considered for purposes of any Federal law a major Federal action significantly affecting the quality of the human environment.

(f) COMMUTERS DEFINED.—For purposes of aircraft operations at Ronald Reagan Washington National Airport under subpart K of part 93 of title 14, Code of Federal Regulations, the term "commuters" means aircraft operations using aircraft having a certificated maximum seating capacity of 76 or less.

(g) ADDITIONAL SLOT EXEMPTIONS.—

(1) INCREASE IN SLOT EXEMPTIONS.—Not later than 90 days after the date of enactment of the FAA Modernization and Reform Act of 2012, the Secretary shall grant, by order 16 exemptions from—

(A) the application of sections 49104(a)(5), 49109, and 41714 to air carriers to operate limited frequencies and aircraft on routes between Ronald Reagan Washington National Airport and airports located beyond the perimeter described in section 49109; and

(B) the requirements of subparts K and S of part 93, Code of Federal Regulations.

(2) NEW ENTRANTS AND LIMITED INCUMBENTS.—Of the slot exemptions made available under paragraph (1), the Secretary shall make 8 available to limited incumbent air carriers or new entrant air carriers (as such terms are defined in section 41714(h)). Such exemptions shall be allocated pursuant to the application process established by the Secretary under subsection (d). The Secretary shall consider the extent to which the exemptions will—

(A) provide air transportation with domestic network benefits in areas beyond the perimeter described in section 49109;

(B) increase competition in multiple markets;

(C) not reduce travel options for communities served by small hub airports and medium hub airports within the perimeter described in section 49109;

(D) not result in meaningfully increased travel delays;

(E) enhance options for nonstop travel to and from the beyond-perimeter airports that will be served as a result of those exemptions;

(F) have a positive impact on the overall level of competition in the markets that will be served as a result of those exemptions; or

(G) produce public benefits, including the likelihood that the service to airports located beyond the perimeter described in section 49109 will result in lower fares, higher capacity, and a variety of service options.

(3) IMPROVED NETWORK SLOTS.—Of the slot exemptions made available under paragraph (1), the Secretary shall make 8 available to incumbent air carriers qualifying for status as a non-limited incumbent carrier at Ronald Reagan Washington National Airport as of the date of enactment of the FAA Modernization and Reform Act of 2012. Each such non-limited incumbent air carrier—

(A) may operate up to a maximum of 2 of the newly authorized slot exemptions;

(B) prior to exercising an exemption made available under paragraph (1), shall discontinue the use of a slot for service between Ronald Reagan Washington National Airport and a large hub airport within the perimeter as described in section 49109, and operate, in place of such service, service between Ronald Reagan Washington National Airport and an airport located beyond the perimeter described in section 49109;

(C) shall be entitled to return of the slot by the Secretary if use of the exemption made available to the carrier under paragraph (1) is discontinued;

(D) shall have sole discretion concerning the use of an exemption made available under paragraph (1), including the initial or any subsequent beyond perimeter destinations to be served; and

(E) shall file a notice of intent with the Secretary and subsequent notices of intent, when appropriate, to inform the Secretary of any change in circumstances concerning the use of any exemption made available under paragraph (1).

(4) NOTICES OF INTENT.—Notices of intent under paragraph (3)(E) shall specify the beyond perimeter destination to be served and the slots the carrier shall discontinue using to serve a large hub airport located within the perimeter.

(5) CONDITIONS.—Beyond-perimeter flight operations carried out by an air carrier using an exemption granted under this subsection shall be subject to the following conditions:

(A) An air carrier may not operate a multi-aisle or widebody aircraft in conducting such operations.

(B) An air carrier granted an exemption under this subsection is prohibited from transferring the rights to its beyond-perimeter exemptions pursuant to section 41714(j).

(h) SCHEDULING PRIORITY.—In administering this section, the Secretary shall—

(1) afford a scheduling priority to operations conducted by new entrant air carriers and limited incumbent air carriers over operations conducted by other air carriers granted additional slot exemptions under subsection (g) for service to airports located beyond the perimeter described in section 49109;

(2) afford a scheduling priority to slot exemptions currently held by new entrant air carriers and limited incumbent air carriers for service to airports located beyond the perimeter described in section 49109, to the extent necessary to protect viability of such service; and

(3) consider applications from foreign air carriers that are certificated by the government of Canada if such consideration is required by the bilateral aviation agreement between the United States and Canada and so long as the conditions and limitations under this section apply to such foreign air carriers.

(i) ADDITIONAL SLOT EXEMPTIONS.—

(1) INCREASE IN SLOT EXEMPTIONS.—Not later than 60 days after the date of enactment of the FAA Reauthorization Act of 2024, the Secretary shall grant, by order, 10 exemptions from—

(A) the application of sections 49104(a)(5), 49109, and 41714 to air carriers to operate limited frequencies and aircraft on routes between Ronald Reagan Washington National Airport and domestic airports located within or beyond the perimeter described in section 49109; and

(B) the requirements of subparts K, S, and T of part 93 of title 14, Code of Federal Regulations.

(2) NON-LIMITED INCUMBENTS.—Of the slot exemptions made available under paragraph (1), the Secretary shall make 8 available to incumbent air carriers qualifying for status as a non-limited incumbent carrier at Ronald Reagan Washington National Airport as of the date of enactment of the FAA Reauthorization Act of 2024.

(3) LIMITED INCUMBENTS.—Of the slot exemptions made available under paragraph (1), the Secretary shall make 2 available to incumbent air carriers qualifying for status as a limited incumbent carrier at Ronald Reagan Washington National Airport as of the date of enactment of the FAA Reauthorization Act of 2024.

(4) ALLOCATION PROCEDURES.—The Secretary shall allocate the 10 slot exemptions provided under paragraph (1) pursuant to the application process established by the Secretary under subsection (d), subject to the following:

(A) LIMITATIONS.—Each air carrier that is eligible under paragraph (2) and paragraph (3) shall be eligible to operate no more and no less than 2 of the newly authorized slot exemptions.

(B) CRITERIA.—The Secretary shall consider the extent to which the exemptions will—

(i) enhance options for nonstop travel to beyond-perimeter airports that do not have nonstop service from Ronald Reagan Washington National Airport as of the date of enactment of the FAA Reauthorization Act of 2024; or

(ii) have a positive impact on the overall level of competition in the markets that will be served as a result of those exemptions.

(5) PROHIBITION.—

(A) IN GENERAL.—The Metropolitan Washington Airports Authority may not assess any penalty or similar levy against an individual air carrier solely for obtaining and operating a slot exemption authorized under this subsection.

(B) RULE OF CONSTRUCTION.—Subparagraph (A) shall not be construed as prohibiting the Metropolitan Washington Airports Authority from assessing and collecting any penalty, fine, or other levy, such as a handling fee or landing fee, that is—

    (i) authorized by the Metropolitan Washington Airports Regulations;

    (ii) agreed to in writing by the air carrier; or

    (iii) charged in the ordinary course of business to an air carrier operating at Ronald Reagan Washington National Airport regardless of whether or not the air carrier obtained a slot exemption authorized under this subsection.

(Added Pub. L. 106–181, title II, §231(e)(1), Apr. 5, 2000, 114 Stat. 112; amended Pub. L. 108–176, title IV, §§425, 426(a), Dec. 12, 2003, 117 Stat. 2555; Pub. L. 112–95, title IV, §414(a), (b), Feb. 14, 2012, 126 Stat. 90, 92; Pub. L. 118–63, title V, §502(a), (b), May 16, 2024, 138 Stat. 1187, 1188.)

§41719. AIR SERVICE TERMINATION NOTICE

(a) IN GENERAL.—An air carrier may not terminate interstate air transportation from a nonhub airport included on the Secretary of Transportation's latest published list of such airports, unless such air carrier has given the Secretary at least 45 days' notice before such termination.

(b) EXCEPTIONS.—The requirements of subsection (a) shall not apply when—

    (1) the carrier involved is experiencing a sudden or unforeseen financial emergency, including natural weather related emergencies, equipment-related emergencies, and strikes;

    (2) the termination of transportation is made for seasonal purposes only;

    (3) the carrier involved has operated at the affected nonhub airport for 180 days or less;

    (4) the carrier involved provides other transportation by jet from another airport serving the same community as the affected nonhub airport; or

    (5) the carrier involved makes alternative arrangements, such as a change of aircraft size, or other types of arrangements with a part 121 or part 135 air carrier, that continues uninterrupted service from the affected nonhub airport.

(c) WAIVERS FOR REGIONAL/COMMUTER CARRIERS.—Before January 1, 1995, the Secretary shall establish terms and conditions under which regional/commuter carriers can be excluded from the termination notice requirement.

(d) DEFINITIONS.—In this section, the following definitions apply:

    (1) PART 121 AIR CARRIER.—The term "part 121 air carrier" means an air carrier to which part 121 of title 14, Code of Federal Regulations, applies.

    (2) PART 135 AIR CARRIER.—The term "part 135 air carrier" means an air carrier to which part 135 of title 14, Code of Federal Regulations, applies.

    (3) REGIONAL/COMMUTER CARRIERS.—The term "regional/commuter carrier" means—

        (A) a part 135 air carrier; or

        (B) a part 121 air carrier that provides air transportation exclusively with aircraft having a seating capacity of no more than 70 passengers.

    (4) TERMINATION.—The term "termination" means the cessation of all service at an airport by an air carrier.

(Added Pub. L. 103–305, title II, §207(a), Aug. 23, 1994, 108 Stat. 1587, §41715; amended Pub. L. 103–429, §6(53), Oct. 31, 1994, 108 Stat. 4385; Pub. L. 104–287, §5(73), Oct. 11, 1996, 110 Stat. 3396; renumbered §41719, Pub. L. 106–181, title II, §231(b)(1), Apr. 5, 2000, 114 Stat. 108; Pub. L. 108–176, title II,

§225(b)(1), Dec. 12, 2003, 117 Stat. 2528.)

§41720. JOINT VENTURE AGREEMENTS

(a) DEFINITIONS.—In this section, the following definitions apply:

(1) JOINT VENTURE AGREEMENT.—The term "joint venture agreement" means an agreement between two or more major air carriers on or after January 1, 1998, with regard to (A) code-sharing, blocked-space arrangements, long-term wet leases (as defined in section 207.1 of title 14, Code of Federal Regulations) of a substantial number (as defined by the Secretary by regulation) of aircraft, or frequent flyer programs, or (B) any other cooperative working arrangement (as defined by the Secretary by regulation) between 2 or more major air carriers that affects more than 15 percent of the total number of available seat miles offered by the major air carriers.

(2) MAJOR AIR CARRIER.—The term "major air carrier" means a passenger air carrier that is certificated under chapter 411 of this title and included in Carrier Group III under criteria contained in section 04 of part 241 of title 14, Code of Federal Regulations.

(b) SUBMISSION OF JOINT VENTURE AGREEMENT.—At least 30 days before a joint venture agreement may take effect, each of the major air carriers that entered into the agreement shall submit to the Secretary—

(1) a complete copy of the joint venture agreement and all related agreements; and

(2) other information and documentary material that the Secretary may require by regulation.

(c) EXTENSION OF WAITING PERIOD.—

(1) IN GENERAL.—The Secretary may extend the 30-day period referred to in subsection (b) until—

(A) in the case of a joint venture agreement with regard to code-sharing, the 150th day following the last day of such period; and

(B) in the case of any other joint venture agreement, the 60th day following the last day of such period.

(2) PUBLICATION OF REASONS FOR EXTENSION.—If the Secretary extends the 30-day period referred to in subsection (b), the Secretary shall publish in the Federal Register the Secretary's reasons for making the extension.

(d) TERMINATION OF WAITING PERIOD.—At any time after the date of submission of a joint venture agreement under subsection (b), the Secretary may terminate the waiting periods referred to in subsections (b) and (c) with respect to the agreement.

(e) REGULATIONS.—The effectiveness of a joint venture agreement may not be delayed due to any failure of the Secretary to issue regulations to carry out this section.

(f) MEMORANDUM TO PREVENT DUPLICATIVE REVIEWS.—Promptly after the date of enactment of this section, the Secretary shall consult with the Assistant Attorney General of the Antitrust Division of the Department of Justice in order to establish, through a written memorandum of understanding, preclearance procedures to prevent unnecessary duplication of effort by the Secretary and the Assistant Attorney General under this section and the antitrust laws of the United States, respectively.

(g) PRIOR AGREEMENTS.—With respect to a joint venture agreement entered into before the date of enactment of this section as to which the Secretary finds that—

(1) the parties submitted the agreement to the Secretary before such date of enactment;

and

(2) the parties submitted all information on the agreement requested by the Secretary, the waiting period described in paragraphs (2) and (3) shall begin on the date, as determined by the Secretary, on which all such information was submitted and end on the last day to which the period could be extended under this section.

(h) LIMITATION ON STATUTORY CONSTRUCTION.—The authority granted to the Secretary under this section shall not in any way limit the authority of the Attorney General to enforce the antitrust laws as defined in the first section of the Clayton Act (15 U.S.C. 12).

(Added Pub. L. 105–277, div. C, title I, §110(f)(1), Oct. 21, 1998, 112 Stat. 2681–588, §41716; renumbered §41720 and amended Pub. L. 106–181, title II, §231(b)(1), title VII, §709, Apr. 5, 2000, 114 Stat. 108, 159.)

§41721. REPORTS BY CARRIERS ON INCIDENTS INVOLVING ANIMALS DURING AIR TRANSPORT

(a) IN GENERAL.—An air carrier that provides scheduled passenger air transportation shall submit monthly to the Secretary a report on any incidents involving the loss, injury, or death of an animal (as defined by the Secretary of Transportation) during air transport provided by the air carrier. The report shall be in such form and contain such information as the Secretary determines appropriate.

(b) TRAINING OF AIR CARRIER EMPLOYEES.—The Secretary shall work with air carriers to improve the training of employees with respect to the air transport of animals and the notification of passengers of the conditions under which the air transport of animals is conducted.

(c) SHARING OF INFORMATION.—The Secretary and the Secretary of Agriculture shall enter into a memorandum of understanding to ensure the sharing of information that the Secretary receives under subsection (a).

(d) PUBLICATION OF DATA.—The Secretary shall publish data on incidents and complaints involving the loss, injury, or death of an animal during air transport in a manner comparable to other consumer complaint and incident data.

(e) AIR TRANSPORT.—For purposes of this section, the air transport of an animal includes the entire period during which an animal is in the custody of an air carrier, from check-in of the animal prior to departure until the animal is returned to the owner or guardian of the animal at the final destination of the animal.

(Added Pub. L. 106–181, title VII, §710(a), Apr. 5, 2000, 114 Stat. 159.)

§41722. DELAY REDUCTION ACTIONS

(a) SCHEDULING REDUCTION MEETINGS.—The Secretary of Transportation may request that air carriers meet with the Administrator of the Federal Aviation Administration to discuss flight reductions at severely congested airports to reduce overscheduling and flight delays during hours of peak operation if—

(1) the Administrator determines that it is necessary to convene such a meeting; and

(2) the Secretary determines that the meeting is necessary to meet a serious transportation need or achieve an important public benefit.

(b) MEETING CONDITIONS.—Any meeting under subsection (a)—

(1) shall be chaired by the Administrator;

(2) shall be open to all scheduled air carriers; and

(3) shall be limited to discussions involving the airports and time periods described in the Administrator's determination.

(c) FLIGHT REDUCTION TARGETS.—Before any such meeting is held, the Administrator shall establish flight reduction targets for the meeting and notify the attending air carriers of those targets not less than 48 hours before the meeting.

(d) DELAY REDUCTION OFFERS.—An air carrier attending the meeting shall make any offer to meet a flight reduction target to the Administrator rather than to another carrier.

(e) TRANSCRIPT.—The Administrator shall ensure that a transcript of the meeting is kept and made available to the public not later than 3 business days after the conclusion of the meeting.

(Added Pub. L. 108–176, title IV, §422(a), Dec. 12, 2003, 117 Stat. 2552.)

§41723. NOTICE CONCERNING AIRCRAFT ASSEMBLY

The Secretary of Transportation shall require, beginning after the last day of the 18-month period following the date of enactment of this section, an air carrier using an aircraft to provide scheduled passenger air transportation to display a notice, on an information placard available to each passenger on the aircraft, that informs the passengers of the nation in which the aircraft was finally assembled.

(Added Pub. L. 108–176, title VIII, §810(a), Dec. 12, 2003, 117 Stat. 2590.)

§41724. MUSICAL INSTRUMENTS

(a) IN GENERAL.—

(1) SMALL INSTRUMENTS AS CARRY-ON BAGGAGE.—An air carrier providing air transportation shall permit a passenger to carry a violin, guitar, or other musical instrument in the aircraft cabin, without charging the passenger a fee in addition to any standard fee that carrier may require for comparable carry-on baggage, if—

(A) the instrument can be stowed safely in a suitable baggage compartment in the aircraft cabin or under a passenger seat, in accordance with the requirements for carriage of carry-on baggage or cargo established by the Administrator; and

(B) there is space for such stowage at the time the passenger boards the aircraft.

(2) LARGER INSTRUMENTS AS CARRY-ON BAGGAGE.—An air carrier providing air transportation shall permit a passenger to carry a musical instrument that is too large to meet the requirements of paragraph (1) in the aircraft cabin, without charging the passenger a fee in addition to the cost of the additional ticket described in subparagraph (E), if—

(A) the instrument is contained in a case or covered so as to avoid injury to other passengers;

(B) the weight of the instrument, including the case or covering, does not exceed 165 pounds or the applicable weight restrictions for the aircraft;

(C) the instrument can be stowed in accordance with the requirements for carriage of carry-on baggage or cargo established by the Administrator;

(D) neither the instrument nor the case contains any object not otherwise permitted to be carried in an aircraft cabin because of a law or regulation of the United States;

and

(E) the passenger wishing to carry the instrument in the aircraft cabin has purchased an additional seat to accommodate the instrument.

(3) LARGE INSTRUMENTS AS CHECKED BAGGAGE.—An air carrier shall transport as baggage a musical instrument that is the property of a passenger traveling in air transportation that may not be carried in the aircraft cabin if—

(A) the sum of the length, width, and height measured in inches of the outside linear dimensions of the instrument (including the case) does not exceed 150 inches or the applicable size restrictions for the aircraft;

(B) the weight of the instrument does not exceed 165 pounds or the applicable weight restrictions for the aircraft; and

(C) the instrument can be stowed in accordance with the requirements for carriage of carry-on baggage or cargo established by the Administrator.

(b) REGULATIONS.—Not later than 2 years after the date of enactment of this section, the Secretary shall issue final regulations to carry out subsection (a).

(c) EFFECTIVE DATE.—The requirements of this section shall become effective on the date of issuance of the final regulations under subsection (b).

(Added Pub. L. 112–95, title IV, §403(a), Feb. 14, 2012, 126 Stat. 84.)

§41725. PROHIBITION ON CERTAIN CELL PHONE VOICE COMMUNICATIONS

(a) PROHIBITION.—The Secretary of Transportation shall issue regulations—

(1) to prohibit an individual on an aircraft from engaging in voice communications using a mobile communications device during a flight of that aircraft in scheduled passenger interstate or intrastate air transportation; and

(2) that exempt from the prohibition described in paragraph (1) any—

(A) member of the flight crew on duty on an aircraft;

(B) flight attendant on duty on an aircraft; and

(C) Federal law enforcement officer acting in an official capacity.

(b) DEFINITIONS.—In this section, the following definitions apply:

(1) FLIGHT.—The term "flight" means, with respect to an aircraft, the period beginning when the aircraft takes off and ending when the aircraft lands.

(2) MOBILE COMMUNICATIONS DEVICE.—

(A) IN GENERAL.—The term "mobile communications device" means any portable wireless telecommunications equipment utilized for the transmission or reception of voice data.

(B) LIMITATION.—The term "mobile communications device" does not include a phone installed on an aircraft.

(Added Pub. L. 115–254, div. B, title IV, §403(a), Oct. 5, 2018, 132 Stat. 3328.)

§41726. STROLLERS

(a) IN GENERAL.—Except as provided in subsection (b), a covered air carrier shall not deny a passenger the ability to check a stroller at the departure gate if the stroller is being used by a passenger to transport a child traveling on the same flight as the passenger.

(b) EXCEPTION.—Subsection (a) shall not apply in instances where the size or weight of the stroller poses a safety or security risk.

(c) COVERED AIR CARRIER DEFINED.—In this section, the term "covered air carrier" means an air carrier or a foreign air carrier as those terms are defined in section 40102 of title 49, United States Code.

(Added Pub. L. 115–254, div. B, title IV, §412(a), Oct. 5, 2018, 132 Stat. 3331.)

§41727. PASSENGER RIGHTS [1]

(a) GUIDELINES.—The Secretary of Transportation shall require each covered air carrier to submit a summarized 1-page document that describes the rights of passengers in air transportation, including guidelines for the following:

(1) Compensation (regarding rebooking options, refunds, meals, and lodging) for flight delays of various lengths.

(2) Compensation (regarding rebooking options, refunds, meals, and lodging) for flight diversions.

(3) Compensation (regarding rebooking options, refunds, meals, and lodging) for flight cancellations.

(4) Compensation for mishandled baggage, including delayed, damaged, pilfered, or lost baggage.

(5) Voluntary relinquishment of a ticketed seat due to overbooking or priority of other passengers.

(6) Involuntary denial of boarding and forced removal for whatever reason, including for safety and security reasons.

(b) FILING OF SUMMARIZED GUIDELINES.—Not later than 90 days after each air carrier submits its guidelines to the Secretary under subsection (a), the air carrier shall make available such 1-page document in a prominent location on its website.

(Added and amended Pub. L. 118–63, title V, §510(a), May 16, 2024, 138 Stat. 1193.)

[1] *So in original. Probably should not be capitalized.*

§41728. AIRLINE PASSENGERS WITH DISABILITIES BILL OF RIGHTS

(a) AIRLINE PASSENGERS WITH DISABILITIES BILL OF RIGHTS.—The Secretary of Transportation shall develop a document, to be known as the "Airline Passengers with Disabilities Bill of Rights", using plain language to describe the basic protections and responsibilities of covered air carriers,[1] their employees and contractors, and people with disabilities under section 41705.

(b) CONTENT.—In developing the Airline Passengers with Disabilities Bill of Rights under subsection (a), the Secretary shall include, at a minimum, plain language descriptions of protections and responsibilities provided in law related to the following:

(1) The right of passengers with disabilities to be treated with dignity and respect.

(2) The right of passengers with disabilities to receive timely assistance, if requested, from properly trained covered air carrier and contractor personnel.

(3) The right of passengers with disabilities to travel with wheelchairs, mobility aids, and other assistive devices, including necessary medications and medical supplies, including stowage of such wheelchairs, aids, and devices.

(4) The right of passengers with disabilities to receive seating accommodations, if requested, to accommodate a disability.

(5) The right of passengers with disabilities to receive announcements in an accessible format.

(6) The right of passengers with disabilities to speak with a complaint resolution officer or to file a complaint with a covered air carrier or the Department of Transportation.

(c) RULE OF CONSTRUCTION.—The development of the Airline Passengers with Disabilities Bill of Rights under subsections (a) and (b) shall not be construed as expanding or restricting the rights available to passengers with disabilities on the day before the date of enactment of the FAA Reauthorization Act of 2018 pursuant to any statute or regulation.

(d) CONSULTATIONS.—In developing the Airline Passengers with Disabilities Bill of Rights under subsection (a), the Secretary of Transportation shall consult with stakeholders, including disability organizations and covered air carriers and their contractors.

(e) DISPLAY.—Each covered air carrier shall include the Airline Passengers with Disabilities Bill of Rights—

(1) on a publicly available internet website of the covered air carrier; and

(2) in any pre-flight notifications or communications provided to passengers who alert the covered air carrier in advance of the need for accommodations relating to a disability.

(f) TRAINING.—Covered air carriers and contractors of covered air carriers shall submit to the Secretary of Transportation plans that ensure that employees of covered air carriers and their contractors receive training on the protections and responsibilities described in the Airline Passengers with Disabilities Bill of Rights. The Secretary shall review such plans to ensure the plans address the matters described in subsection (b).

(Added and amended Pub. L. 118–63, title V, §510(b), May 16, 2024, 138 Stat. 1194.)

[1] *See Definition note below.*

§41729. COVID–19 VACCINATION STATUS

(a) IN GENERAL.—An air carrier (as such term is defined in section 40102) may not deny service to any individual solely based on the vaccination status of the individual with respect to COVID–19.

(b) RULE OF CONSTRUCTION.—Nothing in this section shall be construed to apply to the regulation of intrastate travel, transportation, or movement, including the intrastate transportation of passengers.

(Added Pub. L. 118–63, title XI, §1107(a), May 16, 2024, 138 Stat. 1417.)

SUBCHAPTER II—SMALL COMMUNITY AIR SERVICE

§41731. DEFINITIONS

(a) GENERAL.—In this subchapter—

(1) "eligible place" means a place in the United States that—

(A)(i)(I) was an eligible point under section 419 of the Federal Aviation Act of 1958 before October 1, 1988;

(II) received scheduled air transportation at any time after January 1, 1990; and

(III) is not listed in Department of Transportation Orders 89–9–37 and 89–12–52 as a place ineligible for compensation under this subchapter; or

(ii) was determined, on or after October 1, 1988, and before the date of the enactment of the FAA Extension, Safety, and Security Act of 2016 (Public Law 114–190), under this subchapter by the Secretary of Transportation to be eligible to receive subsidized small community air service under section 41736(a);

(B) had an average of 10 enplanements per service day or more, as determined by the Secretary, during the most recent fiscal year beginning after September 30, 2012;

(C) had an average subsidy per passenger, as determined by the Secretary—

(i) of less than $1,000 during the most recent fiscal year beginning before October 1, 2026, regardless of driving miles to the nearest large or medium hub airport;

(ii) of less than $850 during the most recent fiscal year beginning after September 30, 2026, regardless of driving miles to the nearest medium or large hub airport; and

(iii) of less than $650 during the most recent fiscal year for locations that are less than 175 miles from the nearest large or medium hub airport; and

(D) is a community that, at any time during the period between September 30, 2010, and September 30, 2011, inclusive—

(i) received essential air service for which compensation was provided to an air carrier under this subchapter; or

(ii) received a 140-day notice of intent to terminate essential air service and the Secretary required the air carrier to continue to provide such service to the community.

(2) "enhanced essential air service" means scheduled air transportation to an eligible place of a higher level or quality than basic essential air service described in section 41732 of this title.

(b) LIMITATION ON AUTHORITY TO DECIDE A PLACE NOT AN ELIGIBLE PLACE.—The Secretary may not decide that a place described in subsection (a)(1) of this section is not an eligible place on any basis that is not specifically stated in this subchapter.

(c) EXCEPTION FOR LOCATIONS IN ALASKA AND HAWAII.—Subparagraphs (B), (C), and (D) of subsection (a)(1) shall not apply with respect to locations in the State of Alaska or the State of Hawaii.

(d) EXCEPTIONS FOR LOCATIONS MORE THAN 175 DRIVING MILES FROM THE NEAREST LARGE OR MEDIUM HUB AIRPORT.—Subsection (a)(1)(B) shall not apply with respect to locations that are more than 175 driving miles from the nearest large or medium hub airport.

(e) WAIVERS.—

(1) IN GENERAL.—The Secretary may waive, on an annual basis, subsections (a)(1)(B) and (a)(1)(C)(iii) with respect to an eligible place if such place demonstrates to the Secretary's satisfaction that the reason the eligibility requirements of such subsections are not met is due to a temporary decline in demand.

(2) LIMITATION.—Beginning with fiscal year 2027, the Secretary may not provide a waiver of subsection (a)(1)(B) to any location—

(A) in more than 2 consecutive fiscal years; or

(B) in more than 5 fiscal years within 25 consecutive years.

(3) LIMITATION.—Beginning in fiscal year 2027, the Secretary may not provide a

waiver of subsection (a)(1)(C)(iii) to any location—

(A) in more than 2 consecutive fiscal years; or

(B) in more than 5 fiscal years within 25 consecutive years.

(f) DEFINITION.—For purposes of subsection (a)(1)(B), the term "enplanements" means the number of passengers enplaning, at an eligible place, on flights operated by the subsidized essential air service carrier.

(Pub. L. 103–272, §1(e), July 5, 1994, 108 Stat. 1143; Pub. L. 106–181, title II, §208, Apr. 5, 2000, 114 Stat. 95; Pub. L. 108–176, title II, §225(b)(2), Dec. 12, 2003, 117 Stat. 2529; Pub. L. 112–27, §6, Aug. 5, 2011, 125 Stat. 271; Pub. L. 112–95, title IV, §§421, 422, Feb. 14, 2012, 126 Stat. 96, 97; Pub. L. 115–254, div. B, title IV, §453(a), Oct. 5, 2018, 132 Stat. 3348; Pub. L. 118–63, title V, §561(a)(1)–(3), May 16, 2024, 138 Stat. 1214.)

§41732. BASIC ESSENTIAL AIR SERVICE

(a) GENERAL.—Basic essential air service provided under section 41733 of this title is scheduled air transportation of passengers and cargo—

(1) to a medium or large hub airport less than 650 miles from an eligible place (unless such airport or eligible place are located in a noncontiguous State); or

(2) to a small hub or nonhub airport, when in Alaska or when the nearest medium or large hub airport is more than 400 miles from an eligible place.

(b) MINIMUM REQUIREMENTS.—Basic essential air service shall include at least the following:

(1)(A) for a place not in Alaska, 2 daily round trips 6 days a week, with not more than one intermediate stop on each flight; or

(B) for a place in Alaska, a level of service at least equal to that provided in 1976 or 2 round trips a week, whichever is greater, except that the Secretary of Transportation and the appropriate State authority of Alaska may agree to a different level of service after consulting with the affected community.

(2) flights at reasonable times considering the needs of passengers with connecting flights at the airport and at prices that are not excessive compared to the generally prevailing prices of other air carriers for like service between similar places.

(3) service provided in aircraft with at least 2 engines and using 2 pilots, unless scheduled air transportation has not been provided to the place in aircraft with at least 2 engines and using 2 pilots for at least 60 consecutive operating days at any time since October 31, 1978.

(c) WAIVERS.—Notwithstanding section 41733(e), upon request by an eligible place, the Secretary may waive, in whole or in part, subsections (a) and (b) of this section or subsections (a) through (c) of section 41734. A waiver issued under this subsection shall remain in effect for a limited period of time, as determined by the Secretary.

(Pub. L. 103–272, §1(e), July 5, 1994, 108 Stat. 1144; Pub. L. 115–254, div. B, title IV, §456, Oct. 5, 2018, 132 Stat. 3350; Pub. L. 118–63, title V, §561(b)(1), (c), May 16, 2024, 138 Stat. 1214, 1215.)

§41733. LEVEL OF BASIC ESSENTIAL AIR SERVICE

(a) DECISIONS MADE BEFORE OCTOBER 1, 1988.—For each eligible place for which a decision was made before October 1, 1988, under section 419 of the Federal Aviation Act of 1958, establishing the level of essential air transportation, the level of basic essential air service for that place shall be the level established by the Secretary of Transportation for that place by not later than December 29, 1988.

(b) DECISIONS NOT MADE BEFORE OCTOBER 1, 1988.—(1) The Secretary shall decide on the level of basic essential air service for each eligible place for which a decision was not made before October 1, 1988, establishing the level of essential air transportation, when the Secretary receives notice that service to that place will be provided by only one air carrier. The Secretary shall make the decision by the last day of the 6-month period beginning on the date the Secretary receives the notice. The Secretary may impose notice requirements necessary to carry out this subsection. Before making a decision, the Secretary shall consider the views of any interested community and the appropriate State authority of the State in which the community is located.

(2) Until the Secretary has made a decision on a level of basic essential air service for an eligible place under this subsection, the Secretary, on petition by an appropriate representative of the place, as defined by the Secretary, shall prohibit an air carrier from ending, suspending, or reducing air transportation to that place that appears to deprive the place of basic essential air service.

(c) AVAILABILITY OF COMPENSATION.—(1) If the Secretary decides that basic essential air service will not be provided to an eligible place without compensation, the Secretary shall provide notice that an air carrier may apply to provide basic essential air service to the place for compensation under this section. In selecting an applicant, the Secretary shall consider, among other factors—

(A) the demonstrated reliability of the applicant in providing scheduled air service;

(B) the contractual, marketing, code-share, or interline arrangements the applicant has made with a larger air carrier serving the hub airport;

(C) the preferences of the actual and potential users of air transportation at the eligible place, including the views of the elected officials representing the users;

(D) whether the air carrier has included a plan in its proposal to market its services to the community;

(E) for an eligible place in Alaska, the experience of the applicant in providing, in Alaska, scheduled air service, or significant patterns of non-scheduled air service under an exemption granted under section 40109(a) and (c)–(h) of this title; and

(F) the total compensation proposed by the air carrier for providing scheduled air service under this section.

(2) Under guidelines prescribed under section 41737(a) of this title, the Secretary shall pay the rate of compensation for providing basic essential air service under this section and section 41734 of this title.

(d) COMPENSATION PAYMENTS.—The Secretary shall pay compensation under this section at times and in the way the Secretary decides is appropriate. The Secretary shall end payment of compensation to an air carrier for providing basic essential air service to an eligible place when the Secretary decides the compensation is no longer necessary to maintain basic essential air service to the place.

(e) REVIEW.—The Secretary shall review periodically the level of basic essential air service for each eligible place. Based on the review and consultations with an interested community and the appropriate State authority of the State in which the community is located, the Secretary may make appropriate adjustments in the level of service, to the extent such adjustments are to a level not less than the basic essential air service level established under subsection (a) for the airport that serves the community.

(f) NOTICE TO COMMUNITIES PRIOR TO TERMINATION OF ELIGIBILITY.—

(1) IN GENERAL.—The Secretary shall notify each community receiving basic essential air service for which compensation is being paid under this subchapter on or before the 45th day before issuing any final decision to end the payment of such compensation due to a determination by the Secretary that providing such service requires a rate of subsidy per passenger in excess of the subsidy cap.

(2) PROCEDURES TO AVOID TERMINATION.—The Secretary shall establish, by order, procedures by which each community notified of an impending loss of subsidy under paragraph (1) may work directly with an air carrier to ensure that the air carrier is able to submit a proposal to the Secretary to provide essential air service to such community for an amount of compensation that would not exceed the subsidy cap.

(3) ASSISTANCE PROVIDED.—The Secretary shall provide, by order, information to each community notified under paragraph (1) regarding—

(A) the procedures established pursuant to paragraph (2); and

(B) the maximum amount of compensation that could be provided under this subchapter to an air carrier serving such community that would comply with basic essential air service and the subsidy cap.

(g) PROPOSALS OF STATE AND LOCAL GOVERNMENTS TO RESTORE ELIGIBILITY.—

(1) IN GENERAL.—If the Secretary, after the date of enactment of this subsection, ends payment of compensation to an air carrier for providing basic essential air service to an eligible place because the Secretary has determined that providing such service requires a rate of subsidy per passenger in excess of the subsidy cap or that the place is no longer an eligible place pursuant to section 41731(a)(1)(B), a State or local government may submit to the Secretary a proposal for restoring compensation for such service. Such proposal shall be a joint proposal of the State or local government and an air carrier.

(2) DETERMINATION BY SECRETARY.—The Secretary shall issue an order restoring the eligibility of the otherwise eligible place to receive basic essential air service by an air carrier for compensation under subsection (c) if—

(A) a State or local government submits to the Secretary a proposal under paragraph (1); and

(B) the Secretary determines that—

(i) the rate of subsidy per passenger under the proposal does not exceed the subsidy cap;

(ii) the proposal is likely to result in an average number of enplanements per day that will satisfy the requirement in section 41731(a)(1)(B); and

(iii) the proposal is consistent with the legal and regulatory requirements of the essential air service program.

(h) SUBSIDY CAP DEFINED.—In this section, the term "subsidy cap" means the subsidy-per-passenger cap established under section 41731(a)(1)(C).

(i) COMMUNITY PETITION FOR REVIEW.—

(1) PETITION.—An appropriate representative of an eligible place, as defined by the Secretary, may submit to the Secretary a petition expressing no confidence in the air carrier providing basic essential air service under this section and requesting a review by

the Secretary. A petition submitted under this subsection shall demonstrate that the air carrier—

(A) is unwilling or unable to meet the operational specifications outlined in the order issued by the Secretary specifying the terms of basic essential air service to such place;

(B) is experiencing reliability challenges with the potential to adversely affect air service to such place; or

(C) is no longer able to provide service to such place at the rate of compensation specified by the Secretary.

(2) REVIEW.—Not later than 2 months after the date on which the Secretary receives a petition under paragraph (1), the Secretary shall review the operational performance of the air carrier providing basic essential air service to such place that submitted such petition and determine whether such air carrier is fully complying with the obligations specified in the order issued by the Secretary specifying the terms of basic essential air service to such place.

(3) TERMINATION.—If based on a review under paragraph (2), the Secretary determines noncompliance by an air carrier with an order specifying the terms for basic essential air service to the community, the Secretary may—

(A) terminate the order issued to the air carrier; and

(B) issue a notice pursuant to subsection (c) that an air carrier may apply to provide basic essential air service to such place for compensation under this section and select an applicant pursuant to such subsection.

(4) CONTINUATION OF SERVICE.—If the Secretary makes a determination under paragraph (3) to terminate an order issued to an air carrier under this section, the Secretary shall ensure continuity in air service to the affected place.

(Pub. L. 103–272, §1(e), July 5, 1994, 108 Stat. 1145; Pub. L. 106–181, title II, §209(b), Apr. 5, 2000, 114 Stat. 95; Pub. L. 112–95, title IV, §§423–425, Feb. 14, 2012, 126 Stat. 97, 98; Pub. L. 118–63, title V, §§561(d), 565(a), May 16, 2024, 138 Stat. 1215, 1218.)

§41734. ENDING, SUSPENDING, AND REDUCING BASIC ESSENTIAL AIR SERVICE

(a) NOTICE REQUIRED.—Subject to subsection (d), an air carrier may end, suspend, or reduce air transportation to an eligible place below the level of basic essential air service established for that place under section 41733 of this title only after giving the Secretary of Transportation, the appropriate State authority, and the affected communities at least 140 days' notice before ending, suspending, or reducing that transportation.

(b) CONTINUATION OF SERVICE FOR 30 DAYS AFTER NOTICE PERIOD.—If at the end of the notice period under subsection (a) of this section the Secretary has not found another air carrier to provide basic essential air service to the eligible place, the Secretary shall require the carrier providing notice to continue to provide basic essential air service to the place for an additional 30-day period or until another carrier begins to provide basic essential air service to the place, whichever occurs first.

(c) CONTINUATION OF SERVICE FOR ADDITIONAL 30-DAY PERIODS.—If at the end of the 30-day period under subsection (b) of this section the Secretary decides another air carrier will not provide basic essential air service to the place on a continuing basis, the Secretary shall require the carrier providing service to continue to provide service for additional

30-day periods until another carrier begins providing service on a continuing basis. At the end of each 30-day period, the Secretary shall decide if another carrier will provide service on a continuing basis.

(d) CONTINUATION OF COMPENSATION AFTER NOTICE PERIOD.—

(1) IN GENERAL.—If an air carrier receiving compensation under section 41733 for providing basic essential air service to an eligible place is required to continue to provide service to such place under this section after the 140-day notice period under subsection (a), the Secretary—

(A) shall provide the carrier with compensation sufficient to pay to the carrier the amount required by the then existing contract for performing the basic essential air service that was being provided when the 140-day notice was given under subsection (a);

(B) may pay an additional amount that represents a reasonable return on investment; and

(C) may pay an additional return that recognizes the demonstrated additional lost profits from opportunities foregone and the likelihood that those lost profits increase as the period during which the carrier or provider is required to provide the service continues.

(2) AUTHORITY.—The Secretary may incorporate contract termination penalties or conditions on compensation into a contract for an air carrier to provide service to an eligible place that take effect in the event an air carrier provides notice that it is ending, suspending, or reducing basic essential air service.

(e) COMPENSATION TO AIR CARRIERS ORIGINALLY PROVIDING SERVICE WITHOUT COMPENSATION.—If the Secretary requires an air carrier providing basic essential air service to an eligible place without compensation under section 41733 of this title to continue providing that service after the 140-day notice period required by subsection (a), the Secretary may provide the air carrier with compensation after the end of the 140-day notice period to pay for the fully allocated actual cost to the air carrier of performing the basic essential air service that was being provided when the 140-day notice was given under subsection (a) plus a reasonable return on investment that is at least 5 percent of operating costs.

(f) FINDING REPLACEMENT CARRIERS.—When the Secretary requires an air carrier to continue to provide basic essential air service to an eligible place, the Secretary shall continue to make every effort to find another air carrier to provide at least that basic essential air service to the place on a continuing basis.

(g) TRANSFER OF AUTHORITY.—If an air carrier, providing basic essential air service under section 41733 of this title between an eligible place and an airport at which the Administrator of the Federal Aviation Administration limits the number of instrument flight rule takeoffs and landings of aircraft, provides notice under subsection (a) of this section of an intention to end, suspend, or reduce that service and another carrier is found to provide the service, the Secretary shall require the carrier providing notice to transfer any operational authority the carrier has to land or take off at that airport related to the service to the eligible place to the carrier that will provide the service, if—

(1) the carrier that will provide the service needs the authority; and

(2) the authority to be transferred is being used to provide air service to another

[§41735. Repealed. Pub. L. 118–63, title V, §561(g), May 16, 2024, 138 Stat. 1216]

CHAPTER 417—OPERATIONS O1
CARRIER;

eligible place.

(h) NONCONSIDERATION OF SLOT AVAILABILITY.—In determining what is basic essential air service and in selecting an air carrier to provide such service, the Secretary shall not consider as a factor whether slots at a high density airport are available for providing such service.

(i) EXEMPTION FROM HOLD-IN REQUIREMENTS.—If, after the date of enactment of this subsection, an air carrier commences air transportation to an eligible place that is not receiving scheduled passenger air service as a result of the failure of the eligible place to meet requirements contained in an appropriations Act, the air carrier shall not be subject to the requirements of subsections (b) and (c) with respect to such air transportation.

(Pub. L. 103–272, §1(e), July 5, 1994, 108 Stat. 1146; Pub. L. 103–305, title II, §206(c), Aug. 23, 1994, 108 Stat. 1587; Pub. L. 103–429, §6(81), Oct. 31, 1994, 108 Stat. 4388; Pub. L. 108–176, title IV, §401, Dec. 12, 2003, 117 Stat. 2542; Pub. L. 112–95, title IV, §426(b)(1), Feb. 14, 2012, 126 Stat. 98; Pub. L. 118–63, title V, §561(f), May 16, 2024, 138 Stat. 1215.)

[§41735. REPEALED. PUB. L. 118–63, TITLE V, §561(G), MAY 16, 2024, 138 STAT. 1216]

Section, Pub. L. 103–272, §1(e), July 5, 1994, 108 Stat. 1148, related to enhanced essential air service.

§41736. AIR TRANSPORTATION TO NONELIGIBLE PLACES

(a) PROPOSALS AND DECISIONS.—(1) A State or local government may propose to the Secretary of Transportation that the Secretary provide compensation to an air carrier to provide air transportation to a place that is not an eligible place under this subchapter. Not later than 90 days after receiving a proposal under this section, the Secretary shall—

(A) decide whether to designate the place as eligible to receive compensation under this section; and

(B)(i) approve the proposal if the State or local government or a person is willing and able to pay 50 percent of the compensation for providing the transportation, and notify the State or local government of the approval; or

(ii) disapprove the proposal if the Secretary decides the proposal is not reasonable under paragraph (2) of this subsection, and notify the State or local government of the disapproval and the reasons for the disapproval.

(2) In deciding whether a proposal is reasonable, the Secretary shall consider, among other factors—

(A) the traffic-generating potential of the place;

(B) the cost to the United States Government of providing the proposed transportation; and

(C) the distance of the place from the closest hub airport.

(b) APPROVAL FOR CERTAIN AIR TRANSPORTATION.—Notwithstanding subsection (a)(1)(B) of this section, the Secretary shall approve a proposal under this section to compensate an air carrier for providing air transportation to a place in the 48 contiguous States or the District of Columbia and designate the place as eligible for compensation under this section if—

(1) at any time before October 23, 1978, the place was served by a carrier holding a

certificate under section 401 of the Federal Aviation Act of 1958;

(2) the place is more than 50 miles from the nearest small hub airport or an eligible place;

(3) the place is more than 150 miles from the nearest hub airport; and

(4) the State or local government submitting the proposal or a person is willing and able to pay 25 percent of the cost of providing the compensated transportation.

Paragraph (4) does not apply to any community approved for service under this section during the period beginning October 1, 1991, and ending December 31, 1997.

(c) LEVEL OF AIR TRANSPORTATION.—(1) If the Secretary designates a place under subsection (a)(1) of this section as eligible for compensation under this section, the Secretary shall decide, not later than 6 months after the date of the designation, on the level of air transportation to be provided under this section. Before making a decision, the Secretary shall consider the views of any interested community, the appropriate State authority of the State in which the place is located, and the State or local government or person agreeing to pay compensation for the transportation under subsection (b)(4) of this section.

(2) After making the decision under paragraph (1) of this subsection, the Secretary shall provide notice that any air carrier that is willing to provide the level of air transportation established under paragraph (1) for a place may submit an application to provide the transportation. In selecting an applicant, the Secretary shall consider, among other factors—

(A) the factors listed in section 41733(c)(1) of this title; and

(B) the views of the State or local government or person agreeing to pay compensation for the transportation.

(d) COMPENSATION PAYMENTS.—(1) The Secretary shall pay compensation under this section when and in the way the Secretary decides is appropriate. The Secretary shall continue to pay compensation under this section only as long as—

(A) the air carrier maintains the level of air transportation established by the Secretary under subsection (c)(1) of this section;

(B) the State or local government or person agreeing to pay compensation for transportation under this section continues to pay that compensation; and

(C) the Secretary decides the compensation is necessary to maintain the transportation to the place.

(2) The Secretary may require the State or local government or person agreeing to pay compensation under this section to make advance payments or provide other security to ensure that timely payments are made.

(e) REVIEW.—The Secretary shall review periodically the level of air transportation provided under this section. Based on the review and consultation with any interested community, the appropriate State authority of the State in which the community is located, and the State or local government or person paying compensation under this section, the Secretary may make appropriate adjustments in the level of transportation.

(f) WITHDRAWAL OF ELIGIBILITY DESIGNATIONS.—After providing notice and an opportunity for interested persons to comment, the Secretary may withdraw the designation of a place under subsection (a)(1) of this section as eligible to receive compensation under this section if the place has received air transportation under this section for at least 2 years and the Secretary decides the withdrawal would be in the public interest. The Secretary by regulation shall prescribe standards for deciding whether the withdrawal of a designation under this subsection is in the public interest. The standards shall include the factors listed in subsection (a)(2) of this section.

(g) ENDING, SUSPENDING, AND REDUCING AIR TRANSPORTATION.—An air carrier providing air transportation for compensation under this section may end, suspend, or reduce that transportation below the level of transportation established by the Secretary under this section only after giving the Secretary, the affected community, and the State or local government or person paying compensation under this section at least 30 days' notice before ending, suspending, or reducing the transportation.

(h) SUNSET.—

(1) PROPOSALS.—No proposal under subsection (a) may be accepted by the Secretary after the date of enactment of this subsection.

(2) PROGRAM.—The Secretary may not provide any compensation under this section after the date that is 2 years after the date of enactment of this subsection.

(Pub. L. 103–272, §1(e), July 5, 1994, 108 Stat. 1149; Pub. L. 106–181, title II, §202, Apr. 5, 2000, 114 Stat. 91; Pub. L. 115–254, div. B, title IV, §453(b), Oct. 5, 2018, 132 Stat. 3348.)

§41737. COMPENSATION GUIDELINES, LIMITATIONS, AND CLAIMS

(a) COMPENSATION GUIDELINES.—(1) The Secretary of Transportation shall prescribe guidelines governing the rate of compensation payable under this subchapter. The guidelines shall be used to determine the reasonable amount of compensation required to ensure the continuation of air service or air transportation under this subchapter. The guidelines shall—

(A) provide for a reduction in compensation when an air carrier does not provide service or transportation agreed to be provided;

(B) consider amounts needed by an air carrier to promote public use of the service or transportation for which compensation is being paid;

(C) include expense elements based on representative costs of air carriers providing scheduled air transportation of passengers, property, and mail on aircraft of the type the Secretary decides is appropriate for providing the service or transportation for which compensation is being provided;

(D) include provisions under which the Secretary may encourage an air carrier to improve air service for which compensation is being paid under this subchapter by incorporating financial incentives in an essential air service contract based on specified performance goals, including goals related to improving on-time performance, reducing the number of flight cancellations, establishing reasonable fares (including joint fares beyond the hub airport), establishing convenient connections to flights providing service beyond hub airports, and increasing marketing efforts; and

(E) include provisions under which the Secretary may execute a long-term essential air service contract to encourage an air carrier to provide air service to an eligible place if it would be in the public interest to do so.

(2) Promotional amounts described in paragraph (1)(B) of this subsection shall be a special, segregated element of the compensation provided to a carrier under this subchapter.

(b) REQUIRED FINDING.—The Secretary may pay compensation to an air carrier for providing air service or air transportation under this subchapter only if the Secretary finds the carrier is able to provide the service or transportation in a reliable way.

(c) CLAIMS.—Not later than 15 days after receiving a written claim from an air carrier for compensation under this subchapter, the Secretary shall—

(1) pay or deny the United States Government's share of a claim; and

(2) if denying the claim, notify the carrier of the denial and the reasons for the denial.

(d) AUTHORITY TO MAKE AGREEMENTS AND INCUR OBLIGATIONS.—The Secretary may make agreements and incur obligations from the Airport and Airway Trust Fund established under section 9502 of the Internal Revenue Code of 1986 (26 U.S.C. 9502) to pay compensation under this subchapter. An agreement by the Secretary under this subsection is a contractual obligation of the Government to pay the Government's share of the compensation.

(e) ADJUSTMENTS TO ACCOUNT FOR SIGNIFICANTLY INCREASED COSTS.—

(1) IN GENERAL.—If the Secretary determines that air carriers are experiencing significantly increased costs in providing air service or air transportation for which compensation is being paid under this subchapter, the Secretary may increase the rates of compensation payable under this subchapter without regard to any agreement or requirement relating to the renegotiation of contracts or any notice requirement under section 41734.

(2) READJUSTMENT IF COSTS SUBSEQUENTLY DECLINE.—If an adjustment is made under paragraph (1), and total unit costs subsequently decrease to at least the total unit cost reflected in the compensation rate, then the Secretary may reverse the adjustment previously made under paragraph (1) without regard to any agreement or requirement relating to the renegotiation of contracts or any notice requirement under section 41734.

(3) SIGNIFICANTLY INCREASED COSTS DEFINED.—In this subsection, the term "significantly increased costs" means a total unit cost increase (but not increases in individual unit costs) of 10 percent or more in relation to the total unit cost reflected in the compensation rate, based on the carrier's internal audit of its financial statements if such cost increase is incurred for a period of at least 2 consecutive months.

(Pub. L. 103–272, §1(e), July 5, 1994, 108 Stat. 1151; Pub. L. 108–176, title IV, §402(a), Dec. 12, 2003, 117 Stat. 2543; Pub. L. 112–95, title IV, §427(a), Feb. 14, 2012, 126 Stat. 99; Pub. L. 118–63, title V, §561(h), May 16, 2024, 138 Stat. 1216.)

§41738. FITNESS OF AIR CARRIERS

Notwithstanding section 40109(a) and (c)–(h) of this title, an air carrier may provide air service to an eligible place or air transportation to a place designated under section 41736 of this title only when the Secretary of Transportation decides that—

(1) the carrier is fit, willing, and able to perform the service or transportation; and

(2) aircraft used to provide the service or transportation, and operations related to the service or transportation, conform to the safety standards prescribed by the Administrator of the Federal Aviation Administration.

(Pub. L. 103–272, §1(e), July 5, 1994, 108 Stat. 1152.)

§41739. AIR CARRIER OBLIGATIONS

If at least 2 air carriers make an agreement to operate under or use a single carrier designator code to provide air transportation, the carrier whose code is being used shares

[§41740. Repealed. Pub. L. 118–63, title V, §561(i), May 16, 2024, 138 Stat. 1216]

CHAPTER 417—OPERATIONS OF
CARRIERS

responsibility with the other carriers for the quality of transportation provided the public under the code by the other carriers.

(Pub. L. 103–272, §1(e), July 5, 1994, 108 Stat. 1152.)

[§41740. REPEALED. PUB. L. 118–63, TITLE V, §561(I), MAY 16, 2024, 138 STAT. 1216]

Section, Pub. L. 103–272, §1(e), July 5, 1994, 108 Stat. 1152; Pub. L. 108–176, title IV, §403, Dec. 12, 2003, 117 Stat. 2543, related to joint proposals by 2 or more air carriers for providing air service or air transportation under this subchapter.

§41741. INSURANCE

The Secretary of Transportation may pay an air carrier compensation under this subchapter only when the carrier files with the Secretary an insurance policy or self-insurance plan approved by the Secretary. The policy or plan must be sufficient to pay for bodily injury to, or death of, an individual, or for loss of or damage to property of others, resulting from the operation of aircraft, but not more than the amount of the policy or plan limits.

(Pub. L. 103–272, §1(e), July 5, 1994, 108 Stat. 1152.)

§41742. ESSENTIAL AIR SERVICE AUTHORIZATION

(a) IN GENERAL.—

(1) AUTHORIZATION.—Out of the amounts received by the Federal Aviation Administration credited to the account established under section 45303 of this title or otherwise provided to the Administration, the sum of $50,000,000 for each fiscal year is authorized and shall be made available immediately for obligation and expenditure to carry out the essential air service program under this subchapter.

(2) ADDITIONAL FUNDS.—In addition to amounts authorized under paragraph (1), there is authorized to be appropriated out of the Airport and Airway Trust Fund (established under section 9502 of the Internal Revenue Code of 1986) $348,544,000 for fiscal year 2024, $340,000,000 for fiscal year 2025, $342,000,000 for fiscal year 2026, $342,000,000 for fiscal year 2027, and $350,000,000 for fiscal year 2028 to carry out the essential air service program under this subchapter of which not more than $12,000,000 per fiscal year may be used for the marketing incentive program for communities and for State marketing assistance.

(3) AUTHORIZATION FOR ADDITIONAL EMPLOYEES.—In addition to amounts authorized under paragraphs (1) and (2), there are authorized to be appropriated such sums as may be necessary for the Secretary of Transportation to hire and employ 4 additional employees for the office responsible for carrying out the essential air service program.

(b) DISTRIBUTION OF ADDITIONAL FUNDS.—Notwithstanding any other provision of law, in any fiscal year in which funds credited to the account established under section 45303, including the funds derived from fees imposed under the authority contained in section 45301(a), exceed the $50,000,000 made available under subsection (a)(1), such funds shall be made available immediately for obligation and expenditure to carry out the essential air service program under this subchapter.

(c) AVAILABILITY OF FUNDS.—The funds made available under this section shall remain available until expended.

(Pub. L. 103–272, §1(e), July 5, 1994, 108 Stat. 1152; Pub. L. 104–264, title II, §278(c), Oct. 9, 1996, 110 Stat. 3249; Pub. L. 106–181, title II, §209(a), Apr. 5, 2000, 114 Stat. 95; Pub. L. 108–176, title IV, §404, Dec. 12, 2003, 117 Stat. 2543; Pub. L. 112–30, title II, §209, Sept. 16, 2011, 125 Stat. 359; Pub. L. 112–91, §9, Jan. 31, 2012, 126 Stat. 5; Pub. L. 112–95, title IV, §428, Feb. 14, 2012, 126 Stat. 99; Pub. L. 114–55, title I, §107, Sept. 30, 2015, 129 Stat. 524; Pub. L. 114–141, title I, §107, Mar. 30, 2016, 130 Stat. 324; Pub. L. 114–190, title I, §1107, July 15, 2016, 130 Stat. 618; Pub. L. 115–63, title I, §104(a), Sept. 29, 2017, 131 Stat. 1170; Pub. L. 115–141, div. M, title I, §104(a), Mar. 23, 2018, 132 Stat. 1047; Pub. L. 115–254, div. B, title IV, §451(a), Oct. 5, 2018, 132 Stat. 3347; Pub. L. 118–15, div. B, title II, §2206(a), Sept. 30, 2023, 137 Stat. 85; Pub. L. 118–34, title I, §106(a), Dec. 26, 2023, 137 Stat. 1115; Pub. L. 118–41, title I, §106(a), Mar. 8, 2024, 138 Stat. 23; Pub. L. 118–63, title V, §566, May 16, 2024, 138 Stat. 1219.)

§41743. AIRPORTS NOT RECEIVING SUFFICIENT SERVICE

(a) SMALL COMMUNITY AIR SERVICE DEVELOPMENT PROGRAM.—The Secretary of Transportation shall establish a program that meets the requirements of this section for improving air carrier service to airports not receiving sufficient air carrier service.

(b) APPLICATION REQUIRED.—In order to participate in the program established under subsection (a), a community or consortium of communities shall submit an application to the Secretary in such form, at such time, and containing such information as the Secretary may require, including—

(1) an assessment of the need of the community or consortium for access, or improved access, to the national air transportation system; and

(2) an analysis of the application of the criteria in subsection (c) to that community or consortium.

(c) CRITERIA FOR PARTICIPATION.—In selecting communities, or consortia of communities, for participation in the program established under subsection (a), the Secretary shall apply the following criteria:

(1) SIZE.—On the date of submission of the relevant application under subsection (b), the airport serving the community or consortium—

(A) is not larger than a small hub airport, as determined using the Department of Transportation's most recently published classification; and

(B) has—

(i) insufficient air carrier service; or

(ii) unreasonably high air fares.

(2) CHARACTERISTICS.—The airport presents characteristics, such as geographic diversity or unique circumstances, that will demonstrate the need for, and feasibility of, the program established under subsection (a).

(3) STATE LIMIT.—Not more than 4 communities or consortia of communities, or a combination thereof, from the same State may be selected to participate in the program in any fiscal year.

(4) OVERALL LIMIT.—

(A) IN GENERAL.—No more than 40 communities or consortia of communities, or a combination thereof, may be selected to participate in the program in each year for which funds are appropriated for the program.

(B) SAME PROJECTS.—Except as provided in subparagraph (C), no community, consortia of communities, or combination thereof may participate in the program in support of the same project more than once in a 5-year period, but any community, consortia of communities, or combination thereof may apply, subsequent to such participation, to participate in the program in support of a different project at any time.

(C) EXCEPTION.—The Secretary may waive the limitation under subparagraph (B) related to projects that are the same if the Secretary determines that the community or consortium spent little or no money on its previous project or encountered industry or environmental challenges, due to circumstances that were reasonably beyond the control of the community or consortium.

(5) PRIORITIES.—The Secretary shall give priority to communities or consortia of communities where—

(A) air fares are higher than the average air fares for all communities;

(B) the community has demonstrated support from at least 1 air carrier to provide service;

(C) the community or consortium will provide a portion of the cost of the activity to be assisted under the program from local sources other than airport revenues;

(D) the community or consortium has established, or will establish, a public-private partnership to facilitate air carrier service to the public;

(E) the assistance will provide material benefits to a broad segment of the travelling public, including business, educational institutions, and other enterprises, whose access to the national air transportation system is limited;

(F) the assistance will be used to help restore scheduled passenger air service that has been terminated or substantially reduced (as measured by enplanements, capacity (seats), schedule, connections, or routes);

(G) the assistance will be used in a timely fashion; and

(H) multiple communities cooperate to submit a regional or multistate application to consolidate air service into one regional airport.

(d) TYPES OF ASSISTANCE.—The Secretary may use amounts made available under this section—

(1) to provide assistance to an air carrier to subsidize service to and from an underserved airport for a period not to exceed 3 years, which shall begin with each new grant, including same-project new grants, and which shall be calculated on a non-consecutive basis for air carriers that provide air service that is seasonal;

(2) to provide assistance to an underserved airport, or an airport where air service has been terminated or substantially reduced, to obtain service to and from the underserved airport; and

(3) to provide assistance to an underserved airport to implement such other measures as the Secretary, in consultation with such airport, considers appropriate to improve air service both in terms of the cost of such service to consumers and the availability of such service, including improving air service through marketing and promotion of air service and enhanced utilization of airport facilities.

(e) AUTHORITY TO MAKE AGREEMENTS.—

(1) IN GENERAL.—The Secretary may make agreements to provide assistance under this section. The Secretary may amend the scope of a grant agreement at the request of the community or consortium and any participating air carrier, and may limit the scope

[§41744. Repealed. Pub. L. 118–63, title V, §561(j), May 16, 2024, 138 Stat. 1216]

CHAPTER 417—OPERATIONS OF CARRIERS

of a grant agreement to only the elements using grant assistance or to only the elements achieved, if the Secretary determines that the amendment is reasonably consistent with the original purpose of the project or the community's current air service needs.

(2) AUTHORIZATION OF APPROPRIATIONS.—There is authorized to be appropriated to the Secretary $15,000,000 for each of fiscal years 2024 through 2028, to carry out this section. Such sums shall remain available until expended.

(f) DESIGNATION OF RESPONSIBLE OFFICIAL.—The Secretary shall designate an employee of the Department of Transportation—

(1) to function as a facilitator between small communities and air carriers;

(2) to carry out this section;

(3) to ensure that the Bureau of Transportation Statistics collects data on passenger information to assess the service needs of small communities;

(4) to work with and coordinate efforts with other Federal, State, and local agencies to increase the viability of service to small communities; and

(5) to provide policy recommendations to the Secretary and Congress that will ensure that small communities have access to quality, affordable air transportation services.

(Added Pub. L. 106–181, title II, §203(a), Apr. 5, 2000, 114 Stat. 92; amended Pub. L. 108–11, title II, §2708, Apr. 16, 2003, 117 Stat. 601; Pub. L. 108–176, title II, §225(b)(3), title IV, §412, Dec. 12, 2003, 117 Stat. 2529, 2551; Pub. L. 110–330, §5(b), Sept. 30, 2008, 122 Stat. 3718; Pub. L. 111–69, §5(b), Oct. 1, 2009, 123 Stat. 2055; Pub. L. 111–249, §5(b), Sept. 30, 2010, 124 Stat. 2628; Pub. L. 112–30, title II, §205(b), Sept. 16, 2011, 125 Stat. 358; Pub. L. 112–91, §5(b), Jan. 31, 2012, 126 Stat. 4; Pub. L. 112–95, title IV, §429, Feb. 14, 2012, 126 Stat. 100; Pub. L. 114–190, title I, §1102(e), July 15, 2016, 130 Stat. 617; Pub. L. 115–63, title I, §104(b), Sept. 29, 2017, 131 Stat. 1170; Pub. L. 115–141, div. M, title I, §104(b), Mar. 23, 2018, 132 Stat. 1047; Pub. L. 115–254, div. B, title IV, §455, Oct. 5, 2018, 132 Stat. 3349; Pub. L. 118–15, div. B, title II, §2206(b), Sept. 30, 2023, 137 Stat. 85; Pub. L. 118–34, title I, §106(b), Dec. 26, 2023, 137 Stat. 1115; Pub. L. 118–41, title I, §106(b), Mar. 8, 2024, 138 Stat. 23; Pub. L. 118–63, title V, §562, May 16, 2024, 138 Stat. 1217.)

[§41744. REPEALED. PUB. L. 118–63, TITLE V, §561(J), MAY 16, 2024, 138 STAT. 1216]

Section, added Pub. L. 106–181, title II, §204(a), Apr. 5, 2000, 114 Stat. 93; amended Pub. L. 108–176, title II, §225(b)(4), Dec. 12, 2003, 117 Stat. 2529, related to preservation of basic essential air service at single carrier dominated hub airports.

§41745. COMMUNITY AND REGIONAL CHOICE PROGRAMS

(a) ALTERNATE ESSENTIAL AIR SERVICE PILOT PROGRAM.—

(1) ESTABLISHMENT.—The Secretary of Transportation shall establish an alternate essential air service pilot program in accordance with the requirements of this section.

(2) ASSISTANCE TO ELIGIBLE PLACES.—In carrying out the program, the Secretary, instead of paying compensation to an air carrier to provide essential air service to an eligible place, may provide assistance directly to a unit of local government having jurisdiction over the eligible place or a State within the boundaries of which the eligible place is located.

(3) USE OF ASSISTANCE.—A unit of local government or State receiving assistance for an eligible place under the program may use the assistance for any of the following purposes:

(A) To provide assistance to air carriers that will use smaller equipment to provide the service and to consider increasing the frequency of service using such smaller equipment if the Secretary determines that passenger safety would not be compromised by the use of such smaller equipment and if the State or unit of local government waives the minimum service requirements under section 41732(b).

(B) To provide assistance to an air carrier to provide on-demand air taxi service to and from the eligible place.

(C) To provide assistance to a person to provide scheduled or on-demand surface transportation to and from the eligible place and an airport in another place.

(D) In combination with other units of local government in the same region, to provide transportation services to and from all the eligible places in that region at an airport or other transportation center that can serve all the eligible places in that region.

(E) To pay for other transportation or related services that the Secretary may permit.

(b) APPLICATIONS.—

(1) IN GENERAL.—An entity seeking to participate in a program under this section shall submit to the Secretary an application in such form and containing such information as the Secretary may require.

(2) REQUIRED INFORMATION.—At a minimum, the application shall include—

(A) a statement of the amount of compensation or assistance required; and

(B) a description of how the compensation or assistance will be used.

(c) PARTICIPATION REQUIREMENTS.—An eligible place for which compensation or assistance is provided under this section in a fiscal year shall not be eligible in that fiscal year for the essential air service that it would otherwise be entitled to under this subchapter.

(d) SUBSEQUENT PARTICIPATION.—A unit of local government participating in the program under this subsection (a) in a fiscal year shall not be prohibited from participating in the basic essential air service program under this subchapter in a subsequent fiscal year if such unit is otherwise eligible to participate in such program.

(e) FUNDING.—Amounts appropriated or otherwise made available to carry out the essential air service program under this subchapter shall be available to carry out this section.

(Added Pub. L. 108–176, title IV, §405, Dec. 12, 2003, 117 Stat. 2544; amended Pub. L. 118–63, title V, §561(k), May 16, 2024, 138 Stat. 1216.)

§41746. TRACKING SERVICE

The Secretary of Transportation shall require a carrier that provides essential air service to an eligible place and that receives compensation for such service under this subchapter to report not less than semiannually—

(1) the percentage of flights to and from the place that arrive on time as defined by the Secretary; and

(2) such other information as the Secretary considers necessary to evaluate service provided to passengers traveling to and from such place.

(Added Pub. L. 108–176, title IV, §407, Dec. 12, 2003, 117 Stat. 2545.)

[§41747. Repealed. Pub. L. 112–95, title IV, §430, Feb. 14, 2012, 126 Stat. 100]

CHAPTER 417—OPERATIONS OF CARRIERS

[§41747. Repealed. Pub. L. 112–95, title IV, §430, Feb. 14, 2012, 126 Stat. 100]

Section, added Pub. L. 108–176, title IV, §408(a), Dec. 12, 2003, 117 Stat. 2546, related to the EAS local participation program.

[§41748. Repealed. Pub. L. 118–63, title V, §561(l), May 16, 2024, 138 Stat. 1217]

Section, added Pub. L. 108–176, title IV, §410(b), Dec. 12, 2003, 117 Stat. 2548, established a marketing incentive program for eligible places that received subsidized service by an air carrier under section 41733.

Another section 410(b) of Pub. L. 108–176 amended the table of sections at the beginning of this chapter.

SUBCHAPTER III—REGIONAL AIR SERVICE INCENTIVE PROGRAM

§41761. Purpose

The purpose of this subchapter is to improve service by jet aircraft to underserved markets by providing assistance, in the form of Federal credit instruments, to commuter air carriers that purchase regional jet aircraft for use in serving those markets.

(Added Pub. L. 106–181, title II, §210(a), Apr. 5, 2000, 114 Stat. 96.)

§41762. Definitions

In this subchapter, the following definitions apply:

(1) Air carrier.—The term "air carrier" means any air carrier holding a certificate of public convenience and necessity issued by the Secretary of Transportation under section 41102.

(2) Aircraft purchase.—The term "aircraft purchase" means the purchase of commercial transport aircraft, including spare parts normally associated with the aircraft.

(3) Capital reserve subsidy amount.—The term "capital reserve subsidy amount" means the amount of budget authority sufficient to cover estimated long-term cost to the United States Government of a Federal credit instrument, calculated on a net present value basis, excluding administrative costs and any incidental effects on Government receipts or outlays in accordance with provisions of the Federal Credit Reform Act of 1990 (2 U.S.C. 661 et seq.).

(4) Commuter air carrier.—The term "commuter air carrier" means an air carrier that primarily operates aircraft designed to have a maximum passenger seating capacity of 75 or less in accordance with published flight schedules.

(5) Federal credit instrument.—The term "Federal credit instrument" means a secured loan, loan guarantee, or line of credit authorized to be made under this subchapter.

(6) Financial obligation.—The term "financial obligation" means any note, bond, debenture, or other debt obligation issued by an obligor in connection with the financing of an aircraft purchase, other than a Federal credit instrument.

(7) LENDER.—The term "lender" means any non-Federal qualified institutional buyer (as defined by section 230.144A(a) of title 17, Code of Federal Regulations (or any successor regulation) known as Rule 144A(a) of the Security and Exchange Commission and issued under the Security Act of 1933 (15 U.S.C. 77a et seq.)), including—

(A) a qualified retirement plan (as defined in section 4974(c) of the Internal Revenue Code of 1986) that is a qualified institutional buyer; and

(B) a governmental plan (as defined in section 414(d) of the Internal Revenue Code of 1986) that is a qualified institutional buyer.

(8) LINE OF CREDIT.—The term "line of credit" means an agreement entered into by the Secretary with an obligor under section 41763(d) to provide a direct loan at a future date upon the occurrence of certain events.

(9) LOAN GUARANTEE.—The term "loan guarantee" means any guarantee or other pledge by the Secretary under section 41763(c) to pay all or part of any of the principal of and interest on a loan or other debt obligation issued by an obligor and funded by a lender.

(10) NEW ENTRANT AIR CARRIER.—The term "new entrant air carrier" means an air carrier that has been providing air transportation according to a published schedule for less than 5 years, including any person that has received authority from the Secretary to provide air transportation but is not providing air transportation.

(11) OBLIGOR.—The term "obligor" means a party primarily liable for payment of the principal of or interest on a Federal credit instrument, which party may be a corporation, partnership, joint venture, trust, or governmental entity, agency, or instrumentality.

(12) REGIONAL JET AIRCRAFT.—The term "regional jet aircraft" means a civil aircraft—

(A) powered by jet propulsion; and

(B) designed to have a maximum passenger seating capacity of not less than 30 nor more than 75.

(13) SECURED LOAN.—The term "secured loan" means a direct loan funded by the Secretary in connection with the financing of an aircraft purchase under section 41763(b).

(14) UNDERSERVED MARKET.—The term "underserved market" means a passenger air transportation market (as defined by the Secretary) that—

(A) is served (as determined by the Secretary) by a nonhub airport or a small hub airport;

(B) is not within a 40-mile radius of an airport that each year has at least .25 percent of the total annual boardings in the United States; and

(C) the Secretary determines does not have sufficient air service.

(Added Pub. L. 106–181, title II, §210(a), Apr. 5, 2000, 114 Stat. 96; amended Pub. L. 108–176, title II, §225(b)(5), Dec. 12, 2003, 117 Stat. 2529.)

§41763. FEDERAL CREDIT INSTRUMENTS

(a) IN GENERAL.—Subject to this section and section 41766, the Secretary of Transportation may enter into agreements with one or more obligors to make available Federal credit instruments, the proceeds of which shall be used to finance aircraft purchases.

(b) Secured Loans.—
  (1) Terms and limitations.—
    (A) In general.—A secured loan under this section with respect to an aircraft purchase shall be on such terms and conditions and contain such covenants, representatives, warranties, and requirements (including requirements for audits) as the Secretary determines appropriate.
    (B) Maximum amount.—No secured loan may be made under this section—
      (i) that extends to more than 50 percent of the purchase price (including the value of any manufacturer credits, post-purchase options, or other discounts) of the aircraft, including spare parts, to be purchased; or
      (ii) that, when added to the remaining balance on any other Federal credit instruments made under this subchapter, provides more than $100,000,000 of outstanding credit to any single obligor.
    (C) Final payment date.—The final payment on the secured loan shall not be due later than 18 years after the date of execution of the loan agreement.
    (D) Subordination.—The secured loan may be subordinate to claims of other holders of obligations in the event of bankruptcy, insolvency, or liquidation of the obligor as determined appropriate by the Secretary.
    (E) Fees.—The Secretary, subject to appropriations, may establish fees at a level sufficient to cover all or a portion of the administrative costs to the United States Government of making a secured loan under this section. The proceeds of such fees shall be deposited in an account to be used by the Secretary for the purpose of administering the program established under this subchapter and shall be available upon deposit until expended.
  (2) Repayment.—
    (A) Schedule.—The Secretary shall establish a repayment schedule for each secured loan under this section based on the projected cash flow from aircraft revenues and other repayment sources.
    (B) Commencement.—Scheduled loan repayments of principal and interest on a secured loan under this section shall commence no later than 3 years after the date of execution of the loan agreement.
  (3) Prepayment.—
    (A) Use of excess revenue.—After satisfying scheduled debt service requirements on all financial obligations and secured loans and all deposit requirements under the terms of any trust agreement, bond resolution, or similar agreement securing financial obligations, the secured loan may be prepaid at anytime without penalty.
    (B) Use of proceeds of refinancing.—The secured loan may be prepaid at any time without penalty from proceeds of refinancing from non-Federal funding sources.
(c) Loan Guarantees.—
  (1) In general.—A loan guarantee under this section with respect to a loan made for an aircraft purchase shall be made in such form and on such terms and conditions and contain such covenants, representatives, warranties, and requirements (including requirements for audits) as the Secretary determines appropriate.
  (2) Maximum amount.—No loan guarantee shall be made under this section—
    (A) that extends to more than the unpaid interest and 50 percent of the unpaid

principal on any loan;

(B) that, for any loan or combination of loans, extends to more than 50 percent of the purchase price (including the value of any manufacturer credits, post-purchase options, or other discounts) of the aircraft, including spare parts, to be purchased with the loan or loan combination;

(C) on any loan with respect to which terms permit repayment more than 15 years after the date of execution of the loan; or

(D) that, when added to the remaining balance on any other Federal credit instruments made under this subchapter, provides more than $100,000,000 of outstanding credit to any single obligor.

(3) FEES.—The Secretary, subject to appropriations, may establish fees at a level sufficient to cover all or a portion of the administrative costs to the United States Government of making a loan guarantee under this section. The proceeds of such fees shall be deposited in an account to be used by the Secretary for the purpose of administering the program established under this subchapter and shall be available upon deposit until expended.

(d) LINES OF CREDIT.—

(1) IN GENERAL.—Subject to the requirements of this subsection, the Secretary may enter into agreements to make available lines of credit to one or more obligors in the form of direct loans to be made by the Secretary at future dates on the occurrence of certain events for any aircraft purchase selected under this section.

(2) TERMS AND LIMITATIONS.—

(A) IN GENERAL.—A line of credit under this subsection with respect to an aircraft purchase shall be on such terms and conditions and contain such covenants, representatives, warranties, and requirements (including requirements for audits) as the Secretary determines appropriate.

(B) MAXIMUM AMOUNT.—

(i) TOTAL AMOUNT.—The amount of any line of credit shall not exceed 50 percent of the purchase price (including the value of any manufacturer credits, post-purchase options, or other discounts) of the aircraft, including spare parts.

(ii) 1–YEAR DRAWS.—The amount drawn in any year shall not exceed 20 percent of the total amount of the line of credit.

(C) DRAWS.—Any draw on the line of credit shall represent a direct loan.

(D) PERIOD OF AVAILABILITY.—The line of credit shall be available not more than 5 years after the aircraft purchase date.

(E) RIGHTS OF THIRD-PARTY CREDITORS.—

(i) AGAINST UNITED STATES GOVERNMENT.—A third-party creditor of the obligor shall not have any right against the United States Government with respect to any draw on the line of credit.

(ii) ASSIGNMENT.—An obligor may assign the line of credit to one or more lenders or to a trustee on the lender's behalf.

(F) SUBORDINATION.—A direct loan under this subsection may be subordinate to claims of other holders of obligations in the event of bankruptcy, insolvency, or liquidation of the obligor as determined appropriate by the Secretary.

(G) FEES.—The Secretary, subject to appropriations, may establish fees at a level sufficient to cover all of a portion of the administrative costs to the United States Government of providing a line of credit under this subsection. The proceeds of such fees shall be deposited in an account to be used by the Secretary for the purpose of administering the program established under this subchapter and shall be available upon deposit until expended.

(3) REPAYMENT.—

(A) SCHEDULE.—The Secretary shall establish a repayment schedule for each direct loan under this subsection.

(B) COMMENCEMENT.—Scheduled loan repayments of principal or interest on a direct loan under this subsection shall commence no later than 3 years after the date of the first draw on the line of credit and shall be repaid, with interest, not later than 18 years after the date of the first draw.

(e) RISK ASSESSMENT.—Before entering into an agreement under this section to make available a Federal credit instrument, the Secretary, in consultation with the Director of the Office of Management and Budget, shall determine an appropriate capital reserve subsidy amount for the Federal credit instrument based on such credit evaluations as the Secretary deems necessary.

(f) CONDITIONS.—Subject to subsection (h), the Secretary may only make a Federal credit instrument available under this section if the Secretary finds that—

(1) the aircraft to be purchased with the Federal credit instrument is a regional jet aircraft needed to improve the service and efficiency of operation of a commuter air carrier or new entrant air carrier;

(2) the commuter air carrier or new entrant air carrier enters into a legally binding agreement that requires the carrier to use the aircraft to provide service to underserved markets; and

(3) the prospective earning power of the commuter air carrier or new entrant air carrier, together with the character and value of the security pledged, including the collateral value of the aircraft being acquired and any other assets or pledges used to secure the Federal credit instrument, furnish—

(A) reasonable assurances of the air carrier's ability and intention to repay the Federal credit instrument within the terms established by the Secretary—

(i) to continue its operations as an air carrier; and

(ii) to the extent that the Secretary determines to be necessary, to continue its operations as an air carrier between the same route or routes being operated by the air carrier at the time of the issuance of the Federal credit instrument; and

(B) reasonable protection to the United States.

(g) LIMITATION ON COMBINED AMOUNT OF FEDERAL CREDIT INSTRUMENTS.—The Secretary shall not allow the combined amount of Federal credit instruments available for any aircraft purchase under this section to exceed—

(1) 50 percent of the cost of the aircraft purchase; or

(2) $100,000,000 for any single obligor.

(h) REQUIREMENT.—Subject to subsection (i), no Federal credit instrument may be made under this section for the purchase of any regional jet aircraft that does not comply with the stage 3 noise levels of part 36 of title 14 of the Code of Federal Regulations, as in effect on January 1, 1999.

(i) OTHER LIMITATIONS.—No Federal credit instrument shall be made by the Secretary under this section for the purchase of a regional jet aircraft unless the commuter air carrier or new entrant air carrier enters into a legally binding agreement that requires the carrier to provide scheduled passenger air transportation to the underserved market for which the aircraft is purchased for a period of not less than 36 consecutive months after the date that aircraft is placed in service.

(Added Pub. L. 106–181, title II, §210(a), Apr. 5, 2000, 114 Stat. 97.)

§41764. USE OF FEDERAL FACILITIES AND ASSISTANCE

(a) USE OF FEDERAL FACILITIES.—To permit the Secretary of Transportation to make use of such expert advice and services as the Secretary may require in carrying out this subchapter, the Secretary may use available services and facilities of other agencies and instrumentalities of the United States Government—

(1) with the consent of the appropriate Federal officials; and

(2) on a reimbursable basis.

(b) ASSISTANCE.—The head of each appropriate department or agency of the United States Government shall exercise the duties and powers of that head in such manner as to assist in carrying out the policy specified in section 41761.

(c) OVERSIGHT.—The Secretary shall make available to the Comptroller General of the United States such information with respect to any Federal credit instrument made under this subchapter as the Comptroller General may require to carry out the duties of the Comptroller General under chapter 7 of title 31, United States Code.

(Added Pub. L. 106–181, title II, §210(a), Apr. 5, 2000, 114 Stat. 101.)

§41765. ADMINISTRATIVE EXPENSES

In carrying out this subchapter, the Secretary shall use funds made available by appropriations to the Department of Transportation for the purpose of administration, in addition to the proceeds of any fees collected under this subchapter, to cover administrative expenses of the Federal credit instrument program under this subchapter.

(Added Pub. L. 106–181, title II, §210(a), Apr. 5, 2000, 114 Stat. 101.)

§41766. FUNDING

Of the amounts appropriated under section 106(k) for each of fiscal years 2001 through 2003, such sums as may be necessary may be used to carry out this subchapter, including administrative expenses.

(Added Pub. L. 106–181, title II, §210(a), Apr. 5, 2000, 114 Stat. 101.)

§41767. TERMINATION

(a) AUTHORITY TO ISSUE FEDERAL CREDIT INSTRUMENTS.—The authority of the Secretary of Transportation to issue Federal credit instruments under section 41763 shall terminate on the date that is 5 years after the date of the enactment of this subchapter.

(b) CONTINUATION OF AUTHORITY TO ADMINISTER PROGRAM FOR EXISTING FEDERAL CREDIT INSTRUMENTS.—On and after the termination date, the Secretary shall continue to administer the program established under this subchapter for Federal credit instruments issued under this subchapter before the termination date until all obligations associated with such instruments have been satisfied.

(Added Pub. L. 106–181, title II, §210(a), Apr. 5, 2000, 114 Stat. 101.)

CHAPTER 419—TRANSPORTATION OF MAIL

[1] Section catchline amended by Pub. L. 110–405 without corresponding amendment of chapter analysis.

[2] Section repealed by Pub. L. 110–405 without corresponding amendment of chapter analysis.

§41901. GENERAL AUTHORITY

(a) TITLE 39.—The United States Postal Service may provide for the transportation of mail by aircraft in interstate air transportation under section 5402(e) and (f) of title 39, and in foreign air transportation under section 5402(b) and (c) of title 39.

(b) AUTHORITY TO PRESCRIBE PRICES.—Except as provided in section 5402 of title 39, on the initiative of the Secretary of Transportation or on petition by the Postal Service or an air carrier, the Secretary shall prescribe and publish—

(1) after notice and an opportunity for a hearing on the record, reasonable prices to be paid by the Postal Service for the transportation of mail by aircraft between places in Alaska, the facilities used in and useful for the transportation of mail, and the services related to the transportation of mail for each carrier holding a certificate that authorizes that transportation;

(2) the methods used, whether by aircraft-mile, pound-mile, weight, space, or a combination of those or other methods, to determine the prices for each air carrier or class of air carriers; and

(3) the effective date of the prices.

(c) OTHER TRANSPORTATION.—In prescribing prices under subsection (b) of this section, the Secretary may include transportation other than by aircraft that is incidental to transportation of mail by aircraft or necessary because of emergency conditions related to aircraft operations.

(d) AUTHORITY TO PRESCRIBE DIFFERENT PRICES.—Considering conditions peculiar to transportation by aircraft and to particular air carriers or classes of air carriers, the Secretary may prescribe different prices under this section for different air carriers or classes of air carriers and for different classes of service. In prescribing a price for a carrier under this section, the Secretary shall consider, among other factors, the following:

(1) the condition that the carrier may hold and operate under a certificate authorizing the transportation of mail only by providing necessary and adequate facilities and service for the transportation of mail.

(2) standards related to the character and quality of service to be provided that are prescribed by or under law.

(e) STATEMENTS ON PRICES.—A petition for prescribing a reasonable price under this section must include a statement of the price the petitioner believes is reasonable.

(f) STATEMENTS ON REQUIRED SERVICES.—The Postal Service shall introduce as part of the record in every proceeding under this section a comprehensive statement of the services to be required of the air carrier and other information the Postal Service has that the Secretary considers material to the proceeding.

(Pub. L. 103–272, §§1(e), 4(k)(1), (2), July 5, 1994, 108 Stat. 1153, 1370; Pub. L. 104–52, title VI, §631(c), Nov. 19, 1995, 109 Stat. 505; Pub. L. 106–31, title VI, §6003, May 21, 1999, 113 Stat. 113; Pub. L. 107–206, title III, §3002(e)(2), Aug. 2, 2002, 116 Stat. 924; Pub. L. 110–405, §2(b)(1), (2), Oct. 13, 2008, 122 Stat. 4289.)

§41902. SCHEDULES FOR CERTAIN TRANSPORTATION OF MAIL

(a) REQUIREMENT.—Except as provided in section 41905 of this title and section 5402 of title 39, an air carrier may transport mail by aircraft between places in Alaska only under a schedule designated or required to be established under subsection (c) of this section for the transportation of mail.

(b) STATEMENTS ON PLACES AND SCHEDULES.—Every air carrier shall file with the United States Postal Service a statement showing—

(1) the places between which the carrier is authorized to transport mail in Alaska;

(2) every schedule of aircraft regularly operated by the carrier between places described in paragraph (1) and every change in each schedule; and

(3) for each schedule, the places served by the carrier and the time of arrival at, and departure from, each such place.

(c) DESIGNATING AND ADDITIONAL SCHEDULES.—The Postal Service may—

(1) designate any schedule of an air carrier filed under subsection (b)(2) of this section for the transportation of mail between the places between which the carrier is authorized by its certificate to transport mail; and

(2) require the carrier to establish additional schedules for the transportation of mail between those places.

(d) CHANGING SCHEDULES.—A schedule designated or required to be established for the transportation of mail under subsection (c) of this section may be changed only after 10 days' notice of the change is filed as provided in subsection (b)(2) of this section. The Postal Service may disapprove a proposed change in a schedule or amend or modify the schedule or proposed change.

(Pub. L. 103–272, §§1(e), 4(k)(1), (3), July 5, 1994, 108 Stat. 1153, 1370; Pub. L. 103–429, §7(a)(3)(D), Oct.

31, 1994, 108 Stat. 4389; Pub. L. 106–31, title VI, §6003, May 21, 1999, 113 Stat. 113; Pub. L. 110–405, §2(b)(3), Oct. 13, 2008, 122 Stat. 4289; Pub. L. 115–254, div. B, title V, §539(f), Oct. 5, 2018, 132 Stat. 3370.)

§41903. Duty to provide certain transportation of mail

(a) Air Carriers.—Subject to subsection (b) of this section, an air carrier authorized by its certificate to transport mail by aircraft between places in Alaska shall—

(1) provide facilities and services necessary and adequate to provide that transportation; and

(2) transport mail between the places authorized in the certificate for transportation of mail when required, and under regulations prescribed, by the United States Postal Service.

(b) Maximum Mail Load.—The Secretary of Transportation may prescribe the maximum mail load for a schedule or for an aircraft or type of aircraft for the transportation of mail by aircraft between places in Alaska. If the Postal Service tenders to an air carrier mail exceeding the maximum load for transportation by the carrier under a schedule designated or required to be established for the transportation of mail under section 41902(c) of this title, the carrier, as nearly in accordance with the schedule as the Secretary decides is possible, shall—

(1) provide facilities sufficient to transport the mail to the extent the Secretary decides the carrier reasonably is able to do so; and

(2) transport that mail.

(Pub. L. 103–272, §§1(e), 4(k)(1), July 5, 1994, 108 Stat. 1154, 1370; Pub. L. 106–31, title VI, §6003, May 21, 1999, 113 Stat. 113; Pub. L. 110–405, §2(b)(4), Oct. 13, 2008, 122 Stat. 4289.)

§41904. Noncitizens transporting mail

When the United States Postal Service decides that it may be necessary to have a person not a citizen of the United States transport mail by aircraft between two points outside the United States, the Postal Service may make an arrangement with the person, without advertising, to provide the transportation. Nothing in this section shall affect the authority of the Postal Service to make arrangements with noncitizens for the carriage of mail in foreign air transportation under subsections 5402(b) and (c) of title 39.

(Pub. L. 103–272, §1(e), July 5, 1994, 108 Stat. 1155; Pub. L. 110–405, §2(b)(5), Oct. 13, 2008, 122 Stat. 4289.)

§41905. Emergency mail transportation

(a) Contract Authority.—In an emergency caused by a flood, fire, or other disaster, the United States Postal Service may make a contract without advertising to transport mail by aircraft to or from a locality affected by the emergency when the available facilities of persons authorized to transport mail to or from the locality are inadequate to meet the requirements of the Postal Service during the emergency. The contract may be only for periods necessary to maintain mail service because of the inadequacy of the facilities. Payment for transportation provided under the contract shall be made at prices provided in the contract.

(b) Transportation Not Air Transportation.—Transportation provided under a contract made under subsection (a) of this section is not air transportation within the meaning of this part.

(Pub. L. 103–272, §1(e), July 5, 1994, 108 Stat. 1155, §41906; renumbered §41905, Pub. L. 110–405, §2(b)(7)(B), Oct. 13, 2008, 122 Stat. 4289.)

§41906. Duty to oppose unreasonable prices under the Universal Postal Union Convention

The Secretary of State and the United States Postal Service shall—

(1) take appropriate action to ensure that the prices paid for transporting mail under the Universal Postal Union Convention are not higher than reasonable prices for transporting mail; and

(2) oppose any existing or proposed Universal Postal Union price that is higher than a reasonable price for transporting mail.

(Pub. L. 103–272, §1(e), July 5, 1994, 108 Stat. 1156, §41909; renumbered §41906, Pub. L. 110–405, §2(b)(7)(B), Oct. 13, 2008, 122 Stat. 4289.)

§41907. Weighing mail

The United States Postal Service may weigh mail transported by aircraft between places in Alaska and make statistical and administrative computations necessary in the interest of mail service. When the Secretary of Transportation decides that additional or more frequent weighings of mail are advisable or necessary to carry out this part, the Postal Service shall provide the weighings, but it is not required to provide them for continuous periods of more than 30 days.

(Pub. L. 103–272, §1(e), July 5, 1994, 108 Stat. 1157, §41910; renumbered §41907 and amended Pub. L. 110–405, §2(b)(6), (7)(B), Oct. 13, 2008, 122 Stat. 4289; Pub. L. 115–254, div. B, title V, §539(g), Oct. 5, 2018, 132 Stat. 3370.)

§41908. Effect on foreign postal arrangements

This part does not—

(1) affect an arrangement made by the United States Government with the postal administration of a foreign country related to the transportation of mail by aircraft; or

(2) impair the authority of the United States Postal Service to make such an arrangement.

(Pub. L. 103–272, §1(e), July 5, 1994, 108 Stat. 1157, §41912; renumbered §41908, Pub. L. 110–405, §2(b)(7)(B), Oct. 13, 2008, 122 Stat. 4289.)

[§41909. Renumbered §41906]

[§41910. Renumbered §41907]

[§41911. Repealed. Pub. L. 110–405, §2(b)(7)(A), Oct. 13, 2008, 122 Stat. 4289]

Section, Pub. L. 103–272, §1(e), July 5, 1994, 108 Stat. 1157, related to evidence of providing mail service.

[§41912. RENUMBERED §41908]

§§42101 to 42106. Repealed. Pub. L. 105–220, title I, §199(a)(6), Aug. 7, 1998, 112 Stat. 1059]

CHAPTER 421—LABOR-MANAGEMENT
PROVISIONS

CHAPTER 421—LABOR-MANAGEMENT PROVISIONS

SUBCHAPTER I—EMPLOYEE PROTECTION PROGRAM [1]

SUBCHAPTER II—MUTUAL AID AGREEMENTS AND LABOR REQUIREMENTS OF AIR CARRIERS

SUBCHAPTER III—WHISTLEBLOWER PROTECTION PROGRAM

[1] *Subchapter I repealed by Pub. L. 105–220 without corresponding amendment of chapter analysis.*

[SUBCHAPTER I—REPEALED]

[§§42101 TO 42106. REPEALED. PUB. L. 105–220, TITLE I, §199(A)(6), AUG. 7, 1998, 112 STAT. 1059]

Section 42101, Pub. L. 103–272, §1(e), July 5, 1994, 108 Stat. 1157, defined terms in subchapter.

Section 42102, Pub. L. 103–272, §1(e), July 5, 1994, 108 Stat. 1158, related to payments to eligible protected employees.

Section 42103, Pub. L. 103–272, §1(e), July 5, 1994, 108 Stat. 1159, related to duty to hire protected employees.

Section 42104, Pub. L. 103–272, §1(e), July 5, 1994, 108 Stat. 1159; Pub. L. 104–287, §5(9), Oct. 11, 1996, 110 Stat. 3389, related to congressional review of regulations.

Section 42105, Pub. L. 103–272, §1(e), July 5, 1994, 108 Stat. 1160, related to Airline Employees Protective Account.

Section 42106, Pub. L. 103–272, §1(e), July 5, 1994, 108 Stat. 1160, provided ending effective date for subchapter.

SUBCHAPTER II—MUTUAL AID AGREEMENTS AND LABOR REQUIREMENTS OF AIR CARRIERS

§42111. MUTUAL AID AGREEMENTS

An air carrier that will receive payments from another air carrier under an agreement between the air carriers for the time the one air carrier is not providing foreign air transportation, or is providing reduced levels of foreign air transportation, because of a labor strike must file a true copy of the agreement with the Secretary of Transportation and have it approved by the Secretary under section 41309 of this title. Notwithstanding section 41309, the Secretary shall approve the agreement only if it provides that—

(1) the air carrier will receive payments of not more than 60 percent of direct operating expenses, including interest expenses, but not depreciation or amortization expenses;

(2) benefits may be paid for not more than 8 weeks, and may not be for losses incurred during the first 30 days of a strike; and

(3) on request of the striking employees, the dispute will be submitted to binding arbitration under the Railway Labor Act (45 U.S.C. 151 et seq.).

(Pub. L. 103–272, §1(e), July 5, 1994, 108 Stat. 1160.)

§42112. LABOR REQUIREMENTS OF AIR CARRIERS

(a) DEFINITIONS.—In this section—

(1) "copilot" means an employee whose duties include assisting or relieving the pilot in manipulating an aircraft and who is qualified to serve as, and has in effect an airman certificate authorizing the employee to serve as, a copilot.

(2) "pilot" means an employee who is—

(A) responsible for manipulating or who manipulates the flight controls of an aircraft when under way, including the landing and takeoff of an aircraft; and

(B) qualified to serve as, and has in effect an airman certificate authorizing the employee to serve as, a pilot.

(b) DUTIES OF AIR CARRIERS.—An air carrier shall—

(1) maintain rates of compensation, maximum hours, and other working conditions and relations for its pilots and copilots who are providing interstate air transportation in the 48 contiguous States and the District of Columbia to conform with decision number 83, May 10, 1934, National Labor Board, notwithstanding any limitation in that decision on the period of its effectiveness;

(2) maintain rates of compensation for its pilots and copilots who are providing foreign air transportation or air transportation only in one territory or possession of the United States; and

(3) comply with title II of the Railway Labor Act (45 U.S.C. 181 et seq.) as long as it holds its certificate.

(c) MINIMUM ANNUAL RATE OF COMPENSATION.—A minimum annual rate under subsection (b)(2) of this section may not be less than the annual rate required to be paid for comparable service to a pilot or copilot under subsection (b)(1) of this section.

(d) COLLECTIVE BARGAINING.—This section does not prevent pilots or copilots of an air carrier from obtaining by collective bargaining higher rates of compensation or more favorable working conditions or relations.

(Pub. L. 103–272, §1(e), July 5, 1994, 108 Stat. 1160.)

SUBCHAPTER III—WHISTLEBLOWER PROTECTION PROGRAM

§42121. Protection of employees providing air safety information

(a) Prohibited Discrimination.—A holder of a certificate under section 44704 or 44705 of this title, or a contractor, subcontractor, or supplier of such holder, may not discharge an employee or otherwise discriminate against an employee with respect to compensation, terms, conditions, or privileges of employment because the employee (or any person acting pursuant to a request of the employee)—

(1) provided, caused to be provided, or is about to provide (with any knowledge of the employer) or cause to be provided to the employer or Federal Government information relating to any violation or alleged violation of any order, regulation, or standard of the Federal Aviation Administration or any other provision of Federal law relating to aviation safety under this subtitle or any other law of the United States;

(2) has filed, caused to be filed, or is about to file (with any knowledge of the employer) or cause to be filed a proceeding relating to any violation or alleged violation of any order, regulation, or standard of the Federal Aviation Administration or any other provision of Federal law relating to aviation safety under this subtitle or any other law of the United States;

(3) testified or is about to testify in such a proceeding; or

(4) assisted or participated or is about to assist or participate in such a proceeding.

(b) Department of Labor and Federal Aviation Administration Complaint Procedure.—

(1) Filing and notification.—A person who believes that he or she has been discharged or otherwise discriminated against by any person in violation of subsection (a) may, not later than 90 days after the date on which such violation occurs, file (or have any person file on his or her behalf) a complaint with the Secretary of Labor alleging such discharge or discrimination. Upon receipt of such a complaint, the Secretary of Labor shall notify, in writing, the person named in the complaint and the Administrator of the Federal Aviation Administration of the filing of the complaint, of the allegations contained in the complaint, of the substance of evidence supporting the complaint, and of the opportunities that will be afforded to such person under paragraph (2).

(2) Investigation; preliminary order.—

(A) In general.—Not later than 60 days after the date of receipt of a complaint filed under paragraph (1) and after affording the person named in the complaint an opportunity to submit to the Secretary of Labor a written response to the complaint and an opportunity to meet with a representative of the Secretary to present statements from witnesses, the Secretary of Labor shall conduct an investigation and determine whether there is reasonable cause to believe that the complaint has merit and notify, in writing, the complainant and the person alleged to have committed a violation of subsection (a) of the Secretary's findings. If the Secretary of Labor concludes that there is a reasonable cause to believe that a violation of subsection (a) has occurred, the Secretary shall accompany the Secretary's findings with a preliminary order providing the relief prescribed by paragraph (3)(B). Not later than 30 days after the date of notification of findings under this paragraph, either the person alleged to have committed the violation or the complainant may file objections to the findings or preliminary order, or both, and request a hearing on the record. The filing of such objections shall not operate to stay any reinstatement remedy contained in the preliminary order. Such hearings shall be conducted expeditiously. If a hearing is not requested in such 30-day period, the preliminary order shall be deemed a final order that is not subject to judicial review.

(B) REQUIREMENTS.—

(i) REQUIRED SHOWING BY COMPLAINANT.—The Secretary of Labor shall dismiss a complaint filed under this subsection and shall not conduct an investigation otherwise required under subparagraph (A) unless the complainant makes a prima facie showing that any behavior described in paragraphs (1) through (4) of subsection (a) was a contributing factor in the unfavorable personnel action alleged in the complaint.

(ii) SHOWING BY EMPLOYER.—Notwithstanding a finding by the Secretary that the complainant has made the showing required under clause (i), no investigation otherwise required under subparagraph (A) shall be conducted if the employer demonstrates, by clear and convincing evidence, that the employer would have taken the same unfavorable personnel action in the absence of that behavior.

(iii) CRITERIA FOR DETERMINATION BY SECRETARY.—The Secretary may determine that a violation of subsection (a) has occurred only if the complainant demonstrates that any behavior described in paragraphs (1) through (4) of subsection (a) was a contributing factor in the unfavorable personnel action alleged in the complaint.

(iv) PROHIBITION.—Relief may not be ordered under subparagraph (A) if the employer demonstrates by clear and convincing evidence that the employer would have taken the same unfavorable personnel action in the absence of that behavior.

(3) FINAL ORDER.—

(A) DEADLINE FOR ISSUANCE; SETTLEMENT AGREEMENTS.—Not later than 120 days after the date of conclusion of a hearing under paragraph (2), the Secretary of Labor shall issue a final order providing the relief prescribed by this paragraph or denying the complaint. At any time before issuance of a final order, a proceeding under this subsection may be terminated on the basis of a settlement agreement entered into by the Secretary of Labor, the complainant, and the person alleged to have committed the violation.

(B) REMEDY.—If, in response to a complaint filed under paragraph (1), the Secretary of Labor determines that a violation of subsection (a) has occurred, the Secretary of Labor shall order the person who committed such violation to—

(i) take affirmative action to abate the violation;

(ii) reinstate the complainant to his or her former position together with the compensation (including back pay) and restore the terms, conditions, and privileges associated with his or her employment; and

(iii) provide compensatory damages to the complainant.

If such an order is issued under this paragraph, the Secretary of Labor, at the request of the complainant, shall assess against the person against whom the order is issued a sum equal to the aggregate amount of all costs and expenses (including attorneys' and expert witness fees) reasonably incurred, as determined by the Secretary of Labor, by the complainant for, or in connection with, the bringing the complaint upon which the order was issued.

(C) FRIVOLOUS COMPLAINTS.—If the Secretary of Labor finds that a complaint under paragraph (1) is frivolous or has been brought in bad faith, the Secretary of Labor may award to the prevailing employer a reasonable attorney's fee not exceeding $1,000.

(4) REVIEW.—

(A) APPEAL TO COURT OF APPEALS.—Any person adversely affected or aggrieved by an order issued under paragraph (3) may obtain review of the order in the United States Court of Appeals for the circuit in which the violation, with respect to which the order was issued, allegedly occurred or the circuit in which the complainant resided on the date of such violation. The petition for review must be filed not later than 60 days after the date of the issuance of the final order of the Secretary of Labor. Review shall conform to chapter 7 of title 5, United States Code. The commencement of proceedings under this subparagraph shall not, unless ordered by the court, operate as a stay of the order.

(B) LIMITATION ON COLLATERAL ATTACK.—An order of the Secretary of Labor with respect to which review could have been obtained under subparagraph (A) shall not be subject to judicial review in any criminal or other civil proceeding.

(5) ENFORCEMENT OF ORDER.—Whenever any person has failed to comply with an order issued under paragraph (3), the Secretary of Labor and the Administrator of the Federal Aviation Administration shall consult with each other to determine the most appropriate action to be taken, in which—

(A) the Secretary of Labor may file a civil action in the United States district court for the district in which the violation was found to occur to enforce such order, for which, in actions brought under this paragraph, the district courts shall have jurisdiction to grant all appropriate relief including, injunctive relief and compensatory damages; and

(B) the Administrator of the Federal Aviation Administration may assess a civil penalty pursuant to section 46301.

(6) ENFORCEMENT OF ORDER BY PARTIES.—

(A) COMMENCEMENT OF ACTION.—A person on whose behalf an order was issued under paragraph (3) may commence a civil action against the person to whom such order was issued to require compliance with such order. The appropriate United States district court shall have jurisdiction, without regard to the amount in controversy or the citizenship of the parties, to enforce such order.

(B) ATTORNEY FEES.—The court, in issuing any final order under this paragraph, may award costs of litigation (including reasonable attorney and expert witness fees) to any party whenever the court determines such award is appropriate.

(c) MANDAMUS.—Any nondiscretionary duty imposed by this section shall be enforceable in a mandamus proceeding brought under section 1361 of title 28, United States Code.

(d) NONAPPLICABILITY TO DELIBERATE VIOLATIONS.—Subsection (a) shall not apply with respect to an employee of a holder of a certificate issued under section 44704 or 44705, or a contractor or subcontractor thereof, who, acting without direction from such certificate-holder, contractor, or subcontractor (or such person's agent), deliberately causes a violation of any requirement relating to aviation safety under this subtitle or any other law of the United States.

(e) CONTRACTOR DEFINED.—In this section, the term "contractor" means—

(1) a person that performs safety-sensitive functions by contract for an air carrier or commercial operator; or

(2) a person that performs safety-sensitive functions related to the design or production of an aircraft, aircraft engine, propeller, appliance, or component thereof by contract for a holder of a certificate issued under section 44704.

(Added Pub. L. 106–181, title V, §519(a), Apr. 5, 2000, 114 Stat. 145; amended Pub. L. 116–260, div. V, title I, §118, Dec. 27, 2020, 134 Stat. 2337; Pub. L. 118–63, title III, §370, May 16, 2024, 138 Stat. 1139.)

CHAPTER 423—PASSENGER AIR SERVICE IMPROVEMENTS

§42301. Emergency contingency plans

(a) Submission of Air Carrier and Airport Plans.—Not later than 90 days after the date of enactment of this section, each of the following air carriers and airport operators shall submit to the Secretary of Transportation for review and approval an emergency contingency plan in accordance with the requirements of this section:

(1) An air carrier providing covered air transportation at a commercial airport.

(2) An operator of a commercial airport.

(3) An operator of an airport used by an air carrier described in paragraph (1) for diversions.

(b) Air Carrier Plans.—

(1) Plans for individual airports.—An air carrier shall submit an emergency contingency plan under subsection (a) for—

(A) each airport at which the carrier provides covered air transportation; and

(B) each airport at which the carrier has flights for which the carrier has primary responsibility for inventory control.

(2) Contents.—An emergency contingency plan submitted by an air carrier for an airport under subsection (a) shall contain a description of how the carrier will—

(A) provide adequate food, potable water, restroom facilities, comfortable cabin temperatures, and access to medical treatment for passengers onboard an aircraft at the airport when the departure of a flight is delayed or the disembarkation of passengers is delayed;

(B) share facilities and make gates available at the airport in an emergency; and

(C) allow passengers to deplane following an excessive tarmac delay in accordance with paragraph (3).

(3) Deplaning following an excessive tarmac delay.—For purposes of paragraph (2)(C), an emergency contingency plan submitted by an air carrier under subsection (a) shall incorporate the following requirements:

(A) A passenger shall have the option to deplane an aircraft and return to the airport terminal when there is an excessive tarmac delay.

(B) The option described in subparagraph (A) shall be offered to a passenger even if a flight in covered air transportation is diverted to a commercial airport other than the originally scheduled airport.

(C) In providing the option described in subparagraph (A), the air carrier shall begin to return the aircraft to a suitable disembarkation point—

(i) in the case of a flight in interstate air transportation, not later than 3 hours after the main aircraft door is closed in preparation for departure; and

(ii) in the case of a flight in foreign air transportation, not later than 4 hours after the main aircraft door is closed in preparation for departure.

(D) Notwithstanding the requirements described in subparagraphs (A), (B), and (C), a passenger shall not have an option to deplane an aircraft and return to the airport terminal in the case of an excessive tarmac delay if—

(i) an air traffic controller with authority over the aircraft advises the pilot in command that permitting a passenger to deplane would significantly disrupt airport operations; or

(ii) the pilot in command determines that permitting a passenger to deplane would jeopardize passenger safety or security.

(c) AIRPORT PLANS.—An emergency contingency plan submitted by an airport operator under subsection (a) shall contain a description of how the operator, to the maximum extent practicable, will—

(1) provide for the deplanement of passengers following excessive tarmac delays;

(2) provide for the sharing of facilities and make gates available at the airport in an emergency; and

(3) provide a sterile area following excessive tarmac delays for passengers who have not yet cleared United States Customs and Border Protection.

(d) UPDATES.—

(1) AIR CARRIERS.—An air carrier shall update each emergency contingency plan submitted by the carrier under subsection (a) every 3 years and submit the update to the Secretary for review and approval.

(2) AIRPORTS.—An airport operator shall update each emergency contingency plan submitted by the operator under subsection (a) every 5 years and submit the update to the Secretary for review and approval.

(e) APPROVAL.—

(1) IN GENERAL.—Not later than 60 days after the date of the receipt of an emergency contingency plan submitted under subsection (a) or an update submitted under subsection (d), the Secretary shall review and approve or, if necessary, require modifications to the plan or update to ensure that the plan or update will effectively address emergencies and provide for the health and safety of passengers.

(2) FAILURE TO APPROVE OR REQUIRE MODIFICATIONS.—If the Secretary fails to approve or require modifications to a plan or update under paragraph (1) within the timeframe specified in that paragraph, the plan or update shall be deemed to be approved.

(3) ADHERENCE REQUIRED.—An air carrier or airport operator shall adhere to an emergency contingency plan of the carrier or operator approved under this section.

(f) MINIMUM STANDARDS.—The Secretary shall establish, as necessary or desirable, minimum standards for elements in an emergency contingency plan required to be submitted under this section.

(g) PUBLIC ACCESS.—An air carrier or airport operator required to submit an emergency contingency plan under this section shall ensure public access to the plan after its approval under this section on the Internet Web site of the carrier or operator or by such other means as determined by the Secretary.

(h) REPORTS.—Not later than 30 days after any flight experiences an excessive tarmac delay, the air carrier responsible for such flight shall submit a written description of the incident and its resolution to the Aviation Consumer Protection Division of the Department of Transportation.

(i) DEFINITIONS.—In this section, the following definitions apply:

(1) COMMERCIAL AIRPORT.—The term "commercial airport" means a large hub, medium hub, small hub, or nonhub airport.

(2) COVERED AIR TRANSPORTATION.—The term "covered air transportation" means scheduled or public charter passenger air transportation provided by an air carrier that operates an aircraft that as originally designed has a passenger capacity of 30 or more seats.

(3) TARMAC DELAY.—The term "tarmac delay" means the period during which passengers are on board an aircraft on the tarmac—

(A) awaiting takeoff after the aircraft doors have been closed or after passengers have been boarded if the passengers have not been advised they are free to deplane; or

(B) awaiting deplaning after the aircraft has landed.

(4) EXCESSIVE TARMAC DELAY.—The term "excessive tarmac delay" means a tarmac delay of more than—

(A) 3 hours for a flight in interstate air transportation; or

(B) 4 hours for a flight in foreign air transportation.

(Added Pub. L. 112–95, title IV, §415(a), Feb. 14, 2012, 126 Stat. 93; amended Pub. L. 114–190, title II, §2308(a), (b), July 15, 2016, 130 Stat. 648.)

§42302. CONSUMER COMPLAINTS

(a) IN GENERAL.—The Secretary of Transportation shall—

(1) maintain an accessible website through the Office of Aviation Consumer Protection to accept the submission of complaints from airline passengers regarding air travel service problems; and

(2) take appropriate actions to notify the public of such accessible website.

(b) NOTICE TO PASSENGERS ON THE INTERNET.—An air carrier or foreign air carrier providing scheduled air transportation using any aircraft that as originally designed has a passenger capacity of 30 or more passenger seats shall include on the accessible website of the carrier—

(1) the accessible website, e-mail address, or telephone number of the air carrier for the submission of complaints by passengers about air travel service problems; and

(2) the accessible website maintained pursuant to subsection (a).

(c) USE OF ADDITIONAL OR ALTERNATIVE TECHNOLOGIES.—The Secretary shall periodically evaluate the benefits of using mobile phone applications or other widely used technologies to—

(1) provide additional or alternative means for air passengers to submit complaints; and

(2) provide such additional or alternative means as the Secretary determines

appropriate.

(d) AIR AMBULANCE PROVIDERS.—Each air ambulance provider shall include the accessible website, or a link to such accessible website, maintained pursuant to subsection (a) and the contact information for the Aviation Consumer Advocate established by section 424 of the FAA Reauthorization Act of 2018 (49 U.S.C. 42302 note) on—

(1) any invoice, bill, or other communication provided to a passenger or customer of such provider; and

(2) the accessible website and any related mobile device application of such provider.

(Added Pub. L. 112–95, title IV, §415(a), Feb. 14, 2012, 126 Stat. 95; amended Pub. L. 115–254, div. B, title IV, §§405, 419(a), 423(a), Oct. 5, 2018, 132 Stat. 3329, 3336, 3337; Pub. L. 118–63, title V, §520, May 16, 2024, 138 Stat. 1200.)

§42303. USE OF INSECTICIDES IN PASSENGER AIRCRAFT

(a) INFORMATION TO BE PROVIDED ON THE INTERNET.—The Secretary of Transportation shall establish, and make available to the general public, an Internet Web site that contains a listing of countries that may require an air carrier or foreign air carrier to treat an aircraft passenger cabin with insecticides prior to a flight in foreign air transportation to that country or to apply an aerosol insecticide in an aircraft cabin used for such a flight when the cabin is occupied with passengers.

(b) REQUIRED DISCLOSURES.—An air carrier, foreign air carrier, or ticket agent selling, in the United States, a ticket for a flight in foreign air transportation to a country listed on the internet website established under subsection (a) shall—

(1) disclose, on its own internet website or through other means, that the destination country may require the air carrier or foreign air carrier to treat an aircraft passenger cabin with insecticides prior to the flight or to apply an aerosol insecticide in an aircraft cabin used for such a flight when the cabin is occupied with passengers; and

(2) refer the purchaser of the ticket to the internet website established under subsection (a) for additional information.

(Added Pub. L. 112–95, title IV, §415(a), Feb. 14, 2012, 126 Stat. 95; amended Pub. L. 115–254, div. B, title IV, §404, Oct. 5, 2018, 132 Stat. 3329.)

§42304. WIDESPREAD DISRUPTIONS

(a) GENERAL REQUIREMENTS.—In the event of a widespread disruption, a covered air carrier shall immediately publish, via a prominent link on the air carrier's public internet website, a clear statement indicating whether, with respect to a passenger of the air carrier whose travel is interrupted as a result of the widespread disruption, the air carrier will—

(1) provide for hotel accommodations;

(2) arrange for ground transportation;

(3) provide meal vouchers;

(4) arrange for air transportation on another air carrier or foreign air carrier to the passenger's destination; and

(5) provide for sleeping facilities inside the airport terminal.

(b) DEFINITIONS.—In this section, the following definitions apply:

(1) WIDESPREAD DISRUPTION.—The term "widespread disruption" means, with respect to a covered air carrier, the interruption of all or the overwhelming majority of the air

carrier's systemwide flight operations, including flight delays and cancellations, as the result of the failure of 1 or more computer systems or computer networks of the air carrier.

(2) COVERED AIR CARRIER.—The term "covered air carrier" means an air carrier that provides scheduled passenger air transportation by operating an aircraft that as originally designed has a passenger capacity of 30 or more seats.

(c) SAVINGS PROVISION.—Nothing in this section may be construed to modify, abridge, or repeal any obligation of an air carrier under section 42301.

(Added Pub. L. 115–254, div. B, title IV, §428(a), Oct. 5, 2018, 132 Stat. 3341.)

§42305. REFUNDS FOR CANCELLED OR SIGNIFICANTLY DELAYED OR CHANGED FLIGHTS

(a) IN GENERAL.—In the case of a passenger that holds a nonrefundable ticket on a scheduled flight to, from, or within the United States, an air carrier or a foreign air carrier shall, upon request as set forth in subsection (f), provide a full refund, including any taxes and ancillary fees, for the fare such carrier collected for any cancelled flight or significantly delayed or changed flight where the passenger chooses not to—

(1) fly on the significantly delayed or changed flight or accept rebooking on an alternative flight; or

(2) accept any voucher, credit, or other form of compensation offered by the air carrier or foreign air carrier pursuant to subsection (c).

(b) TIMING OF REFUND.—Any refund required under subsection (a) shall be issued by the air carrier or foreign air carrier—

(1) in the case of a ticket purchased with a credit card, not later than 7 business days after the earliest date the refund was requested as set forth in subsection (f); or

(2) in the case of a ticket purchased with cash or another form of payment, not later than 20 days after the earliest date the refund was requested as set forth in subsection (f).

(c) ALTERNATIVE TO REFUND.—An air carrier and a foreign air carrier may offer a voucher, credit, or other form of compensation as an explicit alternative to providing a refund required by subsection (a) but only if—

(1) the offer includes a clear and conspicuous notice of—

(A) the terms of the offer; and

(B) the passenger's right to a full refund under this section;

(2) the voucher, credit, or other form of compensation offered explicitly as an alternative to providing a refund required by subsection (a) remains valid and redeemable by the consumer for a period of at least 5 years from the date on which such voucher, credit, or other form of compensation is issued;

(3) upon the issuance of such voucher, credit, or other form of compensation, an air carrier, foreign air carrier, or ticket agent, where applicable, notifies the recipient of the expiration date of the voucher, credit, or other form of compensation; and

(4) upon request by an individual who self-identifies as having a disability (as defined in section 382.3 of title 14, Code of Federal Regulations), an air carrier, foreign air carrier, or ticket agent provides a notification under paragraph (3) in an electronic format that is accessible to the recipient.

(d) SIGNIFICANTLY DELAYED OR CHANGED FLIGHT DEFINED.—In this section, the term "significantly delayed or changed flight" includes, at a minimum, a flight where the passenger arrives at a destination airport—

(1) in the case of a domestic flight, 3 or more hours after the original scheduled arrival time; and

(2) in the case of an international flight, 6 or more hours after the original scheduled arrival time.

(e) APPLICATION TO TICKET AGENTS.—

(1) IN GENERAL.—Not later than 1 year after the date of enactment of this section, the Secretary shall issue a final rule to apply refund requirements to ticket agents in the case of cancelled flights and significantly delayed or changed flights.

(2) TRANSFER OF FUNDS.—The Secretary shall issue regulations requiring air carriers and foreign air carriers to promptly transfer funds to a ticket agent if—

(A) the Secretary has determined that the ticket agent is responsible for providing the refund; and

(B) the ticket agent does not possess the funds of the passenger.

(3) TIMING AND ALTERNATIVES.—A refund provided by a ticket agent shall comply with the requirements in subsections (b) and (c) of this section.

(f) REFUND.—An air carrier and a foreign air carrier shall consider a passenger to have requested a refund if—

(1) a flight is cancelled and a passenger is not offered an alternative flight or any voucher, credit, or other form of compensation by the air carrier or foreign air carrier pursuant to subsection (c);

(2) a passenger rejects the significantly delayed or changed flight, rebooking on an alternative flight, or any voucher, credit, or other form of compensation offered by the air carrier or foreign air carrier pursuant to subsection (c); or

(3) a passenger does not respond to an offer of—

(A) a significantly delayed or changed flight or an alternative flight and the flight departs without the passenger; or

(B) a voucher, credit, or other form of compensation by the date on which the cancelled flight was scheduled to depart or the date that the significantly delayed or changed flight departs.

(g) REFUND NOTIFICATION.—An air carrier and a foreign air carrier shall update their passenger notification systems to ensure passengers owed a refund under this section are notified of their right to receive a refund.

(Added Pub. L. 118–63, title V, §503(a), May 16, 2024, 138 Stat. 1188.)

§42306. KNOW YOUR RIGHTS POSTERS

(a) IN GENERAL.—Each large hub airport, medium hub airport, and small hub airport with scheduled passenger service shall prominently display posters that clearly and concisely outline the rights of airline passengers under Federal law with respect to, at a minimum—

(1) flight delays and cancellations;

(2) refunds;

(3) bumping of passengers from flights and the oversale of flights; and

(4) lost, delayed, or damaged baggage.

(b) LOCATION.—Posters described in subsection (a) shall be displayed in conspicuous locations throughout the airport, including ticket counters, security checkpoints, and boarding gates.

(c) ACCESSIBILITY ASSISTANCE.—Each large hub airport, medium hub airport, and small hub airport with scheduled passenger service shall ensure that passengers with a disability (as such term is defined in section 382.3 of title 14, Code of Federal Regulations) who identify themselves as having such a disability are notified of the availability of accessibility assistance and shall assist such passengers in connecting to the appropriate entities to obtain the same information required in this section that is provided to other passengers.

(Added Pub. L. 118–63, title V, §504(a), May 16, 2024, 138 Stat. 1190.)

§42307. REQUIREMENT TO MAINTAIN A LIVE CUSTOMER CHAT OR MONITORED TEXT MESSAGING NUMBER

(a) REQUIREMENT.—

(1) IN GENERAL.—A covered air carrier that operates a domestic or international flight to, from, or within the United States shall maintain—

(A) a customer service telephone line staffed by live agents;

(B) a customer chat option that allows for customers to speak to a live agent within a reasonable time, to the greatest extent practicable; or

(C) a monitored text messaging number that enables customers to communicate and speak with a live agent directly.

(2) PROVISION OF SERVICES.—The services required under paragraph (1) shall be provided to customers without charge for the use of such services, and shall be available at all times.

(b) RULEMAKING AUTHORITY.—The Secretary shall promulgate such rules as may be necessary to carry out this section.

(c) COVERED AIR CARRIER DEFINED.—In this section, the term "covered air carrier" means an air carrier that sells tickets for scheduled passenger air transportation on an aircraft that, as originally designed, has a passenger capacity of 30 or more seats.

(d) EFFECTIVE DATE.—Beginning on the date that is 120 days after the date of enactment of this section, a covered air carrier shall comply with the requirement specified in subsection (a) without regard to whether the Secretary has promulgated any rules to carry out this section as of the date that is 120 days after such date of enactment.

(Added Pub. L. 118–63, title V, §505(b)(1), May 16, 2024, 138 Stat. 1191.)

§42308. DOT AIRLINE CUSTOMER SERVICE DASHBOARDS

(a) REQUIREMENT TO ESTABLISH AND MAINTAIN PUBLICLY AVAILABLE DASHBOARDS.—The Secretary of Transportation shall establish, maintain, and make publicly available the following online dashboards for purposes of keeping aviation consumers informed with respect to certain policies of, and services provided by, large air carriers (as such term is defined by the Secretary) to the extent that such policies or services exceed what is required by Federal law:

(1) DELAY AND CANCELLATION DASHBOARD.—A dashboard that displays information regarding the services and compensation provided by each large air carrier to mitigate

any passenger inconvenience caused by a delay or cancellation due to circumstances in the control of such carrier.

(2) EXPLANATION OF CIRCUMSTANCES.—The website on which such dashboard is displayed shall explain the circumstances under which a delay or cancellation is not due to circumstances in the control of the large air carrier (such as a delay or cancellation due to a weather event or an instruction from the Federal Aviation Administration Air Traffic Control System Command Center) consistent with section 234.4 of title 14, Code of Federal Regulations.

(3) FAMILY SEATING DASHBOARD.—A dashboard that displays information regarding which large air carriers guarantee that each child shall be seated adjacent to an adult accompanying the child without charging any additional fees.

(4) SEAT SIZE DASHBOARD.—A dashboard that displays information regarding aircraft seat size for each large air carrier, including the pitch, width, and length of a seat in economy class for the aircraft models and configurations most commonly flown by such carrier.

(5) FAMILY SEATING SUNSET.—The requirement in subsection (a)(3) shall cease to be effective on the date on which the rule in section 516 of the FAA Reauthorization Act of 2024 is effective.

(b) ACCESSIBILITY REQUIREMENT.—In developing the dashboards required in subsection (a), the Secretary shall, in order to ensure the dashboards are accessible and contain pertinent information for passengers with disabilities, consult with the Air Carrier Access Act Advisory Committee, the Architectural and Transportation Barriers Compliance Board, any other relevant department or agency to determine appropriate accessibility standards, and disability organizations, including advocacy and nonprofit organizations that represent or provide services to individuals with disabilities.

(c) LIMITATION ON DASHBOARDS.—After the rule required in section 516 of the FAA Reauthorization Act of 2024 is effective, the Secretary may not establish or maintain more than 4 different customer service dashboards at any given time.

(d) PROVISION OF INFORMATION.—Each large air carrier shall provide to the Secretary such information as the Secretary requires to carry out this section.

(e) SUNSET.—This section shall cease to be effective on October 1, 2028.

(Added Pub. L. 118–63, title V, §506(a)(1), May 16, 2024, 138 Stat. 1192.)

CHAPTER 441—REGISTRATION AND RECORDATION OF AIRCRAFT

§44101. Operation of aircraft

(a) Registration Requirement.—Except as provided in subsection (b) of this section, a person may operate an aircraft only when the aircraft is registered under section 44103 of this title.

(b) Exceptions.—A person may operate an aircraft in the United States that is not registered—

(1) when authorized under section 40103(d) or 41703 of this title;

(2) when it is an aircraft of the national defense forces of the United States and is identified in a way satisfactory to the Administrator of the Federal Aviation Administration; and

(3) for a reasonable period of time after a transfer of ownership, under regulations prescribed by the Administrator.

(Pub. L. 103–272, §1(e), July 5, 1994, 108 Stat. 1161.)

§44102. Registration requirements

(a) Eligibility.—An aircraft may be registered under section 44103 of this title only when the aircraft is—

(1) not registered under the laws of a foreign country and is owned by—

(A) a citizen of the United States;

(B) an individual citizen of a foreign country lawfully admitted for permanent residence in the United States; or

(C) a corporation not a citizen of the United States when the corporation is organized and doing business under the laws of the United States or a State, and the aircraft is based and primarily used in the United States; or

(2) an aircraft of—

(A) the United States Government; or

(B) a State, the District of Columbia, a territory or possession of the United States, or a political subdivision of a State, territory, or possession.

(b) DUTY TO DEFINE CERTAIN TERM.—In carrying out subsection (a)(1)(C) of this section, the Secretary of Transportation shall define "based and primarily used in the United States".

(Pub. L. 103–272, §1(e), July 5, 1994, 108 Stat. 1161.)

§44103. REGISTRATION OF AIRCRAFT

(a) GENERAL.—(1) On application of the owner of an aircraft that meets the requirements of section 44102 of this title, the Administrator of the Federal Aviation Administration shall—

(A) register the aircraft; and

(B) issue a certificate of registration to its owner.

(2) The Administrator may prescribe the extent to which an aircraft owned by the holder of a dealer's certificate of registration issued under section 44104(2) of this title also is registered under this section.

(b) CONTROLLED SUBSTANCE VIOLATIONS.—(1) The Administrator may not issue an owner's certificate of registration under subsection (a)(1) of this section to a person whose certificate is revoked under section 44106 of this title during the 5-year period beginning on the date of the revocation, except—

(A) as provided in section 44106(e)(2) of this title; or

(B) that the Administrator may issue the certificate to the person after the one-year period beginning on the date of the revocation if the Administrator decides that the aircraft otherwise meets the requirements of section 44102 of this title and that denial of a certificate for the 5-year period—

(i) would be excessive considering the nature of the offense or the act committed and the burden the denial places on the person; or

(ii) would not be in the public interest.

(2) A decision of the Administrator under paragraph (1)(B)(i) or (ii) of this subsection is within the discretion of the Administrator. That decision or failure to make a decision is not subject to administrative or judicial review.

(c) CERTIFICATES AS EVIDENCE.—A certificate of registration issued under this section is—

(1) conclusive evidence of the nationality of an aircraft for international purposes, but not conclusive evidence in a proceeding under the laws of the United States; and

(2) not evidence of ownership of an aircraft in a proceeding in which ownership is or may be in issue.

(d) CERTIFICATES AVAILABLE FOR INSPECTION.—An operator of an aircraft shall make available for inspection a certificate of registration for the aircraft when requested by a United States Government, State, or local law enforcement officer.

(e) VALIDITY OF AIRCRAFT REGISTRATION DURING RENEWAL.—

(1) IN GENERAL.—An aircraft may be operated on or after the expiration date found on the certificate of registration issued for such aircraft under this section as if it were not expired if the operator of such aircraft has aboard the aircraft—

(A) documentation validating that—

(i) an aircraft registration renewal application form (AC Form 8050–1B, or a succeeding form) has been submitted to the Administrator for such aircraft but not yet approved or denied; and

(ii) such aircraft is compliant with maintenance, inspections, and any other requirements for the aircraft's airworthiness certificate issued under section 44704(d); and

(B) the most recent aircraft registration.

(2) PROOF OF PENDING RENEWAL APPLICATION.—The Administrator shall provide an applicant for renewal of registration under this section with documentation described in paragraph (1)(A). Such documentation shall—

(A) be made electronically available to the applicant immediately upon submitting an aircraft registration renewal application to the Civil Aviation Registry for an aircraft;

(B) notify the applicant of the operational allowance described in paragraph (1);

(C) deem an aircraft's airworthiness certificate issued under section 44704(d) as valid provided that the applicant confirms acknowledgment of the requirements of paragraph (1)(A)(ii);

(D) confirm the applicant acknowledged the limitations described in paragraph (3)(A) and (3)(B); and

(E) include identifying information pertaining to such aircraft and to the registered owner.

(3) RULE OF CONSTRUCTION.—Nothing in this subsection shall be construed to permit any person to operate an aircraft—

(A) with an expired registration, except as specifically provided for under this subsection; or

(B) if the Administrator has denied an application to renew the registration of such aircraft.

(Pub. L. 103–272, §1(e), July 5, 1994, 108 Stat. 1162; Pub. L. 118–63, title VIII, §812(a), May 16, 2024, 138 Stat. 1326.)

§44104. REGISTRATION OF AIRCRAFT COMPONENTS AND DEALERS' CERTIFICATES OF REGISTRATION

The Administrator of the Federal Aviation Administration may prescribe regulations—

(1) in the interest of safety for registering and identifying an aircraft engine, propeller, or appliance; and

(2) in the public interest for issuing, suspending, and revoking a dealer's certificate of registration under this chapter and for its use by a person manufacturing, distributing, or selling aircraft.

(Pub. L. 103–272, §1(e), July 5, 1994, 108 Stat. 1162.)

§44105. SUSPENSION AND REVOCATION OF AIRCRAFT CERTIFICATES

The Administrator of the Federal Aviation Administration may suspend or revoke a certificate of registration issued under section 44103 of this title when the aircraft no longer meets the requirements of section 44102 of this title.

(Pub. L. 103–272, §1(e), July 5, 1994, 108 Stat. 1163.)

§44106. REVOCATION OF AIRCRAFT CERTIFICATES FOR CONTROLLED SUBSTANCE VIOLATIONS

(a) DEFINITION.—In this section, "controlled substance" has the same meaning given that term in section 102 of the Comprehensive Drug Abuse Prevention and Control Act of 1970 (21 U.S.C. 802).

(b) REVOCATIONS.—(1) The Administrator of the Federal Aviation Administration shall issue an order revoking the certificate of registration for an aircraft issued to an owner under section 44103 of this title and any other certificate of registration that the owner of the aircraft holds under section 44103, if the Administrator finds that—

(A) the aircraft was used to carry out, or facilitate, an activity that is punishable by death or imprisonment for more than one year under a law of the United States or a State related to a controlled substance (except a law related to simple possession of a controlled substance); and

(B) the owner of the aircraft permitted the use of the aircraft knowing that the aircraft was to be used for the activity described in clause (A) of this paragraph.

(2) An aircraft owner that is not an individual is deemed to have permitted the use of the aircraft knowing that the aircraft was to be used for the activity described in paragraph (1)(A) of this subsection only if a majority of the individuals who control the owner of the aircraft or who are involved in forming the major policy of the owner permitted the use of the aircraft knowing that the aircraft was to be used for the activity described in paragraph (1)(A).

(c) ADVICE TO HOLDERS AND OPPORTUNITY TO ANSWER.—Before the Administrator revokes a certificate under subsection (b) of this section, the Administrator shall—

(1) advise the holder of the certificate of the charges or reasons on which the Administrator bases the proposed action; and

(2) provide the holder of the certificate an opportunity to answer the charges and state why the certificate should not be revoked.

(d) APPEALS.—(1) A person whose certificate is revoked by the Administrator under subsection (b) of this section may appeal the revocation order to the National Transportation Safety Board. The Board shall affirm or reverse the order after providing notice and a hearing on the record. In conducting the hearing, the Board is not bound by the findings of fact of the Administrator.

(2) When a person files an appeal with the Board under this subsection, the order of the Administrator revoking the certificate is stayed. However, if the Administrator advises the Board that safety in air transportation or air commerce requires the immediate effectiveness of the order—

(A) the order remains effective; and

(B) the Board shall dispose of the appeal not later than 60 days after notification by the Administrator under this paragraph.

(3) A person substantially affected by an order of the Board under this subsection may seek judicial review of the order under section 46110 of this title. The Administrator shall be made a party to that judicial proceeding.

(e) ACQUITTAL.—(1) The Administrator may not revoke, and the Board may not affirm a revocation of, a certificate of registration under this section on the basis of an activity described in subsection (b)(1)(A) of this section if the holder of the certificate is acquitted of all charges related to a controlled substance in an indictment or information arising from the activity.

(2) If the Administrator has revoked a certificate of registration of a person under this section because of an activity described in subsection (b)(1)(A) of this section, the Administrator shall reissue a certificate to the person if the person—

(A) subsequently is acquitted of all charges related to a controlled substance in an indictment or information arising from the activity; and

(B) otherwise meets the requirements of section 44102 of this title.

(Pub. L. 103–272, §1(e), July 5, 1994, 108 Stat. 1163.)

§44107. RECORDATION OF CONVEYANCES, LEASES, AND SECURITY INSTRUMENTS

(a) ESTABLISHMENT OF SYSTEM.—The Administrator of the Federal Aviation Administration shall establish a system for recording—

(1) conveyances that affect an interest in civil aircraft of the United States;

(2) leases and instruments executed for security purposes, including conditional sales contracts, assignments, and amendments, that affect an interest in—

(A) a specifically identified aircraft engine having at least 550 rated takeoff horsepower or its equivalent;

(B) a specifically identified aircraft propeller capable of absorbing at least 750 rated takeoff shaft horsepower;

(C) an aircraft engine, propeller, or appliance maintained for installation or use in an aircraft, aircraft engine, or propeller, by or for an air carrier holding a certificate issued under section 44705 of this title; and

(D) spare parts maintained by or for an air carrier holding a certificate issued under section 44705 of this title; and

(3) releases, cancellations, discharges, and satisfactions related to a conveyance, lease, or instrument recorded under paragraph (1) or (2).

(b) GENERAL DESCRIPTION REQUIRED.—A lease or instrument recorded under subsection (a)(2)(C) or (D) of this section only has to describe generally the engine, propeller, appliance, or spare part by type and designate its location.

(c) ACKNOWLEDGMENT.—Except as the Administrator otherwise may provide, a conveyance, lease, or instrument may be recorded under subsection (a) of this section only after it has been acknowledged before—

(1) a notary public; or

(2) another officer authorized under the laws of the United States, a State, the District of Columbia, or a territory or possession of the United States to acknowledge deeds.

(d) RECORDS AND INDEXES.—The Administrator shall—

(1) keep a record of the time and date that each conveyance, lease, and instrument is filed and recorded with the Administrator; and

(2) record each conveyance, lease, and instrument filed with the Administrator, in the order of their receipt, and index them by—

(A) the identifying description of the aircraft, aircraft engine, or propeller, or location specified in a lease or instrument recorded under subsection (a)(2)(C) or (D) of this section; and

(B) the names of the parties to each conveyance, lease, and instrument.

(e) INTERNATIONAL REGISTRY.—

(1) DESIGNATION OF UNITED STATES ENTRY POINT.—As permitted under the Cape Town Treaty, the Federal Aviation Administration Civil Aviation Registry is designated as the United States Entry Point to the International Registry relating to—

(A) civil aircraft of the United States;

(B) an aircraft for which a United States identification number has been assigned but only with regard to a notice filed under paragraph (2); and

(C) aircraft engines.

(2) SYSTEM FOR FILING NOTICE OF PROSPECTIVE INTERESTS.—

(A) ESTABLISHMENT.—The Administrator shall establish a system for filing notices of prospective assignments and prospective international interests in, and prospective sales of, aircraft or aircraft engines described in paragraph (1) under the Cape Town Treaty.

(B) MAINTENANCE OF VALIDITY.—A filing of a notice of prospective assignment, interest, or sale under this paragraph and the registration with the International Registry relating to such assignment, interest, or sale shall not be valid after the 60th day following the date of the filing unless documents eligible for recording under subsection (a) relating to such notice are filed for recordation on or before such 60th day.

(3) AUTHORIZATION FOR REGISTRATION OF AIRCRAFT.—A registration with the International Registry relating to an aircraft described in paragraph (1) (other than subparagraph (C)) is valid only if (A) the person seeking the registration first files documents eligible for recording under subsection (a) and relating to the registration with the United States Entry Point, and (B) the United States Entry Point authorizes the registration.

(Pub. L. 103–272, §1(e), July 5, 1994, 108 Stat. 1164; Pub. L. 108–297, §3, Aug. 9, 2004, 118 Stat. 1096.)

§44108. VALIDITY OF CONVEYANCES, LEASES, AND SECURITY INSTRUMENTS

(a) VALIDITY BEFORE FILING.—Until a conveyance, lease, or instrument executed for security purposes that may be recorded under section 44107(a)(1) or (2) of this title is filed for recording, the conveyance, lease, or instrument is valid only against—

(1) the person making the conveyance, lease, or instrument;

(2) that person's heirs and devisees; and

(3) a person having actual notice of the conveyance, lease, or instrument.

(b) PERIOD OF VALIDITY.—When a conveyance, lease, or instrument is recorded under section 44107 of this title, the conveyance, lease, or instrument is valid from the date of filing against all persons, without other recordation, except that—

(1) a lease or instrument recorded under section 44107(a)(2)(A) or (B) of this title is valid for a specifically identified engine or propeller without regard to a lease or instrument previously or subsequently recorded under section 44107(a)(2)(C) or (D); and

(2) a lease or instrument recorded under section 44107(a)(2)(C) or (D) of this title is valid only for items at the location designated in the lease or instrument.

(c) APPLICABLE LAWS.—(1) The validity of a conveyance, lease, or instrument that may be recorded under section 44107 of this title is subject to the laws of the State, the District of Columbia, or the territory or possession of the United States at which the conveyance, lease, or instrument is delivered, regardless of the place at which the subject of the conveyance, lease, or instrument is located or delivered. If the conveyance, lease, or instrument specifies the place at which delivery is intended, it is presumed that the conveyance, lease, or instrument was delivered at the specified place.

(2) This subsection does not take precedence over the Convention on the International Recognition of Rights in Aircraft (4 U.S.T. 1830) or the Cape Town Treaty, as applicable.

(d) NONAPPLICATION.—This section does not apply to—

(1) a conveyance described in section 44107(a)(1) of this title that was made before August 22, 1938; or

(2) a lease or instrument described in section 44107(a)(2) of this title that was made before June 20, 1948.

(Pub. L. 103–272, §1(e), July 5, 1994, 108 Stat. 1165; Pub. L. 108–297, §5, Aug. 9, 2004, 118 Stat. 1097.)

§44109. REPORTING TRANSFER OF OWNERSHIP

(a) FILING NOTICES.—A person having an ownership interest in an aircraft for which a certificate of registration was issued under section 44103 of this title shall file a notice with the Secretary of the Treasury that the Secretary requires by regulation, not later than 15 days after a sale, conditional sale, transfer, or conveyance of the interest.

(b) EXEMPTIONS.—The Secretary—

(1) shall prescribe regulations that establish guidelines for exempting a person or class from subsection (a) of this section; and

(2) may exempt a person or class under the regulations.

(Pub. L. 103–272, §1(e), July 5, 1994, 108 Stat. 1166.)

§44110. INFORMATION ABOUT AIRCRAFT OWNERSHIP AND RIGHTS

The Administrator of the Federal Aviation Administration may provide by regulation for—

(1) endorsing information on each certificate of registration issued under section 44103 of this title and each certificate issued under section 44704 of this title about ownership of the aircraft for which each certificate is issued; and

(2) recording transactions affecting an interest in, and for other records, proceedings, and details necessary to decide the rights of a party related to, a civil aircraft of the United States, aircraft engine, propeller, appliance, or spare part.

(Pub. L. 103–272, §1(e), July 5, 1994, 108 Stat. 1166.)

§44111. MODIFICATIONS IN REGISTRATION AND RECORDATION SYSTEM FOR

AIRCRAFT NOT PROVIDING AIR TRANSPORTATION

(a) APPLICATION.—This section applies only to aircraft not used to provide air transportation.

(b) AUTHORITY TO MAKE MODIFICATIONS.—The Administrator of the Federal Aviation Administration shall make modifications in the system for registering and recording aircraft necessary to make the system more effective in serving the needs of—

(1) buyers and sellers of aircraft;

(2) officials responsible for enforcing laws related to the regulation of controlled substances (as defined in section 102 of the Comprehensive Drug Abuse Prevention and Control Act of 1970 (21 U.S.C. 802)); and

(3) other users of the system.

(c) NATURE OF MODIFICATIONS.—Modifications made under subsection (b) of this section—

(1) may include a system of titling aircraft or registering all aircraft, even aircraft not operated;

(2) shall ensure positive, verifiable, and timely identification of the true owner; and

(3) shall address at least each of the following deficiencies in and abuses of the existing system:

(A) the registration of aircraft to fictitious persons.

(B) the use of false or nonexistent addresses by persons registering aircraft.

(C) the use by a person registering an aircraft of a post office box or "mail drop" as a return address to evade identification of the person's address.

(D) the registration of aircraft to entities established to facilitate unlawful activities.

(E) the submission of names of individuals on applications for registration of aircraft that are not identifiable.

(F) the ability to make frequent legal changes in the registration markings assigned to aircraft.

(G) the use of false registration markings on aircraft.

(H) the illegal use of "reserved" registration markings on aircraft.

(I) the large number of aircraft classified as being in "self-reported status".

(J) the lack of a system to ensure timely and adequate notice of the transfer of ownership of aircraft.

(K) the practice of allowing temporary operation and navigation of aircraft without the issuance of a certificate of registration.

(d) REGULATIONS.—(1) The Administrator of the Federal Aviation Administration shall prescribe regulations to carry out this section and provide a written explanation of how the regulations address each of the deficiencies and abuses described in subsection (c) of this section. In prescribing the regulations, the Administrator of the Federal Aviation Administration shall consult with the Administrator of Drug Enforcement, the Commissioner of U.S. Customs and Border Protection, other law enforcement officials of the United States Government, representatives of State and local law enforcement officials, representatives of the general aviation aircraft industry, representatives of users of general aviation aircraft, and other interested persons.

(2) Regulations prescribed under this subsection shall require that—

(A) each individual listed in an application for registration of an aircraft provide with the application the individual's driver's license number; and

(B) each person (not an individual) listed in an application for registration of an aircraft provide with the application the person's taxpayer identifying number.

(Pub. L. 103–272, §1(e), July 5, 1994, 108 Stat. 1166; Pub. L. 114–125, title VIII, §802(d)(2), Feb. 24, 2016, 130 Stat. 210.)

§44112. Limitation of liability

(a) Definitions.—In this section—

(1) "lessor" means a person leasing for at least 30 days a civil aircraft, aircraft engine, or propeller.

(2) "owner" means a person that owns a civil aircraft, aircraft engine, or propeller.

(3) "secured party" means a person having a security interest in, or security title to, a civil aircraft, aircraft engine, or propeller under a conditional sales contract, equipment trust contract, chattel or corporate mortgage, or similar instrument.

(b) Liability.—A lessor, owner, or secured party is liable for personal injury, death, or property loss or damage only when a civil aircraft, aircraft engine, or propeller is in the actual possession or operational control of the lessor, owner, or secured party, and the personal injury, death, or property loss or damage occurs because of—

(1) the aircraft, engine, or propeller; or

(2) the flight of, or an object falling from, the aircraft, engine, or propeller.

(Pub. L. 103–272, §1(e), July 5, 1994, 108 Stat. 1167; Pub. L. 115–254, div. B, title V, §514, Oct. 5, 2018, 132 Stat. 3358.)

§44113. Definitions

In this chapter, the following definitions apply:

(1) Cape Town Treaty.—The term "Cape Town Treaty" means the Convention on International Interests in Mobile Equipment, as modified by the Protocol to the Convention on International Interests in Mobile Equipment on Matters Specific to Aircraft Equipment, signed at Rome on May 9, 2003.

(2) United States Entry Point.—The term "United States Entry Point" means the Federal Aviation Administration Civil Aviation Registry.

(3) International Registry.—The term "International Registry" means the registry established under the Cape Town Treaty.

(Added Pub. L. 108–297, §6(a), Aug. 9, 2004, 118 Stat. 1097.)

§44114. Privacy

(a) In General.—Notwithstanding any other provision of law, including section 552(b)(3) of title 5, the Administrator of the Federal Aviation Administration shall establish and update as necessary a process by which, upon request of a private aircraft owner or operator, the Administrator withholds the registration number and other similar identifiable data or information, except for physical markings required by law, of the aircraft of the owner or operator from any broad dissemination or display (except in furnished data or information made available to or from a Government agency pursuant to a government contract, subcontract, or agreement, including for traffic management purposes) for the noncommercial flights of the owner or operator.

(b) WITHHOLDING PERSONALLY IDENTIFIABLE INFORMATION ON THE AIRCRAFT REGISTRY.—Not later than 2 years after the enactment of this Act and notwithstanding any other provision of law, including section 552(b)(3) of title 5, the Administrator shall establish a procedure by which, upon request of a private aircraft owner or operator, the Administrator shall withhold from broad dissemination or display by the FAA (except in furnished data or information made available to or from a Government agency pursuant to a government contract, subcontract, or agreement, including for traffic management purposes) the personally identifiable information of such individual, including on a publicly available website of the FAA.

(c) ICAO AIRCRAFT IDENTIFICATION CODE.—

(1) IN GENERAL.—The Administrator shall establish a program for aircraft owners and operators to apply for a new ICAO aircraft identification code.

(2) LIMITATIONS.—In carrying out the program described in paragraph (1), the Administrator shall require—

(A) each applicant to attest to a safety or security need in applying for a new ICAO aircraft identification code; and

(B) each approved applicant who obtains a new ICAO aircraft identification code to comply with all applicable aspects of, or related to, part 45 of title 14, Code of Federal Regulations, including updating an aircraft's registration number and N–Number to reflect such aircraft's new ICAO aircraft identification code.

(d) DEFINITIONS.—In this section:

(1) ADS–B.—The term "ADS–B" means automatic dependent surveillance-broadcast.

(2) ICAO.—The term "ICAO" means the International Civil Aviation Organization.

(3) PERSONALLY IDENTIFIABLE INFORMATION.—The term "personally identifiable information" means—

(A) the mailing address or registration address of an individual;

(B) an electronic address (including an email address) of an individual; or [1]

(C) the telephone number of an individual.[1]

(D) the names of the aircraft owner or operator, if the owner or operator is an individual.

(Added Pub. L. 118–63, title VIII, §803(a), May 16, 2024, 138 Stat. 1321.)

---

[1] So in original.

CHAPTER 443—INSURANCE

§44301. DEFINITIONS

In this chapter—

(1) "aircraft manufacturer" means any company or other business entity, the majority ownership and control of which is by United States citizens, that manufactures aircraft or aircraft engines.

(2) "American aircraft" means—

(A) a civil aircraft of the United States; and

(B) an aircraft owned or chartered by, or made available to—

(i) the United States Government; or

(ii) a State, the District of Columbia, a territory or possession of the United States, or a political subdivision of the State, territory, or possession.

(3) "insurance carrier" means a person authorized to do aviation insurance business in a State, including a mutual or stock insurance company and a reciprocal insurance association.

(Pub. L. 103–272, §1(e), July 5, 1994, 108 Stat. 1168; Pub. L. 108–176, title I, §106(a)(2), Dec. 12, 2003, 117 Stat. 2498.)

§44302. GENERAL AUTHORITY

(a) INSURANCE AND REINSURANCE.—(1) Subject to subsection (c) of this section and section 44305(a) of this title, the Secretary of Transportation may provide insurance and reinsurance against loss or damage arising out of any risk from the operation of an American aircraft or foreign-flag aircraft.

(2) An aircraft may be insured or reinsured for not more than its reasonable value as determined by the Secretary in accordance with reasonable business practices in the commercial aviation insurance industry. Insurance or reinsurance may be provided only when the Secretary decides that the insurance cannot be obtained on reasonable terms from an insurance carrier.

(b) REIMBURSEMENT OF INSURANCE COST INCREASES.—

(1) IN GENERAL.—The Secretary may reimburse an air carrier for the increase in the

cost of insurance, with respect to a premium for coverage ending before October 1, 2002, against loss or damage arising out of any risk from the operation of an American aircraft over the insurance premium that was in effect for a comparable operation during the period beginning September 4, 2001, and ending September 10, 2001, as the Secretary may determine. Such reimbursement is subject to subsections (a)(2), (c), and (d) of this section and to section 44303.

(2) PAYMENT FROM REVOLVING FUND.—A reimbursement under this subsection shall be paid from the revolving fund established by section 44307.

(3) FURTHER CONDITIONS.—The Secretary may impose such further conditions on insurance for which the increase in premium is subject to reimbursement under this subsection as the Secretary may deem appropriate in the interest of air commerce.

(4) TERMINATION OF AUTHORITY.—The authority to reimburse air carriers under this subsection shall expire 180 days after the date of enactment of this paragraph.

(c) PRESIDENTIAL APPROVAL.—The Secretary may provide insurance or reinsurance under subsection (a) of this section, or reimburse an air carrier under subsection (b) of this section, only with the approval of the President. The President may approve the insurance or reinsurance or the reimbursement only after deciding that the continued operation of the American aircraft or foreign-flag aircraft to be insured or reinsured is necessary in the interest of air commerce or national security or to carry out the foreign policy of the United States Government.

(d) CONSULTATION.—The President may require the Secretary to consult with interested departments, agencies, and instrumentalities of the Government before providing insurance or reinsurance or reimbursing an air carrier under this chapter.

(e) ADDITIONAL INSURANCE.—With the approval of the Secretary, a person having an insurable interest in an aircraft may insure with other underwriters in an amount that is more than the amount insured with the Secretary. However, the Secretary may not benefit from the additional insurance. This subsection does not prevent the Secretary from making contracts of coinsurance.

(f) EXTENSION OF POLICIES.—

(1) IN GENERAL.—The Secretary shall extend through December 11, 2014, the termination date of any insurance policy that the Department of Transportation issued to an air carrier under subsection (a) and that is in effect on the date of enactment of this subsection on no less favorable terms to the air carrier than existed on June 19, 2002; except that the Secretary shall amend the insurance policy, subject to such terms and conditions as the Secretary may prescribe, to add coverage for losses or injuries to aircraft hulls, passengers, and crew at the limits carried by air carriers for such losses and injuries as of such date of enactment and at an additional premium comparable to the premium charged for third-party casualty coverage under such policy.

(2) SPECIAL RULES.—Notwithstanding paragraph (1)—

(A) in no event shall the total premium paid by the air carrier for the policy, as amended, be more than twice the premium that the air carrier was paying to the Department of Transportation for its third party policy as of June 19, 2002; and

(B) the coverage in such policy shall begin with the first dollar of any covered loss that is incurred.

(g) AIRCRAFT MANUFACTURERS.—

(1) In general.—The Secretary may provide to an aircraft manufacturer insurance for loss or damage resulting from operation of an aircraft by an air carrier and involving war or terrorism.

(2) Amount.—Insurance provided by the Secretary under this subsection shall be for loss or damage in excess of the greater of the amount of available primary insurance or $50,000,000.

(3) Terms and conditions.—Insurance provided by the Secretary under this subsection shall be subject to the terms and conditions set forth in this chapter and such other terms and conditions as the Secretary may prescribe.

(Pub. L. 103–272, §1(e), July 5, 1994, 108 Stat. 1168; Pub. L. 105–137, §2(a), Dec. 2, 1997, 111 Stat. 2640; Pub. L. 107–42, title II, §201(a), Sept. 22, 2001, 115 Stat. 234; Pub. L. 107–296, title XII, §1202, Nov. 25, 2002, 116 Stat. 2286; Pub. L. 108–11, title IV, §4001(a), Apr. 16, 2003, 117 Stat. 606; Pub. L. 108–176, title I, §106(a)(1), Dec. 12, 2003, 117 Stat. 2498; Pub. L. 108–447, div. H, title I, §106(a), Dec. 8, 2004, 118 Stat. 3204; Pub. L. 109–115, div. A, title I, §108(a), Nov. 30, 2005, 119 Stat. 2402; Pub. L. 110–161, div. K, title I, §114(a), Dec. 26, 2007, 121 Stat. 2381; Pub. L. 110–253, §3(c)(6), June 30, 2008, 122 Stat. 2418; Pub. L. 110–330, §5(c), Sept. 30, 2008, 122 Stat. 3718; Pub. L. 111–12, §5(b), Mar. 30, 2009, 123 Stat. 1458; Pub. L. 111–69, §5(c), Oct. 1, 2009, 123 Stat. 2055; Pub. L. 111–116, §5(b), Dec. 16, 2009, 123 Stat. 3032; Pub. L. 111–117, div. A, title I, §114(a), Dec. 16, 2009, 123 Stat. 3042; Pub. L. 111–153, §5(b), Mar. 31, 2010, 124 Stat. 1085; Pub. L. 111–161, §5(b), Apr. 30, 2010, 124 Stat. 1127; Pub. L. 111–197, §5(b), July 2, 2010, 124 Stat. 1354; Pub. L. 111–216, title I, §104(b), Aug. 1, 2010, 124 Stat. 2349; Pub. L. 111–249, §5(c), Sept. 30, 2010, 124 Stat. 2628; Pub. L. 111–329, §5(b), Dec. 22, 2010, 124 Stat. 3567; Pub. L. 112–7, §5(b), Mar. 31, 2011, 125 Stat. 32; Pub. L. 112–16, §5(b), May 31, 2011, 125 Stat. 219; Pub. L. 112–21, §5(b), June 29, 2011, 125 Stat. 234; Pub. L. 112–27, §5(b), Aug. 5, 2011, 125 Stat. 271; Pub. L. 112–30, title II, §205(c), Sept. 16, 2011, 125 Stat. 358; Pub. L. 112–91, §5(c), Jan. 31, 2012, 126 Stat. 4; Pub. L. 112–95, title VII, §701, Feb. 14, 2012, 126 Stat. 118; Pub. L. 113–46, div. A, §152, Oct. 17, 2013, 127 Stat. 565; Pub. L. 113–76, div. L, title I, §119E(a), Jan. 17, 2014, 128 Stat. 582; Pub. L. 113–164, §148(a), Sept. 19, 2014, 128 Stat. 1874; Pub. L. 113–235, div. L, §102(a), Dec. 16, 2014, 128 Stat. 2767.)

§44302a. Temporary insurance

(a) In General.—The Secretary may provide insurance or reinsurance under this section to or for an air carrier for 1 coverage period not to exceed 90 days. Except as otherwise provided in this section, such insurance or reinsurance shall be subject to the requirements of this chapter.

(b) Restrictions.—A policy for insurance or reinsurance issued under this section—

(1) may not be issued unless the insurance carrier of the air carrier has unilaterally terminated the air carrier's war risk liability coverage pursuant to—

(A) notice under the policy;

(B) an endorsement to the policy; or

(C) an automatic termination provision in the policy or any endorsement thereto; and

(2) may cover hull, comprehensive, and third party liability risks.

(c) Premium.—A premium for insurance or reinsurance provided under this section shall be calculated based on a prorated amount equivalent to the premium that was in effect under the terminated insurance carrier policy.

(d) Approval.—A policy for insurance or reinsurance provided under this section—

(1) shall be exempt from the requirements of section 44302(c); and

(2) may provide coverage to the extent allowed under section 44303, as determined by the Secretary, notwithstanding any determination by the President in subsection (a)(1) of

such section.

(Added Pub. L. 117–328, div. Q, §103(a), Dec. 29, 2022, 136 Stat. 5252.)

§44303. COVERAGE

(a) IN GENERAL.—The Secretary of Transportation may provide insurance and reinsurance, or reimburse insurance costs, as authorized under sections 44302 and 44302a of this title for the following:

(1) an American aircraft or foreign-flag aircraft engaged in aircraft operations the President decides are necessary in the interest of air commerce or national security or to carry out the foreign policy of the United States Government.

(2) property transported or to be transported on aircraft referred to in clause (1) of this section, including—

(A) shipments by express or registered mail;

(B) property owned by citizens or residents of the United States;

(C) property—

(i) imported to, or exported from, the United States; and

(ii) bought or sold by a citizen or resident of the United States under a contract putting the risk of loss or obligation to provide insurance against risk of loss on the citizen or resident; and

(D) property transported between—

(i) a place in a State or the District of Columbia and a place in a territory or possession of the United States;

(ii) a place in a territory or possession of the United States and a place in another territory or possession of the United States; or

(iii) 2 places in the same territory or possession of the United States.

(3) the personal effects and baggage of officers and members of the crew of an aircraft referred to in clause (1) of this section and of other individuals employed or transported on that aircraft.

(4) officers and members of the crew of an aircraft referred to in clause (1) of this section and other individuals employed or transported on that aircraft against loss of life, injury, or detention.

(5) statutory or contractual obligations or other liabilities, customarily covered by insurance, of an aircraft referred to in clause (1) of this section or of the owner or operator of that aircraft.

(6) loss or damage of an aircraft manufacturer resulting from operation of an aircraft by an air carrier and involving war or terrorism.

(b) AIR CARRIER LIABILITY FOR THIRD PARTY CLAIMS ARISING OUT OF ACTS OF TERRORISM.—For acts of terrorism committed on or to an air carrier during the period beginning on September 22, 2001, and ending on December 11, 2014, the Secretary may certify that the air carrier was a victim of an act of terrorism and in the Secretary's judgment, based on the Secretary's analysis and conclusions regarding the facts and circumstances of each case, shall not be responsible for losses suffered by third parties (as referred to in section 205.5(b)(1) of title 14, Code of Federal Regulations) that exceed $100,000,000, in the aggregate, for all claims by such parties arising out of such act. If the Secretary so certifies, the air carrier shall not be liable for an amount that exceeds

$100,000,000, in the aggregate, for all claims by such parties arising out of such act, and the Government shall be responsible for any liability above such amount. No punitive damages may be awarded against an air carrier (or the Government taking responsibility for an air carrier under this subsection) under a cause of action arising out of such act. The Secretary may extend the provisions of this subsection to an aircraft manufacturer (as defined in section 44301) of the aircraft of the air carrier involved.

(Pub. L. 103–272, §1(e), July 5, 1994, 108 Stat. 1169; Pub. L. 107–42, title II, §201(b)(1), Sept. 22, 2001, 115 Stat. 235; Pub. L. 107–296, title XII, §1201, Nov. 25, 2002, 116 Stat. 2286; Pub. L. 108–11, title IV, §4001(b), Apr. 16, 2003, 117 Stat. 606; Pub. L. 108–176, title I, §106(a)(3), (b), Dec. 12, 2003, 117 Stat. 2499; Pub. L. 108–447, div. H, title I, §106(b), Dec. 8, 2004, 118 Stat. 3204; Pub. L. 109–115, div. A, title I, §108(b), Nov. 30, 2005, 119 Stat. 2402; Pub. L. 110–161, div. K, title I, §114(b), Dec. 26, 2007, 121 Stat. 2381; Pub. L. 110–253, §3(c)(7), June 30, 2008, 122 Stat. 2418; Pub. L. 110–330, §5(d), Sept. 30, 2008, 122 Stat. 3718; Pub. L. 111–12, §5(c), Mar. 30, 2009, 123 Stat. 1458; Pub. L. 111–69, §5(d), Oct. 1, 2009, 123 Stat. 2055; Pub. L. 111–116, §5(c), Dec. 16, 2009, 123 Stat. 3032; Pub. L. 111–117, div. A, title I, §114(b), Dec. 16, 2009, 123 Stat. 3043; Pub. L. 111–153, §5(c), Mar. 31, 2010, 124 Stat. 1085; Pub. L. 111–161, §5(c), Apr. 30, 2010, 124 Stat. 1127; Pub. L. 111–197, §5(c), July 2, 2010, 124 Stat. 1354; Pub. L. 111–216, title I, §104(c), Aug. 1, 2010, 124 Stat. 2349; Pub. L. 111–249, §5(d), Sept. 30, 2010, 124 Stat. 2628; Pub. L. 111–329, §5(c), Dec. 22, 2010, 124 Stat. 3567; Pub. L. 112–7, §5(c), Mar. 31, 2011, 125 Stat. 32; Pub. L. 112–16, §5(c), May 31, 2011, 125 Stat. 219; Pub. L. 112–21, §5(c), June 29, 2011, 125 Stat. 234; Pub. L. 112–27, §5(c), Aug. 5, 2011, 125 Stat. 271; Pub. L. 112–30, title II, §205(d), Sept. 16, 2011, 125 Stat. 358; Pub. L. 112–91, §5(d), Jan. 31, 2012, 126 Stat. 4; Pub. L. 112–95, title VII, §702, Feb. 14, 2012, 126 Stat. 118; Pub. L. 113–46, div. A, §153, Oct. 17, 2013, 127 Stat. 565; Pub. L. 113–76, div. L, title I, §119E(b), Jan. 17, 2014, 128 Stat. 582; Pub. L. 113–164, §148(b), Sept. 19, 2014, 128 Stat. 1874; Pub. L. 113–235, div. L, §102(b), Dec. 16, 2014, 128 Stat. 2767; Pub. L. 117–328, div. Q, §103(b)(1), Dec. 29, 2022, 136 Stat. 5252.)

§44304. REINSURANCE

To the extent the Secretary of Transportation is authorized to provide insurance under this chapter, the Secretary may reinsure any part of the insurance provided by an insurance carrier. The Secretary may reinsure with, transfer to, or transfer back to, any insurance carrier any insurance or reinsurance provided by the Secretary under this chapter.

(Pub. L. 103–272, §1(e), July 5, 1994, 108 Stat. 1169; Pub. L. 107–42, title II, §201(c), Sept. 22, 2001, 115 Stat. 235; Pub. L. 112–95, title VII, §703, Feb. 14, 2012, 126 Stat. 118.)

§44305. INSURING UNITED STATES GOVERNMENT PROPERTY

(a) GENERAL.—With the approval of the President, a department, agency, or instrumentality of the United States Government may obtain—

(1) insurance under this chapter, including insurance for risks from operating an aircraft in intrastate or interstate air commerce, but not including insurance on valuables subject to sections 17302 and 17303 of title 40; and

(2) insurance for risks arising from providing goods or services directly related to and necessary for operating an aircraft covered by insurance obtained under clause (1) of this subsection if the aircraft is operated—

(A) in carrying out a contract of the department, agency, or instrumentality; or

(B) to transport military forces or materiel on behalf of the United States under an agreement between the Government and the government of a foreign country.

(b) PREMIUM WAIVERS AND INDEMNIFICATION.—With the approval required under subsection (a) of this section, the Secretary of Transportation may provide the insurance without premium at the request of the Secretary of Defense or the head of a department, agency, or instrumentality designated by the President when the Secretary of Defense or the designated head agrees to indemnify the Secretary of Transportation against all losses covered by the insurance. The Secretary of Defense and any designated head may make indemnity agreements with the Secretary of Transportation under this section. If such an agreement is countersigned by the President or the President's designee, the agreement shall constitute, for purposes of section 44302(c), a determination that continuation of the aircraft operations to which the agreement applies is necessary to carry out the foreign policy of the United States.

(Pub. L. 103–272, §1(e), July 5, 1994, 108 Stat. 1170; Pub. L. 105–137, §3, Dec. 2, 1997, 111 Stat. 2640; Pub. L. 107–42, title II, §201(e), Sept. 22, 2001, 115 Stat. 236; Pub. L. 107–217, §3(n)(6), Aug. 21, 2002, 116 Stat. 1303.)

§44306. PREMIUMS AND LIMITATIONS ON COVERAGE AND CLAIMS

(a) PREMIUMS BASED ON RISK.—To the extent practical, the premium charged for insurance or reinsurance under this chapter shall be based on consideration of the risk involved.

(b) ALLOWANCES IN SETTING PREMIUM RATES FOR REINSURANCE.—In setting premium rates for reinsurance, the Secretary may make allowances to the insurance carrier for expenses incurred in providing services and facilities that the Secretary considers good business practices, except for payments by the insurance carrier for the stimulation or solicitation of insurance business.

(c) TIME LIMITS.—The Secretary of Transportation may provide insurance and reinsurance under this chapter for a period of not more than 1 year. The period may be extended for additional periods of not more than 1 year each only if the President decides, before each additional period, that the continued operation of the aircraft to be insured or reinsured is necessary in the interest of air commerce or national security or to carry out the foreign policy of the United States Government.

(d) MAXIMUM INSURED AMOUNT.—The insurance policy on an aircraft insured or reinsured under this chapter shall specify a stated amount that is not more than the value of the aircraft, as determined by the Secretary in accordance with reasonable business practices in the commercial aviation insurance industry. A claim under the policy may not be paid for more than that stated amount.

(Pub. L. 103–272, §1(e), July 5, 1994, 108 Stat. 1170; Pub. L. 105–137, §2(b), Dec. 2, 1997, 111 Stat. 2640; Pub. L. 107–42, title II, §201(d), Sept. 22, 2001, 115 Stat. 235; Pub. L. 107–71, title I, §§124(b), 147, Nov. 19, 2001, 115 Stat. 631, 645; Pub. L. 107–296, title XII, §1203, Nov. 25, 2002, 116 Stat. 2287; Pub. L. 108–176, title I, §106(c), (e), Dec. 12, 2003, 117 Stat. 2499.)

§44307. REVOLVING FUND

(a) EXISTENCE, DISBURSEMENTS, APPROPRIATIONS, AND DEPOSITS.—(1) There is a revolving fund in the Treasury. The Secretary of the Treasury shall disburse from the fund payments to carry out this chapter.

(2) Necessary amounts to carry out this chapter may be appropriated to the fund. The amounts appropriated and other amounts received in carrying out this chapter shall be

deposited in the fund.

(b) INVESTMENT.—On request of the Secretary of Transportation, the Secretary of the Treasury may invest any part of the amounts in the revolving fund in interest-bearing securities of the United States Government. The interest on, and the proceeds from the sale or redemption of, the securities shall be deposited in the fund.

(c) EXCESS AMOUNTS.—The balance in the revolving fund in excess of an amount the Secretary of Transportation determines is necessary for the requirements of the fund and for reasonable reserves to maintain the solvency of the fund shall be deposited at least annually in the Treasury as miscellaneous receipts.

(d) EXPENSES.—The Secretary of Transportation shall deposit annually an amount in the Treasury as miscellaneous receipts to cover the expenses the Government incurs when the Secretary of Transportation uses appropriated amounts in carrying out this chapter. The deposited amount shall equal an amount determined by multiplying the average monthly balance of appropriated amounts retained in the revolving fund by a percentage that is at least the current average rate payable on marketable obligations of the Government. The Secretary of the Treasury shall determine annually in advance the percentage applied.

(Pub. L. 103–272, §1(e), July 5, 1994, 108 Stat. 1170.)

§44308. ADMINISTRATIVE

(a) COMMERCIAL PRACTICES.—The Secretary of Transportation may carry out this chapter consistent with commercial practices of the aviation insurance business.

(b) ISSUANCE OF POLICIES AND DISPOSITION OF CLAIMS.—(1) The Secretary may issue insurance policies to carry out this chapter. The Secretary may prescribe the forms, amounts insured under the policies, and premiums charged. Any such policy may authorize the binding arbitration of claims made thereunder in such manner as may be agreed to by the Secretary and any commercial insurer that may be responsible for any part of a loss to which such policy relates. The Secretary may change an amount of insurance or a premium for an existing policy only with the consent of the insured.

(2) For a claim under insurance authorized by this chapter, the Secretary may—

(A) settle and pay the claim made for or against the United States Government;

(B) pay the amount of a binding arbitration award made under paragraph (1); and

(C) pay the amount of a judgment entered against the Government.

(c) UNDERWRITING AGENT.—(1) The Secretary may, and when practical shall, employ an insurance carrier or group of insurance carriers to act as an underwriting agent. The Secretary may use the agent, or a claims adjuster who is independent of the underwriting agent, to adjust claims under this chapter, but claims may be paid only when approved by the Secretary.

(2) The Secretary may pay reasonable compensation to an underwriting agent for servicing insurance the agent writes for the Secretary. Compensation may include payment for reasonable expenses incurred by the agent but may not include a payment by the agent for stimulation or solicitation of insurance business.

(3) Except as provided by this subsection, the Secretary may not pay an insurance broker or other person acting in a similar capacity any consideration for arranging insurance when the Secretary directly insures any part of the risk.

(d) BUDGET.—The Secretary shall submit annually a budget program for carrying out this chapter as provided for wholly owned Government corporations under chapter 91 of title 31.

(e) ACCOUNTS.—The Secretary shall maintain a set of accounts for audit under chapter 35 of title 31. Notwithstanding chapter 35, the Comptroller General shall allow credit for expenditures under this chapter made consistent with commercial practices in the aviation insurance business when shown to be necessary because of the business activities authorized by this chapter.

(Pub. L. 103–272, §1(e), July 5, 1994, 108 Stat. 1171; Pub. L. 104–316, title I, §127(e), Oct. 19, 1996, 110 Stat. 3840; Pub. L. 105–137, §4, Dec. 2, 1997, 111 Stat. 2640; Pub. L. 112–95, title VII, §704, Feb. 14, 2012, 126 Stat. 118.)

§44309. CIVIL ACTIONS

(a) LOSSES.—

(1) ACTIONS AGAINST UNITED STATES.—A person may bring a civil action in a district court of the United States or in the United States Court of Federal Claims against the United States Government when—

(A) a loss insured under this chapter is in dispute; or

(B)(i) the person is subrogated under a contract between the person and a party insured under this chapter (other than section 44305(b)) to the rights of the insured party against the United States Government; and

(ii) the person has paid to the insured party, with the approval of the Secretary of Transportation, an amount for a physical damage loss that the Secretary has determined is a loss covered by insurance issued under this chapter (other than section 44305(b)).

(2) LIMITATION.—A civil action involving the same matter (except the action authorized by this subsection) may not be brought against an agent, officer, or employee of the Government carrying out this chapter. A civil action shall not be instituted against the United States under this chapter unless the claimant first presents the claim to the Secretary of Transportation and such claim is finally denied by the Secretary in writing and notice of the denial of such claim is sent by certified or registered mail.

(3) PROCEDURE.—To the extent applicable, the procedure in an action brought under section 1346(a)(2) of title 28, United States Code, applies to an action under this subsection.

(b) VENUE AND JOINDER.—(1) A civil action under subsection (a) of this section may be brought in the judicial district for the District of Columbia or in the judicial district in which the plaintiff or the agent of the plaintiff resides if the plaintiff resides in the United States. If the plaintiff does not reside in the United States, the action may be brought in the judicial district for the District of Columbia or in the judicial district in which the Attorney General agrees to accept service.

(2) An interested person may be joined as a party to a civil action brought under subsection (a) of this section initially or on motion of either party to the action.

(c) TIME REQUIREMENTS.—(1) Except as provided under paragraph (2), an insurance claim made under this chapter against the United States shall be forever barred unless it is presented in writing to the Secretary of Transportation within two years after the date on which the loss event occurred. Any civil action arising out of the denial of such a claim shall be filed by not later than six months after the date of the mailing, by certified or registered mail, of notice of final denial of the claim by the Secretary.

(2)(A) For claims based on liability to persons with whom the insured has no privity of contract, an insurance claim made under the authority of this chapter against the United States shall be forever barred unless it is presented in writing to the Secretary of Transportation by not later than the earlier of—

 (i) the date that is 60 days after the date on which final judgment is entered by a tribunal of competent jurisdiction; or

 (ii) the date that is six years after the date on which the loss event occurred.

(B) Any civil action arising out of the denial of such claim shall be filed by not later than six months after the date of mailing, by certified or registered mail, of notice of final denial of the claim by the Secretary.

(3) A claim made under this chapter shall be deemed to be administratively denied if the Secretary fails to make a final disposition of the claim before the date that is 6 months after the date on which the claim is presented to the Secretary, unless the Secretary makes a different agreement with the claimant when there is good cause for an agreement.

(d) INTERPLEADER.—(1) If the Secretary admits the Government owes money under an insurance claim under this chapter and there is a dispute about the person that is entitled to payment, the Government may bring a civil action of interpleader in a district court of the United States against the persons that may be entitled to payment. The action may be brought in the judicial district for the District of Columbia or in the judicial district in which any party resides.

(2) The district court may order a party not residing or found in the judicial district in which the action is brought to appear in a civil action under this subsection. The order shall be served in a reasonable manner decided by the district court. If the court decides an unknown person might assert a claim under the insurance that is the subject of the action, the court may order service on that person by publication in the Federal Register.

(3) Judgment in a civil action under this subsection discharges the Government from further liability to the parties to the action and to all other persons served by publication under paragraph (2) of this subsection.

(Pub. L. 103–272, §1(e), July 5, 1994, 108 Stat. 1172; Pub. L. 105–277, div. C, title I, §110(c)(1), Oct. 21, 1998, 112 Stat. 2681–587; Pub. L. 113–291, div. A, title X, §1074(a), Dec. 19, 2014, 128 Stat. 3518.)

§44310. ENDING EFFECTIVE DATE

(a) IN GENERAL.—The authority of the Secretary of Transportation to provide insurance and reinsurance under any provision of this chapter other than sections 44302a and 44305 is not effective after December 11, 2014.

(b) INSURANCE OF UNITED STATES GOVERNMENT PROPERTY.—The authority of the Secretary of Transportation to provide insurance and reinsurance for a department, agency, or instrumentality of the United States Government under section 44305 is not effective after September 30, 2028.

(Pub. L. 103–272, §1(e), July 5, 1994, 108 Stat. 1173; Pub. L. 105–85, div. A, title X, §1088(a), Nov. 18, 1997, 111 Stat. 1921; Pub. L. 105–137, §5(a), Dec. 2, 1997, 111 Stat. 2641; Pub. L. 105–277, div. C, title I, §110(c)(2), Oct. 21, 1998, 112 Stat. 2681–588; Pub. L. 106–6, §6, Mar. 31, 1999, 113 Stat. 10; Pub. L. 106–31, title VI, §6002(f), May 21, 1999, 113 Stat. 113; Pub. L. 106–181, title VII, §711, Apr. 5, 2000,

114 Stat. 160; Pub. L. 108–11, title IV, §4001(c), Apr. 16, 2003, 117 Stat. 606; Pub. L. 108–176, title I, §106(d), Dec. 12, 2003, 117 Stat. 2499; Pub. L. 110–181, div. A, title III, §378, Jan. 28, 2008, 122 Stat. 85; Pub. L. 113–46, div. A, §154, Oct. 17, 2013, 127 Stat. 565; Pub. L. 113–66, div. A, title X, §1093, Dec. 26, 2013, 127 Stat. 878; Pub. L. 113–76, div. L, title I, §119E(c), Jan. 17, 2014, 128 Stat. 582; Pub. L. 113–164, §148(c), Sept. 19, 2014, 128 Stat. 1874; Pub. L. 113–235, div. L, §102(c), Dec. 16, 2014, 128 Stat. 2767; Pub. L. 114–328, div. A, title X, §1046, Dec. 23, 2016, 130 Stat. 2395; Pub. L. 116–92, div. A, title III, §374, Dec. 20, 2019, 133 Stat. 1332; Pub. L. 117–328, div. Q, §103(b)(2), Dec. 29, 2022, 136 Stat. 5252; Pub. L. 118–15, div. B, title II, §2202(a), Sept. 30, 2023, 137 Stat. 82; Pub. L. 118–34, title I, §102(a), Dec. 26, 2023, 137 Stat. 1113; Pub. L. 118–41, title I, §102(a), Mar. 8, 2024, 138 Stat. 21; Pub. L. 118–63, title I, §104(a), May 16, 2024, 138 Stat. 1034.)

CHAPTER 445—FACILITIES, PERSONNEL, AND RESEARCH

§44501. PLANS AND POLICY

(a) LONG RANGE PLANS AND POLICY REQUIREMENTS.—The Administrator of the Federal Aviation Administration shall make long range plans and policy for the orderly development and use of the navigable airspace, and the orderly development of air navigation facilities and services, that will best meet the needs of, and serve the interests of, civil aeronautics and the national defense, except for needs of the armed forces that are peculiar to air warfare and primarily of military concern.

(b) AIRWAY CAPITAL INVESTMENT PLAN.—The Administrator of the Federal Aviation Administration shall review, revise, and publish a national airways system plan, known as the Airway Capital Investment Plan, before the beginning of each fiscal year. The plan shall set forth—

(1) for a 10-year period, the research, engineering, procurement, and development programs and the facilities, services, and equipment that the Administrator considers necessary for a system of airways, air traffic services, and navigation aids that will—

(A) meet the forecasted needs of civil aeronautics;

(B) meet the requirements that the Secretary of Defense establishes for the support of the national defense; and

(C) provide the highest degree of safety in air commerce;

(2) for the first and second years of the plan, detailed annual estimates of—

(A) the number, type, location, and cost of acquiring, operating, and maintaining required facilities and services;

(B) the cost of research, engineering, procurement, and development required to improve safety, system capacity, and efficiency; and

(C) personnel levels required for the activities described in subparagraphs (A) and (B);

(3) for the third, fourth, and fifth years of the plan, estimates of the total cost of each major program for the 3-year period, and additional major research programs, acquisition of systems, services, and facilities, and changes in personnel levels that may be required to meet long range objectives and that may have significant impact on future funding requirements;

(4) a 10-year investment plan that considers long range objectives that the Administrator considers necessary to—

(A) ensure that safety is given the highest priority in providing for a safe and efficient airway system; and

(B) meet the current and projected growth of the aerospace industry and the requirements of interstate commerce, the United States Postal Service, and the national defense; and

(5) a list of capital projects that are part of the Next Generation Air Transportation System and funded by amounts appropriated under section 48101(a).

(c) NATIONAL AVIATION RESEARCH PLAN.—(1) The Administrator of the Federal Aviation Administration shall prepare and publish annually a national aviation research plan and submit the plan to the Committee on Commerce, Science, and Transportation of the Senate and the Committee on Science of the House of Representatives. The plan shall be submitted not later than the date that is 30 days after the date of submission of the President's budget to Congress. If such report cannot be prepared and submitted by the date that is 30 days after the date of submission of the President's budget to Congress, the Administrator shall submit, before such date, a letter to the Chairman and Ranking Member of the Committee on Commerce, Science, and Transportation of the Senate and the Committee of [1] Science, Space, and Technology of the House of Representatives stating the reason for delayed submission, impacts of the delay, and actions taken to address circumstances that led to the delay.

(2)(A) The plan shall describe, for a 5-year period, the research, engineering, and development that the Administrator of the Federal Aviation Administration considers necessary—

(i) to ensure the continued capacity, safety, and efficiency of aviation in the United States, considering emerging technologies and forecasted needs of civil aeronautics; and

(ii) to provide the highest degree of safety in air travel.

(B) The plan shall—

(i) provide estimates by year of the schedule, cost, and work force levels for each active and planned major research and development project under sections 44504, 44505, 44507, 44509, 44511–44513, and 44912 of this title, including activities carried out under cooperative agreements with other Federal departments and agencies;

(ii) specify the goals and the priorities for allocation of resources among the major categories of research and development activities, including the rationale for the priorities identified;

(iii) identify the allocation of resources among long-term research, near-term research, and development activities;

(iv) identify the individual research and development projects in each funding category that are described in the annual budget request;

(v) highlight the research and development activities that address specific recommendations of the research advisory committee established under section 44508 of this title, and document the recommendations of the committee that are not accepted, specifying the reasons for nonacceptance; and

(vi) highlight the research and development technology transfer activities that promote technology sharing among government, industry, and academia through the Stevenson-Wydler Technology Innovation Act of 1980.

(3) Subject to section 44912(d)(2) and regulations prescribed under such section, the Administrator of the Federal Aviation Administration shall submit to the committees named in paragraph (1) of this subsection an annual report on the accomplishments of the research completed during the prior fiscal year, including a description of the dissemination to the private sector of research results and a description of any new technologies developed. The report shall be submitted with the plan required under paragraph (1) and be organized to allow comparison with the plan in effect for the prior fiscal year. The report shall be prepared in accordance with requirements of section 1116 of title 31.

(Pub. L. 103–272, §1(e), July 5, 1994, 108 Stat. 1173; Pub. L. 104–264, title XI, §1105, Oct. 9, 1996, 110 Stat. 3279; Pub. L. 104–287, §5(74), Oct. 11, 1996, 110 Stat. 3396; Pub. L. 106–181, title IX, §902(a), Apr. 5, 2000, 114 Stat. 195; Pub. L. 112–95, title I, §105, Feb. 14, 2012, 126 Stat. 17; Pub. L. 118–63, title VI, §618(a), title X, §1004(a), title XI, §1101(j), May 16, 2024, 138 Stat. 1230, 1386, 1413.)

[1] *So in original. Probably should be "on".*

§44502. GENERAL FACILITIES AND PERSONNEL AUTHORITY

(a) GENERAL AUTHORITY.—(1) The Administrator of the Federal Aviation Administration may—

(A) acquire, establish, improve, operate, and maintain air navigation facilities; and

(B) provide facilities and personnel to regulate and protect air traffic.

(2) The cost of site preparation work associated with acquiring, establishing, or improving an air navigation facility under paragraph (1)(A) of this subsection shall be charged to amounts available for that purpose appropriated under section 48101(a) of this title. The Secretary of Transportation may make an agreement with an airport owner or sponsor (as defined in section 47102 of this title) so that the owner or sponsor will provide the work and be paid or reimbursed by the Secretary from the appropriated amounts.

(3) The Secretary of Transportation may authorize a department, agency, or instrumentality of the United States Government to carry out any duty or power under this subsection with the consent of the head of the department, agency, or instrumentality.

(4) PURCHASE OF INSTRUMENT LANDING SYSTEM.—

(A) ESTABLISHMENT OF PROGRAM.—The Secretary shall purchase precision approach instrument landing system equipment for installation at airports on an expedited basis.

(B) AUTHORIZATION.—No less than $30,000,000 of the amounts appropriated under section 48101(a) for each of fiscal years 2000 through 2002 shall be used for the purpose of carrying out this paragraph, including acquisition under new or existing contracts, site preparation work, installation, and related expenditures.

(5) IMPROVEMENTS ON LEASED PROPERTIES.—The Administrator may make improvements to real property leased for no or nominal consideration for an air navigation facility, regardless of whether the cost of making the improvements exceeds the cost of leasing the real property, if—

(A) the improvements primarily benefit the Government;

(B) the improvements are essential for accomplishment of the mission of the Federal Aviation Administration; and

(C) the interest of the United States Government in the improvements is protected.

(b) CERTIFICATION OF NECESSITY.—Except for Government money expended under this part or for a military purpose, Government money may be expended to acquire, establish, construct, operate, repair, alter, or maintain an air navigation facility only if the Administrator of the Federal Aviation Administration certifies in writing that the facility is reasonably necessary for use in air commerce or for the national defense. An interested person may apply for a certificate for a facility to be acquired, established, constructed, operated, repaired, altered, or maintained by or for the person.

(c) ENSURING CONFORMITY WITH PLANS AND POLICIES.—(1) To ensure conformity with plans and policies for, and allocation of, airspace by the Administrator of the Federal Aviation Administration under section 40103(b)(1) of this title, a military airport, military landing area, or missile or rocket site may be acquired, established, or constructed, or a runway may be altered substantially, only if the Administrator of the Federal Aviation Administration is given reasonable prior notice so that the Administrator of the Federal Aviation Administration may advise the appropriate committees of Congress and interested departments, agencies, and instrumentalities of the Government on the effect of the acquisition, establishment, construction, or alteration on the use of airspace by aircraft. A disagreement between the Administrator of the Federal Aviation Administration and the Secretary of Defense or the Administrator of the National Aeronautics and Space Administration may be appealed to the President for a final decision.

(2) To ensure conformity, an airport or landing area not involving the expenditure of Government money may be established or constructed, or a runway may be altered substantially, only if the Administrator of the Federal Aviation Administration is given reasonable prior notice so that the Administrator may provide advice on the effects of the establishment, construction, or alteration on the use of airspace by aircraft.

(d) PUBLIC USE AND EMERGENCY ASSISTANCE.—(1) The head of a department, agency, or instrumentality of the Government having jurisdiction over an air navigation facility owned or operated by the Government may provide, under regulations the head of the department, agency, or instrumentality prescribes, for public use of the facility.

(2) The head of a department, agency, or instrumentality of the Government having jurisdiction over an airport or emergency landing field owned or operated by the Government may provide, under regulations the head of the department, agency, or instrumentality prescribes, for assistance, and the sale of fuel, oil, equipment, and supplies, to an aircraft, but only when necessary, because of an emergency, to allow the aircraft to continue to the nearest airport operated by private enterprise. The head of the department, agency, or instrumentality shall provide for the assistance and sale at the prevailing local fair market value as determined by the head of the department, agency, or instrumentality. An amount that the head decides is equal to the cost of the assistance provided and the fuel,

oil, equipment, and supplies sold shall be credited to the appropriation from which the cost was paid. The balance shall be credited to miscellaneous receipts.

(e) TRANSFERS OF AIR TRAFFIC SYSTEMS.—

(1) IN GENERAL.—Subject to paragraph (4), an airport in a non-contiguous State may transfer, without consideration, to the Administrator of the Federal Aviation Administration, an eligible air traffic system or equipment that conforms to performance specifications of the Administrator if a Government airport aid program, airport development aid program, or airport improvement project grant was used to assist in purchasing the system or equipment.

(2) ACCEPTANCE.—The Administrator shall accept the eligible air traffic system or equipment and operate and maintain it under criteria of the Administrator.

(3) DEFINITION.—In this subsection, the term "eligible air traffic system or equipment" means—

(A) an instrument landing system consisting of a glide slope and localizer (if the Administrator has determined that a satellite navigation system cannot provide a suitable approach to an airport);

(B) an Automated Weather Observing System weather observation system;

(C) a Remote Communication Air/Ground and Remote Communication Outlet communications facility; or

(D) a Medium Intensity Approach Lighting System with Runway Alignment Indicator Lights.

(4) EXCEPTION.—The requirement under paragraph (1) that an eligible air traffic system or equipment be purchased in part using a Government airport aid program, airport development aid program, or airport improvement project grant shall not apply if the air traffic system or equipment is installed at an airport that is categorized as a basic or local general aviation airport under the most recently published national plan of integrated airport systems under section 47103.

(f) AIRPORT SPACE.—

(1) RESTRICTION.—The Administrator may not require an airport owner or sponsor (as defined in section 47102) to provide to the Federal Aviation Administration without cost any of the following:

(A) Building construction, maintenance, utilities, or expenses for services relating to air traffic control, air navigation, or weather reporting.

(B) Space in a facility owned by the airport owner or sponsor for services relating to air traffic control, air navigation, or weather reporting.

(2) RULE OF CONSTRUCTION.—Nothing in this subsection may be construed to affect—

(A) any agreement the Secretary may have or make with an airport owner or sponsor for the airport owner or sponsor to provide any of the items described in paragraph (1)(A) or (1)(B) at below-market rates; or

(B) any grant assurance that requires an airport owner or sponsor to provide land to the Administration without cost for an air traffic control facility.

(Pub. L. 103–272, §1(e), July 5, 1994, 108 Stat. 1175; Pub. L. 103–305, title I, §120(a), Aug. 23, 1994, 108 Stat. 1581; Pub. L. 103–429, §6(54), Oct. 31, 1994, 108 Stat. 4385; Pub. L. 104–287, §5(75), Oct. 11, 1996, 110 Stat. 3396; Pub. L. 106–181, title I, §153, title VII, §712, Apr. 5, 2000, 114 Stat. 87, 160; Pub. L. 115–254, div. B, title I, §147, Oct. 5, 2018, 132 Stat. 3213; Pub. L. 118–63, title VII, §728(a), May 16, 2024, 138 Stat. 1271.)

§44503. REDUCING NONESSENTIAL EXPENDITURES

The Secretary of Transportation shall attempt to reduce the capital, operating, maintenance, and administrative costs of the national airport and airway system to the maximum extent practicable consistent with the highest degree of aviation safety. At least annually, the Secretary shall consult with and consider the recommendations of users of the system on ways to reduce nonessential expenditures of the United States Government for aviation. The Secretary shall give particular attention to a recommendation that may reduce, with no adverse effect on safety, future personnel requirements and costs to the Government required to be recovered from user charges.

(Pub. L. 103–272, §1(e), July 5, 1994, 108 Stat. 1176.)

§44504. IMPROVED AIRCRAFT, AIRCRAFT ENGINES, PROPELLERS, AND APPLIANCES

(a) DEVELOPMENTAL WORK AND SERVICE TESTING.—The Administrator of the Federal Aviation Administration may conduct or supervise developmental work and service testing to improve aircraft, aircraft engines, propellers, and appliances.

(b) RESEARCH.—The Administrator shall conduct or supervise research—

(1) to develop technologies and analyze information to predict the effects of aircraft design, maintenance, testing, wear, and fatigue on the life of aircraft, including nonstructural aircraft systems, and air safety;

(2) to develop methods of analyzing and improving aircraft maintenance technology and practices, including nondestructive evaluation of aircraft structures;

(3) to assess the fire and smoke resistance of aircraft material;

(4) to develop improved fire and smoke resistant material for aircraft interiors;

(5) to develop and improve fire and smoke containment systems for inflight aircraft fires;

(6) to develop advanced aircraft fuels with low flammability and technologies that will contain aircraft fuels to minimize post-crash fire hazards;

(7) to develop technologies and methods to assess the risk of and prevent defects, failures, and malfunctions of products, parts, processes, and articles manufactured for use in aircraft, aircraft engines, propellers, and appliances that could result in a catastrophic failure of an aircraft; and

(8) in conjunction with other Federal agencies, as appropriate, to develop technologies and methods to assess the risk of and prevent defects, failures, and malfunctions of products, parts, and processes for use in all classes of unmanned aircraft systems that could result in a catastrophic failure of the unmanned aircraft that would endanger other aircraft in the national airspace system.

(c) AUTHORITY TO BUY ITEMS OFFERING SPECIAL ADVANTAGES.—In carrying out this section, the Administrator, by negotiation or otherwise, may buy or exchange experimental aircraft, aircraft engines, propellers, and appliances that the Administrator decides may offer special advantages to aeronautics.

(Pub. L. 103–272, §1(e), July 5, 1994, 108 Stat. 1176; Pub. L. 106–181, title IX, §904, Apr. 5, 2000, 114 Stat. 196; Pub. L. 112–95, title IX, §903(a), Feb. 14, 2012, 126 Stat. 138.)

§44505. Systems, procedures, facilities, services, and devices

(a) General Requirements.—(1) The Administrator of the Federal Aviation Administration shall—

(A) develop, alter, test, and evaluate systems, procedures, facilities, services, and devices, and define their performance characteristics, to meet the needs for safe and efficient navigation and traffic control of civil and military aviation, except for needs of the armed forces that are peculiar to air warfare and primarily of military concern; and

(B) select systems, procedures, facilities, services, and devices that will best serve those needs and promote maximum coordination of air traffic control and air defense systems.

(2) The Administrator may make contracts to carry out this subsection without regard to section 3324(a) and (b) of title 31.

(3) When a substantial question exists under paragraph (1) of this subsection about whether a matter is of primary concern to the armed forces, the Administrator shall decide whether the Administrator or the Secretary of the appropriate military department has responsibility. The Administrator shall be given technical information related to each research and development project of the armed forces that potentially applies to, or potentially conflicts with, the common system to ensure that potential application to the common system is considered properly and that potential conflicts with the system are eliminated.

(b) Research on Human Factors and Simulation Models.—The Administrator shall conduct or supervise research—

(1) to develop a better understanding of the relationship between human factors and aviation accidents and between human factors and air safety;

(2) to enhance air traffic controller, mechanic, and flight crew performance;

(3) to develop a human-factor analysis of the hazards associated with new technologies to be used by air traffic controllers, mechanics, and flight crews;

(4) to identify innovative and effective corrective measures for human errors that adversely affect air safety;

(5) to develop or procure dynamic simulation models and tools of the air traffic control system and airport design and operating procedures that will provide analytical technology—

(A) to predict airport and air traffic control safety and capacity problems;

(B) to evaluate planned research projects; and

(C) to test proposed revisions in airport and air traffic control operations programs;

(6) to develop a better understanding of the relationship between human factors and unmanned aircraft system safety; and

(7) to develop or procure dynamic simulation models and tools for integrating all classes of unmanned aircraft systems into the national airspace system without any degradation of existing levels of safety for all national airspace system users.

(c) Research on Developing and Maintaining a Safe and Efficient System.—The Administrator shall conduct or supervise research on—

(1) airspace and airport planning and design;

(2) airport capacity enhancement techniques;

(3) human performance in the air transportation environment;

(4) aviation safety and security;

(5) the supply of trained air transportation personnel, including pilots and mechanics; and

(6) other aviation issues related to developing and maintaining a safe and efficient air transportation system.

(d) RESEARCH ON DESIGN FOR CERTIFICATION.—

(1) RESEARCH.—Not later than 1 year after the date of enactment of the FAA Modernization and Reform Act of 2012, the Administrator shall conduct research on methods and procedures to improve both confidence in and the timeliness of certification of new technologies for their introduction into the national airspace system.

(2) RESEARCH PLAN.—Not later than 6 months after the date of enactment of the FAA Modernization and Reform Act of 2012, the Administrator shall develop a plan for the research under paragraph (1) that contains objectives, proposed tasks, milestones, and a 5-year budgetary profile.

(3) REVIEW.—The Administrator shall enter into an arrangement with the National Research Council to conduct an independent review of the plan developed under paragraph (2) and shall provide the results of that review to the Committee on Science, Space, and Technology of the House of Representatives and the Committee on Commerce, Science, and Transportation of the Senate not later than 18 months after the date of enactment of the FAA Modernization and Reform Act of 2012.

(e) COOPERATIVE AGREEMENTS.—The Administrator may enter into cooperative agreements on a cost-shared basis with Federal and non-Federal entities that the Administrator may select in order to conduct, encourage, and promote aviation research, engineering, and development, including the development of prototypes and demonstration models.

(Pub. L. 103–272, §1(e), July 5, 1994, 108 Stat. 1177; Pub. L. 103–305, title III, §307, Aug. 23, 1994, 108 Stat. 1593; Pub. L. 112–95, title IX, §§903(b), 905, Feb. 14, 2012, 126 Stat. 138, 139; Pub. L. 118–63, title VI, §618(b)(1), May 16, 2024, 138 Stat. 1231.)

§44506. AIR TRAFFIC CONTROLLERS

(a) RESEARCH ON EFFECT OF AUTOMATION ON PERFORMANCE.—To develop the means necessary to establish appropriate selection criteria and training methodologies for the next generation of air traffic controllers, the Administrator of the Federal Aviation Administration shall conduct research to study the effect of automation on the performance of the next generation of air traffic controllers and the air traffic control system. The research shall include investigating—

(1) methods for improving and accelerating future air traffic controller training through the application of advanced training techniques, including the use of simulation technology;

(2) the role of automation in the air traffic control system and its physical and psychological effects on air traffic controllers;

(3) the attributes and aptitudes needed to function well in a highly automated air traffic control system and the development of appropriate testing methods for identifying individuals with those attributes and aptitudes;

(4) innovative methods for training potential air traffic controllers to enhance the

benefits of automation and maximize the effectiveness of the air traffic control system; and

(5) new technologies and procedures for exploiting automated communication systems, including Mode S Transponders, to improve information transfers between air traffic controllers and aircraft pilots.

(b) RESEARCH ON HUMAN FACTOR ASPECTS OF AUTOMATION.—The Administrators of the Federal Aviation Administration and National Aeronautics and Space Administration may make an agreement for the use of the National Aeronautics and Space Administration's unique human factor facilities and expertise in conducting research activities to study the human factor aspects of the highly automated environment for the next generation of air traffic controllers. The research activities shall include investigating—

(1) human perceptual capabilities and the effect of computer-aided decision making on the workload and performance of air traffic controllers;

(2) information management techniques for advanced air traffic control display systems; and

(3) air traffic controller workload and performance measures, including the development of predictive models.

(c) COLLEGIATE TRAINING INITIATIVE.—(1) The Administrator of the Federal Aviation Administration may maintain the Collegiate Training Initiative program by making new agreements and continuing existing agreements with institutions of higher education (as defined by the Administrator) under which the institutions prepare students for the position of air traffic controller with the Department of Transportation (as defined in section 2109 of title 5). The Administrator may establish standards for the entry of institutions into the program and for their continued participation.

(2)(A) The Administrator of the Federal Aviation Administration may appoint an individual who has successfully completed a course of training in a program described in paragraph (1) of this subsection to the position of air traffic controller noncompetitively in the excepted service (as defined in section 2103 of title 5). An individual appointed under this paragraph serves at the pleasure of the Administrator, subject to section 7511 of title 5. However, an appointment under this paragraph may be converted from one in the excepted service to a career conditional or career appointment in the competitive civil service (as defined in section 2102 of title 5) when the individual achieves full performance level air traffic controller status, as decided by the Administrator.

(B) The authority under subparagraph (A) of this paragraph to make appointments in the excepted service expires on October 6, 1997, except that the Administrator of the Federal Aviation Administration may extend the authority for one or more successive one-year periods.

(d) AIR TRAFFIC CONTROL SPECIALIST QUALIFICATION TRAINING.—

(1) APPOINTMENT OF AIR TRAFFIC CONTROL SPECIALISTS.—The Administrator is authorized to appoint a qualified air traffic control specialist candidate for placement in an airport traffic control facility if the candidate has—

(A) received a control tower operator certification (referred to in this subsection as a "CTO" certificate); and

(B) satisfied all other applicable qualification requirements for an air traffic control specialist position, including successful completion of orientation training at the

Federal Aviation Administration Academy.

(2) COMPENSATION AND BENEFITS.—An individual appointed under paragraph (1) shall receive the same compensation and benefits, and be treated in the same manner as, any other individual appointed as a developmental air traffic controller.

(3) REPORT.—Not later than 2 years after the date of enactment of the FAA Modernization and Reform Act of 2012, the Administrator shall submit to Congress a report that evaluates the effectiveness of the air traffic control specialist qualification training provided pursuant to this section, including the graduation rates of candidates who received a CTO certificate and are working in airport traffic control facilities.

(4) ADDITIONAL APPOINTMENTS.—If the Administrator determines that air traffic control specialists appointed pursuant to this subsection are more successful in carrying out the duties of an air traffic controller than air traffic control specialists hired from the general public without any such certification, the Administrator shall increase, to the maximum extent practicable, the number of appointments of candidates who possess such certification.

(5) REIMBURSEMENT FOR TRAVEL EXPENSES ASSOCIATED WITH CERTIFICATIONS.—

(A) IN GENERAL.—Subject to subparagraph (B), the Administrator may accept reimbursement from an educational entity that provides training to an air traffic control specialist candidate to cover reasonable travel expenses of the Administrator associated with issuing certifications to such candidates.

(B) TREATMENT OF REIMBURSEMENTS.—Notwithstanding section 3302 of title 31, any reimbursement authorized to be collected under subparagraph (A) shall—

(i) be credited as offsetting collections to the account that finances the activities and services for which the reimbursement is accepted;

(ii) be available for expenditure only to pay the costs of activities and services for which the reimbursement is accepted, including all costs associated with collecting such reimbursement; and

(iii) remain available until expended.

(e) STAFFING REPORT.—The Administrator of the Federal Aviation Administration shall submit annually to the Committee on Transportation and Infrastructure of the House of Representatives and the Committee on Commerce, Science, and Transportation of the Senate a report containing—

(1) the staffing standards used to determine the number of fully certified air traffic controllers needed to operate the air traffic control system of the United States;

(2) for each air traffic control facility operated by the Federal Aviation Administration—

(A) the current certified professional controller staffing levels;

(B) the operational staffing targets for certified professional controllers;

(C) the anticipated certified professional controller attrition for each of the next 3 years; and

(D) the number of certified professional controller trainees;

(3) a 3-year projection of the number of controllers needed to be employed to operate the system to meet the standards; and

(4) a detailed plan for employing the controllers, including projected budget requests.

(f) HIRING OF CERTAIN AIR TRAFFIC CONTROL SPECIALISTS.—

(1) CONSIDERATION OF APPLICANTS.—

(A) ENSURING SELECTION OF MOST QUALIFIED APPLICANTS.—In appointing individuals to the position of air traffic controller, the Administrator shall give preferential consideration to qualified individuals maintaining 52 consecutive weeks of air traffic control experience involving the full-time active separation of air traffic after receipt of an air traffic certification or air traffic control facility rating within 5 years of application while serving at—

(i) a Federal Aviation Administration air traffic control facility;

(ii) a civilian or military air traffic control facility of the Department of Defense (including a facility of the National Guard); or

(iii) a tower operating under contract with the Federal Aviation Administration under section 47124.

(B) CONSIDERATION OF ADDITIONAL APPLICANTS.—

(i) IN GENERAL.—After giving preferential consideration to applicants under subparagraph (A), the Administrator shall consider additional applicants for the position of air traffic controller by giving further preferential consideration, within each qualification category based upon pre-employment testing results (including application of veterans' preference as required under section $40122(g)(2)(B)$), to pool 1 applicants described in clause (ii) before pool 2 applicants described in clause (iii).

(ii) POOL 1.—Pool 1 applicants are individuals who—

(I) have successfully completed air traffic controller training and graduated from an institution participating in the Collegiate Training Initiative program maintained under subsection $(c)(1)$ and who have received from the institution—

(aa) an appropriate recommendation; or

(bb) an endorsement certifying that the individual would have met the requirements in effect as of December 31, 2013, for an appropriate recommendation;

(II) are eligible for a veterans recruitment appointment pursuant to section 4214 of title 38 and provide a Certificate of Release or Discharge from Active Duty within 120 days of the announcement closing;

(III) are eligible veterans (as defined in section 4211 of title 38) maintaining aviation experience obtained in the course of the individual's military experience; or

(IV) are preference eligible veterans (as defined in section 2108 of title 5).

(iii) POOL 2.—Pool 2 applicants are individuals who apply under a vacancy announcement recruiting from all United States citizens.

(C) SPECIAL RULE.—

(i) IN GENERAL.—Notwithstanding subparagraph (B), after giving preferential consideration to applicants under subparagraph (A) and if, after consulting with the labor organization recognized as the exclusive representative of air traffic controllers under section 7111 of title 5, the Administrator determines there are unique circumstances affecting a covered facility that warrant a vacancy announcement with a limited area of consideration, the Administrator may consider applicants for the position of air traffic controller who apply under a vacancy announcement recruiting from the local commuting area for that covered facility.

(ii) BIOGRAPHICAL ASSESSMENTS.—The Administrator shall not use any biographical assessment with respect to an applicant under this subparagraph who would otherwise qualify as a Pool 1 applicant under subparagraph (B)(ii).

(iii) COVERED FACILITY DEFINED.—In this subparagraph the term "covered facility" means a radar facility with at least 1,000,000 operations annually that is located in a metropolitan statistical area (as defined by the Office of Management and Budget) with a population estimate by the Bureau of the Census of more than 15,000,000 (as of July 1, 2016).

(2) USE OF BIOGRAPHICAL ASSESSMENTS.—

(A) BIOGRAPHICAL ASSESSMENTS.—The Administrator shall not use any biographical assessment when hiring under paragraph (1)(A) or paragraph (1)(B).

(B) RECONSIDERATION OF APPLICANTS DISQUALIFIED ON BASIS OF BIOGRAPHICAL ASSESSMENTS.—

(i) IN GENERAL.—If an individual described in paragraph (1)(A) or paragraph (1)(B)(ii), who applied for the position of air traffic controller with the Administration in response to Vacancy Announcement FAA–AMC–14–ALLSRCE–33537 (issued on February 10, 2014), was disqualified from the position as a result of a biographical assessment, the Administrator shall provide the applicant an opportunity to reapply for the position as soon as practicable under the revised hiring practices.

(ii) WAIVER OF AGE RESTRICTION.—The Administrator shall waive any maximum age restriction for the position of air traffic controller with the Administration that would otherwise disqualify an individual from the position if the individual—

(I) is reapplying for the position pursuant to clause (i) on or before December 31, 2017; and

(II) met the maximum age requirement on the date of the individual's previous application for the position during the interim hiring process.

(3) MAXIMUM ENTRY AGE FOR EXPERIENCED CONTROLLERS.—Notwithstanding section 3307 of title 5, except for individuals covered by the program described in paragraph (4), the maximum limit of age for an original appointment to a position as an air traffic controller shall be 35 years of age for those maintaining 52 weeks of air traffic control experience involving the full-time active separation of air traffic after receipt of an air traffic certification or air traffic control facility rating in a civilian or military air traffic control facility.

(4) RETIRED MILITARY CONTROLLERS.—The Administrator may establish a program to provide an original appointment to a position as an air traffic controller for individuals who—

(A) are on terminal leave pending retirement from active duty military service or have retired from active duty military service within 5 years of applying for the appointment; and

(B) have held either an air traffic certification or air traffic control facility rating according to Administration standards within 5 years of applying for the appointment.

(Pub. L. 103–272, §1(e), July 5, 1994, 108 Stat. 1178; Pub. L. 104–287, §5(9), Oct. 11, 1996, 110 Stat. 3389; Pub. L. 112–95, title VI, §607, Feb. 14, 2012, 126 Stat. 114; Pub. L. 114–190, title II, §2106(a), July

15, 2016, 130 Stat. 620; Pub. L. 115–141, div. M, title I, §108, Mar. 23, 2018, 132 Stat. 1047; Pub. L. 116–92, div. A, title XI, §§1132, 1133, Dec. 20, 2019, 133 Stat. 1615, 1616; Pub. L. 118–63, title IV, §§433, 437(e)(2), May 16, 2024, 138 Stat. 1174, 1178.)

§44507. REGIONS AND CENTERS

The Civil Aeromedical Institute established by section 106(j) of this title may—

(1) conduct civil aeromedical research, including research related to—

(A) the protection and survival of aircraft occupants;

(B) medical accident investigation and airman medical certification;

(C) toxicology and the effects of drugs on human performance;

(D) the impact of disease and disability on human performance;

(E) vision and its relationship to human performance and equipment design;

(F) human factors of flight crews, air traffic controllers, mechanics, inspectors, airway facility technicians, and other individuals involved in operating and maintaining aircraft and air traffic control equipment; and

(G) agency work force optimization, including training, equipment design, reduction of errors, and identification of candidate tasks for automation;

(2) make comments to the Administrator of the Federal Aviation Administration on human factors aspects of proposed air safety regulations;

(3) make comments to the Administrator on human factors aspects of proposed training programs, equipment requirements, standards, and procedures for aviation personnel;

(4) advise, assist, and represent the Federal Aviation Administration in the human factors aspects of joint projects between the Administration and the National Aeronautics and Space Administration, other departments, agencies, and instrumentalities of the United States Government, industry, and governments of foreign countries; and

(5) provide medical consultation services to the Administrator about medical certification of airmen.

(Pub. L. 103–272, §1(e), July 5, 1994, 108 Stat. 1179; Pub. L. 115–254, div. B, title V, §524(a), Oct. 5, 2018, 132 Stat. 3363; Pub. L. 118–63, title II, §206(h), May 16, 2024, 138 Stat. 1046.)

§44508. RESEARCH ADVISORY COMMITTEE

(a) ESTABLISHMENT AND DUTIES.—(1) There is a research advisory committee in the Federal Aviation Administration. The committee shall—

(A) provide advice and recommendations to the Administrator of the Federal Aviation Administration and Congress about needs, objectives, plans, approaches, content, and accomplishments of all aviation research and development activities and programs carried out, including those under sections 44504, 44505, 44507, 44511–44513, and 44912 of this title;

(B) assist in ensuring that the research is coordinated with similar research being conducted outside the Administration;

(C) review the operations of the regional centers of air transportation excellence established under section 44513 of this title; and

(D) annually review the allocation made by the Administrator of the amounts authorized by section 48102(a) of this title among the major categories of research and development activities carried out by the Administration and provide advice and recommendations to the Administrator on whether such allocation is appropriate to meet the needs and objectives identified under subparagraph (A).

(2) The Administrator may establish subordinate committees to provide advice on specific areas of research conducted under sections 44504, 44505, 44507, 44511–44513, and 44912 of this title.

(b) MEMBERS, CHAIRMAN, PAY, AND EXPENSES.—(1) The committee is composed of not more than 30 members appointed by the Administrator from among individuals who are not employees of the Administration and who are specially qualified to serve on the committee because of their education, training, or experience. In appointing members of the committee, the Administrator shall ensure that the regional centers of air transportation excellence, universities, corporations, associations, consumers, and other departments, agencies, and instrumentalities of the United States Government are represented.

(2) The Administrator shall designate the chairman of the committee.

(3) A member of the committee serves without pay. However, the Administrator may allow a member, when attending meetings of the committee or a subordinate committee, expenses as authorized under section 5703 of title 5.

(c) SUPPORT STAFF, INFORMATION, AND SERVICES.—The Administrator shall provide support staff for the committee. On request of the committee, the Administrator shall provide information, administrative services, and supplies that the Administrator considers necessary for the committee to carry out its duties and powers.

(d) NONAPPLICATION.—Section 1013 of title 5 does not apply to the committee.

(e) USE AND LIMITATION OF AMOUNTS.—(1) Not more than .1 percent of the amounts made available to conduct research under sections 44504, 44505, 44507, 44511–44513, and 44912 of this title may be used by the Administrator to carry out this section.

(2) A limitation on amounts available for obligation by or for the committee does not apply to amounts made available to carry out this section.

(f) WRITTEN REPLY.—

(1) IN GENERAL.—Not later than 60 days after receiving any recommendation from the research advisory committee, the Administrator shall provide a written reply to the research advisory committee that, at a minimum—

(A) clearly states whether the Administrator accepts or rejects the recommendation;

(B) explains the rationale for the Administrator's decision;

(C) sets forth the timeframe in which the Administrator will implement the recommendation; and

(D) describes the steps the Administrator will take to implement the recommendation.

(2) TRANSPARENCY.—The written reply to the research advisory committee, when transmitted to the research advisory committee, shall be—

(A) made publicly available on the research advisory committee website; and

(B) transmitted to the Committee on Science, Space, and Technology of the House of Representatives and the Committee on Commerce, Science, and Transportation of the Senate.

(3) NATIONAL AVIATION RESEARCH PLAN.—The national aviation research plan required under section 44501(c) shall include a summary of all research advisory committee

recommendations and a description of the status of their implementation.

(Pub. L. 103–272, §1(e), July 5, 1994, 108 Stat. 1180; Pub. L. 104–264, title XI, §1104, Oct. 9, 1996, 110 Stat. 3279; Pub. L. 115–254, div. B, title VII, §712, Oct. 5, 2018, 132 Stat. 3410; Pub. L. 117–286, §4(a)(313), Dec. 27, 2022, 136 Stat. 4340; Pub. L. 118–63, title XI, §1101(l), May 16, 2024, 138 Stat. 1414.)

§44509. Demonstration projects

The Secretary of Transportation may carry out under this chapter demonstration projects that the Secretary considers necessary for research and development activities under this chapter.

(Pub. L. 103–272, §1(e), July 5, 1994, 108 Stat. 1181.)

§44510. Repealed. Pub. L. 118–63, title IV, §401(a), May 16, 2024, 138 Stat. 1148

Section, Pub. L. 103–272, §1(e), July 5, 1994, 108 Stat. 1181, related to airway science curriculum grants.

§44511. Aviation research grants

(a) General Authority.—The Administrator of the Federal Aviation Administration may make grants to institutions of higher education and nonprofit research organizations to conduct aviation research in areas the Administrator considers necessary for the long-term growth of civil aviation.

(b) Applications.—An institution of higher education or nonprofit research organization interested in receiving a grant under this section may submit an application to the Administrator. The application must be in the form and contain the information the Administrator requires.

(c) Solicitation, Review, and Evaluation Process.—The Administrator shall establish a solicitation, review, and evaluation process that ensures—

(1) providing grants under this section for proposals having adequate merit and relevancy to the mission of the Administration;

(2) a fair geographical distribution of grants under this section; and

(3) the inclusion of historically black institutions of higher education and other minority nonprofit research organizations for grant consideration under this section.

(d) Records.—Each person receiving a grant under this section shall maintain records that the Administrator requires as being necessary to facilitate an effective audit and evaluation of the use of money provided under the grant.

(e) Annual Report.—The Administrator shall submit an annual report to the Committee on Science of the House of Representatives and the Committee on Commerce, Science, and Transportation of the Senate on carrying out this section.

(f) Airport Cooperative Research Program.—

(1) Establishment.—The Secretary of Transportation shall maintain an airport cooperative research program to—

(A) identify problems that are shared by airport operating agencies and can be solved through applied research but that are not being adequately addressed by existing Federal research programs; and

(B) fund research to address those problems.

(2) GOVERNANCE.—The Secretary of Transportation shall appoint an independent governing board for the research program established under this subsection. The governing board shall be appointed from candidates nominated by national associations representing public airport operating agencies, airport executives, State aviation officials, and the scheduled airlines, and shall include representatives of appropriate Federal agencies. Section 1013 of title 5 shall not apply to the governing board.

(3) IMPLEMENTATION.—The Secretary of Transportation shall enter into an arrangement with the National Academy of Sciences to provide staff support to the governing board established under paragraph (2) and to carry out projects proposed by the governing board that the Secretary considers appropriate.

(4) REPORT.—Not later than September 30, 2012, the Secretary shall transmit to the Congress a report on the program.

(Pub. L. 103–272, §1(e), July 5, 1994, 108 Stat. 1181; Pub. L. 104–287, §5(74), Oct. 11, 1996, 110 Stat. 3396; Pub. L. 108–176, title VII, §712, Dec. 12, 2003, 117 Stat. 2586; Pub. L. 112–95, title IX, §906, Feb. 14, 2012, 126 Stat. 139; Pub. L. 117–286, §4(a)(314), Dec. 27, 2022, 136 Stat. 4340.)

§44512. CATASTROPHIC FAILURE PREVENTION RESEARCH GRANTS

(a) GENERAL AUTHORITY.—The Administrator of the Federal Aviation Administration may make grants to institutions of higher education and nonprofit research organizations—

(1) to conduct aviation research related to the development of technologies and methods to assess the risk of, and prevent, defects, failures, and malfunctions of products, parts, processes, and articles manufactured for use in aircraft, aircraft engines, propellers, and appliances that could result in a catastrophic failure of an aircraft; and

(2) to establish centers of excellence for continuing the research.

(b) SOLICITATION, APPLICATION, REVIEW, AND EVALUATION PROCESS.—The Administrator shall establish a solicitation, application, review, and evaluation process that ensures providing grants under this section for proposals having adequate merit and relevancy to the research described in subsection (a) of this section.

(Pub. L. 103–272, §1(e), July 5, 1994, 108 Stat. 1182.)

§44513. REGIONAL CENTERS OF AIR TRANSPORTATION EXCELLENCE

(a) GENERAL AUTHORITY.—The Administrator of the Federal Aviation Administration may make grants to institutions of higher education to establish and operate regional centers of air transportation excellence. The locations shall be distributed in a geographically fair way.

(b) RESPONSIBILITIES.—(1) The responsibilities of each center established under this section shall include—

(A) conducting research on—

(i) airspace and airport planning and design;

(ii) airport capacity enhancement techniques;

(iii) human performance in the air transportation environment;

(iv) aviation safety and security;

(v) the supply of trained air transportation personnel, including pilots and mechanics; and

(vi) other aviation issues related to developing and maintaining a safe and efficient air transportation system; and

(B) interpreting, publishing, and disseminating the results of the research.

(2) In conducting research described in paragraph (1)(A) of this subsection, each center may make contracts with nonprofit research organizations and other appropriate persons.

(c) APPLICATIONS.—An institution of higher education interested in receiving a grant under this section may submit an application to the Administrator. The application must be in the form and contain the information that the Administrator requires by regulation.

(d) SELECTION CRITERIA.—The Administrator shall select recipients of grants under this section on the basis of the following criteria:

(1) the extent to which the needs of the State in which the applicant is located are representative of the needs of the region for improved air transportation services and facilities.

(2) the demonstrated research and extension resources available to the applicant to carry out this section.

(3) the ability of the applicant to provide leadership in making national and regional contributions to the solution of both long-range and immediate air transportation problems.

(4) the extent to which the applicant has an established air transportation program.

(5) the demonstrated ability of the applicant to disseminate results of air transportation research and educational programs through a statewide or regionwide continuing education program.

(6) the projects the applicant proposes to carry out under the grant.

(e) EXPENDITURE AGREEMENTS.—A grant may be made under this section in a fiscal year only if the recipient makes an agreement with the Administrator that the Administrator requires to ensure that the recipient will maintain its total expenditures from all other sources for establishing and operating the center and related research activities at a level at least equal to the average level of those expenditures in the 2 fiscal years of the recipient occurring immediately before November 5, 1990.

(f) GOVERNMENT'S SHARE OF COSTS.—The United States Government's share of establishing and operating a center and all related research activities that grant recipients carry out shall not exceed 50 percent of the costs, except that the Administrator may increase such share to a maximum of 75 percent of the costs for a fiscal year if the Administrator determines that a center would be unable to carry out the authorized activities described in this section without additional funds.

(g) ALLOCATING AMOUNTS.—The Administrator shall allocate amounts made available to carry out this section in a geographically fair way.

(h) ANNUAL REPORT.—The Administrator shall transmit annually to the Committee on Science, Space, and Technology of the House of Representatives and the Committee on Commerce, Science, and Transportation of the Senate at the time of the President's budget request a report that lists—

(1) the research projects that have been initiated by each center in the preceding year;

(2) the amount of funding for each research project and the funding source;

(3) the institutions participating in each research project and their shares of the overall funding for each research project; and

(4) the level of cost-sharing for each research project.

(Pub. L. 103–272, §1(e), July 5, 1994, 108 Stat. 1182; Pub. L. 112–95, title IX, §907, Feb. 14, 2012, 126 Stat. 140.)

§44514. Repealed. Pub. L. 118–63, title III, §337, May 16, 2024, 138 Stat. 1093

Section, Pub. L. 103–272, §1(e), July 5, 1994, 108 Stat. 1183, related to closing, reopening, and reducing hours of certain flight service stations and establishment of manned auxiliary flight service stations.

§44515. Repealed. Pub. L. 118–63, title IV, §401(a), May 16, 2024, 138 Stat. 1148

Section, Pub. L. 103–272, §1(e), July 5, 1994, 108 Stat. 1184, related to grants for advanced training facilities for maintenance technicians for air carrier aircraft.

§44516. Human factors program

(a) Human Factors Training.—

(1) Air traffic controllers.—The Administrator of the Federal Aviation Administration shall—

(A) address the problems and concerns raised by the National Research Council in its report "The Future of Air Traffic Control" on air traffic control automation; and

(B) respond to the recommendations made by the National Research Council.

(2) Pilots and flight crews.—The Administrator shall work with representatives of the aviation industry and appropriate aviation programs associated with universities to develop specific training curricula to address critical safety problems, including problems of pilots—

(A) in recovering from loss of control of an aircraft, including handling unusual attitudes and mechanical malfunctions;

(B) in deviating from standard operating procedures, including inappropriate responses to emergencies and hazardous weather;

(C) in awareness of altitude and location relative to terrain to prevent controlled flight into terrain; and

(D) in landing and approaches, including nonprecision approaches and go-around procedures.

(b) Test Program.—The Administrator shall establish a test program in cooperation with air carriers to use model Jeppesen approach plates or other similar tools to improve precision-like landing approaches for aircraft.

(c) Report.—Not later than 1 year after the date of the enactment of this section, the Administrator shall transmit to the Committee on Commerce, Science, and Transportation of the Senate and the Committee on Transportation and Infrastructure of the House of Representatives a report on the status of the Administration's efforts to encourage the adoption and implementation of advanced qualification programs for air carriers under this section.

(d) Advanced Qualification Program Defined.—In this section, the term "advanced qualification program" means an alternative method for qualifying, training, certifying, and ensuring the competency of flight crews and other commercial aviation operations personnel subject to the training and evaluation requirements of parts 121 and 135 of title 14, Code of Federal Regulations.

(Added Pub. L. 106–181, title VII, §713(a), Apr. 5, 2000, 114 Stat. 160.)

§44517. PROGRAM TO PERMIT COST SHARING OF AIR TRAFFIC MODERNIZATION PROJECTS

(a) IN GENERAL.—Subject to the requirements of this section, the Secretary may carry out a program under which the Secretary may make grants to project sponsors for not more than 10 eligible projects per fiscal year for the purpose of improving aviation safety and enhancing mobility of the Nation's air transportation system by encouraging non-Federal investment in critical air traffic control equipment and software.

(b) FEDERAL SHARE.—The Federal share of the cost of an eligible project carried out under the program shall not exceed 33 percent. The non-Federal share of the cost of an eligible project shall be provided from non-Federal sources, including revenues collected pursuant to section 40117.

(c) LIMITATION ON GRANT AMOUNTS.—No eligible project may receive more than $5,000,000 in Federal funds under the program.

(d) FUNDING.—The Secretary shall use amounts appropriated under section 48101(a) to carry out the program.

(e) DEFINITIONS.—In this section, the following definitions apply:

(1) ELIGIBLE PROJECT.—The term "eligible project" means a project to purchase equipment or software relating to the Nation's air traffic control system that is certified or approved by the Administrator of the Federal Aviation Administration and that promotes safety, efficiency, or mobility. Such projects may include—

(A) airport-specific air traffic facilities and equipment, including local area augmentation systems, instrument landing systems, weather and wind shear detection equipment, and lighting improvements;

(B) automation tools to effect improvements in airport capacity, including passive final approach spacing tools and traffic management advisory equipment; and

(C) equipment and software that enhance airspace control procedures or assist in en route surveillance, including oceanic and offshore flight tracking.

(2) PROJECT SPONSOR.—The term "project sponsor" means any major user of the national airspace system, as determined by the Secretary, including a public-use airport or a joint venture between a public-use airport and one or more air carriers.

(f) TRANSFERS OF EQUIPMENT.—Notwithstanding any other provision of law, and upon agreement by the Administrator, a project sponsor may transfer, without consideration, to the Federal Aviation Administration, facilities, equipment, or automation tools, the purchase of which was assisted by a grant made under this section, if such facilities, equipment or tools meet Federal Aviation Administration operation and maintenance criteria.

(g) GUIDELINES.—The Administrator shall issue advisory guidelines on the implementation of the program. The guidelines shall not be subject to administrative rulemaking requirements under subchapter II of chapter 5 of title 5.

(Added Pub. L. 108–176, title I, §183(a), Dec. 12, 2003, 117 Stat. 2516.)

§44518. ADVANCED MATERIALS CENTER OF EXCELLENCE

(a) IN GENERAL.—

(1) CONTINUED OPERATIONS.—The Administrator shall—

(A) continue operation of the Advanced Materials Center of Excellence (referred to in this section as the "Center"); and

(B) make a determination on whether to award a grant to the Center not later than 90 days after the date on which the grants officer of the Federal Aviation Administration recommends a proposal for award of such grant to the Administrator.

(2) PURPOSES.—The Center shall—

(A) focus on applied research and training on the safe use of composites and advanced materials, and related manufacturing practices, in airframe structures; and

(B) conduct research and development into aircraft structure crash worthiness and passenger safety, as well as address safe and accessible air travel of individuals with a disability (as defined in section 382.3 of title 14, Code of Federal Regulations (or any successor regulation)), including materials required to facilitate safe wheelchair restraint systems on commercial aircraft.

(b) RESPONSIBILITIES.—The Center shall—

(1) promote and facilitate collaboration among member universities, academia, the Administration, the commercial aircraft industry, including manufacturers, commercial air carriers, and suppliers, and other appropriate stakeholders for the purposes under subsection (a) and the activities described in paragraphs (2) through (4);

(2) carry out research and development activities to advance technology, improve engineering practices, and facilitate continuing education in relevant areas of study, which shall include—

(A) all structural materials, including—

(i) metallic and non-metallic based additive materials, ceramic materials, carbon fiber polymers, and thermoplastic composites;

(ii) the long-term material and structural behavior of such materials; and

(iii) evaluating the resiliency and long-term durability of advanced materials in high temperature conditions and in engines for applications in advanced aircraft; and

(B) structural technologies, such as additive manufacturing, to be used in applications within the commercial aircraft industry, including traditional fixed-wing aircraft, rotorcraft, and emerging aircraft types such as advanced air mobility aircraft; and

(3) conduct research activities for the purpose of improving the safety and certification of aviation structures, materials, and additively manufactured aviation products and components; and

(4) conducting [1] research activities to advance the safe movement of all passengers, including individuals with a disability (as defined in section 382.3 of title 14, Code of Federal Regulations (or any successor regulation)), and individuals using personal wheelchairs in flight, that takes into account the modeling, engineering, testing, operating, and training issues significant to all passengers and relevant stakeholders.

(c) AUTHORIZATION OF APPROPRIATIONS.—Out of amounts appropriated under section 48102(a), the Administrator may expend not more than $10,000,000 for each of fiscal years 2021 through 2023 to carry out this section. Amounts appropriated under the preceding sentence for each fiscal year shall remain available until expended.

(Added Pub. L. 115–254, div. B, title VII, §762(a), Oct. 5, 2018, 132 Stat. 3428; amended Pub. L. 116–260, div. V, title I, §134, Dec. 27, 2020, 134 Stat. 2356; Pub. L. 118–63, title X, §1005, May 16, 2024, 138 Stat. 1387.)

> [1] So in original. Probably should be "conduct".

§44519. CERTIFICATION PERSONNEL CONTINUING EDUCATION AND TRAINING

(a) IN GENERAL.—The Administrator of the Federal Aviation Administration shall—

(1) develop a program for regular recurrent training of engineers, inspectors, and other subject-matter experts employed in the Aircraft Certification Service of the Administration in accordance with the training strategy developed pursuant to section 231 of the FAA Reauthorization Act of 2018 (Public Law 115–254; 132 Stat. 3256);

(2) to the maximum extent practicable, implement measures, including assignments in multiple divisions of the Aircraft Certification Service, to ensure that such engineers and other subject-matter experts in the Aircraft Certification Service have access to diverse professional opportunities that expand their knowledge and skills;

(3) develop a program to provide continuing education and training to Administration personnel who hold positions involving aircraft certification and flight standards, including human factors specialists, engineers, flight test pilots, inspectors, and, as determined appropriate by the Administrator, industry personnel who may be responsible for compliance activities including designees; and

(4) in consultation with outside experts, develop—

(A) an education and training curriculum on current and new aircraft technologies, human factors, project management, and the roles and responsibilities associated with oversight of designees; and

(B) recommended practices for compliance with Administration regulations.

(b) IMPLEMENTATION.—The Administrator shall, to the maximum extent practicable, ensure that actions taken pursuant to subsection (a)—

(1) permit engineers, inspectors, and other subject matter experts to continue developing knowledge of, and expertise in, new and emerging technologies in systems design, flight controls, principles of aviation safety, system oversight, and certification project management;

(2) minimize the likelihood of an individual developing an inappropriate bias toward a designer or manufacturer of aircraft, aircraft engines, propellers, or appliances;

(3) are consistent with any applicable collective bargaining agreements; and

(4) account for gaps in knowledge and skills (as identified by the Administrator in consultation with the exclusive bargaining representatives certified under section 7111 of title 5, United States Code) between Administration employees and private-sector employees for each group of Administration employees covered under this section.

(c) AUTHORIZATION OF APPROPRIATIONS.—There is authorized to be appropriated to the Administrator, $10,000,000 for each of fiscal years 2021 through 2028 to carry out this section. Amounts appropriated under the preceding sentence for any fiscal year shall remain available until expended.

(Added Pub. L. 116–260, div. V, title I, §112(a), Dec. 27, 2020, 134 Stat. 2331; amended Pub. L. 118–63, title III, §306(d), May 16, 2024, 138 Stat. 1072.)

§44520. CENTER OF EXCELLENCE FOR ALTERNATIVE JET FUELS AND ENVIRONMENT

(a) IN GENERAL.—The Administrator shall continue operation of the Center of Excellence for Alternative Jet Fuels and Environment (in this section referred to as the "Center").

(b) RESPONSIBILITIES.—The Center shall—

(1) focus on research to—

(A) assist in the development, qualification, and certification of the use of aviation fuel from alternative and renewable sources (such as biomass, next-generation feedstocks, alcohols, organic acids, hydrogen, bioderived chemicals and gaseous carbon) for commercial aircraft;

(B) assist in informing the safe use of alternative aviation fuels in commercial aircraft that also apply electrified aircraft propulsion systems;

(C) reduce community exposure to civilian aircraft noise and pollutant emissions;

(D) inform decision making to support United States leadership on international aviation environmental issues, including the development of domestic and international standards; and

(E) improve and expand the scientific understanding of civil aviation noise and pollutant emissions and their impacts, as well as support the development of improved modeling approaches and tools;

(2) examine the use of novel technologies and other forms of innovation to reduce noise, emissions, and fuel burn in commercial aircraft; and

(3) support collaboration with other Federal agencies, industry stakeholders, research institutions, and other relevant entities to accelerate the research, development, testing, evaluation, and demonstration programs and facilitate United States sustainability and competitiveness in aviation.

(c) GRANT AUTHORITY.—The Administrator shall carry out the work of the Center through the use of grants or other measures, as determined appropriate by the Administrator pursuant to section 44513, including through interagency agreements and coordination with other Federal agencies.

(d) PARTICIPATION.—

(1) PARTICIPATION OF EDUCATIONAL AND RESEARCH INSTITUTIONS.—In carrying out the responsibilities described in subsection (b), the Center shall include, as appropriate, participation by—

(A) institutions of higher education and research institutions that—

(i) have existing facilities for research, development, and testing; and

(ii) leverage private sector partnerships;

(B) other Federal agencies;

(C) consortia with experience across the alternative fuels supply chain, including with research, feedstock development and production, small-scale development, testing, and technology evaluation related to the creation, processing, production, and transportation of alternative aviation fuel; and

(D) consortia with experience in innovative technologies to reduce noise, emissions, and fuel burn in commercial aircraft.

(2) USE OF NASA FACILITIES.—The Center shall, in consultation with the Administrator of NASA, consider using, on a reimbursable basis, the existing and available capacity in aeronautics research facilities at the Langley Research Center, the NASA John H. Glenn Center at the Neil A. Armstrong Test Facility, and other appropriate facilities of the National Aeronautics and Space Administration.

(Added Pub. L. 118–63, title X, §1017(a), May 16, 2024, 138 Stat. 1396.)

CHAPTER 447—SAFETY REGULATION

[1] *So in original. Does not conform to section catchline.*

§44701. GENERAL REQUIREMENTS

(a) PROMOTING SAFETY.—The Administrator of the Federal Aviation Administration shall promote safe flight of civil aircraft in air commerce by prescribing—

(1) minimum standards required in the interest of safety for appliances and for the design, material, construction, quality of work, cybersecurity, and performance of aircraft, aircraft engines, and propellers;

(2) regulations and minimum standards in the interest of safety for—

(A) inspecting, servicing, and overhauling aircraft, aircraft engines, propellers, and appliances;

(B) equipment and facilities for, and the timing and manner of, the inspecting, servicing, and overhauling; and

(C) a qualified private person, instead of an officer or employee of the Administration, to examine and report on the inspecting, servicing, and overhauling;

(3) regulations required in the interest of safety for the reserve supply of aircraft, aircraft engines, propellers, appliances, and aircraft fuel and oil, including the reserve supply of fuel and oil carried in flight;

(4) regulations in the interest of safety for the maximum hours or periods of service of airmen and other employees of air carriers; and

(5) regulations and minimum standards for cybersecurity and other practices, methods, and procedures the Administrator finds necessary for safety in air commerce and national security.

(b) PRESCRIBING MINIMUM SAFETY STANDARDS.—The Administrator may prescribe minimum safety standards for—

(1) an air carrier to whom a certificate is issued under section 44705 of this title; and

(2) operating an airport serving any passenger operation of air carrier aircraft designed for at least 31 passenger seats.

(c) REDUCING AND ELIMINATING ACCIDENTS.—The Administrator shall carry out this chapter in a way that best tends to reduce or eliminate the possibility or recurrence of accidents in air transportation. However, the Administrator is not required to give preference either to air transportation or to other air commerce in carrying out this chapter.

(d) CONSIDERATIONS AND CLASSIFICATION OF REGULATIONS AND STANDARDS.—When prescribing a regulation or standard under subsection (a) or (b) of this section or any of sections 44702–44716 of this title, the Administrator shall—

    (1) consider—

        (A) the duty of an air carrier to provide service with the highest possible degree of safety in the public interest; and

        (B) differences between air transportation and other air commerce; and

    (2) classify a regulation or standard appropriate to the differences between air transportation and other air commerce.

(e) BILATERAL EXCHANGES OF SAFETY OVERSIGHT RESPONSIBILITIES.—

    (1) IN GENERAL.—Notwithstanding the provisions of this chapter, the Administrator, pursuant to Article 83 bis of the Convention on International Civil Aviation and by a bilateral agreement with the aeronautical authorities of another country, may exchange with that country all or part of their respective functions and duties with respect to registered aircraft under the following articles of the Convention: Article 12 (Rules of the Air); Article 31 (Certificates of Airworthiness); or Article 32a (Licenses of Personnel).

    (2) RELINQUISHMENT AND ACCEPTANCE OF RESPONSIBILITY.—The Administrator relinquishes responsibility with respect to the functions and duties transferred by the Administrator as specified in the bilateral agreement, under the Articles listed in paragraph (1) for United States-registered aircraft described in paragraph (4)(A) transferred abroad and accepts responsibility with respect to the functions and duties under those Articles for aircraft registered abroad and described in paragraph (4)(B) that are transferred to the United States.

    (3) CONDITIONS.—The Administrator may predicate, in the agreement, the transfer of functions and duties under this subsection on any conditions the Administrator deems necessary and prudent, except that the Administrator may not transfer responsibilities for United States registered aircraft described in paragraph (4)(A) to a country that the Administrator determines is not in compliance with its obligations under international law for the safety oversight of civil aviation.

    (4) REGISTERED AIRCRAFT DEFINED.—In this subsection, the term "registered aircraft" means—

        (A) aircraft registered in the United States and operated pursuant to an agreement for the lease, charter, or interchange of the aircraft or any similar arrangement by an operator that has its principal place of business or, if it has no such place of business, its permanent residence in another country; and

        (B) aircraft registered in a foreign country and operated under an agreement for the lease, charter, or interchange of the aircraft or any similar arrangement by an operator that has its principal place of business or, if it has no such place of business, its permanent residence in the United States.

    (5) FOREIGN AIRWORTHINESS DIRECTIVES.—

        (A) ACCEPTANCE.—Subject to subparagraph (D), the Administrator may accept an airworthiness directive, as defined in section 39.3 of title 14, Code of Federal Regulations, issued by an aeronautical safety authority of a foreign country, and leverage that authority's regulatory process, if—

            (i) the country is the state of design for the product that is the subject of the airworthiness directive;

            (ii) the United States has a bilateral safety agreement relating to aircraft certification with the country;

(iii) as part of the bilateral safety agreement with the country, the Administrator has determined that such aeronautical safety authority has an aircraft certification system relating to safety that produces a level of safety equivalent to the level produced by the system of the Federal Aviation Administration;

(iv) the aeronautical safety authority of the country utilizes an open and transparent notice and comment process in the issuance of airworthiness directives; and

(v) the airworthiness directive is necessary to provide for the safe operation of the aircraft subject to the directive.

(B) ALTERNATIVE APPROVAL PROCESS.—Notwithstanding subparagraph (A), the Administrator may issue a Federal Aviation Administration airworthiness directive instead of accepting an airworthiness directive otherwise eligible for acceptance under such subparagraph, if the Administrator determines that such issuance is necessary for safety or operational reasons due to the complexity or unique features of the Federal Aviation Administration airworthiness directive or the United States aviation system.

(C) ALTERNATIVE MEANS OF COMPLIANCE.—The Administrator may—

(i) accept an alternative means of compliance, with respect to an airworthiness directive accepted under subparagraph (A), that was approved by the aeronautical safety authority of the foreign country that issued the airworthiness directive; or

(ii) notwithstanding subparagraph (A), and at the request of any person affected by an airworthiness directive accepted under such subparagraph, approve an alternative means of compliance with respect to the airworthiness directive.

(D) LIMITATION.—The Administrator may not accept an airworthiness directive issued by an aeronautical safety authority of a foreign country if the airworthiness directive addresses matters other than those involving the safe operation of an aircraft.

(f) EXEMPTIONS.—The Administrator may grant an exemption from a requirement of a regulation prescribed under subsection (a) or (b) of this section or any of sections 44702–44716 of this title if the Administrator finds the exemption is in the public interest.

(g) EXCLUSIVE RULEMAKING AUTHORITY.—Notwithstanding any other provision of law and except as provided in section 40131, the Administrator, in consultation with the heads of such other agencies as the Administrator determines necessary, shall have exclusive authority to prescribe regulations for purposes of assuring the cybersecurity of civil aircraft, aircraft engines, propellers, and appliances.

(h) POLICIES, ORDERS, AND GUIDANCE.—

(1) CONSISTENCY OF APPLICATION.—The Administrator shall ensure consistency in the application of policies, orders, and guidance of the Administration by—

(A) audits of the application and interpretation of such material by Administration personnel from person to person and office to office;

(B) updating policies, orders, and guidance to resolve inconsistencies and clarify demonstrated ambiguities, such as through repeated inconsistent interpretation; and

(C) ensuring officials are properly documenting findings and decisions throughout a project to decrease the occurrence of duplicative work and inconsistent findings by subsequent officials assigned to the same project.

(2) ALTERATIONS.—The Administrator shall consult as appropriate with regulated

entities who will be impacted by proposed changes to the content or application of policies, orders, and guidance before making such changes.

(3) AUTHORITIES AND REGULATIONS.—The Administrator shall issue policies, orders, and guidance documents that are related to a law or regulation or clarify the intent of or compliance with specific laws and regulations.

(Pub. L. 103–272, §1(e), July 5, 1994, 108 Stat. 1185; Pub. L. 103–429, §6(55), Oct. 31, 1994, 108 Stat. 4385; Pub. L. 106–181, title VII, §714, Apr. 5, 2000, 114 Stat. 161; Pub. L. 115–254, div. B, title II, §242, Oct. 5, 2018, 132 Stat. 3258; Pub. L. 118–63, title III, §392, title VIII, §822, May 16, 2024, 138 Stat. 1143, 1331.)

§44702. ISSUANCE OF CERTIFICATES

(a) GENERAL AUTHORITY AND APPLICATIONS.—The Administrator of the Federal Aviation Administration may issue airman certificates, design organization certificates, type certificates, production certificates, airworthiness certificates, air carrier operating certificates, airport operating certificates, air agency certificates, and air navigation facility certificates under this chapter. An application for a certificate must—

(1) be under oath when the Administrator requires; and

(2) be in the form, contain information, and be filed and served in the way the Administrator prescribes.

(b) CONSIDERATIONS.—When issuing a certificate under this chapter, the Administrator shall—

(1) consider—

(A) the duty of an air carrier to provide service with the highest possible degree of safety in the public interest; and

(B) differences between air transportation and other air commerce; and

(2) classify a certificate according to the differences between air transportation and other air commerce.

(c) PRIOR CERTIFICATION.—The Administrator may authorize an aircraft, aircraft engine, propeller, or appliance for which a certificate has been issued authorizing the use of the aircraft, aircraft engine, propeller, or appliance in air transportation to be used in air commerce without another certificate being issued.

(d) DELEGATION.—(1) Subject to regulations, supervision, and review the Administrator may prescribe, the Administrator may delegate to a qualified private person, or to an employee under the supervision of that person, a matter related to—

(A) the examination, testing, and inspection necessary to issue a certificate under this chapter; and

(B) issuing the certificate.

(2) The Administrator may rescind a delegation under this subsection at any time for any reason the Administrator considers appropriate.

(3) A person affected by an action of a private person under this subsection may apply for reconsideration of the action by the Administrator. On the Administrator's own initiative, the Administrator may reconsider the action of a private person at any time. If the Administrator decides on reconsideration that the action is unreasonable or unwarranted, the Administrator shall change, modify, or reverse the action. If the Administrator decides the action is warranted, the Administrator shall affirm the action.

(4)(A) With respect to a critical system design feature of a transport category airplane, the Administrator may not delegate any finding of compliance with applicable airworthiness standards or review of any system safety assessment required for the issuance of a certificate, including a type certificate, or amended or supplemental type certificate, under section 44704, until the Administrator has reviewed and validated any underlying assumptions related to human factors.

(B) The requirement under subparagraph (A) shall not apply if the Administrator determines the matter involved is a routine task.

(C) For purposes of subparagraph (A), the term critical system design feature includes any feature (including a novel or unusual design feature) for which the failure of such feature, either independently or in combination with other failures, could result in catastrophic or hazardous failure conditions, as those terms are defined by the Administrator.

(Pub. L. 103–272, §1(e), July 5, 1994, 108 Stat. 1186; Pub. L. 108–176, title II, §227(a), Dec. 12, 2003, 117 Stat. 2531; Pub. L. 116–260, div. V, title I, §106, Dec. 27, 2020, 134 Stat. 2320.)

§44703. AIRMAN CERTIFICATES

(a) GENERAL.—The Administrator of the Federal Aviation Administration shall issue an airman certificate to an individual when the Administrator finds, after investigation, that the individual is qualified for, and physically able to perform the duties related to, the position to be authorized by the certificate.

(b) CONTENTS.—(1) An airman certificate shall—

(A) be numbered and recorded by the Administrator of the Federal Aviation Administration;

(B) contain the name, address, and description of the individual to whom the certificate is issued;

(C) contain terms the Administrator decides are necessary to ensure safety in air commerce, including terms on the duration of the certificate, periodic or special examinations, and tests of physical fitness;

(D) specify the capacity in which the holder of the certificate may serve as an airman with respect to an aircraft; and

(E) designate the class the certificate covers.

(2) A certificate issued to a pilot serving in scheduled air transportation shall have the designation "airline transport pilot" of the appropriate class.

(c) PUBLIC INFORMATION.—

(1) IN GENERAL.—Subject to paragraph (2) and notwithstanding any other provision of law, the information contained in the records of contents of any airman certificate issued under this section that is limited to an airman's name, address, and ratings held shall be made available to the public after the 120th day following the date of the enactment of the Wendell H. Ford Aviation Investment and Reform Act for the 21st Century.

(2) OPPORTUNITY TO WITHHOLD INFORMATION.—Before making any information concerning an airman available to the public under paragraph (1), the airman shall be given an opportunity to elect that the information not be made available to the public.

(3) DEVELOPMENT AND IMPLEMENTATION OF PROGRAM.—Not later than 60 days after the date of the enactment of the Wendell H. Ford Aviation Investment and Reform Act

for the 21st Century, the Administrator shall develop and implement, in cooperation with representatives of the aviation industry, a one-time written notification to airmen to set forth the implications of making information concerning an airman available to the public under paragraph (1) and to carry out paragraph (2). The Administrator shall also provide such written notification to each individual who becomes an airman after such date of enactment.

(d) APPEALS.—(1) An individual whose application for the issuance or renewal of an airman certificate has been denied may appeal the denial to the National Transportation Safety Board, except if the individual holds a certificate that—

    (A) is suspended at the time of denial; or

    (B) was revoked within one year from the date of the denial.

(2) The Board shall conduct a hearing on the appeal at a place convenient to the place of residence or employment of the applicant. The Board is not bound by findings of fact of the Administrator of the Federal Aviation Administration. At the end of the hearing, the Board shall decide whether the individual meets the applicable regulations and standards. The Administrator is bound by that decision.

(3) A person who is substantially affected by an order of the Board under this subsection, or the Administrator if the Administrator decides that an order of the Board will have a significant adverse impact on carrying out this subtitle, may seek judicial review of the order under section 46110. The Administrator shall be made a party to the judicial review proceedings. The findings of fact of the Board in any such case are conclusive if supported by substantial evidence.

(e) RESTRICTIONS AND PROHIBITIONS.—The Administrator of the Federal Aviation Administration may—

    (1) restrict or prohibit issuing an airman certificate to an alien; or

    (2) make issuing the certificate to an alien dependent on a reciprocal agreement with the government of a foreign country.

(f) CONTROLLED SUBSTANCE VIOLATIONS.—The Administrator of the Federal Aviation Administration may not issue an airman certificate to an individual whose certificate is revoked under section 44710 of this title except—

    (1) when the Administrator decides that issuing the certificate will facilitate law enforcement efforts; and

    (2) as provided in section 44710(e)(2) of this title.

(g) MODIFICATIONS IN SYSTEM.—(1) The Administrator of the Federal Aviation Administration shall make modifications in the system for issuing airman certificates necessary to make the system more effective in serving the needs of airmen and officials responsible for enforcing laws related to the regulation of controlled substances (as defined in section 102 of the Comprehensive Drug Abuse Prevention and Control Act of 1970 (21 U.S.C. 802)) and related to combating acts of terrorism. The modifications shall ensure positive and verifiable identification of each individual applying for or holding a certificate and shall address at least each of the following deficiencies in, and abuses of, the existing system:

    (A) the use of fictitious names and addresses by applicants for those certificates.

    (B) the use of stolen or fraudulent identification in applying for those certificates.

    (C) the use by an applicant of a post office box or "mail drop" as a return address to evade identification of the applicant's address.

(D) the use of counterfeit and stolen airman certificates by pilots.

(E) the absence of information about physical characteristics of holders of those certificates.

(2) The Administrator of the Federal Aviation Administration shall prescribe regulations to carry out paragraph (1) of this subsection and provide a written explanation of how the regulations address each of the deficiencies and abuses described in paragraph (1). In prescribing the regulations, the Administrator of the Federal Aviation Administration shall consult with the Administrator of Drug Enforcement, the Commissioner of U.S. Customs and Border Protection, other law enforcement officials of the United States Government, representatives of State and local law enforcement officials, representatives of the general aviation aircraft industry, representatives of users of general aviation aircraft, and other interested persons.

(3) For purposes of this section, the term "acts of terrorism" means an activity that involves a violent act or an act dangerous to human life that is a violation of the criminal laws of the United States or of any State, or that would be a criminal violation if committed within the jurisdiction of the United States or of any State, and appears to be intended to intimidate or coerce a civilian population to influence the policy of a government by intimidation or coercion or to affect the conduct of a government by assassination or kidnaping.

(4) The Administrator is authorized and directed to work with State and local authorities, and other Federal agencies, to assist in the identification of individuals applying for or holding airmen certificates.

(h) RECORDS OF EMPLOYMENT OF PILOT APPLICANTS.—

(1) IN GENERAL.—Subject to paragraph (14), before allowing an individual to begin service as a pilot, an air carrier shall request and receive the following information:

(A) FAA RECORDS.—From the Administrator of the Federal Aviation Administration, records pertaining to the individual that are maintained by the Administrator concerning—

(i) current airman certificates (including airman medical certificates) and associated type ratings, including any limitations to those certificates and ratings; and

(ii) summaries of legal enforcement actions resulting in a finding by the Administrator of a violation of this title or a regulation prescribed or order issued under this title that was not subsequently overturned.

(B) AIR CARRIER AND OTHER RECORDS.—From any air carrier or other person (except a branch of the United States Armed Forces, the National Guard, or a reserve component of the United States Armed Forces) that has employed the individual as a pilot of a civil or public aircraft at any time during the 5-year period preceding the date of the employment application of the individual, or from the trustee in bankruptcy for such air carrier or person—

(i) records pertaining to the individual that are maintained by an air carrier (other than records relating to flight time, duty time, or rest time) under regulations set forth in—

(I) section 121.683 of title 14, Code of Federal Regulations;

(II) paragraph (A) of section VI, appendix I, part 121 of such title;

(III) paragraph (A) of section IV, appendix J, part 121 of such title;

(IV) section 125.401 of such title; and

(V) section 135.63(a)(4) of such title; and

(ii) other records pertaining to the individual's performance as a pilot that are maintained by the air carrier or person concerning—

(I) the training, qualifications, proficiency, or professional competence of the individual, including comments and evaluations made by a check airman designated in accordance with section 121.411, 125.295, or 135.337 of such title;

(II) any disciplinary action taken with respect to the individual that was not subsequently overturned; and

(III) any release from employment or resignation, termination, or disqualification with respect to employment.

(C) NATIONAL DRIVER REGISTER RECORDS.—In accordance with section 30305(b)(8) of this title, from the chief driver licensing official of a State, information concerning the motor vehicle driving record of the individual.

(2) WRITTEN CONSENT; RELEASE FROM LIABILITY.—An air carrier making a request for records under paragraph (1)—

(A) shall be required to obtain written consent to the release of those records from the individual that is the subject of the records requested; and

(B) may, notwithstanding any other provision of law or agreement to the contrary, require the individual who is the subject of the records to request to execute a release from liability for any claim arising from the furnishing of such records to or the use of such records by such air carrier (other than a claim arising from furnishing information known to be false and maintained in violation of a criminal statute).

(3) 5-YEAR REPORTING PERIOD.—A person shall not furnish a record in response to a request made under paragraph (1) if the record was entered more than 5 years before the date of the request, unless the information concerns a revocation or suspension of an airman certificate or motor vehicle license that is in effect on the date of the request.

(4) REQUIREMENT TO MAINTAIN RECORDS.—The Administrator and air carriers shall maintain pilot records described in paragraphs (1)(A) and (1)(B) for a period of at least 5 years.

(5) RECEIPT OF CONSENT; PROVISION OF INFORMATION.—A person shall not furnish a record in response to a request made under paragraph (1) without first obtaining a copy of the written consent of the individual who is the subject of the records requested; except that, for purposes of paragraph (15), the Administrator may allow an individual designated by the Administrator to accept and maintain written consent on behalf of the Administrator for records requested under paragraph (1)(A). A person who receives a request for records under this subsection shall furnish a copy of all of such requested records maintained by the person not later than 30 days after receiving the request.

(6) RIGHT TO RECEIVE NOTICE AND COPY OF ANY RECORD FURNISHED.—A person who receives a request for records under paragraph (1) shall provide to the individual who is the subject of the records—

(A) on or before the 20th day following the date of receipt of the request, written notice of the request and of the individual's right to receive a copy of such records;

and

(B) in accordance with paragraph (10), a copy of such records, if requested by the individual.

(7) REASONABLE CHARGES FOR PROCESSING REQUESTS AND FURNISHING COPIES.—A person who receives a request under paragraph (1) or (6) may establish a reasonable charge for the cost of processing the request and furnishing copies of the requested records.

(8) STANDARD FORMS.—The Administrator shall promulgate—

(A) standard forms that may be used by an air carrier to request records under paragraph (1); and

(B) standard forms that may be used by an air carrier to—

(i) obtain the written consent of the individual who is the subject of a request under paragraph (1); and

(ii) inform the individual of—

(I) the request; and

(II) the individual right of that individual to receive a copy of any records furnished in response to the request.

(9) RIGHT TO CORRECT INACCURACIES.—An air carrier that maintains or requests and receives the records of an individual under paragraph (1) shall provide the individual with a reasonable opportunity to submit written comments to correct any inaccuracies contained in the records before making a final hiring decision with respect to the individual.

(10) RIGHT OF PILOT TO REVIEW CERTAIN RECORDS.—Notwithstanding any other provision of law or agreement, an air carrier shall, upon written request from a pilot who is or has been employed by such carrier, make available, within a reasonable time, but not later than 30 days after the date of the request, to the pilot for review, any and all employment records referred to in paragraph (1)(B)(i) or (ii) pertaining to the employment of the pilot.

(11) PRIVACY PROTECTIONS.—An air carrier that receives the records of an individual under paragraph (1) may use such records only to assess the qualifications of the individual in deciding whether or not to hire the individual as a pilot. The air carrier shall take such actions as may be necessary to protect the privacy of the pilot and the confidentiality of the records, including ensuring that information contained in the records is not divulged to any individual that is not directly involved in the hiring decision.

(12) PERIODIC REVIEW.—Not later than 18 months after the date of the enactment of the Pilot Records Improvement Act of 1996, and at least once every 3 years thereafter, the Administrator shall transmit to Congress a statement that contains, taking into account recent developments in the aviation industry—

(A) recommendations by the Administrator concerning proposed changes to Federal Aviation Administration records, air carrier records, and other records required to be furnished under subparagraphs (A) and (B) of paragraph (1); or

(B) reasons why the Administrator does not recommend any proposed changes to the records referred to in subparagraph (A).

(13) REGULATIONS.—The Administrator shall prescribe such regulations as may be

necessary—

(A) to protect—

(i) the personal privacy of any individual whose records are requested under paragraph (1) and disseminated under paragraph (15); and

(ii) the confidentiality of those records;

(B) to preclude the further dissemination of records received under paragraph (1) by the person who requested those records; and

(C) to ensure prompt compliance with any request made under paragraph (1).

(14) SPECIAL RULES WITH RESPECT TO CERTAIN PILOTS.—

(A) PILOTS OF CERTAIN SMALL AIRCRAFT.—Notwithstanding paragraph (1), an air carrier, before receiving information requested about an individual under paragraph (1), may allow the individual to begin service for a period not to exceed 90 days as a pilot of an aircraft with a maximum payload capacity (as defined in section 119.3 of title 14, Code of Federal Regulations) of 7,500 pounds or less, or a helicopter, on a flight that is not a scheduled operation (as defined in such section). Before the end of the 90-day period, the air carrier shall obtain and evaluate such information. The contract between the carrier and the individual shall contain a term that provides that the continuation of the individual's employment, after the last day of the 90-day period, depends on a satisfactory evaluation.

(B) GOOD FAITH EXCEPTION.—Notwithstanding paragraph (1), an air carrier, without obtaining information about an individual under paragraph (1)(B) from an air carrier or other person that no longer exists or from a foreign government or entity that employed the individual, may allow the individual to begin service as a pilot if the air carrier required to request the information has made a documented good faith attempt to obtain such information.

(15) ELECTRONIC ACCESS TO FAA RECORDS.—For the purpose of increasing timely and efficient access to Federal Aviation Administration records described in paragraph (1), the Administrator may allow, under terms established by the Administrator, an individual designated by the air carrier to have electronic access to a specified database containing information about such records. The terms shall limit such access to instances in which information in the database is required by the designated individual in making a hiring decision concerning a pilot applicant and shall require that the designated individual provide assurances satisfactory to the Administrator that information obtained using such access will not be used for any purpose other than making the hiring decision.

(16) APPLICABILITY.—This subsection shall cease to be effective on the date specified in regulations issued under subsection (i).

(i) FAA PILOT RECORDS DATABASE.—

(1) IN GENERAL.—Before allowing an individual to begin service as a pilot, an air carrier shall access and evaluate, in accordance with the requirements of this subsection, information pertaining to the individual from the pilot records database established under paragraph (2).

(2) PILOT RECORDS DATABASE.—Not later than April 30, 2017, the Administrator shall establish and make available for use an electronic database (in this subsection referred to as the "database") containing the following records:

(A) FAA RECORDS.—From the Administrator—

(i) records that are maintained by the Administrator concerning current airman certificates, including airman medical certificates and associated type ratings and information on any limitations to those certificates and ratings;

(ii) records that are maintained by the Administrator concerning any failed attempt of an individual to pass a practical test required to obtain a certificate or type rating under part 61 of title 14, Code of Federal Regulations; and

(iii) summaries of legal enforcement actions resulting in a finding by the Administrator of a violation of this title or a regulation prescribed or order issued under this title that was not subsequently overturned.

(B) AIR CARRIER AND OTHER RECORDS.—From any air carrier or other person (except a branch of the Armed Forces, the National Guard, or a reserve component of the Armed Forces) that has employed an individual as a pilot of a civil or public aircraft, or from the trustee in bankruptcy for the air carrier or person—

(i) records pertaining to the individual that are maintained by the air carrier (other than records relating to flight time, duty time, or rest time) or person, including records under regulations set forth in—

(I) section 121.683 of title 14, Code of Federal Regulations;

(II) section 121.111(a) of such title;

(III) section 121.219(a) of such title;

(IV) section 125.401 of such title; and

(V) section 135.63(a)(4) of such title; and

(ii) other records pertaining to the individual's performance as a pilot that are maintained by the air carrier or person concerning—

(I) the training, qualifications, proficiency, or professional competence of the individual, including comments and evaluations made by a check airman designated in accordance with section 121.411, 125.295, or 135.337 of such title;

(II) any disciplinary action taken with respect to the individual that was not subsequently overturned; and

(III) any release from employment or resignation, termination, or disqualification with respect to employment.

(C) NATIONAL DRIVER REGISTER RECORDS.—In accordance with section 30305(b)(8) of this title, from the chief driver licensing official of a State, information concerning the motor vehicle driving record of the individual.

(3) WRITTEN CONSENT; RELEASE FROM LIABILITY.—An air carrier—

(A) shall obtain the written consent of an individual before accessing records pertaining to the individual under paragraph (1); and

(B) may, notwithstanding any other provision of law or agreement to the contrary, require an individual with respect to whom the carrier is accessing records under paragraph (1) to execute a release from liability for any claim arising from accessing the records or the use of such records by the air carrier in accordance with this section (other than a claim arising from furnishing information known to be false and maintained in violation of a criminal statute).

(4) REPORTING.—

(A) REPORTING BY ADMINISTRATOR.—The Administrator shall enter data described in paragraph (2)(A) into the database promptly to ensure that an individual's records are current.

(B) Reporting by air carriers and other persons.—

(i) In general.—Air carriers and other persons shall report data described in paragraphs (2)(B) and (2)(C) to the Administrator promptly for entry into the database.

(ii) Data to be reported.—Air carriers and other persons shall report, at a minimum, under clause (i) the following data described in paragraph (2)(B):

(I) Records that are generated by the air carrier or other person after the date of enactment of this paragraph.

(II) Records that the air carrier or other person is maintaining, on such date of enactment, pursuant to subsection (h)(4).

(5) Requirement to maintain records.—The Administrator—

(A) shall maintain all records entered into the database under paragraph (2) pertaining to an individual until the date of receipt of notification that the individual is deceased; and

(B) may remove the individual's records from the database after that date.

(6) Receipt of consent.—The Administrator shall not permit an air carrier to access records pertaining to an individual from the database under paragraph (1) without the air carrier first demonstrating to the satisfaction of the Administrator that the air carrier has obtained the written consent of the individual.

(7) Right of pilot to review certain records and correct inaccuracies.—Notwithstanding any other provision of law or agreement, the Administrator, upon receipt of written request from an individual—

(A) shall make available, not later than 30 days after the date of the request, to the individual for review all records referred to in paragraph (2) pertaining to the individual; and

(B) shall provide the individual with a reasonable opportunity to submit written comments to correct any inaccuracies contained in the records.

(8) Reasonable charges for processing requests and furnishing copies.—

(A) In general.—The Administrator may establish a reasonable charge for the cost of processing a request under paragraph (1) or (7) and for the cost of furnishing copies of requested records under paragraph (7).

(B) Crediting appropriations.—Funds received by the Administrator pursuant to this paragraph shall—

(i) be credited to the appropriation current when the amount is received;

(ii) be merged with and available for the purposes of such appropriation; and

(iii) remain available until expended.

(9) Privacy protections.—

(A) Use of records.—An air carrier that accesses records pertaining to an individual under paragraph (1) may use the records only to assess the qualifications of the individual in deciding whether or not to hire the individual as a pilot. The air carrier shall take such actions as may be necessary to protect the privacy of the individual and the confidentiality of the records accessed, including ensuring that information contained in the records is not divulged to any individual that is not directly involved in the hiring decision.

(B) Disclosure of information.—

(i) In general.—Except as provided by clause (ii), information collected by the Administrator under paragraph (2) shall be exempt from the disclosure requirements of section 552(b)(3)(B) of title 5.

(ii) Exceptions.—Clause (i) shall not apply to—

(I) deidentified, summarized information to explain the need for changes in policies and regulations;

(II) information to correct a condition that compromises safety;

(III) information to carry out a criminal investigation or prosecution;

(IV) information to comply with section 44905, regarding information about threats to civil aviation; and

(V) such information as the Administrator determines necessary, if withholding the information would not be consistent with the safety responsibilities of the Federal Aviation Administration.

(10) Periodic review.—Not later than 18 months after the date of enactment of this paragraph, and at least once every 3 years thereafter, the Administrator shall transmit to Congress a statement that contains, taking into account recent developments in the aviation industry—

(A) recommendations by the Administrator concerning proposed changes to Federal Aviation Administration records, air carrier records, and other records required to be included in the database under paragraph (2); or

(B) reasons why the Administrator does not recommend any proposed changes to the records referred to in subparagraph (A).

(11) Regulations for protection and security of records.—The Administrator shall prescribe such regulations as may be necessary—

(A) to protect and secure—

(i) the personal privacy of any individual whose records are accessed under paragraph (1); and

(ii) the confidentiality of those records; and

(B) to preclude the further dissemination of records received under paragraph (1) by the person who accessed the records.

(12) Good faith exception.—Notwithstanding paragraph (1), an air carrier may allow an individual to begin service as a pilot, without first obtaining information described in paragraph (2)(B) from the database pertaining to the individual, if—

(A) the air carrier has made a documented good faith attempt to access the information from the database; and

(B) the air carrier has received written notice from the Administrator that the information is not contained in the database because the individual was employed by an air carrier or other person that no longer exists or by a foreign government or other entity that has not provided the information to the database.

(13) Limitations on electronic access to records.—

(A) Access by individuals designated by air carriers.—For the purpose of increasing timely and efficient access to records described in paragraph (2), the Administrator may allow, under terms established by the Administrator, an individual designated by an air carrier to have electronic access to the database.

(B) Terms.—The terms established by the Administrator under subparagraph (A) for allowing a designated individual to have electronic access to the database shall limit such access to instances in which information in the database is required by the designated individual in making a hiring decision concerning a pilot applicant and shall require that the designated individual provide assurances satisfactory to the Administrator that—

(i) the designated individual has received the written consent of the pilot applicant to access the information; and

(ii) information obtained using such access will not be used for any purpose other than making the hiring decision.

(14) Authorized expenditures.—Of amounts appropriated under section 106(k)(1), a total of $6,000,000 for fiscal years 2010 through 2013 may be used to carry out this subsection.

(15) Regulations.—

(A) In general.—The Administrator shall issue regulations to carry out this subsection.

(B) Effective date.—The regulations shall specify the date on which the requirements of this subsection take effect and the date on which the requirements of subsection (h) cease to be effective.

(C) Exceptions.—Notwithstanding subparagraph (B)—

(i) the Administrator shall begin to establish the database under paragraph (2) not later than 90 days after the date of enactment of this paragraph;

(ii) the Administrator shall maintain records in accordance with paragraph (5) beginning on the date of enactment of this paragraph; and

(iii) air carriers and other persons shall maintain records to be reported to the database under paragraph (4)(B) in the period beginning on such date of enactment and ending on the date that is 5 years after the requirements of subsection (h) cease to be effective pursuant to subparagraph (B).

(16) Special rule.—During the one-year period beginning on the date on which the requirements of this section become effective pursuant to paragraph (15)(B), paragraph (7)(A) shall be applied by substituting "45 days" for "30 days".

(j) Limitations on Liability; Preemption of State Law.—

(1) Limitation on liability.—No action or proceeding may be brought by or on behalf of an individual who has applied for or is seeking a position with an air carrier as a pilot and who has signed a release from liability, as provided for under subsection (h)(2) or (i)(3), against—

(A) the air carrier requesting the records of that individual under subsection (h)(1) or accessing the records of that individual under subsection (i)(1);

(B) a person who has complied with such request;

(C) a person who has entered information contained in the individual's records; or

(D) an agent or employee of a person described in subparagraph (A) or (B);

in the nature of an action for defamation, invasion of privacy, negligence, interference with contract, or otherwise, or under any Federal or State law with respect to the furnishing or use of such records in accordance with subsection (h) or (i).

(2) Preemption.—No State or political subdivision thereof may enact, prescribe,

issue, continue in effect, or enforce any law (including any regulation, standard, or other provision having the force and effect of law) that prohibits, penalizes, or imposes liability for furnishing or using records in accordance with subsection (h) or (i).

(3) PROVISION OF KNOWINGLY FALSE INFORMATION.—Paragraphs (1) and (2) shall not apply with respect to a person who furnishes information in response to a request made under subsection (h)(1) or who furnished information to the database established under subsection (i)(2), that—

(A) the person knows is false; and

(B) was maintained in violation of a criminal statute of the United States.

(4) PROHIBITION ON ACTIONS AND PROCEEDINGS AGAINST AIR CARRIERS.—

(A) HIRING DECISIONS.—An air carrier may refuse to hire an individual as a pilot if the individual did not provide written consent for the air carrier to receive records under subsection (h)(2)(A) or (i)(3)(A) or did not execute the release from liability requested under subsection (h)(2)(B) or (i)(3)(B).

(B) ACTIONS AND PROCEEDINGS.—No action or proceeding may be brought against an air carrier by or on behalf of an individual who has applied for or is seeking a position as a pilot with the air carrier if the air carrier refused to hire the individual after the individual did not provide written consent for the air carrier to receive records under subsection (h)(2)(A) or (i)(3)(A) or did not execute a release from liability requested under subsection (h)(2)(B) or (i)(3)(B).

(k) LIMITATION ON STATUTORY CONSTRUCTION.—Nothing in subsection (h) or (i) shall be construed as precluding the availability of the records of a pilot in an investigation or other proceeding concerning an accident or incident conducted by the Administrator, the National Transportation Safety Board, or a court.

(l) TEMPORARY AIRMAN CERTIFICATE.—An individual may obtain a temporary airman certificate from the Administrator after requesting a permanent replacement airman certificate issued under this section. A temporary airman certificate shall be—

(1) made available—

(A) electronically to the individual immediately upon submitting an online application for a replacement certificate to the Administrator; or

(B) physically to the individual at a flight standards district office—

(i) if the individual submits an online application for a replacement certificate; or

(ii) if the individual applies for a permanent replacement certificate other than by online application and such application has been received by the Federal Aviation Administration; and

(2) destroyed upon receipt of the permanent replacement airman certificate from the Administrator.

(Pub. L. 103–272, §1(e), July 5, 1994, 108 Stat. 1186; Pub. L. 106–181, title VII, §715, Apr. 5, 2000, 114 Stat. 162; Pub. L. 107–71, title I, §§129, 138(b), 140(a), Nov. 19, 2001, 115 Stat. 633, 640, 641; Pub. L. 111–216, title II, §203, Aug. 1, 2010, 124 Stat. 2352; Pub. L. 111–249, §6(3), (4), Sept. 30, 2010, 124 Stat. 2629; Pub. L. 112–95, title III, §§301(a), 310(c), Feb. 14, 2012, 126 Stat. 56, 65; Pub. L. 112–153, §2(c)(1), Aug. 3, 2012, 126 Stat. 1160; Pub. L. 114–125, title VIII, §802(d)(2), Feb. 24, 2016, 130 Stat. 210; Pub. L. 114–190, title II, §2101, July 15, 2016, 130 Stat. 619; Pub. L. 118–63, title VIII, §813, May 16, 2024, 138 Stat. 1327.)

§44704. TYPE CERTIFICATES, PRODUCTION CERTIFICATES, AIRWORTHINESS

CERTIFICATES, AND DESIGN AND PRODUCTION ORGANIZATION CERTIFICATES

(a) TYPE CERTIFICATES.—

(1) ISSUANCE, INVESTIGATIONS, AND TESTS.—The Administrator of the Federal Aviation Administration shall issue a type certificate for an aircraft, aircraft engine, or propeller, or for an appliance specified under paragraph (2)(A) of this subsection when the Administrator finds that the aircraft, aircraft engine, propeller, or appliance is properly designed and manufactured, performs properly, and meets the regulations and minimum standards prescribed under section 44701(a) of this title. On receiving an application for a type certificate, the Administrator shall investigate the application and may conduct a hearing. The Administrator shall make, or require the applicant to make, tests the Administrator considers necessary in the interest of safety.

(2) SPECIFICATIONS.—The Administrator may—

(A) specify in regulations those appliances that reasonably require a type certificate in the interest of safety;

(B) include in a type certificate terms required in the interest of safety; and

(C) record on the certificate a numerical specification of the essential factors related to the performance of the aircraft, aircraft engine, or propeller for which the certificate is issued.

(3) SPECIAL RULES FOR NEW AIRCRAFT AND APPLIANCES.—Except as provided in paragraph (4), if the holder of a type certificate agrees to permit another person to use the certificate to manufacture a new aircraft, aircraft engine, propeller, or appliance, the holder shall provide the other person with written evidence, in a form acceptable to the Administrator, of that agreement. Such other person may manufacture a new aircraft, aircraft engine, propeller, or appliance based on a type certificate only if such other person is the holder of the type certificate or has permission from the holder.

(4) LIMITATION FOR AIRCRAFT MANUFACTURED BEFORE AUGUST 5, 2004.—Paragraph (3) shall not apply to a person who began the manufacture of an aircraft before August 5, 2004, and who demonstrates to the satisfaction of the Administrator that such manufacture began before August 5, 2004, if the name of the holder of the type certificate for the aircraft does not appear on the airworthiness certificate or identification plate of the aircraft. The holder of the type certificate for the aircraft shall not be responsible for the continued airworthiness of the aircraft. A person may invoke the exception provided by this paragraph with regard to the manufacture of only one aircraft.

(5) RELEASE OF DATA.—

(A) IN GENERAL.—Notwithstanding any other provision of law, the Administrator may make available upon request, to a person seeking to maintain the airworthiness or develop product improvements of an aircraft, engine, propeller, or appliance, engineering data in the possession of the Administration relating to a type certificate or a supplemental type certificate for such aircraft, engine, propeller, or appliance, without the consent of the owner of record, if the Administrator determines that—

(i) the certificate containing the requested data has been inactive for 3 or more years, except that the Administrator may reduce this time if required to address an unsafe condition associated with the product;

(ii) after using due diligence, the Administrator is unable to find the owner of record, or the owner of record's heir, of the type certificate or supplemental type certificate; and

(iii) making such data available will enhance aviation safety.

(B) ENGINEERING DATA DEFINED.—In this section, the term "engineering data" as used with respect to an aircraft, engine, propeller, or appliance means type design drawing and specifications for the entire aircraft, engine, propeller, or appliance or change to the aircraft, engine, propeller, or appliance, including the original design data, and any associated supplier data for individual parts or components approved as part of the particular certificate for the aircraft, engine, propeller, or appliance.

(C) REQUIREMENT TO MAINTAIN DATA.—The Administrator shall maintain engineering data in the possession of the Administration relating to a type certificate or a supplemental type certificate that has been inactive for 3 or more years.

(6) SUBMISSION OF DATA.—When an applicant submits design data to the Administrator for a finding of compliance as part of an application for a type certificate, the applicant shall certify to the Administrator that—

(A) the submitted design data demonstrates compliance with the applicable airworthiness standards; and

(B) any airworthiness standards not complied with are compensated for by factors that provide an equivalent level of safety, as agreed upon by the Administrator.

(b) SUPPLEMENTAL TYPE CERTIFICATES.—

(1) ISSUANCE.—The Administrator may issue a type certificate designated as a supplemental type certificate for a change to an aircraft, aircraft engine, propeller, or appliance.

(2) CONTENTS.—A supplemental type certificate issued under paragraph (1) shall consist of the change to the aircraft, aircraft engine, propeller, or appliance with respect to the previously issued type certificate for the aircraft, aircraft engine, propeller, or appliance.

(3) REQUIREMENT.—If the holder of a supplemental type certificate agrees to permit another person to use the certificate to modify an aircraft, aircraft engine, propeller, or appliance, the holder shall provide the other person with written evidence, in a form acceptable to the Administrator, of that agreement. A person may change an aircraft, aircraft engine, propeller, or appliance based on a supplemental type certificate only if the person requesting the change is the holder of the supplemental type certificate or has permission from the holder to make the change.

(c) PRODUCTION CERTIFICATES.—The Administrator shall issue a production certificate authorizing the production of a duplicate of an aircraft, aircraft engine, propeller, or appliance for which a type certificate has been issued when the Administrator finds the duplicate will conform to the certificate. On receiving an application, the Administrator shall inspect, and may require testing of, a duplicate to ensure that it conforms to the requirements of the certificate. The Administrator may include in a production certificate terms required in the interest of safety.

(d) AIRWORTHINESS CERTIFICATES.—(1) The registered owner of an aircraft may apply to the Administrator for an airworthiness certificate for the aircraft. The Administrator shall issue an airworthiness certificate when the Administrator finds that the aircraft conforms to its type certificate and, after inspection, is in condition for safe operation. The

Administrator shall register each airworthiness certificate and may include appropriate information in the certificate. The certificate number or other individual designation the Administrator requires shall be displayed on the aircraft. The Administrator may include in an airworthiness certificate terms required in the interest of safety.

(2) A person applying for the issuance or renewal of an airworthiness certificate for an aircraft for which ownership has not been recorded under section 44107 or 44110 of this title must submit with the application information related to the ownership of the aircraft the Administrator decides is necessary to identify each person having a property interest in the aircraft and the kind and extent of the interest.

(3) Nonconformity with approved type design.—

(A) In general.—Consistent with the requirements of paragraph (1), a holder of a production certificate for an aircraft may not present a nonconforming aircraft, either directly or through the registered owner of such aircraft or a person described in paragraph (2), to the Administrator for issuance of an initial airworthiness certificate.

(B) Civil penalty.—Notwithstanding section 46301, a production certificate holder who knowingly violates subparagraph (A) shall be liable to the Administrator for a civil penalty of not more than $1,000,000 for each nonconforming aircraft.

(C) Penalty considerations.—In determining the amount of a civil penalty under subparagraph (B), the Administrator shall consider—

(i) the nature, circumstances, extent, and gravity of the violation, including the length of time the nonconformity was known by the holder of a production certificate but not disclosed; and

(ii) with respect to the violator, the degree of culpability, any history of prior violations, and the size of the business concern.

(D) Nonconforming aircraft defined.—In this paragraph, the term "nonconforming aircraft" means an aircraft that does not conform to the approved type design for such aircraft type.

(e) Disclosure of Safety Critical Information.—

(1) In general.—Notwithstanding a delegation described in section 44702(d), the Administrator shall require an applicant for, or holder of, a type certificate for a transport category airplane covered under part 25 of title 14, Code of Federal Regulations, to submit safety critical information with respect to such airplane to the Administrator in such form, manner, or time as the Administrator may require. Such safety critical information shall include—

(A) any design and operational details, intended functions, and failure modes of any system that, without being commanded by the flight crew, commands the operation of any safety critical function or feature required for control of an airplane during flight or that otherwise changes the flight path or airspeed of an airplane;

(B) the design and operational details, intended functions, failure modes, and mode annunciations of autopilot and autothrottle systems, if applicable;

(C) any failure or operating condition that the applicant or holder anticipates or has concluded would result in an outcome with a severity level of hazardous or catastrophic, as defined in the appropriate Administration airworthiness requirements and guidance applicable to transport category airplanes defining risk severity;

(D) any adverse handling quality that fails to meet the requirements of applicable regulations without the addition of a software system to augment the flight controls of the airplane to produce compliant handling qualities; and

(E) a system safety assessment with respect to a system described in subparagraph (A) or (B) or with respect to any component or other system for which failure or erroneous operation of such component or system could result in an outcome with a severity level of hazardous or catastrophic, as defined in the appropriate Administration airworthiness requirements and guidance applicable to transport category airplanes defining risk severity.

(2) ONGOING COMMUNICATIONS.—

(A) NEWLY DISCOVERED INFORMATION.—The Administrator shall require that an applicant for, or holder of, a type certificate disclose to the Administrator, in such form, manner, or time as the Administrator may require, any newly discovered information or design or analysis change that would materially alter any submission to the Administrator under paragraph (1).

(B) SYSTEM DEVELOPMENT CHANGES.—The Administrator shall establish multiple milestones throughout the certification process at which a proposed airplane system will be assessed to determine whether any change to such system during the certification process is such that such system should be considered novel or unusual by the Administrator.

(3) FLIGHT MANUALS.—The Administrator shall ensure that an airplane flight manual and a flight crew operating manual (as appropriate or applicable) for an airplane contains a description of the operation of a system described in paragraph (1)(A) and flight crew procedures for responding to a failure or aberrant operation of such system.

(4) CIVIL PENALTY.—

(A) AMOUNT.—Notwithstanding section 46301, an applicant for, or holder of, a type certificate that knowingly violates paragraph (1), (2), or (3) of this subsection shall be liable to the Administrator for a civil penalty of not more than $1,000,000 for each violation.

(B) PENALTY CONSIDERATIONS.—In determining the amount of a civil penalty under subparagraph (A), the Administrator shall consider—

(i) the nature, circumstances, extent, and gravity of the violation, including the length of time that such safety critical information was known but not disclosed; and

(ii) with respect to the violator, the degree of culpability, any history of prior violations, and the size of the business concern.

(5) REVOCATION AND CIVIL PENALTY FOR INDIVIDUALS.—

(A) IN GENERAL.—The Administrator shall revoke any airline transport pilot certificate issued under section 44703 held by any individual who, while acting on behalf of an applicant for, or holder of, a type certificate, knowingly makes a false statement with respect to any of the matters described in subparagraphs (A) through (E) of paragraph (1).

(B) AUTHORITY TO IMPOSE CIVIL PENALTY.—The Administrator may impose a civil penalty under section 46301 for each violation described in subparagraph (A).

(6) RULE OF CONSTRUCTION.—Nothing in this subsection shall be construed to affect or otherwise inhibit the authority of the Administrator to deny an application by an

applicant for a type certificate or to revoke or amend a type certificate of a holder of such certificate.

(7) DEFINITION OF TYPE CERTIFICATE.—In this subsection, the term "type certificate"—

(A) means a type certificate issued under subsection (a) or an amendment to such certificate; and

(B) does not include a supplemental type certificate issued under subsection (b).

(f) HEARING REQUIREMENT.—The Administrator may find that a person has violated subsection (d)(3) or paragraph (1), (2), or (3) of subsection (e) and impose a civil penalty under the applicable subsection only after notice and an opportunity for a hearing. The Administrator shall provide a person—

(1) written notice of the violation and the amount of penalty; and

(2) the opportunity for a hearing under subpart G of part 13 of title 14, Code of Federal Regulations.

(g) CERTIFICATION DISPUTE RESOLUTION.—

(1) DISPUTE RESOLUTION PROCESS AND APPEALS.—

(A) IN GENERAL.—Not later than 60 days after the date of enactment of this subsection, the Administrator shall issue an order establishing—

(i) an effective, timely, and milestone-based issue resolution process for type certification activities under subsection (a); and

(ii) a process by which a decision, finding of compliance or noncompliance, or other act of the Administration, with respect to compliance with design requirements, may be appealed by a covered person directly involved with the certification activities in dispute on the basis that such decision, finding, or act is erroneous or inconsistent with this chapter, regulations, or guidance materials promulgated by the Administrator, or other requirements.

(B) ESCALATION.—The order issued under subparagraph (A) shall provide processes for—

(i) resolution of technical issues at pre-established stages of the certification process, as agreed to by the Administrator and the type certificate applicant;

(ii) automatic elevation to appropriate management personnel of the Administration and the type certificate applicant of any major certification process milestone that is not completed or resolved within a specific period of time agreed to by the Administrator and the type certificate applicant;

(iii) resolution of a major certification process milestone elevated pursuant to clause (ii) within a specific period of time agreed to by the Administrator and the type certificate applicant;

(iv) initial review by appropriate Administration employees of any appeal described in subparagraph (A)(ii); and

(v) subsequent review of any further appeal by appropriate management personnel of the Administration and the Associate Administrator for Aviation Safety.

(C) DISPOSITION.—

(i) WRITTEN DECISION.—The Associate Administrator for Aviation Safety shall issue a written decision that states the grounds for the decision of the Associate Administrator on—

(I) each appeal submitted under subparagraph (A)(ii); and

(II) An appeal to the Associate Administrator submitted under subparagraph (B)(v).

(ii) REPORT TO CONGRESS.—Not later than December 31 of each calendar year through calendar year 2028, the Administrator shall submit to the Committee on Transportation and Infrastructure of the House of Representatives and the Committee on Commerce, Science, and Transportation of the Senate a report summarizing each appeal resolved under this subsection.

(D) FINAL REVIEW.—

(i) IN GENERAL.—A written decision of the Associate Administrator under subparagraph (C) may be appealed to the Administrator for a final review and determination.

(ii) DECLINE TO REVIEW.—The Administrator may decline to review an appeal initiated pursuant to clause (i).

(iii) JUDICIAL REVIEW.—No decision under this paragraph (including a decision to decline to review an appeal) shall be subject to judicial review.

(2) PROHIBITED CONTACTS.—

(A) PROHIBITION GENERALLY.—During the course of an appeal under this subsection, no covered official may engage in an ex parte communication (as defined in section 551 of title 5) with an individual representing or acting on behalf of an applicant for, or holder of, a certificate under this section in relation to such appeal unless such communication is disclosed pursuant to subparagraph (B).

(B) DISCLOSURE.—If, during the course of an appeal under this subsection, a covered official engages in, receives, or is otherwise made aware of an ex parte communication, the covered official shall disclose such communication in the public record at the time of the issuance of the written decision under paragraph (1)(C), including the time and date of the communication, subject of communication, and all persons engaged in such communication.

(3) DEFINITIONS.—In this subsection:

(A) COVERED PERSON.—The term "covered person" means either—

(i) an employee of the Administration whose responsibilities relate to the certification of aircraft, engines, propellers, or appliances; or

(ii) an applicant for, or holder of, a type certificate or amended type certificate issued under this section.

(B) COVERED OFFICIAL.—The term "covered official" means the following officials:

(i) The Executive Director or any Deputy Director of the Aircraft Certification Service.

(ii) The Deputy Executive Director for Regulatory Operations of the Aircraft Certification Service.

(iii) The Director or Deputy Director of the Compliance and Airworthiness Division of the Aircraft Certification Service.

(iv) The Director or Deputy Director of the System Oversight Division of the Aircraft Certification Service.

(v) The Director or Deputy Director of the Policy and Innovation Division of the Aircraft Certification Service.

(vi) The Executive Director or any Deputy Executive Director of the Flight Standards Service.

(vii) The Associate Administrator or Deputy Associate Administrator for Aviation Safety.

(viii) The Deputy Administrator of the Federal Aviation Administration.

(ix) The Administrator of the Federal Aviation Administration.

(x) Any similarly situated or successor FAA management position to those described in clauses (i) through (ix), as determined by the Administrator.

(C) MAJOR CERTIFICATION PROCESS MILESTONE.—The term "major certification process milestone" means a milestone related to the type certification basis, type certification plan, type inspection authorization, issue paper, or other major type certification activity agreed to by the Administrator and the type certificate applicant.

(4) RULE OF CONSTRUCTION.—Nothing in this subsection shall apply to the communication of a good-faith complaint by any individual alleging—

(A) gross misconduct;

(B) a violation of title 18; or

(C) a violation of any of the provisions of part 2635 or 6001 of title 5, Code of Federal Regulations.

(Pub. L. 103–272, §1(e), July 5, 1994, 108 Stat. 1188; Pub. L. 104–264, title IV, §403, Oct. 9, 1996, 110 Stat. 3256; Pub. L. 108–176, title II, §227(b)(2), (e)(1), title VIII, §811, Dec. 12, 2003, 117 Stat. 2531, 2532, 2590; Pub. L. 109–59, title IV, §4405, Aug. 10, 2005, 119 Stat. 1776; Pub. L. 112–95, title III, §§302, 303(a), (c)(1), Feb. 14, 2012, 126 Stat. 56, 57; Pub. L. 115–254, div. B, title II, §214, Oct. 5, 2018, 132 Stat. 3250; Pub. L. 116–260, div. V, title I, §§105(a), (b), 110, 120, Dec. 27, 2020, 134 Stat. 2317, 2328, 2343; Pub. L. 118–63, title III, §§306(c), 343(a), title XI, §1101(k), May 16, 2024, 138 Stat. 1072, 1101, 1414.)

§44705. AIR CARRIER OPERATING CERTIFICATES

The Administrator of the Federal Aviation Administration shall issue an air carrier operating certificate to a person desiring to operate as an air carrier when the Administrator finds, after investigation, that the person properly and adequately is equipped and able to operate safely under this part and regulations and standards prescribed under this part. An air carrier operating certificate shall—

(1) contain terms necessary to ensure safety in air transportation; and

(2) specify the places to and from which, and the airways of the United States over which, a person may operate as an air carrier.

(Pub. L. 103–272, §1(e), July 5, 1994, 108 Stat. 1189.)

§44706. AIRPORT OPERATING CERTIFICATES

(a) GENERAL.—The Administrator of the Federal Aviation Administration shall issue an airport operating certificate to a person desiring to operate an airport—

(1) that serves an air carrier operating aircraft designed for at least 31 passenger seats;

(2) that is not located in the State of Alaska and serves any scheduled passenger operation of an air carrier operating aircraft designed for more than 9 passenger seats but less than 31 passenger seats; and

(3) that the Administrator requires to have a certificate;

if the Administrator finds, after investigation, that the person properly and adequately is equipped and able to operate safely under this part and regulations and standards prescribed under this part.

(b) TERMS.—An airport operating certificate issued under this section shall contain terms necessary to ensure safety in air transportation. Unless the Administrator decides that it is not in the public interest, the terms shall include conditions related to—

(1) operating and maintaining adequate safety equipment, including firefighting and rescue equipment capable of rapid access to any part of the airport used for landing, takeoff, or surface maneuvering of an aircraft; and

(2) friction treatment for primary and secondary runways that the Secretary of Transportation decides is necessary.

(c) EXEMPTIONS.—The Administrator may exempt from the requirements of this section, related to firefighting and rescue equipment, an operator of an airport described in subsection (a) of this section having less than .25 percent of the total number of passenger boardings each year at all airports described in subsection (a) when the Administrator decides that the requirements are or would be unreasonably costly, burdensome, or impractical.

(d) COMMUTER AIRPORTS.—In developing the terms required by subsection (b) for airports covered by subsection (a)(2), the Administrator shall identify and consider a reasonable number of regulatory alternatives and select from such alternatives the least costly, most cost-effective or the least burdensome alternative that will provide comparable safety at airports described in subsections (a)(1) and (a)(2).

(e) EFFECTIVE DATE.—Any regulation establishing the terms required by subsection (b) for airports covered by subsection (a)(2) shall not take effect until such regulation, and a report on the economic impact of the regulation on air service to the airports covered by the rule, has been submitted to Congress and 120 days have elapsed following the date of such submission.

(f) LIMITATION ON STATUTORY CONSTRUCTION.—Nothing in this title may be construed as requiring a person to obtain an airport operating certificate if such person does not desire to operate an airport described in subsection (a).

(Pub. L. 103–272, §1(e), July 5, 1994, 108 Stat. 1189; Pub. L. 104–264, title IV, §404, Oct. 9, 1996, 110 Stat. 3256.)

§44707. EXAMINING AND RATING AIR AGENCIES

The Administrator of the Federal Aviation Administration may examine and rate the following air agencies:

(1) civilian schools giving instruction in flying or repairing, altering, and maintaining aircraft, aircraft engines, propellers, and appliances, on the adequacy of instruction, the suitability and airworthiness of equipment, and the competency of instructors.

(2) repair stations and shops that repair, alter, and maintain aircraft, aircraft engines, propellers, and appliances, on the adequacy and suitability of the equipment, facilities, and materials for, and methods of, repair and overhaul, and the competency of the individuals doing the work or giving instruction in the work.

(3) other air agencies the Administrator decides are necessary in the public interest.

(Pub. L. 103–272, §1(e), July 5, 1994, 108 Stat. 1190.)

§44708. Inspecting and rating air navigation facilities

The Administrator of the Federal Aviation Administration may inspect, classify, and rate an air navigation facility available for the use of civil aircraft on the suitability of the facility for that use.

(Pub. L. 103–272, §1(e), July 5, 1994, 108 Stat. 1190.)

§44709. Amendments, modifications, suspensions, and revocations of certificates

(a) Reinspection and Reexamination.—

(1) In general.—The Administrator of the Federal Aviation Administration may reinspect at any time a civil aircraft, aircraft engine, propeller, appliance, design organization, production certificate holder, air navigation facility, or air agency, or reexamine an airman holding a certificate issued under section 44703 of this title.

(2) Notification of reexamination of airman.—Before taking any action to reexamine an airman under paragraph (1) the Administrator shall provide to the airman—

(A) a reasonable basis, described in detail, for requesting the reexamination; and

(B) any information gathered by the Federal Aviation Administration, that the Administrator determines is appropriate to provide, such as the scope and nature of the requested reexamination, that formed the basis for that justification.

(b) Actions of the Administrator.—The Administrator may issue an order amending, modifying, suspending, or revoking—

(1) any part of a certificate issued under this chapter if—

(A) the Administrator decides after conducting a reinspection, reexamination, or other investigation that safety in air commerce or air transportation and the public interest require that action; or

(B) the holder of the certificate has violated an aircraft noise or sonic boom standard or regulation prescribed under section 44715(a) of this title; and

(2) an airman certificate when the holder of the certificate is convicted of violating section 13(a) of the Fish and Wildlife Act of 1956 (16 U.S.C. 742j–1(a)).

(c) Advice to Certificate Holders and Opportunity To Answer.—Before acting under subsection (b) of this section, the Administrator shall advise the holder of the certificate of the charges or other reasons on which the Administrator relies for the proposed action. Except in an emergency, the Administrator shall provide the holder an opportunity to answer the charges and be heard why the certificate should not be amended, modified, suspended, or revoked.

(d) Appeals.—(1) A person adversely affected by an order of the Administrator under this section may appeal the order to the National Transportation Safety Board. After notice and an opportunity for a hearing, the Board may amend, modify, or reverse the order when the Board finds—

(A) if the order was issued under subsection (b)(1)(A) of this section, that safety in air commerce or air transportation and the public interest do not require affirmation of the order; or

(B) if the order was issued under subsection (b)(1)(B) of this section—

(i) that control or abatement of aircraft noise or sonic boom and the public health and welfare do not require affirmation of the order; or

(ii) the order, as it is related to a violation of aircraft noise or sonic boom standards and regulations, is not consistent with safety in air commerce or air transportation.

(2) The Board may modify a suspension or revocation of a certificate to imposition of a civil penalty.

(3) When conducting a hearing under this subsection, the Board is not bound by findings of fact of the Administrator.

(e) EFFECTIVENESS OF ORDERS PENDING APPEAL.—

(1) IN GENERAL.—When a person files an appeal with the Board under subsection (d), the order of the Administrator is stayed.

(2) EXCEPTION.—Notwithstanding paragraph (1), the order of the Administrator is effective immediately if the Administrator advises the Board that an emergency exists and safety in air commerce or air transportation requires the order to be effective immediately.

(3) REVIEW OF EMERGENCY ORDER.—A person affected by the immediate effectiveness of the Administrator's order under paragraph (2) may petition for a review by the Board, under procedures promulgated by the Board, of the Administrator's determination that an emergency exists. Any such review shall be requested not later than 48 hours after the order is received by the person. If the Board finds that an emergency does not exist that requires the immediate application of the order in the interest of safety in air commerce or air transportation, the order shall be stayed, notwithstanding paragraph (2). The Board shall dispose of a review request under this paragraph not later than 5 days after the date on which the request is filed.

(4) FINAL DISPOSITION.—The Board shall make a final disposition of an appeal under subsection (d) not later than 60 days after the date on which the appeal is filed.

(f) JUDICIAL REVIEW.—A person substantially affected by an order of the Board under this section, or the Administrator when the Administrator decides that an order of the Board under this section will have a significant adverse impact on carrying out this part, may obtain judicial review of the order under section 46110 of this title. The Administrator shall be made a party to the judicial review proceedings. Findings of fact of the Board are conclusive if supported by substantial evidence.

(Pub. L. 103–272, §1(e), July 5, 1994, 108 Stat. 1190; Pub. L. 106–181, title VII, §716, Apr. 5, 2000, 114 Stat. 162; Pub. L. 108–176, title II, §227(c), Dec. 12, 2003, 117 Stat. 2532; Pub. L. 112–153, §2(c)(2), Aug. 3, 2012, 126 Stat. 1161; Pub. L. 115–254, div. B, title III, §393(a), Oct. 5, 2018, 132 Stat. 3325.)

§44710. REVOCATIONS OF AIRMAN CERTIFICATES FOR CONTROLLED
SUBSTANCE VIOLATIONS

(a) DEFINITION.—In this section, "controlled substance" has the same meaning given that term in section 102 of the Comprehensive Drug Abuse Prevention and Control Act of 1970 (21 U.S.C. 802).

(b) REVOCATION.—(1) The Administrator of the Federal Aviation Administration shall issue an order revoking an airman certificate issued an individual under section 44703 of this title after the individual is convicted, under a law of the United States or a State related to a controlled substance (except a law related to simple possession of a controlled substance), of an offense punishable by death or imprisonment for more than one year if the Administrator finds that—

(A) an aircraft was used to commit, or facilitate the commission of, the offense; and

(B) the individual served as an airman, or was on the aircraft, in connection with committing, or facilitating the commission of, the offense.

(2) The Administrator shall issue an order revoking an airman certificate issued an individual under section 44703 of this title if the Administrator finds that—

(A) the individual knowingly carried out an activity punishable, under a law of the United States or a State related to a controlled substance (except a law related to simple possession of a controlled substance), by death or imprisonment for more than one year;

(B) an aircraft was used to carry out or facilitate the activity; and

(C) the individual served as an airman, or was on the aircraft, in connection with carrying out, or facilitating the carrying out of, the activity.

(3) The Administrator has no authority under paragraph (1) of this subsection to review whether an airman violated a law of the United States or a State related to a controlled substance.

(c) ADVICE TO HOLDERS AND OPPORTUNITY TO ANSWER.—Before the Administrator revokes a certificate under subsection (b) of this section, the Administrator must—

(1) advise the holder of the certificate of the charges or reasons on which the Administrator relies for the proposed revocation; and

(2) provide the holder of the certificate an opportunity to answer the charges and be heard why the certificate should not be revoked.

(d) APPEALS.—(1) An individual whose certificate is revoked by the Administrator under subsection (b) of this section may appeal the revocation order to the National Transportation Safety Board. The Board shall affirm or reverse the order after providing notice and an opportunity for a hearing on the record. When conducting the hearing, the Board is not bound by findings of fact of the Administrator.

(2) When an individual files an appeal with the Board under this subsection, the order of the Administrator revoking the certificate is stayed. However, if the Administrator advises the Board that safety in air transportation or air commerce requires the immediate effectiveness of the order—

(A) the order remains effective; and

(B) the Board shall make a final disposition of the appeal not later than 60 days after the Administrator so advises the Board.

(3) An individual substantially affected by an order of the Board under this subsection, or the Administrator when the Administrator decides that an order of the Board will have a significant adverse effect on carrying out this part, may obtain judicial review of the order under section 46110 of this title. The Administrator shall be made a party to the judicial review proceedings. Findings of fact of the Board are conclusive if supported by substantial evidence.

(e) ACQUITTAL.—(1) The Administrator may not revoke, and the Board may not affirm a revocation of, an airman certificate under subsection (b)(2) of this section on the basis of an activity described in subsection (b)(2)(A) if the holder of the certificate is acquitted of all charges related to a controlled substance in an indictment or information arising from the activity.

(2) If the Administrator has revoked an airman certificate under this section because of an activity described in subsection (b)(2)(A) of this section, the Administrator shall reissue a certificate to the individual if—

(A) the individual otherwise satisfies the requirements for a certificate under section 44703 of this title; and

(B)(i) the individual subsequently is acquitted of all charges related to a controlled substance in an indictment or information arising from the activity; or

(ii) the conviction on which a revocation under subsection (b)(1) of this section is based is reversed.

(f) WAIVERS.—The Administrator may waive the requirement of subsection (b) of this section that an airman certificate of an individual be revoked if—

(1) a law enforcement official of the United States Government or of a State requests a waiver; and

(2) the Administrator decides that the waiver will facilitate law enforcement efforts.

(Pub. L. 103–272, §1(e), July 5, 1994, 108 Stat. 1191; Pub. L. 112–153, §2(c)(3), Aug. 3, 2012, 126 Stat. 1161.)

§44711. PROHIBITIONS AND EXEMPTION

(a) PROHIBITIONS.—A person may not—

(1) operate a civil aircraft in air commerce without an airworthiness certificate in effect or in violation of a term of the certificate;

(2) serve in any capacity as an airman with respect to a civil aircraft, aircraft engine, propeller, or appliance used, or intended for use, in air commerce—

(A) without an airman certificate authorizing the airman to serve in the capacity for which the certificate was issued; or

(B) in violation of a term of the certificate or a regulation prescribed or order issued under section 44701(a) or (b) or any of sections 44702–44716 of this title;

(3) employ for service related to civil aircraft used in air commerce an airman who does not have an airman certificate authorizing the airman to serve in the capacity for which the airman is employed;

(4) operate as an air carrier without an air carrier operating certificate or in violation of a term of the certificate;

(5) operate aircraft in air commerce in violation of a regulation prescribed or certificate issued under section 44701(a) or (b) or any of sections 44702–44716 of this title;

(6) operate a seaplane or other aircraft of United States registry on the high seas in violation of a regulation under section 3 of the International Navigational Rules Act of 1977 (33 U.S.C. 1602);

(7) violate a term of an air agency, design organization certificate, or production certificate or a regulation prescribed or order issued under section 44701(a) or (b) or any of sections 44702–44716 of this title related to the holder of the certificate;

(8) operate an airport without an airport operating certificate required under section 44706 of this title or in violation of a term of the certificate;

(9) manufacture, deliver, sell, or offer for sale any aviation fuel or additive in violation of a regulation prescribed under section 44714 of this title;

(10) work as an aircraft dispatcher outside of a physical location designated as a dispatching center or flight following center of an air carrier, except as provided under section 44747; or

(11) violate section 44732 or any regulation issued thereunder.

(b) EXEMPTION.—On terms the Administrator of the Federal Aviation Administration prescribes as being in the public interest, the Administrator may exempt a foreign aircraft and airmen serving on the aircraft from subsection (a) of this section. However, an exemption from observing air traffic regulations may not be granted.

(c) PROHIBITION ON EMPLOYMENT OF CONVICTED COUNTERFEIT PART TRAFFICKERS.—No person subject to this chapter may knowingly employ anyone to perform a function related to the procurement, sale, production, or repair of a part or material, or the installation of a part into a civil aircraft, who has been convicted in a court of law of a violation of any Federal law relating to the installation, production, repair, or sale of a counterfeit or fraudulently-represented aviation part or material.

(d) POST-EMPLOYMENT RESTRICTIONS FOR INSPECTORS AND ENGINEERS.—

(1) PROHIBITION.—A person holding a certificate issued under part 21 or 119 of title 14, Code of Federal Regulations, may not knowingly employ, or make a contractual arrangement that permits, an individual to act as an agent or representative of such person in any matter before the Administration if the individual, in the preceding 2-year period—

(A) served as, or was responsible for oversight of—

(i) a flight standards inspector of the Administration; or

(ii) an employee of the Administration with responsibility for certification functions with respect to a holder of a certificate issued under section 44704(a); and

(B) had responsibility to inspect, or oversee inspection of, the operations of such person.

(2) WRITTEN AND ORAL COMMUNICATIONS.—For purposes of paragraph (1), an individual shall be considered to be acting as an agent or representative of a certificate holder in a matter before the Administration if the individual makes any written or oral communication on behalf of the certificate holder to the Administration (or any of its officers or employees) in connection with a particular matter, whether or not involving a specific party and without regard to whether the individual has participated in, or had responsibility for, the particular matter while serving as an individual covered under paragraph (1).

(Pub. L. 103–272, §1(e), July 5, 1994, 108 Stat. 1193; Pub. L. 103–429, §6(56), Oct. 31, 1994, 108 Stat. 4385; Pub. L. 106–181, title V, §505(b), Apr. 5, 2000, 114 Stat. 136; Pub. L. 108–176, title II, §227(d), Dec. 12, 2003, 117 Stat. 2532; Pub. L. 112–95, title III, §§307(b), 342(a), Feb. 14, 2012, 126 Stat. 61, 79; Pub. L. 116–260, div. V, title I, §111(b), Dec. 27, 2020, 134 Stat. 2330; Pub. L. 118–63, title IV, §420(a)(1), May 16, 2024, 138 Stat. 1164.)

§44712. EMERGENCY LOCATOR TRANSMITTERS

(a) INSTALLATION.—An emergency locator transmitter must be installed on a fixed-wing powered civil aircraft for use in air commerce.

(b) NONAPPLICATION.—Prior to January 1, 2002, subsection (a) does not apply to—

(1) turbojet-powered aircraft;

(2) aircraft when used in scheduled flights by scheduled air carriers holding certificates issued by the Secretary of Transportation under subpart II of this part;

(3) aircraft when used in training operations conducted entirely within a 50 mile radius of the airport from which the training operations begin;

(4) aircraft when used in flight operations related to design and testing, the manufacture, preparation, and delivery of the aircraft, or the aerial application of a substance for an agricultural purpose;

(5) aircraft holding certificates from the Administrator of the Federal Aviation Administration for research and development;

(6) aircraft when used for showing compliance with regulations, crew training, exhibition, air racing, or market surveys; and

(7) aircraft equipped to carry only one individual.

(c) NONAPPLICATION BEGINNING ON JANUARY 1, 2002.—

(1) IN GENERAL.—Subject to paragraph (2), on and after January 1, 2002, subsection (a) does not apply to—

(A) aircraft when used in scheduled flights by scheduled air carriers holding certificates issued by the Secretary of Transportation under subpart II of this part;

(B) aircraft when used in training operations conducted entirely within a 50-mile radius of the airport from which the training operations begin;

(C) aircraft when used in flight operations related to the design and testing, manufacture, preparation, and delivery of aircraft;

(D) aircraft when used in research and development if the aircraft holds a certificate from the Administrator of the Federal Aviation Administration to carry out such research and development;

(E) aircraft when used in showing compliance with regulations, crew training, exhibition, air racing, or market surveys;

(F) aircraft when used in the aerial application of a substance for an agricultural purpose;

(G) aircraft with a maximum payload capacity of more than 18,000 pounds when used in air transportation; or

(H) aircraft equipped to carry only one individual.

(2) DELAY IN IMPLEMENTATION.—The Administrator of the Federal Aviation Administration may continue to implement subsection (b) rather than subsection (c) for a period not to exceed 2 years after January 1, 2002, if the Administrator finds such action is necessary to promote—

(A) a safe and orderly transition to the operation of civil aircraft equipped with an emergency locator; or

(B) other safety objectives.

(d) COMPLIANCE.—An aircraft meets the requirement of subsection (a) if it is equipped with an emergency locator transmitter that transmits on the 121.5/243 megahertz frequency or the 406 megahertz frequency or with other equipment approved by the Secretary for meeting the requirement of subsection (a).

(e) REMOVAL.—The Administrator shall prescribe regulations specifying the conditions under which an aircraft subject to subsection (a) of this section may operate when its emergency locator transmitter has been removed for inspection, repair, alteration, or replacement.

(Pub. L. 103–272, §1(e), July 5, 1994, 108 Stat. 1194; Pub. L. 106–181, title V, §501(a), Apr. 5, 2000, 114 Stat. 131.)

§44713. INSPECTION AND MAINTENANCE

(a) GENERAL EQUIPMENT REQUIREMENTS.—An air carrier shall make, or cause to be made, any inspection, repair, or maintenance of equipment used in air transportation as required by this part or regulations prescribed or orders issued by the Administrator of the Federal Aviation Administration under this part. A person operating, inspecting, repairing, or maintaining the equipment shall comply with those requirements, regulations, and orders.

(b) DUTIES OF INSPECTORS.—The Administrator of the Federal Aviation Administration shall employ inspectors who shall—

(1) inspect aircraft, aircraft engines, propellers, and appliances designed for use in air transportation, during manufacture and when in use by an air carrier in air transportation, to enable the Administrator to decide whether the aircraft, aircraft engines, propellers, or appliances are in safe condition and maintained properly; and

(2) advise and cooperate with the air carrier during that inspection and maintenance.

(c) UNSAFE AIRCRAFT, ENGINES, PROPELLERS, AND APPLIANCES.—When an inspector decides that an aircraft, aircraft engine, propeller, or appliance is not in condition for safe operation, the inspector shall notify the air carrier in the form and way prescribed by the Administrator of the Federal Aviation Administration. For 5 days after the carrier is notified, the aircraft, engine, propeller, or appliance may not be used in air transportation or in a way that endangers air transportation unless the Administrator or the inspector decides the aircraft, engine, propeller, or appliance is in condition for safe operation.

(d) MODIFICATIONS IN SYSTEM.—(1) The Administrator of the Federal Aviation Administration shall make modifications in the system for processing forms for major repairs or alterations to fuel tanks and fuel systems of aircraft not used to provide air transportation that are necessary to make the system more effective in serving the needs of users of the system, including officials responsible for enforcing laws related to the regulation of controlled substances (as defined in section 102 of the Comprehensive Drug Abuse Prevention and Control Act of 1970 (21 U.S.C. 802)). The modifications shall address at least each of the following deficiencies in, and abuses of, the existing system:

(A) the lack of a special identification feature to allow the forms to be distinguished easily from other major repair and alteration forms.

(B) the excessive period of time required to receive the forms at the Airmen and Aircraft Registry of the Administration.

(C) the backlog of forms waiting for processing at the Registry.

(D) the lack of ready access by law enforcement officials to information contained on the forms.

(2) The Administrator of the Federal Aviation Administration shall prescribe regulations to carry out paragraph (1) of this subsection and provide a written explanation of how the regulations address each of the deficiencies and abuses described in paragraph (1). In prescribing the regulations, the Administrator of the Federal Aviation Administration shall consult with the Administrator of Drug Enforcement, the Commissioner of U.S. Customs

and Border Protection, other law enforcement officials of the United States Government, representatives of State and local law enforcement officials, representatives of the general aviation aircraft industry, representatives of users of general aviation aircraft, and other interested persons.

(e) AUTOMATED SURVEILLANCE TARGETING SYSTEMS.—

(1) IN GENERAL.—The Administrator shall give high priority to developing and deploying a fully enhanced safety performance analysis system that includes automated surveillance to assist the Administrator in prioritizing and targeting surveillance and inspection activities of the Federal Aviation Administration.

(2) DEADLINES FOR DEPLOYMENT.—

(A) INITIAL PHASE.—The initial phase of the operational deployment of the system developed under this subsection shall begin not later than December 31, 1997.

(B) FINAL PHASE.—The final phase of field deployment of the system developed under this subsection shall begin not later than December 31, 1999. By that date, all principal operations and maintenance inspectors of the Administration, and appropriate supervisors and analysts of the Administration shall have been provided access to the necessary information and resources to carry out the system.

(3) INTEGRATION OF INFORMATION.—In developing the system under this section, the Administration shall consider the near-term integration of accident and incident data into the safety performance analysis system under this subsection.

(Pub. L. 103–272, §1(e), July 5, 1994, 108 Stat. 1194; Pub. L. 104–264, title IV, §407(b), Oct. 9, 1996, 110 Stat. 3258; Pub. L. 114–125, title VIII, §802(d)(2), Feb. 24, 2016, 130 Stat. 210.)

§44714. AVIATION FUEL STANDARDS

The Administrator of the Federal Aviation Administration shall prescribe—

(1) standards for the composition or chemical or physical properties of an aircraft fuel or fuel additive to control or eliminate aircraft emissions the Administrator of the Environmental Protection Agency decides under section 231 of the Clean Air Act (42 U.S.C. 7571) endanger the public health or welfare; and

(2) regulations providing for carrying out and enforcing those standards.

(Pub. L. 103–272, §1(e), July 5, 1994, 108 Stat. 1195.)

§44715. CONTROLLING AIRCRAFT NOISE AND SONIC BOOM

(a) STANDARDS AND REGULATIONS.—(1)(A) To relieve and protect the public health and welfare from aircraft noise and sonic boom, the Administrator of the Federal Aviation Administration, as he deems necessary, shall prescribe—

(i) standards to measure aircraft noise and sonic boom; and

(ii) regulations to control and abate aircraft noise and sonic boom.

(B) The Administrator, as the Administrator deems appropriate, shall provide for the participation of a representative of the Environmental Protection Agency on such advisory committees or associated working groups that advise the Administrator on matters related to the environmental effects of aircraft and aircraft engines.

(2) The Administrator of the Federal Aviation Administration may prescribe standards and regulations under this subsection only after consulting with the Administrator of the Environmental Protection Agency. The standards and regulations shall be applied when

issuing, amending, modifying, suspending, or revoking a certificate authorized under this chapter.

(3) An original type certificate may be issued under section 44704(a) of this title for an aircraft for which substantial noise abatement can be achieved only after the Administrator of the Federal Aviation Administration prescribes standards and regulations under this section that apply to that aircraft.

(b) Considerations and Consultation.—When prescribing a standard or regulation under this section, the Administrator of the Federal Aviation Administration shall—

(1) consider relevant information related to aircraft noise and sonic boom;

(2) consult with appropriate departments, agencies, and instrumentalities of the United States Government and State and interstate authorities;

(3) consider whether the standard or regulation is consistent with the highest degree of safety in air transportation or air commerce in the public interest;

(4) consider whether the standard or regulation is economically reasonable, technologically practicable, and appropriate for the applicable aircraft, aircraft engine, appliance, or certificate; and

(5) consider the extent to which the standard or regulation will carry out the purposes of this section.

(c) Proposed Regulations of Administrator of Environmental Protection Agency.—The Administrator of the Environmental Protection Agency shall submit to the Administrator of the Federal Aviation Administration proposed regulations to control and abate aircraft noise and sonic boom (including control and abatement through the use of the authority of the Administrator of the Federal Aviation Administration) that the Administrator of the Environmental Protection Agency considers necessary to protect the public health and welfare. The Administrator of the Federal Aviation Administration shall consider those proposed regulations and shall publish them in a notice of proposed regulations not later than 30 days after they are received. Not later than 60 days after publication, the Administrator of the Federal Aviation Administration shall begin a hearing at which interested persons are given an opportunity for oral and written presentations. Not later than 90 days after the hearing is completed and after consulting with the Administrator of the Environmental Protection Agency, the Administrator of the Federal Aviation Administration shall—

(1) prescribe regulations as provided by this section—

(A) substantially the same as the proposed regulations submitted by the Administrator of the Environmental Protection Agency; or

(B) that amend the proposed regulations; or

(2) publish in the Federal Register—

(A) a notice that no regulation is being prescribed in response to the proposed regulations of the Administrator of the Environmental Protection Agency;

(B) a detailed analysis of, and response to, all information the Administrator of the Environmental Protection Agency submitted with the proposed regulations; and

(C) a detailed explanation of why no regulation is being prescribed.

(d) Consultation and Reports.—(1) If the Administrator of the Environmental Protection Agency believes that the action of the Administrator of the Federal Aviation Administration under subsection (c)(1)(B) or (2) of this section does not protect the public health and welfare from aircraft noise or sonic boom, consistent with the considerations in subsection (b) of this section, the Administrator of the Environmental Protection Agency shall consult with the Administrator of the Federal Aviation Administration and may request a report on the advisability of prescribing the regulation as originally proposed. The request, including a detailed statement of the information on which the request is based, shall be published in the Federal Register.

(2) The Administrator of the Federal Aviation Administration shall report to the Administrator of the Environmental Protection Agency within the time, if any, specified in the request. However, the time specified must be at least 90 days after the date of the request. The report shall—

(A) be accompanied by a detailed statement of the findings of the Administrator of the Federal Aviation Administration and the reasons for the findings;

(B) identify any statement related to an action under subsection (c) of this section filed under section 102(2)(C) of the National Environmental Policy Act of 1969 (42 U.S.C. 4332(2)(C));

(C) specify whether and where that statement is available for public inspection; and

(D) be published in the Federal Register unless the request proposes specific action by the Administrator of the Federal Aviation Administration and the report indicates that action will be taken.

(e) SUPPLEMENTAL REPORTS.—The Administrator of the Environmental Protection Agency may request the Administrator of the Federal Aviation Administration to file a supplemental report if the report under subsection (d) of this section indicates that the proposed regulations under subsection (c) of this section, for which a statement under section 102(2)(C) of the Act (42 U.S.C. 4332(2)(C)) is not required, should not be prescribed. The supplemental report shall be published in the Federal Register within the time the Administrator of the Environmental Protection Agency specifies. However, the time specified must be at least 90 days after the date of the request. The supplemental report shall contain a comparison of the environmental effects, including those that cannot be avoided, of the action of the Administrator of the Federal Aviation Administration and the proposed regulations of the Administrator of the Environmental Protection Agency.

(f) EXEMPTIONS.—An exemption from a standard or regulation prescribed under this section may be granted only if, before granting the exemption, the Administrator of the Federal Aviation Administration consults with the Administrator of the Environmental Protection Agency. However, if the Administrator of the Federal Aviation Administration finds that safety in air transportation or air commerce requires an exemption before the Administrator of the Environmental Protection Agency can be consulted, the exemption may be granted. The Administrator of the Federal Aviation Administration shall consult with the Administrator of the Environmental Protection Agency as soon as practicable after the exemption is granted.

(Pub. L. 103–272, §1(e), July 5, 1994, 108 Stat. 1196; Pub. L. 104–264, title IV, §406(a), Oct. 9, 1996, 110 Stat. 3257.)

§44716. COLLISION AVOIDANCE SYSTEMS

(a) DEVELOPMENT AND CERTIFICATION.—The Administrator of the Federal Aviation Administration shall—

(1) complete the development of the collision avoidance system known as TCAS–II so that TCAS–II can operate under visual and instrument flight rules and can be upgraded to the performance standards applicable to the collision avoidance system known as TCAS–III;

(2) develop and carry out a schedule for developing and certifying TCAS–II that will result in certification not later than June 30, 1989; and

(3) submit to Congress monthly reports on the progress being made in developing and certifying TCAS–II.

(b) INSTALLATION AND OPERATION.—The Administrator shall require by regulation that, not later than 30 months after the date certification is made under subsection (a)(2) of this section, TCAS–II be installed and operated on each civil aircraft that has a maximum passenger capacity of at least 31 seats and is used to provide air transportation of passengers, including intrastate air transportation of passengers. The Administrator may extend the deadline in this subsection for not more than 2 years if the Administrator finds the extension is necessary to promote—

(1) a safe and orderly transition to the operation of a fleet of civil aircraft described in this subsection equipped with TCAS–II; or

(2) other safety objectives.

(c) OPERATIONAL EVALUATION.—Not later than December 30, 1990, the Administrator shall establish a one-year program to collect and assess safety and operational information from civil aircraft equipped with TCAS–II for the operational evaluation of TCAS–II. The Administrator shall encourage foreign air carriers that operate civil aircraft equipped with TCAS–II to participate in the program.

(d) AMENDING SCHEDULE FOR WINDSHEAR EQUIPMENT.—The Administrator shall consider the feasibility and desirability of amending the schedule for installing airborne low-altitude windshear equipment to make the schedule compatible with the schedule for installing TCAS–II.

(e) DEADLINE FOR DEVELOPMENT AND CERTIFICATION.—(1) The Administrator shall complete developing and certifying TCAS–III as soon as possible.

(2) Necessary amounts may be appropriated from the Airport and Airway Trust Fund established under section 9502 of the Internal Revenue Code of 1986 (26 U.S.C. 9502) to carry out this subsection.

(f) INSTALLING AND USING TRANSPONDERS.—The Administrator shall prescribe regulations requiring that, not later than December 30, 1990, operating transponders with automatic altitude reporting capability be installed and used for aircraft operating in designated terminal airspace where radar service is provided for separation of aircraft. The Administrator may provide for access to that airspace (except terminal control areas and airport radar service areas) by nonequipped aircraft if the Administrator finds the access will not interfere with the normal traffic flow.

(g) CARGO COLLISION AVOIDANCE SYSTEMS.—

(1) IN GENERAL.—The Administrator shall require by regulation that, no later than December 31, 2002, collision avoidance equipment be installed on each cargo aircraft with a maximum certificated takeoff weight in excess of 15,000 kilograms.

(2) EXTENSION OF DEADLINE.—The Administrator may extend the deadline established by paragraph (1) by not more than 2 years if the Administrator finds that the extension is

needed to promote—

    (A) a safe and orderly transition to the operation of a fleet of cargo aircraft equipped with collision avoidance equipment; or

    (B) other safety or public interest objectives.

    (3) COLLISION AVOIDANCE EQUIPMENT DEFINED.—In this subsection, the term "collision avoidance equipment" means equipment that provides protection from mid-air collisions using technology that provides—

    (A) cockpit-based collision detection and conflict resolution guidance, including display of traffic; and

    (B) a margin of safety of at least the same level as provided by the collision avoidance system known as TCAS–II.

(Pub. L. 103–272, §1(e), July 5, 1994, 108 Stat. 1198; Pub. L. 106–181, title V, §502, Apr. 5, 2000, 114 Stat. 132.)

§44717. AGING AIRCRAFT

    (a) INSPECTIONS AND REVIEWS.—The Administrator of the Federal Aviation Administration shall prescribe regulations that ensure the continuing airworthiness of aging aircraft. The regulations prescribed under subsection (a) of this section—

    (1) at least shall require the Administrator to make inspections, and review the maintenance and other records, of each aircraft an air carrier uses to provide air transportation that the Administrator decides may be necessary to enable the Administrator to decide whether the aircraft is in safe condition and maintained properly for operation in air transportation;

    (2) at least shall require an air carrier to demonstrate to the Administrator, as part of the inspection, that maintenance of the aircraft's age-sensitive parts and components has been adequate and timely enough to ensure the highest degree of safety;

    (3) shall require the air carrier to make available to the Administrator the aircraft and any records about the aircraft that the Administrator requires to carry out a review; and

    (4) shall establish procedures to be followed in carrying out an inspection.

    (b) WHEN AND HOW INSPECTIONS AND REVIEWS SHALL BE CARRIED OUT.—(1) Inspections and reviews required under subsection (a)(1) of this section shall be carried out as part of each heavy maintenance check of the aircraft conducted after the 14th year in which the aircraft has been in service.

    (2) Inspections under subsection (a)(1) of this section shall be carried out as provided under section 44701(a)(2)(B) and (C) of this title.

    (c) AIRCRAFT MAINTENANCE SAFETY PROGRAMS.—The Administrator shall establish—

    (1) a program to verify that air carriers are maintaining their aircraft according to maintenance programs approved by the Administrator;

    (2) a program—

    (A) to provide inspectors and engineers of the Administration with training necessary to conduct auditing inspections of aircraft operated by air carriers for corrosion and metal fatigue; and

    (B) to enhance participation of those inspectors and engineers in those inspections; and

    (3) a program to ensure that air carriers demonstrate to the Administrator their

commitment and technical competence to ensure the airworthiness of aircraft that the carriers operate.

(d) FOREIGN AIR TRANSPORTATION.—(1) The Administrator shall take all possible steps to encourage governments of foreign countries and relevant international organizations to develop standards and requirements for inspections and reviews that—

(A) will ensure the continuing airworthiness of aging aircraft used by foreign air carriers to provide foreign air transportation to and from the United States; and

(B) will provide passengers of those foreign air carriers with the same level of safety that will be provided passengers of air carriers by carrying out this section.

(2) Not later than September 30, 1994, the Administrator shall report to Congress on carrying out this subsection.

(Pub. L. 103–272, §1(e), July 5, 1994, 108 Stat. 1199.)

§44718. STRUCTURES INTERFERING WITH AIR COMMERCE OR NATIONAL SECURITY

(a) NOTICE.—By regulation or by order when necessary, the Secretary of Transportation shall require a person to give adequate public notice, in the form and way the Secretary prescribes, of the construction, alteration, establishment, or expansion, or the proposed construction, alteration, establishment, or expansion, of a structure or sanitary landfill when the notice will promote—

(1) safety in air commerce;

(2) the efficient use and preservation of the navigable airspace and of airport traffic capacity at public-use airports; or

(3) the interests of national security, as determined by the Secretary of Defense.

(b) STUDIES.—

(1) IN GENERAL.—Under regulations prescribed by the Secretary, if the Secretary decides that constructing or altering a structure may result in an obstruction of the navigable airspace, an interference with air or space navigation facilities and equipment or the navigable airspace, or, after consultation with the Secretary of Defense, an adverse impact on military operations and readiness, the Secretary of Transportation shall conduct an aeronautical study to decide the extent of any adverse impact on the safe and efficient use of the airspace, facilities, or equipment. In conducting the study, the Secretary shall—

(A) consider factors relevant to the efficient and effective use of the navigable airspace, including—

(i) the impact on arrival, departure, and en route procedures for aircraft operating under visual flight rules;

(ii) the impact on arrival, departure, and en route procedures for aircraft operating under instrument flight rules;

(iii) the impact on existing public-use airports and aeronautical facilities;

(iv) the impact on planned public-use airports and aeronautical facilities;

(v) the cumulative impact resulting from the proposed construction or alteration of a structure when combined with the impact of other existing or proposed structures;

(vi) the impact on launch and reentry for launch and reentry vehicles arriving or departing from a launch site or reentry site licensed by the Secretary of Transportation; and

(vii) other factors relevant to the efficient and effective use of navigable airspace; and

(B) include the finding made by the Secretary of Defense under subsection (f).

(2) REPORT.—On completing the study, the Secretary of Transportation shall issue a report disclosing the extent of the—

(A) adverse impact on the safe and efficient use of the navigable airspace that the Secretary finds will result from constructing or altering the structure; and

(B) unacceptable risk to the national security of the United States, as determined by the Secretary of Defense under subsection (f).

(3) SEVERABILITY.—A determination by the Secretary of Transportation on hazard to air navigation under this section shall remain independent of a determination of unacceptable risk to the national security of the United States by the Secretary of Defense under subsection (f).

(c) BROADCAST APPLICATIONS AND TOWER STUDIES.—In carrying out laws related to a broadcast application and conducting an aeronautical study related to broadcast towers, the Administrator of the Federal Aviation Administration and the Federal Communications Commission shall take action necessary to coordinate efficiently—

(1) the receipt and consideration of, and action on, the application; and

(2) the completion of any associated aeronautical study.

(d) LIMITATION ON CONSTRUCTION OF LANDFILLS.—

(1) IN GENERAL.—No person shall construct or establish a municipal solid waste landfill (as defined in section 258.2 of title 40, Code of Federal Regulations, as in effect on the date of the enactment of this subsection) that receives putrescible waste (as defined in section 257.3–8 of such title) within 6 miles of a public airport that has received grants under chapter 471 and is primarily served by general aviation aircraft and regularly scheduled flights of aircraft designed for 60 passengers or less unless the State aviation agency of the State in which the airport is located requests that the Administrator of the Federal Aviation Administration exempt the landfill from the application of this subsection and the Administrator determines that such exemption would have no adverse impact on aviation safety.

(2) LIMITATION ON APPLICABILITY.—Paragraph (1) shall not apply in the State of Alaska and shall not apply to the construction, establishment, expansion, or modification of, or to any other activity undertaken with respect to, a municipal solid waste landfill if the construction or establishment of the landfill was commenced on or before the date of the enactment of this subsection.

(e) REVIEW OF AERONAUTICAL STUDIES.—The Administrator of the Federal Aviation Administration shall develop procedures to allow the Department of Defense and the Department of Homeland Security to review and comment on an aeronautical study conducted pursuant to subsection (b) prior to the completion of the study.

(f) NATIONAL SECURITY FINDING.—As part of an aeronautical study conducted under subsection (b) and in accordance with section 183a(e) of title 10, the Secretary of Defense shall—

(1) make a finding on whether the construction, alteration, establishment, or expansion

of a structure or sanitary landfill included in the study would result in an unacceptable risk to the national security of the United States; and

(2) transmit the finding to the Secretary of Transportation for inclusion in the report required under subsection (b)(2).

(g) SPECIAL RULE FOR IDENTIFIED GEOGRAPHIC AREAS.—In the case of a proposed structure to be located within a geographic area identified under section 183a(d)(2)(B) of title 10, the Secretary of Transportation may not issue a determination pursuant to this section until the Secretary of Defense issues a finding under section 183a(e) of title 10, the Secretary of Defense advises the Secretary of Transportation that no finding under section 183a(e) of title 10 will be forthcoming, or 180 days have lapsed since the project was filed with the Secretary of Transportation pursuant to this section, whichever occurs first.

(h) DEFINITIONS.—In this section, the terms "adverse impact on military operations and readiness" and "unacceptable risk to the national security of the United States" have the meaning given those terms in section 183a(h) of title 10.

(Pub. L. 103–272, §1(e), July 5, 1994, 108 Stat. 1200; Pub. L. 104–264, title XII, §1220(a), Oct. 9, 1996, 110 Stat. 3286; Pub. L. 106–181, title V, §503(b), Apr. 5, 2000, 114 Stat. 133; Pub. L. 112–81, div. A, title III, §332, Dec. 31, 2011, 125 Stat. 1369; Pub. L. 114–248, §1(a), Nov. 28, 2016, 130 Stat. 998; Pub. L. 114–328, div. A, title III, §341(a)(1)–(4)(A), Dec. 23, 2016, 130 Stat. 2079–2081; Pub. L. 115–91, div. A, title III, §311(b)(2), (3), (e), Dec. 12, 2017, 131 Stat. 1347, 1348; Pub. L. 115–232, div. A, title X, §1081(e)(2), Aug. 13, 2018, 132 Stat. 1986; Pub. L. 115–254, div. B, title V, §539(h), Oct. 5, 2018, 132 Stat. 3371; Pub. L. 118–63, title XI, §1101(m), May 16, 2024, 138 Stat. 1414.)

§44719. STANDARDS FOR NAVIGATIONAL AIDS

The Secretary of Transportation shall prescribe regulations on standards for installing navigational aids, including airport control towers. For each type of facility, the regulations shall consider at a minimum traffic density (number of aircraft operations without consideration of aircraft size), terrain and other obstacles to navigation, weather characteristics, passengers served, and potential aircraft operating efficiencies.

(Pub. L. 103–272, §1(e), July 5, 1994, 108 Stat. 1201.)

§44720. METEOROLOGICAL SERVICES

(a) RECOMMENDATIONS.—The Administrator of the Federal Aviation Administration shall make recommendations to the Secretary of Commerce on providing meteorological services necessary for the safe and efficient movement of aircraft in air commerce. In providing the services, the Secretary shall cooperate with the Administrator and give complete consideration to those recommendations.

(b) PROMOTING SAFETY AND EFFICIENCY.—To promote safety and efficiency in air navigation to the highest possible degree, the Secretary shall—

(1) observe, measure, investigate, and study atmospheric phenomena, and maintain meteorological stations and offices, that are necessary or best suited for finding out in advance information about probable weather conditions;

(2) provide reports to the Administrator, to persons engaged in civil aeronautics that are designated by the the Administrator, and to other persons designated by the Secretary in a way and with a frequency that best will result in safety in, and facilitating, air navigation;

(3) cooperate with persons engaged in air commerce in meteorological services, maintain reciprocal arrangements with those persons in carrying out this clause, and collect and distribute weather reports available from aircraft in flight;

(4) maintain and coordinate international exchanges of meteorological information required for the safety and efficiency of air navigation;

(5) in cooperation with other departments, agencies, and instrumentalities of the United States Government, meteorological services of foreign countries, and persons engaged in air commerce, participate in developing an international basic meteorological reporting network, including the establishment, operation, and maintenance of reporting stations on the high seas, in polar regions, and in foreign countries;

(6) coordinate meteorological requirements in the United States to maintain standard observations, to promote efficient use of facilities, and to avoid duplication of services unless the duplication tends to promote the safety and efficiency of air navigation; and

(7) promote and develop meteorological science and foster and support research projects in meteorology through the use of private and governmental research facilities and provide for publishing the results of the projects unless publication would not be in the public interest.

(Pub. L. 103–272, §1(e), July 5, 1994, 108 Stat. 1201; Pub. L. 118–63, title XI, §1101(n), May 16, 2024, 138 Stat. 1414.)

§44721. Aeronautical charts and related products and services

(a) Publication.—

(1) In general.—The Administrator of the Federal Aviation Administration may arrange for the publication of aeronautical maps and charts necessary for the safe and efficient movement of aircraft in air navigation, using the facilities and assistance of departments, agencies, and instrumentalities of the United States Government as far as practicable.

(2) Navigation routes.—In carrying out paragraph (1), the Administrator shall update and arrange for the publication of clearly defined routes for navigating through a complex terminal airspace area and to and from an airport located in such an area, if the Administrator decides that publication of the routes would promote safety in air navigation. The routes shall be developed in consultation with pilots and other users of affected airports and shall be for the optional use of pilots operating under visual flight rules.

(b) Indemnification.—The Government shall make an agreement to indemnify any person that publishes a map or chart for use in aeronautics from any part of a claim arising out of the depiction by the person on the map or chart of a defective or deficient flight procedure or airway if the flight procedure or airway was—

(1) prescribed by the Administrator;

(2) depicted accurately on the map or chart; and

(3) not obviously defective or deficient.

(c) Authority of Office of Aeronautical Charting and Cartography.—Effective October 1, 2000, the Administrator is vested with and shall exercise the functions, powers, and duties of the Secretary of Commerce and other officers of the Department of Commerce that relate to the Office of Aeronautical Charting and Cartography to provide aeronautical charts and related products and services for the safe and efficient navigation of air commerce, under the following authorities:

(1) Sections 1 through 9 of the Act entitled "An Act to define the functions and duties of the Coast and Geodetic Survey, and for other purposes", approved August 6, 1947 (33 U.S.C. 883a–883h).

(2) Section 6082 of the Consolidated Omnibus Budget Reconciliation Act of 1985 (33 U.S.C. 883j).

(d) AUTHORITY.—In order that full public benefit may be derived from the dissemination of data resulting from activities under this section and of related data from other sources, the Administrator may—

(1) develop, process, disseminate and publish digital and analog data, information, compilations, and reports;

(2) compile, print, and disseminate aeronautical charts and related products and services of the United States and its territories and possessions;

(3) compile, print, and disseminate aeronautical charts and related products and services covering international airspace as are required primarily by United States civil aviation; and

(4) compile, print, and disseminate nonaeronautical navigational, transportation or public-safety-related products and services when in the best interests of the Government.

(e) CONTRACTS, COOPERATIVE AGREEMENTS, GRANTS, AND OTHER AGREEMENTS.—

(1) CONTRACTS.—The Administrator is authorized to contract with qualified organizations for the performance of any part of the authorized functions of the Office of Aeronautical Charting and Cartography when the Administrator deems such procedure to be in the public interest and will not compromise public safety.

(2) COOPERATIVE AGREEMENTS, GRANTS, AND OTHER AGREEMENTS.—The Administrator is authorized to enter into cooperative agreements, grants, reimbursable agreements, memoranda of understanding and other agreements, with a State, subdivision of a State, Federal agency, public or private organization, or individual, to carry out the purposes of this section.

(f) SPECIAL SERVICES AND PRODUCTS.—

(1) IN GENERAL.—The Administrator is authorized, at the request of a State, subdivision of a State, Federal agency, public or private organization, or individual, to conduct special services, including making special studies, or developing special publications or products on matters relating to navigation, transportation, or public safety.

(2) FEES.—The Administrator shall assess a fee for any special service provided under paragraph (1). A fee shall be not more than the actual or estimated full cost of the service. A fee may be reduced or waived for research organizations, educational organizations, or non-profit organizations, when the Administrator determines that reduction or waiver of the fee is in the best interest of the Government by furthering public safety.

(g) SALE AND DISSEMINATION OF AERONAUTICAL PRODUCTS.—

(1) IN GENERAL.—Aeronautical products created or maintained under the authority of this section shall be sold at prices established annually by the Administrator consistent with the following:

(A) MAXIMUM PRICE.—Subject to subparagraph (B), the price of an aeronautical product sold to the public shall be not more than necessary to recover all costs attributable to: (i) data base management and processing; (ii) compilation; (iii) printing or other types of reproduction; and (iv) dissemination of the product.

(B) ADJUSTMENT OF PRICE.—The Administrator shall adjust the price of an aeronautical product and service sold to the public as necessary to avoid any adverse impact on aviation safety attributable to the price specified under this paragraph.

(C) COSTS ATTRIBUTABLE TO ACQUISITION OF AERONAUTICAL DATA.—A price established under this paragraph may not include costs attributable to the acquisition of aeronautical data.

(D) CONTINUATION OF PRICES.—The price of any product created under subsection (d) may correspond to the price of a comparable product produced by a department of the United States Government as that price was in effect on September 30, 2000, and may remain in effect until modified by regulation under section 9701 of title 31, United States Code.

(2) PUBLICATION OF PRICES.—The Administrator shall publish annually the prices at which aeronautical products are sold to the public.

(3) DISTRIBUTION.—The Administrator may distribute aeronautical products and provide aeronautical services—

(A) without charge to each foreign government or international organization with which the Administrator or a Federal department or agency has an agreement for exchange of these products or services without cost;

(B) at prices the Administrator establishes, to the departments and officers of the United States requiring them for official use; and

(C) at reduced or no charge where, in the judgment of the Administrator, furnishing the aeronautical product or service to a recipient is a reasonable exchange for voluntary contribution of information by the recipient to the activities under this section.

(4) FEES.—The fees provided for in this subsection are for the purpose of reimbursing the Government for the costs of creating, printing and disseminating aeronautical products and services under this section. The collection of fees authorized by this section does not alter or expand any duty or liability of the Government under existing law for the performance of functions for which fees are collected, nor does the collection of fees constitute an express or implied undertaking by the Government to perform any activity in a certain manner.

(5) CREDITING AMOUNTS RECEIVED.—Notwithstanding any other provision of law, amounts received for the sale of products created and services performed under this section shall be fully credited to the account of the Federal Aviation Administration that funded the provision of the products or services and shall remain available until expended.

(Pub. L. 103–272, §1(e), July 5, 1994, 108 Stat. 1202; Pub. L. 106–181, title VI, §603(a), Apr. 5, 2000, 114 Stat. 150; Pub. L. 106–424, §17(a), Nov. 1, 2000, 114 Stat. 1888; Pub. L. 118–63, title XI, §1101(o), May 16, 2024, 138 Stat. 1414.)

§44722. AIRCRAFT OPERATIONS IN WINTER CONDITIONS

The Administrator of the Federal Aviation Administration shall prescribe regulations requiring procedures to improve safety of aircraft operations during winter conditions. In deciding on the procedures to be required, the Administrator shall consider at least aircraft and air traffic control modifications, the availability of different types of deicing fluids (considering their efficacy and environmental limitations), the types of deicing equipment available, and the feasibility and desirability of establishing timeframes within which deicing must occur under certain types of inclement weather.

(Pub. L. 103–272, §1(e), July 5, 1994, 108 Stat. 1202.)

§44723. ANNUAL REPORT

Not later than January 1 of each year, the Secretary of Transportation shall submit to Congress a comprehensive report on the safety enforcement activities of the Federal Aviation Administration during the fiscal year ending the prior September 30th. The report shall include—

(1) a comparison of end-of-year staffing levels by operations, maintenance, and avionics inspector categories to staffing goals and a statement on how staffing standards were applied to make allocations between air carrier and general aviation operations, maintenance, and avionics inspectors;

(2) schedules showing the range of inspector experience by various inspector work force categories, and the number of inspectors in each of the categories who are considered fully qualified;

(3) schedules showing the number and percentage of inspectors who have received mandatory training by individual course, and the number of inspectors by work force categories, who have received all mandatory training;

(4) a description of the criteria used to set annual work programs, an explanation of how these criteria differ from criteria used in the prior fiscal year and how the annual work programs ensure compliance with appropriate regulations and safe operating practices;

(5) a comparison of actual inspections performed during the fiscal year to the annual work programs by field location and, for any field location completing less than 80 percent of its planned number of inspections, an explanation of why annual work program plans were not met;

(6) a statement of the adequacy of Administration internal management controls available to ensure that field managers comply with Administration policies and procedures, including those on inspector priorities, district office coordination, minimum inspection standards, and inspection followup;

(7) the status of efforts made by the Administration to update inspector guidance documents and regulations to include technological, management, and structural changes taking place in the aviation industry, including a listing of the backlog of all proposed regulatory amendments;

(8) a list of the specific operational measures of effectiveness used to evaluate—

(A) the progress in meeting program objectives;

(B) the quality of program delivery; and

(C) the nature of emerging safety problems;

(9) a schedule showing the number of civil penalty cases closed during the 2 prior fiscal years, including the total initial and final penalties imposed, the total number of

dollars collected, the range of dollar amounts collected, the average case processing time, and the range of case processing time;

(10) a schedule showing the number of enforcement actions taken (except civil penalties) during the 2 prior fiscal years, including the total number of violations cited, and the number of cited violation cases closed by certificate suspensions, certificate revocations, warnings, and no action taken; and

(11) schedules showing the safety record of the aviation industry during the fiscal year for air carriers and general aviation, including—

(A) the number of inspections performed when deficiencies were identified compared with inspections when no deficiencies were found;

(B) the frequency of safety deficiencies for each air carrier; and

(C) an analysis based on data of the general status of air carrier and general aviation compliance with aviation regulations.

(Pub. L. 103–272, §1(e), July 5, 1994, 108 Stat. 1202.)

§44724. MANIPULATION OF FLIGHT CONTROLS

(a) PROHIBITION.—No pilot in command of an aircraft may allow an individual who does not hold—

(1) a valid private pilots certificate issued by the Administrator of the Federal Aviation Administration under part 61 of title 14, Code of Federal Regulations; and

(2) the appropriate medical certificate issued by the Administrator under part 67 of such title,

to manipulate the controls of an aircraft if the pilot knows or should have known that the individual is attempting to set a record or engage in an aeronautical competition or aeronautical feat, as defined by the Administrator.

(b) REVOCATION OF AIRMEN CERTIFICATES.—The Administrator shall issue an order revoking a certificate issued to an airman under section 44703 of this title if the Administrator finds that while acting as a pilot in command of an aircraft, the airman has permitted another individual to manipulate the controls of the aircraft in violation of subsection (a).

(c) PILOT IN COMMAND DEFINED.—In this section, the term "pilot in command" has the meaning given such term by section 1.1 of title 14, Code of Federal Regulations.

(Added Pub. L. 104–264, title VI, §602(a)(1), Oct. 9, 1996, 110 Stat. 3263.)

§44725. LIFE-LIMITED AIRCRAFT PARTS

(a) IN GENERAL.—The Administrator of the Federal Aviation Administration shall conduct a rulemaking proceeding to require the safe disposition of life-limited parts removed from an aircraft. The rulemaking proceeding shall ensure that the disposition deter installation on an aircraft of a life-limited part that has reached or exceeded its life limits.

(b) SAFE DISPOSITION.—For the purposes of this section, safe disposition includes any of the following methods:

(1) The part may be segregated under circumstances that preclude its installation on an aircraft.

(2) The part may be permanently marked to indicate its used life status.

(3) The part may be destroyed in any manner calculated to prevent reinstallation in an aircraft.

(4) The part may be marked, if practicable, to include the recordation of hours, cycles, or other airworthiness information. If the parts are marked with cycles or hours of usage, that information must be updated every time the part is removed from service or when the part is retired from service.

(5) Any other method approved by the Administrator.

(c) DEADLINES.—In conducting the rulemaking proceeding under subsection (a), the Administrator shall—

(1) not later than 180 days after the date of the enactment of this section, issue a notice of proposed rulemaking; and

(2) not later than 180 days after the close of the comment period on the proposed rule, issue a final rule.

(d) PRIOR-REMOVED LIFE-LIMITED PARTS.—No rule issued under subsection (a) shall require the marking of parts removed from aircraft before the effective date of the rules issued under subsection (a), nor shall any such rule forbid the installation of an otherwise airworthy life-limited part.

(Added Pub. L. 106–181, title V, §504(a), Apr. 5, 2000, 114 Stat. 134.)

§44726. DENIAL AND REVOCATION OF CERTIFICATE FOR COUNTERFEIT PARTS VIOLATIONS

(a) DENIAL OF CERTIFICATE.—

(1) IN GENERAL.—Except as provided in paragraph (2) of this subsection and subsection (e)(2), the Administrator of the Federal Aviation Administration may not issue a certificate under this chapter to any person—

(A) convicted in a court of law of a violation of a law of the United States relating to the installation, production, repair, or sale of a counterfeit or fraudulently-represented aviation part or material;

(B) whose certificate is revoked under subsection (b); or

(C) subject to a controlling or ownership interest of an individual described in subparagraph (A) or (B).

(2) EXCEPTION.—Notwithstanding paragraph (1), the Administrator may issue a certificate under this chapter to a person described in paragraph (1) if issuance of the certificate will facilitate law enforcement efforts.

(b) REVOCATION OF CERTIFICATE.—

(1) IN GENERAL.—Except as provided in subsections (f) and (g), the Administrator shall issue an order revoking a certificate issued under this chapter if the Administrator finds that the holder of the certificate or an individual who has a controlling or ownership interest in the holder—

(A) was convicted in a court of law of a violation of a law of the United States relating to the installation, production, repair, or sale of a counterfeit or fraudulently-represented aviation part or material; or

(B) knowingly, and with the intent to defraud, carried out or facilitated an activity punishable under a law described in paragraph (1)(A).

(2) NO AUTHORITY TO REVIEW VIOLATION.—In carrying out paragraph (1), the

Administrator may not review whether a person violated a law described in paragraph (1)(A).

(c) NOTICE REQUIREMENT.—Before the Administrator revokes a certificate under subsection (b), the Administrator shall—

(1) advise the holder of the certificate of the reason for the revocation; and

(2) provide the holder of the certificate an opportunity to be heard on why the certificate should not be revoked.

(d) APPEAL.—The provisions of section 44710(d) apply to the appeal of a revocation order under subsection (b). For the purpose of applying that section to the appeal, "person" shall be substituted for "individual" each place it appears.

(e) ACQUITTAL OR REVERSAL.—

(1) IN GENERAL.—The Administrator may not revoke, and the National Transportation Safety Board may not affirm a revocation of, a certificate under subsection (b)(1)(B) if the holder of the certificate or the individual referred to in subsection (b)(1) is acquitted of all charges directly related to the violation.

(2) REISSUANCE.—The Administrator may reissue a certificate revoked under subsection (b) of this section to the former holder if—

(A) the former holder otherwise satisfies the requirements of this chapter for the certificate; and

(B)(i) the former holder or the individual referred to in subsection (b)(1), is acquitted of all charges related to the violation on which the revocation was based; or

(ii) the conviction of the former holder or such individual of the violation on which the revocation was based is reversed.

(f) WAIVER.—The Administrator may waive revocation of a certificate under subsection (b) if—

(1) a law enforcement official of the United States Government requests a waiver; and

(2) the waiver will facilitate law enforcement efforts.

(g) AMENDMENT OF CERTIFICATE.—If the holder of a certificate issued under this chapter is other than an individual and the Administrator finds that—

(1) an individual who had a controlling or ownership interest in the holder committed a violation of a law for the violation of which a certificate may be revoked under this section or knowingly, and with intent to defraud, carried out or facilitated an activity punishable under such a law; and

(2) the holder satisfies the requirements for the certificate without regard to that individual,

then the Administrator may amend the certificate to impose a limitation that the certificate will not be valid if that individual has a controlling or ownership interest in the holder. A decision by the Administrator under this subsection is not reviewable by the Board.

(Added Pub. L. 106–181, title V, §505(a)(1), Apr. 5, 2000, 114 Stat. 134; amended Pub. L. 108–176, title V, §501, Dec. 12, 2003, 117 Stat. 2556.)

§44727. RUNWAY SAFETY AREAS

(a) AIRPORTS IN ALASKA.—An airport owner or operator in the State of Alaska shall not be required to reduce the length of a runway or declare the length of a runway to be less than the actual pavement length in order to meet standards of the Federal Aviation Administration applicable to runway safety areas.

(b) STUDY.—

(1) IN GENERAL.—The Secretary shall conduct a study of runways at airports in States other than Alaska to determine which airports are affected by standards of the Federal Aviation Administration applicable to runway safety areas and to assess how operations at those airports would be affected if the owner or operator of the airport is required to reduce the length of a runway or declare the length of a runway to be less than the actual pavement length in order to meet such standards.

(2) REPORT.—Not later than 9 months after the date of enactment of this section, the Secretary shall transmit to the Committee on Commerce, Science, and Transportation of the Senate and the Committee on Transportation and Infrastructure of the House of Representatives a report containing the results of the study.

(Added Pub. L. 108–176, title V, §502(a), Dec. 12, 2003, 117 Stat. 2557.)

§44728. FLIGHT ATTENDANT CERTIFICATION

(a) CERTIFICATE REQUIRED.—

(1) IN GENERAL.—No person may serve as a flight attendant aboard an aircraft of an air carrier unless that person holds a certificate of demonstrated proficiency from the Administrator of the Federal Aviation Administration. Upon the request of the Administrator or an authorized representative of the National Transportation Safety Board or another Federal agency, a person who holds such a certificate shall present the certificate for inspection within a reasonable period of time after the date of the request.

(2) SPECIAL RULE FOR CURRENT FLIGHT ATTENDANTS.—An individual serving as a flight attendant on the effective date of this section may continue to serve aboard an aircraft as a flight attendant until completion by that individual of the required recurrent or requalification training and subsequent certification under this section.

(3) TREATMENT OF FLIGHT ATTENDANT AFTER NOTIFICATION.—On the date that the Administrator is notified by an air carrier that an individual has the demonstrated proficiency to be a flight attendant, the individual shall be treated for purposes of this section as holding a certificate issued under the section.

(b) ISSUANCE OF CERTIFICATE.—The Administrator shall issue a certificate of demonstrated proficiency under this section to an individual after the Administrator is notified by the air carrier that the individual has successfully completed all the training requirements for flight attendants approved by the Administrator.

(c) DESIGNATION OF PERSON TO DETERMINE SUCCESSFUL COMPLETION OF TRAINING.—In accordance with part 183 of title 14, Code of Federal Regulations, the director of operations of an air carrier is designated to determine that an individual has successfully completed the training requirements approved by the Administrator for such individual to serve as a flight attendant.

(d) SPECIFICATIONS RELATING TO CERTIFICATES.—Each certificate issued under this section shall—

(1) be numbered and recorded by the Administrator;

(2) contain the name, address, and description of the individual to whom the certificate is issued;

(3) be similar in size and appearance to certificates issued to airmen;

(4) contain the airplane group for which the certificate is issued; and

(5) be issued not later than 120 days after the Administrator receives notification from the air carrier of demonstrated proficiency and, in the case of an individual serving as flight attendant on the effective date of this section, not later than 1 year after such effective date.

(e) APPROVAL OF TRAINING PROGRAMS.—Air carrier flight attendant training programs shall be subject to approval by the Administrator. All flight attendant training programs approved by the Administrator in the 1-year period ending on the date of enactment of this section shall be treated as providing a demonstrated proficiency for purposes of meeting the certification requirements of this section.

(f) MINIMUM LANGUAGE SKILLS.—

(1) IN GENERAL.—No person may serve as a flight attendant aboard an aircraft of an air carrier, unless that person has demonstrated to an individual qualified to determine proficiency the ability to read, speak, and write English well enough to—

(A) read material written in English and comprehend the information;

(B) speak and understand English sufficiently to provide direction to, and understand and answer questions from, English-speaking individuals;

(C) write incident reports and statements and log entries and statements; and

(D) carry out written and oral instructions regarding the proper performance of their duties.

(2) FOREIGN FLIGHTS.—The requirements of paragraph (1) do not apply to a flight attendant serving solely between points outside the United States.

(g) FLIGHT ATTENDANT DEFINED.—In this section, the term "flight attendant" means an individual working as a flight attendant in the cabin of an aircraft that has 20 or more seats and is being used by an air carrier to provide air transportation.

(Added Pub. L. 108–176, title VIII, §814(a), Dec. 12, 2003, 117 Stat. 2590; amended Pub. L. 112–95, title III, §304(a), Feb. 14, 2012, 126 Stat. 58; Pub. L. 115–254, div. B, title V, §539(i), Oct. 5, 2018, 132 Stat. 3371; Pub. L. 118–63, title XI, §1101(p), May 16, 2024, 138 Stat. 1414.)

§44729. AGE STANDARDS FOR PILOTS

(a) IN GENERAL.—Subject to the limitation in subsection (c), a pilot may serve in multicrew covered operations described in subsection (b)(1) until attaining 65 years of age. Air carriers that employ pilots who serve in covered operations described in subsection (b)(2) may elect to implement an age restriction to prohibit employed pilots from serving in such covered operations after attaining 70 years of age by delivering written notice to the Administrator of the Federal Aviation Administration. Such election—

(1) shall take effect 1 year after the date of delivery of written notice of the election; and

(2) may not be terminated after the date on which such election takes effect by the air carrier.

(b) COVERED OPERATIONS DEFINED.—In this section, the term "covered operations" means—

(1) operations under part 121 of title 14, Code of Federal Regulations; or

(2) operations by a person that—

(A) holds an air carrier certificate issued pursuant to part 119 of title 14, Code of Federal Regulations, to conduct operations under part 135 of such title;

(B) holds management specifications under subpart K of title 91 of title 14, Code of Federal Regulations; and

(C) performed an aggregate total of at least 75,000 turbojet operations in calendar year 2019 or any subsequent year.

(c) LIMITATION FOR INTERNATIONAL FLIGHTS.—

(1) APPLICABILITY OF ICAO STANDARD.—A pilot who has attained 60 years of age may serve as pilot-in-command in covered operations between the United States and another country only if there is another pilot in the flight deck crew who has not yet attained 60 years of age.

(2) SUNSET OF LIMITATION.—Paragraph (1) shall cease to be effective on such date as the Convention on International Civil Aviation provides that a pilot who has attained 60 years of age may serve as pilot-in-command in international commercial operations without regard to whether there is another pilot in the flight deck crew who has not attained age 60.

(d) SUNSET OF AGE 60 RETIREMENT RULE.—On and after the date of enactment of this section, section 121.383(c) of title 14, Code of Federal Regulations, shall cease to be effective.

(e) APPLICABILITY.—

(1) NONRETROACTIVITY.—No person who has attained 60 years of age before the date of enactment of this section may serve as a pilot for an air carrier engaged in covered operations unless—

(A) such person is in the employment of that air carrier in such operations on such date of enactment as a required flight deck crew member; or

(B) such person is newly hired by an air carrier as a pilot on or after such date of enactment without credit for prior seniority or prior longevity for benefits or other terms related to length of service prior to the date of rehire under any labor agreement or employment policies of the air carrier.

(2) PROTECTION FOR COMPLIANCE.—An action taken in conformance with this section, taken in conformance with a regulation issued to carry out this section, or taken prior to the date of enactment of this section in conformance with section 121.383(c) of title 14, Code of Federal Regulations (as in effect before such date of enactment), may not serve as a basis for liability or relief in a proceeding, brought under any employment law or regulation, before any court or agency of the United States or of any State or locality.

(f) AMENDMENTS TO LABOR AGREEMENTS AND BENEFIT PLANS.—Any amendment to a labor agreement or benefit plan of an air carrier that is required to conform with the requirements of this section or a regulation issued to carry out this section, and is applicable to pilots represented for collective bargaining, shall be made by agreement of the air carrier and the designated bargaining representative of the pilots of the air carrier.

(g) MEDICAL STANDARDS AND RECORDS.—

(1) MEDICAL EXAMINATIONS AND STANDARDS.—Except as provided by paragraph (2), a person serving as a pilot for an air carrier engaged in covered operations shall not be subject to different medical standards, or different, greater, or more frequent medical examinations, on account of age unless the Secretary determines (based on data received

or studies published after the date of enactment of this section) that different medical standards, or different, greater, or more frequent medical examinations, are needed to ensure an adequate level of safety in flight.

(2) DURATION OF FIRST-CLASS MEDICAL CERTIFICATE.—No person who has attained 60 years of age may serve as a pilot of an air carrier engaged in covered operations unless the person has a first-class medical certificate. Such a certificate shall expire on the last day of the 6-month period following the date of examination shown on the certificate.

(h) SAFETY.—

(1) TRAINING.—Each air carrier engaged in covered operations shall continue to use pilot training and qualification programs approved by the Federal Aviation Administration, with specific emphasis on initial and recurrent training and qualification of pilots who have attained 60 years of age, to ensure continued acceptable levels of pilot skill and judgment.

(2) GAO REPORT.—Not later than 24 months after the date of enactment of this section, the Comptroller General shall submit to the Committee on Transportation and Infrastructure of the House of Representatives and the Committee on Commerce, Science, and Transportation of the Senate a report concerning the effect, if any, on aviation safety of the modification to pilot age standards made by subsection (a).

(Added Pub. L. 110–135, §2(a), Dec. 13, 2007, 121 Stat. 1450; amended Pub. L. 112–95, title III, §305, Feb. 14, 2012, 126 Stat. 58; Pub. L. 117–328, div. Q, §107(a), (b), Dec. 29, 2022, 136 Stat. 5257, 5258.)

§44730. HELICOPTER AIR AMBULANCE OPERATIONS

(a) COMPLIANCE REGULATIONS.—

(1) IN GENERAL.—Except as provided in paragraph (2), a part 135 certificate holder providing air ambulance services shall comply, whenever medical personnel are onboard the aircraft, with regulations pertaining to weather minimums and flight and duty time under part 135.

(2) EXCEPTION.—If a certificate holder described in paragraph (1) is operating, or carrying out training, under instrument flight rules, the weather reporting requirement at the destination shall not apply if authorized by the Administrator of the Federal Aviation Administration.

(b) FINAL RULE.—Not later than June 1, 2012, the Administrator shall issue a final rule, with respect to the notice of proposed rulemaking published in the Federal Register on October 12, 2010 (75 Fed. Reg. 62640), to improve the safety of flight crewmembers, medical personnel, and passengers onboard helicopters providing air ambulance services under part 135.

(c) MATTERS TO BE ADDRESSED.—In conducting the rulemaking proceeding under subsection (b), the Administrator shall consider, or address through other means, the following:

(1) Flight request and dispatch procedures, including performance-based flight dispatch procedures.

(2) Pilot training standards, including establishment of training standards in—

(A) preventing controlled flight into terrain; and

(B) recovery from inadvertent flight into instrument meteorological conditions.

(3) Safety-enhancing technology and equipment, including—

(A) helicopter terrain awareness and warning systems;

(B) radar altimeters; and

(C) devices that perform the function of flight data recorders and cockpit voice recorders, to the extent feasible.

(4) Such other matters as the Administrator considers appropriate.

(d) MINIMUM REQUIREMENTS.—In issuing a final rule under subsection (b), the Administrator, at a minimum, shall consider, or address through other means, the following:

(1) FLIGHT RISK EVALUATION PROGRAM.—The Administrator shall ensure that a part 135 certificate holder providing helicopter air ambulance services—

(A) establishes a flight risk evaluation program, based on FAA Notice 8000.301 issued by the Administration on August 1, 2005, including any updates thereto;

(B) as part of the flight risk evaluation program, develops a checklist for use by pilots in determining whether a flight request should be accepted; and

(C) requires the pilots of the certificate holder to use the checklist.

(2) OPERATIONAL CONTROL CENTER.—The Administrator shall ensure that a part 135 certificate holder providing helicopter air ambulance services using 10 or more helicopters has an operational control center that meets such requirements as the Administrator may prescribe.

(e) SUBSEQUENT ACTIONS.—

(1) IN GENERAL.—Upon completion of the rulemaking required under subsection (b), the Administrator shall address through a follow-on rulemaking, or through such other means that the Administrator considers appropriate, the following:

(A) Pilot training standards, including—

(i) mandatory training requirements, including a minimum time for completing the training requirements;

(ii) training subject areas, such as communications procedures and appropriate technology use; and

(iii) establishment of training standards in—

(I) crew resource management;

(II) flight risk evaluation;

(III) operational control of the pilot in command; and

(IV) use of flight simulation training devices and line-oriented flight training.

(B) Use of safety equipment that should be worn or used by flight crewmembers and medical personnel on a flight, including the possible use of shoulder harnesses, helmets, seatbelts, and fire resistant clothing to enhance crash survivability.

(2) LIMITATION ON CONSTRUCTION.—Nothing in this subsection shall be construed to require the Administrator to propose or finalize any rule that would derogate or supersede the rule required to be finalized under subsection (b).

(f) DEFINITIONS.—In this section, the following definitions apply:

(1) PART 135.—The term "part 135" means part 135 of title 14, Code of Federal Regulations.

(2) PART 135 CERTIFICATE HOLDER.—The term "part 135 certificate holder" means a person holding an operating certificate issued under part 119 of title 14, Code of Federal Regulations, that is authorized to conduct civil helicopter air ambulance operations under part 135.

(Added Pub. L. 112–95, title III, §306(a), Feb. 14, 2012, 126 Stat. 58; amended Pub. L. 118–63, title III, §301(a), May 16, 2024, 138 Stat. 1066.)

§44731. COLLECTION OF DATA ON HELICOPTER AIR AMBULANCE OPERATIONS

(a) IN GENERAL.—The Administrator of the Federal Aviation Administration shall require a part 135 certificate holder providing helicopter air ambulance services to submit to the Administrator, annually, a report containing, at a minimum, the following data:

(1) The number of helicopters that the certificate holder uses to provide helicopter air ambulance services and the base locations of the helicopters.

(2) The number of hours flown by the helicopters operated by the certificate holder.

(3) The number of patients transported and the number of patient transport requests for a helicopter providing air ambulance services that were accepted or declined by the certificate holder and the type of each such flight request (such as scene response, interfacility transport, or organ transport).

(4) The number of accidents, if any, involving helicopters operated by the certificate holder while providing air ambulance services and a description of the accidents.

(5) The number of hours flown under instrument flight rules by helicopters operated by the certificate holder.

(6) The number of hours flown at night by helicopters operated by the certificate holder.

(7) The number of incidents, if any, in which a helicopter was not directly dispatched and arrived to transport patients but was not utilized for patient transport.

(b) REPORTING PERIOD.—Data contained in a report submitted by a part 135 certificate holder under subsection (a) shall relate to such reporting period as the Administrator determines appropriate.

(c) DATABASE.—Not later than 180 days after the date of enactment of this section, the Administrator shall develop a method to collect and store the data collected under subsection (a), including a method to protect the confidentiality of any trade secret or proprietary information provided in response to this section.

(d) IMPLEMENTATION.—In carrying out this section, the Administrator, in collaboration with part 135 certificate holders providing helicopter air ambulance services, shall—

(1) propose and develop a method to collect and store the data submitted under subsection (a), including a method to protect the confidentiality of any trade secret or proprietary information submitted;

(2) make publicly available, in part or in whole, on a website of the Federal Aviation Administration, the database developed pursuant to subsection (c); and

(3) analyze the data submitted under subsection (a) periodically and use such data to inform efforts to improve the safety of helicopter air ambulance operations.

(e) DEFINITIONS.—In this section, the terms "part 135" and "part 135 certificate holder" have the meanings given such terms in section 44730.

(Added Pub. L. 112–95, title III, §306(a), Feb. 14, 2012, 126 Stat. 60; amended Pub. L. 115–254, div. B, title III, §314(d), Oct. 5, 2018, 132 Stat. 3266; Pub. L. 118–63, title III, §301(c), May 16, 2024, 138 Stat. 1066.)

§44732. Prohibition on personal use of electronic devices on flight deck

(a) IN GENERAL.—It is unlawful for a flight crewmember of an aircraft used to provide air transportation under part 121 of title 14, Code of Federal Regulations, to use a personal wireless communications device or laptop computer while at the flight crewmember's duty station on the flight deck of such an aircraft while the aircraft is being operated.

(b) EXCEPTIONS.—Subsection (a) shall not apply to the use of a personal wireless communications device or laptop computer for a purpose directly related to operation of the aircraft, or for emergency, safety-related, or employment-related communications, in accordance with procedures established by the air carrier and the Administrator of the Federal Aviation Administration.

(c) ENFORCEMENT.—In addition to the penalties provided under section 46301 applicable to any violation of this section, the Administrator of the Federal Aviation Administration may enforce compliance with this section under section 44709 by amending, modifying, suspending, or revoking a certificate under this chapter.

(d) PERSONAL WIRELESS COMMUNICATIONS DEVICE DEFINED.—In this section, the term "personal wireless communications device" means a device through which personal wireless services (as defined in section 332(c)(7)(C)(i) of the Communications Act of 1934 (47 U.S.C. 332(c)(7)(C)(i))) are transmitted.

(Added Pub. L. 112–95, title III, §307(a), Feb. 14, 2012, 126 Stat. 61.)

§44733. Oversight of repair stations located outside the United States

(a) IN GENERAL.—The Administrator of the Federal Aviation Administration shall establish and implement a safety assessment system for all part 145 repair stations based on the type, scope, and complexity of work being performed. The system shall—

(1) ensure that repair stations located outside the United States are subject to appropriate inspections based on identified risks and consistent with existing United States requirements;

(2) consider inspection results and findings submitted by foreign civil aviation authorities operating under a maintenance safety or maintenance implementation agreement with the United States; and

(3) require all maintenance safety or maintenance implementation agreements to provide an opportunity for the Administration to conduct independent inspections of part 145 repair stations when safety concerns warrant such inspections.

(b) NOTICE TO CONGRESS OF NEGOTIATIONS.—The Administrator shall notify the Committee on Commerce, Science, and Transportation of the Senate and the Committee on Transportation and Infrastructure of the House of Representatives not later than 30 days after initiating formal negotiations with foreign aviation authorities or other appropriate foreign government agencies on a new maintenance safety or maintenance implementation agreement.

(c) ANNUAL REPORT.—The Administrator shall publish an annual report on the Administration's oversight of part 145 repair stations and implementation of the safety assessment system required under subsection (a). The report shall—

(1) describe in detail any improvements in the Administration's ability to identify and track where part 121 air carrier repair work is performed;

(2) include a staffing model to determine the best placement of inspectors and the number of inspectors needed;

(3) describe the training provided to inspectors; and

(4) include an assessment of the quality of monitoring and surveillance by the Administration of work performed by its inspectors and the inspectors of foreign authorities operating under a maintenance safety or maintenance implementation agreement.

(d) ALCOHOL AND CONTROLLED SUBSTANCES TESTING PROGRAM REQUIREMENTS.—

(1) IN GENERAL.—The Secretary of State and the Secretary of Transportation, acting jointly, shall request the governments of foreign countries that are members of the International Civil Aviation Organization to establish international standards for alcohol and controlled substances testing of persons that perform safety-sensitive maintenance functions on commercial air carrier aircraft.

(2) APPLICATION TO PART 121 AIRCRAFT WORK.—Not later than 1 year after the date of enactment of this section, the Administrator shall promulgate a proposed rule requiring that all part 145 repair station employees responsible for safety-sensitive maintenance functions on part 121 air carrier aircraft are subject to an alcohol and controlled substances testing program determined acceptable by the Administrator and consistent with the applicable laws of the country in which the repair station is located.

(e) ANNUAL INSPECTIONS.—The Administrator shall ensure that part 145 repair stations located outside the United States are inspected annually, without prior notice to such repair stations, by Federal Aviation Administration safety inspectors, without regard to where the station is located, in a manner consistent with United States obligations under international agreements and the applicable laws of the country in which the repair station is located. The Administrator may carry out announced or unannounced inspections in addition to the annual unannounced inspection required under this subsection based on identified risks and in a manner consistent with United States obligations under international agreements and the applicable laws of the country in which the part 145 repair station is located.

(f) RISK-BASED OVERSIGHT.—

(1) IN GENERAL.—Not later than 90 days after the date of enactment of the FAA Extension, Safety, and Security Act of 2016, the Administrator shall take measures to ensure that the safety assessment system established under subsection (a)—

(A) places particular consideration on inspections of part 145 repair stations located outside the United States that conduct scheduled heavy maintenance work on part 121 air carrier aircraft; and

(B) accounts for the frequency and seriousness of any corrective actions that part 121 air carriers must implement to aircraft following such work at such repair stations.

(2) INTERNATIONAL AGREEMENTS.—The Administrator shall take the measures required under paragraph (1)—

(A) in accordance with United States obligations under applicable international agreements; and

(B) in a manner consistent with the applicable laws of the country in which a repair station is located.

(3) ACCESS TO DATA.—The Administrator may access and review such information or data in the possession of a part 121 air carrier as the Administrator may require in carrying out paragraph (1)(B).

(g) DATA ANALYSIS.—

(1) IN GENERAL.—Each fiscal year in which a part 121 air carrier has had heavy maintenance work performed on an aircraft owned or operated by such carrier, such carrier shall provide to the Administrator, not later than the end of the following fiscal year, a report containing the information described in paragraph (2).

(2) INFORMATION REQUIRED.—A report under paragraph (1) shall contain the following:

(A) The location where any heavy maintenance work on aircraft was performed outside the United States.

(B) A description of the work performed at each such location.

(C) The date of completion of the work performed at each such location.

(D) A list of all failures, malfunctions, or defects affecting the safe operation of such aircraft identified by the air carrier not later than 30 days after the date on which an aircraft is returned to service, organized by reference to aircraft registration number, that—

(i) requires corrective action after the aircraft is approved for return to service; and

(ii) results from such work performed on such aircraft.

(E) The certificate number of the person approving such aircraft or on-wing aircraft engine for return to service following completion of the work performed at each such location.

(3) ANALYSIS.—The Administrator shall—

(A) analyze information provided under this subsection and sections 121.703, 121.705, 121.707, and 145.221 of title 14, Code of Federal Regulations, or any successor provisions of such title, to detect safety issues associated with heavy maintenance work on aircraft performed outside the United States; and

(B) require appropriate actions by an air carrier or repair station in response to any safety issue identified by the analysis conducted under subparagraph (A).

(4) CONFIDENTIALITY.—Information provided under this subsection shall be subject to the same protections given to voluntarily provided safety or security related information under section 40123.

(h) APPLICATIONS AND PROHIBITION.—

(1) IN GENERAL.—The Administrator may not approve any new application under part 145 of title 14, Code of Federal Regulations, from a person located or headquartered in a country that the Administration, through the International Aviation Safety Assessment program, has classified as Category 2.

(2) EXCEPTION.—Paragraph (1) shall not apply to an application for the renewal of a certificate issued under part 145 of title 14, Code of Federal Regulations.

(3) MAINTENANCE IMPLEMENTATION PROCEDURES AGREEMENT.—The Administrator may elect not to enter into a new maintenance implementation procedures agreement with a country classified as Category 2, for as long as the country remains classified as Category 2.

(4) PROHIBITION ON CONTINUED HEAVY MAINTENANCE WORK.—No part 121 air carrier may enter into a new contract for heavy maintenance work with a person located or headquartered in a country that the Administrator, through the International Aviation Safety Assessment program, has classified as Category 2, for as long as such country remains classified as Category 2.

(i) MINIMUM QUALIFICATIONS FOR MECHANICS AND OTHERS WORKING ON U.S. REGISTERED AIRCRAFT.—

(1) IN GENERAL.—Not later than 18 months after the date of enactment of this subsection, the Administrator shall require that, at each covered repair station—

(A) all supervisory personnel of such station are appropriately certificated as a mechanic or repairman under part 65 of title 14, Code of Federal Regulations, or under an equivalent certification or licensing regime, as determined by the Administrator; and

(B) all personnel of such station authorized to approve an article for return to service are appropriately certificated as a mechanic or repairman under part 65 of such title, or under an equivalent certification or licensing regime, as determined by the Administrator.

(2) AVAILABLE FOR CONSULTATION.—Not later than 18 months after the date of enactment of this subsection, the Administrator shall require any individual who is responsible for approving an article for return to service or who is directly in charge of heavy maintenance work performed on aircraft operated by a part 121 air carrier be available for consultation while work is being performed at a covered repair station.

(j) DEFINITIONS.—In this section, the following definitions apply:

(1) COVERED REPAIR STATION.—The term "covered repair station" means a facility that—

(A) is located outside the United States;

(B) is a part 145 repair station; and

(C) performs heavy maintenance work on aircraft operated by a part 121 air carrier.

(2) HEAVY MAINTENANCE WORK.—The term "heavy maintenance work" means a C-check, a D-check, or equivalent maintenance operation with respect to the airframe of a transport-category aircraft (including on-wing aircraft engines).

(3) PART 121 AIR CARRIER.—The term "part 121 air carrier" means an air carrier that holds a certificate issued under part 121 of title 14, Code of Federal Regulations.

(4) PART 145 REPAIR STATION.—The term "part 145 repair station" means a repair station that holds a certificate issued under part 145 of title 14, Code of Federal Regulations.

(Added Pub. L. 112–95, title III, §308(a), Feb. 14, 2012, 126 Stat. 62; amended Pub. L. 114–190, title II, §2112(a), July 15, 2016, 130 Stat. 627; Pub. L. 118–63, title III, §302(a)(1), (2), May 16, 2024, 138 Stat. 1067, 1069.)

§44734. TRAINING OF FLIGHT ATTENDANTS

(a) TRAINING REQUIRED.—In addition to other training required under this chapter, each air carrier shall provide to flight attendants employed or contracted by such air carrier initial and annual training regarding—

(1) serving alcohol to passengers;

(2) recognizing intoxicated passengers;

(3) dealing with disruptive passengers; and

(4) recognizing and responding to potential human trafficking victims.

(b) SITUATIONAL TRAINING.—In carrying out the training required under subsection (a), each air carrier shall provide to flight attendants situational training on the proper method for dealing with intoxicated passengers who act in a belligerent manner.

(c) DEFINITIONS.—In this section, the following definitions apply:

(1) AIR CARRIER.—The term "air carrier" means a person, including a commercial enterprise, that has been issued an air carrier operating certificate under section 44705.

(2) FLIGHT ATTENDANT.—The term "flight attendant" has the meaning given that term in section 44728(g).

(Added Pub. L. 112–95, title III, §309(a), Feb. 14, 2012, 126 Stat. 64; amended Pub. L. 114–190, title II, §2113, July 15, 2016, 130 Stat. 628.)

§44735. LIMITATION ON DISCLOSURE OF SAFETY INFORMATION

(a) IN GENERAL.—Except as provided by subsection (c), a report, data, or other information described in subsection (b) shall not be disclosed to the public by the Administrator of the Federal Aviation Administration pursuant to section 552(b)(3)(B) of title 5—

(1) if the report, data, or other information is submitted to the Federal Aviation Administration voluntarily and is not required to be submitted to the Administrator under any other provision of law;

(2) if the report, data, or other information is submitted to the Federal Aviation Administration pursuant to section 102(e) of the Aircraft Certification, Safety, and Accountability Act; or

(3) if the report, data, or other information is submitted for any purpose relating to the development and implementation of a safety management system, including a system required by regulation.

(b) APPLICABILITY.—The limitation established by subsection (a) shall apply to the following:

(1) Reports, data, or other information developed under the Aviation Safety Action Program.

(2) Reports, data, or other information produced or collected under the Flight Operational Quality Assurance Program.

(3) Reports, data, or other information developed under the Line Operations Safety Audit Program.

(4) Reports, data, or other information produced or collected for purposes of developing and implementing a safety management system acceptable to the Administrator.

(5) Reports, analyses, and directed studies, based in whole or in part on reports, data, or other information described in paragraphs (1) through (4), including those prepared under the Aviation Safety Information Analysis and Sharing Program (or any successor program).

(c) EXCEPTION FOR DE-IDENTIFIED INFORMATION.—

(1) IN GENERAL.—The limitation established by subsection (a) shall not apply to a

report, data, or other information if the information contained in the report, data, or other information has been de-identified.

(2) DE-IDENTIFIED DEFINED.—In this subsection, the term "de-identified" means the process by which all information that is likely to establish the identity of the specific persons or entities submitting reports, data, or other information is removed from the reports, data, or other information.

(d) OTHER AGENCIES.—

(1) IN GENERAL.—The limitation established under subsection (a) shall apply to the head of any other Federal agency who receives reports, data, or other information described in such subsection from the Administrator.

(2) RULE OF CONSTRUCTION.—This section shall not be construed to limit the accident or incident investigation authority of the National Transportation Safety Board under chapter 11, including the requirement to not disclose voluntarily provided safety-related information under section 1114.

(Added Pub. L. 112–95, title III, §310(a), Feb. 14, 2012, 126 Stat. 64; amended Pub. L. 116–260, div. V, title I, §102(g), Dec. 27, 2020, 134 Stat. 2311; Pub. L. 118–63, title III, §305, May 16, 2024, 138 Stat. 1071.)

§44736. ORGANIZATION DESIGNATION AUTHORIZATIONS

(a) DELEGATIONS OF FUNCTIONS.—

(1) IN GENERAL.—Except as provided in paragraph (3), when overseeing an ODA holder, the Administrator of the FAA shall—

(A) require, based on an application submitted by the ODA holder and approved by the Administrator (or the Administrator's designee), a procedures manual that addresses all procedures and limitations regarding the functions to be performed by the ODA holder; and

(B) conduct regular oversight activities by inspecting the ODA holder's delegated functions and taking action based on validated inspection findings.

(2) DUTIES OF ODA HOLDERS.—An ODA holder shall—

(A) perform each specified function delegated to the ODA holder in accordance with the approved procedures manual for the delegation;

(B) make the procedures manual available to each member of the appropriate ODA unit; and

(C) cooperate fully with oversight activities conducted by the Administrator in connection with the delegation.

(3) EXISTING ODA HOLDERS.—With regard to an ODA holder operating under a procedures manual approved by the Administrator before the date of enactment of the FAA Reauthorization Act of 2018, the Administrator shall conduct regular oversight activities by inspecting the ODA holder's delegated functions and taking action based on validated inspection findings.

(b) ODA OFFICE.—

(1) ESTABLISHMENT.—The Administrator of the FAA shall identify, within the FAA Office of Aviation Safety, a centralized policy office to be known as the Organization Designation Authorization Office or the ODA Office.

(2) PURPOSE.—The purpose of the ODA Office shall be to provide oversight and ensure the consistency of the FAA's audit functions under the ODA program across the

FAA.

(3) FUNCTIONS.—The ODA Office shall—

(A)(i) require, as appropriate, an ODA holder to establish a corrective action plan to regain authority for any retained limitations;

(ii) require, as appropriate, an ODA holder to notify the ODA Office when all corrective actions have been accomplished; and

(iii) when appropriate, make a reassessment to determine if subsequent performance in carrying out any retained limitation warrants continued retention and, if such reassessment determines performance meets objectives, lift such limitation immediately;

(B) develop a more consistent approach to audit priorities, procedures, and training under the ODA program;

(C) review, in a timely fashion, a random sample of limitations on delegated authorities under the ODA program to determine if the limitations are appropriate;

(D) ensure national consistency in the interpretation and application of the requirements of the ODA program, including any limitations, and in the performance of the ODA program;

(E) at the request of an ODA holder, review and, when appropriate, approve new limitations to ODA functions;

(F) ensure the ODA holders procedures manual contains procedures and policies based on best practices established by the Administrator; and

(G) convene a forum not less than every 2 years between ODA holders, unit members, and other organizational representatives and relevant experts, in order to—

(i) share best practices;

(ii) instill professionalism, ethics, and personal responsibilities in unit members; and

(iii) foster open and transparent communication between Administration safety specialists, ODA holders, and unit members.

(c) DEFINITIONS.—In this section, the following definitions apply:

(1) FAA.—The term "FAA" means the Federal Aviation Administration.

(2) ODA HOLDER.—The term "ODA holder" means an entity authorized to perform functions pursuant to a delegation made by the Administrator of the FAA under section 44702(d).

(3) ODA UNIT.—The term "ODA unit" means a group of 2 or more individuals who perform, under the supervision of an ODA holder, authorized functions under an ODA.

(4) ORGANIZATION.—The term "organization" means a firm, partnership, corporation, company, association, joint-stock association, or governmental entity.

(5) ORGANIZATION DESIGNATION AUTHORIZATION; ODA.—The term "Organization Designation Authorization" or "ODA" means an authorization by the FAA under section 44702(d) for an organization composed of 1 or more ODA units to perform approved functions on behalf of the FAA.

(d) AUDITS.—

(1) IN GENERAL.—The Administrator shall perform a periodic audit of each ODA unit and its procedures.

(2) DURATION.—An audit required under paragraph (1) shall be performed with

respect to an ODA holder once every 7 years (or more frequently as determined appropriate by the Administrator).

(3) RECORDS.—The ODA holder shall maintain, for a period to be determined by the Administrator, a record of—

(A) each audit conducted under this subsection; and

(B) any corrective actions resulting from each such audit.

(e) FEDERAL AVIATION SAFETY ADVISORS.—

(1) IN GENERAL.—In the case of an ODA holder, the Administrator shall assign FAA aviation safety personnel with appropriate expertise to be advisors to the ODA unit members that are authorized to make findings of compliance on behalf of the Administrator. The advisors shall—

(A) communicate with assigned unit members on an ongoing basis to ensure that the assigned unit members are knowledgeable of relevant FAA policies and acceptable methods of compliance; and

(B) monitor the performance of the assigned unit members to ensure consistency with such policies.

(2) APPLICABILITY.—Paragraph (1) shall only apply to an ODA holder that is—

(A) a manufacturer that holds both a type and a production certificate for—

(i) transport category airplanes with a maximum takeoff gross weight greater than 150,000 pounds; or

(ii) airplanes produced and delivered to operators operating under part 121 of title 14, Code of Federal Regulations, for air carrier service under such part 121; or

(B) a manufacturer of engines for an airplane described in subparagraph (A).

(f) COMMUNICATION WITH THE FAA.—Neither the Administrator nor an ODA holder may prohibit—

(1) an ODA unit member from communicating with, or seeking the advice of, the Administrator or FAA staff; or

(2) the Administrator or FAA staff from communicating with an ODA unit member.

(g) ETHICS TRAINING REQUIREMENT FOR ODA HOLDERS.—

(1) IN GENERAL.—Not later than 1 year after the date of enactment of this subsection, the Administrator of the Federal Aviation Administration shall review and ensure each ODA holder authorized by the Administrator under section 44702(d) has in effect a recurrent training program for all ODA unit members that covers—

(A) unit member professional obligations and responsibilities;

(B) the ODA holder's code of ethics as required to be established under section 102(f) of the Aircraft Certification, Safety, and Accountability Act (49 U.S.C. 44701 note);

(C) procedures for reporting safety concerns, as described in the respective approved procedures manual for the delegation;

(D) the prohibition against and reporting procedures for interference from a supervisor or other ODA member described in section 44742; and

(E) any additional information the Administrator considers relevant to maintaining ethical and professional standards across all ODA holders and unit members.

(2) FAA REVIEW.—

(A) REVIEW OF TRAINING PROGRAM.—The Organization Designation Authorization

Office of the Administration established under subsection (b) shall review each ODA holders' recurrent training program to ensure such program includes—

(i) all elements described in paragraph (1); and

(ii) training to instill professionalism and clear understanding among ODA unit members about the purpose of and procedures associated with safety management systems, including the provisions of the third edition of the Safety Management Manual issued by the International Civil Aviation Organization (Doc 9859) (or any successor edition).

(B) CHANGES TO PROGRAM.—Such Office may require changes to the training program considered necessary to maintain ethical and professional standards across all ODA holders and unit members.

(3) TRAINING.—As part of the recurrent training program required under paragraph (1), not later than 60 business days after being designated as an ODA unit member, and annually thereafter, each ODA unit member shall complete the ethics training required by the ODA holder of the respective ODA unit member in order to exercise the functions delegated under the ODA.

(4) ACCOUNTABILITY.—The Administrator shall establish such processes or requirements as are necessary to ensure compliance with paragraph (3).

(Added Pub. L. 115–254, div. B, title II, §212(a), Oct. 5, 2018, 132 Stat. 3247; amended Pub. L. 116–260, div. V, title I, §§107(b)(1), (c), 125(b), Dec. 27, 2020, 134 Stat. 2324, 2325, 2347; Pub. L. 118–63, title III, §§303, 304(a), May 16, 2024, 138 Stat. 1069, 1070.)

§44737. HELICOPTER FUEL SYSTEM SAFETY

(a) PROHIBITION.—

(1) IN GENERAL.—A person may not operate a covered helicopter in United States airspace unless the design of the helicopter is certified by the Administrator of the Federal Aviation Administration to—

(A) comply with the requirements applicable to the category of the helicopter under paragraphs (1), (2), (3), (5), and (6) of section 27.952(a), section 27.952(c), section 27.952(f), section 27.952(g), section 27.963(g) (but allowing for a minimum puncture force of 250 pounds if successfully drop tested in-structure), and section 27.975(b) or paragraphs (1), (2), (3), (5), and (6) of section 29.952(a), section 29.952(c), section 29.952(f), section 29.952(g), section 29.963(b) (but allowing for a minimum puncture force of 250 pounds if successfully drop tested in-structure), and 29.975(a)(7) of title 14, Code of Federal Regulations, as in effect on the date of enactment of this section; or

(B) employ other means acceptable to the Administrator to provide an equivalent level of fuel system crash resistance.

(2) COVERED HELICOPTER DEFINED.—In this subsection, the term "covered helicopter" means a helicopter not otherwise required to comply with section 27.952, section 27.963, and section 27.975, or section 29.952, section 29.963, and section 29.975 of title 14, Code of Federal Regulations as in effect on the date of enactment of this section for which manufacture was completed, as determined by the Administrator, on or after the date that is 18 months after the date of enactment of this section.

(b) ADMINISTRATIVE PROVISIONS.—The Administrator shall—

(1) expedite the certification and validation of United States and foreign type designs and retrofit kits that improve fuel system crashworthiness; and

(2) not later than 180 days after the date of enactment of this section, and periodically thereafter, issue a bulletin to—

(A) inform helicopter owners and operators of available modifications to improve fuel system crashworthiness; and

(B) urge that such modifications be installed as soon as practicable.

(c) RULE OF CONSTRUCTION.—Nothing in this section may be construed to affect the operation of a helicopter by the Department of Defense.

(d) EXCEPTION.—A helicopter issued an experimental certificate under section 21.191 of title 14, Code of Federal Regulations (or any successor regulations), or operating under a Special Flight Permit issued under section 21.197 of title 14, Code of Federal Regulations (or any successor regulations), is excepted from the requirements of this section.

(Added Pub. L. 115–254, div. B, title III, §317(a), Oct. 5, 2018, 132 Stat. 3268; amended Pub. L. 118–63, title VIII, §825, May 16, 2024, 138 Stat. 1332.)

§44738. TRAINING ON HUMAN TRAFFICKING FOR CERTAIN STAFF

In addition to other training requirements, each air carrier shall provide training to ticket counter agents, gate agents, and other air carrier workers whose jobs require regular interaction with passengers on recognizing and responding to potential human trafficking victims.

(Added Pub. L. 115–254, div. B, title IV, §408(a), Oct. 5, 2018, 132 Stat. 3330.)

§44739. PETS ON AIRPLANES

(a) PROHIBITION.—It shall be unlawful for any person to place a live animal in an overhead storage compartment of an aircraft operated under part 121 of title 14, Code of Federal Regulations.

(b) CIVIL PENALTY.—The Administrator may impose a civil penalty under section 46301 for each violation of this section.

(Added Pub. L. 115–254, div. B, title IV, §417(a), Oct. 5, 2018, 132 Stat. 3334.)

§44740. SPECIAL RULE FOR CERTAIN AIRCRAFT OPERATIONS

(a) IN GENERAL.—The operator of an aircraft with a special airworthiness certification in the experimental category may—

(1) operate the aircraft for the purpose of conducting a space support vehicle flight (as that term is defined in section 50902 of title 51); and

(2) conduct such flight under such certificate carrying persons or property for compensation or hire—

(A) notwithstanding any rule or term of a certificate issued by the Administrator of the Federal Aviation Administration that would prohibit flight for compensation or hire; or

(B) without obtaining a certificate issued by the Administrator to conduct air carrier or commercial operations.

(b) LIMITED APPLICABILITY.—Subsection (a) shall apply only to a space support vehicle flight that satisfies each of the following:

(1) The aircraft conducting the space support vehicle flight—

(A) takes flight and lands at a single site that is operated by an entity licensed for operation under chapter 509 of title 51;

(B) is owned or operated by a launch or reentry vehicle operator licensed under chapter 509 of title 51, or on behalf of a launch or reentry vehicle operator licensed under chapter 509 of title 51;

(C) is a launch vehicle, a reentry vehicle, or a component of a launch or reentry vehicle licensed for operations pursuant to chapter 509 of title 51; and

(D) is used only to simulate space flight conditions in support of—

(i) training for potential space flight participants, government astronauts, or crew (as those terms are defined in chapter 509 of title 51);

(ii) the testing of hardware to be used in space flight; or

(iii) research and development tasks, which require the unique capabilities of the aircraft conducting the flight.

(c) RULES OF CONSTRUCTION.—

(1) SPACE SUPPORT VEHICLES.—Section 44711(a)(1) shall not apply to a person conducting a space support vehicle flight under this section only to the extent that a term of the experimental certificate under which the person is operating the space support vehicle prohibits the carriage of persons or property for compensation or hire.

(2) AUTHORITY OF ADMINISTRATOR.—Nothing in this section shall be construed to limit the authority of the Administrator of the Federal Aviation Administration to exempt a person from a regulatory prohibition on the carriage of persons or property for compensation or hire subject to terms and conditions other than those described in this section.

(Added Pub. L. 115–254, div. B, title V, §581(b)(1), Oct. 5, 2018, 132 Stat. 3398, §44737; renumbered §44740 and amended Pub. L. 116–260, div. V, title I, §107(d)(1), (3), Dec. 27, 2020, 134 Stat. 2326.)

§44741. APPROVAL OF ORGANIZATION DESIGNATION AUTHORIZATION UNIT MEMBERS

(a) IN GENERAL.—Beginning January 1, 2022, each individual who is selected on or after such date to become an ODA unit member by an ODA holder engaged in the design of an aircraft, aircraft engine, propeller, or appliance and performs an authorized function pursuant to a delegation by the Administrator of the Federal Aviation Administration under section 44702(d)—

(1) shall be—

(A) an employee, a contractor, or a consultant of the ODA holder; or

(B) the employee of a supplier of the ODA holder; and

(2) may not become a member of such unit unless approved by the Administrator pursuant to this section.

(b) PROCESS AND TIMELINE.—

(1) IN GENERAL.—The Administrator shall maintain an efficient process for the review and approval of an individual to become an ODA unit member under this section.

(2) PROCESS.—An ODA holder described in subsection (a) may submit to the Administrator an application for an individual to be approved to become an ODA unit

member under this section. The application shall be submitted in such form and manner as the Administrator determines appropriate. The Administrator shall require an ODA holder to submit with such an application information sufficient to demonstrate an individual's qualifications under subsection (c).

(3) TIMELINE.—The Administrator shall approve or reject an individual that is selected by an ODA holder to become an ODA unit member under this section not later than 30 days after the receipt of an application by an ODA holder.

(4) DOCUMENTATION OF APPROVAL.—Upon approval of an individual to become an ODA unit member under this section, the Administrator shall provide such individual a letter confirming that such individual has been approved by the Administrator under this section to be an ODA unit member.

(5) REAPPLICATION.—An ODA holder may submit an application under this subsection for an individual to become an ODA unit member under this section regardless of whether an application for such individual was previously rejected by the Administrator.

(c) QUALIFICATIONS.—

(1) IN GENERAL.—The Administrator shall issue minimum qualifications for an individual to become an ODA unit member under this section. In issuing such qualifications, the Administrator shall consider existing qualifications for Administration employees with similar duties and whether such individual—

(A) is technically proficient and qualified to perform the authorized functions sought;

(B) has no recent record of serious enforcement action, as determined by the Administrator, taken by the Administrator with respect to any certificate, approval, or authorization held by such individual;

(C) is of good moral character (as such qualification is applied to an applicant for an airline transport pilot certificate issued under section 44703);

(D) possesses the knowledge of applicable design or production requirements in this chapter and in title 14, Code of Federal Regulations, necessary for performance of the authorized functions sought;

(E) possesses a high degree of knowledge of applicable design or production principles, system safety principles, or safety risk management processes appropriate for the authorized functions sought; and

(F) meets such testing, examination, training, or other qualification standards as the Administrator determines are necessary to ensure the individual is competent and capable of performing the authorized functions sought.

(2) PREVIOUSLY REJECTED APPLICATION.—In reviewing an application for an individual to become an ODA unit member under this section, if an application for such individual was previously rejected, the Administrator shall ensure that the reasons for the prior rejection have been resolved or mitigated to the Administrator's satisfaction before making a determination on the individual's reapplication.

(d) RESCISSION OF APPROVAL.—The Administrator may rescind an approval of an individual as an ODA unit member granted pursuant to this section at any time and for any reason the Administrator considers appropriate. The Administrator shall develop procedures to provide for notice and opportunity to appeal rescission decisions made by the Administrator. Such decisions by the Administrator are not subject to judicial review.

(e) CONDITIONAL SELECTIONS.—

(1) IN GENERAL.—Subject to the requirements of this subsection, the Administrator may authorize an ODA holder to conditionally designate an individual to perform the functions of an ODA unit member for a period of not more than 30 days (beginning on the date an application for such individual is submitted under subsection (b)(2)).

(2) REQUIRED DETERMINATION.—The Administrator may not make an authorization under paragraph (1) unless—

(A) the ODA holder has instituted, to the Administrator's satisfaction, systems and processes to ensure the integrity and reliability of determinations by conditionally-designated ODA unit members; and

(B) the ODA holder has instituted a safety management system in accordance with regulations issued by the Administrator under section 102 of the Aircraft Certification, Safety, and Accountability Act.

(3) FINAL DETERMINATION.—The Administrator shall approve or reject the application for an individual designated under paragraph (1) in accordance with the timeline and procedures described in subsection (b).

(4) REJECTION AND REVIEW.—If the Administrator rejects the application submitted under subsection (b)(2) for an individual conditionally designated under paragraph (1), the Administrator shall review and approve or disapprove any decision pursuant to any authorized function performed by such individual during the period such individual served as a conditional designee.

(5) PROHIBITIONS.—Notwithstanding the requirements of paragraph (2), the Administrator may prohibit an ODA holder from making conditional designations of individuals as ODA unit members under this subsection at any time for any reason the Administrator considers appropriate. The Administrator may prohibit any conditionally designated individual from performing an authorized function at any time for any reason the Administrator considers appropriate.

(f) RECORDS AND BRIEFINGS.—

(1) IN GENERAL.—Beginning on the date described in subsection (a), an ODA holder shall maintain, for a period to be determined by the Administrator and with proper protections to ensure the security of sensitive and personal information—

(A) any data, applications, records, or manuals required by the ODA holder's approved procedures manual, as determined by the Administrator;

(B) the names, responsibilities, qualifications, and example signature of each member of the ODA unit who performs an authorized function pursuant to a delegation by the Administrator under section 44702(d);

(C) training records for ODA unit members and ODA administrators; and

(D) any other data, applications, records, or manuals determined appropriate by the Administrator.

(2) CONGRESSIONAL BRIEFING.—The Administrator shall provide biannual briefings each fiscal year through September 30, 2028 to the Committee on Transportation and Infrastructure of the House of Representatives and the Committee on Commerce, Science, and Transportation of the Senate on the implementation and effects of this section, including—

(A) the Administration's performance in completing reviews of individuals and approving or denying such individuals within the timeline required under subsection (b)(3);

(B) for any individual rejected by the Administrator under subsection (b) during the preceding 6-month period, the reasoning or basis for such rejection; and

(C) any resource, staffing, or other challenges within the Administration associated with implementation of this section.

(g) SPECIAL REVIEW OF QUALIFICATIONS.—

(1) IN GENERAL.—Not later than 30 days after the issuance of minimum qualifications under subsection (c), the Administrator shall initiate a review of the qualifications of each individual who on the date on which such minimum qualifications are issued is an ODA unit member of a holder of a type certificate for a transport airplane to ensure such individual meets the minimum qualifications issued by the Administrator under subsection (c).

(2) UNQUALIFIED INDIVIDUAL.—For any individual who is determined by the Administrator not to meet such minimum qualifications pursuant to the review conducted under paragraph (1), the Administrator—

(A) shall determine whether the lack of qualification may be remedied and, if so, provide such individual with an action plan or schedule for such individual to meet such qualifications; or

(B) may, if the Administrator determines the lack of qualification may not be remedied, take appropriate action, including prohibiting such individual from performing an authorized function.

(3) DEADLINE.—The Administrator shall complete the review required under paragraph (1) not later than 18 months after the date on which such review was initiated.

(4) SAVINGS CLAUSE.—An individual approved to become an ODA unit member of a holder of a type certificate for a transport airplane under subsection (a) shall not be subject to the review under this subsection.

(h) PROHIBITION.—The Administrator may not authorize an organization or ODA holder to approve an individual selected by an ODA holder to become an ODA unit member under this section.

(i) DEFINITIONS.—

(1) GENERAL APPLICABILITY.—The definitions contained in section 44736(c) shall apply to this section.

(2) TRANSPORT AIRPLANE.—The term "transport airplane" means a transport category airplane designed for operation by an air carrier or foreign air carrier type-certificated with a passenger seating capacity of 30 or more or an all-cargo or combi derivative of such an airplane.

(j) AUTHORIZATION OF APPROPRIATIONS.—There is authorized to be appropriated to carry out this section $3,000,000 for each of fiscal years 2021 through 2028.

(Added Pub. L. 116–260, div. V, title I, §107(a), Dec. 27, 2020, 134 Stat. 2320; amended Pub. L. 118–63, title III, §306(a), May 16, 2024, 138 Stat. 1071.)

§44742. INTERFERENCE WITH THE DUTIES OF ORGANIZATION DESIGNATION AUTHORIZATION UNIT MEMBERS

(a) IN GENERAL.—The Administrator of the Federal Aviation Administration shall continuously seek to eliminate or minimize interference by an ODA holder that affects the performance of authorized functions by ODA unit members.

(b) PROHIBITION.—

(1) IN GENERAL.—It shall be unlawful for any individual who is a supervisory employee of an ODA holder that manufactures a transport category airplane to commit an act of interference with an ODA unit member's performance of authorized functions.

(2) CIVIL PENALTY.—

(A) INDIVIDUALS.—An individual shall be subject to a civil penalty under section 46301(a)(1) for each violation under paragraph (1).

(B) SAVINGS CLAUSE.—Nothing in this paragraph shall be construed as limiting or constricting any other authority of the Administrator to pursue an enforcement action against an individual or organization for violation of applicable Federal laws or regulations of the Administration.

(c) REPORTING.—

(1) REPORTS TO ODA HOLDER.—An ODA unit member of an ODA holder that manufactures a transport category airplane shall promptly report any instances of interference to the office of the ODA holder that is designated to receive such reports.

(2) REPORTS TO THE FAA.—

(A) IN GENERAL.—The ODA holder office described in paragraph (1) shall investigate reports and submit to the office of the Administration designated by the Administrator to accept and review such reports any instances of interference reported under paragraph (1).

(B) CONTENTS.—The Administrator shall prescribe parameters for the submission of reports to the Administration under this paragraph, including the manner, time, and form of submission. Such report shall include the results of any investigation conducted by the ODA holder in response to a report of interference, a description of any action taken by the ODA holder as a result of the report of interference, and any other information or potentially mitigating factors the ODA holder or the Administrator deems appropriate.

(d) DEFINITIONS.—

(1) GENERAL APPLICABILITY.—The definitions contained in section 44736(c) shall apply to this section.

(2) INTERFERENCE.—In this section, the term "interference" means—

(A) blatant or egregious statements or behavior, such as harassment, beratement, or threats, that a reasonable person would conclude was intended to improperly influence or prejudice an ODA unit member's performance of his or her duties; or

(B) the presence of non-ODA unit duties or activities that conflict with the performance of authorized functions by ODA unit members.

(Added Pub. L. 116–260, div. V, title I, §107(a), Dec. 27, 2020, 134 Stat. 2323.)

§44743. PILOT TRAINING REQUIREMENTS

(a) IN GENERAL.—

(1) ADMINISTRATOR'S DETERMINATION.—In establishing any pilot training requirements with respect to a new transport airplane, the Administrator of the Federal Aviation Administration shall independently review any proposal by the manufacturer of such

airplane with respect to the scope, format, or minimum level of training required for operation of such airplane.

(2) ASSURANCES AND MARKETING REPRESENTATIONS.—Before the Administrator has established applicable training requirements, an applicant for a new or amended type certificate for an airplane described in paragraph (1) may not, with respect to the scope, format, or magnitude of pilot training for such airplane—

(A) make any assurance or other contractual commitment, whether verbal or in writing, to a potential purchaser of such airplane unless a clear and conspicuous disclaimer (as defined by the Administrator) is included regarding the status of training required for operation of such airplane; or

(B) provide financial incentives (including rebates) to a potential purchaser of such airplane regarding the scope, format, or magnitude of pilot training for such airplane.

(b) PILOT RESPONSE TIME.—Beginning on the day after the date on which regulations are issued under section 119(c)(6) of the Aircraft Certification, Safety, and Accountability Act, the Administrator may not issue a new or amended type certificate for an airplane described in subsection (a) unless the applicant for such certificate has demonstrated to the Administrator that the applicant has accounted for realistic assumptions regarding the time for pilot responses to non-normal conditions in designing the systems and instrumentation of such airplane. Such assumptions shall—

(1) be based on test data, analysis, or other technical validation methods; and

(2) account for generally accepted scientific consensus among experts in human factors regarding realistic pilot response time.

(c) DEFINITION.—In this section, the term "transport airplane" means a transport category airplane designed for operation by an air carrier or foreign air carrier type-certificated with a passenger seating capacity of 30 or more or an all-cargo or combi derivative of such an airplane.

(Added Pub. L. 116–260, div. V, title I, §119(a), Dec. 27, 2020, 134 Stat. 2338.)

§44744. FLIGHT CREW ALERTING

(a) IN GENERAL.—Beginning on December 27, 2022, the Administrator may not issue a type certificate for a transport category airplane unless such airplane incorporates a flight crew alerting system that, at a minimum—

(1) displays and differentiates among warnings, cautions, and advisories; and

(2) includes functions to assist the flight crew in prioritizing corrective actions and responding to systems failures.

(b) LIMITATION.—The prohibition in subsection (a) shall not apply to any application for an original or amended type certificate that was submitted to the Administrator prior to December 27, 2020.

(c) SAFETY ENHANCEMENTS.—

(1) RESTRICTION ON AIRWORTHINESS CERTIFICATE ISSUANCE.—Beginning on the date that is 1 year after the date on which the Administrator issues a type certificate for the Boeing 737-10, the Administrator may not issue an original airworthiness certificate for any Boeing 737 MAX aircraft unless the Administrator finds that the type design for the aircraft includes safety enhancements that have been approved by the Administrator.

(2) RESTRICTION ON OPERATION.—Beginning on the date that is 3 years after the date

on which the Administrator issues a type certificate for the Boeing 737-10, no person may operate a Boeing 737 MAX aircraft unless—

    (A) the type design for the aircraft includes safety enhancements approved by the Administrator; and

    (B) the aircraft was—

        (i) produced in conformance with such type design; or

        (ii) altered in accordance with such type design.

  (d) DEFINITIONS.—In this section:

    (1) BOEING 737 MAX AIRCRAFT.—The term "Boeing 737 MAX aircraft" means any—

    (A) Model 737 series aircraft designated as a 737-7, 737-8, 737-8200, 737-9, or 737-10; or

    (B) other variant of a model described in subparagraph (A).

    (2) SAFETY ENHANCEMENT.—The term "safety enhancement" means any design change to the flight crew alerting system approved by the Administrator for the Boeing 737-10, including—

    (A) a—

        (i) synthetic enhanced angle-of-attack system; and

        (ii) means to shut off stall warning and overspeed alerts; or

    (B) any design changes equivalent to subparagraph (A) determined appropriate by the Administrator.

(Added Pub. L. 117–328, div. O, title V, §501(a), Dec. 29, 2022, 136 Stat. 5230.)

§44745. DON YOUNG ALASKA AVIATION SAFETY INITIATIVE

  (a) IN GENERAL.—The Administrator of the Federal Aviation Administration shall redesignate the FAA Alaska Aviation Safety Initiative of the Administration as the Don Young Alaska Aviation Safety Initiative (in this section referred to as the "Initiative"), under which the Administrator shall carry out the provisions of this section and take such other actions as the Administrator determines appropriate to improve aviation safety in Alaska and covered locations.

  (b) OBJECTIVE.—The objective of the Initiative shall be to work cooperatively with aviation stakeholders and other stakeholders towards the goal of—

    (1) reducing the rate of fatal aircraft accidents in Alaska and covered locations by 90 percent from 2019 to 2033; and

    (2) by January 1, 2033, eliminating fatal accidents of aircraft operated by an air carrier that operates under part 135 of title 14, Code of Federal Regulations.

  (c) LEADERSHIP.—

    (1) IN GENERAL.—The Administrator shall designate the Regional Administrator for the Alaskan Region of the Administration to serve as the Director of the Initiative.

    (2) COVERED LOCATIONS.—The Administrator shall select a designee within the Aviation Safety Organization to implement relevant requirements of this section in covered locations.

    (3) REPORTING CHAIN.—In all matters relating to the Initiative, the Director of the Initiative shall report directly to the Administrator.

    (4) COORDINATION.—The Director of the Initiative shall coordinate with the heads of other offices and lines of business of the Administration, including the other regional

administrators, to carry out the Initiative.

(d) AUTOMATED WEATHER SYSTEMS.—

(1) REQUIREMENT.—The Administrator shall ensure, to the greatest extent practicable, that a covered automated weather system is installed and operated at each covered airport not later than December 31, 2030.

(2) WAIVER.—In complying with the requirement under paragraph (1), the Administrator may waive any positive benefit-cost ratio requirement for the installation and operation of a covered automated weather system.

(3) PRIORITIZATION.—In developing the installation timeline of a covered automated weather system at a covered airport pursuant to this subsection, the Administrator shall—

(A) coordinate and consult with the governments with jurisdiction over Alaska and covered locations, covered airports, air carriers operating in Alaska or covered locations, private pilots based in Alaska or a covered location, and such other members of the aviation community in Alaska or covered locations; and

(B) prioritize early installation at covered airports that would enable the greatest number of instrument flight rule operations by air carriers operating under part 121 or 135 of title 14, Code of Federal Regulations.

(4) RELIABILITY.—

(A) IN GENERAL.—Pertaining to both Federal and non-Federal systems in Alaska, the Administrator shall be responsible for ensuring—

(i) the reliability of covered automated weather systems; and

(ii) the availability of weather information from such systems.

(B) SPECIFICATIONS.—The Administrator shall establish data availability and equipment reliability specifications for covered automated weather systems.

(C) SYSTEM RELIABILITY AND RESTORATION PLAN.—Not later than 2 years after the date of enactment of this section, the Administrator shall establish an automated weather system reliability and restoration plan for Alaska. Such plan shall document the Administrator's strategy for ensuring covered automated weather system reliability, including the availability of weather information from such system, and for restoring service in as little time as possible.

(D) TELECOMMUNICATIONS OR OTHER FAILURES.—If a covered automated weather system in Alaska is unable to broadly disseminate weather information due to a telecommunications failure or a failure other than an equipment failure, the Administrator shall take such actions as may be necessary to restore the full functionality and connectivity of the covered automated weather system. The Administrator shall take actions under this subparagraph with the same urgency as the Administrator would take an action to repair a covered automated weather system equipment failure or data fidelity issue.

(E) RELIABILITY DATA.—In tabulating data relating to the operational status of covered automated weather systems (including individually or collectively), the Administrator may not consider a covered automated weather system that is functioning nominally but is unable to broadly disseminate weather information telecommunications failure or a failure other than an equipment failure as functioning reliably.

(5) INVENTORY.—

(A) MAINTENANCE IMPROVEMENTS.—

(i) IN GENERAL.—Not later than 18 months after the date of enactment of the FAA Reauthorization Act of 2024, the Administrator shall identify and implement reasonable alternative actions to improve maintenance of FAA-owned weather observing systems that experience frequent service outages, including associated surface communication outages, at covered airports.

(ii) SPARE PARTS AVAILABILITY.—The actions identified by the Administrator in clause (i) shall improve spare parts availability, including consideration of storage of more spare parts in the region in which the systems are located.

(B) NOTICE OF OUTAGES.—Not later than 18 months after the date of enactment of the FAA Reauthorization Act of 2024, the Administrator shall update FAA Order 7930.2 Notices to Air Missions, or any successive order, to incorporate weather system outages for automated weather observing systems and automated surface observing systems associated with Service A Outages at covered airports.

(6) VISUAL WEATHER OBSERVATION SYSTEM.—

(A) DEPLOYMENT.—Not later than 3 years after the date of enactment of the FAA Reauthorization Act of 2024, the Administrator shall take such actions as may be necessary to—

(i) deploy visual weather observation systems;

(ii) ensure that such systems are capable of meeting the definition of a covered automated weather system in Alaska; and

(iii) develop standard operation specifications for visual weather operation systems.

(B) MODIFICATION OF SPECIFICATIONS.—Upon the request of an aircraft operator, the Administrator shall issue or modify the standard operation specifications for visual weather observation systems developed under subparagraph (A) to allow such systems to be used to satisfy the requirements for supplemental noncertified local weather observations under section 322 of the FAA Reauthorization Act of 2018 (Public Law 115–254).

(e) WEATHER CAMERAS.—

(1) IN GENERAL.—The Director shall continuously assess the state of the weather camera systems in Alaska and covered locations to ensure the operational sufficiency and reliability of such systems.

(2) APPLICATIONS.—The Director shall—

(A) accept applications from persons to install weather cameras; and

(B) consult with the governments with jurisdiction over Alaska and covered locations, covered airports, air carriers operating in Alaska or covered locations, private pilots based in Alaska or covered locations, and such other members of the aviation community in Alaska and covered locations as the Administrator determines appropriate to solicit additional locations at which to install and operate weather cameras.

(3) PRESUMPTION.—Unless the Director has clear and compelling evidence to the contrary, the Director shall presume that the installation of a weather camera at a covered airport in Alaska, or that is recommended by a government with jurisdiction over a covered location, is cost beneficial and will improve aviation safety.

(f) COOPERATION WITH OTHER AGENCIES.—In carrying out this section, the Administrator shall cooperate with the heads of other Federal or State agencies with responsibilities affecting aviation safety in Alaska and covered locations, including the collection and dissemination of weather data.

(g) SURVEILLANCE AND COMMUNICATION.—

(1) IN GENERAL.—The Director shall take such actions as may be necessary to—

(A) encourage and incentivize the equipage of aircraft that operate under part 135 of title 14, Code of Federal Regulations, with automatic dependent surveillance and broadcast out equipment; and

(B) improve aviation surveillance and communications in Alaska and covered locations.

(2) REQUIREMENT.—Not later than December 31, 2030, the Administrator shall ensure that automatic dependent surveillance and broadcast coverage is available at 5,000 feet above ground level throughout each covered location and Alaska.

(3) WAIVER.—The Administrator shall waive any positive benefit-cost ratio requirement for—

(A) the installation and operation of equipment and facilities necessary to implement the requirement under paragraph (2); and

(B) the provision of additional ground-based transmitters for automatic dependent surveillance-broadcasts to provide a minimum operational network in Alaska along major flight routes.

(4) SERVICE AREAS.—The Director shall continuously identify additional automatic dependent surveillance–broadcast service areas in which the deployment of automatic dependent surveillance–broadcast receivers and equipment would improve aviation safety.

(h) OTHER PROJECTS.—The Director shall continue to build upon other initiatives recommended in the reports of the FAA Alaska Aviation Safety Initiative of the Administration published before the date of enactment of this section.

(i) ANNUAL REPORT.—

(1) IN GENERAL.—Beginning on the date that is 1 year after the date of enactment of the FAA Reauthorization Act of 2024, and annually thereafter, the Administrator shall submit to the Committee on Transportation and Infrastructure of the House of Representatives and the Committee on Commerce, Science, and Transportation of the Senate a report on the Initiative, including an itemized description of how the Administration budget meets the goals of the Initiative.

(2) STAKEHOLDER COMMENTS.—The Director shall append stakeholder comments, organized by topic, to each report submitted under paragraph (1) in the same manner as appendix 3 of the report titled "FAA Alaska Aviation Safety Initiative FY21 Final Report", dated September 30, 2021.

(j) FUNDING.—

(1) IN GENERAL.—Notwithstanding any other provision of law, for each of fiscal years 2025 through 2028—

(A) the Administrator may, upon application from the government with jurisdiction over a covered airport and in coordination with the State or territory in which a covered airport is located, use amounts apportioned under subsection (d)(2)(B) or subsection (e) of section 47114 to carry out the Initiative; or

(B) the sponsor of a covered airport that receives an apportionment under subsection (d)(2)(A) or subsection (e) of section 47114 may use such apportionment for any purpose contained in this section.

(2) SUPPLEMENTAL FUNDING.—Out of amounts made available under section 106(k) and section 48101, not more than a total of $25,000,000 for each of fiscal years 2025 through 2028 is authorized to be expended to carry out the Initiative.

(k) DEFINITIONS.—In this section:

(1) COVERED AIRPORT.—The term "covered airport" means an airport in Alaska or a covered location that is included in the national plan of integrated airport systems required under section 47103 and that has a status other than unclassified in such plan.

(2) COVERED AUTOMATED WEATHER SYSTEM.—The term "covered automated weather system" means an automated or visual weather reporting facility that enables a pilot to begin an instrument procedure approach to an airport under section 91.1039 or 135.225 of title 14, Code of Federal Regulations.

(3) COVERED LOCATION.—The term "covered location" means Hawaii, Puerto Rico, American Samoa, Guam, the Northern Mariana Islands, and the Virgin Islands.

(l) CONFORMITY.—The Administrator shall conduct all activities required under this section in conformity with section 44720.

(Added Pub. L. 118–63, title III, §342(a), May 16, 2024, 138 Stat. 1095.)

§44746. FLIGHT DATA RECOVERY FROM OVERWATER OPERATIONS

(a) IN GENERAL.—Not later than 18 months after the date of enactment of this section, the Administrator of the Federal Aviation Administration shall complete a rulemaking proceeding to require that, not later than 5 years after the date of enactment of this section, all applicable aircraft are—

(1) fitted with a means, in the event of an accident, to recover mandatory flight data parameters in a manner that does not require the underwater retrieval of the cockpit voice recorder or flight data recorder;

(2) equipped with a tamper-resistant method to broadcast sufficient information to a ground station to establish the location where an applicable aircraft terminates flight as the result of such an event; and

(3) equipped with an airframe low-frequency underwater locating device that functions for at least 90 days and that can be detected by appropriate equipment.

(b) APPLICABLE AIRCRAFT DEFINED.—In this section, the term "applicable aircraft" means an aircraft manufactured on or after January 1, 2028, that is—

(1) operated under part 121 of title 14, Code of Federal Regulations;

(2) required by regulation to have a cockpit voice recorder and a flight data recorder; and

(3) used in extended overwater operations.

(Added Pub. L. 118–63, title III, §352(a), May 16, 2024, 138 Stat. 1112.)

§44747. Aviation Safety Oversight Measures Carried Out by Foreign Countries

(a) Assessment.—

(1) In general.—On a regular basis, the Administrator, in consultation with the Secretary of Transportation and the Secretary of State, shall assess aviation safety oversight measures carried out by any foreign country—

(A) from which a foreign air carrier is conducting foreign air transportation to and from the United States;

(B) from which a foreign air carrier seeks to conduct foreign air transportation to and from the United States;

(C) whose air carriers carry or seek to carry the code of a United States air carrier; or

(D) as determined appropriate by the Administrator.

(2) Consultation and criteria.—In conducting an assessment described in paragraph (1), the Administrator shall—

(A) consult with the appropriate authorities of the government of the foreign country;

(B) determine the efficacy with which such foreign country carries out and complies with its aviation safety oversight responsibilities consistent with—

(i) the Convention on International Civil Aviation (in this section referred to as the "Chicago Convention");

(ii) international aviation safety standards; and

(iii) recommended practices set forth by the International Civil Aviation Organization;

(C) use a standard approach and methodology that will result in an analysis of the aviation safety oversight activities of such foreign country that are carried out to meet the minimum standards contained in Annexes 1, 6, and 8 to the Chicago Convention in effect on the date of the assessment, or any such successor documents; and

(D) identify instances of noncompliance pertaining to the aviation safety oversight activities of such foreign country consistent with the Chicago Convention, international aviation safety standards, and recommended practices set forth by the International Civil Aviation Organization.

(3) Findings of noncompliance.—In any case in which the assessment described in subsection (a)(1) finds an instance of non-compliance, the Administrator shall—

(A) notify the foreign country that is the subject of such finding;

(B) not later than 90 days after transmission of such notification, request and initiate final discussions with the foreign country to recommend actions by which the foreign country can mitigate the noncompliance; and

(C) after the discussions described in subparagraph (B) have concluded, determine whether or not the noncompliance finding has been corrected;

(b) Uncorrected Non-compliance.—If the Administrator finds that such foreign country has not corrected the non-compliance by the close of such final discussions—

(1) the Administrator shall notify the Secretary of Transportation and the Secretary of State that the condition of noncompliance remains; and

(2) the Administrator, after consulting with informing the Secretary of Transportation

and the Secretary of State, shall notify the foreign country of such finding; and

(3) notwithstanding section 40105(b), the Administrator, after consulting with the appropriate civil aviation authority of such foreign country and notifying the Secretary of Transportation and the Secretary of State, may withhold, revoke, or prescribe conditions on the operating authority of a foreign air carrier that—

(A) provides or seeks to provide foreign air transportation to and from the United States; or

(B) carries or seeks to carry the code of an air carrier.

(c) AUTHORITY.—Notwithstanding subsections (a) and (b), the Administrator retains the ability to take immediate safety oversight actions if the Administrator, in consultation with the Secretary of Transportation and the Secretary of State, as needed, determines that a condition exists that threatens the safety of passengers, aircraft, or crew traveling to or from such foreign country. In this event that the Administrator makes a determination under this subsection, the Administrator shall immediately notify the Secretary of State of such determination so that the Secretary of State may issue a travel advisory with respect to such foreign country.

(d) PUBLIC NOTIFICATION.—

(1) IN GENERAL.—In any case in which the Administrator provides notification to a foreign country under subsection (b)(2), the Administrator shall—

(A) recommend the actions necessary to bring such foreign country into compliance with the international standards contained in the Chicago Convention;

(B) publish the identity of such foreign country on the website of the Federal Aviation Administration, in the Federal Register, and through other mediums appropriate to provide notice to the public; and

(C) brief the Committee on Transportation and Infrastructure of the House of Representatives and the Committee on Commerce, Science, and Transportation of the Senate on the identity of such foreign country and a summary of any critical safety information resulting from an assessment described in subsection (a)(1).

(2) COMPLIANCE.—If the Administrator finds that a foreign country subsequently corrects all outstanding noncompliances, the Administrator, after consulting with the appropriate civil aviation authority of such foreign country and notifying the Secretary of Transportation and the Secretary of State, shall take actions as necessary to ensure the updated compliance status is reflected, including in the mediums invoked in paragraph (1)(B).

(e) ACCURACY OF THE IASA LIST.—A foreign country that does not have foreign air carrier activity, as described in subsection (a)(1), for an extended period of time, as determined by the Administrator, shall be removed for inactivity from the public listings described in subsection (d)(1)(B), after informing the Secretary of Transportation and the Secretary of State.

(f) CONSISTENCY.—

(1) IN GENERAL.—The Administration shall use data, tools, and methods that ensure transparency and repeatability of assessments conducted under this section.

(2) TRAINING.—The Administrator shall ensure that Administration personnel are properly and adequately trained to carry out the assessments set forth in this section, including with respect to the standards, methodology, and material used to make

determinations under this section.

(Added Pub. L. 118–63, title III, §369(a), May 16, 2024, 138 Stat. 1137.)

§44748. AIRCRAFT DISPATCHING

(a) AIRCRAFT DISPATCHING CERTIFICATE.—No person may serve as an aircraft dispatcher for an air carrier unless such person holds the appropriate aircraft dispatcher certificate issued by the Administrator of the Federal Aviation Administration.

(b) PROOF OF CERTIFICATION.—Upon the request of the Administrator or an authorized representative of the National Transportation Safety Board, or other appropriate Federal agency, a person who holds such a certificate, and is performing dispatching, shall present the certificate for inspection.

(c) DISPATCH CENTERS AND FLIGHT FOLLOWING CENTERS.—

(1) ESTABLISHMENT.—Each air carrier shall establish and maintain sufficient dispatch centers and flight following centers necessary to maintain operational control of each flight of the air carrier at all times.

(2) REQUIREMENTS.—An air carrier shall ensure that each dispatch center and flight following center of the air carrier—

(A) has a sufficient number of aircraft dispatchers on duty at the dispatch center or flight following center to ensure proper operational control of each flight of the air carrier at all times;

(B) has the necessary equipment, in good repair, to maintain proper operational control of each flight of the air carrier at all times; and

(C) includes the presence of physical security and cybersecurity protections to prevent unauthorized access to the dispatch center or flight following center or to the operations of either such center.

(d) PROHIBITION.—

(1) IN GENERAL.—Except as provided in paragraph (2), an air carrier may not dispatch aircraft from any location other than the dispatch center or flight following center of the air carrier.

(2) EMERGENCY AUTHORITY.—In the event of an emergency or other event that renders a dispatch center or a flight following center inoperable, an air carrier may dispatch aircraft from a location other than the dispatch center or flight following center of the air carrier for a period of time not to exceed 14 consecutive days per location without approval of the Administrator.

(Added Pub. L. 118–63, title IV, §420(b)(1), May 16, 2024, 138 Stat. 1164.)

CHAPTER 448—UNMANNED AIRCRAFT SYSTEMS

§44801. DEFINITIONS

In this chapter, the following definitions apply:

(1) ACTIVELY TETHERED UNMANNED AIRCRAFT SYSTEM.—The term "actively tethered unmanned aircraft system" means an unmanned aircraft system in which the unmanned aircraft component—

(A) weighs 55 pounds or less, including payload but not including the tether;

(B) is physically attached to a ground station with a taut, appropriately load-rated tether that provides continuous power to the unmanned aircraft and is unlikely to be separated from the unmanned aircraft;

(C) is controlled and retrieved by such ground station through physical manipulation of the tether;

(D) is able to maintain safe flight control in the event of a power or flight control failure during flight; and

(E) is programmed to initiate a controlled landing in the event of a tether separation.

(2) APPROPRIATE COMMITTEES OF CONGRESS.—The term "appropriate committees of Congress" means the Committee on Commerce, Science, and Transportation of the Senate and the Committee on Transportation and Infrastructure of the House of Representatives.

(3) ARCTIC.—The term "Arctic" means the United States zone of the Chukchi Sea, Beaufort Sea, and Bering Sea north of the Aleutian chain.

(4) CERTIFICATE OF WAIVER; CERTIFICATE OF AUTHORIZATION.—The terms "certificate of waiver" and "certificate of authorization" mean a Federal Aviation Administration grant of approval for a specific flight operation.

(5) COUNTER-UAS SYSTEM.—The term "counter-UAS system" means a system or

device capable of lawfully and safely disabling, disrupting, or seizing control of an unmanned aircraft or unmanned aircraft system.

(6) PERMANENT AREAS.—The term "permanent areas" means areas on land or water that provide for launch, recovery, and operation of small unmanned aircraft.

(7) PUBLIC UNMANNED AIRCRAFT SYSTEM.—The term "public unmanned aircraft system" means an unmanned aircraft system that meets the qualifications and conditions required for operation of a public aircraft.

(8) SENSE AND AVOID CAPABILITY.—The term "sense and avoid capability" means the capability of an unmanned aircraft to remain a safe distance from and to avoid collisions with other airborne aircraft, structures on the ground, and other objects.

(9) SMALL UNMANNED AIRCRAFT.—The term "small unmanned aircraft" means an unmanned aircraft weighing less than 55 pounds, including the weight of anything attached to or carried by the aircraft.

(10) TEST RANGE.—The term "test range" means a defined geographic area where research and development are conducted as authorized by the Administrator of the Federal Aviation Administration, and includes the test ranges designated by the Administrator under section 44803.

(11) UNMANNED AIRCRAFT.—The term "unmanned aircraft" means an aircraft that is operated without the possibility of direct human intervention from within or on the aircraft.

(12) UNMANNED AIRCRAFT SYSTEM.—The term "unmanned aircraft system" means an unmanned aircraft and associated elements (including communication links and the components that control the unmanned aircraft) that are required for the operator to operate safely and efficiently in the national airspace system.

(13) UTM.—The term "UTM" means an unmanned aircraft system traffic management system or service."

(Added Pub. L. 115–254, div. B, title III, §341(a), Oct. 5, 2018, 132 Stat. 3284; amended Pub. L. 118–63, title IX, §§925(b)(1), 926(c), May 16, 2024, 138 Stat. 1360, 1361.)

§44802. INTEGRATION OF CIVIL UNMANNED AIRCRAFT SYSTEMS INTO NATIONAL AIRSPACE SYSTEM

(a) REQUIRED PLANNING FOR INTEGRATION.—

(1) COMPREHENSIVE PLAN.—Not later than November 10, 2012,[1] the Secretary of Transportation, in consultation with representatives of the aviation industry, Federal agencies that employ unmanned aircraft systems technology in the national airspace system, and the unmanned aircraft systems industry, shall develop a comprehensive plan to safely accelerate the integration of civil unmanned aircraft systems into the national airspace system.

(2) CONTENTS OF PLAN.—The plan required under paragraph (1) shall contain, at a minimum, recommendations or projections on—

(A) the rulemaking to be conducted under subsection (b), with specific recommendations on how the rulemaking will—

(i) define the acceptable standards for operation and certification of civil unmanned aircraft systems;

(ii) ensure that any civil unmanned aircraft system includes a sense-and-avoid capability; and

(iii) establish standards and requirements for the operator and pilot of a civil unmanned aircraft system, including standards and requirements for registration and licensing;

(B) the best methods to enhance the technologies and subsystems necessary to achieve the safe and routine operation of civil unmanned aircraft systems in the national airspace system;

(C) a phased-in approach to the integration of civil unmanned aircraft systems into the national airspace system;

(D) a timeline for the phased-in approach described under subparagraph (C);

(E) creation of a safe airspace designation for cooperative manned and unmanned flight operations in the national airspace system;

(F) establishment of a process to develop certification, flight standards, and air traffic requirements for civil unmanned aircraft systems at test ranges where such systems are subject to testing;

(G) the best methods to ensure the safe operation of civil unmanned aircraft systems and public unmanned aircraft systems simultaneously in the national airspace system; and

(H) incorporation of the plan into the annual NextGen Implementation Plan document (or any successor document) of the Federal Aviation Administration.

(3) DEADLINE.—The plan required under paragraph (1) shall provide for the safe integration of civil unmanned aircraft systems into the national airspace system as soon as practicable, but not later than September 30, 2015.[1]

(4) REPORT TO CONGRESS.—Not later than February 14, 2013,[1] the Secretary shall submit to Congress a copy of the plan required under paragraph (1).

(5) ROADMAP.—Not later than February 14, 2013,[1] the Secretary shall approve and make available in print and on the Administration's internet website a 5-year roadmap for the introduction of civil unmanned aircraft systems into the national airspace system, as coordinated by the Unmanned Aircraft Program Office of the Administration. The Secretary shall update, in coordination with the Administrator of the National Aeronautics and Space Administration (NASA) and relevant stakeholders, including those in industry and academia, the roadmap annually. The roadmap shall include, at a minimum—

(A) cost estimates, planned schedules, and performance benchmarks, including specific tasks, milestones, and timelines, for unmanned aircraft systems integration into the national airspace system, including an identification of—

(i) the role of the unmanned aircraft systems test ranges established under subsection (c) and the Unmanned Aircraft Systems Center of Excellence;

(ii) performance objectives for unmanned aircraft systems that operate in the national airspace system; and

(iii) research and development priorities for tools that could assist air traffic controllers as unmanned aircraft systems are integrated into the national airspace system, as appropriate;

(B) a description of how the Administration plans to use research and development, including research and development conducted through NASA's Unmanned Aircraft Systems Traffic Management initiatives, to accommodate, integrate, and provide for the evolution of unmanned aircraft systems in the national airspace system;

(C) an assessment of critical performance abilities necessary to integrate unmanned aircraft systems into the national airspace system, and how these performance abilities can be demonstrated; and

(D) an update on the advancement of technologies needed to integrate unmanned aircraft systems into the national airspace system, including decisionmaking by adaptive systems, such as sense-and-avoid capabilities and cyber physical systems security.

(b) RULEMAKING.—Not later than 18 months after the date on which the plan required under subsection (a)(1) is submitted to Congress under subsection (a)(4), the Secretary shall publish in the Federal Register—

(1) a final rule on small unmanned aircraft systems that will allow for civil operation of such systems in the national airspace system, to the extent the systems do not meet the requirements for expedited operational authorization under section 44807;

(2) a notice of proposed rulemaking to implement the recommendations of the plan required under subsection (a)(1), with the final rule to be published not later than 16 months after the date of publication of the notice; and

(3) an update to the Administration's most recent policy statement on unmanned aircraft systems, contained in Docket No. FAA–2006–25714.

(Added Pub. L. 115–254, div. B, title III, §341(a), Oct. 5, 2018, 132 Stat. 3285.)

[1] *See Prior Provisions note below.*

§44803. UNMANNED AIRCRAFT SYSTEM TEST RANGES

(a) TEST RANGES.—

(1) IN GENERAL.—The Administrator of the Federal Aviation Administration shall carry out and update, as appropriate, a program for the use of unmanned aircraft system (in this section referred to as UAS) test ranges to—

(A) enable a broad variety of development, testing, and evaluation activities related to UAS and associated technologies; and

(B) the extent consistent with aviation safety and efficiency, support the safe integration of unmanned aircraft systems into the national airspace system.

(2) DESIGNATIONS.—

(A) EXISTING TEST RANGES.—Test ranges designated under this section shall include the 7 test ranges established under the following:

(i) Section 332(c) of the FAA Modernization and Reform Act of 2012 (49 U.S.C. 40101 note), as in effect on the day before the date of enactment of the FAA Reauthorization Act of 2018 (Public Law 115–254).

(ii) Any other test ranges designated pursuant to the amendment made by section 2201(b) of the FAA Extension, Safety, and Security Act of 2016 (49 U.S.C. 40101 note) after the date of enactment of such Act.

(B) NEW TEST RANGES.—If the Administrator finds that it is in the best interest of enabling safe UAS integration into the national airspace system, the Administrator may select and designate as a test range under this section up to 2 additional test ranges in accordance with the requirements of this section through a competitive selection process.

(C) LIMITATION.—Not more than 9 test ranges designated under this section shall be part of the program established under this section at any given time.

(3) ELIGIBILITY.—Test ranges selected by the Administrator pursuant to (2)(B) shall—

(A) be an instrumentality of a State, local, Tribal, or territorial government or other public entity;

(B) be approved by the chief executive officer of the State, local, territorial, or Tribal government for the principal place of business of the applicant, prior to seeking designation by the Administrator;

(C) undertake and ensure testing and evaluation of innovative concepts, technologies, and operations that will offer new safety benefits, including developing and retaining an advanced aviation industrial base within the United States; and

(D) meet any other requirements established by the Administrator.

(b) AIRSPACE REQUIREMENTS.—

(1) IN GENERAL.—In carrying out the program under subsection (a), the Administrator may establish, upon the request of a test range sponsor designated by the Administrator under subsection (a), a restricted area, special use airspace, or other similar type of airspace pursuant to part 73 of title 14, Code of Federal Regulations, for purposes of—

(A) accommodating hazardous development, testing, and evaluation activities to inform the safe integration of unmanned aircraft systems into the national airspace system; or

(B) other activities authorized by the Administrator pursuant to subsection (f).

(2) NEPA REVIEW.—The Administrator may require that each test range sponsor designated by the Administrator under subsection (a) provide a draft environmental review consistent with the National Environmental Policy Act of 1969 (42 U.S.C. 4321 et seq.), subject to the supervision of and adoption by the Administrator, with respect to any request for the establishment of a restricted area, special use airspace, or other similar type of airspace under this subsection.

(3) INACTIVE RESTRICTED AREA OR SPECIAL USE AIRSPACE.—

(A) IN GENERAL.—In the event a restricted area, special use airspace, or other similar type of airspace established under paragraph (1) is not needed to meet the needs of the using agency (as described in subparagraph (B)), any related airspace restrictions, limitations, or designations shall be inactive.

(B) USING AGENCY.—For purposes of this subsection, a test range sponsor designated by the Administrator under subsection (a) shall be considered the using agency with respect to a restricted area established by the Administrator under this subsection.

(4) APPROVAL AUTHORITY.—The Administrator shall have the authority to approve access by a participating or nonparticipating operator to a test range or restricted area, special use airspace, or other similar type of airspace established by the Administrator under this subsection.

(c) PROGRAM REQUIREMENTS.—In carrying out the program under subsection (a), the Administrator—

(1) may develop operational standards and air traffic requirements for flight operations at test ranges;

(2) shall coordinate with, and leverage the resources of, the Administrator of the National Aeronautics and Space Administration and other relevant Federal agencies, as determined appropriate by the Administrator;

(3) shall address both civil and public aircraft operations;

(4) shall provide for verification of the safety of flight systems and related navigation procedures as such systems and procedures relate to the continued development of regulations and standards for integration of unmanned aircraft systems into the national airspace system;

(5) shall engage test range sponsors, as necessary and with available resources, in projects for development, testing, and evaluation of flight systems, including activities conducted pursuant to section 1042 of the FAA Reauthorization Act of 2024, to facilitate the development of regulations and the validation of standards by the Administrator for the safe integration of unmanned aircraft systems into the national airspace system, which may include activities related to—

(A) developing and enforcing geographic and altitude limitations;

(B) providing for alerts regarding any hazards or limitations on flight, including prohibition on flight, as necessary;

(C) developing or validating sense and avoid capabilities;

(D) developing or validating technology to support communications, navigation, and surveillance;

(E) testing or validating operational concepts and technologies related to beyond visual line of sight operations, autonomous operations, nighttime operations, operations over people, operations involving multiple unmanned aircraft systems by a single pilot or operator, and unmanned aircraft systems traffic management capabilities or services;

(F) improving privacy protections through the use of advances in unmanned aircraft systems;

(G) conducting counter-UAS testing capabilities, with the approval of the Administrator; and

(H) other relevant topics for which development, testing or evaluation are needed;

(6) shall develop data sharing and collection requirements for test ranges to support the unmanned aircraft systems integration efforts of the Administration and coordinate periodically with all test range sponsors to ensure the test range sponsors know—

(A) what data should be collected;

(B) how data can be de-identified to flow more readily to the Administration;

(C) what procedures should be followed; and

(D) what development, testing, and evaluation would advance efforts to safely integrate unmanned aircraft systems into the national airspace system;

(7) shall allow test range sponsors to receive Federal funding, including in-kind contributions, other than from the Federal Aviation Administration, in furtherance of research, development, testing, and evaluation objectives; and

(8) shall use modeling and simulation tools to assist in the testing, evaluation, verification, and validation of unmanned aircraft systems.

(d) EXEMPTION.—Except as provided in subsection (f), the requirements of section 44711, including any related implementing regulations, shall not apply to persons approved by the test range sponsor for operation at a test range designated by the Administrator under this section.

(e) RESPONSIBILITIES OF TEST RANGE SPONSORS.—The sponsor of each test range designated by the Administrator under subsection (a) shall—

(1) provide access to all interested private and public entities seeking to carry out research, development, testing and evaluation activities at the test range designated pursuant to this section, to the greatest extent practicable, consistent with safety and any operating procedures established by the test range sponsor, including access by small business concerns (as such term is defined in section 3 of the Small Business Act (15 U.S.C. 632));

(2) ensure all activities remain within the geographical boundaries and altitude limitations established for any restricted area, special use airspace, or other similar type of airspace covering the test range;

(3) ensure no activity is conducted at the designated test range in a careless or reckless manner;

(4) establish safe operating procedures for all operators approved for activities at the test range, including provisions for maintaining operational control and ensuring protection of persons and property on the ground, subject to approval by the Administrator;

(5) exercise direct oversight of all operations conducted at the test range;

(6) consult with the Administrator on the nature of planned activities at the test range and whether temporary segregation of the airspace is required to contain such activities consistent with aviation safety;

(7) protect proprietary technology, sensitive data, or sensitive research of any civil or private entity when using the test range;

(8) maintain detailed records of all ongoing and completed activities conducted at the test range and all operators conducting such activities, for inspection by, and reporting to, the Administrator, as required by agreement between the Administrator and the test range sponsor;

(9) make all original records available for inspection upon request by the Administrator; and

(10) provide recommendations, on a quarterly basis until the program terminates, to the Administrator to further enable public and private development, testing, and evaluation activities at the test ranges to contribute to the safe integration of unmanned aircraft systems into the national airspace system.

(f) TESTING.—

(1) IN GENERAL.—The Administrator may authorize a sponsor of a test range designated under subsection (a) to host research, development, testing, and evaluation activities, including activities conducted pursuant to section 1042 of the FAA Reauthorization Act of 2024, as appropriate, other than activities directly related to the integration of unmanned aircraft systems into the national airspace system, so long as the activity is necessary to inform the development of regulations, standards, or policy for integrating new types of flight systems into the national airspace system.

(2) WAIVER.— In carrying out this section, the Administrator may waive the requirements of section 44711 (including any related implementing regulations) to the extent the Administrator determines such waiver is consistent with aviation safety.

(g) COLLABORATIVE RESEARCH AND DEVELOPMENT AGREEMENTS.—The Administrator may use the transaction authority under section 106(l)(6), including in coordination with the Center of Excellence for Unmanned Aircraft Systems, to enter into collaborative research and development agreements or to direct research, development, testing, and evaluation related to unmanned aircraft systems, including activities conducted pursuant to section 1042 of the FAA Reauthorization Act of 2024, as appropriate, at any test range designated under subsection (a).

(h) AUTHORIZATION OF APPROPRIATIONS.—

(1) ESTABLISHMENT.—Out of amounts authorized to be appropriated under section 106(k), $6,000,000 for each of fiscal years 2025 through 2028, shall be available to the Administrator for the purposes of—

(A) providing matching funds to commercial entities that contract with a UAS test range to demonstrate or validate technologies that the FAA considers essential to the safe integration of UAS into the national airspace system; and

(B) supporting or performing such demonstration and validation activities described in subparagraph (A) at a test range designated under the section.

(2) DISBURSEMENT.—Funding provided under this subsection shall be divided evenly among all UAS test ranges designated under this section, for the purpose of providing matching funds to commercial entities described in paragraph (1) and available until expended.

(i) TERMINATION.—The program under this section shall terminate on September 30, 2028.

(Added Pub. L. 118–63, title IX, §925(a), May 16, 2024, 138 Stat. 1356.)

§44804. UNMANNED AIRCRAFT IN THE ARCTIC

(a) IN GENERAL.—The Secretary of Transportation shall develop a plan and initiate a process to work with relevant Federal agencies and national and international communities to designate permanent areas in the Arctic where unmanned aircraft may operate 24 hours per day for research and commercial purposes.

(b) PLAN CONTENTS.—The plan under subsection (a) shall include the development of processes to facilitate the safe operation of unmanned aircraft beyond the visual line of sight.

(c) REQUIREMENTS.—Each permanent area designated under subsection (a) shall enable over-water flights from the surface to at least 2,000 feet in altitude, with ingress and egress routes from selected coastal launch sites.

(d) AGREEMENTS.—To implement the plan under subsection (a), the Secretary may enter into an agreement with relevant national and international communities.

(e) AIRCRAFT APPROVAL.—

(1) IN GENERAL.—Subject to paragraph (2), not later than 1 year after the entry into force of an agreement necessary to effectuate the purposes of this section, the Secretary shall work with relevant national and international communities to establish and implement a process for approving the use of a unmanned aircraft in the designated

permanent areas in the Arctic without regard to whether the unmanned aircraft is used as a public aircraft, a civil aircraft, or a model aircraft.

(2) EXISTING PROCESS.—The Secretary may implement an existing process to meet the requirements under paragraph (1).

(Added Pub. L. 115–254, div. B, title III, §344(a), Oct. 5, 2018, 132 Stat. 3290; amended Pub. L. 118–63, title IX, §902(a), May 16, 2024, 138 Stat. 1341.)

§44805. SMALL UNMANNED AIRCRAFT SAFETY STANDARDS

(a) FAA PROCESS FOR ACCEPTANCE AND AUTHORIZATION.—The Administrator of the Federal Aviation Administration shall establish a process for—

(1) accepting risk-based consensus safety standards related to the design, production, and modification of small unmanned aircraft systems;

(2) authorizing the operation of a small unmanned aircraft system make and model designed, produced, or modified in accordance with the consensus safety standards accepted under paragraph (1);

(3) authorizing a manufacturer to self-certify a small unmanned aircraft system make or model that complies with consensus safety standards accepted under paragraph (1); and

(4) certifying a manufacturer of small unmanned aircraft systems, or an employee of such manufacturer, that has demonstrated compliance with the consensus safety standards accepted under paragraph (1) and met any other qualifying criteria, as determined by the Administrator, to alternatively satisfy the requirements of paragraph (1).

(b) CONSIDERATIONS.—Before accepting consensus safety standards under subsection (a), the Administrator of the Federal Aviation Administration shall consider the following:

(1) Technologies or standards related to geographic limitations, altitude limitations, and sense and avoid capabilities.

(2) Using performance-based requirements.

(3) Assessing varying levels of risk posed by different small unmanned aircraft systems and their operation and tailoring performance-based requirements to appropriately mitigate risk.

(4) Predetermined action to maintain safety in the event that a communications link between a small unmanned aircraft and its operator is lost or compromised.

(5) Detectability and identifiability to pilots, the Federal Aviation Administration, and air traffic controllers, as appropriate.

(6) Means to prevent tampering with or modification of any system, limitation, or other safety mechanism or standard under this section or any other provision of law, including a means to identify any tampering or modification that has been made.

(7) Consensus identification standards under section 2202 of the FAA Extension, Safety, and Security Act of 2016 (Public Law 114–190; 130 Stat. 615).

(8) To the extent not considered previously by the consensus body that crafted consensus safety standards, cost-benefit and risk analyses of consensus safety standards that may be accepted pursuant to subsection (a) for newly designed small unmanned aircraft systems.

(9) Applicability of consensus safety standards to small unmanned aircraft systems

that are not manufactured commercially.

(10) Any technology or standard related to small unmanned aircraft systems that promotes aviation safety.

(11) Any category of unmanned aircraft systems that should be exempt from the consensus safety standards based on risk factors.

(c) NONAPPLICABILITY OF OTHER LAWS.—The process for authorizing the operation of small unmanned aircraft systems under subsection (a) may allow for operation of any applicable small unmanned aircraft systems within the national airspace system without requiring—

(1) airworthiness certification requirements under section 44704 of this title; or

(2) type certification under part 21 of title 14, Code of Federal Regulations.

(d) REVOCATION.—The Administrator may suspend or revoke the authorizations in subsection (a) if the Administrator determines that the manufacturer or the small unmanned aircraft system is no longer in compliance with the standards accepted by the Administrator under subsection (a)(1) or with the manufacturer's statement of compliance under subsection (f).

(e) REQUIREMENTS.—With regard to an authorization under the processes in subsection (a), the Administrator may require a manufacturer of small unmanned aircraft systems to provide the Federal Aviation Administration with the following:

(1) The aircraft system's operating instructions.

(2) The aircraft system's recommended maintenance and inspection procedures.

(3) The manufacturer's statement of compliance described in subsection (f).

(4) Upon request, a sample aircraft to be inspected by the Federal Aviation Administration to ensure compliance with the consensus safety standards accepted by the Administrator under subsection (a).

(f) MANUFACTURER'S STATEMENT OF COMPLIANCE FOR SMALL UAS.—A manufacturer's statement of compliance shall—

(1) identify the aircraft make, model, range of serial numbers, and any applicable consensus safety standards used and accepted by the Administrator;

(2) state that the aircraft make and model meets the provisions of the consensus safety standards identified in paragraph (1);

(3) state that the aircraft make and model conforms to the manufacturer's design data and is manufactured in a way that ensures consistency across units in the production process in order to meet the applicable consensus safety standards accepted by the Administrator;

(4) state that the manufacturer will make available to the Administrator, operators, or customers—

(A) the aircraft's operating instructions, which conform to the consensus safety standards identified in paragraph (1); and

(B) the aircraft's recommended maintenance and inspection procedures, which conform to the consensus safety standards identified in paragraph (1);

(5) state that the manufacturer will monitor safety-of-flight issues and take action to ensure it meets the consensus safety standards identified in paragraph (1) and report these issues and subsequent actions to the Administrator;

(6) state that at the request of the Administrator, the manufacturer will provide

reasonable access for the Administrator to its facilities for the purposes of overseeing compliance with this section; and

(7) state that the manufacturer, in accordance with the consensus safety standards accepted by the Federal Aviation Administration, has—

(A) ground and flight tested random samples of the aircraft;

(B) found the sample aircraft performance acceptable; and

(C) determined that the make and model of aircraft is suitable for safe operation.

(g) PROHIBITIONS.—

(1) FALSE STATEMENTS OF COMPLIANCE.—It shall be unlawful for any person to knowingly submit a statement of compliance described in subsection (f) that is fraudulent or intentionally false.

(2) INTRODUCTION INTO INTERSTATE COMMERCE.—Unless the Administrator determines operation of an unmanned aircraft system may be conducted without an airworthiness certificate or permission, authorization, or approval under subsection (a), it shall be unlawful for any person to knowingly introduce or deliver for introduction into interstate commerce any small unmanned aircraft system that is manufactured after the date that the Administrator accepts consensus safety standards under this section unless—

(A) the make and model has been authorized for operation under subsection (a); or

(B) the aircraft has alternatively received design and production approval issued by the Federal Aviation Administration.

(h) EXCLUSIONS.—The Administrator may exempt from the requirements of this section small unmanned aircraft systems that are not capable of navigating beyond the visual line of sight of the operator through advanced flight systems and technology, if the Administrator determines that such an exemption does not pose a risk to the safety of the national airspace system.

(Added Pub. L. 115–254, div. B, title III, §345(a), Oct. 5, 2018, 132 Stat. 3291; amended Pub. L. 118–63, title IX, §903, May 16, 2024, 138 Stat. 1341.)

§44806. PUBLIC UNMANNED AIRCRAFT SYSTEMS AND PUBLIC SAFETY USE OF TETHERED UNMANNED AIRCRAFT SYSTEMS

(a) GUIDANCE.—The Secretary of Transportation shall issue guidance regarding the operation of a public unmanned aircraft system—

(1) to streamline and expedite the process for the issuance of a certificate of authorization or a certificate of waiver;

(2) to facilitate the capability of public agencies to develop and use test ranges, subject to operating restrictions required by the Federal Aviation Administration, to test and operate public unmanned aircraft systems; and

(3) to provide guidance on a public agency's responsibilities when operating an unmanned aircraft without a civil airworthiness certificate issued by the Administration.

(b) AGREEMENTS WITH GOVERNMENT AGENCIES.—

(1) IN GENERAL.—The Secretary shall enter into an agreement with each appropriate public agency to simplify the process for issuing a certificate of waiver or a certificate of authorization with respect to an application for authorization to operate a public unmanned aircraft system in the national airspace system.

(2) CONTENTS.—An agreement under paragraph (1) shall—

(A) with respect to an application described in paragraph (1)—

(i) provide for an expedited review of the application;

(ii) require a decision by the Administrator on approval or disapproval not later than 60 business days after the date of submission of the application; and

(iii) allow for an expedited appeal if the application is disapproved;

(B) allow for a one-time approval of similar operations carried out during a fixed period of time; and

(C) allow a government public safety agency to operate an unmanned aircraft weighing 4.4 pounds or less if that unmanned aircraft is operated—

(i) within or beyond the visual line of sight of the operator;

(ii) less than 400 feet above the ground;

(iii) during daylight conditions;

(iv) within Class G airspace; and

(v) outside of 5 statute miles from any airport, heliport, seaplane base, spaceport, or other location with aviation activities.

(c) PUBLIC SAFETY USE OF ACTIVELY TETHERED UNMANNED AIRCRAFT SYSTEMS.—

(1) IN GENERAL.—The Administrator of the Federal Aviation Administration shall permit, and may issue guidance regarding, the use of actively tethered unmanned aircraft systems by a public safety organization for such systems that are—

(A) operated—

(i) at or below an altitude of 150 feet above ground level within class B, C, D, E, or G airspace, but not at a greater altitude than the ceiling depicted on the UAS Facility Maps published by the Federal Aviation Administration, where applicable;

(ii) within zero-grid airspaces as depicted on such UAS Facility Maps, only if operated in life-saving or emergency situations and with prior notification to the Administration in a manner determined by the Administrator; or

(iii) above 150 feet above ground level within class B, C, D, E, or G airspace only with prior authorization from the Administrator;

(B) not flown directly over non-participating persons;

(C) operated within visual line of sight of the operator; and

(D) operated in a manner that does not interfere with and gives way to any other aircraft.

(2) REQUIREMENTS.—Public actively tethered unmanned aircraft systems may be operated—

(A) without any requirement to obtain a certificate of authorization, certificate of waiver, or other approval by the Federal Aviation Administration;

(B) without requiring airman certification under section 44703 of this title or any rule or regulation relating to airman certification; and

(C) without requiring airworthiness certification under section 44704 of this title or any rule or regulation relating to aircraft certification.

(3) SAFETY STANDARDS.—Actively tethered unmanned aircraft systems operated within the scope of the guidance issued pursuant to paragraph (1) shall be exempt from the requirements of section 44805 of this title.

(4) SAVINGS PROVISION.—Nothing in this subsection shall be construed to preclude the

Administrator of the Federal Aviation Administration from issuing new regulations for public actively tethered unmanned aircraft systems in order to ensure the safety of the national airspace system.

(d) FEDERAL AGENCY COORDINATION TO ENHANCE THE PUBLIC HEALTH AND SAFETY CAPABILITIES OF PUBLIC UNMANNED AIRCRAFT SYSTEMS.—The Administrator shall assist Federal civilian Government agencies that operate unmanned aircraft systems within civil-controlled airspace, in operationally deploying and integrating sense and avoid capabilities, as necessary to operate unmanned aircraft systems safely within the national airspace system.

(e) DEFINITION.—In this section, the term "public safety organization" means an entity that primarily engages in activities related to the safety and well-being of the general public, including law enforcement, fire departments, emergency medical services, and other organizations that protect and serve the public in matters of safety and security.

(Added Pub. L. 115–254, div. B, title III, §346(a), Oct. 5, 2018, 132 Stat. 3294; amended Pub. L. 118–63, title IX, §926(a), May 16, 2024, 138 Stat. 1360.)

§44807. SPECIAL AUTHORITY FOR CERTAIN UNMANNED AIRCRAFT SYSTEMS

(a) IN GENERAL.—Notwithstanding any other requirement of this chapter or chapter 447, the Administrator of the Federal Aviation Administration shall use a risk-based approach to determine how unmanned aircraft systems may operate safely in the national airspace system notwithstanding completion of the comprehensive plan and rulemaking required by section 44802 or the guidance required by section 44806.

(b) ASSESSMENT OF UNMANNED AIRCRAFT SYSTEMS.—In making the determination under subsection (a), the Administrator shall determine, at a minimum—

(1) how such unmanned aircraft systems, if any, as a result of their size, weight, speed, operational capability, proximity to airports and populated areas, operation over people, and operation within or beyond the visual line of sight, or operation during the day or night, do not create a hazard to users of the national airspace system or the public; and

(2) whether a certificate under section 44703 or section 44704 of this title, or a certificate of waiver or certificate of authorization, is required for the operation of unmanned aircraft systems identified under paragraph (1) of this subsection.

(c) REQUIREMENTS FOR SAFE OPERATION.—

(1) IN GENERAL.—In carrying out this section, the Administrator shall establish requirements, or a process to accept proposed requirements, for the safe and efficient operation of unmanned aircraft systems in the national airspace system, including operations related to testing and evaluation of proprietary systems.

(2) EXPEDITED EXEMPTIONS AND APPROVALS.—The Administrator shall, taking into account the statutory mandate to ensure safe and efficient use of the national airspace system, issue approvals—

(A) to enable low-risk beyond visual line of sight operations, including, at a minimum, package delivery operations, extended visual line of sight operations, or shielded operations within 100 feet of the ground or a structure; or

(B) that are aligned with Administration exemptions or approvals that enable beyond visual line of sight operations with the use of acoustics, ground based radar, automatic dependent surveillance–broadcast, and other technological solutions.

(3) TREATMENT OF MITIGATION MEASURES.—To the extent that an operation under this section will be conducted exclusively within the airspace of a Mode C Veil, such operation shall be treated as satisfying the requirements of section 91.113(b) of title 14, Code of Federal Regulations, if the operation employs—

(A) automatic dependent surveillance–broadcast in-based detect and avoid capabilities;

(B) air traffic control communication and coordination;

(C) aeronautical information management systems acceptable to the Administrator, such as notices to air missions, to notify other airspace users of such operations; or

(D) any other risk mitigations as set by the Administrator.

(4) RULE OF CONSTRUCTION.—Nothing in this subsection shall be construed to—

(A) provide an unmanned aircraft operating pursuant to this section the right of way over a manned aircraft; or

(B) limit the authority of the Administrator to impose requirements, conditions, or limitations on operations conducted under this section in order to address safety concerns.

(d) SUNSET.—The authority under this section for the Secretary to determine if certain unmanned aircraft systems may operate safely in the national airspace system terminates effective September 30, 2033.

(e) AUTHORITY.—The Administrator may exercise the authorities described in this section, including waiving applicable parts of title 14, Code of Federal Regulations, without initiating a rulemaking or imposing the requirements of part 11 of title 14, Code of Federal Regulations, to the extent consistent with aviation safety.

(Added Pub. L. 115–254, div. B, title III, §347(a), Oct. 5, 2018, 132 Stat. 3296; amended Pub. L. 118–15, div. B, title II, §2202(c), Sept. 30, 2023, 137 Stat. 83; Pub. L. 118–34, title I, §102(c), Dec. 26, 2023, 137 Stat. 1113; Pub. L. 118–41, title I, §102(c), Mar. 8, 2024, 138 Stat. 21; Pub. L. 118–63, title IX, §927(a), (b), May 16, 2024, 138 Stat. 1362.)

§44808. CARRIAGE OF PROPERTY BY SMALL UNMANNED AIRCRAFT SYSTEMS FOR COMPENSATION OR HIRE

(a) IN GENERAL.—Not later than 1 year after the date of enactment of the FAA Reauthorization Act of 2018, the Administrator of the Federal Aviation Administration shall update existing regulations to authorize the carriage of property by operators of small unmanned aircraft systems for compensation or hire within the United States.

(b) CONTENTS.—Any rulemaking conducted under subsection (a) shall provide for the following:

(1) Use performance-based requirements.

(2) Consider varying levels of risk to other aircraft and to persons and property on the ground posed by different unmanned aircraft systems and their operation and tailor performance-based requirements to appropriately mitigate risk.

(3) Consider the unique characteristics of highly automated, small unmanned aircraft systems.

(4) Include requirements for the safe operation of small unmanned aircraft systems that, at a minimum, address—

(A) airworthiness of small unmanned aircraft systems;

(B) qualifications for operators and the type and nature of the operations;

(C) operating specifications governing the type and nature of the unmanned aircraft system air carrier operations; and

(D) the views of State, local, and tribal officials related to potential impacts of the carriage of property by operators of small unmanned aircraft systems for compensation or hire within the communities to be served.

(5) SMALL UAS.—The Secretary may amend part 298 of title 14, Code of Federal Regulations, to update existing regulations to establish economic authority for the carriage of property by small unmanned aircraft systems for compensation or hire. Such authority shall only require—

(A) registration with the Department of Transportation;

(B) authorization from the Federal Aviation Administration to conduct operations; and

(C) compliance with chapters 401, 411, and 417.

(6) AVAILABILITY OF CURRENT CERTIFICATION PROCESSES.—Pending completion of the rulemaking required in subsection (a) of this section, a person may seek an air carrier operating certificate and certificate of public convenience and necessity, or an exemption from such certificate, using existing processes.

(Added Pub. L. 115–254, div. B, title III, §348(a), Oct. 5, 2018, 132 Stat. 3297.)

§44809. EXCEPTION FOR LIMITED RECREATIONAL OPERATIONS OF UNMANNED AIRCRAFT

(a) IN GENERAL.—Except as provided in subsection (e), and notwithstanding chapter 447 of title 49, United States Code, a person may operate a small unmanned aircraft without specific certification or operating authority from the Federal Aviation Administration if the operation adheres to all of the following limitations:

(1) The aircraft is flown strictly for recreational purposes.

(2) The aircraft is operated in accordance with or within the programming of a community-based organization's set of safety guidelines that are developed in coordination with the Federal Aviation Administration.

(3) The aircraft is flown within the visual line of sight of the person operating the aircraft or a visual observer co-located and in direct communication with the operator.

(4) The aircraft is operated in a manner that does not interfere with and gives way to any manned aircraft.

(5) In Class B, Class C, or Class D airspace or within the lateral boundaries of the surface area of Class E airspace designated for an airport, the operator obtains prior authorization from the Administrator or designee before operating and complies with all airspace restrictions and prohibitions.

(6) Except for circumstances when the Administrator establishes alternative altitude ceilings or as otherwise authorized in section (c), in Class G airspace, the aircraft is flown from the surface to not more than 400 feet above ground level and complies with all airspace and flight restrictions and prohibitions established under this subtitle, such as special use airspace designations and temporary flight restrictions.

(7) The operator has passed an aeronautical knowledge and safety test described in subsection (g) and maintains proof of test passage to be made available to the

Administrator or law enforcement upon request.

(8) The aircraft is registered and marked in accordance with chapter 441 of this title and proof of registration is made available to the Administrator or a designee of the Administrator or law enforcement upon request.

(b) OTHER OPERATIONS.—Unmanned aircraft operations that do not conform to the limitations in subsection (a) must comply with all statutes and regulations generally applicable to unmanned aircraft and unmanned aircraft systems.

(c) OPERATIONS AT FIXED SITES.—

(1) IN GENERAL.—The Administrator shall establish a process to approve, and publicly disseminate the location of, fixed sites at which a person may carry out recreational unmanned aircraft system operations.

(2) OPERATING PROCEDURES.—

(A) CONTROLLED AIRSPACE.—Persons operating unmanned aircraft under paragraph (1) from a fixed site within Class B, Class C, or Class D airspace or within the lateral boundaries of the surface area of Class E airspace designated for an airport, or a community-based organization sponsoring operations within such airspace, shall make the location of the fixed site known to the Administrator and shall establish a mutually agreed upon operating procedure with the air traffic control facility.

(B) ALTITUDE.—The Administrator, in coordination with community-based organizations sponsoring operations at fixed sites, shall develop a process to approve requests for recreational unmanned aircraft systems operations at fixed sites that exceed the maximum altitude contained in a UAS Facility Map published by the Federal Aviation Administration.

(C) UNCONTROLLED AIRSPACE.—Subject to compliance with all airspace and flight restrictions and prohibitions established under this subtitle, including special use airspace designations and temporary flight restrictions, persons operating unmanned aircraft systems from a fixed site designated under the process described in paragraph (1) may operate within Class G airspace—

(i) up to 400 feet above ground level, without prior authorization from the Administrator; and

(ii) above 400 feet above ground level, with prior authorization from the Administrator.

(3) UNMANNED AIRCRAFT WEIGHING 55 POUNDS OR GREATER.—A person may operate an unmanned aircraft weighing 55 pounds or greater, including the weight of anything attached to or carried by the aircraft, if—

(A) the unmanned aircraft complies with standards and limitations developed by a community-based organization and approved by the Administrator; and

(B) the aircraft is operated from a fixed site as described in paragraph (1).

(4) FAA-RECOGNIZED IDENTIFICATION AREAS.—In implementing subpart C of part 89 of title 14, Code of Federal Regulations, the Administrator shall prioritize the review and adjudication of requests to establish FAA Recognized Identification Areas at fixed sites established under this section.

(d) SAVINGS CLAUSE.—NOTHING IN THIS SUBSECTION SHALL BE CONSTRUED AS EXPANDING THE AUTHORITY OF THE ADMINISTRATOR TO REQUIRE A PERSON OPERATING AN UNMANNED AIRCRAFT UNDER THIS SECTION TO SEEK PERMISSIVE AUTHORITY OF THE ADMINISTRATOR,

BEYOND THAT REQUIRED IN THIS SECTION, PRIOR TO OPERATION IN THE NATIONAL AIRSPACE SYSTEM.

(e) STATUTORY CONSTRUCTION.—Nothing in this section shall be construed to limit the authority of the Administrator to pursue an enforcement action against a person operating any unmanned aircraft who endangers the safety of the national airspace system.

(f) EXCEPTIONS.—Nothing in this section prohibits the Administrator from promulgating rules generally applicable to unmanned aircraft, including those unmanned aircraft eligible for the exception set forth in this section, relating to—

(1) the operational parameters for unmanned aircraft in subsection (a);

(2) the registration and marking of unmanned aircraft;

(3) the standards for remotely identifying owners and operators of unmanned aircraft systems and associated unmanned aircraft; and

(4) other standards consistent with maintaining the safety and security of the national airspace system.

(g) AERONAUTICAL KNOWLEDGE AND SAFETY TEST.—

(1) IN GENERAL.—The Administrator, in consultation with manufacturers of unmanned aircraft systems, community-based organizations, and other industry stakeholders, shall develop, maintain, and update, as necessary, an aeronautical knowledge and safety test. Such test shall be administered electronically by the Administrator or a person designated by the Administrator.

(2) REQUIREMENTS.—The Administrator shall ensure the aeronautical knowledge and safety test is designed to adequately demonstrate an operator's—

(A) understanding of aeronautical safety knowledge; and

(B) knowledge of Federal Aviation Administration regulations and requirements pertaining to the operation of an unmanned aircraft system in the national airspace system.

(h) COMMUNITY-BASED ORGANIZATION DEFINED.—In this section, the term "community-based organization" means a membership-based association entity that—

(1) is recognized by the Administrator of the Federal Aviation Administration;

(2) is described in section 501(c)(3) of the Internal Revenue Code of 1986;

(3) is exempt from tax under section 501(a) of the Internal Revenue Code of 1986;

(4) the mission of which is demonstrably the furtherance of model aviation;

(5) provides a comprehensive set of safety guidelines for all aspects of model aviation addressing the assembly and operation of model aircraft and that emphasize safe aeromodelling operations within the national airspace system and the protection and safety of individuals and property on the ground, and may provide a comprehensive set of safety rules and programming for the operation of unmanned aircraft that have the advanced flight capabilities enabling active, sustained, and controlled navigation of the aircraft beyond visual line of sight of the operator;

(6) provides programming and support for any local charter organizations, affiliates, or clubs; and

(7) provides assistance and support in the development and operation of locally designated model aircraft flying sites.

(i) RECOGNITION OF COMMUNITY-BASED ORGANIZATIONS.—In collaboration with aeromodelling stakeholders, the Administrator shall publish an advisory circular within 180 days of the date of enactment of this section that identifies the criteria and process required for recognition of community-based organizations.

(Added Pub. L. 115–254, div. B, title III, §349(a), Oct. 5, 2018, 132 Stat. 3298; amended Pub. L. 118–63, title IX, §928(a), May 16, 2024, 138 Stat. 1363.)

§44810. AIRPORT SAFETY AND AIRSPACE HAZARD MITIGATION AND ENFORCEMENT

(a) COORDINATION.—The Administrator of the Federal Aviation Administration shall work with the Secretary of Defense, the Secretary of Homeland Security, and the heads of other relevant Federal departments and agencies for the purpose of ensuring that technologies or systems that are developed, tested, or deployed by Federal departments and agencies to detect and mitigate potential risks posed by errant or hostile unmanned aircraft system operations do not adversely impact or interfere with safe airport operations, navigation, air traffic services, or the safe and efficient operation of the national airspace system.

(b) PLAN.—

(1) IN GENERAL.—The Administrator shall develop a plan for the certification, permitting, authorizing, or allowing of the deployment of technologies or systems for the detection and mitigation of unmanned aircraft systems.

(2) CONTENTS.—The plan shall provide for the development of policies, procedures, or protocols that will allow appropriate officials of the Federal Aviation Administration to utilize such technologies or systems to take steps to detect and mitigate potential airspace safety risks posed by unmanned aircraft system operations.

(3) AVIATION RULEMAKING COMMITTEE.—The Administrator shall charter an aviation rulemaking committee to make recommendations for such a plan and any standards that the Administrator determines may need to be developed with respect to such technologies or systems. The Federal Advisory Committee Act (5 U.S.C. App.) [1] shall not apply to an aviation rulemaking committee chartered under this paragraph.

(4) NON-DELEGATION.—The plan shall not delegate any authority granted to the Administrator under this section to other Federal, State, local, territorial, or tribal agencies, or an airport sponsor, as defined in section 47102 of title 49, United States Code.

(c) AIRSPACE HAZARD MITIGATION PROGRAM.—In order to test and evaluate technologies or systems that detect and mitigate potential aviation safety risks posed by unmanned aircraft, the Administrator shall deploy such technologies or systems at 5 airports, including 1 airport that ranks in the top 10 of the FAA's most recent Passenger Boarding Data, and any other location the Administrator determines appropriate.

(d) AUTHORITY.—Under the testing and evaluation in subsection (c), the Administrator shall use unmanned aircraft detection and mitigation systems to detect and mitigate the unauthorized operation of an unmanned aircraft that poses a risk to aviation safety.

(e) AIP FUNDING ELIGIBILITY.—Upon the certification, permitting, authorizing, or allowing of such technologies and systems that have been successfully tested under this section, an airport sponsor may apply for a grant under subchapter I of chapter 471 to purchase an unmanned aircraft detection and mitigation system. For purposes of this subsection, purchasing an unmanned aircraft detection and mitigation system shall be considered airport development (as defined in section 47102).

(f) BRIEFING.—The Administrator shall annually brief the appropriate committees of Congress, including the Committee on Judiciary [1] of the House of Representatives and the Committee on the Judiciary of the Senate, on the implementation of this section.

(g) APPLICABILITY OF OTHER LAWS.—Section 46502 of this title, section 32 of title 18, United States Code (commonly known as the Aircraft Sabotage Act), section 1031 of title 18, United States Code (commonly known as the Computer Fraud and Abuse Act of 1986), sections 2510–2522 of title 18, United States Code (commonly known as the Wiretap Act), and sections 3121–3127 of title 18, United States Code (commonly known as the Pen/ Trap Statute), shall not apply to activities authorized by the Administrator pursuant to subsection [2] (c) and (d).

(h) SUNSET.—This section ceases to be effective September 30, 2028.

(i) NON-DELEGATION.—The Administrator shall not delegate any authority granted to the Administrator under this section to other Federal, State, local, territorial, or tribal agencies, or an airport sponsor, as defined in section 47102 of title 49, United States Code. The Administrator may partner with other Federal agencies under this section, subject to any restrictions contained in such agencies' authority to operate counter unmanned aircraft systems.

(Added Pub. L. 115–254, div. B, title III, §383(a), Oct. 5, 2018, 132 Stat. 3321; amended Pub. L. 118–15, div. B, title II, §2202(d), Sept. 30, 2023, 137 Stat. 83; Pub. L. 118–34, title I, §102(d), Dec. 26, 2023, 137 Stat. 1113; Pub. L. 118–41, title I, §102(d), Mar. 8, 2024, 138 Stat. 21; Pub. L. 118–63, title IX, §904, May 16, 2024, 138 Stat. 1341.)

[1] *So in original. Probably should be preceded by "the".*

[2] *So in original. Probably should be "subsections".*

§44811. BEYOND VISUAL LINE OF SIGHT OPERATIONS FOR UNMANNED AIRCRAFT SYSTEMS

(a) PROPOSED RULE.—Not later than 4 months after the date of enactment of the FAA Reauthorization Act of 2024, the Administrator shall issue a notice of proposed rulemaking establishing a performance-based regulatory pathway for unmanned aircraft systems (in this section referred to as "UAS") to operate beyond visual line of sight (in this section referred to as "BVLOS").

(b) REQUIREMENTS.—The proposed rule required under subsection (a) shall, at a minimum, establish the following:

(1) Acceptable levels of risk for BVLOS UAS operations, including the levels developed pursuant to section 931 of the FAA Reauthorization Act of 2024.

(2) Standards for remote pilots or UAS operators for BVLOS operations, taking into account varying levels of automated control and management of UAS flights.

(3) An approval or acceptance process for UAS and associated elements (as defined by the Administrator), which may leverage the creation of a special airworthiness certificate or a manufacturer's declaration of compliance to a Federal Aviation Administration accepted means of compliance. Such process—

(A) shall not require, but may allow for, the use of type or production certification;

(B) shall consider the airworthiness of any UAS that—

(i) is within a maximum gross weight or kinetic energy, as determined by the Administrator; and

(ii) operates within a maximum speed limit as determined by the Administrator;

(C) may require such systems to operate in the national airspace system at altitude limits determined by the Administrator; and

(D) may require such systems to operate at standoff distances from the radius of a structure or the structure's immediate uppermost limit, as determined by the Administrator.

(4) Operating rules for UAS that have been approved or accepted as described in paragraph (3).

(5) Protocols, if appropriate, for networked information exchange, such as network-based remote identification, in support of BVLOS operations.

(6) The safety of manned aircraft operating in the national airspace system and consider the maneuverability and technology limitations of certain aircraft, including hot air balloons.

(c) FINAL RULE.—Not later than 16 months after publishing the proposed rule under subsection (a), the Administrator shall issue a final rule based on such proposed rule.

(d) SAVINGS CLAUSE.—Nothing in this section shall be construed to require the agency to rescope any rulemaking efforts related to UAS BVLOS operations that are ongoing as of the date of enactment of the FAA Reauthorization Act of 2024.

(Added Pub. L. 118–63, title IX, §930(a), May 16, 2024, 138 Stat. 1366.)

§44812. TEMPORARY FLIGHT RESTRICTIONS FOR UNMANNED AIRCRAFT

(a) IN GENERAL.—

(1) TEMPORARY FLIGHT RESTRICTIONS.—The Administrator of the Federal Aviation Administration shall, upon the request by an eligible entity, temporarily restrict unmanned aircraft operations over eligible large public gatherings.

(2) DENIAL.—Notwithstanding paragraph (1), the Administrator may deny a request for a temporary flight restriction sought under paragraph (1) if—

(A) the temporary flight restriction would be inconsistent with aviation safety or security, would create a hazard to people or property on the ground, or would unnecessarily interfere with the efficient use of the airspace;

(B) the entity seeking the temporary flight restriction does not comply with the requirements in subsection (b);

(C) the eligibility requirements in subsections (c) and (d) have not been met;

(D) a flight restriction exists to the airspace overlying the same location as the temporary flight restriction sought under this section; or

(E) the Administrator determines appropriate for any other reason.

(b) REQUIREMENTS.—

(1) ADVANCE NOTICE.—Eligible entities may only request a temporary flight restriction under subsection (a) not less than 30 calendar days prior to the eligible large public gathering.

(2) REQUIRED INFORMATION.—Eligible entities seeking a temporary flight restriction under this section shall provide the Administrator with all relevant information,

including the following:

(A) Geographic boundaries of the stadium or other venue hosting the eligible large public gathering, as applicable.

(B) The dates and anticipated starting and ending times for the large public gathering.

(C) Points of contact for the requesting eligible entity and the on-scene incident command responsible for securing the large public gathering.

(D) Any other information the Administrator considers necessary to establish the restriction.

(c) ELIGIBLE LARGE PUBLIC GATHERINGS.—

(1) IN GENERAL.—To be eligible for a temporary flight restriction under this section, large public gatherings hosted in a stadium or other venue shall—

(A) be hosted in a stadium or other venue that—

(i) has previously hosted events qualifying for the application of special security instructions in accordance with section 521 of the Transportation, Treasury, and Independent Agencies Appropriations Act, 2004 (Public Law 108–199); and

(ii) is not enclosed;

(B) have an estimated attendance of at least 30,000 people; and

(C) be advertised in the public domain.

(2) ADDITIONAL GATHERINGS.—To be eligible for a temporary flight restriction under this section, large public gatherings hosted in a venue other than a stadium or other venue described in paragraph (1)(A) shall—

(A) have an estimated attendance of at least 100,000 people;

(B) be primarily outdoors;

(C) have a defined and static geographical boundary; and

(D) be advertised in the public domain.

(d) ELIGIBLE ENTITIES.—An entity eligible to request a temporary flight restriction under subsection (a) shall be a credentialed law enforcement organization of the Federal Government or a State, local, Tribal, or territorial government.

(e) TIMELINESS.—The Administrator shall make every practicable effort to assess eligibility and establish temporary flight restrictions under subsection (a) in a timely fashion.

(f) PUBLIC INFORMATION.—Any temporary flight restriction designated under this section shall be published by the Administrator in a publicly accessible manner at least 2 days prior to the start of the eligible large public gathering.

(g) PROHIBITION ON OPERATIONS.—No person may operate an unmanned aircraft within a temporary flight restriction established under this section unless—

(1) the Administrator authorizes the operation for operational or safety purposes;

(2) the operation is being conducted for safety, security, or compliance oversight purposes and is authorized by the Administrator; or

(3) the aircraft operation is conducted with the approval of the eligible entity.

(h) SAVINGS CLAUSE.—Nothing in this section may be construed as prohibiting the Administrator from authorizing the operation of an aircraft, including an unmanned aircraft system, over, under, or within a specified distance from an eligible large public gathering for which a temporary flight restriction has been established under this section or cancelling a temporary flight restriction established under this section.

(i) RULE OF CONSTRUCTION.—Nothing in this section shall be construed to prevent the Administrator from using existing processes or procedures to meet the intent of this section.

(Added Pub. L. 118–63, title IX, §935(a), May 16, 2024, 138 Stat. 1370.)

§44813. CENTER OF EXCELLENCE FOR UNMANNED AIRCRAFT SYSTEMS

(a) IN GENERAL.—The Administrator of the Federal Aviation Administration shall continue operation of the Center of Excellence for Unmanned Aircraft Systems (referred to in this section as the "Center").

(b) RESPONSIBILITIES.—The Center shall carry out the following responsibilities:

(1) Conduct applied research and training on the safe and efficient integration of unmanned aircraft systems and advanced air mobility into the national airspace system.

(2) Promote and facilitate collaboration among academia, the Federal Aviation Administration, Federal agency partners, and industry stakeholders (including manufacturers, operators, service providers, standards development organizations, carriers, and suppliers), with respect to the safe and efficient integration of unmanned aircraft systems and advanced air mobility into the national airspace system.

(3) Establish goals set to advance technology, improve engineering practices, and facilitate continuing education with respect to the safe and efficient integration of unmanned aircraft systems and advanced air mobility into the national airspace system.

(c) PROGRAM PARTICIPATION.—The Administrator shall ensure the participation in the Center of institutions of higher education (as defined in section 101 of the Higher Education Act of 1965 (20 U.S.C. 1001)) and research institutions that provide accredited bachelor's degree programs in aeronautical sciences that provide pathways to commercial pilot certifications and that include a focus on pilot training for women aviators.

(d) LEVERAGING OF CERTAIN CAPACITY AND CAPABILITIES.—The Administrator shall, in carrying out research necessary to validate consensus safety standards accepted pursuant to section 44805, to the maximum extent practicable, leverage the research and testing capacity and capabilities of—

(1) the Center;

(2) the test ranges designated under section 44803;

(3) existing Federal and non-Federal test ranges and testbeds;

(4) the National Aeronautics and Space Administration; and

(5) the William J. Hughes Technical Center for Advanced Aerospace.

(Added Pub. L. 118–63, title X, §1006(a), May 16, 2024, 138 Stat. 1388.)

§44814. ASSUREd SAFE CREDENTIALING AUTHORITY

(a) IN GENERAL.—Not later than 6 months after the date of enactment of this section, the Administrator of the Federal Aviation Administration shall establish a credentialing authority for the program of record of the Federal Aviation Administration (referred to in this section as "ASSUREd Safe") under the Center of Excellence for Unmanned Aircraft Systems.

(b) PURPOSES.—ASSUREd Safe shall offer services throughout the United States, and to allies and partners of the United States, including—

(1) online and in-person standards, education, and testing for the use of unmanned aircraft systems by first responders for emergency and disaster management operations;

(2) uniform communications standards, operational standards, and reporting standards for civilian, military, and international allies and partners; and

(3) any other relevant standards development related to operation of unmanned aircraft systems, as determined appropriate by the Administrator.

(c) COORDINATION.—The Administrator shall ensure that the Center of Excellence for Unmanned Aircraft Systems coordinates with the National Institute of Standards and Technology and the Federal Emergency Management Agency on establishment of ASSUREd Safe, and on any services offered by ASSUREd Safe.

(Added Pub. L. 118–63, title X, §1007(a), May 16, 2024, 138 Stat. 1389.)

CHAPTER 449—SECURITY

SUBCHAPTER I—REQUIREMENTS

SUBCHAPTER II—ADMINISTRATION AND PERSONNEL

[1] *Section catchline amended by Pub. L. 115–254 without corresponding amendment of chapter analysis.*

SUBCHAPTER I—REQUIREMENTS

§44901. SCREENING PASSENGERS AND PROPERTY

(a) IN GENERAL.—The Administrator of the Transportation Security Administration shall provide for the screening of all passengers and property, including United States mail, cargo, carry-on and checked baggage, and other articles, that will be carried aboard a passenger aircraft operated by an air carrier or foreign air carrier in air transportation or intrastate air transportation. In the case of flights and flight segments originating in the United States, the screening shall take place before boarding and shall be carried out by a Federal Government employee (as defined in section 2105 of title 5), except as otherwise provided in section 44920 and except for identifying passengers and baggage for screening under the CAPPS and known shipper programs and conducting positive bag-match programs.

(b) SUPERVISION OF SCREENING.—All screening of passengers and property at airports in the United States where screening is required under this section shall be supervised by uniformed Federal personnel of the Transportation Security Administration who shall have the power to order the dismissal of any individual performing such screening.

(c) CHECKED BAGGAGE.—A system must be in operation to screen all checked baggage at all airports in the United States as soon as practicable.

(d) EXPLOSIVES DETECTION SYSTEMS.—

(1) IN GENERAL.—The Administrator of the Transportation Security Administration shall take all necessary action to ensure that—

(A) explosives detection systems are deployed as soon as possible to ensure that all United States airports described in section 44903(c) have sufficient explosives detection systems to screen all checked baggage, and that as soon as such systems are in place at an airport, all checked baggage at the airport is screened by those systems; and

(B) all systems deployed under subparagraph (A) are fully utilized; and

(C) if explosives detection equipment at an airport is unavailable, all checked baggage is screened by an alternative means.

(2) PRECLEARANCE AIRPORTS.—

(A) IN GENERAL.—For a flight or flight segment originating at an airport outside the United States and traveling to the United States with respect to which checked baggage has been screened in accordance with an aviation security preclearance agreement between the United States and the country in which such airport is located, the Administrator of the Transportation Security Administration may, in coordination with U.S. Customs and Border Protection, determine whether such baggage must be re-screened in the United States by an explosives detection system before such baggage continues on any additional flight or flight segment.

(B) AVIATION SECURITY PRECLEARANCE AGREEMENT DEFINED.—In this paragraph, the term "aviation security preclearance agreement" means an agreement that delineates and implements security standards and protocols that are determined by the Administrator of the Transportation Security Administration, in coordination with U.S. Customs and Border Protection, to be comparable to those of the United States and therefore sufficiently effective to enable passengers to deplane into sterile areas of airports in the United States.

(C) RESCREENING REQUIREMENT.—If the Administrator of the Transportation Security Administration determines that the government of a foreign country has not maintained security standards and protocols comparable to those of the United States at airports at which preclearance operations have been established in accordance with this paragraph, the Administrator shall ensure that Transportation Security Administration personnel rescreen passengers arriving from such airports and their property in the United States before such passengers are permitted into sterile areas of airports in the United States.

(D) REPORT.—The Administrator of the Transportation Security Administration shall submit to the Committee on Homeland Security of the House of Representatives, the Committee on Commerce, Science, and Transportation of the Senate, and the Committee on Homeland Security and Governmental Affairs of the Senate an annual report on the re-screening of baggage under this paragraph. Each such report shall include the following for the year covered by the report:

(i) A list of airports outside the United States from which a flight or flight segment traveled to the United States for which the Administrator determined, in accordance with the authority under subparagraph (A), that checked baggage was not required to be re-screened in the United States by an explosives detection system before such baggage continued on an additional flight or flight segment.

(ii) The amount of Federal savings generated from the exercise of such authority.

(e) MANDATORY SCREENING WHERE EDS NOT YET AVAILABLE.—As soon as practicable and until the requirements of subsection (b)(1)(A) are met, the Administrator of the Transportation Security Administration shall require alternative means for screening any piece of checked baggage that is not screened by an explosives detection system. Such alternative means may include 1 or more of the following:

(1) A bag-match program that ensures that no checked baggage is placed aboard an aircraft unless the passenger who checked the baggage is aboard the aircraft.

(2) Manual search.

(3) Search by canine explosives detection units in combination with other means.

(4) Other means or technology approved by the Administrator.

(f) CARGO DEADLINE.—A system must be in operation to screen, inspect, or otherwise ensure the security of all cargo that is to be transported in all-cargo aircraft in air transportation and intrastate air transportation as soon as practicable.

(g) AIR CARGO ON PASSENGER AIRCRAFT.—

(1) IN GENERAL.—The Secretary of Homeland Security shall establish a system to screen 100 percent of cargo transported on passenger aircraft operated by an air carrier or foreign air carrier in air transportation or intrastate air transportation to ensure the security of all such passenger aircraft carrying cargo.

(2) MINIMUM STANDARDS.—The system referred to in paragraph (1) shall require, at a minimum, that equipment, technology, procedures, personnel, or other methods approved by the Administrator of the Transportation Security Administration, are used to screen cargo carried on passenger aircraft described in paragraph (1) to provide a level of security commensurate with the level of security for the screening of passenger checked baggage.

(3) REGULATIONS.—The Secretary of Homeland Security shall issue a final rule as a permanent regulation to implement this subsection in accordance with the provisions of chapter 5 of title 5.

(4) SCREENING DEFINED.—In this subsection the term "screening" means a physical examination or non-intrusive methods of assessing whether cargo poses a threat to transportation security. Methods of screening include x-ray systems, explosives detection systems, explosives trace detection, explosives detection canine teams certified by the Transportation Security Administration, or a physical search together with manifest verification. The Administrator may approve additional methods to ensure that the cargo does not pose a threat to transportation security and to assist in meeting the requirements of this subsection. Such additional cargo screening methods shall not include solely performing a review of information about the contents of cargo or verifying the identity of a shipper of the cargo that is not performed in conjunction with other security methods authorized under this subsection, including whether a known shipper is registered in the known shipper database. Such additional cargo screening methods may include a program to certify the security methods used by shippers pursuant to paragraphs (1) and (2) and alternative screening methods pursuant to exemptions referred to in subsection (b) of section 1602 of the Implementing Recommendations of the 9/11 Commission Act of 2007.

(h) DEPLOYMENT OF ARMED PERSONNEL.—

(1) IN GENERAL.—The Administrator of the Transportation Security Administration shall order the deployment of law enforcement personnel authorized to carry firearms at each airport security screening location to ensure passenger safety and national security.

(2) MINIMUM REQUIREMENTS.—Except at airports required to enter into agreements under subsection (c), the Administrator of the Transportation Security Administration shall order the deployment of at least 1 law enforcement officer at each airport security screening location. At the 100 largest airports in the United States, in terms of annual passenger enplanements for the most recent calendar year for which data are available,

the Administrator shall order the deployment of additional law enforcement personnel at airport security screening locations if the Administrator determines that the additional deployment is necessary to ensure passenger safety and national security.

(i) EXEMPTIONS AND ADVISING CONGRESS ON REGULATIONS.—The Administrator of the Transportation Security Administration—

(1) may exempt from this section air transportation operations, except scheduled passenger operations of an air carrier providing air transportation under a certificate issued under section 41102 of this title or a permit issued under section 41302 of this title; and

(2) shall advise Congress of a regulation to be prescribed under this section at least 30 days before the effective date of the regulation, unless the Administrator decides an emergency exists requiring the regulation to become effective in fewer than 30 days and notifies Congress of that decision.

(j) BLAST-RESISTANT CARGO CONTAINERS.—

(1) IN GENERAL.—The Administrator of the Transportation Security Administration shall—

(A) evaluate the results of the blast-resistant cargo container pilot program that was initiated before August 3, 2007; and

(B) prepare and distribute through the Aviation Security Advisory Committee to the appropriate Committees [1] of Congress and air carriers a report on that evaluation which may contain nonclassified and classified sections.

(2) ACQUISITION, MAINTENANCE, AND REPLACEMENT.—Upon completion and consistent with the results of the evaluation that paragraph (1)(A) requires, the Administrator shall—

(A) develop and implement a program, as the Administrator determines appropriate, to acquire, maintain, and replace blast-resistant cargo containers;

(B) pay for the program; and

(C) make available blast-resistant cargo containers to air carriers pursuant to paragraph (3).

(3) DISTRIBUTION TO AIR CARRIERS.—The Administrator shall make available, beginning not later than July 1, 2008, blast-resistant cargo containers to air carriers for use on a risk managed basis as determined by the Administrator.

(k) GENERAL AVIATION AIRPORT SECURITY PROGRAM.—

(1) IN GENERAL.—The Administrator of the Transportation Security Administration shall—

(A) develop a standardized threat and vulnerability assessment program for general aviation airports (as defined in section 47134(m)); and

(B) implement a program to perform such assessments on a risk-managed basis at general aviation airports.

(2) GRANT PROGRAM.—The Administrator shall initiate and complete a study of the feasibility of a program, based on a risk-managed approach, to provide grants to operators of general aviation airports (as defined in section 47134(m)) [1] for projects to upgrade security at such airports. If the Administrator determines that such a program is feasible, the Administrator shall establish such a program.

(3) APPLICATION TO GENERAL AVIATION AIRCRAFT.—The Administrator shall develop a

risk-based system under which—

(A) general aviation aircraft, as identified by the Administrator, in coordination with the Administrator of the Federal Aviation Administration, are required to submit passenger information and advance notification requirements for United States Customs and Border Protection before entering United States airspace; and

(B) such information is checked against appropriate databases.

(4) AUTHORIZATION OF APPROPRIATIONS.—There are authorized to be appropriated to the Administrator of the Transportation Security Administration such sums as may be necessary to carry out paragraphs (2) and (3).

(l) LIMITATIONS ON USE OF ADVANCED IMAGING TECHNOLOGY FOR SCREENING PASSENGERS.—

(1) DEFINITIONS.—In this subsection, the following definitions apply:

(A) ADVANCED IMAGING TECHNOLOGY.—The term "advanced imaging technology"—

(i) means a device used in the screening of passengers that creates a visual image of an individual showing the surface of the skin and revealing other objects on the body; and

(ii) may include devices using backscatter x-rays or millimeter waves and devices referred to as "whole-body imaging technology" or "body scanning machines".

(B) APPROPRIATE CONGRESSIONAL COMMITTEES.—The term "appropriate congressional committees" means—

(i) the Committee on Commerce, Science, and Transportation and the Committee on Homeland Security and Governmental Affairs of the Senate; and

(ii) the Committee on Homeland Security of the House of Representatives.

(C) AUTOMATIC TARGET RECOGNITION SOFTWARE.—The term "automatic target recognition software" means software installed on an advanced imaging technology that produces a generic image of the individual being screened that is the same as the images produced for all other screened individuals.

(2) USE OF ADVANCED IMAGING TECHNOLOGY.—The Administrator of the Transportation Security Administration shall ensure that any advanced imaging technology used for the screening of passengers under this section—

(A) is equipped with and employs automatic target recognition software; and

(B) complies with such other requirements as the Administrator determines necessary to address privacy considerations.

(3) EXTENSION.—

(A) IN GENERAL.—The Administrator of the Transportation Security Administration may extend the deadline specified in paragraph (2), if the Administrator determines that—

(i) an advanced imaging technology equipped with automatic target recognition software is not substantially as effective at screening passengers as an advanced imaging technology without such software; or

(ii) additional testing of such software is necessary.

(B) DURATION OF EXTENSIONS.—The Administrator of the Transportation Security Administration may issue one or more extensions under subparagraph (A). The duration of each extension may not exceed one year.

(4) Reports.—

(A) In general.—Not later than 60 days after the date on which the Administrator of the Transportation Security Administration issues any extension under paragraph (3), the Administrator shall submit to the appropriate congressional committees a report on the implementation of this subsection.

(B) Elements.—A report submitted under subparagraph (A) shall include the following:

(i) A description of all matters the Administrator of the Transportation Security Administration considers relevant to the implementation of the requirements of this subsection.

(ii) The status of compliance by the Transportation Security Administration with such requirements.

(iii) If the Administration is not in full compliance with such requirements—

(I) the reasons for the noncompliance; and

(II) a timeline depicting when the Administrator of the Transportation Security Administration expects the Administration to achieve full compliance.

(C) Security classification.—To the greatest extent practicable, a report prepared under subparagraph (A) shall be submitted in an unclassified format. If necessary, the report may include a classified annex.

(Pub. L. 103–272, §1(e), July 5, 1994, 108 Stat. 1204; Pub. L. 107–71, title I, §§101(f)(7), 110(b), Nov. 19, 2001, 115 Stat. 603, 614; Pub. L. 107–296, title IV, §425, Nov. 25, 2002, 116 Stat. 2185; Pub. L. 110–53, title XVI, §§1602(a), 1609, 1617, Aug. 3, 2007, 121 Stat. 477, 484, 488; Pub. L. 112–95, title VIII, §826, Feb. 14, 2012, 126 Stat. 132; Pub. L. 112–218, §2, Dec. 20, 2012, 126 Stat. 1593; Pub. L. 114–125, title VIII, §815, Feb. 24, 2016, 130 Stat. 220; Pub. L. 115–254, div. K, title I, §§1937(b)(3), 1991(d)(1), Oct. 5, 2018, 132 Stat. 3579, 3627.)

[1] So in original. Probably should be "committees".

§44902. Refusal to transport passengers and property

(a) Mandatory Refusal.—The Administrator of the Transportation Security Administration shall prescribe regulations requiring an air carrier, intrastate air carrier, or foreign air carrier to refuse to transport—

(1) a passenger who does not consent to a search under section 44901(a) of this title establishing whether the passenger is carrying unlawfully a dangerous weapon, explosive, or other destructive substance; or

(2) property of a passenger who does not consent to a search of the property establishing whether the property unlawfully contains a dangerous weapon, explosive, or other destructive substance.

(b) Permissive Refusal.—Subject to regulations of the Administrator of the Transportation Security Administration, an air carrier, intrastate air carrier, or foreign air carrier may refuse to transport a passenger or property the carrier decides is, or might be, inimical to safety.

(c) Agreeing to Consent to Search.—An agreement to carry passengers or property in air transportation or intrastate air transportation by an air carrier, intrastate air carrier, or foreign air carrier is deemed to include an agreement that the passenger or property will not be carried if consent to search the passenger or property for a purpose referred to in this section is not given.

(Pub. L. 103–272, §1(e), July 5, 1994, 108 Stat. 1204; Pub. L. 107–71, title I, §101(f)(7), (9), Nov. 19, 2001, 115 Stat. 603; Pub. L. 115–254, div. K, title I, §1991(d)(2), Oct. 5, 2018, 132 Stat. 3630.)

§44903. AIR TRANSPORTATION SECURITY

(a) DEFINITIONS.—In this section:

(1) ADMINISTRATOR.—The term "Administrator" means the Administrator of the Transportation Security Administration.

(2) LAW ENFORCEMENT PERSONNEL.—The term "law enforcement personnel" means individuals—

(A) authorized to carry and use firearms;

(B) vested with the degree of the police power of arrest the Administrator considers necessary to carry out this section; and

(C) identifiable by appropriate indicia of authority.

(b) PROTECTION AGAINST VIOLENCE AND PIRACY.—The Administrator shall prescribe regulations to protect passengers and property on an aircraft operating in air transportation or intrastate air transportation against an act of criminal violence or aircraft piracy. When prescribing a regulation under this subsection, the Administrator shall—

(1) consult with the Secretary of Transportation, the Attorney General, the heads of other departments, agencies, and instrumentalities of the United States Government, and State and local authorities;

(2) consider whether a proposed regulation is consistent with—

(A) protecting passengers; and

(B) the public interest in promoting air transportation and intrastate air transportation;

(3) to the maximum extent practicable, require a uniform procedure for searching and detaining passengers and property to ensure—

(A) their safety; and

(B) courteous and efficient treatment by an air carrier, an agent or employee of an air carrier, and Government, State, and local law enforcement personnel carrying out this section; and

(4) consider the extent to which a proposed regulation will carry out this section.

(c) SECURITY PROGRAMS.—(1) The Administrator shall prescribe regulations under subsection (b) of this section that require each operator of an airport regularly serving an air carrier holding a certificate issued by the Secretary of Transportation to establish an air transportation security program that provides a law enforcement presence and capability at each of those airports that is adequate to ensure the safety of passengers. The regulations shall authorize the operator to use the services of qualified State, local, and private law enforcement personnel. When the Administrator decides, after being notified by an operator in the form the Administrator prescribes, that not enough qualified State, local, and private law enforcement personnel are available to carry out subsection (b), the Administrator may authorize the operator to use, on a reimbursable basis, personnel employed by the Administrator, or by another department, agency, or instrumentality of the Government with the consent of the head of the department, agency, or instrumentality, to supplement State, local, and private law enforcement personnel. When deciding whether additional personnel are needed, the Administrator shall consider the number of passengers boarded at the airport, the extent of anticipated risk of criminal violence or aircraft piracy at the airport or to the air carrier aircraft operations at the airport, and the availability of qualified State or local law enforcement personnel at the airport.

(2)(A) The Administrator may approve a security program of an airport operator, or an amendment in an existing program, that incorporates a security program of an airport tenant (except an air carrier separately complying with part 108 or 129 of title 14, Code of Federal Regulations) having access to a secured area of the airport, if the program or amendment incorporates—

 (i) the measures the tenant will use, within the tenant's leased areas or areas designated for the tenant's exclusive use under an agreement with the airport operator, to carry out the security requirements imposed by the Administrator on the airport operator under the access control system requirements of section 107.14 of title 14, Code of Federal Regulations, or under other requirements of part 107 of title 14; and

 (ii) the methods the airport operator will use to monitor and audit the tenant's compliance with the security requirements and provides that the tenant will be required to pay monetary penalties to the airport operator if the tenant fails to carry out a security requirement under a contractual provision or requirement imposed by the airport operator.

(B) If the Administrator approves a program or amendment described in subparagraph (A) of this paragraph, the airport operator may not be found to be in violation of a requirement of this subsection or subsection (b) of this section when the airport operator demonstrates that the tenant or an employee, permittee, or invitee of the tenant is responsible for the violation and that the airport operator has complied with all measures in its security program for securing compliance with its security program by the tenant.

(C) MAXIMUM USE OF CHEMICAL AND BIOLOGICAL WEAPON DETECTION EQUIPMENT.—The Secretary of Transportation may require airports to maximize the use of technology and equipment that is designed to detect or neutralize potential chemical or biological weapons.

(3) PILOT PROGRAMS.—The Administrator shall establish pilot programs in no fewer than 20 airports to test and evaluate new and emerging technology for providing access control and other security protections for closed or secure areas of the airports. Such technology may include biometric or other technology that ensures only authorized access to secure areas.

(d) AUTHORIZING INDIVIDUALS TO CARRY FIREARMS AND MAKE ARRESTS.—With the approval of the Attorney General and the Secretary of State, the Administrator may authorize an individual who carries out air transportation security duties—

 (1) to carry firearms; and

 (2) to make arrests without warrant for an offense against the United States committed in the presence of the individual or for a felony under the laws of the United States, if the individual reasonably believes the individual to be arrested has committed or is committing a felony.

(e) EXCLUSIVE RESPONSIBILITY OVER PASSENGER SAFETY.—The Administrator has the exclusive responsibility to direct law enforcement activity related to the safety of passengers on an aircraft involved in an offense under section 46502 of this title from the moment all external doors of the aircraft are closed following boarding until those doors are opened to allow passengers to leave the aircraft. When requested by the Administrator, other departments, agencies, and instrumentalities of the Government shall provide assistance necessary to carry out this subsection.

(f) GOVERNMENT AND INDUSTRY CONSORTIA.—The Administrator may establish at airports such consortia of government and aviation industry representatives as the Administrator may designate to provide advice on matters related to aviation security and safety. Such consortia shall not be considered Federal advisory committees for purposes of chapter 10 of title 5.

(g) IMPROVEMENT OF SECURED-AREA ACCESS CONTROL.—

(1) ENFORCEMENT.—

(A) ADMINISTRATOR TO PUBLISH SANCTIONS.—The Administrator shall publish in the Federal Register a list of sanctions for use as guidelines in the discipline of employees for infractions of airport access control requirements. The guidelines shall incorporate a progressive disciplinary approach that relates proposed sanctions to the severity or recurring nature of the infraction and shall include measures such as remedial training, suspension from security-related duties, suspension from all duties without pay, and termination of employment.

(B) USE OF SANCTIONS.—Each airport operator, air carrier, and security screening company shall include the list of sanctions published by the Administrator in its security program. The security program shall include a process for taking prompt disciplinary action against an employee who commits an infraction of airport access control requirements.

(2) IMPROVEMENTS.—The Administrator shall—

(A) work with airport operators and air carriers to implement and strengthen existing controls to eliminate airport access control weaknesses;

(B) require airport operators and air carriers to develop and implement comprehensive and recurring training programs that teach employees their roles in airport security, the importance of their participation, how their performance will be evaluated, and what action will be taken if they fail to perform;

(C) require airport operators and air carriers to develop and implement programs that foster and reward compliance with airport access control requirements and discourage and penalize noncompliance in accordance with guidelines issued by the Administrator to measure employee compliance;

(D) on an ongoing basis, assess and test for compliance with access control requirements, report annually findings of the assessments, and assess the effectiveness of penalties in ensuring compliance with security procedures and take any other appropriate enforcement actions when noncompliance is found;

(E) improve and better administer the Administrator's security database to ensure its efficiency, reliability, and usefulness for identification of systemic problems and allocation of resources;

(F) improve the execution of the Administrator's quality control program; and

(G) work with airport operators to strengthen access control points in secured areas (including air traffic control operations areas, maintenance areas, crew lounges, baggage handling areas, concessions, and catering delivery areas) to ensure the security of passengers and aircraft and consider the deployment of biometric or similar technologies that identify individuals based on unique personal characteristics.

(h) IMPROVED AIRPORT PERIMETER ACCESS SECURITY.—

(1) IN GENERAL.—The Administrator, in consultation with the airport operator and law enforcement authorities, may order the deployment of such personnel at any secure area of the airport as necessary to counter the risk of criminal violence, the risk of aircraft piracy at the airport, the risk to air carrier aircraft operations at the airport, or to meet national security concerns.

(2) SECURITY OF AIRCRAFT AND GROUND ACCESS TO SECURE AREAS.—In determining where to deploy such personnel, the Administrator shall consider the physical security needs of air traffic control facilities, parked aircraft, aircraft servicing equipment, aircraft supplies (including fuel), automobile parking facilities within airport perimeters or adjacent to secured facilities, and access and transition areas at airports served by other means of ground or water transportation.

(3) DEPLOYMENT OF FEDERAL LAW ENFORCEMENT PERSONNEL.—The Secretary of Homeland Security may enter into a memorandum of understanding or other agreement with the Attorney General or the head of any other appropriate Federal law enforcement agency to deploy Federal law enforcement personnel at an airport in order to meet aviation safety and security concerns.

(4) AIRPORT PERIMETER SCREENING.—The Administrator—

(A) shall require screening or inspection of all individuals, goods, property, vehicles, and other equipment before entry into a secured area of an airport in the United States described in section 44903(c); [1]

(B) shall prescribe specific requirements for such screening and inspection that will assure at least the same level of protection as will result from screening of passengers and their baggage;

(C) shall establish procedures to ensure the safety and integrity of—

(i) all persons providing services with respect to aircraft providing passenger air transportation or intrastate air transportation and facilities of such persons at an airport in the United States described in subsection (c);

(ii) all supplies, including catering and passenger amenities, placed aboard such aircraft, including the sealing of supplies to ensure easy visual detection of tampering; and

(iii) all persons providing such supplies and facilities of such persons;

(D) shall require vendors having direct access to the airfield and aircraft to develop security programs; and

(E) shall issue guidance for the use of biometric or other technology that positively verifies the identity of each employee and law enforcement officer who enters a secure area of an airport.

(5) USE OF BIOMETRIC TECHNOLOGY IN AIRPORT ACCESS CONTROL SYSTEMS.—In issuing guidance under paragraph (4)(E), the Administrator in consultation with representatives of the aviation industry, the biometric identifier industry, and the National Institute of Standards and Technology, shall establish, at a minimum—

(A) comprehensive technical and operational system requirements and performance standards for the use of biometric identifier technology in airport access control systems (including airport perimeter access control systems) to ensure that the biometric identifier systems are effective, reliable, and secure;

(B) a list of products and vendors that meet the requirements and standards set forth in subparagraph (A);

(C) procedures for implementing biometric identifier systems—

(i) to ensure that individuals do not use an assumed identity to enroll in a biometric identifier system; and

(ii) to resolve failures to enroll, false matches, and false non-matches; and

(D) best practices for incorporating biometric identifier technology into airport access control systems in the most effective manner, including a process to best utilize existing airport access control systems, facilities, and equipment and existing data networks connecting airports.

(6) USE OF BIOMETRIC TECHNOLOGY FOR ARMED LAW ENFORCEMENT TRAVEL.—

(A) IN GENERAL.—The Secretary of Homeland Security, in consultation with the Attorney General, shall—

(i) implement this paragraph by publication in the Federal Register; and

(ii) establish a national registered armed law enforcement program, that shall be federally managed, for law enforcement officers needing to be armed when traveling by commercial aircraft.

(B) PROGRAM REQUIREMENTS.—The program shall—

(i) establish a credential or a system that incorporates biometric technology and other applicable technologies;

(ii) establish a system for law enforcement officers who need to be armed when traveling by commercial aircraft on a regular basis and for those who need to be armed during temporary travel assignments;

(iii) comply with other uniform credentialing initiatives, including the Homeland Security Presidential Directive 12;

(iv) apply to all Federal, State, local, tribal, and territorial government law enforcement agencies; and

(v) establish a process by which the travel credential or system may be used to verify the identity, using biometric technology, of a Federal, State, local, tribal, or territorial law enforcement officer seeking to carry a weapon on board a commercial aircraft, without unnecessarily disclosing to the public that the individual is a law enforcement officer.

(C) PROCEDURES.—In establishing the program, the Secretary of Homeland Security shall develop procedures—

(i) to ensure that a law enforcement officer of a Federal, State, local, tribal, or territorial government flying armed has a specific reason for flying armed and the reason is within the scope of the duties of such officer;

(ii) to preserve the anonymity of the armed law enforcement officer;

(iii) to resolve failures to enroll, false matches, and false nonmatches relating to the use of the law enforcement travel credential or system;

(iv) to determine the method of issuance of the biometric credential to law enforcement officers needing to be armed when traveling by commercial aircraft;

(v) to invalidate any law enforcement travel credential or system that is lost, stolen, or no longer authorized for use;

(vi) to coordinate the program with the Federal Air Marshal Service, including the force multiplier program of the Service; and

(vii) to implement a phased approach to launching the program, addressing the immediate needs of the relevant Federal agent population before expanding to other law enforcement populations.

(7) DEFINITIONS.—In this subsection, the following definitions apply:

(A) BIOMETRIC IDENTIFIER INFORMATION.—The term "biometric identifier information" means the distinct physical or behavioral characteristics of an individual that are used for unique identification, or verification of the identity, of an individual.

(B) BIOMETRIC IDENTIFIER.—The term "biometric identifier" means a technology that enables the automated identification, or verification of the identity, of an individual based on biometric information.

(C) FAILURE TO ENROLL.—The term "failure to enroll" means the inability of an individual to enroll in a biometric identifier system due to an insufficiently distinctive biometric sample, the lack of a body part necessary to provide the biometric sample, a system design that makes it difficult to provide consistent biometric identifier information, or other factors.

(D) FALSE MATCH.—The term "false match" means the incorrect matching of one individual's biometric identifier information to another individual's biometric identifier information by a biometric identifier system.

(E) FALSE NON-MATCH.—The term "false non-match" means the rejection of a valid identity by a biometric identifier system.

(F) SECURE AREA OF AN AIRPORT.—The term "secure area of an airport" means the sterile area and the Secure Identification Display Area of an airport (as such terms are defined in section 1540.5 of title 49, Code of Federal Regulations, or any successor regulation to such section).

(i) AUTHORITY TO ARM FLIGHT DECK CREW WITH LESS-THAN-LETHAL WEAPONS.—

(1) IN GENERAL.—If the Administrator, after receiving the recommendations of the National Institute of Justice, determines, with the approval of the Attorney General and the Secretary of State, that it is appropriate and necessary and would effectively serve the public interest in avoiding air piracy, the Administrator may authorize members of the flight deck crew on any aircraft providing air transportation or intrastate air transportation to carry a less-than-lethal weapon while the aircraft is engaged in providing such transportation.

(2) USAGE.—If the Administrator grants authority under paragraph (1) for flight deck crew members to carry a less-than-lethal weapon while engaged in providing air transportation or intrastate air transportation, the Administrator shall—

(A) prescribe rules requiring that any such crew member be trained in the proper use of the weapon; and

(B) prescribe guidelines setting forth the circumstances under which such weapons may be used.

(3) REQUEST OF AIR CARRIERS TO USE LESS-THAN-LETHAL WEAPONS.—If the Administrator receives a request from an air carrier for authorization to allow pilots of the air carrier to carry less-than-lethal weapons, the Administrator shall respond to that request within 90 days.

(j) SHORT-TERM ASSESSMENT AND DEPLOYMENT OF EMERGING SECURITY TECHNOLOGIES AND PROCEDURES.—

(1) IN GENERAL.—The Administrator shall periodically recommend to airport operators commercially available measures or procedures to prevent access to secure airport areas by unauthorized persons.

(2) SECURE FLIGHT PROGRAM.—

(A) IN GENERAL.—The Administrator shall ensure that the Secure Flight program, or any successor program—

(i) is used to evaluate all passengers before they board an aircraft; and

(ii) includes procedures to ensure that individuals selected by the program and their carry-on and checked baggage are adequately screened.

(B) MODIFICATIONS.—The Administrator may modify any requirement under the Secure Flight program for flights that originate and terminate within the same State, if the Administrator determines that—

(i) the State has extraordinary air transportation needs or concerns due to its isolation and dependence on air transportation; and

(ii) the routine characteristics of passengers, given the nature of the market, regularly triggers primary selectee status.

(C) ADVANCED AIRLINE PASSENGER PRESCREENING.—

(i) COMMENCEMENT OF TESTING.—The Administrator shall commence testing of an advanced passenger prescreening system that will allow the Department of Homeland Security to assume the performance of comparing passenger information, as defined by the Administrator, to the automatic selectee and no fly lists, utilizing all appropriate records in the consolidated and integrated terrorist watchlist maintained by the Federal Government.

(ii) ASSUMPTION OF FUNCTION.—The Administrator, or the designee of the Administrator, shall begin to assume the performance of the passenger prescreening function of comparing passenger information to the automatic selectee and no fly lists and utilize all appropriate records in the consolidated and integrated terrorist watchlist maintained by the Federal Government in performing that function.

(iii) REQUIREMENTS.—In assuming performance of the function under clause (ii), the Administrator shall—

(I) establish a procedure to enable airline passengers, who are delayed or prohibited from boarding a flight because the advanced passenger prescreening system determined that they might pose a security threat, to appeal such determination and correct information contained in the system;

(II) ensure that Federal Government databases that will be used to establish the identity of a passenger under the system will not produce a large number of false positives;

(III) establish an internal oversight board to oversee and monitor the manner in which the system is being implemented;

(IV) establish sufficient operational safeguards to reduce the opportunities for abuse;

(V) implement substantial security measures to protect the system from unauthorized access;

(VI) adopt policies establishing effective oversight of the use and operation of the system; and

(VII) ensure that there are no specific privacy concerns with the technological architecture of the system.

(iv) PASSENGER INFORMATION.—After the completion of the testing of the advanced passenger prescreening system, the Administrator, by order or interim final rule—

(I) shall require air carriers to supply to the Administrator the passenger information needed to begin implementing the advanced passenger prescreening system; and

(II) shall require entities that provide systems and services to air carriers in the operation of air carrier reservations systems to provide to air carriers passenger information in possession of such entities, but only to the extent necessary to comply with subclause (I).

(v) INCLUSION OF DETAINEES ON NO FLY LIST.—The Administrator, in coordination with the Terrorist Screening Center, shall include on the No Fly List any individual who was a detainee held at the Naval Station, Guantanamo Bay, Cuba, unless the President certifies in writing to Congress that the detainee poses no threat to the United States, its citizens, or its allies. For purposes of this clause, the term "detainee" means an individual in the custody or under the physical control of the United States as a result of armed conflict.

(D) SCREENING OF EMPLOYEES AGAINST WATCHLIST.—The Administrator, in coordination with the Secretary of Transportation and the Administrator of the Federal Aviation Administration, shall ensure that individuals are screened against all appropriate records in the consolidated and integrated terrorist watchlist maintained by the Federal Government before—

(i) being certificated by the Federal Aviation Administration;

(ii) being granted unescorted access to the secure area of an airport; or

(iii) being granted unescorted access to the air operations area (as defined in section 1540.5 of title 49, Code of Federal Regulations, or any successor regulation to such section) of an airport.

(E) AIRCRAFT CHARTER CUSTOMER AND LESSEE PRESCREENING.—

(i) IN GENERAL.—The Administrator Administrator [2] shall establish a process by which operators of aircraft to be used in charter air transportation with a maximum takeoff weight greater than 12,500 pounds and lessors of aircraft with a maximum takeoff weight greater than 12,500 pounds may—

(I) request the Department of Homeland Security to use the advanced passenger prescreening system to compare information about any individual seeking to charter an aircraft with a maximum takeoff weight greater than 12,500 pounds, any passenger proposed to be transported aboard such aircraft, and any individual seeking to lease an aircraft with a maximum takeoff weight greater than 12,500 pounds to the automatic selectee and no fly lists, utilizing all appropriate records in the consolidated and integrated terrorist watchlist maintained by the Federal Government; and

(II) refuse to charter or lease an aircraft with a maximum takeoff weight greater than 12,500 pounds to or transport aboard such aircraft any persons identified on such watch list.

(ii) REQUIREMENTS.—The requirements of subparagraph (C)(iii) shall apply to this subparagraph.

(iii) NO FLY AND AUTOMATIC SELECTEE LISTS.—The Secretary of Homeland Security, in consultation with the Terrorist Screening Center, shall design and review, as necessary, guidelines, policies, and operating procedures for the collection, removal, and updating of data maintained, or to be maintained, in the no fly and automatic selectee lists.

(F) APPLICABILITY.—Section 607 of the Vision 100—Century of Aviation Reauthorization Act (49 U.S.C. 44903 note; 117 Stat. 2568) shall not apply to the advanced passenger prescreening system established under subparagraph (C).

(G) APPEAL PROCEDURES.—

(i) IN GENERAL.—The Administrator shall establish a timely and fair process for individuals identified as a threat under one or more of subparagraphs (C), (D), and (E) to appeal to the Transportation Security Administration the determination and correct any erroneous information.

(ii) RECORDS.—The process shall include the establishment of a method by which the Administrator will be able to maintain a record of air passengers and other individuals who have been misidentified and have corrected erroneous information. To prevent repeated delays of misidentified passengers and other individuals, the Transportation Security Administration record shall contain information determined by the Administrator to authenticate the identity of such a passenger or individual.

(H) DEFINITION.—In this paragraph, the term "secure area of an airport" means the sterile area and the Secure Identification Display Area of an airport (as such terms are defined in section 1540.5 of title 49, Code of Federal Regulations, or any successor regulation to such section).

(k) LIMITATION ON LIABILITY FOR ACTS TO THWART CRIMINAL VIOLENCE OR AIRCRAFT PIRACY.—An individual shall not be liable for damages in any action brought in a Federal or State court arising out of the acts of the individual in attempting to thwart an act of criminal violence or piracy on an aircraft if that individual reasonably believed that such an act of criminal violence or piracy was occurring or was about to occur.

(l) AIR CHARTER PROGRAM.—

(1) IN GENERAL.—The Administrator shall implement an aviation security program for charter air carriers (as defined in section 40102(a)) with a maximum certificated takeoff weight of more than 12,500 pounds.

(2) EXEMPTION FOR ARMED FORCES CHARTERS.—

(A) IN GENERAL.—Paragraph (1) and the other requirements of this chapter do not apply to passengers and property carried by aircraft when employed to provide charter transportation to members of the armed forces.

(B) SECURITY PROCEDURES.—The Secretary of Defense, in consultation with the Secretary of Homeland Security and the Secretary of Transportation, shall establish security procedures relating to the operation of aircraft when employed to provide charter transportation to members of the armed forces to or from an airport described in section 44903(c).

(C) ARMED FORCES DEFINED.—In this paragraph, the term "armed forces" has the meaning given that term by section 101(a)(4) of title 10.

(m) SECURITY SCREENING FOR MEMBERS OF THE ARMED FORCES.—

(1) IN GENERAL.—The Administrator, in consultation with the Department of Defense, shall develop and implement a plan to provide expedited security screening services for a member of the armed forces, and, to the extent possible, any accompanying family member, if the member of the armed forces, while in uniform, presents documentation indicating official orders for air transportation departing from a primary airport (as defined in section 47102).

(2) PROTOCOLS.—In developing the plan, the Administrator shall consider—

(A) leveraging existing security screening models used to reduce passenger wait times;

(B) establishing standard guidelines for the screening of military uniform items, including combat boots; and

(C) incorporating any new screening protocols into an existing trusted passenger program, as established pursuant to section 109(a)(3) of the Aviation and Transportation Security Act (49 U.S.C. 114 note), or into the development of any new credential or system that incorporates biometric technology and other applicable technologies to verify the identity of individuals traveling in air transportation.

(3) RULE OF CONSTRUCTION.—Nothing in this subsection shall affect the authority of the Administrator to require additional screening of a member of the armed forces if intelligence or law enforcement information indicates that additional screening is necessary.

(4) REPORT TO CONGRESS.—The Administrator shall submit to the appropriate committees of Congress a report on the implementation of the plan.

(n) PASSENGER EXIT POINTS FROM STERILE AREA.—

(1) IN GENERAL.—The Secretary of Homeland Security shall ensure that the Transportation Security Administration is responsible for monitoring passenger exit points from the sterile area of airports at which the Transportation Security Administration provided such monitoring as of December 1, 2013.

(2) STERILE AREA DEFINED.—In this section, the term "sterile area" has the meaning given that term in section 1540.5 of title 49, Code of Federal Regulations (or any corresponding similar regulation or ruling).

(Pub. L. 103–272, §1(e), July 5, 1994, 108 Stat. 1205; Pub. L. 106–181, title VII, §717, Apr. 5, 2000, 114 Stat. 163; Pub. L. 106–528, §§4, 6, Nov. 22, 2000, 114 Stat. 2520, 2521; Pub. L. 107–71, title I, §§101(f)(7)–(9), 106(a), (c), (d), 120, 126(b), 136, 144, Nov. 19, 2001, 115 Stat. 603, 608–610, 629, 632, 636, 644; Pub. L. 107–296, title XIV, §§1405, 1406, Nov. 25, 2002, 116 Stat. 2307; Pub. L. 108–176, title VI, §606(a), Dec. 12, 2003, 117 Stat. 2568; Pub. L. 108–458, title IV, §§4011(a), 4012(a)(1), Dec. 17, 2004, 118 Stat. 3712, 3714; Pub. L. 110–53, title XVI, §1615(a), Aug. 3, 2007, 121 Stat. 486; Pub. L. 111–83, title V, §553, Oct. 28, 2009, 123 Stat. 2179; Pub. L. 112–86, §2(a), Jan. 3, 2012, 125 Stat. 1874; Pub. L. 113–67, div. A, title VI, §603, Dec. 26, 2013, 127 Stat. 1188; Pub. L. 115–254, div. K, title I, §1991(d)(3), Oct. 5, 2018, 132 Stat. 3630; Pub. L. 117–286, §4(a)(316), Dec. 27, 2022, 136 Stat. 4340.)

[1] So in original. Probably should be "subsection (c)".

[2] So in original.

§44904. Domestic Air Transportation System Security

(a) Assessing Threats.—The Administrator of the Transportation Security Administration and the Director of the Federal Bureau of Investigation jointly shall assess current and potential threats to the domestic air transportation system. The assessment shall include consideration of the extent to which there are individuals with the capability and intent to carry out terrorist or related unlawful acts against that system and the ways in which those individuals might carry out those acts. The Administrator of the Transportation Security Administration and the Director jointly shall decide on and carry out the most effective method for continuous analysis and monitoring of security threats to that system.

(b) Assessing Security.—In coordination with the Director, the Administrator of the Transportation Security Administration shall carry out periodic threat and vulnerability assessments on security at each airport that is part of the domestic air transportation system. Each assessment shall include consideration of—

(1) the adequacy of security procedures related to the handling and transportation of checked baggage and cargo;

(2) space requirements for security personnel and equipment;

(3) separation of screened and unscreened passengers, baggage, and cargo;

(4) separation of the controlled and uncontrolled areas of airport facilities; and

(5) coordination of the activities of security personnel of the Transportation Security Administration, the United States Customs Service, the Immigration and Naturalization Service, and air carriers, and of other law enforcement personnel.

(c) Modal Security Plan for Aviation.—In addition to the requirements set forth in subparagraphs (B) through (F) of section 114(s)(3), the modal security plan for aviation prepared under section 114(s) shall—

(1) establish a damage mitigation and recovery plan for the aviation system in the event of a terrorist attack; and

(2) include a threat matrix document that outlines each threat to the United States civil aviation system and the corresponding layers of security in place to address such threat.

(d) Operational Criteria.—The Administrator of the Transportation Security Administration shall issue operational criteria to protect airport infrastructure and operations against the threats identified in the plans prepared under section 114(s)(1) and shall approve best practices guidelines for airport assets.

(e) Improving Security.—The Administrator of the Transportation Security Administration shall take necessary actions to improve domestic air transportation security by correcting any deficiencies in that security discovered in the assessments, analyses, and monitoring carried out under this section.

(Pub. L. 103–272, §1(e), July 5, 1994, 108 Stat. 1207; Pub. L. 107–71, title I, §101(f)(1), (7), (9), Nov. 19, 2001, 115 Stat. 603; Pub. L. 108–458, title IV, §4001(b), Dec. 17, 2004, 118 Stat. 3712; Pub. L. 115–254, div. K, title I, §1991(d)(4), Oct. 5, 2018, 132 Stat. 3632.)

§44905. Information about Threats to Civil Aviation

(a) Providing Information.—Under guidelines the Administrator of the Transportation Security Administration prescribes, an air carrier, airport operator, ticket agent, or individual employed by an air carrier, airport operator, or ticket agent, receiving information (except a communication directed by the United States Government) about a threat to civil aviation shall provide the information promptly to the Administrator.

(b) FLIGHT CANCELLATION.—If a decision is made that a particular threat cannot be addressed in a way adequate to ensure, to the extent feasible, the safety of passengers and crew of a particular flight or series of flights, the Administrator of the Transportation Security Administration shall cancel the flight or series of flights.

(c) GUIDELINES ON PUBLIC NOTICE.—(1) The President shall develop guidelines for ensuring that public notice is provided in appropriate cases about threats to civil aviation. The guidelines shall identify officials responsible for—

(A) deciding, on a case-by-case basis, if public notice of a threat is in the best interest of the United States and the traveling public;

(B) ensuring that public notice is provided in a timely and effective way, including the use of a toll-free telephone number; and

(C) canceling the departure of a flight or series of flights under subsection (b) of this section.

(2) The guidelines shall provide for consideration of—

(A) the specificity of the threat;

(B) the credibility of intelligence information related to the threat;

(C) the ability to counter the threat effectively;

(D) the protection of intelligence information sources and methods;

(E) cancellation, by an air carrier or the Administrator of the Transportation Security Administration, of a flight or series of flights instead of public notice;

(F) the ability of passengers and crew to take steps to reduce the risk to their safety after receiving public notice of a threat; and

(G) other factors the Administrator of the Transportation Security Administration considers appropriate.

(d) GUIDELINES ON NOTICE TO CREWS.—The Administrator of the Transportation Security Administration shall develop guidelines for ensuring that notice in appropriate cases of threats to the security of an air carrier flight is provided to the flight crew and cabin crew of that flight.

(e) LIMITATION ON NOTICE TO SELECTIVE TRAVELERS.—Notice of a threat to civil aviation may be provided to selective potential travelers only if the threat applies only to those travelers.

(f) RESTRICTING ACCESS TO INFORMATION.—In cooperation with the departments, agencies, and instrumentalities of the Government that collect, receive, and analyze intelligence information related to aviation security, the Administrator of the Transportation Security Administration shall develop procedures to minimize the number of individuals who have access to information about threats. However, a restriction on access to that information may be imposed only if the restriction does not diminish the ability of the Government to carry out its duties and powers related to aviation security effectively, including providing notice to the public and flight and cabin crews under this section.

(g) DISTRIBUTION OF GUIDELINES.—The guidelines developed under this section shall be distributed for use by appropriate officials of the Department of Transportation, the Department of State, the Department of Justice, and air carriers.

(Pub. L. 103–272, §1(e), July 5, 1994, 108 Stat. 1207; Pub. L. 107–71, title I, §101(f)(7), (9), Nov. 19, 2001, 115 Stat. 603; Pub. L. 115–254, div. K, title I, §1991(d)(5), Oct. 5, 2018, 132 Stat. 3632.)

§44906. FOREIGN AIR CARRIER SECURITY PROGRAMS

The Administrator of the Transportation Security Administration shall continue in effect the requirement of section 129.25 of title 14, Code of Federal Regulations, that a foreign air carrier must adopt and use a security program approved by the Administrator. The Administrator shall not approve a security program of a foreign air carrier under section 129.25, or any successor regulation, unless the security program requires the foreign air carrier in its operations to and from airports in the United States to adhere to the identical security measures that the Administrator requires air carriers serving the same airports to adhere to. The foregoing requirement shall not be interpreted to limit the ability of the Administrator to impose additional security measures on a foreign air carrier or an air carrier when the Administrator determines that a specific threat warrants such additional measures. The Administrator shall prescribe regulations to carry out this section.

(Pub. L. 103–272, §1(e), July 5, 1994, 108 Stat. 1208; Pub. L. 104–132, title III, §322, Apr. 24, 1996, 110 Stat. 1254; Pub. L. 107–71, title I, §101(f)(7), (9), Nov. 19, 2001, 115 Stat. 603; Pub. L. 115–254, div. K, title I, §1991(d)(6), Oct. 5, 2018, 132 Stat. 3632.)

§44907. SECURITY STANDARDS AT FOREIGN AIRPORTS

(a) ASSESSMENT.—(1) At intervals the Secretary of Transportation considers necessary, the Secretary shall assess the effectiveness of the security measures maintained at—

    (A) a foreign airport—

        (i) served by an air carrier;

        (ii) from which a foreign air carrier serves the United States; or

        (iii) that poses a high risk of introducing danger to international air travel; and

    (B) other foreign airports the Secretary considers appropriate.

(2) The Secretary of Transportation shall conduct an assessment under paragraph (1) of this subsection—

    (A) in consultation with appropriate aeronautic authorities of the government of a foreign country concerned and each air carrier serving the foreign airport for which the Secretary is conducting the assessment;

    (B) to establish the extent to which a foreign airport effectively maintains and carries out security measures, including the screening and vetting of airport workers; and

    (C) by using a standard that will result in an analysis of the security measures at the airport based at least on the standards and appropriate recommended practices contained in Annex 17 to the Convention on International Civil Aviation in effect on the date of the assessment.

(3) Each report to Congress required under section 44938(b) of this title shall contain a summary of the assessments conducted under this subsection.

(b) CONSULTATION.—In carrying out subsection (a) of this section, the Secretary of Transportation shall consult with the Secretary of State—

    (1) on the terrorist threat that exists in each country; and

    (2) to establish which foreign airports are not under the de facto control of the government of the foreign country in which they are located and pose a high risk of introducing danger to international air travel.

(c) NOTIFYING FOREIGN AUTHORITIES.—When the Secretary of Transportation, after conducting an assessment under subsection (a) of this section, decides that an airport does not maintain and carry out effective security measures, the Secretary of Transportation, after advising the Secretary of State, shall notify the appropriate authorities of the government of the foreign country of the decision and recommend the steps necessary to bring the security measures in use at the airport up to the standard used by the Secretary of Transportation in making the assessment.

(d) ACTIONS WHEN AIRPORTS NOT MAINTAINING AND CARRYING OUT EFFECTIVE SECURITY MEASURES.—(1) When the Secretary of Transportation decides under this section that an airport does not maintain and carry out effective security measures—

(A) the Secretary of Transportation shall—

(i) publish the identity of the airport in the Federal Register;

(ii) have the identity of the airport posted and displayed prominently at all United States airports at which scheduled air carrier operations are provided regularly; and

(iii) notify the news media of the identity of the airport;

(B) each air carrier and foreign air carrier providing transportation between the United States and the airport shall provide written notice of the decision, on or with the ticket, to each passenger buying a ticket for transportation between the United States and the airport;

(C) notwithstanding section 40105(b) of this title, the Secretary of Transportation, after consulting with the appropriate aeronautic authorities of the foreign country concerned and each air carrier serving the airport and with the approval of the Secretary of State, may withhold, revoke, or prescribe conditions on the operating authority of an air carrier or foreign air carrier that uses that airport to provide foreign air transportation; and

(D) the President may prohibit an air carrier or foreign air carrier from providing transportation between the United States and any other foreign airport that is served by aircraft flying to or from the airport with respect to which a decision is made under this section.

(2)(A) Paragraph (1) of this subsection becomes effective—

(i) 90 days after the government of a foreign country is notified under subsection (c) of this section if the Secretary of Transportation finds that the government has not brought the security measures at the airport up to the standard the Secretary used in making an assessment under subsection (a) of this section; or

(ii) immediately on the decision of the Secretary of Transportation under subsection (c) of this section if the Secretary of Transportation decides, after consulting with the Secretary of State, that a condition exists that threatens the safety or security of passengers, aircraft, or crew traveling to or from the airport.

(B) The Secretary of Transportation immediately shall notify the Secretary of State of a decision under subparagraph (A)(ii) of this paragraph so that the Secretary of State may issue a travel advisory required under section 44908(a) of this title.

(3) The Secretary of Transportation promptly shall submit to Congress a report (and classified annex if necessary) on action taken under paragraph (1) or (2) of this subsection, including information on attempts made to obtain the cooperation of the government of a foreign country in meeting the standard the Secretary used in assessing the airport under subsection (a) of this section.

(4) An action required under paragraph (1)(A) and (B) of this subsection is no longer

required only if the Secretary of Transportation, in consultation with the Secretary of State, decides that effective security measures are maintained and carried out at the airport. The Secretary of Transportation shall notify Congress when the action is no longer required to be taken.

(e) SUSPENSIONS.—Notwithstanding sections 40105(b) and 40106(b) of this title, the Secretary of Transportation, with the approval of the Secretary of State and without notice or a hearing, shall suspend the right of an air carrier or foreign air carrier to provide foreign air transportation, and the right of a person to operate aircraft in foreign air commerce, to or from a foreign airport when the Secretary of Transportation decides that—

(1) a condition exists that threatens the safety or security of passengers, aircraft, or crew traveling to or from that airport; and

(2) the public interest requires an immediate suspension of transportation between the United States and that airport.

(f) CONDITION OF CARRIER AUTHORITY.—This section is a condition to authority the Secretary of Transportation grants under this part to an air carrier or foreign air carrier.

(Pub. L. 103–272, §1(e), July 5, 1994, 108 Stat. 1209; Pub. L. 115–254, div. K, title I, §1954, Oct. 5, 2018, 132 Stat. 3595.)

§44908. TRAVEL ADVISORY AND SUSPENSION OF FOREIGN ASSISTANCE

(a) TRAVEL ADVISORIES.—On being notified by the Administrator of the Transportation Security Administration that the Administrator of the Transportation Security Administration has decided under section 44907(d)(2)(A)(ii) of this title that a condition exists that threatens the security of passengers, aircraft, or crew traveling to or from a foreign airport that the Administrator of the Transportation Security Administration has decided under section 44907 of this title does not maintain and carry out effective security measures, the Secretary of State—

(1) immediately shall issue a travel advisory for that airport; and

(2) shall publicize the advisory widely.

(b) SUSPENDING ASSISTANCE.—The President shall suspend assistance provided under the Foreign Assistance Act of 1961 (22 U.S.C. 2151 et seq.) or the Arms Export Control Act (22 U.S.C. 2751 et seq.) to a country in which is located an airport with respect to which section 44907(d)(1) of this title becomes effective if the Secretary of State decides the country is a high terrorist threat country. The President may waive this subsection if the President decides, and reports to Congress, that the waiver is required because of national security interests or a humanitarian emergency.

(c) ACTIONS NO LONGER REQUIRED.—An action required under this section is no longer required only if the Administrator of the Transportation Security Administration has made a decision as provided under section 44907(d)(4) of this title. The Administrator shall notify Congress when the action is no longer required to be taken.

(Pub. L. 103–272, §1(e), July 5, 1994, 108 Stat. 1211; Pub. L. 105–277, div. G, subdiv. B, title XXII, §2224(a), Oct. 21, 1998, 112 Stat. 2681–819; Pub. L. 115–254, div. K, title I, §1991(d)(7), Oct. 5, 2018, 132 Stat. 3632.)

§44909. PASSENGER MANIFESTS

(a) AIR CARRIER REQUIREMENTS.—(1) The Secretary of Transportation shall require each air carrier to provide a passenger manifest for a flight to an appropriate representative of the Secretary of State—

(A) not later than one hour after that carrier is notified of an aviation disaster outside the United States involving that flight; or

(B) if it is not technologically feasible or reasonable to comply with clause (A) of this paragraph, then as expeditiously as possible, but not later than 3 hours after the carrier is so notified.

(2) The passenger manifest should include the following information:

(A) the full name of each passenger.

(B) the passport number of each passenger, if required for travel.

(C) the name and telephone number of a contact for each passenger.

(3) In carrying out this subsection, the Secretary of Transportation shall consider the necessity and feasibility of requiring air carriers to collect passenger manifest information as a condition for passengers boarding a flight of the carrier.

(b) FOREIGN AIR CARRIER REQUIREMENTS.—The Secretary of Transportation shall consider imposing a requirement on foreign air carriers comparable to that imposed on air carriers under subsection (a)(1) and (2) of this section.

(c) FLIGHTS IN FOREIGN AIR TRANSPORTATION TO THE UNITED STATES.—

(1) IN GENERAL.—Each air carrier and foreign air carrier operating a passenger flight in foreign air transportation to the United States shall provide to the Commissioner of U.S. Customs and Border Protection by electronic transmission a passenger and crew manifest containing the information specified in paragraph (2). Carriers may use the advanced passenger information system established under section 431 of the Tariff Act of 1930 (19 U.S.C. 1431) to provide the information required by the preceding sentence.

(2) INFORMATION.—A passenger and crew manifest for a flight required under paragraph (1) shall contain the following information:

(A) The full name of each passenger and crew member.

(B) The date of birth and citizenship of each passenger and crew member.

(C) The sex of each passenger and crew member.

(D) The passport number and country of issuance of each passenger and crew member if required for travel.

(E) The United States visa number or resident alien card number of each passenger and crew member, as applicable.

(F) Such other information as the Administrator of the Transportation Security Administration, in consultation with the Commissioner of U.S. Customs and Border Protection, determines is reasonably necessary to ensure aviation safety.

(3) PASSENGER NAME RECORDS.—The carriers shall make passenger name record information available to the Customs Service upon request.

(4) TRANSMISSION OF MANIFEST.—Subject to paragraphs (5) and (6), a passenger and crew manifest required for a flight under paragraph (1) shall be transmitted to the Customs Service in advance of the aircraft landing in the United States in such manner, time, and form as the Customs Service prescribes.

(5) TRANSMISSION OF MANIFESTS TO OTHER FEDERAL AGENCIES.—Upon request, information provided to the Administrator of the Transportation Security Administration or the Customs Service under this subsection may be shared with other Federal agencies

for the purpose of protecting national security.

(6) PRESCREENING INTERNATIONAL PASSENGERS.—

(A) IN GENERAL.—The Secretary of Homeland Security, or the designee of the Secretary, shall issue a notice of proposed rulemaking that will allow the Department of Homeland Security to compare passenger information for any international flight to or from the United States against the consolidated and integrated terrorist watchlist maintained by the Federal Government before departure of the flight.

(B) APPEAL PROCEDURES.—

(i) IN GENERAL.—The Secretary of Homeland Security shall establish a timely and fair process for individuals identified as a threat under subparagraph (A) to appeal to the Department of Homeland Security the determination and correct any erroneous information.

(ii) RECORDS.—The process shall include the establishment of a method by which the Secretary of Homeland Security will be able to maintain a record of air passengers and other individuals who have been misidentified and have corrected erroneous information. To prevent repeated delays of misidentified passengers and other individuals, the Department of Homeland Security record shall contain information determined by the Secretary of Homeland Security to authenticate the identity of such a passenger or individual.

(Pub. L. 103–272, §1(e), July 5, 1994, 108 Stat. 1211; Pub. L. 106–181, title VII, §718, Apr. 5, 2000, 114 Stat. 163; Pub. L. 107–71, title I, §115, Nov. 19, 2001, 115 Stat. 623; Pub. L. 108–458, title IV, §4012(a)(2), Dec. 17, 2004, 118 Stat. 3717; Pub. L. 114–125, title VIII, §802(d)(2), Feb. 24, 2016, 130 Stat. 210; Pub. L. 115–254, div. K, title I, §1991(d)(8), Oct. 5, 2018, 132 Stat. 3633.)

§44910. AGREEMENTS ON AIRCRAFT SABOTAGE, AIRCRAFT HIJACKING, AND AIRPORT SECURITY

The Secretary of State shall seek multilateral and bilateral agreement on strengthening enforcement measures and standards for compliance related to aircraft sabotage, aircraft hijacking, and airport security.

(Pub. L. 103–272, §1(e), July 5, 1994, 108 Stat. 1212.)

§44911. INTELLIGENCE

(a) DEFINITION.—In this section, "intelligence community" means the intelligence and intelligence-related activities of the following units of the United States Government:

(1) the Department of State.

(2) the Department of Defense.

(3) the Department of the Treasury.

(4) the Department of Energy.

(5) the Departments of the Army, Navy, and Air Force.

(6) the Central Intelligence Agency.

(7) the National Security Agency.

(8) the Defense Intelligence Agency.

(9) the Federal Bureau of Investigation.

(10) the Drug Enforcement Administration.

(b) POLICIES AND PROCEDURES ON REPORT AVAILABILITY.—The head of each unit in the intelligence community shall prescribe policies and procedures to ensure that intelligence reports about terrorism are made available, as appropriate, to the heads of other units in the intelligence community, the Secretary of Transportation, and the Administrator of the Transportation Security Administration.

(c) UNIT FOR STRATEGIC PLANNING ON TERRORISM.—The heads of the units in the intelligence community shall place greater emphasis on strategic intelligence efforts by establishing a unit for strategic planning on terrorism.

(d) DESIGNATION OF INTELLIGENCE OFFICER.—At the request of the Secretary of Homeland Security, the Director of Central Intelligence shall designate at least one intelligence officer of the Central Intelligence Agency to serve in a senior position in the Office of the Secretary.

(e) WRITTEN WORKING AGREEMENTS.—The heads of units in the intelligence community, the Secretary of Homeland Security, and the Administrator of the Transportation Security Administration shall review and, as appropriate, revise written working agreements between the intelligence community and the Administrator of the Transportation Security Administration.

(Pub. L. 103–272, §1(e), July 5, 1994, 108 Stat. 1212; Pub. L. 107–71, title I, §§101(f)(7), (9), 102(b), (c), Nov. 19, 2001, 115 Stat. 603, 605; Pub. L. 115–254, div. K, title I, §1991(d)(9), Oct. 5, 2018, 132 Stat. 3633.)

§44912. RESEARCH AND DEVELOPMENT

(a) PROGRAM REQUIREMENT.—(1) The Administrator shall establish and carry out a program to accelerate and expand the research, development, and implementation of technologies and procedures to counteract terrorist acts against civil aviation. The program shall provide for developing and having in place new equipment and procedures necessary to meet the technological challenges presented by terrorism. The program shall include research on, and development of, technological improvements and ways to enhance human performance.

(2) In designing and carrying out the program established under this subsection, the Administrator shall—

(A) consult and coordinate activities with other departments, agencies, and instrumentalities of the United States Government doing similar research;

(B) identify departments, agencies, and instrumentalities that would benefit from that research; and

(C) seek cost-sharing agreements with those departments, agencies, and instrumentalities.

(3) In carrying out the program established under this subsection, the Administrator shall review and consider the annual reports the Secretary of Transportation submits to Congress on transportation security and intelligence.

(4)(A) In carrying out the program established under this subsection, the Administrator shall designate an individual to be responsible for engineering, research, and development with respect to security technology under the program.

(B) The individual designated under subparagraph (A) shall use appropriate systems engineering and risk management models in making decisions regarding the allocation of funds for engineering, research, and development with respect to security technology under the program.

(C) The individual designated under subparagraph (A) shall, on an annual basis, submit to the Administrator a report on activities under this paragraph during the preceding year. Each report shall include, for the year covered by such report, information on—

(i) progress made in engineering, research, and development with respect to security technology;

(ii) the allocation of funds for engineering, research, and development with respect to security technology; and

(iii) engineering, research, and development with respect to any technologies drawn from other agencies, including the rationale for engineering, research, and development with respect to such technologies.

(5) The Administrator may—

(A) make grants to institutions of higher learning and other appropriate research facilities with demonstrated ability to carry out research described in paragraph (1) of this subsection, and fix the amounts and terms of the grants; and

(B) make cooperative agreements with governmental authorities the Administrator decides are appropriate.

(b) REVIEW OF THREATS.—(1) The Administrator shall periodically review threats to civil aviation, with particular focus on—

(A) a comprehensive systems analysis (employing vulnerability analysis, threat attribute definition, and technology roadmaps) of the civil aviation system, including—

(i) the destruction, commandeering, or diversion of civil aircraft or the use of civil aircraft as a weapon; and

(ii) the disruption of civil aviation service, including by cyber attack;

(B) explosive material that presents the most significant threat to civil aircraft;

(C) the minimum amounts, configurations, and types of explosive material that can cause, or would reasonably be expected to cause, catastrophic damage to aircraft in air transportation;

(D) the amounts, configurations, and types of explosive material that can be detected reliably by existing, or reasonably anticipated, near-term explosive detection technologies;

(E) the potential release of chemical, biological, or similar weapons or devices either within an aircraft or within an airport;

(F) the feasibility of using various ways to minimize damage caused by explosive material that cannot be detected reliably by existing, or reasonably anticipated, near-term explosive detection technologies;

(G) the ability to screen passengers, carry-on baggage, checked baggage, and cargo; and

(H) the technologies that might be used in the future to attempt to destroy or otherwise threaten commercial aircraft and the way in which those technologies can be countered effectively.

(2) The Administrator shall use the results of the review under this subsection to develop the focus and priorities of the program established under subsection (a) of this section.

(c) SCIENTIFIC ADVISORY PANEL.—(1) The Administrator shall establish a scientific advisory panel to review, comment on, advise the progress of, and recommend modifications in, the program established under subsection (a) of this section, including the need for long-range research programs to detect and prevent catastrophic damage to commercial aircraft, commercial aviation facilities, commercial aviation personnel and passengers, and other components of the commercial aviation system by the next generation of terrorist weapons.

(2)(A) The advisory panel shall consist of individuals who have scientific and technical expertise in—

(i) the development and testing of effective explosive detection systems;

(ii) aircraft structure and experimentation to decide on the type and minimum weights of explosives that an effective explosive detection technology must be capable of detecting;

(iii) technologies involved in minimizing airframe damage to aircraft from explosives; and

(iv) other scientific and technical areas the Administrator considers appropriate.

(B) In appointing individuals to the advisory panel, the Administrator should consider individuals from academia and the national laboratories, as appropriate.

(3) The Administrator shall organize the advisory panel into teams capable of undertaking the review of policies and technologies upon request.

(4) Biennially, the Administrator shall review the composition of the advisory panel in order to ensure that the expertise of the individuals on the panel is suited to the current and anticipated duties of the panel.

(d) SECURITY AND RESEARCH AND DEVELOPMENT ACTIVITIES.—

(1) IN GENERAL.—The Administrator shall conduct research (including behavioral research) and development activities appropriate to develop, modify, test, and evaluate a system, procedure, facility, or device to protect passengers and property against acts of criminal violence, aircraft piracy, and terrorism and to ensure security.

(2) DISCLOSURE.—

(A) IN GENERAL.—Notwithstanding section 552 of title 5, the Administrator shall prescribe regulations prohibiting disclosure of information obtained or developed in ensuring security under this title if the Secretary of Homeland Security decides disclosing the information would—

(i) be an unwarranted invasion of personal privacy;

(ii) reveal a trade secret or privileged or confidential commercial or financial information; or

(iii) be detrimental to transportation safety.

(B) INFORMATION TO CONGRESS.—Subparagraph (A) does not authorize information to be withheld from a committee of Congress authorized to have the information.

(C) RULE OF CONSTRUCTION.—Nothing in subparagraph (A) shall be construed to authorize the designation of information as sensitive security information (as defined in section 15.5 of title 49, Code of Federal Regulations)—

(i) to conceal a violation of law, inefficiency, or administrative error;

(ii) to prevent embarrassment to a person, organization, or agency;

(iii) to restrain competition; or

(iv) to prevent or delay the release of information that does not require protection in the interest of transportation security, including basic scientific research information not clearly related to transportation security.

(D) Privacy act.—Section 552a of title 5 shall not apply to disclosures that the Administrator of the Transportation Security Administration may make from the systems of records of the Transportation Security Administration to any Federal law enforcement, intelligence, protective service, immigration, or national security official in order to assist the official receiving the information in the performance of official duties.

(3) Transfers of duties and powers prohibited.—Except as otherwise provided by law, the Administrator may not transfer a duty or power under this section to another department, agency, or instrumentality of the United States Government.

(e) Definition of Administrator.—In this section, the term "Administrator" means the Administrator of the Transportation Security Administration.

(Pub. L. 103–272, §1(e), July 5, 1994, 108 Stat. 1212; Pub. L. 107–71, title I, §§101(f)(7), (9), 112, Nov. 19, 2001, 115 Stat. 603, 620; Pub. L. 115–254, div. K, title I, §1991(d)(10), Oct. 5, 2018, 132 Stat. 3633.)

§44913. Explosive detection

(a) Deployment and Purchase of Equipment.—(1) A deployment or purchase of explosive detection equipment under section 108.7(b)(8) or 108.20 of title 14, Code of Federal Regulations, or similar regulation is required only if the Administrator of the Transportation Security Administration (referred to in this section as "the Administrator") certifies that the equipment alone, or as part of an integrated system, can detect under realistic air carrier operating conditions the amounts, configurations, and types of explosive material that would likely be used to cause catastrophic damage to commercial aircraft. The Administrator shall base the certification on the results of tests conducted under protocols developed in consultation with expert scientists outside of the Transportation Security Administration. Those tests shall be completed not later than April 16, 1992.

(2) Until such time as the Administrator determines that equipment certified under paragraph (1) is commercially available and has successfully completed operational testing as provided in paragraph (1), the Administrator shall facilitate the deployment of such approved commercially available explosive detection devices as the Administrator determines will enhance aviation security significantly. The Administrator shall require that equipment deployed under this paragraph be replaced by equipment certified under paragraph (1) when equipment certified under paragraph (1) becomes commercially available. The Administrator is authorized, based on operational considerations at individual airports, to waive the required installation of commercially available equipment under paragraph (1) in the interests of aviation security. The Administrator may permit the requirements of this paragraph to be met at airports by the deployment of dogs or other appropriate animals to supplement equipment for screening passengers, baggage, mail, or cargo for explosives or weapons.

(3) This subsection does not prohibit the Administrator from purchasing or deploying explosive detection equipment described in paragraph (1) of this subsection.

(b) Grants.—The Administrator may provide grants to continue the Explosive Detection K-9 Team Training Program to detect explosives at airports and on aircraft.

(Pub. L. 103–272, §1(e), July 5, 1994, 108 Stat. 1214; Pub. L. 104–264, title III, §305(a), Oct. 9, 1996, 110 Stat. 3252; Pub. L. 104–287, §5(9), Oct. 11, 1996, 110 Stat. 3389; Pub. L. 107–71, title I, §101(f)(2), (7), (9), Nov. 19, 2001, 115 Stat. 603; Pub. L. 115–254, div. K, title I, §1991(d)(11), Oct. 5, 2018, 132 Stat. 3635.)

§44914. AIRPORT CONSTRUCTION GUIDELINES

In consultation with the Department of Transportation, air carriers, airport authorities, and others the Administrator of the Transportation Security Administration considers appropriate, the Administrator shall develop guidelines for airport design and construction to allow for maximum security enhancement. In developing the guidelines, the Administrator shall consider the results of the assessment carried out under section 44904(a) of this title.

(Pub. L. 103–272, §1(e), July 5, 1994, 108 Stat. 1214; Pub. L. 107–71, title I, §101(f)(7), (9), Nov. 19, 2001, 115 Stat. 603; Pub. L. 115–254, div. K, title I, §1991(d)(12), Oct. 5, 2018, 132 Stat. 3635.)

§44915. EXEMPTIONS

The Administrator of the Transportation Security Administration may exempt from sections 44901, 44903(a)–(c) and (e), 44906, 44935, and 44936 of this title airports in Alaska served only by air carriers that—

(1) hold certificates issued under section 41102 of this title;

(2) operate aircraft with certificates for a maximum gross takeoff weight of less than 12,500 pounds; and

(3) board passengers, or load property intended to be carried in an aircraft cabin, that will be screened under section 44901 of this title at another airport in Alaska before the passengers board, or the property is loaded on, an aircraft for a place outside Alaska.

(Pub. L. 103–272, §1(e), July 5, 1994, 108 Stat. 1215; Pub. L. 107–71, title I, §101(f)(7), (9), Nov. 19, 2001, 115 Stat. 603; Pub. L. 115–254, div. K, title I, §1991(d)(13), Oct. 5, 2018, 132 Stat. 3635.)

§44916. ASSESSMENTS AND EVALUATIONS

(a) PERIODIC ASSESSMENTS.—The Administrator of the Transportation Security Administration shall require each air carrier and airport (including the airport owner or operator in cooperation with the air carriers and vendors serving each airport) that provides for intrastate, interstate, or foreign air transportation to conduct periodic vulnerability assessments of the security systems of that air carrier or airport, respectively. The Transportation Security Administration shall perform periodic audits of such assessments.

(b) INVESTIGATIONS.—The Administrator of the Transportation Security Administration shall conduct periodic and unannounced inspections of security systems of airports and air carriers to determine the effectiveness and vulnerabilities of such systems. To the extent allowable by law, the Administrator may provide for anonymous tests of those security systems.

(Added Pub. L. 104–264, title III, §312(a), Oct. 9, 1996, 110 Stat. 3253; amended Pub. L. 107–71, title I, §101(f)(3), (7), Nov. 19, 2001, 115 Stat. 603; Pub. L. 115–254, div. K, title I, §1991(d)(14), Oct. 5, 2018, 132 Stat. 3635.)

§44917. DEPLOYMENT OF FEDERAL AIR MARSHALS

(a) IN GENERAL.—The Administrator of the Transportation Security Administration under the authority provided by section 44903(d)—

(1) may provide for deployment of Federal air marshals on every passenger flight of air carriers in air transportation or intrastate air transportation;

(2) shall provide for deployment of Federal air marshals on every such flight determined by the Administrator to present high security risks;

(3) shall provide for appropriate training, supervision, and equipment of Federal air marshals;

(4) shall require air carriers providing flights described in paragraph (1) to provide seating for a Federal air marshal on any such flight without regard to the availability of seats on the flight and at no cost to the United States Government or the marshal;

(5) may require air carriers to provide, on a space-available basis, to an off-duty Federal air marshal a seat on a flight to the airport nearest the marshal's home at no cost to the marshal or the United States Government if the marshal is traveling to that airport after completing his or her security duties;

(6) may enter into agreements with Federal, State, and local agencies under which appropriately-trained law enforcement personnel from such agencies, when traveling on a flight of an air carrier, will carry a firearm and be prepared to assist Federal air marshals;

(7) shall establish procedures to ensure that Federal air marshals are made aware of any armed or unarmed law enforcement personnel on board an aircraft;

(8) may appoint—

(A) an individual who is a retired law enforcement officer;

(B) an individual who is a retired member of the Armed Forces; and

(C) an individual who has been furloughed from an air carrier crew position in the 1-year period beginning on September 11, 2001,

as a Federal air marshal, regardless of age, if the individual otherwise meets the background and fitness qualifications required for Federal air marshals;

(9) shall require the Federal Air Marshal Service to utilize a risk-based strategy when allocating resources between international and domestic flight coverage, including when initially setting its annual target numbers of average daily international and domestic flights to cover;

(10) shall require the Federal Air Marshal Service to utilize a risk-based strategy to support domestic allocation decisions;

(11) shall require the Federal Air Marshal Service to utilize a risk-based strategy to support international allocation decisions; and

(12) shall ensure that the seating arrangements of Federal air marshals on aircraft are determined in a manner that is risk-based and most capable of responding to current threats to aviation security.

(b) INTERIM MEASURES.—Until the Under Secretary [1] completes implementation of subsection (a), the Under Secretary [1] may use, after consultation with and concurrence of the heads of other Federal agencies and departments, personnel from those agencies and departments, on a nonreimbursable basis, to provide air marshal service.

(c) TRAINING FOR FOREIGN LAW ENFORCEMENT PERSONNEL.—

(1) IN GENERAL.—The Administrator of the Transportation Security Administration, after consultation with the Secretary of State, may direct the Federal Air Marshal Service to provide appropriate air marshal training to law enforcement personnel of foreign countries.

(2) WATCHLIST SCREENING.—The Federal Air Marshal Service may only provide

appropriate air marshal training to law enforcement personnel of foreign countries after comparing the identifying information and records of law enforcement personnel of foreign countries against all appropriate records in the consolidated and integrated terrorist watchlists maintained by the Federal Government.

(3) FEES.—The Administrator of the Transportation Security Administration shall establish reasonable fees and charges to pay expenses incurred in carrying out this subsection. Funds collected under this subsection shall be credited to the account in the Treasury from which the expenses were incurred and shall be available to the Administrator of the Transportation Security Administration for purposes for which amounts in such account are available.

(Added Pub. L. 107–71, title I, §105(a), Nov. 19, 2001, 115 Stat. 606; amended Pub. L. 108–458, title IV, §4018, Dec. 17, 2004, 118 Stat. 3721; Pub. L. 115–254, div. K, title I, §§1959(c)(5), (d)(1), 1991(d)(15), Oct. 5, 2018, 132 Stat. 3599, 3635.)

> [1] So in original. Probably should be "Administrator".

§44918. CREW TRAINING

(a) BASIC SECURITY TRAINING.—

(1) IN GENERAL.—Each air carrier providing scheduled passenger air transportation shall carry out a training program for flight and cabin crew members to prepare the crew members for potential threat conditions and unruly passenger behavior.

(2) PROGRAM ELEMENTS.—An air carrier training program under this subsection shall include, at a minimum, elements that address each of the following:

(A) Recognize suspicious behavior and activities and determine the seriousness of any occurrence of such behavior and activities.

(B) Crew communication and coordination.

(C) The proper commands to give passengers and attackers.

(D) Appropriate responses to defend oneself.

(E) Use of protective devices assigned to crew members (to the extent such devices are required by the Administrator of the Federal Aviation Administration or the Administrator of the Transportation Security Administration).

(F) Psychology of terrorists to cope with hijacker behavior and passenger responses.

(G) Situational training exercises regarding various threat conditions.

(H) De-escalation training based on recommendations issued by the Air Carrier Training Aviation Rulemaking Committee.

(I) Methods to subdue and restrain an active attacker.

(J) The proper conduct of a cabin search, including explosive device recognition.

(K) Any other subject matter considered appropriate by the Administrator of the Transportation Security Administration.

(3) APPROVAL.—An air carrier training program under this subsection shall be subject to approval by the Administrator of the Transportation Security Administration.

(4) MINIMUM STANDARDS.—Not later than 180 days after the date of enactment of the FAA Reauthorization Act of 2024, the Administrator of the Transportation Security Administration, in consultation with the Federal Air Marshal Service and the Aviation Security Advisory Committee, shall establish minimum standards for—

(A) the training provided under this subsection and any for recurrent training; and

(B) the individuals or entities providing such training.

(5) EXISTING PROGRAMS.—Notwithstanding paragraphs (3) and (4), any training program of an air carrier to prepare flight and cabin crew members for potential threat conditions that was approved by the Administrator or the Administrator of the Transportation Security Administration before December 12, 2003, may continue in effect until disapproved or ordered modified by the Administrator of the Transportation Security Administration.

(6) MONITORING.—The Administrator of the Transportation Security Administration, in consultation with the Administrator and the Federal Air Marshal Service, shall monitor air carrier training programs under this subsection and shall periodically review an air carrier's training program to ensure that the program is adequately preparing crew members for potential threat conditions based on changes in the potential or actual threat conditions. In determining when an air carrier's training program should be reviewed under this paragraph, the Administrator of the Transportation Security Administration shall consider complaints from crew members. The Administrator of the Transportation Security Administration shall ensure that employees responsible for monitoring the training programs have the necessary resources and knowledge, including self-defense training expertise and experience.

(7) UPDATES.—The Administrator of the Transportation Security Administration, in consultation with the Administrator, shall order air carriers to modify training programs under this subsection to reflect new or different security threats.

(b) ADVANCED SELF-DEFENSE TRAINING.—

(1) IN GENERAL.—The Administrator of the Transportation Security Administration shall develop and provide a voluntary training program for flight and cabin crew members of air carriers providing scheduled passenger air transportation.

(2) PROGRAM ELEMENTS.—The training program under this subsection shall include both classroom and effective hands-on training in the following elements of self-defense:

(A) Deterring a passenger who might present a threat.

(B) Advanced control, striking, and restraint techniques.

(C) Training to defend oneself against edged or contact weapons.

(D) Methods to subdue and restrain an attacker.

(E) Use of available items aboard the aircraft for self-defense.

(F) Appropriate and effective responses to defend oneself, including the use of force against an attacker.

(G) Any other element of training that the Administrator of the Transportation Security Administration considers appropriate.

(3) PARTICIPATION NOT REQUIRED.—A crew member shall not be required to participate in the training program under this subsection.

(4) COMPENSATION.—Except as provided in paragraph (8), neither the Federal Government nor an air carrier shall be required to compensate a crew member for participating in the training program under this subsection.

(5) FEES.—A crew member shall not be required to pay a fee for the training program under this subsection.

(6) CONSULTATION.—In developing the training program under this subsection, the

Administrator of the Transportation Security Administration shall consult with law enforcement personnel and security experts who have expertise in self-defense training, terrorism experts, representatives of air carriers, the director of self-defense training in the Federal Air Marshal Service, flight attendants, labor organizations representing flight attendants, and educational institutions offering law enforcement training programs.

(7) DESIGNATION OF TSA OFFICIAL.—The Administrator of the Transportation Security Administration shall designate an official in the Transportation Security Administration to be responsible for implementing the training program under this subsection. The official shall consult with air carriers and labor organizations representing crew members before implementing the program to ensure that it is appropriate for situations that may arise on board an aircraft during a flight.

(8) AIR CARRIER ACCOMMODATION.—An air carrier with a crew member participating in the training program under this subsection shall provide a process through which each such crew member may obtain reasonable accommodations.

(c) LIMITATION.—Actions by crew members under this section shall be subject to the provisions of section 44903(k).

(Added Pub. L. 107–71, title I, §107(a), Nov. 19, 2001, 115 Stat. 610; amended Pub. L. 107–296, title XIV, §1403(a), Nov. 25, 2002, 116 Stat. 2305; Pub. L. 108–176, title VI, §603, Dec. 12, 2003, 117 Stat. 2563; Pub. L. 115–254, div. K, title I, §1991(d)(16), Oct. 5, 2018, 132 Stat. 3635; Pub. L. 118–63, title IV, §427, May 16, 2024, 138 Stat. 1169.)

§44919. PRECHECK PROGRAM

(a) IN GENERAL.—The Administrator of the Transportation Security Administration shall continue to administer the PreCheck Program in accordance with section 109(a)(3) of the Aviation and Transportation Security Act (49 U.S.C. 114 note).

(b) EXPANSION.—Not later than 180 days after the date of enactment of the TSA Modernization Act, the Administrator shall enter into an agreement, using other transaction authority under section 114(m) of this title, with at least 2 private sector entities to increase the methods and capabilities available for the public to enroll in the PreCheck Program.

(c) MINIMUM CAPABILITY REQUIREMENTS.—At least 1 agreement under subsection (b) shall include the following capabilities:

(1) Start-to-finish secure online or mobile enrollment capability.

(2) Vetting of an applicant by means other than biometrics, such as a risk assessment, if—

(A) such means—

(i) are evaluated and certified by the Secretary of Homeland Security;

(ii) meet the definition of a qualified anti-terrorism technology under section 865 of the Homeland Security Act of 2002 (6 U.S.C. 444); and

(iii) are determined by the Administrator to provide a risk assessment that is as effective as a fingerprint-based criminal history records check conducted through the Federal Bureau of Investigation with respect to identifying individuals who are not qualified to participate in the PreCheck Program due to disqualifying criminal history; and

(B) with regard to private sector risk assessments, the Secretary has certified that reasonable procedures are in place with regard to the accuracy, relevancy, and proper utilization of information employed in such risk assessments.

(d) ADDITIONAL CAPABILITY REQUIREMENTS.—At least 1 agreement under subsection (b) shall include the following capabilities:

(1) Start-to-finish secure online or mobile enrollment capability.

(2) Vetting of an applicant by means of biometrics if the collection—

(A) is comparable with the appropriate and applicable standards developed by the National Institute of Standards and Technology;

(B) protects privacy and data security, including that any personally identifiable information is collected, retained, used, and shared in a manner consistent with section 552a of title 5, United States Code (commonly known as "Privacy Act of 1974"), and with agency regulations;

(C) is evaluated and certified by the Secretary of Homeland Security; and

(D) is determined by the Administrator to provide a risk assessment that is as effective as a fingerprint-based criminal history records check conducted through the Federal Bureau of Investigation with respect to identifying individuals who are not qualified to participate in the PreCheck Program due to disqualifying criminal history.

(e) TARGET ENROLLMENT.—Subject to subsections (b), (c), and (d), the Administrator shall take actions to expand the total number of individuals enrolled in the PreCheck Program as follows:

(1) 7,000,000 passengers before October 1, 2019.

(2) 10,000,000 passengers before October 1, 2020.

(3) 15,000,000 passengers before October 1, 2021.

(f) MARKETING OF PRECHECK PROGRAM.—Not later than 90 days after the date of enactment of the TSA Modernization Act, the Administrator shall—

(1) enter into at least 2 agreements, using other transaction authority under section 114(m) of this title, to market the PreCheck Program; and

(2) implement a long-term strategy for partnering with the private sector to encourage enrollment in such program.

(g) IDENTITY VERIFICATION ENHANCEMENT.—The Administrator shall—

(1) coordinate with the heads of appropriate components of the Department to leverage Department-held data and technologies to verify the identity and citizenship of individuals enrolling in the PreCheck Program;

(2) partner with the private sector to use biometrics and authentication standards, such as relevant standards developed by the National Institute of Standards and Technology, to facilitate enrollment in the program; and

(3) consider leveraging the existing resources and abilities of airports to collect fingerprints for use in background checks to expedite identity verification.

(h) PRECHECK PROGRAM LANES OPERATION.—The Administrator shall—

(1) ensure that PreCheck Program screening lanes are open and available during peak and high-volume travel times at appropriate airports to individuals enrolled in the PreCheck Program; and

(2) make every practicable effort to provide expedited screening at standard screening lanes during times when PreCheck Program screening lanes are closed to individuals enrolled in the program in order to maintain operational efficiency.

(i) ELIGIBILITY OF MEMBERS OF THE ARMED FORCES FOR EXPEDITED SECURITY

SCREENING.—

(1) IN GENERAL.—Subject to paragraph (3), an individual specified in paragraph (2) is eligible for expedited security screening under the PreCheck Program.

(2) INDIVIDUALS SPECIFIED.—An individual specified in this subsection is any of the following:

(A) A member of the Armed Forces, including a member of a reserve component or the National Guard.

(B) A cadet or midshipman of the United States Military Academy, the United States Naval Academy, the United States Air Force Academy, or the United States Coast Guard Academy.

(C) A family member of an individual specified in subparagraph (A) or (B) who is younger than 12 years old and accompanying the individual.

(3) IMPLEMENTATION.—The eligibility of an individual specified in paragraph (2) for expedited security screening under the PreCheck Program is subject to such policies and procedures as the Administrator may prescribe to carry out this subsection, in consultation with the Secretary of Defense and, with respect to the United States Coast Guard, the Commandant of the United States Coast Guard.

(j) VETTING FOR PRECHECK PROGRAM PARTICIPANTS.—The Administrator shall initiate an assessment to identify any security vulnerabilities in the vetting process for the PreCheck Program, including determining whether subjecting PreCheck Program participants to recurrent fingerprint-based criminal history records checks, in addition to recurrent checks against the terrorist watchlist, could be done in a cost-effective manner to strengthen the security of the PreCheck Program.

(k) ASSURANCE OF SEPARATE PROGRAM.—In carrying out this section, the Administrator shall ensure that the additional private sector application capabilities under subsections (b), (c), and (d) are undertaken in addition to any other related TSA program, initiative, or procurement, including the Universal Enrollment Services program.

(l) Expenditure of Funds.—Any Federal funds expended by the Administrator to expand PreCheck Program enrollment shall be expended in a manner that includes the requirements of this section.

(Added Pub. L. 107–71, title I, §108(a), Nov. 19, 2001, 115 Stat. 611; amended Pub. L. 115–254, div. K, title I, §1937(a), Oct. 5, 2018, 132 Stat. 3576.)

§44920. SCREENING PARTNERSHIP PROGRAM

(a) IN GENERAL.—An airport operator may submit to the Administrator of the Transportation Security Administration an application to carry out the screening of passengers and property at the airport under section 44901 by personnel of a qualified private screening company pursuant to a contract entered into with the Transportation Security Administration.

(b) APPROVAL OF APPLICATIONS.—

(1) IN GENERAL.—Not later than 60 days after the date of receipt of an application submitted by an airport operator under subsection (a), the Administrator shall approve or deny the application.

(2) STANDARDS.—The Administrator shall approve an application submitted by an airport operator under subsection (a) if the Administrator determines that the approval

would not compromise security or detrimentally affect the cost-efficiency or the effectiveness of the screening of passengers or property at the airport.

(3) REPORTS ON DENIALS OF APPLICATIONS.—

(A) IN GENERAL.—If the Administrator denies an application submitted by an airport operator under subsection (a), the Administrator shall provide to the airport operator, not later than 60 days following the date of the denial, a written report that sets forth—

(i) the findings that served as the basis for the denial;

(ii) the results of any cost or security analysis conducted in considering the application; and

(iii) recommendations on how the airport operator can address the reasons for the denial.

(B) SUBMISSION TO CONGRESS.—The Administrator shall submit to the Committee on Commerce, Science, and Transportation of the Senate and the Committee on Homeland Security of the House of Representatives a copy of any report provided to an airport operator under subparagraph (A).

(c) QUALIFIED PRIVATE SCREENING COMPANY.—A private screening company is qualified to provide screening services at an airport under this section if the company will only employ individuals to provide such services who meet all the requirements of this chapter applicable to Federal Government personnel who perform screening services at airports under this chapter and will provide compensation and other benefits to such individuals that are not less than the level of compensation and other benefits provided to such Federal Government personnel in accordance with this chapter.

(d) SELECTION OF CONTRACTS AND STANDARDS FOR PRIVATE SCREENING COMPANIES.—

(1) IN GENERAL.—The Administrator shall, upon approval of the application, provide the airport operator with a list of qualified private screening companies.

(2) CONTRACTS.—The Administrator shall, to the extent practicable, enter into a contract with a private screening company from the list provided under paragraph (1) for the provision of screening at the airport not later than 120 days after the date of approval of an application submitted by the airport operator under subsection (a) if—

(A) the level of screening services and protection provided at the airport under the contract will be equal to or greater than the level that would be provided at the airport by Federal Government personnel under this chapter;

(B) the private screening company is owned and controlled by a citizen of the United States, to the extent that the Administrator determines that there are private screening companies owned and controlled by such citizens; and

(C) the selected qualified private screening company offered contract price is equal to or less than the cost to the Federal Government to provide screening services at the airport.

(3) WAIVERS.—The Administrator may waive the requirement of paragraph (2)(B) for any company that is a United States subsidiary with a parent company that has implemented a foreign ownership, control, or influence mitigation plan that has been approved by the Defense Security Service of the Department of Defense prior to the submission of the application. The Administrator has complete discretion to reject any application from a private screening company to provide screening services at an airport

that requires a waiver under this paragraph.

(e) SUPERVISION OF SCREENING PERSONNEL.—The Administrator shall—

(1) provide Federal Government supervisors to oversee all screening at each airport at which screening services are provided under this section and provide Federal Government law enforcement officers at the airport pursuant to this chapter; and

(2) undertake covert testing and remedial training support for employees of private screening companies providing screening at airports.

(f) TERMINATION OR SUSPENSION OF CONTRACTS.—The Administrator may suspend or terminate, as appropriate, any contract entered into with a private screening company to provide screening services at an airport under this section if the Administrator finds that the company has failed repeatedly to comply with any standard, regulation, directive, order, law, or contract applicable to the hiring or training of personnel to provide such services or to the provision of screening at the airport.

(g) OPERATOR OF AIRPORT.—Notwithstanding any other provision of law, an operator of an airport shall not be liable for any claims for damages filed in State or Federal court (including a claim for compensatory, punitive, contributory, or indemnity damages) relating to—

(1) such airport operator's decision to submit an application to the Secretary of Homeland Security under subsection (a) or such airport operator's decision not to submit an application; and

(2) any act of negligence, gross negligence, or intentional wrongdoing by—

(A) a qualified private screening company or any of its employees in any case in which the qualified private screening company is acting under a contract entered into with the Secretary of Homeland Security or the Secretary's designee; or

(B) employees of the Federal Government providing passenger and property security screening services at the airport.

(3) Nothing in this section shall relieve any airport operator from liability for its own acts or omissions related to its security responsibilities, nor except as may be provided by the Support Anti-Terrorism by Fostering Effective Technologies Act of 2002 shall it relieve any qualified private screening company or its employees from any liability related to its own acts of negligence, gross negligence, or intentional wrongdoing.

(h) EVALUATION OF SCREENING COMPANY PROPOSALS FOR AWARD.—

(1) IN GENERAL.—Except as provided in paragraph (2), notwithstanding any other provision of law, including title 48 of the Code of Federal Regulations and the Federal Advisory Committee Act (5 U.S.C. App.), an airport operator that has applied and been approved to have security screening services carried out by a qualified private screening company under contract with the Administrator may nominate to the head of the contracting activity an individual to participate in the evaluation of proposals for the award of such contract.

(2) PARTICIPATION ON A PROPOSAL EVALUATION COMMITTEE.—Any participation on a proposal evaluation committee under paragraph (1) shall be conducted in accordance with chapter 21 of title 41.

(i) [1] INNOVATIVE SCREENING APPROACHES AND TECHNOLOGIES.—The Administrator shall encourage an airport operator to whom screening services are provided under this section to recommend to the Administrator innovative screening approaches and technologies. Upon receipt of any such recommendations, the Administrator shall review and, if appropriate, test, conduct a pilot project, and, if appropriate, deploy such approaches and technologies.

(i) [1] DEFINITION OF ADMINISTRATOR.—In this section, the term "Administrator" means the Administrator of the Transportation Security Administration.

(Added Pub. L. 107–71, title I, §108(a), Nov. 19, 2001, 115 Stat. 612; amended Pub. L. 109–90, title V, §547, Oct. 18, 2005, 119 Stat. 2089; Pub. L. 112–95, title VIII, §830(a)–(c), Feb. 14, 2012, 126 Stat. 135; Pub. L. 115–254, div. K, title I, §§1946(a), 1991(d)(17), Oct. 5, 2018, 132 Stat. 3585, 3636.)

[1] *So in original. Two subsecs. (i) have been enacted.*

§44921. FEDERAL FLIGHT DECK OFFICER PROGRAM

(a) ESTABLISHMENT.—The Administrator shall establish a program to deputize volunteer pilots of air carriers providing air transportation or intrastate air transportation as Federal law enforcement officers to defend the flight decks of aircraft of such air carriers against acts of criminal violence or air piracy. Such officers shall be known as "Federal flight deck officers".

(b) PROCEDURAL REQUIREMENTS.—

(1) IN GENERAL.—The Administrator shall establish procedural requirements to carry out the program under this section.

(2) COMMENCEMENT OF PROGRAM.—The Administrator shall train and deputize pilots who are qualified to be Federal flight deck officers as Federal flight deck officers under the program.

(3) ISSUES TO BE ADDRESSED.—The procedural requirements established under paragraph (1) shall address the following issues:

(A) The type of firearm to be used by a Federal flight deck officer.

(B) The type of ammunition to be used by a Federal flight deck officer.

(C) The standards and training needed to qualify and requalify as a Federal flight deck officer.

(D) The placement of the firearm of a Federal flight deck officer on board the aircraft to ensure both its security and its ease of retrieval in an emergency.

(E) An analysis of the risk of catastrophic failure of an aircraft as a result of the discharge (including an accidental discharge) of a firearm to be used in the program into the avionics, electrical systems, or other sensitive areas of the aircraft.

(F) The division of responsibility between pilots in the event of an act of criminal violence or air piracy if only 1 pilot is a Federal flight deck officer and if both pilots are Federal flight deck officers.

(G) Procedures for ensuring that the firearm of a Federal flight deck officer does not leave the cockpit if there is a disturbance in the passenger cabin of the aircraft or if the pilot leaves the cockpit for personal reasons.

(H) Interaction between a Federal flight deck officer and a Federal air marshal on board the aircraft.

(I) The process for selection of pilots to participate in the program based on their fitness to participate in the program, including whether an additional background check should be required beyond that required by section 44936(a)(1).

(J) Storage and transportation of firearms between flights, including international flights, to ensure the security of the firearms, focusing particularly on whether such security would be enhanced by requiring storage of the firearm at the airport when the pilot leaves the airport to remain overnight away from the pilot's base airport.

(K) Methods for ensuring that security personnel will be able to identify whether a pilot is authorized to carry a firearm under the program.

(L) Methods for ensuring that pilots (including Federal flight deck officers) will be able to identify whether a passenger is a law enforcement officer who is authorized to carry a firearm aboard the aircraft.

(M) Any other issues that the Administrator considers necessary.

(N) The Administrator's decisions regarding the methods for implementing each of the foregoing procedural requirements shall be subject to review only for abuse of discretion.

(4) PREFERENCE.—In selecting pilots to participate in the program, the Administrator shall give preference to pilots who are former military or law enforcement personnel.

(5) CLASSIFIED INFORMATION.—Notwithstanding section 552 of title 5 but subject to section 40119 of this title, information developed under paragraph (3)(E) shall not be disclosed.

(6) NOTICE TO CONGRESS.—The Administrator shall provide notice to the Committee on Transportation and Infrastructure of the House of Representatives and the Committee on Commerce, Science, and Transportation of the Senate after completing the analysis required by paragraph (3)(E).

(7) MINIMIZATION OF RISK.—If the Administrator determines as a result of the analysis under paragraph (3)(E) that there is a significant risk of the catastrophic failure of an aircraft as a result of the discharge of a firearm, the Administrator shall take such actions as may be necessary to minimize that risk.

(c) TRAINING, SUPERVISION, AND EQUIPMENT.—

(1) IN GENERAL.—The Administrator shall only be obligated to provide the training, supervision, and equipment necessary for a pilot to be a Federal flight deck officer under this section at no expense to the pilot or the air carrier employing the pilot.

(2) TRAINING.—

(A) IN GENERAL.—The Administrator shall base the requirements for the training of Federal flight deck officers under subsection (b) on the training standards applicable to Federal air marshals; except that the Administrator shall take into account the differing roles and responsibilities of Federal flight deck officers and Federal air marshals.

(B) ELEMENTS.—The training of a Federal flight deck officer shall include, at a minimum, the following elements:

(i) Training to ensure that the officer achieves the level of proficiency with a firearm required under subparagraph (C)(i).

(ii) Training to ensure that the officer maintains exclusive control over the officer's firearm at all times, including training in defensive maneuvers.

(iii) Training to assist the officer in determining when it is appropriate to use the officer's firearm and when it is appropriate to use less than lethal force.

(C) TRAINING IN USE OF FIREARMS.—

(i) STANDARD.—In order to be deputized as a Federal flight deck officer, a pilot must achieve a level of proficiency with a firearm that is required by the

Administrator. Such level shall be comparable to the level of proficiency required of Federal air marshals.

(ii) CONDUCT OF TRAINING.—

(I) IN GENERAL.—The training of a Federal flight deck officer in the use of a firearm may be conducted by the Administrator or by a firearms training facility.

(II) ACCESS TO TRAINING FACILITIES.—The Administrator shall designate additional firearms training facilities located in various regions of the United States for Federal flight deck officers for recurrent and requalifying training relative to the number of such facilities available on the day before such [1] date of enactment.

(iii) REQUALIFICATION.—

(I) IN GENERAL.—The Administrator shall require a Federal flight deck officer to requalify to carry a firearm under the program. Such requalification shall occur at an interval required by the Administrator.

(II) USE OF FACILITIES FOR REQUALIFICATION.—The Administrator shall allow a Federal flight deck officer to requalify to carry a firearm under the program through training at a Transportation Security Administration-approved firearms training facility utilizing a Transportation Security Administration-approved contractor and a curriculum developed and approved by the Transportation Security Administration.

(iv) PERIODIC REVIEW.—The Administrator shall periodically review requalification training intervals and assess whether it is appropriate and sufficient to adjust the time between each requalification training to facilitate continued participation in the program under this section while still maintaining effectiveness of the training, and update the training requirements as appropriate.

(D) TRAINING REVIEW.—Not later than 2 years after the date of enactment of the TSA Modernization Act, and biennially thereafter, the Administrator shall review training facilities and training requirements for initial and recurrent training for Federal flight deck officers and evaluate how training requirements, including the length of training, could be streamlined while maintaining the effectiveness of the training, and update the training requirements as appropriate.

(d) DEPUTIZATION.—

(1) IN GENERAL.—The Administrator may deputize, as a Federal flight deck officer under this section, a pilot who submits to the Administrator a request to be such an officer and whom the Administrator determines is qualified to be such an officer.

(2) QUALIFICATION.—

(A) IN GENERAL.—A pilot is qualified to be a Federal flight deck officer under this section if—

(i) the pilot is employed by an air carrier;

(ii) the Administrator determines (in the Administrator's discretion) that the pilot meets the standards established by the Administrator for being such an officer; and

(iii) the Administrator determines that the pilot has completed the training required by the Administrator.

(B) CONSISTENCY WITH REQUIREMENTS FOR CERTAIN MEDICAL CERTIFICATES.—In establishing standards under subparagraph (A)(ii), the Administrator may not establish medical or physical standards for a pilot to become a Federal flight deck officer that are inconsistent with or more stringent than the requirements of the Federal Aviation Administration for the issuance of the required airman medical certificate under part 67 of title 14, Code of Federal Regulations (or any corresponding similar regulation or ruling).

(3) DEPUTIZATION BY OTHER FEDERAL AGENCIES.—The Administrator may request another Federal agency to deputize, as Federal flight deck officers under this section, those pilots that the Administrator determines are qualified to be such officers.

(4) REVOCATION.—The Administrator may (in the Administrator's discretion) revoke the deputization of a pilot as a Federal flight deck officer if the Administrator finds that the pilot is no longer qualified to be such an officer.

(5) TRANSFER FROM INACTIVE TO ACTIVE STATUS.—In accordance with any applicable Transportation Security Administration appeals processes, a pilot deputized as a Federal flight deck officer who moves to inactive status may return to active status upon successful completion of a recurrent training program administered within program guidelines.

(e) COMPENSATION.—

(1) IN GENERAL.—Pilots participating in the program under this section shall not be eligible for compensation from the Federal Government for services provided as a Federal flight deck officer. The Federal Government and air carriers shall not be obligated to compensate a pilot for participating in the program or for the pilot's training or qualification and requalification to carry firearms under the program.

(2) FACILITATION OF TRAINING.—An air carrier shall permit a pilot seeking to be deputized as a Federal flight deck officer or a Federal flight deck officer to take a reasonable amount of leave to participate in initial, recurrent, or requalification training, as applicable, for the program. Leave required under this paragraph may be provided without compensation.

(f) AUTHORITY TO CARRY FIREARMS.—

(1) IN GENERAL.—The Administrator shall authorize a Federal flight deck officer to carry a firearm while engaged in providing air transportation or intrastate air transportation. Notwithstanding subsection (c)(1), the officer may purchase a firearm and carry that firearm aboard an aircraft of which the officer is the pilot in accordance with this section if the firearm is of a type that may be used under the program.

(2) PREEMPTION.—Notwithstanding any other provision of Federal or State law, a Federal flight deck officer, whenever necessary to participate in the program, may carry a firearm in any State and from 1 State to another State.

(3) CARRYING FIREARMS OUTSIDE UNITED STATES.—In consultation with the Secretary of State, the Administrator may take such action as may be necessary to ensure that a Federal flight deck officer may carry a firearm in a foreign country whenever necessary to participate in the program.

(4) CONSISTENCY WITH FEDERAL AIR MARSHAL PROGRAM.—The Administrator shall harmonize, to the extent practicable and in a manner that does not jeopardize existing Federal air marshal agreements, the policies relating to the carriage of firearms on international flights by Federal flight deck officers with the policies of the Federal air marshal program for carrying firearms on such flights and carrying out the duties of a

Federal flight deck officer, notwithstanding Annex 17 of the International Civil Aviation Organization.

(g) AUTHORITY TO USE FORCE.—Notwithstanding section 44903(d), the Administrator shall prescribe the standards and circumstances under which a Federal flight deck officer may use, while the program under this section is in effect, force (including lethal force) against an individual in the defense of the flight deck of an aircraft in air transportation or intrastate air transportation.

(h) LIMITATION ON LIABILITY.—

(1) LIABILITY OF AIR CARRIERS.—An air carrier shall not be liable for damages in any action brought in a Federal or State court arising out of a Federal flight deck officer's use of or failure to use a firearm.

(2) LIABILITY OF FEDERAL FLIGHT DECK OFFICERS.—A Federal flight deck officer shall not be liable for damages in any action brought in a Federal or State court arising out of the acts or omissions of the officer in defending the flight deck of an aircraft against acts of criminal violence or air piracy unless the officer is guilty of gross negligence or willful misconduct.

(3) LIABILITY OF FEDERAL GOVERNMENT.—For purposes of an action against the United States with respect to an act or omission of a Federal flight deck officer in defending the flight deck of an aircraft, the officer shall be treated as an employee of the Federal Government under chapter 171 of title 28, relating to tort claims procedure.

(i) PROCEDURES FOLLOWING ACCIDENTAL DISCHARGES.—If an accidental discharge of a firearm under the pilot program results in the injury or death of a passenger or crew member on an aircraft, the Administrator—

(1) shall revoke the deputization of the Federal flight deck officer responsible for that firearm if the Administrator determines that the discharge was attributable to the negligence of the officer; and

(2) if the Administrator determines that a shortcoming in standards, training, or procedures was responsible for the accidental discharge, may temporarily suspend the program until the shortcoming is corrected.

(j) LIMITATION ON AUTHORITY OF AIR CARRIERS.—No air carrier shall prohibit or threaten any retaliatory action against a pilot employed by the air carrier from becoming a Federal flight deck officer under this section. No air carrier shall—

(1) prohibit a Federal flight deck officer from piloting an aircraft operated by the air carrier; or

(2) terminate the employment of a Federal flight deck officer, solely on the basis of his or her volunteering for or participating in the program under this section.

(k) APPLICABILITY.—This section shall not apply to air carriers operating under part 135 of title 14, Code of Federal Regulations, and to pilots employed by such carriers to the extent that such carriers and pilots are covered by section 135.119 of such title or any successor to such section.

(l) DEFINITIONS.—In this section:

(1) ADMINISTRATOR.—The term "Administrator" means the Administrator of the Transportation Security Administration.

(2) AIR TRANSPORTATION.—The term "air transportation" includes all-cargo air transportation.

(3) FIREARMS TRAINING FACILITY.—The term "firearms training facility" means a private or government-owned gun range approved by the Administrator to provide recurrent or requalification training, as applicable, for the program, utilizing a Transportation Security Administration-approved contractor and a curriculum developed and approved by the Transportation Security Administration.

(4) PILOT.—The term "pilot" means an individual who has final authority and responsibility for the operation and safety of the flight or any other flight deck crew member.

(Added Pub. L. 107–296, title XIV, §1402(a), Nov. 25, 2002, 116 Stat. 2300; amended Pub. L. 108–176, title VI, §609(b), Dec. 12, 2003, 117 Stat. 2570; Pub. L. 115–254, div. K, title I, §1963(a)–(h), Oct. 5, 2018, 132 Stat. 3601–3603.)

[1] So in original.

§44922. DEPUTIZATION OF STATE AND LOCAL LAW ENFORCEMENT OFFICERS

(a) DEPUTIZATION AUTHORITY.—The Administrator of the Transportation Security Administration may deputize a State or local law enforcement officer to carry out Federal airport security duties under this chapter.

(b) FULFILLMENT OF REQUIREMENTS.—A State or local law enforcement officer who is deputized under this section shall be treated as a Federal law enforcement officer for purposes of meeting the requirements of this chapter and other provisions of law to provide Federal law enforcement officers to carry out Federal airport security duties.

(c) AGREEMENTS.—To deputize a State or local law enforcement officer under this section, the Administrator of the Transportation Security Administration shall enter into a voluntary agreement with the appropriate State or local law enforcement agency that employs the State or local law enforcement officer.

(d) REIMBURSEMENT.—

(1) IN GENERAL.—The Administrator of the Transportation Security Administration shall reimburse a State or local law enforcement agency for all reasonable, allowable, and allocable costs incurred by the State or local law enforcement agency with respect to a law enforcement officer deputized under this section.

(2) AUTHORIZATION OF APPROPRIATIONS.—There are authorized to be appropriated such sums as may be necessary to carry out this subsection.

(e) FEDERAL TORT CLAIMS ACT.—A State or local law enforcement officer who is deputized under this section shall be treated as an "employee of the Government" for purposes of sections 1346(b), 2401(b), and chapter 171 of title 28, United States Code, while carrying out Federal airport security duties within the course and scope of the officer's employment, subject to Federal supervision and control, and in accordance with the terms of such deputization.

(f) STATIONING OF OFFICERS.—The Administrator of the Transportation Security Administration may allow law enforcement personnel to be stationed other than at the airport security screening location if that would be preferable for law enforcement purposes and if such personnel would still be able to provide prompt responsiveness to problems occurring at the screening location.

(Added Pub. L. 108–7, div. I, title III, §351(a), Feb. 20, 2003, 117 Stat. 419; amended Pub. L. 115–254, div.

K, title I, §1991(d)(18), Oct. 5, 2018, 132 Stat. 3636.)

§44923. AIRPORT SECURITY IMPROVEMENT PROJECTS

(a) GRANT AUTHORITY.—Subject to the requirements of this section, the Administrator of the Transportation Security Administration shall make grants to airport sponsors—

(1) for projects to replace baggage conveyer systems related to aviation security;

(2) for projects to reconfigure terminal baggage areas as needed to install explosive detection systems;

(3) for projects to enable the Administrator of the Transportation Security Administration to deploy explosive detection systems behind the ticket counter, in the baggage sorting area, or in line with the baggage handling system; and

(4) for other airport security capital improvement projects.

(b) APPLICATIONS.—A sponsor seeking a grant under this section shall submit to the Administrator of the Transportation Security Administration an application in such form and containing such information as the Administrator of the Transportation Security Administration prescribes.

(c) APPROVAL.—The Administrator of the Transportation Security Administration, after consultation with the Secretary of Transportation, may approve an application of a sponsor for a grant under this section only if the Administrator of the Transportation Security Administration determines that the project will improve security at an airport or improve the efficiency of the airport without lessening security.

(d) LETTERS OF INTENT.—

(1) ISSUANCE.—The Administrator of the Transportation Security Administration shall issue a letter of intent to a sponsor committing to obligate from future budget authority an amount, not more than the Federal Government's share of the project's cost, for an airport security improvement project (including interest costs and costs of formulating the project).

(2) SCHEDULE.—A letter of intent under this subsection shall establish a schedule under which the Administrator of the Transportation Security Administration will reimburse the sponsor for the Government's share of the project's costs, as amounts become available, if the sponsor, after the Administrator of the Transportation Security Administration issues the letter, carries out the project without receiving amounts under this section.

(3) NOTICE TO ADMINISTRATOR OF THE TRANSPORTATION SECURITY ADMINISTRATION.—A sponsor that has been issued a letter of intent under this subsection shall notify the Administrator of the Transportation Security Administration of the sponsor's intent to carry out a project before the project begins.

(4) NOTICE TO CONGRESS.—The Administrator of the Transportation Security Administration shall transmit to the Committees on Appropriations and Transportation and Infrastructure of the House of Representatives and the Committees on Appropriations and Commerce, Science [1] and Transportation of the Senate a written notification at least 3 days before the issuance of a letter of intent under this section.

(5) LIMITATIONS.—A letter of intent issued under this subsection is not an obligation of the Government under section 1501 of title 31, and the letter is not deemed to be an administrative commitment for financing. An obligation or administrative commitment

may be made only as amounts are provided in authorization and appropriations laws.

(6) STATUTORY CONSTRUCTION.—Nothing in this subsection shall be construed to prohibit the obligation of amounts pursuant to a letter of intent under this subsection in the same fiscal year as the letter of intent is issued.

(e) FEDERAL SHARE.—The Government's share of the cost of a project under this section shall be 90 percent for a project at a medium or large hub airport and 95 percent for a project at any other airport.

(f) SPONSOR DEFINED.—In this section, the term "sponsor" has the meaning given that term in section 47102.

(g) APPLICABILITY OF CERTAIN REQUIREMENTS.—The requirements that apply to grants and letters of intent issued under chapter 471 (other than section 47102(3)) shall apply to grants and letters of intent issued under this section.

(h) AVIATION SECURITY CAPITAL FUND.—

(1) IN GENERAL.—There is established within the Department of Homeland Security a fund to be known as the Aviation Security Capital Fund. The first $250,000,000 derived from fees received under section 44940(a)(1) in each of fiscal years 2004 through 2028 shall be available to be deposited in the Fund. The Administrator of the Transportation Security Administration shall impose the fee authorized by section 44940(a)(1) so as to collect at least $250,000,000 in each of such fiscal years for deposit into the Fund. Amounts in the Fund shall be available to the Administrator of the Transportation Security Administration to make grants under this section.

(2) ALLOCATION.—Of the amount made available under paragraph (1) for a fiscal year, not less than $200,000,000 shall be allocated to fulfill letters of intent issued under subsection (d).

(3) DISCRETIONARY GRANTS.—Of the amount made available under paragraph (1) for a fiscal year, up to $50,000,000 shall be used to make discretionary grants, including other transaction agreements for airport security improvement projects, with priority given to small hub airports and nonhub airports.

(i) LEVERAGED FUNDING.—For purposes of this section, a grant under subsection (a) to an airport sponsor to service an obligation issued by or on behalf of that sponsor to fund a project described in subsection (a) shall be considered to be a grant for that project.

(Added Pub. L. 108–176, title VI, §605(a), Dec. 12, 2003, 117 Stat. 2566; amended Pub. L. 108–458, title IV, §4019(e)(1), Dec. 17, 2004, 118 Stat. 3722; Pub. L. 110–53, title XVI, §§1603(a), 1604(a), Aug. 3, 2007, 121 Stat. 480; Pub. L. 115–254, div. K, title I, §1991(d)(19), Oct. 5, 2018, 132 Stat. 3636.)

[1] So in original. Probably should be "Science,".

§44924. REPAIR STATION SECURITY

(a) SECURITY REVIEW AND AUDIT.—To ensure the security of maintenance and repair work conducted on air carrier aircraft and components at foreign repair stations, the Administrator of the Transportation Security Administration, in consultation with the Administrator of the Federal Aviation Administration, shall complete a security review and audit of foreign repair stations that are certified by the Administrator of the Federal Aviation Administration under part 145 of title 14, Code of Federal Regulations, and that work on air carrier aircraft and components. The review shall be completed not later than 6 months after the date on which the Administrator of the Transportation Security Administration issues regulations under subsection (f).

(b) ADDRESSING SECURITY CONCERNS.—The Administrator of the Transportation Security Administration shall require a foreign repair station to address the security issues and vulnerabilities identified in a security audit conducted under subsection (a) within 90 days of providing notice to the repair station of the security issues and vulnerabilities so identified and shall notify the Administrator of the Federal Aviation Administration that a deficiency was identified in the security audit.

(c) SUSPENSIONS AND REVOCATIONS OF CERTIFICATES.—

(1) FAILURE TO CARRY OUT EFFECTIVE SECURITY MEASURES.—If, after the 90th day on which a notice is provided to a foreign repair station under subsection (b), the Administrator of the Transportation Security Administration determines that the foreign repair station does not maintain and carry out effective security measures, the Administrator of the Transportation Security Administration shall notify the Administrator of the Federal Aviation Administration of the determination. Upon receipt of the determination, the Administrator of the Federal Aviation Administration shall suspend the certification of the repair station until such time as the Administrator of the Transportation Security Administration determines that the repair station maintains and carries out effective security measures and transmits the determination to the Administrator of the Federal Aviation Administration.

(2) IMMEDIATE SECURITY RISK.—If the Administrator of the Transportation Security Administration determines that a foreign repair station poses an immediate security risk, the Administrator of the Transportation Security Administration shall notify the Administrator of the Federal Aviation Administration of the determination. Upon receipt of the determination, the Administrator of the Federal Aviation Administration shall revoke the certification of the repair station.

(3) PROCEDURES FOR APPEALS.—The Administrator of the Transportation Security Administration, in consultation with the Administrator of the Federal Aviation Administration, shall establish procedures for appealing a revocation of a certificate under this subsection.

(d) FAILURE TO MEET AUDIT DEADLINE.—If the security audits required by subsection (a) are not completed on or before the date that is 6 months after the date on which the Administrator of the Transportation Security Administration issues regulations under subsection (f), the Administrator of the Federal Aviation Administration shall be barred from certifying any foreign repair station (other than a station that was previously certified, or is in the process of certification, by the Administration under this part) until such audits are completed for existing stations.

(e) PRIORITY FOR AUDITS.—In conducting the audits described in subsection (a), the Administrator of the Transportation Security Administration and the Administrator of the Federal Aviation Administration shall give priority to foreign repair stations located in countries identified by the Government as posing the most significant security risks.

(f) REGULATIONS.—The Administrator of the Transportation Security Administration, in consultation with the Administrator of the Federal Aviation Administration, shall issue final regulations to ensure the security of foreign and domestic aircraft repair stations.

(g) REPORT TO CONGRESS.—If the Administrator of the Transportation Security

Administration does not issue final regulations before the deadline specified in subsection (f), the Administrator of the Transportation Security Administration shall transmit to the Committee on Transportation and Infrastructure of the House of Representatives and the Committee on Commerce, Science, and Transportation of the Senate a report containing an explanation as to why the deadline was not met and a schedule for issuing the final regulations.

(Added Pub. L. 108–176, title VI, §611(b)(1), Dec. 12, 2003, 117 Stat. 2571; amended Pub. L. 110–53, title XVI, §1616(b), Aug. 3, 2007, 121 Stat. 488; Pub. L. 115–254, div. K, title I, §1991(d)(20), Oct. 5, 2018, 132 Stat. 3637.)

§44925. Deployment and use of detection equipment at airport screening checkpoints

(a) Weapons and Explosives.—The Secretary of Homeland Security shall give a high priority to developing, testing, improving, and deploying, at airport screening checkpoints, equipment that detects nonmetallic, chemical, biological, and radiological weapons, and explosives, in all forms, on individuals and in their personal property. The Secretary shall ensure that the equipment alone, or as part of an integrated system, can detect under realistic operating conditions the types of weapons and explosives that terrorists would likely try to smuggle aboard an air carrier aircraft.

(b) Strategic Plan for Deployment and Use of Explosive Detection Equipment at Airport Screening Checkpoints.—

(1) In general.—The Administrator of the Transportation Security Administration shall submit to the appropriate congressional committees a strategic plan to promote the optimal utilization and deployment of explosive detection equipment at airports to screen individuals and their personal property. Such equipment includes walk-through explosive detection portals, document scanners, shoe scanners, and backscatter x-ray scanners. The plan may be submitted in a classified format.

(2) Content.—The strategic plan shall include, at minimum—

(A) a description of current efforts to detect explosives in all forms on individuals and in their personal property;

(B) a description of the operational applications of explosive detection equipment at airport screening checkpoints;

(C) a deployment schedule and a description of the quantities of equipment needed to implement the plan;

(D) a description of funding needs to implement the plan, including a financing plan that provides for leveraging of non-Federal funding;

(E) a description of the measures taken and anticipated to be taken in carrying out subsection (d); and

(F) a description of any recommended legislative actions.

(c) Portal Detection Systems.—There is authorized to be appropriated to the Secretary of Homeland Security for the use of the Transportation Security Administration $250,000,000, in addition to any amounts otherwise authorized by law, for research, development, and installation of detection systems and other devices for the detection of biological, chemical, radiological, and explosive materials.

(d) Interim Action.—Until measures are implemented that enable the screening of all passengers for explosives, the Administrator of the Transportation Security Administration shall provide, by such means as the Administrator of the Transportation Security Administration considers appropriate, explosives detection screening for all passengers identified for additional screening and their personal property that will be carried aboard a passenger aircraft operated by an air carrier or foreign air carrier in air transportation or intrastate air transportation.

(Added Pub. L. 108–458, title IV, §4013(a), Dec. 17, 2004, 118 Stat. 3719; amended Pub. L. 110–53, title XVI, §1607(b), Aug. 3, 2007, 121 Stat. 483; Pub. L. 115–254, div. K, title I, §1991(d)(21), Oct. 5, 2018, 132 Stat. 3637.)

§44926. APPEAL AND REDRESS PROCESS FOR PASSENGERS WRONGLY DELAYED OR PROHIBITED FROM BOARDING A FLIGHT

(a) IN GENERAL.—The Secretary of Homeland Security shall establish a timely and fair process for individuals who believe they have been delayed or prohibited from boarding a commercial aircraft because they were wrongly identified as a threat under the regimes utilized by the Transportation Security Administration, United States Customs and Border Protection, or any other office or component of the Department of Homeland Security.

(b) OFFICE OF APPEALS AND REDRESS.—

(1) ESTABLISHMENT.—The Secretary shall establish in the Department an Office of Appeals and Redress to implement, coordinate, and execute the process established by the Secretary pursuant to subsection (a). The Office shall include representatives from the Transportation Security Administration, United States Customs and Border Protection, and such other offices and components of the Department as the Secretary determines appropriate.

(2) RECORDS.—The process established by the Secretary pursuant to subsection (a) shall include the establishment of a method by which the Office, under the direction of the Secretary, will be able to maintain a record of air carrier passengers and other individuals who have been misidentified and have corrected erroneous information.

(3) INFORMATION.—To prevent repeated delays of a misidentified passenger or other individual, the Office shall—

(A) ensure that the records maintained under this subsection contain information determined by the Secretary to authenticate the identity of such a passenger or individual;

(B) furnish to the Transportation Security Administration, United States Customs and Border Protection, or any other appropriate office or component of the Department, upon request, such information as may be necessary to allow such office or component to assist air carriers in improving their administration of the advanced passenger prescreening system and reduce the number of false positives; and

(C) require air carriers and foreign air carriers take action to identify passengers determined, under the process established under subsection (a), to have been wrongly identified.

(4) HANDLING OF PERSONALLY IDENTIFIABLE INFORMATION.—The Secretary, in conjunction with the Chief Privacy Officer of the Department shall—

(A) require that Federal employees of the Department handling personally identifiable information of passengers (in this paragraph referred to as "PII") complete mandatory privacy and security training prior to being authorized to handle PII;

(B) ensure that the records maintained under this subsection are secured by encryption, one-way hashing, other data anonymization techniques, or such other equivalent security technical protections as the Secretary determines necessary;

(C) limit the information collected from misidentified passengers or other individuals to the minimum amount necessary to resolve a redress request;

(D) require that the data generated under this subsection shall be shared or transferred via a secure data network, that has been audited to ensure that the anti-hacking and other security related software functions properly and is updated as necessary;

(E) ensure that any employee of the Department receiving the data contained within the records handles the information in accordance with the section 552a of title 5, United States Code, and the Federal Information Security Management Act of 2002 (Public Law 107–296);

(F) only retain the data for as long as needed to assist the individual traveler in the redress process; and

(G) conduct and publish a privacy impact assessment of the process described within this subsection and transmit the assessment to the Committee on Homeland Security of the House of Representatives, the Committee on Commerce, Science, and Transportation of the Senate, and Committee on Homeland Security and Governmental Affairs of the Senate.

(5) INITIATION OF REDRESS PROCESS AT AIRPORTS.—The Office shall establish at each airport at which the Department has a significant presence a process to provide information to air carrier passengers to begin the redress process established pursuant to subsection (a).

(Added Pub. L. 110–53, title XVI, §1606(a), Aug. 3, 2007, 121 Stat. 482; amended Pub. L. 115–254, div. K, title I, §1991(d)(22), Oct. 5, 2018, 132 Stat. 3637.)

§44927. EXPEDITED SCREENING FOR SEVERELY INJURED OR DISABLED MEMBERS OF THE ARMED FORCES AND SEVERELY INJURED OR DISABLED VETERANS

(a) PASSENGER SCREENING.—The Administrator of the Transportation Security Administration, in consultation with the Secretary of Defense, the Secretary of Veterans Affairs, and organizations identified by the Secretaries of Defense and Veterans Affairs that advocate on behalf of severely injured or disabled members of the Armed Forces and severely injured or disabled veterans, shall develop and implement a process to support and facilitate the ease of travel and to the extent possible provide expedited passenger screening services for severely injured or disabled members of the Armed Forces and severely injured or disabled veterans through passenger screening. The process shall be designed to offer the individual private screening to the maximum extent practicable.

(b) OPERATIONS CENTER.—As part of the process under subsection (a), the Administrator of the Transportation Security Administration shall maintain an operations center to provide support and facilitate the movement of severely injured or disabled members of the Armed Forces and severely injured or disabled veterans through passenger screening prior to boarding a passenger aircraft operated by an air carrier or foreign air carrier in air transportation or intrastate air transportation.

(c) PROTOCOLS.—The Administrator of the Transportation Security Administration shall—

(1) establish and publish protocols, in consultation with the Secretary of Defense, the Secretary of Veterans Affairs, and the organizations identified under subsection (a), under which a severely injured or disabled member of the Armed Forces or severely injured or disabled veteran, or the family member or other representative of such member or veteran, may contact the operations center maintained under subsection (b) and request the expedited passenger screening services described in subsection (a) for that member or veteran; and

(2) upon receipt of a request under paragraph (1), require the operations center to notify the appropriate Federal Security Director of the request for expedited passenger screening services, as described in subsection (a), for that member or veteran.

(d) TRAINING.—The Administrator of the Transportation Security Administration shall integrate training on the protocols established under subsection (c) into the training provided to all employees who will regularly provide the passenger screening services described in subsection (a).

(e) RULE OF CONSTRUCTION.—Nothing in this section shall affect the authority of the Administrator of the Transportation Security Administration to require additional screening of a severely injured or disabled member of the Armed Forces, a severely injured or disabled veteran, or their accompanying family members or nonmedical attendants, if intelligence, law enforcement, or other information indicates that additional screening is necessary.

(f) REPORTS.—Each year, the Administrator of the Transportation Security Administration shall submit to Congress a report on the implementation of this section. Each report shall include each of the following:

(1) Information on the training provided under subsection (d).

(2) Information on the consultations between the Administrator of the Transportation Security Administration and the organizations identified under subsection (a).

(3) The number of people who accessed the operations center during the period covered by the report.

(4) Such other information as the Administrator of the Transportation Security Administration determines is appropriate.

(Added Pub. L. 113–27, §2(a), Aug. 9, 2013, 127 Stat. 503; amended Pub. L. 115–254, div. K, title I, §1991(d)(23), Oct. 5, 2018, 132 Stat. 3637.)

§44928. HONOR FLIGHT PROGRAM

The Administrator of the Transportation Security Administration shall establish, in collaboration with the Honor Flight Network or other not-for-profit organization that honors veterans, a process for providing expedited and dignified passenger screening services for veterans traveling on an Honor Flight Network private charter, or such other not-for-profit organization that honors veterans, to visit war memorials built and dedicated to honor the service of such veterans.

(Added Pub. L. 113–221, §2(a), Dec. 16, 2014, 128 Stat. 2094.)

§44929. DONATION OF SCREENING EQUIPMENT TO PROTECT THE UNITED STATES

(a) IN GENERAL.—Subject to subsection (b), the Administrator is authorized to donate security screening equipment to a foreign last point of departure airport operator if such equipment can be reasonably expected to mitigate a specific vulnerability to the security of the United States or United States citizens.

(b) CONDITIONS.—Before donating any security screening equipment to a foreign last point of departure airport operator the Administrator shall—

(1) ensure that the screening equipment has been restored to commercially available settings;

(2) ensure that no TSA-specific security standards or algorithms exist on the screening equipment; and

(3) verify that the appropriate officials have an adequate system—

(A) to properly maintain and operate the screening equipment; and

(B) to document and track any removal or disposal of the screening equipment to ensure the screening equipment does not come into the possession of terrorists or otherwise pose a risk to security.

(c) REPORTS.—Not later than 30 days before any donation of security screening equipment under subsection (a), the Administrator shall provide to the Committee on Commerce, Science, and Transportation and the Committee on Homeland Security and Governmental Affairs of the Senate and the Committee on Homeland Security of the House of Representatives a detailed written explanation of the following:

(1) The specific vulnerability to the United States or United States citizens that will be mitigated by such donation.

(2) An explanation as to why the recipient of such donation is unable or unwilling to purchase security screening equipment to mitigate such vulnerability.

(3) An evacuation plan for sensitive technologies in case of emergency or instability in the country to which such donation is being made.

(4) How the Administrator will ensure the security screening equipment that is being donated is used and maintained over the course of its life by the recipient.

(5) The total dollar value of such donation.

(6) How the appropriate officials will document and track any removal or disposal of the screening equipment by the recipient to ensure the screening equipment does not come into the possession of terrorists or otherwise pose a risk to security.

(Added Pub. L. 115–254, div. K, title I, §1955(a)(1), Oct. 5, 2018, 132 Stat. 3595.)

SUBCHAPTER II—ADMINISTRATION AND PERSONNEL

§44931. AUTHORITY TO EXEMPT

The Secretary of Homeland Security may grant an exemption from a regulation prescribed in carrying out sections 44901, 44903, 44906, 44909(c), and 44935–44937 of this title when the Secretary decides the exemption is in the public interest.

(Added Pub. L. 115–254, div. K, title I, §1991(j)(1), Oct. 5, 2018, 132 Stat. 3645.)

§44932. ADMINISTRATIVE

(a) GENERAL AUTHORITY.—The Secretary of Homeland Security or the Administrator of the Transportation Security Administration may take action the Secretary or the Administrator considers necessary to carry out this chapter and chapters 461, 463, and 465 of this title, including conducting investigations, prescribing regulations, standards, and procedures, and issuing orders.

(b) INDEMNIFICATION.—The Administrator of the Transportation Security Administration may indemnify an officer or employee of the Transportation Security Administration against a claim or judgment arising out of an act that the Administrator decides was committed within the scope of the official duties of the officer or employee.

(Added Pub. L. 115–254, div. K, title I, §1991(j)(1), Oct. 5, 2018, 132 Stat. 3645.)

§44933. FEDERAL SECURITY MANAGERS [1]

(a) ESTABLISHMENT, DESIGNATION, AND STATIONING.—The Administrator of the Transportation Security Administration shall establish the position of Federal Security Director at each airport in the United States described in section 44903(c). The Administrator of the Transportation Security Administration shall designate individuals as Federal Security Directors for, and station those Federal Security Directors at, those airports.

(b) DUTIES AND POWERS.—The Federal Security Director at each airport shall—

(1) oversee the screening of passengers and property at the airport; and

(2) carry out other duties prescribed by the Administrator of the Transportation Security Administration.

(c) INFORMATION SHARING.—Not later than 1 year after the date of the enactment of the TSA Modernization Act, the Administrator shall—

(1) require each Federal Security Director of an airport to meet at least quarterly with the airport director, airport security coordinator, and law enforcement agencies serving each such airport to discuss incident management protocols, including the resolution of screening anomalies at passenger screening checkpoints; and

(2) require each Federal Security Director at an airport to inform, consult, and coordinate, as appropriate, with the respective airport security coordinator in a timely manner on security matters impacting airport operations and to establish and maintain operational protocols with such airport operators to ensure coordinated responses to security matters.

(Pub. L. 103–272, §1(e), July 5, 1994, 108 Stat. 1216; Pub. L. 107–71, title I, §§101(f)(4), 103, Nov. 19, 2001, 115 Stat. 603, 605; Pub. L. 115–254, div. K, title I, §§1989(a), 1991(d)(24), Oct. 5, 2018, 132 Stat. 3624, 3637.)

[1] So in original. Probably should be "Directors".

§44934. FOREIGN SECURITY LIAISON OFFICERS

(a) ESTABLISHMENT, DESIGNATION, AND STATIONING.—The Administrator of the Transportation Security Administration shall establish the position of Foreign Security Liaison Officer for each airport outside the United States at which the Administrator decides an Officer is necessary for air transportation security. In coordination with the Secretary of State, the Administrator shall designate an Officer for each of those airports. In coordination with the Secretary of State, the Administrator shall designate an Officer for each of those airports where extraordinary security measures are in place. The Secretary of State shall give high priority to stationing those Officers.

(b) DUTIES AND POWERS.—An Officer reports directly to the Administrator of the Transportation Security Administration. The Officer at each airport shall—

(1) serve as the liaison of the Administrator to foreign security authorities (including governments of foreign countries and foreign airport authorities) in carrying out United States Government security requirements at that airport; and

(2) to the extent practicable, carry out duties and powers referred to in section 44933(b) of this title.

(c) COORDINATION OF ACTIVITIES.—The activities of each Officer shall be coordinated with the chief of the diplomatic mission of the United States to which the Officer is assigned. Activities of an Officer under this section shall be consistent with the duties and powers of the Secretary of State and the chief of mission to a foreign country under section 103 of the Omnibus Diplomatic Security and Antiterrorism Act of 1986 (22 U.S.C. 4802) and section 207 of the Foreign Service Act of 1980 (22 U.S.C. 3927).

(Pub. L. 103–272, §1(e), July 5, 1994, 108 Stat. 1217; Pub. L. 107–71, title I, §101(f)(4), (5), (7), (9), Nov. 19, 2001, 115 Stat. 603; Pub. L. 115–254, div. K, title I, §1991(d)(25), Oct. 5, 2018, 132 Stat. 3638.)

§44935. EMPLOYMENT STANDARDS AND TRAINING

(a) EMPLOYMENT STANDARDS.—The Administrator shall prescribe standards for the employment and continued employment of, and contracting for, air carrier personnel and, as appropriate, airport security personnel. The standards shall include—

(1) minimum training requirements for new employees;

(2) retraining requirements;

(3) minimum staffing levels;

(4) minimum language skills; and

(5) minimum education levels for employees, when appropriate.

(b) REVIEW AND RECOMMENDATIONS.—In coordination with air carriers, airport operators, and other interested persons, the Administrator shall review issues related to human performance in the aviation security system to maximize that performance. When the review is completed, the Administrator shall recommend guidelines and prescribe appropriate changes in existing procedures to improve that performance.

(c) SECURITY PROGRAM TRAINING, STANDARDS, AND QUALIFICATIONS.—(1) The Administrator—

(A) may train individuals employed to carry out a security program under section 44903(c) of this title; and

(B) shall prescribe uniform training standards and uniform minimum qualifications for individuals eligible for that training.

(2) The Administrator may authorize reimbursement for travel, transportation, and subsistence expenses for security training of non-United States Government domestic and foreign individuals whose services will contribute significantly to carrying out civil aviation security programs. To the extent practicable, air travel reimbursed under this

paragraph shall be on air carriers.

(d) EDUCATION AND TRAINING STANDARDS FOR SECURITY COORDINATORS, SUPERVISORY PERSONNEL, AND PILOTS.—(1) The Administrator shall prescribe standards for educating and training—

(A) ground security coordinators;

(B) security supervisory personnel; and

(C) airline pilots as in-flight security coordinators.

(2) The standards shall include initial training, retraining, and continuing education requirements and methods. Those requirements and methods shall be used annually to measure the performance of ground security coordinators and security supervisory personnel.

(e) SECURITY SCREENERS.—

(1) TRAINING PROGRAM.—The Administrator shall establish a program for the hiring and training of security screening personnel.

(2) HIRING.—

(A) QUALIFICATIONS.—The Administrator shall establish qualification standards for individuals to be hired by the United States as security screening personnel. Notwithstanding any other provision of law, those standards shall require, at a minimum, an individual—

(i) to have a satisfactory or better score on a Federal security screening personnel selection examination;

(ii) to be a citizen of the United States or a national of the United States, as defined in section 101(a)(22) of the Immigration and Nationality Act (8 U.S.C. 1101(a)(22));

(iii) to meet, at a minimum, the requirements set forth in subsection (f);

(iv) to meet such other qualifications as the Administrator may establish; and

(v) to have the ability to demonstrate daily a fitness for duty without any impairment due to illegal drugs, sleep deprivation, medication, or alcohol.

(B) BACKGROUND CHECKS.—The Administrator shall require that an individual to be hired as a security screener undergo an employment investigation (including a criminal history record check) under section 44936(a)(1).

(C) DISQUALIFICATION OF INDIVIDUALS WHO PRESENT NATIONAL SECURITY RISKS.—The Administrator, in consultation with the heads of other appropriate Federal agencies, shall establish procedures, in addition to any background check conducted under section 44936, to ensure that no individual who presents a threat to national security is employed as a security screener.

(3) EXAMINATION; REVIEW OF EXISTING RULES.—The Administrator shall develop a security screening personnel examination for use in determining the qualification of individuals seeking employment as security screening personnel. The Administrator shall also review, and revise as necessary, any standard, rule, or regulation governing the employment of individuals as security screening personnel.

(f) EMPLOYMENT STANDARDS FOR SCREENING PERSONNEL.—

(1) SCREENER REQUIREMENTS.—Notwithstanding any other provision of law, an individual may not be deployed as a security screener unless that individual meets the following requirements:

(A) The individual shall possess a high school diploma, a general equivalency diploma, or experience that the Administrator has determined to be sufficient for the individual to perform the duties of the position.

(B) The individual shall possess basic aptitudes and physical abilities, including color perception, visual and aural acuity, physical coordination, and motor skills, to the following standards:

(i) Screeners operating screening equipment shall be able to distinguish on the screening equipment monitor the appropriate imaging standard specified by the Administrator.

(ii) Screeners operating any screening equipment shall be able to distinguish each color displayed on every type of screening equipment and explain what each color signifies.

(iii) Screeners shall be able to hear and respond to the spoken voice and to audible alarms generated by screening equipment in an active checkpoint environment.

(iv) Screeners performing physical searches or other related operations shall be able to efficiently and thoroughly manipulate and handle such baggage, containers, and other objects subject to security processing.

(v) Screeners who perform pat-downs or hand-held metal detector searches of individuals shall have sufficient dexterity and capability to thoroughly conduct those procedures over an individual's entire body.

(C) The individual shall be able to read, speak, and write English well enough to—

(i) carry out written and oral instructions regarding the proper performance of screening duties;

(ii) read English language identification media, credentials, airline tickets, and labels on items normally encountered in the screening process;

(iii) provide direction to and understand and answer questions from English-speaking individuals undergoing screening; and

(iv) write incident reports and statements and log entries into security records in the English language.

(D) The individual shall have satisfactorily completed all initial, recurrent, and appropriate specialized training required by the security program, except as provided in paragraph (3).

(2) VETERANS PREFERENCE.—The Administrator shall provide a preference for the hiring of an individual as a security screener if the individual is a member or former member of the armed forces and if the individual is entitled, under statute, to retired, retirement, or retainer pay on account of service as a member of the armed forces.

(3) EXCEPTIONS.—An individual who has not completed the training required by this section may be deployed during the on-the-job portion of training to perform functions if that individual—

(A) is closely supervised; and

(B) does not make independent judgments as to whether individuals or property may enter a sterile area or aircraft without further inspection.

(4) REMEDIAL TRAINING.—No individual employed as a security screener may perform a screening function after that individual has failed an operational test related to that function until that individual has successfully completed the remedial training specified

in the security program.

(5) ANNUAL PROFICIENCY REVIEW.—The Administrator shall provide that an annual evaluation of each individual assigned screening duties is conducted and documented. An individual employed as a security screener may not continue to be employed in that capacity unless the evaluation demonstrates that the individual—

(A) continues to meet all qualifications and standards required to perform a screening function;

(B) has a satisfactory record of performance and attention to duty based on the standards and requirements in the security program; and

(C) demonstrates the current knowledge and skills necessary to courteously, vigilantly, and effectively perform screening functions.

(6) OPERATIONAL TESTING.—In addition to the annual proficiency review conducted under paragraph (5), the Administrator shall provide for the operational testing of such personnel.

(g) TRAINING.—

(1) USE OF OTHER AGENCIES.—The Administrator may enter into a memorandum of understanding or other arrangement with any other Federal agency or department with appropriate law enforcement responsibilities, to provide personnel, resources, or other forms of assistance in the training of security screening personnel.

(2) TRAINING PLAN.—The Administrator shall develop a plan for the training of security screening personnel. The plan shall require, at a minimum, that a security screener—

(A) has completed 40 hours of classroom instruction or successfully completed a program that the Administrator determines will train individuals to a level of proficiency equivalent to the level that would be achieved by such classroom instruction;

(B) has completed 60 hours of on-the-job instructions; and

(C) has successfully completed an on-the-job training examination prescribed by the Administrator.

(3) EQUIPMENT-SPECIFIC TRAINING.—An individual employed as a security screener may not use any security screening device or equipment in the scope of that individual's employment unless the individual has been trained on that device or equipment and has successfully completed a test on the use of the device or equipment.

(h) TECHNOLOGICAL TRAINING.—

(1) IN GENERAL.—The Administrator shall require training to ensure that screeners are proficient in using the most up-to-date new technology and to ensure their proficiency in recognizing new threats and weapons.

(2) PERIODIC ASSESSMENTS.—The Administrator shall make periodic assessments to determine if there are dual use items and inform security screening personnel of the existence of such items.

(3) CURRENT LISTS OF DUAL USE ITEMS.—Current lists of dual use items shall be part of the ongoing training for screeners.

(4) DUAL USE DEFINED.—For purposes of this subsection, the term "dual use" item means an item that may seem harmless but that may be used as a weapon.

(i) LIMITATION ON RIGHT TO STRIKE.—An individual that screens passengers or property, or both, at an airport under this section may not participate in a strike, or assert the right to strike, against the person (including a governmental entity) employing such individual to perform such screening.

(j) UNIFORMS.—The Administrator shall require any individual who screens passengers and property pursuant to section 44901 to be attired while on duty in a uniform approved by the Administrator.

(k) ACCESSIBILITY OF COMPUTER-BASED TRAINING FACILITIES.—The Administrator shall work with air carriers and airports to ensure that computer-based training facilities intended for use by security screeners at an airport regularly serving an air carrier holding a certificate issued by the Secretary of Transportation are conveniently located for that airport and easily accessible.

(l) [1] INITIAL AND RECURRING TRAINING.—

(1) IN GENERAL.—The Administrator shall establish a training program for new security screening personnel located at the Transportation Security Administration Academy.

(2) RECURRING TRAINING.—

(A) IN GENERAL.—Not later than 180 days after the date of enactment of the TSA Modernization Act, the Administrator shall establish recurring training for security screening personnel regarding updates to screening procedures and technologies, including, in response to weaknesses identified in covert tests at airports—

(i) methods to identify the verification of false or fraudulent travel documents; and

(ii) training on emerging threats.

(B) CONTENTS.—The training under subparagraph (A) shall include—

(i) internal controls for monitoring and documenting compliance of transportation security officers with such training requirements; and

(ii) such other matters as identified by the Administrator with regard to such training.

(l) [1] DEFINITION OF ADMINISTRATOR.—In this section, the term "Administrator" means the Administrator of the Transportation Security Administration.

(Pub. L. 103–272, §1(e), July 5, 1994, 108 Stat. 1217; Pub. L. 106–528, §3, Nov. 22, 2000, 114 Stat. 2519; Pub. L. 107–71, title I, §§101(f)(7), (9), 111(a), Nov. 19, 2001, 115 Stat. 603, 616; Pub. L. 107–296, title XVI, §1603, Nov. 25, 2002, 116 Stat. 2313; Pub. L. 115–254, div. K, title I, §§1948(a), 1991(d)(26), Oct. 5, 2018, 132 Stat. 3587, 3638.)

[1] *So in original. Two subsecs. (l) have been enacted.*

§44936. EMPLOYMENT INVESTIGATIONS AND RESTRICTIONS

(a) EMPLOYMENT INVESTIGATION REQUIREMENT.—(1)(A) The Administrator shall require by regulation that an employment investigation, including a criminal history record check and a review of available law enforcement data bases and records of other governmental and international agencies to the extent determined practicable by the Administrator, shall be conducted of each individual employed in, or applying for, a position as a security screener under section 44935(e) or a position in which the individual has unescorted access, or may permit other individuals to have unescorted access, to—

(i) aircraft of an air carrier or foreign air carrier; or

(ii) a secured area of an airport in the United States the Administrator designates that serves an air carrier or foreign air carrier.

(B) The Administrator shall require by regulation that an employment investigation (including a criminal history record check and a review of available law enforcement data bases and records of other governmental and international agencies to the extent determined practicable by the Administrator) be conducted for—

(i) individuals who are responsible for screening passengers or property under section 44901 of this title;

(ii) supervisors of the individuals described in clause (i);

(iii) individuals who regularly have escorted access to aircraft of an air carrier or foreign air carrier or a secured area of an airport in the United States the Administrator designates that serves an air carrier or foreign air carrier; and

(iv) such other individuals who exercise security functions associated with baggage or cargo, as the Administrator determines is necessary to ensure air transportation security.

(C) EXEMPTION.—An employment investigation, including a criminal history record check, shall not be required under this subsection for an individual who is exempted under section 107.31(m)(1) or (2) of title 14, Code of Federal Regulations, as in effect on November 22, 2000. The Administrator shall work with the International Civil Aviation Organization and with appropriate authorities of foreign countries to ensure that individuals exempted under this subparagraph do not pose a threat to aviation or national security.

(2) An air carrier, foreign air carrier, airport operator, or government that employs, or authorizes or makes a contract for the services of, an individual in a position described in paragraph (1) of this subsection shall ensure that the investigation the Administrator requires is conducted.

(3) The Administrator shall provide for the periodic audit of the effectiveness of criminal history record checks conducted under paragraph (1) of this subsection.

(b) PROHIBITED EMPLOYMENT.—(1) Except as provided in paragraph (3) of this subsection, an air carrier, foreign air carrier, airport operator, or government may not employ, or authorize or make a contract for the services of, an individual in a position described in subsection (a)(1) of this section if—

(A) the investigation of the individual required under this section has not been conducted; or

(B) the results of that investigation establish that, in the 10-year period ending on the date of the investigation, the individual was convicted (or found not guilty by reason of insanity) of—

(i) a crime referred to in section 46306, 46308, 46312, 46314, or 46315 or chapter 465 of this title or section 32 of title 18;

(ii) murder;

(iii) assault with intent to murder;

(iv) espionage;

(v) sedition;

(vi) treason;

(vii) rape;

(viii) kidnapping;

(ix) unlawful possession, sale, distribution, or manufacture of an explosive or weapon;

(x) extortion;

(xi) armed or felony unarmed robbery;

(xii) distribution of, or intent to distribute, a controlled substance;

(xiii) a felony involving a threat;

(xiv) a felony involving—

(I) willful destruction of property;

(II) importation or manufacture of a controlled substance;

(III) burglary;

(IV) theft;

(V) dishonesty, fraud, or misrepresentation;

(VI) possession or distribution of stolen property;

(VII) aggravated assault;

(VIII) bribery; and

(IX) illegal possession of a controlled substance punishable by a maximum term of imprisonment of more than 1 year, or any other crime classified as a felony that the Administrator determines indicates a propensity for placing contraband aboard an aircraft in return for money; or

(xv) conspiracy to commit any of the acts referred to in clauses (i) through (xiv).

(2) The Administrator may specify other factors that are sufficient to prohibit the employment of an individual in a position described in subsection (a)(1) of this section.

(3) An air carrier, foreign air carrier, airport operator, or government may employ, or authorize or contract for the services of, an individual in a position described in subsection (a)(1) of this section without carrying out the investigation required under this section, if the Administrator approves a plan to employ the individual that provides alternate security arrangements.

(c) FINGERPRINTING AND RECORD CHECK INFORMATION.—(1) If the Administrator requires an identification and criminal history record check, to be conducted by the Attorney General, as part of an investigation under this section, the Administrator shall designate an individual to obtain fingerprints and submit those fingerprints to the Attorney General. The Attorney General may make the results of a check available to an individual the Administrator designates. Before designating an individual to obtain and submit fingerprints or receive results of a check, the Administrator shall consult with the Attorney General. All Federal agencies shall cooperate with the Administrator and the Administrator's designee in the process of collecting and submitting fingerprints.

(2) The Administrator shall prescribe regulations on—

(A) procedures for taking fingerprints; and

(B) requirements for using information received from the Attorney General under paragraph (1) of this subsection—

(i) to limit the dissemination of the information; and

(ii) to ensure that the information is used only to carry out this section.

(3) If an identification and criminal history record check is conducted as part of an investigation of an individual under this section, the individual—

(A) shall receive a copy of any record received from the Attorney General; and

(B) may complete and correct the information contained in the check before a final employment decision is made based on the check.

(d) FEES AND CHARGES.—The Administrator and the Attorney General shall establish reasonable fees and charges to pay expenses incurred in carrying out this section. The employer of the individual being investigated shall pay the costs of a record check of the individual. Money collected under this section shall be credited to the account in the Treasury from which the expenses were incurred and are available to the Administrator and the Attorney General for those expenses.

(e) WHEN INVESTIGATION OR RECORD CHECK NOT REQUIRED.—This section does not require an investigation or record check when the investigation or record check is prohibited by a law of a foreign country.

(f) DEFINITION OF ADMINISTRATOR.—In this section, the term "Administrator" means the Administrator of the Transportation Security Administration.

(Pub. L. 103–272, §1(e), July 5, 1994, 108 Stat. 1218; Pub. L. 104–264, title III, §§304(a), 306, title V, §502(a), Oct. 9, 1996, 110 Stat. 3251, 3252, 3259; Pub. L. 105–102, §2(25), Nov. 20, 1997, 111 Stat. 2205; Pub. L. 105–142, §1, Dec. 5, 1997, 111 Stat. 2650; Pub. L. 106–181, title V, §508, Apr. 5, 2000, 114 Stat. 140; Pub. L. 106–528, §2(c), (d), Nov. 22, 2000, 114 Stat. 2517, 2518; Pub. L. 107–71, title I, §§101(f)(7), (9), 111(b), 138(a), (b)(1), 140(a)(1), Nov. 19, 2001, 115 Stat. 603, 620, 639–641; Pub. L. 115–254, div. K, title I, §1991(d)(27), Oct. 5, 2018, 132 Stat. 3638.)

§44937. PROHIBITION ON TRANSFERRING DUTIES AND POWERS

Except as specifically provided by law, the Administrator of the Transportation Security Administration may not transfer a duty or power under section 44903(a), (b), (c), or (e), 44906, 44912, 44935, 44936, or 44938(b)(3) of this title to another department, agency, or instrumentality of the United States Government.

(Pub. L. 103–272, §1(e), July 5, 1994, 108 Stat. 1219; Pub. L. 103–429, §6(57), Oct. 31, 1994, 108 Stat. 4385; Pub. L. 107–71, title I, §101(f)(7), (9), Nov. 19, 2001, 115 Stat. 603; Pub. L. 115–254, div. K, title I, §1991(d)(28), Oct. 5, 2018, 132 Stat. 3639.)

§44938. REPORTS

(a) TRANSPORTATION SECURITY.—Not later than March 31 of each year, the Secretary of Homeland Security shall submit to Congress a report on transportation security with recommendations the Secretary considers appropriate. The report shall be prepared in conjunction with the biennial report the Administrator of the Transportation Security Administration submits under subsection (b) of this section in each year the Administrator of the Transportation Security Administration submits the biennial report, but may not duplicate the information submitted under subsection (b) or section 44907(a)(3) of this title. The Secretary may submit the report in classified and unclassified parts. The report shall include—

(1) an assessment of trends and developments in terrorist activities, methods, and other threats to transportation;

(2) an evaluation of deployment of explosive detection devices;

(3) recommendations for research, engineering, and development activities related to transportation security, except research engineering and development activities related to aviation security to the extent those activities are covered by the national aviation research plan required under section 44501(c) of this title;

(4) identification and evaluation of cooperative efforts with other departments, agencies, and instrumentalities of the United States Government;

(5) an evaluation of cooperation with foreign transportation and security authorities;

(6) the status of the extent to which the recommendations of the President's Commission on Aviation Security and Terrorism have been carried out and the reasons for any delay in carrying out those recommendations;

(7) a summary of the activities of the Director of Intelligence and Security in the 12-month period ending on the date of the report;

(8) financial and staffing requirements of the Director;

(9) an assessment of financial and staffing requirements, and attainment of existing staffing goals, for carrying out duties and powers of the Administrator of the Transportation Security Administration related to security; and

(10) appropriate legislative and regulatory recommendations.

(b) SCREENING AND FOREIGN AIR CARRIER AND AIRPORT SECURITY.—The Administrator of the Transportation Security Administration shall submit biennially to Congress a report—

(1) on the effectiveness of procedures under section 44901 of this title;

(2) that includes a summary of the assessments conducted under section 44907(a)(1) and (2) of this title; and

(3) that includes an assessment of the steps being taken, and the progress being made, in ensuring compliance with section 44906 of this title for each foreign air carrier security program at airports outside the United States—

(A) at which the Administrator of the Transportation Security Administration decides that Foreign Security Liaison Officers are necessary for air transportation security; and

(B) for which extraordinary security measures are in place.

(Pub. L. 103–272, §1(e), July 5, 1994, 108 Stat. 1220; Pub. L. 103–305, title V, §502, Aug. 23, 1994, 108 Stat. 1595; Pub. L. 105–362, title XV, §1502(b), Nov. 10, 1998, 112 Stat. 3295; Pub. L. 107–71, title I, §101(f)(7), (9), Nov. 19, 2001, 115 Stat. 603; Pub. L. 115–254, div. K, title I, §1991(d)(29), Oct. 5, 2018, 132 Stat. 3639.)

§44939. TRAINING TO OPERATE CERTAIN AIRCRAFT

(a) WAITING PERIOD.—A person operating as a flight instructor, pilot school, or aviation training center or subject to regulation under this part may provide training in the operation of any aircraft having a maximum certificated takeoff weight of more than 12,500 pounds to an alien (as defined in section 101(a)(3) of the Immigration and Nationality Act (8 U.S.C. 1101(a)(3))) or to any other individual specified by the Secretary of Homeland Security only if—

(1) that person has first notified the Secretary that the alien or individual has requested such training and submitted to the Secretary, in such form as the Secretary may prescribe, the following information about the alien or individual:

(A) full name, including any aliases used by the applicant or variations in spelling of the applicant's name;

(B) passport and visa information;

(C) country of citizenship;

(D) date of birth;

(E) dates of training; and

(F) fingerprints collected by, or under the supervision of, a Federal, State, or local law enforcement agency or by another entity approved by the Federal Bureau of Investigation or the Secretary of Homeland Security, including fingerprints taken by United States Government personnel at a United States embassy or consulate; and

(2) the Secretary has not directed, within 30 days after being notified under paragraph (1), that person not to provide the requested training because the Secretary has determined that the individual presents a risk to aviation or national security.

(b) INTERRUPTION OF TRAINING.—If the Secretary of Homeland Security, more than 30 days after receiving notification under subsection (a) from a person providing training described in subsection (a), determines that the individual presents a risk to aviation or national security, the Secretary shall immediately notify the person providing the training of the determination and that person shall immediately terminate the training.

(c) NOTIFICATION.—A person operating as a flight instructor, pilot school, or aviation training center or subject to regulation under this part may provide training in the operation of any aircraft having a maximum certificated takeoff weight of 12,500 pounds or less to an alien (as defined in section 101(a)(3) of the Immigration and Nationality Act (8 U.S.C. 1101(a)(3))) or to any other individual specified by the Secretary of Homeland Security only if that person has notified the Secretary that the individual has requested such training and furnished the Secretary with that individual's identification in such form as the Secretary may require.

(d) EXPEDITED PROCESSING.—The Secretary of Homeland Security shall establish a process to ensure that the waiting period under subsection (a) shall not exceed 5 days for an alien (as defined in section 101(a)(3) of the Immigration and Nationality Act (8 U.S.C. 1101(a)(3))) who—

(1) holds an airman's certification of a foreign country that is recognized by an agency of the United States, including a military agency, that permits an individual to operate a multi-engine aircraft that has a certificated takeoff weight of more than 12,500 pounds;

(2) is employed by a foreign air carrier that is certified under part 129 of title 14, Code of Federal Regulations, and that has a security program approved under section 1546 of title 49, Code of Federal Regulations;

(3) is an individual that has unescorted access to a secured area of an airport designated under section 44936(a)(1)(A)(ii); or

(4) is an individual that is part of a class of individuals that the Secretary has determined that providing aviation training to presents minimal risk to aviation or national security because of the aviation training already possessed by such class of individuals.

(e) TRAINING.—In subsection (a), the term "training" means training received from an instructor in an aircraft or aircraft simulator and does not include recurrent training, ground training, or demonstration flights for marketing purposes.

(f) NONAPPLICABILITY TO CERTAIN FOREIGN MILITARY PILOTS.—The procedures and processes required by subsections (a) through (d) shall not apply to a foreign military pilot endorsed by the Department of Defense for flight training in the United States and seeking training described in subsection (e) in the United States.

(g) Fee.—

(1) In general.—The Secretary of Homeland Security may assess a fee for an investigation under this section, which may not exceed $100 per individual (exclusive of the cost of transmitting fingerprints collected at overseas facilities) during fiscal years 2003 and 2004. For fiscal year 2005 and thereafter, the Secretary may adjust the maximum amount of the fee to reflect the costs of such an investigation.

(2) Offset.—Notwithstanding section 3302 of title 31, any fee collected under this section—

(A) shall be credited to the account in the Treasury from which the expenses were incurred and shall be available to the Secretary for those expenses; and

(B) shall remain available until expended.

(h) Interagency Cooperation.—The Attorney General, the Director of Central Intelligence, and the Administrator of the Federal Aviation Administration shall cooperate with the Secretary in implementing this section.

(i) Security Awareness Training for Employees.—The Secretary shall require flight schools to conduct a security awareness program for flight school employees to increase their awareness of suspicious circumstances and activities of individuals enrolling in or attending flight school.

(Added Pub. L. 107–71, title I, §113(a), Nov. 19, 2001, 115 Stat. 622; amended Pub. L. 108–176, title VI, §612(a), Dec. 12, 2003, 117 Stat. 2572; Pub. L. 115–254, div. K, title I, §1991(d)(30), Oct. 5, 2018, 132 Stat. 3639.)

§44940. Security service fee

(a) General Authority.—

(1) Passenger fees.—The Administrator of the Transportation Security Administration shall impose a uniform fee, on passengers of air carriers and foreign air carriers in air transportation and intrastate air transportation originating at airports in the United States, to pay for the following costs of providing civil aviation security services:

(A) Salary, benefits, overtime, retirement and other costs of screening personnel, their supervisors and managers, and Federal law enforcement personnel deployed at airport security screening locations under section 44901.

(B) The costs of training personnel described in subparagraph (A), and the acquisition, operation, and maintenance of equipment used by such personnel.

(C) The costs of performing background investigations of personnel described in subparagraphs (A), (D), (F), and (G).

(D) The costs of the Federal air marshals program.

(E) The costs of performing civil aviation security research and development under this title.

(F) The costs of Federal Security Managers under section 44903.

(G) The costs of deploying Federal law enforcement personnel pursuant to section 44903(h).

(H) The costs of security-related capital improvements at airports.

(I) The costs of training pilots and flight attendants under sections 44918 and 44921.

(2) Determination of costs.—

(A) In general.—The amount of the costs under paragraph (1) shall be determined by the Administrator of the Transportation Security Administration and shall not be subject to judicial review.

(B) DEFINITION OF FEDERAL LAW ENFORCEMENT PERSONNEL.—For purposes of paragraph (1)(A), the term "Federal law enforcement personnel" includes State and local law enforcement officers who are deputized under section 44922.

(b) SCHEDULE OF FEES.—In imposing fees under subsection (a), the Administrator of the Transportation Security Administration shall ensure that the fees are reasonably related to the Transportation Security Administration's costs of providing services rendered.

(c) LIMITATION ON FEE.—

(1) AMOUNT.—Fees imposed under subsection (a)(1) shall be $5.60 per one-way trip in air transportation or intrastate air transportation that originates at an airport in the United States, except that the fee imposed per round trip shall not exceed $11.20.

(2) DEFINITION OF ROUND TRIP.—In this subsection, the term "round trip" means a trip on an air travel itinerary that terminates or has a stopover at the origin point (or co-terminal).

(3) OFFSETTING COLLECTIONS.—Beginning on October 1, 2027, fees collected under subsection (a)(1) for any fiscal year shall be credited as offsetting collections to appropriations made for aviation security measures carried out by the Transportation Security Administration, to remain available until expended.

(d) IMPOSITION OF FEE.—

(1) IN GENERAL.—Notwithstanding section 9701 of title 31 and the procedural requirements of section 553 of title 5, the Administrator of the Transportation Security Administration shall impose the fee under subsection (a)(1) through the publication of notice of such fee in the Federal Register and begin collection of the fee as soon as possible.

(2) SPECIAL RULES PASSENGER FEES.—A fee imposed under subsection (a)(1) through the procedures under paragraph (1) of this subsection shall apply only to tickets sold after the date on which such fee is imposed. If a fee imposed under subsection (a)(1) through the procedures under paragraph (1) of this subsection on transportation of a passenger of a carrier described in subsection (a)(1) is not collected from the passenger, the amount of the fee shall be paid by the carrier.

(3) SUBSEQUENT MODIFICATION OF FEE.—After imposing a fee in accordance with paragraph (1), the Administrator of the Transportation Security Administration may modify, from time to time through publication of notice in the Federal Register, the imposition or collection of such fee, or both.

(4) LIMITATION ON COLLECTION.—No fee may be collected under this section, other than subsection (i), except to the extent that the expenditure of the fee to pay the costs of activities and services for which the fee is imposed is provided for in advance in an appropriations Act or in section 44923.

(e) ADMINISTRATION OF FEES.—

(1) FEES PAYABLE TO ADMINISTRATOR.—All fees imposed and amounts collected under this section are payable to the Administrator of the Transportation Security Administration.

(2) FEES COLLECTED BY AIR CARRIER.—A fee imposed under subsection (a)(1) shall be collected by the air carrier or foreign air carrier that sells a ticket for transportation

described in subsection (a)(1).

(3) DUE DATE FOR REMITTANCE.—A fee collected under this section shall be remitted on the last day of each calendar month by the carrier collecting the fee. The amount to be remitted shall be for the calendar month preceding the calendar month in which the remittance is made.

(4) INFORMATION.—The Administrator of the Transportation Security Administration may require the provision of such information as the Administrator of the Transportation Security Administration decides is necessary to verify that fees have been collected and remitted at the proper times and in the proper amounts.

(5) FEE NOT SUBJECT TO TAX.—For purposes of section 4261 of the Internal Revenue Code of 1986 (26 U.S.C. 4261), a fee imposed under this section shall not be considered to be part of the amount paid for taxable transportation.

(6) COST OF COLLECTING FEE.—No portion of the fee collected under this section may be retained by the air carrier or foreign air carrier for the costs of collecting, handling, or remitting the fee except for interest accruing to the carrier after collection and before remittance.

(f) RECEIPTS CREDITED AS OFFSETTING COLLECTIONS.—Notwithstanding section 3302 of title 31, any fee collected under this section—

(1) shall be credited as offsetting collections to the account that finances the activities and services for which the fee is imposed;

(2) shall be available for expenditure only to pay the costs of activities and services for which the fee is imposed; and

(3) shall remain available until expended.

(g) REFUNDS.—The Administrator of the Transportation Security Administration may refund any fee paid by mistake or any amount paid in excess of that required.

(h) EXEMPTIONS.—The Administrator of the Transportation Security Administration may exempt from the passenger fee imposed under subsection (a)(1) any passenger enplaning at an airport in the United States that does not receive screening services under section 44901 for that segment of the trip for which the passenger does not receive screening.

(i) DEPOSIT OF RECEIPTS IN GENERAL FUND.—

(1) IN GENERAL.—Beginning in fiscal year 2014, out of fees received in a fiscal year under subsection (a)(1), after amounts are made available in the fiscal year under section 44923(h), the next funds derived from such fees in the fiscal year, in the amount specified for the fiscal year in paragraph (4), shall be credited as offsetting receipts and deposited in the general fund of the Treasury.

(2) FEE LEVELS.—The Secretary of Homeland Security shall impose the fee authorized by subsection (a)(1) so as to collect in a fiscal year at least the amount specified in paragraph (4) for the fiscal year for making deposits under paragraph (1).

(3) RELATIONSHIP TO OTHER PROVISIONS.—Subsections (b) and (f) shall not apply to amounts to be used for making deposits under this subsection.

(4) FISCAL YEAR AMOUNTS.—For purposes of paragraphs (1) and (2), the fiscal year amounts are as follows:

(A) $1,320,000,000 for fiscal year 2018.
(B) $1,360,000,000 for fiscal year 2019.
(C) $1,400,000,000 for fiscal year 2020.

(D) $1,440,000,000 for fiscal year 2021.

(E) $1,480,000,000 for fiscal year 2022.

(F) $1,520,000,000 for fiscal year 2023.

(G) $760,000,000 for fiscal year 2024.

(H) $1,600,000,000 for fiscal year 2025.

(M) [1] $1,640,000,000 for fiscal year 2026.

(N) [1] $1,680,000,000 for fiscal year 2027.

(Added Pub. L. 107–71, title I, §118(a), Nov. 19, 2001, 115 Stat. 625; amended Pub. L. 108–7, div. I, title III, §351(b), Feb. 20, 2003, 117 Stat. 420; Pub. L. 108–176, title VI, §605(b)(1), (2), Dec. 12, 2003, 117 Stat. 2568; Pub. L. 110–53, title XVI, §1601, Aug. 3, 2007, 121 Stat. 477; Pub. L. 110–161, div. E, title V, §540, Dec. 26, 2007, 121 Stat. 2079; Pub. L. 113–67, div. A, title VI, §601(a)(1), (2), (b), (c), Dec. 26, 2013, 127 Stat. 1187; Pub. L. 113–294, §1(a), Dec. 19, 2014, 128 Stat. 4009; Pub. L. 114–41, title III, §3001, July 31, 2015, 129 Stat. 460; Pub. L. 115–123, div. C, title II, §30202, Feb. 9, 2018, 132 Stat. 126; Pub. L. 115–254, div. K, title I, §§1940, 1991(d)(31), Oct. 5, 2018, 132 Stat. 3582, 3639; Pub. L. 118–47, div. G, title I, §108(a), Mar. 23, 2024, 138 Stat. 857.)

[1] *So in original.*

§44941. IMMUNITY FOR REPORTING SUSPICIOUS ACTIVITIES

(a) IN GENERAL.—Any air carrier or foreign air carrier or any employee of an air carrier or foreign air carrier who makes a voluntary disclosure of any suspicious transaction relevant to a possible violation of law or regulation, relating to air piracy, a threat to aircraft or passenger safety, or terrorism, as defined by section 3077 of title 18, United States Code, to any employee or agent of the Department of Transportation, the Department of Homeland Security, the Department of Justice, any Federal, State, or local law enforcement officer, or any airport or airline security officer shall not be civilly liable to any person under any law or regulation of the United States, any constitution, law, or regulation of any State or political subdivision of any State, for such disclosure.

(b) APPLICATION.—Subsection (a) shall not apply to—

(1) any disclosure made with actual knowledge that the disclosure was false, inaccurate, or misleading; or

(2) any disclosure made with reckless disregard as to the truth or falsity of that disclosure.

(Added Pub. L. 107–71, title I, §125(a), Nov. 19, 2001, 115 Stat. 631; amended Pub. L. 115–254, div. K, title I, §1991(d)(32), Oct. 5, 2018, 132 Stat. 3640.)

§44942. PERFORMANCE GOALS AND OBJECTIVES

(a) SHORT TERM TRANSITION.—

(1) IN GENERAL.—The Administrator of the Transportation Security Administration may, in consultation with other relevant Federal agencies and Congress—

(A) establish acceptable levels of performance for aviation security, including screening operations and access control; and

(B) provide Congress with an action plan, containing measurable goals and milestones, that outlines how those levels of performance will be achieved.

(2) BASICS OF ACTION PLAN.—The action plan shall clarify the responsibilities of the Transportation Security Administration, the Federal Aviation Administration, and any

other agency or organization that may have a role in ensuring the safety and security of the civil air transportation system.

(b) Long-Term Results-Based Management.—

(1) Performance plan.—

(A) Each year, consistent with the requirements of the Government Performance and Results Act of 1993 (GPRA), the Secretary of Homeland Security and the Administrator of the Transportation Security Administration shall agree on a performance plan for the succeeding 5 years that establishes measurable goals and objectives for aviation security. The plan shall identify action steps necessary to achieve such goals.

(B) In addition to meeting the requirements of GPRA, the performance plan should clarify the responsibilities of the Secretary of Homeland Security, the Administrator of the Transportation Security Administration, and any other agency or organization that may have a role in ensuring the safety and security of the civil air transportation system.

(2) Performance report.—Each year, consistent with the requirements of GPRA, the Administrator of the Transportation Security Administration shall prepare and submit to Congress an annual report including an evaluation of the extent goals and objectives were met. The report shall include the results achieved during the year relative to the goals established in the performance plan.

(Added Pub. L. 107–71, title I, §130, Nov. 19, 2001, 115 Stat. 633; amended Pub. L. 115–254, div. K, title I, §1991(d)(33), Oct. 5, 2018, 132 Stat. 3640.)

§44943. Performance management system

(a) Establishing a Fair and Equitable System for Measuring Staff Performance.—The Administrator of the Transportation Security Administration shall establish a performance management system which strengthens the organization's effectiveness by providing for the establishment of goals and objectives for managers, employees, and organizational performance consistent with the performance plan.

(b) Establishing Management Accountability for Meeting Performance Goals.—

(1) In general.—Each year, the Secretary of Homeland Security and Administrator of the Transportation Security Administration shall enter into an annual performance agreement that shall set forth organizational and individual performance goals for the Administrator of the Transportation Security Administration.

(2) Goals.—Each year, the Administrator of the Transportation Security Administration and each senior manager who reports to the Administrator shall enter into an annual performance agreement that sets forth organization and individual goals for those managers. All other employees hired under the authority of the Administrator shall enter into an annual performance agreement that sets forth organization and individual goals for those employees.

(c) Performance-Based Service Contracting.—To the extent contracts, if any, are used to implement the Aviation and Transportation Security Act (Public Law 107–71; 115 Stat. 597), the Administrator of the Transportation Security Administration shall, to the extent practical, maximize the use of performance-based service contracts. These contracts should be consistent with guidelines published by the Office of Federal Procurement Policy.

(Added Pub. L. 107–71, title I, §130, Nov. 19, 2001, 115 Stat. 634; amended Pub. L. 115–254, div. K, title I, §1991(d)(34), Oct. 5, 2018, 132 Stat. 3640.)

§44944. Voluntary provision of emergency services

(a) Program for Provision of Voluntary Services.—

(1) Program.—The Administrator of the Transportation Security Administration shall carry out a program to permit qualified law enforcement officers, firefighters, and emergency medical technicians to provide emergency services on commercial air flights during emergencies.

(2) Requirements.—The Administrator of the Transportation Security Administration shall establish such requirements for qualifications of providers of voluntary services under the program under paragraph (1), including training requirements, as the Administrator of the Transportation Security Administration considers appropriate.

(3) Confidentiality of registry.—If as part of the program under paragraph (1) the Administrator of the Transportation Security Administration requires or permits registration of law enforcement officers, firefighters, or emergency medical technicians who are willing to provide emergency services on commercial flights during emergencies, the Administrator of the Transportation Security Administration shall take appropriate actions to ensure that the registry is available only to appropriate airline personnel and otherwise remains confidential.

(4) Consultation.—The Administrator of the Transportation Security Administration shall consult with the Administrator of the Federal Aviation Administration, appropriate representatives of the commercial airline industry, and organizations representing community-based law enforcement, firefighters, and emergency medical technicians, in carrying out the program under paragraph (1), including the actions taken under paragraph (3).

(b) Exemption From Liability.—An individual shall not be liable for damages in any action brought in a Federal or State court that arises from an act or omission of the individual in providing or attempting to provide assistance in the case of an in-flight emergency in an aircraft of an air carrier if the individual meets such qualifications as the Administrator of the Transportation Security Administration shall prescribe for purposes of this section.

(c) Exception.—The exemption under subsection (b) shall not apply in any case in which an individual provides, or attempts to provide, assistance described in that paragraph in a manner that constitutes gross negligence or willful misconduct.

(Added Pub. L. 107–71, title I, §131(a), Nov. 19, 2001, 115 Stat. 635; amended Pub. L. 115–254, div. K, title I, §1991(d)(35), Oct. 5, 2018, 132 Stat. 3641.)

§44945. Disposition of unclaimed money and clothing

(a) Disposition of Unclaimed Money.—Notwithstanding section 3302 of title 31, unclaimed money recovered at any airport security checkpoint shall be retained by the Transportation Security Administration and shall remain available until expended for the purpose of providing civil aviation security as required in this chapter.

(b) Disposition of Unclaimed Clothing.—

(1) IN GENERAL.—In disposing of unclaimed clothing recovered at any airport security checkpoint, the Administrator of the Transportation Security Administration shall make every reasonable effort, in consultation with the Secretary of Veterans Affairs, to transfer the clothing to the local airport authority or other local authorities for donation to charity, including local veterans organizations or other local charitable organizations for distribution to homeless or needy veterans and veteran families.

(2) AGREEMENTS.—In implementing paragraph (1), the Administrator of the Transportation Security Administration may enter into agreements with airport authorities.

(3) OTHER CHARITABLE ARRANGEMENTS.—Nothing in this subsection shall prevent an airport or the Transportation Security Administration from donating unclaimed clothing to a charitable organization of their choosing.

(4) LIMITATION.—Nothing in this subsection shall create a cost to the Government.

(Added Pub. L. 108–334, title V, §515(a), Oct. 18, 2004, 118 Stat. 1317; amended Pub. L. 112–271, §2(a), Jan. 14, 2013, 126 Stat. 2446; Pub. L. 115–254, div. K, title I, §1991(d)(36), Oct. 5, 2018, 132 Stat. 3641.)

§44946. AVIATION SECURITY ADVISORY COMMITTEE

(a) ESTABLISHMENT.—The Administrator shall establish within the Transportation Security Administration an aviation security advisory committee.

(b) DUTIES.—

(1) IN GENERAL.—The Administrator shall consult the Advisory Committee, as appropriate, on aviation security matters, including on the development, refinement, and implementation of policies, programs, rulemaking, and security directives pertaining to aviation security, while adhering to sensitive security guidelines.

(2) RECOMMENDATIONS.—

(A) IN GENERAL.—The Advisory Committee shall develop, at the request of the Administrator, recommendations for improvements to aviation security.

(B) RECOMMENDATIONS OF SUBCOMMITTEES.—Recommendations agreed upon by the subcommittees established under this section shall be approved by the Advisory Committee before transmission to the Administrator.

(3) PERIODIC REPORTS.—The Advisory Committee shall periodically submit to the Administrator—

(A) reports on matters identified by the Administrator; and

(B) reports on other matters identified by a majority of the members of the Advisory Committee.

(4) ANNUAL REPORT.—The Advisory Committee shall submit to the Administrator an annual report providing information on the activities, findings, and recommendations of the Advisory Committee, including its subcommittees, for the preceding year. Not later than 6 months after the date that the Administrator receives the annual report, the Administrator shall publish a public version describing the Advisory Committee's activities and such related matters as would be informative to the public consistent with the policy of section 552(b) of title 5.

(5) FEEDBACK.—Not later than 90 days after receiving recommendations transmitted by the Advisory Committee under paragraph (2) or (4), the Administrator shall respond in writing to the Advisory Committee with feedback on each of the recommendations,

an action plan to implement any of the recommendations with which the Administrator concurs, and a justification for why any of the recommendations have been rejected.

(6) CONGRESSIONAL NOTIFICATION.—Not later than 30 days after providing written feedback to the Advisory Committee under paragraph (5), the Administrator shall notify the Committee on Commerce, Science, and Transportation of the Senate and the Committee on Homeland Security of the House of Representatives on such feedback, and provide a briefing upon request.

(7) REPORT TO CONGRESS.—Prior to briefing the Committee on Commerce, Science, and Transportation of the Senate and the Committee on Homeland Security of the House of Representatives under paragraph (6), the Administrator shall submit to such committees a report containing information relating to the recommendations transmitted by the Advisory Committee in accordance with paragraph (4).

(c) MEMBERSHIP.—

(1) APPOINTMENT.—

(A) IN GENERAL.—The Administrator shall appoint the members of the Advisory Committee.

(B) COMPOSITION.—The membership of the Advisory Committee shall consist of individuals representing not more than 34 member organizations. Each organization shall be represented by 1 individual (or the individual's designee).

(C) REPRESENTATION.—The membership of the Advisory Committee shall include representatives of air carriers, all-cargo air transportation, indirect air carriers, labor organizations representing air carrier employees, labor organizations representing transportation security officers, aircraft manufacturers, airport operators, airport construction and maintenance contractors, labor organizations representing employees of airport construction and maintenance contractors, general aviation, privacy organizations, the travel industry, airport-based businesses (including minority-owned small businesses), businesses that conduct security screening operations at airports, aeronautical repair stations, passenger advocacy groups, the aviation security technology industry (including screening technology and biometrics), victims of terrorist acts against aviation, and law enforcement and security experts.

(2) TERM OF OFFICE.—

(A) TERMS.—The term of each member of the Advisory Committee shall be two years, but a member may continue to serve until a successor is appointed. A member of the Advisory Committee may be reappointed.

(B) REMOVAL.—The Administrator may review the participation of a member of the Advisory Committee and remove such member for cause at any time.

(3) PROHIBITION ON COMPENSATION.—The members of the Advisory Committee shall not receive pay, allowances, or benefits from the Government by reason of their service on the Advisory Committee.

(4) MEETINGS.—

(A) IN GENERAL.—The Administrator shall require the Advisory Committee to meet at least semiannually and may convene additional meetings as necessary.

(B) PUBLIC MEETINGS.—At least 1 of the meetings described in subparagraph (A) shall be open to the public.

(C) ATTENDANCE.—The Advisory Committee shall maintain a record of the persons present at each meeting.

(5) MEMBER ACCESS TO SENSITIVE SECURITY INFORMATION.—Not later than 60 days after the date of a member's appointment, the Administrator shall determine if there is cause for the member to be restricted from possessing sensitive security information. Without such cause, and upon the member voluntarily signing a non-disclosure agreement, the member may be granted access to sensitive security information that is relevant to the member's advisory duties. The member shall protect the sensitive security information in accordance with part 1520 of title 49, Code of Federal Regulations.

(6) CHAIRPERSON.—A stakeholder representative on the Advisory Committee who is elected by the appointed membership of the Advisory Committee shall chair the Advisory Committee.

(d) SUBCOMMITTEES.—

(1) MEMBERSHIP.—The Advisory Committee chairperson, in coordination with the Administrator, may establish within the Advisory Committee any subcommittee that the Administrator and Advisory Committee determine to be necessary. The Administrator and the Advisory Committee shall create subcommittees to address aviation security issues, including the following:

(A) AIR CARGO SECURITY.—The implementation of the air cargo security programs established by the Transportation Security Administration to screen air cargo on passenger aircraft and all-cargo aircraft in accordance with established cargo screening mandates.

(B) GENERAL AVIATION.—General aviation facilities, general aviation aircraft, and helicopter operations at general aviation and commercial service airports.

(C) PERIMETER AND ACCESS CONTROL.—Recommendations on airport perimeter security, exit lane security and technology at commercial service airports, and access control issues.

(D) SECURITY TECHNOLOGY.—Security technology standards and requirements, including their harmonization internationally, technology to screen passengers, passenger baggage, carry-on baggage, and cargo, and biometric technology.

(2) RISK-BASED SECURITY.—All subcommittees established by the Advisory Committee chairperson in coordination with the Administrator shall consider risk-based security approaches in the performance of their functions that weigh the optimum balance of costs and benefits in transportation security, including for passenger screening, baggage screening, air cargo security policies, and general aviation security matters.

(3) MEETINGS AND REPORTING.—Each subcommittee shall meet at least quarterly and submit to the Advisory Committee for inclusion in the annual report required under subsection (b)(4) information, including recommendations, regarding issues within the subcommittee.

(4) SUBCOMMITTEE CHAIRS.—Each subcommittee shall be co-chaired by a Government official and an industry official.

(e) SUBJECT MATTER EXPERTS.—Each subcommittee under this section shall include subject matter experts with relevant expertise who are appointed by the respective subcommittee chairpersons.

(f) NONAPPLICABILITY OF CHAPTER 10 OF TITLE 5.—Chapter 10 of title 5 shall not apply to the Advisory Committee and its subcommittees.

(g) DEFINITIONS.—In this section:

(1) ADMINISTRATOR.—The term "Administrator" means the Administrator of the Transportation Security Administration.

(2) ADVISORY COMMITTEE.—The term "Advisory Committee" means the aviation security advisory committee established under subsection (a).

(3) PERIMETER SECURITY.—

(A) IN GENERAL.—The term "perimeter security" means procedures or systems to monitor, secure, and prevent unauthorized access to an airport, including its airfield and terminal.

(B) INCLUSIONS.—The term "perimeter security" includes the fence area surrounding an airport, access gates, and access controls.

(Added Pub. L. 113–238, §2(a), Dec. 18, 2014, 128 Stat. 2842; amended Pub. L. 114–190, title III, §3411, July 15, 2016, 130 Stat. 662; Pub. L. 115–254, div. K, title I, §1991(d)(37), Oct. 5, 2018, 132 Stat. 3641; Pub. L. 117–286, §4(a)(317), Dec. 27, 2022, 136 Stat. 4340.)

§44947. AIR CARGO SECURITY DIVISION

(a) ESTABLISHMENT.—Not later than 90 days after the date of enactment of the TSA Modernization Act, the Administrator shall establish an air cargo security division to carry out and engage with stakeholders regarding the implementation of air cargo security programs established by the Administration.

(b) LEADERSHIP; STAFFING.—The air cargo security division established pursuant to subsection (a) shall be headed by an individual in the executive service within the TSA and be staffed by not fewer than 4 full-time equivalents, including the head of the division.

(c) STAFFING.—The Administrator of the Transportation Security Administration shall staff the air cargo security division with existing TSA personnel.

(Added Pub. L. 115–254, div. K, title I, §1943(a), Oct. 5, 2018, 132 Stat. 3584.)

§44948. NATIONAL DEPLOYMENT OFFICE

(a) ESTABLISHMENT.—There is established within the Transportation Security Administration a National Deployment Office, to be headed by an individual with supervisory experience. Such individual shall be designated by the Administrator of the Transportation Security Administration.

(b) DUTIES.—The individual designated as the head of the National Deployment Office shall be responsible for the following:

(1) Maintaining a National Deployment Force within the Transportation Security Administration, including transportation security officers, supervisory transportation security officers and lead transportation security officers, to provide the Administration with rapid and efficient response capabilities and augment the Department of Homeland Security's homeland security operations to mitigate and reduce risk, including for the following:

(A) Airports temporarily requiring additional security personnel due to an emergency, seasonal demands, hiring shortfalls, severe weather conditions, passenger volume mitigation, equipment support, or other reasons.

(B) Special events requiring enhanced security including National Special Security

Events, as determined by the Secretary of Homeland Security.

(C) Response in the aftermath of any manmade disaster, including any terrorist attack.

(D) Other such situations, as determined by the Administrator.

(2) Educating transportation security officers regarding how to participate in the Administration's National Deployment Force.

(3) Recruiting officers to serve on the National Deployment Force, in accordance with a staffing model to be developed by the Administrator.

(4) Approving 1-year appointments for officers to serve on the National Deployment Force, with an option to extend upon officer request and with the approval of the appropriate Federal Security Director.

(5) Training officers to serve on the National Deployment Force.

(Added Pub. L. 115–254, div. K, title I, §1988(a), Oct. 5, 2018, 132 Stat. 3622.)

CHAPTER 451—ALCOHOL AND CONTROLLED SUBSTANCES TESTING

§45101. DEFINITION

In this chapter, "controlled substance" means any substance under section 102 of the Comprehensive Drug Abuse Prevention and Control Act of 1970 (21 U.S.C. 802) specified by the Administrator of the Federal Aviation Administration.

(Pub. L. 103–272, §1(e), July 5, 1994, 108 Stat. 1221.)

§45102. ALCOHOL AND CONTROLLED SUBSTANCES TESTING PROGRAMS

(a) PROGRAM FOR EMPLOYEES OF AIR CARRIERS AND FOREIGN AIR CARRIERS.—(1) In the interest of aviation safety, the Administrator of the Federal Aviation Administration shall prescribe regulations that establish a program requiring air carriers and foreign air carriers to conduct preemployment, reasonable suspicion, random, and post-accident testing of airmen, crew members, airport security screening personnel, and other air carrier employees responsible for safety-sensitive functions (as decided by the Administrator) for the use of a controlled substance in violation of law or a United States Government regulation; and to conduct reasonable suspicion, random, and post-accident testing of airmen, crew members, airport security screening personnel, and other air carrier employees responsible for safety-sensitive functions (as decided by the Administrator) for the use of alcohol in violation of law or a United States Government regulation. The regulations shall permit air carriers and foreign air carriers to conduct preemployment testing of airmen, crew members, airport security screening personnel, and other air carrier employees responsible for safety-sensitive functions (as decided by the Administrator) for the use of alcohol.

(2) When the Administrator considers it appropriate in the interest of safety, the Administrator may prescribe regulations for conducting periodic recurring testing of airmen, crewmembers, airport security screening personnel, and other air carrier employees responsible for safety-sensitive functions for the use of alcohol or a controlled substance in violation of law or a Government regulation.

(b) PROGRAM FOR EMPLOYEES OF THE FEDERAL AVIATION ADMINISTRATION.—(1) The Administrator shall establish a program of preemployment, reasonable suspicion, random, and post-accident testing for the use of a controlled substance in violation of law or a United States Government regulation for employees of the Administration whose duties include responsibility for safety-sensitive functions and shall establish a program of reasonable suspicion, random, and post-accident testing for the use of alcohol in violation of law or a United States Government regulation for such employees. The Administrator may establish a program of preemployment testing for the use of alcohol for such employees.

(2) When the Administrator considers it appropriate in the interest of safety, the Administrator may prescribe regulations for conducting periodic recurring testing of employees of the Administration responsible for safety-sensitive functions for use of alcohol or a controlled substance in violation of law or a Government regulation.

(c) SANCTIONS.—In prescribing regulations under the programs required by this section, the Administrator shall require, as the Administrator considers appropriate, the suspension or revocation of any certificate issued to an individual referred to in this section, or the disqualification or dismissal of the individual, under this chapter when a test conducted and confirmed under this chapter indicates the individual has used alcohol or a controlled substance in violation of law or a Government regulation.

(Pub. L. 103–272, §1(e), July 5, 1994, 108 Stat. 1221; Pub. L. 104–59, title III, §342(d), Nov. 28, 1995, 109 Stat. 609; Pub. L. 107–71, title I, §139(1), Nov. 19, 2001, 115 Stat. 640.)

§45103. PROHIBITED SERVICE

(a) USE OF ALCOHOL OR A CONTROLLED SUBSTANCE.—An individual may not use alcohol or a controlled substance after October 28, 1991, in violation of law or a United States Government regulation and serve as an airman, crewmember, airport security screening employee, air carrier employee responsible for safety-sensitive functions (as decided by the Administrator of the Federal Aviation Administration), or employee of the Administration with responsibility for safety-sensitive functions.

(b) REHABILITATION REQUIRED TO RESUME SERVICE.—Notwithstanding subsection (a) of this section, an individual found to have used alcohol or a controlled substance after October 28, 1991, in violation of law or a Government regulation may serve as an airman, crewmember, airport security screening employee, air carrier employee responsible for safety-sensitive functions (as decided by the Administrator), or employee of the Administration with responsibility for safety-sensitive functions only if the individual completes a rehabilitation program described in section 45105 of this title.

(c) PERFORMANCE OF PRIOR DUTIES PROHIBITED.—An individual who served as an airman, crewmember, airport security screening employee, air carrier employee responsible for safety-sensitive functions (as decided by the Administrator), or employee of the Administration with responsibility for safety-sensitive functions and who was found by the Administrator to have used alcohol or a controlled substance after October 28, 1991, in violation of law or a Government regulation may not carry out the duties related to air transportation that the individual carried out before the finding of the Administrator if the individual—

(1) used the alcohol or controlled substance when on duty;

(2) began or completed a rehabilitation program described in section 45105 of this title before using the alcohol or controlled substance; or

(3) refuses to begin or complete a rehabilitation program described in section 45105 of this title after a finding by the Administrator under this section.

(Pub. L. 103–272, §1(e), July 5, 1994, 108 Stat. 1222; Pub. L. 107–71, title I, §139(2), Nov. 19, 2001, 115

Stat. 640.)

§45104. TESTING AND LABORATORY REQUIREMENTS

In carrying out section 45102 of this title, the Administrator of the Federal Aviation Administration shall develop requirements that—

(1) promote, to the maximum extent practicable, individual privacy in the collection of specimens;

(2) for laboratories and testing procedures for controlled substances, incorporate the Department of Health and Human Services scientific and technical guidelines dated April 11, 1988, and any amendments to those guidelines, including mandatory guidelines establishing—

(A) comprehensive standards for every aspect of laboratory controlled substances testing and laboratory procedures to be applied in carrying out this chapter, including standards requiring the use of the best available technology to ensure the complete reliability and accuracy of controlled substances tests and strict procedures governing the chain of custody of specimens collected for controlled substances testing;

(B) the minimum list of controlled substances for which individuals may be tested; and

(C) appropriate standards and procedures for periodic review of laboratories and criteria for certification and revocation of certification of laboratories to perform controlled substances testing in carrying out this chapter;

(3) require that a laboratory involved in controlled substances testing under this chapter have the capability and facility, at the laboratory, of performing screening and confirmation tests;

(4) provide that all tests indicating the use of alcohol or a controlled substance in violation of law or a United States Government regulation be confirmed by a scientifically recognized method of testing capable of providing quantitative information about alcohol or a controlled substance;

(5) provide that each specimen be subdivided, secured, and labeled in the presence of the tested individual and that a part of the specimen be retained in a secure manner to prevent the possibility of tampering, so that if the individual's confirmation test results are positive the individual has an opportunity to have the retained part tested by a 2d confirmation test done independently at another certified laboratory if the individual requests the 2d confirmation test not later than 3 days after being advised of the results of the first confirmation test;

(6) ensure appropriate safeguards for testing to detect and quantify alcohol in breath and body fluid samples, including urine and blood, through the development of regulations that may be necessary and in consultation with the Secretary of Health and Human Services;

(7) provide for the confidentiality of test results and medical information (except information about alcohol or a controlled substance) of employees, except that this clause does not prevent the use of test results for the orderly imposition of appropriate sanctions under this chapter; and

(8) ensure that employees are selected for tests by nondiscriminatory and impartial methods, so that no employee is harassed by being treated differently from other

employees in similar circumstances.

(Pub. L. 103–272, §1(e), July 5, 1994, 108 Stat. 1222.)

§45105. REHABILITATION

(a) PROGRAM FOR EMPLOYEES OF AIR CARRIERS AND FOREIGN AIR CARRIERS.—The Administrator of the Federal Aviation Administration shall prescribe regulations establishing requirements for rehabilitation programs that at least provide for the identification and opportunity for treatment of employees of air carriers and foreign air carriers referred to in section 45102(a)(1) of this title who need assistance in resolving problems with the use of alcohol or a controlled substance in violation of law or a United States Government regulation. Each air carrier and foreign air carrier is encouraged to make such a program available to all its employees in addition to the employees referred to in section 45102(a)(1). The Administrator shall decide on the circumstances under which employees shall be required to participate in a program. This subsection does not prevent an air carrier or foreign air carrier from establishing a program under this subsection in cooperation with another air carrier or foreign air carrier.

(b) PROGRAM FOR EMPLOYEES OF THE FEDERAL AVIATION ADMINISTRATION.—The Administrator shall establish and maintain a rehabilitation program that at least provides for the identification and opportunity for treatment of employees of the Administration whose duties include responsibility for safety-sensitive functions who need assistance in resolving problems with the use of alcohol or a controlled substance.

(Pub. L. 103–272, §1(e), July 5, 1994, 108 Stat. 1223; Pub. L. 103–429, §6(58), Oct. 31, 1994, 108 Stat. 4385.)

§45106. RELATIONSHIP TO OTHER LAWS, REGULATIONS, STANDARDS, AND ORDERS

(a) EFFECT ON STATE AND LOCAL GOVERNMENT LAWS, REGULATIONS, STANDARDS, OR ORDERS.—A State or local government may not prescribe, issue, or continue in effect a law, regulation, standard, or order that is inconsistent with regulations prescribed under this chapter. However, a regulation prescribed under this chapter does not preempt a State criminal law that imposes sanctions for reckless conduct leading to loss of life, injury, or damage to property.

(b) INTERNATIONAL OBLIGATIONS AND FOREIGN LAWS.—(1) In prescribing regulations under this chapter, the Administrator of the Federal Aviation Administration—

(A) shall establish only requirements applicable to foreign air carriers that are consistent with international obligations of the United States; and

(B) shall consider applicable laws and regulations of foreign countries.

(2) The Secretaries of State and Transportation jointly shall request the governments of foreign countries that are members of the International Civil Aviation Organization to strengthen and enforce existing standards to prohibit crewmembers in international civil aviation from using alcohol or a controlled substance in violation of law or a United States Government regulation.

(c) OTHER REGULATIONS ALLOWED.—This section does not prevent the Administrator from continuing in effect, amending, or further supplementing a regulation prescribed before October 28, 1991, governing the use of alcohol or a controlled substance by airmen, crewmembers, airport security screening employees, air carrier employees responsible for safety-sensitive functions (as decided by the Administrator), or employees of the Administration with responsibility for safety-sensitive functions.

(Pub. L. 103–272, §1(e), July 5, 1994, 108 Stat. 1224; Pub. L. 107–71, title I, §139(3), Nov. 19, 2001, 115 Stat. 640.)

§45107. Transportation Security Administration

(a) Transfer of Functions Relating to Testing Programs With Respect to Airport Security Screening Personnel.—The authority of the Administrator of the Federal Aviation Administration under this chapter with respect to programs relating to testing of airport security screening personnel are transferred to the Administrator of the Transportation Security Administration. Notwithstanding section 45102(a), the regulations prescribed under section 45102(a) shall require testing of such personnel by their employers instead of by air carriers and foreign air carriers.

(b) Applicability of Chapter With Respect to Employees of Administration.—The provisions of this chapter that apply with respect to employees of the Federal Aviation Administration whose duties include responsibility for safety-sensitive functions shall apply with respect to employees of the Transportation Security Administration whose duties include responsibility for security-sensitive functions.

(Added Pub. L. 107–71, title I, §139(4), Nov. 19, 2001, 115 Stat. 640; amended Pub. L. 115–254, div. K, title I, §1991(e), Oct. 5, 2018, 132 Stat. 3642.)

CHAPTER 453—FEES

§45301. GENERAL PROVISIONS

(a) SCHEDULE OF FEES.—The Administrator of the Federal Aviation Administration shall establish a schedule of new fees, and a collection process for such fees, for the following services provided by the Administration:

(1) Air traffic control and related services provided to aircraft other than military and civilian aircraft of the United States Government or of a foreign government that neither take off from, nor land in, the United States.

(2) Services (other than air traffic control services) provided to a foreign government or services provided to any entity obtaining services outside the United States, except that the Administrator shall not impose fees in any manner for production-certification related service performed outside the United States pertaining to aeronautical products manufactured outside the United States.

(b) ESTABLISHMENT AND ADJUSTMENT OF FEES.—

(1) IN GENERAL.—In establishing and adjusting fees under this section, the Administrator shall ensure that the fees are reasonably related to the Administration's costs, as determined by the Administrator, of providing the services rendered.

(2) SERVICES FOR WHICH COSTS MAY BE RECOVERED.—Services for which costs may be recovered under this section include the costs of air traffic control, navigation, weather services, training, and emergency services that are available to facilitate safe transportation over the United States and the costs of other services provided by the Administrator, or by programs financed by the Administrator, to flights that neither take off nor land in the United States.

(3) LIMITATIONS ON JUDICIAL REVIEW.—Notwithstanding section 702 of title 5 or any other provision of law, the following actions and other matters shall not be subject to judicial review:

(A) The establishment or adjustment of a fee by the Administrator under this section.

(B) The validity of a determination of costs by the Administrator under paragraph (1), and the processes and procedures applied by the Administrator when reaching such determination.

(C) An allocation of costs by the Administrator under paragraph (1) to services provided, and the processes and procedures applied by the Administrator when establishing such allocation.

(4) AIRCRAFT ALTITUDE.—Nothing in this section shall require the Administrator to

take into account aircraft altitude in establishing any fee for aircraft operations in en route or oceanic airspace.

(5) COSTS DEFINED.—In this subsection, the term "costs" includes operation and maintenance costs, leasing costs, and overhead expenses associated with the services provided and the facilities and equipment used in providing such services.

(c) USE OF EXPERTS AND CONSULTANTS.—In developing the system, the Administrator may consult with such nongovernmental experts as the Administrator may employ and the Administrator may utilize the services of experts and consultants under section 3109 of title 5 without regard to the limitation imposed by the last sentence of section 3109(b) of such title, and may contract on a sole source basis, notwithstanding any other provision of law to the contrary. Notwithstanding any other provision of law to the contrary, the Administrator may retain such experts under a contract awarded on a basis other than a competitive basis and without regard to any such provisions requiring competitive bidding or precluding sole source contract authority.

(d) PRODUCTION-CERTIFICATION RELATED SERVICE DEFINED.—In this section, the term "production-certification related service" has the meaning given that term in appendix C of part 187 of title 14, Code of Federal Regulations.

(e) ADJUSTMENT OF FEES.—In addition to adjustments under subsection (b), the Administrator may periodically adjust the fees established under this section.

(Added Pub. L. 104–264, title II, §273(a), Oct. 9, 1996, 110 Stat. 3239; amended Pub. L. 106–181, title VII, §719, Apr. 5, 2000, 114 Stat. 163; Pub. L. 107–71, title I, §119(d), Nov. 19, 2001, 115 Stat. 629; Pub. L. 112–95, title I, §121, Feb. 14, 2012, 126 Stat. 19; Pub. L. 115–254, div. B, title V, §539(k), Oct. 5, 2018, 132 Stat. 3371; Pub. L. 118–63, title XI, §1101(r), May 16, 2024, 138 Stat. 1414.)

§45302. FEES INVOLVING AIRCRAFT NOT PROVIDING AIR TRANSPORTATION

(a) APPLICATION.—This section applies only to aircraft not used to provide air transportation.

(b) GENERAL AUTHORITY AND MAXIMUM FEES.—The Administrator of the Federal Aviation Administration may impose fees to pay for the costs of issuing airman certificates to pilots and certificates of registration of aircraft and processing forms for major repairs and alterations of fuel tanks and fuel systems of aircraft. The following fees may not be more than the amounts specified:

(1) $12 for issuing an airman's certificate to a pilot.

(2) $25 for registering an aircraft after the transfer of ownership.

(3) $15 for renewing an aircraft registration.

(4) $7.50 for processing a form for a major repair or alteration of a fuel tank or fuel system of an aircraft.

(c) ADJUSTMENTS.—The Administrator shall adjust the maximum fees established by subsection (b) of this section for changes in the Consumer Price Index of All Urban Consumers published by the Secretary of Labor.

(d) CREDIT TO ACCOUNT AND AVAILABILITY.—Money collected from fees imposed under this section shall be credited to the account in the Treasury from which the Administrator incurs expenses in carrying out chapter 441 and sections 44701–44716 of this title (except sections 44701(c), 44703(g)(2), and 44713(d)(2)). The money is available to the Administrator to pay expenses for which the fees are collected.

(e) EFFECTIVE DATE.—

(1) IN GENERAL.—A fee may not be imposed under this section before the date on which the regulations prescribed under sections 44111(d), 44703(g)(2), and 44713(d)(2) of this title take effect.

(2) EFFECT OF IMPOSITION OF OTHER FEES.—A fee may not be imposed for a service or activity under this section during any period in which a fee for the same service or activity is imposed under section 45305.

(Pub. L. 103–272, §1(e), July 5, 1994, 108 Stat. 1225; Pub. L. 103–429, §6(59), Oct. 31, 1994, 108 Stat. 4385; Pub. L. 112–95, title I, §122(c), Feb. 14, 2012, 126 Stat. 20; Pub. L. 115–254, div. B, title V, §539(j), Oct. 5, 2018, 132 Stat. 3371.)

§45303. ADMINISTRATIVE PROVISIONS

(a) FEES PAYABLE TO ADMINISTRATOR.—All fees imposed and amounts collected under this chapter for services performed, or materials furnished, by the Federal Aviation Administration are payable to the Administrator of the Federal Aviation Administration.

(b) REFUNDS.—The Administrator may refund any fee paid by mistake or any amount paid in excess of that required.

(c) RECEIPTS CREDITED TO ACCOUNT.—Notwithstanding section 3302 of title 31, all fees and amounts collected by the Administration, except insurance premiums and other fees charged for the provision of insurance and deposited in the Aviation Insurance Revolving Fund and interest earned on investments of such Fund, and except amounts which on September 30, 1996, are required to be credited to the general fund of the Treasury (whether imposed under this section or not)—

(1) shall be credited to a separate account established in the Treasury and made available for Administration activities;

(2) shall be available immediately for expenditure but only for congressionally authorized and intended purposes; and

(3) shall remain available until expended.

(d) ANNUAL BUDGET REPORT BY ADMINISTRATOR.—The Administrator shall, on the same day each year as the President submits the annual budget to Congress, provide to the Committee on Commerce, Science, and Transportation of the Senate and the Committee on Transportation and Infrastructure of the House of Representatives—

(1) a list of fee collections by the Administration during the preceding fiscal year;

(2) a list of activities by the Administration during the preceding fiscal year that were supported by fee expenditures and appropriations;

(3) budget plans for significant programs, projects, and activities of the Administration, including out-year funding estimates;

(4) any proposed disposition of surplus fees by the Administration; and

(5) such other information as those committees consider necessary.

(e) DEVELOPMENT OF COST ACCOUNTING SYSTEM.—The Administration shall develop a cost accounting system that adequately and accurately reflects the investments, operating and overhead costs, revenues, and other financial measurement and reporting aspects of its operations.

(f) COMPENSATION TO CARRIERS FOR ACTING AS COLLECTION AGENTS.—The Administration shall prescribe regulations to ensure that any air carrier required, pursuant to the Air Traffic Management System Performance Improvement Act of 1996 or any amendments made by that Act, to collect a fee imposed on another party by the Administrator may collect from such other party an additional uniform amount that the Administrator determines reflects the necessary and reasonable expenses (net of interest accruing to the carrier after collection and before remittance) incurred in collecting and handling the fee.

(g) DATA TRANSPARENCY.—

(1) AIR TRAFFIC SERVICES INITIAL DATA REPORT.—

(A) INITIAL REPORT.—Not later than 6 months after the date of enactment of the FAA Reauthorization Act of 2018, the Administrator and the Chief Operating Officer of the Air Traffic Organization shall, based upon the most recently available full fiscal year data, complete the following calculations for each segment of air traffic services users:

(i) The total costs allocable to the use of air traffic services for that segment during such fiscal year.

(ii) The total revenues received from that segment during such fiscal year.

(B) VALIDATION OF MODEL.—

(i) REVIEW AND DETERMINATION.—Not later than 3 months after completion of the initial report required under subparagraph (A), the inspector general of the Department of Transportation shall review and determine the validity of the model used by the Administrator and the Chief Operating Officer to complete the calculations required under subparagraph (A).

(ii) VALIDATION PROCESS.—In the event that the inspector general determines that the model used by the Administrator and the Chief Operating Officer to complete the calculations required by subparagraph (A) is not valid—

(I) the inspector general shall provide the Administrator and Chief Operating Officer recommendations on how to revise the model;

(II) the Administrator and the Chief Operating Officer shall complete the calculations required by subparagraph (A) utilizing the revised model and resubmit the revised initial report required under subparagraph (A) to the inspector general; and

(III) not later than 3 months after completion of the revised initial report required under subparagraph (A), the inspector general shall review and determine the validity of the revised model used by the Administrator and the Chief Operating Officer to complete the calculations required by subparagraph (A).

(iii) ACCESS TO DATA.—The Administrator and the Chief Operating Officer shall provide the inspector general of the Department of Transportation with unfettered access to all data produced by the cost accounting system operated and maintained pursuant to subsection (e).

(C) REPORT TO CONGRESS.—Not later than 60 days after completion of the review and receiving a determination that the model used is valid under subparagraph (B), the Administrator and the Chief Operating Officer shall submit to the Committee on Transportation and Infrastructure, the Committee on Appropriations, and the Committee on Ways and Means of the House of Representatives, and the Committee on Commerce, Science, and Transportation, the Committee on Appropriations, and the Committee on Finance of the Senate a report describing the results of the calculations completed under subparagraph (A).

(D) PUBLICATION.—Not later than 60 days after submission of the report required under subparagraph (C), the Administrator and Chief Operating Officer shall publish the initial report, including any revision thereto if required as a result of the validation process for the model.

(2) AIR TRAFFIC SERVICES BIENNIAL DATA REPORTING.—

(A) BIENNIAL DATA REPORTING.—Not later than March 31, 2019, and biennially thereafter for 14 years, the Administrator and the Chief Operating Officer shall, using the validated model, complete the following calculations for each segment of air traffic services users for the most recent full fiscal year:

(i) The total costs allocable to the use of the air traffic services for that segment.

(ii) The total revenues received from that segment.

(B) REPORT TO CONGRESS.—Not later than 15 days after completing the calculations under subparagraph (A), the Administrator and the Chief Operating Officer shall complete and submit to the Committee on Transportation and Infrastructure, the Committee on Appropriations, and the Committee on Ways and Means of the House of Representatives, and the Committee on Commerce, Science, and Transportation, the Committee on Appropriations, and the Committee on Finance of the Senate a report containing the results of such calculations.

(C) PUBLICATION.—Not later than 60 days after completing the calculations pursuant to subparagraph (A), the Administrator and the Chief Operating Officer shall publish the results of such calculations.

(3) SEGMENTS OF AIR TRAFFIC SERVICES USERS.—

(A) IN GENERAL.—For purposes of this subsection, each of the following shall constitute a separate segment of air traffic services users:

(i) Passenger air carriers conducting operations under part 121 of title 14, Code of Federal Regulations.

(ii) All-cargo air carriers conducting operations under part 121 of such title.

(iii) Operators covered by part 125 of such title.

(iv) Air carriers and operators of piston-engine aircraft operating under part 135 of such title.

(v) Air carriers and operators of turbine-engine aircraft operating under part 135 of such title.

(vi) Foreign air carriers providing passenger air transportation.

(vii) Foreign air carriers providing all-cargo air transportation.

(viii) Operators of turbine-engine aircraft operating under part 91 of such title, excluding those operating under subpart (K) of such part.

(ix) Operators of piston-engine aircraft operating under part 91 of such title, excluding those operating under subpart (K) of such part.

(x) Operators covered by subpart (K) of part 91 of such title.

(xi) Operators covered by part 133 of such title.

(xii) Operators covered by part 136 of such title.

(xiii) Operators covered by part 137 of such title.

(xiv) Operators of public aircraft that qualify under section 40125.

(xv) Operators of aircraft that neither take off from, nor land in, the United States.

(B) ADDITIONAL SEGMENTS.—The Secretary may identify and include additional segments of air traffic users under subparagraph (A) as revenue and air traffic services cost data become available for that additional segment of air traffic services users.

(4) DEFINITIONS.—For purposes of this subsection:

(A) AIR TRAFFIC SERVICES.—The term "air traffic services" means services—

(i) used for the monitoring, directing, control, and guidance of aircraft or flows of aircraft and for the safe conduct of flight, including communications, navigation, and surveillance services and provision of aeronautical information; and

(ii) provided directly, or contracted for, by the Federal Aviation Administration.

(B) AIR TRAFFIC SERVICES USER.—The term "air traffic services user" means any individual or entity using air traffic services provided directly, or contracted for, by the Federal Aviation Administration within United States airspace or international airspace delegated to the United States.

(Added Pub. L. 104–264, title II, §276(a)(2), Oct. 9, 1996, 110 Stat. 3247; amended Pub. L. 115–254, div. B, title V, §519, Oct. 5, 2018, 132 Stat. 3359; Pub. L. 118–63, title VI, §607, May 16, 2024, 138 Stat. 1225.)

§45304. MAXIMUM FEES FOR PRIVATE PERSON SERVICES

The Administrator of the Federal Aviation Administration may establish maximum fees that private persons may charge for services performed under a delegation to the person under section 44702(d) of this title.

(Pub. L. 103–272, §1(e), July 5, 1994, 108 Stat. 1225, §45303; renumbered §45304, Pub. L. 104–264, title II, §276(a)(1), Oct. 9, 1996, 110 Stat. 3247.)

§45305. REGISTRATION, CERTIFICATION, AND RELATED FEES

(a) GENERAL AUTHORITY AND FEES.—Subject to subsection (c), the Administrator of the Federal Aviation Administration shall establish and collect a fee for each of the following services and activities of the Administration that does not exceed the estimated costs of the service or activity:

(1) Registering an aircraft.

(2) Reregistering, replacing, or renewing an aircraft registration certificate.

(3) Issuing an original dealer's aircraft registration certificate.

(4) Issuing an additional dealer's aircraft registration certificate (other than the original).

(5) Issuing a special registration number.

(6) Issuing a renewal of a special registration number reservation.

(7) Recording a security interest in an aircraft or aircraft part.

(8) Issuing an airman certificate.

(9) Issuing a replacement airman certificate.

(10) Issuing an airman medical certificate.

(11) Providing a legal opinion pertaining to aircraft registration or recordation.

(b) CERTIFICATION SERVICES.—Subject to subsection (c), and notwithstanding section 45301(a), the Administrator may establish and collect a fee from a foreign government or entity for services related to certification, regardless of where the services are provided, if

the fee—
(1) is established and collected in a manner consistent with aviation safety agreements; and

(2) does not exceed the estimated costs of the services.

(c) LIMITATION ON COLLECTION.—No fee may be collected under this section unless the expenditure of the fee to pay the costs of activities and services for which the fee is imposed is provided for in advance in an appropriations Act.

(d) FEES CREDITED AS OFFSETTING COLLECTIONS.—

(1) IN GENERAL.—Notwithstanding section 3302 of title 31, any fee authorized to be collected under this section shall—

(A) be credited as offsetting collections to the account that finances the activities and services for which the fee is imposed;

(B) be available for expenditure only to pay the costs of activities and services for which the fee is imposed, including all costs associated with collecting the fee; and

(C) remain available until expended.

(2) CONTINUING APPROPRIATIONS.—The Administrator may continue to assess, collect, and spend fees established under this section during any period in which the funding for the Federal Aviation Administration is provided under an Act providing continuing appropriations in lieu of the Administration's regular appropriations.

(3) ADJUSTMENTS.—The Administrator shall adjust a fee established under subsection (a) for a service or activity if the Administrator determines that the actual cost of the service or activity is higher or lower than was indicated by the cost data used to establish such fee.

(Added Pub. L. 112–95, title I, §122(a), Feb. 14, 2012, 126 Stat. 19; amended Pub. L. 115–254, div. B, title II, §244, Oct. 5, 2018, 132 Stat. 3260.)

§45306. MANUAL SURCHARGE

(a) IN GENERAL.—Not later 3 years after the date of enactment of the FAA Reauthorization Act of 2018, the Administrator shall impose and collect a surcharge on a Civil Aviation Registry transaction that—

(1) is conducted in person at the Civil Aviation Registry;

(2) could be conducted, as determined by the Administrator, with the same or greater level of efficiency by electronic or other remote means; and

(3) is not related to research or other non-commercial activities.

(b) MAXIMUM SURCHARGE.—A surcharge imposed and collected under subsection (a) shall not exceed twice the maximum fee the Administrator is authorized to charge for the registration of an aircraft, not used to provide air transportation, after the transfer of ownership under section 45302(b)(2).

(c) CREDIT TO ACCOUNT AND AVAILABILITY.—Monies collected from a surcharge imposed under subsection (a) shall be treated as monies collected under section 45302 and subject to the terms and conditions set forth in section 45302(d).

(Added Pub. L. 115–254, div. B, title V, §546(d), Oct. 5, 2018, 132 Stat. 3376.)

§46101. COMPLAINTS AND INVESTIGATIONS

(a) GENERAL.—(1) A person may file a complaint in writing with the Secretary of Transportation (or the Administrator of the Transportation Security Administration with respect to security duties and powers designated to be carried out by the Administrator of the Transportation Security Administration or the Administrator of the Federal Aviation Administration with respect to aviation safety duties and powers designated to be carried out by the Administrator of the Federal Aviation Administration) about a person violating this part or a requirement prescribed under this part. Except as provided in subsection (b) of this section, the Secretary, Administrator of the Transportation Security Administration, or Administrator of the Federal Aviation Administration shall investigate the complaint if a reasonable ground appears to the Secretary, Administrator of the Transportation Security Administration, or Administrator of the Federal Aviation Administration for the investigation.

(2) On the initiative of the Secretary, Administrator of the Transportation Security Administration, or Administrator of the Federal Aviation Administration, as appropriate, the Secretary, Administrator of the Transportation Security Administration, or Administrator of the Federal Aviation Administration may conduct an investigation, if a reasonable ground appears to the Secretary, Administrator of the Transportation Security Administration, or Administrator of the Federal Aviation Administration for the investigation, about—

(A) a person violating this part or a requirement prescribed under this part; or

(B) any question that may arise under this part.

(3) The Secretary of Transportation, Administrator of the Transportation Security Administration, or Administrator of the Federal Aviation Administration may dismiss a complaint without a hearing when the Secretary, Administrator of the Transportation Security Administration, or Administrator of the Federal Aviation Administration is of the opinion that the complaint does not state facts that warrant an investigation or action.

(4) After notice and an opportunity for a hearing and subject to section 40105(b) of this title, the Secretary of Transportation, Administrator of the Transportation Security Administration, or Administrator of the Federal Aviation Administration shall issue an order to compel compliance with this part if the Secretary, Administrator of the Transportation Security Administration, or Administrator of the Federal Aviation Administration finds in an investigation under this subsection that a person is violating this part.

(b) COMPLAINTS AGAINST MEMBERS OF ARMED FORCES.—The Secretary of Transportation, Administrator of the Transportation Security Administration, or Administrator of the Federal Aviation Administration shall refer a complaint against a member of the armed forces of the United States performing official duties to the Secretary of the department concerned for action. Not later than 90 days after receiving the complaint, the Secretary of that department shall inform the Secretary of Transportation, Administrator of the Transportation Security Administration, or Administrator of the Federal Aviation Administration of the action taken on the complaint, including any corrective or disciplinary action taken.

(c) PROHIBITION ON USING ADS–B OUT DATA TO INITIATE AN INVESTIGATION.—

(1) IN GENERAL.—Notwithstanding any other provision of this section, the Administrator of the Federal Aviation Administration may not initiate an investigation (excluding a criminal investigation) of a person based exclusively on automatic dependent surveillance–broadcast data.

(2) RULE OF CONSTRUCTION.—Nothing in this subsection shall prohibit the use of automatic dependent surveillance–broadcast data in an investigation that was initiated for any reason other than the review of automatic dependent surveillance–broadcast data, including if such investigation was initiated as a result of a report or complaint submitted to the Administrator.

(Pub. L. 103–272, §1(e), July 5, 1994, 108 Stat. 1226; Pub. L. 107–71, title I, §140(b)(1)–(3), Nov. 19, 2001, 115 Stat. 641; Pub. L. 115–254, div. K, title I, §1991(f)(1)–(4), Oct. 5, 2018, 132 Stat. 3642; Pub. L. 118–63, title VIII, §829, May 16, 2024, 138 Stat. 1336.)

§46102. PROCEEDINGS

(a) CONDUCTING PROCEEDINGS.—Subject to subchapter II of chapter 5 of title 5, the Secretary of Transportation (or the Administrator of the Transportation Security Administration with respect to security duties and powers designated to be carried out by the Administrator of the Transportation Security Administration or the Administrator of the Federal Aviation Administration with respect to aviation safety duties and powers designated to be carried out by the Administrator of the Federal Aviation Administration) may conduct proceedings in a way conducive to justice and the proper dispatch of business.

(b) APPEARANCE.—A person may appear and be heard before the Secretary, the Administrator of the Transportation Security Administration, and the Administrator of the Federal Aviation Administration in person or by an attorney. The Secretary may appear and participate as an interested party in a proceeding the Administrator of the Federal Aviation Administration conducts under section 40113(a) of this title.

(c) RECORDING AND PUBLIC ACCESS.—Official action taken by the Secretary, Administrator of the Transportation Security Administration, and Administrator of the

Federal Aviation Administration under this part shall be recorded. Proceedings before the Secretary, Administrator of the Transportation Security Administration, and Administrator of the Federal Aviation Administration shall be open to the public on the request of an interested party unless the Secretary, Administrator of the Transportation Security Administration, or Administrator of the Federal Aviation Administration decides that secrecy is required because of national defense.

(d) CONFLICTS OF INTEREST.—The Secretary, the Administrator of the Transportation Security Administration, the Administrator of the Federal Aviation Administration, or an officer or employee of the Federal Aviation Administration may not participate in a proceeding referred to in subsection (a) of this section in which the individual has a pecuniary interest.

(Pub. L. 103–272, §1(e), July 5, 1994, 108 Stat. 1226; Pub. L. 107–71, title I, §140(b)(1), (2), (4)–(6), Nov. 19, 2001, 115 Stat. 641; Pub. L. 115–254, div. K, title I, §1991(f)(1)–(5), Oct. 5, 2018, 132 Stat. 3642.)

§46103. SERVICE OF NOTICE, PROCESS, AND ACTIONS

(a) DESIGNATING AGENTS.—(1) Each air carrier and foreign air carrier shall designate an agent on whom service of notice and process in a proceeding before, and an action of, the Secretary of Transportation (or the Administrator of the Transportation Security Administration with respect to security duties and powers designated to be carried out by the Administrator of the Transportation Security Administration or the Administrator of the Federal Aviation Administration with respect to aviation safety duties and powers designated to be carried out by the Administrator of the Federal Aviation Administration) may be made.

(2) The designation—

(A) shall be in writing and filed with the Secretary, Administrator of the Transportation Security Administration, or Administrator of the Federal Aviation Administration; and

(B) may be changed in the same way as originally made.

(b) SERVICE.—(1) Service may be made—

(A) by personal service;

(B) on a designated agent;

(C) by certified or registered mail to the person to be served or the designated agent of the person;

(D) by electronic or facsimile transmission to the person to be served or the designated agent of the person; or

(E) as designated by regulation or guidance published in the Federal Register.

(2) The date of service made by certified or registered mail is the date of mailing.

(3) The date of service made by an electronic or facsimile method is—

(A) the date an electronic or facsimile transmission is sent; or

(B) the date a notification is sent by an electronic or facsimile method that a notice, process, or action is immediately available and accessible in an electronic database.

(c) SERVING AGENTS.—Service on an agent designated under this section shall be made at the office or usual place of residence of the agent or at the electronic or facsimile address designated by the agent. If an air carrier or foreign air carrier does not have a designated agent, service may be made by posting the notice, process, or action in the office of the

Secretary, Administrator of the Transportation Security Administration, or Administrator of the Federal Aviation Administration.

(Pub. L. 103–272, §1(e), July 5, 1994, 108 Stat. 1227; Pub. L. 107–71, title I, §140(b)(1), (2), Nov. 19, 2001, 115 Stat. 641; Pub. L. 115–254, div. K, title I, §1991(f)(1)–(4), Oct. 5, 2018, 132 Stat. 3642; Pub. L. 118–63, title II, §219, May 16, 2024, 138 Stat. 1057.)

§46104. EVIDENCE

(a) GENERAL.—In conducting a hearing or investigation under this part, the Secretary of Transportation (or the Administrator of the Transportation Security Administration with respect to security duties and powers designated to be carried out by the Administrator of the Transportation Security Administration or the Administrator of the Federal Aviation Administration with respect to aviation safety duties and powers designated to be carried out by the Administrator of the Federal Aviation Administration) may—

(1) subpoena witnesses and records related to a matter involved in the hearing or investigation from any place in the United States to the designated place of the hearing or investigation;

(2) administer oaths;

(3) examine witnesses; and

(4) receive evidence at a place in the United States the Secretary, Administrator of the Transportation Security Administration, or Administrator of the Federal Aviation Administration designates.

(b) COMPLIANCE WITH SUBPOENAS.—If a person disobeys a subpoena, the Secretary, the Administrator of the Transportation Security Administration, the Administrator of the Federal Aviation Administration, or a party to a proceeding before the Secretary, Administrator of the Transportation Security Administration, or Administrator of the Federal Aviation Administration may petition a court of the United States to enforce the subpoena. A judicial proceeding to enforce a subpoena under this section may be brought in the jurisdiction in which the proceeding or investigation is conducted. The court may punish a failure to obey an order of the court to comply with the subpoena as a contempt of court.

(c) DEPOSITIONS.—(1) In a proceeding or investigation, the Secretary, Administrator of the Transportation Security Administration, or Administrator of the Federal Aviation Administration may order a person to give testimony by deposition and to produce records. If a person fails to be deposed or to produce records, the order may be enforced in the same way a subpoena may be enforced under subsection (b) of this section.

(2) A deposition may be taken before an individual designated by the Secretary, Administrator of the Transportation Security Administration, or Administrator of the Federal Aviation Administration and having the power to administer oaths.

(3) Before taking a deposition, the party or the attorney of the party proposing to take the deposition must give reasonable notice in writing to the opposing party or the attorney of record of that party. The notice shall state the name of the witness and the time and place of taking the deposition.

(4) The testimony of a person deposed under this subsection shall be under oath. The person taking the deposition shall prepare, or cause to be prepared, a transcript of the testimony taken. The transcript shall be subscribed by the deponent. Each deposition

shall be filed promptly with the Secretary, Administrator of the Transportation Security Administration, or Administrator of the Federal Aviation Administration.

(5) If the laws of a foreign country allow, the testimony of a witness in that country may be taken by deposition—

(A) by a consular officer or an individual commissioned by the Secretary, Administrator of the Transportation Security Administration, or Administrator of the Federal Aviation Administration or agreed on by the parties by written stipulation filed with the Secretary, Administrator of the Transportation Security Administration, or Administrator of the Federal Aviation Administration; or

(B) under letters rogatory issued by a court of competent jurisdiction at the request of the Secretary, Administrator of the Transportation Security Administration, or Administrator of the Federal Aviation Administration.

(d) WITNESS FEES AND MILEAGE AND CERTAIN FOREIGN COUNTRY EXPENSES.—A witness summoned before the Secretary, Administrator of the Transportation Security Administration, or Administrator of the Federal Aviation Administration or whose deposition is taken under this section and the individual taking the deposition are each entitled to the same fee and mileage that the witness and individual would have been paid for those services in a court of the United States. Under regulations of the Secretary, Administrator of the Transportation Security Administration, or Administrator of the Federal Aviation Administration, the Secretary, Administrator of the Transportation Security Administration, or Administrator of the Federal Aviation Administration shall pay the necessary expenses incident to executing, in another country, a commission or letter rogatory issued at the initiative of the Secretary, Administrator of the Transportation Security Administration, or Administrator of the Federal Aviation Administration.

(e) DESIGNATING EMPLOYEES TO CONDUCT HEARINGS.—When designated by the Secretary, Administrator of the Transportation Security Administration, or Administrator of the Federal Aviation Administration, an employee appointed under section 3105 of title 5 may conduct a hearing, subpoena witnesses, administer oaths, examine witnesses, and receive evidence at a place in the United States the Secretary, Administrator of the Transportation Security Administration, or Administrator of the Federal Aviation Administration designates. On request of a party, the Secretary, Administrator of the Transportation Security Administration, or Administrator of the Federal Aviation Administration shall hear or receive argument.

(Pub. L. 103–272, §1(e), July 5, 1994, 108 Stat. 1227; Pub. L. 107–71, title I, §140(b)(1), (2), (6), Nov. 19, 2001, 115 Stat. 641; Pub. L. 115–254, div. K, title I, §1991(f)(1)–(4), (6), Oct. 5, 2018, 132 Stat. 3642.)

§46105. REGULATIONS AND ORDERS

(a) EFFECTIVENESS OF ORDERS.—Except as provided in this part, a regulation prescribed or order issued by the Secretary of Transportation (or the Administrator of the Transportation Security Administration with respect to security duties and powers designated to be carried out by the Administrator of the Transportation Security Administration or the Administrator of the Federal Aviation Administration with respect to aviation safety duties and powers designated to be carried out by the Administrator of the Federal Aviation Administration) takes effect within a reasonable time prescribed by the Secretary, Administrator of the Transportation Security Administration, or Administrator of the Federal Aviation Administration. The regulation or order remains in effect under its own terms or until superseded. Except as provided in this part, the Secretary, Administrator of the Transportation Security Administration, or Administrator of the Federal Aviation Administration may amend, modify, or suspend an order in the way, and by giving the notice, the Secretary, Administrator of the Transportation Security Administration, or Administrator of the Federal Aviation Administration decides.

(b) CONTENTS AND SERVICE OF ORDERS.—An order of the Secretary, Administrator of the Transportation Security Administration, or Administrator of the Federal Aviation Administration shall include the findings of fact on which the order is based and shall be served on the parties to the proceeding and the persons affected by the order.

(c) EMERGENCIES.—When the Administrator of the Federal Aviation Administration is of the opinion that an emergency exists related to safety in air commerce and requires immediate action, the Administrator, on the initiative of the Administrator or on complaint, may prescribe regulations and issue orders immediately to meet the emergency, with or without notice and without regard to this part and subchapter II of chapter 5 of title 5. The Administrator shall begin a proceeding immediately about an emergency under this subsection and give preference, when practicable, to the proceeding.

(Pub. L. 103–272, §1(e), July 5, 1994, 108 Stat. 1228; Pub. L. 107–71, title I, §140(b)(1), (2), Nov. 19, 2001, 115 Stat. 641; Pub. L. 115–254, div. K, title I, §1991(f)(1)–(4), (7), Oct. 5, 2018, 132 Stat. 3642.)

§46106. ENFORCEMENT BY THE DEPARTMENT OF TRANSPORTATION

The Secretary of Transportation (or the Administrator of the Transportation Security Administration with respect to security duties and powers designated to be carried out by the Administrator of the Transportation Security Administration or the Administrator of the Federal Aviation Administration with respect to aviation safety duties and powers designated to be carried out by the Administrator of the Federal Aviation Administration) may bring a civil action against a person in a district court of the United States to enforce this part or a requirement or regulation prescribed, or an order or any term of a certificate or permit issued, under this part. The action may be brought in the judicial district in which the person does business or the violation occurred.

(Pub. L. 103–272, §1(e), July 5, 1994, 108 Stat. 1229; Pub. L. 107–71, title I, §140(b)(1), (7), Nov. 19, 2001, 115 Stat. 641; Pub. L. 115–254, div. K, title I, §1991(f)(1), (3), Oct. 5, 2018, 132 Stat. 3642.)

§46107. ENFORCEMENT BY THE ATTORNEY GENERAL

(a) CIVIL ACTIONS TO ENFORCE SECTION 40106(b).—The Attorney General may bring a civil action in a district court of the United States against a person to enforce section 40106(b) of this title. The action may be brought in the judicial district in which the person does business or the violation occurred.

(b) CIVIL ACTIONS TO ENFORCE THIS PART.—(1) On request of the Secretary of Transportation (or the Administrator of the Transportation Security Administration with respect to security duties and powers designated to be carried out by the Administrator of the Transportation Security Administration or the Administrator of the Federal Aviation Administration with respect to aviation safety duties and powers designated to be carried out by the Administrator of the Federal Aviation Administration), the Attorney General may bring a civil action in an appropriate court—

(A) to enforce this part or a requirement or regulation prescribed, or an order or any term of a certificate or permit issued, under this part; and

(B) to prosecute a person violating this part or a requirement or regulation prescribed, or an order or any term of a certificate or permit issued, under this part.

(2) The costs and expenses of a civil action shall be paid out of the appropriations for the expenses of the courts of the United States.

(c) PARTICIPATION OF SECRETARY, ADMINISTRATOR OF THE TRANSPORTATION SECURITY ADMINISTRATION, OR ADMINISTRATOR OF THE FEDERAL AVIATION ADMINISTRATION.—On request of the Attorney General, the Secretary, Administrator of the Transportation Security Administration, or Administrator of the Federal Aviation Administration, as appropriate, may participate in a civil action under this part.

(Pub. L. 103–272, §1(e), July 5, 1994, 108 Stat. 1229; Pub. L. 107–71, title I, §140(b)(1), (2), Nov. 19, 2001, 115 Stat. 641; Pub. L. 115–254, div. K, title I, §1991(f)(1)–(4), Oct. 5, 2018, 132 Stat. 3642.)

§46108. ENFORCEMENT OF CERTIFICATE REQUIREMENTS BY INTERESTED PERSONS

An interested person may bring a civil action in a district court of the United States against a person to enforce section 41101(a)(1) of this title. The action may be brought in the judicial district in which the defendant does business or the violation occurred.

(Pub. L. 103–272, §1(e), July 5, 1994, 108 Stat. 1229.)

§46109. JOINDER AND INTERVENTION

A person interested in or affected by a matter under consideration in a proceeding before the Secretary of Transportation (or the Administrator of the Transportation Security Administration with respect to security duties and powers designated to be carried out by the Administrator of the Transportation Security Administration or the Administrator of the Federal Aviation Administration with respect to aviation safety duties and powers designated to be carried out by the Administrator) or civil action to enforce this part or a requirement or regulation prescribed, or an order or any term of a certificate or permit issued, under this part may be joined as a party or permitted to intervene in the proceeding or civil action.

(Pub. L. 103–272, §1(e), July 5, 1994, 108 Stat. 1230; Pub. L. 115–254, div. K, title I, §1991(f)(8), Oct. 5, 2018, 132 Stat. 3642.)

§46110. JUDICIAL REVIEW

(a) FILING AND VENUE.—Except for an order related to a foreign air carrier subject to disapproval by the President under section 41307 or 41509(f) of this title, a person disclosing a substantial interest in an order issued by the Secretary of Transportation (or the Administrator of the Transportation Security Administration with respect to security duties and powers designated to be carried out by the Administrator of the Transportation Security Administration or the Administrator of the Federal Aviation Administration with respect to aviation duties and powers designated to be carried out by the Administrator of the Federal Aviation Administration) in whole or in part under this part, part B, or subsection (l) or (r) of section 114 may apply for review of the order by filing a petition for review in the United

States Court of Appeals for the District of Columbia Circuit or in the court of appeals of the United States for the circuit in which the person resides or has its principal place of business. The petition must be filed not later than 60 days after the order is issued. The court may allow the petition to be filed after the 60th day only if there are reasonable grounds for not filing by the 60th day.

(b) JUDICIAL PROCEDURES.—When a petition is filed under subsection (a) of this section, the clerk of the court immediately shall send a copy of the petition to the Secretary, Administrator of the Transportation Security Administration, or Administrator of the Federal Aviation Administration, as appropriate. The Secretary, Administrator of the Transportation Security Administration, or Administrator of the Federal Aviation Administration shall file with the court a record of any proceeding in which the order was issued, as provided in section 2112 of title 28.

(c) AUTHORITY OF COURT.—When the petition is sent to the Secretary, Administrator of the Transportation Security Administration, or Administrator of the Federal Aviation Administration, the court has exclusive jurisdiction to affirm, amend, modify, or set aside any part of the order and may order the Secretary, Administrator of the Transportation Security Administration, or Administrator of the Federal Aviation Administration to conduct further proceedings. After reasonable notice to the Secretary, Administrator of the Transportation Security Administration, or Administrator of the Federal Aviation Administration, the court may grant interim relief by staying the order or taking other appropriate action when good cause for its action exists. Findings of fact by the Secretary, Administrator of the Transportation Security Administration, or Administrator of the Federal Aviation Administration, if supported by substantial evidence, are conclusive.

(d) REQUIREMENT FOR PRIOR OBJECTION.—In reviewing an order under this section, the court may consider an objection to an order of the Secretary, Administrator of the Transportation Security Administration, or Administrator of the Federal Aviation Administration only if the objection was made in the proceeding conducted by the Secretary, Administrator of the Transportation Security Administration, or Administrator of the Federal Aviation Administration or if there was a reasonable ground for not making the objection in the proceeding.

(e) SUPREME COURT REVIEW.—A decision by a court under this section may be reviewed only by the Supreme Court under section 1254 of title 28.

(Pub. L. 103–272, §1(e), July 5, 1994, 108 Stat. 1230; Pub. L. 107–71, title I, §140(b)(1), (2), Nov. 19, 2001, 115 Stat. 641; Pub. L. 108–176, title II, §228, Dec. 12, 2003, 117 Stat. 2532; Pub. L. 115–254, div. K, title I, §1991(f)(1)–(4), Oct. 5, 2018, 132 Stat. 3642; Pub. L. 118–63, title XI, §1101(s), May 16, 2024, 138 Stat. 1414.)

§46111. CERTIFICATE ACTIONS IN RESPONSE TO A SECURITY THREAT

(a) ORDERS.—The Administrator of the Federal Aviation Administration shall issue an order amending, modifying, suspending, or revoking any part of a certificate issued under this title if the Administrator of the Federal Aviation Administration is notified by the Administrator of the Transportation Security Administration that the holder of the certificate poses, or is suspected of posing, a risk of air piracy or terrorism or a threat to airline or passenger safety. If requested by the Administrator of the Transportation Security Administration, the order shall be effective immediately.

(b) HEARINGS FOR CITIZENS.—An individual who is a citizen of the United States who is adversely affected by an order of the Administrator of the Federal Aviation Administration under subsection (a) is entitled to a hearing on the record.

(c) HEARINGS.—When conducting a hearing under this section, the administrative law judge shall not be bound by findings of fact or interpretations of laws and regulations of the Administrator of the Federal Aviation Administration or the Administrator of the Transportation Security Administration.

(d) APPEALS.—An appeal from a decision of an administrative law judge as the result of a hearing under subsection (b) shall be made to the Transportation Security Oversight Board established by section 115. The Board shall establish a panel to review the decision. The members of this panel (1) shall not be employees of the Transportation Security Administration, (2) shall have the level of security clearance needed to review the determination made under this section, and (3) shall be given access to all relevant documents that support that determination. The panel may affirm, modify, or reverse the decision.

(e) REVIEW.—A person substantially affected by an action of a panel under subsection (d), or the Administrator of the Transportation Security Administration when the Administrator of the Transportation Security Administration decides that the action of the panel under this section will have a significant adverse impact on carrying out this part, may obtain review of the order under section 46110. The Administrator of the Transportation Security Administration and the Administrator of the Federal Aviation Administration shall be made a party to the review proceedings. Findings of fact of the panel are conclusive if supported by substantial evidence.

(f) EXPLANATION OF DECISIONS.—An individual who commences an appeal under this section shall receive a written explanation of the basis for the determination or decision and all relevant documents that support that determination to the maximum extent that the national security interests of the United States and other applicable laws permit.

(g) CLASSIFIED EVIDENCE.—

(1) IN GENERAL.—The Administrator of the Transportation Security Administration, in consultation with the Administrator of the Federal Aviation Administration and the Director of Central Intelligence, shall issue regulations to establish procedures by which the Administrator of the Transportation Security Administration, as part of a hearing conducted under this section, may provide an unclassified summary of classified evidence upon which the order of the Administrator of the Federal Aviation Administration was based to the individual adversely affected by the order.

(2) REVIEW OF CLASSIFIED EVIDENCE BY ADMINISTRATIVE LAW JUDGE.—

(A) REVIEW.—As part of a hearing conducted under this section, if the order of the Administrator of the Federal Aviation Administration issued under subsection (a) is based on classified information (as defined in section 1(a) of the Classified Information Procedures Act (18 U.S.C. App.)), such information may be submitted by the Administrator of the Transportation Security Administration to the reviewing administrative law judge, pursuant to appropriate security procedures, and shall be reviewed by the administrative law judge ex parte and in camera.

(B) SECURITY CLEARANCES.—Pursuant to existing procedures and requirements, the Administrator of the Transportation Security Administration shall, in coordination, as necessary, with the heads of other affected departments or agencies, ensure that administrative law judges reviewing orders of the Administrator of the Federal Aviation Administration under this section possess security clearances appropriate for their work under this section.

(3) UNCLASSIFIED SUMMARIES OF CLASSIFIED EVIDENCE.—As part of a hearing conducted under this section and upon the request of the individual adversely affected by an order of the Administrator of the Federal Aviation Administration under subsection (a), the Administrator of the Transportation Security Administration shall provide to the individual and reviewing administrative law judge, consistent with the procedures established under paragraph (1), an unclassified summary of any classified information upon which the order of the Administrator of the Federal Aviation Administration is based.

(Added Pub. L. 108–176, title VI, §601(a), Dec. 12, 2003, 117 Stat. 2561; amended Pub. L. 115–254, div. B, title V, §539(l), div. K, title I, §1991(f)(9), Oct. 5, 2018, 132 Stat. 3371, 3643.)

CHAPTER 463—PENALTIES

§46301. CIVIL PENALTIES

(a) GENERAL PENALTY.—(1) A person is liable to the United States Government for a civil penalty of not more than $75,000 (or $1,100 if the person is an individual or small business concern) for violating—

(A) chapter 401 (except sections 40103(a) and (d), 40105, 40116, and 40117), chapter 411, chapter 413 (except sections 41307 and 41310(b)–(f)), chapter 415 (except sections 41502, 41505, and 41507–41509), chapter 417 (except sections 41703, 41704, 41710, 41713, and 41714), chapter 419, subchapter II or III of chapter 421, chapter 423, chapter 441 (except section 44109), section 44502(b) or (c), chapter 447 (except sections 44717 and 44719–44723), chapter 448, chapter 449 (except sections 44902, 44903(d), 44904, 44907(a)–(d)(1)(A) and (d)(1)(C)–(f), and 44908), chapter 451, section 47107(a)(22) (including any assurance made under such section), section 47107(b) (including any assurance made under such section), or section 47133 of this title;

(B) a regulation prescribed or order issued under any provision to which clause (A) of this paragraph applies;

(C) any term of a certificate or permit issued under section 41102, 41103, or 41302 of this title; or

(D) a regulation of the United States Postal Service under this part.

(2) A separate violation occurs under this subsection for each day the violation (other than a violation of section 41719) continues or, if applicable, for each flight involving the violation (other than a violation of section 41719).

(3) PENALTY FOR DIVERSION OF AVIATION REVENUES.—The amount of a civil penalty assessed under this section for a violation of section 47107(b) of this title (or any assurance made under such section) or section 47133 of this title may be increased above the otherwise applicable maximum amount under this section to an amount not to exceed 3 times the amount of revenues that are used in violation of such section.

(4) AVIATION SECURITY VIOLATIONS.—Notwithstanding paragraph (1) of this subsection, the maximum civil penalty for violating chapter 449 shall be $10,000; except that the maximum civil penalty shall be $25,000 in the case of a person operating an aircraft for the transportation of passengers or property for compensation (except an individual serving as an airman).

(5) PENALTIES APPLICABLE TO INDIVIDUALS AND SMALL BUSINESS CONCERNS.—

(A) An individual (except an airman serving as an airman) or small business concern is liable to the Government for a civil penalty of not more than $10,000 for violating—

(i) chapter 401 (except sections 40103(a) and (d), 40105, 40106(b), 40116, and 40117), section 44502 (b) or (c), chapter 447 (except sections 44717–44723), chapter 448, chapter 449 (except sections 44902, 44903(d), 44904, and 44907–44909), chapter 451, or section 46314(a) of this title; or

(ii) a regulation prescribed or order issued under any provision to which clause (i) applies.

(B) A civil penalty of not more than $10,000 may be imposed for each violation under paragraph (1) committed by an individual or small business concern related to—

(i) the transportation of hazardous material;

(ii) the registration or recordation under chapter 441 of an aircraft not used to provide air transportation;

(iii) a violation of section 44718(d), relating to the limitation on construction or establishment of landfills;

(iv) a violation of section 44725, relating to the safe disposal of life-limited aircraft parts; or

(v) a violation of section 40127 or section 41705, relating to discrimination.

(C) Notwithstanding paragraph (1), the maximum civil penalty for a violation of section 41719 committed by an individual or small business concern shall be $5,000 instead of $1,000.

(D) Notwithstanding paragraph (1), the maximum civil penalty for a violation of section 41712 (including a regulation prescribed or order issued under such section) or any other regulation prescribed by the Secretary of Transportation by an individual or small business concern that is intended to afford consumer protection to commercial air transportation passengers shall be $2,500 for each violation.

(6) FAILURE TO COLLECT AIRPORT SECURITY BADGES.—Notwithstanding paragraph (1), any employer (other than a governmental entity or airport operator) who employs an employee to whom an airport security badge or other identifier used to obtain access to a secure area of an airport is issued before, on, or after the date of enactment of this

paragraph and who does not collect or make reasonable efforts to collect such badge from the employee on the date that the employment of the employee is terminated and does not notify the operator of the airport of such termination within 24 hours of the date of such termination shall be liable to the Government for a civil penalty not to exceed $10,000.

(7) Penalties relating to harm to passengers with disabilities.—

(A) Penalty for bodily harm or damage to wheelchair or other mobility aid.—The amount of a civil penalty assessed under this section for a violation of section 41705 that involves damage to a passenger's wheelchair or other mobility aid or injury to a passenger with a disability may be increased above the otherwise applicable maximum amount under this section for a violation of section 41705 to an amount not to exceed 3 times the maximum penalty otherwise allowed.

(B) Each act constitutes separate offense.—Notwithstanding paragraph (2), a separate violation of section 41705 occurs for each act of discrimination prohibited by that section.

(8) Failure to Continue Offering Aviation Fuel [1].—Notwithstanding paragraph (1), the maximum civil penalty for a violation of section 47107(a)(22) (including any assurance made under such section) committed by a person, including if the person is an individual or a small business concern, shall be $5,000 for each day that the person is in violation of that section.

(b) Smoke Alarm Device Penalty.—(1) A passenger may not tamper with, disable, or destroy a smoke alarm device located in a lavatory on an aircraft providing air transportation or intrastate air transportation.

(2) An individual violating this subsection is liable to the Government for a civil penalty of not more than $2,000.

(c) Procedural Requirements.—(1) The Secretary of Transportation may impose a civil penalty for the following violations only after notice and an opportunity for a hearing:

(A) a violation of subsection (b) of this section or chapter 411, chapter 413 (except sections 41307 and 41310(b)–(f)), chapter 415 (except sections 41502, 41505, and 41507–41509), chapter 417 (except sections 41703, 41704, 41710, 41713, and 41714), chapter 419, subchapter II of chapter 421, chapter 423, or section 44909 of this title.

(B) a violation of a regulation prescribed or order issued under any provision to which clause (A) of this paragraph applies.

(C) a violation of any term of a certificate or permit issued under section 41102, 41103, or 41302 of this title.

(D) a violation under subsection (a)(1) of this section related to the transportation of hazardous material.

(2) The Secretary shall give written notice of the finding of a violation and the civil penalty under paragraph (1) of this subsection.

(d) Administrative Imposition of Penalties.—(1) In this subsection—

(A) "flight engineer" means an individual who holds a flight engineer certificate issued under part 63 of title 14, Code of Federal Regulations.

(B) "mechanic" means an individual who holds a mechanic certificate issued under part 65 of title 14, Code of Federal Regulations.

(C) "pilot" means an individual who holds a pilot certificate issued under part 61 of title 14, Code of Federal Regulations.

 (D) "repairman" means an individual who holds a repairman certificate issued under part 65 of title 14, Code of Federal Regulations.

 (2) The Administrator of the Federal Aviation Administration may impose a civil penalty for a violation of chapter 401 (except sections 40103(a) and (d), 40105, 40106(b), 40116, and 40117), section 42121, chapter 441 (except section 44109), section 44502(b) or (c), chapter 447 (except sections 44717 and 44719–44723), chapter 448, chapter 451, section 46301(b), section 46302 (for a violation relating to section 46504), section 46318, section 46319, section 46320, or section 47107(b) (as further defined by the Secretary of Transportation under section 47107(k) and including any assurance made under section 47107(b)) of this title or a regulation prescribed or order issued under any of those provisions. The Secretary of Homeland Security may impose a civil penalty for a violation of chapter 449 (except sections 44902, 44903(d), 44907(a)–(d)(1)(A), 44907(d)(1)(C)–(f), 44908, and 44909), section 46302 (except for a violation relating to section 46504), or section 46303 of this title or a regulation prescribed or order issued under any of those provisions. The Secretary of Homeland Security or Administrator of the Federal Aviation Administration shall give written notice of the finding of a violation and the penalty.

 (3) In a civil action to collect a civil penalty imposed by the Secretary of Homeland Security or Administrator of the Federal Aviation Administration under this subsection, the issues of liability and the amount of the penalty may not be reexamined.

 (4) Notwithstanding paragraph (2) of this subsection, the district courts of the United States have exclusive jurisdiction of a civil action involving a penalty the Secretary of Homeland Security or Administrator of the Federal Aviation Administration initiates if—

  (A) the amount in controversy is more than—

   (i) $400,000 if the violation was committed by any person other than an individual or small business concern before the date of enactment of the FAA Reauthorization Act of 2024;

   (ii) $50,000 if the violation was committed by an individual or small business concern before the date of enactment of the FAA Reauthorization Act of 2024;

   (iii) $1,200,000 if the violation was committed by a person other than an individual or small business concern on or after the date of enactment of the FAA Reauthorization Act of 2024; or

   (iv) $100,000 if the violation was committed by an individual on or after the date of enactment of the FAA Reauthorization Act of 2024;

  (B) the action is in rem or another action in rem based on the same violation has been brought;

  (C) the action involves an aircraft subject to a lien that has been seized by the Government; or

  (D) another action has been brought for an injunction based on the same violation.

 (5)(A) The Administrator of the Federal Aviation Administration may issue an order imposing a penalty under this subsection against an individual acting as a pilot, flight engineer, mechanic, or repairman only after advising the individual of the charges or any reason the Administrator of the Federal Aviation Administration relied on for the proposed penalty and providing the individual an opportunity to answer the charges and be heard about why the order shall not be issued.

 (B) An individual acting as a pilot, flight engineer, mechanic, or repairman may appeal an order imposing a penalty under this subsection to the National Transportation Safety Board. After notice and an opportunity for a hearing on the record, the Board shall affirm, modify, or reverse the order. The Board may modify a civil penalty imposed to a suspension or revocation of a certificate.

(C) When conducting a hearing under this paragraph, the Board is not bound by findings of fact of the Administrator of the Federal Aviation Administration but is bound by all validly adopted interpretations of laws and regulations the Administrator of the Federal Aviation Administration carries out and of written agency policy guidance available to the public related to sanctions to be imposed under this section unless the Board finds an interpretation is arbitrary, capricious, or otherwise not according to law.

(D) When an individual files an appeal with the Board under this paragraph, the order of the Administrator of the Federal Aviation Administration is stayed.

(6) An individual substantially affected by an order of the Board under paragraph (5) of this subsection, or the Administrator of the Federal Aviation Administration when the Administrator of the Federal Aviation Administration decides that an order of the Board under paragraph (5) will have a significant adverse impact on carrying out this part, may obtain judicial review of the order under section 46110 of this title. The Administrator of the Federal Aviation Administration shall be made a party to the judicial review proceedings. Findings of fact of the Board are conclusive if supported by substantial evidence.

(7)(A) The Administrator of the Federal Aviation Administration may impose a penalty on a person (except an individual acting as a pilot, flight engineer, mechanic, or repairman) only after notice and an opportunity for a hearing on the record.

(B) In an appeal from a decision of an administrative law judge as the result of a hearing under subparagraph (A) of this paragraph, the Administrator of the Federal Aviation Administration shall consider only whether—

(i) each finding of fact is supported by a preponderance of reliable, probative, and substantial evidence;

(ii) each conclusion of law is made according to applicable law, precedent, and public policy; and

(iii) the judge committed a prejudicial error that supports the appeal.

(C) Except for good cause, a civil action involving a penalty under this paragraph may not be initiated later than 2 years after the violation occurs.

(D) In the case of a violation of section 47107(b) of this title or any assurance made under such section—

(i) a civil penalty shall not be assessed against an individual;

(ii) a civil penalty may be compromised as provided under subsection (f); and

(iii) judicial review of any order assessing a civil penalty may be obtained only pursuant to section 46110 of this title.

(8) The maximum civil penalty the Administrator of the Transportation Security Administration, Administrator of the Federal Aviation Administration, or Board may impose under this subsection is—

(A) $400,000 if the violation was committed by a person other than an individual or small business concern before the date of enactment of the FAA Reauthorization Act of 2024;

(B) $50,000 if the violation was committed by an individual or small business concern before the date of enactment of the FAA Reauthorization Act of 2024;

(C) $1,200,000 if the violation was committed by a person other than an individual or small business concern on or after the date of enactment of the FAA Reauthorization Act of 2024; or

(D) $100,000 if the violation was committed by an individual on or after the date of enactment of the FAA Reauthorization Act of 2024.

(9) This subsection applies only to a violation occurring after August 25, 1992.

(e) PENALTY CONSIDERATIONS.—In determining the amount of a civil penalty under subsection (a)(3) of this section related to transportation of hazardous material, the Secretary of Transportation shall consider—

(1) the nature, circumstances, extent, and gravity of the violation;

(2) with respect to the violator, the degree of culpability, any history of prior violations, the ability to pay, and any effect on the ability to continue doing business; and

(3) other matters that justice requires.

(f) COMPROMISE AND SETOFF.—(1)(A) The Secretary may compromise the amount of a civil penalty imposed for violating—

(i) chapter 401 (except sections 40103(a) and (d), 40105, 40116, and 40117), chapter 441 (except section 44109), section 44502(b) or (c), chapter 447 (except sections 44717 and 44719–44723), chapter 448, chapter 449 (except sections 44902, 44903(d), 44904, 44907(a)–(d)(1)(A) and (d)(1)(C)–(f), 44908, and 44909), or chapter 451 of this title; or

(ii) a regulation prescribed or order issued under any provision to which clause (i) of this subparagraph applies.

(B) The Postal Service may compromise the amount of a civil penalty imposed under subsection (a)(1)(D) of this section.

(2) The Government may deduct the amount of a civil penalty imposed or compromised under this subsection from amounts it owes the person liable for the penalty.

(g) JUDICIAL REVIEW.—An order of the Secretary or the Administrator of the Federal Aviation Administration imposing a civil penalty may be reviewed judicially only under section 46110 of this title.

(h) NONAPPLICATION.—(1) This section does not apply to the following when performing official duties:

(A) a member of the armed forces of the United States.

(B) a civilian employee of the Department of Defense subject to the Uniform Code of Military Justice.

(2) The appropriate military authority is responsible for taking necessary disciplinary action and submitting to the Secretary (or the Administrator of the Transportation Security Administration with respect to security duties and powers designated to be carried out by the Administrator of the Transportation Security Administration or the Administrator of the Federal Aviation Administration with respect to aviation safety duties and powers designated to be carried out by the Administrator of the Federal Aviation Administration) a timely report on action taken.

(i) SMALL BUSINESS CONCERN DEFINED.—In this section, the term "small business concern" has the meaning given that term in section 3 of the Small Business Act (15 U.S.C. 632).

(Pub. L. 103–272, §1(e), July 5, 1994, 108 Stat. 1231; Pub. L. 103–305, title I, §112(c), title II, §207(c), Aug. 23, 1994, 108 Stat. 1575, 1588; Pub. L. 103–429, §6(60), Oct. 31, 1994, 108 Stat. 4385; Pub. L. 104–264, title V, §502(c), title VIII, §804(b), title XII, §1220(b), Oct. 9, 1996, 110 Stat. 3263, 3271, 3286; Pub. L. 104–287, §5(77), Oct. 11, 1996, 110 Stat. 3396; Pub. L. 105–102, §3(c)(4), Nov. 20, 1997, 111 Stat. 2215; Pub. L. 106–181, title II, §222, title V, §§503(c), 504(b), 519(c), title VII, §§707(b), 720, Apr. 5, 2000, 114 Stat. 102, 133, 134, 149, 158, 163; Pub. L. 106–424, §15, Nov. 1, 2000, 114 Stat. 1888; Pub. L. 107–71, title I, §140(d)(1)–(4), Nov. 19, 2001, 115 Stat. 642; Pub. L. 107–296, title XVI, §1602, Nov. 25, 2002, 116 Stat. 2312; Pub. L. 108–176, title V, §503(a)–(c), Dec. 12, 2003, 117 Stat. 2557, 2558; Pub. L. 108–458, title IV, §4027(a), Dec. 17, 2004, 118 Stat. 3727; Pub. L. 110–53, title XIII, §1302(b), Aug. 3, 2007, 121 Stat. 392; Pub. L. 110–161, div. E, title V, §542, Dec. 26, 2007, 121 Stat. 2079; Pub. L. 112–74, div. D, title V, §564(a), Dec. 23, 2011, 125 Stat. 981; Pub. L. 112–95, title IV, §415(b), title VIII, §803, Feb. 14, 2012, 126 Stat. 96, 119; Pub. L. 113–188, title XV, §1501(b)(2)(B), Nov. 26, 2014, 128 Stat. 2024; Pub. L. 114–190, title II, §2205(b), July 15, 2016, 130 Stat. 631; Pub. L. 115–254, div. B, title III, §372(e), title IV, §436, div. K, title I, §1991(g)(1), Oct. 5, 2018, 132 Stat. 3312, 3344, 3643; Pub. L. 118–63, title III, §§345, 371, title V, §§504(b), 507(a), title VII, §770(b), title XI, §1101(t), May 16, 2024, 138 Stat. 1102, 1139, 1191, 1193, 1295, 1414.)

[1] *So in original. Words following initial word in par. heading probably should not be capitalized.*

§46302. FALSE INFORMATION

(a) CIVIL PENALTY.—A person that, knowing the information to be false, gives, or causes to be given, under circumstances in which the information reasonably may be believed, false information about an alleged attempt being made or to be made to do an act that would violate section 46502(a), 46504, 46505, or 46506 of this title, is liable to the United States Government for a civil penalty of not more than $10,000 for each violation.

(b) COMPROMISE AND SETOFF.—(1) The Secretary of Homeland Security and, for a violation relating to section 46504, the Secretary of Transportation, may compromise the amount of a civil penalty imposed under subsection (a) of this section.

(2) The Government may deduct the amount of a civil penalty imposed or compromised under this section from amounts it owes the person liable for the penalty.

(Pub. L. 103–272, §1(e), July 5, 1994, 108 Stat. 1234; Pub. L. 108–458, title IV, §4027(b), Dec. 17, 2004, 118 Stat. 3727.)

§46303. CARRYING A WEAPON

(a) CIVIL PENALTY.—An individual who, when on, or attempting to board, an aircraft in, or intended for operation in, air transportation or intrastate air transportation, has on or about the individual or the property of the individual a concealed dangerous weapon that is or would be accessible to the individual in flight is liable to the United States Government for a civil penalty of not more than $10,000 for each violation.

(b) COMPROMISE AND SETOFF.—(1) The Secretary of Homeland Security may compromise the amount of a civil penalty imposed under subsection (a) of this section.

(2) The Government may deduct the amount of a civil penalty imposed or compromised under this section from amounts it owes the individual liable for the penalty.

(c) NONAPPLICATION.—This section does not apply to—

(1) a law enforcement officer of a State or political subdivision of a State, or an officer or employee of the Government, authorized to carry arms in an official capacity; or

(2) another individual the Administrator of the Federal Aviation Administration or the Secretary of Homeland Security by regulation authorizes to carry arms in an official

capacity.

(Pub. L. 103–272, §1(e), July 5, 1994, 108 Stat. 1234; Pub. L. 107–71, title I, §140(d)(5), Nov. 19, 2001, 115 Stat. 642; Pub. L. 108–458, title IV, §4027(c), Dec. 17, 2004, 118 Stat. 3727.)

§46304. LIENS ON AIRCRAFT

(a) AIRCRAFT SUBJECT TO LIENS.—When an aircraft is involved in a violation referred to in section 46301(a)(1)(A)–(C) of this title and the violation is by the owner of, or individual commanding, the aircraft, the aircraft is subject to a lien for the civil penalty.

(b) SEIZURE.—An aircraft subject to a lien under this section may be seized summarily and placed in the custody of a person authorized to take custody of it under regulations of the Secretary of Transportation (or the Administrator of the Federal Aviation Administration with respect to aviation safety duties and powers designated to be carried out by the Administrator of the Federal Aviation Administration). A report on the seizure shall be submitted to the Attorney General. The Attorney General promptly shall bring a civil action in rem to enforce the lien or notify the Secretary or Administrator that the action will not be brought.

(c) RELEASE.—An aircraft seized under subsection (b) of this section shall be released from custody when—

(1) the civil penalty is paid;

(2) a compromise amount agreed on is paid;

(3) the aircraft is seized under a civil action in rem to enforce the lien;

(4) the Attorney General gives notice that a civil action will not be brought under subsection (b) of this section; or

(5) a bond (in an amount and with a surety the Secretary or Administrator prescribes), conditioned on payment of the penalty or compromise, is deposited with the Secretary or Administrator.

(Pub. L. 103–272, §1(e), July 5, 1994, 108 Stat. 1235; Pub. L. 108–176, title V, §503(d)(2), Dec. 12, 2003, 117 Stat. 2559; Pub. L. 115–254, div. K, title I, §1991(g)(2), Oct. 5, 2018, 132 Stat. 3644.)

§46305. ACTIONS TO RECOVER CIVIL PENALTIES

A civil penalty under this chapter may be collected by bringing a civil action against the person subject to the penalty, a civil action in rem against an aircraft subject to a lien for a penalty, or both. The action shall conform as nearly as practicable to a civil action in admiralty, regardless of the place an aircraft in a civil action in rem is seized. However, a party may demand a jury trial of an issue of fact in an action involving a civil penalty under this chapter (except a penalty imposed by the Secretary of Transportation that formerly was imposed by the Civil Aeronautics Board) if the value of the matter in controversy is more than $20. Issues of fact tried by a jury may be reexamined only under common law rules.

(Pub. L. 103–272, §1(e), July 5, 1994, 108 Stat. 1235.)

§46306. REGISTRATION VIOLATIONS INVOLVING AIRCRAFT NOT PROVIDING AIR TRANSPORTATION

(a) APPLICATION.—This section applies only to aircraft not used to provide air transportation.

(b) GENERAL CRIMINAL PENALTY.—Except as provided by subsection (c) of this section, a person shall be fined under title 18, imprisoned for not more than 3 years, or both, if the person—

(1) knowingly and willfully forges or alters a certificate authorized to be issued under this part;

(2) knowingly sells, uses, attempts to use, or possesses with the intent to use, such a certificate;

(3) knowingly and willfully displays or causes to be displayed on an aircraft a mark that is false or misleading about the nationality or registration of the aircraft;

(4) obtains a certificate authorized to be issued under this part by knowingly and willfully falsifying or concealing a material fact, making a false, fictitious, or fraudulent statement, or making or using a false document knowing it contains a false, fictitious, or fraudulent statement or entry;

(5) owns an aircraft eligible for registration under section 44102 of this title and knowingly and willfully operates, attempts to operate, or allows another person to operate the aircraft when—

(A) the aircraft is not registered under section 44103 of this title or the certificate of registration is suspended or revoked; or

(B) the owner knows or has reason to know that the other person does not have proper authorization to operate or navigate the aircraft without registration for a period of time after transfer of ownership;

(6) knowingly and willfully operates or attempts to operate an aircraft eligible for registration under section 44102 of this title knowing that—

(A) the aircraft is not registered under section 44103 of this title;

(B) the certificate of registration is suspended or revoked; or

(C) the person does not have proper authorization to operate or navigate the aircraft without registration for a period of time after transfer of ownership;

(7) knowingly and willfully serves or attempts to serve in any capacity as an airman without an airman's certificate authorizing the individual to serve in that capacity;

(8) knowingly and willfully employs for service or uses in any capacity as an airman an individual who does not have an airman's certificate authorizing the individual to serve in that capacity; or

(9) operates an aircraft with a fuel tank or fuel system that has been installed or modified knowing that the tank, system, installation, or modification does not comply with regulations and requirements of the Administrator of the Federal Aviation Administration.

(c) CONTROLLED SUBSTANCE CRIMINAL PENALTY.—(1) In this subsection, "controlled substance" has the same meaning given that term in section 102 of the Comprehensive Drug Abuse Prevention and Control Act of 1970 (21 U.S.C. 802).

(2) A person violating subsection (b) of this section shall be fined under title 18, imprisoned for not more than 5 years, or both, if the violation is related to transporting a controlled substance by aircraft or aiding or facilitating a controlled substance violation and the transporting, aiding, or facilitating—

(A) is punishable by death or imprisonment of more than one year under a law of the United States or a State; or

(B) that is provided is related to an act punishable by death or imprisonment for more than one year under a law of the United States or a State related to a controlled substance (except a law related to simple possession of a controlled substance).

(3) A term of imprisonment imposed under paragraph (2) of this subsection shall be served in addition to, and not concurrently with, any other term of imprisonment imposed on the individual.

(d) SEIZURE AND FORFEITURE.—(1) The Administrator of Drug Enforcement or the Commissioner of U.S. Customs and Border Protection may seize and forfeit under the customs laws an aircraft whose use is related to a violation of subsection (b) of this section, or to aid or facilitate a violation, regardless of whether a person is charged with the violation.

(2) An aircraft's use is presumed to have been related to a violation of, or to aid or facilitate a violation of—

(A) subsection (b)(1) of this section if the aircraft certificate of registration has been forged or altered;

(B) subsection (b)(3) of this section if there is an external display of false or misleading registration numbers or country of registration;

(C) subsection (b)(4) of this section if—

(i) the aircraft is registered to a false or fictitious person; or

(ii) the application form used to obtain the aircraft certificate of registration contains a material false statement;

(D) subsection (b)(5) of this section if the aircraft was operated when it was not registered under section 44103 of this title; or

(E) subsection (b)(9) of this section if the aircraft has a fuel tank or fuel system that was installed or altered—

(i) in violation of a regulation or requirement of the Administrator of the Federal Aviation Administration; or

(ii) if a certificate required to be issued for the installation or alteration is not carried on the aircraft.

(3) The Administrator of the Federal Aviation Administration, the Administrator of Drug Enforcement, and the Commissioner shall agree to a memorandum of understanding to establish procedures to carry out this subsection.

(e) RELATIONSHIP TO STATE LAWS.—This part does not prevent a State from establishing a criminal penalty, including providing for forfeiture and seizure of aircraft, for a person that—

(1) knowingly and willfully forges or alters an aircraft certificate of registration;

(2) knowingly sells, uses, attempts to use, or possesses with the intent to use, a fraudulent aircraft certificate of registration;

(3) knowingly and willfully displays or causes to be displayed on an aircraft a mark that is false or misleading about the nationality or registration of the aircraft; or

(4) obtains an aircraft certificate of registration from the Administrator of the Federal Aviation Administration by—

(A) knowingly and willfully falsifying or concealing a material fact;

(B) making a false, fictitious, or fraudulent statement; or

(C) making or using a false document knowing it contains a false, fictitious, or fraudulent statement or entry.

(Pub. L. 103–272, §1(e), July 5, 1994, 108 Stat. 1235; Pub. L. 104–287, §5(78), Oct. 11, 1996, 110 Stat. 3397; Pub. L. 114–125, title VIII, §802(d)(2), Feb. 24, 2016, 130 Stat. 210.)

§46307. Violation of national defense airspace

A person that knowingly or willfully violates section 40103(b)(3) of this title or a regulation prescribed or order issued under section 40103(b)(3) shall be fined under title 18, imprisoned for not more than one year, or both.

(Pub. L. 103–272, §1(e), July 5, 1994, 108 Stat. 1237.)

§46308. Interference with air navigation

A person shall be fined under title 18, imprisoned for not more than 5 years, or both, if the person—

(1) with intent to interfere with air navigation in the United States, exhibits in the United States a light or signal at a place or in a way likely to be mistaken for a true light or signal established under this part or for a true light or signal used at an air navigation facility;

(2) after a warning from the Administrator of the Federal Aviation Administration, continues to maintain a misleading light or signal; or

(3) knowingly interferes with the operation of a true light or signal.

(Pub. L. 103–272, §1(e), July 5, 1994, 108 Stat. 1238.)

§46309. Concession and price violations

(a) Criminal Penalty for Offering, Granting, Giving, or Helping To Obtain Concessions and Lower Prices.—An air carrier, foreign air carrier, ticket agent, or officer, agent, or employee of an air carrier, foreign air carrier, or ticket agent shall be fined under title 18 if the air carrier, foreign air carrier, ticket agent, officer, agent, or employee—

(1) knowingly and willfully offers, grants, or gives, or causes to be offered, granted, or given, a rebate or other concession in violation of this part; or

(2) by any means knowingly and willfully assists, or willingly allows, a person to obtain transportation or services subject to this part at less than the price lawfully in effect.

(b) Criminal Penalty for Receiving Rebates, Privileges, and Facilities.—A person shall be fined under title 18 if the person by any means—

(1) knowingly and willfully solicits, accepts, or receives a rebate of a part of a price lawfully in effect for the foreign air transportation of property, or a service related to the foreign air transportation; or

(2) knowingly solicits, accepts, or receives a privilege or facility related to a matter the Secretary of Transportation requires be specified in a currently effective tariff applicable to the foreign air transportation of property.

(Pub. L. 103–272, §1(e), July 5, 1994, 108 Stat. 1238.)

§46310. Reporting and recordkeeping violations

(a) General Criminal Penalty.—An air carrier or an officer, agent, or employee of an air carrier shall be fined under title 18 for intentionally—

   (1) failing to make a report or keep a record under this part;

   (2) falsifying, mutilating, or altering a report or record under this part; or

   (3) filing a false report or record under this part.

   (b) SAFETY REGULATION CRIMINAL PENALTY.—An air carrier or an officer, agent, or employee of an air carrier shall be fined under title 18, imprisoned for not more than 5 years, or both, for intentionally falsifying or concealing a material fact, or inducing reliance on a false statement of material fact, in a report or record under section 44701(a) or (b) or any of sections 44702–44716 of this title.

(Pub. L. 103–272, §1(e), July 5, 1994, 108 Stat. 1238; Pub. L. 103–429, §6(56), Oct. 31, 1994, 108 Stat. 4385.)

§46311. UNLAWFUL DISCLOSURE OF INFORMATION

   (a) CRIMINAL PENALTY.—The Secretary of Transportation, the Administrator of the Transportation Security Administration with respect to security duties and powers designated to be carried out by the Administrator of the Transportation Security Administration, or the Administrator of the Federal Aviation Administration with respect to aviation safety duties and powers designated to be carried out by the Administrator of the Federal Aviation Administration, or an officer or employee of the Secretary, Administrator of the Transportation Security Administration, or Administrator of the Federal Aviation Administration shall be fined under title 18, imprisoned for not more than 2 years, or both, if the Secretary, Administrator of the Transportation Security Administration, Administrator of the Federal Aviation Administration, officer, or employee knowingly and willfully discloses information that—

   (1) the Secretary, Administrator of the Transportation Security Administration, Administrator of the Federal Aviation Administration, officer, or employee acquires when inspecting the records of an air carrier; or

   (2) is withheld from public disclosure under section 40115 of this title.

   (b) NONAPPLICATION.—Subsection (a) of this section does not apply if—

   (1) the officer or employee is directed by the Secretary, Administrator of the Transportation Security Administration, or Administrator of the Federal Aviation Administration to disclose information that the Secretary, Administrator of the Transportation Security Administration, or Administrator of the Federal Aviation Administration had ordered withheld; or

   (2) the Secretary, Administrator of the Transportation Security Administration, Administrator of the Federal Aviation Administration, officer, or employee is directed by a court of competent jurisdiction to disclose the information.

   (c) WITHHOLDING INFORMATION FROM CONGRESS.—This section does not authorize the Secretary, Administrator of the Transportation Security Administration, or Administrator of the Federal Aviation Administration to withhold information from a committee of Congress authorized to have the information.

(Pub. L. 103–272, §1(e), July 5, 1994, 108 Stat. 1239; Pub. L. 107–71, title I, §140(d)(6), Nov. 19, 2001, 115 Stat. 642; Pub. L. 115–254, div. K, title I, §1991(g)(3), Oct. 5, 2018, 132 Stat. 3644.)

§46312. Transporting hazardous material

(a) In General.—A person shall be fined under title 18, imprisoned for not more than 5 years, or both, if the person, in violation of a regulation or requirement related to the transportation of hazardous material prescribed by the Secretary of Transportation under this part or chapter 51—

(1) willfully delivers, or causes to be delivered, property containing hazardous material to an air carrier or to an operator of a civil aircraft for transportation in air commerce; or

(2) recklessly causes the transportation in air commerce of the property.

(b) Knowledge of Regulations.—For purposes of subsection (a), knowledge by the person of the existence of a regulation or requirement related to the transportation of hazardous material prescribed by the Secretary under this part or chapter 51 is not an element of an offense under this section but shall be considered in mitigation of the penalty.

(Pub. L. 103–272, §1(e), July 5, 1994, 108 Stat. 1239; Pub. L. 106–181, title V, §507, Apr. 5, 2000, 114 Stat. 140; Pub. L. 109–59, title VII, §7128(a), Aug. 10, 2005, 119 Stat. 1909.)

§46313. Refusing to appear or produce records

A person not obeying a subpoena or requirement of the Secretary of Transportation (or the Administrator of the Transportation Security Administration with respect to security duties and powers designated to be carried out by the Administrator of the Transportation Security Administration or the Administrator of the Federal Aviation Administration with respect to aviation safety duties and powers designated to be carried out by the Administrator of the Federal Aviation Administration) to appear and testify or produce records shall be fined under title 18, imprisoned for not more than one year, or both.

(Pub. L. 103–272, §1(e), July 5, 1994, 108 Stat. 1239; Pub. L. 107–71, title I, §140(d)(7), Nov. 19, 2001, 115 Stat. 642; Pub. L. 115–254, div. K, title I, §1991(g)(4), Oct. 5, 2018, 132 Stat. 3644.)

§46314. Entering aircraft or airport area in violation of security requirements

(a) Prohibition.—A person may not knowingly and willfully enter, in violation of security requirements prescribed under section 44901, 44903(b) or (c), or 44906 of this title, an aircraft or an airport area that serves an air carrier or foreign air carrier.

(b) Criminal Penalty.—(1) A person violating subsection (a) of this section shall be fined under title 18, imprisoned for not more than one year, or both.

(2) A person violating subsection (a) of this section with intent to evade security procedures or restrictions or with intent to commit, in the aircraft or airport area, a felony under a law of the United States or a State shall be fined under title 18, imprisoned for not more than 10 years, or both.

(c) Notice of Penalties.—

(1) In general.—Each operator of an airport in the United States that is required to establish an air transportation security program pursuant to section 44903(c) shall ensure that signs that meet such requirements as the Secretary of Homeland Security may prescribe providing notice of the penalties imposed under section 46301(a)(5)(A)(i) and subsection (b) of this section are displayed near all screening locations, all locations

where passengers exit the sterile area, and such other locations at the airport as the Secretary of Homeland Security determines appropriate.

(2) EFFECT OF SIGNS ON PENALTIES.—An individual shall be subject to a penalty imposed under section 46301(a)(5)(A)(i) or subsection (b) of this section without regard to whether signs are displayed at an airport as required by paragraph (1).

(Pub. L. 103–272, §1(e), July 5, 1994, 108 Stat. 1239; Pub. L. 112–74, div. D, title V, §564(b), (c), Dec. 23, 2011, 125 Stat. 981.)

§46315. LIGHTING VIOLATIONS INVOLVING TRANSPORTING CONTROLLED SUBSTANCES BY AIRCRAFT NOT PROVIDING AIR TRANSPORTATION

(a) APPLICATION.—This section applies only to aircraft not used to provide air transportation.

(b) CRIMINAL PENALTY.—A person shall be fined under title 18, imprisoned for not more than 5 years, or both, if—

(1) the person knowingly and willfully operates an aircraft in violation of a regulation or requirement of the Administrator of the Federal Aviation Administration related to the display of navigation or anticollision lights;

(2) the person is knowingly transporting a controlled substance by aircraft or aiding or facilitating a controlled substance offense; and

(3) the transporting, aiding, or facilitating—

(A) is punishable by death or imprisonment for more than one year under a law of the United States or a State; or

(B) is provided in connection with an act punishable by death or imprisonment for more than one year under a law of the United States or a State related to a controlled substance (except a law related to simple possession of a controlled substance).

(Pub. L. 103–272, §1(e), July 5, 1994, 108 Stat. 1240.)

§46316. GENERAL CRIMINAL PENALTY WHEN SPECIFIC PENALTY NOT PROVIDED

(a) CRIMINAL PENALTY.—Except as provided by subsection (b) of this section, when another criminal penalty is not provided under this chapter, a person that knowingly and willfully violates this part, a regulation prescribed or order issued by the Secretary of Transportation (or the Administrator of the Transportation Security Administration with respect to security duties and powers designated to be carried out by the Administrator of the Transportation Security Administration or the Administrator of the Federal Aviation Administration with respect to aviation safety duties and powers designated to be carried out by the Administrator of the Federal Aviation Administration) under this part, or any term of a certificate or permit issued under section 41102, 41103, or 41302 of this title shall be fined under title 18. A separate violation occurs for each day the violation continues.

(b) NONAPPLICATION.—Subsection (a) of this section does not apply to chapter 401 (except sections 40103(a) and (d), 40105, 40116, and 40117), chapter 441 (except section 44109), chapter 445, chapter 447 (except section 44718(a)), and chapter 449 (except sections 44902, 44903(d), 44904, and 44907–44909) of this title.

(Pub. L. 103–272, §1(e), July 5, 1994, 108 Stat. 1240; Pub. L. 104–287, §5(79), Oct. 11, 1996, 110 Stat.

3397; Pub. L. 105–102, §3(d)(1)(D), Nov. 20, 1997, 111 Stat. 2215; Pub. L. 107–71, title I, §140(d)(7), Nov. 19, 2001, 115 Stat. 642; Pub. L. 115–254, div. K, title I, §1991(g)(5), Oct. 5, 2018, 132 Stat. 3645.)

§46317. CRIMINAL PENALTY FOR PILOTS OPERATING IN AIR TRANSPORTATION WITHOUT AN AIRMAN'S CERTIFICATE

(a) GENERAL CRIMINAL PENALTY.—An individual shall be fined under title 18 or imprisoned for not more than 3 years, or both, if that individual—

(1) knowingly and willfully serves or attempts to serve in any capacity as an airman operating an aircraft in air transportation without an airman's certificate authorizing the individual to serve in that capacity; or

(2) knowingly and willfully employs for service or uses in any capacity as an airman to operate an aircraft in air transportation an individual who does not have an airman's certificate authorizing the individual to serve in that capacity.

(b) CONTROLLED SUBSTANCE CRIMINAL PENALTY.—

(1) CONTROLLED SUBSTANCES DEFINED.—In this subsection, the term "controlled substance" has the meaning given that term in section 102 of the Comprehensive Drug Abuse Prevention and Control Act of 1970 (21 U.S.C. 802).

(2) CRIMINAL PENALTY.—An individual violating subsection (a) shall be fined under title 18 or imprisoned for not more than 5 years, or both, if the violation is related to transporting a controlled substance by aircraft or aiding or facilitating a controlled substance violation and that transporting, aiding, or facilitating—

(A) is punishable by death or imprisonment of more than 1 year under a Federal or State law; or

(B) is related to an act punishable by death or imprisonment for more than 1 year under a Federal or State law related to a controlled substance (except a law related to simple possession (as that term is used in section 46306(c)) of a controlled substance).

(3) TERMS OF IMPRISONMENT.—A term of imprisonment imposed under paragraph (2) shall be served in addition to, and not concurrently with, any other term of imprisonment imposed on the individual subject to the imprisonment.

(Added Pub. L. 106–181, title V, §509(a), Apr. 5, 2000, 114 Stat. 141.)

§46318. INTERFERENCE WITH CABIN OR FLIGHT CREW

(a) GENERAL RULE.—An individual who physically or sexually assaults or threatens to physically or sexually assault a member of the flight crew or cabin crew of a civil aircraft or any other individual on the aircraft, or takes any action that poses an imminent threat to the safety of the aircraft or other individuals on the aircraft is liable to the United States Government for a civil penalty of not more than $35,000.

(b) COMPROMISE AND SETOFF.—

(1) COMPROMISE.—The Secretary may compromise the amount of a civil penalty imposed under this section.

(2) SETOFF.—The United States Government may deduct the amount of a civil penalty imposed or compromised under this section from amounts the Government owes the person liable for the penalty.

(Added Pub. L. 106–181, title V, §511(a), Apr. 5, 2000, 114 Stat. 142; amended Pub. L. 115–254, div. B, title III, §339(a), Oct. 5, 2018, 132 Stat. 3282.)

§46319. PERMANENT CLOSURE OF AN AIRPORT WITHOUT PROVIDING SUFFICIENT NOTICE

(a) PROHIBITION.—A public agency (as defined in section 47102) may not permanently close an airport listed in the national plan of integrated airport systems under section 47103 without providing written notice to the Administrator of the Federal Aviation Administration at least 30 days before the date of the closure.

(b) PUBLICATION OF NOTICE.—The Administrator shall publish each notice received under subsection (a) in the Federal Register.

(c) CIVIL PENALTY.—A public agency violating subsection (a) shall be liable for a civil penalty of $10,000 for each day that the airport remains closed without having given the notice required by this section.

(Added Pub. L. 108–176, title I, §185(a), Dec. 12, 2003, 117 Stat. 2517.)

§46320. INTERFERENCE WITH WILDFIRE SUPPRESSION, LAW ENFORCEMENT, OR EMERGENCY RESPONSE EFFORT BY OPERATION OF UNMANNED AIRCRAFT

(a) IN GENERAL.—Except as provided in subsection (b), an individual who operates an unmanned aircraft and in so doing knowingly or recklessly interferes with a wildfire suppression, law enforcement, or emergency response effort is liable to the United States Government for a civil penalty of not more than $20,000.

(b) EXCEPTIONS.—This section does not apply to the operation of an unmanned aircraft conducted by a unit or agency of the United States Government or of a State, tribal, or local government (including any individual conducting such operation pursuant to a contract or other agreement entered into with the unit or agency) for the purpose of protecting the public safety and welfare, including firefighting, law enforcement, or emergency response.

(c) COMPROMISE AND SETOFF.—

(1) COMPROMISE.—The United States Government may compromise the amount of a civil penalty imposed under this section.

(2) SETOFF.—The United States Government may deduct the amount of a civil penalty imposed or compromised under this section from the amounts the Government owes the person liable for the penalty.

(d) DEFINITIONS.—In this section, the following definitions apply:

(1) WILDFIRE.—The term "wildfire" has the meaning given that term in section 2 of the Emergency Wildfire Suppression Act (42 U.S.C. 1856m).

(2) WILDFIRE SUPPRESSION.—The term "wildfire suppression" means an effort to contain, extinguish, or suppress a wildfire.

(Added Pub. L. 114–190, title II, §2205(a), July 15, 2016, 130 Stat. 630.)

CHAPTER 465—SPECIAL AIRCRAFT JURISDICTION OF THE UNITED STATES

§46501. Definitions

In this chapter—

(1) "aircraft in flight" means an aircraft from the moment all external doors are closed following boarding—

(A) through the moment when one external door is opened to allow passengers to leave the aircraft; or

(B) until, if a forced landing, competent authorities take over responsibility for the aircraft and individuals and property on the aircraft.

(2) "special aircraft jurisdiction of the United States" includes any of the following aircraft in flight:

(A) a civil aircraft of the United States.

(B) an aircraft of the armed forces of the United States.

(C) another aircraft in the United States.

(D) another aircraft outside the United States—

(i) that has its next scheduled destination or last place of departure in the United States, if the aircraft next lands in the United States;

(ii) on which an individual commits an offense (as defined in the Convention for the Suppression of Unlawful Seizure of Aircraft) if the aircraft lands in the United States with the individual still on the aircraft; or

(iii) against which an individual commits an offense (as defined in subsection (d) or (e) of article I, section I of the Convention for the Suppression of Unlawful Acts against the Safety of Civil Aviation) if the aircraft lands in the United States with the individual still on the aircraft.

(E) any other aircraft leased without crew to a lessee whose principal place of business is in the United States or, if the lessee does not have a principal place of business, whose permanent residence is in the United States.

(3) an individual commits an offense (as defined in the Convention for the Suppression of Unlawful Seizure of Aircraft) when the individual, when on an aircraft in flight—

(A) by any form of intimidation, unlawfully seizes, exercises control of, or attempts to seize or exercise control of, the aircraft; or

(B) is an accomplice of an individual referred to in subclause (A) of this clause.

(Pub. L. 103–272, §1(e), July 5, 1994, 108 Stat. 1240.)

§46502. Aircraft Piracy

(a) In Special Aircraft Jurisdiction.—(1) In this subsection—

(A) "aircraft piracy" means seizing or exercising control of an aircraft in the special aircraft jurisdiction of the United States by force, violence, threat of force or violence, or any form of intimidation, and with wrongful intent.

(B) an attempt to commit aircraft piracy is in the special aircraft jurisdiction of the United States although the aircraft is not in flight at the time of the attempt if the aircraft would have been in the special aircraft jurisdiction of the United States had the aircraft piracy been completed.

(2) An individual committing or attempting or conspiring to commit aircraft piracy—

(A) shall be imprisoned for at least 20 years; or

(B) notwithstanding section 3559(b) of title 18, if the death of another individual results from the commission or attempt, shall be put to death or imprisoned for life.

(b) Outside Special Aircraft Jurisdiction.—(1) An individual committing or conspiring to commit an offense (as defined in the Convention for the Suppression of Unlawful Seizure of Aircraft) on an aircraft in flight outside the special aircraft jurisdiction of the United States—

(A) shall be imprisoned for at least 20 years; or

(B) notwithstanding section 3559(b) of title 18, if the death of another individual results from the commission or attempt, shall be put to death or imprisoned for life.

(2) There is jurisdiction over the offense in paragraph (1) if—

(A) a national of the United States was aboard the aircraft;

(B) an offender is a national of the United States; or

(C) an offender is afterwards found in the United States.

(3) For purposes of this subsection, the term "national of the United States" has the meaning prescribed in section 101(a)(22) of the Immigration and Nationality Act (8 U.S.C. 1101(a)(22)).

(Pub. L. 103–272, §1(e), July 5, 1994, 108 Stat. 1241; Pub. L. 103–429, §6(61), Oct. 31, 1994, 108 Stat. 4385; Pub. L. 104–132, title VII, §§721(a), 723(b), Apr. 24, 1996, 110 Stat. 1298, 1300.)

§46503. Interference with security screening personnel

(a) In General.—An individual in an area within a commercial service airport in the United States who, by assaulting a Federal, airport, or air carrier employee who has security duties within the airport, interferes with the performance of the duties of the employee or lessens the ability of the employee to perform those duties, shall be fined under title 18, imprisoned for not more than 10 years, or both. If the individual used a dangerous weapon in committing the assault or interference, the individual may be imprisoned for any term of years or life imprisonment.

(b) Airport and Air Carrier Employees.—For purposes of this section, an airport or air carrier employee who has security duties within the airport includes an airport or air carrier employee performing ticketing, check-in, baggage claim, or boarding functions.

(Added Pub. L. 107–71, title I, §114(a), Nov. 19, 2001, 115 Stat. 623; amended Pub. L. 118–63, title IV, §436, May 16, 2024, 138 Stat. 1176.)

§46504. INTERFERENCE WITH FLIGHT CREW MEMBERS AND ATTENDANTS

An individual on an aircraft in the special aircraft jurisdiction of the United States who, by assaulting or intimidating a flight crew member or flight attendant of the aircraft, interferes with the performance of the duties of the member or attendant or lessens the ability of the member or attendant to perform those duties, or attempts or conspires to do such an act, shall be fined under title 18, imprisoned for not more than 20 years, or both. However, if a dangerous weapon is used in assaulting or intimidating the member or attendant, the individual shall be imprisoned for any term of years or for life.

(Pub. L. 103–272, §1(e), July 5, 1994, 108 Stat. 1244; Pub. L. 107–56, title VIII, §811(i), Oct. 26, 2001, 115 Stat. 382.)

§46505. CARRYING A WEAPON OR EXPLOSIVE ON AN AIRCRAFT

(a) DEFINITION.—In this section, "loaded firearm" means a starter gun or a weapon designed or converted to expel a projectile through an explosive, that has a cartridge, a detonator, or powder in the chamber, magazine, cylinder, or clip.

(b) GENERAL CRIMINAL PENALTY.—An individual shall be fined under title 18, imprisoned for not more than 10 years, or both, if the individual—

(1) when on, or attempting to get on, an aircraft in, or intended for operation in, air transportation or intrastate air transportation, has on or about the individual or the property of the individual a concealed dangerous weapon that is or would be accessible to the individual in flight;

(2) has placed, attempted to place, or attempted to have placed a loaded firearm on that aircraft in property not accessible to passengers in flight; or

(3) has on or about the individual, or has placed, attempted to place, or attempted to have placed on that aircraft, an explosive or incendiary device.

(c) CRIMINAL PENALTY INVOLVING DISREGARD FOR HUMAN LIFE.—An individual who willfully and without regard for the safety of human life, or with reckless disregard for the safety of human life, violates subsection (b) of this section, shall be fined under title 18, imprisoned for not more than 20 years, or both, and, if death results to any person, shall be imprisoned for any term of years or for life.

(d) NONAPPLICATION.—Subsection (b)(1) of this section does not apply to—

(1) a law enforcement officer of a State or political subdivision of a State, or an officer or employee of the United States Government, authorized to carry arms in an official capacity;

(2) another individual the Administrator of the Federal Aviation Administration or the Administrator of the Transportation Security Administration by regulation authorizes to carry a dangerous weapon in air transportation or intrastate air transportation; or

(3) an individual transporting a weapon (except a loaded firearm) in baggage not accessible to a passenger in flight if the air carrier was informed of the presence of the weapon.

(e) CONSPIRACY.—If two or more persons conspire to violate subsection (b) or (c), and one or more of such persons do any act to effect the object of the conspiracy, each of the parties to such conspiracy shall be punished as provided in such subsection.

(Pub. L. 103–272, §1(e), July 5, 1994, 108 Stat. 1244; Pub. L. 104–132, title VII, §705(b), Apr. 24, 1996, 110 Stat. 1295; Pub. L. 107–56, title VIII, §§810(g), 811(j), Oct. 26, 2001, 115 Stat. 381, 382; Pub. L. 107–71, title I, §140(d)(8), Nov. 19, 2001, 115 Stat. 642; Pub. L. 115–254, div. K, title I, §1991(h)(1), Oct. 5, 2018, 132 Stat. 3645.)

§46506. Application of certain criminal laws to acts on aircraft

An individual on an aircraft in the special aircraft jurisdiction of the United States who commits an act that—

(1) if committed in the special maritime and territorial jurisdiction of the United States (as defined in section 7 of title 18) would violate section 113, 114, 661, 662, 1111, 1112, 1113, or 2111 or chapter 109A of title 18, shall be fined under title 18, imprisoned under that section or chapter, or both; or

(2) if committed in the District of Columbia would violate section 9 of the Act of July 29, 1892 (D.C. Code §22-1112), shall be fined under title 18, imprisoned under section 9 of the Act, or both.

(Pub. L. 103–272, §1(e), July 5, 1994, 108 Stat. 1245.)

§46507. False information and threats

An individual shall be fined under title 18, imprisoned for not more than 5 years, or both, if the individual—

(1) knowing the information to be false, willfully and maliciously or with reckless disregard for the safety of human life, gives, or causes to be given, under circumstances in which the information reasonably may be believed, false information about an alleged attempt being made or to be made to do an act that would violate section 46502(a), 46504, 46505, or 46506 of this title; or

(2)(A) threatens to violate section 46502(a), 46504, 46505, or 46506 of this title, or causes a threat to violate any of those sections to be made; and

(B) has the apparent determination and will to carry out the threat.

(Pub. L. 103–272, §1(e), July 5, 1994, 108 Stat. 1245.)

PART B
AIRPORT DEVELOPMENT AND NOISE

PART B—AIRPORT DEVELOPMENT AND NOISE

CHAPTER 471—AIRPORT DEVELOPMENT

SUBCHAPTER I—AIRPORT IMPROVEMENT

SUBCHAPTER II—SURPLUS PROPERTY FOR PUBLIC AIRPORTS

SUBCHAPTER III—AVIATION DEVELOPMENT STREAMLINING

[1] *So in original. Does not conform to section catchline.*

SUBCHAPTER I—AIRPORT IMPROVEMENT

§47101. POLICIES

(a) GENERAL.—It is the policy of the United States—

(1) that the safe operation of the airport and airway system is the highest aviation priority;

(2) that projects, activities, and actions that prevent runway incursions serve to—

(A) improve airport surface surveillance; and

(B) mitigate surface safety risks that are essential to ensuring the safe operation of the airport and airway system;

(3) that aviation facilities be constructed and operated to minimize current and projected noise impact on nearby communities;

(4) to give special emphasis to developing reliever airports;

(5) that appropriate provisions should be made to make the development and enhancement of cargo hub airports easier;

(6) to encourage the development of intermodal connections on airport property between aeronautical and other transportation modes and systems to serve air transportation passengers and cargo efficiently and effectively and promote economic development;

(7) that airport development projects under this subchapter provide for the protection and enhancement of natural resources and the quality of the environment of the United States;

(8) that airport construction and improvement projects that increase the capacity of facilities to accommodate passenger and cargo traffic be undertaken to the maximum feasible extent so that safety and efficiency increase and delays decrease;

(9) to ensure that nonaviation usage of the navigable airspace be accommodated but not allowed to decrease the safety and capacity of the airspace and airport system;

(10) that artificial restrictions on airport capacity—

(A) are not in the public interest;

(B) should be imposed to alleviate air traffic delays only after other reasonably available and less burdensome alternatives have been tried; and

(C) should not discriminate unjustly between categories and classes of aircraft;

(11) that special emphasis should be placed on converting appropriate former military air bases to civil use and identifying and improving additional joint-use facilities;

(12) that the airport improvement program should be administered to encourage projects that employ innovative technology (including integrated in-pavement lighting systems for runways and taxiways and other runway and taxiway incursion prevention devices), concepts, and approaches that will promote safety, capacity, and efficiency improvements in the construction of airports and in the air transportation system (including the development and use of innovative concrete and other materials in the construction of airport facilities to minimize initial laydown costs, minimize time out of service, and maximize lifecycle durability) and to encourage and solicit innovative technology proposals and activities in the expenditure of funding pursuant to this subchapter;

(13) that airport fees, rates, and charges must be reasonable and may only be used for purposes not prohibited by this subchapter; and

(14) that airports should be as self-sustaining as possible under the circumstances existing at each particular airport and in establishing new fees, rates, and charges, and generating revenues from all sources, airport owners and operators should not seek to create revenue surpluses that exceed the amounts to be used for airport system purposes and for other purposes for which airport revenues may be spent under section 47107(b)(1) of this title, including reasonable reserves and other funds to facilitate financing and cover contingencies.

(b) NATIONAL TRANSPORTATION POLICY.—(1) It is a goal of the United States to develop a national intermodal transportation system that transports passengers and property in an efficient manner. The future economic direction of the United States depends on its ability to confront directly the enormous challenges of the global economy, declining productivity growth, energy vulnerability, air pollution, and the need to rebuild the infrastructure of the

United States.

(2) United States leadership in the world economy, the expanding wealth of the United States, the competitiveness of the industry of the United States, the standard of living, and the quality of life are at stake.

(3) A national intermodal transportation system is a coordinated, flexible network of diverse but complementary forms of transportation that transports passengers and property in the most efficient manner. By reducing transportation costs, these intermodal systems will enhance the ability of the industry of the United States to compete in the global marketplace.

(4) All forms of transportation, including aviation and other transportation systems of the future, will be full partners in the effort to reduce energy consumption and air pollution while promoting economic development.

(5) An intermodal transportation system consists of transportation hubs that connect different forms of appropriate transportation and provides users with the most efficient means of transportation and with access to commercial centers, business locations, population centers, and the vast rural areas of the United States, as well as providing links to other forms of transportation and to intercity connections.

(6) Intermodality and flexibility are paramount issues in the process of developing an integrated system that will obtain the optimum yield of United States resources.

(7) The United States transportation infrastructure must be reshaped to provide the economic underpinnings for the United States to compete in the 21st century global economy. The United States can no longer rely on the sheer size of its economy to dominate international economic rivals and must recognize fully that its economy is no longer a separate entity but is part of the global marketplace. The future economic prosperity of the United States depends on its ability to compete in an international marketplace that is teeming with competitors but in which a full one-quarter of the economic activity of the United States takes place.

(8) The United States must make a national commitment to rebuild its infrastructure through development of a national intermodal transportation system. The United States must provide the foundation for its industries to improve productivity and their ability to compete in the global economy with a system that will transport passengers and property in an efficient manner.

(c) CAPACITY EXPANSION AND NOISE ABATEMENT.—It is in the public interest to recognize the effects of airport capacity expansion projects on aircraft noise. Efforts to increase capacity through any means can have an impact on surrounding communities. Noncompatible land uses around airports must be reduced and efforts to mitigate noise must be given a high priority.

(d) CONSISTENCY WITH AIR COMMERCE AND SAFETY POLICIES.—Each airport and airway program should be carried out consistently with section 40101(a), (b), (d), and (f) of this title to foster competition, prevent unfair methods of competition in air transportation, maintain essential air transportation, and prevent unjust and discriminatory practices, including as the practices may be applied between categories and classes of aircraft.

(e) ADEQUACY OF NAVIGATION AIDS AND AIRPORT FACILITIES.—This subchapter should be carried out to provide adequate navigation aids and airport facilities for places at which scheduled commercial air service is provided. The facilities provided may include—

(1) reliever airports; and

(2) heliports designated by the Secretary of Transportation to relieve congestion at commercial service airports by diverting aircraft passengers from fixed-wing aircraft to helicopter carriers.

(f) MAXIMUM USE OF SAFETY FACILITIES.—This subchapter should be carried out consistently with a comprehensive airspace system plan, giving highest priority to commercial service airports, to maximize the use of safety facilities, including installing, operating, and maintaining, to the extent possible with available money and considering other safety needs—

(1) electronic or visual vertical guidance on each runway;

(2) grooving or friction treatment of each primary and secondary runway;

(3) distance-to-go signs for each primary and secondary runway;

(4) a precision approach system, a vertical visual guidance system, and a full approach light system for each primary runway;

(5) a nonprecision instrument approach for each secondary runway;

(6) runway end identifier lights on each runway that does not have an approach light system;

(7) a surface movement radar system at each category III airport;

(8) a taxiway lighting and sign system;

(9) runway edge lighting and marking;

(10) radar approach coverage for each airport terminal area; and

(11) runway and taxiway incursion prevention devices, including integrated in-pavement lighting systems for runways and taxiways.

(g) INTERMODAL PLANNING.—To carry out the policy of subsection (a)(6) of this section, the Secretary of Transportation shall take each of the following actions:

(1) COORDINATION IN DEVELOPMENT OF AIRPORT PLANS AND PROGRAMS.—Cooperate with State and local officials in developing airport plans and programs that are based on overall transportation needs. The airport plans and programs shall be developed in coordination with other transportation planning and considering comprehensive long-range land-use plans and overall social, economic, environmental (including long-term resilience from the impact of natural hazards and severe weather events), system performance, and energy conservation objectives. The process of developing airport plans and programs shall be continuing, cooperative, and comprehensive to the degree appropriate to the complexity of the transportation problems.

(2) GOALS FOR AIRPORT MASTER AND SYSTEM PLANS.—Encourage airport sponsors and State and local officials to develop airport master plans and airport system plans that—

(A) foster effective coordination between aviation planning and metropolitan planning;

(B) include an evaluation of aviation needs within the context of multimodal planning;

(C) consider passenger convenience, airport ground access, and access to airport facilities;

(D) are integrated with metropolitan plans to ensure that airport development proposals include adequate consideration of land use and ground transportation access; and

(E) consider the impact of hazardous weather events on long-term operational resilience.

(3) REPRESENTATION OF AIRPORT OPERATORS ON MPO'S.—Encourage metropolitan planning organizations, particularly in areas with populations greater than 200,000, to establish membership positions for airport operators.

(h) CONSULTATION.—To carry out the policy of subsection (a)(7) of this section, the Secretary of Transportation may consult with the Secretary of the Interior and the Administrator of the Environmental Protection Agency about any project included in a project grant application involving the location of an airport or runway, or a major runway extension, that may have a significant effect on—

(1) natural resources, including fish and wildlife;

(2) natural, scenic, and recreation assets;

(3) water and air quality; or

(4) another factor affecting the environment.

(Pub. L. 103–272, §1(e), July 5, 1994, 108 Stat. 1246; Pub. L. 103–305, title I, §§104, 110, Aug. 23, 1994, 108 Stat. 1571, 1573; Pub. L. 103–429, §6(62), Oct. 31, 1994, 108 Stat. 4385; Pub. L. 104–264, title I, §141, Oct. 9, 1996, 110 Stat. 3220; Pub. L. 106–181, title I, §§121(a), (b), 137(a), Apr. 5, 2000, 114 Stat. 74, 85; Pub. L. 112–95, title I, §131, Feb. 14, 2012, 126 Stat. 21; Pub. L. 118–63, title III, §347(a)(1), (2), title VII, §§701, 781, May 16, 2024, 138 Stat. 1104, 1245, 1302.)

§47102. DEFINITIONS

In this subchapter—

(1) "air carrier" has the meaning given such term in section 40102.

(2) "airport"—

(A) means—

(i) an area of land or water used or intended to be used for the landing and taking off of aircraft;

(ii) an appurtenant area used or intended to be used for airport buildings or other airport facilities or rights of way; and

(iii) airport buildings and facilities located in any of those areas; and

(B) includes a heliport.

(3) "airport development" means the following activities, if undertaken by the sponsor, owner, or operator of a public-use airport:

(A) constructing, repairing, or improving a public-use airport, including—

(i) removing, lowering, relocating, marking, and lighting an airport hazard;

(ii) preparing a plan or specification, including carrying out a field investigation; and

(iii) a secondary runway at a nonhub airport that is equivalent in size and type to the primary runway of such airport.

(B) acquiring for, or installing at, a public-use airport—

(i) a navigation aid or another aid (including a precision approach system) used by aircraft for landing at or taking off from the airport, including preparing the site as required by the acquisition or installation;

(ii) safety or security equipment, including explosive detection devices, universal access systems, and emergency call boxes, the Secretary requires by regulation for, or approves as contributing significantly to, the safety or security of individuals and property at the airport and integrated in-pavement lighting systems for runways and taxiways and other runway and taxiway incursion prevention devices;

(iii) equipment to remove snow, to measure runway surface friction, or for aviation-related weather reporting, including closed circuit weather surveillance equipment and fuel infrastructure for such equipment to remove snow if the airport is located in Alaska;

(iv) firefighting and rescue equipment at an airport that serves scheduled passenger operations of air carrier aircraft designed for more than 9 passenger seats;

(v) aircraft deicing equipment and structures (except aircraft deicing fluids and storage facilities for the equipment and fluids);

(vi) interactive training systems;

(vii) windshear detection equipment that is certified by the Administrator of the Federal Aviation Administration;

(viii) stainless steel adjustable lighting extensions approved by the Administrator;

(ix) engineered materials arresting systems as described in the Advisory Circular No. 150/5220–22 published by the Federal Aviation Administration on August 21, 1998, including any revision to the circular;

(x) replacement of baggage conveyor systems, and reconfiguration of terminal baggage areas, that the Secretary determines are necessary to install bulk explosive detection devices; except that such activities shall be eligible for funding under this subchapter only using amounts apportioned under section 47114; and

(xi) a medium intensity approach lighting system with runway alignment indicator lights.

(C) acquiring an interest in land or airspace, including land for future airport development, that is needed—

(i) to carry out airport development described in subclause (A) or (B) of this clause; or

(ii) to remove or mitigate an existing airport hazard or prevent or limit the creation of a new airport hazard.

(D) acquiring land for, or constructing, a burn area training structure on or off the airport to provide live fire drill training for aircraft rescue and firefighting personnel required to receive the training under regulations the Secretary prescribes, including basic equipment and minimum structures to support the training under standards the Administrator of the Federal Aviation Administration prescribes.

(E) relocating an air traffic control tower and any navigational aid (including radar) if the relocation is necessary to carry out a project approved by the Secretary under this subchapter or under section 40117.

(F) constructing, reconstructing, repairing, or improving an airport, or purchasing capital equipment for an airport, if necessary for compliance with the responsibilities of the operator or owner of the airport under the Americans with Disabilities Act of 1990 (42 U.S.C. 12101 et seq.), the Clean Air Act (42 U.S.C. 7401 et seq.), and the Federal Water Pollution Control Act (33 U.S.C. 1251 et seq.), except constructing or purchasing capital equipment that would benefit primarily a revenue-producing area of the airport used by a nonaeronautical business.

(G) acquiring land for, or work necessary to construct, a pad suitable for deicing aircraft before takeoff at a commercial service airport, including constructing or reconstructing paved areas, drainage collection structures, treatment and discharge systems, appropriate lighting, paved access for deicing vehicles and aircraft, and including acquiring glycol recovery vehicles, but not including acquiring aircraft deicing fluids or constructing or reconstructing storage facilities for aircraft deicing equipment or fluids.

(H) routine work to preserve and extend the useful life of runways, taxiways, and aprons at nonhub airports and airports that are not primary airports, under guidelines issued by the Administrator of the Federal Aviation Administration.

(I) constructing, reconstructing, or improving an airport, or purchasing nonrevenue generating capital equipment to be owned by an airport, for the purpose of transferring passengers, cargo, or baggage between the aeronautical and ground transportation modes on airport property.

(J) constructing an air traffic control tower or acquiring and installing air traffic control, communications, and related equipment at an air traffic control tower under the terms specified in section 47124(b)(4).

(K) work necessary to construct or modify airport facilities to provide low-emission fuel systems, gate electrification, and other related air quality improvements at a commercial service airport.

(L) a project by a commercial service airport for the acquisition of airport-owned vehicles or ground support equipment equipped with low-emission technology if the vehicles are;

    (i) used exclusively on airport property; or

    (ii) used exclusively to transport passengers and employees between the airport and the airport's consolidated rental car facility or an intermodal surface transportation facility adjacent to the airport.

(M) construction of mobile refueler parking within a fuel farm at a nonprimary airport meeting the requirements of section 112.8 of title 40, Code of Federal Regulations.

(N) terminal development under section 47119(a).

(O) acquiring and installing facilities and equipment to provide air conditioning, heating, or electric power from terminal-based, nonexclusive use facilities to aircraft parked at a public use airport for the purpose of reducing energy use or harmful emissions as compared to the provision of such air conditioning, heating, or electric power from aircraft-based systems.

(P) an on-airport project to improve reliability and efficiency of the power supply of the airport or meet current and future electrical power demand and to prevent power disruptions to the airfield, passenger terminal, and any other airport facilities, including the acquisition and installation of electrical generators, renewable energy generation and storage infrastructure (including necessary substation upgrades to support such infrastructure), separation of the airport's main power supply from its redundant power supply, the construction or modification of airport facilities to install a microgrid (as defined in section 641 of the United States Energy Storage Competitiveness Act of 2007 (42 U.S.C. 17231)), and smart glass (including electrochromic glass).

(Q) converting or retrofitting vehicles and ground support equipment into eligible zero-emission vehicles and equipment (as defined in section 47136) and for acquiring, by purchase or lease, eligible zero-emission vehicles and equipment.

(R) predevelopment planning, including financial, legal, or procurement consulting services, related to an application or proposed application for an exemption under section 47134.

(S) acquisition of advanced digital construction management systems and related technology used in the planning, design and engineering, construction, and maintenance of airport facilities when such systems or technologies are acquired to carry out a project approved by the Secretary under this subchapter.

(T) improvements, or planning for improvements (including monitoring equipment or services), that would be necessary to sustain commercial service flight operations or permit the resumption of such flight operations following a natural disaster (including an earthquake, flooding, high water, wildfires, hurricane, storm surge, tidal wave, tornado, tsunami, wind driven water, sea level rise, tropical storm, cyclone, land instability, or winter storm) at—

(i) a primary airport; or

(ii) a nonprimary airport that is designated as a Federal staging area or incident support base by the Administrator of the Federal Emergency Management Agency.

(U) a project to comply with rulemakings and recommendations on airport cybersecurity standards from the aviation rulemaking committee convened under section 395 of the FAA Reauthorization Act of 2024.

(V) reconstructing or rehabilitating an existing crosswind runway (regardless of the wind coverage of the primary runway) if the reconstruction or rehabilitation of such crosswind runway is in the most recently approved airport layout plan of the sponsor.

(W) constructing or acquiring such airport-owned infrastructure or equipment, notwithstanding revenue producing capability of such infrastructure or equipment, as may be required for—

(i) the on-airport distribution or storage of unleaded aviation gasoline for piston-driven aircraft, including on-airport construction or expansion of pipelines, storage tanks, low-emission fuel systems, and airport-owned fuel trucks providing exclusively unleaded aviation fuels (unless the Secretary determines that an alternative fuel may be safely used in such fuel truck for a limited time); or

(ii) fueling systems for type certificated hydrogen-powered aircraft.

(X) constructing, reconstructing, or rehabilitating a taxiway or taxilane that serves non-exclusive use aeronautical facilities, including aircraft storage facilities, except for the 50 feet of pavement immediately in front of an ineligible building.

(Y) any other activity (excluding terminal development) that the Secretary concludes will reasonably improve the safety of the airport.

(4) "airport hazard" means a structure or object of natural growth located on or near a public-use airport, or a use of land near the airport, that obstructs or otherwise is hazardous to the landing or taking off of aircraft at or from the airport.

(5) "airport planning" means planning as defined by requirements the Secretary prescribes and includes—

(A) integrated airport system planning and catchment area analyses;

(B) developing an environmental management system;

(C) developing a plan for recycling and minimizing the generation of airport solid waste, consistent with applicable State and local recycling laws, including the cost of a waste audit; and

(D) assessing current and future electrical power demand for airport airside and landside activities.

(6) "amount made available under section 48103" or "amount newly made available" means the amount authorized for grants under section 48103 as that amount may be limited in that year by a subsequent law, but as determined without regard to grant obligation recoveries made in that year or amounts covered by section 47107(f).

(7) "commercial service airport" means a public airport in a State that the Secretary determines has at least 2,500 passenger boardings each year and is receiving scheduled passenger aircraft service.

(8) "general aviation airport" means a public-use airport that is located in a State and that, as determined by the Secretary—

(A) does not have scheduled service; or

(B) has scheduled service with less than 2,500 passenger boardings each year.

(9) "integrated airport system planning" means developing for planning purposes information and guidance to decide the extent, kind, location, and timing of airport development needed in a specific area to establish a viable, balanced, and integrated system of public-use airports, including—

(A) identifying system needs;

(B) developing an estimate of systemwide development costs;

(C) conducting studies, surveys, and other planning actions, including those related to airport access, needed to decide which aeronautical needs should be met by a system of airports; and

(D) standards prescribed by a State, except standards for safety of approaches, for airport development at nonprimary public-use airports.

(10) "landed weight" means the weight of aircraft transporting only cargo in intrastate, interstate, and foreign air transportation, as the Secretary determines under regulations the Secretary prescribes.

(11) "large hub airport" means a commercial service airport that has at least 1.0 percent of the passenger boardings.

(12) "low-emission technology" means technology for vehicles and equipment whose emission performance is the best achievable under emission standards established by the Environmental Protection Agency and that relies exclusively on alternative fuels that are substantially nonpetroleum based, as defined by the Department of Energy, but not excluding hybrid systems or natural gas powered vehicles.

(13) "medium hub airport" means a commercial service airport that has at least 0.25 percent but less than 1.0 percent of the passenger boardings.

(14) "nonhub airport" means a commercial service airport that has less than 0.05 percent of the passenger boardings.

(15) "passenger boardings"—

(A) means, unless the context indicates otherwise, revenue passenger boardings in the United States in the prior calendar year on an aircraft in service in air commerce, as the Secretary determines under regulations the Secretary prescribes; and

(B) includes passengers who continue on an aircraft in international flight that stops at an airport in the 48 contiguous States, Alaska, or Hawaii for a nontraffic purpose.

(16) "primary airport" means a commercial service airport the Secretary determines to have more than 10,000 passenger boardings each year.

(17) "project" means a project, separate projects included in one project grant application, or all projects to be undertaken at an airport in a fiscal year, to achieve airport development or airport planning.

(18) "project cost" means a cost involved in carrying out a project.

(19) "project grant" means a grant of money the Secretary makes to a sponsor to carry out at least one project.

(20) "public agency" means—

(A) a State or political subdivision of a State;

(B) a tax-supported organization;

(C) an Indian tribe or pueblo; or

(D) the Republic of the Marshall Islands, Federated States of Micronesia, and Republic of Palau.

(21) "public airport" means an airport used or intended to be used for public purposes—

(A) that is under the control of a public agency; and

(B) of which the area used or intended to be used for the landing, taking off, or surface maneuvering of aircraft is publicly owned.

(22) "public-use airport" means—

(A) a public airport; or

(B) a privately-owned airport used or intended to be used for public purposes that is—

(i) a reliever airport; or

(ii) determined by the Secretary to have at least 2,500 passenger boardings each year and to receive scheduled passenger aircraft service.

(23) "reliever airport" means an airport the Secretary designates to relieve congestion at a commercial service airport and to provide more general aviation access to the overall community.

(24) "revenue producing aeronautical support facilities" means fuel farms, hangar buildings, self-service credit card aeronautical fueling systems, airplane wash racks, major rehabilitation of a hangar owned by a sponsor, or other aeronautical support facilities that the Secretary determines will increase the revenue producing ability of the airport.

(25) "small hub airport" means a commercial service airport that has at least 0.05 percent but less than 0.25 percent of the passenger boardings.

(26) "sponsor" means—

(A) a public agency that submits to the Secretary under this subchapter an application for financial assistance; and

(B) a private owner of a public-use airport that submits to the Secretary under this subchapter an application for financial assistance for the airport.

(27) "State" means a State of the United States, the District of Columbia, Puerto Rico, the Virgin Islands, American Samoa, the Northern Mariana Islands, and Guam.

(28) "terminal development" means—

(A) development of—

(i) an airport passenger terminal building, including terminal gates;

(ii) access roads servicing exclusively airport traffic that leads directly to or from an airport passenger terminal building; and

(iii) walkways that lead directly to or from an airport passenger terminal building; and

(B) the cost of a vehicle for moving passengers and baggage between terminal facilities and between terminal facilities and aircraft.

(Pub. L. 103–272, §1(e), July 5, 1994, 108 Stat. 1248; Pub. L. 103–305, title I, §105, Aug. 23, 1994, 108 Stat. 1572; Pub. L. 104–264, title I, §142(b)(1), Oct. 9, 1996, 110 Stat. 3221; Pub. L. 106–181, title I, §§121(c), 122, 123(b), 137(b), title V, §514(a), Apr. 5, 2000, 114 Stat. 74, 75, 85, 144; Pub. L. 107–71, title I, §119(a)(1), (5), Nov. 19, 2001, 115 Stat. 628, 629; Pub. L. 108–7, div. I, title III, §370(a), Feb. 20, 2003, 117 Stat. 424; Pub. L. 108–176, title I, §§141, 142, 159(b)(1), (d), title VIII, §801(a), Dec. 12, 2003, 117 Stat. 2503, 2510, 2511, 2586; Pub. L. 112–95, title I, §132, Feb. 14, 2012, 126 Stat. 21; Pub. L. 115–254, div. B, title I, §165, Oct. 5, 2018, 132 Stat. 3225; Pub. L. 118–63, title VII, §702, May 16, 2024, 138 Stat. 1246.)

§47103. NATIONAL PLAN OF INTEGRATED AIRPORT SYSTEMS

(a) GENERAL REQUIREMENTS AND CONSIDERATIONS.—The Secretary of Transportation shall maintain the plan for developing public-use airports in the United States, named "the national plan of integrated airport systems". The plan shall include the kind and estimated cost of eligible airport development the Secretary of Transportation considers necessary to provide a safe, efficient, and integrated system of public-use airports adequate to anticipate and meet the needs of civil aeronautics, to meet the national defense requirements of the Secretary of Defense, and to meet identified needs of the United States Postal Service. Airport development included in the plan may not be limited to meeting the needs of any particular classes or categories of public-use airports. In maintaining the plan, the Secretary of Transportation shall consider the needs of each segment of civil aviation and the relationship of the airport system to—

(1) the rest of the transportation system, including connection to the surface transportation network; and

(2) forecasted technological developments in aeronautics.

(b) SPECIFIC REQUIREMENTS.—In maintaining the plan, the Secretary of Transportation shall—

(1) to the extent possible and as appropriate, consult with departments, agencies, and instrumentalities of the United States Government, with public agencies, and with the aviation community; and

(2) make every reasonable effort to address the needs of air cargo operations and rotary wing aircraft operations.

(c) AVAILABILITY OF DOMESTIC MILITARY AIRPORTS AND AIRPORT FACILITIES.—To the extent possible, the Secretary of Defense shall make domestic military airports and airport facilities available for civil use. In advising the Secretary of Transportation under subsection (a) of this section, the Secretary of Defense shall indicate the extent to which domestic military airports and airport facilities are available for civil use.

(d) NON-COMPLIANT AIRPORTS.—

(1) IN GENERAL.—The Secretary shall include in the plan a detailed statement listing airports the Secretary has reason to believe are not in compliance with grant assurances or other requirements with respect to airport lands and shall include—

(A) the circumstances of noncompliance;

(B) the timeline for corrective action with respect to such noncompliance; and

(C) any corrective action the Secretary intends to require to bring the airport sponsor into compliance.

(2) LISTING.—The Secretary is not required to conduct an audit or make a final determination before including an airport on the list referred to in paragraph (1).

(e) PUBLICATION.—The Secretary of Transportation shall publish the plan every 2 years.

(Pub. L. 103–272, §1(e), July 5, 1994, 108 Stat. 1251; Pub. L. 112–95, title I, §152(a), Feb. 14, 2012, 126 Stat. 32; Pub. L. 118–63, title II, §218(e), May 16, 2024, 138 Stat. 1055.)

§47104. PROJECT GRANT AUTHORITY

(a) GENERAL AUTHORITY.—To maintain a safe and efficient nationwide system of public-use airports that meets the present and future needs of civil aeronautics, the Secretary of Transportation may make project grants under this subchapter from the Airport and Airway Trust Fund.

(b) INCURRING OBLIGATIONS.—The Secretary may incur obligations to make grants from amounts made available under section 48103 of this title as soon as the amounts are apportioned under section 47114(c) and (d)(2) of this title.

(c) EXPIRATION OF AUTHORITY.—After September 30, 2028, the Secretary may not incur obligations under subsection (b) of this section, except for obligations of amounts—

(1) remaining available after that date under section 47117(b) of this title; or

(2) recovered by the United States Government from grants made under this chapter if the amounts are obligated only for increases under section 47108(b)(2) and (3) of this title in the maximum amount of obligations of the Government for any other grant made under this title.

(Pub. L. 103–272, §1(e), July 5, 1994, 108 Stat. 1252; Pub. L. 103–305, title I, §101(b), Aug. 23, 1994, 108 Stat. 1571; Pub. L. 103–429, §6(63), Oct. 31, 1994, 108 Stat. 4385; Pub. L. 104–264, title I, §101(b), Oct. 9, 1996, 110 Stat. 3216; Pub. L. 105–277, div. C, title I, §110(b)(2), Oct. 21, 1998, 112 Stat. 2681–587; Pub. L. 106–6, §2(b), Mar. 31, 1999, 113 Stat. 10; Pub. L. 106–31, title VI, §6002(b), May 21, 1999, 113 Stat. 113; Pub. L. 106–59, §1(b), Sept. 29, 1999, 113 Stat. 482; Pub. L. 106–181, title I, §101(b), Apr. 5, 2000, 114 Stat. 65; Pub. L. 108–176, title I, §101(b), Dec. 12, 2003, 117 Stat. 2494; Pub. L. 110–190, §4(b), Feb. 28, 2008, 122 Stat. 644; Pub. L. 110–253, §4(b), June 30, 2008, 122 Stat. 2418; Pub. L. 110–330, §4(b), Sept. 30, 2008, 122 Stat. 3718; Pub. L. 111–12, §4(b), Mar. 30, 2009, 123 Stat. 1458; Pub. L. 111–69, §4(b), Oct. 1, 2009, 123 Stat. 2055; Pub. L. 111–116, §4(b), Dec. 16, 2009, 123 Stat. 3032; Pub. L. 111–153, §4(b), Mar. 31, 2010, 124 Stat. 1085; Pub. L. 111–161, §4(b), Apr. 30, 2010, 124 Stat. 1127; Pub. L. 111–197, §4(b), July 2, 2010, 124 Stat. 1354; Pub. L. 111–216, title I, §103, Aug. 1, 2010, 124 Stat. 2349; Pub. L. 111–249, §4(b), Sept. 30, 2010, 124 Stat. 2628; Pub. L. 111–329, §4(b), Dec. 22, 2010, 124 Stat. 3567; Pub. L. 112–7, §4(b), Mar. 31, 2011, 125 Stat. 32; Pub. L. 112–16, §4(b), May 31, 2011, 125 Stat. 219; Pub. L. 112–21, §4(b), June 29, 2011, 125 Stat. 234; Pub. L. 112–27, §4(b), Aug. 5, 2011, 125 Stat. 271; Pub. L. 112–30, title II, §204(b), Sept. 16, 2011, 125 Stat. 358; Pub. L. 112–91, §4(b), Jan. 31, 2012, 126 Stat. 4; Pub. L. 112–95, title I, §101(b), Feb. 14, 2012, 126 Stat. 15; Pub. L. 114–55, title I, §101(b), Sept. 30, 2015, 129 Stat. 523; Pub. L. 114–141, title I, §101(b), Mar. 30, 2016, 130 Stat. 323; Pub. L. 114–190, title I, §1101(b), July 15,

2016, 130 Stat. 617; Pub. L. 115–63, title I, §101(b), Sept. 29, 2017, 131 Stat. 1169; Pub. L. 115–141, div. M, title I, §101(b), Mar. 23, 2018, 132 Stat. 1046; Pub. L. 115–254, div. B, title I, §111(b), Oct. 5, 2018, 132 Stat. 3199; Pub. L. 118–15, div. B, title II, §2201(d), Sept. 30, 2023, 137 Stat. 82; Pub. L. 118–34, title I, §101(d), Dec. 26, 2023, 137 Stat. 1113; Pub. L. 118–41, title I, §101(d), Mar. 8, 2024, 138 Stat. 21; Pub. L. 118–63, title I, §101(b), May 16, 2024, 138 Stat. 1033.)

§47105. PROJECT GRANT APPLICATIONS

(a) SUBMISSION AND CONSULTATION.—(1) An application for a project grant under this subchapter may be submitted to the Secretary of Transportation by—

(A) a sponsor; or

(B) a State, as the only sponsor, for an airport development project benefitting 1 or more airports in the State or for airport planning for projects for 1 or more airports in the State if—

(i) the sponsor of each airport gives written consent that the State be the applicant;

(ii) the Secretary is satisfied there is administrative merit and aeronautical benefit in the State being the sponsor; and

(iii) an acceptable agreement exists that ensures that the State will comply with appropriate grant conditions and other assurances the Secretary requires.

(2) Before deciding to undertake an airport development project at an airport under this subchapter, a sponsor shall consult with the airport users that will be affected by the project.

(3) This subsection does not authorize a public agency that is subject to the laws of a State to apply for a project grant in violation of a law of the State.

(b) CONTENTS AND FORM.—An application for a project grant under this subchapter—

(1) shall describe the project proposed to be undertaken;

(2) may propose a project only for a public-use airport included in the current national plan of integrated airport systems;

(3) may propose airport development only if the development complies with standards the Secretary prescribes or approves, including standards for site location, airport layout, site preparation, paving, lighting, and safety of approaches; and

(4) shall be in the form and contain other information the Secretary prescribes.

(c) STATE STANDARDS FOR AIRPORT DEVELOPMENT.—

(1) IN GENERAL.—The Secretary may approve standards (except standards for safety of approaches) that a State prescribes for airport development at nonprimary public-use airports in the State. On approval under this subsection, a State's standards apply to the nonprimary public-use airports in the State instead of the comparable standards prescribed by the Secretary under subsection (b)(3) of this section. The Secretary, or the State with the approval of the Secretary, may revise standards approved under this subsection.

(2) PAVEMENT STANDARDS.—

(A) TECHNICAL ASSISTANCE.—At the request of a State, the Secretary shall, not later than 30 days after the date of the request, provide technical assistance to the State in developing standards, acceptable to the Secretary under subparagraph (B), for pavement on nonprimary public-use airports in the State.

(B) REQUIREMENTS.—The Secretary shall—

(i) continue to provide technical assistance under subparagraph (A) until the standards are approved under paragraph (1); and

(ii) clearly indicate to the State the standards that are acceptable to the Secretary, considering, at a minimum, local conditions and locally available materials.

(d) CERTIFICATION OF COMPLIANCE.—The Secretary may require a sponsor to certify that the sponsor will comply with this subchapter in carrying out the project. The Secretary may rescind the acceptance of a certification at any time. This subsection does not affect an obligation or responsibility of the Secretary under another law of the United States.

(e) PREVENTIVE MAINTENANCE.—After January 1, 1995, the Secretary may approve an application under this subchapter for the replacement or reconstruction of pavement at an airport only if the sponsor has provided such assurances or certifications as the Secretary may determine appropriate that such airport has implemented an effective airport pavement maintenance-management program. The Secretary may require such reports on pavement condition and pavement management programs as the Secretary determines may be useful.

(f) NOTIFICATION.—The sponsor of an airport for which an amount is apportioned under section 47114(c) of this title shall notify the Secretary of the fiscal year in which the sponsor intends to submit a project grant application for the apportioned amount. The notification shall be given by the time and contain the information the Secretary prescribes.

(Pub. L. 103–272, §1(e), July 5, 1994, 108 Stat. 1253; Pub. L. 103–305, title I, §§106, 107(a), Aug. 23, 1994, 108 Stat. 1572; Pub. L. 115–254, div. B, title I, §183, Oct. 5, 2018, 132 Stat. 3233.)

§47106. PROJECT GRANT APPLICATION APPROVAL CONDITIONED ON SATISFACTION OF PROJECT REQUIREMENTS

(a) PROJECT GRANT APPLICATION APPROVAL.—The Secretary of Transportation may approve an application under this subchapter for a project grant only if the Secretary is satisfied that—

(1) the project is consistent with plans (existing at the time the project is approved) of public agencies authorized by the State in which the airport is located to plan for the development of the area surrounding the airport;

(2) the project will contribute to carrying out this subchapter;

(3) enough money is available to pay the project costs that will not be paid by the United States Government under this subchapter;

(4) the project will be completed without unreasonable delay;

(5) the sponsor has authority to carry out the project as proposed;

(6) if the project is for an airport that has an airport master plan that includes the project, the master plan addresses issues relating to solid waste recycling at the airport, including—

(A) the feasibility of solid waste recycling at the airport;

(B) minimizing the generation of solid waste at the airport;

(C) operation and maintenance requirements;

(D) the review of waste management contracts; and

(E) the potential for cost savings or the generation of revenue; and

(7) if the project is at an airport that is listed as having an unclassified status under the most recent national plan of integrated airport systems (as described in section 47103), the project will be funded with an amount appropriated under section 47114(d)(2)(B) and is—

(A) for maintenance of the pavement of the primary runway;

(B) for obstruction removal for the primary runway;

(C) for the rehabilitation of the primary runway; or

(D) for a project that the Secretary considers necessary for the safe operation of the airport.

(b) AIRPORT DEVELOPMENT PROJECT GRANT APPLICATION APPROVAL.—The Secretary may approve an application under this subchapter for an airport development project grant for an airport only if the Secretary is satisfied that—

(1) the sponsor, a public agency, or the Government holds good title to the areas of the airport used or intended to be used for the landing, taking off, or surface maneuvering of aircraft, or that good title will be acquired;

(2) the interests of the community in or near which the project may be located have been given fair consideration; and

(3) the application provides touchdown zone and centerline runway lighting, high intensity runway lighting, or land necessary for installing approach light systems that the Secretary, considering the category of the airport and the kind and volume of traffic using it, decides is necessary for safe and efficient use of the airport by aircraft.

(c) ENVIRONMENTAL REQUIREMENTS.—(1) The Secretary may approve an application under this subchapter for an airport development project involving the location of an airport or runway or a major runway extension—

(A) only if the sponsor certifies to the Secretary that—

(i) an opportunity for a public hearing was given to consider the economic, social, and environmental effects of the location and the location's consistency with the objectives of any planning that the community has carried out;

(ii) the airport management board has voting representation from the communities in which the project is located or has advised the communities that they have the right to petition the Secretary about a proposed project; and

(iii) with respect to an airport development project involving the location of an airport, runway, or major runway extension at a medium or large hub airport, the airport sponsor has made available to and has provided upon request to the metropolitan planning organization in the area in which the airport is located, if any, a copy of the proposed amendment to the airport layout plan to depict the project and a copy of any airport master plan in which the project is described or depicted; and

(B) if the application is found to have a significant adverse effect on natural resources, including fish and wildlife, natural, scenic, and recreation assets, water and air quality, or another factor affecting the environment, only after finding that no possible and prudent alternative to the project exists and that every reasonable step has been taken to minimize the adverse effect.

(2) The Secretary may approve an application under this subchapter for an airport development project that does not involve the location of an airport or runway, or a major runway extension, at an existing airport without requiring an environmental impact statement related to noise for the project if—

(A) completing the project would allow operations at the airport involving aircraft complying with the noise standards prescribed for "stage 3" aircraft in section 36.1 of title 14, Code of Federal Regulations, to replace existing operations involving aircraft that do not comply with those standards; and

(B) the project meets the other requirements under this subchapter.

(3) At the Secretary's request, the sponsor shall give the Secretary a copy of the transcript of any hearing held under paragraph (1)(A) of this subsection.

(4) The Secretary may make a finding under paragraph (1)(B) of this subsection only after completely reviewing the matter. The review and finding must be a matter of public record.

(d) WITHHOLDING APPROVAL.—(1) The Secretary may withhold approval of an application under this subchapter for amounts apportioned under section 47114(c) and (e) of this title for violating an assurance or requirement of this subchapter only if—

(A) the Secretary provides the sponsor an opportunity for a hearing; and

(B) not later than 180 days after the later of the date of the application or the date the Secretary discovers the noncompliance, the Secretary finds that a violation has occurred.

(2) The 180-day period may be extended by—

(A) agreement between the Secretary and the sponsor; or

(B) the hearing officer if the officer decides an extension is necessary because the sponsor did not follow the schedule the officer established.

(3) A person adversely affected by an order of the Secretary withholding approval may obtain review of the order by filing a petition in the United States Court of Appeals for the District of Columbia Circuit or in the court of appeals of the United States for the circuit in which the project is located. The action must be brought not later than 60 days after the order is served on the petitioner.

(e) REPORTS RELATING TO CONSTRUCTION OF CERTAIN NEW HUB AIRPORTS.—At least 90 days prior to the approval under this subchapter of a project grant application for construction of a new hub airport that is expected to have 0.25 percent or more of the total annual enplanements in the United States, the Secretary shall submit to Congress a report analyzing the anticipated impact of such proposed new airport on—

(1) the fees charged to air carriers (including landing fees), and other costs that will be incurred by air carriers, for using the proposed airport;

(2) air transportation that will be provided in the geographic region of the proposed airport; and

(3) the availability and cost of providing air transportation to rural areas in such geographic region.

(f) COMPETITION PLANS.—

(1) PROHIBITION.—Beginning in fiscal year 2001, no passenger facility charge may be approved for a covered airport under section 40117 and no grant may be made under this subchapter for a covered airport unless the airport has submitted to the Secretary a written competition plan in accordance with this subsection.

(2) CONTENTS.—A competition plan under this subsection shall include information on the availability of airport gates and related facilities, leasing and sub-leasing arrangements, gate-use requirements, gate-assignment policy, financial constraints, airport controls over air- and ground-side capacity, and whether the airport intends to build or acquire gates that would be used as common facilities.

(3) SPECIAL RULE FOR FISCAL YEAR 2002.—This subsection does not apply to any passenger facility fee approved, or grant made, in fiscal year 2002 if the fee or grant is to be used to improve security at a covered airport.

(4) COVERED AIRPORT DEFINED.—In this subsection, the term "covered airport" means a commercial service airport—

(A) that has more than .25 percent of the total number of passenger boardings each year at all such airports; and

(B) at which one or two air carriers control more than 50 percent of the passenger boardings.

(g) CONSULTATION WITH SECRETARY OF HOMELAND SECURITY.—The Secretary shall consult with the Secretary of Homeland Security before approving an application under this subchapter for an airport development project grant for activities described in section 47102(3)(B)(ii) only as they relate to security equipment or section 47102(3)(B)(x) only as they relate to installation of bulk explosive detection system.

(h) EVALUATION OF AIRPORT MASTER PLANS.—When evaluating the master plan of an airport for purposes of this subchapter, the Secretary shall take into account—

(1) the role the airport plays with respect to medical emergencies and evacuations; and

(2) the role the airport plays in emergency or disaster preparedness in the community served by the airport.

(Pub. L. 103–272, §1(e), July 5, 1994, 108 Stat. 1254; Pub. L. 103–305, title I, §§108, 109, Aug. 23, 1994, 108 Stat. 1573; Pub. L. 106–181, title I, §155(b), Apr. 5, 2000, 114 Stat. 88; Pub. L. 107–71, title I, §123(a), Nov. 19, 2001, 115 Stat. 630; Pub. L. 107–296, title IV, §426(b), Nov. 25, 2002, 116 Stat. 2187; Pub. L. 108–176, title I, §187, title III, §305, Dec. 12, 2003, 117 Stat. 2518, 2539; Pub. L. 112–95, title I, §§111(c)(2)(A)(i), 133, 134, Feb. 14, 2012, 126 Stat. 18, 22; Pub. L. 115–254, div. B, title I, §§148(a), 149, Oct. 5, 2018, 132 Stat. 3214, 3215; Pub. L. 118–63, title VII, §712(c)(1), May 16, 2024, 138 Stat. 1256.)

§47107. PROJECT GRANT APPLICATION APPROVAL CONDITIONED ON ASSURANCES ABOUT AIRPORT OPERATIONS

(a) GENERAL WRITTEN ASSURANCES.—The Secretary of Transportation may approve a project grant application under this subchapter for an airport development project only if the Secretary receives written assurances, satisfactory to the Secretary, that—

(1) the airport will be available for public use on reasonable conditions and without unjust discrimination;

(2) air carriers making similar use of the airport will be subject to substantially comparable charges—

(A) for facilities directly and substantially related to providing air transportation; and

(B) regulations and conditions, except for differences based on reasonable classifications, such as between—

(i) tenants and nontenants; and

(ii) signatory and nonsignatory carriers;

(3) the airport operator will not withhold unreasonably the classification or status of tenant or signatory from an air carrier that assumes obligations substantially similar to those already imposed on air carriers of that classification or status;

(4) a person providing, or intending to provide, aeronautical services to the public will not be given an exclusive right to use the airport, with a right given to only one fixed-base operator to provide services at an airport deemed not to be an exclusive right if—

(A) the right would be unreasonably costly, burdensome, or impractical for more than one fixed-base operator to provide the services; and

(B) allowing more than one fixed-base operator to provide the services would require reducing the space leased under an existing agreement between the one fixed-base operator and the airport owner or operator;

(5) fixed-base operators similarly using the airport will be subject to the same charges;

(6) an air carrier using the airport may service itself or use any fixed-base operator allowed by the airport operator to service any carrier at the airport;

(7) the airport and facilities on or connected with the airport will be operated and maintained suitably, with consideration given to climatic and flood conditions;

(8) a proposal to close the airport temporarily for a nonaeronautical purpose must first be approved by the Secretary;

(9) appropriate action will be taken to ensure that terminal airspace required to protect instrument and visual operations to the airport (including operations at established minimum flight altitudes) will be cleared and protected by mitigating existing, and preventing future, airport hazards;

(10) appropriate action, including the adoption of zoning laws, has been or will be taken to the extent reasonable to restrict the use of land next to or near the airport to uses that are compatible with normal airport operations;

(11) each of the airport's facilities developed with financial assistance from the United States Government and each of the airport's facilities usable for the landing and taking off of aircraft always will be available without charge for use by Government aircraft in common with other aircraft, except that if the use is substantial, the Government may be charged a reasonable share, proportionate to the use, of the cost of operating and maintaining the facility used;

(12) the airport owner or operator will provide, without charge to the Government, property interests of the sponsor in land or water areas or buildings that the Secretary decides are desirable for, and that will be used for, constructing at Government expense, facilities for carrying out activities related to air traffic control or navigation;

(13) the airport owner or operator will maintain a schedule of charges for use of facilities and services at the airport—

(A) that will make the airport as self-sustaining as possible under the circumstances existing at the airport, including volume of traffic and economy of collection; and

(B) without including in the rate base used for the charges the Government's share of costs for any project for which a grant is made under this subchapter or was made under the Federal Airport Act or the Airport and Airway Development Act of 1970;

(14) the project accounts and records will be kept using a standard system of accounting that the Secretary, after consulting with appropriate public agencies, prescribes;

(15) the airport owner or operator will submit any annual or special airport financial and operations reports to the Secretary that the Secretary reasonably requests and make such reports available to the public;

(16) the airport owner or operator will maintain a current layout plan of the airport that meets the following requirements:

(A) the plan will be in a form the Secretary prescribes;

(B) subject to subsection (x), the Secretary will review and approve or disapprove the plan and any revision or modification of the plan before the plan, revision, or modification takes effect;

(C) the owner or operator will not make or allow any alteration in the airport or any of its facilities unless the alteration—

(i) is outside the scope of the Secretary's review and approval authority as set forth in subsection (x); or

(ii) complies with the portions of the plan approved by the Secretary; and

(D) when an alteration in the airport or its facility is made that is within the scope of the Secretary's review and approval authority as set forth in subparagraph (B), and does not conform with the portions of the plan approved by the Secretary, and the Secretary decides that the alteration adversely affects the safety, utility, or efficiency of aircraft operations, or of any property on or off the airport that is owned, leased, or financed by the Government, then the owner or operator will, if requested by the Secretary—

(i) eliminate the adverse effect in a way the Secretary approves; or

(ii) bear all cost of relocating the property or its replacement to a site acceptable to the Secretary and of restoring the property or its replacement to the level of safety, utility, efficiency, and cost of operation that existed before the alteration was made, except in the case of a relocation or replacement of an existing airport facility that meets the conditions of section 47110(d);

(17) if any phase of such project has received funds under this subchapter, each contract and subcontract for program management, construction management, planning studies, feasibility studies, architectural services, preliminary engineering, design, engineering, surveying, mapping, and related services will be awarded in the same way that a contract for architectural and engineering services is negotiated under chapter 11 of title 40 or an equivalent qualifications-based requirement prescribed for or by the sponsor;

(18) the airport and each airport record will be available for inspection by the Secretary on reasonable request, and a report of the airport budget will be available to the public at reasonable times and places;

(19) the airport owner or operator will submit to the Secretary and make available to the public an annual report listing in detail—

(A) all amounts paid by the airport to any other unit of government and the purposes for which each such payment was made; and

(B) all services and property provided to other units of government and the amount of compensation received for provision of each such service and property;

(20) the airport owner or operator will permit, to the maximum extent practicable, intercity buses or other modes of transportation to have access to the airport, but the sponsor does not have any obligation under this paragraph, or because of it, to fund special facilities for intercity bus service or for other modes of transportation;

(21) if the airport owner or operator and a person who owns an aircraft agree that a hangar is to be constructed at the airport for the aircraft at the aircraft owner's expense, the airport owner or operator will grant to the aircraft owner for the hangar a long-term lease that is subject to such terms and conditions on the hangar as the airport owner or operator may impose; and

(22) the airport owner or operator may not restrict or prohibit the sale or self-fueling of any 100-octane low lead aviation gasoline for purchase or use by operators of general aviation aircraft if such aviation gasoline was available at such airport at any time during calendar year 2022, until the earlier of—

(A) December 31, 2030; or

(B) the date on which the airport or any retail fuel seller at such airport makes available an unleaded aviation gasoline that—

(i) has been authorized for use by the Administrator of the Federal Aviation Administration as a replacement for 100-octane low lead aviation gasoline for use in nearly all piston-engine aircraft and engine models; and

(ii) meets either an industry consensus standard or other standard that facilitates the safe use, production, and distribution of such unleaded aviation gasoline, as determined appropriate by the Administrator.

(b) WRITTEN ASSURANCES ON USE OF REVENUE.—(1) The Secretary of Transportation may approve a project grant application under this subchapter for an airport development project only if the Secretary receives written assurances, satisfactory to the Secretary, that local taxes on aviation fuel (except taxes in effect on December 30, 1987) and the revenues generated by a public airport will be expended for the capital or operating costs of—

(A) the airport;

(B) the local airport system; or

(C) other local facilities owned or operated by the airport owner or operator and directly and substantially related to the air transportation of passengers or property.

(2) Paragraph (1) of this subsection does not apply if a provision enacted not later than September 2, 1982, in a law controlling financing by the airport owner or operator, or a covenant or assurance in a debt obligation issued not later than September 2, 1982, by the owner or operator, provides that the revenues, including local taxes on aviation fuel at public airports, from any of the facilities of the owner or operator, including the airport, be used to support not only the airport but also the general debt obligations or other facilities of the owner or operator.

(3) This subsection does not prevent the use of a State tax on aviation fuel to support a State aviation program or the use of airport revenue on or off the airport for a noise mitigation purpose.

(c) WRITTEN ASSURANCES ON ACQUIRING LAND.—(1) In this subsection, land is needed for an airport purpose (except a noise compatibility purpose) if—

(A)(i) the land may be needed for an aeronautical purpose (including runway protection zone) or serves as noise buffer land; and

(ii) revenue from interim uses of the land contributes to the financial self-sufficiency of the airport; and

(B) for land purchased with a grant the owner or operator received not later than December 30, 1987, the Secretary of Transportation or the department, agency, or instrumentality of the Government that made the grant was notified by the owner or operator of the use of the land and did not object to the use and the land is still being used for that purpose.

(2) The Secretary of Transportation may approve an application under this subchapter for an airport development project grant only if the Secretary receives written assurances,

satisfactory to the Secretary, that if an airport owner or operator has received or will receive a grant for acquiring land and—

(A) if the land was or will be acquired for a noise compatibility purpose (including land serving as a noise buffer either by being undeveloped or developed in a way that is compatible with using the land for noise buffering purposes)—

(i) the owner or operator will dispose of the land at fair market value at the earliest practicable time after the land no longer is needed for a noise compatibility purpose;

(ii) the disposition will be subject to retaining or reserving an interest in the land necessary to ensure that the land will be used in a way that is compatible with noise levels associated with operating the airport; and

(iii) the part of the proceeds from disposing of the land that is proportional to the Government's share of the cost of acquiring the land will be reinvested in another project at the airport or transferred to another airport as the Secretary prescribes under paragraph (4); or

(B) if the land was or will be acquired for an airport purpose (except a noise compatibility purpose)—

(i) the owner or operator, when the land no longer is needed for an airport purpose, will dispose of the land at fair market value or make available to the Secretary an amount equal to the Government's proportional share of the fair market value;

(ii) the disposition will be subject to retaining or reserving an interest in the land necessary to ensure that the land will be used in a way that is compatible with noise levels associated with operating the airport; and

(iii) the part of the proceeds from disposing of the land that is proportional to the Government's share of the cost of acquiring the land will be reinvested in another project at the airport or transferred to another airport as the Secretary prescribes under paragraph (4).

(3) Proceeds referred to in paragraph (2)(A)(iii) and (B)(iii) of this subsection and deposited in the Airport and Airway Trust Fund are available as provided in subsection (f) of this section.

(4) In approving the reinvestment or transfer of proceeds under paragraph (2)(A)(iii) or (2)(B)(iii), the Secretary shall give preference, in descending order, to the following actions:

(A) Reinvestment in an approved noise compatibility project.

(B) Reinvestment in an approved project that is eligible for funding under section 47117(e).

(C) Reinvestment in an approved airport development project that is eligible for funding under section 47114, 47115, or 47117.

(D) Transfer to a sponsor of another public airport to be reinvested in an approved noise compatibility project at that airport.

(E) Payment to the Secretary for deposit in the Airport and Airway Trust Fund established under section 9502 of the Internal Revenue Code of 1986.

(5)(A) A lease at fair market value by an airport owner or operator of land acquired for a noise compatibility purpose using a grant provided under this subchapter shall not be considered a disposal for purposes of paragraph (2).

(B) The airport owner or operator may use revenues from a lease described in subparagraph (A) for an approved airport development project that is eligible for funding under section 47114, 47115, or 47117.

(C) The Secretary shall coordinate with each airport owner or operator to ensure that leases described in subparagraph (A) are consistent with noise buffering purposes.

(D) The provisions of this paragraph apply to all land acquired before, on, or after the date of enactment of this paragraph.

(d) ASSURANCES OF CONTINUATION AS PUBLIC-USE AIRPORT.—The Secretary of Transportation may approve an application under this subchapter for an airport development project grant for a privately owned public-use airport only if the Secretary receives appropriate assurances that the airport will continue to function as a public-use airport during the economic life (that must be at least 10 years) of any facility at the airport that was developed with Government financial assistance under this subchapter.

(e) WRITTEN ASSURANCES OF OPPORTUNITIES FOR SMALL BUSINESS CONCERNS.—(1) The Secretary of Transportation may approve a project grant application under this subchapter for an airport development project only if the Secretary receives written assurances, satisfactory to the Secretary, that the airport owner or operator will take necessary action to ensure, to the maximum extent practicable, that at least 10 percent of all businesses at the airport selling consumer products or providing consumer services to the public are small business concerns (as defined by regulations of the Secretary) owned and controlled by a socially and economically disadvantaged individual (as defined in section 47113(a) of this title) or qualified HUBZone small business concerns (as defined in section 31(b) of the Small Business Act).

(2) An airport owner or operator may meet the percentage goal of paragraph (1) of this subsection by including any business operated through a management contract or subcontract. The dollar amount of a management contract or subcontract with a disadvantaged business enterprise shall be added to the total participation by disadvantaged business enterprises in airport concessions and to the base from which the airport's percentage goal is calculated. The dollar amount of a management contract or subcontract with a non-disadvantaged business enterprise and the gross revenue of business activities to which the management contract or subcontract pertains may not be added to this base.

(3) Except as provided in paragraph (4) of this subsection, an airport owner or operator may meet the percentage goal of paragraph (1) of this subsection by including the purchase from disadvantaged business enterprises of goods and services used in businesses conducted at the airport, but the owner or operator and the businesses conducted at the airport shall make good faith efforts to explore all available options to achieve, to the maximum extent practicable, compliance with the goal through direct ownership arrangements, including joint ventures and franchises.

(4)(A) In complying with paragraph (1) of this subsection, an airport owner or operator shall include the revenues of car rental firms at the airport in the base from which the percentage goal in paragraph (1) is calculated.

(B) An airport owner or operator may require a car rental firm to meet a requirement under paragraph (1) of this subsection by purchasing or leasing goods or services from a disadvantaged business enterprise. If an owner or operator requires such a purchase or lease, a car rental firm shall be permitted to meet the requirement by including purchases or leases of vehicles from any vendor that qualifies as a small business concern owned and controlled by a socially and economically disadvantaged individual or as a qualified HUBZone small business concern (as defined in section 31(b) of the Small Business Act).

(C) This subsection does not require a car rental firm to change its corporate structure to provide for direct ownership arrangements to meet the requirements of this subsection.

(5) This subsection does not preempt—

(A) a State or local law, regulation, or policy enacted by the governing body of an airport owner or operator; or

(B) the authority of a State or local government or airport owner or operator to adopt or enforce a law, regulation, or policy related to disadvantaged business enterprises.

(6) An airport owner or operator may provide opportunities for a small business concern owned and controlled by a socially and economically disadvantaged individual or a qualified HUBZone small business concern (as defined in section 31(b) of the Small Business Act) to participate through direct contractual agreement with that concern.

(7) An air carrier that provides passenger or property-carrying services or another business that conducts aeronautical activities at an airport may not be included in the percentage goal of paragraph (1) of this subsection for participation of small business concerns at the airport.

(8) Not later than April 29, 1993, the Secretary of Transportation shall prescribe regulations to carry out this subsection.

(f) AVAILABILITY OF AMOUNTS.—An amount deposited in the Airport and Airway Trust Fund under—

(1) subsection (c)(2)(A)(iii) of this section is available to the Secretary of Transportation to make a grant for airport development or airport planning under section 47104 of this title;

(2) subsection (c)(2)(B)(iii) of this section is available to the Secretary—

(A) to make a grant for a purpose described in section 47115(b) of this title; and

(B) for use under section 47114(d)(2) of this title at another airport in the State in which the land was disposed of under subsection (c)(2)(B)(ii) of this section; and

(3) subsection (c)(2)(B)(iii) of this section is in addition to an amount made available to the Secretary under section 48103 of this title and not subject to apportionment under section 47114 of this title.

(g) ENSURING COMPLIANCE.—(1) To ensure compliance with this section, the Secretary of Transportation—

(A) shall prescribe requirements for sponsors that the Secretary considers necessary; and

(B) may make a contract with a public agency.

(2) The Secretary of Transportation may approve an application for a project grant only if the Secretary is satisfied that the requirements prescribed under paragraph (1)(A) of this subsection have been or will be met.

(h) MODIFYING ASSURANCES AND REQUIRING COMPLIANCE WITH ADDITIONAL ASSURANCES.—

(1) IN GENERAL.—Subject to paragraph (2), before modifying an assurance required of a person receiving a grant under this subchapter and in effect after December 29, 1987, or to require compliance with an additional assurance from the person, the Secretary of Transportation must—

(A) publish notice of the proposed modification in the Federal Register; and

(B) provide an opportunity for comment on the proposal.

(2) PUBLIC NOTICE BEFORE WAIVER OF AERONAUTICAL LAND-USE ASSURANCE.—Before modifying an assurance under subsection (c)(2)(B) that requires any property to be used for an aeronautical purpose, the Secretary must provide notice to the public not less than 30 days before making such modification.

(i) RELIEF FROM OBLIGATION TO PROVIDE FREE SPACE.—When a sponsor provides a property interest in a land or water area or a building that the Secretary of Transportation uses to construct a facility at Government expense, the Secretary may relieve the sponsor from an obligation in a contract made under this chapter, the Airport and Airway Development Act of 1970, or the Federal Airport Act to provide free space to the Government in an airport building, to the extent the Secretary finds that the free space no longer is needed to carry out activities related to air traffic control or navigation.

(j) USE OF REVENUE IN HAWAII.—(1) In this subsection—

(A) "duty-free merchandise" and "duty-free sales enterprise" have the same meanings given those terms in section 555(b)(8) of the Tariff Act of 1930 (19 U.S.C. 1555(b)(8)).

(B) "highway" and "Federal-aid system" have the same meanings given those terms in section 101(a) of title 23.

(2) Notwithstanding subsection (b)(1) of this section, Hawaii may use, for a project for construction or reconstruction of a highway on a Federal-aid system that is not more than 10 miles by road from an airport and that will facilitate access to the airport, revenue from the sales at off-airport locations in Hawaii of duty-free merchandise under a contract between Hawaii and a duty-free sales enterprise. However, the revenue resulting during a Hawaiian fiscal year may be used only if the amount of the revenue, plus amounts Hawaii receives in the fiscal year from all other sources for costs Hawaii incurs for operating all airports it operates and for debt service related to capital projects for the airports (including interest and amortization of principal costs), is more than 150 percent of the projected costs for the fiscal year.

(3)(A) Revenue from sales referred to in paragraph (2) of this subsection in a Hawaiian fiscal year that Hawaii may use may not be more than the amount that is greater than 150 percent as determined under paragraph (2).

(B) The maximum amount of revenue Hawaii may use under paragraph (2) of this subsection is $250,000,000.

(4) If a fee imposed or collected for rent, landing, or service from an aircraft operator by an airport operated by Hawaii is increased during the period from May 4, 1990, through December 31, 1994, by more than the percentage change in the Consumer Price Index of All Urban Consumers for Honolulu, Hawaii, that the Secretary of Labor publishes during that period and if revenue derived from the fee increases because the fee increased, the amount under paragraph (3)(B) of this subsection shall be reduced by the amount of the projected revenue increase in the period less the part of the increase attributable to changes in the Index in the period.

(5) Hawaii shall determine costs, revenue, and projected revenue increases referred to in this subsection and shall submit the determinations to the Secretary of Transportation. A determination is approved unless the Secretary disapproves it not later than 30 days after it is submitted.

(6) Hawaii is not eligible for a grant under section 47115 of this title in a fiscal year in which Hawaii uses under paragraph (2) of this subsection revenue from sales referred to in paragraph (2). Hawaii shall repay amounts it receives in a fiscal year under a grant it is not eligible to receive because of this paragraph to the Secretary of Transportation for deposit in the discretionary fund established under section 47115.

(7)(A) This subsection applies only to revenue from sales referred to in paragraph (2) of this subsection from May 5, 1990, through December 30, 1994, and to amounts in the Airport Revenue Fund of Hawaii that are attributable to revenue before May 4, 1990, on sales referred to in paragraph (2).

(B) Revenue from sales referred to in paragraph (2) of this subsection from May 5, 1990, through December 30, 1994, may be used under paragraph (2) in any Hawaiian fiscal year, including a Hawaiian fiscal year beginning after December 31, 1994.

(k) POLICIES AND PROCEDURES TO ENSURE ENFORCEMENT AGAINST ILLEGAL DIVERSION OF AIRPORT REVENUE.—

(1) IN GENERAL.—Not later than 90 days after August 23, 1994, the Secretary of Transportation shall establish policies and procedures that will assure the prompt and effective enforcement of subsections (a)(13) and (b) of this section and grant assurances made under such subsections. Such policies and procedures shall recognize the exemption provision in subsection (b)(2) of this section and shall respond to the information contained in the reports of the Inspector General of the Department of Transportation on airport revenue diversion and such other relevant information as the Secretary may by law consider.

(2) REVENUE DIVERSION.—Policies and procedures to be established pursuant to paragraph (1) of this subsection shall prohibit, at a minimum, the diversion of airport revenues (except as authorized under subsection (b) of this section) through—

(A) direct payments or indirect payments, other than payments reflecting the value of services and facilities provided to the airport;

(B) use of airport revenues for general economic development, marketing, and promotional activities unrelated to airports or airport systems;

(C) payments in lieu of taxes or other assessments that exceed the value of services provided; or

(D) payments to compensate nonsponsoring governmental bodies for lost tax revenues exceeding stated tax rates.

(3) EFFORTS TO BE SELF-SUSTAINING.—With respect to subsection (a)(13) of this section, policies and procedures to be established pursuant to paragraph (1) of this subsection shall take into account, at a minimum, whether owners and operators of airports, when entering into new or revised agreements or otherwise establishing rates, charges, and fees, have undertaken reasonable efforts to make their particular airports as self-sustaining as possible under the circumstances existing at such airports.

(4) ADMINISTRATIVE SAFEGUARDS.—Policies and procedures to be established pursuant to paragraph (1) shall mandate internal controls, auditing requirements, and increased levels of Department of Transportation personnel sufficient to respond fully and promptly to complaints received regarding possible violations of subsections (a)(13) and (b) of this section and grant assurances made under such subsections and to alert the Secretary to such possible violations.

(5) STATUTE OF LIMITATIONS.—In addition to the statute of limitations specified in subsection (m)(7), with respect to project grants made under this chapter—

(A) any request by a sponsor or any other governmental entity to any airport for additional payments for services conducted off of the airport or for reimbursement for capital contributions or operating expenses shall be filed not later than 6 years after the date on which the expense is incurred; and

(B) any amount of airport funds that are used to make a payment or reimbursement as described in subparagraph (A) after the date specified in that subparagraph shall be considered to be an illegal diversion of airport revenues that is subject to subsection (m).

(l) AUDIT CERTIFICATION.—

(1) IN GENERAL.—The Secretary of Transportation, acting through the Administrator of the Federal Aviation Administration, shall include a provision in the compliance supplement provisions to require a recipient of a project grant (or any other recipient of Federal financial assistance that is provided for an airport) to include as part of an annual audit conducted under sections 7501 through 7505 of title 31, a review concerning the funding activities with respect to an airport that is the subject of the project grant (or other Federal financial assistance) and the sponsors, owners, or operators (or other recipients) involved.

(2) CONTENT OF REVIEW.—A review conducted under paragraph (1) shall provide reasonable assurances that funds paid or transferred to sponsors are paid or transferred in a manner consistent with the applicable requirements of this chapter and any other applicable provision of law (including regulations promulgated by the Secretary or the Administrator).

(m) RECOVERY OF ILLEGALLY DIVERTED FUNDS.—

(1) IN GENERAL.—Not later than 180 days after the issuance of an audit or any other report that identifies an illegal diversion of airport revenues (as determined under subsections (b) and (k) and section 47133), the Secretary, acting through the Administrator, shall—

(A) review the audit or report;

(B) perform appropriate factfinding; and

(C) conduct a hearing and render a final determination concerning whether the illegal diversion of airport revenues asserted in the audit or report occurred.

(2) NOTIFICATION.—Upon making such a finding, the Secretary, acting through the Administrator, shall provide written notification to the sponsor and the airport of—

(A) the finding; and

(B) the obligations of the sponsor to reimburse the airport involved under this paragraph.

(3) ADMINISTRATIVE ACTION.—The Secretary may withhold any amount from funds that would otherwise be made available to the sponsor, including funds that would otherwise be made available to a State, municipality, or political subdivision thereof (including any multimodal transportation agency or transit authority of which the sponsor is a member entity) as part of an apportionment or grant made available pursuant to this title, if the sponsor—

(A) receives notification that the sponsor is required to reimburse an airport; and

(B) has had an opportunity to reimburse the airport, but has failed to do so.

(4) CIVIL ACTION.—If a sponsor fails to pay an amount specified under paragraph (3) during the 180-day period beginning on the date of notification and the Secretary is unable to withhold a sufficient amount under paragraph (3), the Secretary, acting through the Administrator, may initiate a civil action under which the sponsor shall be liable for civil penalty in an amount equal to double the illegal diversion in question plus interest (as determined under subsection (n)).

(5) DISPOSITION OF PENALTIES.—

(A) AMOUNTS WITHHELD.—The Secretary or the Administrator shall transfer any amounts withheld under paragraph (3) to the Airport and Airway Trust Fund.

(B) CIVIL PENALTIES.—With respect to any amount collected by a court in a civil action under paragraph (4), the court shall cause to be transferred to the Airport and Airway Trust Fund any amount collected as a civil penalty under paragraph (4).

(6) REIMBURSEMENT.—The Secretary, acting through the Administrator, shall, as soon as practicable after any amount is collected from a sponsor under paragraph (4), cause to be transferred from the Airport and Airway Trust Fund to an airport affected by a diversion that is the subject of a civil action under paragraph (4), reimbursement in an amount equal to the amount that has been collected from the sponsor under paragraph (4) (including any amount of interest calculated under subsection (n)).

(7) STATUTE OF LIMITATIONS.—No person may bring an action for the recovery of funds illegally diverted in violation of this section (as determined under subsections (b) and (k)) or section 47133 after the date that is 6 years after the date on which the diversion occurred.

(n) INTEREST.—

(1) IN GENERAL.—Except as provided in paragraph (2), the Secretary, acting through the Administrator, shall charge a minimum annual rate of interest on the amount of any illegal diversion of revenues referred to in subsection (m) in an amount equal to double the average investment interest rate for tax and loan accounts of the Department of the Treasury (as determined by the Secretary of the Treasury) for the applicable calendar year, rounded to the nearest whole percentage point.

(2) ADJUSTMENT OF INTEREST RATES.—If, with respect to a calendar quarter, the average investment interest rate for tax and loan accounts of the Department of the Treasury exceeds the average investment interest rate for the immediately preceding calendar quarter, rounded to the nearest whole percentage point, the Secretary of the Treasury may adjust the interest rate charged under this subsection in a manner that reflects that change.

(3) ACCRUAL.—Interest assessed under subsection (m) shall accrue from the date of the actual illegal diversion of revenues referred to in subsection (m).

(4) DETERMINATION OF APPLICABLE RATE.—The applicable rate of interest charged under paragraph (1) shall—

(A) be the rate in effect on the date on which interest begins to accrue under paragraph (3); and

(B) remain at a rate fixed under subparagraph (A) during the duration of the indebtedness.

(o) PAYMENT BY AIRPORT TO SPONSOR.—If, in the course of an audit or other review conducted under this section, the Secretary or the Administrator determines that an airport owes a sponsor funds as a result of activities conducted by the sponsor or expenditures by the sponsor for the benefit of the airport, interest on that amount shall be determined in the same manner as provided in paragraphs (1) through (4) of subsection (n), except that the amount of any interest assessed under this subsection shall be determined from the date on which the Secretary or the Administrator makes that determination.

(p) Notwithstanding any written assurances prescribed in subsections (a) through (o), a general aviation airport with more than 300,000 annual operations may be exempt from having to accept scheduled passenger air carrier service, provided that the following conditions are met:

(1) No scheduled passenger air carrier has provided service at the airport within 5 years prior to January 1, 2002.

(2) The airport is located within or underneath the Class B airspace of an airport that maintains an airport operating certificate pursuant to section 44706 of title 49.

(3) The certificated airport operating under section 44706 of title 49 does not contribute to significant passenger delays as defined by DOT/FAA in the "Airport Capacity Benchmark Report 2001".

(q) An airport that meets the conditions of paragraphs (1) through (3) of subsection (p) is not subject to section 47524 of title 49 with respect to a prohibition on all scheduled passenger service.

(r) COMPETITION DISCLOSURE REQUIREMENT.—

(1) IN GENERAL.—The Secretary of Transportation may approve an application under this subchapter for an airport development project grant for a large hub airport or a medium hub airport only if the Secretary receives assurances that the airport sponsor will provide the information required by paragraph (2) at such time and in such form as the Secretary may require.

(2) COMPETITIVE ACCESS.—On February 1 and August 1 of each year, an airport that during the previous 6-month period has been unable to accommodate one or more requests by an air carrier for access to gates or other facilities at that airport in order to provide service to the airport or to expand service at the airport shall transmit a report to the Secretary that—

(A) describes the requests;

(B) provides an explanation as to why the requests could not be accommodated; and

(C) provides a time frame within which, if any, the airport will be able to accommodate the requests.

(3) SUNSET PROVISION.—This subsection shall cease to be effective beginning October 1, 2028.

(s) AGREEMENTS GRANTING THROUGH-THE-FENCE ACCESS TO GENERAL AVIATION AIRPORTS.—

(1) IN GENERAL.—Subject to paragraph (2), a sponsor of a general aviation airport shall not be considered to be in violation of this subtitle, or to be in violation of a grant assurance made under this section or under any other provision of law as a condition for the receipt of Federal financial assistance for airport development, solely because the sponsor enters into an agreement that grants to a person that owns residential real property adjacent to or near the airport access to the airfield of the airport for the

following:

    (A) Aircraft of the person.

    (B) Aircraft authorized by the person.

  (2) THROUGH-THE-FENCE AGREEMENTS.—

    (A) IN GENERAL.—An agreement described in paragraph (1) between an airport sponsor and a property owner (or an association representing such property owner) shall be a written agreement that prescribes the rights, responsibilities, charges, duration, and other terms the airport sponsor determines are necessary to establish and manage the airport sponsor's relationship with the property owner.

    (B) TERMS AND CONDITIONS.—An agreement described in paragraph (1) between an airport sponsor and a property owner (or an association representing such property owner) shall require the property owner, at minimum—

      (i) to pay airport access charges that, as determined by the airport sponsor, are comparable to those charged to tenants and operators on-airport making similar use of the airport;

      (ii) to bear the cost of building and maintaining the infrastructure that, as determined by the airport sponsor, is necessary to provide aircraft located on the property adjacent to or near the airport access to the airfield of the airport;

      (iii) to maintain the property for residential, noncommercial use for the duration of the agreement;

      (iv) to prohibit access to the airport from other properties through the property of the property owner; and

      (v) to prohibit any aircraft refueling from occurring on the property.

  (3) EXEMPTION.—The terms and conditions of paragraph (2) shall not apply to an agreement described in paragraph (1) made before the enactment of the FAA Modernization and Reform Act of 2012 (Public Law 112–95) that the Secretary determines does not comply with such terms and conditions but involves property that is subject to deed or lease restrictions that are considered perpetual and that cannot readily be brought into compliance. However, if the Secretary determines that the airport sponsor and residential property owners are able to make any modification to such an agreement on or after the date of enactment of this paragraph, the exemption provided by this paragraph shall no longer apply.

(t) RENEWAL OF CERTAIN LEASES.—

  (1) IN GENERAL.—Notwithstanding subsection (a)(13), an airport owner or operator who renews a covered lease shall not be treated as violating a written assurance requirement under this section as a result of such renewal.

  (2) COVERED LEASE DEFINED.—In this subsection, the term "covered lease" means a lease—

    (A) originally entered into before October 7, 2016;

    (B) under which a nominal lease rate is provided;

    (C) under which the lessee is a Federal or State government entity; and

    (D) that—

      (i) supports the operation of military aircraft by the Air Force or Air National Guard—

        (I) at the airport; or

(II) remotely from the airport; or

(ii) is for the use of nonaeronautical land or facilities of the airport by the National Guard.

(u) CONSTRUCTION OF RECREATIONAL AIRCRAFT.—

(1) IN GENERAL.—The construction of a covered aircraft shall be treated as an aeronautical activity for purposes of—

(A) determining an airport's compliance with a grant assurance made under this section or any other provision of law; and

(B) the receipt of Federal financial assistance for airport development.

(2) COVERED AIRCRAFT DEFINED.—In this subsection, the term "covered aircraft" means an aircraft—

(A) used or intended to be used exclusively for recreational purposes; and

(B) constructed or under construction by a private individual at a general aviation airport.

(v) COMMUNITY USE OF AIRPORT LAND.—

(1) IN GENERAL.—Notwithstanding subsections (a)(13), (b), and (c) and section 47133, and subject to paragraph (2), the sponsor of a public-use airport shall not be considered to be in violation of this subtitle, or to be found in violation of a grant assurance made under this section, or under any other provision of law, as a condition for the receipt of Federal financial assistance for airport development, solely because the sponsor has—

(A) entered into an agreement, including a revised agreement, with a local government providing for the use of airport property for an interim compatible recreational purpose at below fair market value; or

(B) permanently restricted the use of airport property to compatible recreational and public park use without paying or otherwise obtaining payment of fair market value for the property.

(2) RESTRICTIONS.—

(A) INTERIM COMPATIBLE RECREATIONAL PURPOSE.—Paragraph (1) shall apply, with respect to a sponsor that has taken the action described in subparagraph (A) of such paragraph, only—

(i) to an agreement regarding airport property that was initially entered into before the publication of the Federal Aviation Administration's Policy and Procedures Concerning the Use of Airport Revenue, dated February 16, 1999;

(ii) if the agreement between the sponsor and the local government is subordinate to any existing or future agreements between the sponsor and the Secretary, including agreements related to a grant assurance under this section;

(iii) to airport property that was purchased using funds from a Federal grant for acquiring land issued prior to January 1, 1989;

(iv) if the airport sponsor has provided a written statement to the Administrator that the property made available for a recreational purpose will not be needed for any aeronautical purpose during the next 10 years;

(v) if the agreement includes a term of not more than 2 years to prepare the airport property for the interim compatible recreational purpose and not more than 10 years of use for that purpose;

(vi) if the recreational purpose will not impact the aeronautical use of the airport;

(vii) if the airport sponsor provides a certification that the sponsor is not responsible for preparation, startup, operations, maintenance, or any other costs associated with the recreational purpose; and

(viii) if the recreational purpose is consistent with Federal land use compatibility criteria under section 47502.

(B) RECREATIONAL USE.—Paragraph (1) shall apply, with respect to a sponsor that has taken the action described in subparagraph (B) of such paragraph, only—

(i) to airport property that was purchased using funds from a Federal grant for acquiring land issued prior to January 1, 1989;

(ii) to airport property that has been continuously leased or licensed through a written agreement with a governmental entity or non-profit entity for recreational or public park uses since July 1, 2003;

(iii) if the airport sponsor has provided a written statement to the Administrator that the recreational or public park use does not impact the aeronautical use of the airport and that the property to be permanently restricted for recreational or public park use is not needed for any aeronautical use at the time the written statement is provided and is not expected to be needed for any aeronautical use at any time after such statement is provided;

(iv) if the airport sponsor provides a certification to the Administrator that the sponsor is not responsible for operations, maintenance, or any other costs associated with the recreational or public park use;

(v) if the recreational purpose is consistent with Federal land use compatibility criteria under section 47502; and

(vi) if the airport sponsor will—

(I) lease the property to a local government entity or non-profit entity to operate and maintain the property at no cost to the airport sponsor; or

(II) transfer title to the property to a local government entity subject to a permanent deed restriction ensuring compatible airport use under regulations issued pursuant to section 47502.

(3) REVENUE FROM CERTAIN SALES OF AIRPORT PROPERTY.—Notwithstanding any other provision of law, an airport sponsor leasing or selling a portion of airport property as described in paragraph (2)(B)(vi) may—

(A) lease or sell such portion of airport property for less than fair market value; and

(B) subject to the requirements of subsection (b), retain the revenue from the lease or sale of such portion of airport property for use in accordance with section 47133.

(4) SECRETARY REVIEW AND APPROVAL.—Notwithstanding any other provision of law, and subject to the sponsor providing a written statement certifying such sponsor meets the requirements under this subsection, no actions permitted under this subsection shall require the review or approval of the Secretary of Transportation.

(5) STATUTORY CONSTRUCTION.—Nothing in this subsection may be construed as permitting a diversion of airport revenue for the capital or operating costs associated with the community use of airport land.

(6) AERONAUTICAL USE; AERONAUTICAL PURPOSE DEFINED.—In this subsection, the terms "aeronautical use" and "aeronautical purpose"—

(A) mean all activities that involve or are directly related to the operation of aircraft, including activities that make the operation of aircraft possible and safe;

(B) include services located at an airport that are directly and substantially related to the movement of passengers, baggage, mail, and cargo; and

(C) do not include any uses of an airport that are not described in subparagraph (A) or (B), including any aviation-related uses that do not need to be located at an airport, such as flight kitchens and airline reservation centers.

(W) MOTHERS' ROOMS.—

(1) IN GENERAL.—The Secretary of Transportation may approve an application under this subchapter for an airport development project grant only if the Secretary receives written assurances that the airport owner or operator will maintain—

(A) a lactation area in the sterile area of each passenger terminal building of the airport; and

(B) a baby changing table in at least one men's and at least one women's restroom in each passenger terminal building of the airport.

(2) APPLICABILITY.—

(A) AIRPORT SIZE.—

(i) IN GENERAL.—The requirements in paragraph (1) shall only apply to applications submitted by the airport sponsor of—

(I) a medium or large hub airport in fiscal year 2021 and each fiscal year thereafter; and

(II) an applicable small hub airport in fiscal year 2023 and each fiscal year thereafter.

(ii) APPLICABLE SMALL HUB AIRPORT DEFINED.—In clause (i)(II), the term "applicable small hub airport" means an airport designated as a small hub airport during—

(I) the 3-year period consisting of 2020, 2021, and 2022; or

(II) any consecutive 3-year period beginning after 2020.

(B) PREEXISTING FACILITIES.—On application by an airport sponsor, the Secretary may determine that a lactation area in existence on October 5, 2018, complies with the requirement in paragraph (1)(A), notwithstanding the absence of one of the facilities or characteristics referred to in the definition of the term "lactation area" in this subsection.

(C) SPECIAL RULE.—The requirement in paragraph (1)(A) shall not apply with respect to a project grant application for a period of time, determined by the Secretary, if the Secretary determines that construction or maintenance activities make it impracticable or unsafe for the lactation area to be located in the sterile area of the building.

(3) DEFINITION.—In this section, the term—

(A) "lactation area" means a room or similar accommodation that—

(i) provides a location for members of the public to express breast milk that is shielded from view and free from intrusion from the public;

(ii) has a door that can be locked;

(iii) includes a place to sit, a table or other flat surface, a sink or sanitizing equipment, and an electrical outlet;

(iv) is readily accessible to and usable by individuals with disabilities, including individuals who use wheelchairs; and

(v) is not located in a restroom; and

(B) "sterile area" has the same meaning given that term in section 1540.5 of title 49, Code of Federal Regulations.

(x) SCOPE OF AIRPORT LAYOUT PLAN REVIEW AND APPROVAL AUTHORITY OF SECRETARY.—

(1) AUTHORITY OVER PROJECTS ON LAND ACQUIRED WITHOUT FEDERAL ASSISTANCE.—For purposes of subsection (a)(16)(B), with respect to any project proposed on land acquired by an airport owner or operator without Federal assistance, the Secretary may review and approve or disapprove only the portions of the plan (or any subsequent revision to the plan) that—

(A) materially impact the safe and efficient operation of aircraft at, to, or from the airport;

(B) adversely affect the safety of people or property on the ground as a result of aircraft operations; or

(C) adversely affect the value of prior Federal investments to a significant extent.

(2) LIMITATION ON NON-AERONAUTICAL REVIEW.—

(A) IN GENERAL.—The Secretary may not require an airport to seek approval for (including in the submission of an airport layout plan), or directly or indirectly regulate or place conditions on (including through any grant assurance), any project that is not subject to paragraph (1).

(B) REVIEW AND APPROVAL AUTHORITY.—If only a portion of a project proposed by an airport owner or operator is subject to the review and approval of the Secretary under subsection (a)(16)(B), the Secretary shall not extend review and approval authority to other non-aeronautical portions of the project.

(3) NOTICE.—

(A) IN GENERAL.—An airport owner or operator shall submit to the Secretary a notice of intent to proceed with a proposed project (or a portion thereof) that is outside of the review and approval authority of the Secretary, as described in this subsection, if the project was not on the most recently submitted airport layout plan of the airport.

(B) FAILURE TO OBJECT.—If not later than 45 days after receiving the notice of intent described in subparagraph (A), the Secretary fails to object to such notice, the proposed project (or portion thereof) shall be deemed as being outside the scope of the review and approval authority of the Secretary under subsection (a)(16)(B).

(y) UNIVERSAL CHANGING STATION.—

(1) IN GENERAL.—In fiscal year 2030 and each fiscal year thereafter, the Secretary of Transportation may approve an application under this subchapter for an airport development project grant only if the Secretary receives written assurances that the airport owner or operator will install or maintain (in compliance with the requirements of section 35.133 of title 28, Code of Federal Regulations), as applicable—

(A) at least 1 private, single-use room with a universal changing station that—

(i) meets the standards established under paragraph (2)(A); and

(ii) is accessible to all individuals for purposes of use by an individual with a disability in each passenger terminal building of the airport; and

(B) signage at or near the entrance to the changing station indicating the location of the changing station.

(2) STANDARDS REQUIRED.—Not later than 2 years after the date of enactment of this subsection, the United States Access Board shall—

(A) establish—

(i) comprehensive accessible design standards for universal changing tables; and

(ii) standards on the privacy, accessibility, and sanitation equipment of the room in which such table is located, required to be installed, or maintained under this subsection; and

(B) in establishing the standards under subparagraph (A), consult with entities with appropriate expertise relating to the use of universal changing stations used by individuals with disabilities.

(3) APPLICABILITY.—

(A) AIRPORT SIZE.—The requirement in paragraph (1) shall only apply to applications submitted by the airport sponsor of a medium or large hub airport.

(B) SPECIAL RULE.—The requirement in paragraph (1) shall not apply with respect to a project grant application for a period of time, determined by the Secretary, if the Secretary determines that construction or maintenance activities make it impracticable or unsafe for the universal changing station to be located in the sterile area of the building.

(4) EXCEPTION.—Upon application by an airport sponsor, the Secretary may determine that a universal changing station in existence before the date of enactment of the FAA Reauthorization Act of 2024, complies with the requirements of paragraph (1) (including the standards established under paragraph (2)(A)), notwithstanding the absence of 1 or more of the standards or characteristics required under such paragraph.

(5) DEFINITION.—In this section:

(A) DISABILITY.—The term "disability" has the meaning given that term in section 3 of the Americans with Disabilities Act of 1990 (42 U.S.C. 12102).

(B) STERILE AREA.—The term "sterile area" has the same meaning given that term in section 1540.5 of title 49, Code of Federal Regulations.

(C) UNIVERSAL CHANGING STATION.—The term "universal changing station" means a universal or adult changing station that meets the standards established by the United States Access Board under paragraph (2)(A).

(D) UNITED STATES ACCESS BOARD.—The term "United States Access Board" means the Architectural and Transportation Barriers Compliance Board established under section 502(a)(1) of the Rehabilitation Act of 1973 (29 U.S.C. 792(a)(1)).

(Pub. L. 103–272, §1(e), July 5, 1994, 108 Stat. 1256; Pub. L. 103–305, title I, §§111(a), (c), 112(a), Aug. 23, 1994, 108 Stat. 1573, 1574; Pub. L. 104–264, title I, §143, title VIII, §805(a), (b)(2), Oct. 9, 1996, 110 Stat. 3221, 3271, 3274; Pub. L. 104–287, §5(9), (80), Oct. 11, 1996, 110 Stat. 3389, 3397; Pub. L. 105–135, title VI, §604(h)(1), Dec. 2, 1997, 111 Stat. 2634; Pub. L. 106–181, title I, §125(a), Apr. 5, 2000, 114 Stat. 75; Pub. L. 107–217, §3(n)(7), Aug. 21, 2002, 116 Stat. 1303; Pub. L. 108–7, div. I, title III, §321(a), Feb. 20, 2003, 117 Stat. 411; Pub. L. 108–11, title II, §2702, Apr. 16, 2003, 117 Stat. 600; Pub. L. 108–176, title I, §§144, 164, 165, title IV, §424, Dec. 12, 2003, 117 Stat. 2503, 2513, 2514, 2554; Pub. L. 110–330, §5(e), Sept. 30, 2008, 122 Stat. 3718; Pub. L. 111–12, §5(d), Mar. 30, 2009, 123 Stat. 1458; Pub. L. 111–69, §5(e), Oct. 1, 2009, 123 Stat. 2055; Pub. L. 111–116, §5(d), Dec. 16, 2009, 123 Stat. 3032; Pub. L. 111–153, §5(d), Mar. 31, 2010, 124 Stat. 1085; Pub. L. 111–161, §5(d), Apr. 30, 2010, 124 Stat. 1127; Pub. L. 111–197, §5(d), July 2, 2010, 124 Stat. 1354; Pub. L. 111–216, title I, §104(d), Aug. 1, 2010, 124 Stat. 2349; Pub. L. 111–249, §5(e), Sept. 30, 2010, 124 Stat. 2628; Pub. L. 111–329, §5(d), Dec. 22, 2010, 124 Stat. 3567; Pub.

CHAPTER 471—AIRPORT DEVELOPMENT

L. 112–7, §5(d), Mar. 31, 2011, 125 Stat. 32; Pub. L. 112–16, §5(d), May 31, 2011, 125 Stat. 219; Pub. L. 112–21, §5(d), June 29, 2011, 125 Stat. 234; Pub. L. 112–27, §5(d), Aug. 5, 2011, 125 Stat. 271; Pub. L. 112–30, title II, §205(e), Sept. 16, 2011, 125 Stat. 358; Pub. L. 112–91, §5(e), Jan. 31, 2012, 126 Stat. 4; Pub. L. 112–95, title I, §§135, 136(a), title IV, §404, Feb. 14, 2012, 126 Stat. 22, 23, 85; Pub. L. 113–188, title XV, §1501(b)(1), (2)(A), Nov. 26, 2014, 128 Stat. 2023, 2024; Pub. L. 114–55, title I, §102(a), Sept. 30, 2015, 129 Stat. 523; Pub. L. 114–141, title I, §102(a), Mar. 30, 2016, 130 Stat. 323; Pub. L. 114–190, title I, §1102(a), July 15, 2016, 130 Stat. 617; Pub. L. 114–238, §1, Oct. 7, 2016, 130 Stat. 972; Pub. L. 115–63, title I, §102(a), Sept. 29, 2017, 131 Stat. 1169; Pub. L. 115–91, div. A, title XVII, §1701(a)(4)(G)(i), Dec. 12, 2017, 131 Stat. 1796; Pub. L. 115–141, div. M, title I, §102(a), Mar. 23, 2018, 132 Stat. 1046; Pub. L. 115–254, div. B, title I, §§131, 132(a), 163(d), 185, Oct. 5, 2018, 132 Stat. 3203–3205, 3224, 3234; Pub. L. 116–190, §2, Oct. 30, 2020, 134 Stat. 974; Pub. L. 118–15, div. B, title II, §2202(e), Sept. 30, 2023, 137 Stat. 83; Pub. L. 118–34, title I, §102(e), Dec. 26, 2023, 137 Stat. 1113; Pub. L. 118–41, title I, §102(e), Mar. 8, 2024, 138 Stat. 21; Pub. L. 118–63, title VII, §§703(a), 704–706, 743(b), 770(a), 774(a), May 16, 2024, 138 Stat. 1248, 1249, 1280, 1295, 1297.)

§47108. PROJECT GRANT AGREEMENTS

(a) OFFER AND ACCEPTANCE.—On approving a project grant application under this subchapter, the Secretary of Transportation shall offer the sponsor a grant to pay the United States Government's share of the project costs allowable under section 47110 of this title. The Secretary may impose terms on the offer that the Secretary considers necessary to carry out this subchapter and regulations prescribed under this subchapter. An offer shall state the obligations to be assumed by the sponsor and the maximum amount the Government will pay for the project from the amounts authorized under chapter 481 of this title (except sections 48102(e), 48106, 48107, and 48110). At the request of the sponsor, an offer of a grant for a project that will not be completed in one fiscal year shall provide for the obligation of amounts apportioned or to be apportioned to a sponsor under section 47114(c) or 47114(d)(2)(A) for the fiscal years necessary to pay the Government's share of the cost of the project. An offer that is accepted in writing by the sponsor is an agreement binding on the Government and the sponsor. The Government may pay or be obligated to pay a project cost only after a grant agreement for the project is signed.

(b) INCREASING GOVERNMENT SHARE.—

(1) IN GENERAL.—Except as provided in paragraph (2) or (3), the amount stated in an offer as the maximum amount the Government will pay may not be increased when the offer has been accepted in writing.

(2) EXCEPTION.—For a project receiving assistance under a grant approved under this chapter or chapter 475, the amount may be increased—

(A) for an airport development project, by not more than 15 percent; and

(B) to acquire an interest in land for an airport (except a primary airport), based on creditable appraisals at the time of the acquisition or a court award in a condemnation proceeding, by not more than the greater of—

(i) 15 percent; or

(ii) 25 percent of the total increase in allowable project costs attributable to acquiring an interest in land.

(3) PRICE ADJUSTMENT PROVISIONS.—

(A) IN GENERAL.—The Secretary may incorporate a provision in a project grant agreement under which the Secretary agrees to pay more than the maximum amount otherwise specified in the agreement if the Secretary finds that commodity or labor prices have increased since the agreement was made.

(B) DECREASE IN COSTS.—A provision incorporated in a project grant agreement under this paragraph shall ensure that the Secretary realizes any financial benefit associated with a decrease in material or labor costs for the project.

(c) CHANGING WORKSCOPE.—With the consent of the sponsor, the Secretary may amend a grant agreement made under this subchapter to change the workscope of a project financed under the grant if the amendment does not result in an increase in the maximum amount the Government may pay under subsection (b) of this section.

(d) CHANGE IN AIRPORT STATUS.—

(1) CHANGES TO NONPRIMARY AIRPORT STATUS.—If the status of a primary airport changes to a nonprimary airport at a time when a development project under a multiyear agreement under subsection (a) is not yet completed, the project shall remain eligible for funding from discretionary funds under section 47115 at the funding level and under the terms provided by the agreement, subject to the availability of funds.

(2) CHANGES TO NONCOMMERCIAL SERVICE AIRPORT STATUS.—If the status of a commercial service airport changes to a noncommercial service airport at a time when a terminal development project under a phased-funding arrangement is not yet completed, the project shall remain eligible for funding from discretionary funds under section 47115 at the funding level and under the terms provided by the arrangement subject to the availability of funds.

(3) CHANGES TO NONHUB PRIMARY STATUS.—If the status of a nonhub primary airport changes to a small hub primary airport at a time when the airport has received discretionary funds under this chapter for a terminal development project in accordance with section 47119(a), and the project is not yet completed, the project shall remain eligible for funding from the discretionary fund and the small airport fund to pay costs allowable under section 47119(a). Such project shall remain eligible for such funds for three fiscal years after the start of construction of the project, or if the Secretary determines that a further extension of eligibility is justified, until the project is completed.

(Pub. L. 103–272, §1(e), July 5, 1994, 108 Stat. 1262; Pub. L. 106–181, title I, §135(c), Apr. 5, 2000, 114 Stat. 84; Pub. L. 108–176, title I, §149(a), Dec. 12, 2003, 117 Stat. 2505; Pub. L. 109–115, div. A, title I, §176(a), Nov. 30, 2005, 119 Stat. 2427; Pub. L. 112–95, title I, §152(e)(2), Feb. 14, 2012, 126 Stat. 34; Pub. L. 118–63, title VII, §707, May 16, 2024, 138 Stat. 1251.)

§47109. UNITED STATES GOVERNMENT'S SHARE OF PROJECT COSTS

(a) GENERAL.—Except as otherwise provided in this section, the United States Government's share of allowable project costs is—

(1) 75 percent for a project at a medium or large hub airport;

(2) not more than 90 percent for a project funded by a grant issued to and administered by a State under section 47128, relating to the State block grant program;

(3) 90 percent for a project at any other airport;

(4) 70 percent for a project funded by the Administrator from the discretionary fund under section 47115 at an airport receiving an exemption under section 47134; and

(5) 95 percent for a project that—

(A) the Administrator determines is a successive phase of a multiphase construction project for which the sponsor received a grant in fiscal year 2011; and

    (B) for which the United States Government's share of allowable project costs would otherwise be capped at 90 percent under paragraph (2) or (3).

(b) INCREASED GOVERNMENT SHARE.—If, under subsection (a) of this section, the Government's share of allowable costs of a project in a State containing unappropriated and unreserved public lands and nontaxable Indian lands (individual and tribal) of more than 5 percent of the total area of all lands in the State, is less than the share applied on June 30, 1975, under section 17(b) of the Airport and Airway Development Act of 1970, the Government's share under subsection (a) of this section shall be increased by the lesser of—

    (1) 25 percent;

    (2) one-half of the percentage that the area of unappropriated and unreserved public lands and nontaxable Indian lands in the State is of the total area of the State; or

    (3) the percentage necessary to increase the Government's share to the percentage that applied on June 30, 1975, under section 17(b) of the Act.

(c) GRANDFATHER RULE.—

    (1) IN GENERAL.—In the case of any project approved after September 30, 2003, at a small hub airport or nonhub airport that is located in a State containing unappropriated and unreserved public lands and nontaxable Indian lands (individual and tribal) of more than 5 percent of the total area of all lands in the State, the Government's share of allowable costs of the project shall be increased by the same ratio as the basic share of allowable costs of a project divided into the increased (Public Lands States) share of allowable costs of a project as shown on documents of the Federal Aviation Administration dated August 3, 1979, at airports for which the general share was 80 percent on August 3, 1979. This subsection shall apply only if—

        (A) the State contained unappropriated and unreserved public lands and nontaxable Indian lands of more than 5 percent of the total area of all lands in the State on August 3, 1979; and

        (B) the application under subsection (b), does not increase the Government's share of allowable costs of the project.

    (2) The Government's share of allowable project costs determined under this subsection shall not exceed the lesser of 93.75 percent or the highest percentage Government share applicable to any project in any State under subsection (b), except that at a primary non-hub and non-primary commercial service airport located in a State as set forth in paragraph (1) of this subsection that is within 15 miles of another State as set forth in paragraph (1) of this subsection, the Government's share shall be an average of the Government share applicable to any project in each of the States.

(d) SPECIAL RULE FOR PRIVATELY OWNED RELIEVER AIRPORTS.—If a privately owned reliever airport contributes any lands, easements, or rights-of-way to carry out a project under this subchapter, the current fair market value of such lands, easements, or rights-of-way shall be credited toward the non-Federal share of allowable project costs.

(e) SPECIAL RULE FOR TRANSITION FROM SMALL HUB TO MEDIUM HUB STATUS.—If the status of a small hub airport changes to a medium hub airport, the Government's share of allowable project costs for the airport may not exceed 90 percent for the first 2 fiscal years after such change in hub status.

(f) SPECIAL RULE FOR ECONOMICALLY DISTRESSED COMMUNITIES.—The Government's share of allowable project costs shall be 95 percent for a project at an airport that—

 (1) is receiving essential air service for which compensation was provided to an air carrier under subchapter II of chapter 417; and

 (2) is located in an area that meets one or more of the criteria established in section 301(a) of the Public Works and Economic Development Act of 1965 (42 U.S.C. 3161(a)), as determined by the Secretary of Commerce.

 (g) SPECIAL RULE FOR COVERED EQUIPMENT.—

 (1) IN GENERAL.—The Government's share of allowable project costs for covered equipment and its installation shall be 100 percent.

 (2) DEFINITION OF COVERED EQUIPMENT.—For purposes of this subsection, the term "covered equipment" means aqueous film forming foam input-based testing equipment that is eligible for Airport Improvement Program funding based on Federal Aviation Administration PGL 21–01, titled "Extension of Eligibility for stand-alone acquisition of input-based testing equipment and truck modification", dated October 5, 2021 (or any other successor program guidance letter).

 (3) SUNSET.—The higher cost share authority established in this subsection shall terminate on the earlier of—

  (A) 180 days after the date on which the eligibility of covered equipment for Airport Improvement Program funding under the authority described in paragraph (2) terminates or is discontinued by the Administrator; or

  (B) 5 years after the date of enactment of this subsection.

 (h) SPECIAL RULE FOR FISCAL YEARS 2025 AND 2026.—Notwithstanding subsection (a), the Government's share of allowable project costs for a grant made to a nonhub or nonprimary airport in each of fiscal years 2025 and 2026 shall be 95 percent.

(Pub. L. 103–272, §1(e), July 5, 1994, 108 Stat. 1264; Pub. L. 103–305, title I, §114, Aug. 23, 1994, 108 Stat. 1579; Pub. L. 104–264, title I, §149(c), title XII, §1211, Oct. 9, 1996, 110 Stat. 3227, 3282; Pub. L. 106–181, title I, §126, Apr. 5, 2000, 114 Stat. 76; Pub. L. 107–71, title I, §119(a)(4), Nov. 19, 2001, 115 Stat. 629; Pub. L. 108–176, title I, §§162, 163, Dec. 12, 2003, 117 Stat. 2513; Pub. L. 112–95, title I, §137, Feb. 14, 2012, 126 Stat. 24; Pub. L. 113–235, div. K, title I, §119F, Dec. 16, 2014, 128 Stat. 2704; Pub. L. 115–31, div. K, title I, §119E, May 5, 2017, 131 Stat. 734; Pub. L. 115–254, div. B, title I, §134, Oct. 5, 2018, 132 Stat. 3209; Pub. L. 117–254, §2(a), Dec. 20, 2022, 136 Stat. 2361; Pub. L. 118–63, title VII, §708, May 16, 2024, 138 Stat. 1251.)

§47110. ALLOWABLE PROJECT COSTS

 (a) GENERAL AUTHORITY.—Except as provided in section 47111 of this title, the United States Government may pay or be obligated to pay, from amounts appropriated to carry out this subchapter, a cost incurred in carrying out a project under this subchapter only if the Secretary of Transportation decides the cost is allowable.

 (b) ALLOWABLE COST STANDARDS.—A project cost is allowable—

 (1)(A) if the cost necessarily is incurred in carrying out the project in compliance with the grant agreement made for the project under this subchapter, including any cost a sponsor incurs related to an audit the Secretary requires under section 47121(b) or (d) of this title and any cost of moving a Federal facility impeding the project if the rebuilt facility is of an equivalent size and type; or

  (B) if the cost is an incentive payment incurred in carrying out the project described in subparagraph (A) that is to be provided to a contractor upon early completion of a project, if—

   (i) such payment does not exceed the lesser of 5 percent of the initial construction contract amount or $1,000,000;

   (ii) the level of contractor's control of, or access to, the worksite necessary to shorten the duration of the project does not negatively impact the operation of the airport;

   (iii) the contract specifies application of the incentive structure in the event of unforeseeable, non-weather delays beyond the control of the contractor;

   (iv) nothing in any agreement with the contractor prevents the airport operator from retaining responsibility for the safety, efficiency, and capacity of the airport during the execution of the grant agreement; and

   (v) the Secretary determines that the use of an incentive payment is likely to increase airport capacity or efficiency or result in cost savings as a result of shortening the project's duration;

(2)(A) if the cost is incurred after the grant agreement is executed and is for airport development or airport planning carried out after the grant agreement is executed;

(B) if the cost is incurred after June 1, 1989, by the airport operator (regardless of when the grant agreement is executed) as part of a Government-approved noise compatibility program (including project formulation costs) and is consistent with all applicable statutory and administrative requirements;

(C) if the Government's share is paid only with amounts apportioned under paragraphs (1) and (2) of section 47114(c) or section 47114(d)(3)(A) [1] and if the cost is incurred—

   (i) after September 30, 1996;

   (ii) before a grant agreement is executed for the project; and

   (iii) in accordance with an airport layout plan approved by the Secretary and with all statutory and administrative requirements that would have been applicable to the project if the project had been carried out after the grant agreement had been executed; or

(D) if the cost is for airport development and is incurred before execution of the grant agreement, but in the same fiscal year as execution of the grant agreement, and if—

   (i) the cost was incurred before execution of the grant agreement because the airport has a shortened construction season due to climatic conditions in the vicinity of the airport;

   (ii) the cost is in accordance with an airport layout plan approved by the Secretary and with all statutory and administrative requirements that would have been applicable to the project if the project had been carried out after execution of the grant agreement, including submission of a complete grant application to the appropriate regional or district office of the Federal Aviation Administration;

   (iii) the sponsor notifies the Secretary before authorizing work to commence on the project;

   (iv) the sponsor has an alternative funding source available to fund the project; and

   (v) the sponsor's decision to proceed with the project in advance of execution of the grant agreement does not affect the priority assigned to the project by the Secretary for the allocation of discretionary funds;

(3) to the extent the cost is reasonable in amount;

(4) if the cost is not incurred in a project for airport development or airport planning for which other Government assistance has been granted;

(5) if the total costs allowed for the project are not more than the amount stated in the grant agreement as the maximum the Government will pay (except as provided in section 47108(b) of this title);

(6) if the cost is for a project not described in section 47102(3) for acquiring for use at a commercial service airport vehicles and ground support equipment owned by an airport that include low-emission technology, but only to the extent of the incremental cost of equipping such vehicles or equipment with low-emission technology, as determined by the Secretary; and

(7) if the cost is incurred on a measure to improve the efficiency of an airport building (such as a measure designed to meet one or more of the criteria for being considered a high-performance green building as set forth under section 401(13) of the Energy Independence and Security Act of 2007 (42 U.S.C. 17061(13))) and—

    (A) the measure is for a project for airport development;

    (B) the measure is for an airport building that is otherwise eligible for construction assistance under this subchapter; and

    (C) if the measure results in an increase in initial project costs, the increase is justified by expected savings over the life cycle of the project.

(c) CERTAIN PRIOR COSTS AS ALLOWABLE COSTS.—The Secretary may decide that a project cost under subsection (b)(2)(A) of this section incurred before the date the grant agreement is executed is allowable if it is—

(1) necessarily incurred in formulating or preparing for an airport development project, including costs incurred for field surveys, plans and specifications, property interests in land or airspace, utility relocation, work site preparation, and administration or other incidental items that would not have been incurred except for the project; or

(2) necessarily and directly incurred in developing the work scope of an airport planning project.

(d) RELOCATION OF AIRPORT-OWNED FACILITIES.—The Secretary may determine that the costs of relocating or replacing an airport-owned facility are allowable for an airport development project at an airport only if—

(1) the Government's share of such costs will be paid with funds apportioned to the airport sponsor under section 47114 or distributed from the small airport fund under section 47116;

(2) the Secretary determines that the relocation or replacement is required due to a change in the Secretary's design standards; and

(3) the Secretary determines that the change is beyond the control of the airport sponsor.

(e) LETTERS OF INTENT.—(1) The Secretary may issue a letter of intent to the sponsor stating an intention to obligate from future budget authority an amount, not more than the Government's share of allowable project costs, for an airport development project (including costs of formulating the project) at a primary or reliever airport. The letter shall establish a schedule under which the Secretary will reimburse the sponsor for the Government's share of allowable project costs, as amounts become available, if the sponsor, after the Secretary issues the letter, carries out the project without receiving amounts under this subchapter.

(2) Paragraph (1) of this subsection applies to a project—

(A) about which the sponsor notifies the Secretary, before the project begins, of the sponsor's intent to carry out the project;

(B) that will comply with all statutory and administrative requirements that would apply to the project if it were carried out with amounts made available under this subchapter; and

(C) that meets the criteria of section 47115(d) and, if for a project at a medium hub airport or large hub airport, the Secretary decides will enhance system-wide airport capacity significantly.

(3) A letter of intent issued under paragraph (1) of this subsection is not an obligation of the Government under section 1501 of title 31, and the letter is not deemed to be an administrative commitment for financing. An obligation or administrative commitment may be made only as amounts are provided in authorization and appropriation laws.

(4) The total estimated amount of future Government obligations covered by all outstanding letters of intent under paragraph (1) of this subsection may not be more than the amount authorized to carry out section 48103 of this title, less an amount reasonably estimated by the Secretary to be needed for grants under section 48103 that are not covered by a letter.

(5) LETTERS OF INTENT.—The Secretary may not require an eligible agency to impose a passenger facility charge under section 40117 in order to obtain a letter of intent under this section.

(6) LIMITATION ON STATUTORY CONSTRUCTION.—Nothing in this section shall be construed to prohibit the obligation of amounts pursuant to a letter of intent under this subsection in the same fiscal year as the letter of intent is issued.

(7) PARTNERSHIP PROGRAM AIRPORTS.—The Secretary may issue a letter of intent under this subsection to an airport sponsor with an approved application under section 47134(b) if—

(A) the application was approved in fiscal year 2019; and

(B) the project meets all other requirements set forth in this chapter.

(f) NONALLOWABLE COSTS.—Except as provided in subsection (d) of this section and section 47118(f) of this title, a cost is not an allowable airport development project cost if it is for—

(1) constructing a public parking facility for passenger automobiles;

(2) constructing, altering, or repairing part of an airport building, except to the extent the building will be used for facilities or activities directly related to the safety of individuals at the airport;

(3) decorative landscaping; or

(4) providing or installing sculpture or art works.

(g) USE OF DISCRETIONARY FUNDS.—A project for which cost reimbursement is provided under subsection (b)(2)(C) shall not receive priority consideration with respect to the use of discretionary funds made available under section 47115 of this title even if the amounts made available under paragraphs (1) and (2) of section 47114(c) or section 47114(d)(3)(A) are not sufficient to cover the Government's share of the cost of the project.

(h) NONPRIMARY AIRPORTS.—The Secretary may decide that the construction costs of revenue producing aeronautical support facilities are allowable for an airport development project at a nonprimary airport if the Government's share of such costs is paid only with funds apportioned to the airport sponsor under section 47114(c)(1)(D) or section 47114(d)(2)(A) and if the Secretary determines that the sponsor has made adequate provision for financing airside needs of the airport.

(i) SMALL AIRPORT LETTERS OF INTENT.—

(1) IN GENERAL.—The Secretary may issue a letter of intent to a sponsor stating an intention to obligate an amount from future budget authority for an airport development project (including costs of formulating the project) at a nonhub airport or an airport that is not a primary airport.

(2) CONTENTS.—In the letter issued under paragraph (1), the Secretary shall establish a schedule under which the Secretary will reimburse the sponsor for the Government's share of allowable project costs, as amounts become available, if the sponsor, after the Secretary issues the letter, carries out the project without receiving amounts under this subchapter.

(3) LIMITATIONS.—The amount the Secretary intends to obligate in a letter of intent issued under this subsection shall not exceed the larger of—

(A) the Government's share of allowable project costs; or

(B) $10,000,000.

(4) FINANCING.—Allowable project costs under paragraphs (1) and (2) may include costs associated with making payments for debt service on indebtedness incurred to carry out the project.

(5) REQUIREMENTS.—The Secretary shall issue a letter of intent under paragraph (1) only if—

(A) the sponsor notifies the Secretary, before the project begins, of the intent of the sponsor to carry out the project and requests a letter of intent; and

(B) the sponsor agrees to comply with all statutory and administrative requirements that would apply to the project if it were carried out with amounts made available under this subchapter.

(6) ASSESSMENT.—In reviewing a request for a letter of intent under this subsection, the Secretary shall consider the grant history of an airport, the enplanements or operations of an airport, and such other factors as the Secretary determines appropriate.

(7) PRIORITIZATION.—In issuing letters of intent under this subsection, the Secretary shall—

(A) prioritize projects that—

(i) cannot reasonably be funded by an airport sponsor using funds apportioned under section 47114(c), 47114(d)(2)(A), or 47114(d)(6), including funds apportioned under such sections in multiple fiscal years pursuant to section 47117(b)(1); and

(ii) are necessary to the continued safe operation or development of an airport; and

(B) structure the reimbursement schedules under such letters in a manner that minimizes unnecessary or undesirable project segmentation.

(8) NO OBLIGATION OR COMMITMENT.—

(A) IN GENERAL.—A letter of intent issued under this subsection is not an obligation of the Government under section 1501 of title 31, and the letter is not deemed to be an administrative commitment for financing.

(B) OBLIGATION OR COMMITMENT.—An obligation or administrative commitment may be made only as amounts are provided in authorization and appropriation Acts.

(9) LIMITATION ON STATUTORY CONSTRUCTION.—Nothing in this section shall be construed to prohibit the obligation of amounts pursuant to a letter of intent under this subsection in the same fiscal year as the letter of intent is issued.

(Pub. L. 103–272, §1(e), July 5, 1994, 108 Stat. 1264; Pub. L. 103–305, title I, §115, Aug. 23, 1994, 108 Stat. 1579; Pub. L. 103–429, §6(64), Oct. 31, 1994, 108 Stat. 4385; Pub. L. 104–264, title I, §144, Oct. 9, 1996, 110 Stat. 3222; Pub. L. 106–181, title I, §127, Apr. 5, 2000, 114 Stat. 76; Pub. L. 107–71, title I, §119(a)(2), Nov. 19, 2001, 115 Stat. 628; Pub. L. 108–176, title I, §§145, 149(b), 159(c), Dec. 12, 2003, 117 Stat. 2504, 2505, 2511; Pub. L. 109–115, div. A, title I, §176(b), Nov. 30, 2005, 119 Stat. 2427; Pub. L. 112–95, title I, §§111(c)(2)(A)(ii), 138, Feb. 14, 2012, 126 Stat. 18, 25; Pub. L. 115–254, div. B, title I, §184(b), title V, §539(n), Oct. 5, 2018, 132 Stat. 3234, 3371; Pub. L. 117–186, §2, Oct. 10, 2022, 136 Stat. 2199; Pub. L. 118–63, title VII, §§709–710(b)(1), May 16, 2024, 138 Stat. 1252, 1253.)

§47111. PAYMENTS UNDER PROJECT GRANT AGREEMENTS

(a) GENERAL AUTHORITY.—After making a project grant agreement under this subchapter and consulting with the sponsor, the Secretary of Transportation may decide when and in what amounts payments under the agreement will be made. Payments totaling not more than 90 percent of the United States Government's share of the project's estimated allowable costs may be made before the project is completed if the sponsor certifies to the Secretary that the total amount expended from the advance payments at any time will not be more than the cost of the airport development work completed on the project at that time.

(b) RECOVERING PAYMENTS.—If the Secretary determines that the total amount of payments made under a grant agreement under this subchapter is more than the Government's share of the total allowable project costs, the Government may recover the excess amount. If the Secretary finds that a project for which an advance payment was made has not been completed within a reasonable time, the Government may recover any part of the advance payment for which the Government received no benefit.

(c) PAYMENT DEPOSITS.—A payment under a project grant agreement under this subchapter may be made only to an official or depository designated by the sponsor and authorized by law to receive public money.

(d) WITHHOLDING PAYMENTS.—(1) The Secretary may withhold a payment under a grant agreement under this subchapter for more than 180 days after the payment is due only if the Secretary—

(A) notifies the sponsor and provides an opportunity for a hearing; and

(B) finds that the sponsor has violated the agreement.

(2) The 180-day period may be extended by—

(A) agreement of the Secretary and the sponsor; or

(B) the hearing officer if the officer decides an extension is necessary because the sponsor did not follow the schedule the officer established.

(3) A person adversely affected by an order of the Secretary withholding a payment may apply for review of the order by filing a petition in the United States Court of Appeals for the District of Columbia Circuit or in the court of appeals of the United States for the circuit in which the project is located. The petition must be filed not later than 60 days after the

order is served on the petitioner.

(e) ACTION ON GRANT ASSURANCES CONCERNING AIRPORT REVENUES.—If, after notice and opportunity for a hearing, the Secretary finds a violation of section 47107(b) of this title, as further defined by the Secretary under section 47107(k) of this title, or a violation of an assurance made under section 47107(b) of this title, and the Secretary has provided an opportunity for the airport sponsor to take corrective action to cure such violation, and such corrective action has not been taken within the period of time set by the Secretary, the Secretary shall withhold approval of any new grant application for funds under this chapter, or any proposed modification to an existing grant that would increase the amount of funds made available under this chapter to the airport sponsor, and withhold approval of any new application to impose a charge under section 40117 of this title. Such applications may thereafter be approved only upon a finding by the Secretary that such corrective action as the Secretary requires has been taken to address the violation and that the violation no longer exists.

(f) JUDICIAL ENFORCEMENT.—For any violation of this chapter or any grant assurance made under this chapter, the Secretary may apply to the district court of the United States for any district in which the violation occurred for enforcement. Such court shall have jurisdiction to enforce obedience thereto by a writ of injunction or other process, mandatory or otherwise, restraining any person from further violation.

(Pub. L. 103–272, §1(e), July 5, 1994, 108 Stat. 1266; Pub. L. 103–305, title I, §112(b), Aug. 23, 1994, 108 Stat. 1575; Pub. L. 113–188, title XV, §1501(b)(2)(C), Nov. 26, 2014, 128 Stat. 2024; Pub. L. 118–63, title XI, §1101(u), May 16, 2024, 138 Stat. 1414.)

§47112. CARRYING OUT AIRPORT DEVELOPMENT PROJECTS

(a) CONSTRUCTION WORK.—The Secretary of Transportation may inspect and approve construction work for an airport development project carried out under a grant agreement under this subchapter. The construction work must be carried out in compliance with regulations the Secretary prescribes. The regulations shall require the sponsor to make necessary cost and progress reports on the project. The regulations may amend or modify a contract related to the project only if the contract was made with actual notice of the regulations.

(b) PREVAILING WAGES.—A contract for more than $2,000 involving labor for an airport development project carried out under a grant agreement under this subchapter must require contractors to pay labor minimum wage rates as determined by the Secretary of Labor under sections 3141–3144, 3146, and 3147 of title 40. The minimum rates must be included in the bids for the work and in the invitation for those bids.

(c) VETERANS' PREFERENCE.—(1) In this subsection—

(A) "disabled veteran" has the same meaning given that term in section 2108 of title 5.

(B) "Vietnam-era veteran" means an individual who served on active duty (as defined in section 101 of title 38) in the armed forces for more than 180 consecutive days, any part of which occurred after August 4, 1964, and before May 8, 1975, and who was discharged or released from active duty in the armed forces under honorable conditions.

(C) "Afghanistan-Iraq war veteran" means an individual who served on active duty (as defined in section 101 of title 38) in the armed forces in support of Operation Enduring Freedom, Operation Iraqi Freedom, Operation New Dawn, Operation Inherent Resolve,

Operation Freedom's Sentinel, or any successor contingency operation to such operations for more than 180 consecutive days, any part of which occurred after September 11, 2001, and before the date prescribed by presidential proclamation or by law as the last day of Operation Enduring Freedom, Operation Iraqi Freedom, Operation New Dawn, Operation Inherent Resolve, Operation Freedom's Sentinel, or any successor contingency operation to such operations (whichever is later), and who was discharged or released from active duty in the armed forces under honorable conditions.

(D) "Persian Gulf veteran" means an individual who served on active duty in the armed forces in the Southwest Asia theater of operations during the Persian Gulf War for more than 180 consecutive days, any part of which occurred after August 2, 1990, and before the date prescribed by presidential proclamation or by law, and who was discharged or released from active duty in the armed forces under honorable conditions.

(2) A contract involving labor for carrying out an airport development project under a grant agreement under this subchapter must require that preference in the employment of labor (except in executive, administrative, and supervisory positions) be given to Vietnam-era veterans, Persian Gulf veterans, Afghanistan-Iraq war veterans, disabled veterans, and small business concerns (as defined in section 3 of the Small Business Act (15 U.S.C. 632)) owned and controlled by disabled veterans when they are available and qualified for the employment.

(Pub. L. 103–272, §1(e), July 5, 1994, 108 Stat. 1267; Pub. L. 107–217, §3(n)(8), Aug. 21, 2002, 116 Stat. 1303; Pub. L. 112–95, title I, §139, Feb. 14, 2012, 126 Stat. 26; Pub. L. 115–254, div. B, title I, §135, Oct. 5, 2018, 132 Stat. 3209.)

§47113. MINORITY AND DISADVANTAGED BUSINESS PARTICIPATION

(a) DEFINITIONS.—In this section—

(1) "small business concern"—

(A) has the meaning given the term in section 3 of the Small Business Act (15 U.S.C. 632); but

(B) in the case of a concern in the construction industry, a concern shall be considered a small business concern if the concern meets the size standard for the North American Industry Classification System Code 237310, as adjusted by the Small Business Administration;

(2) "socially and economically disadvantaged individual" has the same meaning given that term in section 8(d) of the Act (15 U.S.C. 637(d)) and relevant subcontracting regulations prescribed under section 8(d), except that women are presumed to be socially and economically disadvantaged; and

(3) the term "qualified HUBZone small business concern" has the meaning given that term in section 31(b) of the Small Business Act.

(b) GENERAL REQUIREMENT.—Except to the extent the Secretary decides otherwise, at least 10 percent of amounts available in a fiscal year under section 48103 of this title shall be expended with small business concerns owned and controlled by socially and economically disadvantaged individuals or qualified HUBZone small business concerns.

(c) UNIFORM CRITERIA.—The Secretary shall establish minimum uniform criteria for State governments and airport sponsors to use in certifying whether a small business concern qualifies under this section. The criteria shall include on-site visits, personal interviews, licenses, analyses of stock ownership and bonding capacity, listings of equipment and work completed, resumes of principal owners, financial capacity, and type of work preferred.

(d) SURVEYS AND LISTS.—Each State or airport sponsor annually shall survey and compile a list of small business concerns referred to in subsection (b) of this section and the location of each concern in the State.

(e) MANDATORY TRAINING PROGRAM.—

(1) IN GENERAL.—Not later than 1 year after the date of enactment of this subsection, the Secretary shall establish a mandatory training program for persons described in paragraph (3) to provide streamlined training on certifying whether a small business concern qualifies as a small business concern owned and controlled by socially and economically disadvantaged individuals under this section and section 47107(e).

(2) IMPLEMENTATION.—The training program may be implemented by one or more private entities approved by the Secretary.

(3) PARTICIPANTS.—A person referred to in paragraph (1) is an official or agent of an airport sponsor—

(A) who is required to provide a written assurance under this section or section 47107(e) that the airport owner or operator will meet the percentage goal of subsection (b) of this section or section 47107(e)(1), as the case may be; or

(B) who is responsible for determining whether or not a small business concern qualifies as a small business concern owned and controlled by socially and economically disadvantaged individuals under this section or section 47107(e).

(f) SUPPORTIVE SERVICES.—

(1) IN GENERAL.—The Secretary, in coordination with the Administrator of the Federal Aviation Administration, may, at the request of an airport sponsor, provide assistance under a grant issued under this subchapter to develop, conduct, and administer training programs and assistance programs in connection with any airport improvement project subject to part 26 of title 49, Code of Federal Regulations, for small business concerns referred to in subsection (b) to achieve proficiency to compete, on an equal basis for contracts and subcontracts related to such projects.

(2) ELIGIBLE ENTITIES.—An entity eligible to receive assistance under this section is—

(A) a State;

(B) a political subdivision of a State or local government;

(C) a Tribal government;

(D) an airport sponsor;

(E) a metropolitan planning organization;

(F) a group of entities described in subparagraphs (A) through (E); or

(G) any other organization considered appropriate by the Secretary.

(Pub. L. 103–272, §1(e), July 5, 1994, 108 Stat. 1268; Pub. L. 103–429, §6(65), Oct. 31, 1994, 108 Stat. 4386; Pub. L. 105–135, title VI, §604(h)(2), Dec. 2, 1997, 111 Stat. 2635; Pub. L. 112–95, title I, §140(b), Feb. 14, 2012, 126 Stat. 27; Pub. L. 115–91, div. A, title XVII, §1701(a)(4)(G)(ii), Dec. 12, 2017, 131 Stat. 1796; Pub. L. 115–254, div. B, title I, §150, title V, §539(o), Oct. 5, 2018, 132 Stat. 3215, 3371; Pub. L. 118–63, title VII, §730(b), May 16, 2024, 138 Stat. 1272.)

§47114. APPORTIONMENTS

(a) DEFINITION.—In this section, "amount subject to apportionment" means the amount newly made available under section 48103 of this title for a fiscal year.

(b) APPORTIONMENT DATE.—On the first day of each fiscal year, the Secretary of Transportation shall apportion the amount subject to apportionment for that fiscal year as provided in this section.

(c) AMOUNTS APPORTIONED TO SPONSORS.—

(1) PRIMARY AND COMMERCIAL SERVICE AIRPORTS.—

(A) PRIMARY AIRPORT APPORTIONMENT.—The Secretary shall apportion to the sponsor of each primary airport for each fiscal year an amount equal to—

(i) $15.60 for each of the first 50,000 passenger boardings at the airport during the prior calendar year;

(ii) $10.40 for each of the next 50,000 passenger boardings at the airport during the prior calendar year;

(iii) $5.20 for each of the next 400,000 passenger boardings at the airport during the prior calendar year;

(iv) $1.30 for each of the next 500,000 passenger boardings at the airport during the prior calendar year; and

(v) $1.00 for each additional passenger boarding at the airport during the prior calendar year.

(B) MINIMUM AND MAXIMUM APPORTIONMENTS.—Not less than $1,300,000 nor more than $22,000,000 may be apportioned under subparagraph (A) to an airport sponsor for a primary airport for each fiscal year.

(C) NEW AIRPORT.—Notwithstanding subparagraph (A), the Secretary shall apportion in the first fiscal year following the official opening of a new airport with scheduled passenger air transportation an amount equal to $1,300,000 to the sponsor of such airport.

(D) NONPRIMARY COMMERCIAL SERVICE AIRPORT APPORTIONMENT.—

(i) IN GENERAL.—The Secretary shall apportion to each commercial service airport that is not a primary airport an amount equal to—

(I) $60 for each of the first 2,500 passenger boardings at the airport during the prior calendar year; and

(II) $153.33 for each of the next 7,499 passenger boardings at the airport during the prior calendar year.

(ii) APPLICABILITY.—Paragraphs (4) and (5) of subsection (d) shall apply to funds apportioned under this subparagraph.

(E) PUBLIC AIRPORTS WITH MILITARY USE.—Notwithstanding any other provision of law, a public airport shall be considered a primary airport in each of fiscal years 2025 through 2028 for purposes of this chapter if such airport was—

(i) designated as a primary airport in fiscal year 2017; and

(ii) in use by an air reserve station in the calendar year used to calculate apportionments to airport sponsors in a fiscal year.

(F) SPECIAL RULE FOR FISCAL YEAR 2024.—Notwithstanding any other provision of this paragraph or the absence of scheduled passenger service at an airport, the Secretary shall apportion in fiscal year 2024 to the sponsor of an airport an amount based on the number of passenger boardings at the airport during whichever of the following years that would result in the highest apportioned amount under this paragraph:

    (i) Calendar year 2018.

    (ii) Calendar year 2019.

    (iii) The prior full calendar year prior to fiscal year 2024.

(2) CARGO AIRPORTS.—

    (A) APPORTIONMENT.—Subject to subparagraph (D), the Secretary shall apportion an amount equal to 4 percent of the amount subject to apportionment each fiscal year to the sponsors of airports served by aircraft providing air transportation of only cargo with a total annual landed weight of more than 25,000,000 pounds.

    (B) SUBALLOCATION FORMULA.—Any funds apportioned under subparagraph (A) to sponsors of airports described in subparagraph (A) shall be allocated among those airports in the proportion that the total annual landed weight of aircraft described in subparagraph (A) landing at each of those airports bears to the total annual landed weight of those aircraft landing at all those airports.

    (C) DISTRIBUTION TO OTHER AIRPORTS.—Before apportioning amounts to the sponsors of airports under subparagraph (A) for a fiscal year, the Secretary may set-aside a portion of such amounts for distribution to the sponsors of other airports, selected by the Secretary, that the Secretary finds will be served primarily by aircraft providing air transportation of only cargo.

    (D) DETERMINATION OF LANDED WEIGHT.—Landed weight under this paragraph is the landed weight of aircraft landing at each airport described in subparagraph (A) during the prior calendar year.

(d) AMOUNTS APPORTIONED FOR GENERAL AVIATION AIRPORTS.—

    (1) DEFINITIONS.—In this subsection, the following definitions apply:

    (A) AREA.—The term "area" includes land and water.

    (B) POPULATION.—The term "population" means the population stated in the latest decennial census of the United States.

    (2) APPORTIONMENT.—In any fiscal year in which the total amount made available under section 48103 is $3,200,000,000 or more, rather than making an apportionment under paragraph (2), the Secretary shall apportion 25 percent of the amount subject to apportionment for each fiscal year as follows:

    (A) To each airport, excluding commercial service airports but including reliever airports, in States the lesser of—

    (i) $150,000; or

    (ii) 1/5 of the most recently published estimate of the 5-year costs for airport improvement for the airport, as listed in the national plan of integrated airport systems developed by the Federal Aviation Administration under section 47103.

    (B) Any remaining amount to States as follows:

    (i) 0.62 percent of the remaining amount to Guam, American Samoa, the Commonwealth of the Northern Mariana Islands, and the Virgin Islands.

    (ii) Except as provided in paragraph (4), 49.69 percent of the remaining amount for airports, excluding commercial service airports but including reliever airports, in States not named in clause (i) in the proportion that the population of each of those States bears to the total population of all of those States.

(iii) Except as provided in paragraph (4), 49.69 percent of the remaining amount for airports, excluding commercial service airports but including reliever airports, in States not named in clause (i) in the proportion that the area of each of those States bears to the total area of all of those States.

(C) An airport that has previously been listed as unclassified under the national plan of integrated airport systems that has reestablished the classified status of such airport as of the date of apportionment shall be eligible to accrue apportionment funds pursuant to subparagraph (A) so long as such airport retains such classified status.

(3) AIRPORTS IN NONCONTIGUOUS STATES AND TERRITORIES.—

(A) ALASKA, PUERTO RICO, AND HAWAII.—An amount apportioned under this subsection to Alaska, Puerto Rico, or Hawaii for airports in such State may be made available by the Secretary for any public airport in those respective jurisdictions.

(B) OTHER TERRITORIES.—An amount apportioned under paragraph (2)(B)(i) may be made available by the Secretary for any public-use airport in Guam, American Samoa, the Northern Mariana Islands, or the Virgin Islands if the Secretary determines that there are insufficient qualified grant applications for projects at airports that are otherwise eligible for funding under that paragraph. The Secretary shall prioritize the use of such amounts in the territory the amount was originally apportioned in.

(4) USE OF STATE HIGHWAY SPECIFICATIONS.—The Secretary shall use the highway specifications of a State for airfield pavement construction and improvement using funds made available under this subsection or subsection (c)(1)(D) at nonprimary airports serving aircraft that do not exceed 60,000 pounds gross weight if—

(A) such State requests the use of such specifications; and

(B) the Secretary determines that—

(i) safety will not be negatively affected; and

(ii) the life of the pavement, with necessary maintenance and upkeep, will not be shorter than it would be if constructed using Administration standards.

(5) INTEGRATED AIRPORT SYSTEM PLANNING.—Notwithstanding any other provision of this section, funds made available under this subsection or subsection (c)(1)(D) may be used for integrated airport system planning that encompasses one or more primary airports.

(6) ELIGIBILITY TO RECEIVE PRIMARY AIRPORT MINIMUM APPORTIONMENT AMOUNT.—Notwithstanding any other provision of this subsection, the Secretary may apportion to an airport sponsor in a fiscal year an amount equal to the minimum apportionment available under subsection (c)(1)(B) if the Secretary finds that the airport—

(A) received scheduled or unscheduled air service from a large certificated air carrier (as defined in part 241 of title 14, Code of Federal Regulations, or such other regulations as may be issued by the Secretary under the authority of section 41709) in the calendar year used to calculate the apportionment; and

(B) had more than 10,000 passenger boardings in the calendar year used to calculate the apportionment.

(e) SUPPLEMENTAL APPORTIONMENT FOR ALASKA.—

(1) IN GENERAL.—Notwithstanding subsections (c) and (d) of this section, the

Secretary may apportion amounts for airports in Alaska in the way in which amounts were apportioned in the fiscal year ending September 30, 1980, under section 15(a) of the Act. However, in apportioning amounts for a fiscal year under this subsection, the Secretary shall apportion—

 (A) for each primary airport at least as much as would be apportioned for the airport under subsection (c)(1) of this section; and

 (B) a total amount at least equal to the minimum amount required to be apportioned to airports in Alaska in the fiscal year ending September 30, 1980, under section 15(a)(3)(A) of the Act.

(2) AUTHORITY FOR DISCRETIONARY GRANTS.—This subsection does not prohibit the Secretary from making project grants for airports in Alaska from the discretionary fund under section 47115 of this title.

(3) AIRPORTS ELIGIBLE FOR FUNDS.—An amount apportioned under this subsection may be used for any public airport in Alaska.

(4) SPECIAL RULE.—In any fiscal year in which the total amount made available under section 48103 is $3,200,000,000 or more, the amount that may be apportioned for airports in Alaska under paragraph (1) shall be increased by doubling the amount that would otherwise be apportioned.

(f) REDUCING APPORTIONMENTS.—

(1) IN GENERAL.—Subject to paragraph (3), an amount that would be apportioned under this section (except subsection (c)(2)) in a fiscal year to the sponsor of a medium or large hub airport for which a charge is imposed in the fiscal year under section 40117 of this title shall be reduced by an amount equal to—

 (A) in the case of a charge of $3.00 or less—

  (i) except as provided in clause (ii), 40 percent of the projected revenues from the charge in the fiscal year but not by more than 40 percent of the amount that otherwise would be apportioned under this section; or

  (ii) with respect to an airport in Hawaii, 40 percent of the projected revenues from the charge in the fiscal year but not by more than 40 percent of the excess of—

   (I) the amount that otherwise would be apportioned under this section; over

   (II) the amount equal to the amount specified in subclause (I) multiplied by the percentage of the total passenger boardings at the applicable airport that are comprised of interisland passengers; and

 (B) in the case of a charge of more than $3.00—

  (i) except as provided in clause (ii), 60 percent of the projected revenues from the charge in the fiscal year but not by more than 60 percent of the amount that otherwise would be apportioned under this section; or

  (ii) with respect to an airport in Hawaii, 60 percent of the projected revenues from the charge in the fiscal year but not by more than 60 percent of the excess of—

   (I) the amount that otherwise would be apportioned under this section; over

   (II) the amount equal to the amount specified in subclause (I) multiplied by the percentage of the total passenger boardings at the applicable airport that are comprised of interisland passengers.

(2) EFFECTIVE DATE OF REDUCTION.—

 (A) NEW CHARGE COLLECTION.—A reduction in an apportionment under paragraph

(1) shall not take effect until the first fiscal year following the year in which the collection of the charge imposed under section 40117 has begun.

(B) New categorization.—A reduction in an apportionment under paragraph (1) shall only be applied to an airport if such airport has been designated as a medium or large hub airport for 3 consecutive years.

(g) Supplemental Apportionment for Puerto Rico and United States Territories.—The Secretary shall apportion amounts for airports in Puerto Rico and all other United States territories in accordance with this section. This subsection does not prohibit the Secretary from making project grants for airports in Puerto Rico or other United States territories from the discretionary fund under section 47115.

(Pub. L. 103–272, §1(e), July 5, 1994, 108 Stat. 1268; Pub. L. 103–429, §6(66), Oct. 31, 1994, 108 Stat. 4386; Pub. L. 104–264, title I, §121, Oct. 9, 1996, 110 Stat. 3217; Pub. L. 106–181, title I, §§104(a)–(d), 105(c), Apr. 5, 2000, 114 Stat. 67–71; Pub. L. 108–176, title I, §§146, 147, Dec. 12, 2003, 117 Stat. 2504; Pub. L. 109–115, div. A, title I, §109, Nov. 30, 2005, 119 Stat. 2402; Pub. L. 112–95, title I, §§111(c)(2)(A)(iii), 141–143, Feb. 14, 2012, 126 Stat. 18, 28, 29; Pub. L. 114–190, title II, §2301, July 15, 2016, 130 Stat. 638; Pub. L. 115–63, title I, §102(b), Sept. 29, 2017, 131 Stat. 1169; Pub. L. 115–254, div. B, title I, §§136, 148(b), 151, 164, Oct. 5, 2018, 132 Stat. 3210, 3214, 3215, 3225; Pub. L. 116–260, div. L, title IV, §422, Dec. 27, 2020, 134 Stat. 1909; Pub. L. 118–15, div. B, title II, §2201(e), Sept. 30, 2023, 137 Stat. 82; Pub. L. 118–34, title I, §101(e), Dec. 26, 2023, 137 Stat. 1113; Pub. L. 118–41, title I, §101(e), Mar. 8, 2024, 138 Stat. 21; Pub. L. 118–63, title VII, §§712(a), (b), 713(a), May 16, 2024, 138 Stat. 1254, 1255, 1257.)

§47115. Discretionary fund

(a) Existence and Amounts in Fund.—The Secretary of Transportation has a discretionary fund. The fund consists of—

(1) amounts subject to apportionment for a fiscal year that are not apportioned under section 47114(c)–(e) of this title; and

(2) 12.5 percent of amounts not apportioned under section 47114 of this title because of section 47114(f).

(b) Availability of Amounts.—Subject to subsection (c) of this section and section 47117(e) of this title, the fund is available for making grants for any purpose for which amounts are made available under section 48103 of this title that the Secretary considers most appropriate to carry out this subchapter.

(c) Minimum Percentage for Primary and Reliever Airports.—At least 75 percent of the amount in the fund and distributed by the Secretary in a fiscal year shall be used for making grants—

(1) to preserve and enhance capacity, safety, and security at primary and reliever airports; and

(2) to carry out airport noise compatibility planning and programs at primary and reliever airports.

(d) Considerations.—

(1) For capacity enhancement projects.—In selecting a project for a grant to preserve and improve capacity funded in whole or in part from the fund, the Secretary shall consider—

(A) the effect that the project will have on overall national transportation system capacity;

(B) the benefit and cost of the project, including, in the case of a project at a reliever airport, the number of operations projected to be diverted from a primary airport to the reliever airport as a result of the project, as well as the cost savings projected to be realized by users of the local airport system;

(C) the financial commitment from non-United States Government sources to preserve or improve airport capacity;

(D) the airport improvement priorities of the States to the extent such priorities are not in conflict with subparagraphs (A) and (B);

(E) the projected growth in the number of passengers or aircraft that will be using the airport at which the project will be carried out; and

(F) the ability of the project to foster United States competitiveness in securing global air cargo activity at a United States airport.

(2) FOR ALL PROJECTS.—In selecting a project for a grant under this section, the Secretary shall consider among other factors whether—

(A) funding has been provided for all other projects qualifying for funding during the fiscal year under this chapter that have attained a higher score under the numerical priority system employed by the Secretary in administering the fund; and

(B) the sponsor will be able to commence the work identified in the project application in the fiscal year in which the grant is made or within 6 months after the grant is made, whichever is later.

(e) WAIVING PERCENTAGE REQUIREMENT.—If the Secretary decides the Secretary cannot comply with the percentage requirement of subsection (c) of this section in a fiscal year because there are insufficient qualified grant applications to meet that percentage, the amount the Secretary determines will not be distributed as required by subsection (c) is available for obligation during the fiscal year without regard to the requirement.

(f) CONSIDERATION OF DIVERSION OF REVENUES IN AWARDING DISCRETIONARY GRANTS.—

(1) GENERAL RULE.—Subject to paragraph (2), in deciding whether or not to distribute funds to an airport from the discretionary funds established by subsection (a) of this section and section 47116 of this title, the Secretary shall consider as a factor militating against the distribution of such funds to the airport the fact that the airport is using revenues generated by the airport or by local taxes on aviation fuel for purposes other than capital or operating costs of the airport or the local airports system or other local facilities which are owned or operated by the owner or operator of the airport and directly and substantially related to the actual air transportation of passengers or property.

(2) REQUIRED FINDING.—Paragraph (1) shall apply only when the Secretary finds that the amount of revenues used by the airport for purposes other than capital or operating costs in the airport's fiscal year preceding the date of the application for discretionary funds exceeds the amount of such revenues in the airport's first fiscal year ending after August 23, 1994, adjusted by the Secretary for changes in the Consumer Price Index of All Urban Consumers published by the Bureau of Labor Statistics of the Department of Labor.

(g) MINIMUM AMOUNT TO BE CREDITED.—

(1) GENERAL RULE.—In a fiscal year, there shall be credited to the fund, out of amounts made available under section 48103 of this title, an amount that is at least equal to the sum of—

(A) $148,000,000; plus

(B) the total amount required from the fund to carry out in the fiscal year letters of intent issued before January 1, 1996, under section 47110(e) of this title or the Airport and Airway Improvement Act of 1982.

The amount credited is exclusive of amounts that have been apportioned in a prior fiscal year under section 47114 of this title and that remain available for obligation.

(2) REDUCTION OF APPORTIONMENTS.—In a fiscal year in which the amount credited under subsection (a) is less than the minimum amount to be credited under paragraph (1), the total amount calculated under paragraph (3) shall be reduced by an amount that, when credited to the fund, together with the amount credited under subsection (a), equals such minimum amount.

(3) AMOUNT OF REDUCTION.—For a fiscal year, the total amount available to make a reduction to carry out paragraph (2) is the total of the amounts determined under sections 47114(c)(1)(A), 47114(c)(2), 47114(d), and 47117(e) of this title. Each amount shall be reduced by an equal percentage to achieve the reduction.

(h) PRIORITY FOR LETTERS OF INTENT.—In making grants in a fiscal year with funds made available under this section, the Secretary shall fulfill intentions to obligate under section 47110(e) prior to fulfilling intentions to obligate under section 47110(i).

(i) MARSHALL ISLANDS, MICRONESIA, AND PALAU.—For fiscal years 2024 through 2028, the sponsors of airports located in the Republic of the Marshall Islands, Federated States of Micronesia, and Republic of Palau shall be eligible for grants under this section and section 47116.

(j) AIRPORT SAFETY AND RESILIENT INFRASTRUCTURE DISCRETIONARY PROGRAM.—

(1) IN GENERAL.—The Secretary shall establish a program to provide grants, subject to the conditions of this subsection, for any purpose for which amounts are made available under section 48103 that the Secretary considers most appropriate to carry out this subchapter.

(2) TREATMENT OF GRANTS.—

(A) IN GENERAL.—A grant made under this subsection shall be treated as having been made pursuant to the Secretary's authority under section 47104(a) and from the Secretary's discretionary fund under subsection (a) of this section.

(B) EXCEPTION.—Except as otherwise provided in this subsection, grants made under this subsection shall not be subject to subsection (c), section 47117(e), or any other apportionment formula, special apportionment category, or minimum percentage set forth in this chapter.

(3) ELIGIBILITY AND PRIORITIZATION.—

(A) ELIGIBILITY.—The Secretary may provide grants under this subsection for an airport or terminal development project at any airport that is eligible to receive a grant from the discretionary fund under subsection (a) of this section.

(B) MINIMUM ALLOCATION.—Not less than 50 percent of the amounts available under this subsection shall be used to provide grants at nonprimary, nonhub, and small hub airports.

(C) PRIORITIZATION.—In making grants for projects eligible under subparagraph (D)(iii), the Secretary shall prioritize grants to large and medium hub airports.

(D) ELIGIBILITIES.—In making grants under this subsection, the Secretary shall provide grants to airports for projects that—

    (i) meet the definition of "airport development" under section 47102(3)(T);

    (ii) would otherwise increase the resilience of airport infrastructure against changing flooding or inundation patterns; or

    (iii) reduce runway incursions or increase runway or taxiway safety.

(4) AUTHORIZATION.—

    (A) IN GENERAL.—There is authorized to be appropriated to the Secretary to carry out this subsection the following amounts:

        (i) $532,392,074 for fiscal year 2024.

        (ii) $200,000,000 for fiscal year 2025.

        (iii) $200,000,000 for fiscal year 2026.

        (iv) $200,000,000 for fiscal year 2027.

        (v) $200,000,000 for fiscal year 2028.

    (B) AVAILABILITY.—Sums authorized to be appropriated under subparagraph (A) shall remain available for 3 fiscal years.

(k) PARTNERSHIP PROGRAM AIRPORTS.—

    (1) AUTHORITY.—The Secretary may make grants with funds made available under this section for an airport participating in the program under section 47134 if—

    (A) the Secretary has approved the application of an airport sponsor under section 47134(b) in fiscal year 2019; and

    (B) the grant will—

        (i) satisfy an obligation incurred by an airport sponsor under section 47110(e) or funded by a nonpublic sponsor for an airport development project on the airport; or

        (ii) provide partial Federal reimbursement for airport development (as defined in section 47102) on the airport layout plan initiated in the fiscal year in which the application was approved, or later, for over a period of not more than 10 years.

    (2) NONAPPLICABILITY OF CERTAIN SECTIONS.—Grants made under this subsection shall not be subject to—

    (A) subsection (c) of this section;

    (B) section 47117(e); or

    (C) any other apportionment formula, special apportionment category, or minimum percentage set forth in this chapter.

(l) SPECIAL CARRYOVER ASSUMPTION RULE.—Notwithstanding any other provision of law, in addition to amounts made available under paragraphs (1) and (2) of subsection (a), the Secretary may add to the discretionary fund an amount equal to one-third of the apportionment funds made available under section 47114 that were not required during the previous fiscal year pursuant to section 47117(b)(1) out of the anticipated amount of apportionment funds made available under section 47114 that will not be required during the current fiscal year pursuant to section 47117(b)(1).

(Pub. L. 103–272, §1(e), July 5, 1994, 108 Stat. 1270; Pub. L. 103–305, title I, §112(d), Aug. 23, 1994, 108 Stat. 1576; Pub. L. 103–429, §6(67), Oct. 31, 1994, 108 Stat. 4386; Pub. L. 104–264, title I, §§122, 145, Oct. 9, 1996, 110 Stat. 3218, 3222; Pub. L. 104–287, §5(81), Oct. 11, 1996, 110 Stat. 3397; Pub. L. 106–6, §§5, 8(a), Mar. 31, 1999, 113 Stat. 10, 11; Pub. L. 107–71, title I, §119(a)(3), Nov. 19, 2001, 115 Stat. 628; Pub. L. 108–176, title I, §§148, 188, Dec. 12, 2003, 117 Stat. 2504, 2519; Pub. L. 110–253, §3(c)(5), June 30, 2008, 122 Stat. 2418; Pub. L. 110–330, §5(f), Sept. 30, 2008, 122 Stat. 3718; Pub. L. 111–12, §5(e), Mar. 30, 2009, 123 Stat. 1458; Pub. L. 111–69, §5(f), Oct. 1, 2009, 123 Stat. 2055; Pub. L. 111–116, §5(e),

Dec. 16, 2009, 123 Stat. 3032; Pub. L. 111–153, §5(e), Mar. 31, 2010, 124 Stat. 1085; Pub. L. 111–161, §5(e), Apr. 30, 2010, 124 Stat. 1127; Pub. L. 111–197, §5(e), July 2, 2010, 124 Stat. 1354; Pub. L. 111–216, title I, §104(e), Aug. 1, 2010, 124 Stat. 2349; Pub. L. 111–249, §5(f), Sept. 30, 2010, 124 Stat. 2628; Pub. L. 111–329, §5(e), Dec. 22, 2010, 124 Stat. 3567; Pub. L. 112–7, §5(e), Mar. 31, 2011, 125 Stat. 32; Pub. L. 112–16, §5(e), May 31, 2011, 125 Stat. 219; Pub. L. 112–21, §5(e), June 29, 2011, 125 Stat. 234; Pub. L. 112–27, §5(e), Aug. 5, 2011, 125 Stat. 271; Pub. L. 112–30, title II, §205(f), Sept. 16, 2011, 125 Stat. 358; Pub. L. 112–91, §5(f), Jan. 31, 2012, 126 Stat. 4; Pub. L. 112–95, title I, §144, Feb. 14, 2012, 126 Stat. 29; Pub. L. 114–55, title I, §102(b), Sept. 30, 2015, 129 Stat. 523; Pub. L. 114–141, title I, §102(b), Mar. 30, 2016, 130 Stat. 323; Pub. L. 114–190, title I, §1102(b), July 15, 2016, 130 Stat. 617; Pub. L. 115–63, title I, §102(c), Sept. 29, 2017, 131 Stat. 1169; Pub. L. 115–141, div. M, title I, §102(b), Mar. 23, 2018, 132 Stat. 1046; Pub. L. 115–254, div. B, title I, §§117(a), 158, 184(a), Oct. 5, 2018, 132 Stat. 3201, 3219, 3234; Pub. L. 118–15, div. B, title II, §2202(f), (g), Sept. 30, 2023, 137 Stat. 83; Pub. L. 118–34, title I, §102(f), (g), Dec. 26, 2023, 137 Stat. 1113; Pub. L. 118–41, title I, §102(f), (g), Mar. 8, 2024, 138 Stat. 21; Pub. L. 118–63, title I, §104(b), title VII, §§710(b)(2), 714(a), 715, May 16, 2024, 138 Stat. 1034, 1253, 1257, 1258.)

§47116. SMALL AIRPORT FUND

(a) EXISTENCE AND AMOUNTS IN FUND.—The Secretary of Transportation has a small airport fund. The fund consists of 87.5 percent of amounts not apportioned under section 47114 of this title because of section 47114(f).

(b) DISTRIBUTION OF AMOUNTS.—The Secretary may distribute amounts in the fund in each fiscal year for any purpose for which amounts are made available under section 48103 of this title as follows:

(1) Not more than 25 percent for grants for projects at small hub airports.

(2) Not less than 25 percent for grants to sponsors of public-use airports (except commercial service airports).

(3) Not less than 50 percent for grants to sponsors of commercial service airports that are not larger than a nonhub airport.

(c) AUTHORITY TO RECEIVE GRANT NOT DEPENDENT ON PARTICIPATION IN BLOCK GRANT PILOT PROGRAM.—An airport in a State participating in the State block grant pilot program under section 47128 of this title may receive a grant under this section to the same extent the airport may receive a grant if the State were not participating in the program.

(d) PRIORITY CONSIDERATION FOR CERTAIN PROJECTS.—

(1) CONSTRUCTION OF NEW RUNWAYS.—In making grants to sponsors described in subsection (b)(2), the Secretary shall give priority consideration to multi-year projects for construction of new runways that the Secretary finds are cost beneficial and would increase capacity in a region of the United States.

(2) CONTROL TOWER CONSTRUCTION.—Notwithstanding section 47124(b)(4)(A), the Secretary may provide grants under this section to an airport sponsor participating in the contract tower program under section 47124 for the construction or improvement of a nonapproach control tower, as defined by the Secretary, and for the acquisition and installation of air traffic control, communications, and related equipment to be used in that tower. Such grants shall be subject to the distribution requirements of subsection (b) and the eligibility requirements of section 47124(b)(4)(B).

(e) GENERAL AVIATION TRANSIENT APRONS.—In distributing amounts from the fund described in subsection (a) to sponsors described in subsection [1] (b)(2) and (b)(3), 5 percent of each amount shall be used for projects to construct or rehabilitate aprons intended to be used for itinerant general aviation aircraft parking.

(Pub. L. 103–272, §1(e), July 5, 1994, 108 Stat. 1271; Pub. L. 104–264, title I, §146, Oct. 9, 1996, 110 Stat. 3223; Pub. L. 106–6, §8(b), Mar. 31, 1999, 113 Stat. 11; Pub. L. 106–181, title I, §128, Apr. 5, 2000, 114 Stat. 76; Pub. L. 108–176, title VIII, §801(b), Dec. 12, 2003, 117 Stat. 2587; Pub. L. 115–254, div. B, title I, §§152, 154, Oct. 5, 2018, 132 Stat. 3216, 3217; Pub. L. 118–63, title VII, §716, May 16, 2024, 138 Stat. 1259.)

> [1] So in original. Probably should be "subsections".

§47117. USE OF APPORTIONED AMOUNTS

(a) GRANT PURPOSE.—Except as provided in this section, an amount apportioned under section 47114(c)(1) or (d)(2) of this title is available for making grants for any purpose for which amounts are made available under section 48103 of this title.

(b) PERIOD OF AVAILABILITY.—

(1) IN GENERAL.—An amount apportioned under section 47114 of this title is available to be obligated for grants under the apportionment only during the fiscal year for which the amount was apportioned and the 2 fiscal years immediately after that year or the 3 fiscal years immediately following that year in the case of a nonhub airport or any airport that is not a commercial service airport. Except as provided in paragraph (2), if the amount is not obligated under the apportionment within that time, it shall be added to the discretionary fund.

(2) EXPIRED AMOUNTS APPORTIONED FOR GENERAL AVIATION AIRPORTS.—

(A) IN GENERAL.—Except as provided in subparagraph (B), if an amount apportioned under section 47114(d) is not obligated within the time specified in paragraph (1), that amount shall be added to the discretionary fund under section 47115 of this title, provided that—

(i) amounts made available under paragraph (2)(A) shall be used for grants for projects in accordance with section 47115(d)(2) at airports eligible to receive an apportionment under section 47114(d)(2); and

(ii) amounts made available under paragraph (2)(A) that are not obligated by July 1 of the fiscal year in which the funds will expire shall be made available for all projects in accordance with section 47115(d)(2).

(B) STATE BLOCK GRANT PROGRAM.—If an amount apportioned to an airport under section 47114(d)(2)(A) is not obligated within the time specified in paragraph (1), and the airport is located in a State participating in the State block grant program under section 47128, the amount shall be made available to that State under the same conditions as if the State had been apportioned the amount under section 47114(d)(2)(B).

(c) PRIMARY AIRPORTS.—(1) An amount apportioned to a sponsor of a primary airport under section 47114(c)(1) of this title is available for grants for any public-use airport of the sponsor included in the national plan of integrated airport systems.

(2) WAIVER.—A sponsor of an airport may make an agreement with the Secretary of Transportation waiving the sponsor's claim to any part of the amount apportioned for the airport under sections 47114(c) and 47114(d)(2)(A) if the Secretary agrees to make the waived amount available for a grant for another public-use airport in the same State or geographical area as the airport, as determined by the Secretary.

(d) STATE USE.—An amount apportioned to a State under—

(1) section 47114(d)(2)(B)(i) is available for grants for airports located in the State; and

(2) section 47114(d)(2)(B)(ii) or (iii) is available for grants for airports described in section 47114(d)(2)(B)(ii) or (iii) and located in the State.

(e) SPECIAL APPORTIONMENT CATEGORIES.—(1) The Secretary shall use amounts available to the discretionary fund under section 47115 of this title for each fiscal year as follows:

(A) At least 35 percent, but not more than $200,000,000, for grants for airport noise compatibility planning under section 47505(a)(2), for carrying out noise compatibility programs under section 47504(c), for noise mitigation projects approved in an environmental record of decision for an airport development project under this title, for airport development described in subparagraphs (O), (P), (Q), and (W) of section 47102(3), for airport development described in section 47102(3)(F), 47102(3)(K), or 47102(3)(L), and for water quality mitigation projects to comply with the Act of June 30, 1948 (33 U.S.C. 1251 et seq.), approved in an environmental record of decision for an airport development project under this title. The Secretary may count the amount of grants made for such planning and programs with funds apportioned under section 47114 in that fiscal year in determining whether or not the requirements of the preceding sentence are being met in that fiscal year. The Secretary shall provide not less than two-thirds of amounts under this subparagraph and paragraph (3) for grants to sponsors of small hub, medium hub, and large hub airports.

(B) At least 4 percent to sponsors of current or former military airports designated by the Secretary under section 47118(a) of this title for grants for developing current and former military airports to improve the capacity of the national air transportation system and to sponsors of noncommercial service airports for grants for operational and maintenance expenses at any such airport if the amount of such grants to the sponsor of the airport does not exceed $30,000 in that fiscal year, if the Secretary determines that the airport is adversely affected by the closure or realignment of a military base, and if the sponsor of the airport certifies that the airport would otherwise close if the airport does not receive the grant.

(2) If the Secretary decides that an amount required to be used for grants under paragraph (1) of this subsection cannot be used for a fiscal year because there are insufficient qualified grant applications, the amount the Secretary determines cannot be used is available during the fiscal year for grants for other airports or for other purposes for which amounts are authorized for grants under section 48103 of this title.

(3) SPECIAL RULE.—Beginning in fiscal year 2026, if the amount made available under paragraph (1)(A) was not equal to or greater than $150,000,000 in the preceding fiscal year, the Secretary shall issue grants for projects eligible under paragraph (1)(A) from apportionment funds made available under section 47114 that are not required during the fiscal year pursuant to subsection (b)(1) in an amount that is not less than—

(A) $150,000,000; minus

(B) the amount made available under paragraph (1)(A) in the preceding fiscal year.

(f) DISCRETIONARY USE OF APPORTIONMENTS.—

(1) IN GENERAL.—Subject to paragraph (2), if the Secretary finds that all or part of

an amount of an apportionment under section 47114 is not required during a fiscal year to fund a grant for which the apportionment may be used, the Secretary may use during such fiscal year the amount not so required to make grants for any purpose for which grants may be made under section 48103. The finding may be based on the notifications that the Secretary receives under section 47105(f) or on other information received from airport sponsors.

(2) Restoration of apportionments.—

(A) In general.—If the fiscal year for which a finding is made under paragraph (1) with respect to an apportionment is not the last fiscal year of availability of the apportionment under subsection (b), the Secretary shall restore to the apportionment an amount equal to the amount of the apportionment used under paragraph (1) for a discretionary grant whenever a sufficient amount is made available under section 48103.

(B) Period of availability.—If restoration under this paragraph is made in the fiscal year for which the finding is made or the succeeding fiscal year, the amount restored shall be subject to the original period of availability of the apportionment under subsection (b). If the restoration is made thereafter, the amount restored shall remain available in accordance with subsection (b) for the original period of availability of the apportionment plus the number of fiscal years during which a sufficient amount was not available for the restoration.

(3) Newly available amounts.—

(A) Restored amounts to be unavailable for discretionary grants.—Of an amount newly available under section 48103 of this title, an amount equal to the amounts restored under paragraph (2) shall not be available for discretionary grant obligations under section 47115.

(B) Use of remaining amounts.—Subparagraph (A) does not impair the Secretary's authority under paragraph (1), after a restoration under paragraph (2), to apply all or part of a restored amount that is not required to fund a grant under an apportionment to fund discretionary grants.

(4) Limitations on obligations apply.—Nothing in this subsection shall be construed to authorize the Secretary to incur grant obligations under section 47104 for a fiscal year in an amount greater than the amount made available under section 48103 for such obligations for such fiscal year.

(g) Limiting Authority of Secretary.—The authority of the Secretary to make grants during a fiscal year from amounts that were apportioned for a prior fiscal year and remain available for approved airport development project grants under subsection (b) of this section may be impaired only by a law enacted after September 3, 1982, that expressly limits that authority.

(Pub. L. 103–272, §1(e), July 5, 1994, 108 Stat. 1271; Pub. L. 103–305, title I, §116(a), Aug. 23, 1994, 108 Stat. 1579; Pub. L. 103–429, §6(68), Oct. 31, 1994, 108 Stat. 4387; Pub. L. 104–264, title I, §§123, 124(d), Oct. 9, 1996, 110 Stat. 3219, 3220; Pub. L. 104–287, §5(82), Oct. 11, 1996, 110 Stat. 3397; Pub. L. 105–102, §3(c)(1), (2), Nov. 20, 1997, 111 Stat. 2215; Pub. L. 106–6, §7, Mar. 31, 1999, 113 Stat. 10; Pub. L. 106–31, title VI, §6002(d), May 21, 1999, 113 Stat. 113; Pub. L. 106–181, title I, §§104(e)–(g), 129, title II, §231(f), Apr. 5, 2000, 114 Stat. 70, 77, 114; Pub. L. 108–176, title I, §§149(c), 150, 151, Dec. 12, 2003, 117 Stat. 2505, 2506; Pub. L. 112–95, title I, §145, Feb. 14, 2012, 126 Stat. 30; Pub. L. 115–254, div. B, title I, §§155, 192(b), title V, §539(p), Oct. 5, 2018, 132 Stat. 3217, 3241, 3371; Pub. L. 118–63, title VII, §717, May 16,

2024, 138 Stat. 1259.)

§47118. DESIGNATING CURRENT AND FORMER MILITARY AIRPORTS

(a) GENERAL REQUIREMENTS.—The Secretary of Transportation shall designate current or former military airports for which grants may be made under section 47117(e)(1)(B) of this title. The maximum number of airports bearing such designation at any time is 15. The Secretary may only so designate an airport (other than an airport so designated before August 24, 1994) if—

(1) the airport is a former military installation closed or realigned under—

(A) section 2687 of title 10;

(B) section 201 of the Defense Authorization Amendments and Base Closure and Realignment Act (10 U.S.C. 2687 note); or

(C) section 2905 of the Defense Base Closure and Realignment Act of 1990 (10 U.S.C. 2687 note);

(2) the airport is a military installation with both military and civil aircraft operations; or

(3) the airport is—

(A) a former military installation that, at any time after December 31, 1965, was owned and operated by the Department of Defense; and

(B) a nonhub primary airport.

(b) SURVEY.—Not later than September 30, 1991, the Secretary shall complete a survey of current and former military airports to identify which airports have the greatest potential to improve the capacity of the national air transportation system. The survey shall identify the capital development needs of those airports to make them part of the system and which of those qualify for grants under section 47104 of this title.

(c) CONSIDERATIONS.—In carrying out this section, the Secretary shall consider only current or former military airports for designation under this section if a grant under section 47117(e)(1)(B) would—

(1) reduce delays at an airport with more than 20,000 hours of annual delays in commercial passenger aircraft takeoffs and landings;

(2) enhance airport and air traffic control system capacity in a metropolitan area or reduce current and projected flight delays; or

(3) preserve or enhance minimum airfield infrastructure facilities at former military airports to support emergency diversionary operations for transoceanic flights in locations—

(A) within United States jurisdiction or control; and

(B) where there is a demonstrable lack of diversionary airports within the distance or flight-time required by regulations governing transoceanic flights.

(d) GRANTS.—Grants under section 47117(e)(1)(B) of this title may be made for an airport designated under subsection (a) of this section for the 5 fiscal years following the designation, and for subsequent periods, each not to exceed 5 fiscal years, if the Secretary determines that the airport satisfies the designation criteria under subsection (a) at the beginning of each such subsequent period.

(e) TERMINAL BUILDING FACILITIES.—From amounts the Secretary distributes to an airport under section 47115, $10,000,000 for each of fiscal years 2004 and 2005, and

$7,000,000 for each fiscal year thereafter, is available to the sponsor of a current or former military airport the Secretary designates under this section to construct, improve, or repair a terminal building facility, including terminal gates used for revenue passengers getting on or off aircraft. A gate constructed, improved, or repaired under this subsection—

(1) may not be leased for more than 10 years; and

(2) is not subject to majority in interest clauses.

(f) PARKING LOTS, FUEL FARMS, UTILITIES, HANGARS, AND AIR CARGO TERMINALS.—

(1) CONSTRUCTION.—From amounts the Secretary distributes to an airport under section 47115, $10,000,000 for each of fiscal years 2004 and 2005, and $7,000,000 for each fiscal year thereafter, is available to the sponsor of a current or former military airport the Secretary designates under this section to construct, improve, or repair airport surface parking lots, fuel farms, utilities, and hangars and air cargo terminals of an area that is 50,000 square feet or less.

(2) REIMBURSEMENT.—Upon approval of the Secretary, the sponsor of a current or former military airport the Secretary designates under this section may use an amount apportioned under section 47114, or made available under section 47115 or 47117(e)(1)(B), to the airport for reimbursement of costs incurred by the airport in fiscal years 2003 and 2004 for construction, improvement, or repair described in paragraph (1).

(g) DESIGNATION OF GENERAL AVIATION AIRPORTS.—Notwithstanding any other provision of this section, 3 of the airports bearing designations under subsection (a) may be general aviation airports that were former military installations closed or realigned under a section referred to in subsection (a)(1).

(h) SAFETY-CRITICAL AIRPORTS.—Notwithstanding any other provision of this chapter, a grant under section 47117(e)(1)(B) may be made for a federally owned airport designated under subsection (a) if the grant is for a project that is—

(1) to preserve or enhance minimum airfield infrastructure facilities described in subsection (c)(3); and

(2) necessary to meet the minimum safety and emergency operational requirements established under part 139 of title 14, Code of Federal Regulations.

(Pub. L. 103–272, §1(e), July 5, 1994, 108 Stat. 1273; Pub. L. 103–305, title I, §116(b)–(d), Aug. 23, 1994, 108 Stat. 1579; Pub. L. 104–264, title I, §124(a)–(c), Oct. 9, 1996, 110 Stat. 3219, 3220; Pub. L. 104–287, §5(83), Oct. 11, 1996, 110 Stat. 3397; Pub. L. 106–181, title I, §130, Apr. 5, 2000, 114 Stat. 78; Pub. L. 108–176, title I, §153, Dec. 12, 2003, 117 Stat. 2507; Pub. L. 112–95, title I, §146, Feb. 14, 2012, 126 Stat. 30; Pub. L. 115–254, div. B, title I, §137, Oct. 5, 2018, 132 Stat. 3210.)

§47119. TERMINAL DEVELOPMENT COSTS

(a) TERMINAL DEVELOPMENT PROJECTS.—

(1) IN GENERAL.—The Secretary of Transportation may approve a project for terminal development (including multimodal terminal development) in a nonrevenue-producing public-use area of a commercial service airport—

(A) if the sponsor certifies that the airport, on the date the grant application is submitted to the Secretary, has—

(i) all the safety equipment required for certification of the airport under section 44706;

(ii) all the security equipment required by regulation; and

(iii) provided for access by passengers to the area of the airport for boarding or exiting aircraft that are not air carrier aircraft;

(B) if the cost is directly related to—

(i) moving passengers and baggage in air commerce within the airport, including vehicles for moving passengers between terminal facilities and between terminal facilities and aircraft; or

(ii) installing security cameras in the public area of the interior and exterior of the terminal; and

(C) under terms necessary to protect the interests of the Government.

(2) PROJECT IN REVENUE-PRODUCING AREAS AND NONREVENUE-PRODUCING PARKING LOTS.—In making a decision under paragraph (1), the Secretary may approve as allowable costs the expenses of terminal development in a revenue-producing area and construction, reconstruction, repair, and improvement in a nonrevenue-producing parking lot if—

(A) except as provided in section 47108(e)(3), the airport does not have more than .05 percent of the total annual passenger boardings in the United States; and

(B) the sponsor certifies that any needed airport development project affecting safety, security, or capacity will not be deferred because of the Secretary's approval.

(3) LACTATION AREAS.—In addition to the projects described in paragraph (1), the Secretary may approve a project for terminal development for the construction or installation of a lactation area (as defined in section 47107(w)) at a commercial service airport.

(4) UNIVERSAL CHANGING STATIONS.—In addition to the projects described in paragraph (1), the Secretary may approve a project for terminal development for the construction or installation of a universal changing station (as defined in section 47107(y)) at a commercial service airport.

(b) REPAYING BORROWED MONEY.—

(1) TERMINAL DEVELOPMENT COSTS INCURRED AFTER JUNE 30, 1970, AND BEFORE JULY 12, 1976.—An amount apportioned under section 47114 and made available to the sponsor of a commercial service airport at which terminal development was carried out after June 30, 1970, and before July 12, 1976, is available to repay immediately money borrowed and used to pay the costs for such terminal development if those costs would be allowable project costs under section 47110(d) if they had been incurred after September 3, 1982.

(2) TERMINAL DEVELOPMENT COSTS INCURRED BETWEEN JANUARY 1, 1992, AND OCTOBER 31, 1992.—An amount apportioned under section 47114 and made available to the sponsor of a nonhub airport at which terminal development was carried out between January 1, 1992, and October 31, 1992, is available to repay immediately money borrowed and to pay the costs for such terminal development if those costs would be allowable project costs under section 47110(d).

(3) TERMINAL DEVELOPMENT COSTS AT PRIMARY AIRPORTS.—An amount apportioned under section 47114 or available under subsection (b)(3) to a primary airport—

(A) that was a nonhub airport in the most recent year used to calculate apportionments under section 47114;

(B) that is a designated airport under section 47118 in fiscal year 2003; and

(C) at which terminal development is carried out between January 2003 and August 2004,

is available to repay immediately money borrowed and used to pay the costs for such terminal development if those costs would be allowable project costs under subsection (a).

(4) CONDITIONS FOR GRANT.—An amount is available for a grant under this subsection only if—

(A) the sponsor submits the certification required under subsection (a);

(B) the Secretary decides that using the amount to repay the borrowed money will not defer an airport development project outside the terminal area at that airport; and

(C) amounts available for airport development under this subchapter will not be used for additional terminal development projects at the airport for at least 1 year beginning on the date the grant is used to repay the borrowed money.

(5) APPLICABILITY OF CERTAIN LIMITATIONS.—A grant under this subsection shall be subject to the limitations in subsections (c)(1) and (c)(2).

(c) AVAILABILITY OF AMOUNTS.—In a fiscal year, the Secretary may make available—

(1) to a sponsor of a primary airport, any part of amounts apportioned to the sponsor for the fiscal year under section 47114(c)(1) of this title to pay project costs allowable under subsection (a);

(2) on approval of the Secretary, not more than $200,000 of the amount that may be distributed for the fiscal year from the discretionary fund established under section 47115 of this title—

(A) to a sponsor of a nonprimary commercial service airport to pay project costs allowable under subsection (a); and

(B) to a sponsor of a reliever airport for the types of project costs allowable under subsection (a), including project costs allowable for a commercial service airport that each year does not have more than .05 percent of the total boardings in the United States;

(3) for use by a primary airport that each year does not have more than .05 percent of the total boardings in the United States, any part of amounts that may be distributed for the fiscal year from the discretionary fund and small airport fund to pay project costs allowable under subsection (a);

(4) not more than $25,000,000 to pay project costs allowable for the fiscal year under subsection (a) for projects at commercial service airports that were not eligible for assistance for terminal development during the fiscal year ending September 30, 1980, under section 20(b) of the Airport and Airway Development Act of 1970;

(5) to a sponsor of a nonprimary airport, any part of amounts apportioned to the sponsor for the fiscal year under sections 47114(c) and 47114(d)(2)(A) for project costs allowable under subsection (a); or

(6) not more than $20,000,000 of the amount that may be distributed for the fiscal year from the discretionary fund established under section 47115, to the sponsor of a nonprimary airport to pay costs allowable under subsection (a) for terminal development projects, if the Secretary determines (which may be based on actual and projected enplanement trends, as well as completion of an air service development study, demonstrated commitment by airlines to provide commercial service accommodating

at least 10,000 annual enplanements, the documented commitment of a sponsor to providing the remaining funding to complete the proposed project, and a favorable environmental finding (including all required permits) in support of the proposed project) that the status of the nonprimary airport is reasonably expected to change to primary status based on enplanements for the third calendar year after the issuance of the discretionary grant.

(d) NONHUB AIRPORTS.—With respect to a project at a commercial service airport which annually has less than 0.05 percent of the total enplanements in the United States, the Secretary may approve the use of the amounts described in subsection (a) notwithstanding the requirements of sections 47107(a)(17), 47112, and 47113.

(e) DETERMINATION OF PASSENGER BOARDING AT COMMERCIAL SERVICE AIRPORTS.—For the purpose of determining whether an amount may be distributed for a fiscal year from the discretionary fund in accordance with subsection (b)(2)(A) to a commercial service airport, the Secretary shall make the determination of whether or not a public airport is a commercial service airport on the basis of the number of passenger boardings and type of air service at the public airport in the calendar year that includes the first day of such fiscal year or the preceding calendar year, whichever is more beneficial to the airport.

(f) Limitation on Discretionary Funds.—The Secretary may distribute not more than $30,000,000 from the discretionary fund established under section 47115 for terminal development projects at a nonhub airport or a small hub airport that is eligible to receive discretionary funds under section 47108(e)(3).

(Pub. L. 103–272, §1(e), July 5, 1994, 108 Stat. 1274; Pub. L. 103–305, title I, §117, Aug. 23, 1994, 108 Stat. 1579; Pub. L. 103–429, §6(69), Oct. 31, 1994, 108 Stat. 4387; Pub. L. 106–181, title I, §152(b), Apr. 5, 2000, 114 Stat. 87; Pub. L. 108–176, title I, §§149(d), 166, Dec. 12, 2003, 117 Stat. 2505, 2514; Pub. L. 112–95, title I, §152(b), Feb. 14, 2012, 126 Stat. 33; Pub. L. 115–254, div. B, title I, §§132(b), 138, Oct. 5, 2018, 132 Stat. 3206, 3210; Pub. L. 118–63, title VII, §§718, 774(b), May 16, 2024, 138 Stat. 1260, 1298.)

§47120. GRANT PRIORITY

(a) IN GENERAL.—In making a grant under this subchapter, the Secretary of Transportation may give priority to a project that is consistent with an integrated airport system plan.

(b) DISCRETIONARY FUNDING TO BE USED FOR HIGHER PRIORITY PROJECTS.—The Administrator of the Federal Aviation Administration shall discourage airport sponsors and airports from using entitlement funds for lower priority projects by giving lower priority to discretionary projects submitted by airport sponsors and airports that have used entitlement funds for projects that have a lower priority than the projects for which discretionary funds are being requested.

(Pub. L. 103–272, §1(e), July 5, 1994, 108 Stat. 1274; Pub. L. 106–181, title I, §162, Apr. 5, 2000, 114 Stat. 91.)

§47121. RECORDS AND AUDITS

(a) RECORDS.—A sponsor shall keep the records the Secretary of Transportation requires. The Secretary may require records—

(1) that disclose—

(A) the amount and disposition by the sponsor of the proceeds of the grant;

(B) the total cost of the plan or program for which the grant is given or used; and

(C) the amounts and kinds of costs of the plan or program provided by other sources; and

(2) that make it easier to carry out an audit.

(b) AUDITS AND EXAMINATIONS.—The Secretary and the Comptroller General may audit and examine records of a sponsor that are related to a grant made under this subchapter.

(c) AUTHORITY OF COMPTROLLER GENERAL.—When an independent audit is made of the accounts of a sponsor under this subchapter related to the disposition of the proceeds of the grant or related to the plan or program for which the grant was given or used, the sponsor shall submit a certified copy of the audit to the Secretary not more than 6 months after the end of the fiscal year for which the audit was made. The Comptroller General may report to Congress describing the results of each audit conducted or reviewed by the Comptroller General under this section during the prior fiscal year.

(d) AUDIT REQUIREMENT.—The Secretary may require a sponsor to conduct an appropriate audit as a condition for receiving a grant under this subchapter.

(e) ANNUAL REVIEW.—The Secretary shall review annually the recordkeeping and reporting requirements under this subchapter to ensure that they are the minimum necessary to carry out this subchapter.

(f) WITHHOLDING INFORMATION FROM CONGRESS.—This section does not authorize the Secretary or the Comptroller General to withhold information from a committee of Congress authorized to have the information.

(Pub. L. 103–272, §1(e), July 5, 1994, 108 Stat. 1274; Pub. L. 104–316, title I, §127(f), Oct. 19, 1996, 110 Stat. 3840.)

§47122. ADMINISTRATIVE

(a) GENERAL.—The Secretary of Transportation may take action the Secretary considers necessary to carry out this subchapter, including conducting investigations and public hearings, prescribing regulations and procedures, and issuing orders.

(b) CONDUCTING INVESTIGATIONS AND PUBLIC HEARINGS.—In conducting an investigation or public hearing under this subchapter, the Secretary has the same authority the Secretary has under section 46104 of this title. An action of the Secretary in exercising that authority is governed by the procedures specified in section 46104 and shall be enforced as provided in section 46104.

(Pub. L. 103–272, §1(e), July 5, 1994, 108 Stat. 1275.)

§47123. NONDISCRIMINATION

(a) IN GENERAL.—The Secretary of Transportation shall take affirmative action to ensure that an individual is not excluded because of race, creed, color, national origin, or sex from participating in an activity carried out with money received under a grant under this subchapter. The Secretary shall prescribe regulations necessary to carry out this section. The regulations shall be similar to those in effect under title VI of the Civil Rights Act of 1964 (42 U.S.C. 2000d et seq.). This section is in addition to title VI of the Act.

(b) INDIAN EMPLOYMENT.—

(1) TRIBAL SPONSOR PREFERENCE.—Consistent with section 703(i) of the Civil Rights Act of 1964 (42 U.S.C. 2000e–2(i)), nothing in this section shall preclude the preferential

employment of Indians living on or near a reservation on a project or contract at—

(A) an airport sponsored by an Indian tribal government; or

(B) an airport located on an Indian reservation.

(2) STATE PREFERENCE.—A State may implement a preference for employment of Indians on a project carried out under this subchapter near an Indian reservation.

(3) IMPLEMENTATION.—The Secretary shall consult with Indian tribal governments and cooperate with the States to implement this subsection.

(4) INDIAN TRIBAL GOVERNMENT DEFINED.—In this section, the term "Indian tribal government" has the same meaning given that term in section 102 of the Robert T. Stafford Disaster Relief and Emergency Assistance Act (42 U.S.C. 5122).

(Pub. L. 103–272, §1(e), July 5, 1994, 108 Stat. 1275; Pub. L. 115–254, div. B, title I, §153, Oct. 5, 2018, 132 Stat. 3216.)

§47124. AGREEMENTS FOR STATE AND LOCAL OPERATION OF AIRPORT FACILITIES

(a) GOVERNMENT RELIEF FROM LIABILITY.—The Secretary of Transportation shall ensure that an agreement under this subchapter with a qualified entity (as determined by the Secretary), State, or a political subdivision of a State to allow the entity, State, or subdivision to operate an airport facility relieves the United States Government from any liability arising out of, or related to, acts or omissions of employees of the entity, State, or subdivision in operating the airport facility.

(b) AIR TRAFFIC CONTROL CONTRACT PROGRAM.—

(1) CONTRACT TOWER PROGRAM.—

(A) CONTINUATION.—The Secretary shall continue the low activity (Visual Flight Rules) level I air traffic control tower contract program established under subsection (a) of this section for towers existing on December 30, 1987, and extend the program to other towers as practicable.

(B) SPECIAL RULE.—If the Secretary determines that a tower already operating under the Contract Tower Program has a benefit-to-cost ratio of less than 1.0, the airport sponsor or State or local government having jurisdiction over the airport shall not be required to pay the portion of the costs that exceeds the benefit—

(i) for the 1-year period after such determination is made; or

(ii) if an appeal of such determination is requested, for the 1-year period described in subsection (d)(4)(D).

(C) USE OF EXCESS FUNDS.—If the Secretary finds that all or part of an amount made available to carry out the program continued under this paragraph is not required during a fiscal year, the Secretary may use, during such fiscal year, the amount not so required to carry out the Cost-share Program.

(2) GENERAL AUTHORITY.—

(A) IN GENERAL.—The Secretary may make a contract with a qualified entity (as determined by the Secretary) or, on a sole source basis, with a State or a political subdivision of a State to allow the entity, State, or subdivision to operate an airport traffic control tower classified as a level I (Visual Flight Rules) tower if the Secretary decides that the entity, State, or subdivision has the capability to comply with the requirements of this paragraph. The contract shall require that the entity, State, or subdivision comply with applicable safety regulations in operating the facility and with applicable competition requirements in making a subcontract to perform work to carry out the contract.

(B) SMALL OR MEDIUM HUB AIRPORTS.—In the case of a contract entered into on or after the date of enactment of this subparagraph to operate an airport traffic control tower at a small or medium hub airport, the contract shall require the Secretary, after coordination with the airport sponsor and the entity, State, or subdivision, and not later than 18 months after the date of enactment of the FAA Reauthorization Act of 2024, to provide funding sufficient for the cost of wages and benefits of at least 2 air traffic controllers for each tower operating shift.

(3) COST-SHARE PROGRAM.—

(A) IN GENERAL.—The Secretary shall establish a program to contract for air traffic control services at nonapproach control towers, as defined by the Secretary, that do not qualify for the Contract Tower Program.

(B) PROGRAM COMPONENTS.—In carrying out the Cost-share Program, the Secretary shall—

(i) utilize for purposes of cost-benefit analyses, current, actual, site-specific data, forecast estimates, or airport master plan data provided by a facility owner or operator and verified by the Secretary; and

(ii) approve for participation only facilities willing to fund a pro rata share of the operating costs of the air traffic control tower to achieve a 1-to-1 benefit-to-cost ratio using actual site-specific contract tower operating costs in any case in which there is an operating air traffic control tower or a remote air traffic control tower equipment that has received System Design Approval from the Federal Aviation Administration, as required for eligibility under the Contract Tower Program.

(C) PRIORITY.—In selecting facilities to participate in the Cost-share Program, the Secretary shall give priority to the following facilities:

(i) Air traffic control towers that are participating in the Contract Tower Program but have been notified that they will be terminated from such program because the Secretary has determined that the benefit-to-cost ratio for their continuation in such program is less than 1.0.

(ii) Air traffic control towers that the Secretary determines have a benefit-to-cost ratio of at least .50.

(iii) Air traffic control towers of the Federal Aviation Administration that are closed as a result of the air traffic controllers strike in 1981.

(iv) Air traffic control towers located at airports or points at which an air carrier is receiving compensation under the essential air service program under this chapter.

(v) Air traffic control towers located at airports that are prepared to assume partial responsibility for maintenance costs.

(vi) Air traffic control towers located at airports with safety or operational problems related to topography, weather, runway configuration, or mix of aircraft.

(vii) Air traffic control towers located at an airport at which the community has been operating the tower at its own expense.

(viii) Air traffic control towers at airports with safety or operational problems related to the lack of an existing tower.

(ix) Air traffic control towers at airports with projected commercial and military increases in aircraft or flight operations.

(x) Air traffic control towers at airports with a variety of aircraft operations, including a variety of commercial and military flight operations.

(D) COSTS EXCEEDING BENEFITS.—If the costs of operating an air traffic tower under the Cost-share Program exceed the benefits, the airport sponsor or State or local government having jurisdiction over the airport shall pay the portion of the costs that exceed such benefit, with the maximum allowable local cost share capped at 20 percent. Airports with air service provided under part 121 of title 14, Code of Federal Regulations, and more than 25,000 passenger enplanements in calendar year 2014 shall be exempt from any cost-share requirement under this paragraph.

(E) FUNDING.—Of the amounts appropriated pursuant to section 106(k)(1), not more than $10,350,000 for each of fiscal years 2012 through 2018 may be used to carry out this paragraph.

(F) USE OF EXCESS FUNDS.—If the Secretary finds that all or part of an amount made available under this paragraph is not required during a fiscal year, the Secretary may use, during such fiscal year, the amount not so required to carry out the Contract Tower Program.

(G) BENEFIT-TO-COST CALCULATION.—Not later than 90 days after receiving an application to the Contract Tower Program, the Secretary shall calculate a benefit-to-cost ratio (as described in subsection (d)) for the applicable air traffic control tower for purposes of selecting towers for participation in the Contract Tower Program.

(H) PERIOD FOR COMPLETION OF AN OPERATIONAL READINESS INSPECTION.—The Secretary shall provide airport sponsors acting in good faith 7 years to complete an operational readiness inspection after receiving a benefit-to-cost ratio of air traffic control services for an airport.

(4) CONSTRUCTION OF AIR TRAFFIC CONTROL TOWERS.—

(A) GRANTS.—The Secretary may provide grants to a sponsor of—

(i) a primary airport—

(I) from amounts made available under sections 47114(c)(1) and 47114(c)(2) for the construction or improvement of a nonapproach control tower, as defined by the Secretary, and for the acquisition and installation of air traffic control, communications, and related equipment to be used in that tower;

(II) from amounts made available under sections 47114(c)(1) and 47114(c)(2) for reimbursement for the cost of construction or improvement of a nonapproach control tower, as defined by the Secretary, incurred after October 1, 1996, if the sponsor complied with the requirements of sections 47107(e), 47112(b), and 47112(c) in constructing or improving that tower; and

(III) from amounts made available under sections 47114(c)(1) and 47114(c)(2) for reimbursement for the cost of acquiring and installing in that tower air traffic control, communications, and related equipment that was acquired or installed after October 1, 1996, including remote air traffic control tower equipment certified by the Federal Aviation Administration or remote air traffic control tower equipment that has received System Design Approval from the Federal Aviation Administration; and

(ii) a public-use airport that is not a primary airport—

(I) from amounts made available under subsections (c) and (d) of section 47114 for the construction or improvement of a nonapproach control tower, as defined by the Secretary, and for the acquisition and installation of air traffic control, communications, and related equipment to be used in that tower;

(II) from amounts made available under sections 47114(c) and 47114(d)(2)(A) for reimbursement for the cost of construction or improvement of a nonapproach control tower, as defined by the Secretary, incurred after October 1, 1996, if the sponsor complied with the requirements of sections 47107(e), 47112(b), and 47112(c) in constructing or improving that tower; and

(III) from amounts made available under sections 47114(c) and 47114(d)(2)(A) for reimbursement for the cost of acquiring and installing in that tower air traffic control, communications, and related equipment that was acquired or installed after October 1, 1996, including remote air traffic control tower equipment certified by the Federal Aviation Administration or remote air traffic control tower equipment that has received System Design Approval from the Federal Aviation Administration.

(B) ELIGIBILITY.—An airport sponsor shall be eligible for a grant under this paragraph only if—

(i)(I) the sponsor is a participant in the Federal Aviation Administration Contract Tower Program or the Cost-share Program; or

(II) construction of a nonapproach control tower would qualify the sponsor to be eligible to participate in such program;

(ii) the sponsor certifies that it will pay not less than 10 percent of the cost of the activities for which the sponsor is receiving assistance under this paragraph;

(iii) the Secretary affirmatively accepts the proposed contract tower into a contract tower program under this section and certifies that the Secretary will seek future appropriations to pay the Federal Aviation Administration's cost of the contract to operate the tower to be constructed under this paragraph;

(iv) the sponsor certifies that it will pay its share of the cost of the contract to operate the tower to be constructed under this paragraph; and

(v) in the case of a tower to be constructed under this paragraph from amounts made available under section 47114(d)(2)(B), the Secretary certifies that—

(I) the Federal Aviation Administration has consulted the State within the borders of which the tower is to be constructed and the State supports the construction of the tower as part of its State airport capital plan; and

(II) the selection of the tower for funding is based on objective criteria.

(c) SAFETY AUDITS.—The Secretary shall establish uniform standards and requirements for regular safety assessments of air traffic control towers that receive funding under this section.

(d) CRITERIA TO EVALUATE PARTICIPANTS.—

(1) TIMING OF EVALUATIONS.—

(A) TOWERS PARTICIPATING IN COST-SHARE PROGRAM.—In the case of an air traffic control tower that is operated under the Cost-share Program, the Secretary shall annually calculate a benefit-to-cost ratio with respect to the tower.

(B) TOWERS PARTICIPATING IN CONTRACT TOWER PROGRAM.—In the case of an air traffic control tower that is operated under the Contract Tower Program, the Secretary shall not calculate a benefit-to-cost ratio after the date of enactment of this subsection with respect to the tower unless the Secretary determines that the annual aircraft traffic at the airport where the tower is located has decreased—

(i) by more than 25 percent from the previous year; or

(ii) by more than 55 percent cumulatively in the preceding 3-year period.

(2) COSTS TO BE CONSIDERED.—In establishing a benefit-to-cost ratio under this section with respect to an air traffic control tower, the Secretary shall consider only the following costs:

(A) The Federal Aviation Administration's actual cost of wages and benefits of personnel working at the tower.

(B) The Federal Aviation Administration's actual telecommunications costs directly associated with the tower.

(C) The Federal Aviation Administration's costs of purchasing and installing any air traffic control equipment that would not have been purchased or installed except as a result of the operation of the tower.

(D) The Federal Aviation Administration's actual travel costs associated with maintaining air traffic control equipment that is owned by the Administration and would not be maintained except as a result of the operation of the tower.

(E) Other actual costs of the Federal Aviation Administration directly associated with the tower that would not be incurred except as a result of the operation of the tower (excluding costs for noncontract tower-related personnel and equipment, even if the personnel or equipment is located in the contract tower building).

(3) OTHER CRITERIA TO BE CONSIDERED.—In establishing a benefit-to-cost ratio under this section with respect to an air traffic control tower, the Secretary shall add a 10 percentage point margin of error to the benefit-to-cost ratio determination to acknowledge and account for the direct and indirect economic and other benefits that are not included in the criteria the Secretary used in calculating that ratio.

(4) REVIEW OF COST-BENEFIT DETERMINATIONS.—In issuing a benefit-to-cost ratio determination under this section with respect to an air traffic control tower located at an airport, the Secretary shall implement the following procedures:

(A) The Secretary shall provide the airport (or the State or local government having jurisdiction over the airport) at least 90 days following the date of receipt of the determination to submit to the Secretary a request for an appeal of the determination, together with updated or additional data in support of the appeal.

(B) Upon receipt of a request for an appeal submitted pursuant to subparagraph (A), the Secretary shall—

(i) transmit to the Administrator of the Federal Aviation Administration any updated or additional data submitted in support of the appeal; and

(ii) provide the Administrator not more than 90 days to review the data and provide a response to the Secretary based on the review.

(C) After receiving a response from the Administrator pursuant to subparagraph (B), the Secretary shall—

(i) provide the airport, State, or local government that requested the appeal at least 30 days to review the response; and

(ii) withhold from taking further action in connection with the appeal during that 30-day period.

(D) If, after completion of the appeal procedures with respect to the determination, the Secretary requires the tower to transition into the Cost-share Program, the Secretary shall not require a cost-share payment from the airport, State, or local government for 1 year following the last day of the 30-day period described in subparagraph (C).

(e) DEFINITIONS.—In this section:

(1) CONTRACT TOWER PROGRAM.—The term "Contract Tower Program" means the level I air traffic control tower contract program established under subsection (a) and continued under subsection (b)(1).

(2) COST-SHARE PROGRAM.—The term "Cost-share Program" means the cost-share program established under subsection (b)(3).

(f) IMPROVING CONTROLLER SITUATIONAL AWARENESS.—

(1) IN GENERAL.—Not later than 1 year after the date of enactment of this subsection, the Secretary shall allow air traffic controllers at towers operated under the Contract Tower Program to use approved advanced equipment and technologies to improve operational situational awareness, including Standard Terminal Automation Replacement System radar displays, Automatic Dependent Surveillance-Broadcast, Flight Data Input/Output, and Automatic Terminal Information System.

(2) INSTALLATION AND MAINTENANCE.—Not later than 2 years after the date of enactment of this subsection, the Secretary shall allow airports to—

(A) procure a Standard Terminal Automation Replacement System or any equivalent system through the Federal Aviation Administration, and install and maintain such system using Administration services; or

(B) purchase a Standard Terminal Automation Replacement System, or any equivalent system, and install and maintain such system using services directly from an original equipment manufacturer.

(3) REQUIREMENTS.—To help facilitate the integration of the equipment and technology described in paragraph (1), the Secretary—

(A) shall establish minimum performance and technical standards that ensure the safe use of equipment and technology, including commercial radar displays capable of displaying primary and secondary radar targets, for use by controllers in contract towers to improve situational awareness;

(B) shall identify approved vendors for such equipment and technology, to the maximum extent practicable;

(C) shall establish, in consultation with contract tower operators, an appropriate training program to periodically train air traffic controllers employed by such operators to ensure proper and efficient integration and use of the situational awareness equipment and technology described in paragraph (1) into contract tower operations;

(D) may add Standard Terminal Automation Replacement System equipment or any equivalent system to the minimum level of equipage necessary for Federal contract towers to perform the function of such towers, as applicable; and

(E) shall require that any technology, system, or equipment procured pursuant to this subsection be procured using non-Federal funds, except as made available under a grant issued pursuant to 47124(b)(4).[1]

(g) LIABILITY INSURANCE.—

(1) IN GENERAL.—Not later than 18 months after the date of enactment of this subsection, the Secretary shall consult with aviation industry experts, including air traffic control contractors and aviation insurance professionals, to determine adequate limits of liability for the Contract Tower Program.

(2) INTERIM STEPS.—Not later than 6 months after the date of enactment of this subsection and until the Secretary makes a determination on liability limits under paragraph (1), the Secretary shall require air traffic control contractors to have excess liability insurance (as determined by the Secretary) to ensure continuity of such coverage should a major accident occur.

(3) BRIEFING.—Not later than 24 months after the date of enactment of this subsection, the Secretary shall brief the Committee on Transportation and Infrastructure of the House of Representatives and the Commerce,[2] Science, and Transportation of the Senate on the findings, conclusions, and actions taken and planned to be taken to carry out this subsection.

(h) MILESTONES FOR DESIGN APPROVAL OF REMOTE TOWERS.—

(1) IN GENERAL.—Not later than 180 days after the date of enactment of this subsection, the Administrator of the Federal Aviation Administration shall create a program and publish milestones to achieve system design and operational approval for a remote tower system.

(2) REQUIREMENTS.—In carrying out paragraph (1), the Administrator shall—

(A) rely on support from the Office of Airports of the Federal Aviation Administration and the Air Traffic Organization of the Federal Aviation Administration, including the Air Traffic Services Service Unit and the Technical Operations Service Unit;

(B) consult with relevant stakeholders, as the Administrator determines appropriate;

(C) establish requirements for the system design and operational approval of remote towers, including—

(i) visual siting processes and requirements for electro-optical sensors;

(ii) datalink latency requirements;

(iii) visual presentation design requirements for monitors used to display sensor and camera feeds; and

(iv) any other wireless telecommunications infrastructure requirements to enable the operation of such towers;

(D) use a safety risk management panel process to address any safety issues with respect to a remote tower;

(E) if a remote tower is intended to be installed at a non-towered airport, assess the safety benefits of the remote tower against the lack of an existing tower;

(F) allow the use of surface surveillance technology, either standalone or integrated into the visual automation platform, as a situational awareness tool;

(G) establish protocols for contingency operations and procedures in the event of remote tower technology failures and malfunctions; and

(H) support active testing of a remote tower system that has achieved system design approval by the William J. Hughes Technical Center at an airport that has installed remote tower infrastructure to support such system.

(3) SYSTEM DESIGN APPROVAL AND EVALUATION PROCESS.—Not later than December 31, 2024, the Administrator shall expand the system design approval and evaluation process for a digital or remote tower system to not less than 3 airports at which a digital or remote tower will be installed or operated at airports not located at the William J. Hughes Technical Center and using the criteria under section 161 of the FAA Reauthorization Act of 2018 (49 U.S.C. 47104 note), to the extent the Administrator has willing technology providers and airports interested in the installation and operation of such towers.

(4) PRESERVATION OF EXISTING DESIGN APPROVALS.—Nothing in this subsection shall be construed to invalidate any system design approval activity carried out by the William J. Hughes Technical Center prior to the date of enactment of this subsection.

(5) PRIORITIZATION FOR REMOTE TOWER CERTIFICATION.—In carrying out the program established under paragraph (1), the Administrator shall prioritize system design and operational approval for a remote tower system at—

(A) airports that do not have a permanent air traffic control tower at the time of application;

(B) airports that would provide small and rural community air service; or

(C) airports that have been newly accepted as of the date of enactment of this subsection into the Contract Tower Program.

(Pub. L. 103–272, §1(e), July 5, 1994, 108 Stat. 1276; Pub. L. 106–181, title I, §131, Apr. 5, 2000, 114 Stat. 78; Pub. L. 108–7, div. I, title III, §370(b)(1), (2), Feb. 20, 2003, 117 Stat. 425, 426; Pub. L. 108–176, title I, §105, Dec. 12, 2003, 117 Stat. 2498; Pub. L. 112–55, div. C, title I, §119, Nov. 18, 2011, 125 Stat. 649; Pub. L. 112–95, title I, §147, Feb. 14, 2012, 126 Stat. 30; Pub. L. 113–76, div. L, title I, §118, Jan. 17, 2014, 128 Stat. 581; Pub. L. 113–235, div. K, title I, §118, Dec. 16, 2014, 128 Stat. 2704; Pub. L. 114–55, title I, §102(c), Sept. 30, 2015, 129 Stat. 523; Pub. L. 114–141, title I, §102(c), Mar. 30, 2016, 130 Stat. 323; Pub. L. 114–190, title I, §1102(c), July 15, 2016, 130 Stat. 617; Pub. L. 115–63, title I, §102(d), Sept. 29, 2017, 131 Stat. 1169; Pub. L. 115–141, div. M, title I, §102(c), Mar. 23, 2018, 132 Stat. 1046; Pub. L. 115–254, div. B, title I, §133(a)–(c), Oct. 5, 2018, 132 Stat. 3206–3208; Pub. L. 118–63, title VI, §§620, 621(a), (c), 625(b), (c), title VII, §712(c)(2), title XI, §1101(v), May 16, 2024, 138 Stat. 1234, 1235, 1237, 1242, 1256, 1414.)

[1] So in original. Probably should be preceded by "section".

[2] So in original. Probably should be preceded by "Committee on".

§47124A. ACCESSIBILITY OF CERTAIN FLIGHT DATA

(a) DEFINITIONS.—In this section:

(1) ADMINISTRATION.—The term "Administration" means the Federal Aviation Administration.

(2) ADMINISTRATOR.—The term "Administrator" means the Administrator of the Federal Aviation Administration.

(3) APPLICABLE INDIVIDUAL.—The term "applicable individual" means an individual who is the subject of an investigation initiated by the Administrator related to a covered flight record.

(4) CONTRACT TOWER.—The term "contract tower" means an air traffic control tower providing air traffic control services pursuant to a contract with the Administration under section 47124.

(5) COVERED FLIGHT RECORD.—The term "covered flight record" means any air traffic data (as defined in section 2(b)(4)(B) of the Pilot's Bill of Rights (49 U.S.C. 44703 note)), created, maintained, or controlled by any program of the Administration, including any program of the Administration carried out by employees or contractors of the Administration, such as contract towers, flight service stations, and controller training programs.

(b) PROVISION OF COVERED FLIGHT RECORD TO ADMINISTRATION.—

(1) REQUESTS.—Whenever the Administration receives a written request for a covered flight record from an applicable individual and the covered flight record is not in the possession of the Administration, the Administrator shall request the covered flight record from the contract tower or other contractor of the Administration in possession of the covered flight record.

(2) PROVISION OF RECORDS.—Any covered flight record created, maintained, or controlled by a contract tower or another contractor of the Administration that maintains covered flight records shall be provided to the Administration if the Administration requests the record pursuant to paragraph (1).

(3) NOTICE OF PROPOSED CERTIFICATE ACTION.—If the Administrator has issued, or subsequently issues, a Notice of Proposed Certificate Action relying on evidence contained in the covered flight record and the individual who is the subject of an investigation has requested the record, the Administrator shall promptly produce the record and extend the time the individual has to respond to the Notice of Proposed Certificate Action until the covered flight record is provided.

(c) IMPLEMENTATION.—

(1) IN GENERAL.—Not later than 180 days after the date of enactment of the Fairness for Pilots Act, the Administrator shall promulgate regulations or guidance to ensure compliance with this section.

(2) COMPLIANCE BY CONTRACTORS.—

(A) IN GENERAL.—Compliance with this section by a contract tower or other contractor of the Administration that maintains covered flight records shall be included as a material term in any contract between the Administration and the contract tower or contractor entered into or renewed on or after the date of enactment of the Fairness for Pilots Act.

(B) NONAPPLICABILITY.—Subparagraph (A) shall not apply to any contract or agreement in effect on the date of enactment of the Fairness for Pilots Act unless the contract or agreement is renegotiated, renewed, or modified after that date.

(d) PROTECTION OF CERTAIN DATA.—The Administrator of the Federal Aviation Administration may withhold information that would otherwise be required to be made available under section [1] only if—

(1) the Administrator determines, based on information in the possession of the Administrator, that the Administrator may withhold the information in accordance with section 552a of title 5, United States Code; or

(2) the information is submitted pursuant to a voluntary safety reporting program

covered by section 40123 of title 49, United States Code.

(Added Pub. L. 115–254, div. B, title III, §395(a), Oct. 5, 2018, 132 Stat. 3326.)

¹ So in original. Probably should be "this section".

§47125. CONVEYANCES OF UNITED STATES GOVERNMENT LAND

(a) CONVEYANCES TO PUBLIC AGENCIES.—Except as provided in subsection (b) of this section, the Secretary of Transportation shall request the head of the department, agency, or instrumentality of the United States Government owning or controlling land or airspace to convey a property interest in the land or airspace to the public agency sponsoring the project or owning or controlling the airport when necessary to carry out a project under this subchapter at a public airport, to operate a public airport, or for the future development of an airport under the national plan of integrated airport systems. The head of the department, agency, or instrumentality shall decide whether the requested conveyance is consistent with the needs of the department, agency, or instrumentality and shall notify the Secretary of that decision not later than 4 months after receiving the request. If the head of the department, agency, or instrumentality decides that the requested conveyance is consistent with its needs, the head of the department, agency, or instrumentality, with the approval of the Attorney General and without cost to the Government, shall make the conveyance. A conveyance may be made only on the condition that the property interest conveyed reverts to the Government, at the option of the Secretary, to the extent it is not developed for an airport purpose or used consistently with the conveyance. Before waiving a condition that property be used for an aeronautical purpose under the preceding sentence, the Secretary must provide notice to the public not less than 30 days before waiving such condition.

(b) NONAPPLICATION.—Except as specifically provided by law, subsection (a) of this section does not apply to land or airspace owned or controlled by the Government within—

(1) a national park, national monument, national recreation area, or similar area under the administration of the National Park Service;

(2) a unit of the National Wildlife Refuge System or similar area under the jurisdiction of the United States Fish and Wildlife Service; or

(3) a national forest or Indian reservation.

(c) WAIVING RESTRICTIONS.—

(1) IN GENERAL.—Subject to paragraph (2), the Secretary may grant to an airport, city, or county a waiver of any of the terms, conditions, reservations, or restrictions contained in a deed under which the United States conveyed to the airport, city, or county an interest in real property for airport purposes pursuant to section 16 of the Federal Airport Act (60 Stat. 179), section 23 of the Airport and Airway Development Act of 1970 (84 Stat. 232), or this section.

(2) CONDITIONS.—Any waiver granted by the Secretary pursuant to paragraph (1) shall be subject to the following conditions:

(A) The applicable airport, city, county, or other political subdivision shall agree that in conveying any interest in the real property which the United States conveyed to the airport, city, or county, the airport, city, or county will receive consideration for such interest that is equal to its current fair market value.

(B) Any consideration received by the airport, city, or county under subparagraph

(A) shall be used exclusively for the development, improvement, operation, or maintenance of a public airport by the airport, city, or county.

(C) Such waiver—

(i) will not significantly impair the aeronautical purpose of an airport;

(ii) will not result in the permanent closure of an airport (unless the Secretary determines that the waiver will directly facilitate the construction of a replacement airport); or

(iii) is necessary to protect or advance the civil aviation interests of the United States.

(D) Any other conditions required by the Secretary.

(3) ANNUAL REPORTING.—The Secretary shall include a list and description of each waiver granted pursuant to paragraph (1) in the plan required under section 47103.

(Pub. L. 103–272, §1(e), July 5, 1994, 108 Stat. 1276; Pub. L. 106–181, title I, §125(b), Apr. 5, 2000, 114 Stat. 75; Pub. L. 118–63, title VII, §719(a), May 16, 2024, 138 Stat. 1260.)

§47126. CRIMINAL PENALTIES FOR FALSE STATEMENTS

A person (including an officer, agent, or employee of the United States Government or a public agency) shall be fined under title 18, imprisoned for not more than 5 years, or both, if the person, with intent to defraud the Government, knowingly makes—

(1) a false statement about the kind, quantity, quality, or cost of the material used or to be used, or the quantity, quality, or cost of work performed or to be performed, in connection with the submission of a plan, map, specification, contract, or estimate of project cost for a project included in a grant application submitted to the Secretary of Transportation for approval under this subchapter;

(2) a false statement or claim for work or material for a project included in a grant application approved by the Secretary under this subchapter; or

(3) a false statement in a report or certification required under this subchapter.

(Pub. L. 103–272, §1(e), July 5, 1994, 108 Stat. 1277.)

§47127. GROUND TRANSPORTATION DEMONSTRATION PROJECTS

(a) GENERAL AUTHORITY.—To improve the airport and airway system of the United States consistent with regional airport system plans financed under section 13(b) of the Airport and Airway Development Act of 1970, the Secretary of Transportation may carry out ground transportation demonstration projects to improve ground access to air carrier airport terminals. The Secretary may carry out a demonstration project independently or by grant or contract, including an agreement with another department, agency, or instrumentality of the United States Government.

(b) PRIORITY.—In carrying out this section, the Secretary shall give priority to a demonstration project that—

(1) affects an airport in an area with an operating regional rapid transit system with existing facilities reasonably near the airport;

(2) includes connection of the airport terminal to that system;

(3) is consistent with and supports a regional airport system plan adopted by the planning agency for the region and submitted to the Secretary; and

(4) improves access to air transportation for individuals residing or working in the

region by encouraging the optimal balance of use of airports in the region.

(Pub. L. 103–272, §1(e), July 5, 1994, 108 Stat. 1277.)

§47128. STATE BLOCK GRANT PROGRAM

(a) GENERAL REQUIREMENTS.—The Secretary of Transportation shall issue guidance to carry out a State block grant program. The guidance shall provide that the Secretary may designate not more than 20 qualified States for each fiscal year to assume administrative responsibility for all airport grant amounts available under this subchapter, except for amounts designated for use at primary airports.

(b) APPLICATIONS AND SELECTION.—A State wishing to participate in the program must submit an application to the Secretary. The Secretary shall select a State on the basis of its application only after—

(1) deciding the State has an organization capable of effectively administering a block grant made under this section;

(2) deciding the State uses a satisfactory airport system planning process;

(3) deciding the State uses a programming process acceptable to the Secretary;

(4) finding that the State has agreed to comply with United States Government standard requirements for administering the block grant, including the National Environmental Policy Act of 1969 (42 U.S.C. 4321 et seq.), State and local environmental policy acts, Executive orders, agency regulations and guidance, and other Federal environmental requirements; and

(5) finding that the State has agreed to provide the Secretary with program information the Secretary requires.

(c) SAFETY AND SECURITY NEEDS AND NEEDS OF SYSTEM.—Before deciding whether a planning process is satisfactory or a programming process is acceptable under subsection (b)(2) or (b)(3) of this section, the Secretary shall ensure that the process provides for meeting critical safety and security needs and that the programming process ensures that the needs of the national airport system will be addressed in deciding which projects will receive money from the Government. In carrying out this subsection, the Secretary shall permit a State to use the priority system of the State if such system is not inconsistent with the national priority system.

(d) ENVIRONMENTAL ANALYSIS AND COORDINATION REQUIREMENTS.—A Federal agency, other than the Federal Aviation Administration, that is responsible for issuing an approval, license, or permit to ensure compliance with a Federal environmental requirement applicable to a project or activity to be carried out by a State using amounts from a block grant made under this section shall—

(1) coordinate and consult with the State;

(2) use the environmental analysis prepared by the State for the project or activity if such analysis is adequate; and

(3) as necessary, consult with the State to describe the supplemental analysis the State must provide to meet applicable Federal requirements.

(e) TRAINING FOR PARTICIPATING STATES.—

(1) IN GENERAL.—The Secretary shall provide to each State participating in the block grant program under this section training or updated training materials for the administrative responsibilities assumed by the State under such program at no cost to the

State.

(2) Timing.—The training or updated training materials provided under paragraph (1) shall be provided at least once during each 2-year period and at any time there is a material change in the program.

(f) Roles and Responsibilities of Participating States.—

(1) Airports.—Unless a State participating in the block grant program under this section expressly agrees in a memorandum of agreement, the Secretary shall not require the State to manage functions and responsibilities for airport actions or projects that do not relate to such program.

(2) Program documentation.—

(A) In general.—Any grant agreement providing funds to be administered under such program shall be consistent with the most recently executed memorandum of agreement between the State and the Federal Aviation Administration.

(B) Parity.—The Administrator of the Federal Aviation Administration shall provide parity to participating States and shall only require the same type of information and level of detail for any program agreements and documentation that the Administrator would perform with respect to such action if the State did not participate in the program.

(3) Responsibilities.—Unless the State expressly agrees to retain responsibility, the Administrator shall retain responsibility for the following:

(A) Grant compliance investigations, determinations, and enforcement.

(B) Obstruction evaluation and airport airspace analysis, determinations, and enforcement off airport property.

(C) Non-rulemaking analysis, determinations, and enforcement for proposed improvements on airport properties not associated with this subchapter, or off airport property.

(D) Land use determinations, compatibility planning, and airport layout plan review and approval (consistent with section 47107(x)) for projects not funded by amounts available under this subchapter.

(E) Nonaeronautical and special event recommendations and approvals.

(F) Instrument approach procedure evaluations and determinations.

(G) Environmental review for projects not funded by amounts available under this subchapter.

(H) Review and approval of land leases, land releases, changes in on-airport land-use designation, and through-the-fence agreements.

(Pub. L. 103–272, §1(e), July 5, 1994, 108 Stat. 1277; Pub. L. 103–429, §6(70), Oct. 31, 1994, 108 Stat. 4387; Pub. L. 104–264, title I, §147(a)–(c)(1), Oct. 9, 1996, 110 Stat. 3223; Pub. L. 104–287, §5(84), Oct. 11, 1996, 110 Stat. 3397; Pub. L. 105–102, §3(d)(1)(E), Nov. 20, 1997, 111 Stat. 2215; Pub. L. 106–181, title I, §138, Apr. 5, 2000, 114 Stat. 85; Pub. L. 112–95, title V, §502, Feb. 14, 2012, 126 Stat. 103; Pub. L. 115–254, div. B, title I, §139, Oct. 5, 2018, 132 Stat. 3210; Pub. L. 118–63, title VII, §720(a), (b), May 16, 2024, 138 Stat. 1262.)

§47129. Resolution of disputes concerning airport fees

(a) Authority To Request Secretary's Determination.—

(1) In general.—The Secretary of Transportation shall issue a determination as to whether a fee imposed upon one or more air carriers or foreign air carriers (as those terms

are defined in section 40102) by the owner or operator of an airport is reasonable if—

(A) a written request for such determination is filed with the Secretary by such owner or operator; or

(B) a written complaint requesting such determination is filed with the Secretary by an affected air carrier or foreign air carrier within 60 days after such carrier receives written notice of the establishment or increase of such fee.

(2) CALCULATION OF FEE.—A fee subject to a determination of reasonableness under this section may be calculated pursuant to either a compensatory or residual fee methodology or any combination thereof.

(3) SECRETARY NOT TO SET FEE.—In determining whether a fee is reasonable under this section, the Secretary may only determine whether the fee is reasonable or unreasonable and shall not set the level of the fee.

(4) FEES IMPOSED BY PRIVATELY-OWNED AIRPORTS.—In evaluating the reasonableness of a fee imposed by an airport receiving an exemption under section 47134 of this title, the Secretary shall consider whether the airport has complied with section 47134(c)(4).

(b) PROCEDURAL REGULATIONS.—Not later than 90 days after August 23, 1994, the Secretary shall publish in the Federal Register final regulations, policy statements, or guidelines establishing—

(1) the procedures for acting upon any written request or complaint filed under subsection (a)(1); and

(2) the standards or guidelines that shall be used by the Secretary in determining under this section whether an airport fee is reasonable.

(c) DECISIONS BY SECRETARY.—The final regulations, policy statements, or guidelines required in subsection (b) shall provide the following:

(1) Not more than 120 days after an air carrier or foreign air carrier files with the Secretary a written complaint relating to an airport fee, the Secretary shall issue a final order determining whether such fee is reasonable.

(2) Within 30 days after such complaint is filed with the Secretary, the Secretary shall dismiss the complaint if no significant dispute exists or shall assign the matter to an administrative law judge; and thereafter the matter shall be handled in accordance with part 302 of title 14, Code of Federal Regulations, or as modified by the Secretary to ensure an orderly disposition of the matter within the 120-day period and any specifically applicable provisions of this section.

(3) The administrative law judge shall issue a recommended decision within 60 days after the complaint is assigned or within such shorter period as the Secretary may specify.

(4) If the Secretary, upon the expiration of 120 days after the filing of the complaint, has not issued a final order, the decision of the administrative law judge shall be deemed to be the final order of the Secretary.

(5) Any party to the dispute may seek review of a final order of the Secretary under this subsection in the Circuit Court of Appeals for the District of Columbia Circuit or the court of appeals in the circuit where the airport which gives rise to the written complaint is located.

(6) Any findings of fact in a final order of the Secretary under this subsection, if supported by substantial evidence, shall be conclusive if challenged in a court pursuant to this subsection. No objection to such a final order shall be considered by the court unless

objection was urged before an administrative law judge or the Secretary at a proceeding under this subsection or, if not so urged, unless there were reasonable grounds for failure to do so.

(d) PAYMENT UNDER PROTEST; GUARANTEE OF AIR CARRIER AND FOREIGN AIR CARRIER ACCESS.—

(1) PAYMENT UNDER PROTEST.—

(A) IN GENERAL.—Any fee increase or newly established fee which is the subject of a complaint that is not dismissed by the Secretary shall be paid by the complainant air carrier or foreign air carrier to the airport under protest.

(B) REFERRAL OR CREDIT.—Any amounts paid under this subsection by a complainant air carrier or foreign air carrier to the airport under protest shall be subject to refund or credit to the air carrier or foreign air carrier in accordance with directions in the final order of the Secretary within 30 days of such order.

(C) ASSURANCE OF TIMELY REPAYMENT.—In order to assure the timely repayment, with interest, of amounts in dispute determined not to be reasonable by the Secretary, the airport shall obtain a letter of credit, or surety bond, or other suitable credit facility, equal to the amount in dispute that is due during the 120-day period established by this section, plus interest, unless the airport and the complainant air carrier or foreign air carrier agree otherwise.

(D) DEADLINE.—The letter of credit, or surety bond, or other suitable credit facility shall be provided to the Secretary within 20 days of the filing of the complaint and shall remain in effect for 30 days after the earlier of 120 days or the issuance of a timely final order by the Secretary determining whether such fee is reasonable.

(2) GUARANTEE OF AIR CARRIER AND FOREIGN AIR CARRIER ACCESS.—Contingent upon an air carrier's or foreign air carrier's compliance with the requirements of paragraph (1) and pending the issuance of a final order by the Secretary determining the reasonableness of a fee that is the subject of a complaint filed under subsection (a)(1)(B), an owner or operator of an airport may not deny an air carrier or foreign air carrier currently providing air service at the airport reasonable access to airport facilities or service, or otherwise interfere with an air carrier's or foreign air carrier's prices, routes, or services, as a means of enforcing the fee.

(e) APPLICABILITY.—This section does not apply to—

(1) a fee imposed pursuant to a written agreement with air carriers or foreign air carriers using the facilities of an airport;

(2) a fee imposed pursuant to a financing agreement or covenant entered into prior to August 23, 1994; or

(3) any other existing fee not in dispute as of August 23, 1994.

(f) EFFECT ON EXISTING AGREEMENTS.—Nothing in this section shall adversely affect—

(1) the rights of any party under any existing written agreement between an air carrier or foreign air carrier and the owner or operator of an airport; or

(2) the ability of an airport to meet its obligations under a financing agreement, or covenant, that is in force as of August 23, 1994.

(g) DEFINITION.—In this section, the term "fee" means any rate, rental charge, landing fee, or other service charge for the use of airport facilities.

(Added Pub. L. 103–305, title I, §113(a)(2), Aug. 23, 1994, 108 Stat. 1577; amended Pub. L. 104–264, title

I, §149(d), Oct. 9, 1996, 110 Stat. 3227; Pub. L. 104–287, §5(85), Oct. 11, 1996, 110 Stat. 3397; Pub. L. 112–95, title I, §148(a), Feb. 14, 2012, 126 Stat. 31.)

§47130. AIRPORT SAFETY DATA COLLECTION

Notwithstanding any other provision of law, the Administrator of the Federal Aviation Administration may award a contract, using sole source or limited source authority, or enter into a cooperative agreement with, or provide a grant from amounts made available under section 48103 to, a private company or entity for the collection of airport safety data. In the event that a grant is provided under this section, the United States Government's share of the cost of the data collection shall be 100 percent.

(Added Pub. L. 103–305, title I, §118(a), Aug. 23, 1994, 108 Stat. 1580; amended Pub. L. 108–176, title I, §154, Dec. 12, 2003, 117 Stat. 2507.)

[§47131. REPEALED. PUB. L. 118–63, TITLE II, §218(D), MAY 16, 2024, 138 STAT. 1055]

Section, Pub. L. 103–272, §1(e), July 5, 1994, 108 Stat. 1278, §47129; renumbered §47131, Pub. L. 103–305, title I, §113(a)(1), Aug. 23, 1994, 108 Stat. 1577; amended Pub. L. 106–181, title VII, §722, Apr. 5, 2000, 114 Stat. 165; Pub. L. 112–95, title I, §152(c), Feb. 14, 2012, 126 Stat. 34, related to annual report submitted to Congress on activities carried out under this subchapter during the prior fiscal year.

[§47132. REPEALED. PUB. L. 106–181, TITLE I, §123(A)(1), APR. 5, 2000, 114 STAT. 74]

Section, added Pub. L. 104–264, title I, §142(a), Oct. 9, 1996, 110 Stat. 3221, temporarily directed the Administrator of the Federal Aviation Administration to issue guidelines to carry out not more than 10 pavement maintenance pilot projects.

§47133. RESTRICTION ON USE OF REVENUES

(a) PROHIBITION.—Local taxes on aviation fuel (except taxes in effect on December 30, 1987) or the revenues generated by an airport that is the subject of Federal assistance may not be expended for any purpose other than the capital or operating costs of—
 (1) the airport;
 (2) the local airport system; or
 (3) any other local facility that is owned or operated by the person or entity that owns or operates the airport that is directly and substantially related to the air transportation of passengers or property.
(b) EXCEPTIONS.—
 (1) PRIOR LAWS AND AGREEMENTS.—Subsection (a) shall not apply if a provision enacted not later than September 2, 1982, in a law controlling financing by the airport owner or operator, or a covenant or assurance in a debt obligation issued not later than September 2, 1982, by the owner or operator, provides that the revenues, including local taxes on aviation fuel at public airports, from any of the facilities of the owner or operator, including the airport, be used to support not only the airport but also the general debt obligations or other facilities of the owner or operator.

(2) SALE OF PRIVATE AIRPORT TO PUBLIC SPONSOR.—In the case of a privately owned airport, subsection (a) shall not apply to the proceeds from the sale of the airport to a public sponsor if—

(A) the sale is approved by the Secretary;

(B) funding is provided under this subchapter for any portion of the public sponsor's acquisition of airport land; and

(C) an amount equal to the remaining unamortized portion of any airport improvement grant made to that airport for purposes other than land acquisition, amortized over a 20-year period, plus an amount equal to the Federal share of the current fair market value of any land acquired with an airport improvement grant made to that airport on or after October 1, 1996, is repaid to the Secretary by the private owner.

(3) TREATMENT OF REPAYMENTS.—Repayments referred to in paragraph (2)(C) shall be treated as a recovery of prior year obligations.

(c) RULE OF CONSTRUCTION.—Nothing in this section may be construed to prevent the use of a State tax on aviation fuel to support a State aviation program or the use of airport revenue on or off the airport for a noise mitigation purpose.

(Added Pub. L. 104–264, title VIII, §804(a), Oct. 9, 1996, 110 Stat. 3271; amended Pub. L. 112–95, title I, §149(a), Feb. 14, 2012, 126 Stat. 32.)

§47134. AIRPORT INVESTMENT PARTNERSHIP PROGRAM

(a) SUBMISSION OF APPLICATIONS.—If a sponsor intends to sell or lease a general aviation airport or lease any other type of airport for a long term to a person (other than a public agency), the sponsor and purchaser or lessee may apply to the Secretary of Transportation for exemptions under this section.

(b) APPROVAL OF APPLICATIONS.—The Secretary may approve applications submitted under subsection (a) granting exemptions from the following provisions:

(1) USE OF REVENUES.—

(A) IN GENERAL.—The Secretary may grant an exemption to a sponsor from the provisions of sections 47107(b) and 47133 of this title (and any other law, regulation, or grant assurance) to the extent necessary to permit the sponsor to recover from the sale or lease of the airport such amount as may be approved—

(i) in the case of a primary airport, by at least 65 percent of the scheduled air carriers serving the airport and by scheduled and nonscheduled air carriers whose aircraft landing at the airport during the preceding calendar year, had a total landed weight during the preceding calendar year of at least 65 percent of the total landed weight of all aircraft landing at the airport during such year; or

(ii) in the case of a nonprimary airport, by the Secretary after the airport has consulted with at least 65 percent of the owners of aircraft based at that airport, as determined by the Secretary.

(B) OBJECTION TO EXEMPTION.—An air carrier shall be deemed to have approved a sponsor's application for an exemption under subparagraph (A) unless the air carrier has submitted an objection, in writing, to the sponsor within 60 days of the filing of the sponsor's application with the Secretary, or within 60 days of the service of the application upon that air carrier, whichever is later.

(C) Landed weight defined.—In this paragraph, the term "landed weight" means the weight of aircraft transporting passengers or cargo, or both, in intrastate, interstate, and foreign air transportation, as the Secretary determines under regulations the Secretary prescribes.

(2) Repayment requirements.—If the Secretary grants an exemption to a sponsor pursuant to paragraph (1), the Secretary shall grant an exemption to the sponsor from the provisions of sections 47107 and 47152 of this title (and any other law, regulation, or grant assurance) to the extent necessary to waive any obligation of the sponsor to repay to the Federal Government any grants, or to return to the Federal Government any property, received by the airport under this title, the Airport and Airway Improvement Act of 1982, or any other law.

(3) Compensation from airport operations.—If the Secretary grants an exemption to a sponsor pursuant to paragraph (1), the Secretary shall grant an exemption to the corresponding purchaser or lessee from the provisions of sections 47107(b) and 47133 of this title (and any other law, regulation, or grant assurance) to the extent necessary to permit the purchaser or lessee to earn compensation from the operations of the airport.

(4) Benefit-cost analysis.—

(A) In general.—Prior to approving an application submitted under subsection (a), the Secretary may require a benefit-cost analysis.

(B) Finding.—If a benefit-cost analysis is required, the Secretary shall issue a preliminary and conditional finding, which shall—

(i) be issued not later than 60 days after the date on which the sponsor submits all information required by the Secretary;

(ii) be based upon a collaborative review process that includes the sponsor or a representative of the sponsor;

(iii) not constitute the issuance of a Federal grant or obligation to issue a grant under this chapter or other provision of law; and

(iv) not constitute any other obligation on the part of the Federal Government until the conditions specified in the final benefit-cost analysis are met.

(c) Terms and Conditions.—The Secretary may approve an application under subsection (b) only if the Secretary finds that the sale or lease agreement includes provisions satisfactory to the Secretary to ensure the following:

(1) The airport will continue to be available for public use on reasonable terms and conditions and without unjust discrimination.

(2) The operation of the airport will not be interrupted in the event that the purchaser or lessee becomes insolvent or seeks or becomes subject to any State or Federal bankruptcy, reorganization, insolvency, liquidation, or dissolution proceeding or any petition or similar law seeking the dissolution or reorganization of the purchaser or lessee or the appointment of a receiver, trustee, custodian, or liquidator for the purchaser or lessee or a substantial part of the purchaser or lessee's property, assets, or business.

(3) The purchaser or lessee will maintain, improve, and modernize the facilities of the airport through capital investments and will submit to the Secretary a plan for carrying out such maintenance, improvements, and modernization.

(4) Every fee of the airport imposed on an air carrier on the day before the date of the lease of the airport will not increase faster than the rate of inflation unless a higher

amount is approved—

    (A) by at least 65 percent of the air carriers serving the airport; and

    (B) by air carriers whose aircraft landing at the airport during the preceding calendar year had a total landed weight during the preceding calendar year of at least 65 percent of the total landed weight of all aircraft landing at the airport during such year.

    (5) The percentage increase in fees imposed on general aviation aircraft at the airport will not exceed the percentage increase in fees imposed on air carriers at the airport.

    (6) Safety and security at the airport will be maintained at the highest possible levels.

    (7) The adverse effects of noise from operations at the airport will be mitigated to the same extent as at a public airport.

    (8) Any adverse effects on the environment from airport operations will be mitigated to the same extent as at a public airport.

    (9) Any collective bargaining agreement that covers employees of the airport and is in effect on the date of the sale or lease of the airport will not be abrogated by the sale or lease.

(d) PROGRAM PARTICIPATION.—

    (1) MULTIPLE AIRPORTS.—The Secretary may consider applications under this section submitted by a public airport sponsor for multiple airports under the control of the sponsor if all airports under the control of the sponsor are located in the same State.

    (2) PARTIAL PRIVATIZATION.—A purchaser or lessee may be an entity in which a sponsor has an interest.

(e) REQUIRED FINDING THAT APPROVAL WILL NOT RESULT IN UNFAIR METHODS OF COMPETITION.—The Secretary may approve an application under subsection (b) only if the Secretary finds that the approval will not result in unfair and deceptive practices or unfair methods of competition.

(f) INTERESTS OF GENERAL AVIATION USERS.—In approving an application of an airport under this section, the Secretary shall ensure that the interests of general aviation users of the airport are not adversely affected.

(g) PASSENGER FACILITY FEES; APPORTIONMENTS; SERVICE CHARGES.—Notwithstanding that the sponsor of an airport receiving an exemption under subsection (b) is not a public agency, the sponsor shall not be prohibited from—

    (1) imposing a passenger facility charge under section 40117 of this title;

    (2) receiving apportionments under section 47114 of this title; or

    (3) collecting reasonable rental charges, landing fees, and other service charges from aircraft operators under section 40116(e)(2) of this title.

(h) EFFECTIVENESS OF EXEMPTIONS.—An exemption granted under subsection (b) shall continue in effect only so long as the facilities sold or leased continue to be used for airport purposes.

(i) REVOCATION OF EXEMPTIONS.—The Secretary may revoke an exemption issued to a purchaser or lessee of an airport under subsection (b)(3) if, after providing the purchaser or lessee with notice and an opportunity to be heard, the Secretary determines that the purchaser or lessee has knowingly violated any of the terms specified in subsection (c) for the sale or lease of the airport.

(j) NONAPPLICATION OF PROVISIONS TO AIRPORTS OWNED BY PUBLIC AGENCIES.—The provisions of this section requiring the approval of air carriers in determinations concerning the use of revenues, and imposition of fees, at an airport shall not be extended so as to apply to any airport owned by a public agency that is not participating in the program established by this section.

(k) AUDITS.—The Secretary may conduct periodic audits of the financial records and operations of an airport receiving an exemption under this section.

(l) PREDEVELOPMENT LIMITATION.—A grant to an airport sponsor under this subchapter for predevelopment planning costs relating to the preparation of an application or proposed application under this section may not exceed $750,000 per application or proposed application.

(Added Pub. L. 104–264, title I, §149(a)(1), Oct. 9, 1996, 110 Stat. 3224; amended Pub. L. 108–176, title I, §155(a), Dec. 12, 2003, 117 Stat. 2508; Pub. L. 112–95, title I, §§111(c)(2)(A)(iv), 156, Feb. 14, 2012, 126 Stat. 18, 36; Pub. L. 115–254, div. B, title I, §160(a), Oct. 5, 2018, 132 Stat. 3220; Pub. L. 118–63, title VII, §738, May 16, 2024, 138 Stat. 1276.)

§47135. INNOVATIVE FINANCING TECHNIQUES

(a) AUTHORITY.—

(1) IN GENERAL.—The Secretary of Transportation may approve an application by an airport sponsor to use grants received under this subchapter for innovative financing techniques related to an airport development project that is located at an airport that is not a large hub airport.

(2) APPROVAL.—The Secretary may approve not more than 30 applications described under paragraph (1) in a fiscal year.

(b) PURPOSES.—The purpose of grants made under this section shall be to—

(1) provide information on the benefits and difficulties of using innovative financing techniques for airport development projects;

(2) lower the total cost of an airport development project; or

(3) expedite the delivery or completion of an airport development project without reducing safety or causing environmental harm.

(c) LIMITATIONS.—

(1) NO GUARANTEES.—In no case shall the implementation of an innovative financing technique under this section be used in a manner giving rise to a direct or indirect guarantee of any airport debt instrument by the United States Government.

(2) TYPES OF TECHNIQUES.—In this section, innovative financing techniques are limited to—

(A) payment of interest;

(B) commercial bond insurance and other credit enhancement associated with airport bonds for eligible airport development;

(C) flexible non-Federal matching requirements;

(D) use of funds apportioned under section 47114 for the payment of principal and interest of terminal development for costs incurred before the date of the enactment of this section; and

(E) any other techniques that the Secretary determines are consistent with the purposes of this section.

(Added Pub. L. 106–181, title I, §132(a), Apr. 5, 2000, 114 Stat. 80; amended Pub. L. 108–176, title I, §156, Dec. 12, 2003, 117 Stat. 2508; Pub. L. 118–63, title VII, §721, May 16, 2024, 138 Stat. 1264.)

§47136. ZERO-EMISSION AIRPORT VEHICLES AND INFRASTRUCTURE

(a) IN GENERAL.—The Secretary of Transportation may establish a pilot program under which the sponsors of public-use airports may use funds made available under this chapter or section 48103 for use at such airports to carry out—

(1) activities associated with the acquisition, by purchase or lease, and operation of eligible zero-emission vehicles and equipment, including removable power sources for such vehicles; and

(2) the construction or modification of infrastructure to facilitate the delivery of fuel, power or services necessary for the use of such vehicles.

(b) ELIGIBILITY.—A public-use airport is eligible for participation in the program if the eligible vehicles or equipment are—

(1) used exclusively on airport property; or

(2) used exclusively to transport passengers and employees between the airport and—

(A) nearby facilities which are owned or controlled by the airport or which otherwise directly support the functions or services provided by the airport; or

(B) an intermodal surface transportation facility adjacent to the airport.

(c) SELECTION CRITERIA.—In selecting from among applicants for participation in the program, the Secretary shall give priority consideration to applicants that—

(1) will achieve the greatest air quality benefits measured by the amount of emissions reduced per dollar of funds expended under the program; and

(2) provide a long-term management plan for eligible vehicles and equipment that includes the existing and future infrastructure requirements of the airport related to such vehicles and equipment.

(d) FEDERAL SHARE.—The Federal share of the cost of a project carried out under the program shall be the Federal share specified in section 47109.

(e) TECHNICAL ASSISTANCE.—

(1) IN GENERAL.—The sponsor of a public-use airport may use not more than 10 percent of the amounts made available to the sponsor under the program in any fiscal year for—

(A) technical assistance; and

(B) project management support to assist the airport with the solicitation, acquisition, and deployment of zero-emission vehicles, related equipment, and supporting infrastructure.

(2) PROVIDERS OF TECHNICAL ASSISTANCE.—To receive the technical assistance or project management support described in paragraph (1), participants in the program may use—

(A) a nonprofit organization selected by the Secretary; or

(B) a university transportation center receiving grants under section 5505 in the region of the airport.

(f) MATERIALS IDENTIFYING BEST PRACTICES.—The Secretary may create and make available materials identifying best practices for carrying out activities funded under the program based on previous related projects and other sources.

(g) ALLOWABLE PROJECT COST.—The allowable project cost for the acquisition of a zero-emission vehicle shall be the total cost of purchasing or leasing the vehicle, including the cost of technical assistance or project management support described in subsection (e).

(h) Flexible Procurement.—A sponsor of a public-use airport may use funds made available under the program to acquire, by purchase or lease, a zero-emission vehicle and a removable power source in separate transactions, including transactions by which the airport purchases the vehicle and leases the removable power source.

(i) Testing Required.—

(1) In general.—A sponsor of a public-use airport may not use funds made available under the program to acquire a zero-emission vehicle unless that make, model, or type of vehicle has been tested by a Federal vehicle testing facility acceptable to the Secretary.

(2) Penalties for false statements.—A certification of compliance under paragraph (1) shall be considered a certification required under this subchapter for purposes of section 47126.

(j) Definitions.—In this section, the following definitions apply:

(1) Eligible zero-emission vehicle and equipment.—The term "eligible zero-emission vehicle and equipment" means a zero-emission vehicle, equipment related to such a vehicle, or ground support equipment that includes zero-emission technology that is—

(A) used exclusively on airport property; or

(B) used exclusively to transport passengers and employees between the airport and—

(i) nearby facilities which are owned or controlled by the airport or which otherwise directly support the functions or services provided by the airport; or

(ii) an intermodal surface transportation facility adjacent to the airport.

(2) Removable power source.—The term "removable power source" means a power source that is separately installed in, and removable from, a zero-emission vehicle and may include a battery, a fuel cell, an ultra-capacitor, or other power source used in a zero-emission vehicle.

(3) Zero-emission vehicle.—The term "zero-emission vehicle" means—

(A) a zero-emission vehicle as defined in section 88.102–94 of title 40, Code of Federal Regulations; or

(B) a vehicle that produces zero exhaust emissions of any criteria pollutant (or precursor pollutant) under any possible operational modes and conditions.

(Added Pub. L. 112–95, title V, §511(a), Feb. 14, 2012, 126 Stat. 107, §47136a; renumbered §47136 and amended Pub. L. 115–254, div. B, title I, §§166(b)(1), 192(a), Oct. 5, 2018, 132 Stat. 3226, 3239; Pub. L. 118–63, title VII, §722, May 16, 2024, 138 Stat. 1265.)

[§47136a. Renumbered §47136]

§47137. Airport security program

(a) General Authority.—To improve security at public airports in the United States, the Secretary of Transportation shall carry out not less than one project to test and evaluate innovative aviation security systems and related technology.

(b) Priority.—In carrying out this section, the Secretary shall give the highest priority to a request from an eligible sponsor for a grant to undertake a project that—

(1) evaluates and tests the benefits of innovative aviation security systems or related technology, including explosives detection systems, for the purpose of improving

aviation and aircraft physical security, access control, and passenger and baggage screening; and

(2) provides testing and evaluation of airport security systems and technology in an operational, testbed environment.

(c) MATCHING SHARE.—Notwithstanding section 47109, the United States Government's share of allowable project costs for a project under this section shall be 100 percent.

(d) TERMS AND CONDITIONS.—The Secretary may establish such terms and conditions as the Secretary determines appropriate for carrying out a project under this section, including terms and conditions relating to the form and content of a proposal for a project, project assurances, and schedule of payments.

(e) ADMINISTRATION.—The Secretary, in cooperation with the Secretary of Homeland Security, shall administer the program authorized by this section.

(f) ELIGIBLE SPONSOR DEFINED.—In this section, the term "eligible sponsor" means a nonprofit corporation composed of a consortium of public and private persons, including a sponsor of a primary airport, with the necessary engineering and technical expertise to successfully conduct the testing and evaluation of airport and aircraft related security systems.

(g) AUTHORIZATION OF APPROPRIATIONS.—Of the amounts made available to the Secretary under section 47115 in a fiscal year, the Secretary shall make available not less than $5,000,000 for the purpose of carrying out this section.

(Added Pub. L. 106–181, title I, §134(a), Apr. 5, 2000, 114 Stat. 83; amended Pub. L. 108–176, title I, §157, Dec. 12, 2003, 117 Stat. 2508.)

§47138. PILOT PROGRAM FOR PURCHASE OF AIRPORT DEVELOPMENT RIGHTS

(a) IN GENERAL.—The Secretary of Transportation shall establish a pilot program to support the purchase, by a State or political subdivision of a State, of development rights associated with, or directly affecting the use of, privately owned public use airports located in that State. Under the program, the Secretary may make a grant to a State or political subdivision of a State from funds apportioned under section 47114 for the purchase of such rights.

(b) GRANT REQUIREMENTS.—

(1) IN GENERAL.—The Secretary may not make a grant under subsection (a) unless the grant is made—

(A) to enable the State or political subdivision to purchase development rights in order to ensure that the airport property will continue to be available for use as a public airport; and

(B) subject to a requirement that the State or political subdivision acquire an easement or other appropriate covenant requiring that the airport shall remain a public use airport in perpetuity.

(2) MATCHING REQUIREMENT.—The amount of a grant under the program may not exceed 90 percent of the costs of acquiring the development rights.

(c) GRANT STANDARDS.—The Secretary shall prescribe standards for grants under subsection (a), including—

(1) grant application and approval procedures; and

(2) requirements for the content of the instrument recording the purchase of the

development rights.

(d) RELEASE OF PURCHASED RIGHTS AND COVENANT.—Any development rights purchased under the program shall remain the property of the State or political subdivision unless the Secretary approves the transfer or disposal of the development rights after making a determination that the transfer or disposal of that right is in the public interest.

(e) LIMITATION.—The Secretary may not make a grant under the pilot program for the purchase of development rights at more than 10 airports.

(Added Pub. L. 108–176, title I, §152(a), Dec. 12, 2003, 117 Stat. 2506.)

§47139. EMISSION CREDITS FOR AIR QUALITY PROJECTS

(a) IN GENERAL.—The Administrator of the Environmental Protection Agency, in consultation with the Secretary of Transportation, shall issue guidance on how to ensure that airport sponsors may receive appropriate emission reduction credits for carrying out projects, including projects described in sections 40117(a)(3)(G), 47102(3)(K), and 47102(3)(L). Such guidance shall include, at a minimum, the following considerations:

(1) The provision of credits is consistent with the Clean Air Act (42 U.S.C. 7402 et seq.).

(2) Credits generated by the emissions reductions are kept by the airport sponsor, including for an airport outside of a nonattainment area or maintenance area, and may be used for purposes of any current or future general conformity determination under the Clean Air Act, as offsets under the Environmental Protection Agency's new source review program for projects on the airport or associated with the airport, or as part of a State implementation plan.

(3) Credits are calculated and provided to airports on a consistent basis nationwide.

(4) Credits are provided to airport sponsors in a timely manner.

(5) The establishment of a method to assure the Secretary that, for any specific airport project for which funding is being requested, the appropriate credits will be granted.

(b) STATE AUTHORITY UNDER CAA.—Nothing in this section shall be construed as overriding existing State law or regulation pursuant to section 116 of the Clean Air Act (42 U.S.C. 7416).

(Added Pub. L. 108–176, title I, §158(a), Dec. 12, 2003, 117 Stat. 2508; amended Pub. L. 112–95, title I, §§111(c)(2)(A)(v), 152(d), Feb. 14, 2012, 126 Stat. 18, 34; Pub. L. 115–254, div. B, title I, §166(b)(2), Oct. 5, 2018, 132 Stat. 3226; Pub. L. 118–63, title VII, §782, May 16, 2024, 138 Stat. 1302.)

§47140. MEETING CURRENT AND FUTURE ENERGY POWER DEMAND

(a) IN GENERAL.—The Secretary of Transportation shall establish a program under which the Secretary shall—

(1) encourage the sponsor of each public-use airport to—

(A) conduct airport planning that assesses the airport's—

(i) current and future energy power requirements, including—

(I) heating and cooling;

(II) on-road airport vehicles and ground support equipment;

(III) gate electrification;

(IV) electric aircraft charging; and

(V) vehicles and equipment used to transport passengers and employees

between the airport and—
    (aa) nearby facilities owned or controlled by the airport or which otherwise directly support the functions or services provided by the airport; or
    (bb) an intermodal surface transportation facility adjacent to the airport; and
    (ii) existing energy infrastructure condition, location, and capacity, including base load and backup power, to meet the current and future electrical power demand as identified in this subparagraph; and
    (B) conduct airport development to improve energy efficiency, increase peak load savings at the airport, and meet future electrical power demands as identified in subparagraph (A); and
    (2) reimburse the airport sponsor for the costs incurred in conducting the assessment under paragraph (1)(A).

(b) GRANTS.—The Secretary shall make grants to airport sponsors from amounts made available under section 48103 to assist such sponsors that have completed the assessment described in subsection (a)(1)—
    (1) to acquire or construct equipment that will improve energy efficiency at the airport; and
    (2) to pursue an airport development project described in subsection (a)(1)(B).

(c) APPLICATION.—To be eligible for a grant under paragraph (1),[1] the sponsor of a public-use airport shall submit an application, including a certification that no safety projects are being deferred by requesting a grant under this section, to the Secretary at such time, in such manner, and containing such information as the Secretary may require.

(Added Pub. L. 112–95, title V, §512(a), Feb. 14, 2012, 126 Stat. 109, §47140a; renumbered §47140 and amended Pub. L. 115–254, div. B, title I, §§166(b)(1), 171, Oct. 5, 2018, 132 Stat. 3226, 3227; Pub. L. 118–63, title VII, §742(a), May 16, 2024, 138 Stat. 1278.)

[1] So in original. Probably should be "subsection (b)".

[§47140A. RENUMBERED §47140]

§47141. COMPATIBLE LAND USE PLANNING AND PROJECTS BY STATE AND LOCAL GOVERNMENTS

(a) IN GENERAL.—The Secretary of Transportation may make grants, from amounts set aside under section 47117(e)(1)(A), to States and units of local government for development and implementation of land use compatibility plans and implementation of land use compatibility projects resulting from those plans for the purposes of making the use of land areas around large hub airports and medium hub airports compatible with aircraft operations. The Secretary may make a grant under this section for a land use compatibility plan or a project resulting from such plan only if—
    (1) the airport operator has not submitted a noise compatibility program to the Secretary under section 47504 or has not updated such program within the preceding 10 years; and
    (2) the land use plan or project meets the requirements of this section.

(b) ELIGIBILITY.—In order to receive a grant under this section, a State or unit of local government must—

(1) have the authority to plan and adopt land use control measures, including zoning, in the planning area in and around a large or medium hub airport;

(2) enter into an agreement with the airport owner or operator that the development of the land use compatibility plan will be done cooperatively; and

(3) provide written assurance to the Secretary that it will achieve, to the maximum extent possible, compatible land uses consistent with Federal land use compatibility criteria under section 47502(3) and that those compatible land uses will be maintained.

(c) ASSURANCES.—The Secretary shall require a State or unit of local government to which a grant may be made under this section for a land use plan or a project resulting from such plan to provide—

(1) assurances satisfactory to the Secretary that the plan—

(A) is reasonably consistent with the goal of reducing existing noncompatible land uses and preventing the introduction of additional noncompatible land uses;

(B) addresses ways to achieve and maintain compatible land uses, including zoning, building codes, and any other land use compatibility measures under section 47504(a)(2) that are within the authority of the State or unit of local government to implement;

(C) uses noise contours provided by the airport operator that are consistent with the airport operation and planning, including any noise abatement measures adopted by the airport operator as part of its own noise mitigation efforts;

(D) does not duplicate, and is not inconsistent with, the airport operator's noise compatibility measures for the same area; and

(E) has been approved jointly by the airport owner or operator and the State or unit of local government; and

(2) such other assurances as the Secretary determines to be necessary to carry out this section.

(d) GUIDELINES.—The Secretary shall establish guidelines to administer this section in accordance with the purposes and conditions described in this section. The Secretary may require a State or unit of local government to which a grant may be made under this section to provide progress reports and other information as the Secretary determines to be necessary to carry out this section.

(e) ELIGIBLE PROJECTS.—The Secretary may approve a grant under this section to a State or unit of local government for a project resulting from a land use compatibility plan only if the Secretary is satisfied that the project is consistent with the guidelines established by the Secretary under this section, the State or unit of local government has provided the assurances required by this section, the State or unit of local government has implemented (or has made provision to implement) those elements of the plan that are not eligible for Federal financial assistance, and that the project is not inconsistent with applicable Federal Aviation Administration standards.

(f) SUNSET.—This section shall not be in effect after May 10, 2024.

(Added Pub. L. 108–176, title I, §160(a), Dec. 12, 2003, 117 Stat. 2511; amended Pub. L. 110–253, §3(c)(2), June 30, 2008, 122 Stat. 2417; Pub. L. 110–330, §5(g), Sept. 30, 2008, 122 Stat. 3718; Pub. L. 111–12, §5(f), Mar. 30, 2009, 123 Stat. 1458; Pub. L. 111–69, §5(g), Oct. 1, 2009, 123 Stat. 2055; Pub. L. 111–116, §5(f), Dec. 16, 2009, 123 Stat. 3032; Pub. L. 111–153, §5(f), Mar. 31, 2010, 124 Stat. 1085; Pub. L. 111–161, §5(f), Apr. 30, 2010, 124 Stat. 1127; Pub. L. 111–197, §5(f), July 2, 2010, 124 Stat. 1354; Pub. L. 111–216, title I, §104(f), Aug. 1, 2010, 124 Stat. 2349; Pub. L. 111–249, §5(g), Sept. 30, 2010, 124 Stat. 2628; Pub.

L. 111–329, §5(f), Dec. 22, 2010, 124 Stat. 3567; Pub. L. 112–7, §5(f), Mar. 31, 2011, 125 Stat. 32; Pub. L. 112–16, §5(f), May 31, 2011, 125 Stat. 219; Pub. L. 112–21, §5(f), June 29, 2011, 125 Stat. 234; Pub. L. 112–27, §5(f), Aug. 5, 2011, 125 Stat. 271; Pub. L. 112–30, title II, §205(g), Sept. 16, 2011, 125 Stat. 358; Pub. L. 112–91, §5(g), Jan. 31, 2012, 126 Stat. 4; Pub. L. 112–95, title I, §153, Feb. 14, 2012, 126 Stat. 34; Pub. L. 114–55, title I, §102(d), Sept. 30, 2015, 129 Stat. 523; Pub. L. 114–141, title I, §102(d), Mar. 30, 2016, 130 Stat. 323; Pub. L. 114–190, title I, §1102(d), July 15, 2016, 130 Stat. 617; Pub. L. 115–63, title I, §102(e), Sept. 29, 2017, 131 Stat. 1169; Pub. L. 115–141, div. M, title I, §102(d), Mar. 23, 2018, 132 Stat. 1046; Pub. L. 115–254, div. B, title I, §117(b), Oct. 5, 2018, 132 Stat. 3201; Pub. L. 118–15, div. B, title II, §2202(h), Sept. 30, 2023, 137 Stat. 83; Pub. L. 118–34, title I, §102(h), Dec. 26, 2023, 137 Stat. 1113; Pub. L. 118–41, title I, §102(h), Mar. 8, 2024, 138 Stat. 21.)

§47142. ALTERNATIVE PROJECT DELIVERY

(a) IN GENERAL.—The Secretary of Transportation may approve an application of an airport sponsor under this section to authorize the airport sponsor to award a covered project delivery contract using a selection process permitted under applicable State or local law if—

(1) the Administrator approves the application using criteria established by the Administrator;

(2) the covered project delivery contract is in a form that is approved by the Administrator;

(3) the Administrator is satisfied that the contract will be executed pursuant to competitive procedures and contains a schematic design adequate for the Administrator to approve the grant;

(4) use of a covered project delivery contract is projected to be cost effective and expedite the project;

(5) the Administrator is satisfied that there will be no conflict of interest; and

(6) the Administrator is satisfied that the selection process will be as open, fair, and objective as the competitive bid system and that at least 3 or more bids will be submitted for each project under the selection process.

(b) REIMBURSEMENT OF COSTS.—The Administrator may reimburse an airport sponsor for design and construction costs incurred before a grant is made pursuant to this section if the project is approved by the Administrator in advance and is carried out in accordance with all administrative and statutory requirements that would have been applicable under this chapter if the project were carried out after a grant agreement had been executed.

(c) PILOT PROGRAM.—

(1) PILOT PROGRAM.—Not later than 270 days after the date of enactment of this section, the Secretary shall establish a pilot program under which the Administrator may award grants for integrated project delivery contracts, as described in subsection (d)(2), to carry out up to 5 building construction projects at airports in the United States with a grant awarded under section 47104.

(2) APPLICATION.—

(A) ELIGIBILITY.—A sponsor of an airport may submit to the Secretary an application, in such time and manner and containing such information as the Secretary may require, to carry out a building construction project under the pilot program that would otherwise be eligible for assistance under this chapter.

(B) APPROVAL.—The Secretary may approve the application of a sponsor of an airport submitted under paragraph (1) to authorize such sponsor to award an integrated project delivery contract using a selection process permitted under applicable State or local law if—

    (i) the Secretary approves the application using criteria established by the Secretary;

    (ii) the integrated project delivery contract is in a form that is approved by the Secretary;

    (iii) the Secretary is satisfied that the contract will be executed pursuant to competitive procedures and contains a schematic design and any other material that the Secretary determines sufficient to approve the grant;

    (iv) the Secretary is satisfied that the use of an integrated project delivery contract will be cost effective and expedite the project;

    (v) the Secretary is satisfied that there will be no conflict of interest; and

    (vi) the Secretary is satisfied that the contract selection process will be open, fair, and objective and that not less than 2 sets of proposals will be submitted for each team entity under the selection process.

(3) REIMBURSEMENT OF COSTS.—

(A) IN GENERAL.—The Secretary may reimburse a sponsor of an airport for any design or construction costs incurred before a grant is made pursuant to this section if—

    (i) the project funding is approved by the Secretary in advance;

    (ii) the project is carried out in accordance with all administrative and statutory requirements under this chapter; and

    (iii) the project is carried out under this chapter after a grant agreement has been executed.

(B) ACCOUNTING.—Reimbursement of costs shall be based on transparent cost accounting or open book cost accounting.

(d) COVERED PROJECT DELIVERY CONTRACT DEFINED.—In this section, the term "covered project delivery contract" means—

(1) an agreement that provides for both design and construction of a project by a contractor through alternative project delivery methods, including construction manager-at-risk and progressive design build; or

(2) a single contract for the delivery of a whole project that—

(A) includes, at a minimum, the sponsor, builder, and architect-engineer as parties that are subject to the terms of the contract;

(B) aligns the interests of all the parties to the contract with respect to the project costs and project outcomes; and

(C) includes processes to ensure transparency and collaboration among all parties to the contract relating to project costs and project outcomes.

(Added Pub. L. 108–176, title I, §181(a), Dec. 12, 2003, 117 Stat. 2515; amended Pub. L. 118–63, title VII, §723(a), May 16, 2024, 138 Stat. 1265.)

§47143. NON-MOVEMENT AREA SURVEILLANCE SURFACE DISPLAY SYSTEMS PILOT PROGRAM

(a) IN GENERAL.—The Administrator of the Federal Aviation Administration may carry out a pilot program to support non-Federal acquisition and installation of qualifying non-movement area surveillance surface display systems and sensors if—

(1) the Administrator determines that such systems and sensors would improve safety or capacity in the National Airspace System; and

(2) the non-movement area surveillance surface display systems and sensors supplement existing movement area systems and sensors at the selected airports established under other programs administered by the Administrator.

(b) PROJECT GRANTS.—

(1) IN GENERAL.—For purposes of carrying out the pilot program, the Administrator may make a project grant out of funds apportioned under paragraph (1) or paragraph (2) of section 47114(c) to not more than 5 eligible sponsors to acquire and install qualifying non-movement area surveillance surface display systems and sensors. The airports selected to participate in the pilot program shall have existing Administration movement area systems and airlines that are participants in Federal Aviation Administration's airport collaborative decision-making process.

(2) DATA EXCHANGE PROCESSES.—As part of the pilot program carried out under this section, the Administrator may establish data exchange processes to allow airport participation in the Administration's airport collaborative decision-making process and fusion of the non-movement surveillance data with the Administration's movement area systems.

(c) SUNSET.—This section shall cease to be effective on October 1, 2028.

(d) DEFINITIONS.—In this section:

(1) NON-MOVEMENT AREA.—The term "non-movement area" means the portion of the airfield surface that is not under the control of air traffic control.

(2) NON-MOVEMENT AREA SURVEILLANCE SURFACE DISPLAY SYSTEMS AND SENSORS.—The term "non-movement area surveillance surface display systems and sensors" means a non-Federal surveillance system that uses on-airport sensors that track vehicles or aircraft that are equipped with transponders in the non-movement area.

(3) QUALIFYING NON-MOVEMENT AREA SURVEILLANCE SURFACE DISPLAY SYSTEM AND SENSORS.—The term "qualifying non-movement area surveillance surface display system and sensors" means a non-movement area surveillance surface display system that—

(A) provides the required transmit and receive data formats consistent with the National Airspace System architecture at the appropriate service delivery point;

(B) is on-airport; and

(C) is airport operated.

(Added Pub. L. 115–254, div. B, title I, §140(a), Oct. 5, 2018, 132 Stat. 3210; amended Pub. L. 118–15, div. B, title II, §2202(i), Sept. 30, 2023, 137 Stat. 83; Pub. L. 118–34, title I, §102(i), Dec. 26, 2023, 137 Stat. 1113; Pub. L. 118–41, title I, §102(i), Mar. 8, 2024, 138 Stat. 21; Pub. L. 118–63, title VII, §724, May 16, 2024, 138 Stat. 1267.)

§47144. USE OF FUNDS FOR REPAIRS FOR RUNWAY SAFETY REPAIRS

(a) IN GENERAL.—The Secretary of Transportation may make project grants under this subchapter to an airport described in subsection (b) from funds under section 47114 apportioned to that airport or funds available for discretionary grants to that airport under section 47115 to conduct airport development to repair the runway safety area of the airport damaged as a result of a natural disaster in order to maintain compliance with the regulations of the Federal Aviation Administration relating to runway safety areas, without regard to whether construction of the runway safety area damaged was carried out using amounts the airport received under this subchapter.

(b) AIRPORTS DESCRIBED.—An airport is described in this subsection if—

(1) the airport is a public-use airport;

(2) the airport is listed in the National Plan of Integrated Airport Systems of the Federal Aviation Administration;

(3) the runway safety area of the airport was damaged as a result of a natural disaster;

(4) the airport was denied funding under the Robert T. Stafford Disaster Relief and Emergency Assistance Act (42 U.S.C. 5121 et seq.) with respect to the disaster;

(5) the operator of the airport has exhausted all legal remedies, including legal action against any parties (or insurers thereof) whose action or inaction may have contributed to the need for the repair of the runway safety area;

(6) there is still a demonstrated need for the runway safety area to accommodate current or imminent aeronautical demand; and

(7) the cost of repairing or replacing the runway safety area is reasonable in relation to the anticipated operational benefit of repairing the runway safety area, as determined by the Administrator of the Federal Aviation Administration.

(Added Pub. L. 115–31, div. K, title I, §119F(a), May 5, 2017, 131 Stat. 734; amended Pub. L. 118–63, title XI, §1101(w), May 16, 2024, 138 Stat. 1414.)

§47145. PILOT PROGRAM FOR AIRPORT ACCESSIBILITY

(a) IN GENERAL.—The Secretary of Transportation shall establish and carry out a pilot program to award grants to sponsors to carry out capital projects to upgrade the accessibility of commercial service airports for individuals with disabilities by increasing the number of commercial service airports, airport terminals, or airport facilities that meet or exceed the standards and regulations under the Americans with Disabilities Act of 1990 (42 U.S.C. 12131 et seq.) and the Rehabilitation Act of 1973 (29 U.S.C. 701 note) .

(b) USE OF FUNDS.—

(1) IN GENERAL.—Subject to paragraph (2), a sponsor shall use a grant awarded under this section—

(A) for a project to repair, improve, or relocate the infrastructure of an airport, airport terminal, or airport facility to increase accessibility for individuals with disabilities, or as part of a plan to increase accessibility for individuals with disabilities;

(B) to develop or modify a plan (as described in subsection (e)) for a project that increases accessibility for individuals with disabilities, including—

(i) assessments of accessibility or assessments of planned modifications to an airport, airport terminal, or airport facility for passenger use, performed by the disability advisory committee of the recipient airport (if applicable), the protection and advocacy system for individuals with disabilities in the applicable State, a center for independent living, or a disability organization, including an advocacy or nonprofit organization that represents or provides services to individuals with disabilities; or

(ii) coordination by the disability advisory committee of the recipient airport with a protection and advocacy system, center for independent living, or such disability organization; or

(C) to carry out any other project that meets or exceeds the standards and regulations described in subsection (a).

(2) LIMITATION.—Eligible costs for a project funded with a grant awarded under this section shall be limited to the costs associated with carrying out the purpose authorized under subsection (a).

(c) ELIGIBILITY.—A sponsor may use a grant under this section to upgrade a commercial service airport that is accessible to and usable by individuals with disabilities—

(1) consistent with the current (as of the date of the upgrade) standards and regulations described in subsection (a); and

(2) even if the related service, program, or activity, when viewed in the entirely of the service, program, or activity, is readily accessible and usable as so described.

(d) SELECTION CRITERIA.—In making grants to sponsors under this section, the Secretary shall give priority to sponsors that are proposing—

(1) a capital project to upgrade the accessibility of a commercial service airport that is not accessible to and usable by individuals with disabilities consistent with standards and regulations described in subsection (a); or

(2) to meet or exceed the Airports Council International accreditation under the Accessibility Enhancement Accreditation, through the incorporation of universal design principles.

(e) ACCESSIBILITY COMMITMENT.—A sponsor that receives a grant under this section shall adopt a plan under which the sponsor commits to pursuing airport accessibility projects that—

(1) enhance the passenger experience and maximize accessibility of commercial service airports, airport terminals, or airport facilities for individuals with disabilities, including by—

(A) upgrading bathrooms, counters, or pumping rooms;

(B) increasing audio and visual accessibility on information boards, security gates, or paging systems;

(C) updating airport terminals to increase the availability of accessible seating and power outlets for durable medical equipment (such as powered wheelchairs);

(D) updating airport websites and other information communication technology to be accessible for individuals with disabilities; or

(E) increasing the number of elevators, including elevators that move power wheelchairs to an aircraft;

(2) improve the operations of, provide efficiencies of service to, and enhance the use of commercial service airports for individuals with disabilities;

(3) establish a disability advisory committee if the airport is a small, medium, or large hub airport; and

(4) make improvements in personnel, infrastructure, and technology that can assist passenger self-identification regarding disability and needing assistance.

(f) COORDINATION WITH DISABILITY ADVOCACY ENTITIES.—In administering grants under this section, the Secretary shall encourage—

(1) engagement with disability advocacy entities (such as the disability advisory

committee of the sponsor) and a protection and advocacy system for individuals with disabilities in the applicable State, a center for independent living, or a disability organization, including an advocacy or nonprofit organization that represents or provides services to individuals with disabilities; and

(2) assessments of accessibility or assessments of planned modifications to commercial service airports to the extent merited by the scope of the capital project of the sponsor proposed to be assisted under this section, taking into account any such assessment already conducted by the Federal Aviation Administration.

(g) FEDERAL SHARE OF COSTS.—The Government's share of allowable project costs for a project carried out with a grant under this section shall be the Government's share of allowable project costs specified under section 47109.

(h) DEFINITIONS.—In this section:

(1) CENTER FOR INDEPENDENT LIVING.—The term "center for independent living" has the meaning given such term in section 702 of the Rehabilitation Act of 1973 (29 U.S.C. 796a).

(2) DISABILITY ADVISORY COMMITTEE.—The term "disability advisory committee" means a body of stakeholders (including airport staff, airline representatives, and individuals with disabilities) that provide to airports and appropriate transportation authorities input from individuals with disabilities, including identifying opportunities for removing barriers, expanding accessibility features, and improving accessibility for individuals with disabilities at airports.

(3) PROTECTION AND ADVOCACY SYSTEM.—The term "protection and advocacy system" means a system established in accordance with section 143 of the Developmental Disabilities Assistance and Bill of Rights Act of 2000 (42 U.S.C. 15043).

(i) FUNDING.—Notwithstanding any other provision of this chapter, for each of fiscal years 2025 through 2028, the Secretary may use up to $20,000,000 of the amounts that would otherwise be used to make grants from the discretionary fund under section 47115 for each such fiscal year to carry out this section.

(Added Pub. L. 118–63, title VII, §725(a), May 16, 2024, 138 Stat. 1267.)

§47146. GENERAL AVIATION PROGRAM RUNWAY EXTENSION PILOT PROGRAM

(a) ESTABLISHMENT.—The Secretary of Transportation shall establish and carry out a pilot program to provide grants to general aviation airports to increase the usable runway length capability at such airports in order to—

(1) expand access to such airports for larger aircraft; and

(2) support the development and economic viability of such airports.

(b) GRANTS.—

(1) IN GENERAL.—For the purpose of carrying out the pilot program established in subsection (a), the Secretary shall make grants to not more than 2 sponsors of general aviation airports per fiscal year.

(2) USE OF FUNDS.—A sponsor of a general aviation airport shall use a grant awarded under this section to plan, design, or construct a project to extend an existing primary runway by not greater than 1,000 feet in order to accommodate large turboprop or turbojet aircraft that cannot be accommodated with the existing runway length.

(3) ELIGIBILITY.—To be eligible to receive a grant under this section, a sponsor of a

general aviation airport shall submit an application to the Secretary at such time, in such form, and containing such information as the Secretary may require.

(4) SELECTION.—In selecting an applicant for a grant under this section, the Secretary shall prioritize projects that demonstrate that the existing runway length at the airport is—

(A) inadequate to support the near-term operations of 1 or more business entities operating at the airport as of the date of submission of such application;

(B) a direct aircraft operational impediment to airport economic viability, job creation or retention, or local economic development; and

(C) not located within 20 miles of another National Plan of Integrated Airport Systems airport with comparable runway length.

(c) PROJECT JUSTIFICATION.—A project that demonstrates the criteria described in subsection (b) shall be considered a justified cost with respect to the pilot program, notwithstanding—

(1) any benefit-cost analysis required under section 47115(d); or

(2) a project justification determination described in section 3 of chapter 3 of FAA Order 5100.38D, Airport Improvement Program Handbook (dated September 30, 2014) (or any successor document).

(d) FEDERAL SHARE.—The Government's share of allowable project costs for a project carried out with a grant under this section shall be the Government's share of allowable project costs specified under section 47109.

(e) REPORT TO CONGRESS.—Not later than 5 years after the establishment of the pilot program under subsection (a), the Secretary shall submit to the Committee on Commerce, Science, and Transportation of the Senate and the Committee on Transportation and Infrastructure of the House of Representatives a report that evaluates the pilot program, including—

(1) information regarding the level of applicant interest in grants for increasing runway length;

(2) the number of large aircraft that accessed each general aviation airport that received a grant under the pilot program in comparison to the number of such aircraft that accessed the airport prior to the date of enactment of the FAA Reauthorization Act of 2024, based on data provided to the Secretary by the airport sponsor not later than 6 months before the submission date described in this subsection; and

(3) a description, provided to the Secretary by the airport sponsor not later than 6 months before the submission date described in this subsection, of the economic development opportunities supported by increasing the runway length at general aviation airports.

(f) FUNDING.—For each of fiscal years 2025 through 2028, the Secretary may use funds under section 47116(b)(2) to carry out this section.

(Added Pub. L. 118–63, title VII, §726(a), May 16, 2024, 138 Stat. 1269.)

SUBCHAPTER II—SURPLUS PROPERTY FOR PUBLIC AIRPORTS

§47151. Authority to transfer an interest in surplus property

(a) GENERAL AUTHORITY.—Subject to sections 47152 and 47153 of this title, a department, agency, or instrumentality of the executive branch of the United States Government or a wholly owned Government corporation may convey to a State, political subdivision of a State, or tax-supported organization any interest in surplus property—

(1) that the Secretary of Transportation decides is—

(A) desirable for developing, improving, operating, or maintaining a public airport (as defined in section 47102 of this title);

(B) reasonably necessary to fulfill the immediate and foreseeable future requirements for developing, improving, operating, or maintaining a public airport; or

(C) needed for developing sources of revenue from nonaviation businesses at a public airport; and

(2) if the Administrator of General Services approves the conveyance and decides the interest is not best suited for industrial use.

(b) ENSURING COMPLIANCE.—Only the Secretary may ensure compliance with an instrument conveying an interest in surplus property under this subchapter. The Secretary may amend the instrument to correct the instrument or to make the conveyance comply with law.

(c) DISPOSING OF INTERESTS NOT CONVEYED UNDER THIS SUBCHAPTER.—An interest in surplus property that could be used at a public airport but that is not conveyed under this subchapter shall be disposed of under other applicable law.

(d) WAIVER OF CONDITION.—The Secretary may not waive any condition imposed on an interest in surplus property conveyed under subsection (a) that such interest be used for an aeronautical purpose unless the Secretary provides public notice not less than 30 days before the issuance of such waiver and determines that such waiver—

(1) will not significantly impair the aeronautical purpose of an airport;

(2) will not result in the permanent closure of an airport (unless the Secretary determines that the waiver will directly facilitate the construction of a replacement airport); or

(3) is necessary to protect or advance the civil aviation interests of the United States.

(e) REQUESTS BY PUBLIC AGENCIES.—Except with respect to a request made by another department, agency, or instrumentality of the executive branch of the United States Government, such a department, agency, or instrumentality shall give priority consideration to a request made by a public agency (as defined in section 47102) for surplus property described in subsection (a) for use at a public airport.

(Pub. L. 103–272, §1(e), July 5, 1994, 108 Stat. 1278; Pub. L. 106–181, title I, §§125(c), 135(d)(1), 136, Apr. 5, 2000, 114 Stat. 75, 84, 85; Pub. L. 112–95, title I, §152(f), Feb. 14, 2012, 126 Stat. 34; Pub. L. 118–63, title VII, §719(b)(1), May 16, 2024, 138 Stat. 1261.)

§47152. Terms of conveyances

Except as provided in section 47153 of this title, the following terms apply to a conveyance of an interest in surplus property under this subchapter:

(1) A State, political subdivision of a State, or tax-supported organization receiving the interest may use, lease, salvage, or dispose of the interest for other than airport purposes only after the Secretary of Transportation gives written consent that the interest can be used, leased, salvaged, or disposed of without materially and adversely affecting the development, improvement, operation, or maintenance of the airport at which the property is located.

(2) The interest shall be used and maintained for public use and benefit without unreasonable discrimination.

(3) A right may not be vested in a person, excluding others in the same class from using the airport at which the property is located—

(A) to conduct an aeronautical activity requiring the operation of aircraft; or

(B) to engage in selling or supplying aircraft, aircraft accessories, equipment, or supplies (except gasoline and oil), or aircraft services necessary to operate aircraft (including maintaining and repairing aircraft, aircraft engines, propellers, and appliances).

(4) The State, political subdivision, or tax-supported organization accepting the interest shall clear and protect the aerial approaches to the airport by mitigating existing, and preventing future, airport hazards.

(5) During a national emergency declared by the President or Congress, the United States Government is entitled to use, control, or possess, without charge, any part of the public airport at which the property is located. However, the Government shall—

(A) pay the entire cost of maintaining the part of the airport it exclusively uses, controls, or possesses during the emergency;

(B) contribute a reasonable share, consistent with the Government's use, of the cost of maintaining the property it uses nonexclusively, or over which the Government has nonexclusive control or possession, during the emergency; and

(C) pay a fair rental for use, control, or possession of improvements to the airport made without Government assistance.

(6) The Government is entitled to the nonexclusive use, without charge, of the landing area of an airport at which the property is located. The Secretary may limit the use of the landing area if necessary to prevent unreasonable interference with use by other authorized aircraft. However, the Government shall—

(A) contribute a reasonable share, consistent with the Government's use, of the cost of maintaining and operating the landing area; and

(B) pay for damages caused by its use of the landing area if its use of the landing area is substantial.

(7) The State, political subdivision, or tax-supported organization accepting the interest shall release the Government from all liability for damages arising under an agreement that provides for Government use of any part of an airport owned, controlled, or operated by the State, political subdivision, or tax-supported organization on which, adjacent to which, or in connection with which, the property is located.

(8) When a term under this section is not satisfied, any part of the interest in the property reverts to the Government, at the option of the Government, as the property then exists.

(Pub. L. 103–272, §1(e), July 5, 1994, 108 Stat. 1279; Pub. L. 106–181, title I, §135(d)(2), Apr. 5, 2000, 114 Stat. 85.)

§47153. Waiving and adding terms

(a) General Authority.—(1) The Secretary of Transportation may waive, without charge, a term of a conveyance of an interest in property under this subchapter if the Secretary decides that—

(A) the property no longer serves the purpose for which it was conveyed; or

(B) the waiver will not prevent carrying out the purpose for which the conveyance was made and is necessary to advance the civil aviation interests of the United States.

(2) The Secretary of Transportation shall waive a term under paragraph (1) of this subsection on terms the Secretary considers necessary to protect or advance the civil aviation interests of the United States.

(b) Waivers and Inclusion of Additional Terms on Request.—On request of the Secretary of Transportation or the Secretary of a military department, a department, agency, or instrumentality of the executive branch of the United States Government or a wholly owned Government corporation may waive a term required by section 47152 of this title or add another term if the appropriate Secretary decides it is necessary to protect or advance the interests of the United States in civil aviation or for national defense.

(c) Restrictions on Waiver.—Notwithstanding subsections (a) and (b), the Secretary may not waive any term under this section that an interest in land be used for an aeronautical purpose unless—

(1) the Secretary provides public notice not less than 30 days before the issuance of a waiver; and

(2) the Secretary determines that such waiver—

(A) will not significantly impair the aeronautical purpose of an airport;

(B) will not result in the permanent closure of an airport (unless the Secretary determines that the waiver will directly facilitate the construction of a replacement airport); or

(C) is necessary to protect or advance the civil aviation interests of the United States.

(Pub. L. 103–272, §1(e), July 5, 1994, 108 Stat. 1280; Pub. L. 106–181, title I, §§125(d), 135(d)(3), Apr. 5, 2000, 114 Stat. 76, 85; Pub. L. 118–63, title VII, §719(b)(2), May 16, 2024, 138 Stat. 1261.)

SUBCHAPTER III—AVIATION DEVELOPMENT STREAMLINING

§47171. Expedited, coordinated environmental review process

(a) Aviation Project Review Process.—The Secretary of Transportation shall implement an expedited and coordinated environmental review process for airport capacity enhancement projects, terminal development projects, general aviation airport construction or improvement projects, and aviation safety projects that—

(1) provides for streamlined coordination among the Federal, regional, State, and local agencies concerned with the preparation of environmental impact statements or environmental assessments under the National Environmental Policy Act of 1969 (42

U.S.C. 4321 et seq.);

(2) provides that all environmental reviews, analyses, opinions, permits, licenses, and approvals that must be issued or made by a Federal agency or airport sponsor for such a project will be conducted concurrently, to the maximum extent practicable; and

(3) provides that any environmental review, analysis, opinion, permit, license, or approval that must be issued or made by a Federal agency or airport sponsor for such a project will be completed within a time period established by the Secretary, in cooperation with the agencies identified under subsection (d) with respect to the project.

(b) AVIATION PROJECTS SUBJECT TO A STREAMLINED ENVIRONMENTAL REVIEW PROCESS.—

(1) IN GENERAL.—Any airport capacity enhancement project, terminal development project, or general aviation airport construction or improvement project shall be subject to the coordinated and expedited environmental review process requirements set forth in this section.

(2) PROJECT DESIGNATION CRITERIA.—

(A) IN GENERAL.—The Secretary may designate an aviation safety project for priority environmental review.

(B) REQUIREMENTS.—A designated project shall be subject to the coordinated and expedited environmental review process requirements set forth in this section.

(C) GUIDELINES.—

(i) IN GENERAL.—The Secretary shall establish guidelines for the designation of an aviation safety project or aviation security project for priority environmental review.

(ii) CONSIDERATION.—Guidelines established under clause (i) shall provide for consideration of—

(I) the importance or urgency of the project;

(II) the potential for undertaking the environmental review under existing emergency procedures under the National Environmental Policy Act of 1969 (42 U.S.C. 4321 et seq.);

(III) the need for cooperation and concurrent reviews by other Federal or State agencies; and

(IV) the prospect for undue delay if the project is not designated for priority review.

(c) HIGH PRIORITY OF AND AGENCY PARTICIPATION IN COORDINATED REVIEWS.—

(1) HIGH PRIORITY FOR ENVIRONMENTAL REVIEWS.—Each Federal agency with jurisdiction over an environmental review, analysis, opinion, permit, license, or approval shall accord any such review, analysis, opinion, permit, license, or approval involving a project described or designated under subsection (b) the highest possible priority and conduct the review, analysis, opinion, permit, license, or approval expeditiously.

(2) AGENCY PARTICIPATION.—Each Federal agency described in subsection (d) shall formulate and implement administrative, policy, and procedural mechanisms to enable the agency to participate in the coordinated environmental review process under this section and to ensure completion of environmental reviews, analyses, opinions, permits, licenses, and approvals described in subsection (a) in a timely and environmentally responsible manner.

(d) IDENTIFICATION OF JURISDICTIONAL AGENCIES.—With respect to a project described or designated under subsection (b), the Secretary shall identify, as soon as practicable, all Federal and State agencies that may have jurisdiction over environmental-related matters that may be affected by the project or may be required by law to conduct an environmental-related review or analysis of the project or determine whether to issue an environmental-related permit, license, or approval for the project.

(e) STATE AUTHORITY.—Under a coordinated review process being implemented under this section by the Secretary with respect to a project at an airport within the boundaries of a State, the Governor of the State, consistent with State law, may choose to participate in such process and provide that all State agencies that have jurisdiction over environmental-related matters that may be affected by the project or may be required by law to conduct an environmental-related review or analysis of the project or determine whether to issue an environmental-related permit, license, or approval for the project, be subject to the process.

(f) MEMORANDUM OF UNDERSTANDING.—The coordinated review process developed under this section may be incorporated into a memorandum of understanding for a project between the Secretary and the heads of other Federal and State agencies identified under subsection (d) with respect to the project and, if applicable, the airport sponsor.

(g) USE OF INTERAGENCY ENVIRONMENTAL IMPACT STATEMENT TEAMS.—

(1) IN GENERAL.—The Secretary may utilize an interagency environmental impact statement team to expedite and coordinate the coordinated environmental review process for a project under this section. When utilizing an interagency environmental impact statement team, the Secretary shall invite Federal, State and Tribal agencies with jurisdiction by law, and may invite such agencies with special expertise, to participate on an interagency environmental impact statement team.

(2) RESPONSIBILITY OF INTERAGENCY ENVIRONMENTAL IMPACT STATEMENT TEAM.—Under a coordinated environmental review process being implemented under this section, the interagency environmental impact statement team shall assist the Federal Aviation Administration in the preparation of the environmental impact statement. To facilitate timely and efficient environmental review, the team shall agree on agency or Tribal points of contact, protocols for communication among agencies, and deadlines for necessary actions by each individual agency (including the review of environmental analyses, the conduct of required consultation and coordination, and the issuance of environmental opinions, licenses, permits, and approvals). The members of the team may formalize their agreement in a written memorandum.

(h) LEAD AGENCY RESPONSIBILITY.—The Federal Aviation Administration shall be the lead agency for projects described in subsection (b)(1) and shall be responsible for defining the scope and content of the environmental impact statement, consistent with regulations issued by the Council on Environmental Quality. Any other Federal agency or State agency that is participating in a coordinated environmental review process under this section shall give substantial deference, to the extent consistent with applicable law and policy, to the aviation expertise of the Federal Aviation Administration.

(i) EFFECT OF FAILURE TO MEET DEADLINE.—

(1) NOTIFICATION OF CONGRESS AND CEQ.— If the Secretary determines that a Federal agency, State agency, or airport sponsor that is participating in a coordinated review process under this section with respect to a project has not met a deadline established under subsection (a)(3) for the project, the Secretary shall notify, within 30 days of the

date of such determination, the Committee on Commerce, Science, and Transportation of the Senate, the Committee on Transportation and Infrastructure of the House of Representatives, the Council on Environmental Quality, and the agency or sponsor involved about the failure to meet the deadline.

(2) AGENCY REPORT.—Not later than 30 days after date of receipt of a notice under paragraph (1), the agency or sponsor involved shall submit a report to the Secretary, the Committee on Transportation and Infrastructure of the House of Representatives, the Committee on Commerce, Science, and Transportation of the Senate, and the Council on Environmental Quality explaining why the agency or sponsor did not meet the deadline and what actions it intends to take to complete or issue the required review, analysis, opinion, permit, license, or approval.

(j) PURPOSE AND NEED.—

(1) IN GENERAL.—For any environmental review, analysis, opinion, permit, license, or approval that must be issued or made by a Federal or State agency that is participating in a coordinated review process under this section and that requires an analysis of purpose and need for the project, the agency, notwithstanding any other provision of law, shall be bound by the project purpose and need as defined by the Secretary.

(2) DEADLINE.—The Secretary shall define the purpose and need of a project not later than 45 days after—

(A) the submission of the appropriately completed proposed purpose and need description of the airport sponsor; and

(B) any appropriately completed proposed revision to a development project that affects the purpose and need description previously prepared or accepted by the Federal Aviation Administration.

(3) ASSISTANCE.—The Secretary shall provide all airport sponsors with technical assistance in drafting purpose and need statements and necessary supporting documentation for projects involving Federal approvals from more than 1 Federal agency.

(k) ALTERNATIVES ANALYSIS.—The Secretary shall determine the reasonable alternatives to a project described or designated under subsection (b). Any other Federal agency, or State agency that is participating in a coordinated review process under this section with respect to the project shall—

(1) consider only those alternatives to the project that the Secretary has determined are reasonable; and

(2) limit the comments of the agency to—

(A) subject matter areas within the special expertise of the agency; and

(B) changes necessary to ensure the agency is carrying out the obligations of that agency under the National Environmental Policy Act of 1969 (42 U.S.C. 4321 et seq.) and other applicable law.

(l) SOLICITATION AND CONSIDERATION OF COMMENTS.—In applying subsections (j) and (k), the Secretary shall solicit and consider comments from interested persons and governmental entities in accordance with the National Environmental Policy Act of 1969 (42 U.S.C. 4321 et seq.) and section 1503 of title 40, Code of Federal Regulations.

(m) COORDINATION AND SCHEDULE.—

(1) COORDINATION PLAN.—

(A) IN GENERAL.—Not later than 90 days after the date of publication of a notice of intent to prepare an environmental impact statement or the initiation of an environmental assessment, the Secretary of Transportation shall establish a plan for coordinating public and agency participation in and comment on the environmental review process for a project described or designated under subsection (b). The coordination plan may be incorporated into a memorandum of understanding.

(B) CLOUD-BASED, INTERACTIVE DIGITAL PLATFORMS.—The Secretary is encouraged to utilize cloud-based, interactive digital platforms to meet community engagement and agency coordination requirements under subparagraph (A).

(C) SCHEDULE.—

(i) IN GENERAL.—The Secretary shall establish as part of such coordination plan, after consultation with and the concurrence of each participating agency for the project and with the State in which the project is located (and, if the State is not the project sponsor, with the project sponsor), a schedule for—

(I) interim milestones and deadlines for agency activities necessary to complete the environmental review; and

(II) completion of the environmental review process for the project.

(ii) FACTORS FOR CONSIDERATION.—In establishing the schedule under clause (i), the Secretary shall consider factors such as—

(I) the responsibilities of participating agencies under applicable laws;

(II) resources available to the cooperating agencies;

(III) overall size and complexity of the project;

(IV) the overall time required by an agency to conduct an environmental review and make decisions under applicable Federal law relating to a project (including the issuance or denial of a permit or license) and the cost of the project; and

(V) the sensitivity of the natural and historic resources that could be affected by the project.

(iii) MAXIMUM PROJECT SCHEDULE.—To the maximum extent practicable and consistent with applicable Federal law, the Secretary shall develop, in concurrence with the project sponsor, a maximum schedule for the project described or designated under subsection (b) that is not more than 2 years for the completion of the environmental review process for such projects, as measured from, as applicable, the date of publication of a notice of intent to prepare an environmental impact statement to the record of decision.

(iv) DISPUTE RESOLUTION.—

(I) IN GENERAL.—Any issue or dispute that arises between the Secretary and participating agencies (or amongst participating agencies) during the environmental review process shall be addressed expeditiously to avoid delay.

(II) RESPONSIBILITIES.—The Secretary and participating agencies shall—

(aa) implement the requirements of this section consistent with any dispute resolution process established in an applicable law, regulation, or legally binding agreement to the maximum extent permitted by law; and

(bb) seek to resolve issues or disputes at the earliest possible time at the project level through agency employees who have day-to-day involvement in the project.

(III) SECRETARY RESPONSIBILITIES.—

(aa) IN GENERAL.—The Secretary shall make information available to each cooperating and participating agency and project sponsor as early as practicable in the environmental review regarding the environmental, historic, and socioeconomic resources located within the project area and the general locations of the alternatives under consideration.

(bb) SOURCES OF INFORMATION.—The information described in item (aa) may be based on existing data sources, including geographic information systems mapping.

(IV) COOPERATING AND PARTICIPATING AGENCY RESPONSIBILITIES.—Each cooperating and participating agency shall—

(aa) identify, as early as practicable, any issues of concern regarding any potential environmental impacts of the project, including any issues that could substantially delay or prevent an agency from completing any environmental review or authorization required for the project; and

(bb) communicate any issues described in item (aa) to the project sponsor.

(V) ELEVATION FOR MISSED MILESTONE.—If a dispute between the Secretary and participating agencies (or amongst participating agencies) causes a milestone to be missed or extended, or the Secretary anticipates that a permitting timetable milestone will be missed or will need to be extended, the dispute shall be elevated to an official designated by the relevant agency for resolution. The elevation of a dispute shall take place as soon as practicable after the Secretary becomes aware of the dispute or potential missed milestone.

(VI) EXCEPTION.—Disputes that do not impact the ability of an agency to meet a milestone may be elevated as appropriate.

(VII) FURTHER EVALUATION.—If a resolution has not been reached at the end of the 30-day period after a relevant milestone date or extension date after a dispute has been elevated to the designated official, the relevant agencies shall elevate the dispute to senior agency leadership for resolution.

(D) CONSISTENCY WITH OTHER TIME PERIODS.—A schedule under subparagraph (C) shall be consistent with any other relevant time periods established under Federal law.

(E) MODIFICATION.—

(i) IN GENERAL.—Except as provided in clause (ii), the Secretary may lengthen or shorten a schedule established under subparagraph (C) for good cause. The Secretary may consider a decision by the project sponsor to change, modify, expand, or reduce the scope of a project as good cause for purposes of this clause.

(ii) LIMITATIONS.—

(I) LENGTHENED SCHEDULE.—The Secretary may lengthen a schedule under clause (i) for a cooperating Federal agency by not more than 1 year after the latest deadline established for the project described or designated under subsection (b) by the Secretary.

(II) SHORTENED SCHEDULE.—The Secretary may not shorten a schedule under clause (i) if doing so would impair the ability of a cooperating Federal agency to conduct necessary analyses or otherwise carry out relevant obligations of the

Federal agency for the project.

(F) FAILURE TO MEET DEADLINE.—If a cooperating Federal agency fails to meet a deadline established under subparagraph (D)(ii)(I) [1]—

(i) the cooperating Federal agency shall, not later than 10 days after failing to meet the deadline, submit to the Secretary a report that describes the reasons why the deadline was not met; and

(ii) the Secretary shall—

(I) submit to the Committee on Transportation and Infrastructure of the House of Representatives and the Committee on Commerce, Science, and Transportation of the Senate a copy of the report under clause (i); and

(II) make the report under clause (i) publicly available on a website of the Department of Transportation.

(G) DISSEMINATION.—A copy of a schedule under subparagraph (C), and of any modifications to the schedule under subparagraph (E), shall be—

(i) provided to all participating agencies and to the State department of transportation of the State in which the project is located (and, if the State is not the project sponsor, to the project sponsor); and

(ii) made available to the public.

(2) COMMENT DEADLINES.—The Secretary shall establish the following deadlines for comment during the environmental review process for a project:

(A) For comments by agencies and the public on a draft environmental impact statement, a period of not more than 60 days after publication in the Federal Register of notice of the date of public availability of such statement, unless—

(i) a different deadline is established by agreement of the lead agency, the project sponsor, and all participating agencies; or

(ii) the deadline is extended by the lead agency for good cause.

(B) For all other comment periods established by the lead agency for agency or public comments in the environmental review process, a period of not more than 45 days from availability of the materials on which comment is requested, unless—

(i) a different deadline is established by agreement of the Secretary, the project sponsor, and all participating agencies; or

(ii) the deadline is extended by the lead agency for good cause.

(3) DEADLINES FOR DECISIONS UNDER OTHER LAWS.—In any case in which a decision under any Federal law relating to a project described or designated under subsection (b) (including the issuance or denial of a permit or license) is required to be made by the later of the date that is 180 days after the date on which the Secretary made all final decisions of the lead agency with respect to the project or 180 days after the date on which an application was submitted for the permit or license, the Secretary shall submit to the Committee on Transportation and Infrastructure of the House of Representatives and the Committee on Commerce, Science, and Transportation of the Senate and publish on a website of the Department of Transportation—

(A) as soon as practicable after the 180-day period, an initial notice of the failure of the Federal agency to make the decision; and

(B) every 60 days thereafter until such date as all decisions of the Federal agency relating to the project have been made by the Federal agency, an additional notice that describes the number of decisions of the Federal agency that remain outstanding as of the date of the additional notice.

(4) INVOLVEMENT OF THE PUBLIC.—Nothing in this subsection shall reduce any time period provided for public comment in the environmental review process under existing Federal law, including a regulation.

(n) CONCURRENT REVIEWS AND SINGLE NEPA DOCUMENT.—

(1) CONCURRENT REVIEWS.—Each participating agency and cooperating agency under the expedited and coordinated environmental review process established under this section shall—

(A) carry out the obligations of such agency under other applicable law concurrently, and in conjunction, with the review required under the National Environmental Policy Act of 1969 (42 U.S.C. 4321 et seq.), unless doing so would impair the ability of such agency to conduct needed analysis or otherwise carry out such obligations; and

(B) formulate and implement administrative, policy, and procedural mechanisms to enable the agency to ensure completion of the environmental review process in a timely, coordinated, and environmentally responsible manner.

(2) SINGLE NEPA DOCUMENT.—

(A) IN GENERAL.—To the maximum extent practicable and consistent with Federal law, all Federal permits and reviews for a project shall rely on a single environmental document prepared under the National Environmental Policy Act of 1969 (42 U.S.C. 4321 et seq.) under the leadership of the Secretary.

(B) USE OF DOCUMENT.—

(i) IN GENERAL.—To the maximum extent practicable, the Secretary shall develop an environmental document sufficient to satisfy the requirements for any Federal approval or other Federal action required for the project, including permits issued by other Federal agencies.

(ii) COOPERATION OF PARTICIPATING AGENCIES.—In carrying out this subparagraph, other participating agencies shall cooperate with the lead agency and provide timely information.

(C) TREATMENT AS PARTICIPATING AND COOPERATING AGENCIES.—A Federal agency required to make an approval or take an action for a project, as described in this paragraph, shall work with the Secretary to ensure that the agency making the approval or taking the action is treated as being both a participating and cooperating agency for the project.

(D) EXCEPTIONS.—The Secretary may waive the application of subparagraph (A) with respect to a project if—

(i) the project sponsor requests that agencies issue separate environmental documents;

(ii) the obligations of a cooperating agency or participating agency under the National Environmental Policy Act of 1969 (42 U.S.C. 4321 et seq.) have already been satisfied with respect to the project; or

(iii) the Secretary determines that reliance on a single environmental document (as described in subparagraph (A)) would not facilitate timely completion of the environmental review process for the project.

(3) Participating agency responsibilities.—An agency participating in the expedited and coordinated environmental review process under this section shall—

(A) provide comments, responses, studies, or methodologies on areas within the special expertise or jurisdiction of the agency; and

(B) use the process to address any environmental issues of concern to the agency.

(o) Environmental Impact Statement.—

(1) In general.—In preparing a final environmental impact statement under the National Environmental Policy Act of 1969 (42 U.S.C. 4321 et seq.) for a project described or designated under subsection (b), if the Secretary modifies the statement in response to comments that are minor and are confined to factual corrections or explanations of why the comments do not warrant additional agency response, the Secretary may write on errata sheets attached to the statement instead of rewriting the draft statement, subject to the condition that the errata sheets—

(A) cite the sources, authorities, and reasons that support the position of the agency; and

(B) if appropriate, indicate the circumstances that would trigger agency reappraisal or further response.

(2) Single document.—To the maximum extent practicable, for a project subject to a coordinated review process under this section, the Secretary shall expeditiously develop a single document that consists of a final environmental impact statement and a record of decision, unless—

(A) the final environmental impact statement or record of decision makes substantial changes to the project that are relevant to environmental or safety concerns; or

(B) there is a significant new circumstance or information relevant to environmental concerns that bears on the proposed action or the environmental impacts of the proposed action.

(3) Length of environmental document.—

(A) In general.—Except as provided in subparagraph (B), an environmental impact statement shall not exceed 150 pages, not including any citations or appendices.

(B) Extraordinary complexity.—An environmental impact statement for a proposed agency action of extraordinary complexity shall not exceed 300 pages, not including any citations or appendices.

(p) Integration of Planning and Environmental Review.—

(1) In general.—Subject to paragraph (5) and to the maximum extent practicable and appropriate, the following agencies may adopt or incorporate by reference, and use a planning product in proceedings relating to, any class of action in the environmental review process of a project described or designated under subsection (b):

(A) The lead agency for a project, with respect to an environmental impact statement, environmental assessment, categorical exclusion, or other document prepared under the National Environmental Policy Act of 1969 (42 U.S.C. 4321 et seq.).

(B) A cooperating agency with responsibility under Federal law with respect to the process for and completion of any environmental permit, approval, review, or study required for a project under any Federal law other than the National Environmental Policy Act of 1969 (42 U.S.C. 4321 et seq.), if consistent with such Act.

(2) IDENTIFICATION.—If a lead or cooperating agency makes a determination to adopt or incorporate by reference and use a planning product under paragraph (1), such agency shall identify the agencies that participated in the development of the planning products.

(3) ADOPTION OR INCORPORATION BY REFERENCE OF PLANNING PRODUCTS.—Such agency may—

(A) adopt or incorporate by reference an entire planning product under paragraph (1); or

(B) select portions of a planning project under paragraph (1) for adoption or incorporation by reference.

(4) TIMING.—The adoption or incorporation by reference of a planning product under paragraph (1) may—

(A) be made at the time the lead and cooperating agencies decide the appropriate scope of environmental review for the project; or

(B) occur later in the environmental review process, as appropriate.

(5) CONDITIONS.—Such agency in the environmental review process may adopt or incorporate by reference a planning product under this section if such agency determines, with the concurrence of the lead agency, if appropriate, and, if the planning product is necessary for a cooperating agency to issue a permit, review, or approval for the project, with the concurrence of the cooperating agency, if appropriate, that the following conditions have been met:

(A) The planning product was developed through a planning process conducted pursuant to applicable Federal law.

(B) The planning product was developed in consultation with appropriate Federal and State resource agencies and Indian Tribes.

(C) The planning process included broad multidisciplinary consideration of systems-level or corridor-wide transportation needs and potential effects, including effects on the human and natural environment.

(D) The planning process included public notice that the planning products produced in the planning process may be adopted during any subsequent environmental review process in accordance with this section.

(E) During the environmental review process, the such agency has—

(i) made the planning documents available for public review and comment by members of the general public and Federal, State, local, and Tribal governments that may have an interest in the proposed project;

(ii) provided notice of the intention of the such agency to adopt or incorporate by reference the planning product; and

(iii) considered any resulting comments.

(F) There is no significant new information or new circumstance that has a reasonable likelihood of affecting the continued validity or appropriateness of the planning product or portions thereof.

(G) The planning product has a rational basis and is based on reliable and reasonably current data and reasonable and scientifically acceptable methodologies.

(H) The planning product is documented in sufficient detail to support the decision or the results of the analysis and to meet requirements for use of the information in the environmental review process.

(I) The planning product is appropriate for adoption or incorporation by reference and use in the environmental review process for the project and is incorporated in accordance with, and is sufficient to meet the requirements of, the National Environmental Policy Act of 1969 (42 U.S.C. 4321 et seq.) and section 1502.21 of title 40, Code of Federal Regulations.

(6) EFFECT OF ADOPTION OR INCORPORATION BY REFERENCE.—Any planning product or portions thereof adopted or incorporated by reference by such agency in accordance with this subsection may be—

(A) incorporated directly into an environmental review process document or other environmental document; and

(B) relied on and used by other Federal agencies in carrying out reviews of the project.

(q) REPORT ON NEPA DATA.—

(1) IN GENERAL.—The Secretary shall carry out a process to track, and annually submit to the Committee on Transportation and Infrastructure of the House of Representatives, the Committee on Commerce, Science, and Transportation of the Senate, the Committee on Natural Resources of the House of Representatives, and the Committee on Environment and Public Works of the Senate a report on projects described in subsection (b)(1) that contains the information described in paragraph (3).

(2) TIME TO COMPLETE.—For purposes of paragraph (3), the NEPA process—

(A) for an environmental impact statement—

(i) begins on the date on which a notice of intent is published in the Federal Register; and

(ii) ends on the date on which the Secretary issues a record of decision, including, if necessary, a revised record of decision; and

(B) for an environmental assessment—

(i) begins on the date on which the Secretary makes a determination to prepare an environmental assessment; and

(ii) ends on the date on which the Secretary issues a finding of no significant impact or determines that preparation of an environmental impact statement is necessary.

(3) INFORMATION DESCRIBED.—The information referred to in paragraph (1) is, with respect to the Federal Aviation Administration—

(A) the number of proposed actions for which a categorical exclusion was applied by the Secretary during the reporting period;

(B) the number of proposed actions for which a documented categorical exclusion was applied by the Secretary during the reporting period;

(C) the number of proposed actions pending on the date on which the report is submitted for which the issuance of a documented categorical exclusion by the Secretary is pending;

(D) the number of proposed actions for which an environmental assessment was issued by the Secretary during the reporting period;

(E) the length of time the Administration took to complete each environmental assessment described in subparagraph (D);

(F) the number of proposed actions pending on the date on which the report is submitted for which an environmental assessment is being drafted by the Secretary;

(G) the number of proposed actions for which a final environmental impact statement was completed by the Secretary during the reporting period;

(H) the length of time that the Secretary took to complete each environmental impact statement described in subparagraph (G);

(I) the number of proposed actions pending on the date on which the report is submitted for which an environmental impact statement is being drafted; and

(J) for the proposed actions reported under subparagraphs (F) and (I), the percentage of such proposed actions for which—

(i) project funding has been identified; and

(ii) all other Federal, State, and local activities that are required to allow the proposed action to proceed are completed.

(4) DEFINITIONS.—In this section:

(A) ENVIRONMENTAL ASSESSMENT.—The term "environmental assessment" has the meaning given such term in section 1508.1 of title 40, Code of Federal Regulations (or a successor regulation).

(B) ENVIRONMENTAL IMPACT STATEMENT.—The term "environmental impact statement" means a detailed statement required under section 102(2)(C) of the National Environmental Policy Act of 1969 (42 U.S.C. 4332(2)(C)).

(C) NEPA PROCESS.—The term "NEPA process" means the entirety of the development and documentation of the analysis required under the National Environmental Policy Act of 1969 (42 U.S.C. 4321 et seq.), including the assessment and analysis of any impacts, alternatives, and mitigation of a proposed action, and any interagency participation and public involvement required to be carried out before the Secretary undertakes a proposed action.

(D) PROPOSED ACTION.—The term "proposed action" means an action (within the meaning of the National Environmental Policy Act of 1969 (42 U.S.C. 4321 et seq.)) under this title that the Secretary proposes to carry out.

(E) REPORTING PERIOD.—The term "reporting period" means the fiscal year prior to the fiscal year in which a report is issued under subsection (a).

(Added Pub. L. 108–176, title III, §304(a), Dec. 12, 2003, 117 Stat. 2534; amended Pub. L. 115–254, div. B, title I, §191(a), title V, §539(q), Oct. 5, 2018, 132 Stat. 3238, 3371; Pub. L. 118–63, title VII, §783, May 16, 2024, 138 Stat. 1302.)

[1] So in original. Probably should be "subparagraph (E)(ii)(I)".

§47172. AIR TRAFFIC PROCEDURES FOR AIRPORT CAPACITY ENHANCEMENT PROJECTS AT CONGESTED AIRPORTS

(a) IN GENERAL.—The Administrator of the Federal Aviation Administration may consider prescribing flight procedures to avoid or minimize potentially significant adverse noise impacts of an airport capacity enhancement project at a congested airport that involves the construction of new runways or the reconfiguration of existing runways during the environmental planning process for the project. If the Administrator determines that noise mitigation flight procedures are consistent with safe and efficient use of the navigable airspace, the Administrator may commit, at the request of the airport sponsor and in a manner consistent with applicable Federal law, to prescribing such procedures in any record of decision approving the project.

(b) MODIFICATION.—Notwithstanding any commitment by the Administrator under subsection (a), the Administrator may initiate changes to such procedures if necessary to maintain safety and efficiency in light of new information or changed circumstances.

(Added Pub. L. 108–176, title III, §304(a), Dec. 12, 2003, 117 Stat. 2537.)

§47173. AIRPORT FUNDING OF FAA STAFF

(a) ACCEPTANCE OF SPONSOR-PROVIDED FUNDS.—Notwithstanding any other provision of law, the Administrator of the Federal Aviation Administration may accept funds from an airport sponsor, including funds provided to the sponsor under section 47114(c), to hire additional staff or obtain the services of consultants—

(1) to facilitate the timely processing, review, and completion of environmental activities associated with an airport development project;

(2) to conduct special environmental studies related to an airport project funded with Federal funds;

(3) to conduct special studies or reviews to support approved noise compatibility measures described in part 150 of title 14, Code of Federal Regulations;

(4) to conduct special studies or reviews to support environmental mitigation in a record of decision or finding of no significant impact by the Federal Aviation Administration; and

(5) to facilitate the timely processing, review, and completion of environmental activities associated with new or amended flight procedures, including performance-based navigation procedures, such as required navigation performance procedures and area navigation procedures.

(b) ADMINISTRATIVE PROVISION.—Instead of payment from an airport sponsor from funds apportioned to the sponsor under section 47114, the Administrator, with agreement of the sponsor, may transfer funds that would otherwise be apportioned to the sponsor under section 47114 to the account used by the Administrator for activities described in subsection (a).

(c) RECEIPTS CREDITED AS OFFSETTING COLLECTIONS.—Notwithstanding section 3302 of title 31, any funds accepted under this section, except funds transferred pursuant to subsection (b)—

(1) shall be credited as offsetting collections to the account that finances the activities and services for which the funds are accepted;

(2) shall be available for expenditure only to pay the costs of activities and services for which the funds are accepted; and

(3) shall remain available until expended.

(d) MAINTENANCE OF EFFORT.—No funds may be accepted pursuant to subsection (a), or transferred pursuant to subsection (b), in any fiscal year in which the Federal Aviation Administration does not allocate at least the amount it expended in fiscal year 2002 (excluding amounts accepted pursuant to section 337 of the Department of Transportation and Related Agencies Appropriations Act, 2002 (115 Stat. 862)) for the activities described in subsection (a).

(Added Pub. L. 108–176, title III, §304(a), Dec. 12, 2003, 117 Stat. 2537; amended Pub. L. 112–95, title V, §503, Feb. 14, 2012, 126 Stat. 103.)

§47174. AUTHORIZATION OF APPROPRIATIONS

In addition to the amounts authorized to be appropriated under section 106(k), there is authorized to be appropriated to the Secretary of Transportation, out of the Airport and Airway Trust Fund established under section 9502 of the Internal Revenue Code of 1986 (26 U.S.C. 9502), $4,200,000 for fiscal year 2004 and for each fiscal year thereafter to facilitate the timely processing, review, and completion of environmental activities associated with airport capacity enhancement projects at congested airports.

(Added Pub. L. 108–176, title III, §304(a), Dec. 12, 2003, 117 Stat. 2538.)

§47175. DEFINITIONS

In this subchapter, the following definitions apply:

(1) AIRPORT CAPACITY ENHANCEMENT PROJECT.—The term "airport capacity enhancement project" means—

(A) a project for construction or extension of a runway, including any land acquisition, taxiway, or safety area associated with the runway or runway extension;or

(B) such other airport development projects as the Secretary may designate as facilitating a reduction in air traffic congestion and delays.

(2) AIRPORT SPONSOR.—The term "airport sponsor" has the meaning given the term "sponsor" under section 47102.

(3) AVIATION SAFETY PROJECT.—The term "aviation safety project" means an aviation project that—

(A) has as its primary purpose reducing the risk of injury to persons or damage to aircraft and property, as determined by the Administrator;

(B) is needed to respond to a recommendation from the National Transportation Safety Board, as determined by the Administrator; or

(C) is necessary for an airport to comply with part 139 of title 14, Code of Federal Regulations (relating to airport certification).

(4) CONGESTED AIRPORT.—The term "congested airport" means an airport that accounted for at least 1 percent of all delayed aircraft operations in the United States in the most recent year for which such data is available and an airport listed in table 1 of the Federal Aviation Administration's Airport Capacity Benchmark Report 2004 or any successor report.

(5) FEDERAL AGENCY.—The term "Federal agency" means a department or agency of the United States Government.

(6) GENERAL AVIATION AIRPORT CONSTRUCTION OR IMPROVEMENT PROJECT.—The term "general aviation airport construction or improvement project" means—

(A) a project for the construction or extension of a runway, including any land acquisition, helipad, taxiway, safety area, apron, or navigational aids associated with the runway or runway extension, at a general aviation airport, a reliever airport, or a commercial service airport that is not a primary airport (as such terms are defined in section 47102); and

(B) any other airport development project that the Secretary designates as facilitating aviation capacity building projects at a general aviation airport.

(7) JOINT USE AIRPORT.—The term "joint use airport" means an airport owned by the Department of Defense, at which both military and civilian aircraft make shared use of the airfield.

(8) TERMINAL DEVELOPMENT.—The term "terminal development" has the meaning given such term in section 47102.

(Added Pub. L. 108–176, title III, §304(a), Dec. 12, 2003, 117 Stat. 2538; amended Pub. L. 112–95, title I, §152(g), Feb. 14, 2012, 126 Stat. 34; Pub. L. 115–254, div. B, title I, §191(b), Oct. 5, 2018, 132 Stat. 3239; Pub. L. 118–63, title VII, §784, May 16, 2024, 138 Stat. 1313.)

CHAPTER 473—INTERNATIONAL AIRPORT FACILITIES

§47301. DEFINITIONS

In this chapter—

(1) "airport property" means an interest in property used or useful in operating and maintaining an airport.

(2) "airway property" means an interest in property used or useful in operating and maintaining a ground installation, facility, or equipment desirable for the orderly and safe operation of air traffic, including air navigation, air traffic control, airway communication, and meteorological facilities.

(3) "foreign territory" means an area—

(A) over which no government or a government of a foreign country has sovereignty;

(B) temporarily under military occupation by the United States Government; or

(C) occupied or administered by the Government or a government of a foreign country under an international agreement.

(4) "territory outside the continental United States" means territory outside the 48 contiguous States and the District of Columbia.

(Pub. L. 103–272, §1(e), July 5, 1994, 108 Stat. 1280.)

§47302. PROVIDING AIRPORT AND AIRWAY PROPERTY IN FOREIGN TERRITORIES

(a) GENERAL AUTHORITY.—Subject to the concurrence of the Secretary of State and the consideration of objectives of the International Civil Aviation Organization—

(1) the Secretary of Transportation may acquire, establish, and construct airport property and airway property (except meteorological facilities) in foreign territory; and

(2) the Secretary of Commerce may acquire, establish, and construct meteorological facilities in foreign territory.

(b) SPECIFIC APPROPRIATIONS REQUIRED.—Except for airport property transferred under section 47304(b) of this title, an airport (as defined in section 40102(a) of this title) may be acquired, established, or constructed under subsection (a) of this section only if amounts have been appropriated specifically for the airport.

(c) ACCEPTING FOREIGN PAYMENTS.—The Secretary of Transportation or Commerce, as appropriate, may accept payment from a government of a foreign country or international organization for facilities or services sold or provided the government or organization under this chapter. The amount received may be credited to the appropriation current when the expenditures are or were paid, the appropriation current when the amount is received, or both.

(Pub. L. 103–272, §1(e), July 5, 1994, 108 Stat. 1281.)

§47303. Training foreign citizens

Subject to the concurrence of the Secretary of State, the Secretary of Transportation or Commerce, as appropriate, may train a foreign citizen in a subject related to aeronautics and essential to the orderly and safe operation of civil aircraft. The training may be provided—

(1) directly by the appropriate Secretary or jointly with another department, agency, or instrumentality of the United States Government;

(2) through a public or private agency of the United States (including a State or municipal educational institution); or

(3) through an international organization.

(Pub. L. 103–272, §1(e), July 5, 1994, 108 Stat. 1281.)

§47304. Transfer of airport and airway property

(a) General Authority.—When requested by the government of a foreign country or an international organization, the Secretary of Transportation or Commerce, as appropriate, may transfer to the government or organization airport property and airway property operated and maintained under this chapter by the appropriate Secretary in foreign territory. The transfer shall be on terms the appropriate Secretary considers proper, including consideration agreed on through negotiations with the government or organization.

(b) Property Installed or Controlled by Military.—Subject to terms to which the parties agree, the Secretary of a military department may transfer without charge to the Secretary of Transportation airport property and airway property (except meteorological facilities), and to the Secretary of Commerce meteorological facilities, that the Secretary of the military department installed or controls in territory outside the continental United States. The transfer may be made if consistent with the needs of national defense and—

(1) the Secretary of the military department finds that the property or facility is no longer required exclusively for military purposes; and

(2) the Secretary of Transportation or Commerce, as appropriate, decides that the transfer is or may be necessary to carry out this chapter.

(c) Republic of Panama.—(1) The Secretary of Transportation may provide, operate, and maintain facilities and services for air navigation, airway communications, and air traffic control in the Republic of Panama subject to—

(A) the approval of the Secretary of Defense; and

(B) each obligation assumed by the United States Government under an agreement between the Government and the Republic of Panama.

(2) The Secretary of a military department may transfer without charge to the Secretary of Transportation property located in the Republic of Panama when the Secretary of Transportation decides that the transfer may be useful in carrying out this chapter.

(3) Subsection (b) of this section (related to the Secretary of Transportation) and section 47302(a) and (b) of this title do not apply in carrying out this subsection.

(d) Retaking Property for Military Requirement.—(1) When necessary for a military requirement, the Secretary of a military department immediately may retake property (with any improvements to it) transferred by the Secretary under subsection (b) or (c) of this section. The Secretary shall pay reasonable compensation to each person (or its successor in interest) that made an improvement to the property that was not made at the expense of the Government. The Secretary or a delegate of the Secretary shall decide on the amount of compensation.

(2) On the recommendation of the Secretary of Transportation or Commerce, as appropriate, the Secretary of a military department may decide not to act under paragraph (1) of this subsection.

(Pub. L. 103–272, §1(e), July 5, 1994, 108 Stat. 1281.)

§47305. Administrative

(a) General Authority.—The Secretary of Transportation shall consolidate, operate, protect, maintain, and improve airport property and airway property (except meteorological facilities), and the Secretary of Commerce may consolidate, operate, protect, maintain, and improve meteorological facilities, that the appropriate Secretary has acquired and that are located in territory outside the continental United States. In carrying out this section, the appropriate Secretary may—

(1) adapt the property or facility to the needs of civil aeronautics;

(2) lease the property or facility for not more than 20 years;

(3) make a contract, or provide directly, for facilities and services;

(4) make reasonable charges for aeronautical services; and

(5) acquire an interest in property.

(b) Crediting Appropriations.—Money received from the direct sale or charge that the Secretary of Transportation or Commerce, as appropriate, decides is equivalent to the cost of facilities and services sold or provided under subsection (a)(3) and (4) of this section is credited to the appropriation from which the cost was paid. The balance shall be deposited in the Treasury as miscellaneous receipts.

(c) Using Other Government Facilities and Services.—To carry out this chapter and to use personnel and facilities of the United States Government most advantageously and without unnecessary duplication, the Secretary of Transportation or Commerce, as appropriate, shall request, when practicable, to use a facility or service of an appropriate department, agency, or instrumentality of the Government on a reimbursable basis. A department, agency, or instrumentality receiving a request under this section may provide the facility or service.

(d) Advertising Not Required.—Section 6101(b) to (d) of title 41 does not apply to a lease or contract made by the Secretary of Transportation or Commerce under this chapter.

(Pub. L. 103–272, §1(e), July 5, 1994, 108 Stat. 1282; Pub. L. 111–350, §5(o)(9), Jan. 4, 2011, 124 Stat. 3854.)

[§47306. Repealed. Pub. L. 118–63, title VII, §727, May 16, 2024, 138 Stat. 1271]

Section, Pub. L. 103–272, §1(e), July 5, 1994, 108 Stat. 1283, related to criminal

[§47306. Repealed. Pub. L. 118–63, title VII, §727, May 16, 2024, 138 Stat. 1271]

CHAPTER 473—INTERNATIONAL
AIRPORT FACILITIES

penalty for knowingly and willfully violating a regulation prescribed by the Secretary of Transportation to carry out this chapter.

CHAPTER 475—NOISE

SUBCHAPTER I—NOISE ABATEMENT

SUBCHAPTER II—NATIONAL AVIATION NOISE POLICY

SUBCHAPTER I—NOISE ABATEMENT

§47501. DEFINITIONS

In this subchapter—

(1) "airport" means a public-use airport as defined in section 47102 of this title.

(2) "airport operator" means—

(A) for an airport serving air carriers that have certificates from the Secretary of Transportation, any person holding an airport operating certificate issued under section 44706 of this title; and

(B) for any other airport, the person operating the airport.

(Pub. L. 103–272, §1(e), July 5, 1994, 108 Stat. 1284.)

§47502. Noise measurement and exposure systems and identifying land use compatible with noise exposure

After consultation with the Administrator of the Environmental Protection Agency and United States Government, State, and interstate agencies that the Secretary of Transportation considers appropriate, the Secretary shall by regulation—

(1) establish a single system of measuring noise that—

(A) has a highly reliable relationship between projected noise exposure and surveyed reactions of individuals to noise; and

(B) is applied uniformly in measuring noise at airports and the surrounding area;

(2) establish a single system for determining the exposure of individuals to noise resulting from airport operations, including noise intensity, duration, frequency, and time of occurrence; and

(3) identify land uses normally compatible with various exposures of individuals to noise.

(Pub. L. 103–272, §1(e), July 5, 1994, 108 Stat. 1284.)

§47503. Noise exposure maps

(a) Submission and Preparation.—An airport operator may submit to the Secretary of Transportation a noise exposure map showing the noncompatible uses in each area of the map on the date the map is submitted, a description of estimated aircraft operations during a forecast period that is at least 5 years in the future and how those operations will affect the map. The map shall—

(1) be prepared in consultation with public agencies and planning authorities in the area surrounding the airport; and

(2) comply with regulations prescribed under section 47502 of this title.

(b) Revised Maps.—

(1) In general.—An airport operator that submits a noise exposure map under subsection (a) shall submit a revised map to the Secretary if, in an area surrounding an airport, a change in the operation of the airport would establish a substantial new noncompatible use, or would significantly reduce noise over existing noncompatible uses, that is not reflected in either the existing conditions map or forecast map currently on file with the Federal Aviation Administration.

(2) Timing.—A submission under paragraph (1) shall be required only if the relevant change in the operation of the airport occurs during—

(A) the forecast period of the applicable noise exposure map submitted by an airport operator under subsection (a); or

(B) the implementation period of the airport operator's noise compatibility program.

(Pub. L. 103–272, §1(e), July 5, 1994, 108 Stat. 1284; Pub. L. 108–176, title III, §324, Dec. 12, 2003, 117 Stat. 2542; Pub. L. 115–254, div. B, title I, §174, Oct. 5, 2018, 132 Stat. 3228.)

§47504. NOISE COMPATIBILITY PROGRAMS

(a) SUBMISSIONS.—(1) An airport operator that submitted a noise exposure map and related information under section 47503(a) of this title may submit a noise compatibility program to the Secretary of Transportation after—

(A) consulting with public agencies and planning authorities in the area surrounding the airport, United States Government officials having local responsibility for the airport, and air carriers using the airport; and

(B) notice and an opportunity for a public hearing.

(2) A program submitted under paragraph (1) of this subsection shall state the measures the operator has taken or proposes to take to reduce existing noncompatible uses and prevent introducing additional noncompatible uses in the area covered by the map. The measures may include—

(A) establishing a preferential runway system;

(B) restricting the use of the airport by a type or class of aircraft because of the noise characteristics of the aircraft;

(C) constructing barriers and acoustical shielding and soundproofing public buildings;

(D) using flight procedures to control the operation of aircraft to reduce exposure of individuals to noise in the area surrounding the airport; and

(E) acquiring land, air rights, easements, development rights, and other interests to ensure that the property will be used in ways compatible with airport operations.

(b) APPROVALS.—(1) The Secretary shall approve or disapprove a program submitted under subsection (a) of this section (except as the program is related to flight procedures referred to in subsection (a)(2)(D) of this section) not later than 180 days after receiving it. The Secretary shall approve the program (except as the program is related to flight procedures referred to in subsection (a)(2)(D)) if the program—

(A) does not place an unreasonable burden on interstate or foreign commerce;

(B) is reasonably consistent with achieving the goal of reducing noncompatible uses and preventing the introduction of additional noncompatible uses; and

(C) provides for necessary revisions because of a revised map submitted under section 47503(b) of this title.

(2) A program (except as the program is related to flight procedures referred to in subsection (a)(2)(D) of this section) is deemed to be approved if the Secretary does not act within the 180-day period.

(3) The Secretary shall submit any part of a program related to flight procedures referred to in subsection (a)(2)(D) of this section to the Administrator of the Federal Aviation Administration. The Administrator shall approve or disapprove that part of the program.

(4) The Secretary shall not approve in fiscal years 2004 through 2007 a program submitted under subsection (a) if the program requires the expenditure of funds made available under section 48103 for mitigation of aircraft noise less than 65 DNL.

(c) GRANTS.—(1) The Secretary may incur obligations to make grants from amounts available under section 48103 of this title to carry out a project under a part of a noise compatibility program approved under subsection (b) of this section. A grant may be made to—

(A) an airport operator submitting the program; and

(B) a unit of local government in the area surrounding the airport, if the Secretary decides the unit is able to carry out the project.

(2) SOUNDPROOFING AND ACQUISITION OF CERTAIN RESIDENTIAL BUILDINGS AND PROPERTIES.—The Secretary may incur obligations to make grants from amounts made available under section 48103 of this title—

(A) for projects to soundproof residential buildings—

(i) if the airport operator received approval for a grant for a project to soundproof residential buildings pursuant to section 301(d)(4)(B) of the Airport and Airway Safety and Capacity Expansion Act of 1987;

(ii) if the airport operator submits updated noise exposure contours, as required by the Secretary; and

(iii) if the Secretary determines that the proposed projects are compatible with the purposes of this chapter;

(B) to an airport operator and unit of local government referred to in paragraph (1)(A) or (1)(B) of this subsection to soundproof residential buildings located on residential properties, and to acquire residential properties, at which noise levels are not compatible with normal operations of an airport—

(i) if the airport operator amended an existing local aircraft noise regulation during calendar year 1993 to increase the maximum permitted noise levels for scheduled air carrier aircraft as a direct result of implementation of revised aircraft noise departure procedures mandated for aircraft safety purposes by the Administrator of the Federal Aviation Administration for standardized application at airports served by scheduled air carriers;

(ii) if the airport operator submits updated noise exposure contours, as required by the Secretary; and

(iii) if the Secretary determines that the proposed projects are compatible with the purposes of this chapter;

(C) to an airport operator and unit of local government referred to in paragraph (1)(A) or (1)(B) of this subsection to carry out any part of a program developed before February 18, 1980, or before implementing regulations were prescribed, if the Secretary decides the program is substantially consistent with reducing existing noncompatible uses and preventing the introduction of additional noncompatible uses and the purposes of this chapter will be furthered by promptly carrying out the program;

(D) to an airport operator and unit of local government referred to in paragraph (1)(A) or (1)(B) of this subsection to soundproof a building in the noise impact area surrounding the airport that is used primarily for educational or medical purposes and that the Secretary decides is adversely affected by airport noise;

(E) to an airport operator of a congested airport (as defined in section 47175) and a unit of local government referred to in paragraph (1)(B) of this subsection to carry out a project to mitigate noise in the area surrounding the airport if the project is included as a commitment in a record of decision of the Federal Aviation Administration for an airport capacity enhancement project (as defined in section 47175) even if that airport has not met the requirements of part 150 of title 14, Code of Federal Regulations; and

(F) to an airport operator of a congested airport (as defined in section 47175) and a unit of local government referred to in paragraph (1)(B) to carry out a project to mitigate noise, if the project—

(i) consists of—

(I) replacement windows, doors, and the installation of through-the-wall air conditioning units; or

(II) a contribution of the equivalent costs to be used for reconstruction if reconstruction is the preferred local solution;

(ii) is located at a school near the airport; and

(iii) is included in a memorandum of agreement entered into before September 30, 2002, even if the airport has not met the requirements of part 150 of title 14, Code of Federal Regulations, and only if the financial limitations of the memorandum are applied.

(3) An airport operator may agree to make a grant made under paragraph (1)(A) of this subsection available to a public agency in the area surrounding the airport if the Secretary decides the agency is able to carry out the project.

(4) The Government's share of a project for which a grant is made under this subsection is the greater of—

(A) 80 percent of the cost of the project; or

(B) the Government's share that would apply if the amounts available for the project were made available under subchapter I of chapter 471 of this title for a project at the airport.

(5) The provisions of subchapter I of chapter 471 of this title related to grants apply to a grant made under this chapter, except—

(A) section 47109(a) and (b) of this title; and

(B) any provision that the Secretary decides is inconsistent with, or unnecessary to carry out, this chapter.

(6) AIRCRAFT NOISE PRIMARILY CAUSED BY MILITARY AIRCRAFT.—The Secretary may make a grant under this subsection for a project even if the purpose of the project is to mitigate the effect of noise primarily caused by military aircraft at an airport.

(d) GOVERNMENT RELIEF FROM LIABILITY.—The Government is not liable for damages from aviation noise because of action taken under this section.

(e) GRANTS FOR ASSESSMENT OF FLIGHT PROCEDURES.—

(1) IN GENERAL.—In accordance with subsection (c)(1), the Secretary may make a grant to an airport operator to assist in completing environmental review and assessment activities for proposals to implement flight procedures at such airport that have been approved as part of an airport noise compatibility program under subsection (b).

(2) ADDITIONAL STAFF.—The Administrator may accept funds from an airport operator, including funds provided to the operator under paragraph (1), to hire additional staff or obtain the services of consultants in order to facilitate the timely processing, review, and completion of environmental activities associated with proposals to implement flight procedures at such airport that have been approved as part of an airport noise compatibility program under subsection (b).

(3) RECEIPTS CREDITED AS OFFSETTING COLLECTIONS.—Notwithstanding section 3302

of title 31, any funds accepted under this section—

    (A) shall be credited as offsetting collections to the account that finances the activities and services for which the funds are accepted;

    (B) shall be available for expenditure only to pay the costs of activities and services for which the funds are accepted; and

    (C) shall remain available until expended.

(f) DETERMINATION OF FAIR MARKET VALUE OF RESIDENTIAL PROPERTIES.—In approving a project to acquire residential real property using financial assistance made available under this section or chapter 471, the Secretary shall ensure that the appraisal of the property to be acquired disregards any decrease or increase in the fair market value of the real property caused by the project for which the property is to be acquired, or by the likelihood that the property would be acquired for the project, other than that due to physical deterioration within the reasonable control of the owner.

(Pub. L. 103–272, §1(e), July 5, 1994, 108 Stat. 1285; Pub. L. 103–305, title I, §119, Aug. 23, 1994, 108 Stat. 1580; Pub. L. 103–429, §6(71), Oct. 31, 1994, 108 Stat. 4387; Pub. L. 106–181, title I, §154, Apr. 5, 2000, 114 Stat. 88; Pub. L. 108–176, title I, §189, title III, §306, Dec. 12, 2003, 117 Stat. 2519, 2539; Pub. L. 112–95, title V, §§504, 505, Feb. 14, 2012, 126 Stat. 104; Pub. L. 115–232, div. A, title X, §1044, Aug. 13, 2018, 132 Stat. 1958.)

§47505. AIRPORT NOISE COMPATIBILITY PLANNING GRANTS

(a) GENERAL AUTHORITY.—The Secretary of Transportation may make a grant to a sponsor of an airport to develop, for planning purposes, information necessary to prepare and submit—

    (1) a noise exposure map and related information under section 47503 of this title, including the cost of obtaining the information; or

    (2) a noise compatibility program under section 47504 of this title.

(b) AVAILABILITY OF AMOUNTS AND GOVERNMENT'S SHARE OF COSTS.—A grant under subsection (a) of this section may be made from amounts available under section 48103 of this title. The United States Government's share of the grant is the percent for which a project for airport development at an airport would be eligible under section 47109(a) and (b) of this title.

(Pub. L. 103–272, §1(e), July 5, 1994, 108 Stat. 1286.)

§47506. LIMITATIONS ON RECOVERING DAMAGES FOR NOISE

(a) GENERAL LIMITATIONS.—A person acquiring an interest in property after February 18, 1980, in an area surrounding an airport for which a noise exposure map has been submitted under section 47503 of this title and having actual or constructive knowledge of the existence of the map may recover damages for noise attributable to the airport only if, in addition to any other elements for recovery of damages, the person shows that—

    (1) after acquiring the interest, there was a significant—

        (A) change in the type or frequency of aircraft operations at the airport;

        (B) change in the airport layout;

        (C) change in flight patterns; or

        (D) increase in nighttime operations; and

    (2) the damages resulted from the change or increase.

(b) CONSTRUCTIVE KNOWLEDGE.—Constructive knowledge of the existence of a map under subsection (a) of this section shall be imputed, at a minimum, to a person if—

(1) before the person acquired the interest, notice of the existence of the map was published at least 3 times in a newspaper of general circulation in the county in which the property is located; or

(2) the person is given a copy of the map when acquiring the interest.

(Pub. L. 103–272, §1(e), July 5, 1994, 108 Stat. 1286.)

§47507. NONADMISSIBILITY OF NOISE EXPOSURE MAP AND RELATED INFORMATION AS EVIDENCE

No part of a noise exposure map or related information described in section 47503 of this title that is submitted to, or prepared by, the Secretary of Transportation and no part of a list of land uses the Secretary identifies as normally compatible with various exposures of individuals to noise may be admitted into evidence or used for any other purpose in a civil action asking for relief for noise resulting from the operation of an airport.

(Pub. L. 103–272, §1(e), July 5, 1994, 108 Stat. 1287.)

§47508. NOISE STANDARDS FOR AIR CARRIERS AND FOREIGN AIR CARRIERS PROVIDING FOREIGN AIR TRANSPORTATION

(a) GENERAL REQUIREMENTS.—The Secretary of Transportation shall require each air carrier and foreign air carrier providing foreign air transportation to comply with noise standards—

(1) the Secretary prescribed for new subsonic aircraft in regulations of the Secretary in effect on January 1, 1977; or

(2) of the International Civil Aviation Organization that are substantially compatible with standards of the Secretary for new subsonic aircraft in regulations of the Secretary at parts 36 and 91 of title 14, Code of Federal Regulations, prescribed between January 2, 1977, and January 1, 1982.

(b) COMPLIANCE AT PHASED RATE.—The Secretary shall require each air carrier and foreign air carrier providing foreign air transportation to comply with the noise standards at a phased rate similar to the rate for aircraft registered in the United States.

(c) NONDISCRIMINATION.—The requirement for air carriers providing foreign air transportation may not be more stringent than the requirement for foreign air carriers.

(Pub. L. 103–272, §1(e), July 5, 1994, 108 Stat. 1287.)

§47509. RESEARCH PROGRAM ON QUIET AIRCRAFT TECHNOLOGY FOR PROPELLER AND ROTOR DRIVEN AIRCRAFT

(a) ESTABLISHMENT.—The Administrator of the Federal Aviation Administration and the Administrator of the National Aeronautics and Space Administration shall conduct a study to identify technologies for noise reduction of propeller driven aircraft and rotorcraft.

(b) GOAL.—The goal of the study conducted under subsection (a) is to determine the status of research and development now underway in the area of quiet technology for propeller driven aircraft and rotorcraft, including technology that is cost beneficial, and to determine whether a research program to supplement existing research activities is necessary.

(c) PARTICIPATION.—In conducting the study required under subsection (a), the Administrator of the Federal Aviation Administration and the Administrator of the National Aeronautics and Space Administration shall encourage the participation of the Department of Defense, the Department of the Interior, the airtour industry, the aviation industry, academia and other appropriate groups.

(d) REPORT.—Not less than 280 days after August 23, 1994, the Administrator of the Federal Aviation Administration and the Administrator of the National Aeronautics and Space Administration shall transmit to Congress a report on the results of the study required under subsection (a).

(e) RESEARCH AND DEVELOPMENT PROGRAM.—If the Administrator of the Federal Aviation Administration and the Administrator of the National Aeronautics and Space Administration determine that additional research and development is necessary and would substantially contribute to the development of quiet aircraft technology, then the agencies shall conduct an appropriate research program in consultation with the entities listed in subsection (c) to develop safe, effective, and economical noise reduction technology (including technology that can be applied to existing propeller driven aircraft and rotorcraft) that would result in aircraft that operate at substantially reduced levels of noise to reduce the impact of such aircraft and rotorcraft on the resources of national parks and other areas.

(Added Pub. L. 103–305, title III, §308(a), Aug. 23, 1994, 108 Stat. 1593; amended Pub. L. 104–287, §5(86), Oct. 11, 1996, 110 Stat. 3398.)

§47510. TRADEOFF ALLOWANCE

Notwithstanding another law or a regulation prescribed or order issued under that law, the tradeoff provisions contained in appendix C of part 36 of title 14, Code of Federal Regulations, apply in deciding whether an aircraft complies with subpart I of part 91 of title 14.

(Added Pub. L. 103–429, §6(72)(A), Oct. 31, 1994, 108 Stat. 4387.)

§47511. CLEEN ENGINE AND AIRFRAME TECHNOLOGY PARTNERSHIP

(a) IN GENERAL.—The Administrator of the Federal Aviation Administration shall enter into a cost-sharing cooperative agreement, using a competitive process, with institutions, entities, or consortiums to carry out a program for the development, maturation, and testing of certifiable CLEEN aircraft, engine technologies, and jet fuels for civil airplanes.

(b) CLEEN ENGINE AND AIRFRAME TECHNOLOGY DEFINED.—In this section, the term "CLEEN aircraft and engine technology" means continuous lower energy, emissions, and noise aircraft and engine technology.

(c) PERFORMANCE OBJECTIVE.—The Administrator shall establish the performance objectives for the program in terms of the specific objectives to reduce fuel burn, emissions and noise.

(d) SELECTION.—In carrying out the program, the Administrator may provide that not less than 2 of the cooperative agreements entered into under this section involve the participation of an entity that is a small business concern (as defined in section 3 of the Small Business Act (15 U.S.C. 632)), provided that the submitted technology proposal of the entity meets, at a minimum, FAA Acquisition Management System requirements and requisite technology readiness levels for entry into the agreement, as determined by the Administrator.

(Added Pub. L. 115–254, div. B, title VII, §743(a), Oct. 5, 2018, 132 Stat. 3413; amended Pub. L. 118–63, title X, §1008, May 16, 2024, 138 Stat. 1389.)

SUBCHAPTER II—NATIONAL AVIATION NOISE POLICY

§47521. FINDINGS

Congress finds that—

(1) aviation noise management is crucial to the continued increase in airport capacity;

(2) community noise concerns have led to uncoordinated and inconsistent restrictions on aviation that could impede the national air transportation system;

(3) a noise policy must be carried out at the national level;

(4) local interest in aviation noise management shall be considered in determining the national interest;

(5) community concerns can be alleviated through the use of new technology aircraft and the use of revenues, including those available from passenger facility charges, for noise management;

(6) revenues controlled by the United States Government can help resolve noise problems and carry with them a responsibility to the national airport system;

(7) revenues derived from a passenger facility charge may be applied to noise management and increased airport capacity; and

(8) a precondition to the establishment and collection of a passenger facility charge is the prescribing by the Secretary of Transportation of a regulation establishing procedures for reviewing airport noise and access restrictions on operations of stage 2 and stage 3 aircraft.

(Pub. L. 103–272, §1(e), July 5, 1994, 108 Stat. 1287; Pub. L. 112–95, title I, §111(c)(2)(A)(vi), (B), Feb. 14, 2012, 126 Stat. 18.)

§47522. DEFINITIONS

In this subchapter—

(1) "air carrier", "air transportation", and "United States" have the same meanings given those terms in section 40102(a) of this title.

(2) "stage 3 noise levels" means the stage 3 noise levels in part 36 of title 14, Code of Federal Regulations, in effect on November 5, 1990.

(Pub. L. 103–272, §1(e), July 5, 1994, 108 Stat. 1288.)

§47523. NATIONAL AVIATION NOISE POLICY

(a) GENERAL REQUIREMENTS.—Not later than July 1, 1991, the Secretary of Transportation shall establish by regulation a national aviation noise policy that considers this subchapter, including the phaseout and nonaddition of stage 2 aircraft as provided in this subchapter and dates for carrying out that policy and reporting requirements consistent with this subchapter and law existing as of November 5, 1990.

(b) DETAILED ECONOMIC ANALYSIS.—The policy shall be based on a detailed economic analysis of the impact of the phaseout date for stage 2 aircraft on competition in the airline industry, including—

(1) the ability of air carriers to achieve capacity growth consistent with the projected rate of growth for the airline industry;

(2) the impact of competition in the airline and air cargo industries;

(3) the impact on nonhub and small community air service; and

(4) the impact on new entry into the airline industry.

(Pub. L. 103–272, §1(e), July 5, 1994, 108 Stat. 1288.)

§47524. AIRPORT NOISE AND ACCESS RESTRICTION REVIEW PROGRAM

(a) GENERAL REQUIREMENTS.—The national aviation noise policy established under section 47523 of this title shall provide for establishing by regulation a national program for reviewing airport noise and access restrictions on the operation of stage 2 and stage 3 aircraft. The program shall provide for adequate public notice and opportunity for comment on the restrictions.

(b) STAGE 2 AIRCRAFT.—Except as provided in subsection (d) of this section, an airport noise or access restriction may include a restriction on the operation of stage 2 aircraft proposed after October 1, 1990, only if the airport operator publishes the proposed restriction and prepares and makes available for public comment at least 180 days before the effective date of the proposed restriction—

(1) an analysis of the anticipated or actual costs and benefits of the existing or proposed restriction;

(2) a description of alternative restrictions;

(3) a description of the alternative measures considered that do not involve aircraft restrictions; and

(4) a comparison of the costs and benefits of the alternative measures to the costs and benefits of the proposed restriction.

(c) STAGE 3 AIRCRAFT.—(1) Except as provided in subsection (d) of this section, an airport noise or access restriction on the operation of stage 3 aircraft not in effect on October 1, 1990, may become effective only if the restriction has been agreed to by the airport proprietor and all aircraft operators or has been submitted to and approved by the Secretary of Transportation after an airport or aircraft operator's request for approval as provided by the program established under this section. Restrictions to which this paragraph applies include—

(A) a restriction on noise levels generated on either a single event or cumulative basis;

(B) a restriction on the total number of stage 3 aircraft operations;

(C) a noise budget or noise allocation program that would include stage 3 aircraft;

(D) a restriction on hours of operations; and

(E) any other restriction on stage 3 aircraft.

(2) Not later than 180 days after the Secretary receives an airport or aircraft operator's request for approval of an airport noise or access restriction on the operation of a stage 3 aircraft, the Secretary shall approve or disapprove the restriction. The Secretary may approve the restriction only if the Secretary finds on the basis of substantial evidence that—

(A) the restriction is reasonable, nonarbitrary, and nondiscriminatory;

(B) the restriction does not create an unreasonable burden on interstate or foreign commerce;

(C) the restriction is not inconsistent with maintaining the safe and efficient use of the navigable airspace;

(D) the restriction does not conflict with a law or regulation of the United States;

(E) an adequate opportunity has been provided for public comment on the restriction; and

(F) the restriction does not create an unreasonable burden on the national aviation system.

(3) Paragraphs (1) and (2) of this subsection do not apply if the Administrator of the Federal Aviation Administration, before November 5, 1990, has formed a working group (outside the process established by part 150 of title 14, Code of Federal Regulations) with a local airport operator to examine the noise impact of air traffic control procedure changes at the airport. However, if an agreement on noise reductions at that airport is made between the airport proprietor and one or more air carriers or foreign air carriers that constitute a majority of the carrier use of the airport, this paragraph applies only to a local action to enforce the agreement.

(4) The Secretary may reevaluate an airport noise or access restriction previously agreed to or approved under this subsection on request of an aircraft operator able to demonstrate to the satisfaction of the Secretary that there has been a change in the noise environment of the affected airport that justifies a reevaluation. The Secretary shall establish by regulation procedures for conducting a reevaluation. A reevaluation—

(A) shall be based on the criteria in paragraph (2) of this subsection; and

(B) may be conducted only after 2 years after a decision under paragraph (2) of this subsection has been made.

(d) NONAPPLICATION.—Subsections (b) and (c) of this section do not apply to—

(1) a local action to enforce a negotiated or executed airport noise or access agreement between the airport operator and the aircraft operators in effect on November 5, 1990;

(2) a local action to enforce a negotiated or executed airport noise or access restriction agreed to by the airport operator and the aircraft operators before November 5, 1990;

(3) an intergovernmental agreement including an airport noise or access restriction in effect on November 5, 1990;

(4) a subsequent amendment to an airport noise or access agreement or restriction in effect on November 5, 1990, that does not reduce or limit aircraft operations or affect aircraft safety;

(5)(A) an airport noise or access restriction adopted by an airport operator not later than October 1, 1990, and stayed as of October 1, 1990, by a court order or as a result of litigation, if any part of the restriction is subsequently allowed by a court to take effect; or

(B) a new restriction imposed by an airport operator to replace any part of a restriction described in subclause (A) of this clause that is disallowed by a court, if the new restriction would not prohibit aircraft operations in effect on November 5, 1990; or

(6) a local action that represents the adoption of the final part of a program of a staged airport noise or access restriction if the initial part of the program was adopted during 1988 and was in effect on November 5, 1990.

(e) GRANT LIMITATIONS.—Beginning on the 91st day after the Secretary prescribes a regulation under subsection (a) of this section, a sponsor of a facility operating under an airport noise or access restriction on the operation of stage 3 aircraft that first became effective after October 1, 1990, is eligible for a grant under section 47104 of this title and is eligible to impose a passenger facility charge under section 40117 of this title only if the restriction has been—

(1) agreed to by the airport proprietor and aircraft operators;

(2) approved by the Secretary as required by subsection (c)(1) of this section; or

(3) rescinded.

(Pub. L. 103–272, §1(e), July 5, 1994, 108 Stat. 1288; Pub. L. 112–95, title I, §111(c)(2)(A)(vii), Feb. 14, 2012, 126 Stat. 18.)

§47525. DECISION ABOUT AIRPORT NOISE AND ACCESS RESTRICTIONS ON CERTAIN STAGE 2 AIRCRAFT

The Secretary of Transportation shall conduct a study and decide on the application of section 47524(a)–(d) of this title to airport noise and access restrictions on the operation of stage 2 aircraft with a maximum weight of not more than 75,000 pounds. In making the decision, the Secretary shall consider—

(1) noise levels produced by those aircraft relative to other aircraft;

(2) the benefits to general aviation and the need for efficiency in the national air transportation system;

(3) the differences in the nature of operations at airports and the areas immediately surrounding the airports;

(4) international standards and agreements on aircraft noise; and

(5) other factors the Secretary considers necessary.

(Pub. L. 103–272, §1(e), July 5, 1994, 108 Stat. 1291.)

§47526. LIMITATIONS FOR NONCOMPLYING AIRPORT NOISE AND ACCESS RESTRICTIONS

Unless the Secretary of Transportation is satisfied that an airport is not imposing an airport noise or access restriction not in compliance with this subchapter, the airport may not—

(1) receive money under subchapter I of chapter 471 of this title; or

(2) impose a passenger facility charge under section 40117 of this title.

(Pub. L. 103–272, §1(e), July 5, 1994, 108 Stat. 1291; Pub. L. 112–95, title I, §111(c)(2)(A)(viii), Feb. 14, 2012, 126 Stat. 18.)

§47527. LIABILITY OF THE UNITED STATES GOVERNMENT FOR NOISE DAMAGES

When a proposed airport noise or access restriction is disapproved under this subchapter, the United States Government shall assume liability for noise damages only to the extent that a taking has occurred as a direct result of the disapproval. The United States Court of Federal Claims has exclusive jurisdiction of a civil action under this section.

(Pub. L. 103–272, §1(e), July 5, 1994, 108 Stat. 1291.)

§47528. Prohibition on operating certain aircraft not complying with stage 3 noise levels

(a) Prohibition.—Except as provided in subsection (b) or (f) of this section and section 47530 of this title, a person may operate after December 31, 1999, a civil subsonic turbojet (for which an airworthiness certificate other than an experimental certificate has been issued by the Administrator) with a maximum weight of more than 75,000 pounds to or from an airport in the United States only if the Secretary of Transportation finds that the aircraft complies with the stage 3 noise levels.

(b) Waivers.—(1) If, not later than July 1, 1999, at least 85 percent of the aircraft used by an air carrier or foreign air carrier to provide air transportation comply with the stage 3 noise levels, the carrier may apply for a waiver of subsection (a) of this section for the remaining aircraft used by the carrier to provide air transportation. The application must be filed with the Secretary not later than January 1, 1999, or, in the case of a foreign air carrier, the 15th day following the date of the enactment of the Wendell H. Ford Aviation Investment and Reform Act for the 21st Century and must include a plan with firm orders for making all aircraft used by the carrier to provide air transportation comply with the noise levels not later than December 31, 2003.

(2) The Secretary may grant a waiver under this subsection if the Secretary finds it would be in the public interest. In making the finding, the Secretary shall consider the effect of granting the waiver on competition in the air carrier industry and on small community air service.

(3) A waiver granted under this subsection may not permit the operation of stage 2 aircraft in the United States after December 31, 2003.

(c) Schedule for Phased-In Compliance.—The Secretary shall establish by regulation a schedule for phased-in compliance with subsection (a) of this section. The phase-in period shall begin on November 5, 1990, and end before December 31, 1999. The regulations shall establish interim compliance dates. The schedule for phased-in compliance shall be based on—

(1) a detailed economic analysis of the impact of the phaseout date for stage 2 aircraft on competition in the airline industry, including—

(A) the ability of air carriers to achieve capacity growth consistent with the projected rate of growth for the airline industry;

(B) the impact of competition in the airline and air cargo industries;

(C) the impact on nonhub and small community air service; and

(D) the impact on new entry into the airline industry; and

(2) an analysis of the impact of aircraft noise on individuals residing near airports.

(d) Annual Report.—Beginning with calendar year 1992—

(1) each air carrier shall submit to the Secretary an annual report on the progress the carrier is making toward complying with the requirements of this section and regulations prescribed under this section; and

(2) the Secretary shall submit to Congress an annual report on the progress being made toward that compliance.

(e) Hawaiian Operations.—(1) In this subsection, "turnaround service" means a flight between places only in Hawaii.

(2)(A) An air carrier or foreign air carrier may not operate in Hawaii, or between a place in Hawaii and a place outside the 48 contiguous States, a greater number of stage 2 aircraft with a maximum weight of more than 75,000 pounds than it operated in Hawaii, or between a place in Hawaii and a place outside the 48 contiguous States, on November 5, 1990.

(B) An air carrier that provided turnaround service in Hawaii on November 5, 1990, using stage 2 aircraft with a maximum weight of more than 75,000 pounds may include in the number of aircraft authorized under subparagraph (A) of this paragraph all stage 2 aircraft with a maximum weight of more than 75,000 pounds that were owned or leased by that carrier on that date, whether or not the aircraft were operated by the carrier on that date.

(3) An air carrier may provide turnaround service in Hawaii using stage 2 aircraft with a maximum weight of more than 75,000 pounds only if the carrier provided the service on November 5, 1990.

(4) An air carrier operating stage 2 aircraft under this subsection may transport stage 2 aircraft to or from the 48 contiguous States on a nonrevenue basis in order—

(A) to perform maintenance (including major alterations) or preventative maintenance on aircraft operated, or to be operated, within the limitations of paragraph (2)(B); or

(B) conduct operations within the limitations of paragraph (2)(B).

(f) AIRCRAFT MODIFICATION, DISPOSAL, SCHEDULED HEAVY MAINTENANCE, OR LEASING.—

(1) IN GENERAL.—The Secretary shall permit a person to operate after December 31, 1999, a stage 2 aircraft in nonrevenue service through the airspace of the United States or to or from an airport in the contiguous 48 States in order to—

(A) sell, lease, or use the aircraft outside the contiguous 48 States;

(B) scrap the aircraft;

(C) obtain modifications to the aircraft to meet stage 3 noise levels;

(D) perform scheduled heavy maintenance or significant modifications on the aircraft at a maintenance facility located in the contiguous 48 States;

(E) deliver the aircraft to an operator leasing the aircraft from the owner or return the aircraft to the lessor;

(F) prepare or park or store the aircraft in anticipation of any of the activities described in subparagraphs (A) through (E); or

(G) divert the aircraft to an alternative airport in the contiguous 48 States on account of weather, mechanical, fuel, air traffic control, or other safety reasons while conducting a flight in order to perform any of the activities described in subparagraphs (A) through (F).

(2) PROCEDURE TO BE PUBLISHED.—Not later than 30 days after the date of the enactment of this subsection, the Secretary shall establish and publish a procedure to implement paragraph (1) through the use of categorical waivers, ferry permits, or other means.

(g) STATUTORY CONSTRUCTION.—Nothing in this section may be construed as interfering with, nullifying, or otherwise affecting determinations made by the Federal Aviation Administration, or to be made by the Administration with respect to applications under part 161 of title 14, Code of Federal Regulations, that were pending on November 1, 1999.

(Pub. L. 103–272, §1(e), July 5, 1994, 108 Stat. 1291; Pub. L. 106–113, div. B, §1000(a)(5) [title II, §231(a), (b)(1)], Nov. 29, 1999, 113 Stat. 1536, 1501A–300, 1501A–301; Pub. L. 106–181, title VII, §721(a)–(c)(1), (d), Apr. 5, 2000, 114 Stat. 164, 165.)

§47529. Nonaddition Rule

(a) General Limitations.—Except as provided in subsection (b) of this section and section 47530 of this title, a person may operate a civil subsonic turbojet aircraft with a maximum weight of more than 75,000 pounds that is imported into the United States after November 4, 1990, only if the aircraft—

 (1) complies with the stage 3 noise levels; or

 (2) was purchased by the person importing the aircraft into the United States under a legally binding contract made before November 5, 1990.

(b) Exemptions.—The Secretary of Transportation may provide an exemption from subsection (a) of this section to permit a person to obtain modifications to an aircraft to meet the stage 3 noise levels.

(c) Aircraft Deemed Not Imported.—In this section, an aircraft is deemed not to have been imported into the United States if the aircraft—

 (1) was owned on November 5, 1990, by—

  (A) a corporation, trust, or partnership organized under the laws of the United States or a State (including the District of Columbia);

  (B) an individual who is a citizen of the United States; or

  (C) an entity that is owned or controlled by a corporation, trust, partnership, or individual described in subclause (A) or (B) of this clause; and

 (2) enters the United States not later than 6 months after the expiration of a lease agreement (including any extension) between an owner described in clause (1) of this subsection and a foreign carrier.

(Pub. L. 103–272, §1(e), July 5, 1994, 108 Stat. 1292.)

§47530. Nonapplication of Sections 47528(a)–(d) and 47529 to Aircraft Outside the 48 Contiguous States

Sections 47528(a)–(d) and 47529 of this title do not apply to aircraft used only to provide air transportation outside the 48 contiguous States. A civil subsonic turbojet aircraft with a maximum weight of more than 75,000 pounds that is imported into a noncontiguous State or a territory or possession of the United States after November 4, 1990, may be used to provide air transportation in the 48 contiguous States only if the aircraft complies with the stage 3 noise levels.

(Pub. L. 103–272, §1(e), July 5, 1994, 108 Stat. 1293.)

§47531. Penalties

A person violating section 47528, 47529, 47530, or 47534 of this title or a regulation prescribed under any of those sections is subject to the same civil penalties and procedures under chapter 463 of this title as a person violating section 44701(a) or (b) or any of sections 44702–44716 of this title.

(Pub. L. 103–272, §1(e), July 5, 1994, 108 Stat. 1293; Pub. L. 103–429, §6(73), Oct. 31, 1994, 108 Stat. 4388; Pub. L. 112–95, title V, §506(b)(1), Feb. 14, 2012, 126 Stat. 106.)

§47532. Judicial Review

An action taken by the Secretary of Transportation under any of sections 47528–47531 or 47534 of this title is subject to judicial review as provided under section 46110 of this title.

(Pub. L. 103–272, §1(e), July 5, 1994, 108 Stat. 1293; Pub. L. 103–429, §6(74), Oct. 31, 1994, 108 Stat. 4388; Pub. L. 112–95, title V, §506(b)(2), Feb. 14, 2012, 126 Stat. 106.)

§47533. RELATIONSHIP TO OTHER LAWS

Except as provided by section 47524 of this title, this subchapter does not affect—

(1) law in effect on November 5, 1990, on airport noise or access restrictions by local authorities;

(2) any proposed airport noise or access restriction at a general aviation airport if the airport proprietor has formally initiated a regulatory or legislative process before October 2, 1990; or

(3) the authority of the Secretary of Transportation to seek and obtain legal remedies the Secretary considers appropriate, including injunctive relief.

(Pub. L. 103–272, §1(e), July 5, 1994, 108 Stat. 1293.)

§47534. PROHIBITION ON OPERATING CERTAIN AIRCRAFT WEIGHING 75,000 POUNDS OR LESS NOT COMPLYING WITH STAGE 3 NOISE LEVELS

(a) PROHIBITION.—Except as otherwise provided by this section, after December 31, 2015, a person may not operate a civil subsonic jet airplane with a maximum weight of 75,000 pounds or less, and for which an airworthiness certificate (other than an experimental certificate) has been issued, to or from an airport in the United States unless the Secretary of Transportation finds that the aircraft complies with stage 3 noise levels.

(b) AIRCRAFT OPERATIONS OUTSIDE 48 CONTIGUOUS STATES.—Subsection (a) shall not apply to aircraft operated only outside the 48 contiguous States.

(c) TEMPORARY OPERATIONS.—The Secretary may allow temporary operation of an aircraft otherwise prohibited from operation under subsection (a) to or from an airport in the contiguous United States by granting a special flight authorization for one or more of the following circumstances:

(1) To sell, lease, or use the aircraft outside the 48 contiguous States.

(2) To scrap the aircraft.

(3) To obtain modifications to the aircraft to meet stage 3 noise levels.

(4) To perform scheduled heavy maintenance or significant modifications on the aircraft at a maintenance facility located in the contiguous 48 States.

(5) To deliver the aircraft to an operator leasing the aircraft from the owner or return the aircraft to the lessor.

(6) To prepare, park, or store the aircraft in anticipation of any of the activities described in paragraphs (1) through (5).

(7) To provide transport of persons and goods in the relief of an emergency situation.

(8) To divert the aircraft to an alternative airport in the 48 contiguous States on account of weather, mechanical, fuel, air traffic control, or other safety reasons while conducting a flight in order to perform any of the activities described in paragraphs (1) through (7).

(d) REGULATIONS.—The Secretary may prescribe such regulations or other guidance as may be necessary for the implementation of this section.

(e) STATUTORY CONSTRUCTION.—

(1) AIP GRANT ASSURANCES.—Noncompliance with subsection (a) shall not be construed as a violation of section 47107 or any regulations prescribed thereunder.

(2) PENDING APPLICATIONS.—Nothing in this section may be construed as interfering with, nullifying, or otherwise affecting determinations made by the Federal Aviation Administration, or to be made by the Administration, with respect to applications under part 161 of title 14, Code of Federal Regulations, that were pending on the date of enactment of this section.

(Added Pub. L. 112–95, title V, §506(a), Feb. 14, 2012, 126 Stat. 105.)

PART C
FINANCING

PART C—FINANCING

CHAPTER 481—AIRPORT AND AIRWAY TRUST FUND AUTHORIZATIONS

§48101. AIR NAVIGATION FACILITIES AND EQUIPMENT

(a) GENERAL AUTHORIZATION OF APPROPRIATIONS.—Not more than a total of the following amounts may be appropriated to the Secretary of Transportation out of the Airport and Airway Trust Fund established under section 9502 of the Internal Revenue Code of 1986 (26 U.S.C. 9502) to acquire, establish, and improve air navigation facilities under section 44502(a)(1)(A) of this title:

(1) $3,191,250,000 for fiscal year 2024.

(2) $3,575,000,000 for fiscal year 2025.

(3) $3,625,000,000 for fiscal year 2026.

(4) $3,675,000,000 for fiscal year 2027.

(5) $3,725,000,000 for fiscal year 2028.

(b) AVAILABILITY OF AMOUNTS.—Amounts appropriated under this section remain available until expended.

(c) AUTHORIZED EXPENDITURES.—Of the amounts appropriated under subsection (a), such sums as may be necessary may be used for the following:

(1) The implementation and use of upgrades to the current automated surface observation system/automated weather observing system, if the upgrade is successfully demonstrated.

(2) The acquisition and construction of remote towers (as defined in section 161 of the FAA Reauthorization Act of 2018).

(3) The remediation and elimination of identified cybersecurity vulnerabilities in the air traffic control system.

(4) The construction of facilities dedicated to improving the cybersecurity of the National Airspace System.

(5) Systems associated with the Data Communications program.

(6) The infrastructure, sustainment, and the elimination of the deferred maintenance backlog of air navigation facilities and other facilities for which the Federal Aviation Administration is responsible.

(7) The modernization and digitization of the Civil Aviation Registry.

(8) The construction of necessary Priority 1 National Airspace System facilities.

(9) Cost-beneficial construction, rehabilitation, or retrofitting programs designed to reduce Federal Aviation Administration facility operating costs.

(d) LIFE-CYCLE COST ESTIMATES.—The Administrator of the Federal Aviation Administration shall establish life-cycle cost estimates for any air traffic control modernization project the total life-cycle costs of which equal or exceed $50,000,000.

(Pub. L. 103–272, §1(e), July 5, 1994, 108 Stat. 1294; Pub. L. 103–305, title I, §102(a), Aug. 23, 1994, 108 Stat. 1571; Pub. L. 104–264, title I, §102(a), (b)(1), Oct. 9, 1996, 110 Stat. 3216; Pub. L. 106–6, §3, Mar. 31, 1999, 113 Stat. 10; Pub. L. 106–181, title I, §102, Apr. 5, 2000, 114 Stat. 65; Pub. L. 108–176, title I, §102, Dec. 12, 2003, 117 Stat. 2494; Pub. L. 110–330, §7, Sept. 30, 2008, 122 Stat. 3719; Pub. L. 111–12, §7, Mar. 30, 2009, 123 Stat. 1458; Pub. L. 111–69, §7, Oct. 1, 2009, 123 Stat. 2056; Pub. L. 111–116, §7, Dec. 16, 2009, 123 Stat. 3033; Pub. L. 111–153, §7, Mar. 31, 2010, 124 Stat. 1086; Pub. L. 111–161, §7, Apr. 30, 2010, 124 Stat. 1128; Pub. L. 111–197, §7, July 2, 2010, 124 Stat. 1354; Pub. L. 111–216, title I, §106, Aug. 1, 2010, 124 Stat. 2350; Pub. L. 112–30, title II, §207, Sept. 16, 2011, 125 Stat. 359; Pub. L. 112–91, §7, Jan. 31, 2012, 126 Stat. 4; Pub. L. 112–95, title I, §102, Feb. 14, 2012, 126 Stat. 16; Pub. L. 114–55, title I, §104, Sept. 30, 2015, 129 Stat. 524; Pub. L. 114–141, title I, §104, Mar. 30, 2016, 130 Stat. 323; Pub. L. 114–190, title I, §1104, July 15, 2016, 130 Stat. 618; Pub. L. 115–63, title I, §105, Sept. 29, 2017, 131 Stat. 1170; Pub. L. 115–141, div. M, title I, §105, Mar. 23, 2018, 132 Stat. 1047; Pub. L. 115–254, div. B, title I, §112, Oct. 5, 2018, 132 Stat. 3200; Pub. L. 118–15, div. B, title II, §2204, Sept. 30, 2023, 137 Stat. 84; Pub. L. 118–34, title I, §104, Dec. 26, 2023, 137 Stat. 1114; Pub. L. 118–41, title I, §104, Mar. 8, 2024, 138 Stat. 23; Pub. L. 118–63, title I, §102, May 16, 2024, 138 Stat. 1034.)

§48102. RESEARCH AND DEVELOPMENT

(a) AUTHORIZATION OF APPROPRIATIONS.—Not more than the following amounts may be appropriated to the Secretary of Transportation out of the Airport and Airway Trust Fund established under section 9502 of the Internal Revenue Code of 1986 (26 U.S.C. 9502) for conducting civil aviation research and development under sections 44504, 44505, 44507, 44509, and 44511–44513 of this title:

(1) for fiscal year 2004, $346,317,000, including—

(A) $65,000,000 for Improving Aviation Safety;

(B) $24,000,000 for Weather Safety Research;

(C) $27,500,000 for Human Factors and Aeromedical Research;

(D) $30,000,000 for Environmental Research and Development, of which $20,000,000 shall be for research activities related to reducing community exposure to civilian aircraft noise or emissions;

(E) $7,000,000 for Research Mission Support;

(F) $10,000,000 for the Airport Cooperative Research Program;

(G) $1,500,000 for carrying out subsection (h) of this section;

(H) \$42,800,000 for Advanced Technology Development and Prototyping;
(I) \$30,300,000 for Safe Flight 21;
(J) \$90,800,000 for the Center for Advanced Aviation System Development;
(K) \$9,667,000 for Airports Technology-Safety; and
(L) \$7,750,000 for Airports Technology-Efficiency;
(2) for fiscal year 2005, \$356,192,000, including—
  (A) \$65,705,000 for Improving Aviation Safety;
  (B) \$24,260,000 for Weather Safety Research;
  (C) \$27,800,000 for Human Factors and Aeromedical Research;
  (D) \$30,109,000 for Environmental Research and Development, of which \$20,000,000 shall be for research activities related to reducing community exposure to civilian aircraft noise or emissions;
  (E) \$7,076,000 for Research Mission Support;
  (F) \$10,000,000 for the Airport Cooperative Research Program;
  (G) \$1,650,000 for carrying out subsection (h) of this section;
  (H) \$43,300,000 for Advanced Technology Development and Prototyping;
  (I) \$31,100,000 for Safe Flight 21;
  (J) \$95,400,000 for the Center for Advanced Aviation System Development;
  (K) \$2,200,000 for Free Flight Phase 2;
  (L) \$9,764,000 for Airports Technology-Safety; and
  (M) \$7,828,000 for Airports Technology-Efficiency;
(3) for fiscal year 2006, \$352,157,000, including—
  (A) \$66,447,000 for Improving Aviation Safety;
  (B) \$24,534,000 for Weather Safety Research;
  (C) \$28,114,000 for Human Factors and Aeromedical Research;
  (D) \$30,223,000 for Environmental Research and Development, of which \$20,000,000 shall be for research activities related to reducing community exposure to civilian aircraft noise or emissions;
  (E) \$7,156,000 for Research Mission Support;
  (F) \$10,000,000 for the Airport Cooperation Research Program;
  (G) \$1,815,000 for carrying out subsection (h) of this section;
  (H) \$42,200,000 for Advanced Technology Development and Prototyping;
  (I) \$23,900,000 for Safe Flight 21;
  (J) \$100,000,000 for the Center for Advanced Aviation System Development;
  (K) \$9,862,000 for Airports Technology-Safety; and
  (L) \$7,906,000 for Airports Technology-Efficiency;
(4) for fiscal year 2007, \$356,261,000, including—
  (A) \$67,244,000 for Improving Aviation Safety;
  (B) \$24,828,000 for Weather Safety Research;
  (C) \$28,451,000 for Human Factors and Aeromedical Research;
  (D) \$30,586,000 for Environmental Research and Development, of which \$20,000,000 shall be for research activities related to reducing community exposure to civilian aircraft noise or emissions;
  (E) \$7,242,000 for Research Mission Support;
  (F) \$10,000,000 for the Airport Cooperation Research Program;

    (G) $1,837,000 for carrying out subsection (h) of this section;

    (H) $42,706,000 for Advanced Technology Development and Prototyping;

    (I) $24,187,000 for Safe Flight 21;

    (J) $101,200,000 for the Center for Advanced Aviation System Development;

    (K) $9,980,000 for Airports Technology-Safety; and

    (L) $8,000,000 for Airports Technology-Efficiency;

  (5) $171,000,000 for fiscal year 2009;

  (6) $190,500,000 for fiscal year 2010;

  (7) $170,000,000 for fiscal year 2011;

  (8) $168,000,000 for each of fiscal years 2012 through 2015;

  (9) $166,000,000 for each of fiscal years 2016 and 2017;

  (10) $189,000,000 for fiscal year 2018;

  (11) $194,000,000 for fiscal year 2019;

  (12) $199,000,000 for fiscal year 2020;

  (13) $204,000,000 for fiscal year 2021;

  (14) $209,000,000 for fiscal year 2022;

  (15) $214,000,000 for fiscal year 2023;

  (16) $280,000,000 for fiscal year 2024;

  (17) $311,000,000 for fiscal year 2025;

  (18) $323,000,000 for fiscal year 2026;

  (19) $334,000,000 for fiscal year 2027; and

  (20) $345,000,000 for fiscal year 2028.

  (b) RESEARCH PRIORITIES.—(1) The Administrator shall prioritize safety in considering the advice and recommendations of the research advisory committee established by section 44508 of this title in establishing priorities among major categories of research and development activities carried out by the Federal Aviation Administration.

  (2) As safety related activities shall be the highest research priority, at least 70 percent of the amount appropriated under subsection (a) of this section shall be for safety research and development projects.

  (3) At least 15 percent of the amount appropriated under subsection (a) of this section shall be for long-term research projects.

  (c) TRANSFERS BETWEEN CATEGORIES.—(1) Not more than 10 percent of the net amount authorized for a category of projects and activities in a fiscal year under subsection (a) of this section may be transferred to or from that category in that fiscal year.

  (2) The Secretary may transfer more than 10 percent of an authorized amount to or from a category only after—

    (A) submitting a written explanation of the proposed transfer to the Committees on Science and Appropriations of the House of Representatives and the Committees on Commerce, Science, and Transportation and Appropriations of the Senate; and

    (B) 30 days have passed after the explanation is submitted or each Committee notifies the Secretary in writing that it does not object to the proposed transfer.

  (d) AIRPORT CAPACITY RESEARCH AND DEVELOPMENT.—(1) Of the amounts made available under subsection (a) of this section, at least $25,000,000 may be appropriated each fiscal year for research and development under section 44505(a) and (c) of this title on preserving and enhancing airport capacity, including research and development on improvements to airport design standards, maintenance, safety, operations, and environmental concerns.

(2) The Administrator shall submit to the Committees on Science and Transportation and Infrastructure of the House of Representatives and the Committee on Commerce, Science, and Transportation of the Senate a report on expenditures made under paragraph (1) of this subsection for each fiscal year. The report shall be submitted not later than 60 days after the end of the fiscal year.

(e) AIR TRAFFIC CONTROLLER PERFORMANCE RESEARCH.—Necessary amounts may be appropriated to the Secretary out of amounts in the Fund available for research and development to conduct research under section 44506(a) and (b) of this title.

(f) AVAILABILITY OF AMOUNTS.—Amounts appropriated under subsection (a) of this section remain available until expended.

(g) ANNUAL SUBMISSION OF THE NATIONAL AVIATION RESEARCH PLAN.—The Administrator shall submit the national aviation research plan to Congress no later than the date that is 30 days after the date of submission of the President's budget request to Congress for that fiscal year, as required under section 44501(c).

(h) RESEARCH GRANTS PROGRAM INVOLVING UNDERGRADUATE STUDENTS.—

(1) ESTABLISHMENT.—The Administrator of the Federal Aviation Administration shall establish a program to utilize undergraduate and technical colleges, including Historically Black Colleges and Universities and Hispanic Serving Institutions, in research on subjects of relevance to the Federal Aviation Administration. Grants may be awarded under this subsection for—

(A) research projects to be carried out at primarily undergraduate institutions and technical colleges;

(B) research projects that combine research at primarily undergraduate institutions and technical colleges with other research supported by the Federal Aviation Administration;

(C) research on future training requirements on projected changes in regulatory requirements for aircraft maintenance and power plant licensees; or

(D) research on the impact of new technologies and procedures, particularly those related to aircraft flight deck and air traffic management functions, on training requirements for pilots and air traffic controllers.

(2) NOTICE OF CRITERIA.—Within 6 months after the date of the enactment of the FAA Research, Engineering, and Development Authorization Act of 1998, the Administrator of the Federal Aviation Administration shall establish and publish in the Federal Register criteria for the submittal of proposals for a grant under this subsection, and for the awarding of such grants.

(3) PRINCIPAL CRITERIA.—The principal criteria for the awarding of grants under this subsection shall be—

(A) the relevance of the proposed research to technical research needs identified by the Federal Aviation Administration;

(B) the scientific and technical merit of the proposed research; and

(C) the potential for participation by undergraduate students in the proposed research.

(4) COMPETITIVE, MERIT-BASED EVALUATION.—Grants shall be awarded under this

subsection on the basis of evaluation of proposals through a competitive, merit-based process.

(Pub. L. 103–272, §1(e), July 5, 1994, 108 Stat. 1294; Pub. L. 103–305, title III, §302, Aug. 23, 1994, 108 Stat. 1589; Pub. L. 104–264, title XI, §§1102, 1103, Oct. 9, 1996, 110 Stat. 3278; Pub. L. 104–287, §5(9), (74), Oct. 11, 1996, 110 Stat. 3389, 3396; Pub. L. 105–155, §§2, 3, Feb. 11, 1998, 112 Stat. 5; Pub. L. 106–181, title IX, §901, Apr. 5, 2000, 114 Stat. 194; Pub. L. 108–176, title VII, §§701, 707, Dec. 12, 2003, 117 Stat. 2574, 2582; Pub. L. 110–330, §8, Sept. 30, 2008, 122 Stat. 3719; Pub. L. 111–12, §8, Mar. 30, 2009, 123 Stat. 1459; Pub. L. 111–69, §8, Oct. 1, 2009, 123 Stat. 2056; Pub. L. 111–116, §8, Dec. 16, 2009, 123 Stat. 3033; Pub. L. 111–153, §8, Mar. 31, 2010, 124 Stat. 1086; Pub. L. 111–161, §8, Apr. 30, 2010, 124 Stat. 1128; Pub. L. 111–197, §8, July 2, 2010, 124 Stat. 1355; Pub. L. 111–216, title I, §107, Aug. 1, 2010, 124 Stat. 2350; Pub. L. 112–30, title II, §208, Sept. 16, 2011, 125 Stat. 359; Pub. L. 112–91, §8, Jan. 31, 2012, 126 Stat. 4; Pub. L. 112–95, title IX, §901(a), (b), Feb. 14, 2012, 126 Stat. 137; Pub. L. 114–55, title I, §105, Sept. 30, 2015, 129 Stat. 524; Pub. L. 114–141, title I, §105, Mar. 30, 2016, 130 Stat. 324; Pub. L. 114–190, title I, §1105, July 15, 2016, 130 Stat. 618; Pub. L. 115–63, title I, §106, Sept. 29, 2017, 131 Stat. 1170; Pub. L. 115–141, div. M, title I, §106, Mar. 23, 2018, 132 Stat. 1047; Pub. L. 115–254, div. B, title VII, §703, Oct. 5, 2018, 132 Stat. 3409; Pub. L. 118–15, div. B, title II, §2205, Sept. 30, 2023, 137 Stat. 84; Pub. L. 118–34, title I, §105, Dec. 26, 2023, 137 Stat. 1115; Pub. L. 118–41, title I, §105, Mar. 8, 2024, 138 Stat. 23; Pub. L. 118–63, title X, §§1002, 1004(b), May 16, 2024, 138 Stat. 1386.)

§48103. AIRPORT PLANNING AND DEVELOPMENT AND NOISE COMPATIBILITY PLANNING AND PROGRAMS

(a) IN GENERAL.—There shall be available to the Secretary of Transportation out of the Airport and Airway Trust Fund established under section 9502 of the Internal Revenue Code of 1986 to make grants for airport planning and airport development under section 47104, airport noise compatibility planning under section 47505(a)(2), and carrying out noise compatibility programs under section 47504(c)—

(1) $3,350,000,000 for fiscal year 2018;
(2) $3,350,000,000 for fiscal year 2019;
(3) $3,350,000,000 for fiscal year 2020;
(4) $3,350,000,000 for fiscal year 2021;
(5) $3,350,000,000 for fiscal year 2022;
(6) $3,350,000,000 for fiscal year 2023;
(7) $3,350,000,000 for fiscal year 2024;
(8) $4,000,000,000 for fiscal year 2025;
(9) $4,000,000,000 for fiscal year 2026;
(10) $4,000,000,000 for fiscal year 2027; and
(11) $4,000,000,000 for fiscal year 2028.

(b) AVAILABILITY OF AMOUNTS.—Amounts made available under subsection (a) shall remain available until expended.

(Pub. L. 103–272, §1(e), July 5, 1994, 108 Stat. 1296; Pub. L. 103–305, title I, §101(a), Aug. 23, 1994, 108 Stat. 1570; Pub. L. 104–264, title I, §101(a), Oct. 9, 1996, 110 Stat. 3216; Pub. L. 105–277, div. C, title I, §110(b)(1), Oct. 21, 1998, 112 Stat. 2681–587; Pub. L. 106–6, §2(a), Mar. 31, 1999, 113 Stat. 10; Pub. L. 106–31, title VI, §6002(a), May 21, 1999, 113 Stat. 113; Pub. L. 106–59, §1(a), Sept. 29, 1999, 113 Stat. 482; Pub. L. 106–181, title I, §101(a), Apr. 5, 2000, 114 Stat. 65; Pub. L. 108–176, title I, §101(a), Dec. 12, 2003, 117 Stat. 2494; Pub. L. 110–190, §4(a)(1), Feb. 28, 2008, 122 Stat. 643; Pub. L. 110–253, §4(a), June 30, 2008, 122 Stat. 2418; Pub. L. 110–330, §4(a)(1), Sept. 30, 2008, 122 Stat. 3717; Pub. L. 111–12, §4(a), Mar. 30, 2009, 123 Stat. 1457; Pub. L. 111–69, §4(a)(1), Oct. 1, 2009, 123 Stat. 2054; Pub. L. 111–116, §4(a)(1), Dec. 16, 2009, 123 Stat. 3031; Pub. L. 111–153, §4(a)(1), Mar. 31, 2010, 124 Stat. 1084; Pub. L.

111–161, §4(a)(1), Apr. 30, 2010, 124 Stat. 1126; Pub. L. 111–197, §4(a)(1), July 2, 2010, 124 Stat. 1353; Pub. L. 111–249, §4(a)(1), Sept. 30, 2010, 124 Stat. 2627; Pub. L. 111–329, §4(a)(1), Dec. 22, 2010, 124 Stat. 3566; Pub. L. 112–7, §4(a)(1), Mar. 31, 2011, 125 Stat. 31; Pub. L. 112–16, §4(a)(1), May 31, 2011, 125 Stat. 218; Pub. L. 112–21, §4(a)(1), June 29, 2011, 125 Stat. 233; Pub. L. 112–27, §4(a)(1), Aug. 5, 2011, 125 Stat. 270; Pub. L. 112–30, title II, §204(a)(1), Sept. 16, 2011, 125 Stat. 357; Pub. L. 112–91, §4(a)(1), Jan. 31, 2012, 126 Stat. 3; Pub. L. 112–95, title I, §101(a), Feb. 14, 2012, 126 Stat. 15; Pub. L. 114–55, title I, §101(a)(1), Sept. 30, 2015, 129 Stat. 522; Pub. L. 114–141, title I, §101(a)(1), Mar. 30, 2016, 130 Stat. 322; Pub. L. 114–190, title I, §1101(a), July 15, 2016, 130 Stat. 617; Pub. L. 115–63, title I, §101(a)(1), Sept. 29, 2017, 131 Stat. 1169; Pub. L. 115–141, div. M, title I, §101(a), Mar. 23, 2018, 132 Stat. 1046; Pub. L. 115–254, div. B, title I, §111(a), Oct. 5, 2018, 132 Stat. 3199; Pub. L. 118–15, div. B, title II, §2201(a), Sept. 30, 2023, 137 Stat. 82; Pub. L. 118–34, title I, §101(a), Dec. 26, 2023, 137 Stat. 1112; Pub. L. 118–41, title I, §101(a), Mar. 8, 2024, 138 Stat. 20; Pub. L. 118–63, title I, §101(a), May 16, 2024, 138 Stat. 1033.)

§48104. OPERATIONS AND MAINTENANCE

The balance of the money available in the Airport and Airway Trust Fund established under section 9502 of the Internal Revenue Code of 1986 (26 U.S.C. 9502) may be appropriated to the Secretary of Transportation out of the Fund for—

(1) direct costs the Secretary incurs to flight check, operate, and maintain air navigation facilities referred to in section 44502(a)(1)(A) of this title safely and efficiently; and

(2) the costs of services provided under international agreements related to the joint financing of air navigation services assessed against the United States Government.

(Pub. L. 103–272, §1(e), July 5, 1994, 108 Stat. 1296; Pub. L. 103–305, title I, §102(b), Aug. 23, 1994, 108 Stat. 1571; Pub. L. 104–264, title I, §103(b), (d)(1), Oct. 9, 1996, 110 Stat. 3216; Pub. L. 104–287, §5(87), Oct. 11, 1996, 110 Stat. 3398; Pub. L. 106–181, title I, §106(d), Apr. 5, 2000, 114 Stat. 73; Pub. L. 115–254, div. B, title V, §539(r), Oct. 5, 2018, 132 Stat. 3371.)

§48105. WEATHER REPORTING SERVICES

To sustain the aviation weather reporting programs of the Federal Aviation Administration, the Secretary of Transportation may expend from amounts available under section 48104 of this title not more than the following amounts:

(1) for the fiscal year ending September 30, 1993, $35,596,000.

(2) for the fiscal year ending September 30, 1994, $37,800,000.

(3) for the fiscal year ending September 30, 1995, $39,000,000.

(4) $39,000,000 for each of fiscal years 2019 through 2023.

(5) $60,000,000 for each of fiscal years 2024 through 2028.

(Pub. L. 103–272, §1(e), July 5, 1994, 108 Stat. 1296; Pub. L. 115–254, div. B, title I, §114, Oct. 5, 2018, 132 Stat. 3201; Pub. L. 118–15, div. B, title II, §2202(j), Sept. 30, 2023, 137 Stat. 83; Pub. L. 118–34, title I, §102(j), Dec. 26, 2023, 137 Stat. 1113; Pub. L. 118–41, title I, §102(j), Mar. 8, 2024, 138 Stat. 22; Pub. L. 118–63, title I, §104(c), May 16, 2024, 138 Stat. 1035.)

§48106. AIRWAY SCIENCE CURRICULUM GRANTS

Amounts are available from the Airport and Airway Trust Fund established under section 9502 of the Internal Revenue Code of 1986 (26 U.S.C. 9502) to carry out section 44510 [1] of this title. The amounts remain available until expended.

(Pub. L. 103–272, §1(e), July 5, 1994, 108 Stat. 1296.)

§48107. CIVIL AVIATION SECURITY RESEARCH AND DEVELOPMENT

After the review under section 44912(b) of this title is completed, necessary amounts may be appropriated to the Secretary of Transportation out of the Airport and Airway Trust Fund established under section 9502 of the Internal Revenue Code of 1986 (26 U.S.C. 9502) to make grants under section 44912(a)(4)(A).

(Pub. L. 103–272, §1(e), July 5, 1994, 108 Stat. 1297.)

§48108. AVAILABILITY AND USES OF AMOUNTS

(a) AVAILABILITY OF AMOUNTS.—Amounts equal to the amounts authorized under sections 48101–48105 of this title remain in the Airport and Airway Trust Fund established under section 9502 of the Internal Revenue Code of 1986 (26 U.S.C. 9502) until appropriated for the purposes of sections 48101–48105.

(b) LIMITATIONS ON USES.—(1) Amounts in the Fund may be appropriated only to carry out a program or activity referred to in this chapter.

(2) Amounts in the Fund may be appropriated for administrative expenses of the Department of Transportation or a component of the Department only to the extent authorized by section 48104 of this title.

(c) LIMITATION ON OBLIGATING OR EXPENDING AMOUNTS.—In a fiscal year beginning after September 30, 1998, the Secretary of Transportation may obligate or expend an amount appropriated out of the Fund under section 48104 of this title only if a law expressly amends section 48104.

(Pub. L. 103–272, §1(e), July 5, 1994, 108 Stat. 1297; Pub. L. 103–305, title I, §102(c), Aug. 23, 1994, 108 Stat. 1571; Pub. L. 104–264, title I, §103(c), Oct. 9, 1996, 110 Stat. 3216.)

§48109. SUBMISSION OF BUDGET INFORMATION AND LEGISLATIVE RECOMMENDATIONS AND COMMENTS

When the Administrator of the Federal Aviation Administration submits to the Secretary of Transportation, the President, or the Director of the Office of Management and Budget any budget information, legislative recommendation, or comment on legislation about amounts authorized in section 48101 or 48102 of this title, the Administrator concurrently shall submit a copy of the information, recommendation, or comment to the Speaker of the House of Representatives, the Committees on Transportation and Infrastructure and Appropriations of the House, the President of the Senate, and the Committees on Commerce, Science, and Transportation and Appropriations of the Senate.

(Pub. L. 103–272, §1(e), July 5, 1994, 108 Stat. 1297; Pub. L. 104–287, §5(9), Oct. 11, 1996, 110 Stat. 3389.)

§48110. FACILITIES FOR ADVANCED TRAINING OF MAINTENANCE TECHNICIANS FOR AIR CARRIER AIRCRAFT

For the fiscal years ending September 30, 1993–1995, amounts necessary to carry out section 44515 of this title may be appropriated to the Secretary of Transportation out of the Airport and Airway Trust Fund established under section 9502 of the Internal Revenue Code of 1986 (26 U.S.C. 9502). The amounts remain available until expended.

(Pub. L. 103–272, §1(e), July 5, 1994, 108 Stat. 1297.)

§48111. FUNDING PROPOSALS

(a) INTRODUCTION IN THE SENATE.—Within 15 days (not counting any day on which the Senate is not in session) after a funding proposal is submitted to the Senate by the Secretary of Transportation under section 274(c) of the Air Traffic Management System Performance Improvement Act of 1996, an implementing bill with respect to such funding proposal shall be introduced in the Senate by the majority leader of the Senate, for himself and the minority leader of the Senate, or by Members of the Senate designated by the majority leader and minority leader of the Senate.

(b) CONSIDERATION IN THE SENATE.—An implementing bill introduced in the Senate under subsection (a) shall be referred to the Committee on Commerce, Science, and Transportation. The Committee on Commerce, Science, and Transportation shall report the bill with its recommendations within 60 days following the date of introduction of the bill. Upon the reporting of the bill by the Committee on Commerce, Science, and Transportation, the reported bill shall be referred sequentially to the Committee on Finance for a period of 60 legislative days.

(c) DEFINITIONS.—For purposes of this section, the following definitions apply:

(1) IMPLEMENTING BILL.—The term "implementing bill" means only a bill of the Senate which is introduced as provided in subsection (a) with respect to one or more Federal Aviation Administration funding proposals which contain changes in existing laws or new statutory authority required to implement such funding proposal or proposals.

(2) FUNDING PROPOSAL.—The term "funding proposal" means a proposal to provide interim or permanent funding for operations of the Federal Aviation Administration.

(d) RULES OF THE SENATE.—The provisions of this section are enacted—

(1) as an exercise of the rulemaking power of the Senate and as such they are deemed a part of the rules of the Senate and they supersede other rules only to the extent that they are inconsistent therewith; and

(2) with full recognition of the constitutional right of the Senate to change the rules (so far as relating to the procedure of the Senate) at any time, in the same manner and to the same extent as in the case of any other rule of the Senate.

(Added Pub. L. 104–264, title II, §275(a), Oct. 9, 1996, 110 Stat. 3246.)

[§48112. REPEALED. PUB. L. 115–254, DIV. B, TITLE I, §115, OCT. 5, 2018, 132 STAT. 3201]

Section, added Pub. L. 106–181, title I, §107(a), Apr. 5, 2000, 114 Stat. 73, related to adjustment to AIP program funding.

§48113. REPROGRAMMING NOTIFICATION REQUIREMENT

Before reprogramming any amounts appropriated under section 106(k), 48101(a), or 48103, for which notification of the Committees on Appropriations of the Senate and the House of Representatives is required, the Secretary of Transportation shall transmit a written explanation of the proposed reprogramming to the Committee on Commerce, Science, and Transportation of the Senate and the Committee on Transportation and Infrastructure of the House of Representatives.

(Added Pub. L. 106–181, title I, §108(a), Apr. 5, 2000, 114 Stat. 73.)

§48114. FUNDING FOR AVIATION PROGRAMS

(a) AUTHORIZATION OF APPROPRIATIONS.—

(1) AIRPORT AND AIRWAY TRUST FUND GUARANTEE.—

(A) IN GENERAL.—The total budget resources made available from the Airport and Airway Trust Fund each fiscal year pursuant to sections 48101, 48102, 48103, and 106(k) shall—

(i) in fiscal year 2013, be equal to 90 percent of the estimated level of receipts plus interest credited to the Airport and Airway Trust Fund for that fiscal year; and

(ii) in fiscal years 2014 through 2018, be equal to the sum of—

(I) 90 percent of the estimated level of receipts plus interest credited to the Airport and Airway Trust Fund for that fiscal year; and

(II) the actual level of receipts plus interest credited to the Airport and Airway Trust Fund for the second preceding fiscal year minus the total amount made available for obligation from the Airport and Airway Trust Fund for the second preceding fiscal year.

Such amounts may be used only for the aviation investment programs listed in subsection (b)(1).

(B) GUARANTEE.—No funds may be appropriated or limited for aviation investment programs listed in subsection (b)(1) unless the amount described in subparagraph (A) has been provided.

(2) ADDITIONAL AUTHORIZATIONS OF APPROPRIATIONS FROM THE GENERAL FUND.—In any fiscal year through fiscal year 2018, if the amount described in paragraph (1) is appropriated, there is further authorized to be appropriated from the general fund of the Treasury such sums as may be necessary for the Federal Aviation Administration Operations account.

(b) DEFINITIONS.—In this section, the following definitions apply:

(1) TOTAL BUDGET RESOURCES.—The term "total budget resources" means the total amount made available from the Airport and Airway Trust Fund for the sum of obligation limitations and budget authority made available for a fiscal year for the following budget accounts that are subject to the obligation limitation on contract authority provided in this title and for which appropriations are provided pursuant to authorizations contained in this title:

(A) 69–8106–0–7–402 (Grants in Aid for Airports).

(B) 69–8107–0–7–402 (Facilities and Equipment).

(C) 69–8108–0–7–402 (Research and Development).

(D) 69–8104–0–7–402 (Trust Fund Share of Operations).

(2) ESTIMATED LEVEL OF RECEIPTS PLUS INTEREST.—The term "estimated level of receipts plus interest" means the level of excise taxes and interest credited to the Airport and Airway Trust Fund under section 9502 of the Internal Revenue Code of 1986 for a fiscal year as set forth in the President's budget baseline projection as defined in section 257 of the Balanced Budget and Emergency Deficit Control Act of 1985 (Public Law 99–177) (Treasury identification code 20–8103–0–7–402) for that fiscal year submitted pursuant to section 1105 of title 31, United States Code.

(c) Enforcement of Guarantees.—

(1) Total airport and airway trust fund funding.—It shall not be in order in the House of Representatives or the Senate to consider any bill, joint resolution, amendment, motion, or conference report that would cause total budget resources in a fiscal year for aviation investment programs described in subsection (b) to be less than the amount required by subsection (a)(1)(A) for such fiscal year.

(2) Capital priority.—It shall not be in order in the House of Representatives or the Senate to consider any bill, joint resolution, amendment, motion, or conference report that provides an appropriation (or any amendment thereto) for any fiscal year through fiscal year 2018 for Research and Development or Operations if the sum of the obligation limitation for Grants-in-Aid for Airports and the appropriation for Facilities and Equipment for such fiscal year is below the sum of the authorized levels for Grants-in-Aid for Airports and for Facilities and Equipment for such fiscal year.

(Added Pub. L. 108–176, title I, §104(a), Dec. 12, 2003, 117 Stat. 2496; amended Pub. L. 112–95, title I, §104, Feb. 14, 2012, 126 Stat. 16; Pub. L. 114–55, title I, §106(a), Sept. 30, 2015, 129 Stat. 524; Pub. L. 114–190, title I, §1106(a), July 15, 2016, 130 Stat. 618; Pub. L. 115–63, title I, §107(a), Sept. 29, 2017, 131 Stat. 1170; Pub. L. 115–254, div. B, title I, §116, Oct. 5, 2018, 132 Stat. 3201.)

CHAPTER 482—ADVANCE APPROPRIATIONS FOR AIRPORT AND AIRWAY TRUST FACILITIES

§48201. ADVANCE APPROPRIATIONS

(a) MULTIYEAR AUTHORIZATIONS.—Beginning with fiscal year 1999, any authorization of appropriations for an activity for which amounts are to be appropriated from the Airport and Airway Trust Fund established under section 9502 of the Internal Revenue Code of 1986 shall provide funds for a period of not less than 3 fiscal years unless the activity for which appropriations are authorized is to be concluded before the end of that period.

(b) MULTIYEAR APPROPRIATIONS.—Beginning with fiscal year 1999, amounts appropriated from the Airport and Airway Trust Fund shall be appropriated for periods of 3 fiscal years rather than annually.

(Added Pub. L. 104–264, title II, §277(a), Oct. 9, 1996, 110 Stat. 3248.)

[CHAPTER 483—REPEALED]

[§48301. REPEALED. PUB. L. 115–254, DIV. K, TITLE I, §1991(I)(1), OCT. 5, 2018, 132 STAT. 3645]

Section, added Pub. L. 107–71, title I, §118(c)(1), Nov. 19, 2001, 115 Stat. 627; amended Pub. L. 108–458, title IV, §4029, Dec. 17, 2004, 118 Stat. 3727; Pub. L. 110–53, title XVI, §1618, Aug. 3, 2007, 121 Stat. 489, related to aviation security funding.

PART D
PUBLIC AIRPORTS

PART D—PUBLIC AIRPORTS

CHAPTER 491—METROPOLITAN WASHINGTON AIRPORTS

§49101. FINDINGS

Congress finds that—

(1) the 2 federally owned airports in the metropolitan area of the District of Columbia constitute an important and growing part of the commerce, transportation, and economic patterns of Virginia, the District of Columbia, and the surrounding region;

(2) Baltimore/Washington International Airport, owned and operated by Maryland, is an air transportation facility that provides service to the greater Metropolitan Washington region together with the 2 federally owned airports, and timely Federal-aid grants to Baltimore/Washington International Airport will provide additional capacity to meet the growing air traffic needs and to compete with other airports on a fair basis;

(3) the United States Government has a continuing but limited interest in the operation of the 2 federally owned airports, which serve the travel and cargo needs of the entire Metropolitan Washington region as well as the District of Columbia as the national seat of government;

(4) operation of the Metropolitan Washington Airports by an independent local authority will facilitate timely improvements at both airports to meet the growing demand of interstate air transportation occasioned by the Airline Deregulation Act of 1978 (Public Law 95–504; 92 Stat. 1705);

(5) all other major air carrier airports in the United States are operated by public entities at the State, regional, or local level;

(6) any change in status of the 2 airports must take into account the interest of nearby communities, the traveling public, air carriers, general aviation, airport employees, and other interested groups, as well as the interests of the United States Government and State governments involved;

(7) in recognition of a perceived limited need for a Federal role in the management of these airports and the growing local interest, the Secretary of Transportation has

recommended a transfer of authority from the Federal to the local/State level that is consistent with the management of major airports elsewhere in the United States;

(8) an operating authority with representation from local jurisdictions, similar to authorities at all major airports in the United States, will improve communications with local officials and concerned residents regarding noise at the Metropolitan Washington Airports;

(9) a commission of congressional, State, and local officials and aviation representatives has recommended to the Secretary that transfer of the federally owned airports be as a unit to an independent authority to be created by Virginia and the District of Columbia; and

(10) the Federal interest in these airports can be provided through a lease mechanism which provides for local control and operation.

(Added Pub. L. 105–102, §2(26), Nov. 20, 1997, 111 Stat. 2206.)

§49102. PURPOSE

(a) GENERAL.—The purpose of this chapter is to authorize the transfer of operating responsibility under long-term lease of the 2 Metropolitan Washington Airport properties as a unit, including access highways and other related facilities, to a properly constituted independent airport authority created by Virginia and the District of Columbia, in order to achieve local control, management, operation, and development of these important transportation assets.

(b) INCLUSION OF BALTIMORE/WASHINGTON INTERNATIONAL AIRPORT NOT PRECLUDED.—This chapter does not prohibit the Airports Authority and Maryland from making an agreement to make Baltimore/Washington International Airport part of a regional airports authority, subject to terms agreed to by the Airports Authority, the Secretary of Transportation, Virginia, the District of Columbia, and Maryland.

(Added Pub. L. 105–102, §2(26), Nov. 20, 1997, 111 Stat. 2207.)

§49103. DEFINITIONS

In this chapter—

(1) "Airports Authority" means the Metropolitan Washington Airports Authority, a public authority created by Virginia and the District of Columbia consistent with the requirements of section 49106 of this title.

(2) "employee" means any permanent Federal Aviation Administration personnel employed by the Metropolitan Washington Airports on June 7, 1987.

(3) "Metropolitan Washington Airports" means Ronald Reagan Washington National Airport and Washington Dulles International Airport.

(4) "Washington Dulles International Airport" means the airport constructed under the Act of September 7, 1950 (ch. 905, 64 Stat. 770), and includes the Dulles Airport Access Highway and Right-of-way, including the extension between Interstate Routes I–495 and I–66.

(5) "Ronald Reagan Washington National Airport" means the airport described in the Act of June 29, 1940 (ch. 444, 54 Stat. 686).

(Added Pub. L. 105–102, §2(26), Nov. 20, 1997, 111 Stat. 2207; amended Pub. L. 105–154, §2(a)(1)(D),

Feb. 6, 1998, 112 Stat. 3.)

§49104. LEASE OF METROPOLITAN WASHINGTON AIRPORTS

(a) GENERAL.—The lease between the Secretary of Transportation and the Metropolitan Washington Airports Authority under section 6005(a) of the Metropolitan Washington Airports Act of 1986 (Public Law 99–500; 100 Stat. 1783–375; Public Law 99–591; 100 Stat. 3341–378), for the Metropolitan Washington Airports must provide during its 50-year term at least the following:

(1) The Airports Authority shall operate, maintain, protect, promote, and develop the Metropolitan Washington Airports as a unit and as primary airports serving the Metropolitan Washington area.

(2)(A) In this paragraph, "airport purposes" means a use of property interests (except a sale) for—

(i) aviation business or activities;

(ii) activities necessary or appropriate to serve passengers or cargo in air commerce;

(iii) nonprofit, public use facilities that are not inconsistent with the needs of aviation; or

(iv) a business or activity not inconsistent with the needs of aviation that has been approved by the Secretary.

(B) During the period of the lease, the real property constituting the Metropolitan Washington Airports shall be used only for airport purposes.

(C) If the Secretary decides that any part of the real property leased to the Airports Authority under this chapter is used for other than airport purposes, the Secretary shall—

(i) direct that the Airports Authority take appropriate measures to have that part of the property be used for airport purposes; and

(ii) retake possession of the property if the Airports Authority fails to have that part of the property be used for airport purposes within a reasonable period of time, as the Secretary decides.

(3) The Airports Authority is subject to section 47107(a)–(c) and (e) of this title and to the assurances and conditions required of grant recipients under the Airport and Airway Improvement Act of 1982 (Public Law 97–248; 96 Stat. 671) as in effect on June 7, 1987. Notwithstanding section 47107(b) of this title, all revenues generated by the Metropolitan Washington Airports shall be expended for the capital and operating costs of the Metropolitan Washington Airports.

(4) In acquiring by contract supplies or services for an amount estimated to be more than $200,000, or awarding concession contracts, the Airports Authority to the maximum extent practicable shall obtain complete and open competition through the use of published competitive procedures. By a vote of 7 members, the Airports Authority may grant exceptions to the requirements of this paragraph.

(5)(A) Except as provided in subparagraph (B) of this paragraph, all regulations of the Metropolitan Washington Airports (14 CFR part 159) become regulations of the Airports Authority as of June 7, 1987, and remain in effect until modified or revoked by the Airports Authority under procedures of the Airports Authority.

(B) Sections 159.59(a) and 159.191 of title 14, Code of Federal Regulations, do not become regulations of the Airports Authority.

(C) The Airports Authority may not increase or decrease the number of instrument flight rule takeoffs and landings authorized by the High Density Rule (14 CFR 93.121 et seq.) at Ronald Reagan Washington National Airport on October 18, 1986, and may not impose a limitation on the number of passengers taking off or landing at Ronald Reagan Washington National Airport.

(D) Subparagraph (C) does not apply to any increase in the number of instrument flight rule takeoffs and landings necessary to implement exemptions granted by the Secretary under section 41718.

(6)(A) Except as specified in subparagraph (B) of this paragraph, the Airports Authority shall assume all rights, liabilities, and obligations of the Metropolitan Washington Airports on June 7, 1987, including leases, permits, licenses, contracts, agreements, claims, tariffs, accounts receivable, accounts payable, and litigation related to those rights and obligations, regardless whether judgment has been entered, damages awarded, or appeal taken. The Airports Authority must cooperate in allowing representatives of the Attorney General and the Secretary adequate access to employees and records when needed for the performance of duties and powers related to the period before June 7, 1987. The Airports Authority shall assume responsibility for the Federal Aviation Administration's Master Plans for the Metropolitan Washington Airports.

(B) The procedure for disputes resolution contained in any contract entered into on behalf of the United States Government before June 7, 1987, continues to govern the performance of the contract unless otherwise agreed to by the parties to the contract. Claims for monetary damages founded in tort, by or against the Government as the owner and operator of the Metropolitan Washington Airports, arising before June 7, 1987, shall be adjudicated as if the lease had not been entered into.

(C) The Administration is responsible for reimbursing the Employees' Compensation Fund, as provided in section 8147 of title 5, for compensation paid or payable after June 7, 1987, in accordance with chapter 81 of title 5 for any injury, disability, or death due to events arising before June 7, 1987, whether or not a claim was filed or was final on that date.

(D) The Airports Authority shall continue all collective bargaining rights enjoyed by employees of the Metropolitan Washington Airports before June 7, 1987.

(7) The Comptroller General may conduct periodic audits of the activities and transactions of the Airports Authority in accordance with generally accepted management principles, and under regulations the Comptroller General may prescribe. An audit shall be conducted where the Comptroller General considers it appropriate. All records and property of the Airports Authority shall remain in possession and custody of the Airports Authority.

(8) The Airports Authority shall develop a code of ethics and financial disclosure to ensure the integrity of all decisions made by its board of directors and employees. The code shall include standards by which members of the board will decide, for purposes of section 49106(d) of this title, what constitutes a substantial financial interest and the circumstances under which an exception to the conflict of interest prohibition may be granted.

(9) A landing fee imposed for operating an aircraft or revenues derived from parking automobiles—

(A) at Washington Dulles International Airport may not be used for maintenance or operating expenses (excluding debt service, depreciation, and amortization) at Ronald Reagan Washington National Airport; and

(B) at Ronald Reagan Washington National Airport may not be used for maintenance or operating expenses (excluding debt service, depreciation, and amortization) at Washington Dulles International Airport.

(10) The Airports Authority shall compute the fees and charges for landing general aviation aircraft at the Metropolitan Washington Airports on the same basis as the landing fees for air carrier aircraft, except that the Airports Authority may require a minimum landing fee that is not more than the landing fee for aircraft weighing 12,500 pounds.

(11) The Secretary shall include other terms applicable to the parties to the lease that are consistent with, and carry out, this chapter.

(b) PAYMENTS.—Under the lease, the Airports Authority must pay to the general fund of the Treasury annually an amount, computed using the GNP Price Deflator, equal to $3,000,000 in 1987 dollars. The Secretary and the Airports Authority may renegotiate the level of lease payments attributable to inflation costs every 10 years.

(c) ENFORCEMENT OF LEASE PROVISIONS.—The district courts of the United States have jurisdiction to compel the Airports Authority and its officers and employees to comply with the terms of the lease. The Attorney General or an aggrieved party may bring an action on behalf of the Government.

(d) EXTENSION OF LEASE.—The Secretary and the Airports Authority may at any time negotiate an extension of the lease.

(Added Pub. L. 105–102, §2(26), Nov. 20, 1997, 111 Stat. 2207; amended Pub. L. 105–154, §2(a)(1)(D), Feb. 6, 1998, 112 Stat. 3; Pub. L. 106–181, title II, §231(e)(2), Apr. 5, 2000, 114 Stat. 113; Pub. L. 112–95, title IV, §414(e), Feb. 14, 2012, 126 Stat. 92.)

§49105. CAPITAL IMPROVEMENTS, CONSTRUCTION, AND REHABILITATION

(a) SENSE OF CONGRESS.—It is the sense of Congress that the Metropolitan Washington Airports Authority—

(1) should pursue the improvement, construction, and rehabilitation of the facilities at Washington Dulles International Airport and Ronald Reagan Washington National Airport simultaneously; and

(2) to the extent practicable, should cause the improvement, construction, and rehabilitation proposed by the Secretary of Transportation to be completed at Washington Dulles International Airport and Ronald Reagan Washington National Airport within 5 years after March 30, 1988.

(b) SECRETARY'S ASSISTANCE.—The Secretary shall assist the 3 airports serving the District of Columbia metropolitan area in planning for operational and capital improvements at those airports and shall accelerate consideration of applications for United States Government financial assistance by whichever of the 3 airports is most in need of increasing airside capacity.

(Added Pub. L. 105–102, §2(26), Nov. 20, 1997, 111 Stat. 2210; amended Pub. L. 105–154, §2(a)(1)(D), Feb. 6, 1998, 112 Stat. 3.)

§49106. METROPOLITAN WASHINGTON AIRPORTS AUTHORITY

(a) STATUS.—The Metropolitan Washington Airports Authority shall be—

(1) a public body corporate and politic with the powers and jurisdiction—

(A) conferred upon it jointly by the legislative authority of Virginia and the District of Columbia or by either of them and concurred in by the legislative authority of the other jurisdiction; and

(B) that at least meet the specifications of this section;

(2) independent of Virginia and its local governments, the District of Columbia, and the United States Government; and

(3) a political subdivision constituted only to operate and improve the Metropolitan Washington Airports as primary airports serving the Metropolitan Washington area.

(b) GENERAL AUTHORITY.—(1) The Airports Authority shall be authorized—

(A) to acquire, maintain, improve, operate, protect, and promote the Metropolitan Washington Airports for public purposes;

(B) to issue bonds from time to time in its discretion for public purposes, including paying any part of the cost of airport improvements, construction, and rehabilitation and the acquisition of real and personal property, including operating equipment for the airports;

(C) to acquire real and personal property by purchase, lease, transfer, or exchange;

(D) to exercise the powers of eminent domain in Virginia that are conferred on it by Virginia;

(E) to levy fees or other charges; and

(F) to make and maintain agreements with employee organizations to the extent that the Federal Aviation Administration was authorized to do so on October 18, 1986.

(2) Bonds issued under paragraph (1)(B) of this subsection—

(A) are not a debt of Virginia, the District of Columbia, or a political subdivision of Virginia or the District of Columbia; and

(B) may be secured by the Airports Authority's revenues generally, or exclusively from the income and revenues of certain designated projects whether or not any part of the projects are financed from the proceeds of the bonds.

(c) BOARD OF DIRECTORS.—(1) The Airports Authority shall be governed by a board of directors composed of the following 17 members:

(A) 7 members appointed by the Governor of Virginia;

(B) 4 members appointed by the Mayor of the District of Columbia;

(C) 3 members appointed by the Governor of Maryland; and

(D) 3 members appointed by the President with the advice and consent of the Senate.

(2) The chairman of the board shall be appointed from among the members by majority vote of the members and shall serve until replaced by majority vote of the members.

(3) Members of the board shall be appointed to the board for 6 years, except that of the members first appointed by the President after October 9, 1996, one shall be appointed for 4 years. Any member of the board shall be eligible for reappointment for 1 additional term. A member shall not serve after the expiration of the member's term(s).

(4) A member of the board—

(A) may not hold elective or appointive political office;

(B) serves without compensation except for reasonable expenses incident to board functions; and

(C) must reside within the Washington Standard Metropolitan Statistical Area, except that a member of the board appointed by the President must be a registered voter of a State other than Maryland, Virginia, or the District of Columbia.

(5) A vacancy in the board shall be filled in the manner in which the original appointment was made. A member appointed to fill a vacancy occurring before the expiration of the term for which the member's predecessor was appointed shall be appointed only for the remainder of that term.

(6)(A) Not more than 2 of the members of the board appointed by the President may be of the same political party.

(B) In carrying out their duties on the board, members appointed by the President shall ensure that adequate consideration is given to the national interest.

(C) A member appointed by the President may be removed by the President for cause. A member appointed by the Mayor of the District of Columbia, the Governor of Maryland or the Governor of Virginia may be removed or suspended from office only for cause and in accordance with the laws of the jurisdiction from which the member is appointed.

(7) Ten votes are required to approve bond issues and the annual budget.

(d) CONFLICTS OF INTEREST.—Members of the board and their immediate families may not be employed by or otherwise hold a substantial financial interest in any enterprise that has or is seeking a contract or agreement with the Airports Authority or is an aeronautical, aviation services, or airport services enterprise that otherwise has interests that can be directly affected by the Airports Authority. The official appointing a member may make an exception if the financial interest is completely disclosed when the member is appointed and the member does not participate in board decisions that directly affect the interest.

(e) CERTAIN ACTIONS TO BE TAKEN BY REGULATION.—An action of the Airports Authority changing, or having the effect of changing, the hours of operation of, or the type of aircraft serving, either of the Metropolitan Washington Airports may be taken only by regulation of the Airports Authority.

(f) ADMINISTRATIVE.—To assist the Secretary in carrying out this chapter, the Secretary may hire 2 staff individuals to be paid by the Airports Authority. The Airports Authority shall provide clerical and support staff that the Secretary may require.

(g) REVIEW OF CONTRACTING PROCEDURES.—The Comptroller General shall review contracts of the Airports Authority to decide whether the contracts were awarded by procedures that follow sound Government contracting principles and comply with section 49104(a)(4) of this title. The Comptroller General shall submit periodic reports of the conclusions reached as a result of the review to the Committee on Transportation and Infrastructure of the House of Representatives and the Committee on Commerce, Science, and Transportation of the Senate.

(Added Pub. L. 105–102, §2(26), Nov. 20, 1997, 111 Stat. 2210; amended Pub. L. 105–225, §7(c)(1)(A), (B), Aug. 12, 1998, 112 Stat. 1511; Pub. L. 106–181, title II, §231(i), Apr. 5, 2000, 114 Stat. 115; Pub. L. 112–55, div. C, title I, §191, Nov. 18, 2011, 125 Stat. 671; Pub. L. 118–63, title XI, §1101(x), May 16, 2024, 138 Stat. 1414.)

§49107. FEDERAL EMPLOYEES AT METROPOLITAN WASHINGTON AIRPORTS

(a) LABOR AGREEMENTS.—(1) The Metropolitan Washington Airports Authority shall

[§49108. Repealed. Pub. L. 112–95, title I, §150, Feb. 14, 2012, 126 Stat. 32]

CHAPTER 491—METROPOLITAN
WASHINGTON AIRPORTS

adopt all labor agreements that were in effect on June 7, 1987. Unless the parties otherwise agree, the agreements must be renegotiated before June 7, 1992.

(2) Employee protection arrangements made under this section shall ensure, during the 50-year lease term, the continuation of all collective bargaining rights enjoyed by transferred employees retained by the Airports Authority.

(b) Civil Service Retirement.—Any Federal employee who transferred to the Airports Authority and who on June 6, 1987, was subject to subchapter III of chapter 83 or chapter 84 of title 5, is subject to subchapter III of chapter 83 or chapter 84 for so long as continually employed by the Airports Authority without a break in service. For purposes of subchapter III of chapter 83 and chapter 84, employment by the Airports Authority without a break in continuity of service is deemed to be employment by the United States Government. The Airports Authority is the employing agency for purposes of subchapter III of chapter 83 and chapter 84 and shall contribute to the Civil Service Retirement and Disability Fund amounts required by subchapter III of chapter 83 and chapter 84.

(c) Access to Records.—The Airports Authority shall allow representatives of the Secretary of Transportation adequate access to employees and employee records of the Airports Authority when needed to carry out a duty or power related to the period before June 7, 1987. The Secretary shall provide the Airports Authority access to employee records of transferring employees for appropriate purposes.

(Added Pub. L. 105–102, §2(26), Nov. 20, 1997, 111 Stat. 2212; amended Pub. L. 105–225, §7(c)(1)(C), Aug. 12, 1998, 112 Stat. 1511.)

[§49108. Repealed. Pub. L. 112–95, title I, §150, Feb. 14, 2012, 126 Stat. 32]

Section, added Pub. L. 105–102, §2(26), Nov. 20, 1997, 111 Stat. 2213; amended Pub. L. 106–181, title II, §231(h), Apr. 5, 2000, 114 Stat. 115; Pub. L. 108–176, title VIII, §804, Dec. 12, 2003, 117 Stat. 2587; Pub. L. 110–330, §5(h), Sept. 30, 2008, 122 Stat. 3718; Pub. L. 111–12, §5(g), Mar. 30, 2009, 123 Stat. 1458; Pub. L. 111–69, §5(h), Oct. 1, 2009, 123 Stat. 2055; Pub. L. 111–116, §5(g), Dec. 16, 2009, 123 Stat. 3032; Pub. L. 111–153, §5(g), Mar. 31, 2010, 124 Stat. 1085; Pub. L. 111–161, §5(g), Apr. 30, 2010, 124 Stat. 1127; Pub. L. 111–197, §5(g), July 2, 2010, 124 Stat. 1354; Pub. L. 111–216, title I, §104(g), Aug. 1, 2010, 124 Stat. 2350; Pub. L. 111–249, §5(h), Sept. 30, 2010, 124 Stat. 2628; Pub. L. 111–329, §5(g), Dec. 22, 2010, 124 Stat. 3567; Pub. L. 112–7, §5(g), Mar. 31, 2011, 125 Stat. 32; Pub. L. 112–16, §5(g), May 31, 2011, 125 Stat. 219; Pub. L. 112–21, §5(g), June 29, 2011, 125 Stat. 234; Pub. L. 112–27, §5(g), Aug. 5, 2011, 125 Stat. 271; Pub. L. 112–30, title II, §205(h), Sept. 16, 2011, 125 Stat. 358; Pub. L. 112–91, §5(h), Jan. 31, 2012, 126 Stat. 4, related to limitations on Secretary of Transportation's authority to approve an application of the Metropolitan Washington Airports Authority.

§49109. Nonstop flights

An air carrier may not operate an aircraft nonstop in air transportation between Ronald Reagan Washington National Airport and another airport that is more than 1,250 statute miles away from Ronald Reagan Washington National Airport.

(Added Pub. L. 105–102, §2(26), Nov. 20, 1997, 111 Stat. 2213; amended Pub. L. 105–154, §2(a)(1)(D), Feb. 6, 1998, 112 Stat. 3.)

§49110. Use of Dulles Airport Access Highway

The Metropolitan Washington Airports Authority shall continue in effect and enforce section 4.2(1) and (2) of the Metropolitan Washington Airports Regulations, as in effect on February 1, 1995. The district courts of the United States have jurisdiction to compel the Airports Authority and its officers and employees to comply with this section. The Attorney General or an aggrieved party may bring an action on behalf of the United States Government.

(Added Pub. L. 105–102, §2(26), Nov. 20, 1997, 111 Stat. 2213.)

§49111. Relationship to and effect of other laws

(a) Same Powers and Restrictions Under Other Laws.—To ensure that the Metropolitan Washington Airports Authority has the same proprietary powers and is subject to the same restrictions under United States law as any other airport except as otherwise provided in this chapter, during the period that the lease authorized by section 6005 of the Metropolitan Washington Airports Act of 1986 (Public Law 99–500; 100 Stat. 1783–375; Public Law 99–591; 100 Stat. 3341–378) is in effect—

(1) the Metropolitan Washington Airports are deemed to be public airports for purposes of chapter 471 of this title; and

(2) the Act of June 29, 1940 (ch. 444, 54 Stat. 686), the First Supplemental Civil Functions Appropriations Act, 1941 (ch. 780, 54 Stat. 1030), and the Act of September 7, 1950 (ch. 905, 64 Stat. 770), do not apply to the operation of the Metropolitan Washington Airports, and the Secretary of Transportation is relieved of all responsibility under those Acts.

(b) Inapplicability of Certain Laws.—The Metropolitan Washington Airports and the Airports Authority are not subject to the requirements of any law solely by reason of the retention by the United States Government of the fee simple title to those airports.

(c) Police Power.—Virginia shall have concurrent police power authority over the Metropolitan Washington Airports, and the courts of Virginia may exercise jurisdiction over Ronald Reagan Washington National Airport.

(d) Planning.—(1) The authority of the National Capital Planning Commission under section 8722 of title 40 does not apply to the Airports Authority.

(2) The Airports Authority shall consult with—

(A) the Commission and the Advisory Council on Historic Preservation before undertaking any major alterations to the exterior of the main terminal at Washington Dulles International Airport; and

(B) the Commission before undertaking development that would alter the skyline of Ronald Reagan Washington National Airport when viewed from the opposing shoreline of the Potomac River or from the George Washington Parkway.

(Added Pub. L. 105–102, §2(26), Nov. 20, 1997, 111 Stat. 2213; amended Pub. L. 105–154, §2(a)(1)(D), Feb. 6, 1998, 112 Stat. 3; Pub. L. 105–225, §7(c)(1)(D), Aug. 12, 1998, 112 Stat. 1511; Pub. L. 106–181, title II, §231(j)(1), Apr. 5, 2000, 114 Stat. 115; Pub. L. 107–217, §3(n)(9), Aug. 21, 2002, 116 Stat. 1303.)

§49112. Separability and effect of judicial order

(a) Separability.—If any provision of this chapter, or the application of a provision of this chapter to a person or circumstance, is held invalid, the remainder of this chapter and the application of the provision to other persons or circumstances is not affected.

(b) EFFECT OF JUDICIAL ORDER.—Any action of the Airports Authority that was required to be submitted to the Board of Review under section 6007(f)(4) of the Metropolitan Washington Airports Act of 1986 (Public Law 99–500; 100 Stat. 1783–380; Public Law 99–599; 100 Stat. 3341–383) before October 9, 1996, remains in effect and may not be set aside only because of a judicial order invalidating certain functions of the Board.

(Added Pub. L. 105–102, §2(26), Nov. 20, 1997, 111 Stat. 2214; amended Pub. L. 118–63, title XI, §1101(y), May 16, 2024, 138 Stat. 1415.)

PART E
MISCELLANEOUS

PART E—MISCELLANEOUS

CHAPTER 501—BUY-AMERICAN PREFERENCES

§50101. BUYING GOODS PRODUCED IN THE UNITED STATES

(a) PREFERENCE.—The Secretary of Transportation may obligate an amount that may be appropriated to carry out section 106(k), 44502(a)(2), or 44509, subchapter I of chapter 471, or chapter 481 (except sections 48102(e), 48106, 48107, and 48110) of this title for a project only if steel and manufactured goods used in the project are produced in the United States.

(b) WAIVER.—The Secretary may waive subsection (a) of this section if the Secretary finds that—

(1) applying subsection (a) would be inconsistent with the public interest;

(2) the steel and goods produced in the United States are not produced in a sufficient and reasonably available amount or are not of a satisfactory quality;

(3) when procuring a facility or equipment under section 44502(a)(2) or 44509, subchapter I of chapter 471, or chapter 481 (except sections 48102(e), 48106, 48107, and 48110) of this title—

(A) the cost of components and subcomponents produced in the United States is more than 60 percent of the cost of all components of the facility or equipment; and

(B) final assembly of the facility or equipment has occurred in the United States; or

(4) including domestic material will increase the cost of the overall project by more than 25 percent.

(c) LABOR COSTS.—In this section, labor costs involved in final assembly are not included in calculating the cost of components.

(d) LIMITATION ON CERTAIN ROLLING STOCK PROCUREMENTS.—

(1) IN GENERAL.—Financial assistance made available under the provisions described in subsection (a) shall not be used in awarding a contract or subcontract to an entity on or after the date of enactment of this subsection for the procurement of rolling stock for use in an airport-related project if the manufacturer of the rolling stock—

(A) is incorporated in or has manufacturing facilities in the United States; and

(B) is owned or controlled by, is a subsidiary of, or is otherwise related legally or financially to a corporation based in a country that—

(i) is identified as a nonmarket economy country (as defined in section 771(18) of the Tariff Act of 1930 (19 U.S.C. 1677(18))) as of the date of enactment of this subsection;

(ii) was identified by the United States Trade Representative in the most recent report required by section 182 of the Trade Act of 1974 (19 U.S.C. 2242) as a foreign country included on the priority watch list defined in subsection (g)(3) of that section; and

(iii) is subject to monitoring by the Trade Representative under section 306 of the Trade Act of 1974 (19 U.S.C. 2416).

(2) EXCEPTION.—

(A) IN GENERAL.—For purposes of paragraph (1), the term "otherwise related legally or financially" does not include—

(i) a minority relationship or investment; or

(ii) relationship with or investment in a subsidiary, joint venture, or other entity based in a country described in paragraph (1)(B) that does not export rolling stock or components of rolling stock for use in the United States.

(B) CORPORATION BASED IN PEOPLE'S REPUBLIC OF CHINA.—Notwithstanding subparagraph (A)(i), for purposes of paragraph (1), the term "otherwise related legally or financially" includes a minority relationship or investment if the relationship or investment involves a corporation based in the People's Republic of China.

(3) INTERNATIONAL AGREEMENTS.—This subsection shall be applied in a manner consistent with the obligations of the United States under international agreements.

(4) WAIVER.—

(A) IN GENERAL.—The Secretary may waive the limitation described in paragraph (1) using the criteria described in subsection (b).

(B) NOTIFICATION.—Not later than 10 days after issuing a waiver under subparagraph (A), the Secretary shall notify the Committee on Transportation and Infrastructure of the House of Representatives and the Committee on Commerce, Science, and Transportation of the Senate.

(Pub. L. 103–272, §1(e), July 5, 1994, 108 Stat. 1298, §49101; renumbered §50101 and amended Pub. L. 104–287, §5(88)(D), (89), Oct. 11, 1996, 110 Stat. 3398; Pub. L. 118–63, title VII, §768(a), May 16, 2024, 138 Stat. 1293.)

§50102. RESTRICTING CONTRACT AWARDS BECAUSE OF DISCRIMINATION AGAINST UNITED STATES GOODS OR SERVICES

A person or enterprise domiciled or operating under the laws of a foreign country may not make a contract or subcontract under section 106(k), 44502(a)(2), or 44509, subchapter I of chapter 471, or chapter 481 (except sections 48102(e), 48106, 48107, and 48110) of this title or subtitle B of title IX of the Omnibus Budget Reconciliation Act of 1990 (Public Law 101–508, 104 Stat. 1388–353) if the government of that country unfairly maintains, in government procurement, a significant and persistent pattern of discrimination against United States goods or services that results in identifiable harm to United States businesses, that the President identifies under section 305(g)(1)(A) of the Trade Agreements Act of 1979 (19 U.S.C. 2515(g)(1)(A)).

(Pub. L. 103–272, §1(e), July 5, 1994, 108 Stat. 1298, §49102; renumbered §50102 and amended Pub. L. 104–287, §5(88)(D), (89), Oct. 11, 1996, 110 Stat. 3398; Pub. L. 118–63, title VII, §768(b)(1), May 16, 2024, 138 Stat. 1294.)

§50103. Contract preference for domestic firms

(a) Definitions.—In this section—

(1) "domestic firm" means a business entity incorporated, and conducting business, in the United States.

(2) "foreign firm" means a business entity not described in clause (1) of this subsection.

(b) Preference.—Subject to subsections (c) and (d) of this section, the Administrator of the Federal Aviation Administration may make, with a domestic firm, a contract related to a grant made under section 44511, 44512, or 44513 of this title that, under competitive procedures, would be made with a foreign firm, if—

(1) the Administrator decides, and the Secretary of Commerce and the United States Trade Representative concur, that the public interest requires making the contract with the domestic firm, considering United States international obligations and trade relations;

(2) the difference between the bids submitted by the foreign firm and the domestic firm is not more than 6 percent;

(3) the final product of the domestic firm will be assembled completely in the United States; and

(4) at least 51 percent of the final product of the domestic firm will be produced in the United States.

(c) Nonapplication.—Subsection (b) of this section does not apply if—

(1) compelling national security considerations require that subsection (b) of this section not apply; or

(2) the Trade Representative decides that making the contract would violate the multilateral trade agreements (as defined in section 3501(4) of title 19) or an international agreement to which the United States is a party.

(d) Application to Certain Grants.—This section applies only to a contract related to a grant made under section 44511, 44512, or 44513 of this title for which—

(1) an amount is authorized by section 48102(a), (b), or (d) of this title to be made available for the fiscal years ending September 30, 1991, and September 30, 1992; and

(2) a solicitation for bid is issued after November 5, 1990.

(e) Report.—The Administrator shall submit a report to Congress on—

(1) contracts to which this section applies that are made with foreign firms in the fiscal years ending September 30, 1991, and September 30, 1992;

(2) the number of contracts that meet the requirements of subsection (b) of this section, but that the Trade Representative decides would violate the multilateral trade agreements (as defined in section 3501(4) of title 19) or an international agreement to which the United States is a party; and

(3) the number of contracts made under this section.

(Pub. L. 103–272, §1(e), July 5, 1994, 108 Stat. 1298, §49103; renumbered §50103, Pub. L. 104–287, §5(88)(D), Oct. 11, 1996, 110 Stat. 3398; amended Pub. L. 106–36, title I, §1002(i), June 25, 1999, 113 Stat. 134.)

§50104. Restriction on airport projects using products or services of foreign countries denying fair market opportunities

(a) Definition and Rules for Construing Section.—In this section—

(1) "project" has the same meaning given that term in section 47102 of this title.

(2) each foreign instrumentality and each territory and possession of a foreign country administered separately for customs purposes is a separate foreign country.

(3) an article substantially produced or manufactured in a foreign country is a product of the country.

(4) a service provided by a person that is a national of a foreign country or that is controlled by a national of a foreign country is a service of the country.

(b) LIMITATION ON USE OF AVAILABLE AMOUNTS.—(1) An amount made available under subchapter I of chapter 471 of this title may not be used for a project that uses a product or service of a foreign country during any period the country is on the list maintained by the United States Trade Representative under subsection (d)(1) of this section.

(2) Paragraph (1) of this subsection does not apply when the Secretary of Transportation decides that—

(A) applying paragraph (1) to the product, service, or project is not in the public interest;

(B) a product or service of the same class or type and of satisfactory quality is not produced or offered in the United States, or in a foreign country not listed under subsection (d)(1) of this section, in a sufficient and reasonably available amount; and

(C) the project cost will increase by more than 20 percent if the product or service is excluded.

(c) DECISIONS ON DENIAL OF FAIR MARKET OPPORTUNITIES.—Not later than 30 days after a report is submitted to Congress under section 181(b) of the Trade Act of 1974 (19 U.S.C. 2241(b)), the Trade Representative, for a construction project of more than $500,000 for which the government of a foreign country supplies any part of the amount, shall decide whether the foreign country denies fair market opportunities for products and suppliers of the United States in procurement or for United States bidders. In making the decision, the Trade Representative shall consider information obtained in preparing the report and other information the Trade Representative considers relevant.

(d) LIST OF COUNTRIES DENYING FAIR MARKET OPPORTUNITIES.—(1) The Trade Representative shall maintain a list of each foreign country the Trade Representative finds under subsection (c) of this section is denying fair market opportunities. The country shall remain on the list until the Trade Representative decides the country provides fair market opportunities.

(2) The Trade Representative shall publish in the Federal Register—

(A) annually the list required under paragraph (1) of this subsection; and

(B) any modification of the list made before the next list is published.

(Pub. L. 103–272, §1(e), July 5, 1994, 108 Stat. 1299, §49104; renumbered §50104 and amended Pub. L. 104–287, §5(88)(D), (89), Oct. 11, 1996, 110 Stat. 3398; Pub. L. 118–63, title VII, §768(b)(2), May 16, 2024, 138 Stat. 1294.)

§50105. FRAUDULENT USE OF "MADE IN AMERICA" LABEL

If the Secretary of Transportation decides that a person intentionally affixed a "Made in America" label to goods sold in or shipped to the United States that are not made in the United States, the Secretary shall declare the person ineligible, for not less than 3 nor more than 5 years, to receive a contract or grant from the United States Government related to a contract made under section 106(k), 44502(a)(2), or 44509, subchapter I of chapter 471, or chapter 481 (except sections 48102(e), 48106, 48107, and 48110) of this title or subtitle B of title IX of the Omnibus Budget Reconciliation Act of 1990 (Public Law 101–508, 104 Stat. 1388–353). The Secretary may bring a civil action to enforce this section in any district court of the United States.

(Pub. L. 103–272, §1(e), July 5, 1994, 108 Stat. 1300, §49105; renumbered §50105 and amended Pub. L. 104–287, §5(88)(D), (89), Oct. 11, 1996, 110 Stat. 3398; Pub. L. 118–63, title VII, §768(b)(3), May 16, 2024, 138 Stat. 1295.)

* * * * * * *

POPULAR TITLE NAMES

POPULAR TITLE NAMES

Act of June 29, 1940--(Washington Airports)
54 stat. 686
Act of October 31, 1945
Chapter 443 of 79th Congress
59 Stat. 553
Act of September 7, 1950--(Washington Airports)
Chapter 905 of 81st Congress 64
Stat. 770
Air Transportation Safety and System Stabilization Act
Pub. L. 107 42, Sept. 22, 2001,
115 Stat. 230 (49 U.S.C. 40101 note)
Aircraft Certification, Safety, and Accountability Act
Pub. L. 116 260, div. V, title I, Dec. 27, 2020,
134 Stat. 2309
Short title, see 49 U.S.C. 40101 note
Airline Safety and Federal Aviation Administration Extension Act of 2010
Pub. L. 111 216, Aug. 1, 2010,
124 Stat. 2348
Short title, see 49 U.S.C. 40101 note
Airport and Airway Improvement Act of 1982
Pub. L. 97 248, title V, Sept. 3, 1982,
96 Stat. 671
Airport Security Improvement Act of 2000
Pub. L. 106 528, Nov. 22, 2000, 1
14 Stat. 2517
Short title, see 49 U.S.C. 40101 note
Atomic Energy Defense Act
Pub. L. 107 314, div. D, as added Pub. L. 108 136, div. C, title XXXI, § 3141(b), Nov. 24, 2003,
117 Stat. 1753 (50 U.S.C. 2501 et seq.)
Short title, see 50 U.S.C. 2501 note
Aviation and Transportation Security Act
Pub. L. 107 71, Nov. 19, 2001, 1
15 Stat. 597
Short title, see 49 U.S.C. 40101 note
Aviation Medical Assistance Act of 1998

Pub. L. 105 170, Apr. 24, 1998,
112 Stat. 47 (49 U.S.C. 44701 note)

Bob Stump National Defense Authorization Act for Fiscal Year 2003
Pub. L. 107 314, Dec. 2, 2002,
116 Stat. 2458

Cape Town Treaty Implementation Act of 2004
Pub. L. 108 297, Aug. 9, 2004,
118 Stat. 1095
Short title, see 49 U.S.C. 40101 note

Clean Air Act
July 14, 1955, ch. 360,
69 Stat. 322 (42 U.S.C. 7401 et seq.)
Short title, see 42 U.S.C. 7401 note

Consolidated Appropriations Act, 2021
Pub. L. 116 260, Dec. 27, 2020,
134 Stat. 1182

Consolidated Appropriations Resolution, 2003
Pub. L. 108 7, Feb. 20, 2003,
117 Stat. 11

Death on the High Seas Act
Title 46, chapter 303 (§ 30301 et seq.) Mar. 30, 1920, ch. 111,
41 Stat. 537
Short title, see 46 U.S.C. 30301

Department of Housing and Urban Development Appropriations Act, 2006
Pub. L. 109 115, div. A, title III, Nov. 30, 2005,
119 Stat. 2440

Department of Transportation and Related Agencies Appropriations Act, 2000
Pub. L. 106 69, Oct. 9, 1999,
113 Stat. 986

European Union Emissions Trading Scheme Prohibition Act of 2011
Pub. L. 112 200, Nov. 27, 2012,
126 Stat. 1477 (49 U.S.C. 40101 note)

FAA Extension, Safety, and Security Act of 2016
Pub. L. 114 190, July 15, 2016, 1
30 Stat. 615
Short title, see 49 U.S.C. 40101 note

FAA Modernization and Reform Act of 2012
Pub. L. 112 95, Feb. 14, 2012,
126 Stat. 11
Short title, see 49 U.S.C. 40101 note

FAA Reauthorization Act of 2018
Pub. L. 115 254, Oct. 5, 2018,
132 Stat. 3186
Short title, see 49 U.S.C. 40101 note

Fairness for Pilots Act

Pub. L. 115-254, div. B, title III, subtitle C (Secs. 391-396), Oct. 5, 2018,132 Stat.
3323
Short title, see 49 U.S.C. 40101 note

FAA Reauthorization Act of 2024
Pub. L. 118 63, May 16, 2024,
138 Stat. 1025
Short title, see 49 U.S.C. 40101 note

Federal Airport Act
May 13, 1946, ch. 251,
60 Stat. 170

Federal Aviation Act of 1958
Pub. L. 85 726, Aug. 23, 1958,
72 Stat. 731

Federal Aviation Reauthorization Act of 1996
Pub. L. 104 264, Oct. 9, 1996,
110 Stat. 3213
Short title, see 49 U.S.C. 40101 note

General Aviation Revitalization Act of 1994
Pub. L. 103 298, Aug. 17, 1994,
108 Stat. 1552 (49 U.S.C. 40101 note)

Homeland Security Act of 2002
Pub. L. 107 296, Nov. 25, 2002,
116 Stat. 2135 (6 U.S.C. 101 et seq.)
Short title, see 6 U.S.C. 101 note

Implementing Recommendations of the 9/11 Commission Act of 2007
Pub. L. 110 53, Aug. 3, 2007,
121 Stat. 266
Short title, see 6 U.S.C. 101 note

Intelligence Reform and Terrorism Prevention Act of 2004
Pub. L. 108 458, Dec. 17, 2004,
118 Stat. 3638
Short title, see 50 U.S.C. 3001 note

International Air Transportation Competition Act of 1979
Pub. L. 96 192, Feb. 15, 1980,
94 Stat. 35

International Security and Development Cooperation Act of 1985
Pub. L. 99 83, Aug. 8, 1985,
99 Stat. 190
Short title, see 22 U.S.C. 2151 note

John S. McCain National Defense Authorization Act for Fiscal Year 2019
Pub. L. 115 232, Aug. 13, 2018,
132 Stat. 1636

MAP 21 Also known as *Moving Ahead for Progress in the 21st Century Act*
Pub. L. 112 141, July 6, 2012,
126 Stat. 405

Short title, see 23 U.S.C. 101 note

Moving Ahead for Progress in the 21st Century Act also known as *MAP 21*
    Pub. L. 112 141, July 6, 2012, 126 Stat. 405
    Short title, see 23 U.S.C. 101 note

Narcotics Control Trade Act
    Pub. L. 93 618, title VIII, as added Pub. L. 99 570, title IX, § 9001, Oct. 27, 1986,
    100 Stat. 3207 164 (19 U.S.C. 2491 et seq.)
    Short title, see 19 U.S.C. 2491

National Defense Authorization Act for Fiscal Year 2016
    Pub. L. 114 92, Nov. 25, 2015,
    129 Stat. 726

National Defense Authorization Act for Fiscal Year 2017
    Pub. L. 114 328, Dec. 23, 2016,
    130 Stat. 2000

National Emission Standards Act
    July 14, 1955, ch. 360, title II, as added Pub. L. 89 272, Title I, § 101(8), Oct. 20,
      1965,
    79 Stat. 992
    Short title, see 42 .S.C. 7401 note

National Parks Air Tour Management Act of 2000
    Pub. L. 106 181, title VIII, Apr. 5, 2000,
    114 Stat. 185
    Short title, see 49 U.S.C. 40128 note

National Transportation Safety Board Amendments Act of 2000
    Pub. L. 106 424, Nov. 1, 2000,
    114 Stat. 1883
    Short title, see 49 U.S.C. 1101 note

National Transportation Safety Board Reauthorization Act of 2003
    Pub. L. 108 168, Dec. 6, 2003,
    117 Stat. 2032
    Short title, see 49 U.S.C. 1101 note134 Stat. 1182

National Transportation Safety Board Reauthorization Act of 2006
    Pub. L. 109 443, Dec. 21, 2006,
    120 Stat. 3297
    Short title, see 49 U.S.C. 1101 note

NOTAM Improvement Act of 2023
    Pub. L. 118 4, June 3,,2023, 137 Stat. 7
    Short title, see 49,U.S.C. 40101 note

Railway Labor Act
    May 20, 1926, ch. 347, 44 Stat. 577
    (45 U.S.C. 151 et seq.)
    Short title, see 45,U.S.C. 151

Safe, Accountable, Flexible, Efficient Transportation, Equity Act: A Legacy for Users
    Also known as *SAFETEA LU*
    Pub. L. 109 59, Aug. 10, 2005,

119 Stat. 1144

Short title, see 23 U.S.C. 101 note

SAFETEA LU Also known as *Safe, Accountable, Flexible, Efficient Transportation Equity Act: A Legacy for Users*

Pub. L. 109 59, Aug. 10, 2005,

119 Stat. 1144

Short title, see 23 U.S.C. 101 note

September 11th Victim Compensation Fund of 2001

Pub. L. 107 42, title IV, Sept. 22, 2001,

115 Stat. 237 (49 U.S.C. 40101 note)

TICKETS Act Also known as the *Transparency Improvements and Compensation to Keep Every Ticketholder Safe Act of 2018*

Pub. L. 115-254, div. B, title IV, Sec. 425, Oct. 5, 2018,

132 Stat. 3338 (49 U.S.C. note prec. 42301)

Trade Act of 1974

Pub. L. 93 618, Jan. 3, 1975,

88 Stat. 1978 (19 U.S.C. 2101 et seq.)

Short title, see 19 U.S.C. 2101

Transparency Improvements and Compensation to Keep Every Ticketholder Safe Act of 2018 Also known as the *TICKETS Act*

Pub. L. 115-254, div. B, title IV, Sec. 425, Oct. 5, 2018,

132 Stat. 3338 (49 U.S.C. note prec. 42301)

Trust Fund Code of 1981

Aug. 16, 1954, ch. 736, § 1(d) [Internal Revenue Title, subtitle I], as added Pub. L. 97 119, title I, § 103(a), Dec. 29, 1981,

95 Stat. 1636 (26 U.S.C. 9500 et seq.)

Vision 100 Century of Aviation Reauthorization Act

Pub. L. 108 176, Dec. 12, 2003,

117 Stat. 2490

Short title, see 49 U.S.C. 40101 note

Wendell H. Ford Aviation Investment and Reform Act for the 21st Century

Pub. L. 106 181, Apr. 5, 2000,

114 Stat. 61

Short title, see 49 U.S.C. 40101 note

INDEX

Index

B

C

Q

T